File Name	LINDO	STORM	QSB**
		CHAPTER 7	
EX7_1A.DAT	Yes	Linear and Integer Programming	Linear Programming
EX7_1B.DAT	Yes	Linear and Integer Programming	Linear Programming
EX7_1C.DAT	Yes	Linear and Integer Programming	Linear Programming
DIET.DAT	Yes	Linear and Integer Programming	Linear Programming
DIET_B.DAT	Yes	Linear and Integer Programming	Linear Programming
DIET_C.DAT	Yes	Linear and Integer Programming	Linear Programming
DIET_D.DAT	Yes	Linear and Integer Programming	Linear Programming
		CHAPTER 8	
EX8_1.DAT*	Yes	Linear and Integer Programming	Integer Programming
EX8_2.DAT	Yes	Linear and Integer Programming	Integer Programming
EX8_3.DAT[a]	Yes	Linear and Integer Programming	Integer Programming
EX8_4.DAT*	Yes	Linear and Integer Programming	Integer Programming
EX8_5.DAT	Yes	Linear and Integer Programming	Integer Programming
EX8_10.DAT	Yes	Linear and Integer Programming	Integer Programming
CREW.DAT	Yes	Linear and Integer Programming	Integer Programming
		CHAPTER 9	
MTI_1.DAT	No	Flow Networks	Transportation and Transshipment
CCCTR.DAT*	No	Transportation	Transportation and Transshipment
MAG_1.DAT	No	Transportation	Transportation and Transshipment
RICH_1.DAT	No	Transportation	Transportation and Transshipment
MAG_2.DAT	No	Transportation	Transportation and Transshipment
MAG_3.DAT	No	Transportation	Transportation and Transshipment
MAG_4.DAT	No	Transportation	Capacitated Network Flow Modeling
RICH_2.DAT	No	Transportation	Capacitated Network Flow Modeling
MTI_2.DAT	No	Transportation	Capacitated Network Flow Modeling
EX9_6.DAT	No	Assignment	Assignment and Traveling Salesman
GDTIRE.DAT	No	Transportation	Transportation and Transshipment
SGEX_4.DAT	No	Distant Networks	Assignment and Traveling Salesman
SGEX_8.DAT	No	Distant Networks	Assignment and Traveling Salesman

MANAGEMENT SCIENCE

The Art of Decision Making

KAMLESH MATHUR

AND

DANIEL SOLOW

Department of Operations Research
Weatherhead School of Management
Case Western Reserve University

PRENTICE HALL, Englewood Cliffs, New Jersey 07632

Library of Congress Cataloging-in-Publication Data

Mathur, Kamlesh.
    Management science: the art of decision making / Kamlesh Mathur,
Daniel Solow.
        p.   cm.
    Includes index.
    ISBN 0–13–052143–4
    1. Management—Mathematical models.   2. Decision-making—
Mathematical models.   3. Management science.   I. Solow, Daniel.
II. Title.
HD30.25.M374   1994
    658.4′03—dc20   93–17365
                                                                          CIP

Acquisitions Editor: *Valerie Ashton*
Development Editor: *Stephen Deitmer*
Production Editor: *Edith Pullman*
Interior and Cover Designer: *Rosemarie Paccione*
Manufacturing Buyers: *Trudy Pisciotti and Herb Klein*
Supplements Coordinator: *Maureen Hull*
Editorial Assistant: *Eileen Deguzman*

Cover Art: Illustration by *Warren Gebert*

LINDO® is registered in the U.S. Patent and Trademark Office
SIMAN® is registered in the U.S. Patent and Trademark Office
STORM® is registered in the U.S. Patent and Trademark Office
@RISK™ is a trademark of Palisade Corporation

Printed in the United States of America

10   9   8   7   6   5   4   3   2   1

0-13-052143-4

Prentice-Hall International (UK) Limited, *London*
Prentice-Hall of Australia Pty. Limited, *Sydney*
Prentice-Hall Canada Inc., *Toronto*
Prentice-Hall Hispanoamericana, S.A., *Mexico*
Prentice-Hall of India Private Limited, *New Delhi*
Prentice-Hall of Japan, Inc., *Tokyo*
Simon & Schuster Asia Pte. Ltd., *Singapore*
Editora Prentice-Hall do Brasil, Ltda., *Rio de Janeiro*

To our wives for their patience and support

BRIEF CONTENTS

PART 2 STOCHASTIC MODELS

CONTENTS

■ CHAPTER 7   Multiobjective Optimization Using Goal Programming   240

■ CHAPTER 10   PROJECT MANAGEMENT: CPM AND PERT   455

PART 2 STOCHASTIC MODELS

■ CHAPTER 11   DECISION ANALYSIS   527

CHAPTER 14   COMPUTER SIMULATION: THE GENERAL METHODOLOGY   700

PREFACE

Management Science: The Art of Decision Making is an introductory text for an under-graduate or graduate course in Quantitative Methods, Operations Research, Manage-ment Science, Decision Science, or similar course. Why another management science text?

From our experience teaching hundreds of business undergraduate and MBA students over the past 15 years at Case Western Reserve University, we have found that existing texts do not provide an adequate discussion of the supporting *thinking process* involved in formulating and solving management science problems. Rather, these books present numerous examples and algorithms, hoping the students will somehow absorb the underlying ideas through osmosis. Without having learned this thinking process explicitly, many students are unable to solve *new* problems—that is, problems that are even slightly different from the ones they see in their text or hear in the classroom.

Our primary objective in writing this book is to correct this deficiency by teaching this thinking process in a systematic and explicit way. One example of this is our Chapter 2, in which we present model-building tools that students can use in formu-lating virtually any deterministic problem, be it a linear programming, an integer programming, a nonlinear programming, or a network problem. Consider, also, our approach to teaching algorithms. Most existing texts present algorithms as a collection of individual techniques, with little or no relation to each other. To correct this prob-lem, we present, in a unifying and easily understandable manner, the concept of a general *Finite-Improvement Algorithm* in Chapter 5. Doing so provides the student with the basic ideas behind many of the algorithms and solution procedures taught later in the text, including the simplex algorithm (in Chapter 6), the transportation and transshipment algorithms (in Chapter 9), and others.

■ EMPHASIS ON MODEL BUILDING

Perhaps our most significant contribution to the teaching of management science is in the area of model building. Many instructors would agree that this is the most impor-tant aspect of management science, for although there are numerous computer pack-ages for *solving* a model, there are no general packages for *building* a model. In teaching students how to build models, we are teaching them how to think about management science problems.

Most texts attempt to teach problem formulation and model building by present-ing a series of problem statements and then a complete mathematical model, with little or no discussion as to *how* the model was developed. This approach makes it difficult for students to formulate mathematical models for *new* problems that are different from the ones they have seen. We overcome this deficiency by illustrating and emphasizing the *thinking process* involved in problem formulation. In Chapters 2 and 3, general model-building techniques are presented, such as *decomposing* an objective function into a sum, difference, or product of individual terms; *working through a specific numerical example,* to identify the form of an objective function or constraints; *grouping,* to identify group of related constraints; and the use of *schematic diagrams* to visualize important aspects of the problem. These techniques are then used repeatedly, where appropriate, each time a problem is formulated. Although model building is an art that comes only with practice, these techniques provide students with systematic tools they can use to formulate new problems on their own.

■ MODULAR DESIGN

All management science courses now cover, to varying degrees, problem formulation, solution procedures, mathematical development, and use of computer packages. Other texts often place primary emphasis on one or two of these areas at the expense of the others. For each management science topic, we provide a balance among these areas in a modular way so that instructors with different course objectives can use our book. We now describe these modules.

1. **Problem Formulation** is described first, by using the systematic model-building techniques presented in Chapters 2 and 3. This formulation process is illustrated with many examples designed to show the variety of business problems to which the management science topic can be applied.

2. Next, a **conceptual approach** to each solution procedure is presented. With the advent of efficient computer packages for solving management science problems, there is a tendency for books to treat the associated algorithms as a "black box." Doing so often leads a manager not to use the full capabilities of a solution technique, or even to misuse the technique completely. Our objective in this area is to ensure that future managers understand the *basic ideas* behind the algorithms, without necessarily having to learn all of the mathematical details. We accomplish this by providing a conceptual approach that requires no mathematical sophistication.

3. A more complete **mathematical development** then provides the details of the solution method. (The one exception is the exclusion of the detailed description of the algebraic steps of the simplex algorithm. Market survey information indicates that only a few management science courses have the time to cover this topic. However, a supplement on the mathematical details of the simplex algorithm is available from the publisher, on request.)

4. The next section presents and interprets the results of **using computer packages** to solve previously formulated (and other) problems. A wide variety of different software packages is illustrated, including: STORM®, LINDO®, EXCEL™, QSB™, @RISK™, and SIMAN®. In many cases, we show that different software packages provide similar solutions, although the specific format varies. This book, therefore, can be used in conjunction with any software you choose.

These four modules are sequenced in such a way that you may cover the section on computer solutions without having taught the mathematical details of the algorithm.

■ PEDAGOGICAL FEATURES: AN EMPHASIS ON THE MANAGERIAL PERSPECTIVE

Regardless of which topics you cover in class, *Management Science: The Art of Decision Making* emphasizes the manager's perspective and the important—sometimes essential—role that management science plays in business decision making. Throughout each chapter, including the coverage of the mathematical and computational ideas, our primary focus is on the managerial perspective. We accomplish this through the use of realistic problems of different size and complexity, actual computer output generated in solving the problem, and consistent discussion of the economic interpretation of the solution. Almost all chapters feature a special section called *Additional Managerial Considerations* (set off with a blue tint), devoted to topics that are of particular importance to managers. In these sections, we may discuss the what-happens-if questions that managers can ask. We may also talk about the assumptions and limitations of the techniques under investigation, examine issues in the practical difficulties of data collection, and so on. Our goal is to place the student in the role of the person making the business decision.

Another important feature included in most chapters is the *Case Study*. Each Case Study illustrates an *innovative* application of the material in the chapter to solving a large-scale business problem. Thus, Case Studies extend the explicit teaching of the thinking process while widening the student's vision of the application of management science in decision making.

A *Critical-Thinking Project* appears after the exercises near the end of each chapter. The projects are designed to provide students with practice in handling more realistic, complex problems. Because we want to promote communication skills, the projects also require that students write managerial reports. Moreover, we have designed the projects to be solved by groups of students, with the goal of promoting collaborative learning. But of course, instructors may assign the projects on an individual basis.

Where appropriate, we present the Critical-Thinking Project in two parts: formulation and solution. It is our experience that students often make mistakes in the formulations, which in turn render the solutions to the subsequent managerial questions meaningless. What we suggest is that students turn in their formulations, which the instructors can then grade. Then, when assigning the solution part of the project, the instructors can hand out a correct formulation (available in the *Solutions Manual*) to the students.

■ ADDITIONAL PEDAGOGICAL SUPPORT

A flip through any chapter reveals the attention we have paid to supporting the student with numerous pedagogical tools. *Key features* throughout the running text highlight the most important points for a student's first reading of the chapter and also serve as sign posts guiding the student in reviewing the material.

Key terms are bold faced at their first use in the running text. They also appear in the margin with their full definition.

A disk is included inside the back cover that contains data files for solving all in-text problems with STORM, LINDO, and/or QSB, where appropriate. The corresponding file name for each problem is identified in the text margin next to that problem. End papers present a table listing every data file we offer. The student need only read across in this table to find the appropriate module to use with each software package. No other book offers the student this support.

At the back of the book, answers are presented to selected exercises. We have taken this support for the student an important step further. We also provide fully worked-out solutions to these selected exercises in an accompanying supplement. More than just an answer, these solutions show the student *how* the answer is obtained. A student can use these key exercises as self-teaching problems. These key exercises are identified with a special key symbol in the margin. The instructor may want to assign the unmarked exercises as homework.

■ SUPPLEMENTS

A successful course requires more than a well-written book. The following supplemental teaching and learning aids are available from Prentice Hall to accompany *Management Science: The Art of Decision Making.*

Instructor's Solutions Manual, prepared by Kamlesh Mathur and Daniel Solow of Case Western Reserve University, contains fully worked-out solutions to all problems, helpful information regarding the use of the Critical-Thinking Projects, and general teaching tips.

Teaching Transparency Masters, prepared by John Day of Ohio University, contains approximately 200 detailed teaching transparencies for use in the classroom. This packet also contains 50 four-color transparencies of key artwork from the text.

Applications Pack, prepared by Rick Hesse of Mercer University, contains additional videocases (there are videocases at the end of each chapter in the text). These videocases build on video clips from ABC News, COMAP, and corporations themselves (see Management Science Video Library, described below). Other features of the Applications Pack include chapter "road maps," articles from the journal *Interfaces,* Critical-Thinking Projects solutions, and additional transparency masters.

Student Resource Manual prepared by Kamlesh Mathur and Daniel Solow of Case Western Reserve University is a unique student supplement that contains fully worked-out solutions to keyed problems in the text; additional network problems (Maximum Flow, Shortest Path, Minimum Cost Spanning Tree, and Traveling Salesperson); coverage of the Simplex Algorithm; and reviews of Probability Theory, Statistical Estimation, and Linear Equations.

Test Item File, prepared by Dave Russell of Western New England College, contains additional tests and questions as well as fully worked-out solutions. It is available for both IBM and Macintosh computers.

Management Science Video Library, prepared by Rick Hesse of Mercer University, contains five-to-fifteen-minute video clips that accompany the videocases that appear at the end of each chapter and in the *Applications Pack.* This video material is drawn from ABC News programs—a Prentice Hall exclusive—as well as from COMAP (the Consortium for Mathematics and Its Applications) and from individual corporations.

■ SOFTWARE

Prentice Hall also distributes some of the leading software packages for the quantitative disciplines. There are two leading packages that are particularly appropriate for use with this text.

Quantitative Systems for Business Plus (QSB+), Version 3.0 by Yih-Long Chang of Georgia Institute of Technology is a text/software package that explores a wide range of problem solving algorithms for management science. Version 3.0 adds new modules on basic statistics, non-linear programming and financial analysis.

Value STORM:MS Quantitative Modeling for Decision Support prepared by Hamilton Emmons, A. Dale Flowers, Chandrashekhar M. Khot and Kamlesh Mathur of Storm Software, Inc. and Case Western Reserve University, is a special version of *Personal STORM Version 3.0* tailored for use in the management science course.

■ ACKNOWLEDGMENTS

We thank the following list of reviewers, whose many constructive comments and suggestions have been included and have lead to an improved version of the book:

S. Christian Albright—Indiana University
James C. Bean—University of Michigan
Richard Clemens—West Virginia Wesleyan College
Gyu C. Kim—Northern Illinois University
Douglas J. Morrice—University of Texas at Austin
Nicholas G. Odrey—Lehigh University
Gary R. Reaves—University of South Carolina
Jeffrey L. Rummel—Duke University
Hossein Soroush—Clemson University
William F. Younkin—University of Miami

We extend special appreciation to David Carhart of Bentley College for his most attentive review of the final text.

No single person had more input to this book than Steve Deitmer, our Development Editor at Prentice Hall. He painstakingly read the book from cover to cover (more than once) from the student's perspective and made us keenly aware when some topic was not explained clearly enough. His stylistic and grammatical comments have been incorporated throughout the text. Luckily for us, his command of English is better than his quantitative skills. Thank you, Steve, for a job well done.

Edie Pullman, our Production Editor at Prentice Hall, and the staff had the challenging task of overseeing the entire production, from the art, the design, and the copy editing (thank you Peter Zurita for doing such a fine and consistent job of copy editing), to keeping the project on schedule. We would hate to see her phone bills. In view of the number and complexity of the figures in this book, a special thanks goes to those involved in the Art Department: Pat Wosczyk, director, Rosemarie Paccione, designer, and Mirella Signoretto, illustrator.

Thanks also to Valerie Ashton, our Acquisitions Editor, and now Editor in Chief at Prentice Hall, who signed us on and took overall responsibility for this project. Others at Prentice Hall that deserve recognition are those in the Business and Economics group, headed by Joyce Turner, as well as the members of the Advertising Department, under the guidance of Lori Cowen.

Special recognition is due Mark Fleischer, a student at the Weatherhead School of Management who, while trying to finish his Ph.D. in Operations Research, spent two years working with us on creating and developing the exercises and preparing the answers that are included in the back of the book and the extensive solutions that make up the Solutions Supplements (both for the student and instructor). He also is responsible for quality of the production of these supplements (he did all the word processing and drawing of the graphs and diagrams). There is definitely a career for him in the publishing business. Thanks for all your help.

Thanks also to our secretaries, Tedda Nathan and Michelle Bolin, for all their typing and administrative help. We are also grateful to have had the support of the Department of Operations Research and especially to Professors Hamilton Emmons, Harvey Salkin, and Sheldon Jacobson for class testing the book in draft form. Finally, we appreciate the use of the hardware facilities at the Weatherhead School of Management at Case Western Reserve University. Danny Solow is also grateful to Waseda University where, as a Visiting Professor in the Toshiba Chair, he was able to complete the work on this book.

INTRODUCTION TO MANAGEMENT SCIENCE

· ·

*D*o you invest in stocks, in bonds, or in both? How do you balance your investment to achieve maximum growth at an acceptable risk? The art and techniques of management science can lead you to an answer, as you will discover in this chapter.

Business managers, both in the service sector and in the manufacturing sector, likewise face problems that they can solve through management science. How does Case Chemicals develop the weekly production plan that maximizes profits? How does American Steel decide on whether to accept the special order from its Japanese customer or its Korean customer? What financial commitment should Star Productions make in launching its new television series?

This book looks at how managers have answered these and many other types of questions by applying management science in their search for the best decision.

■ 1.1 WHAT IS MANAGEMENT SCIENCE?

Management science/Operations research
The use of mathematics and computers to help make rational decisions to complex managerial problems.

In **management science** (sometimes called **operations research**), managers use mathematics and computers to make rational decisions in solving problems. Although some problems are simple enough that a manager can apply personal experience to solve them, in today's complex world many problems cannot be solved this way. Evaluating each alternative is too difficult or time consuming due to the amount and complexity of the information that must be processed or because the number of alternative solutions is so vast that a manager simply cannot evaluate them all to select an appropriate one.

For example, consider the problem faced by Mark, an MBA graduate who has recently taken a job as a financial analyst with a firm on Wall Street. One of the fringe benefits is a retirement plan in which the employee puts 5% of his/her monthly income. The company matches this amount. Monies in this plan are then invested in two funds: a stock fund and a bond fund. The Benefits Department has asked Mark to specify what fraction of these retirement monies to invest in each fund. Mark has analyzed the historical performance of these funds and has learned that the stock fund has grown at an average annual rate of 10%, whereas the more conservative bond fund had averaged a 6% annual return. To diversify his porfolio and to control the risk—he does not want to put all his eggs in one basket—he has identified two guidelines:

1. Neither of the two funds should have more than 75% of the total investment.
2. The amount invested in the stock fund should not exceed twice that invested in the bond fund.

In this problem, there are many different combinations of investment strategies that can be considered. For example,

- Invest 50% in each fund. Because each dollar invested this way returns $0.05 from the $0.50 invested in the stock fund and $0.03 from the $0.50 invested in the bond fund, this strategy earns a total annual return of 8%.
- Invest 60% in the stock fund and 40% in the bond fund. This strategy earns $0.084 for each dollar invested, which is an annual return of 8.4%.
- Invest 70% in the stock fund and 30% in the bond fund. This strategy earns a larger amount—$0.088 for each dollar invested—but, unfortunately, these percentages violate the foregoing guideline (2). The amount of 70% invested in the stock fund exceeds twice the amount invested in the bond fund.

Deterministic problem
A problem in which all necessary information for obtaining a solution is known with certainty.

In this problem, Mark cannot try each and every combination of investment in an attempt to find the best strategy, as there are simply too many options. (In Chapter 4, you will learn that there are an *infinite* number of possible combinations.) Managers increasingly turn to quantitative methods and computers to arrive at the optimal solution to problems involving a large number of alternatives. The study of these various methods and how managers use them in the decision process is the essence of management science.

Management science techniques apply to the following two basic categories of problems:

Stochastic problem
A problem in which some of the information is not known with certainty.

1. **Deterministic problems**, in which all necessary information for obtaining a solution is known with certainty. In Mark's problem, the expected returns for each of the two funds are known.
2. **Stochastic problems**, in which some of the necessary information is not known with certainty, but rather behaves in a *probabilistic* manner. Mark's problem

becomes stochastic if his objective is to maximize the probability of earning at least 8%. This is because the objective now depends on the probabilistic behavior of the returns of the two funds.

Solving a deterministic problem is similar to deciding which airline ticket to buy for flying from New York to Los Angeles today because you can obtain the exact fares from all airlines. In contrast, consider making the same trip 1 month from now. Deciding whether to buy the best available ticket today or to risk waiting for a better fare is a stochastic problem because you do not know the future airfares. Obtaining solutions to these two groups of decision problems—deterministic and stochastic—often requires very different management science techniques. The first eleven chapters focus on deterministic problems and their solution procedures. Stochastic problems are dealt with in the remaining six chapters.

■ 1.2 THE HISTORY OF MANAGEMENT SCIENCE

The field of management science arose during World War II, when there was a critical need to manage scarce resources. The British Air Force formed the first group to develop quantitative methods for solving these operational problems and named their efforts *operational research*. Soon, the American armed forces formed a similar group, consisting of physical scientists and engineers, five of whom later became Nobel laureates. The efforts of these groups, especially in the area of radar detection, are considered vital in winning the air battle of Britain.

After World War II, managers in industry recognized the value of applying similar techniques to their complex decision problems. Early efforts were devoted to developing appropriate models and corresponding procedures for solving problems arising in such areas as the scheduling of petroleum refineries, distribution of products, production planning, market research, and investment planning. These solution procedures were made possible by the advent of high-speed computers because solving the typical operations research problem requires too many computations to be performed practically by hand. The use of management science techniques has grown with the advances in computing to the point where today these techniques are used routinely on a desktop computer to solve many decision problems.

The remainder of this chapter presents the general steps used in applying management science techniques. The rest of the book describes in more detail the different techniques available for solving deterministic and stochastic problems, including how and when to use these techniques, how to interpret the solutions obtained from the computer, and how to evaluate additional issues a manager should consider regarding each method.

■ 1.3 THE METHODOLOGY OF MANAGEMENT SCIENCE

Using quantitative methods to solve problems generally involves many people throughout the organization. The individuals on a project team provide information from their respective areas about various aspects of the problem. The process of *applying* quantitative methods requires the systematic sequence of steps illustrated in Figure 1.1. Each of these steps is described in detail in this section.

1.3.1 Defining the Problem

The first step is to identify, understand, and describe, in precise terms, the problem the organization faces. In some cases, the problem is well-defined and clear. For example, the problem Mark faces in Section 1.1 is quite well-defined. The overall objective is known, as are the limitations (in terms of the investment guidelines) that must be considered in reaching the decision. Mark has also determined the necessary returns for the two funds.

In other situations, the problem may not be so well-defined and may require much discussion and consensus among the members of the project team. For instance, there may be several objectives that conflict. You may want to maximize customer satisfaction yet also minimize total costs. It is unlikely you can accomplish both goals. Corporate decisions as to an overall objective will have to be made. Sometimes quantifying the objective itself is difficult. For example, how do you measure "customer satisfaction"? All of these issues must be resolved and made clear by consensus of the project team during the problem-definition phase.

1.3.2 Developing a Mathematical Model and Collecting Data

After the problem is clearly defined and understood, the next step is to express the problem in a mathematical form—that is, to *formulate a mathematical model*. Once

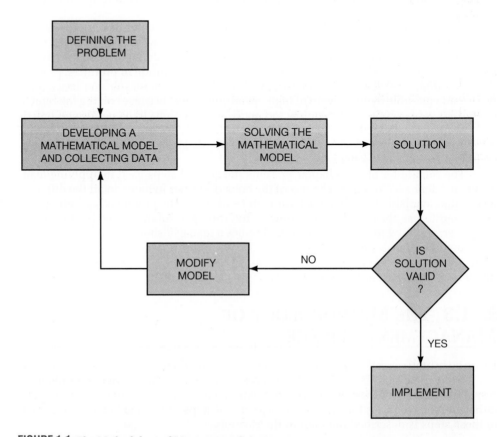

FIGURE 1.1 The Methodology of Management Science.

the model is built, there are many mathematical techniques available for obtaining the best solution, in spite of the vast number of alternatives and/or the complexity involved. To illustrate this formulation process for Mark's deterministic problem, recall that he wants to determine the fraction of his retirement monies to invest in each of the stock and bond funds. To state the problem mathematically, begin by defining two **decision variables**, often simply called **variables** (whose values are not yet known), as follows:

$$S = \text{the fraction to invest in the stock fund}$$

$$B = \text{the fraction to invest in the bond fund}$$

These decision variables are also called **controllable variables** because you have some control over their values. For this problem, you want to choose values for these variables that

1. Maximize the expected annual return.
2. Satisfy all the investment guidelines.

For specific values of S and B, you can express the expected annual return in a mathematical formula. Recall that each dollar invested in the stock fund is expected to return $0.10 and each dollar invested in the bond fund is expected to return $0.06. Hence, a fraction S of a dollar invested in the stock fund is expected to return $0.10 * S$, and a fraction B of a dollar invested in the bond fund is expected to return $0.06 * B$. Thus, the **objective function**—that is, the overall objective expressed in a mathematical form—is to choose values for S and B to

$$\text{Maximize} \quad 0.10S + 0.06B$$

Due to the investment guidelines, you cannot choose "arbitrary" values for these variables. Each guideline gives rise to a **constraint**, which you can also describe by a mathematical formula. The first guideline requires that no one fund has more than 75% of the total amount invested. Therefore, the fractions S and B must each be less than or equal to 0.75. Thus, the upper limits on these two fractions are expressed mathematically as the following two constraints:

$$S \leq 0.75 \quad \text{(upper limit on stock fund)}$$

$$B \leq 0.75 \quad \text{(upper limit on bond fund)}$$

Another constraint is also needed for the second investment guideline. The fraction S invested in the stock fund should not exceed twice the fraction B invested in the bond fund. The corresponding mathematical constraint is

$$S \leq 2B$$

or

$$S - 2B \leq 0 \quad \text{(portfolio-mix constraint)}$$

Finally, each fraction must be nonnegative. This implicit constraint is made explicit in the mathematical model by writing

$$S, \ B \geq 0$$

Decision variable/
Variable/
Controllable variable
A quantity whose value you can control and need to determine in order to solve a decision problem.

Objective function
The overall objective of a decision problem expressed in a mathematical form in terms of the data and the decision variables.

Constraint
A restriction on the values of variables in a mathematical model typically imposed by outside limitations.

By putting together all the pieces, the mathematical model developed so far for this problem is to choose values for the variables S and B so as to

Linear Program
Mark_1.DAT

$$
\begin{array}{llll}
\text{Maximize} & 0.10S + 0.06B & & \\
\text{Subject to} & S & \leq 0.75 & \text{(upper limit on stock fund)} \\
& B \leq 0.75 & & \text{(upper limit on bond fund)} \\
& S - 2B \leq & 0 & \text{(portfolio-mix constraint)} \\
& S \,, \quad B \geq & 0 &
\end{array}
$$

Observe that the objective function and constraints are expressed in terms of the decision variables and other known information. This "other known information" is called **data**. In this case, the data consist of the known annual returns for the two funds and the upper and lower limits on the amounts to invest in each fund. In contrast to the decision variables, whose values you *can* control, you *cannot* control the values of the data. For this reason, the data are often called **uncontrollable parameters**.

Data/Uncontrollable parameter
Known information in a decision problem that you cannot control but that you can use to determine the solution.

For Mark's problem, all the data were provided when the problem was stated, but in most real-world problems, this is not so. Only some data may be identified during problem definition. The need for additional data may be discovered only as problem formulation progresses. Once the data items are identified, you must determine their specific values. In some cases, you may need to use estimates because the exact values are not readily available. Furthermore, obtaining these values can sometimes be more time consuming than developing the model. Keep in mind that the quality of the solution you eventually obtain is only as good as the accuracy of the data.

1.3.3   *Solving the Mathematical Model*

Once a mathematical model of the problem has been formulated, the next step is to *solve* the model—that is, to obtain numerical values for the decision variable. For the investment example, this means obtaining the best values for S and B. How these values are obtained depends on the specific form, or type, of the mathematical model. That is, once you identify what *type* of model you have, you will be able to choose an appropriate management science technique for solving it. These techniques fall into one of two categories:

Optimal method
A method used in management science that yields the best possible values for the decision variables.

1. **Optimal methods**, which yield the best values for the decision variables—that is, those values that simultaneously satisfy all of the constraints and provide the best value for the objective function.
2. **Heuristic methods**, which yield values for the variables that satisfy all the constraints. Although not necessarily optimal, these values provide an acceptable value for the objective function.

Heuristic method
A method used in management science that provides acceptable (though not necessarily optimal) values for the decision variables.

In contrast to the optimal methods, the heuristic methods are computationally more efficient and therefore are used when obtaining optimal solutions is either too time consuming or impossible because the model is too complex.

One objective of this book is to show many different mathematical models and their associated solution procedures. Most of the time, these procedures will be available on a computer, and you will learn how to obtain and interpret the solutions to the model. In fact, using the procedure discussed in Chapter 4, the solution to Mark's investment model in Section 1.3.2 is

$$S = 0.75$$

$$B = 0.75$$

leading to an expected annual return of $0.10S + 0.06B = (0.10 * 0.75) + (0.06 * 0.75) = 0.12$. That is, each dollar invested is expected to return \$0.12. However, you can see that this solution does not make sense because it is impossible to invest 75% in *both* of these funds. The source of this error is identified and corrected in the following section.

1.3.4 Validating, Implementing, and Monitoring the Solution

After solving the mathematical model, it is extremely important to **validate the solution**—that is, to review the solution carefully to see that the values make sense and that the resulting decisions can be implemented. Some of the reasons for doing so are:

1. The mathematical model may not have captured all the limitations of the real problem.
2. Certain aspects of the problem may have been overlooked, deliberately omitted, or simplified.
3. The data may have been incorrectly estimated or recorded, perhaps when entered into the computer.

Validation of the solution The process of reviewing a solution to a mathematical model to ensure that the values make sense and that the resulting decisions can be implemented.

For example, in validating the solution of $S = 0.75$ and $B = 0.75$ for Mark's invesment model, you can see that these values do not make sense. He cannot invest 75% in both funds. In this case, the error is caused by the omission of a constraint to ensure that the fractions S and B add up to 1, that is:

$$S + B = 1.0$$

This constraint means simply that the amount invested in stocks and the amount invested in bonds must add up to the total amount invested. In general, if the solution cannot be implemented, either modify the model to reflect more accurately the limitations of the real problem (and obtain a new solution) or use your experience and judgement to modify the solution provided by the model.

It is also important to realize that even though the model and solution may be valid, you might still be unable to implement a decision based on your results. There may be behavioral or political implications that cannot be included in the model. For example, the result of a model may indicate that it is most cost effective to transfer some workers from the day shift to the night shift. However, such a change may face resistance from employees (or managers) for personal, political, or other reasons. One way to avoid this type of difficulty is to include representatives of all potentially affected groups as a part of the project team.

The results and subsequent implementation must be monitored carefully, not only to ensure that the solution works as planned, but also because the problem and/or data may change over time. For example, the expected returns of the two funds in Mark's investment problem may change at some future point, thus necessitating a change in the model, which in turn may lead to a change in the solution.

1.3.5 Modifying the Model

If during the validation step, you find that the solution cannot be implemented, you may identify constraints that were omitted during the original problem formulation or you may find that some of the original constraints were incorrect and need to be modified. In these cases, you should return to the problem-formulation step and carefully make the appropriate modifications to reflect more accurately the real problem. For example, adding the constraint that the fractions sum to 1 to Mark's original investment model results in the following revised model:

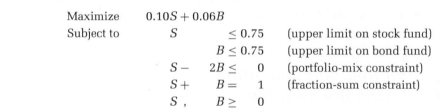

Linear Program
Mark_2.DAT

$$
\begin{array}{lrcll}
\text{Maximize} & 0.10S + 0.06B & & & \\
\text{Subject to} & S & \leq & 0.75 & \text{(upper limit on stock fund)} \\
& B \leq & 0.75 & & \text{(upper limit on bond fund)} \\
& S - 2B \leq & 0 & & \text{(portfolio-mix constraint)} \\
& S + B = & 1 & & \text{(fraction-sum constraint)} \\
& S\,, \quad B \geq & 0 & &
\end{array}
$$

The solution to this new model (obtained by the procedure presented in Chapter 4) is

$$S = 0.6667$$

$$B = 0.3333$$

In other words, it is optimal for Mark to invest two-thirds of his monies in the stock funds and one-third in the bond fund, leading to an expected return of $0.10S + 0.06B = (0.10 * 0.6667) + (0.06 * 0.3333) = 0.08667$. That is, each dollar invested is expected to return \$0.08667.

This process of modifying a model, obtaining the new solution, and validating it may have to be repeated several times before an acceptable and implementable solution is found (see Figure 1.1).

■ 1.4 USES AND ADVANTAGES OF MANAGEMENT SCIENCE MODELS

You have seen how a mathematical model helped Mark reach a decision. In general, mathematical models help managers make two types of decisions: strategic and operational. **Strategic decisions,** generally one-time decisions, have an affect over relatively long time spans. Consider the following decisions you may have to make as a manager:

Strategic decision
A one-time decision involving policies that have long-term consequences for the organization.

- Should an existing system be replaced with a recently proposed new system? For example, should you convert one of three toll booths to an express lane for cars with two or more passengers? As another example, should you open a new production facility?
- Should you change your management policy? For example, should you reorder inventory at regular time intervals rather than when the level drops below some specified amount?

Because the models you build to reach strategic decisions are generally used to make just the one long-term determination, you should not be overly concerned with how much computational effort is needed to obtain the solution. Strategic decisions will most likely have a major impact on the organization, so you should devote most of your efforts to ensuring that the model is valid, that it includes all important aspects of the problem, and that the data are as accurate as possible.

Operational decision
A decision involving short-term planning issues that must generally be made repeatedly.

Operational decisions, conversely, affect ongoing processes over shorter time spans. Consider the following operational decisions you may have to make regularly:

- How can the business most efficiently schedule the work force on a weekly basis?
- What is the optimal monthly production plan?

- What is the most cost-effective shipping plan for distributing products from plants to retail outlets?

In contrast to models for strategic planning, models for operational decisions are used repeatedly. It is therefore worthwhile spending extra time and effort in identifying or developing the most efficient solution procedures, as doing so can result in significant savings in computational costs over time.

Regardless of whether a strategic or operational decision is needed, mathematical models provide the following benefits to managers:

1. A method of determining the best way to accomplish an objective, such as allocating scarce resources.
2. A way to evaluate the impact of a proposed change or a new system without the expense and time of implementing it first.
3. A way to evaluate the *robustness* of the optimal solution by asking **sensitivity questions** of the form "What happens if · · ·?" For example, what happens to Mark's optimal investment plan and annual return if the stock fund is expected to yield only 8% (instead of the original 10%)?
4. A procedure for achieving an objective that benefits the overall organization by including in the model considerations from many different parts of the organization.

Sensitivity question
A question pertaining to how changes in the data of a mathematical model affect the optimal solution.

SUMMARY

The general steps involved in applying management science techniques to solve deterministic and stochastic decision problems are as follows:

1. Defining the problem—by identifying and understanding the problem so you can express it precisely.
2. Developing a mathematical model—often by identifying decision variables, an overall mathematical objective, and constraints.
3. Solving the model—by using an appropriate management science technique.
4. Validating the solution—by using intuition and experience to determine if the solution obtained from the model makes sense and can realistically be implemented. If not, you may need to modify the model appropriately and obtain the new solution.
5. Implementing and monitoring the solution—if unanticipated results are encountered, or if the data change, you will need to modify the model accordingly and validate the new solution.

Now that you know the basic ideas behind the methodology of management science, Chapter 2 provides you with systematic techniques for formulating mathematical models of deterministic problems.

LAUNCHING INTO MANAGEMENT SCIENCE

NASA's greatest mission in the 1960s was to get an astronaut to the Moon and back again safely. This video looks at the enormously complex task that faced the managers of NASA's Apollo project.

Relying on guess work or seat-of-the-pants approaches would not get Apollo off the ground, so NASA plugged into management science to provide the systematic mathematical analysis needed to coordinate this national space effort. NASA needed to take advantage of optimization, the important aspect of management science that leads to finding the best method, the lowest cost, the fastest route, or the most efficient design.

The Apollo project was immense, and to make it succeed meant breaking it down into thousands of manageable pieces, finding the right people and putting them in the right configuration, and coordinating their work so that they functioned without duplication or oversight. Team meetings were a big part of harmonizing these many components and keeping the lines of communication open. Managers used these lines to focus team members on the critical factors—those activities that, if delayed, might delay the entire project—while giving a back seat to those activities that did not have as strong an impact on the schedule.

Team meetings also offered people the chance to pool their talents and tackle a problem together. With several team members offering their perspective on a problem, a solution that might have been overlooked by an individual working alone was more likely to be found.

Along the way, NASA also learned from its mistakes. It gained a large deal of knowledge from the careful analysis of its failures. For example, by studying pieces of rockets that blew up, NASA scientists were able to determine design flaws and suggest improvements, always with an eye on the schedule.

In July 1969, Neil Armstrong stepped out of the *Apollo* 11 landing capsule and onto the Moon. Beyond the physics and the engineering, NASA's reliance on the "hidden" science—management science—to guide the Apollo project's course had paid off. (Total running time is 6:34.)

Questions on the Video

1. What goals and constraints can you identify in NASA's Moon-landing mission? What was the directive from President Kennedy and the Congress?

2. In what way is management science "hidden"? What makes management science different from, say, chemistry, physics, and engineering?

Beyond the Video

1. NASA relied on mathematical tools in directing the Apollo project. How might you direct your investments in the stock market? Contrast an investment strategy based on data analysis, forecasting, and other mathematical tools with a strategy based on hunches and guesses.

2. How does a problem in management science differ from a math homework problem?

Practical Considerations

1. What did you learn from the video about trial and error and problem solving?

2. What did you learn about working in teams?

Source: "For all Practical Purposes," from *The Consortium for Mathematics and Its Applications* (Arlington, MA: 1986), Program 1.

2

THE ART AND SCIENCE OF BUILDING DETERMINISTIC MODELS

. . . .

*H*ow does Case Chemicals determine the mix of products that maximizes profits? How does Cosmic Computer Company figure out the least expensive plan for transporting its microcomputers to retailers while satisfying customer demand? How does Hexxon Oil decide on the shipping network that maximizes the flow of its oil to its storage tanks in Philadelpia? To make the best-informed business decision, you must know how to ask the right question and how to formulate the problem correctly.

In this chapter you will learn how to build the mathematical models that will lead you to the answers to these and other questions.

In the previous chapter, you learned that among the most important steps in problem solving are to identify and then to formulate the decision problem in a mathematical framework. Model building is an art that improves with practice. However, in an effort to make the process more systematic, several problem-formulation techniques are illustrated with numerous examples in this chapter. By applying these techniques, you can formulate not only the problems in this book, but also many others you might encounter in practice.

After correctly formulating a mathematical model, you will want to *solve* it—that is, obtain a solution. Because the solution procedure depends on the specific mathematical characteristics of a model, choosing the appropriate technique means you must identify what characteristics *your* model possesses. This chapter helps you identify these mathematical characteristics and how they are used to classify models. Subsequent chapters deal with the various solution procedures, what classes of problems they can be applied to, and how to interpret and implement the solutions obtained from a computer.

■ 2.1 GENERAL STEPS AND TECHNIQUES OF BUILDING MATHEMATICAL MODELS

In Chapter 1, you learned that the first step in using management science techniques is to identify and describe the problem. The next step is to formulate the problem in a mathematical framework. This section provides systematic steps and techniques that you can apply in formulating your own deterministic models. To illustrate, consider the problem faced by the Production Manager of Case Chemicals.

EXAMPLE 2.1 THE PRODUCTION-PLANNING PROBLEM OF CASE CHEMICALS Case Chemicals produces two solvents, CS-01 and CS-02, at its Cleveland plant. The businesses that buy these solvents use them to dissolve certain toxic substances that arise during particular manufacturing processes. The plant operates 40 hours per week and employs five full-time and two part-time workers, who work 15 hours per week. These people run the seven machines that blend certain chemicals to produce each solvent. The products leave the Blending Department to be refined in the Purification Department, which currently has seven purifiers and employs six full-time workers and one part-time worker, who puts in 10 hours per week.

Case Chemicals has a nearly unlimited supply of the raw materials it needs to produce the two solvents. Case Chemicals can sell any amount of CS-01, but the demand for the more specialized product CS-02 is limited to at most 120,000 gallons per week. As Production Manager, you want to determine the optimal weekly production plan for Case Chemicals. How much of each solvent should Case Chemicals produce to maximize profit? ■

Problem formulation
The process of converting the qualitative description of a problem into mathematical form.

The objective now is to convert this qualitative description of the problem into a mathematical form that can then be solved. This process is called **problem formulation** and generally involves four steps, each of which is described in the following sections.

2.1.1 *Identifying the Decision Variables*

The first step in problem formulation is to identify the decision variables, often simply called *variables*. The values of these variables, once determined, provide the solution to the problem. For Example 2.1, you can identify the decision variables by asking yourself what information you need to provide the production staff—the Blending and Purification departments—so they will know how to proceed. Your answer to this question should be

1. The number of thousands of gallons of CS-01 to produce each week.
2. The number of thousands of gallons of CS-02 to produce each week.

Because the values of these items are not yet known, each decision variable is given a **symbolic name**. You may choose whatever symbolic name you like, but you will find it helpful to select a symbolic name that reminds you of the quantity that the decision variable represents. For the current example, you might create the following variables, corresponding to the two items identified before:

Symbolic name
A descriptive name given to a variable in a mathematical model that aids in understanding the meaning of the variable.

$$CS_1 = \text{the number of thousands of gallons of CS-01 to produce each week}$$

$$CS_2 = \text{the number of thousands of gallons of CS-02 to produce each week}$$

Note that these descriptions are *precise*. They include the *units* associated with the quantities the variables represent (thousands of gallons, in this case). It is not sufficient to define a variable as the "amount" of an item, because to others who read your formulation, the term "amount" can have various meanings (for example, thousands of liters in this instance).

The need to identify the decision variables correctly is critical. Otherwise, formulating a valid model that captures all aspects of the problem is impossible. The choice for these variables is not unique, and there are no fixed rules. However, the following guidelines are useful in identifying a proper set of decision variables *for virtually any problem*.

KEY FEATURES
General Guidelines for Identifying Decision Variables

✔ What items affect costs and/or profits (or, in general, the overall objective)?
✔ What items are you free to choose and/or have some control over?
✔ What decisions do you have to make?
✔ What values, once determined, constitute a solution to the problem? Put yourself in the position of someone who has to implement your solution, and then ask yourself what information is needed.

For Example 2.1, the answers to all of these questions are the same and lead you to identify as the decision variables the number of thousands of gallons of CS-01 and CS-02 to produce each week.

2.1.2 Identifying the Problem Data

The ultimate aim of solving a problem is to provide the actual values for the decision variables you have identified. You need to know certain information to help determine those values. For instance, to determine the actual amounts of the two solvents to produce so as to maximize the corporate profits, you will need to know:

1. The number of hours of labor available in the Blending Department.
2. The number of hours of labor available in the Purification Department.
3. The amount of profit obtained from producing and selling each type of solvent.

These quantities constitute the problem data. In deterministic problems, these values must be known (or attainable) at the time the problem is formulated. For Case Chemicals:

1. As stated in the problem description, the Blending Department has five full-time workers (at 40 hours each) and two part-time workers (at 15 hours each). This is a total of 230 hours of labor per week in the Blending Department.
2. Similarly, the six full-time workers (at 40 hours each) and one part-time worker (at 10 hours) provide a total of 250 hours of labor per week in the Purification Department.
3. The Accounting Department estimates a profit margin of $0.30 per gallon for CS-01 and $0.50 per gallon for CS-02—that is, $300 per thousand gallons of CS-01 and $500 per thousand gallons of CS-02.

In contrast to the decision variables, whose values you *can* control, you *cannot directly control the values of the data.*

KEY FEATURES

The need for some of the problem data may be clear when you specify the problem. Other data may become necessary as you develop the mathematical model and discover that additional information is needed to help determine the values of the decision variables.

2.1.3 Identifying the Objective Function

The next step in problem formulation is expressing the overall organizational objective in a mathematical form using the decision variables and known problem data. This expression, the *objective function,* is usually created in three stages.

1. State the objective in verbal form. For Example 2.1, this objective is

   Maximize the total weekly profit from the production of CS-01 and CS-02

Decomposition
The breaking up of an objective function into the sum, difference, or product of individual quantities.

2. Where appropriate, **decompose** the objective into a sum, difference, or product of individual quantities. For Example 2.1, the total profit can be computed as the sum of the profit from CS-01 and that from CS-02:

   Maximize Profit = (profit from CS-01) + (profit from CS-02)

3. Express the individual quantities mathematically using the decision variables and other known data in the problem.

Working through a specific example
The technique of using specific values for the variables to determine how the objective function is computed.

To accomplish the task in the third stage, it is often useful to choose some specific values for the decision variables and then use those values to determine how the objective function is computed. This technique is referred to as **working through a specific example**. In Example 2.1, suppose that 10 thousand gallons of CS-01 and 20 thousand gallons of CS-02 are produced (so $CS_1 = 10$ and $CS_2 = 20$). The Accounting Department has told you that each thousand gallons of CS-01 contributes $300 to profit and each thousand gallons of CS-02 contributes $500. You can write:

$$\begin{array}{ll} \text{Profit from CS-01} = 300\,(10) = \$\ 3{,}000 \\ + \text{Profit from CS-02} = 500\,(20) = \$10{,}000 \\ \hline \text{Total profit} \qquad\qquad\qquad = \$13{,}000 \end{array}$$

However, the purpose of using specific values for the variables is *not* to obtain the total profit for these values, but rather to help you determine *how* to compute the objective when the values of the variables are not explicitly known. In this problem, you can easily see from the foregoing computations that if CS_1 is the unspecified number of thousands of gallons of CS-01 and CS_2 is the unspecified number of thousands of gallons of CS-02 to produce, then the profit is

$$\begin{array}{ll} \text{Profit from CS-01} = 300CS_1 \\ + \text{Profit from CS-02} = 500CS_2 \\ \hline \text{Total profit} \qquad\quad = 300CS_1 + 500CS_2 \end{array}$$

Thus, the mathematical objective function expressed in terms of the decision variables and the problem data is

$$\text{Maximize} \qquad 300CS_1 + 500CS_2$$

KEY FEATURES

This problem illustrates the following key features:

✔ Creating the objective function by:
  a. Stating the objective in a verbal form.
  b. Where appropriate, decomposing the objective into a sum, difference, and/or product of individual terms.
  c. Expressing the individual terms in (b) using the decision variables and other known problem data.

✔ Working through a specific example to determine how the objective function is expressed in a mathematical form, by choosing specific values for the decision variables and making the necessary computations.

2.1.4 *Identifying the Constraints*

Your objective is to maximize profit. The objective function tells you that the larger the value of the variables, the larger the profit. But the real world puts a limit on what values you can assign these variables. In Example 2.1, the Blending and Purification Departments have certain physical limitations—a limited number of hours of labor available in each. These limitations, as well as any other considerations that impose restrictions on the values of the variables, are the *constraints*. The final step in problem formulation is to identify these constraints and write them in mathematical form.

The constraints are conditions that the decision variables must satisfy to constitute an "acceptable" solution. These constraints typically arise from:

1. Physical limitations (the limited number of hours of labor in the Blending and Purification Departments, for example).
2. Management-imposed restrictions (for example, management may have promised a certain amount of a product to a valued customer).

3. External restrictions (for example, Case Chemicals cannot sell more than 120 thousand gallons of CS-02 per week, and there is no reason to produce more than the amount demanded).

4. Implied relationships between variables (for example, in Mark's investment problem in Section 1.1, the two fractions representing the proportion of monies to invest in the two funds must add up to 1).

5. Logical restrictions on individual variables (for example, the number of cars produced must be a whole number, and Case Chemicals cannot produce a negative amount of solvents).

➡ **KEY FEATURES**

After identifying these constraints, you must express them in mathematical form using the decision variables and other problem data. This process is identical to the one used for specifying the objective function:

✔ Express the constraints in verbal form.
✔ When appropriate, decompose the constraint into a sum, difference, and/or product of individual quantities.
✔ By working through a specific example, express the individual quantities mathematically using the decision variables and other known problem data.

Consider the constraints in Example 2.1.

LABOR CONSTRAINT IN THE BLENDING DEPARTMENT (PHYSICAL LIMITATION)

Verbal form: Total hours used in blending   cannot exceed   230

Decomposition: $\begin{pmatrix} \text{Hours} \\ \text{used} \\ \text{for CS-01} \end{pmatrix} + \begin{pmatrix} \text{Hours} \\ \text{used} \\ \text{for CS-02} \end{pmatrix}$ cannot exceed   230 hours

Mathematics: To express the hours used for CS-01 and CS-02 in the Blending Department, try working through a specific example. For instance, suppose $CS_1 = 15$ thousand and $CS_2 = 10$ thousand gallons. How do you compute the number of hours used in the Blending Department? You need some *additional* information. In particular, you need to know how many hours each thousand gallons of CS-01 and CS-02 require in the Blending Department. These values are problem data (in addition to the data already identified in Section 2.1.2) that you must obtain. Suppose you call the Process Department and gather the following data for the Blending and Purification Departments:

	HOURS PER THOUSAND GALLONS OF	
	CS-01	CS-02
Blending	2	1
Purification	1	2

It is then easy to calculate the hours used in the Blending Department by working through the specific values of $CS_1 = 15$ and $CS_2 = 10$:

$$
\begin{array}{lll}
\text{Hours for 15 thousand gallons of CS-01} & = 2(15) & = 30 \\
+\text{Hours for 10 thousand gallons of CS-02} & = 1(10) & = 10 \\
\hline
\text{Total hours used in blending} & = 2(15) + 1(10) & = 40
\end{array}
$$

The purpose of using this specific numerical example is to help you write a *general* mathematical constraint when the values of the variables (CS_1 and CS_2, in this case) are not known. From the foregoing calculations, you obtain the following general mathematical constraint:

$$2CS_1 + 1CS_2 \leq 230$$

LABOR CONSTRAINT IN THE PURIFICATION DEPARTMENT (PHYSICAL LIMITATION)

Verbal form: Total hours in purification   cannot exceed   250

Decomposition:
$$\begin{pmatrix} \text{Hours} \\ \text{used} \\ \text{for CS-01} \end{pmatrix} + \begin{pmatrix} \text{Hours} \\ \text{used} \\ \text{for CS-02} \end{pmatrix} \quad \text{cannot exceed} \quad 250$$

Mathematics: $1CS_1$ $+$ $2CS_2$ $\leq$ $250.$

BOUND CONSTRAINT (EXTERNAL RESTRICTION)

The restriction that at most 120 thousand gallons of CS-02 can be sold gives rise to the following constraint on the value of CS_2:

$$CS_2 \leq 120$$

NONNEGATIVITY CONSTRAINT (LOGICAL RESTRICTIONS)

Of course, you know that the values of these decision variables must be nonnegative— that is, zero or positive. Such *implicit* constraints that *you* are aware of must be made *explicit* in the mathematical formulation. For this problem, you should include the following constraints:

$$CS_1 \geq 0 \quad \text{and} \quad CS_2 \geq 0 \qquad \text{or } CS_1,\ CS_2 \geq 0$$

By putting together all the pieces from the previous steps, the complete mathematical formulation of the production-planning problem of Case Chemicals is as follows.

MATHEMATICAL FORMULATION FOR THE PROBLEM OF CASE CHEMICALS

$$
\begin{array}{llll}
\text{Maximize} & 300CS_1 + 500CS_2 & & \text{(profit)} \\
\text{Subject to} & 2CS_1 + 1CS_2 \leq 230 & & \text{(blending)} \\
& 1CS_1 + 2CS_2 \leq 250 & & \text{(purification)} \\
& CS_2 \leq 120 & & \text{(bound on CS-02)} \\
& CS_1, CS_2 \geq 0 & & \text{(nonnegativity)}
\end{array}
$$

Linear Program
EX2_1.DAT

where

$$CS_1 = \text{the number of thousands of gallons of CS-01 to produce each week}$$

$$CS_2 = \text{the number of thousands of gallons of CS-02 to produce each week}$$

You will learn the solution procedure for this type of problem in Chapter 4. Applying that procedure results in the optimal solution:

$$CS_1 = 70$$

$$CS_2 = 90$$

That is, the optimal production plan is 70,000 gallons of CS-01 and 90,000 gallons of CS-02, resulting in a weekly profit of $66,000.

In this section, you have learned the steps to take in formulating problems by identifying (1) the decision variables, (2) the problem data, (3) the objective function, and (4) the constraints. To write the objective function and the constraints in a mathematical form, use the variables together with the problem data that you have as you formulate the model. You may not know all the data needed when you first define the problem. The need for additional data may be discovered as you proceed with the problem formulation. These data values must be obtained from appropriate sources within the organization. To save time and space, future problem statements in this book will include all necessary data. The formulation will consist of these three steps:

Step 1. *Identifying* the decision variables.
Step 2. *Identifying* the objective function.
Step 3. *Identifying* the constraints.

The problem in this section involves only two decision variables and a few constraints. Problems of practical importance often contain hundreds or thousands of variables and a similar number of constraints. These more complex problems can also be formulated using the steps you learned in this section.

■ 2.2 ADDITIONAL EXAMPLES OF PROBLEM FORMULATION

Schematic diagram
A drawing used to represent the various components of a problem.

Network problem
A problem that can be represented by circles and arrows connecting them.

In this section, the steps of formulation you learned in Section 2.1 are applied to problems of varying complexity. You will also learn new techniques helpful in identifying the variables, the data, the objective function, and the constraints. For example, one such technique is to draw a **schematic diagram** to represent the various components of the problem. One advantage of doing so is that the most important aspect of these problems can be conveyed with a single picture. One class of problems for which schematic diagrams are particularly helpful are called **network problems**, which can involve the distribution of goods, as illustrated in Sections 2.2.1 and 2.2.2.

2.2.1 *Examples of Network Problems: The Transportation Problem*

Among the many problems a production business faces is determining the best shipping plan for distributing finished goods from the production facilities (factories and plants) to the distribution outlets (customers and retail stores). For instance, how does an oil company best move gasoline from its refineries to its gas stations? The business must develop a *shipping plan* (or a *distribution schedule*) stating the number (or amount) of finished products to ship from each production facility to each distribution outlet. These shipments cannot exceed the available capacities or *supplies* of the production facilities and must also meet all customer *demands*. Often, the best schedule minimizes the total transportation costs. Developing this schedule is called the **transportation problem**.

It is necessary to identify certain information—problem data—to develop the schedule:

1. customer demands
2. plant capacities
3. shipping costs from each plant to each customer

Consider the following problem faced by CCC, the Cosmic Computer Company.

EXAMPLE 2.2 THE DISTRIBUTION PROBLEM OF THE COSMIC COMPUTER COMPANY CCC has three microcomputer assembly plants located in San Francisco, Los Angeles, and Phoenix. The plant in Los Angeles has a monthly production capacity of 2000 units. Each of the plants in San Francisco and Phoenix can turn out a maximum of 1700 units per month. The CCC microcomputers are sold through four retail stores, located in San Diego, Barstow, Tucson, and Dallas. The monthly orders from the retailers are 1700 units in San Diego, 1000 in Barstow, 1500 in Tucson, and 1200 in Dallas. Table 2.1 contains the cost of shipping one microcomputer from each assembly plant to each of the different retail stores. Your job is to formulate a mathematical model for finding the least-cost shipping schedule. ■

TABLE 2.1 *Shipping Costs ($/Unit)*

	STORES			
PLANTS	SAN DIEGO	BARSTOW	TUCSON	DALLAS
San Francisco	5	3	2	6
Los Angeles	4	7	8	10
Phoenix	6	5	3	8

Before formulating this problem mathematically, it is possible to draw a schematic *network diagram* to represent the various components of the problem, as illustrated in Figure 2.1. The seven circles, or **nodes**, represent the three plants and the four retail stores. Each arrow, or **arc**, connects a node corresponding to a plant to a node corresponding to a retail store. The arc indicates that computers can be shipped from that plant to the associated retail store.

In addition to the nodes and arcs, the network diagram includes the problem data. In this case, the numbers next to the nodes corresponding to the plants in Figure 2.1 indicate the production capacities. The numbers next to the nodes corresponding to the retail stores indicate the number of computers requested there. Finally, the numbers next to each arc represent the cost of shipping one computer from the corresponding plant to the associated retail store. All the important aspects of this problem are included in this network diagram, and, as you will see, the diagram simplifies the mathematical formulation that follows.

STEP 1. IDENTIFYING THE DECISION VARIABLES

Following the steps of problem formulation, your first task is to identify the decision variables. To do so, ask yourself these questions:

Transportation problem
The problem of determining the least-cost plan for shipping goods from production facilities to distribution outlets.

Node
A circle in a network diagram that represents an important aspect of a problem, such as the source and destination for goods in a transportation problem.
Arc A line connecting two nodes in a schematic diagram that represents a relationship between those two nodes, such as a possible route for the shipment of goods in a transportation problem.

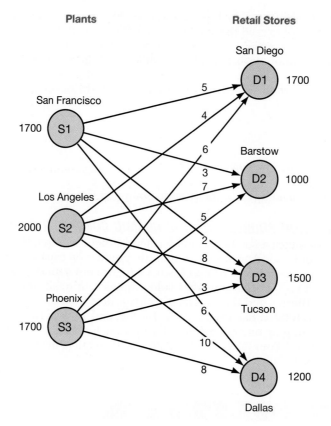

FIGURE 2.1 The Distribution Network of CCC.

1. What items affect costs and/or profits?
2. What items are you free to choose and/or control?
3. What decisions do you have to make?
4. What are the items whose values, when known, constitute a solution (in this case, a shipping schedule)? In other words, what information would you have to provide to the assembly plants so that they would know how to distribute their products?

The answers to all these questions may lead you to identify twelve decision variables, corresponding to the number of microcomputers to ship from each of the three assembly plants to each of the four retail stores. You could refer to them with symbolic names $x_1, x_2, \ldots, x_{12}$. But recall that in working with variables, it is helpful to use a symbolic name that in some way reminds you of the quantity being represented. For example, you could define:

San/Tuc = the number of microcomputers to ship from the assembly plant
in San Francisco to the retail store in Tucson

or

x_{13} = the number of microcomputers to ship from assembly plant #1
(San Francisco) to retail store #3 (Tucson)

or

x_{ST} = the number of microcomputers to ship from the assembly plant
in San Francisco to the retail store in Tucson.

TABLE 2.2 *Decision Variables for Example 2.2*

PLANTS	STORES			
	SAN DIEGO	BARSTOW	TUCSON	DALLAS
San Francisco	x_{SS}	x_{SB}	x_{ST}	x_{SD}
Los Angeles	x_{LS}	x_{LB}	x_{LT}	x_{LD}
Phoenix	x_{PS}	x_{PB}	x_{PT}	x_{PD}

For this example, the last notation is used. The twelve symbolic names are summarized in Table 2.2. In terms of the network diagram in Figure 2.1, each of these decision variables denotes the number of computers to ship along the corresponding arc, as illustrated in Figure 2.2.

STEP 2. IDENTIFYING THE OBJECTIVE FUNCTION

Recalling the procedure used in Section 2.1, you can specify the objective function as follows:

Verbal form: Minimize   total shipping costs from all plants to all stores

Decomposition: Minimize $\begin{pmatrix} \text{Shipping cost} \\ \text{from SF} \end{pmatrix} + \begin{pmatrix} \text{Shipping cost} \\ \text{from LA} \end{pmatrix} + \begin{pmatrix} \text{Shipping cost} \\ \text{from Phoenix} \end{pmatrix}$

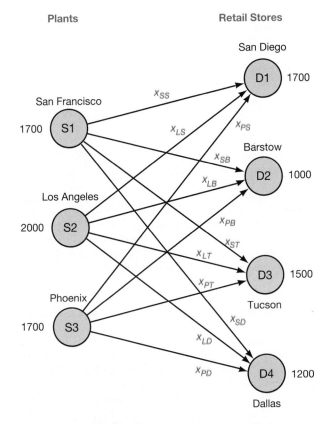

FIGURE 2.2 Decision Variables for the Distribution Problem of CCC.

SPECIFIC EXAMPLE. To obtain a mathematical expression for each of these three shipping costs, work through a specific example. Suppose that the San Francisco plant ships 500 microcomputers to San Diego, 200 to Barstow, 400 to Tucson, and 300 to Dallas. That is, $x_{SS} = 500$, $x_{SB} = 200$, $x_{ST} = 400$, and $x_{SD} = 300$. Recalling the per-unit transportation costs given in Table 2.1,

$$\text{Shipping cost from SF} = 5(500) + 3(200) + 2(400) + 6(300) = 5700$$

In general, when x_{SS}, x_{SB}, x_{ST}, and x_{SD} units are shipped from San Francisco,

$$\text{Shipping cost from SF} = 5x_{SS} + 3x_{SB} + 2x_{ST} + 6x_{SD}$$

Proceeding similarly for the transportation cost from Los Angeles and from Phoenix leads to the following total transportation cost.

MATHEMATICS

$$\text{Minimize } (5x_{SS} + 3x_{SB} + 2x_{ST} + 6x_{SD}) +$$
$$(4x_{LS} + 7x_{LB} + 8x_{LT} + 10x_{LD}) +$$
$$(6x_{PS} + 5x_{PB} + 3x_{PT} + 8x_{PD})$$

STEP 3. IDENTIFYING THE CONSTRAINTS

To identify the constraints, ask yourself the following questions:

1. What prevents you from choosing arbitrary values for the variables? (Looking at the given objective function, you can minimize the cost by setting each variable to zero. What prevents you from doing so?)
2. What physical or logical restrictions are needed so that the values of the variables constitute an acceptable solution?

To answer both these questions, look at Figure 2.2, which should lead you to identify the following *groups* of constraints:

1. The total shipment from each plant should not exceed its capacity. These constraints are associated with each node corresponding to a plant in Figure 2.2.
2. The total shipment received by each retail store should satisfy its demand. These constraints are associated with each node corresponding to a retail store and its demand in Figure 2.2. In this example, "satisfy" will mean "exactly equal to." However, in some situations, it may mean "at least equal to." Whenever such ambiguities may arise, be sure to clarify them before formulating the problem.
3. The shipment from each plant to each retail store should be a nonnegative whole number, often called a nonnegative **integer**, because you cannot ship part of a computer.

Integer
A whole number.

Note that the first two groups of constraints are *physical* restrictions and that the third is a *logical* restriction.

All that remains is to convert these constraints from their verbal description to mathematics using decision variables and problem data. To do so, observe that there is one capacity constraint associated with each of the three nodes in Figure 2.2 corresponding to the three plants. For instance, the number of units shipped from the plant in San Francisco cannot exceed its capacity of 1700. Now, use the technique of decomposition to express the number of units shipped out of San Francisco as a sum of individual terms. From Figure 2.2, the four arcs leaving the node corresponding to the plant in San Francisco provide the following decomposition:

$$
\left\{\begin{array}{l}\text{Number of units} \\ \text{shipped out of San} \\ \text{Francisco}\end{array}\right\} = \left\{\begin{array}{l}\text{number of units} \\ \text{shipped to San Diego}\end{array}\right\} +
$$

$$
\left\{\begin{array}{l}\text{number of units} \\ \text{shipped to Barstow}\end{array}\right\} +
$$

$$
\left\{\begin{array}{l}\text{number of units} \\ \text{shipped to Tucson}\end{array}\right\} +
$$

$$
\left\{\begin{array}{l}\text{number of units} \\ \text{shipped to Dallas}\end{array}\right\}
$$

Thus, the capacity constraint corresponding to this node is

$$
x_{SS} + x_{SB} + x_{ST} + x_{SD} \leq 1700
$$

A similar process, with reference to the network diagram in Figure 2.2, leads to the following group of capacity constraints:

$$
\begin{array}{ll}
x_{SS} + x_{SB} + x_{ST} + x_{SD} \leq 1700 & \text{(San Francisco)} \\
x_{LS} + x_{LB} + x_{LT} + x_{LD} \leq 2000 & \text{(Los Angeles)} \\
x_{PS} + x_{PB} + x_{PT} + x_{PD} \leq 1700 & \text{(Phoenix)}
\end{array}
$$

To identify the demand constraints, observe that there is one such constraint associated with each of the four nodes in Figure 2.2 corresponding to the four retail stores. For instance, the number of units shipped to the retail store in San Diego should be exactly 1700. Now use the technique of decomposition to express the number of units shipped to San Diego as a sum of individual terms. From Figure 2.2, the three arcs entering the node corresponding to the retail store in San Diego provide the following decomposition:

$$
\left\{\begin{array}{l}\text{Number of units} \\ \text{shipped to San Diego}\end{array}\right\} = \left\{\begin{array}{l}\text{number of units shipped} \\ \text{from San Francisco}\end{array}\right\} +
$$

$$
\left\{\begin{array}{l}\text{number of units shipped} \\ \text{from Los Angeles}\end{array}\right\} +
$$

$$
\left\{\begin{array}{l}\text{number of units shipped} \\ \text{from Phoenix}\end{array}\right\}
$$

Thus, the demand constraint corresponding to this node is

$$
x_{SS} + x_{LS} + x_{PS} = 1700
$$

A similar process, again with reference to the network diagram in Figure 2.2, leads to the following group of demand constraints:

$$
\begin{array}{ll}
x_{SS} + x_{LS} + x_{PS} = 1700 & \text{(San Diego)} \\
x_{SB} + x_{LB} + x_{PB} = 1000 & \text{(Barstow)} \\
x_{ST} + x_{LT} + x_{PT} = 1500 & \text{(Tucson)} \\
x_{SD} + x_{LD} + x_{PD} = 1200 & \text{(Dallas)}
\end{array}
$$

Finally, each shipment (decision variable) must be nonnegative and integer:

$$x_{SS},\ x_{SB},\ x_{ST},\ x_{SD},\ x_{LS},\ x_{LB},\ x_{LT},\ x_{LD},$$
$$x_{PS},\ x_{PB},\ x_{PT},\ x_{PD} \geq 0 \text{ and integer}$$

By putting together all the pieces, the complete mathematical model is as follows.

MATHEMATICAL FORMULATION OF THE TRANSPORTATION PROBLEM OF CCC

Integer Program
EX2_2.DAT

Minimize $(5x_{SS} + 3x_{SB} + 2x_{ST} + 6x_{SD}) +$
      $(4x_{LS} + 7x_{LB} + 8x_{LT} + 10x_{LD}) +$
      $(6x_{PS} + 5x_{PB} + 3x_{PT} + 8x_{PD})$

Subject to

CAPACITY CONSTRAINTS

$$x_{SS} +\ x_{SB} +\ x_{ST} +\ x_{SD} \leq 1700 \quad \text{(San Francisco)}$$
$$x_{LS} +\ x_{LB} +\ x_{LT} +\ x_{LD} \leq 2000 \quad \text{(Los Angeles)}$$
$$x_{PS} +\ x_{PB} +\ x_{PT} +\ x_{PD} \leq 1700 \quad \text{(Phoenix)}$$

DEMAND CONSTRAINTS

$$x_{SS} + x_{LS} + x_{PS} = 1700 \quad \text{(San Diego)}$$
$$x_{SB} + x_{LB} + x_{PB} = 1000 \quad \text{(Barstow)}$$
$$x_{ST} + x_{LT} + x_{PT} = 1500 \quad \text{(Tucson)}$$
$$x_{SD} + x_{LD} + x_{PD} = 1200 \quad \text{(Dallas)}$$

LOGICAL CONSTRAINTS

$$x_{SS},\ x_{SB},\ x_{ST},\ x_{SD},\ x_{LS},\ x_{LB},\ x_{LT},\ x_{LD},$$
$$x_{PS},\ x_{PB},\ x_{PT},\ x_{PD} \geq 0 \text{ and integer}$$

You will learn the method to solve this type of problem in Chapter 9. Applying that solution procedure results in the following optimal shipping plan for CCC:

PLANTS	STORES			
	SAN DIEGO	BARSTOW	TUCSON	DALLAS
San Francisco	0	800	0	900
Los Angeles	1700	0	0	300
Phoenix	0	200	1500	0

The total shipping cost associated with this optimal solution is $23,100.

➡ KEY FEATURES

The CCC problem illustrates the following key points in addition to the problem-formulation techniques previously covered.

✔ The use of a schematic diagram, both to illustrate the problem and to help in its mathematical formulation.

✔ The need to resolve ambiguities that arise with regard to interpreting the objective and constraints imposed on the problem. For example, "satisfying demand" may mean *exactly equal to* or *at least*.

✔ The technique of **grouping**, which is the identification of groups of constraints, each of which pertains to one particular aspect of the problem, such as meeting demands. The advantage of grouping is that, after formulating the demand constraint for one retailer, you will find it is easy to formulate all the constraints in that group because they all have the same mathematical structure.

Grouping
The technique of identifying a collection of similar constraints, each of which pertains to one particular aspect of the problem, such as meeting demands.

2.2.2 Examples of Network Problems: The Maximum-Flow Problem

To illustrate the use of a network diagram once again, consider the problem faced by the management of Hexxon Oil Company.

EXAMPLE 2.3 THE MAXIMUM-FLOW PROBLEM OF HEXXON OIL COMPANY Hexxon Oil Company has a large refinery located in Newark, New Jersey. Refined gasoline is shipped from there to storage tanks in Philadelphia through a pipeline network with pumping stations at Sayerville, Easton, Trenton, Bridgewater, and Allentown. The pipeline is built in segments that connect pairs of these cities. Along each segment there is a known maximum number of gallons per hour that can be shipped. Those segments and their respective capacities in gallons per hour are

FROM	TO	CAPACITY
Newark	Sayerville	150,000
Sayreville	Trenton	125,000
Trenton	Philadelphia	130,000
Newark	Bridgewater	80,000
Sayerville	Bridgewater	60,000
Bridgewater	Easton	100,000
Easton	Allentown	75,000
Easton	Trenton	50,000
Allentown	Philadelphia	90,000

Increased driving in the upcoming summer months is expected in the Philadelphia region. Will Hexxon have enough gas to meet increased demand at the service stations? Before increasing the production rate at the refinery, the management of Hexxon wants to know the maximum number of gallons of gasoline per hour that can be shipped through the pipeline network to the storage tanks in Philadelphia. ∎

Prior to formulating this problem mathematically, consider drawing a network diagram to help you visualize the information and problem data. First, identify certain nodes and arcs. In this problem, each city list can be represented by a node. An arc is used to connect those cities for which there is a segment of the pipeline network, as seen in Figure 2.3. There you can also see the capacity of each segment written next to the corresponding arc.

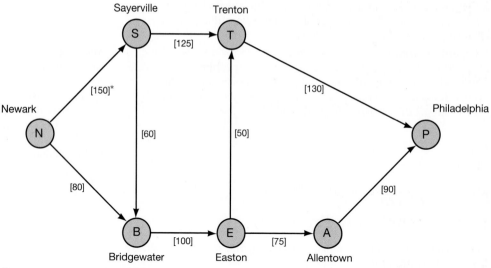

*In thousands of gallons per hour

FIGURE 2.3 Network Representation of the Maximum—Flow Problem of Hexxon Oil Company.

STEP 1. IDENTIFYING THE DECISION VARIABLES

The first step in the formulation is to identify the decision variables. Ask yourself what you are free to control and what constitutes a solution to this problem. The answer is that you must determine the number of gallons of gasoline to ship per hour along each segment of the pipeline. You can define

x_{NS} = the number of gallons of gasoline per hour to ship along the segment from Newark to Sayerville

A similar variable is needed for each of the other eight arcs in the network diagram in Figure 2.3. These nine variables are written next to the arcs in Figure 2.4.

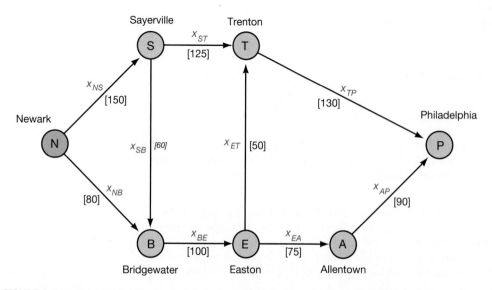

FIGURE 2.4 Decision Variables for the Maximum—Flow Problem of Hexxon Oil Company.

STEP 2. IDENTIFYING THE OBJECTIVE FUNCTION

The next step in the formulation process is to identify the objective function, which in this case is

Maximize the number of gallons of gasoline per hour shipped to Philadelphia

Looking at the network diagram in Figure 2.4 and applying the technique of decomposition, you can see that

$$\left\{ \begin{array}{l} \text{Number of gallons per} \\ \text{hour into Philadephia} \end{array} \right\} = \left\{ \begin{array}{l} \text{number of gallons per} \\ \text{hour from Allentown} \end{array} \right\} + \left\{ \begin{array}{l} \text{number of gallons per} \\ \text{hour from Trenton} \end{array} \right\}$$

In terms of the decision variables, then, the objective function is

$$\text{Maximize} \qquad x_{AP} + x_{TP}$$

STEP 3. IDENTIFYING THE CONSTRAINTS

The technique of grouping can be used to identify the following three groups of constraints.

1. *Bound constraints*, specifying that the shipping rate in each segment of the pipeline should not exceed its capacity. By using the variables and the capacities given in Figure 2.4, these constraints are

$$x_{NS} \leq 150000$$
$$x_{NB} \leq 80000$$
$$x_{SB} \leq 60000$$
$$x_{ST} \leq 125000$$
$$x_{BE} \leq 100000$$
$$x_{EA} \leq 75000$$
$$x_{ET} \leq 50000$$
$$x_{AP} \leq 90000$$
$$x_{TP} \leq 130000$$

2. *Balance constraints*, specifying that at each pumping station, the amount of gasoline per hour shipped out should precisely equal the amount shipped in. For example, looking at the node in Figure 2.4 corresponding to the pumping station at Bridgewater, you can see that

$$\left\{ \begin{array}{l} \text{Amount shipped out of} \\ \text{Bridgewater} \end{array} \right\} = \left\{ \begin{array}{l} \text{amount shipped} \\ \text{from Bridgewater} \\ \text{to Easton} \end{array} \right\}$$

$$= x_{BE}$$

$$\left\{ \begin{array}{l} \text{Amount shipped into} \\ \text{Bridgewater} \end{array} \right\} = \left\{ \begin{array}{l} \text{amount shipped into} \\ \text{Bridgewater from} \\ \text{Newark} \end{array} \right\} + \left\{ \begin{array}{l} \text{amount shipped into} \\ \text{Bridgewater from} \\ \text{Sayerville} \end{array} \right\}$$

$$= x_{NB} + x_{SB}$$

Equating these two amounts provides the following balance constraint for the pumping station at Bridgewater:

$$x_{BE} = x_{NB} + x_{SB}$$

or

$$x_{BE} - x_{NB} - x_{SB} = 0 \text{ (balance at Bridgewater)}$$

Proceeding similarly for each pumping station gives rise to the following four additional balance constraints:

$$
\begin{aligned}
x_{ST} + x_{SB} - x_{NS} &= 0 \quad \text{(balance at Sayerville)} \\
x_{EA} + x_{ET} - x_{BE} &= 0 \quad \text{(balance at Easton)} \\
x_{TP} - x_{ST} - x_{ET} &= 0 \quad \text{(balance at Trenton)} \\
x_{AP} - x_{EA} \phantom{- x_{ET}} &= 0 \quad \text{(balance at Allentown)}
\end{aligned}
$$

3. *Logical constraints*, specifying that the amount shipped in each segment be non-negative.

By putting all the pieces together, the mathematical formulation of the problem of the Hexxon Oil Company is as follows.

MATHEMATICAL FORMULATION OF THE MAXIMUM FLOW PROBLEM OF HEXXON OIL COMPANY

Linear Program
EX2_3.DAT

Maximize $x_{AP} + x_{TP}$

Subject to

BOUND CONSTRAINTS

$$
\begin{aligned}
x_{NS} &\leq 150000 \\
x_{NB} &\leq 80000 \\
x_{SB} &\leq 60000 \\
x_{ST} &\leq 125000 \\
x_{BE} &\leq 100000 \\
x_{EA} &\leq 75000 \\
x_{ET} &\leq 50000 \\
x_{AP} &\leq 90000 \\
x_{TP} &\leq 130000
\end{aligned}
$$

BALANCE CONSTRAINTS

$$
\begin{aligned}
x_{BE} - x_{NB} - x_{SB} &= 0 \quad \text{(balance at Bridgewater)} \\
x_{ST} + x_{SB} - x_{NS} &= 0 \quad \text{(balance at Sayerville)} \\
x_{EA} + x_{ET} - x_{BE} &= 0 \quad \text{(balance at Easton)} \\
x_{TP} - x_{ST} - x_{ET} &= 0 \quad \text{(balance at Trenton)} \\
x_{AP} - x_{EA} \phantom{- x_{ET}} &= 0 \quad \text{(balance at Allentown)}
\end{aligned}
$$

LOGICAL CONSTRAINTS

All variables are nonnegative.

Applying the appropriate solution procedure results in the optimal flows shown in Figure 2.5.

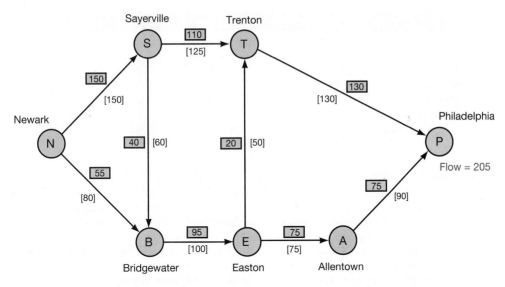

FIGURE 2.5 An Optimal Solution to the Maximum—Flow Problem of Hexxon Oil Company.

This solution results in a maximum flow of 205,000 gallons of oil per hour from the refinery in Newark to the storage tanks in Philadelphia.

Management now knows how much gas the company can pump to Philadelphia. This information is also important in making the decision on what the production rate at the Newark refinery should be. In fact, the maximum flow into Philadelphia puts an upper limit on how much gas should flow out of Newark.

2.2.3 Portfolio Management: The Use of 0–1 Integer Variables

In many problems, managers must make certain *strategic* decisions, such as:

1. Should a new plant or warehouse be constructed?
2. Should a particular project be undertaken?
3. Should a certain security be purchased?
4. Should a new piece of equipment be bought?

These four questions address problems that are different in nature from the transportation problem and the maximum—flow problem. In developing the shipping schedule and the gas flow, you sought a *quantitative* answer: How many? The four foregoing strategic questions posed are *qualitative*: Their answers will be "no" or "yes."

The unknown qualitative decisions—the no or yes answer to these questions—are the items you are free to control and so are incorporated in a mathematical model as decision variables. In formulating a model, these decision variables are restricted to values of 0 (for "no") and 1 (for "yes") and are thus called **0–1 integer variables**. The next example illustrates how these variables are used in developing models.

0–1 integer variable
A decision variable, restricted to have a value of either 0 or 1, used to model "no/yes" decisions.

EXAMPLE 2.4 THE PORTFOLIO-MANAGEMENT PROBLEM OF HIGH-TECH The general partners of High-Tech, a venture-capital investment company, are considering investing in one or more proposals they have received from various entrepreneurial businesses. The Research Department has screened each proposal, and four of the entrepreneurs meet High-Tech's requirement of achieving a sufficiently high return for the

TABLE 2.3	*Investment Data for High-Tech ($ thousands)*				
PROJECTS	YEAR 1	YEAR 2	YEAR 3	YEAR 4	RETURN
Bio-Tech	60	10	10	10	250
Tele-Comm	35	35	35	35	375
Laser-Optics	10	50	50	10	275
Compu-Ware	15	10	10	40	140
Investable Funds	90	80	80	50	

associated risk. These companies are Bio-Tech, Tele-Comm, Laser-Optics, and Compu-Ware. The Research Department at High-Tech has also estimated the total return of these businesses in today's dollars, given in the last column of Table 2.3.

Each of the four projects requires investments of a known amount at the beginning of each of the next 4 years, as given in Table 2.3. The Accounting Department at High-Tech has prepared an estimate of the total funds High-Tech has for investing at the beginning of each of the next 4 years, given in the last row of Table 2.3. Note that unused funds in any year are not available for investment in subsequent years.

As one of the general partners of High-Tech, you have been asked to make recommendations on which, if any, of these projects to invest in so as to achieve the highest total return in today's dollars. You and the other partners have agreed that High-Tech, in an effort to diversify, will not invest in both Tele-Comm and Laser-Optics, which are developing the same type of technology. ■

STEP 1. IDENTIFYING THE DECISION VARIABLES

Ask what you are free to control in this problem and you will realize that you can choose to accept or reject each of the four proposals. You should recognize that these decisions involve a "no" or "yes" decision. It seems reasonable therefore to create a 0–1 integer variable for each project, as follows:

$$B = \begin{cases} 1, & \text{if High-Tech is to invest in Bio-Tech} \\ 0, & \text{if High-Tech is not to invest in Bio-Tech} \end{cases}$$

$$T = \begin{cases} 1, & \text{if High-Tech is to invest in Tele-Comm} \\ 0, & \text{if High-Tech is not to invest in Tele-Comm} \end{cases}$$

$$L = \begin{cases} 1, & \text{if High-Tech is to invest in Laser-Optics} \\ 0, & \text{if High-Tech is not to invest in Laser-Optics} \end{cases}$$

$$C = \begin{cases} 1, & \text{if High-Tech is to invest in Compu-Ware} \\ 0, & \text{if High-Tech is not to invest in Compu-Ware} \end{cases}$$

The choice of 1 for "yes" and 0 for "no" is completely arbitrary. You could also have chosen 1 for "no" and 0 for "yes." However, once you make the choice, you must use it consistently throughout the formulation. In some cases, a particular choice simplifies the subsequent formulation.

STEP 2. IDENTIFYING THE OBJECTIVE FUNCTION

In this case, the objective is to maximize the total return of the investments in today's dollars. The total return can be decomposed into the sum of the returns for each of the four projects, as follows:

$$\text{Total return} = \text{return from Bio-Tech} + \text{return from Tele-Comm} + \text{return from Laser-Optics} + \text{return from Compu-Ware}$$

Work through a specific example. The return from Bio-Tech is $250,000 as given in Table 2.3. However, you will receive this return *only if you decide to invest in Bio-Tech*—that is, if $B = 1$. Otherwise—that is, if $B = 0$—the return from Bio-Tech is 0. These two possibilities can be combined into the following single mathematical expression:

$$\text{Return from Bio-Tech} = 250B$$

If the decision is not to invest—that is, $B = 0$—then $250B = 0$. Otherwise, when the decision is to invest—that is, $B = 1$—then $250B = 250$.

In a similar fashion, the return from each of the remaining three projects is obtained by multiplying the return from Table 2.3 with the 0–1 decision variable corresponding to that project. In summary, the objective function for this problem is to maximize:

$$\begin{aligned} \text{Total return} \quad = \quad & \text{return from Bio-Tech} \quad + \quad \text{return from Tele-Comm} \quad + \\ & \text{return from Laser-Optics} \quad + \quad \text{return from Compu-Ware} \end{aligned}$$

$$= \quad 250B + 375T + 275L + 140C$$

STEP 3. IDENTIFYING THE CONSTRAINTS

Begin by using the technique of grouping to identify the following groups of constraints: (1) yearly cash flow, (2) a guideline to reflect that High-Tech does not want to invest in both Tele-Comm and Laser-Optics, and (3) logical constraints.

YEARLY CASH-FLOW CONSTRAINTS

Ask yourself what prevents you from investing in all the four projects. One constraint is the limited amount of funds available for investment during each of the 4 years (see Table 2.3). In particular, a budget constraint is needed for each of the 4 years to ensure that the total funds invested in selected projects does not exceed the amount of investable funds available that year. For example, for the first year,

$$\text{Total funds invested in selected projects} \; \leq 90$$

By using the technique of decomposition, the total funds invested in selected projects is the sum of the amounts invested in each of the four projects—that is,

$$\begin{aligned} \text{Total funds invested} = \; & (\text{amount invested in Bio-Tech}) \; + \\ & (\text{amount invested in Tele-Comm}) \; + \\ & (\text{amount invested in Laser-Optics}) \; + \\ & (\text{amount invested in Compu-Ware}) \end{aligned}$$

A mathematical expression is needed for each of these amounts in terms of the decision variables and other problem data. Use decomposition again, and work through a specific example. The amount invested in each project is the amount needed for that project during the first year (see Table 2.3) times the corresponding 0–1 variable. Thus, the budget constraint for the first year becomes

$$60B + 35T + 10L + 15C \leq 90 \qquad (\text{budget for year 1})$$

A similar constraint is needed for each of the remaining 3 years. By using the data in Table 2.3, those constraints are

$$10B + 35T + 50L + 10C \leq 80 \qquad \text{(budget for year 2)}$$

$$10B + 35T + 50L + 10C \leq 80 \qquad \text{(budget for year 3)}$$

$$10B + 35T + 10L + 40C \leq 50 \qquad \text{(budget for year 4)}$$

INVESTMENT-GUIDELINE CONSTRAINT

Recall that management has decided not to invest in both Tele-Comm and Laser-Optics. Can you use the variables T and L to write an appropriate mathematical constraint?

A constraint is needed to ensure that if T is 1, then L is 0, and that if L is 1, then T is 0 (or, equivalently, that both variables cannot have value 1). One way to accomplish this is to require that the *product* of these two variables be 0:

$$T * L = 0$$

If one of the variables is positive, the other must be 0. With some thought, you might realize that the following constraint accomplishes the same goal:

$$T + L \leq 1$$

In the latter constraint, if T is 1, L cannot also be 1 and satisfy the inequality (and vice versa). Either of these two constraints is acceptable. The choice should ultimately be based on your ability to find a method for solving the resulting formulation. In this case, the second constraint provides a model that is easier to solve, as you will learn in subsequent chapters on solution techniques.

LOGICAL CONSTRAINTS

As specified in the definitions, each variable must have a value of 0 or 1. This implicit constraint is made explicit as follows:

$$B, \ T, \ L, \text{ and } C = 0 \text{ or } 1$$

Alternatively, you could write these logical constraints as

$$0 \leq B \leq 1 \quad \text{and} \quad B \quad \text{integer}$$
$$0 \leq T \leq 1 \quad \text{and} \quad T \quad \text{integer}$$
$$0 \leq L \leq 1 \quad \text{and} \quad L \quad \text{integer}$$
$$0 \leq C \leq 1 \quad \text{and} \quad C \quad \text{integer}$$

By putting together the pieces, the complete mathematical model is as follows.

MATHEMATICAL FORMULATION FOR THE INVESTMENT PROBLEM OF HIGH-TECH

Integer Program
EX2_4.DAT

$$
\begin{array}{lll}
\text{Maximize} & 250B + 375T + 275L + 140C & \\
\text{Subject to} & 60B + \ 35T + \ 10L + \ 15C \leq 90 & \text{(year 1)} \\
& 10B + \ 35T + \ 50L + \ 10C \leq 80 & \text{(year 2)} \\
& 10B + \ 35T + \ 50L + \ 10C \leq 80 & \text{(year 3)} \\
& 10B + \ 35T + \ 10L + \ 40C \leq 50 & \text{(year 4)} \\
& T + \ L \qquad \qquad \leq \ 1 & \\
& B, \qquad T, \qquad L, \qquad C = 0 \text{ or } 1 &
\end{array}
$$

This formulation is based on defining the variables as done in Step 1. An alternative, but equivalent, formulation can be obtained by defining each decision variable to have a value of 1 for "no," meaning that you will not invest in the associated project, and 0 for "yes," meaning that you will invest. You are asked to develop the corresponding model in an exercise at the end of this chapter. This will show that there is no unique formulation of a problem.

In either case, you will learn the solution procedure for this type of problem in Chapter 8. Applying that procedure results in the recommendation to invest only in the projects of Bio-Tech and Laser-Optics, with an expected return of 525 thousand dollars.

KEY FEATURES

This problem illustrates the following key features, in addition to problem-formulation techniques you already know:

- ✔ The use of 0–1 integer variables to incorporate no/yes decisions.
- ✔ The use of 0–1 integer variables to model either-or constraints by requiring that the sum of two such variables not exceed 1.
- ✔ The possibility of different mathematical expressions for the same constraint.
- ✔ The possibility of different models, depending on the choice and definition of the decision variables.

2.2.4 A Location Problem

Many problems in industry involve choosing a location for facilities—for example, plants and warehouses. The location of facilities can greatly influence the transportation costs. For example, if the assembly plants of the Cosmic Computer Company, in Example 2.2 in Section 2.2.1, were located in different cities, the costs of shipping the computers to the retail stores change. Location decisions can also affect customer satisfaction. Is a store convenient and accessible? Location can be critical to the success of the business. The question to be answered is where "best" to locate facilities to achieve an overall organizational objective, as illustrated in the following example.

EXAMPLE 2.5 THE BLOOD-BANK LOCATION PROBLEM Suppose New York City has five hospitals in Manhattan. The Health Department wants to build a central blood bank to provide daily supplies of blood to each hospital. Hospitals 2 and 4 require morning and afternoon deliveries. The remaining three hospitals require only one delivery per day. As a manager of the department, you have been asked to make a recommendation as to the ideal location of this blood bank, whether that location is actually available for acquisition or not. ■

STEP 1. IDENTIFYING THE DECISION VARIABLES

What are you free to control in this problem? It is clear that you control the location of the blood bank. The real question is how do you *specify* that location. The obvious way to do so is to define a single variable, say, x, whose value is the address of the blood bank. But think carefully about what you are going to *do* with that variable in the problem formulation. If the known address of a hospital is y, for example, you will not be able to use x and y to develop a mathematical expression for the distance from the blood bank to the hospital because addresses alone do not contain enough information.

A more precise set of variables is needed. One way to define a location on a map (as in Figure 2.6) is to describe each point in relation to a fixed point, called the *origin*. Each point on the map consists of two *coordinates*, say (a, b). The first coordinate, a, represents the East–West distance (say, in miles) from the origin, and the second coordinate, b, represents the North–South distance (in miles). Which point you choose as the origin is immaterial as long as you express *all* coordinates relative to that point.

In this example, City Hall in Figure 2.6 is chosen as the origin. Its coordinates are $(0, 0)$. Any other point on the map then consists of two coordinates, (a, b), in which a negative value of a represents the distance from City Hall to the *West* (left) and a positive value of a represents the distance to the *East* (right). Similarly, a negative value of b represents the distance from City Hall to the *South* (down) and a positive value represents the distance to the *North* (up). With this understanding, you can write the known coordinates of the five hospitals in Figure 2.6 relative to City Hall as follows:

$$\text{Location of Hospital } 1 = (a_1, \ b_1)$$
$$\text{Location of Hospital } 2 = (a_2, \ b_2)$$
$$\text{Location of Hospital } 3 = (a_3, \ b_3)$$
$$\text{Location of Hospital } 4 = (a_4, \ b_4)$$
$$\text{Location of Hospital } 5 = (a_5, \ b_5)$$

Returning to the issue of identifying the decision variables, you are free to choose the location of the blood bank—that is, its East–West and North–South distance in miles from City Hall. It is therefore reasonable to define two variables, one for each coordinate of the location of the blood bank:

$$x = \text{the East-West distance in miles from City Hall}$$
$$y = \text{the North-South distance in miles from City Hall}$$

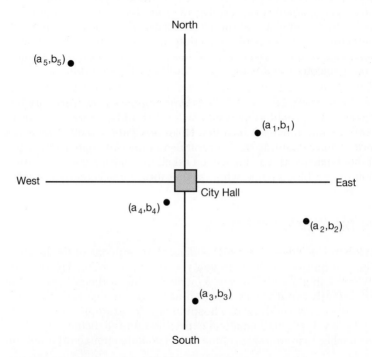

FIGURE 2.6 Location of Hospitals in New York City.

STEP 2. IDENTIFYING THE OBJECTIVE FUNCTION

What is the objective of this problem? Rereading the problem statement, you will discover that the objective is not specified precisely. In general terms, you have been asked to make a recommendation as to an "ideal" location for the blood bank. So the first question that must be addressed is how to measure how "good" a particular location is. For instance, would a blood bank located at coordinates (s, t) be "better" than one located at (x, y)? Some measure of comparison is needed to determine the "best" location. To develop this measure, begin by asking what constitutes a good location. Some possible answers are that the best location

1. Minimizes the sum of the distances from the blood bank to each of the five hospitals.
2. Minimizes the distance to the farthest hospital.
3. Minimizes the total distance traveled in making all the deliveries during one day.

The choice of an objective is up to the decision makers of the organization. In this problem, suppose the third criterion is selected.

The next issue is how to express this objective in terms of the variables and other problem data. Using the technique of decomposition, you can express the objective function as follows:

Minimize total travel distance =

2　*　(distance from the blood bank to Hospital 1) *
　　　(number of deliveries per day to Hospital 1) +

2　*　(distance from the blood bank to Hospital 2) *
　　　(number of deliveries per day to Hospital 2) +

$$\vdots$$

2　*　(distance from the blood bank to Hospital 5) *
　　　(number of deliveries per day to Hospital 5)

The value of 2 in each term arises because each delivery is a round trip.

Now it is necessary to express each individual term using variables and other problem data. Can you do so for the distance from the blood bank to Hospital 1 in Figure 2.6? One difficulty you might encounter is that it is not clear precisely what is meant by "distance." For example, if the deliveries are made by air (for example, by helicopter), the distance is not the same as if the deliveries are made by surface. Suppose deliveries are made by air. In this case, recall the formula for computing a straight-line distance. The distance from the blood bank, located at the unknown coordinates (x, y), to Hospital 1, located at (a_1, b_1), is

$$\text{Distance} = \sqrt{(x - a_1)^2 + (y - b_1)^2}$$

Because each delivery requires a round trip,

$$\text{Round-trip distance} = 2 * \sqrt{(x - a_1)^2 + (y - b_1)^2}$$

Use the same formula for each of the remaining four hospitals, and multiply each distance by the number of daily trips given in the problem description. The overall objective function is

$$\text{Minimize} \quad 2 * \left(\sqrt{(x - a_1)^2 + (y - b_1)^2} \right) +$$

$$4 * \left(\sqrt{(x - a_2)^2 + (y - b_2)^2} \right) +$$

$$2 * \left(\sqrt{(x - a_3)^2 + (y - b_3)^2} \right) +$$

$$4 * \left(\sqrt{(x - a_4)^2 + (y - b_4)^2} \right) +$$

$$2 * \left(\sqrt{(x - a_5)^2 + (y - b_5)^2} \right)$$

STEP 3. IDENTIFYING THE CONSTRAINTS

To identify the constraints, ask what prevents you from choosing arbitrary values for variables x and y. At first glance, you might feel that some restriction on these variables is needed to ensure that they represent a valid location on the map. You would not want the blood bank to be located in Philadelphia. Although you could include such constraints, there is no need to do so in this problem. The reason is that the objective function restricts the values for x and y. When the objective function is in fact minimized, the values for x and y will *automatically* be close to the five hospitals.

There are many other practical considerations regarding the actual location of the blood bank, but they are not included as constraints in this model because the objective is to determine the *ideal* location.

Observe additionally that there are no nonnegativity constraints. The reason for this is that variables x and y are allowed to have negative as well as positive values. Indeed, *this problem has no constraints at all* and is thus referred to as an **unconstrained optimization problem**. The final formulation is as follows.

Unconstrained optimization problem
A mathematical model that has an objective function but no constraints.

MATHEMATICAL FORMULATION OF THE BLOOD-BANK LOCATION PROBLEM

$$\text{Minimize} \quad 2 * \left[\sqrt{(x - a_1)^2 + (y - b_1)^2} \right] +$$

$$4 * \left[\sqrt{(x - a_2)^2 + (y - b_2)^2} \right] +$$

$$2 * \left[\sqrt{(x - a_3)^2 + (y - b_3)^2} \right] +$$

$$4 * \left[\sqrt{(x - a_4)^2 + (y - b_4)^2} \right] +$$

$$2 * \left[\sqrt{(x - a_5)^2 + (y - b_5)^2} \right]$$

To solve this problem requires obtaining specific values for the data representing the location (coordinates) of the five hospitals.

KEY FEATURES

This problem illustrates the following key features beyond the previously taught problem-formulation techniques:

✔ The need to clarify certain aspects of the problem (such as the concept of "distance") before attempting to formulate the problem.

✔ The possibility of specifying the objective function in different ways, based on different criteria, such as the alternative concepts of an ideal location. In such cases, choose the criterion that is most consistent with the overall strategic plan of the organization.

✔ The ability to formulate a problem using symbolic names to represent the data (for example, (a_1, b_1) to represent the location of a hospital). However, to obtain a *solution*, you will need to replace the symbolic names with specific data values. Using symbolic names instead of specific data values enables you:

    a. To formulate a problem without waiting for data values to be collected and

    b. To use the same model for similar problems having different data values. For example, the blood-bank model, with different hospital locations, can be used by the county of Los Angeles also.

✔ The possibility of having **unrestricted variables**—that is, variables whose values can be negative as well as positive.

✔ The possibility of omitting certain constraints that, by the nature of the objective function, are automatically satisfied. Sometimes, you can omit a constraint because that restriction is automatically imposed by some other constraint in the model.

Unrestricted variable
A variable in a decision problem whose value can be positive, negative, or zero.

2.2.5 *The Container-Design Problem*

Another important class of problems focuses on the optimal design of items such as structures (for example, support columns) and equipment (for example, containers). The goal of these problems is to determine the dimensions of a particular object with a known shape and material, subject to certain design specifications. The modeling of these problems often involves engineering mathematics in specifying the objective function and constraints, as illustrated by the following example.

EXAMPLE 2.6 THE DESIGN PROBLEM OF CONTAINERS, INC. Containers, Inc., manufactures all sorts of containers made to order. The company has just received an inquiry from a British firm for reusable six-sided rectangular containers made of a special fiberboard material. The volume of each container must be at least 12,000 cubic centimeters (cm^3). Shipping restrictions on these containers in England require that their girth (that is, length plus width plus height) not exceed 72 cm and that the largest single dimension not exceed 40 cm. The British firm has already obtained a bid of $8.20 per container. The Chief Executive Officer (CEO) of Containers, Inc., has asked you, the Manager of the Production Division, if the company can supply the containers for less and still achieve a 25% profit. You have obtained data indicating that the fiberboard material costs $20 per square meter and that the labor and other variable costs are $1 per container. Do you make a bid for the contract? ■

STEP 1. IDENTIFYING THE DECISION VARIABLES

Recognizing the need for a mathematical model, you first identify the variables. In asking the usual question of what you are free to control in this problem, you should realize that you *cannot* control the shape of the container (it must be rectangular and have six sides) nor the variable costs of $1 per container. However, you *can* control the total cost of the fiberboard used in producing the containers by controlling the *design* of the box. Further reflection should lead you to realize that this design is determined by the dimensions of the container. You could therefore begin by defining L, W, and H to be the length, width, and height of the container, respectively. However, this definition is not precise enough, as it lacks the *units* in which the dimensions are measured. You are free to choose those units, but think about how they will be used and what units are given in the problem data. Because the data are expressed in metric units (centimeters and meters), it is appropriate to use centimeters or meters rather than inches or feet. Arbitrarily choosing centimeters, let

$$L = \text{the length of the container in centimeters}$$
$$W = \text{the width of the container in centimeters}$$
$$H = \text{the height of the container in centimeters}$$

STEP 2. IDENTIFYING THE OBJECTIVE FUNCTION

The overall objective of this problem is to decide whether you can produce the containers with a profit margin of 25% above costs while pricing the containers below the competing bid of $8.20 per container. One approach to solving this problem is to determine the minimum possible cost of the fiberboard used, add $1 for the labor and other variable costs to obtain the total cost per container, and then add 25% to see if the resulting value is less than $8.20. From a modeling point of view, the objective in words is

Minimize the total cost of fiberboard used per container

Now determine a mathematical expression for the cost of the fiberboard used in one container in terms of the decision variables and other problem data. If you are having trouble doing so, then try the technique of working through a specific example. For instance, let $L = 40$ cm, $W = 20$ cm, and $H = 10$ cm. To calculate the total cost, you need to know how much fiberboard is needed to make a container of these dimensions. Looking at Figure 2.7 and using the technique of decomposition, you should realize that

Total cost $=$ sum of the costs for each of the six sides

For each side, the cost is computed as

Cost of a side = (amount of fiberboard needed) $*$ (cost per unit of fiberboard)

In particular, for the side bounded by the length and width, the amount of fiberboard needed is

$$\text{Area of side} = \text{length} * \text{width}$$
$$= (40 \text{ cm})(20 \text{ cm})$$
$$= 800 \text{ cm}^2$$

If you were now to compute the cost of this side as 800 times the unit cost of fiberboard ($20 per square meter), you would obtain an *incorrect* cost of $16,000 for this side. This mistake occurs because of an incorrect mixing of units. The dimensions of the container are defined in terms of *centimeters*, but the cost of fiberboard is given in dollars per *square meter*. One way to correct this situation is to redefine the variables in terms of

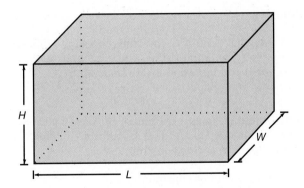

FIGURE 2.7 Dimensions of the Container.

meters instead of centimeters. Alternatively, you can compute the cost of fiberboard in terms of dollars per square centimeter, as will be done here. Observe that 1 square meter equals 100 cm times 100 cm, or 10,000 square centimeters. Thus, a cost of $20 per square meter is equivalent to a cost of $20/10,000 = $0.002 per square centimeter. Hence, the cost for the one side bounded by a length of 40 and a width 20 is

$$\text{Cost for this side} = 0.002 * 40 * 20 = \$1.60$$

Recall that the purpose of working through a specific example is *not* to obtain a numerical answer for this one specific set of values for the variables, but rather to determine how to perform the computations when the values of the variables are not specified. In this case, the cost of this one side, in terms of L and W, is given by

$$\text{Cost of this side} = 0.002 * L * W$$

Having calculated the cost of this one side, you must still calculate the cost of the other five sides. From Figure 2.7, you can see that there are two sides bounded by the length and width. Similarly, there are two sides bounded by the length and height and two sides bounded by the width and height. Therefore, the total cost of constructing the container can be expressed mathematically as follows:

$$\text{Total cost} = \text{sum of the cost of the six sides}$$

$$= 2 * (\text{cost of the side bounded by the length and width}) +$$
$$2 * (\text{cost of the side bounded by the length and height}) +$$
$$2 * (\text{cost of the side bounded by the height and width})$$

$$= 2 * (0.002 * L * W) +$$
$$2 * (0.002 * L * H) +$$
$$2 * (0.002 * H * W)$$

$$= 0.004 * L * W + 0.004 * L * H + 0.004 * H * W$$

The objective function for this problem is to

$$\text{Minimize} \quad 0.004 * L * W + 0.004 * L * H + 0.004 * H * W$$

STEP 3. IDENTIFYING THE CONSTRAINTS

Reread the problem description, and ask what prohibits you from choosing arbitrary values for the dimensions of the container. You should then identify three types of constraints, pertaining to the volume, girth, and largest single dimension.

THE VOLUME CONSTRAINT

The British firm has requested that the container have a volume of at least 12,000 cm^3. Recalling that the volume of a box is calculated as the product of its three dimensions, you can use L, W, and H defined before to express this constraint as

$$L * W * H \geq 12000 \qquad \text{(volume constraint)}$$

THE GIRTH CONSTRAINT

To express the restriction that the girth not exceed 72 cm, recall that the girth is the sum of the three dimensions of the container, so

$$L + W + H \leq 72 \qquad \text{(girth constraint)}$$

RESTRICTION ON THE LARGEST SINGLE DIMENSION

Another constraint given in the problem description is that the largest single dimension not exceed 40 cm. You do not know which dimension is going to be the largest one, so one way to express this constraint is as follows:

$$\text{Maximum } \{L, \ W, \ H\} \leq 40$$

This constraint is correct in this form, but you might realize that there is another equivalent way to express the restriction that the largest dimension not exceed 40 cm. You could require that *each individual dimension* not exceed 40 cm. Thus, the foregoing constraint can be written equally well as the three constraints:

$$L \leq 40$$

$$W \leq 40$$

$$H \leq 40$$

Here, again, you see that it is possible to formulate a problem in more than one way. Compare the two approaches. The first requires one complex mathematical constraint, and the latter requires three simple ones. Both formulations are correct. The choice of which formulation to use should be based on your ability to find a method for solving the resulting problem, as discussed in Section 2.3. For now, the second approach is used because of its simplicity.

MATHEMATICAL FORMULATION OF THE PROBLEM OF CONTAINERS, INC.

Put together all the pieces, including the implicit nonnegativity constraints on each variable, and the final and correct problem formulation is

$$
\begin{aligned}
\text{Minimize} \quad & 0.004 * L * W + \ 0.004 * L * H + 0.004 * H * W \\
\text{Subject to} \quad & L * W * H \geq 12000 && \text{(volume)} \\
& L + W + H \leq 72 && \text{(girth)} \\
& 0 \leq L \leq 40 \\
& 0 \leq W \leq 40 \\
& 0 \leq H \leq 40
\end{aligned}
$$

Note that constraint $0 \leq L \leq 40$ means that L is nonnegative $(0 \leq L)$ and is less than 40 $(L \leq 40)$. In Section 2.3, you will learn that this problem belongs to a general class called *nonlinear programming problems*. The procedure for solving these problems is beyond the scope of this book. However, such methods do exist and are available in some computer packages. Applying such a procedure results in the optimal design in which the length, width, and height are each 22.8943 centimeters. This design incurs a total cost of $7.29, consisting of $6.29 for the fiberboard and an additional dollar of labor and overhead. Adding a 25% profit margin brings the total to $9.11. Because this amount exceeds the competing bid of $8.20, you should recommend to the CEO that the company not bid for this contract.

KEY FEATURES

This problem illustrates the following key features in addition to the previous problem-formulation techniques:

✔ The need to use appropriate units (centimeters, in this example) when defining the variables and to be consistent throughout the formulation in expressing all aspects of the problem in terms of the chosen units.

✔ The possibility of writing constraints in more than one way (such as the constraint that the maximum dimension of the container not exceed 40 cm).

■ 2.3 CLASSIFICATION OF MATHEMATICAL MODELS

Now that you know how to formulate a problem mathematically, the next step is to *solve* the problem–that is, to find values for the decision variables that satisfy all the constraints and, at the same time, that provide the best possible value of the objective function. This task is accomplished by using systematic, step-by-step procedures called **algorithms**. Ultimately, a computer performs these algorithms. Algorithms that solve one mathematical model may or may not solve another. Different algorithms have been designed to solve different *types* of problems. The natural question to ask is, after formulating a particular mathematical model, how do I choose the correct algorithm for solving that problem?

Algorithm
A systematic step-by-step procedure used to solve a mathematical model.

The answer to this question is to identify the *class* of mathematical models to which your particular problem belongs. One or more algorithms exist for solving *all* problems in that class. Once you know the class to which your problem belongs, you will be able to select an associated algorithm for solving that problem.

In this section, you will learn to identify some of these different classes of models according to the mathematical properties that all problems in that class share. You will also learn how to determine the class to which your problem belongs by examining its mathematical properties. Advantages and disadvantages of algorithms associated with each class are discussed briefly here and throughout the rest of this book. The details of how to use the various algorithms in these classes and how to interpret the results obtained from the computer are also presented in subsequent chapters.

2.3.1 Classifications Based on Problem Data

As you learned in Chapter 1, problems in which all the data are *known with certainty*—such as those in this chapter—are deterministic. In the stochastic problems presented in Chapters 11 through 16, some (or all) of the problem data are not known with certainty. The remainder of this section is devoted to classifying deterministic problems based on certain mathematical properties.

2.3.2 Classifications Based on the Constraints

Deterministic problems are classified first on the basis of whether constraints exist. This gives rise to the following two classes:

Unconstrained problem
A problem that has an objective function but no constraints.

Constrained problem
A problem that has one or more constraints.

Additivity
A mathematical property of constraints in which the contribution of each variable to the constraint function is added (or subtracted) to that of each other variable in the constraint.

1. **Unconstrained problems** are those that have no constraints at all.
2. **Constrained problems** are those that have one or more constraints.

The location problem of the blood bank in Example 2.5 in Section 2.2 is an unconstrained problem. All the other examples in Section 2.2 are constrained problems.

Constrained problems are then classified on the basis of the mathematical properties the constraints satisfy. One of the two fundamental mathematical properties of constraints is **additivity**, in which the contribution of each variable to the constraint function is *added* (or *subtracted*) to that of each other variable in the constraint.

To illustrate the property of additivity, recall the following labor constraint from the Blending Department of the problem of Case Chemicals in Section 2.2, in which CS_1 is the number of thousands of gallons of CS-01 to produce and CS_2 is the number of thousands of gallons of CS-02 to produce

$$2CS_1 + CS_2 \leq 230 \tag{1}$$

This constraint satisfies additivity because the contribution of CS_1 to the constraint (namely, $2CS_1$) is added to that of CS_2 (namely, CS_2). Similarly, consider the following balance constraint for the pumping station at Allentown in the maximum-flow problem of Hexxon Oil Company in Example 2.3:

$$x_{AP} - x_{EA} = 0 \tag{2}$$

This constraint satisfies the property of additivity because the contribution of x_{EA} is subtracted from that of x_{AP}.

In contrast, consider the following volume constraint from the design problem of Containers, Inc., in Example 2.6:

$$L * W * H \geq 12000 \tag{3}$$

This constraint does not satisfy additivity because the contributions of L, W, and H are *not* added to each other. Rather, those values are *multiplied* by each other.

Proportionality
A mathematical property of constraints by which if the value of a variable is multiplied by any constant, its contribution to the constraint is multiplied by that same constant.

The second mathematical property of a constraint is that of **proportionality**: If the value of a variable is multiplied by *any* constant, the variable's contribution to the constraint is multiplied by that *same* constant. Foregoing constraint (1) does satisfy proportionality. Suppose that CS_1 has a value of 5. In this case,

$$\text{Contribution of } CS_1 = 2CS_1 = 2(5) = 10$$

If the value of $CS_1 = 5$ is multiplied by any constant—say, c—then:

$$\text{Contribution of } CS_1 = 2CS_1 = 2(5c) = 10c$$

As you can see, if the value of CS_1 is multiplied by any constant c, the contribution of CS_1 to the constraint is also multiplied by c. Because this same property is true for CS_2, this constraint

$$2CS_1 + CS_2 \leq 230$$

satisfies proportionality.

In contrast, consider the constraint:

$$x_1^2 + 2x_2 \geq 10 \qquad (4)$$

Constraint (4) does not satisfy proportionality. To see why, suppose that x_1 has a value of 5:

$$\text{Contribution of } x_1 = x_1^2 = (5)^2 = 25$$

If the value of $x_1 = 5$ is multiplied by a constant—say, 2—then:

$$\text{Contribution of } x_1 = x_1^2 = (2*5)^2 = (2^2)*(5^2) = 4*25$$

As you can see, if the value of x_1 is multiplied by 2, the contribution of x_1 to the constraint is multiplied by 4. Proportionality does not hold.

On the basis of the properties of additivity and proportionality, there are two classifications of constrained problems:

1. **Linear constraints**, in which *all* constraints satisfy both additivity and proportionality.
2. **Nonlinear constraints**, in which some constraint does not satisfy at least one of the properties of additivity and proportionality.

You can recognize whether a particular constraint is linear or not by looking at its *form*. A constraint is linear if, in terms of decision variables $x_1, \ldots, x_n$ (or any symbolic names), it can be written as

$$a_1 x_1 + a_2 x_2 + \cdots + a_n x_n \leq (\geq, =) \, b$$

in which each of $a_1, \ldots, a_n$, and b is a known real number. For example, foregoing constraint (1) is linear because the coefficient of the variable CS_1 is $a_1 = 2$, that of CS_2 is $a_2 = 1$, and $b = 230$. Constraint (2) is also linear because the coefficient of the variable x_{AP} is $a_1 = 1$, that of x_{EA} is $a_2 = -1$, and $b = 0$. In contrast, constraints (3) and (4) are nonlinear.

Linear constraint
A mathematical property of a model in which all constraints satisfy both additivity and proportionality.

Nonlinear constraint
A mathematical property of a model in which some constraint does not satisfy at least one of the properties of additivity or proportionality.

2.3.3 Classifications Based on the Objective Function

The next classification of deterministic models is based on the mathematical properties of the objective function. As with the constraint functions, the objective function can be either linear or nonlinear, giving rise to the following two classes:

1. **Linear objective**, in which the objective function is linear.
2. **Nonlinear objective**, in which the objective function is nonlinear.

For example, the following objective function of the production-planning problem of Case Chemicals is linear:

$$\text{Maximize} \quad 300CS_1 + 500CS_2$$

Linear objective
An objective function that is linear.

Nonlinear objective
An objective function that is not linear.

In contrast, the following objective function of the design problem of Containers, Inc., in Example 2.6 is nonlinear:

$$\text{Minimize} \quad (0.004 * L * W) + (0.004 * L * H) + (0.004 * H * W)$$

Divisibility
The property of a decision variable being able to assume any value—fractional or otherwise—within some interval.

Continuous variable
A variable that satisfies divisibility.

Integer (discrete) variable
A variable that must have an integer value.

2.3.4 Classifications Based on the Variables

The final classification of deterministic problems is based on a mathematical property of the variables. That property is called **divisibility**, which means that a decision variable can, in theory, assume any value—fractional or otherwise—within some interval. For instance, variables CS_1 and CS_2 in the example of Case Chemicals represent the number of thousands of gallons of the solvents to produce. Because in theory it is possible to produce 5.132 thousand gallons, these variables *are* divisible. In contrast, all the variables in the transportation problem of CCC in Example 2.2 in Section 2.2 represent the number of microcomputers to ship. These variables are *not* divisible because it is not possible to ship 1.3 microcomputers—that is, these variables must be assigned *integer* values. The property of divisibility gives rise to the following two classes:

1. the class of **continuous variable** models, in which *all* variables satisfy divisibility.
2. the class of **integer** (or **discrete**) **variable** models, in which one or more variables must have integer values.

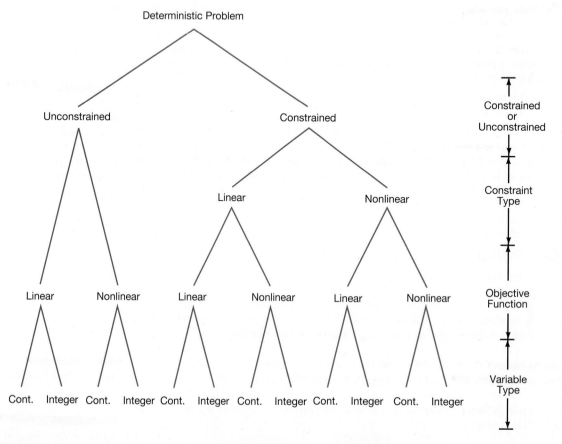

FIGURE 2.8 Classification of Deterministic Models.

The various classifications of deterministic models are summarized in Figure 2.8. As mentioned previously, after formulating a model, you must determine what class it belongs to so that you can choose an appropriate algorithm for solving the problem.

In this section, you have learned to classify a model into a particular group, based on its various mathematical characteristics. This effort helps you choose an appropriate algorithm for obtaining a solution to your model. Additional concerns regarding the model-building process are discussed next.

ADDITIONAL MANAGERIAL CONSIDERATIONS

In this chapter, you have learned how to develop and classify mathematical models for solving certain types of deterministic problems. Throughout the formulation and solution processes, there are several other issues that a manager must consider.

Resolving Ambiguities in the Problem Definition

When a problem is first identified in an organization, often many details and issues are ambiguous. For example:

1. The overall objective may not be clear. For instance, the concept of what is "best" for an organization may have several different meanings.
   a. Should you minimize the total cost of shipping your goods, the total distance traveled in shipping those goods, or the total time needed to deliver those goods?
   b. In an investment problem, is it better to maximize the *total* return on an investment, or the *rate* of return?
   c. What is meant by the "best" location for a blood bank, as in Example 2.5 in Section 2.2?

2. There may be conflicting objectives. For instance, should you minimize costs or maximize customer satisfaction?

3. The use of certain words to describe aspects of the problem can be vague and subject to various interpretations.
   a. Does "meeting demand" mean to ship *exactly* the demand or *at least* the demand, as in Example 2.2 in Section 2.2?
   b. Does the "distance" between two locations mean the distance as traveled by air or through a road network, as in Example 2.5 in Section 2.2?

These questions must be answered before the formulation process can begin. Failure to do so might result in implementing an optimal solution to the wrong problem.

Alternative Problem Formulations

As a manager, you should be aware that there is no single correct formulation for a given problem. Each formulation has its advantages and disadvantages.

There is more than one way to write a mathematical constraint. For instance, recall the constraint of the problem of High-Tech in Example 2.4. The partners agree not to invest in both the projects of Tele-Comm and Laser-Optics. How do you use the associated 0–1 decision variables, T and L, to specify this constraint? Either of the following two approaches is valid:

$$T * L = 0$$
$$T + L \leq 1$$

Observe that the first constraint is nonlinear and the second is linear. This difference is extremely important in choosing an appropriate solution procedure for the resulting model. (See also the constraint specifying that the size of the largest dimension of a container not exceed 40 cm in the design problem of Containers, Inc., in Example 2.6 in Section 2.2.)

The choice of decision variables and their units can vary. For example, when deciding how many of an item to ship from each of two suppliers to a customer having a known demand of D units, you can define *two* variables—say, x and y—to represent the number of units to ship from the two suppliers, respectively. In this case, you would need demand constraints of the form:

$$x + y = D \qquad x, y \geq 0$$

Alternatively, you could define only the variable x as the number of units to ship from the first supplier; this implies that the amount $D - x$ is shipped by the second supplier. Here you would need the demand constraints:

$$x \leq D \qquad x \geq 0$$

The choice for a particular model should be based in part on the following points:

1. Your ability to find an efficient solution procedure for solving the resulting mathematical model.

2. Your ability to communicate an understanding of the problem's formulation. For example, the use of additional variables may make it easier for someone else to understand certain constraints.

3. Your ability to interpret and implement the resulting solution without undue effort. Reconsider the alternatives just discussed for choosing the decision variables to meet the known demand of D units. To implement the solution obtained from solving the model having only the variable x, you still need to calculate the value of $D - x$ to determine how much the second supplier ships to a customer. In contrast, solving the model with both variables x and y provides all the information you need for implementation.

Data-Collection Issues

As described in Section 2.1, the data needed for a problem are identified throughout the formulation process. These data are used to specify the objective function and constraints and must be obtained before the formulation is completed. As a manager, you should be aware that obtaining the values for the data can be time consuming, expensive, or even impossible because the information is simply unavailable. In such cases, you may have to request that the data be obtained at additional time and expense, (if possible), estimate the data to the best of your ability, or restrict the scope of the model so as to include only data that are available.

When data are estimated, be careful how much weight you give to the resulting solution. One way to gauge the reliability of the solution is to ask, "How *sensitive* is the solution to changes in the data?" That is, "What happens to the solution if certain data values are changed individually or together?" You can obtain the answer to these questions by solving the model repeatedly, each time changing the data appropriately. The larger the change in the solution, the more careful you must be in obtaining accurate estimates of the data. Sometimes there are more systematic approaches to answering these questions, as described in Chapter 4.

Implementation Issues

When formulating models, certain simplifications and omissions may have occurred because the data could not be obtained or because certain constraints were not identified during the formulation. Also, you may have had to make certain simplifying assumptions to get to a mathematical model that can be solved by the available computer package. As a result, the mathematical model is generally not a complete and accurate representation of the real problem. Thus, when a model is solved, you must validate the solution. You must review and examine the solution in the context of the original problem—rather than merely as the mathematical result of the formulation—to determine if implementing the solution is practical and makes sense. For example, a solution that recommends reducing the staff by twenty persons or closing down a plant may have implications not accounted for in the mathematical model. In such cases, a manager should use experience, expertise, and common sense either to modify the solution appropriately prior to implementation or to modify the mathematical formulation to reflect more accurately the actual problem and then resolve the new model.

After implementation, it is necessary to monitor the results to see that the solution achieves the objectives the organization expected. Also, the problem data may change over time (for example, the costs of raw material and interest rates), so it is often necessary to resolve the problem using the new data.

SUMMARY

In this chapter, you have learned to formulate and to classify mathematical models for solving deterministic decision problems. Both formulation and classification are reviewed in this section.

Problem Formulation

Formulating a problem means developing a mathematical model for that problem. Once the problem is in a mathematical form, there are many management science techniques available for obtaining the solution. To formulate a problem:

1. Identify the *decision variables*. These values, once determined, provide the solution to the problem. This task is accomplished by asking yourself any of the following questions:
   a. What items are you free to choose and/or control?
   b. What decisions do you have to make?
   c. What values constitute a solution that can be conveyed to someone else?
   d. What items affect costs and/or profits, or the overall objective?
2. Identify the problem *data*. These are known information items needed to develop the mathematical model. Whereas you can control the values of the variables, you *cannot* control the values of the data. You may need to identify problem data throughout the formulation process.
3. Identify the *objective function*. This is a single, overall organizational objective expressed in mathematical terms using the variables and the problem data. This task is accomplished by starting with a verbal statement of the objective and then using any of the following techniques to express this objective in mathematical terms:
   a. *Decomposing* the objective into a sum, difference, and/or product of individual terms.

b. *Working through a specific example.* Use specific values for the variables to determine how to compute the objective function. The goal of this technique is to understand how to express the objective function when the values of the variables are *not specifically known.*

If your problem has more than one objective, you can follow the procedure described in Chapter 7.

4. Identify the physical and logical *constraints.* These are imposed restrictions that prohibit you from choosing arbitrary values for the variables. To express these constraints in mathematical form, apply the same techniques used in identifying the objective function. If the problem has many constraints, try using the technique of *grouping* to identify a group of related constraints (such as meeting the demands of different customers). Each constraint within the group has a similar structure. Do not forget to include explicitly the implied constraints—that is, constraints, such as nonnegativity and the need for integer variables—that you know exist but that are not specifically stated.

Classifying Mathematical Models

Obtaining a solution to a mathematical model requires that you identify the *class* of problems to which it belongs. You can then choose an appropriate solution procedure. In this chapter, you have learned to classify models based on the following mathematical characteristics.

1. Is the problem *deterministic* or *stochastic*? If all the data are *known with certainty,* the problem is deterministic.
2. Is the deterministic problem *constrained* or *unconstrained*?
3. Does the constrained deterministic problem have *linear* or *nonlinear* constraints? If all the constraints can be expressed as a sum or difference of known constants times a single variable, the constraints are linear.
4. Does the deterministic problem have a *linear* or *nonlinear* objective function?
5. Does the deterministic problem have *integer* (whole numbers) or *continuous* variables?

Now that you know how to formulate and to classify mathematical models, the next step is to learn about the various techniques for solving those problems. Chapter 3 presents one class of problems for which there is an efficient solution procedure. The details of this solution procedure are then described in Chapters 4, 5, and 6.

EXERCISES

 EXERCISE 2.1   Identify a set of appropriate decision variables for this exercise. Provide relevant symbolic names and a complete description of each variable. You need not formulate the model.

Florida Citrus, Inc., processes orange juice into frozen concentrate at three plants located in Tampa, Miami, and Jacksonville. Pounds of oranges can be shipped from either of two groves located near Orlando and Gainesville to any plant. Given the cost of shipping and the selling price of the concentrate, the objective, subject to certain supply-and-demand constraints, is to determine how to ship these oranges from the two groves to the three processing plants to maximize total profit.

EXERCISE 2.2   Identify a set of appropriate decision variables for this exercise. Provide relevant symbolic names and a complete description of each variable. You need not formulate the model.

Pension Planners, Inc., manages one particular portfolio consisting of 1800, 1000, and 500 shares of three mutual funds. Given certain assumptions on the economic conditions in the next 2 months, the Portfolio Manager wants to determine the number of shares of each fund to sell or to buy in each of the next 2 months to maximize the expected value of the portfolio.

EXERCISE 2.3 For Exercise 2.1, the grove near Orlando has 20,000 pounds of oranges and the grove near Gainesville has 12,000 pounds of oranges. The plant in Tampa requires at least 8000 pounds of oranges to meet its production quota. The plants in Miami and Jacksonville each require at least 11,000 pounds of oranges. Use the technique of grouping to identify *all* groups of constraints. You need not formulate the constraints; however, specify the *number* of constraints in each group.

EXERCISE 2.4 When determining the number of shares to buy or sell in Exercise 2.2, management never wants to sell more shares than it has. Also, Fund 1 should never have more than twice as many shares as Fund 2 nor should Fund 2 have more than twice the number of shares as Fund 3. Finally, the total amount invested in each fund should not exceed $75,000. Use the technique of grouping to identify *all* groups of constraints. You need not formulate the constraints; however, specify the *number* of constraints in each group.

EXERCISE 2.5 For Exercise 2.1, use the technique of decomposition to express the objective function of maximizing profits given the following cost and revenue data:

	SHIPPING COST ($/ton) TO		
FROM	TAMPA	MIAMI	JACKSONVILLE
Orlando	50	75	60
Gainesville	60	90	45

	REVENUE ($/ton of oranges processed)
Tampa	550
Miami	750
Jacksonville	600

EXERCISE 2.6 For Exercise 2.2, assume that at the end of the second month, the price per share of Fund 1 is expected to be $28, that of Fund 2 $60, and that of Fund 3 $45. Formulate a constraint to ensure that with these prices, the value of the portfolio at the end of the second month is at least $125,000. Illustrate the use of decomposition.

EXERCISE 2.7 World Oil Company can buy two types of crude oil: light oil at a cost of $25 per barrel, and heavy oil at $22 per barrel. Each barrel of crude oil, when refined, yields three products: gasoline, jet fuel, and kerosene. The following table indicates the quantities in barrels of gasoline, jet fuel, and kerosene produced per barrel of each type of crude oil:

	GASOLINE	JET FUEL	KEROSENE
Light crude	0.45	0.18	0.30
Heavy crude	0.35	0.36	0.20

The refinery has contracted to deliver 1,260,000 barrels of gasoline, 900,000 barrels of jet fuel, and 300,000 barrels of kerosene. As the Production Manager, formulate a model to determine the amount of each type of crude oil to purchase that minimizes the total cost while meeting appropriate demands. Define all decision variables. Use the scheme in Section 2.3 to classify your model.

EXERCISE 2.8 Reconsider Exercise 2.7. Each barrel of light crude oil refined produces a waste of 0.07 barrel which is disposed at a cost of $1 per barrel of waste. Similarly, each barrel of heavy crude oil refined produces a waste of 0.09 barrel and costs $1.50 per barrel to dispose. Formulate a new model to incorporate these additional costs using the same data from Exercise 2.7.

EXERCISE 2.9 Carmac Company manufactures compact and subcompact cars. The production of each car requires a certain amount of raw material and labor, as specified in the following table:

	RAW MATERIAL (pounds)	LABOR (hours)
Compact	200	18
Subcompact	150	20
Unit cost ($)	10	70
Total available	80,000	9,000

The Marketing Division has estimated that at most 1500 compacts can be sold at $10,000 each and that at most 200 subcompacts can be sold at $8000 each. As Vice-President of Scheduling, formulate a model to determine how many of each type of car to manufacture so as to maximize the total profit (revenues minus expenses). Define all decision variables. Use the scheme in Section 2.3 to classify your model.

EXERCISE 2.10 Fresh Dairy Farms has two different machines for processing raw milk into low-fat milk, butter, or cheese. The amount of time required on each machine to produce each unit of resulting product and the net profits are provided in the following table:

	LOW-FAT MILK	BUTTER	CHEESE
Machine 1	0.2 min/gal	0.5 min/lb	1.5 min/lb
Machine 2	0.3 min/gal	0.7 min/lb	1.2 min/lb
Net profit	$0.22 /gal	$0.38 /lb	$0.72 /lb

Assuming that 8 hours are available on each machine each day, as Manager of the Production Department, formulate a model to determine a daily production plan that maximizes the net corporate profits and yields a minimum of 300 gallons of low-fat milk, 200 pounds of butter, and 100 pounds of cheese.

EXERCISE 2.11 Each gallon of milk, pound of cheese, and pound of apples provides a known number of milligrams of protein and vitamins A, B, and C. The following table includes those data together with the minimum daily requirements of the nutritional ingredients, as recommended by the U.S. Department of Agriculture. The table also includes the minimum amount of each food that should be included in the meal and its cost.

	MILK (mg/gal)	CHEESE (mg/lb)	APPLES (mg/lb)	MINIMUM DAILY REQUIREMENTS (mg)
Protein	40	30	10	80
Vitamin A	5	50	30	60
Vitamin B	20	30	40	50
Vitamin C	30	50	60	30
Minimum amount	0.5 gal	0.5 lb	0.5 lb	
Unit cost ($)	2.15	2.25	1.25	

As a dietician for a public school, formulate a model to determine the least-cost meal that meets all the daily nutritional requirements. Use the scheme in Section 2.3 to classify your model.

EXERCISE 2.12 An implicit assumption in the investment model of High-Tech in Example 2.4 in Section 2.2.3 is that any funds not used in a year cannot be used in any subsequent year. Modify the problem formulation to allow for carryovers of unused funds from one year to the next by defining the following four new variables and assuming that unused funds earn 10% interest annually:

$$U_1 = \text{the number of unused dollars after year 1}$$

$$U_2 = \text{the number of unused dollars after year 2}$$

$$U_3 = \text{the number of unused dollars after year 3}$$

$$U_4 = \text{the number of unused dollars after year 4}$$

EXERCISE 2.13 Rich Oil Company near Cleveland supplies gasoline to its distributors by truck. The company has recently received a contract to begin supplying 800,000 gallons of gasoline per month to distributors in Cincinnati. The company has $500,000 available to create a fleet consisting of three different types of trucks. The relevant capacity, purchase cost, operating cost, and maximum number of trips for each truck type are given in the following table:

TRUCK TYPE	CAPACITY (gal)	PURCHASE COST ($)	OPERATING COST ($/month)	MAXIMUM TRIPS/MONTH
1	6000	50,000	800	20
2	3000	40,000	650	25
3	2000	25,000	500	30

On the basis of maintenance and driver availability, the firm does not want to buy more than 10 vehicles for its fleet. Also, the company would like to make sure that at least three of the type-3 trucks are purchased. (They are needed for use on short-run/low-demand routes.) Finally, the company does not want more than half of the fleet to be type-1 trucks. As Manager of Operations, formulate a model to determine the composition of the fleet that minimizes the monthly operating costs while meeting the demands, staying within the budget and satisfying the other company requirements. Use the scheme in Section 2.3 to classify your model.

EXERCISE 2.14 World Airlines refuels its aircraft regularly at the four airports it serves. Jet fuel can be purchased from three possible vendors at each airport. The table indicates (1) the delivery (purchase plus shipping) cost per thousand gallons from each vendor to each airport, (2) the available number of thousands of gallons that each vendor can supply every month, and (3) the monthly requirement of jet fuel (in thousands of gallons) at each airport.

| AIRPORT | DELIVERY COSTS | | | REQUIRED AMOUNT OF FUEL |
	Vendor 1	Vendor 2	Vendor 3	
1	900	800	900	150
2	900	1200	1300	250
3	800	1300	500	350
4	1000	1400	1000	480
Maximum supply	300	600	700	

Formulate a model to determine the amounts to purchase and ship from each vendor to each airport so as to minimize the total cost while at least meeting the monthly demand at each airport and not exceeding the supply of any vendor. Use the scheme in Section 2.3 to classify your model.

EXERCISE 2.15   Mason Communication Commission has received requests from four new radio stations to be assigned frequencies. Two radio frequencies interfere if they are within 0.5 megahertz of each other. The following frequencies (in megahertz) are currently available: 100.0, 100.1, 100.3, 100.7, 101.0, 101.1, 101.4, 101.8. Formulate a model to determine if the Commission can assign four new frequencies and, if so, which ones. Use the scheme in Section 2.3 to classify your model. (Hint: You are free to assign or not to assign each frequency, so consider 0–1 variables.)

EXERCISE 2.16   The city of Dakota Heights wants to determine how many postal substations are needed to service its population. The city has been divided into eight postal zones. Five possible locations for the substations have been identified. Each location can service a number of different zones, as indicated in the following table:

LOCATION	ZONES THAT CAN BE SERVICED
1	1, 2, 3
2	1, 4, 5
3	2, 4, 5, 8
4	3, 5, 6, 7
5	6, 7, 8

Formulate a model to determine the fewest number of substations (and their locations) needed to service all eight postal zones. Use the scheme in Section 2.3 to classify your model. (Hint: Define an appropriate variable for each location.)

EXERCISE 2.17   Three divisions of the Twinsburg Company manufacture a product in which each complete unit consists of four units of component A and three units of component B. The two components (A and B) are manufactured from two different raw materials. There are 100 units of raw material 1 and 200 units of raw material 2 available. Each of the three divisions uses a different method for manufacturing the components, resulting in different raw-material requirements and outputs produced. The table gives the raw-material requirements per production run in each division and the number of each component produced by that run.

| | INPUT/RUN (units) | OUTPUT/RUN (units) | | |
| | RAW MATERIAL | COMPONENT | | |
DIVISION	1	2	A	B
1	8	6	7	5
2	5	9	6	9
3	3	8	8	4

For example, each production run at Division 1 requires 8 units of raw material 1 and 6 units of raw material 2. The output from this run is 7 units of A and 5 units of B. As Production Manager, formulate a model to determine the number of production runs for each division that maximizes the total number of completed units of the final product. Use the scheme in Section 2.3 to classify your model.

EXERCISE 2.18 The two products that Case Chemicals makes—CS-01 and CS-02—yield excessive amounts of three different pollutants: A, B, and C. The state government has ordered the company to install and to employ antipollution devices. The following table provides the current daily emissions in kg/1000 liters and the maximum of each pollutant allowed in kg.

POLLUTANT	CS-01	CS-02	MAXIMUM ALLOWED
A	25	40	43
B	10	15	20
C	80	60	50

The Manager of the Production Department has approved the installation of two antipollution devices. The emissions from each product can be handled by either device in any proportion. (The emissions are sent through a device only once—that is, the output of one device cannot be the input to the other or back to itself.) The following table shows the percentage of each pollutant from each product that is removed by each device.

| | DEVICE 1 | | DEVICE 2 | |
POLLUTANT	CS-01	CS-02	CS-01	CS-02
A	40	40	30	20
B	60	60	0	0
C	55	55	65	80

For example, if the emission from CS-01 is sent through Device 1, 40% of pollutant A, 60% of pollutant B, and 55% of pollutant C are removed. Manufacturing considerations dictate that CS-01 and CS-02 be produced in the ratio of 2 to 1. Formulate a model to determine a plan that maximizes the total daily production (amount of CS-01 plus amount of CS-02) while meeting governmental requirements. Use the scheme in Section 2.3 to classify your model.

EXERCISE 2.19 Philadelphia Paint Company produces three types of paints: Standard, Quality, and Premium. The current facilities can produce a maximum of 18,000 gallons of Standard, 10,000 gallons of Quality, and 5000 gallons of Premium per day. Due to economies of scale, the cost for producing each type of paint decreases as the number of gallons produced increases. For example, if x gallons of Standard paint are produced, then the cost per gallon is $a - bx$. The following table provides, for each type of paint, the values of a and b; the selling price per gallon; and the minimum daily demand.

TYPE OF PAINT	VALUES OF a	b	SALES PRICE ($/gal)	MINIMUM DEMAND (gal)
Standard	3	0.0001	6.50	10,000
Quality	4	0.0002	8.50	6,000
Premium	5	0.0003	11.00	2,500

The company can produce a combined total of up to 25,000 gallons of paint per day. As Production Supervisor, formulate a model to determine how much of each paint to produce that maximizes the profit (revenue minus cost). Use the scheme in Section 2.3 to classify your model.

EXERCISE 2.20   Formulate the portfolio-management problem of High-Tech in Example 2.4 in Section 2.2.3 using as the decision variables 1 if High-Tech is not to invest in a project and 0 if it is to invest.

EXERCISE 2.21   Containers, Inc., has received an order to make cylindrical steel drums, with a circular top and bottom. The total volume of the container is to be at least 10 cubic feet. The cost of the steel to make the side of the container is $3 per square foot. The cost for the top and bottom is $3.82 per square foot. As Production Engineer, formulate a model to determine a design that minimizes the cost of steel needed. Use the scheme in Section 2.3 to classify your model. (Hint: Recall that the volume of a cylinder with a height H and a radius R is $\pi R^2 H$, the surface area of the cylinder is $2\pi RH$, and the area of the top and the bottom is πR^2 each, where $\pi = 3.14159$.)

EXERCISE 2.22   Modify Example 2.5 in Section 2.2.4 to determine a location for the blood bank so that the distance to the farthest hospital is as small as possible. (Hint: Create a variable, say, D, to denote the distance to the farthest hospital. Include constraints to ensure that D is greater than or equal to the distance to all hospitals.)

EXERCISE 2.23   ABC Window Company sells windows for homes and apartment buildings through advertising. Management wishes to develop a method for predicting how much annual sales will be for a given annual amount of advertising dollars. Management believes that if X dollars are spent on advertising, then sales volume, Y, will be

$$Y = aX + b$$

The only problem is that management does not yet know the best values to use for a and b. To help determine those values, the Accounting Department has supplied the following historical data ($ thousands) for the past 6 years:

YEAR	ADVERTISING	ACTUAL SALES	PREDICTED SALES
1988	9.4	280.0	$9.4a + b$
1989	10.4	281.5	$10.4a + b$
1990	14.5	337.4	$14.5a + b$
1991	15.8	404.2	$15.8a + b$
1992	16.8	402.1	$16.8a + b$
1993	17.4	452.0	$17.4a + b$

The best values for a and b are the ones that minimize the sum of the squares of the amounts by which the actual sales values in the foregoing table would differ from the predicted sales value. Formulate a model to determine those values. Use the scheme in Section 2.3 to classify your model.

EXERCISE 2.24 The Leather Company produces baseball gloves, footballs, and leather straps using raw leather that is processed on a machine. For the coming week, there are 1000 square meters of leather and 40 hours of machine time available. As Production Manager, you want to determine a production plan for this week in the form of how many of each product to make that maximizes the net corporate profits.

   a. Identify the variables.
   b. Identify and assign a symbolic name to each *additional* data value you would have to obtain to be able to formulate a mathematical model.
   c. Formulate a mathematical model using the variable names from (a) and the symbolic names for the data from (b).

EXERCISE 2.25 Nutritionists at HealthNut Company are designing a new snack made from air-popped popcorn and natural peanut butter. The objective is to minimize the total cost of these ingredients used, but the final product must contain at least 4 grams of protein, not more than 10 grams of carbohydrates, and 2 grams of saturated fat.

   a. Identify the variables.
   b. Identify and assign a symbolic name to each *additional* data value you would have to obtain to be able to formulate a mathematical model.
   c. Formulate a mathematical model using the variable names from (a) and the symbolic names for the data from (b).

EXERCISE 2.26 The Research Division has identified six projects in which High-Tech can choose to invest or not. Each project has been evaluated to determine the amount of capital that must be invested, the expected rate of return, and also a risk factor using a proprietary algorithm. These data are summarized in the following table:

PROJECT	CAPITAL NEEDED ($)	RATE OF RETURN (%)	RISK
1	100,000	10	0.50
2	400,000	5	0.40
3	170,000	20	0.70
4	250,000	15	0.65
5	200,000	7	0.45
6	250,000	30	0.80

The general partners have agreed that the total risk, obtained by adding the risk factors for each project funded, should not exceed 3, and that no more than two projects having a risk factor greater than 0.6 should be undertaken. Using the variables

$$P_i = \begin{cases} 1, & \text{if project } i \text{ is undertaken} \\ 0, & \text{if project } i \text{ is not undertaken} \end{cases} \quad i = 1, \ldots, 6$$

a general partner has formulated the following model to determine which projects to fund so as to maximize the expected 1-year return on the amount invested and stay within a $1 million budget:

Maximize $\quad 10P_1 + 20P_2 + 34P_3 + 37.5P_4 + 14P_5 + 75P_6$

Subject to

$$100P_1 + 400P_2 + 170P_3 + 250P_4 + 200P_5 + 250P_6 \leq 1000$$
$$0.50P_1 + 0.40P_2 + 0.70P_3 + 0.65P_4 + 0.45P_5 + 0.80P_6 \geq 3$$
$$P_1, \quad P_2, \quad P_3, \quad P_4, \quad P_5, \quad P_6 \geq 0$$

Is this model correct? If not, identify and correct all mistakes.

EXERCISE 2.27   Chirality Company must produce at least 600,000 small screws and 400,000 large screws to meet demands for the next 4 weeks. These screws can be produced on two different machines, which are each available for 40 hours per week. The costs and time requirements for producing each size screw on each machine and the selling price of each size screw are given in the following table:

	SMALL SCREWS	LARGE SCREWS
Selling price ($/1000)	27.50	32.50
Cost on Machine 1 ($/1000)	6.25	7.75
Cost on Machine 2 ($/1000)	8.00	9.25
Time on Machine 1 (min/lb)	1.50	1.75
Time on Machine 2 (min/lb)	1.00	1.25

There are about 60 small screws in each pound and 40 large screws in each pound. Using the variables

S_1 = the number of thousands of small screws to produce on Machine 1 during the next 4 weeks

S_2 = the number of thousands of small screws to produce on Machine 2 during the next 4 weeks

L_1 = the number of thousands of large screws to produce on Machine 1 during the next 4 weeks

L_2 = the number of thousands of large screws to produce on Machine 2 during the next 4 weeks

the Production Manager has formulated the following model to maximize the profit and meet the demand with the limited availability of machine time in the next 4 weeks:

$$\text{Maximize} \quad 27.50S_1 + 27.50S_2 + 32.50L_1 + 32.50L_2$$

Subject to

$$
\begin{aligned}
S_1 + S_2 \quad\quad\quad\quad\quad &\geq 600000 \\
L_1 + L_2 &\geq 400000 \\
1.5S_1 \quad\quad + 1.75L_1 \quad\quad &\leq 40 \\
1.0S_2 \quad\quad + 1.25L_2 &\leq 40 \\
S_1, \quad S_2, \quad L_1, \quad L_2 &\geq 0
\end{aligned}
$$

Is this model correct? If not, identify and correct all mistakes.

SQUEEZING PROFITS

New England Apple Products makes sixteen Very Fine juice products from apples, oranges, cranberries, and assorted other fruits. The question New England Apple Products managers must ask is, "What mix of juice products leads to the greatest profit?" The answer may seem to be the common-sense response, "The mix that brings in the most money," but the problem turns out to be quite complex.

What complicates the search for the greatest profit is that the company has limited supplies of ingredients. Managers must make many decisions about how the company uses these limited resources, called constraints. To reach the best overall plan, New England Apple Product managers turned to management science and its tools, including the important mathematical principle of optimization. Managers built a linear, deterministic model and sought their answer through linear programming.

This video examines a simplified version of New England Apple Product's problem. A linear program is built in which only two made-up products—Cranapple and Appleberry—are considered. The demonstration states that the raw materials for these two products are the same—cranberry juice and apple juice—and that the only difference in the two final products lies in the recipe. How does the company make the greatest profit?

We assume the company makes a profit of 3 cents for each gallon of Cranapple juice sold and 4 cents for each gallon of Appleberry sold. Why, then, wouldn't managers decide to sell only Appleberry? Well, the constraints are that the company has a limited number of gallons of the ingredients—the cranberry juice and the apple juice—that go into making these two products. Still another ripple in the problem is that the two recipes call for different proportions of the two ingredients.

Step by step, the complete deterministic model emerges and, by applying a bit of algebra, the optimal solution is found from among many feasible solutions. The next time you're standing in the grocery store aisle reading off the list of ingredients in a juice product—or in many other products, for that matter—remember that one very important ingredient is not mentioned: management science. (Total running time is 5:47.)

Questions on the Video

1. Why can't this model lead to a decision that produces an infinite profit? What constrains the model from producing a solution in which an infinite amount of either product is sold?

2. In what way is linear programming a "hidden ingredient"? Compare the decision reached through linear programming with a decision based on a hunch.

Beyond the Video

1. What other types of blending problems can you envision in business and industry? Might linear programming apply to them all?

2. Consider a refinery that must supply several grades of unleaded gasoline under different brand names to several cut-rate gas stations. Identify the decision variables, constraints, and the objective function in general terms. Break the constraints down into physical limitations, management-imposed restrictions, external restrictions, implied relationships among products, and logical considerations.

Practical Considerations

1. Assume you have modeled a blending problem for your company. How difficult would it be to model another?

2. Again assuming that you have modeled a blending problem, how difficult do you think it would be to gather a complete set of data? How difficult would it be to maintain these data and to update them?

Source: "For All Practical Purposes," from *The Consortium for Mathematics and Its Applications* (Arlington, MA: 1986), Program 3.

APPLICATIONS OF LINEAR PROGRAMMING

$\cdots\cdots\cdots\cdots\cdots\cdots$

*T*he world of business continues to expand globally. For example, through a vigorous sales effort, American Steel has expanded its network of clients to include customers in Japan, Korea, Taiwan, and Mexico. Management feels that diversifying its client list from what had been an exclusive focus on customers in the United States can only improve its business position. The challenge facing American Steel is how to forge a plan that minimizes the costs of buying the ore, producing the steel, and distributing it to these customers.

The Case Study in this chapter examines how American Steel develops a linear program to tackle this problem.

In Chapter 2, you learned to formulate and classify deterministic problems according to the mathematical properties of the variables, objective function, and constraints. One such classification is the **linear programming problem**—that is, a problem in which the objective function and all constraints are linear and all the variables are continuous (allowed to assume fractional values). Special attention is given to linear programming problems because they have wide practical applications in such diverse areas as allocation of scarce resources, purchasing and manufacturing, diet planning, portfolio management, blending, and production planning, as illustrated with the examples in this chapter. In Chapters 4 to 6, you will learn how to obtain the solution to such problems efficiently using a computer.

Linear programming problem
A problem in which the objective function and all constraints are linear and all variables are continuous (allowed to assume fractional values).

■ 3.1 LINEAR PROGRAMMING MODELS FOR PRODUCT-MIX DECISIONS

Managers often need to determine how to allocate various scarce resources—such as labor, raw materials, and capital—to several alternatives that compete for these resources. The final decision is based on the availability of these resources and on achieving an overall objective for the organization. For example, in a production setting, the mix of products to manufacture is ultimately based on an overall corporate objective such as maximizing profits or minimizing total production costs. Linear programming models are often used to help managers make such decisions. Consider the problem faced by the management of BlubberMaid, Inc.

EXAMPLE 3.1 THE PRODUCT-MIX PROBLEM OF BLUBBERMAID, INC. BlubberMaid, Inc., manufactures three rubber-based products: Airtex (a spongy material), Extendex (a stretchy material), and Resistex (a hard material). All three products require the same three chemical polymers and a base. The amount of each ingredient used per pound of final product is given in Table 3.1.

TABLE 3.1 *Ingredients Used in Producing Airtex, Extendex, and Resistex*

PRODUCT	INGREDIENT (oz/lb of product)			
	POLYMER A	POLYMER B	POLYMER C	BASE
Airtex	4	2	4	6
Extendex	3	2	2	9
Resistex	6	3	5	2

For the coming week, BlubberMaid has a commitment to produce at least 1000 pounds of Airtex, 500 pounds of Extendex, and 400 pounds of Resistex, but the company management knows it can sell more of each of the three products. Current inventories of the ingredients are 500 pounds of polymer A, 425 pounds of polymer B, 650 pounds of polymer C, and 1100 pounds of the base. Each pound of Airtex nets the company a profit of $7, each pound of Extendex a profit of $7, and each pound of Resistex a profit of $6. As Manager of the Production Department, you need to determine an optimal production plan for this week. ■

3.1.1 *Identifying the Decision Variables*

Following the steps of problem formulation from Chapter 2, first identify the decision variables. Asking yourself what you can control and what information constitutes a production plan should lead you to identify the following variables:

A = the number of pounds of Airtex to produce this week

E = the number of pounds of Extendex to produce this week

R = the number of pounds of Resistex to produce this week

3.1.2 *Identifying the Objective Function*

For BlubberMaid, the logical objective is to determine how much of each product to make so as to maximize total profit. Applying the technique of decomposition leads to

Total profit = profit from Airtex + profit from Extendex + profit from Resistex

Because each pound of Airtex nets a profit of $7, A pounds of Airtex yields $7A$. Similarly, Extendex and Resistex contribute $7E$ and $6R$, respectively, to the total profit. In terms of the decision variables and the profit data, the objective function is

$$\text{Maximize} \quad 7A + 7E + 6R$$

3.1.3 *Identifying the Constraints*

Applying the technique of grouping should lead you to identify the following three groups of constraints:

1. Resource constraints to ensure that no more of the three polymers and base are used than are available.
2. Demand constraints to ensure that company commitments are met.
3. Logical constraints to specify that all production quantities are nonnegative.

RESOURCE CONSTRAINTS

This group consists of four constraints: one for each of the three polymers and one for the base. For the limited availability of 500 pounds of polymer A:

$$\text{Amount of polymer A used} \ \leq \ 500 \text{ pounds}$$

Using decomposition leads to

Amount of polymer A used = (amount used to produce A pounds of Airtex) +

(amount used to produce E pounds of Extendex) +

(amount used to produce R pounds of Resistex)

To determine the amount of polymer A used in making each product, work through a specific example. For instance, set $A = 100$, $E = 300$, and $R = 200$. According to the data in Table 3.1:

Amount of polymer A used in Airtex $= 4(100) =$ 400

Amount of polymer A used in Extendex $= 3(300) =$ 900

Amount of polymer A used in Resistex $= 6(200) = 1200$

In terms of the decision variables, then, you might think that the appropriate constraint for polymer A is

$$4A + 3E + 6R \leq 500$$

However, this constraint is *not* correct. The reason is that the *units* in the expression on the left-hand side are in *ounces* (see Table 3.1) but the units on the right-hand side are in *pounds*. This discrepancy can be corrected by converting the units of either side to those of the other side. For example, converting the 500 available pounds of polymer A to 8000 ounces (1 pound equals 16 ounces) results in the following constraint:

$$4A + 3E + 6R \leq 8000 \quad \text{(polymer A)}$$

Following similar logic for the remaining three resources results in these constraints:

$$2A + 2E + 3R \leq 6800 \quad \text{(polymer B)}$$
$$4A + 2E + 5R \leq 10400 \quad \text{(polymer C)}$$
$$6A + 9E + 2R \leq 17600 \quad \text{(base)}$$

DEMAND CONSTRAINTS

This group consists of three constraints: one for the minimum requirement on the amount of each of the three products. These constraints are

$$A \geq 1000 \quad \text{(Airtex)}$$
$$E \geq 500 \quad \text{(Extendex)}$$
$$R \geq 400 \quad \text{(Resistex)}$$

LOGICAL CONSTRAINTS

Because all production quantities must be nonnegative, the following logical constraints are needed:

$$A, E, R \geq 0$$

3.1.4 Complete Formulation and Solution of the Product-MixProblem of BlubberMaid, Inc.

As Manager of the Production Department, you put together all the pieces, which results in the following mathematical model of the linear programming problem of BlubberMaid, Inc.:

Maximize $\quad 7A + 7E + 6R$
Subject to

Linear Program
EX3_1.DAT

RESOURCE CONSTRAINTS

$$4A + 3E + 6R \leq 8000 \quad \text{(polymer A)}$$
$$2A + 2E + 3R \leq 6800 \quad \text{(polymer B)}$$
$$4A + 2E + 5R \leq 10400 \quad \text{(polymer C)}$$
$$6A + 9E + 2R \leq 17600 \quad \text{(base)}$$

DEMAND CONSTRAINTS

$$A \qquad\quad \geq \quad 1000 \qquad \text{(Airtex)}$$

$$E \quad \geq \quad 500 \qquad \text{(Extendex)}$$

$$R \geq \quad 400 \qquad \text{(Resistex)}$$

LOGICAL CONSTRAINTS

$$A, \quad E, \quad R \geq \quad 0$$

The optimal solution to this problem, computed using any linear programming software package, is

$$A = 1000.00$$

$$E = 533.33$$

$$R = 400.00$$

with an objective function value of 13,133.33. In other words, the optimal weekly plan is to produce 1000 pounds of Airtex, 533.33 pounds of Extendex, and 400 pounds of Resistex, resulting in a net profit of $13,133.33. You may want to verify this solution with your own linear programming software.

■ 3.2 LINEAR PROGRAMMING MODELS FOR MAKE-OR-BUY DECISIONS

In many production settings, a company may not have enough resources to meet an unexpectedly large demand for one or more products. In such cases, the company can supplement its production capacity by purchasing some of the products from outside suppliers. The central issue in those situations is for the managers to decide how much of each product to produce versus how much to purchase from the outside. A linear programming model is often useful in making such decisions, as illustrated by the following example.

EXAMPLE 3.2 THE MAKE-OR-BUY PROBLEM OF MTV STEEL COMPANY MTV Steel Company produces three sizes of tubes: A, B, and C, that sell, respectively, for $10, $12, and $9 per foot. To manufacture each foot of tube A requires 0.5 minutes of processing time on a particular type of shaping machine. Each foot of tube B needs 0.45 minutes, and each foot of tube C needs 0.6 minutes. After production, each foot of tube, regardless of type, requires 1 ounce of welding material. The total cost is estimated to be $3, $4, and $4 per foot of tubes A, B, and C, respectively.

For the coming week, MTV Steel has received exceptionally large orders totaling 2000 feet for tube A, 4000 feet for tube B, and 5000 feet for tube C. As only 40 hours of machine time are available this week and only 5500 ounces of welding material are in inventory, the Production Department will not be able to meet these demands, which require a total of 97 hours of machine time and 11,000 ounces of welding material. This high level of demand is not anticipated to continue. Rather than expanding the capacity of the production facilities, the management of MTV Steel is considering purchasing some of these tubes from suppliers in Japan at a delivered cost of $6 per foot of tube A, $6 per foot of tube B, and $7 per foot of tube C. These various data are summarized in Table 3.2. As Manager of the Production Department, you have been asked to make recommendations as to how much of each tube type to produce and how much to purchase from Japan so as to meet the demands and maximize the company's profits.

■

TABLE 3.2	*Data for the Make-or-Buy Problem of MTV Steel*					
TYPE	SELLING PRICE ($/ft)	DEMAND (ft)	MACHINE TIME (min/ft)	WELDING MATERIAL (oz/ft)	PRODUCTION COST ($/ft)	PURCHASE COST ($/ft)
A	10	2000	0.50	1	3	6
B	12	4000	0.45	1	4	6
C	9	5000	0.60	1	4	7
Amount available			40 hr	5500 oz		

3.2.1 *Identifying the Decision Variables*

In this problem, you are free to choose how many feet of each type of tube to produce and how many feet to purchase from Japan. This gives rise to the following six decision variables:

$$AP = \text{the number of feet of tube type A to produce}$$
$$BP = \text{the number of feet of tube type B to produce}$$
$$CP = \text{the number of feet of tube type C to produce}$$

$$AJ = \text{the number of feet of tube type A to buy from Japan}$$
$$BJ = \text{the number of feet of tube type B to buy from Japan}$$
$$CJ = \text{the number of feet of tube type C to buy from Japan}$$

3.2.2 *Identifying the Objective Function*

As stated in the problem description, the overall objective is to maximize total profits. Applying decomposition results in

$$\text{Total profits} = \text{(profits from production)} +$$
$$\text{(profits from products purchased from Japan)}$$

Applying decomposition to the profits from production yields

$$\text{Profits from production} = \text{(profits from producing type A tube)} +$$
$$\text{(profits from producing type B tube)} +$$
$$\text{(profits from producing type C tube)}$$

Each of these profits, in turn, is computed as the revenue minus the cost per foot. For example, because tubes of type A sell for $10 per foot but cost $3 to produce, the net profit is $7 per foot. Thus, the profit for producing AP feet of type A tube is $7AP$. A similar computation for type B and C tubes results in

$$\text{Profits from production} = 7AP + 8BP + 5CP$$

Applying a similar decomposition and logic to the products purchased from Japan results in

$$\text{Profits from products purchased from Japan} = 4AJ + 6BJ + 2CJ$$

As you would expect, each foot of tube produced results in a higher profit than each foot purchased from the outside supplier. Combining these two profit components results in the following overall objective function:

$$\text{Maximize} \qquad 7AP + 8BP + 5CP + 4AJ + 6BJ + 2CJ$$

3.2.3 Identifying the Constraints

Applying the technique of grouping should lead you to identify the following three groups of constraints:

1. Resource constraints to ensure that the amount of machine time and welding material used does not exceed available supplies.
2. Demand constraints to ensure that the demand for each type of tube is met.
3. Logical constraints.

RESOURCE CONSTRAINTS

To produce these tubes requires two resources: machine time and welding material. Because these resources are limited, two constraints are needed to ensure that the available supplies are not exceeded. The machine-time constraint is

Total machine time used should not exceed 40 hours

Appplying decomposition leads to

Total machine time used = (machine time used to produce type A tube) +

(machine time used to produce type B tube) +

(machine time used to produce type C tube)

Recall from Table 3.2 that each foot of tube A requires 0.5 minutes of machine time. Thus, to produce AP feet requires $0.5AP$ minutes. Similarly, each foot of tube B requires 0.45 minutes, and each foot of tube C needs 0.6 minutes. The constraint is:

$$0.5AP + 0.45BP + 0.6CP \le 40$$

However, observe that the quantity on the left-hand side is expressed in *minutes* whereas that on the right-hand side is expressed in *hours*. One way to correct this inconsistency is to convert 40 hours into $40 * 60 = 2400$ minutes:

$$0.5AP + 0.45BP + 0.6CP \le 2400 \qquad \text{(machine time)}$$

By turning to the availability of the welding material, the associated constraint is

Total welding material used should not exceed 5500 ounces

Applying decomposition and recalling that each foot of tube, regardless of type, requires 1 ounce of welding material, this resource constraint is

$$AP + BP + CP \le 5500 \qquad \text{(welding material)}$$

DEMAND CONSTRAINTS

This group consists of three constraints, one for the demand associated with each type of tube. For tube A:

Total number of feet of type A tube = 2000 feet

Applying decomposition:

Total number of feet of type A tube = (number of feet of type A produced) +

(number of feet of type A purchased from Japan)

$$= AP + AJ$$

Thus, the demand constraint for type A tube is

$$AP + AJ = 2000 \quad \text{(demand for type A)}$$

A similar logic results in the following demand constraints for types B and C tubes:

$$BP + BJ = 4000 \quad \text{(demand for type B)}$$
$$CP + CJ = 5000 \quad \text{(demand for type C)}$$

LOGICAL CONSTRAINTS

The only logical constraint in this problem is that all variables be nonnegative.

3.2.4 Complete Formulation and Solution of the Make-or-Buy Problem of MTV Steel Company

Putting together the pieces results in the following linear programming model for the problem of MTV Steel Company:

Maximize $\quad 7AP + \quad 8BP + \quad 5CP + 4AJ + 6BJ + 2CJ$
Subject to

Linear Program
EX3_2.DAT

DEMAND CONSTRAINTS

AP			$+\ AJ$		$= 2000$	(demand for type A)
	BP			$+\ BJ$	$= 4000$	(demand for type B)
		CP		$+\ CJ$	$= 5000$	(demand for type C)

RESOURCE CONSTRAINTS

$$0.5AP + 0.45BP + 0.6CP \qquad \le 2400 \quad \text{(machine time)}$$
$$AP + \quad BP + \quad CP \qquad \le 5500 \quad \text{(welding material)}$$

LOGICAL CONSTRAINTS

$$AP \ , \quad BP \ , \quad CP \ , \quad AJ \ , \quad BJ \ , \quad CJ \ge \quad 0$$

The optimal solution to this problem, obtained with any linear programming software package, is

$$AP = 2000.000$$

$$BP = 0.000$$

$$CP = 2333.333$$

$$AJ = 0.000$$

$$BJ = 4000.000$$

$$CJ = 2666.667$$

with a net profit of $55,000. In other words, MTV Steel should produce 2000 feet of type A tube and 2333.333 feet of type C tube while importing 4000 feet of type B tube and 2666.667 feet of type C tube from Japan. You may want to verify this solution with your own linear programming software.

■ 3.3 LINEAR PROGRAMMING MODELS FOR DIET PROBLEMS

Linear programming models can also be applied in the planning of diets. In particular, given a number of food alternatives, each of which yields a known amount of a needed nutrient, you want to determine how much of each food type to include in a diet to ensure minimum nutrient requirements while achieving an overall objective. Such a problem is illustrated in the following example.

EXAMPLE 3.3 THE DIET PROBLEM OF MOUNTAIN VIEW GENERAL HOSPITAL The Nutrition Department of the Mountain View General Hospital prepares 30 dinner menus, one for each day of the month. One meal consists of spaghetti, turkey, scalloped potatoes, spinach, and apple strudel. As Director of the Nutrition Department, you have determined that this meal must provide 63,000 milligrams (mg) of protein, 10 mg of iron, 15 mg of niacin, 1 mg of thiamin, and 50 mg of vitamin C. Each 100 grams of these foods provides the amount of each nutrient and fat indicated in Table 3.3.

TABLE 3.3 *Nutrients Provided by the Various Foods*

	NUTRIENT (mg/100 gm)					
	PROTEIN	IRON	NIACIN	THIAMIN	VITAMIN C	FAT
Spaghetti	5,000	1.1	1.4	0.18	0.0	5,000
Turkey	29,300	1.8	5.4	0.06	0.0	5,000
Potatoes	5,300	0.5	0.9	0.06	10.0	7,900
Spinach	3,000	2.2	0.5	0.07	28.0	300
Apple Strudel	4,000	1.2	0.6	0.15	3.0	14,300

To avoid too much of one type of food, not more than 300 grams of spaghetti, 300 grams of turkey, 200 grams of potatoes, 100 grams of spinach, and 100 grams of apple strudel should be included in the meal. As Director of the Nutrition Department, you want to determine the composition of a meal that meets the nutritional requirements and provides the least amount of fat. ■

3.3.1 *Identifying the Decision Variables*

In this problem, you can control how much of each of the five foods to include in the meal, leading you to define the following five variables:

$$SPAG = \text{the number of 100 grams of spaghetti to include}$$

$$TURK = \text{the number of 100 grams of turkey to include}$$

$$POTA = \text{the number of 100 grams of potatoes to include}$$

$$SPIN = \text{the number of 100 grams of spinach to include}$$

$$APPL = \text{the number of 100 grams of apple strudel to include}$$

For convenience, the units of the variables are chosen to be in hundreds of grams because those are the units used in Table 3.3.

3.3.2 *Identifying the Objective Function*

As stated in the problem description, the overall objective is to minimize the total fat content of the diet. Applying decomposition results in the following:

$$\text{Total fat content} = \text{(fat contributed by spaghetti)} +$$
$$\text{(fat contributed by turkey)} +$$
$$\text{(fat contributed by potatoes)} +$$
$$\text{(fat contributed by spinach)} +$$
$$\text{(fat contributed by apple strudel)}$$

Using the data in the last column of Table 3.3 and working through a specific example should lead you to identify the following overall objective:

$$\text{Minimize} \quad 5000SPAG + 5000TURK + 7900POTA + 300SPIN + 14300APPL$$

3.3.3 *Identifying the Constraints*

Applying the technique of grouping leads you to the following three groups of constraints:

1. Nutrient constraints to ensure that the meal provides the minimum amount of each nutrient.
2. Bound constraints to ensure that not too much of one type of food is included (for example, asking a patient to eat 1000 grams of spinach).
3. Logical constraints to ensure that all variables are nonnegative.

NUTRIENT REQUIREMENTS

This group consists of five constraints, one to ensure the minimum amount of each of the five nutrients. Consider the protein requirement:

$$\text{Total amount of protein in the meal} \geq 63000 \text{ mg}$$

Applying decomposition yields:

Total amount of protein in the meal = (amount of protein from spaghetti) +

(amount of protein from turkey) +

(amount of protein from potatoes) +

(amount of protein from spinach) +

(amount of protein from apple strudel)

Refer to the first column of Table 3.3. Each 100 grams of spaghetti contains 5000 mg of protein. Thus, $SPAG$ hundred grams of this food provides $5000SPAG$ mg of protein to the meal. Similarly, using the remaining data in the first column of Table 3.3 results in the following constraint for protein:

$$5000SPAG + 29300TURK + 5300POTA + 3000SPIN + 4000APPL \geq 63000 \quad \text{(protein)}$$

Although the units of the variables are expressed in hundreds of grams, the units on both sides of the foregoing constraint are in milligrams.

Using the next four columns of data in Table 3.3 results in the following similar constraints for each of the remaining four nutrients:

$$
\begin{aligned}
1.1SPAG + 1.8TURK + 0.5POTA + 2.2SPIN + 1.2APPL &\geq 10 \quad \text{(iron)} \\
1.4SPAG + 5.4TURK + 0.9POTA + 0.5SPIN + 0.6APPL &\geq 15 \quad \text{(niacin)} \\
0.18SPAG + 0.06TURK + 0.06POTA + 0.07SPIN + 0.15APPL &\geq 1 \quad \text{(thiamin)} \\
10POTA + 28SPIN + 3APPL &\geq 50 \quad \text{(vitamin C)}
\end{aligned}
$$

BOUND CONSTRAINTS

These restrictions limit the maximum amount of each food type in the meal. Keeping in mind that the units of the variables are in hundreds of grams, the following five bound constraints arise:

$$
\begin{aligned}
SPAG &\leq 3 \\
TURK &\leq 3 \\
POTA &\leq 2 \\
SPIN &\leq 1 \\
APPL &\leq 1
\end{aligned}
$$

LOGICAL CONSTRAINTS

The only logical constraint in this problem is that all variables be nonnegative.

3.3.4 Complete Formulation and Solution of the Diet Problem of Mountain View General Hospital

All this information results in the following linear programming model for the problem of Mountain View General Hospital:

Minimize

$5000SPAG + 5000TURK + 7900POTA + 300SPIN + 14300APPL$

Subject to

Linear Program
EX3_3.DAT

NUTRIENT CONSTRAINTS

$$
\begin{array}{rcl}
5000SPAG + 29300TURK + 5300POTA + 3000SPIN + 4000APPL & \geq & 63000 \quad \text{(protein)} \\
1.1SPAG + 1.8TURK + 0.5POTA + 2.2SPIN + 1.2APPL & \geq & 10 \quad \text{(iron)} \\
1.4SPAG + 5.4TURK + 0.9POTA + 0.5SPIN + 0.6APPL & \geq & 15 \quad \text{(niacin)} \\
0.18SPAG + 0.06TURK + 0.06POTA + 0.07SPIN + 0.15APPL & \geq & 1 \quad \text{(thiamin)} \\
10POTA + 28SPIN + 3APPL & \geq & 50 \quad \text{(vitamin C)}
\end{array}
$$

BOUND CONSTRAINTS

$$
\begin{array}{rcl}
SPAG & \leq & 3 \\
TURK & \leq & 3 \\
POTA & \leq & 2 \\
SPIN & \leq & 1 \\
APPL & \leq & 1
\end{array}
$$

LOGICAL CONSTRAINTS

$$
SPAG, \quad TURK, \quad POTA, \quad SPIN, \quad APPL \geq 0
$$

The optimal solution to this problem, which results from using any linear programming software package, is

$$
\begin{aligned}
SPAG &= 3.000 \\
TURK &= 2.833 \\
POTA &= 2.000 \\
SPIN &= 1.000 \\
APPL &= 0.667
\end{aligned}
$$

with a total fat content of 54,800 milligrams. In other words, the meal should consist of 300 grams of spaghetti, 283.3 grams of turkey, 200 grams of potatoes, 100 grams of spinach, and 66.7 grams of apple strudel. You may want to verify this solution with your own linear programming software.

■ 3.4 LINEAR PROGRAMMING MODELS FOR PORTFOLIO MANAGEMENT

Recall the portfolio-management problem of High-Tech in Example 2.4 in Section 2.2.3. The decision in that problem is to determine *which* investments to select. That problem required making a "no/yes" decision that resulted in an *integer programming model* with 0–1 variables. As you will see now, an investment decision may also require determining *how much* to invest in each available alternative. A linear programming model can often be formulated for a problem of this nature.

The overall objective of an investor is to gain the highest possible return. But high return comes at a price: risk. An investor must balance return against risk. Often a linear programming model can be formulated to design an investment strategy that achieves the maximum return while satisfying certain risk requirements. Consider the problem faced by the general partners of Pension Planners, Inc.

EXAMPLE 3.4 THE INVESTMENT PROBLEM OF PENSION PLANNERS, INC. The Portfolio Manager of Pension Planners, Inc., has been asked to invest $1,000,000 of a large pension fund. The Investment Research Department has identified six mutual funds with varying investment strategies, resulting in different potential returns and associated risks, as summarized in Table 3.4.

TABLE 3.4 *Risk and Expected Rate of Return for Six Mutual Funds*

	FUND					
	1	2	3	4	5	6
Price ($/share)	45	76	110	17	23	22
Expected return (%)	30	20	15	12	10	7
Risk category	High	High	High	Medium	Medium	Low

One way to control the risk is to limit the amount of money invested in the various funds. To that end, the management of Pension Planners, Inc., has specified the following guidelines:

1. The total amount invested in high-risk funds must be between 50 and 75% of the portfolio.
2. The total amount invested in medium-risk funds must be between 20 and 30% of the portfolio.
3. The total amount invested in low-risk funds must be at least 5% of the portfolio.

A second way to control risk is to diversify—that is, to spread the risk by investing in many different alternatives. The management of Pension Planners, Inc., has specified that the amount invested in the high-risk Funds 1, 2, and 3 should be in the ratio 1:2:3, respectively. The amount invested in the medium-risk Funds 4 and 5 should be 1:2.

With these guidelines, what portfolio should you, the Portfolio Manager, recommend so as to maximize the expected rate of return? ■

3.4.1 *Identifying the Decision Variables*

In this problem, you can control how much to invest in each of the six mutual funds, thus giving rise to six decision variables. As usual, you must specify the units associated with each variable. For example, for Fund 1, you could define any one of the following variables:

F_1 = the number of *shares* of Fund 1 to buy

F_1 = the number of *dollars* to invest in Fund 1

F_1 = the *fraction* of the portfolio to invest in Fund 1

Each choice leads to a different, but equivalent, mathematical model. Here, the last choice is used. In the exercises at the end of this chapter, you are asked to develop the appropriate models corresponding to the other two choices. So, for each of the remaining funds, define:

F_2 = the fraction of the portfolio to invest in Fund 2

F_3 = the fraction of the portfolio to invest in Fund 3

F_4 = the fraction of the portfolio to invest in Fund 4

F_5 = the fraction of the portfolio to invest in Fund 5

F_6 = the fraction of the portfolio to invest in Fund 6

3.4.2 *Identifying the Objective Function*

As stated in the problem description, the overall objective is to maximize the expected rate of return—that is,

$$\text{Expected rate of return} \ = \ \frac{\text{expected total return}}{\text{amount invested}}$$

Applying decomposition to the numerator leads to

$$\text{Expected total return} = (\text{expected return from Fund 1}) +$$
$$(\text{expected return from Fund 2}) +$$
$$(\text{expected return from Fund 3}) +$$
$$(\text{expected return from Fund 4}) +$$
$$(\text{expected return from Fund 5}) +$$
$$(\text{expected return from Fund 6})$$

To determine the expected return from Fund 1, work through a specific example in which 10% of the portfolio is invested in Fund 1—that is, $F_1 = 0.10$. In this case, $0.10 * 1,000,000 = \$100,000$ of the portfolio are invested in Fund 1. According to the data in Table 3.4, these monies are expected to return 30%, or $0.30 * 100,000 = \$30,000$. Thus, in terms of F_1,

$$\text{Expected return from Fund 1} = (\text{amount invested in Fund 1}) *$$
$$(\text{rate of return from Fund 1})$$
$$= (F_1 * 1,000,000) * 0.30$$
$$= 300000 F_1$$

Using a similar logic for the remaining five funds leads to

$$\text{Expected total return} = 300000 F_1 + 200000 F_2 + 150000 F_3 +$$
$$120000 F_4 + 100000 F_5 + \ \ 70000 F_6$$

Dividing this by the total investment of \$1,000,000 provides the rate of return and hence the following objective function:

$$\text{Maximize} \quad 0.30 F_1 + 0.20 F_2 + 0.15 F_3 + 0.12 F_4 + 0.10 F_5 + 0.07 F_6$$

3.4.3 *Identifying the Constraints*

Applying the technique of grouping should lead you to identify the following three groups of constraints:

1. Investment limitations to control the amount invested in each of the three risk categories.
2. Diversification constraints to spread the investment within each risk category.
3. Logical constraints.

INVESTMENT-LIMITATION CONSTRAINTS

This group consists of three subgroups of constraints, one for each category of risk, namely:

1. The total amount invested in high-risk funds must be between 50 and 75% of the portfolio. Because F_1, F_2, and F_3 represent the fraction of the portfolio to invest in high-risk funds, the fraction of the total portfolio invested in high-risk funds is $F_1 + F_2 + F_3$. These constraints are

$$F_1 + F_2 + F_3 \geq 0.50 \qquad \text{(minimum in high risk)}$$

$$F_1 + F_2 + F_3 \leq 0.75 \qquad \text{(maximum in high risk)}$$

2. The total amount invested in medium-risk funds must be between 20 and 30% of the portfolio. Because F_4 and F_5 represent the fraction of the portfolio to invest in medium-risk funds, the fraction of the total portfolio invested in medium-risk funds is $F_4 + F_5$. These constraints are

$$F_4 + F_5 \geq 0.20 \qquad \text{(minimum in medium risk)}$$

$$F_4 + F_5 \leq 0.30 \qquad \text{(maximum in medium risk)}$$

3. The total amount invested in low-risk funds must be at least 5% of the portfolio. Because F_6 is the fraction of the portfolio invested in low-risk funds, this constraint is

$$F_6 \geq 0.05 \qquad \text{(minimum in low risk)}$$

DIVERSIFICATION CONSTRAINTS

This group of constraints is used to control risk by ensuring that the amount invested in the funds within a given risk category is in the specified ratio, as follows:

1. The amount invested in high-risk Funds 1, 2, and 3 should be in the ratio 1:2:3. This constraint specifies that the amount invested in Fund 2 be twice the amount invested in Fund 1:

$$F_2 = 2F_1$$

Rearranging this so that all variables are on the left-hand side, results in

$$-2F_1 + F_2 = 0 \qquad \text{(ratio of } F_1 \text{ to } F_2\text{)}$$

Similarly, the amount invested in Fund 3 is to be three times that invested in Fund 1:

$$F_3 = 3F_1$$

or

$$-3F_1 + F_3 = 0 \qquad \text{(ratio of } F_1 \text{ to } F_3\text{)}$$

2. The amount invested in medium-risk Funds 4 and 5 should be in the ratio of 1:2—that is, the amount invested in Fund 5 should be twice that in Fund 4:

$$F_5 = 2F_4$$

Rearranging this so that all variables are on the left-hand side, results in

$$-2F_4 + F_5 = 0 \qquad \text{(ratio of } F_4 \text{ to } F_5\text{)}$$

LOGICAL CONSTRAINTS

Of course, one set of logical constraints is that each variable be nonnegative. Also because it *is* possible to buy fractional shares of a mutual fund, these variables are allowed to have *any* fractional value, which results in a linear programming problem. Moreover, another logical constraint is needed to ensure that the total portfolio of precisely $1,000,000 is invested. Because the decision variables represent the *fraction* of this portfolio to invest in the various funds, this constraint is

Total fraction of $1,000,000 invested should equal 1

or

$$F_1 + F_2 + F_3 + F_4 + F_5 + F_6 = 1.0 \qquad \text{(total portfolio)}$$

3.4.4 *Complete Formulation and Solution of the Investment Problem of Pension Planners, Inc.*

The entire linear programming model for the general partners of Pension Planners, Inc., follows:

Maximize
$$0.30F_1 + 0.20F_2 + 0.15F_3 + 0.12F_4 + 0.10F_5 + 0.07F_6$$
Subject to

Linear Program
EX3_4.DAT

INVESTMENT-LIMITATION CONSTRAINTS

$F_1 +$	$F_2 +$	F_3				≥ 0.50	(minimum in high risk)
$F_1 +$	$F_2 +$	F_3				≤ 0.75	(maximum in high risk)
			$F_4 +$	F_5		≥ 0.20	(minimum in medium risk)
			$F_4 +$	F_5		≤ 0.30	(maximum in medium risk)
					$F_6 \geq 0.05$		(minimum in low risk)

DIVERSIFICATION CONSTRAINTS

$-2F_1 +$	F_2				$= 0$	(ratio of F_1 to F_2)
$-3F_1 +$		F_3			$= 0$	(ratio of F_1 to F_3)
			$- 2F_4 +$	F_5	$= 0$	(ratio of F_4 to F_5)

LOGICAL CONSTRAINTS

$F_1 +$	$F_2 +$	$F_3 +$	$F_4 +$	$F_5 +$	$F_6 = 1.0$	(total portfolio)
$F_1,$	$F_2,$	$F_3,$	$F_4,$	$F_5,$	$F_6 \geq 0$	

The optimal solution to this problem, which any linear programming software package yields, is:

$F_1 = 0.1250$

$F_2 = 0.2500$

$F_3 = 0.3750$

$F_4 = 0.0667$

$$F_5 = 0.1333$$

$$F_6 = 0.0500$$

with a rate of return of 0.168583. In other words, the amount of money invested in each of the six funds is

$$\text{Amount in Fund 1} = 0.1250 * 1,000,000 = \$ \quad 125,000$$
$$\text{Amount in Fund 2} = 0.2500 * 1,000,000 = \$ \quad 250,000$$
$$\text{Amount in Fund 3} = 0.3750 * 1,000,000 = \$ \quad 375,000$$
$$\text{Amount in Fund 4} = 0.0667 * 1,000,000 = \$ \quad 66,700$$
$$\text{Amount in Fund 5} = 0.1333 * 1,000,000 = \$ \quad 133,300$$
$$\text{Amount in Fund 6} = 0.0500 * 1,000,000 = \$ \quad 50,000$$

$$\text{Total Investment} \qquad\qquad\qquad = \$1,000,000$$

with an expected rate of return of 16.86% (or $168,600 total return). You may want to verify this solution with your own linear programming software.

Recall that the decision variables are defined as the *fraction* of the portfolio to invest, rather than the number of dollars. This approach has a distinct advantage. Should the dollar amount of the portfolio change—a likely event—the current model remains unchanged. You simply need to multiply the fractions obtained in the foregoing solution by the new portfolio size to determine the new amounts to invest in each of the six funds.

■ 3.5 Linear Programming Models for Blending Problems

Another example of the use of a linear programming model is in the blending of various components to produce a final product. For example, how does a refinery blend and process crude oils to produce gasoline? How does a metal-making business blend alloys to produce a new alloy with certain properties? In blending problems, each component contains certain ingredients, such as sulfur in the crude oil or iron in an alloy. The final blend may call for these ingredients to be present in certain amounts. The objective in a blending problem is to determine the amount of each component in the blend that yields the desired product at a minimum cost. Consider the gasoline-blending problem facing the managers at Hexxon Oil Company.

EXAMPLE 3.5 THE GASOLINE-BLENDING PROBLEM OF HEXXON OIL COMPANY
Hexxon Oil Company obtains three types of crude oils from its wells in Mississippi, New Mexico, and Texas. The gasoline obtained from these crude oils is blended together with two additives to obtain the final product. These crude oils and additives contain sulfur, lead, and phosphorus, as shown in Table 3.5. The cost of each component is also presented. Due to by-products and impurities, each gallon of Mississippi crude oil results in only 0.35 gallon of the final product, which contains 0.07% sulfur. Similarly, each gallon of New Mexico crude yields 0.40 gallon of the final product containing 0.08% sulfur and each gallon of Texas crude results in 0.30 gallon of the final product containing 0.10% sulfur. Management has set up the following specifications to control the amounts of sulfur, lead, and phosphorus:

1. Each gallon must have at most 0.07% sulfur.
2. Each gallon must have between 1.25 and 2.5 grams of lead.
3. Each gallon must have between 0.0025 and 0.0045 grams of phosphorus.
4. The total amount of the additives cannot exceed 19% of the blend.

TABLE 3.5 *Composition and Cost of the Blending Components*					
	CRUDE OILS			ADDITIVES	
	MISSISSIPPI	NEW MEXICO	TEXAS	1	2
Sulfur (%)	0.07	0.08	0.10	—	—
Lead (gm/gal)	—	—	—	7	6
Phosphorus (gm/gal)	—	—	—	0.025	0.02
Cost ($/gal)	0.55	0.47	0.33	0.08	0.12

As Production Manager, determine a blending plan that yields an acceptable gasoline at the least cost. ∎

3.5.1 *Identifying the Decision Variables*

You can control how much of each type of crude and each additive to blend when producing a gallon of gasoline. This leads to the following five decision variables:

x_M = the number of gallons of Mississippi crude oil used in making 1 gallon of gasoline

x_N = the number of gallons of New Mexico crude oil used in making 1 gallon of gasoline

x_T = the number of gallons of Texas crude oil used in making 1 gallon of gasoline

A_1 = the number of gallons of Additive 1 used in making 1 gallon of gasoline

A_2 = the number of gallons of Additive 2 used in making 1 gallon of gasoline

3.5.2 *Identifying the Objective Function*

As stated in the problem description, the overall objective is to minimize the cost of the components used in making each gallon of gasoline. Applying decomposition leads to

Total cost = (cost of Mississipi crude oil) + (cost of New Mexico crude oil) +
(cost of Texas crude oil) + (cost of Additive 1) + (cost of Additive 2)

Using the variables and the associated costs in Table 3.5 results in the following objective function:

$$\text{Minimize} \quad 0.55x_M + 0.47x_N + 0.33x_T + 0.08A_1 + 0.12A_2$$

3.5.3 *Identifying the Constraints*

Applying the technique of grouping should lead you to identify the following three groups of constraints:

1. A production constraint to ensure that 1 gallon of gasoline is produced, because the blending plan is for *each* gallon.
2. Blend-composition constraints to ensure that the resulting gasoline meets the sulfur, lead, phosphorus, and additive requirements.
3. Logical constraints.

PRODUCTION CONSTRAINT

This constraint ensures that precisely 1 gallon of gasoline is produced:

$$\text{Amount of gasoline produced } = \text{ 1 gallon}$$

Applying decomposition leads to

Amount of gasoline produced = (amount produced from Mississippi crude oil) +

(amount produced from New Mexico crude oil) +

(amount produced from Texas crude oil) +

(amount of additive 1) + (amount of additive 2)

Recall that each gallon of Mississippi crude yields only 0.35 gallon of gasoline. Thus, x_M gallons of this crude yield $0.35x_M$ gallon of gasoline. Similarly, because each gallon of New Mexico crude oil yield 0.40 gallon of gasoline and each gallon of Texas crude oil results in 0.30 gallon of gasoline, this constraint is

$$0.35x_M + 0.40x_N + 0.30x_T + A_1 + A_2 = 1.0 \qquad \text{(production)}$$

BLEND-COMPOSITION CONSTRAINTS

This group consists of three sets of constraints, one for each of the sulfur, lead, and phosphorus restrictions on the final blend. For example, for sulfur:

$$\text{Proportion of sulfur in the blend } \leq 0.0007 \qquad \text{(that is, } \leq 0.07\%)$$

Applying decomposition,

$$\text{Proportion of sulfur in the blend } = \frac{\text{amount of sulfur in the blend}}{\text{total amount of the blend}}$$

However, from the foregoing production constraint, the total amount of the blend is precisely 1 gallon, so all that need be computed is the amount of sulfur in the blend. Applying decomposition,

Amount of sulfur in the blend = (amount of sulfur from Mississippi crude oil) +

(amount of sulfur from New Mexico crude oil) +

(amount of sulfur from Texas crude oil) +

(amount of sulfur from Additive 1) +

(amount of sulfur from Additive 2)

According to Table 3.5, each gallon of Mississippi crude oil yields 0.35 gallon of gasoline containing 0.07% sulfur. Thus, x_M gallons of this crude oil yield $0.35x_M$ gallon that contains 0.07% sulfur. So

$$\text{Amount of sulfur from Mississippi crude oil } = 0.0007 * 0.35x_M$$

$$= 0.000245x_M$$

Noting that the additives contribute no sulfur, and applying similar logic to the other two crude oils results in the following sulfur constraint:

$$0.35 * 0.0007x_M + 0.40 * 0.0008x_N + 0.30 * 0.001x_T \leq 0.0007$$

or

$$0.000245x_M + 0.00032x_N + 0.0003x_T \leq 0.0007 \quad \text{(sulfur)}$$

There are both lower and upper limits on the amounts of lead and phosphorus in the final blend. Applying the same reasoning as used in developing the sulfur constraint results in the following four constraints for lead and phosphorus:

$$7A_1 + 6A_2 \leq 2.50 \quad \text{(upper limit on lead)}$$
$$7A_1 + 6A_2 \geq 1.25 \quad \text{(lower limit on lead)}$$

$$0.025A_1 + 0.02A_2 \leq 0.0045 \quad \text{(upper limit on phosphorus)}$$
$$0.025A_1 + 0.02A_2 \geq 0.0025 \quad \text{(lower limit on phosphorus)}$$

Finally, there is a restriction that the blend contain at most 19% of additives. Thus, the total of A_1 and A_2 must be at most 0.19 gallon, resulting in the following constraint:

$$A_1 + A_2 \leq 0.19 \quad \text{(upper limit on additives)}$$

LOGICAL CONSTRAINTS

The only logical constraint is that all variables be nonnegative.

3.5.4 Complete Formulation and Solution of the Blending Problem of the Hexxon Oil Company

As Production Manager of Hexxon Oil Company, you put this information together in the following linear programming model:

Minimize $\quad 0.55x_M + 0.47x_N + 0.33x_T + 0.08A_1 + 0.12A_2$

Subject to

Linear Program
EX3_5.DAT

PRODUCTION CONSTRAINT

$$0.35x_M + 0.40x_N + 0.30x_T + A_1 + A_2 = 1.0 \quad \text{(production)}$$

BLEND-COMPOSITION CONSTRAINTS

$$0.000245x_M + 0.00032x_N + 0.0003x_T \leq 0.0007 \quad \text{(sulfur)}$$
$$7A_1 + 6A_2 \leq 2.50 \quad \text{(upper limit on lead)}$$
$$7A_1 + 6A_2 \geq 1.25 \quad \text{(lower limit on lead)}$$
$$0.025A_1 + 0.02A_2 \leq 0.0045 \quad \text{(upper limit on phosphorus)}$$
$$0.025A_1 + 0.02A_2 \geq 0.0025 \quad \text{(lower limit on phosphorus)}$$
$$A_1 + A_2 \leq 0.19 \quad \text{(upper limit on additives)}$$

LOGICAL CONSTRAINT

$$x_M, \ x_N, \ x_T, \ A_1, \ A_2 \geq 0$$

The optimal solution to this problem, which results from using any linear programming software package, is

$$x_M = 0.0000$$

$$x_N = 1.3750$$

$$x_T = 0.8667$$

$$A_1 = 0.1400$$

$$A_2 = 0.0500$$

with an objective function value of 0.94945. In other words, each gallon of final product is made by blending and processing 1.3750 gallons of New Mexico crude oil and 0.8667 gallon of Texas crude oil with 0.14 gallon of Additive 1 and 0.05 gallon of Additive 2, at a total cost of 94.945 cents. You may want to verify this solution with your own linear programming software.

■ 3.6 LINEAR PROGRAMMING MODELS FOR AGGREGATE PRODUCTION PLANNING

Another application of linear programming is in the area of production planning. Managers in production planning must determine how many of one or more items to produce and how many to draw from existing inventories to meet anticipated demands for a specific period of time. Any leftover items are stored in inventory. The overall objective is to minimize total costs, made up of production, inventory, and other charges. Consider the problem facing the management of National Steel Corporation.

EXAMPLE 3.6 THE PRODUCTION-PLANNING PROBLEM OF NATIONAL STEEL COR-PORATION National Steel Corporation (NSC) produces a special-purpose steel used in the aircraft and aerospace industries. The Sales Department of NSC has received orders of 2400, 2200, 2700, and 2500 tons of steel for each of the next 4 months. NSC can meet these demands by producing the steel, by drawing from its inventory, or by using any combination of the two alternatives.

The production costs per ton of steel during each of the next 4 months are projected to be $7400, $7500, $7600, and $7650. Because costs are rising each month—due to inflationary pressures—NSC might be better off producing more steel than it needs in a given month and storing the excess. Production capacity, though, cannot exceed 4000 tons in any one month. The monthly production is finished at the end of the month, at which time the demand is met. Any remaining steel is then stored in inventory at a cost of $120 per ton for each month that it remains there. These data are summarized in Table 3.6.

If the production level is increased from one month to the next, then the company incurs a cost of $50 per ton of increased production to cover the additional labor and/or overtime. Each ton of decreased production incurs a cost of $30 to cover the benefits of unused employees.

TABLE 3.6	*Data for the Production-Planning Problem of NSC*			
	MONTH			
	1	2	3	4
Demand (tons)	2400	2200	2700	2500
Production cost ($/ton)	7400	7500	7600	7650
Inventory cost ($/ton/month)	120	120	120	120

The production level during the previous month was 1800 tons, and the beginning inventory is 1000 tons. Inventory at the end of the fourth month must be at least 1500 tons to cover anticipated demand. Formulate a production plan for NSC that minimizes the total costs over the next 4 months. ■

3.6.1 *Identifying the Decision Variables*

In this problem, you are free to choose how many tons of steel to produce each month to meet demand. Four variables arise:

x_1 = the number of tons of steel to produce during month 1

x_2 = the number of tons of steel to produce during month 2

x_3 = the number of tons of steel to produce during month 3

x_4 = the number of tons of steel to produce during month 4

At first glance, you might think that these are all the variables needed. With these variables, you can always determine the amount in inventory. For example, from the schematic diagram in Figure 3.1, the inventory at the end of the first month is

Inventory at the end of month 1 = beginning inventory + production amount − demand

$$= 1000 + x_1 - 2400$$

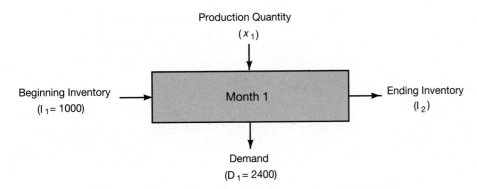

FIGURE 3.1 Relationship Among Inventory Levels, Production, and Demand.

However, writing the inventory at the end of the second, third, and subsequent months is more complicated. For example, for month 2:

Inventory at the end of month 2 = beginning inventory + production amount − demand
$$= (1000 + x_1 - 2400) + x_2 - 2200$$

To simplify, it is expedient to create five more variables to represent the inventory levels *at the beginning* of each month:

$$I_1 = \text{inventory in tons at the beginning of month 1}$$
$$I_2 = \text{inventory in tons at the beginning of month 2}$$
$$I_3 = \text{inventory in tons at the beginning of month 3}$$
$$I_4 = \text{inventory in tons at the beginning of month 4}$$
$$I_5 = \text{inventory in tons at the beginning of month 5}$$

3.6.2 *Identifying the Objective Function*

As stated in the problem description, the overall objective is to minimize the total costs over the 4-month planning horizon. Applying decomposition to identify three different cost components leads to

Total costs = production costs + inventory costs + change-in-production costs

PRODUCTION COSTS

Applying decomposition again identifies the production costs as the sum of the production costs in each of the 4 months. Using the production variables x_1, x_2, x_3, and x_4 together with the per-ton production costs in Table 3.6 yields

$$\text{Production costs} = 7400x_1 + 7500x_2 + 7600x_3 + 7650x_4$$

INVENTORY COSTS

A similar decomposition yields a total inventory cost as the sum of the inventory costs during each of the 4 months. Because the inventory levels change *only* at the end of the month, all inventories at the beginning of the month incur a cost of $120 per ton for that month. Using variables I_1, I_2, I_3, and I_4 yields

$$\text{Inventory costs} = 120I_1 + 120I_2 + 120I_3 + 120I_4$$

Observe that I_5 is not included in this portion because the objective is to minimize total costs over the next 4 months only, and I_5 incurs cost during the fifth month.

CHANGE-IN-PRODUCTION COSTS

To determine the change-in-production costs from one month to the next, work through a specific example in which, say, $x_1 = 100$ and $x_2 = 300$. In this case, there is an increase of $300 - 100 = 200$ tons of steel from month 1 to month 2. Thus, at a cost of $50 per ton of increase,

$$\text{Change-in-production cost} = (300 - 100) * 50 = \$10,000$$

Using this example, you might write the following general expression:

$$\text{Change-in-production cost} = (x_2 - x_1) * 50$$

However, what if $x_1 = 300$ and $x_2 = 100$? That is, what if the production level *decreases*. In this case, the foregoing expression results in a cost of $(100 - 300) * 50 = -\$10,000$ — that is, a *profit* of $10,000, which makes no sense. Instead, at a cost of $30 per ton of decrease, the correct expression is

$$\text{Change-in-production cost} = (300 - 100) * 30$$
$$= \$6000$$

In general, when the production level decreases from month 1 to month 2, the correct expression is

$$\text{Change-in-production cost} = (x_1 - x_2) * 30$$

Combining the expressions for an increase and a decrease results in the following change-in-production costs from month 1 to month 2:

$$\text{Change-in-production costs} = \begin{cases} 50(x_2 - x_1), & \text{if } x_2 \geq x_1 \quad \text{(increase)} \\ 30(x_1 - x_2), & \text{if } x_1 > x_2 \quad \text{(decrease)} \end{cases}$$

Because the values of x_1 and x_2 are as yet unknown, the issue is how to combine these two cases into a single expression.

One approach is to create additional decision variables whose values are precisely the amounts of increased and decreased production from one month to the next. That is,

S_1 = the number of tons of increased production in month 1

D_1 = the number of tons of decreased production in month 1

S_2 = the number of tons of increased production in month 2

D_2 = the number of tons of decreased production in month 2

S_3 = the number of tons of increased production in month 3

D_3 = the number of tons of decreased production in month 3

S_4 = the number of tons of increased production in month 4

D_4 = the number of tons of decreased production in month 4

The values of these variables depend on the production levels. For example, when $x_2 = 300$ and $x_1 = 100$, you want S_2 to be 200 and D_2 to be 0. If $x_2 = 100$ and $x_1 = 300$, you want S_2 to be 0 and D_2 to be 200. The constraints that ensure the proper relationships among these variables are identified in the next section.

With these new variables, when S_1 is positive, D_1 must be 0. Similarly, when D_1 is positive, S_1 must be 0. Thus, the change-in-production costs for the first month are $50S_1 + 30D_1$. Hence, the total change-in-production costs are

$$\text{Change-in-production costs} = (\text{change-in-production cost in month 1}) +$$
$$(\text{change-in-production cost in month 2}) +$$
$$(\text{change-in-production cost in month 3}) +$$
$$(\text{change-in-production cost in month 4})$$
$$= (50S_1 + 30D_1) + (50S_2 + 30D_2) +$$
$$(50S_3 + 30D_3) + (50S_4 + 30D_4)$$

COMPLETE OBJECTIVE FUNCTION

Combining the three cost components results in the following overall objective function:

$$\text{Minimize total costs} = 7400x_1 + 7500x_2 + 7600x_3 + 7650x_4 +$$
$$120I_1 + 120I_2 + 120I_3 + 120I_4 +$$
$$50S_1 + 30D_1 + 50S_2 + 30D_2 + 50S_3 + 30D_3 + 50S_4 + 30D_4$$

3.6.3 *Identifying the Constraints*

Applying the technique of grouping should lead you to identify the following six groups of constraints:

1. Initial and final inventory constraints to ensure the proper beginning and ending inventory levels.
2. Production-bound constraints to ensure that the production in any given month not exceed 4000 tons.
3. Inventory-balance constraints to ensure the proper relationship between the production and inventory variables.
4. The change-in-production constraints to ensure the proper relationship between the production and change-in-production variables.
5. Demand constraints to ensure that demands are met in each month.
6. Logical constraints to ensure all variables are nonnegative.

INITIAL AND FINAL INVENTORY CONSTRAINTS

In words, the two constraints in this group are

1. Initial inventory level is 1000 tons.
2. Final inventory level must be at least 1500 tons.

Because I_1 and I_5 represent the initial and final inventories at the beginning and end of the 4-month planning period, respectively, these constraints are

$$I_1 = 1000 \quad \text{(beginning inventory)}$$
$$I_5 \geq 1500 \quad \text{(ending inventory)}$$

PRODUCTION-BOUND CONSTRAINTS

The production in any month cannot exceed 4000 tons, so the four constraints in this group are

$$x_1 \leq 4000 \quad \text{(bound in month 1)}$$
$$x_2 \leq 4000 \quad \text{(bound in month 2)}$$
$$x_3 \leq 4000 \quad \text{(bound in month 3)}$$
$$x_4 \leq 4000 \quad \text{(bound in month 4)}$$

INVENTORY-BALANCE CONSTRAINTS

This group consists of four constraints to ensure the proper relationship between the hypothetical production and inventory amounts illustrated in Figure 3.2. For example, for month 1:

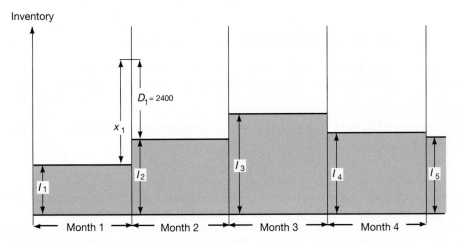

FIGURE 3.2 Inventory Levels of NSC.

Inventory at the end of month 1 = (inventory at the beginning of month 1) +

(amount produced in month 1) −

(demand for month 1)

Because the inventory at the end of month 1 is precisely the beginning inventory in month 2,

$$I_2 = I_1 + x_1 - 2400$$

or

$$-I_2 + I_1 + x_1 = 2400 \qquad \text{(inventory balance in month 1)}$$

A similar constraint is needed for each of the remaining three months, resulting in

$$-I_3 + I_2 + x_2 = 2200 \qquad \text{(inventory balance in month 2)}$$
$$-I_4 + I_3 + x_3 = 2700 \qquad \text{(inventory balance in month 3)}$$
$$-I_5 + I_4 + x_4 = 2500 \qquad \text{(inventory balance in month 4)}$$

CHANGE-IN-PRODUCTION CONSTRAINTS

This group of constraints ensures the proper relationship between the production and change-in-production variables. For instance, consider the change in production from month 1 to month 2. After working through several specific examples, you might conclude that

Production in month 2 = (production in month 1) +

(increase in production in month 2 −

decrease in production in month 2)

Using the variables x_2, x_1, S_2, and D_2 leads to

$$x_2 = x_1 + (S_2 - D_2)$$

or

$$x_2 - x_1 - S_2 + D_2 = 0 \qquad \text{(change in month 2)}$$

For example, when $x_2 = 300$ and $x_1 = 100$, the values of $S_2 = 200$ and $D_2 = 0$ satisfy this constraint, as they should. However, what ensures that if S_2 is positive, then D_2 is in fact 0? For instance, when $x_2 = 300$ and $x_1 = 100$, the values of $S_2 = 250$ and $D_2 = 50$ also satisfies the foregoing constraint. Likewise, if x_2 is less than x_1, what ensures that D_2 is positive and S_2 is 0? It would appear that an additional constraint is necessary, for example:

$$S_2 * D_2 = 0$$

Including such constraints results in a *nonlinear* model, which is substantially more difficult to solve than a linear programming model. It is indeed fortunate that *in this particular problem*, these nonlinear constraints are not needed. This is because the *objective function* serves the same purpose. To see how, consider the numerical example just used:

x_2	x_1	S_2	D_2	CHANGE-IN-PRODUCTION COSTS
300	100	200	0	$(200 * 50) + (\ 0 * 30) = 10000$
300	100	250	50	$(250 * 50) + (50 * 30) = 14000$

Because the objective is to achieve minimum costs, it is *always* less expensive to make one of the two variables S_2 or D_2 have value 0. As a result, *no additional constraints are needed to ensure this relationship.*

A similar constraint for each of the first, third, and fourth months yields

$$\begin{aligned} x_1 - 1800 - S_1 + D_1 &= \quad 0, \qquad \text{or} \\ x_1 \qquad\quad - S_1 + D_1 &= 1800 \qquad \text{(change in month 1)} \end{aligned}$$

$$\begin{aligned} x_3 - \quad x_2 - S_3 + D_3 &= \quad 0 \qquad \text{(change in month 3)} \\ x_4 - \quad x_3 - S_4 + D_4 &= \quad 0 \qquad \text{(change in month 4)} \end{aligned}$$

DEMAND CONSTRAINTS

To ensure that the demands are met, consider month 1. The appropriate constraint is

$$\left(\begin{array}{c} \text{Beginning inventory} \\ \text{in month 1} \end{array} \right) + \left(\begin{array}{c} \text{amount produced} \\ \text{in month 1} \end{array} \right) \geq \left(\begin{array}{c} \text{demand} \\ \text{in month 1} \end{array} \right)$$

Using the decision variables results in

$$I_1 + x_1 \geq 2400$$

or

$$I_1 + x_1 - 2400 \geq 0$$

However, observe from the inventory-balance constraint for month 1 that

$$I_2 = I_1 + x_1 - 2400$$

Thus, the demand constraint for month 1 can also be written as

$$I_2 \geq 0$$

In other words, requiring that each inventory variable be nonnegative ensures that the demand for the previous month is met. Thus, these demand constraints can be included as the logical constraints.

LOGICAL CONSTRAINTS

The only logical constraints are that each production, inventory, and change-in-production variable be nonnegative.

3.6.4 Complete Formulation and Solution of the Production-Planning Problem of NSC

Having developed all the parts to the problem, you, as a Manager at NSC, put together the following linear programming model for the production-planning concern of National Steel Corporation:

Minimize $\quad 7400x_1 + 7500x_2 + 7600x_3 + 7650x_4 +$
$\qquad\quad 120I_1 + 120I_2 + 120I_3 + 120I_4 +$
$\qquad\quad 50S_1 + 30D_1 + 50S_2 + 30D_2 +$
$\qquad\quad 50S_3 + 30D_3 + 50S_4 + 30D_4$

Linear Program
EX3_6.DAT

Subject to

INITIAL AND FINAL INVENTORY CONSTRAINTS

$$
\begin{array}{ll}
I_1 = 1000 & \text{(beginning inventory)} \\
I_5 \geq 1500 & \text{(ending inventory)}
\end{array}
$$

PRODUCTION BOUND CONSTRAINTS

$$
\begin{array}{ll}
x_1 \leq 4000 & \text{(bound in month 1)} \\
x_2 \leq 4000 & \text{(bound in month 2)} \\
x_3 \leq 4000 & \text{(bound in month 3)} \\
x_4 \leq 4000 & \text{(bound in month 4)}
\end{array}
$$

INVENTORY BALANCE CONSTRAINTS

$$
\begin{array}{ll}
-I_2 + I_1 + x_1 = 2400 & \text{(inventory balance in month 1)} \\
-I_3 + I_2 + x_2 = 2200 & \text{(inventory balance in month 2)} \\
-I_4 + I_3 + x_3 = 2700 & \text{(inventory balance in month 3)} \\
-I_5 + I_4 + x_4 = 2500 & \text{(inventory balance in month 4)}
\end{array}
$$

CHANGE-IN-PRODUCTION CONSTRAINTS

$$
\begin{array}{ll}
x_1 \qquad\quad - S_1 + D_1 = 1800 & \text{(change in month 1)} \\
x_2 - x_1 - S_2 + D_2 = \quad 0 & \text{(change in month 2)} \\
x_3 - x_2 - S_3 + D_3 = \quad 0 & \text{(change in month 3)} \\
x_4 - x_3 - S_4 + D_4 = \quad 0 & \text{(change in month 4)}
\end{array}
$$

LOGICAL CONSTRAINTS

$$x_1, x_2, x_3, x_4, I_1, I_2, I_3, I_4, I_5,$$
$$S_1, S_2, S_3, S_4, D_1, D_2, D_3, D_4 \geq 0$$

The optimal solution to this problem, which results from using any linear programming software package, is

$$
\begin{array}{llll}
x_1 = 1800.00 & I_1 = 1000.00 & S_1 = 0.00 & D_1 = 0.00 \\
x_2 = 1800.00 & I_2 = 400.00 & S_2 = 0.00 & D_2 = 0.00 \\
x_3 = 2700.00 & I_3 = 0.00 & S_3 = 900.00 & D_3 = 0.00 \\
x_4 = 4000.00 & I_4 = 0.00 & S_4 = 1300.00 & D_4 = 0.00 \\
                & I_5 = 1500.00 &   &
\end{array}
$$

with an objective function value of 78,218,000. The optimal production plan can be summarized as

	MONTH			
	1	2	3	4
Beginning inventory	1000	400	0	0
Amount produced	1800	1800	2700	4000
Demand	2400	2200	2700	2500
Ending inventory	400	0	0	1500

The total cost is $78,218,000. You may want to verify this solution with your own linear programming software.

➡ ### KEY FEATURES

The Production-Planning Problem of NSC illustrates the key feature of using additional decision variables to make the formulation more manageable and understandable. For example, the five inventory variables I_1, I_2, I_3, I_4, and I_5 serve this purpose, as did the change-in-production variables S_1, D_1, S_2, D_2, S_3, D_3, S_4, and D_4.

In Sections 3.1 through 3.6, you have seen several examples of how linear programming models are formulated to help managers make decisions. These models are built using the techniques and guidelines given in Chapter 2. Unlike the examples presented so far, most real-world problems involve hundreds or thousands of variables and a similar number of constraints. Formulating these large, complex models is accomplished using these same techniques, as you will see in the following case study.

CASE STUDY
GLOBAL PLANNING FOR AMERICAN STEEL COMPANY

All the problems discussed so far have involved only one functional area of an organization. For instance, the transportation problem in Example 2.2 in Section 2.2 involves only the distribution of finished computers given that the production plan has already been decided. Moreover, these models have required very few variables and constraints. Most real-world problems involve many functional areas of the company (sales, production, distribution, and marketing). Formulating such problems requires a large number of variables and constraints—perhaps tens of thousands of variables and thousands of constraints. Teams of people may be involved in formulating these models. Whatever the problem's size, the basic process is the same as the one you have already learned: Identify the decision variables, the data, the objective function, and the constraints.

Additional techniques are sometimes helpful in making the formulation of large-scale problems manageable. Some of these techniques are illustrated in this case study.

The Problem of American Steel Company

American Steel has received annual orders from four countries—Japan, Korea, Taiwan, and Mexico—for two different types of steels it produces: high-grade and low-grade. These steels are produced at its two plants, located in Pittsburgh and Youngstown, using iron ores supplied by two mining companies—Butte Minerals and Cheyenne Mines. The management of American Steel needs an overall annual purchase/production/distribution plan to minimize total costs. Various departments have collected the necessary data regarding the sales commitment, ore availability and cost, production characteristics, and distribution costs of ore and finished steel.

American Steel can obtain up to 1000 tons of Grade-A iron ore from Butte Minerals and up to 2000 tons of Grade-B iron ore from Cheyenne Mines. American Steel can specify how much of each ore is to be shipped to each of its two steel mills. The associated purchase cost and shipping charge per ton are given in Table 3.7.

Each of American Steel's two mills can produce high-grade steel and low-grade steel. High-grade steel requires blending Grade-A and Grade-B iron ore in a ratio of 1 to 2. Low-grade steel requires a ratio of 1 to 3. The Youngstown mill can process up to 1500 tons of iron ore, and the Pittsburgh facility can handle at most 700 tons. The mill at Pittsburgh is a modern facility and has a lower processing cost per ton of steel produced than does the facility at Youngstown, as indicated in Table 3.8.

The finished steel is shipped to Japan, Korea, Taiwan, and Mexico. The International Sales Division of American Steel has received orders for each type of steel, given in Table 3.9. This table also includes the shipping costs per ton for each type of steel.

As Manager of the Management Science Group of American Steel, you have been asked to make recommendations on the purchasing, processing, and shipping functions with the objective of minimizing the total annual cost.

TABLE 3.7 *Ore Purchase and Shipping Costs ($/ton)*

	PURCHASE COST	SHIPPING COST TO	
		PITTSBURGH	YOUNGSTOWN
Butte Minerals	130	10	13
Cheyenne Mines	110	14	17

TABLE 3.8 *Processing Costs ($/ton)*

	MILL	
	PITTSBURGH	YOUNGSTOWN
High-grade steel	32	39
Low-grade steel	27	32

TABLE 3.9 *Demands and Unit Shipping Costs of Steel*

COUNTRY	STEEL TYPE	DEMAND (tons)	SHIPPING COST ($/ton) FROM PITTSBURGH	SHIPPING COST ($/ton) FROM YOUNGSTOWN
Japan	High-grade	400	110	115
	Low-grade	200	100	110
Korea	High-grade	200	140	150
	Low-grade	100	130	145
Taiwan	High-grade	200	130	135
	Low-grade	100	125	127
Mexico	High-grade	150	80	90
	Low-grade	50	80	85

Mathematical Formulation

Your first step is to formulate the mathematical model that, once classified, can be solved by computer using an appropriate algorithm, to be discussed in subsequent chapters. Although the problem and all its data may at first appear overwhelming, you can formulate this problem using the same techniques you learned in Section 2.2. Some additional techniques are also introduced to help make the formulation easier to handle.

IDENTIFYING THE DECISION VARIABLES

One technique for simplifying the process of identifying all the decision variables is to *decompose* the overall problem into a collection of smaller, more manageable subproblems. There are no specific rules for doing this, but one typical approach is to focus on the individual functional areas, as will be done in this example. To that end, consider the *sequence* of operations that are performed:

1. The purchase of the iron ores from the two mining companies and the shipment of the ores to the two steel mills.
2. The processing of the ores at the two mills to produce the two grades of steel.
3. The shipping of the finished steel to the four countries.

Having decomposed the original problem into these three subproblems, you can now proceed to identify the decision variables associated with each function.

DECISION VARIABLES FOR PURCHASING AND SHIPPING
IRON ORE

Asking yourself the usual question of what you can control should lead you to identify the following decision variables pertaining to this functional area:

IBP = the number of tons of Grade-A iron ore to buy from Butte Minerals and ship to the Pittsburgh mill

IBY = the number of tons of Grade-A iron ore to buy from Butte Minerals and ship to the Youngstown mill

ICP = the number of tons of Grade-B iron ore to buy from Cheyenne Mines and ship to the Pittsburgh mill

ICY = the number of tons of Grade-B iron ore to buy from Cheyenne Mines and ship to the Youngstown mill

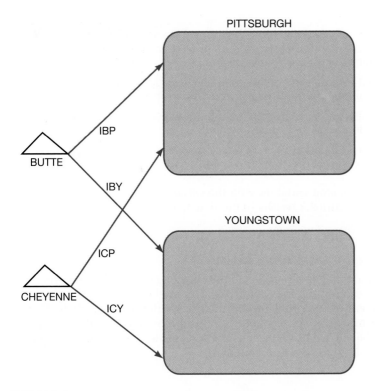

FIGURE 3.3 Schematic Diagram for American Steel: Ore Purchase.

The variables corresponding to this portion of the problem are illustrated in the schematic diagram of Figure 3.3. Schematic diagrams are used throughout this formulation to help identify the relationships among the decision variables for the various functional areas.

DECISION VARIABLES FOR PRODUCING STEEL

Recall that the production of low-grade and high-grade steel at the mills is the second functional area. For this phase, ask yourself what decisions you are free to make. What can you control? One answer is the number of tons of each type steel to produce at each mill. Another answer is the amount of each grade of iron ore to blend. It is possible to develop the model by using either set of decision variables, or both sets. In this case, the formulation is more manageable using both sets. So let

HP = the number of tons of high-grade steel to produce at the Pittsburgh mill

LP = the number of tons of low-grade steel to produce at the Pittsburgh mill

HY = the number of tons of high-grade steel to produce at the Youngstown mill

LY = the number of tons of low-grade steel to produce at the Youngstown mill

$OBPH$ = the number of tons of iron ore from Butte Minerals used to produce high-grade steel at the Pittsburgh mill

$OCPH$ = the number of tons of iron ore from Cheyenne Mines used to produce high-grade steel at the Pittsburgh mill

$OBPL$ = the number of tons of iron ore from Butte Minerals used to produce low-grade steel at the Pittsburgh mill

$OCPL$ = the number of tons of iron ore from Cheyenne Mines used to produce low-grade steel at the Pittsburgh mill

$OBYH$ = the number of tons of iron ore from Butte Minerals used to produce high-grade steel at the Youngstown mill

$OCYH$ = the number of tons of iron ore from Cheyenne Mines used to produce high-grade steel at the Youngstown mill

$OBYL$ = the number of tons of iron ore from Butte Minerals used to produce low-grade steel at the Youngstown mill

$OCYL$ = the number of tons of iron ore from Cheyenne Mines used to produce low-grade steel at the Youngstown mill

Combining these decision variables with the variables corresponding to the purchase of the iron ore in Figure 3.3 results in the schematic diagram of Figure 3.4.

DECISION VARIABLES FOR THE DISTRIBUTION OF STEEL

Recall that the last functional area pertains to the shipping of the final steel products from the two mills to each of the four countries. You might recognize the similarity between this component of the problem and the transportation problem in Section 2.2.1. Think of each mill as a supply point and each country as a demand point. The distribution can be viewed as two transportation problems—one for each type of steel—leading to the following decision variables:

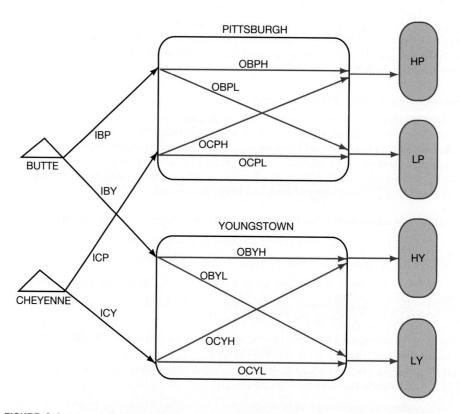

FIGURE 3.4 Schematic Diagram for American Steel: Ore Purchase and Steel Production.

FOR HIGH-GRADE STEEL

$SHPJ$ = the number of tons of high-grade steel to ship from the Pittsburgh mill to Japan

$SHPK$ = the number of tons of high-grade steel to ship from the Pittsburgh mill to Korea

$SHPT$ = the number of tons of high-grade steel to ship from the Pittsburgh mill to Taiwan

$SHPM$ = the number of tons of high-grade steel to ship from the Pittsburgh mill to Mexico

$SHYJ$ = the number of tons of high-grade steel to ship from the Youngstown mill to Japan

$SHYK$ = the number of tons of high-grade steel to ship from the Youngstown mill to Korea

$SHYT$ = the number of tons of high-grade steel to ship from the Youngstown mill to Taiwan

$SHYM$ = the number of tons of high-grade steel to ship from the Youngstown mill to Mexico

FOR LOW-GRADE STEEL

$SLPJ$ = the number of tons of low-grade steel to ship from the Pittsburgh mill to Japan

$SLPK$ = the number of tons of low-grade steel to ship from the Pittsburgh mill to Korea

$SLPT$ = the number of tons of low-grade steel to ship from the Pittsburgh mill to Taiwan

$SLPM$ = the number of tons of low-grade steel to ship from the Pittsburgh mill to Mexico

$SLYJ$ = the number of tons of low-grade steel to ship from the Youngstown mill to Japan

$SLYK$ = the number of tons of low-grade steel to ship from the Youngstown mill to Korea

$SLYT$ = the number of tons of low-grade steel to ship from the Youngstown mill to Taiwan

$SLYM$ = the number of tons of low-grade steel to ship from the Youngstown mill to Mexico

Putting together all of the decision variables for this problem results in the schematic diagram in Figure 3.5. Due to limited space, the symbolic names of most of the shipping variables are not included. This diagram illustrates (1) the three functional areas of this problem, (2) the sequential nature in which the various operations are performed, and (3) a summary of all the variables used in the formulation. Because it provides a concise visual summary of the entire process, you will find this diagram useful throughout the rest of the formulation.

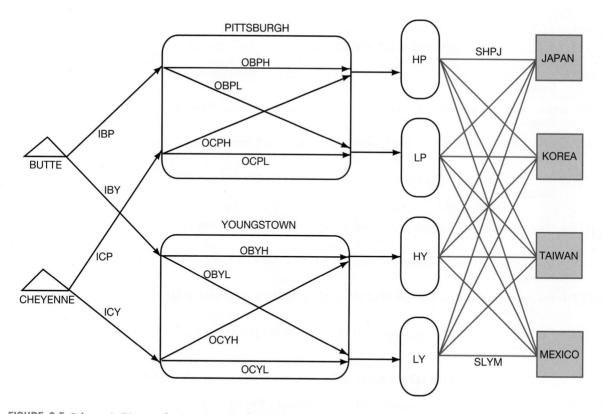

FIGURE 3.5 Schematic Diagram for American Steel: Ore Purchase, Steel Production, and Distribution.

IDENTIFYING THE OBJECTIVE FUNCTION

As stated in the problem description, the overall objective is to minimize the total cost. Applying the technique of decomposition according to the functional areas in Figure 3.5, you have

$$\text{Total cost} = \text{purchase costs} + \text{production costs} + \text{distribution costs}$$

PURCHASE COSTS

Look at Figure 3.5. You can further decompose the purchase costs into the cost of the iron ore plus the shipping cost to each of the mills. Use the decision variables IBP, IBY, ICP, and ICY, and the specific data in Table 3.7 to get

$$\text{Purchase costs} = \text{iron ore costs} + \text{shipping costs}$$
$$= (130IBP + 130IBY + 110ICP + 110ICY) +$$
$$(\ 10IBP + \ 13IBY + \ 14ICP + \ 17ICY)$$
$$= (140IBP + 143IBY + 124ICP + 127ICY)$$

PRODUCTION COSTS

In a similar manner, you can decompose the production costs into the production costs at the Pittsburgh mill plus those at the Youngstown mill. Using HP, LP, HY, and LY together with the data in Table 3.8 leads to

$$\text{Production costs} = (\text{costs at Pittsburgh}) + (\text{costs at Youngstown})$$
$$= (\ 32HP + 27LP\ ) + (\ 39HY + 32LY\ )$$

SHIPPING COSTS

You can decompose the total shipping costs into the shipping costs from the Pittsburgh mill to each of the four countries plus the shipping costs from the Youngstown mill to each of the four countries. Using the appropriate decision variables and the data in Table 3.9 leads to

$$\text{Shipping costs} = \text{(costs from Pittsburgh)} + \text{(costs from Youngstown)}$$
$$= (110SHPJ + 140SHPK + 130SHPT + 80SHPM +$$
$$100SLPJ + 130SLPK + 125SLPT + 80SLPM) +$$
$$(115SHYJ + 150SHYK + 135SHYT + 90SHYM +$$
$$110SLYJ + 145SLYK + 127SLYT + 85SLYM)$$

Combining the three individual cost components, you create the complete objective function:

$$\text{Minimize} \quad (140IBP + 143IBY + 124ICP + 127ICY) +$$
$$(32HP + 27LP) + (39HY + 32LY) +$$
$$(110SHPJ + 140SHPK + 130SHPT + 80SHPM +$$
$$100SLPJ + 130SLPK + 125SLPT + 80SLPM) +$$
$$(115SHYJ + 150SHYK + 135SHYT + 90SHYM +$$
$$110SLYJ + 145SLYK + 127SLYT + 85SLYM)$$

IDENTIFYING THE CONSTRAINTS

Constraints are needed to reflect the appropriate *physical* limitations of the problem and to specify the *logical* relationships among the decision variables of the different functional areas. To develop both types of constraints, use the technique of decomposition and follow the flow of information in Figure 3.5.

PURCHASING CONSTRAINTS

Recalling the physical capacity limitations of the two mines should lead you to identify the following constraints: The total number of tons of iron ore shipped from each mining company cannot exceed the available supply. Use the decision variables of this functional area to formulate these constraints mathematically:

$$IBP + IBY \leq 1000 \quad \text{(Butte Minerals supply)} \tag{1}$$
$$ICP + ICY \leq 2000 \quad \text{(Cheyenne Mines supply)} \tag{2}$$

PRODUCTION CONSTRAINTS

Asking yourself what restrictions apply to the production process will lead you to identify the following groups of constraints:

1. Ore-processing capacities—the total number of tons of ore processed at each mill cannot exceed the mill's capacity.
2. The blending requirements for producing each grade of steel—that is, each grade of steel requires the blending of a certain proportion of each type of iron ore.

Using the decision variables, you can formulate these constraints mathematically as follows:

1. *Ore-Capacity Constraints*

$$OBPH + OBPL + OCPH + OCPL \leq \ 700 \qquad \text{(Pittsburgh mill)} \qquad (3)$$

$$OBYH + OBYL + OCYH + OCYL \leq 1500 \qquad \text{(Youngstown mill)} \qquad (4)$$

2. *Blending Requirements.* According to the problem description, the iron ore from Cheyenne Mines and Butte Minerals must be blended in a ratio of 2 to 1 to produce high-grade steel. Thus, you are led to the following mathematical constraint for high-grade steel at the Pittsburgh mill:

$$OCPH/OBPH = 2/1$$

To make this constraint linear, multiply through by OBPH and then subtract 2OBPH from both sides to obtain

$$OCPH - 2OBPH = 0 \qquad (5)$$

Likewise, the constraint for low-grade steel, requiring a ratio of 3 to 1, is

$$OCPL - 3OBPL = 0 \qquad (6)$$

Similar constraints are needed for the Youngstown mill, so

$$OCYH - 2OBYH = 0 \qquad (7)$$

$$OCYL - 3OBYL = 0 \qquad (8)$$

In addition to these constraints, there are some implicit relationships between the amounts of iron ore purchased from the mines and the amounts of these ores used in the production of steel. For example, from Figure 3.5, you can see that the total amount of ore used in producing the two steels cannot exceed the amount purchased. These implicit constraints must be made explicit:

3. *Production and Purchasing Relationships*

$$OBPH + OBPL - IBP \leq 0 \qquad \text{(ore from Butte used in Pittsburgh)} \qquad (9)$$

$$OCPH + OCPL - ICP \leq 0 \qquad \text{(ore from Cheyenne used in Pittsburgh)} \qquad (10)$$

$$OBYH + OBYL - IBY \leq 0 \qquad \text{(ore from Butte used in Youngstown)} \qquad (11)$$

$$OCYH + OCYL - ICY \leq 0 \qquad \text{(ore from Cheyenne used in Youngstown)} \qquad (12)$$

Another implicit constraint evident from Figure 3.5 is that the total amount of ore used in the production process must equal the total amount of steel produced. This must be the case for each grade of steel at each mill. These implicit constraints can be made explicit as follows:

$$OCPH + OBPH - HP = 0 \qquad \text{(high-grade steel produced at Pittsburgh)} \qquad (13)$$

$$OCPL + OBPL - LP = 0 \qquad \text{(low-grade steel produced at Pittsburgh)} \qquad (14)$$

$$OCYH + OBYH - HY = 0 \qquad \text{(high-grade steel produced at Youngstown)} \qquad (15)$$

$$OCYL + OBYL - LY = 0 \qquad \text{(low-grade steel produced at Youngstown)} \qquad (16)$$

DISTRIBUTION CONSTRAINTS

You still need appropriate constraints to ensure that the demands for the amounts of the two grades of steel supplied by the two mills to each of the four countries are met. You might recognize that this portion is a transportation problem, as described in Section 2.2.1, which should lead to the following mathematical constraints:

1. *Supplies at the Mills*

$$SHPJ + SHPK + SHPT + SHPM - HP \leq 0 \quad \text{(high-grade steel shipped from Pittsburgh)} \quad (17)$$

$$SLPJ + SLPK + SLPT + SLPM - LP \leq 0 \quad \text{(low-grade steel shipped from Pittsburgh)} \quad (18)$$

$$SHYJ + SHYK + SHYT + SHYM - HY \leq 0 \quad \text{(high-grade steel shipped from Youngstown)} \quad (19)$$

$$SLYJ + SLYK + SLYT + SLYM - LY \leq 0 \quad \text{(low-grade steel shipped from Youngstown)} \quad (20)$$

2. *Demands for Steel in the Four Countries*

$$SHPJ + SHYJ \geq 400 \quad \text{(demand for high-grade steel in Japan)} \quad (21)$$

$$SLPJ + SLYJ \geq 200 \quad \text{(demand for low-grade steel in Japan)} \quad (22)$$

$$SHPK + SHYK \geq 200 \quad \text{(demand for high-grade steel in Korea)} \quad (23)$$

$$SLPK + SLYK \geq 100 \quad \text{(demand for low-grade steel in Korea)} \quad (24)$$

$$SHPT + SHYT \geq 200 \quad \text{(demand for high-grade steel in Taiwan)} \quad (25)$$

$$SLPT + SLYT \geq 100 \quad \text{(demand for low-grade steel in Taiwan)} \quad (26)$$

$$SHPM + SHYM \geq 150 \quad \text{(demand for high-grade steel in Mexico)} \quad (27)$$

$$SLPM + SLYM \geq 50 \quad \text{(demand for low-grade steel in Mexico)} \quad (28)$$

The final set of constraints are nonnegativity constraints on all variables. These constraints, together with the objective function and all other constraints formulated before, provide a complete and correct formulation of the problem, which follows.

Mathematical Formulation of the Problem of American Steel Company

Minimize $(140 IBP + 143 IBY + 124 ICP + 127 ICY) +$
$(32 HP + 27 LP) + (39 HY + 32 LY) +$
$(110 SHPJ + 140 SHPK + 130 SHPT + 80 SHPM +$
$100 SLPJ + 130 SLPK + 125 SLPT + 80 SLPM) +$
$(115 SHYJ + 150 SHYK + 135 SHYT + 90 SHYM +$
$110 SLYJ + 145 SLYK + 127 SLYT + 85 SLYM)$

Linear Program
ASC.DAT

Subject to

PURCHASING CONSTRAINTS

$$IBP + IBY \leq 1000 \qquad \text{(Butte Minerals supply)} \tag{1}$$
$$ICP + ICY \leq 2000 \qquad \text{(Cheyenne Mines supply)} \tag{2}$$

PRODUCTION CONSTRAINTS

ORE-CAPACITY CONSTRAINTS

$$OBPH + OBPL + OCPH + OCPL \leq 700 \qquad \text{(Pittsburgh mill)} \tag{3}$$
$$OBYH + OBYL + OCYH + OCYL \leq 1500 \qquad \text{(Youngstown mill)} \tag{4}$$

BLENDING REQUIREMENTS

$$OCPH - 2OBPH = 0 \tag{5}$$
$$OCPL - 3OBPL = 0 \tag{6}$$
$$OCYH - 2OBYH = 0 \tag{7}$$
$$OCYL - 3OBYL = 0 \tag{8}$$

PRODUCTION AND PURCHASING RELATIONSHIPS

$$OBPH + OBPL - IBP \leq 0 \qquad \text{(ore from Butte used in Pittsburgh)} \tag{9}$$
$$OCPH + OCPL - ICP \leq 0 \qquad \text{(ore from Cheyenne used in Pittsburgh)} \tag{10}$$

$$OBYH + OBYL - IBY \leq 0 \qquad \text{(ore from Butte used in Youngstown)} \tag{11}$$
$$OCYH + OCYL - ICY \leq 0 \qquad \text{(ore from Cheyenne used in Youngstown)} \tag{12}$$

PRODUCTION-BALANCE CONSTRAINTS

$$OCPH + OBPH - HP = 0 \qquad \text{(high-grade steel produced at Pittsburgh)} \tag{13}$$
$$OCPL + OBPL - LP = 0 \qquad \text{(low-grade steel produced at Pittsburgh)} \tag{14}$$

$$OCYH + OBYH - HY = 0 \qquad \text{(high-grade steel produced at Youngstown)} \tag{15}$$
$$OCYL + OBYL - LY = 0 \qquad \text{(low-grade steel produced at Youngstown)} \tag{16}$$

DISTRIBUTION CONSTRAINTS

SUPPLIES AT THE MILLS

$$SHPJ + SHPK + SHPT + SHPM - HP \leq 0 \qquad \text{(high-grade steel shipped from Pittsburgh)} \tag{17}$$
$$SLPJ + SLPK + SLPT + SLPM - LP \leq 0 \qquad \text{(low-grade steel shipped from Pittsburgh)} \tag{18}$$

$$SHYJ + SHYK + SHYT + SHYM - HY \leq 0 \qquad \text{(high-grade steel shipped from Youngstown)} \tag{19}$$
$$SLYJ + SLYK + SLYT + SLYM - LY \leq 0 \qquad \text{(low-grade steel shipped from Youngstown)} \tag{20}$$

DEMANDS FOR STEEL IN THE FOUR COUNTRIES

$SHPJ + SHYJ \geq 400$	(demand for high-grade steel in Japan)	(21)
$SLPJ + SLYJ \geq 200$	(demand for low-grade steel in Japan)	(22)
$SHPK + SHYK \geq 200$	(demand for high-grade steel in Korea)	(23)
$SLPK + SLYK \geq 100$	(demand for low-grade steel in Korea)	(24)
$SHPT + SHYT \geq 200$	(demand for high-grade steel in Taiwan)	(25)
$SLPT + SLYT \geq 100$	(demand for low-grade steel in Taiwan)	(26)
$SHPM + SHYM \geq 150$	(demand for high-grade steel in Mexico)	(27)
$SLPM + SLYM \geq 50$	(demand for low-grade steel in Mexico)	(28)

and all variables must be nonnegative.

This section has provided an example of formulating a large and complex problem with many variables and constraints. (The solution to this problem is given in Chapter 6.)

KEY FEATURES

In addition to applying the techniques of Section 2.2, this case study illustrates the key feature of decomposing a problem into smaller, more manageable subproblems. This is often done based on the functional areas of an organization or on a sequence of operations to be performed. A schematic diagram is useful to summarize this decomposition. Then, each subproblem is formulated by identifying the decision variables relevant to that subproblem. After specifying an overall objective function, constraints are needed not only to reflect the restrictions within each subproblem, but also to specify the relationships among the variables from one subproblem to another.

Now that you know how to formulate an appropriate linear programming model, it is time to learn the algorithm available for solving these problems. That study begins in Chapter 4.

SUMMARY

In this chapter, you have seen numerous applications of linear programming problems that arise in such areas as production planning, financial planning, blending decisions, and allocating scarce resources. These applications are limited only by your ability to identify and formulate such problems.

To formulate a linear programming problem, follow these steps, which are discussed in Chapter 2:

1. Identify decision variables.
2. Identify an overall objective function.
3. Identify constraints.

As necessary, identify data that are needed to help solve the problem. After formulating the problem, be sure you have a linear programming problem by verifying that:

1. The objective function is linear.
2. All constraints are linear.
3. All variables are continuous (that is, they can assume all fractional values).

Now that you know various applications of linear programming problems and how to formulate them, the next three chapters provide the details involved in *solving* such problems—that is, in finding the values of the variables that provide the best value of the objective function while satisfying all of the constraints simultaneously.

EXERCISES

 EXERCISE 3.1   Gasahol, Inc., has 14,000 gallons of a gasoline–alcohol mixture stored at its facility in Fresno and 16,000 gallons stored at its facility in Bakersfield. From these facilities, Gasahol must supply Fresh Food Farms (FFF) with 10,000 gallons and American Growers (AG) with 20,000 gallons. The cost for shipping 1 gallon from each storage facility to each customer is

	TO	
FROM	FFF	AG
Fresno	$0.04	$0.06
Bakersfield	$0.05	$0.03

Formulate a linear programming model to determine the least-cost shipping plan that meets the supply-and-demand constraints.

EXERCISE 3.2   HealthNut Company is developing a new peanut butter and chocolate candy bar. The candy must have at least 5 grams of protein but not more than 5 grams of carbohydrates and 3 grams of saturated fats. Develop a linear program to determine the amount of each ingredient to use that meets these nutritional requirements at least total cost, based on the following data:

	PEANUT BUTTER	CHOCOLATE
Cost ($/oz)	0.10	0.18
Protein (g/oz)	4.00	0.80
Carbohydrates (g/oz)	2.50	1.00
Saturated fats (g/oz)	2.00	0.50

 EXERCISE 3.3   HealthNut Company has a machine that grinds raw psyllium seeds into a fine powder at the rate of 30 pounds per hour. The company also uses the machine to make peanut butter from roasted peanuts at the rate of 60 pounds per hour. The set up time to switch the machine from one product to the other is negligible. The monthly demand and inventory holding costs for each product are provided in the following table:

	DEMAND (lb)		HOLDING COSTS ($/lb)	
	PEANUT BUTTER	PSYLLIUM	PEANUT BUTTER	PSYLLIUM
May	400	600	0.10	0.05
June	450	700	0.10	0.05
July	500	650	0.12	0.05

The initial inventory of each product at the beginning of May is 0 and should also be 0 at the end of July. At no time can the inventory of psyllium exceed 1000 pounds nor that of peanut butter exceed 500 pounds. Also, there are 20 hours of machine time available each month. Formulate a linear program to determine a production plan for the months of May, June, and July that minimizes the total holding costs, assuming that demand is met at the end of each month and inventory holding costs are based on the amount in inventory at the beginning of the month.

EXERCISE 3.4 FMR Company has a machine capable of making large-diameter and small-diameter pipes for plumbing contractors. Large pipes are produced at the rate of 200 feet per hour and small pipes at 300 feet per hour. Each hour the machine is used for producing large pipes typically results in 1.5 jams and 3 jams per hour result when producing small pipes. Each jam requires about 5 minutes to reset, during which time the machine cannot produce pipes. Management wants an equal number of feet of both sizes of pipe and as much total pipe as possible. Formulate a model to determine how much of an 8-hour day should be allocated to producing large pipes and how much to small pipes. For the decision variables, use the number of hours of machine time to devote to making small and large pipes.

EXERCISE 3.5 Repeat Exercise 3.4 using the fraction of 8 hours of machine time to devote to making small and large pipes as the decision variables.

EXERCISE 3.6 Repeat Exercise 3.4 using the number of feet of small and large pipes to make in 8 hours of machine time as the decision variables.

EXERCISE 3.7 Sulfur, charcoal, and saltpeter are mixed to produce gunpowder at Explosives, Inc. The final product must contain at least 10%, but not more than 20%, charcoal by weight. The amount of saltpeter cannot exceed 50% of the amount of charcoal used. To avoid an inadvertent explosion, the sum of 50% of the sulfur plus 60% of the charcoal plus 30% of the saltpeter used cannot exceed 35% of the final product. Sulfur is by far the most expensive component. Formulate a model to determine how much of each ingredient should be used in making each pound of gunpowder that satisfies the constraints while requiring the least amount of sulfur.

EXERCISE 3.8 Case Chemicals dilutes each liter of concentrated sulfuric acid with 20 liters of distilled water to produce H_2SO_4. Similarly, each liter of concentrated hydrochloric acid is diluted with 30 liters of distilled water to produce HCl. These two products are each sold to high schools at $0.10 per 100-milliliter (that is, 0.1-liter) bottle. The company currently has 50,000 empty bottles in inventory. Assume that there is virtually an unlimited amount of distilled water costing $0.15 per liter and that the following data are available:

	SULFURIC ACID	HYDROCHLORIC ACID
Cost ($/liter)	12.00	18.00
Supply (liters)	200.00	150.00

Formulate a model to determine how much of each concentrated acid to dilute to maximize the total profits. Can you solve this model as a linear program? Explain.

EXERCISE 3.9 ManuMania Company uses a base and two gum products, all in equal amounts, to make its Gooey Gum. The company can produce a combined total of up to 800 pounds of the base and two gum products. Alternatively, it can purchase these ingredients on the open market at the following dollars per pound:

PRODUCT	PRODUCTION COST	PURCHASE COST
Base	1.75	3.00
GP-1	2.00	3.25
GP-2	2.25	3.75

Formulate a model to determine the least-cost production/purchasing plan to meet a demand of 1200 pounds of Gooey Gum.

EXERCISE 3.10   Each week, Florida Citrus, Inc., uses a single machine for 150 hours to distill orange juice and grapefruit juice into concentrates stored in two separate 1000-gallon tanks before being frozen. The machine can process 25 gallons of orange juice per hour but only 20 gallons of grapefruit juice. Each gallon of orange juice costs $1.50 and loses 30% in water content when distilled into a concentrate. The orange juice concentrate then sells for $6.00 per gallon. Each gallon of grapefruit juice costs $2.00 and loses 25% in water content when distilled into a concentrate. The grapefruit juice concentrate then sells for $8.00 per gallon. Formulate a linear programming model to determine a production plan to maximize the profit for the coming week using the variables:

OJ = the number of gallons of orange juice to use this week

GJ = the number of gallons of grapefruit juice to use this week

EXERCISE 3.11   For Exercise 3.10, formulate a linear programming model to determine a production plan to maximize the profit for the coming week using the variables:

OC = the number of gallons of orange-juice concentrate to produce this week

GC = the number of gallons of grapefruit-juice concentrate to produce this week

EXERCISE 3.12   For Exercise 3.10, formulate a linear programming model to determine a production plan to maximize the profit for the coming week using the variables:

OT = the number of hours of machine time to use this week for distilling orange juice

GT = the number of hours of machine time to use this week for distilling grapefruit juice

EXERCISE 3.13   Oklahoma Oil, Inc., must transport 100,000 barrels from each of its three oil fields to its storage tank in Oklahoma City. Oil can be trucked directly from the fields to the storage tank at a cost of $0.03 per barrel per mile. Up to 150,000 barrels of oil also can be sent from the fields via a pipeline to a central hub in Tulsa at a cost of $0.02 per barrel per mile and then trucked to Oklahoma City for $1 per barrel. Formulate a model to determine the least-cost shipping plan, given the following distances in miles:

	TO	
FROM	OKLAHOMA CITY	TULSA
Oil Field 1	150	50
Oil Field 2	170	65
Oil Field 3	190	80

EXERCISE 3.14 Cajun World mixes six spices to make a product for blackening fish. The following table provides the cost of each spice and the minimum and maximum percentages by weight that can be used in the final product:

SPICE	COST ($/gm)	MINIMUM (%)	MAXIMUM (%)
Cayenne	0.020	18	20
Black pepper	0.025	15	18
Fennel seeds	0.082	12	14
Onion powder	0.025	16	20
Garlic	0.028	12	15
Oregano	0.075	14	18

Formulate a linear program to determine the amount of each spice to use in making each kilogram of product that minimizes the total cost.

EXERCISE 3.15 Incredible Indelible Ink Company mixes three additives, A_1, A_2, and A_3, to a base in different proportions to obtain different colors of ink. Red ink is obtained by mixing A_1, A_2, and A_3 in the ratio of 3:1:2, blue ink in the ratio of 2:3:4, and green ink in the ratio of 1:2:3. After these additives are mixed, an equal amount of base is added for each color. The company currently has 1000 gallons of A_1, 1500 of A_2, 2000 of A_3, and 4000 of base. Given that the selling price per gallon for each type of ink is the same, develop a model to determine how these resources should be used to obtain the maximum revenue.

EXERCISE 3.16 The Department of Energy of Lilliput is currently in the process of developing a national energy plan for the next year. Lilliput can generate energy from any one of five sources: coal, natural gas, nuclear materials, hydroelectric projects, and petroleum. The data on the energy resources, generation capacities measured in megawatt-hours (MW-hr), and unit costs of generation are given in Table 3.10.

Lilliput needs 50,000 MW-hr of energy for domestic use, and the country has a commitment to produce 10,000 MW-hr for export. Furthermore, to conserve the energy resources and to protect the environment, the government has passed the following regulations:

1. The generation from nuclear materials should not exceed 20% of the total energy generated by Lilliput.
2. At least 80% of the capacity of the coal plants should be utilized.
3. The effluents let off into the atmosphere should not exceed the limits specified in Table 3.11.
4. The amount of energy generated from natural gas should be at least 30% of that generated from petroleum.

Formulate a linear program to determine a least-cost energy plan.

TABLE 3.10 *Generation Capacities and Costs*

ENERGY SOURCE	TOTAL CAPACITY (MW-hr)	GENERATING COST ($/MW-hr)
Coal	45,000	6.0
Natural gas	15,000	5.5
Nuclear	45,000	4.5
Hydroelectric	24,000	5.0
Petroleum	48,000	7.0

TABLE 3.11   *Pollution Data for Generating Energy*

| ENERGY SOURCE | POLLUTANT (gm/MW-hr) | | | |
	SULFUR DIOXIDE	CARBON MONOXIDE	DUST PARTICLES	SOLID WASTE
Coal	1.5	1.2	0.7	0.4
Natural gas	0.2	0.5	—	—
Nuclear	—	0.1	0.2	0.7
Hydroelectric	—	—	—	—
Petroleum	0.4	0.8	0.5	0.1
Maximum kg allowed	75	60	30	25

EXERCISE 3.17   Fresh Food Farms, Inc., has 50 acres of land on which to plant any amount of corn, soybeans, lettuce, cotton, and broccoli. The following table shows the relevant information pertaining to the yield, the cost for planting, the expected selling price, and the water requirements of each crop:

CROP	YIELD (kg/acre)	COST ($/kg)	SELLING PRICE ($/kg)	WATER REQUIRED (liters/kg)
Corn	640	1.00	1.70	8.75
Soybeans	500	0.50	1.30	5.00
Lettuce	400	0.40	1.00	2.25
Cotton	300	0.25	1.00	4.25
Broccoli	350	0.60	1.30	3.50

For the coming season, there are 100,000 liters of water available and the company has contracted to sell at least 5120 kilograms of corn. Formulate a linear program to determine an optimal planting strategy for Fresh Food Farms, Inc. Use the number of acres of each crop to plant as the decision variables.

EXERCISE 3.18   Repeat Exercise 3.17 using the number of kilograms of each crop to produce as the decision variables.

EXERCISE 3.19   Formulate the investment problem of Pension Planners, Inc., described in Section 3.4, using the following decision variables:

$$F_1 = \text{the number of shares of Fund 1 to buy}$$

$$F_2 = \text{the number of shares of Fund 2 to buy}$$

$$F_3 = \text{the number of shares of Fund 3 to buy}$$

$$F_4 = \text{the number of shares of Fund 4 to buy}$$

$$F_5 = \text{the number of shares of Fund 5 to buy}$$

$$F_6 = \text{the number of shares of Fund 6 to buy}$$

EXERCISE 3.20   Repeat Exercise 3.19 using the following decision variables:

$$F_1 = \text{the number of dollars to invest in Fund 1}$$

$$F_2 = \text{the number of dollars to invest in Fund 2}$$

$$F_3 = \text{the number of dollars to invest in Fund 3}$$

$$F_4 = \text{the number of dollars to invest in Fund 4}$$

$$F_5 = \text{the number of dollars to invest in Fund 5}$$

$$F_6 = \text{the number of dollars to invest in Fund 6}$$

EXERCISE 3.21   Repeat Exercise 3.19 using the following decision variables:

$$H = \text{the fraction of the portfolio to invest in high-risk funds}$$

$$M = \text{the fraction of the portfolio to invest in medium-risk funds}$$

$$L = \text{the fraction of the portfolio to invest in low-risk funds}$$

CRITICAL-THINKING PROJECTS: PROBLEM FORMULATIONS

NOTE TO INSTRUCTORS

Each Critical-Thinking Project has two parts. In the first part, students formulate the problem. In the second part, students address managerial considerations. For consistency, you may wish to have all your students base their responses to the managerial concerns of a project on a single, specific formulation. The *Solutions Manual* accompanying this book provides a formulation for each critical-thinking project, which you may choose to pass out to students after they complete their own formulation. (See the Preface for more information on the Critical-Thinking Projects.)

Formulate a *single* mathematical model for each of the following critical-thinking projects. These models can be linear, integer, or even nonlinear programming problems. Whenever possible, draw a schematic diagram or network to represent the problem. Check with your instructor for additional information and guidelines.

CRITICAL-THINKING PROJECT A
THE BLENDING PROBLEM OF HEXXON OIL COMPANY

Mr. Sam Barton, Production Manager at Hexxon Oil Company, has been asked by Mr. James Arden, Vice-President of Production, to formulate a new daily production plan for the three brands of gasoline the company sells: Regular (90 octane), Unleaded (96 octane), and Supreme (100 octane). In their meeting, Mr. Arden brought the data in Table 3.12, consisting of the projected daily demands for these three gasolines in barrels

TABLE 3.12 *Selling Prices and Demands for Gasoline*			
BRAND OF GASOLINE	MINIMUM OCTANE RATING	SELLING PRICE ($/bbl)	DEMAND (bbl/day)
Regular	90	16.50	2000
Unleaded	96	18.00	4000
Supreme	100	22.50	3000

TABLE 3.13   *Data on the Constituents for Blending Gasoline*

BLENDING CONSTITUENT	OCTANE RATING	COST ($/bbl)	SUPPLY (bbl/day)
1	102	15.00	2500
2	96	12.00	3000
3	93	9.00	3500
4	110	24.00	2000

(bbl) and their respective selling prices, prepared by Ms. Jean Ferraro in the Accounting Department. When Mr. Arden wanted to achieve the highest possible daily profit, Mr. Barton said that he would have to meet with Mr. Allen, the Production Supervisor, to discuss the availability and costs of the constituents used in making the three brands of gasoline. He would then get back to Mr. Arden with a production plan.

When Mr. Barton discussed the problem on the phone with the Production Supervisor, Mr. Allen said he would obtain the necessary information pertaining to the four constituents used in making the three brands of gasoline. At their meeting the next day, he brought the data in Table 3.13, which include, for each constituent: (a) the octane rating, (b) the cost ($/bbl), and (c) the maximum supply available (bbl/day).

Mr. Allen reminded Mr. Barton that each of the three brands of gasoline must meet the minimum standard for octane rating (see Table 3.12). When asked precisely how this is accomplished, Mr. Allen explained that the octane rating of a mixture consisting of x_1, x_2, x_3, and x_4 barrels of the four constituents is the ratio of $102x_1 + 96x_2 + 93x_3 + 110x_4$ to the total number of barrels of the mixture, namely, $x_1 + x_2 + x_3 + x_4$.

1. Formulate a production model for Mr. Barton that maximizes the daily profits and satisfies all constraints.
2. Ms. Jean Ferraro in the Accounting Department has discovered that the costs of the constituents given in Table 3.13 were not exactly correct. Formulate the new objective function on the basis of the following memo she sent to Mr. Barton:

> TO: Mr. S. Barton, Production Manager
> FROM: Ms. J. Ferraro, Head of Accounting
> RE: Cost of Blending Constituent 1 to Make Supreme Gasoline
>
> Please note that the cost of blending x barrels of Constituent 1 when making Supreme gas should be 13.50 + 0.001x per barrel, instead of $15.00 per barrel.

CRITICAL-THINKING PROJECT B
THE PRODUCTION PROBLEM OF ASA STEEL COMPANY

ASA is a large steel company that produces five different types of iron plates at its eight factories. At a recent strategic-planning meeting, management allocated the budgets in Table 3.14 to each of the eight factories for the next fiscal year. These budgets were based, in part, on the fixed demands in Table 3.15 for the five iron plates provided by the Sales Department. As Vice-President of Production, you, Mr. Leroy Adams, have been asked to determine a production plan for each of the eight factories.

In preparation to formulate such a plan, you asked your associate, Mr. James Dietz, to obtain production costs for each of the five iron plates at each of the eight factories.

TABLE 3.14	Budget Assigned to Each Factory ($ 000)							
Factory	1	2	3	4	5	6	7	8
Budget	900	1050	950	1050	1000	1600	950	1050

TABLE 3.15	Demand for Each Type of Iron Plate (tons)				
Plate type	1	2	3	4	5
Demand	450	800	500	650	180

At your next meeting, Mr. Dietz brought the cost data in Table 3.16. He also pointed out that, as external suppliers, ASA has three subcontractors from which it can purchase precisely the amounts of different types of iron plates at the prices shown in Table 3.17. Mr. Dietz reminded you that contractual obligations require that if a particular subcontractor is chosen, ASA must purchase *all* of its supplies of all five types of iron plates at the indicated prices. You can, of course, choose to purchase from either none, one, two, or all three subcontractors. When you relayed this information to Mr. Charles Bentley, the CEO, he approved the use of subcontractors if it would lower the total costs, and informed you that the cost for buying iron plates from subcontractors would not affect the budgets of any of the factories (see Table 3.14).

As Production Manager, formulate a model to determine a production plan for each of the eight factories and which subcontractor(s), if any, to buy iron plates from to minimize the total costs while staying within each factory's budget and meeting the given demands.

TABLE 3.16	Cost of Producing 1 Ton of Each Iron Plate Type i at Factory j ($ 000)							
				FACTORY NO.				
PLATE TYPE	1	2	3	4	5	6	7	8
1	5	3	4	3	3	4	6	4
2	3	4	6	2	5	3	6	4
3	7	6	5	8	4	3	4	5
4	6	6	6	5	3	5	5	4
5	8	9	8	7	10	9	8	6

TABLE 3.17	Cost per Ton and Amount of Each Plate Type Available from Each Subcontractor					
	SUBCONTRACTOR 1		SUBCONTRACTOR 2		SUBCONTRACTOR 3	
PLATE TYPE	COST[a]	AMOUNT[b]	COST[a]	AMOUNT[b]	COST[a]	AMOUNT[b]
1	5	40	4	10	5	20
2	5	20	8	80	6	40
3	5	30	6	50	6	10
4	3	40	4	20	5	10
5	5	20	3	10	4	50

[a]Cost ($ 000) to purchase 1 ton of plate type *i* from a subcontractor.

[b]For any subcontractor used, all of its available amounts of all five types of iron plates must be purchased at the indicated costs.

CRITICAL-THINKING PROJECT C

THE DELIVERY PROBLEM OF HEXXON OIL COMPANY

You, Ms. Tina Chen, Production Manager of Hexxon Oil Company, received a call from Mr. Peter Finch, Vice-President of Production, who needs to ship at least 1.5 million barrels of oil to the refinery in New Orleans (Refinery 1), 1.6 million barrels to the refinery in Houston (Refinery 2), and 1.4 million barrels to the refinery in Mobile (Refinery 3) for the next production quarter. You told him that you would develop a plan of least cost to transport the oil by tanker from the port in Mexico and via a pipeline from the facility in Alaska.

     Making phone calls to these two facilities, you learned that there are up to 3.5 million barrels of oil at the port in Mexico and up to 1.2 million barrels at the facility in Alaska. To transport the oil from Mexico to the refineries, you can lease at most three tankers, A, B, and C, each with a capacity of 1.6 million barrels. In discussions with Ms. Yuki Ando in the Accounting Department, you learned that the cost of transporting the oil by tanker consists of an insurance cost against spills and a fixed lease cost. The insurance cost is $0.25/barrel/1000 miles traveled plus a surcharge that depends on the age of the tanker. Ms. Ando provided the following data for each tanker:

TANKER	BASE CHARGE ($/bbl/1000 mi)	SURCHARGE ($/bbl/1000 mi)	FIXED COST ($)
A	0.25	0.0000	200,000
B	0.25	0.1250	100,000
C	0.25	0.0625	150,000

     She was also able to provide the approximate distances from the port in Mexico to each of the refineries and the total cost for pumping a barrel of oil from Alaska to each of the three refineries. These data follow:

	DISTANCE FROM THE MEXICAN PORT (mi)	COST TO SHIP BY PIPELINE FROM ALASKA ($/bbl)
Refinery 1	2500	1.40
Refinery 2	2000	1.25
Refinery 3	1800	1.20

     As Manager of the Production Department, formulate a single model to determine the least-cost way to ship all the needed oil from both Alaska and the port in Mexico to the three refineries. Keep in mind that you can determine which, if any, tankers to use and which refineries to send them to, but a tanker can go to no more than one refinery.

CRITICAL-THINKING PROJECT D

THE DELIVERY PROBLEM OF GASAHOL, INC.

Gasahol, Inc., produces a special fuel consisting of a mixture of gasoline and alcohol at each of three plants, located in Denver, Oklahoma City, and St. Louis. This fuel is supplied to customers in Dallas, Kansas City, Phoenix, San Francisco, and Los Angeles. Gasahol, Inc., can also subcontract to GasMix, Inc., a California-based company, to produce and deliver a combined total of up to 18,000 gallons of the same product to customers in Los Angeles and San Francisco. As Vice-President, one of your responsibilities is to determine a least-cost production and shipping plan.

Speaking to the production managers at each plant, you have obtained their production capacities and costs per gallon, as follows:

PLANT	CAPACITY (gal)	COST ($/gal)
Denver	14,000	0.55
Oklahoma	16,000	0.62
St. Louis	20,000	0.48

Mr. Tubb Jones, Manager of the Sales Department, has obtained for you next month's orders for this fuel from each customer. Knowing that Gasahol, Inc., incurs a delivery charge at the rate of $0.01/gallon/100 miles traveled, you have used a road map to find the approximate distances in miles from the plants to the five customers.
These distances and the customer demands are summarized in the following table:

	DISTANCE (mi)				
	DALLAS	KANSAS	PHOENIX	SF	LA
Denver	780	610	810	1260	1030
Oklahoma	210	350	980	1660	1340
St. Louis	660	260	1480	2120	1860
Demand (gal)	11000	10000	9000	12000	18000

Checking your records, you find that your subcontractor, GasMix, Inc., charges a combined production and transportation cost based on the amount shipped (regardless of whether to San Francisco or to Los Angeles) as follows:

PRODUCTION AND TRANSPORTATION PRICE ($/gal)	WHEN THE FOLLOWING AMOUNTS ARE SHIPPED (gal)
0.95	Up to 7,999
0.90	8,000–15,999
0.85	16,000–23,999

As Vice-President of the Production Department of Gasahol, Inc., formulate a single mathematical model to determine the optimal production and shipping plan that precisely meets the demands. Include an appropriate schematic diagram. (Hint: Create an integer variable Y, whose value is 0 if 0–7,999 gallons are shipped by GasMix to San Francisco, 1 if 8,000–15,999 gallons are shipped, and 2 if 16,000–23,999 gallons are shipped. In terms of this variable, the cost for shipping each gallon is $0.95 - 0.05Y$. Create a similar variable, Z, for shipping from GasMix to Los Angeles. Be sure to include constraints to ensure that the amounts shipped by GasMix and the unit shipping costs match those in the foregoing table.)

CRITICAL-THINKING PROJECT E
THE DATA-TRANSMISSION PROBLEM OF TELE COM

Ms. Amy Jenkins, Director of Communications for Tele Com, has just come from a meeting. Upper management has decided that, due to a major new group of clients in Los Angeles and Boston, it is necessary to increase the existing capacity for transmitting data between the offices in these two cities. The current communication network has intermediate offices with computers and retransmission capabilities in Salt Lake City, Phoenix, Denver, Albuquerque, Minneapolis, Houston, Chicago, Atlanta, Cleveland, Washington, D.C., and New York.

As a first step, Ms. Jenkins needs to review the current system. She has obtained from her files the following list of communication links between certain pairs of these cities and the maximum number of bits per day that can be sent through that link:

FROM	TO	MAXIMUM BITS PER DAY (billions)
Los Angeles	Salt Lake	15
Los Angeles	Phoenix	12
Salt Lake	Denver	10
Salt Lake	Albuquerque	10
Phoenix	Albuquerque	12
Denver	Minneapolis	8
Albuquerque	Houston	9
Minneapolis	Chicago	15
Houston	Atlanta	12
Chicago	Cleveland	15
Atlanta	Cleveland	12
Atlanta	Washington	14
Cleveland	Washington	8
Cleveland	Boston	12
Washington	New York	15
New York	Boston	18

Formulate a single mathematical model to determine the maximum number of bits per day that can be transmitted from the Los Angeles to the Boston office through the existing network. (Include a schematic diagram.)

HOT DOG FOR LINEAR PROGRAMMING

So you think linear programming matters only to business managers and space scientists. Well, what's more ordinary than a drive to the local hot dog stand? This video illustrates how linear programming models and the sophisticated simplex technique (discussed in detail in Chapters 4, 5 and 6) touch our lives in three different ways as we drive out to grab a bite for lunch.

Consider the car itself, a General Motors product. GM has 60 different models, and there are countless new features it could offer to its customers. All these possibilities result in a huge number of variations that GM *could* sell. How does it determine the optimal product mix? Evaluating all the various combinations of models and options would take decades even with high-speed computers. But computers at GM are able to determine the optimal product mix by applying the simplex method to LP models.

"Check the oil?" Even the oil that keeps our car's engine running smoothly results from a decision based on a linear programming model. Oil refineries produce more than oil. They can turn out up to 3,000 different products, such as ink, aspirin, guitar strings, perfume, hair coloring, insect repellent, table tennis paddles, carpeting, and even bubble gum. The decision as to which of these products to make in an effort to maximize profit—given that available resources are limited—is again found through linear programming.

And now we're at the hot dog stand. In any week the ingredients in the hot dog made back at the plant may change. Some weeks the hot dogs are mostly beef, and other weeks they are mostly pork. How does the manufacturer decide? You guessed it. A linear programming model provides the information that the managers need for deciding the best mix of ingredients. (Total running time is 1:47.)

Questions on the Video

1. When Henry Ford first produced automobiles, did he face the problem that GM now faces about which body styles and what colors to offer?

2. What makes linear programming necessary in the three examples the video presents?

Beyond the Video

1. List a few categories of features in a car (body style, color, type of roof, sound system, and so on). Within each category, list a few options (for example, the body style could be two-door, four-door, and so on). Multiplying the number of options in each category gives you the total number of possible variations in a car. How hard do you think it is to reach a thousand variations? Comment on why a car manufacturer might find a linear programming model an advantage in considering which variations to produce.

2. Why doesn't a hot dog manufacturer just keep the same recipe every day? What constraints do you think the manufacturer has in its linear programming model?

Practical Considerations

1. Assume GM has 10,000,000 possible car variations. If a high-speed computer can determine the production plan for each variation in one second, how long will it take (in years) to determine the optimal plan? What does this tell you about the need for good mathematical methods?

2. Go to a paint store and get a card that shows different colors on the front. Flip it over, and note the bar coding on the back. What do you think the coding represents? Why do you think this information is in bar-coding format?

Source: "For All Practical Purposes," from *The Consortium for Mathematics and Its Applications* (Arlington, MA: 1986), Program 2.

CHAPTER
4

LINEAR PROGRAMMING: THE GRAPHICAL APPROACH

· ·

*C*ase Chemicals produces two solvents. One solvent sells from hardware stores to weekend carpenters who are stripping old furniture before refinishing it. The other solvent, designed for heavier duty, is sold at automotive supply centers to people who need to dissolve the build-up on carburetors, manifolds, and the like to improve their engine's performance. The question Case Chemicals faces is how much of each solvent should it manufacture to make the most profit? How should Case assign its labor force? Does it make more sense to use part-time workers or full-time workers? In what department should workers be added? And what happens to profits if the price of particular raw materials changes?

This chapter focuses on how Case Chemicals determines its optimal plan—that is, how it maximizes profits—as it answers these and other questions.

You now know how to formulate and identify a linear program. This chapter and the next two show how to solve linear programming problems, both by hand and by computer. In this chapter, linear programs having two variables are examined from a geometric point of view. Although real-world problems have many more variables and cannot be solved geometrically, the insight gained by solving two-variable problems graphically provides a clear understanding of how to solve problems of three or more variables algebraically, which is the method used with computers. The graphical approach is useful not only for finding an optimal solution, but also for obtaining additional information on how sensitive the optimal solution is with regard to changes in problem data.

■ 4.1 THE GEOMETRY OF A LINEAR PROGRAM WITH TWO VARIABLES

In this section, linear programming problems having two variables are solved graphically. Consider the problem faced by the managers of Case Chemicals introduced in Section 2.1 in Chapter 2.

EXAMPLE 4.1 THE PRODUCTION-PLANNING PROBLEM OF CASE CHEMICALS Case Chemicals Company produces two solvents, CS-01 and CS-02, at its Cleveland plant. The plant operates 40 hours per week and employs five full-time and two part-time workers working 15 hours per week to run their seven blending machines that mix certain chemicals to produce each solvent. This work force provides up to 230 hours of available labor in the Blending Department. The products, once blended, are refined in the Purification Department, which currently has seven purifiers and employs six full-time workers and one part-time worker who puts in 10 hours per week. This work force provides up to 250 hours of available labor in the Purification Department. The hours required in the Blending and Purification Departments to produce one thousand gallons of each of the solvents are listed in Table 4.1.

TABLE 4.1	Blending and Purification Requirements (hr/1000 gal)	
	CS-01	CS-02
Blending	2	1
Purification	1	2

Case Chemicals has a nearly unlimited supply of raw materials to produce the two solvents. It can sell any amount of CS-01, but the demand for the more-specialized product CS-02 is limited to at most 120 thousand gallons per week. The Accounting Department estimates a profit margin of $0.30 per gallon of CS-01 and $0.50 per gallon of CS-02. Because all the employees are salaried and thus paid the same amount regardless of how many hours they work, these salaries and the costs of machines are considered fixed and are not included in the computation of the profit margin. As a Production-Planning Manager, you want to determine the optimal weekly manufacturing plan for Case Chemicals. ■

Through the process of problem formulation, you might develop the following mathematical model. Here, x_1 is the number of thousands of gallons of CS-01 to produce, and x_2 is the number of thousands of gallons of CS-02 to produce. The objective function is expressed in hundreds of dollars.

Linear Program
EX4_1.DAT

$$
\begin{array}{rlll}
\text{Maximize} & 3x_1 + 5x_2 & & \\
\text{Subject to} & 2x_1 + x_2 \leq 230 & \text{(blending)} & (1) \\
& x_1 + 2x_2 \leq 250 & \text{(purification)} & (2) \\
& x_2 \leq 120 & \text{(limit on CS-02)} & (3) \\
& x_1 \geq 0 & & (4) \\
& x_2 \geq 0 & & (5)
\end{array}
$$

This model is the same as the one presented in Section 2.1 in Chapter 2, except for the variable names and the units of the objective function.

As the Manager, your objective is to *solve* this problem—that is, to find values for variables x_1 and x_2 that satisfy the five constraints and produce the largest profit margin for the objective function. You will now learn how to solve this problem graphically.

4.1.1 Graphing the Constraints of a Linear Program

Feasible value
Values for decision variables that satisfy all of the constraints.

Infeasible value
Values for decision variables that do not satisfy all of the constraints.

The graphical method for solving a linear program having two variables is best understood by first concentrating on the constraints and subsequently on the objective function. To determine which values of x_1 and x_2 satisfy all the constraints, consider one constraint at a time. Each constraint permits certain values for x_1 and x_2 that satisfy the constraint. These values are called **feasible values.** Those values that do not satisfy the constraint are called **infeasible values.**

For example, constraint (4) in Example 4.1 ($x_1 \geq 0$) permits only nonnegative values for x_1. Constraint (5) ($x_2 \geq 0$) permits only nonnegative values for x_2. Geometrically, these two constraints together permit feasible values for the variables that are to the right of the x_2-axis and above the x_1-axis, as illustrated in Figure 4.1.

Remember that you are looking for those values of x_1 and x_2 that satisfy *all* constraints, not just the nonnegativity constraints. To see graphically which values are

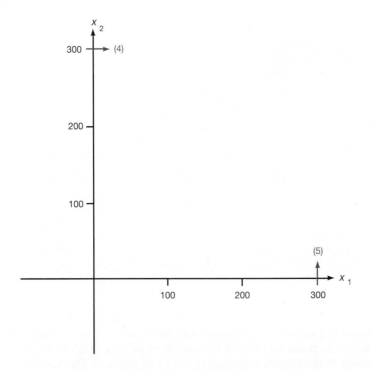

FIGURE 4.1 Feasible Area Based on Constraints (4) and (5).

feasible for constraint (1) in Example 4.1—that is, $2x_1 + x_2 \leq 230$—begin by finding those values of x_1 and x_2 that satisfy the *equality*

$$2x_1 + x_2 = 230$$

Note that an equality sign has replaced the inequality sign. By using the techniques described in Appendix 4A, the graph of this equation is the straight line shown in Figure 4.2.

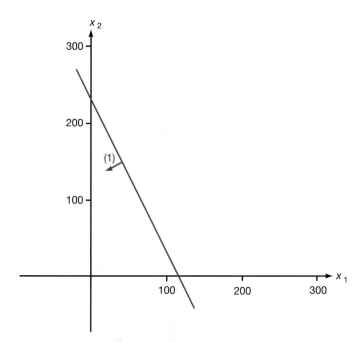

FIGURE 4.2 Feasible Area Based on Constraint (1).

Recall, however, that the feasible values for constraint (1) consist of those values for which $2x_1 + x_2 \leq 230$, not just those for which $2x_1 + x_2 = 230$. What you will discover by trial and error is that all points on the line in Figure 4.2 give rise to feasible values for x_1 and x_2, as does every point on one of the two *sides* of this line. The only question is: Which side? To find out, choose any point *not on the line* and see if the corresponding x_1 and x_2 values satisfy the constraint. If they do, then this point is on the feasible side; otherwise, the point is on the infeasible side.

For example, consider the point $x_1 = 0$, $x_2 = 0$, which is not on the line in Figure 4.2. (If the origin were on the line, another point would be selected.) The point $x_1 = 0$ and $x_2 = 0$ does satisfy the constraint because $2x_1 + x_2 = 2(0) + 0 = 0$, which is $\leq$ 230. Therefore, the feasible values for this constraint consist of the line $2x_1 + x_2 = 230$ together with everything on the same side of this line as the origin, as shown in Figure 4.3. The shaded region in the figure illustrates those values of x_1 and x_2 that are feasible not only for constraint (1), but also for the nonnegativity constraints (4) and (5).

The foregoing process is then repeated for each constraint—that is:

1. Replace the inequality sign in a constraint by an equality sign.
2. Draw the straight line corresponding to the equation in (1); refer to the techniques in Appendix 4A, if necessary.
3. Identify the side of the line in step 2 that satisfies the original inequality.

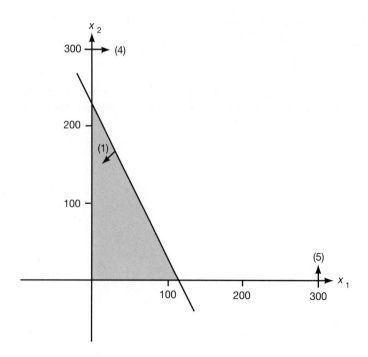

FIGURE 4.3 Feasible Area Based on Constraints (1), (4), and (5).

4. Shade that portion of the graph that satisfies *all* the constraints drawn so far.

This has been done for constraint (2) in Figure 4.4 and finally for constraint (3) in Figure 4.5. Note that in this case these constraints reduce the feasible area.

Feasible region
The set of values for the decision variables in a linear program that satisfies all constraints.

The final shaded area in Figure 4.5 is called the **feasible region** of the linear program. Any point inside the feasible region is a **feasible solution** and gives rise to values for x_1 and x_2 that satisfy all constraints. You can also see that the feasible region is bounded by straight lines that meet at sharp "corner points" labeled A to E in Figure 4.5. These corner points are called **extreme points**.

Feasible solution
A solution in which the decision variables are feasible.

4.1.2 Using the Objective Function to Obtain an Optimal Solution

Extreme point
The corner point of a feasible region.

To solve the linear programming problem in Example 4.1, a feasible point must be found that provides the largest value of the objective function $3x_1 + 5x_2$. Begin by choosing any point inside the feasible region and computing the value of the objective function at that point. In Example 4.1, suppose you choose the feasible point $x_1 = 20$ and $x_2 = 30$. The value of the objective function at that point is $3x_1 + 5x_2 = 3(20) + 5(30) = 210$. You can now ask: Is there another point in the feasible region that provides a *larger* value of the objective function? To find out, first identify all the feasible points that yield the *same* value of the objective function as the current point. In Example 4.1, this means you must find all the points that satisfy $3x_1 + 5x_2 = 210$. This is achieved by drawing the following **objective function line:**

Objective function line
A line used in the graphical method in which all points on the line have the same objective function value.

$$3x_1 + 5x_2 = 210$$

as illustrated by the blue line in Figure 4.6. Any point on this blue line yields an objective function value of 210.

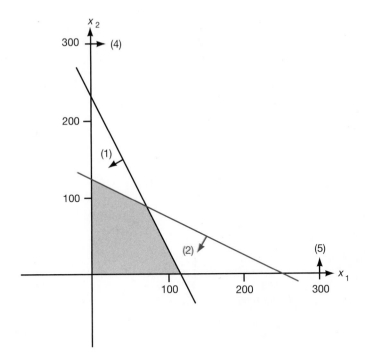

FIGURE 4.4 Feasible Area Based on Constraints (1), (2), (4), and (5).

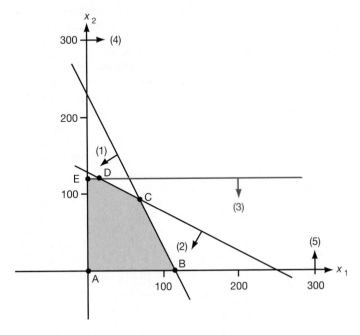

FIGURE 4.5 Feasible Region Based on Constraints (1), (2), (3), (4), and (5).

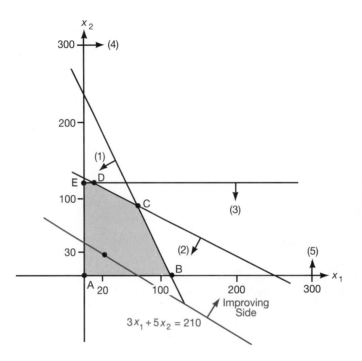

FIGURE 4.6 Drawing the Objective Function Line.

What you will discover, perhaps by trial and error, is that all values of the variables on one side of this line provide a *better* value of the objective function than does the current point; all values on the other side provide a worse value. To determine the "better" side, simply choose any point *not on the objective function line* and see if its x_1 and x_2 values provide a better value for the objective function than the current point whose values are $x_1 = 20$ and $x_2 = 30$. For example, consider the point where $x_1 = 50$ and $x_2 = 50$. The value of the objective function at this point is $3(50) + 5(50) = 400$. Because the objective in this problem is to *maximize*, this value of 400 is better than the previous one of $3(20) + 5(30) = 210$. Thus, the point whose values are $x_1 = 50$ and $x_2 = 50$ *is* on the better side of the objective function line, as indicated by the arrow on the blue line in Figure 4.6. Observe that had the objective of this problem been to *minimize*, the point whose values are $x_1 = 50$ and $x_2 = 50$ would *not* be on the improving side of the objective function line.

Having found the better side of the objective function line, you need locate only one point on this side of the line that is also *in the feasible region*. For example, the point whose values are $x_1 = 50$ and $x_2 = 50$ is such a point. In other words, you have succeeded in finding a new *feasible* point, $x_1 = 50$ and $x_2 = 50$, whose objective function value of 400 is better than that of 210 at the current point $x_1 = 20$ and $x_2 = 30$.

Now, the entire process can be repeated at the new point $x_1 = 50$ and $x_2 = 50$. That is, you can draw the new objective function line through the new point $x_1 = 50$ and $x_2 = 50$:

$$3x_1 + 5x_2 = 400$$

as done in Figure 4.7. An important observation is that the new objective function line is *parallel* to the previous one.

In summary, you have discovered that, starting at an initial feasible point,

1. drawing the objective function line
2. locating its better side, and

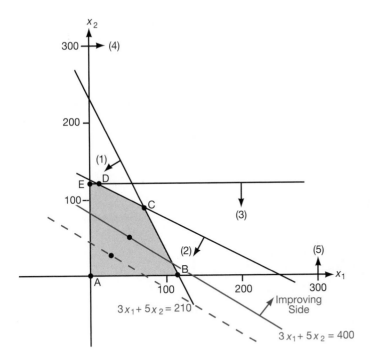

FIGURE 4.7 Drawing the Improved Objective Function Line.

3. moving the objective function line parallel to itself in the improving direction

result in producing points in the feasible region whose objective function values are better and better. In fact, to solve the linear programming problem graphically, you need only move the objective function line parallel to itself in the improving direction *until it is just about to leave the feasible region.* This final point is the **optimal solution** to the linear program. The result of applying this process for Example 4.1, illustrated in Figure 4.8, is that the extreme point C is the optimal solution.

> **Optimal solution**
> The point in the feasible region that has the best objective function value.

Based on the observation that the optimal solution occurs at an extreme point, an alternative approach to solving this linear programming problem is to list all the extreme points of the feasible region, to compute the objective function value at each one, and to select the one with the best value. This is illustrated in the table within Figure 4.8.

4.1.3 *Obtaining Numerical Values for the Optimal Solution*

The optimal solution to the linear program in Example 4.1 is shown graphically in Figure 4.8. One way to obtain the *values* for the variables in this optimal solution is to read them directly from the graph. This visual process, however, is not precise. A more accurate approach is based on the observation that, in Figure 4.8, the optimal solution occurs at the extreme point C. This extreme point lies at the intersection of the two lines corresponding to constraints (1) and (2). These equations are

$$2x_1 + x_2 = 230 \tag{6}$$

$$x_1 + 2x_2 = 250 \tag{7}$$

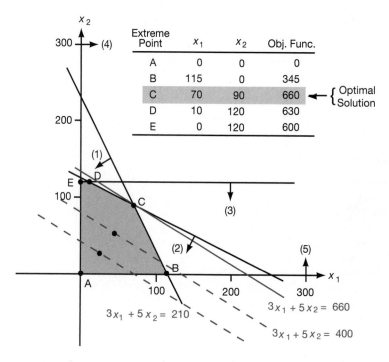

FIGURE 4.8 Finding the Optimal Solution.

You can find the exact values for the optimal solution by solving these two equations in the two unknowns, x_1 and x_2. To see how, use Equation (6) to solve for x_2 in terms of x_1, that is,

$$x_2 = 230 - 2x_1 \tag{8}$$

Now, substitute this expression for x_2 into Equation (7):

$$x_1 + 2(230 - 2x_1) = 250 \tag{9}$$

or

$$-3x_1 + 460 = 250 \tag{10}$$

Now, use Equation (10) to solve for x_1:

$$x_1 = 70$$

Finally, substituting $x_1 = 70$ into Equation (8) yields

$$x_2 = 230 - 2x_1 = 230 - 2(70) = 90$$

This process of solving two equations in two unknowns has led to the *exact* optimal solution of $x_1 = 70$ and $x_2 = 90$ for the linear program in Example 4.1. The corresponding value of the objective function (in hundreds of dollars) at this point is

$$3x_1 + 5x_2 = 3(70) + 5(90) = 660$$

The results for Case Chemicals in the form of a weekly production plan are as follows:

$$\text{Amount of CS-01 to produce} = \quad 70000 \text{ gallons}$$

$$\text{Amount of CS-02 to produce} = \quad 90000 \text{ gallons}$$

$$\text{Weekly profit margin} = \$66000$$

KEY FEATURES

In this section, you have learned that the key features associated with the graphical solution of a linear programming problem with two variables and several inequality constraints are as follows:

✔ Obtain the feasible region by performing the following for each constraint:
  a. Replace the inequality sign with an equality sign.
  b. Draw the resulting line by finding two different points on that line.
  c. Identify the feasible side of the line.

The feasible region then consists of those points that satisfy *all* the constraints simultaneously.

✔ Obtain an optimal solution by performing the following:
  a. Select any point inside the feasible region.
  b. Draw the objective function line through the chosen point.
  c. Determine the improving side of the objective function line.
  d. Move the objective function line parallel to itself in the improving direction until the line is about to leave the feasible region. (The final extreme point is the optimal solution to the linear program.)
  e. Compute the values of the variables at the optimal solution by solving the two equations of the two lines that go through that point.

■ 4.2 LINEAR PROGRAMS HAVING SPECIAL GEOMETRIC PROPERTIES

In Section 4.1, you saw how to solve graphically a linear programming problem with two variables. In Example 4.1, the optimal solution occurred at an extreme point of the feasible region in Figure 4.8. In this section, you will see examples of linear programs for which this is not the case. You will also learn what causes these exceptions and how to interpret them.

4.2.1 *Infeasible Linear Programs*

To examine one type of exception, suppose you are the Manager of the Production-Planning Department of Case Chemicals, and your Sales Manager informs you that she wants to sign a long-term contract for supplying 150,000 gallons of CS-01 each week. To derive a weekly production plan that meets this sales requirement, you have modified the formulation of the linear program in Example 4.1 by adding the new constraint:

$$x_1 \geq 150$$

resulting in the following linear program:

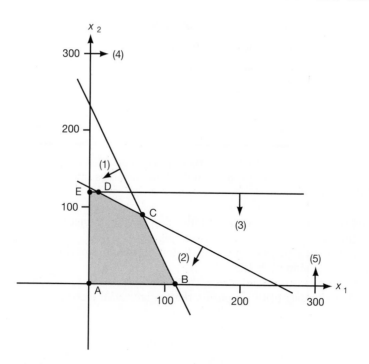

FIGURE 4.9 Feasible Region for Example 4.1.

EXAMPLE 4.2 AN INFEASIBLE LINEAR PROGRAM

Linear Program
EX4_2.DAT

$$
\begin{array}{llrr}
\text{Maximize} & 3x_1 + 5x_2 & & \\
\text{Subject to} & 2x_1 + \ x_2 \le 230 & & (1) \\
& x_1 + 2x_2 \le 250 & & (2) \\
& x_2 \le 120 & & (3) \\
& x_1 \qquad\quad \ge \ \ 0 & & (4) \\
& x_2 \ge \ \ 0 & & (5) \\
& x_1 \qquad\quad \ge 150 & & (6)
\end{array}
$$

■

Constraints (1) through (5) are the same as those in Example 4.1, and the feasible region corresponding to those five constraints is depicted in Figure 4.9. The result of adding the new constraint (6) is illustrated in Figure 4.10. As you can see, there are *no* values of x_1 and x_2 that satisfy the new constraint (6) as well as all the previous ones. This means that, with their current resources, Case Chemicals *cannot* satisfy a contractual agreement to supply 150 thousand gallons of CS-01 per week. If the proposed contract is signed, Case Chemicals will need to obtain additional resources to increase production capabilities. Senior management, therefore, will have to make a strategic decision on the value of this investment.

Infeasible linear program
A linear program in which there are no values of the variables that satisfy all constraints simultaneously.

The linear program in Example 4.2 is called an **infeasible linear program**, which means that no values of the variables satisfy all of the constraints simultaneously—that is, there is no feasible region. For such problems, there is no point in trying to obtain an *optimal* solution because you will not even be able to find a *feasible* solution.

Perhaps the most common cause for a linear program to be infeasible is a mistake in the formulation of the problem. For example, a less-than-or-equal-to constraint may have been written accidentally as a greater-than-or-equal-to constraint. Alternatively,

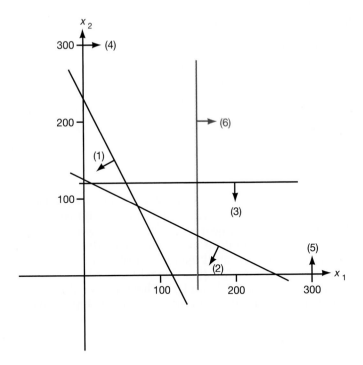

FIGURE 4.10 Graphical Solution to Example 4.2.

a mistake may have been made when the data for a linear program are typed into a computer program. For example, the constraint $x_1 + 2x_2 \leq 230$ may have been entered accidently into the computer as $x_1 + 2x_2 \leq 130$, and this error could result in an infeasible linear program. If you discover that a linear program is infeasible, first check the problem formulation carefully, and then make sure the data have been entered correctly.

Even if there are no mistakes in the problem formulation or the way the data are entered into the computer, a linear program can still be infeasible. These infeasible problems occur in practice when the constraints are too restrictive. Such constraints can arise in any number of ways. For instance, the requirement to produce at least 150 thousand gallons of CS-01 in constraint (6) of Example 4.2 imposes a restriction that cannot be handled by the available resources in the Blending and Purification Departments of Case Chemicals. As another example, the government may impose such severe restrictions on the amount of pollutants a steel plant can emit that no production plan can meet both those requirements and attain a minimum level of profitablility.

4.2.2 *Unbounded Linear Programs*

Consider another example of a linear program whose solution does not occur at an extreme point of the feasible region. Suppose that the inequality signs of constraints (1) and (2) in Example 4.1 are accidentally reversed during problem formulation. The resulting linear program is given in Example 4.3.

EXAMPLE 4.3 AN UNBOUNDED LINEAR PROGRAM

Linear Program
EX4_3.DAT

$$\begin{array}{llrl}
\text{Maximize} & 3x_1 + 5x_2 & & \\
\text{Subject to} & 2x_1 + \ \ x_2 \geq 230 & & (1) \\
& x_1 + 2x_2 \geq 250 & & (2) \\
& x_2 \leq 120 & & (3) \\
& x_1 \qquad \geq \ \ 0 & & (4) \\
& x_2 \geq \ \ 0 & & (5)
\end{array}$$

■

The feasible region of this linear program appears in Figure 4.11, together with the objective function line drawn through the feasible point $x_1 = 100$ and $x_2 = 100$. According to the procedure described in Section 4.1, this linear program is solved graphically by moving the objective function line parallel to itself in the improving direction, indicated by the arrow on that line in Figure 4.11, until the line is just about to leave the feasible region. In this example, the objective function line will *never* leave because the rightmost part of the feasible region has no boundary. Theoretically, this would mean that Case Chemicals can obtain an *infinite* profit, which is clearly impossible.

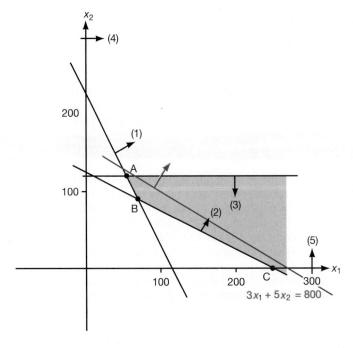

FIGURE 4.11 Graphical Solution to Example 4.3.

Unbounded linear program
A feasible linear program in which the objective function can be improved indefinitely.

Such a problem is said to be an **unbounded linear program**, meaning that the objective function can be improved indefinitely—that is, there are feasible values of the variables that can make the objective function value as large as desired in the case of maximization (or as small as desired in the case of minimization). An unbounded linear program is identified graphically when the objective function line can be moved parallel to itself in the improving direction without ever leaving the feasible region.

The general cause for an unbounded linear program is a mistake in problem formulation. For example, a constraint may have been omitted accidentally. Also, a mistake may have been made in typing the data into a computer program. For instance, the constraint $x_1 + 2x_2 \leq 230$ may have been entered accidentally into the computer as $x_1 + 2x_2 \geq 230$, and this error results in an unbounded linear program. If you discover that a linear program is unbounded, first check the problem formulation carefully, and then make sure the data have been entered correctly. It is important to note that there is a difference between a *feasible region* being unbounded and a *linear program* being unbounded. As illustrated in Figure 4.12, it is possible for the feasible region to be unbounded but the linear program *not* to be unbounded.

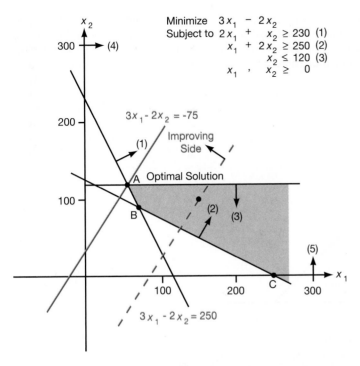

FIGURE 4.12 An Unbounded Feasible Region but Not an Unbounded Linear Program.

KEY FEATURES

So far, you have seen three mutually exclusive types of linear programming problems. Namely, those that are

1. *Optimal*—that is, they have an optimal solution.
2. *Infeasible*—that is, there are no values of the variables that satisfy all of the constraints simultaneously.
3. *Unbounded*—that is, there are feasible values of the variables that make the objective function as large or small as desired.

Every linear program is either optimal, infeasible, or unbounded.

4.2.3 Linear Programs with Redundant Constraints

Redundant constraint
A constraint that is not necessary in the sense that the feasible region is the same whether this constraint is included or not.

In formulating a linear programming problem, you might come across a constraint that is not necessary, in the sense that the feasible region is exactly the same whether you include this constraint or not. Such a constraint is a **redundant constraint**. To illustrate, suppose the following constraint is added to Example 4.1, the Case Chemicals problem:

$$x_1 + x_2 \le 300 \tag{6}$$

The feasible region of the resulting linear program is illustrated in Figure 4.13. Note that constraint (6) does not affect the feasible region. The feasible region in Figure 4.13 with constraint (6) is exactly the same as the one in Figure 4.9, which does not include this constraint. Constraint (6) is, therefore, redundant.

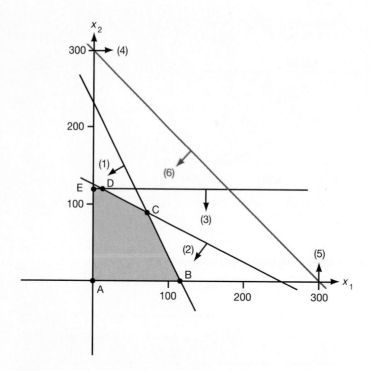

FIGURE 4.13 A Linear Program with a Redundant Constraint.

You may not be aware that a constraint is redundant as you formulate a linear program, but this need not concern you. The optimal solution does not change if a redundant constraint is included. The only effect is that it increases the size of the linear program, which, in turn, may cause a computer program to take extra time to solve the problem. The general rule is: Do not worry about redundant constraints; if you think you need a constraint, include it in the formulation.

4.2.4 *Linear Programs with Alternative Optimal Solutions*

Some linear programs have more than one optimal solution. Each optimal solution is termed an **alternative optimal solution**. Having alternative optimal solutions means only that there are different feasible values for the variables that produce the same best value of the objective function. All optimal solutions are the same in that all are, by definition, the best. However, you may prefer one of these alternative optimal solutions over the others for some secondary reason—perhaps because one solution is easier to implement than the other.

> **Alternative optimal solution**
> Two or more different solutions to linear programs that have the same best value of the objective function.

    To illustrate, suppose the profit margins in Example 4.1 are changed to $0.20 per gallon of CS-01 and $0.40 per gallon of CS-02. The new linear program is given in Example 4.4.

EXAMPLE 4.4 A LINEAR PROGRAM WITH ALTERNATIVE OPTIMAL SOLUTION

$$
\begin{array}{lrll}
\text{Maximize} & 2x_1 + 4x_2 & & \\
\text{Subject to} & 2x_1 +\ x_2 \leq 230 & & (1) \\
& x_1 + 2x_2 \leq 250 & & (2) \\
& x_2 \leq 120 & & (3) \\
& x_1 \quad\quad\ \geq\ 0 & & (4) \\
& x_2 \geq\ 0 & & (5)
\end{array}
$$

■

The graphical solution to this problem is illustrated in Figure 4.14. There you can see that the *two* extreme points C and D are optimal. In fact, all points on the line segment connecting these two extreme points are optimal. Geometrically, the reason this problem has alternative optimal solutions is because the objective function line is parallel to one of the constraints that goes through one of the optimal solutions. In Example 4.4, the objective function line is parallel to constraint (2).

■ 4.3 A GRAPHICAL APPROACH TO SENSITIVITY AND PARAMETRIC ANALYSIS

In a real-world environment, some of the data in a linear programming model may change over time because of the dynamic nature of the business. What happens to the optimal solution if market prices drop? If labor or raw-material costs rise? If additional employees are hired on a production line? A manager in such situations would like to know how sensitive the optimal solution is to these data values.

    Answers to such questions can be used in various ways. For example, if the optimal solution is very sensitive to some coefficients, and if these values are expected to fluctuate over time, then the manager may want to use the model only for short-term planning, or may have to resolve the model periodically as the data change.

    After formulating and solving a linear programming problem, a manager should ask a number of important questions of the form: "What happens if?" For instance:

1. What happens to the optimal solution and the corresponding objective function value if one particular coefficient in the objective function is changed? For example, suppose that, due to recent competition in the market for CS-01, the management of Case Chemicals in Section 4.1 has decided to decrease the sales price of this product by $25 per thousand gallons. This change decreases the profit coefficient

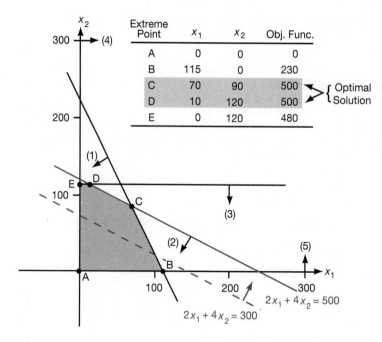

FIGURE 4.14 A Linear Program with Alternative Optimal Solutions.

    of CS-01 from 3 hundred dollars per thousand gallons to 2.75 hundred dollars. How does this change in the objective function coefficient affect the production plan?

2. What happens to the optimal solution and the corresponding objective function value if one particular right-hand-side value in the constraints is changed? For example, suppose that each of the two part-time employees in the Blending Department at Case Chemicals works 10 instead of 15 hours per week. This change reduces the available hours of labor in the Blending Department from 230 to 220. How does this change in the right-hand-side value of the blending constraint affect the production plan and the optimal profit?

Sensitivity analysis
Determining how sensitive the optimal solution and objective function value are with regard to changes in problem data.

These questions deal with the topic of **sensitivity analysis**. You, the Manager, are asking how sensitive the optimal solution and objective function value are with regard to changes in the problem data—that is, the coefficients in the objective function and constraints. How big an impact will a change in any of the data have in the solution?

    These sensitivity questions are important to a manager because the problem data often have to be estimated and are therefore subject to inaccuracies. Before implementing the solution obtained from a linear program, it is to the Manager's advantage to know what might happen if the estimates of the data are slightly off. Sensitivity analysis indicates which coefficients most significantly affect the optimal solution.

    To illustrate another use of sensitivity analysis, suppose that the constraints of a particular linear program deal with the allocation of scarce resources, such as capital, labor, and raw materials. Sensitivity analysis can help determine whether or not it is profitable to acquire additional amounts of resources. In this section, you will learn how to use a graphical approach for answering certain types of sensitivity questions.

4.3.1 Sensitivity Analysis of the Objective Function Coefficients

In this section, a graphical approach is used to determine what happens to the optimal solution and objective function value when *one objective function coefficient is changed.* Such a situation is illustrated in the foregoing first question. As another example, suppose the objective function coefficients in a model have been estimated within a certain known degree of accuracy. For example, suppose that you estimate a coefficient in the objective function—that represents a profit for a particular product—to be $5 per unit to an accuracy of within 10%. After obtaining an optimal solution to a linear program that uses this value of $5 as one of the objective function coefficients, you should realize that its "true" value might be any amount between $4.50 and $5.50 per unit. Sensitivity analysis on this coefficient is used to determine if the optimal solution remains optimal *for all* values of the per-unit profit within this range. If so, then the current estimates are accurate enough; if not, perhaps more accurate estimates should be obtained.

SENSITIVITY ANALYSIS OF THE OBJECTIVE FUNCTION COEFFICIENT FOR x_1

Suppose that, as Manager of Case Chemicals, you have solved the linear program in Example 4.1, which is restated in what follows. Its feasible region and optimal solution are illustrated in Figure 4.15.

$$
\begin{array}{lrl}
\text{Maximize} & 3x_1 + 5x_2 & \\
\text{Subject to} & 2x_1 + x_2 \le 230 & \quad (1) \\
& x_1 + 2x_2 \le 250 & \quad (2) \\
& x_2 \le 120 & \quad (3) \\
& x_1 \ge 0 & \quad (4) \\
& x_2 \ge 0 & \quad (5)
\end{array}
$$

Based on the optimal solution obtained graphically in Section 4.1, the company has been producing 70 thousand gallons of CS-01 and 90 thousand gallons of CS-02.

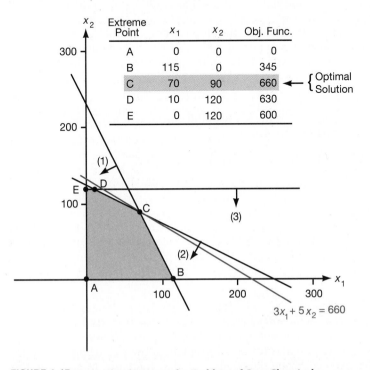

Extreme Point	x_1	x_2	Obj. Func.
A	0	0	0
B	115	0	345
C	70	90	660
D	10	120	630
E	0	120	600

FIGURE 4.15 Optimal Solution to the Problem of Case Chemicals.

Due to recent competition in the market for CS-01, management has decided to decrease the sales price of CS-01 by $25 per thousand gallons. How should the production plan for CS-01 and CS-02 change?

The first step in answering this question is to realize that a decrease of $25 in the sales price of each thousand gallons of CS-01 results in a corresponding decrease in the profit margin of CS-01 from $300 to $275. The question to ask is: What happens to the previous optimal solution of $x_1 = 70$ and $x_2 = 90$ when the coefficient of x_1 in the objective function decreases from 3 to 2.75?

One way to answer this question is to resolve the problem after changing the coefficient of x_1 in the objective function to 2.75. However, sensitivity analysis enables you to answer this and related questions *without having to resolve the problem each time such a question is asked.*

Begin by asking: What happens to the optimal solution of $x_1 = 70$ and $x_2 = 90$ as the coefficient of x_1 in the objective function in Example 4.1 changes from its current value of 3? The blue objective function line in Figures 4.16(a) to 4.16(f) shows the graphical solution to this problem when the coefficient of x_1 in the objective function changes from its current value of 3 to (a) 4, (b) 5, (c) 15, (d) 2.75, (e) 2.0, and (f) 1.0, respectively.

Careful examination of Figure 4.16 should lead you to the conclusion that as the coefficient of x_1 in the objective function changes, the *slope* of the objective function line changes (see Appendix 4A for a discussion of the slope of a line). As long as that slope does not change "too much" (for example, when the coefficient increases from 3 to 4), the current optimal solution at extreme point C remains optimal. However, if the slope changes "too much" (for example, when the coefficient increases from 3 to 15), the current optimal solution no longer remains optimal, as seen in Figure 4.16(c).

You can also observe in Figures 4.16(a) and 4.16(b) that as the coefficient of x_1 increases, the objective function line through the current optimal point gets closer and closer to the line corresponding to constraint (1). As long as the objective function line does not go "beyond" constraint (1), $x_1 = 70$ and $x_2 = 90$ remains optimal. In Figure 4.16(c), however, the objective function line has gone beyond constraint (1), and so $x_1 = 70$ and $x_2 = 90$ is no longer optimal. Thus, the maximum value of the coefficient of x_1 that keeps the current solution optimal is the one that makes the slope of the objective function line precisely the *same* as the slope of constraint (1).

To determine that maximum value numerically, think of the coefficient of x_1 as a variable, say, b, instead of the fixed value 3. Then, the objective function becomes

$$bx_1 + 5x_2$$

To determine the value of b that makes the slope of the objective function equal to that of constraint (1), recall from Appendix 4A that

$$\text{Slope of the objective function line} = -(b/5)$$

$$\text{Slope of constraint (1)} = -(2/1)$$

Equating the two slopes gives

$$-(b/5) = -(2/1)$$

so

$$b = 10$$

This means that *as long as the coefficient of* x_1 *does not increase from its original value of 3* beyond a value of 10, *the current optimal solution remains optimal.*

Even though the current optimal solution may remain optimal, the *objective function value changes.* For instance, when the coefficient of x_1 increases from 3 to 4, the

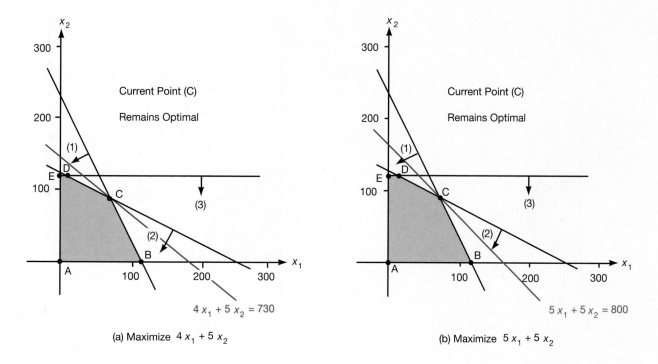

(a) Maximize $4\,x_1 + 5\,x_2$

(b) Maximize $5\,x_1 + 5\,x_2$

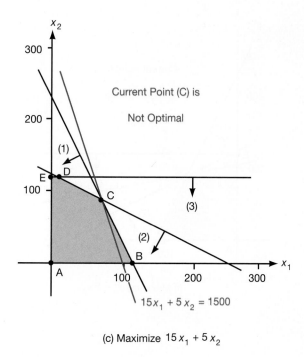

(c) Maximize $15\,x_1 + 5\,x_2$

FIGURE 4.16 Sensitivity Analysis of the Profit Coefficient of x_1.

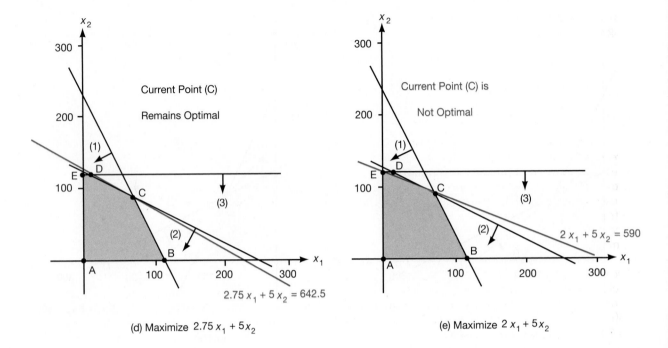

(d) Maximize $2.75\,x_1 + 5\,x_2$

(e) Maximize $2\,x_1 + 5\,x_2$

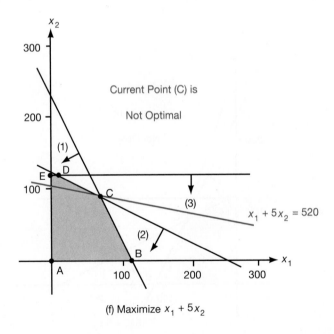

(f) Maximize $x_1 + 5\,x_2$

FIGURE 4.16 *continued*

solution $x_1 = 70$ and $x_2 = 90$ remains optimal. However, the objective function value changes from

$$3x_1 + 5x_2 = 3(70) + 5(90) = 660$$

to

$$4x_1 + 5x_2 = 4(70) + 5(90) = 730$$

Now consider what happens as the value of the objective function coefficient of x_1 *decreases*. Looking at Figures 4.16(d) to 4.16(f), you will notice again that as this value decreases, the slope of the objective function line through the optimal point changes. As long as that slope does not change too much (for example, when the coefficient decreases from 3 to 2.75), the current optimal solution at extreme point C in Figure 4.16(d) remains optimal. However, if the slope changes too much (for example, when the coefficient decreases from 3 to 1.0), the current optimal solution no longer remains optimal, as seen in Figure 4.16(f).

You can also observe in Figures 4.16(d) and 4.16(e) that as the coefficient of x_1 decreases, the objective function line through the current optimal point gets closer and closer to the line corresponding to constraint (2). As long as the objective function line does not go beyond constraint (2), $x_1 = 70$ and $x_2 = 90$ remains optimal. In Figure 4.16(f), however, the objective function line has gone beyond constraint (2), and so $x_1 = 70$ and $x_2 = 90$ is no longer optimal. Thus, the minimum value of the coefficient of x_1 that keeps the current solution optimal is the one that makes the slope of the objective function line precisely the *same* as the slope of constraint (2).

To determine that minimum value numerically, think of the coefficient of x_1 as a variable, say, a, instead of the fixed value 3. Then, the objective function becomes

$$ax_1 + 5x_2$$

To determine the value of a that makes the slope of the objective function equal to that of constraint (2), you have

Slope of the objective function line $= -(a/5)$

Slope of constraint (2) $= -(1/2)$

Equating the two slopes gives

$$-(a/5) = -(1/2)$$

so

$$a = 5/2 = 2.5$$

This means that *as long as the coefficient of x_1 does not decrease from its original value of 3 below a value of 2.5, the current optimal solution remains optimal.* Once again, remember that although the current solution remains optimal throughout this range, the *optimal objective function value changes.*

In summary, if all other data remain unchanged, then as long as the objective function coefficient of x_1 stays within the interval [2.5, 10], the current solution of $x_1 = 70$ and $x_2 = 90$ remains optimal. The value of the objective function at this point, though, changes. The size of this interval indicates how sensitive the optimal solution is to this coefficient. For example, a range of [2.9, 3.1] would indicate that the optimal solution is more sensitive to a change in this objective function coefficient than the previous range of [2.5, 10].

You can now answer the original question of how to change the production plan of Case Chemicals when the price of CS-01 is decreased by $25 per thousand gallons. Although this decrease causes the coefficient of x_1 to decrease from its current value of 3 to 2.75, this new value of 2.75 is above the minimum value of 2.5 computed in the sensitivity analysis. Thus, the previous optimal solution remains optimal, that is, Case Chemicals should *not* change its production plan of 70 thousand gallons of CS-01 and 90 thousand gallons of CS-02 per week. However, the weekly profit margin (in hundreds of dollars) changes:

$$\text{New profit margin} = 2.75x_1 + 5x_2$$
$$= 2.75(70) + 5(90)$$
$$= 642.50$$

That is, their weekly profit margin decreases to $64,250.

SENSITIVITY ANALYSIS OF THE OBJECTIVE FUNCTION COEFFICIENT FOR x_2

You can conduct a similar analysis on the profit coefficient of x_2 in Example 4.1, assuming the coefficient of x_1 remains unchanged at its original value of 3. Think of the objective function coefficient of x_2 as a variable, and then perform algebraic computations similar to those just explained to obtain the appropriate sensitivity range. What you will discover is that if all other data are unchanged, the current optimal solution $x_1 = 70$ and $x_2 = 90$ remains optimal as long as the profit for selling each thousand gallons of CS-02 is within the range [1.5, 6]. The size of this interval indicates how sensitive the optimal solution is to this coefficient.

➡ ### KEY FEATURES

In summary, as long as a coefficient in the objective function lies within some range around its original value (and all other coefficients do not change), the current optimal solution remains optimal. However, the optimal objective function value changes. If the coefficient of interest is changed to a value outside this range, a new optimal solution and objective function value must be found.

4.3.2 *Sensitivity Analysis of the Right-Hand-Side (RHS) Values*

You can apply sensitivity analysis not only to changes in the coefficients in the objective function, but also to changes in the values of the right-hand side of the constraints. For example, as Production Manager of Case Chemicals, you might be interested in any of the following questions.

1. In preparation for potential budget cuts from upper management, you want to know: What happens to the profit margin of Case Chemicals if each of the two part-time employees in the Blending Department works 10 (instead of 15) hours per week?

2. Observing that all available hours of labor in the Blending Department are used under the current production plan, will the profit margin increase if the available hours are increased by making one of the part-time employees in this department full-time while the second one is let go?

3. As an alternative to question 2, by how much will the profit margin increase if one additional full-time worker is hired in the Purification Department?

The first step in answering these questions is to understand how the changes they imply affect the original mathematical model. For example, question 1 deals with a reduction in the total number of hours of labor available per week in the Blending Department from 230 (five full-time workers at 40 hours per week and two part-time workers at 15 hours per week) to 220 (because each of the two part-time employees will now work only 10 hours per week). Question 1 is equivalent to asking: What happens to the optimal objective function value when the value on the right-hand side of constraint (1) is changed from its current value of 230 hours to a new value of 220 hours?

In a similar manner, question 2 also deals with a change in the value of the right-hand side of the first constraint. In particular, if one of the part-time employees in the Blending Department becomes full-time, an additional 25 hours of labor per week becomes available. However, because the second part-time employee is to be let go, 15 hours per week of labor are lost. The net result is that 10 *additional* hours per week of labor are available in the Blending Department. Question 2 is equivalent to asking: What happens to the optimal objective function value when the value on the right-hand side of constraint (1) is changed from its current value of 230 hours to a new value of 240 hours?

Question 3 deals with an increase in the total number of hours of labor available per week in the Purification Department from 250 (six full-time workers at 40 hours per week and one part-time worker at 10 hours per week) to 290 (because of hiring an additional full-time employee). Question 3 is equivalent to asking: What happens to the optimal objective function value when the value on the right-hand side of constraint (2) is changed from 250 hours to 290 hours?

Each of these questions can be rephrased in the following general form:

What happens to the optimal objective function value of a linear program when one of the values on the right-hand side of a constraint is changed and all other data in the problem remain the same?

One way to answer this type of question is to solve a new linear programming problem in which the one right-hand-side value of interest is changed, and everything else is the same. However, the techniques presented in what follows enable you to answer such questions *without having to resolve the entire problem.*

SENSITIVITY ANALYSIS OF THE RIGHT-HAND-SIDE VALUE OF CONSTRAINT (1)

To illustrate the graphical method for answering sensitivity questions pertaining to the right-hand-side value of constraint (1) in the problem of Case Chemicals,

$$2x_1 + x_2 \leq 230$$

look at Figures 4.17(a) to 4.17(f). They show what happens to the optimal solution when the right-hand-side (rhs) value of constraint (1) is changed from 230 to (a) 300, (b) 500, (c) 600, (d) 200, (e) 140, and (f) 130, respectively.

Careful examination of Figure 4.17 leads to the conclusion that even the slightest change in the rhs value of constraint (1) results in a change in the optimal solution. Specifically, as the rhs value of the first constraint changes, *that constraint line moves parallel to itself*—that is, the slope of that constraint line does not change. As long as that line does not move too much—for example, when the rhs value increases from 230 to 300—the optimal solution remains at the intersection of the two lines corresponding to constraints (1) and (2). However, when that value exceeds 500 (for example, 600), the optimal solution is determined by the intersection of the two lines corresponding to constraints (2) and (5) rather than (1) and (2), as seen in Figure 4.17(c).

To see how much the rhs value of constraint (1) can increase before the new constraints (2) and (5) determine the optimal solution, think of the rhs value of constraint (1) as a variable, say, b, instead of the fixed value 230. Thus, the line corresponding to constraint (1) becomes

$$2x_1 + x_2 = b$$

As in Figure 4.17(b), b can be increased until this constraint line goes through point $x_1 = 250$ and $x_2 = 0$. So,

$$2(250) + (0) = b$$

or

$$b = 500$$

This means that as long as the number of hours of labor in the Blending Department of Case Chemicals is not increased above 500, the optimal solution is determined by the intersection of this labor constraint and that of the Purification Department [constraint (2)].

Now, consider what happens when the rhs of constraint (1) is *decreased* from its current value of 230. The line corresponding to constraint (1) now moves parallel to itself but in the opposite direction, as seen in Figure 4.17(e). As it does so, the optimal solution changes. As long as that line does not move too much (for example, when the rhs value decreases from 230 to 200), the optimal solution remains at the intersection of the two lines corresponding to constraints (1) and (2). However, when that value is below 140 (for example, 130), the optimal solution is the *adjacent* extreme point determined by the intersection of the two lines corresponding to constraints (1) and (3) rather than (1) and (2), as seen in Figure 4.17(f).

To see how much the rhs value of constraint (1) can decrease before the new constraints (2) and (4) determine the optimal solution, think of the rhs value of constraint (1) as a variable, say, a, instead of the fixed value 230. Thus, the line corresponding to constraint (1) becomes

$$2x_1 + x_2 = a$$

As in Figure 4.17(e), a can be decreased until this constraint line moves parallel to itself through the extreme point D; namely, $x_1 = 10$ and $x_2 = 120$. So,

$$2(10) + (120) = a$$

or

$$a = 140$$

This means that as long as the number of hours of labor in the Blending Department of Case Chemicals is not decreased below 140, the optimal solution is determined by the intersection of this labor constraint and constraint (2).

From the foregoing calculations, you can conclude that if no other data in the problem change, then as long as the rhs value of constraint (1) remains within the range of [140, 500], the optimal solution lies at the intersection of the two lines corresponding to constraints (1) and (2). *However, even within this range, the specific values of the variables at the optimal solution change.*

Throughout the analysis of the rhs value so far, you have seen how the optimal solution changes. As a Manager of Case Chemicals, you should also be interested in what happens to the total profit—that is, what happens to the value of the objective

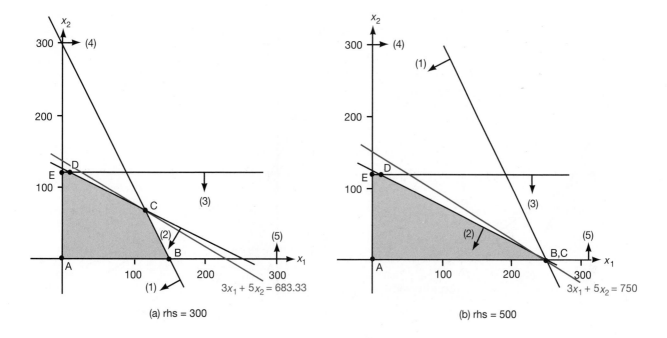

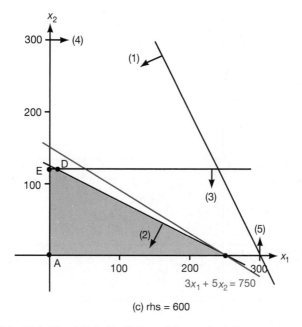

FIGURE 4.17 Sensitivity Analysis of the Right-Hand-Side Coefficient of Constraint (1).

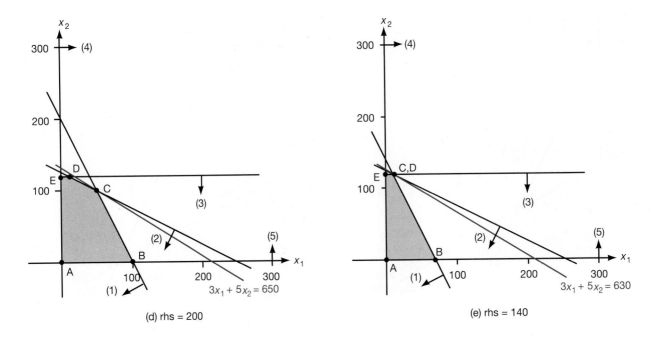

(d) rhs = 200   (e) rhs = 140

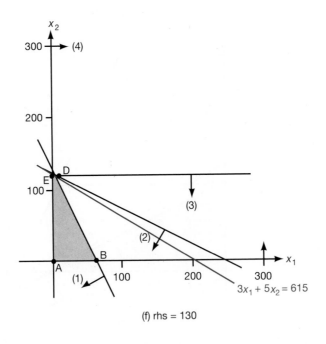

(f) rhs = 130

FIGURE 4.17 *continued*

function at the optimal solution as the rhs value of constraint (1) changes. This information is summarized in Table 4.2 for various values of the rhs for constraint (1). For example, when the rhs of constraint (1) decreases to a value of 140, the optimal solution becomes $x_1 = 10$ and $x_2 = 120$, with an associated objective function value of 630. These rhs values and the associated optimal objective function values are plotted in Figure 4.18.

TABLE 4.2	Optimal Objective Function Values Associated with Changes in the Right-Hand-Side Value of Constraint (1)	
RIGHT-HAND-SIDE VALUE	OPTIMAL SOLUTION	VALUE OF OBJECTIVE FUNCTION
140	$x_1 = 10, \quad x_2 = 120$	630
200	$x_1 = 50, \quad x_2 = 100$	650
230	$x_1 = 70, \quad x_2 = 90$	660
300	$x_1 = 350/3, \quad x_2 = 200/3$	$683\frac{1}{3}$
500	$x_1 = 250, \quad x_2 = 0$	750

From Figure 4.18, you can see that as the rhs value of constraint (1) is increased from 140 to 500, *the value of the objective function at the optimal solution increases in a linear way*. The slope of that line is computed using any two values from Table 4.2. For example:

$$\text{Slope} = \frac{(\text{profit when rhs} = 200) - (\text{profit when rhs} = 140)}{200 - 140} = \frac{650 - 630}{60} = 1/3$$

This means that for each additional hour of labor made available to the Blending Department over and above the current value of 230 up to 500 hours, the corporate profit margin increases by 1/3 of one hundred dollars—that is, $33.33. In other words, the slope of 1/3 reflects the value of this labor resource, and it is called the **shadow**

Shadow (dual) price
The rate of change in the value of the objective function per unit of increase in the value of a right-hand side value within the sensitivity range.

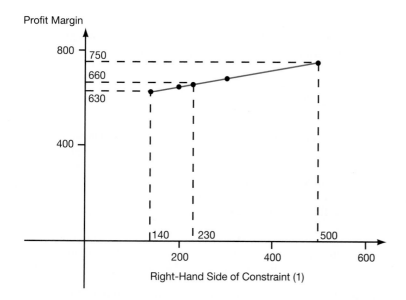

FIGURE 4.18 The Shadow Price of Constraint (1).

price, or **dual price**, of the resource. Observe that the shadow price of 1/3 also indicates that each hour cut from the current level of 230 down to 140 results in a loss of $33.33 in the profit margin.

SENSITIVITY ANALYSIS OF THE RIGHT-HAND-SIDE VALUE OF CONSTRAINT (2)

There is also a shadow price associated with the labor available in the Purification Department [constraint (2)]. Think of the rhs value of constraint (2) as a variable, say, c:

$$x_1 + 2x_2 \leq c$$

By using the same logic, you will discover that as long as this rhs value remains in the interval [115, 295], the optimal solution is determined by the intersection of constraints (1) and (2). Table 4.3 shows how the value of the objective function at the optimal solution changes within this range.

TABLE 4.3 *Optimal Objective Function Values Associated with Changes in the Right-Hand-Side Value of Constraint (2)*

RIGHT-HAND-SIDE VALUE	OPTIMAL SOLUTION		VALUE OF OBJECTIVE FUNCTION
115	$x_1 =$ 115,	$x_2 =$ 0	345
200	$x_1 =$ 260/3,	$x_2 =$ 170/3	$543\frac{1}{3}$
250	$x_1 =$ 70,	$x_2 =$ 90	660
275	$x_1 =$ 185/3,	$x_2 =$ 320/3	$718\frac{1}{3}$
295	$x_1 =$ 55,	$x_2 =$ 120	765

The optimal objective function value varies linearly with the rhs value in this range. The slope of that line is found by choosing any two values for the rhs from Table 4.3. For example,

$$\text{Slope} = \frac{(\text{profit when rhs} = 200) - (\text{profit when rhs} = 115)}{200 - 115} = (543\tfrac{1}{3} - 345)/85 = 2\tfrac{1}{3}$$

For each additional hour of labor made available to the Purification Department over and above the current value of 250 up to 295 hours, the corporate profit margin increases by $233.33. Similarly, each hour that is cut from the current level of 250 down to 115 hours results in a loss of $233.33 in the profit margin.

Having calculated the shadow prices of the two constraints, you can now answer the three questions posed at the beginning of this section, which are repeated here:

1. What happens to the profit margin of Case Chemicals if each of the two part-time employees in the Blending Department works 10 (instead of 15) hours per week (that is, the rhs value of constraint (1) is decreased to 220 from its current value of 230)?

   Because this change is within the range [140, 500], each hour lost decreases the profit margin by the shadow price:

New profit margin = (old profit margin) − (shadow price) *

(decrease in hours of labor)

$$= 660 - \frac{1}{3} * 10$$

$$= 556\frac{2}{3} \quad \text{(that is, \$55,667)}$$

2. What happens to the profit margin if one of the part-time employees in the Blending Department becomes a full-time employee and the second one is let go (that is, the rhs value of constraint (1) is increased to 240)?

Because this change is within the range [140, 500], the profit margin increases at the rate of the shadow price, that is:

New profit margin = (old profit margin) + (shadow price) *

(increase in hours of labor)

$$= 660 + \frac{1}{3} * 10$$

$$= 663\frac{1}{3} \quad \text{(that is, \$66,333)}$$

3. What happens to the profit margin when one additional full-time worker is hired in the Purification Department (that is, the rhs value of constraint (2) is increased to 290 from its current value of 250)?

Because this change is within the range [115, 295], each hour gained increases the profit margin by the shadow price:

New profit margin = (old profit margin) + (shadow price) *

(increase in hours of labor)

$$= 660 + 2\frac{1}{3} * 40$$

$$= 753\frac{1}{3} \quad \text{(that is, \$75,333)}$$

KEY FEATURES

In summary, after finding an optimal solution to your linear program, you can compute, for each resource corresponding to a constraint, a shadow price together with a range within which this price is valid. The shadow prices represent the change in the optimal value of the objective function that results when one additional unit of this resource is available and, therefore, are used to determine if it is profitable to acquire additional resources.

4.3.3 *Parametric Analysis of the Right-Hand-Side Values*

With sensitivity analysis, you are equipped to answer certain "What happens if?" questions, *provided that the changes in the coefficients are within the sensitivity range.* However, what if those changes are outside the range? For example, as a Manager of Case Chemicals, you might be faced with one of the following questions (*but not both simultaneously*):

1. What happens to the weekly profit if the Blending Department is reduced to two full-time workers and one part-time worker at 30 hours per week?

2. What happens to the weekly profit margin if the Purification Department is expanded to nine purifiers with nine full-time workers?

The first step is to realize that both of these questions deal with changes in the rhs values. These questions can be rephrased as follows:

1. What happens to the optimal weekly profit margin if the rhs value of constraint (1) decreases from its current value of 230 to 110 (two full-time workers at 40 hours per week and one part-time worker at 30 hours per week)?
2. What happens to the optimal weekly profit margin if the rhs value of constraint (2) increases from its current value of 250 to 360 (nine full-time workers at 40 hours per week)?

Parametric analysis
Determining how the optimal objective function value changes with any corresponding change in the right-hand side of one particular constraint.

Observe that the new value of 120 for the rhs in question 1 is outside the sensitivity range [140, 500] calculated for constraint (1) in Section 4.3.2. Similarly, the new value of 360 for the rhs in question 2 is outside the sensitivity range [115, 295] for constraint (2). To answer questions pertaining to values of the rhs outside the sensitivity range, the technique of **parametric analysis** is used to compute how the optimal objective function value changes with *any* corresponding change in the rhs of one particular constraint.

To answer the first question graphically, recall that as the rhs value of constraint (1) decreases, that constraint line moves parallel to itself (in this case, toward the origin). In Section 4.3.2, you saw from Figure 4.17 that as long as the rhs value of constraint (1) does not decrease below 140, the optimal solution is determined by the intersection of constraints (1) and (2) and the corresponding shadow price of 1/3 reflects how the optimal objective function value changes within this range.

For a value of the rhs just below 140, you can see in Figure 4.17 that the optimal solution is determined by the intersection of the lines corresponding to constraints (1) and (3) instead of constraints (1) and (2). As a result, below 140, the change in the weekly profit margin per unit of change in the rhs value is determined by constraints (1) and (3) rather than constraints (1) and (2). Thus, the shadow price *changes* at this point. Its new value of 1.5 is obtained using the technique discussed in Section 4.3.2. From Figure 4.19, you can see that the new shadow price of 1.5 is applicable for all values of the rhs of constraint (1) in the range [120, 140]. For example, if the rhs of constraint (1) is decreased by 15 hours below the value of 140, the optimal objective function value is

$$\text{Weekly profit} = (\text{profit at 140 hours}) - (\text{shadow price}) *$$

$$(\text{number of hours above 140})$$

$$= 630 - 1.5 * 15$$

$$= 607.50$$

Similarly, if the value of the rhs of constraint (1) is reduced below 120 but stays above 0, the optimal solution is determined by constraints (1) and (4) instead of constraints (1) and (3), as seen in Figure 4.20. The shadow price for the range [0, 120] is 5.

With increases in the rhs of constraint (1) from its original value of 230, the constraint line moves parallel to itself *away* from the origin. From the sensitivity analysis in Section 4.3.2, you saw that as long as the rhs value does not increase beyond 500, the optimal solution is determined by constraints (1) and (2) and the associated shadow price in this range is 1/3. For any value of the rhs largerthan 500, the optimal solution,

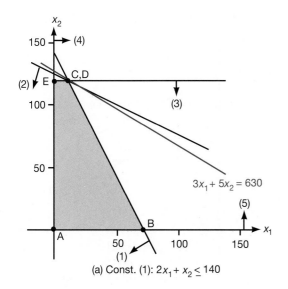

(a) Const. (1): $2x_1 + x_2 \leq 140$

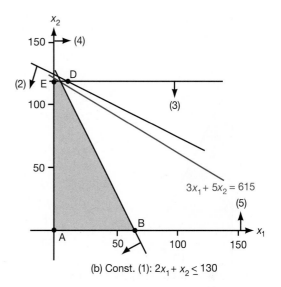

(b) Const. (1): $2x_1 + x_2 \leq 130$

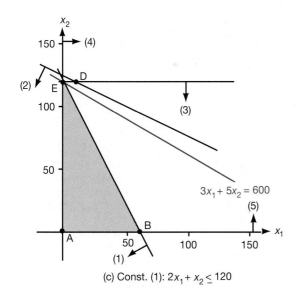

(c) Const. (1): $2x_1 + x_2 \leq 120$

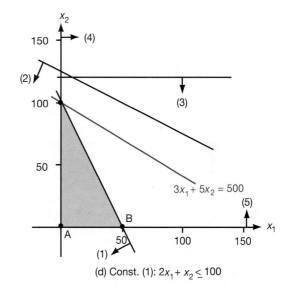

(d) Const. (1): $2x_1 + x_2 \leq 100$

	Optimal Solution		
rhs	x_1	x_2	Obj. Func.
120	0	120	600
130	5	120	615
140	10	120	630

(e) Optimal Solutions in the Range [120,140]

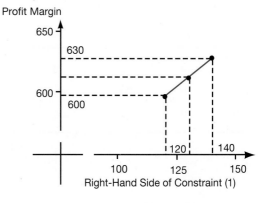

(f) The Shadow Price

FIGURE 4.19 Shadow Price of Constraint (1) in the Range [120, 140].

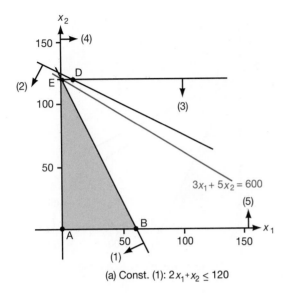

(a) Const. (1): $2x_1 + x_2 \leq 120$

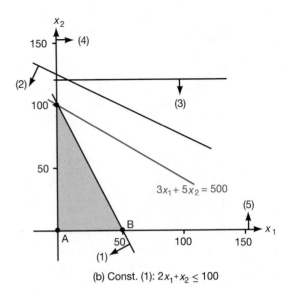

(b) Const. (1): $2x_1 + x_2 \leq 100$

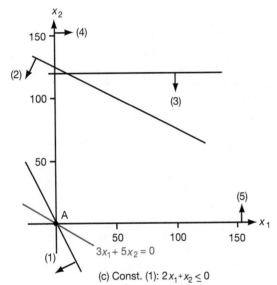

(c) Const. (1): $2x_1 + x_2 \leq 0$

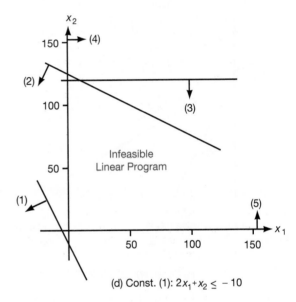

(d) Const. (1): $2x_1 + x_2 \leq -10$

Optimal Solution

rhs	x_1	x_2	Obj. Func.
0	0	0	0
100	0	100	500
120	0	120	600

(e) Optimal Solutions in the Range [0,120]

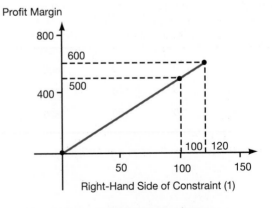

(f) The Shadow Price

FIGURE 4.20 Shadow Price of Constraint (1) in the Range [0, 120].

determined by constraints (2) and (5), remains unchanged, as shown in Figure 4.21. The new shadow price in this range is 0 because the slope of a horizontal line is 0. This means that there is no value in having more than 500 hours in the Blending Department because additional hours result in no additional profit.

This information is summarized in Figure 4.22. Note how the optimal objective function value changes as the rhs of constraint (1) changes. You can use this information to answer question 1. Because the question pertains to a change of the rhs to a value of 110, from the graph in Figure 4.22, you can see that the corresponding optimal profit margin can be computed using the shadow price of 5 as

$$\text{Weekly profit} = (\text{profit at 120 hours}) - (\text{shadow price}) *$$

$$(\text{number of hours below 120})$$

$$= 600 - 5 * (120 - 110)$$

$$= 550$$

In other words, if the number of hours of labor in the Blending Department is reduced to 110, the weekly profit margin drops from \$66,000 to \$55,000. This information should be used together with other factors in making a managerial decision.

To answer question 2, you need a similar analysis for the rhs value of constraint (2). The information resulting from such an analysis is summarized in Figure 4.23. Note how the optimal objective function value changes as the rhs of constraint (2) changes. Question 2 pertains to a change in the rhs to a value of 360. From Figure 4.23, you can see that the corresponding optimal profit margin can be computed using the shadow price of 0:

$$\text{Weekly profit} = (\text{profit at 295 hours}) + (\text{shadow price}) *$$

$$(\text{number of hours above 295})$$

$$= 765 + 0 * (360 - 295)$$

$$= 765$$

In other words, if the number of hours of labor in the Purification Department is increased to 360, the weekly profit margin increases from \$66,000 to \$76,500. This information should be used together with other factors in making a managerial decision. For example, observe that the same profit margin of \$76,500 can be realized if the rhs value of constraint (2) is as low as 295. Management could achieve this value with seven full-time workers and one part-time worker at 15 hours per week. Thus, it may not be necessary to hire nine full-time workers.

In this section, you have learned to ask and answer questions relating to how sensitive the optimal solution and objective function value are to changes in one of the coefficients of the objective function or values of the right-hand side. Such questions are of particular importance to managers who must make decisions when the data for a problem are subject to change or uncertainty.

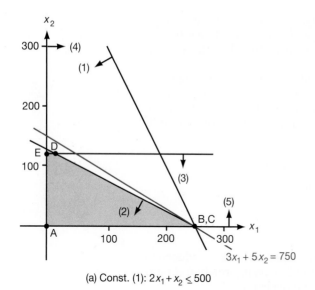

(a) Const. (1): $2x_1 + x_2 \leq 500$

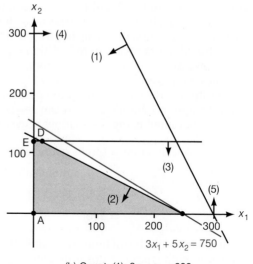

(b) Const. (1): $2x_1 + x_2 \leq 600$

Optimal Solution

rhs	x_1	x_2	Obj. Func.
500	250	0	750
600	250	0	750
.			
.			
.			

(c) Optimal Solutions in the Range [500,∞]

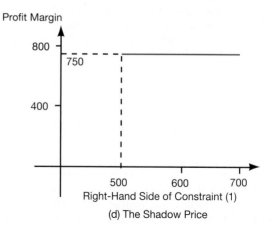

(d) The Shadow Price

FIGURE 4.21 Shadow Price of Constraint (1) in the Range [500, ∞].

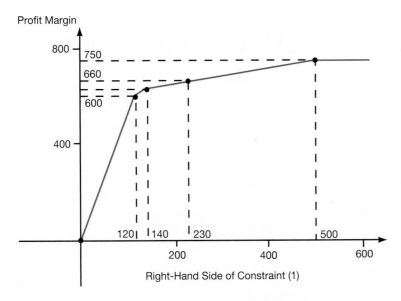

FIGURE 4.22 Parametric Analysis Trade-Off Diagram for Constraint (1).

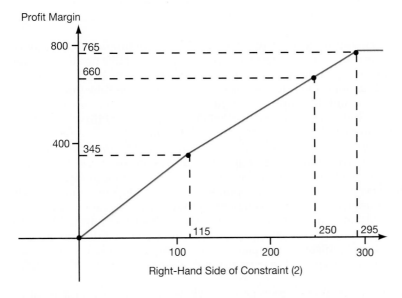

FIGURE 4.23 Parametric Analysis Trade-Off Diagram for Constraint (2).

ADDITIONAL MANAGERIAL CONSIDERATIONS

In Section 4.3, you learned to ask: What happens to the optimal solution and/or objective function value if one of the coefficients in the objective function or if the value of the right-hand side of a constraint is changed (and all other data in the problem remain the same)? Through sensitivity and parametric analysis, you learned to answer these questions using graphical techniques. Other relevant "What happens if?" questions you may want or need to ask include:

1. What happens to the optimal solution and objective function value if one or more coefficients in the constraints are changed (for example, if new technology changes the production rate)?
2. What happens to the optimal solution and objective function value if a new constraint must be added (such as a new labor contract that restricts the hiring of part-time workers)?
3. What happens to the optimal solution and objective function value if a new variable must be added (for example, the introduction of a new product) or deleted (for example, a product is discontinued)?

One approach to answering these questions is to modify the formulation according to the new requirements and then solve the resulting linear program. Although in some circumstances you may have to alter the formulation because the problem has actually changed, you may also want to ask these "What happens if?" questions for planning purposes or to get a better understanding of the relative importance of certain aspects of the problem.

Assume a particular product currently requires 5 hours in production on a given machine. Suppose you ask what happens to the optimal solution if this production time is reduced to 4 hours and you discover a *significant* increase in the profits. It may be worthwhile to search for a way to achieve this reduced production time (for example, by investing in research and development) to pursue new production methods or by purchasing a new machine. As a general rule, you can expect to modify and solve a linear programming problem many times to gain such insights.

Another managerial consideration is the use of *alternative optimal solutions*, if they exist, as described in Section 4.2. Although all optimal solutions provide the same value for the objective function, there may be differences between these solutions that might lead you to choose one alternative over others. For example, one solution might be more practical to implement. For instance, in a production-planning problem like that of Case Chemicals, an optimal solution in which the fraction of available hours of labor used in both departments is approximately the same may be preferred to one in which there is a significant discrepancy. Many computer packages for solving linear programming problems provide a method for obtaining these alternative optimal solutions.

Keep in mind that great care must be used when attempting to implement an optimal solution because (1) the model may not include all constraints, (2) some of the data may be estimates rather than actual values, and/or (3) the model may be only an approximation of the actual problem and may not have included all relevant issues, such as behavioral and/or political aspects. Before implementing, you may have to modify the solution to account for those issues not included in the mathematical model.

SUMMARY

This chapter has taught you how to solve linear programming problems having two variables and several inequality constraints using a graph. You have learned that every linear programming problem belongs to one of the following three mutually exclusive categories:

1. *Optimal* (an optimal solution exists). In this case, the optimal solution occurs at one of the extreme points of the feasible region and can be found by moving the objective function line parallel to itself in a particular direction until that line is just about to leave the feasible region.
2. *Infeasible* (no feasible solution exists). Such problems arise in practice because of incorrect problem formulation or data entry to the computer, or because the constraints are too restrictive.
3. *Unbounded* (the problem is feasible, but any value for the objective function is attainable within the feasible region). Such problems arise in practice because of incorrect problem formulation or data entry to the computer.

You also learned about redundant constraints, which can be included or excluded in the problem formulation without affecting the feasible region. You also examined linear programs with alternative optimal solutions—that is, with more than one optimal solution.

After formulating and solving a linear programming problem, you learned to ask managerial questions like: What happens to the optimal solution and/or objective function value if one of the coefficients in the objective function or if the value of the right-hand side of a constraint is changed, and all other data in the problem remain the same? Through sensitivity and parametric analysis, you learned to answer such questions using a graph and reached the following conclusions:

1. As long as a coefficient in the *objective function* lies within some range around its original value, the current optimal solution remains optimal, although the optimal objective function value changes. If the coefficient of interest is changed to a value outside this range, a new optimal solution and objective function value must be found.
2. Even the smallest change in the *right-hand-side value* of a constraint can cause the optimal solution to change. However, as long as that value lies within some range around its original value, the optimal objective function value changes in a linear way in proportion to the change in the rhs value, according to the shadow price. Even outside of this range, for each value of the right-hand side for which the linear program is feasible, there is a shadow price that can be used to obtain the new optimal objective function value.

Now that you know how to solve linear programming problems having two variables, you can do so for larger problems, using a computer. Geometry cannot be used because when a problem has more than three variables, it is not possible to draw a graph. Furthermore, computers work with linear algebra, not geometry. Chapter 5 presents the essential ideas of the computer method most commonly used for solving linear programming problems.

Appendix 4A
REVIEW OF GRAPHICAL CONCEPTS IN TWO DIMENSIONS

In this appendix, a review of how to draw straight lines on a graph is provided. The properties of the *slope* and *intercept* of a line are also reviewed.

■ 4A.1 DRAWING STRAIGHT LINES ON A GRAPH

Graph

A geometric method for illustrating the relationship between two variables.

A straight line expresses a linear relationship between the values of two variables, say, x_1 and x_2. To visualize this relationship, a **graph** is drawn. The graph consists of a horizontal line (x_1-axis) that corresponds to the values for x_1 and a vertical line (x_2-axis) that corresponds to the values for x_2, as in Figure 4.24. The point O at which the two axes meet is the *origin*, and corresponds to the values $x_1 = x_2 = 0$.

For any *numerical* values of x_1 and x_2—say, $x_1 = 2$ and $x_2 = 3$—there is a corresponding *geometric* point. To find this point, first locate the value of 2 for x_1 on the x_1-axis and draw a vertical line upward. Then locate the value of 3 for x_2 on the x_2-axis and draw a horizontal line. The place where the vertical and horizontal lines intersect is the geometric point that corresponds to the given numerical values of $x_1 = 2$ and $x_2 = 3$, as in Figure 4.24.

Conversely, you can find the numerical values corresponding to any point x_1 and x_2 in the graph. The value for x_1 is found by drawing a vertical line through the given point and then noting where it intersects the x_1-axis; the value for x_2 is found by drawing a horizontal line through the given point and then seeing where it intersects the x_2-axis, as in Figure 4.24.

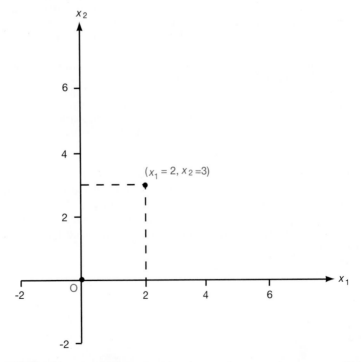

FIGURE 4.24 A Graph of Two Variables.

To draw a straight line whose equation you know, you need only find two *different* points on that line, plot the two points on the graph, and connect them with a straight line. Consider the line

$$x_1 + 2x_2 = 6$$

To find one point on this line, begin by choosing a value for x_1—say, $x_1 = 0$. Substituting this value in the equation above yields $2x_2 = 6$, or $x_2 = 3$. Thus, one point on the line is $x_1 = 0$ and $x_2 = 3$. This point has been plotted on the graph in Figure 4.25. Find a second point on this line by choosing any other *different* values for x_1 or x_2—say, $x_2 = 0$. Substituting this value into the foregoing equation yields $x_1 = 6$. Thus, a second point on the line is $x_1 = 6$ and $x_2 = 0$. This point has also been plotted on the graph in Figure 4.25 together with the straight line that connects the two points, $(0, 3)$ and $(6, 0)$. This line is the graphical representation of the equation.

After drawing several examples of straight lines, you might believe that the easiest way to find two points on a given line is to set x_1 to 0 and use the equation to solve for x_2, and then set x_2 to 0 and solve for x_1 (as is done in the previous example). Indeed, this is often a valid approach. Sometimes, however, this approach will not work. For example, consider the equation

$$x_1 = 4$$

You cannot set x_1 to 0 and solve for x_2 because the coefficient of x_2 in this equation is 0. Instead, you can find two points on this line by setting x_1 to 4 and then choosing two different values for x_2. For example, as shown in Figure 4.25, the following two points are on this line: $(4, 0)$ and $(4, 2)$. Note that this line—as is the line for any equation in which the coefficient of x_2 is 0—is a vertical line.

Take a similar approach to find two points on a line whose x_1 coefficient is 0. You will find that the graph of such a line is horizontal. For example, the line representing the equation $x_2 = 6$ is a horizontal line.

There are other occasions when setting x_1 or x_2 to 0 does not provide two different points you need to draw a line. Consider the equation

$$3x_1 + 2x_2 = 0$$

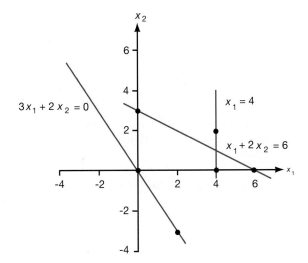

FIGURE 4.25 Plotting Straight Lines on a Graph.

In this example, when you set x_1 to 0 and solve for x_2, you get the point (0, 0). However, when you set x_2 to 0 and solve for x_1, you again get the point (0, 0). In this case, you have not obtained two *different* points on the line. To do so, you must choose a value for x_1 *other than* 0—say, $x_1 = 2$. Doing so and solving for x_2 yields a second point on the line: (2, −3), as seen in Figure 4.25.

KEY FEATURES

In summary, to draw a straight line whose equation you know:

✔ Find two *different* points on the line. (In general, the easiest way to find the two points is to set x_1 to 0 and use the equation to solve for x_2. Then, set x_2 to 0 and solve for x_1. If this method does not produce two different points, then use trial and error to find a second point.)
✔ Plot those points on the graph.
✔ Connect those points with a straight line.

■ 4A.2 THE SLOPE AND INTERCEPT OF A STRAIGHT LINE

From your previous studies, recall that a straight line has a *slope* and an *intercept*. To understand these concepts for the line whose equation is

$$-4x_1 + 2x_2 = 6 \qquad (1)$$

begin by expressing x_2 in terms of x_1. Adding $4x_1$ to both sides of (1) yields

$$2x_2 = 6 + 4x_1 \qquad (2)$$

Dividing both sides of (2) by 2 yields

$$x_2 = 3 + 2x_1 \qquad (3)$$

Intercept
The value of x_2 on a straight line when $x_1 = 0$.

The **intercept** is the value of x_2 when $x_1 = 0$, that is, where this line crosses the x_2-axis (see Figure 4.26). Setting the value of x_1 to 0 and then solving for x_2 in Equation (3) yields

$$\text{Intercept} = \text{value of } x_2 \text{ when } x_1 \text{ is } 0$$
$$= 3$$

Slope
The amount of change in x_2 per unit of increase in x_1 in a straight line.

The **slope** represents the amount of change in x_2 per *unit of increase* in x_1. You already know from the intercept that when $x_1 = 0$, $x_2 = 3$. When x_1 is increased to a value of 1, Equation (3) yields $x_2 = 5$. Thus,

$$\text{Slope} = (\text{value of } x_2 \text{ when } x_1 \text{ is } 1) - (\text{value of } x_2 \text{ when } x_1 \text{ is } 0)$$
$$= 5 - 3$$
$$= 2$$

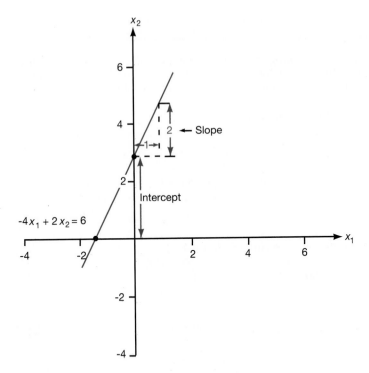

FIGURE 4.26 Intercept and Slope of a Straight Line.

A slope of 2 for this line means that each unit of increase in the value of x_1 results in a corresponding increase of two units in the value of x_2. In general, for a line whose equation is

$$ax_1 + bx_2 = c$$

in which a, b, and c are known, and b is not 0,

$$\text{Intercept} = c/b$$
$$\text{Slope} = -(a/b)$$

Observe that if the slope is positive, an increase in x_1 results in an increase in x_2; if the slope is negative, an increase in x_1 results in a decrease in x_2. In Equation (1), $a = -4$, $b = 2$, and $c = 6$, resulting in

$$\text{Intercept} = c/b = 6/2 = 3$$
$$\text{Slope} = -(a/b) = -(-4/2) = 2$$

EXERCISES

Solve each of the following linear programs using the graphical method (label each constraint accordingly). Indicate whether the problem is infeasible, optimal, or unbounded. For those that are optimal, find the optimal solution and objective function value.

EXERCISE 4.1   (See the foregoing instructions.)

$$
\begin{aligned}
\text{Maximize} \quad & -x_1 + 2x_2 \\
\text{Subject to} \quad & 6x_1 - 2x_2 \le 3 & \text{(a)}\\
& -2x_1 + 3x_2 \le 6 & \text{(b)}\\
& x_1 + x_2 \le 3 & \text{(c)}\\
& x_1, \; x_2 \ge 0
\end{aligned}
$$

EXERCISE 4.2   (See the instructions preceding Exercise 4.1.)

$$
\begin{aligned}
\text{Maximize} \quad & -4x_1 + 8x_2 \\
\text{Subject to} \quad & 6x_1 - 2x_2 \le 3 & \text{(a)}\\
& -2x_1 + 3x_2 \le 6 & \text{(b)}\\
& 2x_1 + 3x_2 \le 24 & \text{(c)}\\
& x_1, \; x_2 \ge 0
\end{aligned}
$$

EXERCISE 4.3   (See the instructions preceding Exercise 4.1.)

$$
\begin{aligned}
\text{Maximize} \quad & 3x_1 + 5x_2 \\
\text{Subject to} \quad & -3x_1 + 2x_2 \le 6 & \text{(a)}\\
& -x_1 + x_2 \le 5 & \text{(b)}\\
& -3x_1 + 8x_2 \ge 12 & \text{(c)}\\
& 3x_1 + 2x_2 \ge 18 & \text{(d)}\\
& x_1, \; x_2 \ge 0
\end{aligned}
$$

EXERCISE 4.4   (See the instructions preceding Exercise 4.1.)

$$
\begin{aligned}
\text{Minimize} \quad & x_1 + x_2 \\
\text{Subject to} \quad & 3x_1 - 5x_2 \ge 30 & \text{(a)}\\
& 3x_1 + 2x_2 \le 9 & \text{(b)}\\
& x_1, \; x_2 \ge 0
\end{aligned}
$$

EXERCISE 4.5   (See the instructions preceding Exercise 4.1.)

$$
\begin{aligned}
\text{Minimize} \quad & 3x_1 + 7x_2 \\
\text{Subject to} \quad & x_1 - x_2 \ge 4 & \text{(a)}\\
& x_1 - 2x_2 \le 10 & \text{(b)}\\
& -2x_1 - x_2 \ge 2 & \text{(c)}\\
& x_1, \; x_2 \ge 0
\end{aligned}
$$

EXERCISE 4.6   (See the instructions preceding Exercise 4.1.)

$$\begin{array}{lll} \text{Maximize} & 2x_1 + 2x_2 & \\ \text{Subject to} & -6x_1 + 10x_2 \geq 15 & \text{(a)} \\ & x_1 + x_2 \geq 7 & \text{(b)} \\ & x_1 \leq 7 & \text{(c)} \\ & x_2 \geq 0 & \end{array}$$

Solve each of the following linear programs graphically (label each constraint accordingly). Describe how the problem differs from the one in which the solution occurs at a single extreme point (see Figure 4.8), such as alternative optimal solutions, redundant constraints, and so on.

EXERCISE 4.7   (See the foregoing instructions.)

$$\begin{array}{lll} \text{Maximize} & -4x_1 + 6x_2 & \\ \text{Subject to} & 6x_1 - 2x_2 \leq 3 & \text{(a)} \\ & -2x_1 + 3x_2 \leq 6 & \text{(b)} \\ & x_1 + x_2 \leq 3 & \text{(c)} \\ & x_1 , x_2 \geq 0 & \end{array}$$

EXERCISE 4.8   (See the instructions preceding Exercise 4.7.)

$$\begin{array}{lll} \text{Maximize} & -x_1 + 2x_2 & \\ \text{Subject to} & 6x_1 - 2x_2 \leq 3 & \text{(a)} \\ & -2x_1 + 3x_2 \leq 6 & \text{(b)} \\ & x_1 + x_2 \leq 3 & \text{(c)} \\ & 2x_1 + 2x_2 \leq 8 & \text{(d)} \\ & 0 \leq x_1 \leq 5 & \text{(e)} \\ & 0 \leq x_2 \leq 5 & \text{(f)} \end{array}$$

EXERCISE 4.9   (See the instructions preceding Exercise 4.7.)

$$\begin{array}{lll} \text{Maximize} & x_1 + 2x_2 & \\ \text{Subject to} & x_1 + x_2 \leq 3 & \text{(a)} \\ & x_1 - 2x_2 \geq 0 & \text{(b)} \\ & x_2 \leq 1 & \text{(c)} \\ & x_1 , x_2 \geq 0 & \end{array}$$

EXERCISE 4.10   (See the instructions preceding Exercise 4.7.)

$$\begin{array}{lll} \text{Maximize} & x_1 + 2x_2 & \\ \text{Subject to} & x_1 + x_2 \leq 3 & \text{(a)} \\ & x_1 - 2x_2 \geq 0 & \text{(b)} \\ & x_2 \geq 1 & \text{(c)} \\ & x_1 , x_2 \geq 0 & \end{array}$$

EXERCISE 4.11 (See the instructions preceding Exercise 4.7.)

$$\begin{array}{ll} \text{Minimize} & 2x_1 + x_2 \\ \text{Subject to} & 5x_1 - 4x_2 \leq 14 \quad \text{(a)} \\ & x_1 - 4x_2 \leq -2 \quad \text{(b)} \\ & 2x_1 + x_2 \geq 5 \quad \text{(c)} \\ & 6x_1 - x_2 \geq 3 \quad \text{(d)} \\ & x_1, \quad x_2 \geq 0 \end{array}$$

EXERCISE 4.12 (See the instructions preceding Exercise 4.7.)

$$\begin{array}{ll} \text{Minimize} & 12x_1 - 2x_2 \\ \text{Subject to} & 5x_1 - 4x_2 \leq 14 \quad \text{(a)} \\ & x_1 - 4x_2 \leq -2 \quad \text{(b)} \\ & 2x_1 + x_2 \geq 5 \quad \text{(c)} \\ & 6x_1 - x_2 \geq 3 \quad \text{(d)} \\ & x_1, \quad x_2 \geq 0 \end{array}$$

EXERCISE 4.13 For the problem of World Oil Company in Exercise 2.7 in Chapter 2, the following model is proposed, in which L is the number of barrels of light crude oil to purchase and H is number of barrels of heavy crude oil to purchase:

$$\begin{array}{ll} \text{Minimize} & 25L + 22H \\ \text{Subject to} & \\ & 0.45L + 0.35H \geq 1260000 \quad \text{(gasoline)} \\ & 0.18L + 0.36H \geq 900000 \quad \text{(jet fuel)} \\ & 0.30L + 0.20H \geq 300000 \quad \text{(kerosene)} \\ & L, \quad H \geq 0 \end{array}$$

a. Solve the problem graphically. What is the optimal purchase plan and the total cost of the crude oil purchased?
b. On the basis of your solution in part (a), how many barrels of each product is produced?

EXERCISE 4.14 Florida Citrus, Inc., has one machine that operates for 150 hours per week distilling orange juice and grapefruit juice into concentrates. The machine can distill at an hourly rate either 25 gallons of orange juice into 17.5 gallons of concentrate or 20 gallons of grapefruit juice into 10 gallons of concentrate. Up to 1000 gallons of each concentrate can be stored in separate tanks after processing. The net profit for each gallon of orange juice processed is $0.55 and that of grapefruit juice is $0.40. Solve the following linear program to determine the number of gallons of orange juice (OJ) and grapefruit juice (GJ) to distill to maximize the net profit:

$$\begin{array}{ll} \text{Maximize} & 0.55OJ + 0.40GJ \\ \text{Subject to} & \\ & 0.04OJ + 0.05GJ \leq 150 \quad \text{(machine time)} \\ & 0.70OJ \leq 1000 \quad \text{(orange concentrate)} \\ & 0.50GJ \leq 1000 \quad \text{(grapefruit concentrate)} \\ & OJ, \quad GJ \geq 0 \end{array}$$

a. Solve the problem graphically. What is the optimal weekly production plan and the total profit?

b. On the basis of your solution in part (a), which of the three resources is binding?

c. From the production plan in part (a), how many gallons of each concentrate are produced?

EXERCISE 4.15 The following model was developed for the Carmac Company in Exercise 2.9 in Chapter 2, in which C is the number of compact cars and S is the number of subcompact cars to produce.

$$\begin{array}{lll}
\text{Maximize} & 6740C + 5100S & \\
\text{Subject to} & & \\
& 200C + 150S \leq 80000 & \text{(raw materials)} \\
& 18C + 20S \leq 9000 & \text{(labor)} \\
& C \leq 1500 & \\
& S \leq 200 & \\
& C\, , S \geq 0 & \text{and integer}
\end{array}$$

Solve this problem graphically, ignoring the integer requirements.

EXERCISE 4.16 Mineral Mining Company sends one truckload of iron and copper ore daily from the mine to the processing plant. The truck has a weight capacity of 10 tons and a volume capacity of 1200 cubic feet. Each pound of iron ore takes up 0.04 cubic feet of space and yields a net profit of $0.30 when processed. Each pound of copper ore uses 0.08 cubic feet of space and provides $0.50 of net profit.

a. Formulate a linear programming problem to determine how much of each ore to load each day so as to maximize the profit.

b. Solve the problem in part (a) graphically. Explain the optimal solution and objective function value in the context of this problem.

EXERCISE 4.17 Graphically determine the sensitivity range of each objective function coefficient at the optimal solution of the linear program in Exercise 4.13. Explain the meaning of each range in the context of the problem.

EXERCISE 4.18 Graphically determine the sensitivity range of each objective function coefficient at the optimal solution of the linear program in Exercise 4.14. Explain the meaning of each range in the context of the problem.

EXERCISE 4.19 Graphically determine the sensitivity range of each objective function coefficient at the optimal solution of the linear program in Exercise 4.15. Explain the meaning of each range in the context of the problem.

EXERCISE 4.20 Graphically determine the sensitivity range of each objective function coefficient at the optimal solution of the linear program in Exercise 4.16. Explain the meaning of each range in the context of the problem.

EXERCISE 4.21 For each constraint that holds with equality at the optimal solution of the linear program in Exercise 4.13, perform the following:

a. Graphically determine the sensitivity range of the right-hand-side value.

b. Compute the shadow price associated with each sensitivity range found in part (a). Explain the meaning of the shadow price in the context of the problem.

EXERCISE 4.22 For each constraint that holds with equality at the optimal solution of the linear program in Exercise 4.14, perform the following:

a. Graphically determine the sensitivity range of the right-hand-side value.

b. Compute the shadow price associated with each sensitivity range found in part (a). Explain the meaning of the shadow price in the context of the problem.

EXERCISE 4.23   For each constraint that holds with equality at the optimal solution of the linear program in Exercise 4.15, perform the following:

a. Graphically determine the sensitivity range of the right-hand-side value.
b. Compute the shadow price associated with each sensitivity range found in part (a). Explain the meaning of the shadow price in the context of the problem.

EXERCISE 4.24   For each constraint that holds with equality at the optimal solution of the linear program in Exercise 4.16, perform the following:

a. Graphically determine the sensitivity range of the right-hand-side value.
b. Compute the shadow price associated with each sensitivity range found in part (a). Explain the meaning of the shadow price in the context of the problem.

EXERCISE 4.25   For the problem of World Oil in Exercise 4.13, use your results from Exercises 4.17 to answer the following managerial questions:

a. Management is expecting an increase in the price of heavy crude oil by as much as $7 per barrel. What impact will this have on the current purchase plan and the total cost? Explain.
b. Contrary to the expectation in part (a), the cost of heavy crude oil has not changed, but that of light crude oil has increased by $4 per barrel. What impact does this have on the current purchase plan and the total cost? Explain.

EXERCISE 4.26   For the problem of Florida Citrus, Inc., in Exercise 4.14, what happens to the optimal solution and net profit if the processing cost for each gallon of grapefruit juice decreases by $0.05? (Use your results from Exercise 4.18.)

EXERCISE 4.27   For the problem of the Carmac Company in Exercise 4.15, which profit margin (the 6740 or the 5100) is most sensitive in the sense that a smaller change up or down affects the optimal production plan? Explain. (Use your results from Exercise 4.19.)

EXERCISE 4.28   For the problem of Mineral Mining Company in Exercise 4.16, management is considering leasing one of the following two new trucks to replace the existing one:

TRUCK TYPE	WEIGHT CAPACITY (lb)	VOLUME CAPACITY (ft)^3	ADDITIONAL COST ($/day)
Tr 22/12	22,000	1,200	100
Tr 20/13	20,000	1,300	150

Should the company replace the old truck and, if so, with which one of the new trucks? Explain. (Use your results from Exercise 4.24.)

Video Case

Video Case

DRAWING CONCLUSIONS

This video case brings us back to the blending department at New England Apple Products. How much Cranapple juice and Appleberry juice should the company produce to maximize its profits? Restating this problem in mathematical terms is half the task, a task we accomplished in Chapter 2. We are ready to tackle the second half: Find the optimal solution graphically.

Because we have a small, 2-variable problem we can graph the possible solutions and understand some important points about linear relationships. The video lists four steps:

1. Plot the constraints
2. Define the feasible set
3. Determine the feasible corner points
4. Find the optimal solution

The first constraint—How much cranberry juice is available?—appears as a line on the graph. Any point on that line is a feasible point; it is a geometric representation of a possible solution to the blending problem. The second constraint—How much apple juice do we have on hand?—is also graphed. These two constraints are combined, and the non-negativity constraint is added.

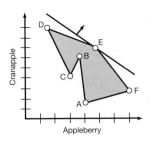

The narrator divides the graph into four sections. We use too much cranberry juice in one section and too much apple juice in another section. In a third section, we use too much of both. Only Area D in the video satisfies all constraints. Some point in Area D—and there are an infinite number of them—is the most profitable. Which point is it?

Because a linear program has linear constraints and a linear objective function, the Corner Principle applies. The Corner Principle states that the optimal solution must be at one of the corner points of the feasible region (Area D). It would be impossible for the optimal solution to appear in the middle of the set because the linear objective function can be moved farther away from the origin to give a better solution. The profit increases infinitely, but the line quickly leaves the feasible are.

We turn to the corners of the feasible region. The amount of Cranapple and Appleberry juice represented at each corner and the profit each combination would bring follow:

I: (0, 0) $0.00 II: (0, 50) $2.00 III: (50, 25) $2.50
IV: (66.7, 0) $2.00

The optimal solution is point III: Make 50 gallons of Cranaaple juice and 25 gallons of Appleberry juice for a profit of $2.50. (Total running time is 4:47.)

QUESTIONS ON THE VIDEO

1. What two points do you need to connect in order to draw each constraint?

2. What constraint is violated in Area B of the graph? In area C?

BEYOND THE VIDEO

1. Why can't an LP feasible region have an indentation like the figure below?

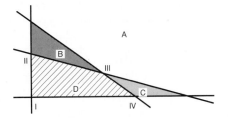

2. What solutions do we get if we reverse the profit margins so that the profit on Cranapple is 4 cents and the Appleberry is 3 cents?

PRACTICAL CONSIDERATIONS

1. Why is it not practical to graph a problem with more than three variables?

2. What practical points do we learn about solving linear programming problems from the graphical solution method?

Source: "For All Practical Purposes," from *The Consortium for Mathematics and its Applications,* (Arlington, MA: 1986), Program 3.

LINEAR PROGRAMMING: A CONCEPTUAL APPROACH TO THE SIMPLEX ALGORITHM

. . . .

*H*aving forged close ties with South American coffee bean exporters, your business, Creative Coffees, is running fairly smoothly. But can you improve profits? Would it make more financial sense to increase production of regular coffee? Or perhaps you would be better off blending more decaf. Decaf brings you greater profit, but preparing decaf from the beans is more complex and more expensive. How do you decide on your strategy?

This chapter moves linear programming from graph paper to a conceptual method that helps decision makers reach answers to such problems with any number of variables.

In Chapter 4, you learned how to solve linear programming problems with two variables *graphically*. When more than three variables are involved, this approach is not possible. Furthermore, real-world linear programs are solved with computers, which use *linear algebra*, not geometry. In this chapter, you will learn the **simplex algorithm**, an algebraic method for solving *all* linear programming problems in a finite number of steps on a computer. You will also learn the intuitive ideas behind this algorithm—including how and why it works.

Simplex algorithm
An algebraic method for solving any linear programming problem in a finite number of steps on a computer.

■ 5.1 WHY THE NEED FOR THE SIMPLEX ALGORITHM

In this section, the problem faced by the management of Creative Coffees is first solved graphically and then used as a springboard in the subsequent development of the simplex algorithm.

EXAMPLE 5.1 THE PRODUCT-MIX PROBLEM OF CREATIVE COFFEES Creative Coffees sells two types of coffees to retail stores: regular and decaf. For the current month, the company has 200 tons of coffee beans in inventory and has scheduled up to 300 hours of processing time for roasting. Each ton of regular coffee requires 1 ton of beans and 1 hour of roasting, and yields a net profit of $3000. Each ton of decaf also requires 1 ton of beans but needs 2 hours of roasting. It yields a net profit of $5000. To maximize the net profit (in thousands of dollars) for the month, the Manager of the Production Department has formulated the following linear program in which x_1 is the number of tons of regular coffee and x_2 is the number of tons of decaf coffee to produce:

$$
\begin{array}{lll}
\text{Maximize} & 3x_1 + 5x_2 & \\
\text{Subject to} & x_1 + x_2 \leq 200 & \text{(bean constraint)} \quad (1)\\
& x_1 + 2x_2 \leq 300 & \text{(time constraint)} \quad (2)\\
& x_1 \,, x_2 \geq 0 & \quad\blacksquare
\end{array}
$$

The feasible region associated with this problem is shown in Figure 5.1. As you learned in Section 4.1, the optimal solution occurs at one of the *extreme points*. One way to obtain an optimal extreme point is to move the objective function line parallel to itself, as described in Section 4.1. Because this graphical approach cannot be generalized for problems with more than three variables, another method is needed for finding the optimal extreme point. From Figure 5.1, there are a *finite number of extreme points* (in particular, four of them, labeled A through D). You can find an optimal extreme point as follows:

1. List all four extreme points—that is, find the values of variables x_1 and x_2 at each extreme point.
2. Compute the objective function value at each extreme point using the associated values of the variables.
3. Select the one with the largest objective function value.

These three steps have been carried out for Example 5.1, and the results are summarized in the table in Figure 5.1. As you can see, the extreme point $x_1 = 100$ and $x_2 = 100$ is the optimal one.

The approach of listing all the extreme points, computing the objective function value at each one, and choosing the best one works well for problems with two variables. However, this approach is impractical for larger problems, so what is needed is a method for finding the best extreme point *without having to list them all*. The simplex algorithm is precisely such a method and its basic idea is described in the next section.

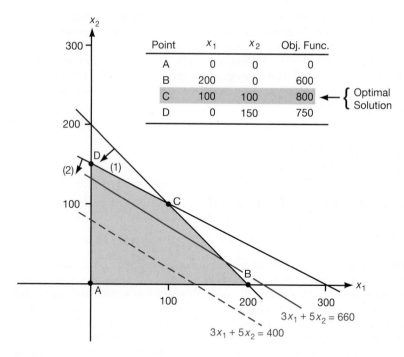

Point	x_1	x_2	Obj. Func.	
A	0	0	0	
B	200	0	600	
C	100	100	800	← { Optimal Solution
D	0	150	750	

FIGURE 5.1 Graphical Solution to Example 5.1.

■ 5.2 THE GENERAL FINITE-IMPROVEMENT ALGORITHM

To develop a systematic, practical method for finding an optimal solution to a linear program, consider the following analogue. Look again at Figure 5.1, and imagine that each extreme point is a ball in a closed box. On each ball is a number—the value of the objective function at the corresponding extreme point. Imagine that the ball corresponding to the optimal extreme point is colored red and all other balls are white. How would you go about finding the optimal solution—that is, the red ball?

Without too much effort, you might develop the following step-by-step algorithm:

Step 0. *Initialization*: Pick a ball out of the box.
Step 1. Is the current ball red? If so, stop with an optimal solution. If not, go to step 2.
Step 2. Throw the current ball away. Pick a new ball from the box and return to step 1.

Iteration
A collection of steps in an algorithm that is repeated.

Observe that this algorithm may repeat steps 1 and 2 many times. Each repetition is called an **iteration**. As long as there are a finite number of balls in the box and one of them is red, this algorithm will eventually produce a red one in a finite number of iterations.

As simple as this idea seems, it forms the very basis of the simplex algorithm (and many otheralgorithms discussed in this book). However, there are two additional key features that make this process computationally efficient:

Test for optimality
A method of determining whether the current solution is optimal.

1. Even though in reality the balls (that is, extreme points) are not colored, there is a computationally efficient way to perform the **test for optimality** in step 1—that is, to determine whether the current ball has the best number.

2. The concept of **improvement** is used in step 2—that is, the new ball picked in step 2 has a "better" number (higher if the objective is to maximize and lower if the objective is to minimize) than the current ball.

Incorporating the test for optimality in step 1 and the process of *moving* to an improved solution in step 2 yields the general finite-improvement algorithm.

Improvement
The process of finding feasible solutions with better and better objective function values in a mathematical model.

> *KEY FEATURES*
>
> The General Finite-Improvement Algorithm
>
> **Step 0.** *Initialization*: Pick a ball out of the box.
> **Step 1.** *Test for Optimality*: Determine if the current ball has the best number on it. If so, stop with an optimal solution. If not, go to step 2.
> **Step 2.** *Moving*: Pick a new ball with a strictly better number. Return to step 1.

This algorithm is referred to as a **finite-improvement algorithm** because

1. Each solution chosen by the algorithm is strictly better, in terms of the objective function, than the previous one (that is, improvement).
2. The algorithm will find an optimal solution in a finite number of iterations because there are only a finite number of possible solutions and, due to improvement, no solution is picked more than once.

Now that you have learned what the steps of a general finite-improvement algorithm are, in the next section these steps are developed in more detail based on the graphical approach to solving linear programming problems.

Finite-improvement algorithm
A systematic method used to find an optimal solution to a mathematical model by generating a finite number of feasible solutions, each of which has a strictly better objective function value than the previous one.

■ 5.3 THE GEOMETRIC FINITE-IMPROVEMENT ALGORITHM FOR LINEAR PROGRAMS

To understand the geometric version of the finite-improvement algorithm described in the last section as it pertains to solving linear programs, consider again Creative Coffees. Each extreme point in the feasible region depicted in Figure 5.2 corresponds to a ball in the finite-improvement algorithm. For example, the extreme point B ($x_1 = 200$ and $x_2 = 0$) whose objective function value is 600 corresponds to one of the balls.

The objective now is to restate steps 0, 1, and 2 of the finite-improvement algorithm in Section 5.2 in terms of the geometry of a linear program. For example, step 0 can be restated as

Step 0. *Initialization*: Find an initial extreme point.

Once an extreme point is obtained (for example, extreme point B in Figure 5.2), the next step (step 1) is to test it for optimality—that is, to see if the objective function of the current extreme point (600, in this case) is the best one. One approach is to compare the objective function value of the current extreme point with that of all other extreme points. However, doing so is impractical because, for real-world problems, there are too many other extreme points. Fortunately, a more practical test has been found.

To understand that test, imagine yourself on the graph at extreme point B and recall that the objective is to maximize the profit. The test for optimality is this: Is it

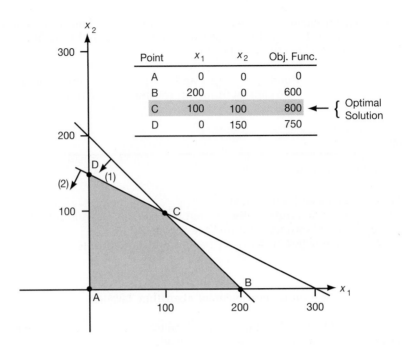

FIGURE 5.2 Feasible Region for Example 5.1.

Edge of the feasible region
The line segment connecting two extreme points of the feasible region.

possible to move from the current extreme point along one of the **edges of the feasible region** to some other **neighboring extreme point** in such a way as to *increase* the objective function value? If the answer is "no," the current extreme point is optimal. If the answer is "yes," the current extreme point is not optimal.

To see that this test for optimality makes sense geometrically, look again at Figure 5.2 and consider any extreme point. Now, draw the objective function line through that extreme point and indicate the improving direction with an arrow (see extreme point B in Figure 5.3). If the extreme point is not optimal, you can see that at least one of the neighboring extreme points (extreme point C in Figure 5.3) is on the improving side of the objective function line. If no neighboring extreme point is on the improving side, the current extreme point is optimal.

Neighboring extreme point
An extreme point of the feasible region that is connected by an edge to the extreme point.

With this observation, step 1 of the finite-improvement algorithm can be restated geometrically as

Step 1. *Test for Optimality*: Given the current extreme point, see if one of the edges leads to a neighboring extreme point with a larger objective function value. If the answer is "no," stop: The current extreme point is optimal. If the answer is "yes," go to step 2: The current extreme point is not optimal.

If step 2 is reached in the finite-improvement algorithm, you know that the current extreme point is not optimal and, in fact, one or more of the edges lead to a neighboring extreme point having a larger objective function value. You can select *any* of these edges and move to the corresponding neighboring extreme point. Thus, step 2 becomes

Step 2. *Moving*: Choose any of the improving edges found in step 1 and move from the current extreme point to the associated neighboring extreme point that has a larger objective function value. Return to step 1.

In summary, the geometric version of the finite-improvement algorithm for solving linear programming problems is as follows:

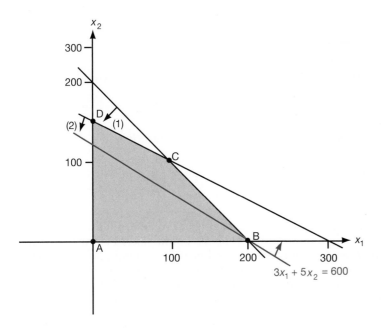

FIGURE 5.3 A Geometric Test for Optimality.

KEY FEATURES

Geometric Finite-Improvement Algorithm for Linear Programming

Step 0. *Initialization*: Find an initial extreme point.
Step 1. *Test for Optimality*: Given the current extreme point, see if one of the edges leads to a neighboring extreme point with a larger objective function value. If the answer is "no," stop: The current extreme point is optimal. If the answer is "yes," go to step 2: The current extreme point is not optimal.
Step 2. *Moving*: Choose any of the improving edges found in step 1 and move from the current extreme point to the associated neighboring extreme point that has a larger objective function value. Return to step 1.

Because the simplex algorithm is algebraic, it is necessary to replace each of these *geometric* steps with a corresponding *algebraic* step. To do so first requires converting a linear programming problem into one specific *form* amenable to algebraic manipulation, as described in the next section.

■ 5.4 STANDARD FORM

As you learned in Chapters 2 and 3, a linear programming problem can come in many *forms*: Its objective can be to maximize or to minimize; it can have equality or inequality (less-than-or-equal-to or greater-than-or-equal-to) constraints; the variables can be nonnegative (≥ 0), nonpositive (≤ 0), or unrestricted. Rather than develop a method for handling each of these different forms, it is easier to design an algorithm to solve only one specific form, called the **standard form**.

Standard form
A particular form of a linear programming problem in which the objective function is to be maximized; there are only equality constraints, and all right-hand sides and variables are nonnegative.

➡ **KEY FEATURES**

The specific form of the algorithm is chosen to enable the computer to perform algebraic manipulations easily. Therefore, throughout this book, standard form will mean a linear program in which

✔ The objective function is to *maximize*.
✔ All right-hand-side values of the constraints are *nonnegative*.
✔ All constraints are *equalities*.
✔ All variables are *nonnegative*.

A natural question to ask is: What happens if *your* problem, after formulation, is not in standard form? After all, most of the problems formulated so far have involved *inequalities*. Most computer programs for solving linear programming problems automatically create an *equivalent* standard-form linear program from your original problem. "Equivalent" means that whatever pertains to the standard-form problem also pertains to the original problem.

1. If the standard-form problem has an optimal solution, so does the original problem. Furthermore, an optimal solution to the standard-form problem can be used to construct an optimal solution to the original problem.
2. If the standard-form problem is infeasible, so is the original problem.
3. If the standard-form problem is unbounded, so is the original problem.

You will now learn how this conversion is accomplished.

5.4.1 An Example of Converting a Linear Program to Standard Form

To illustrate how to create a standard-form linear program, recall the problem of Creative Coffees presented in Section 5.1. After identifying the variables x_1 as the number of tons of regular coffee to produce and x_2 as the number of tons of decaf to produce, you formulate the following linear program:

$$
\begin{array}{lll}
\text{Maximize} & 3x_1 + 5x_2 & \\
\text{Subject to} & x_1 + x_2 \leq 200 & \text{(bean constraint)} \\
& x_1 + 2x_2 \leq 300 & \text{(time constraint)} \\
& x_1\ ,\ \ \ x_2 \geq \ \ \ 0 &
\end{array}
$$

Notice that although the objective function and variable types match those of standard form, the two inequality constraints do not. You need to convert these constraints into *equalities*. Recall that the first constraint means that you cannot use more than 200 tons of beans:

(Tons of beans used for regular coffee) + (tons of beans used for decaf coffee) $\leq$ 200

To create an equivalent equality constraint, observe that another way to express this inequality constraint is

(Tons of beans used for regular coffee) + (tons of beans used for decaf coffee) + (tons of beans left over) = 200

The "tons of beans left over" depend on the values of the variables x_1 and x_2. For example, if $x_1 = 50$ and $x_2 = 70$, then the leftover amount is 80 (that is, $200 - 50 - 70$) tons. Thus, this leftover quantity

1. Is itself a variable that can be denoted by s_1.
2. Must be nonnegative (because a negative value for s_1 would indicate that you have used more than 200 tons of beans).
3. Does not affect the net profit (that is, the coefficient of this variable in the objective function is 0).

In summary, by using the new variable s_1, the corresponding equality constraint is

$$x_1 + x_2 + s_1 = 200$$
$$s_1 \geq 0$$

In a similar way, the inequality constraint corresponding to the roasting time can be converted to an equality constraint by defining a new nonnegative variable s_2 that represents the number of unused hours in roasting. That new equality constraint is

$$x_1 + 2x_2 + s_2 = 300$$
$$s_2 \geq 0$$

By putting the pieces together, the standard-form linear program corresponding to the original coffee problem is

$$
\begin{array}{lll}
\text{Maximize} & 3x_1 + 5x_2 & \\
\text{Subject to} & x_1 + x_2 + s_1 \phantom{{}+{}s_2} = 200 & \text{(bean constraint)} \\
& x_1 + 2x_2 \phantom{{}+{}s_1} + s_2 = 300 & \text{(time constraint)} \\
& x_1 , \quad x_2 , \ s_1 , \ s_2 \geq 0 &
\end{array}
$$

5.4.2 General Rules for Converting a Linear Program to Standard Form

Now, you will learn how to convert *any* linear program into an equivalent one in standard form. Imagine that you have formulated the following linear program:

EXAMPLE 5.2 CONVERTING A LINEAR PROGRAM TO STANDARD FORM

$$
\begin{array}{llcr}
\text{Minimize} & -2x_1 + x_2 - 3x_3 & & \\
\text{Subject to} & x_1 - x_2 + x_3 = 10 & & (1) \\
& -3x_1 - 2x_2 - 2x_3 \geq -15 & & (2) \\
& x_1 \geq 3 & & (3) \\
& x_1 \geq 0 & & (4) \\
& x_2 \leq 0 & & (5) \\
& x_3 \quad \text{unrestricted.} & & (6)
\end{array}
$$

■

CONVERTING A MINIMIZATION OBJECTIVE FUNCTION

To understand how to convert a linear program whose objective function is to be minimized into an equivalent one whose objective function is to be maximized, consider the set of numbers {10, 15, 7, 9}. The smallest number in this set is 7, the third element. Now consider the set {−10, −15, −7, −9} obtained by multiplyng each number by −1. The *largest* number in this set is −7, the third element. In both cases, the same element produces the best value (although one element is the negative of the other). In other words, finding the smallest number in a set is equivalent to

1. Multiplying each element in the set by −1 and then finding the largest element.
2. Multiplying the element found in step 1 by −1.

This same approach is used in converting a minimization objective function into an equivalent maximization one. That is, each coefficient in the objective function is multiplied by −1 to create an equivalent maximization problem. Consider the objective function in Example 5.2:

$$\text{Minimize} \qquad -2x_1 + x_2 - 3x_3$$

The objective function of the corresponding maximization problem is

$$\text{Maximize} \qquad 2x_1 - x_2 + 3x_3$$

and so the entire problem in Example 5.2 becomes

EXAMPLE 5.2(a)

$$
\begin{array}{lrcll}
\text{Maximize} & 2x_1 - x_2 + 3x_3 & & & \\
\text{Subject to} & x_1 - x_2 + x_3 &=& 10 & (1)\\
& -3x_1 - 2x_2 - 2x_3 &\geq& -15 & (2)\\
& x_1 &\geq& 3 & (3)\\
& x_1 &\geq& 0 & (4)\\
& x_2 &\leq& 0 & (5)\\
& x_3 & \text{unrestricted} & & (6)
\end{array}
$$

■

Assume the optimal solution to the maximization problem in Example 5.2(a) turns out to be $x_1 = 3$, $x_2 = -2$, and $x_3 = 5$, with an objective function value of $2x_1 - x_2 + 3x_3 = 2(3) - (-2) + 3(5) = 23$. The same values for these variables are optimal for the original minimization problem. However, the minimization objective function value is -23, the negative of the one in standard form.

CONVERTING NEGATIVE RIGHT-HAND SIDES

In Example 5.2(a), all the right-hand-side values are nonnegative except for the value of -15 associated with constraint (2). To create a standard-form constraint that has a nonnegative right-hand side, multiply both sides of the constraint:

$$-3x_1 - 2x_2 - 2x_3 \geq -15$$

by −1 to obtain

$$3x_1 + 2x_2 + 2x_3 \leq 15$$

Observe that the $\geq$ sign has changed to a $\leq$. In a similar manner, if the original constraint having a negative right-hand side were a less-than-or-equal-to constraint, after multiplying through by −1 you will obtain a greater-than-or-equal-to constraint. If the original constraint is an equality, the new constraint obtained when multiplying through by -1 remains an equality constraint.

By multiplying constraint (2) through by -1, the linear program in Example 5.2(a) becomes the one in Example 5.2(b).

EXAMPLE 5.2(b)

$$
\begin{array}{lll}
\text{Maximize} & 2x_1 - x_2 + 3x_3 & \\
\text{Subject to} & x_1 - x_2 + x_3 = 10 & (1) \\
& 3x_1 + 2x_2 + 2x_3 \leq 15 & (2) \\
& x_1 \geq 3 & (3) \\
& x_1 \geq 0 & (4) \\
& x_2 \leq 0 & (5) \\
& x_3 \quad \text{unrestricted} & (6)
\end{array}
$$

∎

CONVERTING INEQUALITY CONSTRAINTS

Because the first constraint in Example 5.2(b) is an equality constraint, no conversion is needed. To convert the second constraint, recall the example of Creative Coffees in which a less-than-or-equal-to constraint is converted to an equivalent equality constraint by adding a nonnegative variable to the left-hand side to make up the difference. This added variable is called a **slack variable** because it picks up the "slack" between the two sides. For constraint (2) in Example 5.2(b), adding a nonnegative slack variable, s_1, results in

$$
3x_1 + 2x_2 + 2x_3 + s_1 = 15 \qquad (2)
$$
$$
s_1 \geq 0
$$

Slack variable
A nonnegative variable that is added to the left-hand side of a less-than-or-equal-to constraint to obtain an equivalent equality constraint.

Now, consider constraint (3) in Example 5.2(b), which is a greater-than-or-equal-to constraint. In such a constraint, the left-hand side will be greater than or equal to the right-hand side. To make both sides equal, you will need to *subtract* a nonnegative amount from the left-hand side. That is, you will need to subtract a nonnegative **surplus variable.** Constraint (3) is converted to an equality constraint by subtracting a nonnegative surplus variable, s_2, as follows:

$$
x_1 - s_2 = 3 \qquad (3)
$$
$$
s_2 \geq 0
$$

Surplus variable
A nonnegative variable that is subtracted from the left-hand side of a greater-than-or-equal-to constraint to obtain an equivalent equality constraint.

With new constraints (2) and (3) replacing those in Example 5.2(b), the resulting linear program is given in Example 5.2(c).

EXAMPLE 5.2(c)

$$
\begin{array}{lll}
\text{Maximize} & 2x_1 - x_2 + 3x_3 & \\
\text{Subject to} & x_1 - x_2 + x_3 = 10 & (1) \\
& 3x_1 + 2x_2 + 2x_3 + s_1 = 15 & (2) \\
& x_1 - s_2 = 3 & (3) \\
& x_1, \quad s_1, s_2 \geq 0 & (4) \\
& x_2 \leq 0 & (5) \\
& x_3 \quad \text{unrestricted} & (6)
\end{array}
$$

∎

Not all variables are nonnegative, so the linear program in Example 5.2(c) is still not in standard form. Additional conversion is necessary.

CONVERTING NONPOSITIVE AND UNRESTRICTED VARIABLES

Up to now, the variables in all linear programs have been nonnegative. However, in some problems, a variable may be restricted to be *nonpositive* (≤ 0) or may even be *unrestricted* (that is, it can be positive, negative, or 0). For example, suppose you must locate a warehouse in a city. Using a fixed-coordinate system, you define the following two decision variables, relative to the origin:

$$x_1 = \text{the } x\text{-coordinate of the location of the warehouse}$$

$$x_2 = \text{the } y\text{-coordinate of the location of the warehouse}$$

These two variables are unrestricted. A positive value for x_1 indicates a location to the right of the origin; a negative value indicates a location to the left. Similarly, a positive or negative value for x_2 indicates a location above or below the origin, respectively.

Suppose that the location of the warehouse must be to the left of the origin. This restriction is reflected with the constraint:

$$x_1 \leq 0$$

In this case, x_1 is nonpositive and x_2 is unrestricted. You will now see how to convert a problem with both unrestricted and nonpositive variables to standard form. This task is accomplished by replacing those variables with appropriate nonnegative ones, as described in what follows.

CONVERTING UNRESTRICTED VARIABLES

In Example 5.2(c), variable x_3 is unrestricted. To shape such a problem into standard form—which means with nonnegative variables—each unrestricted variable must be replaced with the *difference* of two nonnegative variables. For example, in Example 5.2(c), replace the originial unrestricted variable x_3 everywhere with the difference of two nonnegative variables—whose symbolic names are chosen arbitrarily as x_3^+ and x_3^-—as follows:

$$x_3 = x_3^+ - x_3^-$$
$$x_3^+ , x_3^- \geq 0$$

The way to interpret this substitution is to recall that x_3 can be positive or negative. If x_3 is positive (say, $x_3 = 5$), then x_3^+ will have the same positive value as x_3 (that is, $x_3^+ = 5$) and x_3^- will be 0. If x_3 is negative (say, $x_3 = -7$), then x_3^+ will be 0 and x_3^- will be equal to the absolute value of x_3 (that is, $x_3^- = 7$). Alternatively, given nonnegative values for x_3^+ and x_3^-, the value for x_3 is obtained by computing $x_3 = x_3^+ - x_3^-$.

Substituting $x_3 = x_3^+ - x_3^-$ in Example 5.2(c) yields the linear program in Example 5.2(d).

EXAMPLE 5.2(d)

$$
\begin{array}{lll}
\text{Maximize} & 2x_1 - x_2 + 3x_3^+ - 3x_3^- & \\
\text{Subject to} & x_1 - x_2 + x_3^+ - x_3^- \qquad\qquad = 10 & (1) \\
& 3x_1 + 2x_2 + 2x_3^+ - 2x_3^- + s_1 \qquad = 15 & (2) \\
& x_1 \qquad\qquad\qquad\qquad - s_2 = 3 & (3) \\
& x_1, \qquad x_3^+, \quad x_3^-, \ s_1, \ s_2 \geq 0 & (4) \\
& x_2 \qquad\qquad\qquad\qquad \leq 0 & (5)
\end{array}
$$

■

CONVERTING NONPOSITIVE VARIABLES

In Example 5.2(d), all that remains is to handle the nonpositive variable x_2. Replace x_2 everywhere with the negative of a new nonnegative variable whose symbolic name is arbitrarily chosen as x_2', that is,

$$x_2 = -x_2'$$

$$x_2' \geq 0$$

For example, if in the standard-form problem $x_2' = 4$, the value of the original variable x_2 is $x_2 = -x_2' = -4$.

Substituting $x_2 = -x_2'$ in Example 5.2(d) yields the standard-form linear program in Example 5.2(e).

EXAMPLE 5.2(e) STANDARD-FORM LINEAR PROGRAM FOR EXAMPLE 5.2

$$
\begin{array}{lll}
\text{Maximize} & 2x_1 + x_2' + 3x_3^+ - 3x_3^- & \\
\text{Subject to} & x_1 + x_2' + x_3^+ - x_3^- \qquad\qquad = 10 & (1) \\
& 3x_1 - 2x_2' + 2x_3^+ - 2x_3^- + s_1 \qquad = 15 & (2) \\
& x_1 \qquad\qquad\qquad\qquad - s_2 = 3 & (3) \\
& x_1, \quad x_2', \quad x_3^+, \quad x_3^- \quad s_1, \ s_2 \geq 0 & (4)
\end{array}
$$

■

The linear programming problem in Example 5.2(e) is the standard-form version of the original problem in Example 5.2. This standard-form linear program is equivalent to the original one. Given an optimal solution to the standard-form problem, you can construct an optimal solution to the original problem. Suppose that the optimal solution to the standard-form problem in Example 5.2(e) is

$$x_1 = 3$$

$$x_2' = 2$$

$$x_3^+ = 5$$

$$x_3^- = 0$$

$$s_1 = 0$$

$$s_2 = 0$$

By computing $x_2 = -x_2' = -2$ and $x_3 = x_3^+ - x_3^- = 5 - 0$, the optimal solution to the original problem in Example 5.2 is

$$x_1 = \quad 3$$
$$x_2 = -2$$
$$x_3 = \quad 5$$

Whereas the optimal objective function value for the standard-form problem in Example 5.2(e) is 23, that of the original problem is -23 because the original minimization objective was multiplied by -1 to convert it into a maximization problem.

5.4.3 Summary of the Steps for Converting a Linear Program to Standard Form

To provide a summary of how a linear program is converted to standard form, consider again Example 5.2:

Minimize	$-2x_1 + x_2 - 3x_3$		
Subject to	$x_1 - x_2 + x_3 = 10$		(1)
	$-3x_1 - 2x_2 - 2x_3 \geq -15$		(2)
	$x_1 \geq 3$		(3)
	$x_1 \geq 0$		(4)
	$x_2 \leq 0$		(5)
	x_3 unrestricted		(6)

➡ **KEY FEATURES**

Step 1. *Converting a Minimization Objective Function*
Each coefficient in the objective function is multiplied by -1 to create an equivalent maximization problem.

$$\text{Minimize} \quad -2x_1 + x_2 - 3x_3 \quad \rightarrow \quad \text{Maximize} \quad 2x_1 - x_2 + 3x_3$$

Step 2. *Converting Negative Right-Hand Sides*
Multiply both sides of the constraint having a negative right-hand side by -1 and change the direction of the inequality, if any.

$$-3x_1 - 2x_2 - 2x_3 \geq -15 \quad \rightarrow \quad 3x_1 + 2x_2 + 2x_3 \leq 15$$

Step 3. *Converting Inequality Constraints*
Equality constraints need no conversion. Each less-than-or-equal-to (greater-than-or-equal-to) constraint is converted to an equivalent equality constraint by adding (subtracting) a nonnegative slack (surplus) variable to the left-hand side.

$$3x_1 + 2x_2 + 2x_3 \leq 15 \quad \rightarrow \quad 3x_1 + 2x_2 + 2x_3 + s_1 = 15$$
$$\text{and} \quad s_1 \geq 0 x_1 \geq 3 \quad \rightarrow \quad x_1 - s_2 = 3 \quad \text{and} \quad s_2 \geq 0$$

Step 4. *Converting Nonpositive and Unrestricted Variables*
Replace each unrestricted variable with the *difference* of two new nonnegative variables. Replace each nonpositive variable with the negative of a new nonnegative variable.

$$x_3 \rightarrow x_3^+ - x_3^- \quad \text{and} \quad x_3^+, x_3^- \geq 0$$
$$x_2 \rightarrow \quad -x_2' \quad \text{and} \quad x_2' \geq 0$$

Performing these steps given in the Key Features box above on Example 5.2 results in the equivalent standard-form linear program in Example 5.2(e). The *order* in which these four steps are performed is irrelevant. You will always obtain an equivalent standard-form linear program, whatever the sequence.

Once a linear program is in standard form, it is possible to design an algebraic algorithm for finding an optimal solution. The conceptual steps of this algorithm are presented in the next section.

■ 5.5 The Conceptual Steps of the Simplex Algorithm

In this section, the conceptual steps of the finite-improvement algorithm described in Section 5.2 and the geometric steps presented in Section 5.3 are developed in algebraic terms to solve linear programming problems in standard form. The resulting algorithm is the *simplex algorithm*.

5.5.1 Basic Feasible Solutions: The Algebraic Definition of Extreme Points

The simplex algorithm works with algebra instead of geometry. The first step in designing this algorithm is to develop an algebraic concept corresponding to the geometric concept of an extreme point. That algebraic concept is called a *basic feasible solution* (bfs). In this section, you will learn what a bfs is and how to identify and create one.

Recall the example of Creative Coffees that resulted in the following linear program:

$$
\begin{array}{lll}
\text{Maximize} & 3x_1 + 5x_2 & \\
\text{Subject to} & x_1 + x_2 \leq 200 & \text{(bean constraint)} \\
& x_1 + 2x_2 \leq 300 & \text{(time constraint)} \\
& x_1 , \quad x_2 \geq \quad 0 &
\end{array}
$$

The associated standard-form linear program is

$$
\begin{array}{lll}
\text{Maximize} & 3x_1 + 5x_2 & \\
\text{Subject to} & x_1 + x_2 + s_1 \quad\quad = 200 & \quad (1) \\
& x_1 + 2x_2 \quad\quad + s_2 = 300 & \quad (2) \\
& x_1 , \quad x_2 , \quad s_1 , \quad s_2 \geq \quad 0 & \quad (3)
\end{array}
$$

The feasible region and extreme points associated with this problem are illustrated in Figure 5.1. Although there are many *feasible* solutions, the extreme points are *special* and one of them is *optimal.* Similarly, the associated standard-form linear program has many *feasible* solutions, but the basic feasible solutions—the bfs—are *special* and one of them is *optimal.*

To identify a bfs, observe that in this standard-form linear program, there are more variables than equations. In this case, having two more variables than equations means that there are an *infinite* number of solutions because you can choose arbitrary values for *any two* (number of variables − number of equations) of these variables and use the two equations to obtain the values of the remaining variables. For example, choosing a value of $x_1 = 30$ and $x_2 = 50$ and putting those values into Equations (1) and (2) results in

$$
\begin{aligned}
30 + 50 + s_1 &= 200 \quad &\text{or} \quad & s_1 = 120 \\
30 + 100 \phantom{{}+{}} + s_2 &= 300 \quad &\text{or} \quad & s_2 = 170
\end{aligned}
$$

Observe that, in this case, the values of all variables are nonnegative.

Any number of solutions can be generated by repeating this process with different values for x_1 and x_2. However, these solutions may or may not satisfy the nonnegativity constraints. In general, if a standard-form linear program has n variables and m equations, and $n > m$, you can construct a solution by choosing arbitrary values for $n - m$ of the variables and by using the m equations to find the values of the remaining m variables.

A basic feasible solution, however, is constructed in a special way. As before, begin by choosing two variables (number of variables − number of equations). These variables are called **nonbasic variables**, and their values are set to 0. Solve the two reduced equations to find the values of the remaining two variables, called the **basic variables**. For example, if s_1 and s_2 are chosen as nonbasic variables and set to 0, the reduced equations for the basic variables x_1 and x_2 are

$$
\begin{aligned}
x_1 + x_2 &= 200 \\
x_1 + 2x_2 &= 300
\end{aligned}
$$

Solving these two equations to obtain the values of these basic variables results in the following values:

$$
x_1 = 100; \qquad x_2 = 100
$$

The solution

$$
x_1 = 100; \qquad x_2 = 100; \qquad s_1 = 0; \qquad s_2 = 0
$$

constructed in this specific way is called a **basic solution**. Because this solution also satisfies the nonnegativity constraints, it is called a **basic feasible solution** in which x_1 and x_2 are basic variables and s_1 and s_2 are nonbasic variables.

There are many different ways to choose which variables are to be basic and which are to be nonbasic. Some of these choices result in values for the variables that *are* basic feasible solutions; others do not. In this example, there are six possible choices for selecting two nonbasic variables out of the six variables. These choices together with the corresponding basic solutions are summarized in Table 5.1. Of these six basic solutions, numbers 1, 3, 4, and 6 are basic *feasible* solutions because the values of all the variables are nonnegative.

Nonbasic variable
A chosen set of variables in a standard-form linear program (equal in number to the total number of variables minus the number of equality constraints) whose values are set to 0.

Basic variable
The remaining variables, other than the nonbasic variables, in a standard-form linear program (equal in number to the number of equality constraints).

Basic solution
Values for the variables that satisfy the equality constraints in a standard-form linear program after the nonbasic variables have been set to 0.

Basic feasible solution (bfs)
Values for the variables that satisfy the equality and the nonnegativity constraints in a standard-form linear program after the nonbasic variables have been set to 0.

TABLE 5.1	All Basic Solutions to Example 5.1				
	NONBASIC VARIABLES		BASIC VARIABLES		BFS (*)
1	$x_1 = 0,$	$x_2 = 0$	$s_1 = 200,$	$s_2 = 300$	*
2	$x_1 = 0,$	$s_1 = 0$	$x_2 = 200,$	$s_2 = -100$	
3	$x_1 = 0,$	$s_2 = 0$	$x_2 = 150,$	$s_1 = 50$	*
4	$x_2 = 0,$	$s_1 = 0$	$x_1 = 200,$	$s_2 = 100$	*
5	$x_2 = 0,$	$s_2 = 0$	$x_1 = 300,$	$s_1 = -100$	
6	$s_1 = 0,$	$s_2 = 0$	$x_1 = 100,$	$x_2 = 100$	*

To see the relationship between basic feasible solutions and extreme points, look at the values of x_1 and x_2 corresponding to the four basic feasible solutions in Table 5.1. If you locate those points on the graph in Figure 5.4, you will discover that each basic feasible solution corresponds precisely to one of the four extreme points.

Just as the *graphical* approach to solving a linear program involves finding the best extreme point, so the *algebraic* approach requires finding the best bfs. When the problem has only a few variables and constraints, it might be reasonable to list every basic feasible solution, evaluate the objective function at each one, and choose the best one. Unfortunately, when the number of variables and constraints is large (as in most real-world problems), the number of basic feasible solutions is so large that, even with today's fastest computers, they cannot all be listed in a reasonable amount of time. For example, in a standard-form problem in which there are $m = 20$ equality constraints and $n = 100$ variables, to generate a basic solution, you must choose $n - m = 100 - 20 = 80$ nonbasic variables whose values are set to 0. Thus, you will have $m = 20$ basic

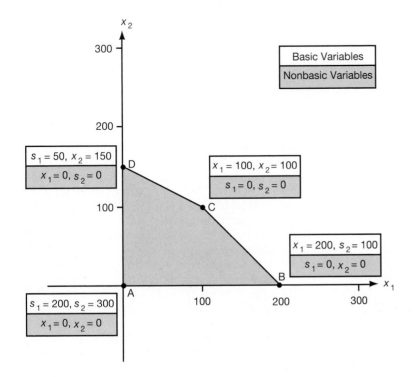

FIGURE 5.4 The Extreme Points and bfs of Example 5.1.

variables whose values are obtained by solving m equations in the m unknown basic variables. In this example, the number of basic solutions is

$$\frac{n!}{(n-m)!\, m!} = \frac{100!}{80!\, 20!} = 5.3598 \times 10^{20}$$

where for any integer k, $k! = (k)(k-1)\ldots(1)$.

    As you can see, even for a linear program of moderate size, it is impractical to list every bfs. However, it is important to note that there are a *finite* number of possible bfs because there are a finite number of ways to choose which variables are to be basic. In Section 5.5.2, you will learn how to use the finite-improvement algorithm presented in Section 5.2 to find an optimal bfs without necessarily having to examine all of them.

5.5.2 An Algebraic Finite-Improvement Algorithm for Linear Programs

Recall the steps of the geometric finite-improvement algorithm for solving linear programming problems presented in Section 5.3:

THE GEOMETRIC FINITE-IMPROVEMENT ALGORITHM FOR LINEAR PROGRAMMING

Step 0. *Initialization*: Find an initial extreme point.
Step 1. *Test for Optimality*: Given the current extreme point, see if one of the edges leads to a neighboring extreme point with a larger objective function value. If the answer is "no," stop: The current extreme point is optimal. If the answer is "yes," go to step 2: The current extreme point is not optimal.
Step 2. *Moving*: Choose any of the improving edges found in step 1 and move from the current extreme point to the associated neighboring extreme point that has a larger objective function value. Return to step 1.

Because the simplex algorithm is algebraic, it is necessary to replace each of these *geometric* steps with a corresponding *algebraic* step. This is accomplished by first replacing the geometric term "extreme point" everywhere with the algebraic term "basic feasible solution." Thus, for example, step 0 becomes:

Step 0. *Initialization*: Find an initial basic feasible solution.

    To develop an algebraic version of the test for optimality, you must first understand the algebraic notions corresponding to an edge and a neighboring extreme point. In Figure 5.4, you can see all the extreme points together with the basic feasible solutions corresponding to those extreme points. Now, choose an extreme point (and bfs) and look at its neighboring extreme points (and bfs). Can you identify a property that is common to all the neighboring bfs in relation to the chosen one? In particular, each neighboring bfs can be obtained from the chosen bfs by *exchanging one basic with one nonbasic variable*. For example, consider extreme point A, at which x_1 and x_2 are nonbasic and s_1 and s_2 are basic. To reach the neighboring extreme point B, along the x_1-axis, you need only exchange the nonbasic variable x_1 with the basic variable s_1.

Adjacent bfs
Any bfs that can be obtained from the current bfs by exchanging one basic and one nonbasic variable.

    Alternatively, to reach the neighboring extreme point D, along the x_2-axis, you need only exchange the other nonbasic variable x_2 with the basic variable s_2. In general, for a linear program with m constraints and n variables, a bfs has m basic variables and $n - m$ nonbasic variables. Each bfs has $n - m$ **adjacent bfs**, namely, one for each choice of a nonbasic variable that could be made basic in exchange for some basic variable, while keeping all other nonbasic variables as nonbasics.

Some of the $n - m$ neighbors of a bfs may have a larger objective function value than the current bfs, and others may not. One way to find a better bfs is to list each adjacent bfs and check its objective function value until a better one is found, if one exists. But this requires a great deal of computational effort. A more efficient method has been devised. For each nonbasic variable in a given bfs, it is possible to compute a single number, called the **reduced cost**.

The value of the reduced cost indicates if the adjacent bfs reached by making this nonbasic variable basic produces a new bfs with a larger objective function value than the current one.

Reduced cost
A number associated with each nonbasic variable in a given basic feasible solution that indicates how much the objective function would improve if that nonbasic variable were increased to a value of 1.

➡ *KEY FEATURES*

To understand the meaning of the reduced cost, recall that, in the current bfs, all nonbasic variables have value 0. If you choose to make a nonbasic variable basic, the value of this variable will become positive. The reduced cost of a nonbasic variable is

Reduced cost = the change in the objective function value for each unit of increase in the value of the nonbasic variable

Thus, a *positive* reduced cost for a nonbasic variable results in an adjacent bfs with a *larger* objective function value when this nonbasic variable is made basic; a *negative* reduced cost results in an adjacent bfs with a *smaller* objective function value.

For example, at the bfs corresponding to extreme point A in Figure 5.4, the reduced cost of the nonbasic variable x_1 happens to be 3. This positive value indicates that the neighboring bfs at extreme point B obtained by making x_1 basic has a larger objective function value than does the one at extreme point A. Similarly, the reduced cost of the nonbasic variable x_2 is 5. Again, this positive value indicates that the neighboring bfs at extreme point D obtained by making x_2 basic has a larger objective function value than does the one at extreme point A.

With the concept of reduced costs, step 1 of the finite-improvement algorithm becomes:

Step 1. *Test for Optimality*: For the current bfs:

    a. Compute the reduced cost of each nonbasic variable.

    b. If all reduced costs are ≤ 0, then the current bfs is optimal; otherwise, go to step 2.

To complete the algebraic version of the simplex algorithm, all that remains is to understand how to "move" to—that is, to compute—the new bfs if the current one is *not* optimal. In fact, when the current bfs fails the test for optimality, you have discovered one or more nonbasic variables with a positive reduced cost. When such a variable is made basic, the objective function value increases. Two questions remain:

    1. Which *nonbasic* variable having a positive reduced cost should you choose, if there is more than one?

    2. If this chosen nonbasic variable is made basic, which *basic* variable is to be made nonbasic?

With regard to the first question, you can choose *any* nonbasic variable with a positive reduced cost. However, the **rule of steepest ascent** has proven efficient in practice and is:

Rule of steepest ascent
The rule used to choose the nonbasic variable with the most positive reduced cost to make basic.

The Rule of Steepest Ascent: Choose the nonbasic variable with the largest positive reduced cost.

With regard to the second question, indeed there is a basic variable to make nonbasic, but for now, step 2 becomes

Step 2. *Moving*:

    a. Use the rule of steepest ascent to select the nonbasic variable to make basic.
    b. Identify a specific basic variable to become nonbasic.
    c. Create the new adjacent bfs by exchanging the chosen nonbasic and basic variables and recomputing the values of all variables in the new bfs. Return to step 1.

By putting together the pieces, the algebraic version of the simplex algorithm is as follows:

➡ **KEY FEATURES**

The Algebraic Finite-Improvement Algorithm for Linear Programming

Step 0. *Initialization*: Find an initial basic feasible solution.
Step 1. *Test for Optimality*: For the current bfs:

    a. Compute the reduced cost of each nonbasic variable.
    b. If all reduced costs are ≤ 0, then the current bfs is optimal; otherwise, go to step 2.

Step 2. *Moving*:

    a. Use the rule of steepest ascent to select the nonbasic variable to make basic.
    b. Identify a specific basic variable to become nonbasic.
    c. Create the new adjacent bfs by exchanging the chosen nonbasic and basic variables and recomputing the values of all variables in the new bfs. Return to step 1.

The algebraic details for performing the steps of this algorithm provide little managerial insight and are therefore omitted from this text. Your efforts are better spent concentrating on interpreting the computer's results, as you will learn to do in Chapter 6.

    This finite-improvement algorithm is based on a linear program that *has* an optimal solution. However, as you learned in Section 4.2 in Chapter 4, a linear program can also be infeasible or unbounded. How do these cases affect the algorithm just described?

    Suppose a linear program is infeasible. Which of the previous steps are affected? The answer is step 0 because you will be unable to find an initial basic feasible solution. The simplex algorithm will detect and report this situation.

    What about unboundedness? For example, look again at the example of an unbounded linear program in Figure 4.11 in Section 4.2. With an unbounded problem, in step 2(b), you will be unable to identify an appropriate basic variable to make nonbasic. Once again, the simplex algorithm detects and reports this situation when it arises.

In this section, you have learned the conceptual steps of the simplex algorithm, which provide an algebraic method for solving *any* linear programming problem in standard form. A summary of the conceptual ideas behind the simplex algorithm follows.

SUMMARY

In this chapter, you have learned the geometric and algebraic conceptual steps of the algorithm most commonly used for solving linear programming problems. The algebraic version is called the *simplex algorithm*. It is designed to solve one specific form of linear program known as *standard form* in which

1. The objective function is to be maximized.
2. All constraints are equalities with nonnegative right-hand-side values.
3. All variables are restricted to be nonnegative.

You learned to convert any linear program into an equivalent one in standard form as follows:

1. Multiply each coefficient of a minimization objective function by −1 to obtain a maximization objective.
2. Add (subtract) a nonnegative slack (surplus) variable to each less-than-or-equal-to (greater-than-or-equal-to) constraint to create an equality constraint.
3. Multiply both sides of a constraint by −1 in the event that the right-hand-side value is negative to create a constraint with a nonnegative right-hand-side value. In so doing, remember to change a ≤ constraint to a ≥ constraint, and vice versa.
4. Replace each *unrestricted* variable with the difference of two nonnegative variables; replace each nonpositive variable with a new nonnegative variable whose value is the negative of the original variable.

Once the problem is in standard form, the simplex algorithm can determine whether the linear program is infeasible, optimal, or unbounded. The algorithm works with basic feasbile solutions (bfs), which are the algebraic versions of extreme points. A bfs is a feasible solution obtained by choosing one *basic* variable for each equality constraint; the remaining variables are *nonbasic* and have value 0. The values of the basic variables are obtained by solving a system of linear equations. The simplex algorithm proceeds by performing the following steps:

Step 0. *Initialization*: Find an initial basic feasible solution or determine that none exists, in which case the problem is infeasible.

Step 1. *Test for Optimality*: For the current bfs:

    a. Compute the reduced cost of each nonbasic variable, which is a single number whose sign indicates whether or not it is advantageous, relative to the objective function, to increase the value of that nonbasic variable.

    b. If all reduced costs are ≤ 0, then the current bfs is optimal; otherwise, go to step 2.

Step 2. *Moving*:

    a. Use the rule of steepest ascent to select the nonbasic variable having the most positive reduced cost to make basic.

    b. Identify a specific basic variable to become nonbasic, or determine that the problem is unbounded.

c. Create the new adjacent bfs by exchanging the chosen nonbasic and basic variables. Recompute the values of all variables in the new bfs. Return to step 1.

In this chapter, you have learned the conceptual steps of the simplex algorithm, which provide an algebraic method for solving *any* linear programming problem in standard form. Ultimately, these steps are performed on a computer. In Chapter 6, you will learn how to use the concepts from this chapter to interpret the information obtained when using the simplex algorithm on a computer.

EXERCISES

EXERCISE 5.1   Convert the linear program in Exercise 4.1 in Chapter 4 to standard form.

EXERCISE 5.2   Convert the linear program in Exercise 4.2 in Chapter 4 to standard form.

EXERCISE 5.3   Convert the following linear program to standard form:

$$
\begin{aligned}
\text{Minimize} \quad & 2x_1 + x_2 - 3x_3 \\
\text{Subject to} \quad & x_1 + 2x_2 - x_3 \le 11 \\
& x_1 - x_2 + x_3 = -1 \\
& -2x_1 - 3x_2 + 4x_3 \ge 8 \\
& x_1 \ge 0 \\
& x_2 \le 0 \\
& x_3 \quad \text{unrestricted}
\end{aligned}
$$

EXERCISE 5.4   Convert the following linear program to standard form:

$$
\begin{aligned}
\text{Maximize} \quad & x_1 + 2x_2 - 4x_3 - 6x_4 \\
\text{Subject to} \quad & -2x_1 + 9x_2 + 9x_3 - x_4 \ge -7 \\
& 6x_1 - 9x_2 + 4x_3 - 7x_4 \le 21 \\
& 6x_1 - 2x_2 - 6x_3 + x_4 = 3 \\
& 7x_1 + 11x_2 - 9x_3 - 21x_4 \ge 0 \\
& x_1, \quad x_3 \ge 0 \\
& x_2, \quad x_4 \le 0
\end{aligned}
$$

EXERCISE 5.5   Convert the linear program in Exercise 4.13 in Chapter 4 to standard form. Explain the meaning of the slack/surplus variables in the context of the problem.

EXERCISE 5.6   Convert the linear program in Exercise 4.16 in Chapter 4 to standard form. Explain the meaning of the slack/surplus variables in the context of the problem.

EXERCISE 5.7   For the following linear program and given basic feasible solution, interpret the meaning of the reduced cost of each nonbasic variable. Is the current basic feasible solution optimal? Explain.

$$
\begin{aligned}
\text{Maximize} \quad & 3x_1 + 5x_2 \\
\text{Subject to} \quad & -2x_1 + 2x_2 + s_1 = 1 \\
& 3x_1 - x_2 + s_2 = 2 \\
& x_1, \quad x_2, \quad s_1, \quad s_2 \ge 0
\end{aligned}
$$

VARIABLE	VALUE	BASIC/NONBASIC	REDUCED COST
x_1	0.6667	Basic	—
x_2	0.0000	Nonbasic	6
s_1	2.3333	Basic	—
s_2	0.0000	Nonbasic	1

EXERCISE 5.8 For the following linear program and given basic feasible solution, interpret the meaning of the reduced cost of each nonbasic variable. Is the current basic feasible solution optimal? Explain.

$$
\begin{aligned}
\text{Minimize} \quad & x_1 + 4x_2 \\
\text{Subject to} \quad & 3x_1 + x_2 + s_1 = 10 \\
& x_1 + x_2 + s_2 = 2 \\
& x_1 + 2x_2 + s_3 = 16 \\
& x_1, \quad x_2, \quad s_1, \quad s_2, \quad s_3 \geq 0
\end{aligned}
$$

VARIABLE	VALUE	BASIC/NONBASIC	REDUCED COST
x_1	2.000	Basic	—
x_2	0.000	Nonbasic	3
s_1	4.000	Basic	—
s_2	0.000	Nonbasic	−1
s_3	14.000	Basic	—

EXERCISE 5.9 Identify the optimal solution and objective function value for the standard-form problem using the given solution to the original linear program.

ORIGINAL LINEAR PROGRAM

$$
\begin{aligned}
\text{Maximize} \quad & 2x_1 + 3x_2 + x_3 \\
\text{Subject to} \quad & -x_1 - x_2 - x_3 = -10 \\
& 2x_1 - x_2 + 3x_3 \geq 5 \\
& x_1 + 2x_2 \leq 8 \\
& x_1, \quad x_2, \quad x_3 \geq 0
\end{aligned}
$$

Optimal solution: $x_1 = 0, x_2 = 4$, and $x_3 = 6$.

STANDARD-FORM LINEAR PROGRAM

$$
\begin{aligned}
\text{Maximize} \quad & 2x_1 + 3x_2 + x_3 \\
\text{Subject to} \quad & x_1 + x_2 + x_3 = 10 \\
& 2x_1 - x_2 + 3x_3 - s_1 = 5 \\
& x_1 + 2x_2 + s_2 = 8 \\
& x_1, \quad x_2, \quad x_3, \quad s_1, \quad s_2 \geq 0
\end{aligned}
$$

EXERCISE 5.10   Identify the optimal solution and objective function value for the original linear program using the given solution to the associated standard-form problem.

ORIGINAL LINEAR PROGRAM

$$
\begin{array}{lrcrcrcr}
\text{Minimize} & 2x_1 & + & 2x_2 & - & x_3 \\
\text{Subject to} & -x_1 & + & x_2 & - & x_3 & \leq & -16 \\
& 2x_1 & & & - & 2x_3 & \geq & 30 \\
& x_1 & + & 2x_2 & & & \geq & 8 \\
& x_1 & , & & & x_3 & \geq & 0 \\
& & & x_2 & & & \leq & 0
\end{array}
$$

STANDARD-FORM LINEAR PROGRAM

$$
\begin{array}{lrcrcrcrcr}
\text{Maximize} & -2x_1 & + & 2x_2' & + & x_3 \\
\text{Subject to} & x_1 & + & x_2' & + & x_3 & - & s_1 & & & = 16 \\
& 2x_1 & & & - & 2x_3 & & & - & s_2 & = 30 \\
& x_1 & - & 2x_2' & & & & & - & s_3 & = 8 \\
& x_1 & , & x_2' & , & x_3 & , & s_1 & , & s_2 & , & s_3 \geq 0
\end{array}
$$

Optimal solution: $x_1 = 15, x_2' = 3.5, x_3 = 0, s_1 = 2.5,$ and $s_2 = s_3 = 0$.

EXERCISE 5.11   Suppose that x_1 and x_2 are the basic variables for the following linear program:

$$
\begin{array}{lrcrcrcr}
\text{Maximize} & & & & & x_3 & - & 5x_4 \\
\text{Subject to} & x_1 & & & + & 2x_3 & + & 8x_4 & = 10 \\
& & & x_2 & - & 2x_3 & + & 2x_4 & = 6 \\
& x_1 & , & x_2 & , & x_3 & , & x_4 & \geq 0
\end{array}
$$

a. Find the values of all the variables and the corresponding objective function value.
b. Find the new basic feasible solution and objective function value obtained by making x_1 nonbasic and x_3 basic.
c. Indicate whether the reduced cost of the nonbasic variable x_3 in the original basic feasible solution in part (a) is positive or negative. Explain.

EXERCISE 5.12   Suppose that x_1 and x_2 are the basic variables for the following linear program:

$$
\begin{array}{lrcrcrcr}
\text{Minimize} & 2x_1 & - & 4x_2 \\
\text{Subject to} & 4x_1 & + & x_2 & + & x_3 & & & = 4 \\
& 4x_1 & + & 6x_2 & & & - & x_4 & = 6 \\
& x_1 & , & x_2 & , & x_3 & , & x_4 & \geq 0
\end{array}
$$

a. Find the values of all the variables and the corresponding objective function value.
b. Find the new basic feasible solution and objective function value obtained by making x_1 nonbasic and x_3 basic.
c. Indicate whether the reduced cost of the nonbasic variable x_3 in the original basic feasible solution in part (a) is positive or negative. Explain.

EXERCISE 5.13   Recall the linear program in Exercise 4.1 in Chapter 4.

a. Draw the feasible region and write the values of the variables next to each extreme point.
b. Put the problem in standard form and list all basic feasible solutions.

c. Identify each basic feasible solution with a corresponding extreme point.

d. Start at the extreme point in which x_1 and x_2 are 0 and perform the steps of the geometric finite-improvement algorithm in Section 5.3. Indicate the sequence of extreme points visited.

EXERCISE 5.14 Perform parts (a) to (d) in Exercise 5.13 for the following linear program:

$$\begin{array}{llll}
\text{Maximize} & x_1 + 2x_2 & & \\
\text{Subject to} & -2x_1 + x_2 \le 3 & & \text{(a)} \\
& x_1 - x_2 \le 2 & & \text{(b)} \\
& x_1, \quad x_2 \ge 0 & &
\end{array}$$

EXERCISE 5.15 Perform parts (a) to (d) in Exercise 5.13 for the following linear program: ⫫O

$$\begin{array}{llll}
\text{Maximize} & 2x_1 + 3x_2 & & \\
\text{Subject to} & -3x_1 + x_2 \le 2 & & \text{(a)} \\
& x_1 - 2x_2 \le 1 & & \text{(b)} \\
& 4x_1 - 2x_2 \le 7 & & \text{(c)} \\
& x_1, \quad x_2 \ge 0 & &
\end{array}$$

EXERCISE 5.16 Perform parts (a) to (d) in Exercise 5.13 for the linear program in Exercise 4.2 in Chapter 4.

EXERCISE 5.17 Indicate by letter which of the four bfs in the list are adjacent to the given bfs. For those that are adjacent, indicate which of the three nonbasic variables in the given bfs becomes basic and which of the two basic variables becomes nonbasic. Given bfs: $x_1 = 0$, $x_2 = 5$, $x_3 = 0$, $x_4 = 0$, and $x_5 = 1$. ⫫O

a. $x_1 = 3$, $x_2 = 0$, $x_3 = 0$, $x_4 = 0$, and $x_5 = 4$.
b. $x_1 = 1$, $x_2 = 0$, $x_3 = 2$, $x_4 = 0$, and $x_5 = 0$.
c. $x_1 = 0$, $x_2 = 0$, $x_3 = 3$, $x_4 = 2$, and $x_5 = 0$.
d. $x_1 = 0$, $x_2 = 2$, $x_3 = 1$, $x_4 = 0$, and $x_5 = 0$.

EXERCISE 5.18 Repeat Exercise 5.17 for the following given bfs: $x_1 = 1$, $x_2 = 0$, $x_3 = 1$, $x_4 = 2$, $x_5 = 0$, and $x_6 = 0$.

a. $x_1 = 0$, $x_2 = 0$, $x_3 = 1$, $x_4 = 0$, $x_5 = 4$, and $x_6 = 5$.
b. $x_1 = 3$, $x_2 = 1$, $x_3 = 5$, $x_4 = 0$, $x_5 = 0$, and $x_6 = 0$.
c. $x_1 = 3$, $x_2 = 0$, $x_3 = 6$, $x_4 = 0$, $x_5 = 0$, and $x_6 = 2$.
d. $x_1 = 1$, $x_2 = 2$, $x_3 = 0$, $x_4 = 0$, $x_5 = 0$, and $x_6 = 3$.

EXERCISE 5.19 Starting with the bfs marked with an asterisk (∗), use the reduced costs of the nonbasic variables to indicate, by letter, the sequence of bfs visited by the simplex algorithm. ⫫O

	BASIC VARIABLES		NONBASIC VARIABLES (REDUCED COST)		
∗.	x_1,	x_2	$x_3(-1)$,	$x_4\ (2)$,	$x_5(-2)$
a.	x_2,	x_3	$x_1\ (2)$,	$x_4(-1)$,	$x_5(-1)$
b.	x_4,	x_5	$x_1(-2)$,	$x_2(-1)$,	$x_3\ (0)$
c.	x_1,	x_3	$x_2(-1)$,	$x_4\ (0)$,	$x_5\ (2)$
d.	x_1,	x_4	$x_3(-1)$,	$x_2(-2)$,	$x_5\ (3)$
e.	x_3,	x_4	$x_1\ (0)$,	$x_2(-1)$,	$x_5\ (2)$

EXERCISE 5.20   Repeat Exercise 5.19 for the following:

	BASIC VARIABLES		NONBASIC VARIABLES (REDUCED COST)		
*.	x_1,	x_2	$x_3(-3)$,	$x_4\ (0)$,	$x_5\ (2)$
a.	x_2,	x_3	$x_1\ (2)$,	$x_4(-1)$,	$x_5(-1)$
b.	x_4,	x_5	$x_1(-2)$,	$x_2(-1)$,	$x_3\ (0)$
c.	x_1,	x_3	$x_2(-1)$,	$x_4\ (1)$,	$x_5(-2)$
d.	x_1,	x_4	$x_3\ (1)$,	$x_2\ (2)$,	$x_5\ (3)$
e.	x_1,	x_5	$x_2\ (0)$,	$x_3\ (2)$,	$x_4(-1)$

EXERCISE 5.21   Consider the following standard-form linear program:

$$\text{Maximize} \quad 3x_1 + x_2 - x_3 + 2x_4$$
$$\text{Subject to} \quad x_1 \qquad\ + x_3 + 2x_4 = 2$$
$$x_2 + x_3 + \ \ x_4 = 3$$
$$x_1\ ,\ x_2\ ,\ x_3\ ,\ \ x_4 \geq 0$$

a. List all basic solutions.
b. Indicate which of these are basic *feasible* solutions (bfs) and compute the corresponding value of the objective function.
c. For each bfs in part (b), indicate the ones that are adjacent to it and, for each adjacent one, indicate which nonbasic variable becomes basic; which basic variable becomes nonbasic; and whether the reduced cost of the nonbasic variable that became basic is positive or negative (Hint: Compare objective function values at the current bfs and the adjacent bfs.)

EXERCISE 5.22   Perform parts (a) to (c) in Exercise 5.21 for the following linear program:

$$\text{Maximize} \quad x_1 - 2x_2 - \ x_3 + x_4$$
$$\text{Subject to} \quad x_1 + 3x_2 + 2x_3 \qquad\ = 5$$
$$x_2 + 2x_3 + x_4 = 6$$
$$x_1\ ,\quad x_2\ ,\quad x_3\ ,\ x_4 \geq 0$$

YOU MAKE THE CALL

How does AT&T route millions of long distance calls every day? How does the company decide how best to use long distance land lines, repeater amplifiers, and satellite terminals?

Large linear programming problems present feasible sets with many extreme points to evaluate, which in turn means many computations must be made. The simplex technique, completely algebraic, lets us take a short cut. We can avoid some extreme points and thus do away with the corresponding calculations. The simplex method visits a very small fraction of the extreme points of the feasible set of solutions, and this efficient method of solving linear programming problems thus eliminates many calculations.

As powerful as the simplex method is, as linear programming problems grow to hundreds of thousands of variables our method must become even more efficient. Narendra Karmarkar, of AT&T's Bell Labs, has developed a mathematical technique for tackling certain structured large linear programming problems. Instead of starting at an extreme point, the Karmarkar method cuts through the feasible region.

As AT&T turns to management science for solving its routing problems, Dr. Tom Cook, Vice President of American Airlines Decision Technologies Divisions, addresses a second industry application. What happens when major weather problems disrupt airports? Many planes and crews are in the wrong place at the wrong time, and a linear programming model must be run immediately to minimize both the cost of the disruption and passenger inconvenience. The simplex method is not efficient for this large a problem. American Airlines is now experimenting with the new KORBX code, sold by AT&T, which features Karmarkar's algorithm. (Total running time: 2:41.)

Questions on the Video

1. What limits geometry-based solution techniques?

2. What is the basic difference between the simplex method and Karmarkar's method?

Beyond the Video

1. From Chapter 3, on applications of linear programming models, identify a homework problem that shows why the simplex method is needed for its solution.

2. Describe in words a resource allocation problem that your university or college may face in coordinating classrooms, students, and instructors. Can the simplex method solve this problem?

Practical Considerations

1. A rule of thumb for the simplex method is that if the size of the problem (n variables times m constraints) increases by a factor of p, the solution time increases by a factor of p^2. Consider a linear programming problem with 1,000 variables and 200 constraints that takes just 2 seconds to solve. How long would it take to solve a similar problem with 300,000 variables and 5,000 constraints?

2. There are many versions of the simplex method. A host of different programs offer various "bells and whistles" for simplex method programs written for main frame computers and personal computers. Look through a current copy of *OR/MS Today* and check the advertisements for several versions. What differences and similarities among programs do you find? What is the price range for these programs?

"For All Practical Purposes," from *The Consortium for Mathematics and Its Applications* (Arlington, MA:1986), Program 2.

LINEAR PROGRAMMING: USING THE COMPUTER

. . . .

*I*n Chapter 3, American Steel Company (ASC) was searching for the plan that would minimize the cost of buying ore, making steel, and shipping its products to its international clients in Korea, Japan, Taiwan, and Mexico. A consulting team called in by ASC management has used its computer package to solve the linear program developed to find that best plan. Before the consulting team can leave the boardroom, management fires off some additional questions. Should ASC expand its steel-making facilities? By how much? Does ASC accept the special order from Japan or from Korea?

The Case Study in this chapter examines how decision makers use the computer to solve problems with many variables and how to interpret the computer's results to formulate the best plan.

Now that you understand how the simplex algorithm solves linear programming problems, you can rely on the computer to perform the detailed computations. As you learned in Chapters 4 and 5, the simplex algorithm not only produces the optimal solution, but also provides additional economic information useful in the decision-making process, such as the values of the shadow prices, reduced costs, slack variables, and sensitivity ranges. All modern linear-programming computer packages provide this information, which you will learn to interpret in this chapter.

■ 6.1 THE EXAMPLE OF CASE CHEMICALS

Recall the problem of Case Chemicals in Section 4.1, in which the two solvents CS-01 and CS-02 are produced at its Cleveland plant. The plant operates 40 hours per week and employs five full-time and two part-time workers in their Blending Department. Each part-timer works 15 hours per week. The products, once blended, are refined in the Purification Department, which employs six full-time workers and one part-time worker, who puts in 10 hours per week. The hours required in the Blending and Purification Departments needed to produce each of the solvents are provided in Table 6.1.

TABLE 6.1 *Blending and Purification Requirements (hr/1000 gal)*		
	CS-01	CS-02
Blending	2	1
Purification	1	2

Case Chemicals has a virtually unlimited supply of raw materials needed to produce the two solvents and can sell any amount of CS-01, but the demand for the more specialized product CS-02 is limited to at most 120,000 gallons per week. The Accounting Department estimates a profit margin of $0.30 per gallon for CS-01 and $0.50 per gallon for CS-02. The cost of labor and machines in both departments are fixed, so they are not considered in the computation of the profit margin.

As Production-Planning Manager, you have developed the following mathematical model whose solution can help determine the production plan that maximizes the weekly profit margin in hundreds of dollars without exceeding the 230 hours of labor available in the Blending Department and the 250 hours of labor available in the Purification Department. The variables x_1 and x_2 are the number of thousands of gallons of CS-01 and CS-02 to produce, respectively.

$$
\begin{array}{lrll}
\text{Maximize} & 3x_1 + 5x_2 & & \\
\text{Subject to} & 2x_1 + x_2 \le 230 & & (1) \\
& x_1 + 2x_2 \le 250 & & (2) \\
& x_2 \le 120 & & (3) \\
& x_1 \quad\quad \ge 0 & & (4) \\
& x_2 \ge 0 & & (5)
\end{array}
$$

Linear Program
EX4_1.DAT

The first step in using any linear programming package to solve a formulated problem is to enter the data in a manner that the specific computer package can read.

```
Title : Case Chemicals
Number of variables        :           2
Number of constraints      :           3
Starting solution given    :          NO
Objective type (MAX/MIN)   :          MAX
ROW LABEL          X1      X2 CONST TYPE      RHS       RANGE
OBJ COEFF          3.      5.      XXXX      XXXX      XXXX
CONSTR    1        2.      1.      <=        230.         .
CONSTR    2        1.      2.      <=        250.         .
CONSTR    3        0.      1.      <=        120.         .
VARBL TYPE        POS     POS      XXXX      XXXX      XXXX
LOWR BOUND         .       .       XXXX      XXXX      XXXX
UPPR BOUND         .       .       XXXX      XXXX      XXXX
INIT SOLN          0.      0.      XXXX      XXXX      XXXX
```

FIGURE 6.1 STORM Input Data for Case Chemicals.

Although some industry standards exist, most packages have their own particular *format* in which these data must be entered. You will need to learn how to enter the data for the linear programming package you are using. This has been done for the STORM package using the data in the problem formulation for Case Chemicals just given, as shown in Figure 6.1 (ignore the last three rows and the last column.) You will notice that, for the STORM package, the nonnegativity constraints (4) and (5) are included in the row labeled VARBL TYPE by declaring both variables as POS (positive). You need not convert the problem to standard form—STORM (and most computer packages) does that automatically.

This problem has few data. In larger problems, it can be a time-consuming task to collect and enter the data and verify that all the values have been typed in their correct locations. In any event, once these data are entered, you can instruct the computer to solve the problem. The results are presented in Section 6.2, along with an explanation of the values obtained from the output.

■ 6.2 INTERPRETING THE OPTIMAL SOLUTION

The computer performed the steps of the simplex algorithm, as described in Section 5.5, to solve the problem of Case Chemicals presented in Section 6.1. The results are given in Figure 6.2.

Recall that the simplex algorithm is designed to solve a problem in *standard form*. Because the input was not in standard form, the computer had to add three slack variables corresponding to the three inequality constraints. The output in the section labeled A pertains to the two original variables. The output in B pertains to the three slack variables. The output in C pertains to the three inequality constraints.

6.2.1 Interpreting the Values of the Original Variables

The column of output labeled "Value" in section A indicates that the optimal solution to this problem is to produce 70 thousand gallons of CS-01 and 90 thousand gallons of CS-02. The column in section A labeled "Cost" provides the original profit coefficients of these two chemicals (3 and 5, respectively). The column labeled "Red. cost" pertains to the reduced costs of these two variables. However, as you may recall from Section

```
                        Case Chemicals
                 OPTIMAL SOLUTION - DETAILED REPORT


               Variable        Value        Cost    Red. cost    Status
  A ->    1        X1        70.0000      3.0000     0.0000      Basic
          2        X2        90.0000      5.0000     0.0000      Basic


          Slack Variables
          3 CONSTR   1        0.0000      0.0000    -0.3333  Lower bound
  B ->    4 CONSTR   2        0.0000      0.0000    -2.3333  Lower bound
          5 CONSTR   3       30.0000      0.0000     0.0000      Basic


Objective Function Value = 660
          Constraint  Type        RHS          Slack    Shadow price


          1   CONSTR   1   <=    230.0000      0.0000       0.3333
  C ->    2   CONSTR   2   <=    250.0000      0.0000       2.3333
          3   CONSTR   3   <=    120.0000     30.0000       0.0000
```

FIGURE 6.2 STORM Optimal-Solution Report for the Problem of Case Chemicals.

5.5.2, reduced costs have meaning only for *nonbasic* variables. From the output in the column labeled "Status" in section A, you can see that both variables x_1 and x_2 are *basic*, and so the reduced costs are 0 and have no relevant meaning.

6.2.2 Interpreting the Values of the Slack Variables

The output in section B contains similar information pertaining to the three slack variables. In particular, from the column labeled "Value," the optimal values of the three slack variables (whose names are those of the corresponding three constraints) are 0, 0, and 30, respectively. What do these values mean in the context of this problem?

Recall that the slack variable for constraint (1) represents the number of unused hours of labor in the Blending Department. Having a value of 0 for this variable in the optimal solution in Figure 6.2 means that there is no slack time—all available hours in the Blending Department are used. Similarly, all hours in the Purification Department are used because the value of its slack variable is also 0. The value of 30 for the third slack variable, corresponding to the constraint $x_2 \leq 120$, indicates that there is a slack of 30 thousand gallons of CS-02—that is, the amount of x_2 to produce is 30 thousand less than the limit of 120 thousand gallons.

Consider to the column labeled "Cost" in Section B. The objective function coefficients of these (and all) slack variables are 0, as indicated. The column labeled "Red. cost" provides reduced costs for the slack variables. For example, the reduced costs for the first slack variable is −0.3333. Recalling the meaning of a reduced cost, as described in Section 5.5, this value of −0.3333 indicates that each unit increase in the value of this slack variable, while keeping all other nonbasic variables at value 0, results in a *decrease* of 0.3333 hundred dollars ($33.33) of profit in the objective function. Because a unit of increase in this slack variable corresponds to using 1 hour less of labor in the Blending Department, using 1 hour less decreases the profits by $33.33.

Similarly, for the second slack variable, the reduced cost of -2.3333 means that each unit increase in the second slack variable, while keeping all other nonbasic variables at value 0, results in a *decrease* of 2.3333 hundred dollars ($233.33) of profit in the objective function. Because a unit of increase in this slack variable corresponds to using 1 hour less of labor in the Purification Department, using 1 hour less decreases the profits by $233.33.

Recall that reduced costs have meaning only for the *nonbasic* variables, such as the first two slack variables, which, as indicated in the STORM output by the term "Lower bound" in the column labeled "Status," are nonbasic. In contrast, the third slack variable is basic (see the column labeled "Status"), and so its reduced cost of 0 has no relevant meaning.

The final row of section B indicates that the optimal production plan results in a profit of $66,000—that is, $3x_1 + 5x_2 = 3(70) + 5(90) = 660$ (hundred dollars).

6.2.3 Interpreting the Output Pertaining to the Constraints

Now, consider the output in section C of Figure 6.2. Each row contains information pertaining to one of the three inequality constraints. The column label "RHS" provides the values of the right-hand side of each constraint as entered in the data. The column labeled "Slack" provides the values of the slack variables whose meanings have already been discussed. Of special interest, however, are the values in the last column labeled "Shadow price." As discussed in Section 4.3.2, the shadow price is the value of the resource pertaining to that constraint. For example, the shadow price of 0.3333 for the first constraint is the additional profit (in hundreds of dollars) that could be obtained by having an additional hour of blending time. That is, the value of 1 additional hour of blending time is worth 0.3333 hundred dollars ($33.33). Similarly, for the second constraint, the shadow price of 2.3333 indicates that each additional hour of purification time increases the profits by 2.3333 hundred dollars ($233.33). Finally, observe that the shadow price of the third constraint is 0. This means that increasing the limit of 120 on the amount of CS-02 produced will result in *no* additional profit. This makes sense, as the amount of 90 thousand gallons of CS-02 used in the current optimal solution is already below the specified limit of 120 thousand gallons.

■ 6.3 INTERPRETING SENSITIVITY OUTPUT FOR CHANGES IN ONE PARAMETER

As you learned in Section 4.3, the simplex algorithm provides much more information than just the optimal solution. With regard to the problem of Case Chemicals, the following sensitivity questions arose:

1. Due to the recent competition in the market for CS-01, management has decided to decrease the sales price of CS-01 by $25 per thousand gallons. How should the production plan for CS-01 and CS-02 change?
2. What happens to the profit margin of Case Chemicals if each of the two part-time employees in the Blending Department works 10 hours per week instead of 15?
3. What happens to the profit margin if one of the part-time employees in the Blending Department becomes a full-time employee and the second one is let go?
4. What happens to the weekly profit if the Blending Department is reduced to two full-time workers and one part-time worker at 30 hours per week?
5. What happens to the profit margin when one additional full-time worker is hired in the Purification Department?
6. What happens to the weekly profit margin if the Purification Department is expanded to nine purifiers with nine full-time workers?

In Section 4.3 these questions are answered using a graphical approach. In this section, they are answered using the output from the STORM computer program used to solve the problem of Case Chemicals. The appropriate output, called a *sensitivity analysis report*, is given in Figure 6.3.

The first question deals with a decrease of $25 in the sales price of CS-01, with a corresponding decrease in the profit margin of CS-01 from $300 to $275. In other words, you want to know what happens to the previous optimal solution of $x_1 = 70$ and $x_2 = 90$ when the coefficient of x_1 in the objective function decreases from 3 to 2.75. The first part of the output report in Figure 6.3, labeled "SENSITIVITY ANALYSIS OF COST COEFFICIENTS," provides the answer. For x_1, the original objective function coefficient is 3.0, as indicated in the column labeled "Current Coeff." The next two columns provide the minimum and maximum values that this coefficient can have and not change the current optimal solution (of $x_1 = 70$ and $x_2 = 90$). In this example, as long as the profit coefficient of x_1 remains in the range of 2.5 to 10.0, which is the allowable minimum value and allowable maximum value, respectively—and as long as all other coefficients remain unchanged—the optimal solution of $x_1 = 70$ and $x_2 = 90$ does not change. A value outside this range, however, may cause a change in the optimal solution. Because the new value of 2.75 for this coefficient is inside the range 2.5 to 10.0, the current solution remains optimal. However, the profit margin changes:

$$\text{New profit margin} = (2.75 * x_1) + (5 * x_2)$$
$$= (2.75 * 70) + (5 * 90)$$
$$= 642.50$$

The second row in Figure 6.3 corresponds to x_2. You can see that as long as the objective function coefficient of x_2 remains in the range of 1.5 to 6.0, the current optimal solution of $x_1 = 70$ and $x_2 = 90$ remains optimal.

All the remaining sensitivity questions pertain to a change in the right-hand-side value of a particular constraint. For example, the second question refers to a decrease in the right-hand side of the first constraint from its original value of 230 to 220. The second part of the report in Figure 6.3 labeled "SENSITIVITY ANALYSIS OF RIGHT-HAND-SIDE VALUES" helps answer this question.

Recall from Section 4.3 that the shadow price of a constraint represents the amount of change in the objective function per unit of increase in the right-hand-side (rhs) value. For the first constraint, which restricts the total hours spent in the Blending Department to less than 230, the shadow price of 0.3333 is given in section

```
                        Case Chemicals
              SENSITIVITY ANALYSIS OF COST COEFFICIENTS
                               Current     Allowable     Allowable
                  Variable     Coeff.      Minimum       Maximum
        1            X1        3.0000       2.5000        10.0000
        2            X2        5.0000       1.5000         6.0000
              SENSITIVITY ANALYSIS OF RIGHT-HAND-SIDE VALUES
                               Current     Allowable     Allowable
        Constraint  Type       Value       Minimum       Maximum
   1    CONSTR   1   <=       230.0000     140.0000       500.0000
   2    CONSTR   2   <=       250.0000     115.0000       295.0000
   3    CONSTR   3   <=       120.0000      90.0000       Infinity
```

FIGURE 6.3 STORM Sensitivity Analysis Report.

C of Figure 6.2. However, *that shadow price is applicable only if the right-hand-side value remains within a certain range.* Indeed, that range is provided in the second part of the report in Figure 6.3 in the columns labeled "Allowable Minimum" and "Allowable Maximum." As long as the blending hour limit is between 140 and 500, the shadow price of 0.3333 is valid. This means that each additional hour of labor in the Blending Department from the current level of 230 hours up to 500 hours increases the profit margin by $33.33. Alternatively, each decreased hour from the current level of 230 hours down to 140 hours decreases the profit margin by $33.33. This information is summarized in Figure 6.4(a).

You can use this information to answer the second question as follows. For the first constraint corresponding to the Blending Department, the new rhs value of 220

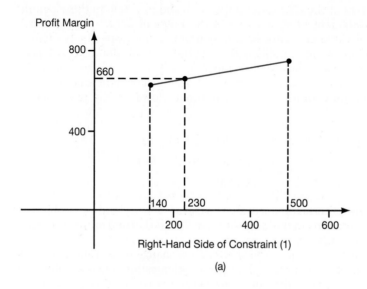

(a)

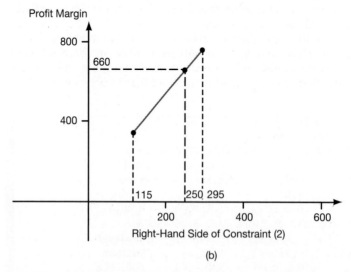

(b)

FIGURE 6.4 Sensitivity Analysis Graphs for (a) Constraint (1) and (b) Constraint (2).

is within the range of 140 to 500, so the shadow price of 0.3333 is valid. The new optimal objective function value corresponding to 220 available hours in the Blending Department is

$$\left\{\begin{array}{l}\text{New objective} \\ \text{function} \\ \text{value}\end{array}\right\} = \left\{\begin{array}{l}\text{Original objective} \\ \text{function value}\end{array}\right\} + \left\{\begin{array}{l}\text{Shadow} \\ \text{price}\end{array}\right\} * \left\{\begin{array}{l}\text{Change in rhs} \\ \text{value}\end{array}\right\}$$

$$= \quad 660 \quad + \quad 0.3333 \quad * \quad (-10)$$

$$= \quad 656.667$$

So, in cutting back from 15 to 10 hours for each part-time worker, the weekly profit margin decreases from \$66,000 to \$65,667.

The third question pertains to an increase in the rhs value of the first constraint, from its original value of 230 to 240. Using the same part of the output report in Figure 6.3, you can see that this new value is within the range 140 to 500, and, therefore, the shadow price of 0.3333 remains valid. The new profit margin is

$$\left\{\begin{array}{l}\text{New objective} \\ \text{function} \\ \text{value}\end{array}\right\} = \left\{\begin{array}{l}\text{Original objective} \\ \text{function value}\end{array}\right\} + \left\{\begin{array}{l}\text{Shadow} \\ \text{price}\end{array}\right\} * \left\{\begin{array}{l}\text{Change in rhs} \\ \text{value}\end{array}\right\}$$

$$= \quad 660 \quad + \quad 0.3333 \quad * \quad (10)$$

$$= \quad 663.333$$

Making one of the part-time workers full-time and letting the other go result in increasing the weekly profit margin from \$66,000 to \$66,333.

The fourth question deals with a decrease in the rhs of the first constraint, from its current value of 230 to 110. Looking at the same part of the report in Figure 6.3, you can see that this value of 110 is outside the range of 140 to 500. The shadow price of 0.3333 is no longer applicable. To answer this question, you will need to use output pertaining to parametric analysis of the rhs values, as discussed in Section 6.5.

The fifth question pertains to a change in the rhs value of the second constraint in the Purification Department. That value is increased from 250 to 290. Looking at the next line of the report in Figure 6.3, you can see that this new value of 290 is within the range of 115 to 295 for the second constraint. Therefore, the shadow price of 2.3333 from Figure 6.2 remains valid. The value of the optimal objective function changes linearly in this range, as shown in Figure 6.4 (b). Hence, the new profit margin is

$$\left\{\begin{array}{l}\text{New objective} \\ \text{function} \\ \text{value}\end{array}\right\} = \left\{\begin{array}{l}\text{Original objective} \\ \text{function value}\end{array}\right\} + \left\{\begin{array}{l}\text{Shadow} \\ \text{price}\end{array}\right\} * \left\{\begin{array}{l}\text{Change in rhs} \\ \text{value}\end{array}\right\}$$

$$= \quad 660 \quad + \quad 2.3333 \quad * \quad (40)$$

$$= \quad 753.333$$

Hiring an additional full-time worker in the Purification Department increases the weekly profit margin from \$66,000 to \$75,333.

The final question pertains to an increase in the rhs of the second constraint from its current value of 250 to 360. However, this value of 360 is outside the range of 115 to 295, as indicated in the report in Figure 6.3, so the shadow price of 2.3333 is not applicable. To answer this question, you will need to use output pertaining to a parametric analysis of the rhs values, as discussed in Section 6.5.

■ 6.4 USING SENSITIVITY OUTPUT FOR MULTIPLE CHANGES IN THE PARAMETERS: THE 100% RULE

Each of the sensitivity questions in Section 6.3 affected only one value in the model of Case Chemicals: either a single objective function coefficient or else a single rhs value of a constraint. Managers are often concerned with what happens to the optimal solution and/or objective function value when *more* than one coefficient changes simultaneously. Consider these questions:

1. Due to recent competition in the market for CS-01, management has decided to decrease the sales price of CS-01 by $25 per thousand gallons. At the same time, management wants to increase the price of CS-02 by $20 per thousand gallons because it has become scarce in the market. How should the production plan for CS-01 and CS-02 change?

2. What happens to the profit margin if one of the part-time employees in the Blending Department becomes a full-time employee and the second one is transferred to the Purification Department?

3. What happens to the optimal solution and the profit margin if *all* the changes in questions 1 and 2 are implemented?

100% rules
Rules that enable you to use sensitivity reports when more than one of the data values in a mathematical model are changed at the same time.

Observe that each of these sensitivity questions results in changes in more than one value in the original model of Case Chemicals. In general, to answer these questions requires changing all affected values in the model and obtaining the new solution. However, you can still use the sensitivity reports to answer these questions if these changes satisfy either one of the following two **100% rules**.

➡ **KEY FEATURES**

The 100% Rule for Changes in the Objective Function Coefficients

If all the changes affect *only* the values of the objective function coefficients, then follow these steps:

a. For each affected coefficient, compute the ratio of the amount by which the value increases (decreases) to the maximum amount of increase (decrease) allowed within the sensitivity range.

b. Add the amounts in (a) and multiply the result by 100 to obtain a total percentage change.

If the total computed in (b) does not exceed 100%, then the current solution remains optimal, although the optimal objective function value changes according to the changes in the affected coefficients.

To see if this rule can be used to answer question 1, observe that this question affects only the values of the objective function coefficients—that is, the question deals with a decrease of $25 in the sales price of CS-01 and an increase in the profit margin of CS-02 by $20. This results in a simultaneous decrease in the profit margin of CS-01 from $300 to $275 and an increase in the profit margin of CS-02 from $500 to $520. You want to know what happens to the previous optimal solution of $x_1 = 70$ and $x_2 = 90$ when the coefficient of x_1 in the objective function decreases from 3 to 2.75 and that of x_2 simultaneously increases from 5 to 5.2.

According to the 100% rule, you must use these changes together with the sensitivity ranges of [2.5, 10] for the objective function coefficient of x_1 and that of [1.5, 6] for that of x_2 given in the sensitivity reports in Figure 6.3 to compute:

$$\text{Ratio for } x_1 = \frac{\text{amount of decrease}}{\text{maximum allowable decrease}}$$
$$= \frac{3 - 2.75}{3 - 2.5}$$
$$= \frac{0.25}{0.50}$$
$$= 0.5$$

$$\text{Ratio for } x_2 = \frac{\text{amount of increase}}{\text{maximum allowable increase}}$$
$$= \frac{5.2 - 5}{6 - 5}$$
$$= \frac{0.2}{1}$$
$$= 0.2$$

Adding these two ratios and multiplying by 100 yields a total change of 70%. Because this value is less than 100%, according to the 100% rule the optimal solution of $x_1 = 70$ and $x_2 = 90$ does not change. However, the profit margin changes:

$$\text{New profit margin} = (2.75 * x_1) + (5.2 * x_2)$$
$$= (2.75 * 70) + (5.2 * 90)$$
$$= 660.50$$

In other words, implementing these price changes does not affect the optimal production plan of 70,000 gallons of CS-01 and 90,000 gallons of CS-02. However, the new weekly profit margin increases slightly to $66,050 from $66,000.

KEY FEATURES
The 100% Rule for Changes in the Right-Hand-Side Values

If all the changes affect *only* the values of the right-hand sides of the constraints, then follow these steps:

a. For each affected value, compute the ratio of the amount by which the value increases (decreases) to the maximum amount of increase (decrease) allowed within the sensitivity range.

b. Add the amounts in (a) and multiply the result by 100 to obtain a total percentage change.

If the total computed in (b) does not exceed 100%, then the change in the optimal objective function value is the sum of the individual changes due to each affected constraint using the corresponding shadow prices. Note, however, that the optimal solution itself *does* change.

To see if this rule can be used to answer question 2, observe that this question affects only the values of the rhs of the constraints—that is, the question deals with an increase of 10 available hours in the Blending Department and an increase of 40 hours in the Purification Department. You want to know what happens to the optimal objective function value when the rhs value of constraint (1) increases from 230 to 240 and that of constraint (2) increases from 250 to 290.

According to the 100% rule, you must use these changes together with the sensitivity ranges of [140, 500] for constraint (1) and [115, 295] for constraint (2) given in the sensitivity reports in Figure 6.3 to compute:

$$\text{Ratio for constraint (1)} = \frac{\text{amount of increase}}{\text{maximum allowable increase}}$$
$$= \frac{240 - 230}{500 - 230}$$
$$= \frac{10}{270}$$
$$= 0.0370$$

$$\text{Ratio for constraint (2)} = \frac{\text{amount of increase}}{\text{maximum allowable increase}}$$
$$= \frac{290 - 250}{295 - 250}$$
$$= \frac{40}{45}$$
$$= 0.8889$$

Adding these two ratios and multiplying by 100 yields a total change of 92.59%. This value is less than 100%, so according to the 100% rule the change in the optimal objective function value is obtained using the shadow prices of 0.3333 for constraint (1) and 2.3333 for constraint (2) given in the report in Figure 6.2, as follows:

$$\text{Change from constraint (1)} = (\text{change in rhs value}) * (\text{shadow price})$$
$$= \quad (240 - 230) \quad * \quad 0.3333$$
$$= 3.333$$
$$\text{Change from constraint (2)} = (\text{change in rhs value}) * (\text{shadow price})$$
$$= \quad (290 - 250) \quad * \quad 2.3333$$
$$= 93.332$$

Thus, the total change in the optimal objective function value is $3.333 + 93.332 = 96.665$, and so the new optimal objective function value is

$$\text{New profit margin} = \text{old profit margin} + \text{change}$$
$$= \quad 660 \quad + 96.665$$
$$= 756.665$$

In other words, implementing all labor changes results in a new increased weekly profit margin of $75,667 instead of $66,000. If you decide to implement these changes, then, to obtain the new production plan, you will need to solve the model with the new rhs values.

Finally, recall the third question: You want to know the effect of changing both the prices and the available labor hours at the same time. Because these changes simultaneously affect both the objective function coefficients as well as the rhs values of the constraints, the 100% rule does not apply. Instead, you will need to change those coefficients to their new values and solve the model again. The result is shown

```
                        Case Chemicals
                 OPTIMAL SOLUTION - DETAILED REPORT
           Variable        Value       Cost     Red. cost   Status
    1           X1        63.3333     2.7500      0.0000     Basic
    2           X2       113.3333     5.2000      0.0000     Basic
    Slack Variables
    3    CONSTR   1        0.0000     0.0000     -0.1000 Lower bound
    4    CONSTR   2        0.0000     0.0000     -2.5500 Lower bound
    5    CONSTR   3        6.6667     0.0000      0.0000     Basic
    Objective Function Value = 763.5
         Constraint  Type      RHS          Slack      Shadow price
    1    CONSTR   1    <=    240.0000       0.0000         0.1000
    2    CONSTR   2    <=    290.0000       0.0000         2.5500
    3    CONSTR   3    <=    120.0000       6.6667         0.0000
```

FIGURE 6.5 STORM Optimal-Solution Report for the Revised Problem of Case Chemicals.

in Figure 6.5. As you can see, the new optimal production plan for Case Chemicals is to produce 63,333 gallons of CS-01 and 113,333 gallons of CS-02, which results in a weekly profit margin of $76,350.

◼ 6.5 INTERPRETING PARAMETRIC ANALYSIS REPORTS

In Section 6.3, the sensitivity analysis report of the right-hand side for the problem of Case Chemicals indicates that the shadow price of 0.3333 for constraint (1) is valid as long as that rhs value remains within the range 140 to 500. Likewise, the shadow price of 2.3333 for constraint (2) is valid as long as the rhs value remains within the range 115 to 295. However, as is the case with questions 4 and 6 in Section 6.3, what happens if a coefficient is changed to a value outside these ranges?

Parametric analysis of the rhs, as described graphically in Section 4.3, provides the answer. The same information is provided in a *parametric analysis report*, as in the STORM outputs shown in Figure 6.6. In Figure 6.6(a), section A indicates what happens when the rhs of the first constraint is increased from its current value of 230. Section B indicates what happens when the rhs is decreased from its current value of 230. Similarly, in Figure 6.6(b), section A indicates what happens when the rhs value of constraint (2) is increased from its current value of 250. Section B indicates what happens when the rhs is decreased from its current value of 250.

The first two lines in section A of Figure 6.6(a) confirm what you have already learned from the sensitivity analysis report—that is, as the rhs value increases from 230 to 500, the optimal objective function value increases from 660 to 750 at the rate of the shadow price of 0.333. (The interpretation of the remaining columns labeled "Leave" and "Enter" are beyond the scope of this book.) The next two lines indicate that an increase in the rhs value beyond 500 has no effect on the optimal objective function value because the shadow price in this range is 0.000.

Section B provides similar information on a decrease in the value of the rhs. The first two lines state that as this rhs value decreases from 230 to 140, the optimal objective function value decreases from 660 to 630 at the rate of the shadow price of 0.333. The next two lines indicate that as this rhs value is further decreased from 140 to 120, the optimal objective function value decreases from 630 to 600 at the rate of the new shadow price of 1.500. The next two lines specify that as the rhs value decreases from 120 to 0, the optimal objective function value decreases from 600 to 0 at a rate of

```
            PARAMETRIC ANALYSIS OF RIGHT-HAND-SIDE VALUE - CONSTR   1
            COEF = 230.000   LWR LIMIT = -Infinity   UPR LIMIT = Infinity
            ----------- Range -------      Shadow    ---- Variable ----
                       From          To     Price      Leave       Enter

          ┌ RHS    230.000     500.000      0.333         X2  SLACK    1
          │ Obj    660.000     750.000
          │
   A ->   │
          │ RHS    500.000    Infinity      0.000   ---- No change  ----
          └ Obj    750.000     750.000

          ┌ RHS    230.000     140.000      0.333  SLACK    3  SLACK    2
          │ Obj    660.000     630.000
          │
          │ RHS    140.000     120.000      1.500         X1  SLACK    3
          │ Obj    630.000     600.000
          │
   B ->   │ RHS    120.000       0.000      5.000         X2
          │ Obj    600.000       0.000
          │
          └ RHS      0.000    -Infinity  ---- Infeasible in this range ----
```

(a)

```
            PARAMETRIC ANALYSIS OF RIGHT-HAND-SIDE VALUE - CONSTR   2
            COEF = 250.000   LWR LIMIT = -Infinity   UPR LIMIT = Infinity
            ----------- Range -------      Shadow    ---- Variable ----
                       From          To     Price      Leave       Enter

          ┌ RHS    250.000     295.000      2.333  SLACK    3  SLACK    2
          │ Obj    660.000     765.000
          │
   A ->   │
          │ RHS    295.000    Infinity      0.000   ---- No change  ----
          └ Obj    765.000     765.000

          ┌ RHS    250.000     115.000      2.333         X2  SLACK  1
          │ Obj    660.000     345.000
          │
   B ->   │ RHS    115.000       0.000      3.000         X1
          │ Obj    345.000       0.000
          │
          └ RHS      0.000    -Infinity  ---- Infeasible in this range ----
```

(b)

FIGURE 6.6 Parametric Analysis Report for (a) Constraint (1) and (b) Constraint (2).

the new shadow price of 5.0. The final line indicates that a negative value of this rhs value results in an infeasible problem.

A graph can summarize this information. In Figure 6.7(a), the horizontal axis represents the value of the rhs value of constraint (1) and the vertical axis represents the corresponding optimal value of the objective function. A similar graph for constraint (2) is presented in Figure 6.7(b).

The graph together with the parametric analysis report are used to help the Manager answer the fourth question posed in Section 6.3: What happens to the optimal weekly profit margin if the Blending Department is reduced to two full-time workers and one part-time worker at 30 hours per week? This question pertains to a decrease in the rhs of constraint (1) from its current value of 230 to 110. Locating this value in section B in Figure 6.6(a) and also in Figure 6.7(a), you can see that 110 lies in the range of 120 to 0, where a shadow price of 5.000 is applicable. In this range, the objective function value decreases from 600 to 0 at the rate of 5.000. Therefore, the new profit margin is

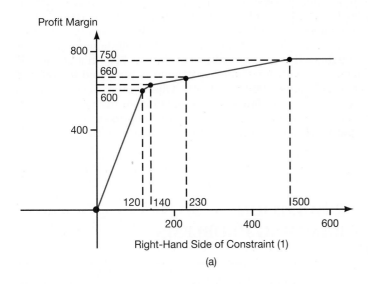

(a)

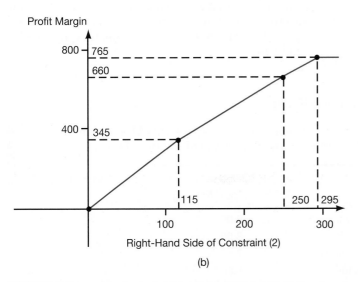

(b)

FIGURE 6.7 Parametric Analysis Diagram for (a) Constraint (1) and (b) Constraint (2).

$$\text{New profit margin} = (\text{profit at 120}) - (\text{shadow price}) *$$

$$(\text{number of hours below 120})$$

$$= 600 - 5 * 10$$

$$= 550$$

So, reducing the number of employees in the Blending Department to two full-time employees and one part-time at 30 hours reduces the weekly profit margin from $66,000 to $55,000. Keep in mind that as the right-hand-side value changes, the production plan also changes. If you decide to implement this change in Blending Department, then, to obtain the new production plan, you will need to solve the model with the new rhs value.

You can conduct a similar analysis on the second constraint. For example, recall question 6 in Section 6.3: What happens to the weekly profit margin if the Purification Department is expanded to nine purifiers with nine full-time workers? This question pertains to an increase in the rhs of constraint (2) from its original value of 250 to 360. Looking at the report for constraint (2) in Figure 6.6(b) and the corresponding graph in Figure 6.7(b), you can see that the new rhs value of 360 is within the range 295 to infinity. In this range, the applicable shadow price is 0. Therefore, the value of the objective function throughout this range remains constant at 765. In summary, if the number of hours of labor in the Purification Department is increased to 360, the weekly profit margin increases from $66,000 to $76,500. Observe that the same profit margin of $76,500 can be realized with as few as 295 hours of labor in the Purification Department. Management can achieve this value with 7 full-time workers and one part-time worker at 15 hours per week. Thus, it may not be necessary to hire 9 full-time workers.

■ 6.6 COMPUTER SOLUTION TO LINEAR PROGRAMMING PROBLEMS USING LINDO

In this section, the linear programming package LINDO is used to solve and analyze another linear programming problem. In Section 6.7, the same problem is solved again with the package EXCEL. The objective is to show that these and most other linear programming software packages provide virtually the same information in terms of the optimal solution, sensitivity, and parametric reports.

6.6.1 Problem Definition

IMC is a money-management company considering investing $100,000 in one or more of the following securities with the anticipated rate of return as follows:

INVESTMENT	PROJECTED RATE OF RETURN (%)
Eastern Oil preferred stock	9.00
Alaskan Oil common stock	8.00
American Steel common stock	7.00
Cleveland municipal bonds	6.00

The management of IMC has imposed the following investment guidelines:

1. Investment in municipal bonds should be at least $20,000.
2. Investment in municipal bonds should not exceed 20% of the total investment in stocks, plus $50,000.
3. Total investment in stocks should not be more than 60% of the total investment.
4. Total investment should not exceed the available funds.

As Portfolio Manager, you want to determine the investment strategy that maximizes the total expected yearly return without violating any of the investment guidelines.

6.6.2 Problem Formulation

Using the formulation techniques from Chapter 2, you are led to define the following four decision variables:

E-OIL = the number of dollars to invest in Eastern Oil preferred stock

A-OIL = the number of dollars to invest in Alaskan Oil common stock

A-STL = the number of dollars to invest in American Steel common stock

CL-MB = the number of dollars to invest in Cleveland municipal bonds

Combining the objective function of maximizing the total expected return and the four constraints as given in the investment guidelines results in the following linear programming problem:

Maximize	0.09E-OIL $+ 0.08$A-OIL $+ 0.07$A-STL $+ 0.06$CL-MB	(1)
Subject to	CL-MB $\geq$ 20000	(2)
	-0.2E-OIL $- 0.2$A-OIL $- 0.2$A-STL $+$ CL-MB $\leq$ 50000	(3)
	0.4E-OIL $+ 0.4$A-OIL $+ 0.4$A-STL $- 0.6$CL-MB $\leq$ 0	(4)
	E-OIL $+$ A-OIL $+$ A-STL $+$ CL-MB $\leq$ 100000	(5)
	E-OIL , A-OIL , A-STL , CL-MB $\geq$ 0	

Linear Program
IMC.DAT

Constraint (4), corresponding to the third investment guideline, is obtained as follows:

Total dollars in stocks ≤ 0.60(total investment)

E-OIL $+$ A-OIL $+$ A-STL ≤ 0.60(E-OIL $+$ A-OIL $+$ A-STL $+$ CL-MB)

Bringing all the variables to the left-hand side results in constraint (4) as given in the problem formulation.

6.6.3 Computer Solution

This investment model can be solved using any available linear programming software package such as LINDO. The first step is to enter the data from the model in the format required by LINDO. As illustrated in Figure 6.8(a), type the problem in precisely the same format as in the given formulation.

You can now instruct the computer to use LINDO to solve the problem by typing the command GO. The solution, shown in Figure 6.8(b), is obtained by typing the command SOLUTION. The first part of the report provides the optimal values of the original variables. The second part provides information pertaining to the constraints.

```
MAX       0.09 EOIL + 0.08 AOIL + 0.07 ASTL + 0.06 CLMB
SUBJECT TO
        CLMB >=    20000
        - 0.2 EOIL - 0.2 AOIL - 0.2 ASTL + CLMB <=    50000
        0.4 EOIL + 0.4 AOIL + 0.4 ASTL - 0.6 CLMB <=      0
              EOIL + AOIL + ASTL + CLMB <=    100000
END
```
(a)

```
LP OPTIMUM FOUND AT STEP        3
        OBJECTIVE FUNCTION VALUE
        1)      7800.0000
   VARIABLE         VALUE         REDUCED COST
      EOIL      60000.000000          .000000
      AOIL          .000000          .010000
      ASTL          .000000          .020000
      CLMB      40000.000000          .000000
      ROW    SLACK OR SURPLUS     DUAL PRICES
       2)      20000.000000          .000000
       3)      22000.000000          .000000
       4)          .000000          .030000
       5)          .000000          .078000
NO. ITERATIONS=        3
```
(b)

FIGURE 6.8 (a) LINDO Input and (b) LINDO Optimal Report for the Problem of IMC.

On the basis of the first part, your recommendation to IMC management is to invest $60,000 in Eastern Oil preferred stock, nothing in either Alaska Oil or American Steel common stock, and $40,000 in Cleveland municipal bonds. As indicated by the optimal objective function value, this portfolio has an expected yearly return of $7,800, which is a rate of return of 7.8%.

In the second part, the constraints are numbered sequentially, starting with the number 2 (number 1 refers to the objective function). For example, in the row labeled 2)—corresponding to the first constraint in the formulation—the value of 20,000 for the surplus variable indicates that the value of the left-hand side of this constraint is 20,000 more than the right-hand side. In other words, the $40,000 invested in Cleveland municipal bonds is $20,000 more than the minimum required. Furthermore, the dual price (also called the shadow price) for this constraint, shown in the last column, is 0.

As another example, in the row labeled 5)—corresponding to the last constraint in the formulation above—the value of 0 for the slack variable indicates that this constraint is binding—that is, all $100,000 is invested using the current plan. Furthermore, the dual price of 0.078 associated with this constraint indicates that each additional dollar IMC can invest (up to an amount given in the sensitivity report, as shown in Figure 6.9) earns an expected rate of return of 7.8%.

6.6.4 Using Sensitivity and Parametric Reports

During the presentation of your results, management raised the following questions:

1. The Manager of Finance warned that recent uncertainty in the oil market might lower the expected rate of return from Eastern Oil stock to 8%. If this happens, should IMC reconsider its investment strategy?

2. The President of IMC may be able to negotiate a long-term loan from a local bank at 7%. Should IMC attempt to obtain this loan? If so, for what amount?

3. The Vice-President of Finance has studied the prospectus of a slightly more risky venture (compared to the four stocks and bond under consideration) that requires an investment of exactly $60,000 and offers a rate of return of 8%. Should IMC consider this alternative, leaving only $40,000 to invest in the stocks and bond under consideration?

To answer the first question, identify what impact this change has on the mathematical model. If the rate of return of Eastern Oil preferred stock goes down to 8%, the coefficient of the variable E-OIL in the objective function changes from 0.09 to 0.08. To determine if this change results in a change in the investment plan, look at the sensitivity analysis report in Figure 6.9 obtained from LINDO by typing the command RANGE. The first part provides sensitivity ranges for the objective function coefficients. The second part provides ranges for each constraint over which the dual prices from the report in Figure 6.8(b) remain valid. LINDO provides these ranges by reporting the maximum allowable increase and decrease from the current values.

Returning to the first question posed, is the new value of 0.08 for the objective function coefficient within the range where the current solution remains optimal? The first line of the LINDO sensitivity analysis report in Figure 6.9 indicates that the current value of 0.09 for this coefficient can increase infinitely or decrease by as much as 0.01 without changing the optimal solution. Thus, the sensitivity range for this coefficient is from $0.09 - 0.01 = 0.08$ to $0.09 + \infty = \infty$. Because the new value of 0.08 for this coefficient *is* within the range of 0.08 to infinity, there is no change in the investment plan. However, the total expected return decreases by 1% of the amount invested in Eastern Oil stock—that is:

$$\text{New return} = 7800 - 0.01(60000)$$

$$= 7800 - 600$$

$$= 7200$$

So, a decrease in the rate of return for Eastern Oil stock to 8% does not affect the investment plan of IMC, but it decreases the return to $7200.

To answer the second question—whether IMC should obtain a loan at 7% interest and, if so, for what amount—ask yourself how this change affects the mathematical

```
RANGES IN WHICH THE BASIS IS UNCHANGED:
                         OBJ COEFFICIENT RANGES
VARIABLE           CURRENT        ALLOWABLE          ALLOWABLE
                   COEF           INCREASE           DECREASE
    EOIL           .090000        INFINITY            .010000
    AOIL           .080000         .010000           INFINITY
    ASTL           .070000         .020000           INFINITY
    CLMB           .060000         .030000            .195000
                         RIGHTHAND SIDE RANGES
    ROW            CURRENT        ALLOWABLE          ALLOWABLE
                   RHS            INCREASE           DECREASE
       2        20000.000000   20000.000000          INFINITY
       3        50000.000000      INFINITY        22000.000000
       4            .000000     20000.000000       18333.330000
       5       100000.000000    78571.430000       50000.000000
```

FIGURE 6.9 LINDO Sensitivity Analysis Reports for the Problem of IMC.

model. The answer is that obtaining additional investment funds through the proposed loan results in an increase in the right-hand side of the last constraint. The dual price of 0.078 associated with this constraint, as shown in the report in Figure 6.8(b), indicates that each additional dollar available for investment returns 7.8 cents. Because this return of 7.8% is more than the cost of the loan at 7%, it is indeed worthwhile for IMC to secure such a loan. But the next issue is for how much? Certainly up to the limit for which this dual price of 0.078 is valid. You can compute that limit from the information in the last line of the second part of the sensitivity report in Figure 6.9. This value is the maximum allowable increase of 78,571.43 over the current value of 100,000—that is, IMC should obtain a loan for *at least* $78,571.43, but should the company obtain more?

The answer to this question depends on what happens to the dual price *outside* this range. As discussed in Section 6.5, the parametric analysis report is used to study the impact of such a change. This report, obtained from LINDO by using the command PARA and specifying a maximum rhs value of 500,000 for this constraint, is shown in Figure 6.10 (a). The information needed to answer the question is provided in the last three columns. For example, the first two rows of the report indicate that from a rhs value of 100,000 up to 178,571, the objective function changes from 7800 up to 13,928.6 at the rate of the dual price of .780000E-01 (that is, 0.078) given in the second row. This indicates that each additional dollar of investment (up to $178,571) will earn IMC 7.8% (the associated dual price of 0.078). The third row indicates that additional funds beyond $178,571 will not increase the total expected return because the associated dual price given in the third row is 0.

On the basis of this information, your recommendation to the President should be to pursue the current negotiations with the bank for a loan of $78,571 (of course, in practice, this amount may be rounded down to $78,000). The interest rate of 7% on this loan will be more than offset by the 7.8% expected return from the investment.

To answer the third question—pertaining to the new investment opportunity requiring an investment of $60,000 and an expected return of 8%—again begin by identifying what impact this change has on the mathematical model. If $60,000 is invested in the new venture, IMC will receive an expected yearly return of 0.08($60,000) = $4800, but will have only $40,000 to invest in the other stocks and bond. Therefore, investing in the new venture results in a reduction in the right-hand side of the last constraint from the original value of $100,000 to $40,000. Because this value of $40,000 is outside the sensitivity range for this constraint of 100,000 + 78,571.43 = 178,571.43 down to 100,000 − 50,000 = 50,000 given in Figure 6.9, parametric analysis is needed.

VAR OUT		VAR IN		PIVOT ROW	RHS VAL	DUAL PRICE BEFORE PIVOT	OBJ VAL
					100000.	.780000E-01	7800.00
SLK	3	SLK	5	3	178571.	.780000E-01	13928.6
					500000.	.000000	13928.6

(a)

VAR OUT		VAR IN		PIVOT ROW	RHS VAL	DUAL PRICE BEFORE PIVOT	OBJ VAL
					100000.	.780000E-01	7800.00
SLK	2	SLK	4	5	50000.0	.780000E-01	3900.00
	EOIL	ART		4	20000.0	.900000E-01	1200.00
					.000000	+INFINITY	INFEASIBLE

(b)

FIGURE 6.10 Parametric Analysis Report for (a) the Last Constraint in the Range 100,000 to 500,000 and (b) the Last Constraint in the Range 0 to 100,000.

The parametric analysis report of LINDO in Figure 6.10(b) is used to study the impact of this change. The dual prices associated with each value of the rhs of the last constraint from 100,000 down to 0 are shown in this report. The desired value of $40,000 is between the rhs values of $50,000 and $20,000 in the second and third rows of the report in Figure 6.10(b). Using the dual price of .900E-01 (that is, 0.09) from the third row corresponding to a rhs value of 20,000 for this constraint, you can compute the optimal yearly return when IMC has only $40,000 to invest as follows:

$$
\begin{Bmatrix} \text{Return with} \\ \$40,000 \end{Bmatrix} = \begin{Bmatrix} \text{Return with} \\ \$20,000 \end{Bmatrix} + \begin{Bmatrix} \text{Shadow price} \\ \text{in this range} \end{Bmatrix} * \begin{Bmatrix} \text{Amount} \\ \text{to invest over} \\ \$20,000 \end{Bmatrix}
$$

$$
\begin{aligned}
&= \quad 1200 \quad + \quad 0.09 \quad * (40{,}000 - 20{,}000) \\
&= \quad 3000
\end{aligned}
$$

Thus, the total return from the new venture and the $40,000 investment in stocks and bonds is $4800 + $3000 = $7800. Because this new investment strategy offers the same yearly return as before, you should recommend that the new venture *not* be considered because of the higher risk associated with the new venture.

In this section you have seen how LINDO provides the optimal solution, dual prices, sensitivity ranges, and parametric reports similar to other packages such as STORM. You have learned to use that information to answer managerial questions of the form: "What happens if?" A similar analysis is presented for EXCEL in the next section.

■ 6.7 COMPUTER SOLUTION TO LINEAR PROGRAMMING PROBLEMS USING EXCEL

In this section, the linear programming package EXCEL 4.0 is used to solve and analyze the linear programming problem of IMC presented in Section 6.5, whose formulation resulted in the following model:

Maximize	0.09E-OIL + 0.08A-OIL + 0.07A-STL + 0.06CL-MB					
Subject to				CL-MB $\geq$	20000	(1)
	$-$0.2E-OIL $-$	0.2A-OIL $-$	0.2A-STL $+$	CL-MB $\leq$	50000	(2)
	0.4E-OIL $+$	0.4A-OIL $+$	0.4A-STL $-$	0.6CL-MB $\leq$	0	(3)
	E-OIL $+$	A-OIL $+$	A-STL $+$	CL-MB $\leq$	100000	(4)
	E-OIL ,	A-OIL ,	A-STL ,	CL-MB $\geq$	0	

Linear Program
IMC.DAT

6.7.1 *Computer Solution*

The first step is to enter the data from the model in the format required by EXCEL. This is accomplished by creating a spreadsheet of your own general design, such as the one illustrated in Figure 6.11. The names of the four variables have been entered in row 1 with their values (initially set to 0) immediately below them. The numbers in row 4 contain the objective function coefficients of each variable. The cell in column H immediately to the right of the = sign in this row computes the objective function based on the values of the variables in row 2. Each remaining row corresponds to one of the four constraints. For example, the last row shows the coefficient of 1 for each of the four variables in that constraint. The cell in column H immediately to the right of the = sign in this row computes the value of the left-hand side of this constraint based on the values of the variables in row 2. The cell in column I in that row is the rhs value

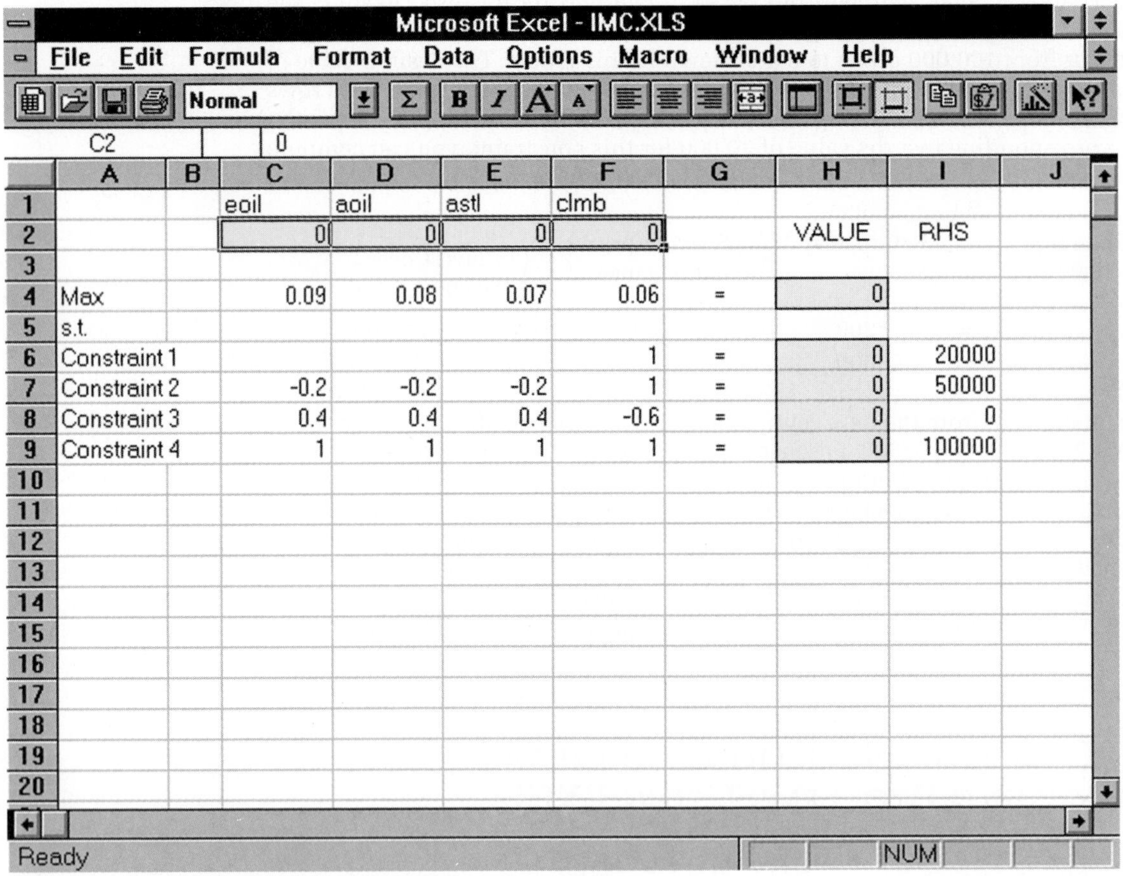

Microsoft Excel - IMC.XLS

	A	B	C	D	E	F	G	H	I
1			eoil	aoil	astl	clmb			
2			0	0	0	0		VALUE	RHS
3									
4	Max		0.09	0.08	0.07	0.06	=	0	
5	s.t.								
6	Constraint 1					1	=	0	20000
7	Constraint 2		-0.2	-0.2	-0.2	1	=	0	50000
8	Constraint 3		0.4	0.4	0.4	-0.6	=	0	0
9	Constraint 4		1	1	1	1	=	0	100000

FIGURE 6.11 EXCEL Input for the Problem of IMC.

(100,000) for this constraint. Observe that the constraint types ($\leq$, $\geq$, or $=$) and the nonnegativity constraints on the variables are not included in this spreadsheet. This information is provided when you subsequently call the built-in command SOLVER. Refer to the EXCEL User Manual for further information on how to create and enter appropriate values in the cells of a spreadsheet and how to use the SOLVER routine.

After preparing the spreadsheet with the appropriate data from the model, you can instruct the computer to use EXCEL to solve the problem by calling the built-in program SOLVER. The spreadsheet is updated with the optimal solution, as shown in Figure 6.12. The optimal values are displayed in row 2 under each respective variable and indicate that IMC should invest \$60,000 in Eastern Oil, nothing in Alaskan Oil, nothing in American Steel, and \$40,000 in Cleveland municipal bonds. This investment strategy results in an expected yearly return of \$7800, as given in the cell in column H immediately to the right of the = sign in the objective function in row 4 in Figure 6.12.

By using these values of the variables, the value of the left-hand side (lhs) of each constraint is provided in the cells in column H immediately to the right of the = sign in Figure 6.12. For example, the value of the lhs of the first constraint is 40,000, which is more than the rhs value of 20,000. Thus, this constraint has a surplus of 40,000 - 20,000 = 20,000, indicating that IMC is investing \$20,000 more in Cleveland municipal bonds than the minimum amount of \$20,000 set by management. In contrast, the value of the

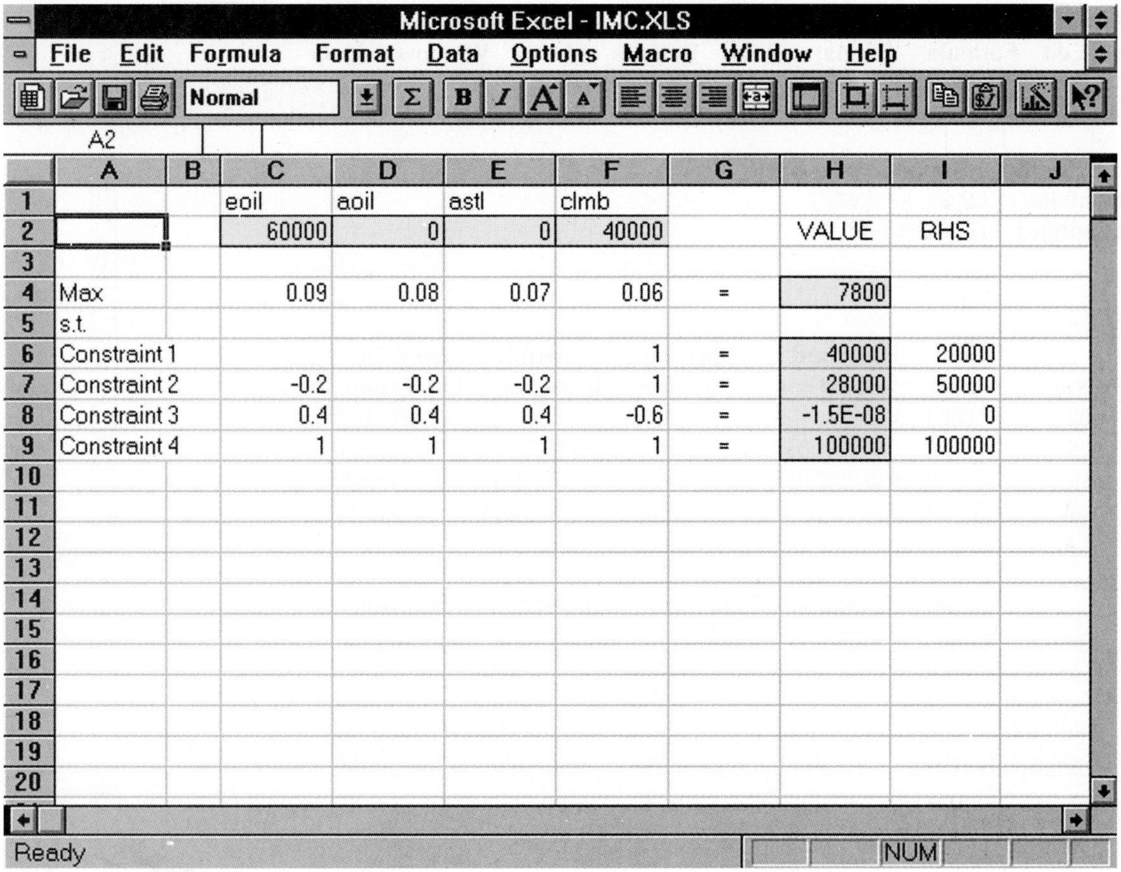

FIGURE 6.12 EXCEL Optimal Report for the Problem of IMC.

lhs of the last constraint is 100,000, which is the same as the rhs. Thus, this constraint has no slack, indicating that IMC is investing all of the available $100,000.

6.7.2 *Performing Sensitivity and Parametric Analysis*

Recall that during the presentation of your results, management raised the following questions:

1. The Manager of Finance warned that recent uncertainty in the oil market might lower the expected rate of return from Eastern Oil stock to 8%. If this happens, should IMC reconsider its investment strategy?

2. The President of IMC may be able to negotiate a long-term loan from a local bank at 7%. Should IMC attempt to obtain this loan? If so, for what amount?

3. The Vice-President of Finance has studied the prospectus of a slightly more risky venture (compared to the four stocks and bond under consideration) that requires an investment of exactly $60,000 and offers a rate of return of 8%. Should IMC consider this alternative, leaving only $40,000 to invest optimally in the stocks and bond under consideration?

To answer the first question, identify what impact this change has on the mathematical model. If the rate of return of Eastern Oil preferred stock goes down to 8%, the

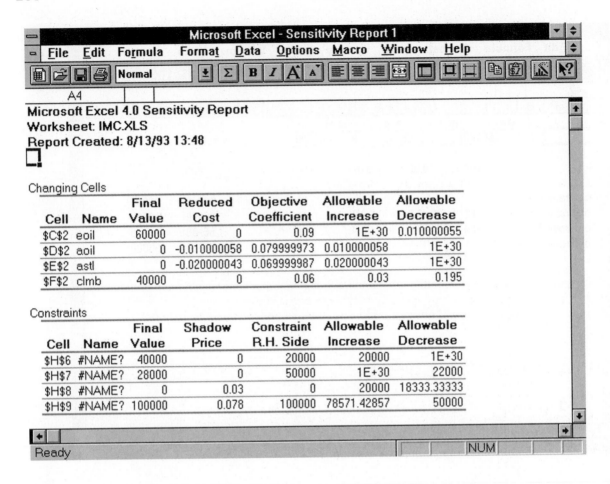

FIGURE 6.13 EXCEL Sensitivity Analysis Reports for the Problem of IMC.

coefficient of the variable E-OIL in the objective function changes from 0.09 to 0.08. To determine if this change results in a change in the investment plan, look at the sensitivity analysis report in Figure 6.13 obtained from EXCEL. The first part provides sensitivity ranges for the objective function coefficients. The second part provides, for each constraint, the shadow price and range over which this price remains valid. EXCEL provides these ranges by reporting the maximum allowable increase and decrease from the current values.

Returning to the first question posed, is the new value of 0.08 for the objective function coefficient within the range where the current solution remains optimal? The first row of the EXCEL sensitivity analysis report in Figure 6.13 indicates that the current value of 0.09 for this coefficient can increase by 1E+30 (virtually, infinity) or decrease by as much as 0.01 without changing the optimal solution. Thus the sensitivity range for this coefficient is from $0.09 - 0.01 = 0.08$ to $0.09 + \infty = \infty$. Because the new value of 0.08 for this coefficient *is* within the range of 0.08 to infinity, there is no change in the investment plan. However, the total expected return decreases by 1% of the amount invested in Eastern Oil stock—that is:

$$\text{New return} = 7800 - 0.01(60000)$$
$$= 7800 - 600$$
$$= 7200$$

So, a decrease in the rate of return for Eastern Oil stock to 8% does not affect the investment plan of IMC, but it decreases the return to $7200.

To answer the second question—whether IMC should obtain a loan at 7% interest and, if so, for what amount—ask yourself how this change affects the mathematical model. The answer is that obtaining additional investment funds through the proposed loan results in an increase in the right-hand side of the last constraint. The shadow price of 0.078 associated with this constraint, as shown in the last row of the report in Figure 6.13, indicates that each additional dollar available for investment returns 7.8 cents. Because this return of 7.8% is more than the cost of the loan at 7%, it is indeed worthwhile for IMC to secure such a loan. But the next issue is for how much? Certainly up to the limit for which this shadow price of 0.078 is valid. You can compute that limit from the information in the second part of the sensitivity report in Figure 6.13. This value is the maximum allowable increase of 78,571.43 over the current value of 100,000—that is, IMC should obtain a loan for *at least* $78,571.43 that will return an additional $0.078 * \$78,571.43 = \$6128.57$, more than offsetting the interest of $0.07 * \$78,571.43 = \$5500$. But should the company obtain a larger loan?

The answer to this question depends on what happens to the shadow price *outside* this range. As discussed in Section 6.5, the parametric analysis report is used to study the impact of such a change. Because this version of EXCEL does not provide parametric analysis, one way to proceed is to experiment by choosing successively larger and larger values of the right-hand side above 178,571.43 in small increments until the

	A	B	C	D	E	F	G	H	I	J
1			eoil	aoil	astl	clmb				
2			20000	0	0	20000		VALUE	RHS	
3										
4	Max		0.09	0.08	0.07	0.06	=	3000		
5	s.t.									
6	Constraint 1					1	=	20000	20000	
7	Constraint 2		-0.2	-0.2	-0.2	1	=	16000	50000	
8	Constraint 3		0.4	0.4	0.4	-0.6	=	-4000	0	
9	Constraint 4		1	1	1	1	=	40000	40000	

FIGURE 6.14 EXCEL Optimal Solution for IMC When Investing $40,000.

additional annual return does not offset the cost of the additional loan. For example, changing the right-hand side of this constraint to 180,000 and resolving the problem will reveal that the optimal objective function value—that is, the total return—is the same as when the right-hand side has a value of 178,571.43. By trying other values of the rhs between 178,571.43 and 180,000 you will discover that none of them results in additional revenue that offsets the interest. Therefore, you should report to the CEO that there is no value in obtaining a loan for more than $78,571.43.

To answer the third question—pertaining to the new investment opportunity requiring an investment of $60,000 and an expected return of 8%—begin again by identifying what impact this change has on the mathematical model. If $60,000 is invested in the new venture, IMC will receive an expected yearly return of 0.08($60,000) = $4800, but will have only $40,000 to invest in other stocks and bonds. Therefore, investing in the new venture results in a reduction in the $100,000 to $40,000. Because this value of $40,000 is outside of the sensitivity range for this constraint of 100,000 + 78,571.43 = 178,571.43 down to 100,000 − 50,000 = 50,000 given in Figure 6.13, parametric analysis is needed. Again, because EXCEL does not provide parametric analysis reports, the impact of this change can be studied only by changing the rhs of the last constraint to 40,000 and resolving the problem. The results are shown in Figure 6.14, where you can see that the annual return IMC can expect on $40,000 is $3000.

Thus, the total return from the new venture and the $40,000 investment in stocks and bonds is $4800 + $3000 = $7800. Because this new investment strategy offers the same yearly return as before, you should recommend that the new venture *not* be considered because of the higher risk associated with the new venture.

In this section, you have seen how the spreadsheet-based package of EXCEL is used to solve linear programming problems and answer associated sensitivity questions. In the next section, the case study formulated in Section 3.6 is solved by computer.

CASE STUDY
COMPUTER SOLUTION

In this section you will interpret computer output for the solution of a much larger linear program. Recall from Chapter 3 the global planning problem of American Steel Company, whose linear programming formulation follows.

Mathematical Formulation

DECISION VARIABLES

IBP = the number of tons of Grade A iron ore to be bought from Butte Minerals and shipped to the Pittsburgh mill

IBY = the number of tons of Grade A iron ore to be bought from Butte Minerals and shipped to the Youngstown mill

ICP = the number of tons of Grade B iron ore to be bought from Cheyenne Mines and shipped to the Pittsburgh mill

ICY = the number of tons of Grade B iron ore to be bought from Cheyenne Mines and shipped to the Youngstown mill

HP = the number of tons of high-grade steel to be produced at the Pittsburgh mill

LP = the number of tons of low-grade steel to be produced at the Pittsburgh mill

HY = the number of tons of high-grade steel to be produced at the Youngstown mill

LY = the number of tons of low-grade steel to be produced at the Youngstown mill

$OBPH$ = the number of tons of iron ore from Butte Minerals used to produce high-grade steel at the Pittsburgh mill

$OCPH$ = the number of tons of iron ore from Cheyenne mines used to produce high-grade steel at the Pittsburgh mill

$OBPL$ = the number of tons of iron ore from Butte Minerals used to produce low-grade steel at the Pittsburgh mill

$OCPL$ = the number of tons of iron ore from Cheyenne Mines used to produce low-grade steel at the Pittsburgh mill

$OBYH$ = the number of tons of iron ore from Butte Minerals used to produce high-grade steel at the Youngstown mill

$OCYH$ = the number of tons of iron ore from Cheyenne Mines used to produce high-grade steel at the Youngstown mill

$OBYL$ = the number of tons of iron ore from Butte Minerals used to produce low-grade steel at the Youngstown mill

$OCYL$ = the number of tons of iron ore from Cheyenne Mines used to produce low-grade steel at the Youngstown mill

FOR HIGH-GRADE STEEL

$SHPJ$ = the number of tons of high-grade steel to be shipped from the Pittsburgh mill to Japan

$SHPK$ = the number of tons of high-grade steel to be shipped from the Pittsburgh mill to Korea

$SHPT$ = the number of tons of high-grade steel to be shipped from the Pittsburgh mill to Taiwan

$SHPM$ = the number of tons of high-grade steel to be shipped from the Pittsburgh mill to Mexico

$SHYJ$ = the number of tons of high-grade steel to be shipped from the Youngstown mill to Japan

$SHYK$ = the number of tons of high-grade steel to be shipped from the Youngstown mill to Korea

$SHYT$ = the number of tons of high-grade steel to be shipped from the Youngstown mill to Taiwan

$SHYM$ = the number of tons of high-grade steel to be shipped from the Youngstown mill to Mexico

FOR LOW-GRADE STEEL

$SLPJ$ = the number of tons of low-grade steel to be shipped from the Pittsburgh mill to Japan

$SLPK$ = the number of tons of low-grade steel to be shipped from the Pittsburgh mill to Korea

$SLPT$ = the number of tons of low-grade steel to be shipped from the Pittsburgh mill to Taiwan

$SLPM$ = the number of tons of low-grade steel to be shipped from the Pittsburgh mill to Mexico

$SLYJ$ = the number of tons of low-grade steel to be shipped from the Youngstown mill to Japan

$SLYK$ = the number of tons of low-grade steel to be shipped from the Youngstown mill to Korea

$SLYT$ = the number of tons of low-grade steel to be shipped from the Youngstown mill to Taiwan

$SLYM$ = the number of tons of low-grade steel to be shipped from the Youngstown mill to Mexico

MATHEMATICAL MODEL

OBJECTIVE FUNCTION

Linear Program
ASC.DAT

Minimize $(140IBP + 143IBY + 124ICP + 127ICY) + (32HP + 27LP) + (39HY + 32LY) + (110SHPJ + 140SHPK + 130SHPT + 80SHPM + 100SLPJ + 130SLPK + 125SLPT + 80SLPM) + (115SHYJ + 150SHYK + 135SHYT + 90SHYM + 110SLYJ + 145SLYK + 127SLYT + 85SLYM)$

Subject to

PURCHASING CONSTRAINTS

$$IBP + IBY \leq 1000 \qquad \text{(Butte Minerals supply)} \qquad (1)$$
$$ICP + ICY \leq 2000 \qquad \text{(Cheyenne Mines supply)} \qquad (2)$$

PRODUCTION CONSTRAINTS

ORE CAPACITY CONSTRAINTS

$$OBPH + OBPL + OCPH + OCPL \leq 700 \qquad \text{(Pittsburgh mill)} \qquad (3)$$
$$OBYH + OBYL + OCYH + OCYL \leq 1500 \qquad \text{(Youngstown mill)} \qquad (4)$$

BLENDING REQUIREMENTS

$$OCPH - 2OBPH = 0 \qquad (5)$$
$$OCPL - 3OBPL = 0 \qquad (6)$$
$$OCYH - 2OBYH = 0 \qquad (7)$$
$$OCYL - 3OBYL = 0 \qquad (8)$$

PRODUCTION AND PURCHASING RELATIONSHIPS

$$OBPH + OBPL - IBP = 0 \qquad \text{(ore from Butte used in Pittsburgh)} \qquad (9)$$
$$OCPH + OCPL - ICP = 0 \qquad \text{(ore from Cheyenne used in Pittsburgh)} \qquad (10)$$
$$OBYH + OBYL - IBY = 0 \qquad \text{(ore from Butte used in Youngstown)} \qquad (11)$$
$$OCYH + OCYL - ICY = 0 \qquad \text{(ore from Cheyenne used in Youngstown)} \qquad (12)$$

PRODUCTION-BALANCE CONSTRAINTS

$$OCPH + OBPH - HP = 0 \qquad \text{(high-grade steel produced at Pittsburgh)} \qquad (13)$$
$$OCPL + OBPL - LP = 0 \qquad \text{(low-grade steel produced at Pittsburgh)} \qquad (14)$$
$$OCYH + OBYH - HY = 0 \qquad \text{(high-grade steel produced at Youngstown)} \qquad (15)$$
$$OCYL + OBYL - LY = 0 \qquad \text{(low-grade steel produced at Youngstown)} \qquad (16)$$

DISTRIBUTION CONSTRAINTS

SUPPLIES AT THE MILLS

$$SHPJ + SHPK + SHPT + SHPM - HP = 0 \quad \text{(high-grade steel shipped from Pittsburgh)} \quad (17)$$

$$SLPJ + SLPK + SLPT + SLPM - LP = 0 \quad \text{(low-grade steel shipped from Pittsburgh)} \quad (18)$$

$$SHYJ + SHYK + SHYT + SHYM - HY = 0 \quad \text{(high-grade steel shipped from Youngstown)} \quad (19)$$

$$SLYJ + SLYK + SLYT + SLYM - LY = 0 \quad \text{(low-grade steel shipped from Youngstown)} \quad (20)$$

DEMANDS FOR STEEL IN THE FOUR COUNTRIES

$$SHPJ + SHYJ \geq 400 \quad \text{(demand for high-grade steel in Japan)} \quad (21)$$
$$SLPJ + SLYJ \geq 200 \quad \text{(demand for low-grade steel in Japan)} \quad (22)$$
$$SHPK + SHYK \geq 200 \quad \text{(demand for high-grade steel in Korea)} \quad (23)$$
$$SLPK + SLYK \geq 100 \quad \text{(demand for low-grade steel in Korea)} \quad (24)$$
$$SHPT + SHYT \geq 200 \quad \text{(demand for high-grade steel in Taiwan)} \quad (25)$$
$$SLPT + SLYT \geq 100 \quad \text{(demand for low-grade steel in Taiwan)} \quad (26)$$
$$SHPM + SHYM \geq 150 \quad \text{(demand for high-grade steel in Mexico)} \quad (27)$$
$$SLPM + SLYM \geq 50 \quad \text{(demand for low-grade steel in Mexico)} \quad (28)$$

and all variables must be nonnegative

Computer Solution

Any linear programming software package can be used to obtain a solution to the foregoing problem. Figure 6.15 provides the optimal solution for American Steel Company (ASC) obtained from the STORM software package. This report is used to produce Tables 6.2 through 6.5, which summarize the optimal plan for the various functional areas of ASC. This optimal plan results in a yearly cost of $392,416.70.

TABLE 6.2 *Ore Purchase and Shipping Plan for ASC*

	PITTSBURGH	YOUNGSTOWN
Butte Minerals	208.3333	220.8333
Cheyenne Mines	491.6667	479.1667
Total	700.0000	700.0000

TABLE 6.3 *Production Plan for the Pittsburgh Mill*

	HIGH-GRADE	LOW-GRADE
Ore from Butte Minerals	133.3333	75.0000
Ore from Cheyenne Mines	266.6667	225.0000
Total steel produced	400.0000	300.0000

TABLE 6.4 *Production Plan for the Youngstown Mill*

	HIGH-GRADE	LOW-GRADE
Ore from Butte Minerals	183.3333	37.5000
Ore from Cheyenne Mines	366.6667	112.5000
Total steel produced	550.0000	150.0000

TABLE 6.5 *Shipping Plan for Pittsburgh and Youngstown*

			TONS SHIPPED FROM	
COUNTRY	STEEL TYPE	DEMAND	PITTSBURGH	YOUNGSTOWN
Japan	High-grade	400	0	400
	Low-grade	200	200	0
Korea	High-grade	200	200	0
	Low-grade	100	100	0
Taiwan	High-grade	200	50	150
	Low-grade	100	0	100
Mexico	High-grade	150	150	0
	Low-grade	50	0	50

Using Sensitivity and Parametric Reports

As you learned earlier, sensitivity and parametric reports help answer "What happens if?" questions. Consider the following questions raised by ASC management:

1. From the output pertaining to constraint (3) in Figure 6.15, management recognizes that the capacity of their Pittsburgh mill is a binding limitation. ASC has an option to increase the capacity of that mill from the current value of 700 tons to either 800 or 1400 tons. To evaluate these expansion alternatives, ASC needs to know the yearly savings under each option.

Changing the capacity of this mill results in a change in the rhs of constraint (3). To evaluate the impact of such a change, parametric analysis is the appropriate report to study. The shadow price in the first pair of lines in the parametric analysis report for constraint (3) shown in Figure 6.16 indicates that as long as the new capacity is between 700 and 850, each unit increase in that capacity decreases the total cost by $15. Thus:

$$\text{Total savings if the Pittsburgh mill's capacity is increased to 800} = (\text{shadow price}) * (\text{increase over 700})$$
$$= \quad 15 \quad * \quad 100$$
$$= \quad 1500$$

Likewise, if the Pittsburgh mill's capacity increases to 1400, the relevant range in the parametric analysis report is 1300 to 1400. This part of the report indicates that the cost decreases to $382,516.70. Thus, the savings is $392,416.70 − $382,516.70 = $9900.

```
                American Steel Company's Global Planning
                   OPTIMAL SOLUTION - DETAILED REPORT
         Variable        Value        Cost     Red. cost    Status
    1       IBP        208.3333     140.0000     0.0000      Basic
    2       IBY        220.8333     143.0000     0.0000      Basic
    3       ICP        491.6667     124.0000     0.0000      Basic
    4       ICY        479.1667     127.0000     0.0000      Basic
    5       HP         400.0000      32.0000     0.0000      Basic
    6       LP         300.0000      27.0000     0.0000      Basic
    7       HY         550.0000      39.0000     0.0000      Basic
    8       LY         150.0000      32.0000     0.0000      Basic
    9       SHPJ         0.0000     110.0000     0.0000 Lower bound
   10       SHPK       200.0000     140.0000     0.0000      Basic
   11       SHPT        50.0000     130.0000     0.0000      Basic
   12       SHPM       150.0000      80.0000     0.0000      Basic
   13       SLPJ       200.0000     100.0000     0.0000      Basic
   14       SLPK       100.0000     130.0000     0.0000      Basic
   15       SLPT         0.0000     125.0000     5.0000 Lower bound
   16       SLPM         0.0000      80.0000     2.0000 Lower bound
   17       SHYJ       400.0000     115.0000     0.0000      Basic
   18       SHYK         0.0000     150.0000     5.0000 Lower bound
   19       SHYT       150.0000     135.0000     0.0000      Basic
   20       SHYM         0.0000      90.0000     5.0000 Lower bound
   21       SLYJ         0.0000     110.0000     3.0000 Lower bound
   22       SLYK         0.0000     145.0000     8.0000 Lower bound
   23       SLYT       100.0000     127.0000     0.0000      Basic
   24       SLYM        50.0000      85.0000     0.0000      Basic
   25       OBPH       133.3333       0.0000     0.0000      Basic
   26       OBPL        75.0000       0.0000     0.0000      Basic
   27       OCPH       266.6667       0.0000     0.0000      Basic
   28       OCPL       225.0000       0.0000     0.0000      Basic
   29       OBYH       183.3333       0.0000     0.0000      Basic
   30       OBYL        37.5000       0.0000     0.0000      Basic
   31       OCYH       366.6667       0.0000     0.0000      Basic
   32       OCYL       112.5000       0.0000     0.0000      Basic
                                                             (cont.)
```

FIGURE 6.15 STORM Optimal Solution to the Global Planning Problem of ASC.

2. The Sales Manager of ASC has just received an offer from both Japan and Korea to buy an additional 200 tons of low-grade steel. For this amount of steel, Japan is willing to pay $60,000, whereas Korea offers $65,000. Because this is a one-time order, the management of ASC does not want to hire additional labor, and the current work force permits ASC to accept only one offer. What is your recommendation?

To answer this question, observe that an additional shipment of 200 tons of low-grade steel to either Japan or Korea results in an increase of 200 in the rhs of constraints (22) or (24), respectively. To evaluate the additional cost for each alternative, refer to the parametric analysis reports given in Figures 6.17 and 6.18.

The parametric analysis report in Figure 6.17 helps determine the impact on the optimal cost when the demand for low-grade steel sent to Japan changes. To calculate the new cost when this demand increases from 200 to 400, use the shadow price of 273 in the range 250 to 1000 as follows:

FIGURE 6.15 (cont.)

American Steel Company's Global Planning
OPTIMAL SOLUTION - DETAILED REPORT

	Variable		Value	Cost	Red. cost	Status
Slack Variables						
33	CONSTR	1	570.8333	0.0000	0.0000	Basic
34	CONSTR	2	1029.1670	0.0000	0.0000	Basic
35	CONSTR	3	0.0000	0.0000	15.0000	Lower bound
36	CONSTR	4	800.0000	0.0000	0.0000	Basic
41	CONSTR	9	0.0000	0.0000	140.0000	Lower bound
42	CONSTR	10	0.0000	0.0000	124.0000	Lower bound
43	CONSTR	11	0.0000	0.0000	143.0000	Lower bound
44	CONSTR	12	0.0000	0.0000	127.0000	Lower bound
49	CONSTR	17	0.0000	0.0000	176.3333	Lower bound
50	CONSTR	18	0.0000	0.0000	170.0000	Lower bound
51	CONSTR	19	0.0000	0.0000	171.3333	Lower bound
52	CONSTR	20	0.0000	0.0000	163.0000	Lower bound
53	CONSTR	21	0.0000	0.0000	286.3333	Lower bound
54	CONSTR	22	0.0000	0.0000	270.0000	Lower bound
55	CONSTR	23	0.0000	0.0000	316.3333	Lower bound
56	CONSTR	24	0.0000	0.0000	300.0000	Lower bound
57	CONSTR	25	0.0000	0.0000	306.3333	Lower bound
58	CONSTR	26	0.0000	0.0000	290.0000	Lower bound
59	CONSTR	27	0.0000	0.0000	256.3333	Lower bound
60	CONSTR	28	0.0000	0.0000	248.0000	Lower bound

Objective Function Value = 392416.7

	Constraint		Type	RHS	Slack	Shadow price
1	CONSTR	1	<=	1000.0000	570.8333	0.0000
2	CONSTR	2	<=	2000.0000	1029.1670	0.0000
3	CONSTR	3	<=	700.0000	0.0000	-15.0000
4	CONSTR	4	<=	1500.0000	800.0000	0.0000
5	CONSTR	5	=	0.0000	0.0000	-5.3333
6	CONSTR	6	=	0.0000	0.0000	-4.0000
7	CONSTR	7	=	0.0000	0.0000	-5.3333
8	CONSTR	8	=	0.0000	0.0000	-4.0000
9	CONSTR	9	>=	0.0000	0.0000	-140.0000
10	CONSTR	10	>=	0.0000	0.0000	-124.0000
11	CONSTR	11	>=	0.0000	0.0000	-143.0000
12	CONSTR	12	>=	0.0000	0.0000	-127.0000
13	CONSTR	13	=	0.0000	0.0000	144.3333
14	CONSTR	14	=	0.0000	0.0000	143.0000
15	CONSTR	15	=	0.0000	0.0000	132.3333
16	CONSTR	16	=	0.0000	0.0000	131.0000
17	CONSTR	17	<=	0.0000	0.0000	-176.3333
18	CONSTR	18	<=	0.0000	0.0000	-170.0000
19	CONSTR	19	<=	0.0000	0.0000	-171.3333
20	CONSTR	20	<=	0.0000	0.0000	-163.0000
21	CONSTR	21	>=	400.0000	0.0000	286.3333
22	CONSTR	22	>=	200.0000	0.0000	270.0000
23	CONSTR	23	>=	200.0000	0.0000	316.3333
24	CONSTR	24	>=	100.0000	0.0000	300.0000
25	CONSTR	25	>=	200.0000	0.0000	306.3333
26	CONSTR	26	>=	100.0000	0.0000	290.0000
27	CONSTR	27	>=	150.0000	0.0000	256.3333
28	CONSTR	28	>=	50.0000	0.0000	248.0000

Objective Function Value = 392416.7

$$\text{New cost} = \text{cost at 250} + (\text{shadow price}) * (\text{amount over 250})$$
$$= 405916.70 + \quad 273 \quad * \quad 150$$
$$= \$446,866.70$$

Comparing this cost with the original one of \$392,416.70 from Figure 6.15 reveals that to meet the additional 200 tons of low-grade steel demanded in Japan results in an increase in the production and shipping costs of \$446,866.70 − \$392,416.70 = \$54,450. However, because this additional demand in Japan will increase revenues by \$60,000, the net gain is \$60,000 − \$54,450 = \$5550.

Similarly, the parametric analysis report in Figure 6.18 helps determine the impact on the optimal cost when the demand for low-grade steel shipped to Korea changes. When this demand increases from 100 to 300, use the shadow price of 303 in the range 150 to 350 to compute the new cost as follows:

$$\text{New cost} = \text{cost at 150} + (\text{shadow price}) * (\text{amount over 150})$$
$$= 407416.70 + \quad 303 \quad * \quad 150$$
$$= \$452,866.70$$

```
              American Steel Company's Global Planning
         PARAMETRIC ANALYSIS OF RIGHT-HAND-SIDE VALUE - CONSTR    3
     COEF = 700.000       LWR LIMIT = -Infinity     UPR LIMIT = Infinity
            -------  Range  -------        Shadow   ----  Variable  ----
                   From          To         Price     Leave       Enter
     RHS      700.000     850.000        -15.000      SHYT        SHPJ
     Obj   392416.700  390166.700
     RHS      850.000    1250.000        -15.000      SHYJ        SLPM
     Obj   390166.700  384166.700
     RHS     1250.000    1300.000        -13.000      SLYM        SLPT
     Obj   384166.700  383516.700
     RHS     1300.000    1400.000        -10.000      SLYT  SLACK    3
     Obj   383516.700  382516.700
     RHS     1400.000    Infinity          0.000  ----  No change  ----
     Obj   382516.700  382516.700
     RHS      700.000     650.000        -15.000      SHPT        SLYJ
     Obj   392416.700  393166.700
     RHS      650.000     450.000        -18.000      SLPJ        SHYK
     Obj   393166.700  396766.700
     RHS      450.000     250.000        -20.000      SHPK        SHYM
     Obj   396766.700  400766.700
     RHS      250.000     100.000        -20.000      OCPH        SLYK
     Obj   400766.700  403766.700
     RHS      100.000       0.000        -23.000      SLPK
     Obj   403766.700  406066.700
     RHS        0.000    -Infinity  ----  Infeasible in this range  ----
```

FIGURE 6.16 STORM Parametric Analysis of Constraint (3).

```
                American Steel Company's Global Planning
            PARAMETRIC ANALYSIS OF RIGHT-HAND-SIDE VALUE - CONSTR  22
         COEF = 200.000       LWR LIMIT = -Infinity      UPR LIMIT = Infinity
            ------- Range -------        Shadow    ---- Variable ----
                 From           To        Price      Leave       Enter
         RHS    200.000      250.000     270.000      SHPT        SLYJ
         Obj  392416.700   405916.700

         RHS    250.000     1000.000     273.000    SLACK    4
         Obj  405916.700   610666.700

         RHS   1000.000     Infinity   ---- Infeasible in this range ----

         RHS    200.000       50.000     270.000      SHYT        SHPJ
         Obj  392416.700   351916.700

         RHS     50.000        0.000     270.000      SLPJ    SLACK   22
         Obj  351916.700   338416.700

         RHS      0.000    -2.048E+40      0.000   ---- No change   ----
         Obj  338416.700   338416.700
```

FIGURE 6.17 STORM Parametric Analysis of Constraint (22).

```
                American Steel Company's Global Planning
            PARAMETRIC ANALYSIS OF RIGHT-HAND-SIDE VALUE - CONSTR  24
         COEF = 100.000       LWR LIMIT = -Infinity      UPR LIMIT = Infinity
            ------- Range -------        Shadow    ---- Variable ----
                 From           To        Price      Leave       Enter
         RHS    100.000      150.000     300.000      SHPT        SLYJ
         Obj  392416.700   407416.700

         RHS    150.000      350.000     303.000      SLPJ        SHYK
         Obj  407416.700   468016.700

         RHS    350.000      550.000     305.000      SHPK        SHYM
         Obj  468016.700   529016.700

         RHS    550.000      700.000     305.000      SHPM        SLYK
         Obj  529016.700   574766.700

         RHS    700.000      900.000     308.000    SLACK    4
         Obj  574766.700   636366.700

         RHS    900.000     Infinity   ---- Infeasible in this range ----

         RHS    100.000        0.000     300.000      SLPK    SLACK   24
         Obj  392416.700   362416.700

         RHS      0.000    -2.048E+40      0.000   ---- No change   ----
         Obj  362416.700   362416.700
```

FIGURE 6.18 STORM Parametric Analysis of Constraint (24).

Comparing this cost with the original one of $392,416.70 from Figure 6.15 reveals that to meet the additional 200 tons of low-grade steel demanded in Korea results in an increase in the production and shipping costs of $452,866.70 − $392,416.70 = $60,450. However, because this additional demand in Korea will increase revenues by $65,000, the net gain is $65,000 − $60,450 = $4550.

Comparing the two alternatives indicates that it is more profitable to ship an additional 200 tons to Japan, even though the offer of $60,000 is $5000 less than the $65,000 offer from Korea. This situation occurs mainly because the lower shipping costs to Japan (compared to Korea) more than offset the smaller revenue from Japan.

3. The Accounting Department of ASC just discovered a mistake in its calculation for the shipping cost from Butte to Pittsburgh. The corrected cost is $25 per ton instead of the previously reported value of $10 per ton. Based on this change, what should the revised plan for ASC be? What is the new monthly cost?

American Steel Company's Global Planning
SENSITIVITY ANALYSIS OF COST COEFFICIENTS

	Variable	Current Coeff.	Allowable Minimum	Allowable Maximum
1	IBP	140.0000	104.0000	164.0000
2	IBY	143.0000	119.0000	179.0000
3	ICP	124.0000	100.0000	146.5000
4	ICY	127.0000	104.5000	151.0000
5	OBPH	0.0000	−9.0000	6.0000
6	OBPL	0.0000	−8.0000	12.0000
7	OCPH	0.0000	−4.5000	3.0000
8	OCPL	0.0000	−2.6667	4.0000
9	OBYH	0.0000	−6.0000	9.0000
10	OBYL	0.0000	−12.0000	8.0000
11	OCYH	0.0000	−3.0000	4.5000
12	OCYL	0.0000	−4.0000	2.6667
13	HP	32.0000	29.0000	34.0000
14	LP	27.0000	25.0000	30.0000
15	HY	39.0000	37.0000	42.0000
16	LY	32.0000	29.0000	34.0000
17	SHPJ	110.0000	110.0000	Infinity
18	SHPK	140.0000	−176.3333	145.0000
19	SHPT	130.0000	127.0000	130.0000
20	SHPM	80.0000	−176.3333	85.0000
21	SLPJ	100.0000	−170.0000	103.0000
22	SLPK	130.0000	−170.0000	138.0000
23	SLPT	125.0000	120.0000	Infinity
24	SLPM	80.0000	78.0000	Infinity
25	SHYJ	115.0000	−171.3333	115.0000
26	SHYK	150.0000	145.0000	Infinity
27	SHYT	135.0000	135.0000	138.0000
28	SHYM	90.0000	85.0000	Infinity
29	SLYJ	110.0000	107.0000	Infinity
30	SLYK	145.0000	137.0000	Infinity
31	SLYT	127.0000	−163.0000	132.0000
32	SLYM	85.0000	−163.0000	87.0000

FIGURE 6.19 STORM Sensitivity Analysis Report for the Problem of ASC.

To answer this question, ask how an increase of $15 in the shipping cost from Butte to Pittsburgh changes the model. Reviewing the derivation of the objective function in the Case Study of Chapter 3 leads you to determine that the only change is an increase in the objective function coefficient of the variable IBP from its current value of 140 to 155. To see if this change requires a change in the current optimal plan, use the sensitivity analysis report for that cost coefficient given in Figure 6.19. Because the new objective function coefficient of 155 for IBP lies within the range of 104 to 164, the current optimal solution in Figure 6.15 remains optimal. However, the optimal objective function value increases by $15 for every ton shipped from Butte to Pittsburgh. Hence:

$$
\begin{aligned}
\text{New cost} = \quad & \text{old cost} \quad + 15 * \text{value of IBP} \\
= \quad & 392416.70 \quad + 15 * 208.3333 \\
= \quad & \$395,541.70
\end{aligned}
$$

The first two questions for ASC presented in this section are answered assuming that the cost coefficient of IBP remains at its current value of 140. If this value is changed to 155 (as indicated in the third question), then the previous answers for the first two questions may no longer be applicable. In this case, you should solve the problem with the new cost coefficient and use the new parametric and sensitivity reports to answer the first two questions again.

➡ ### KEY FEATURES

In this section you have learned how to use the output obtained from a linear programming package to answer "What happens if?" questions. This requires that you identify what impact the proposed change has on the original model and then use the appropriate parametric or sensitivity report to obtain an answer. Keep in mind that these reports are applicable to *one* specific change in the data, *assuming that all other values remain unchanged.*

ADDITIONAL MANAGERIAL CONSIDERATIONS

You have now learned to interpret the output obtained from using a computer package to solve a linear programming problem. As a manager, there are several issues you should be aware of when using such a package.

Problems Associated with the Data

Sparsity
A characteristic of some linear programs in which most (perhaps 95% or more) of the data values are 0.

When a linear program has few variables and constraints, collecting and entering the data in the format required by the computer program are relatively easy tasks. However, in many real-world problems, there can be hundreds or thousands of variables and constraints. A linear program having 100 variables and 200 constraints could have as many as 20,000 values for the data. Fortunately, such large problems usually exhibit a special structure called **sparsity**, meaning that most (perhaps more than 95%) of the data values are 0 and need not be typed into the computer. Nonetheless, as a manager, you should realize that collecting data and verifying that all the information has been correctly entered into the computer can be an enormous task, often requiring more time and effort than formulating the problem.

Alternative Optimal Solutions

As discussed in Chapter 4, a linear program may have more than one optimal solution. It may be worthwhile obtaining these alternative optimal solutions because, even though they have the same objective function value, one solution may be more desirable than the others when implementational issues are considered. For example, an optimal solution that utilizes approximately the same capacity of each steel mill may be preferred by management to an optimal solution in which 10% of the capacity of one mill is used and 75% of the other mill is used. As another example, management may prefer an optimal solution in which each steel mill ships its final products to as few countries as possible.

For the optimal shipping plan of ASC in Figure 6.15, note that the reduced cost for the *nonbasic* variable *SHPJ* (variable number 17 in the report) is 0. Recall the Chapter 5 discussion of the reduced costs. The value of 0 for the reduced cost of the variable *SHPJ* indicates that the objective function increases by 0 for each unit increase in the value of *SHPJ* (keeping all other nonbasic variables at value 0). Thus, the solution obtained by making *SHPJ* basic has the same objective function value as the current one and is therefore an *alternative optimal solution*. In other words, if one or more nonbasic variables in an optimal solution have a reduced cost of 0, an alternative optimal solution can be obtained by making any one of these nonbasic variables basic.

If *SHPJ* is made basic (STORM allows you to select a nonbasic variable to make basic at any iteration as well as at the optimal solution), Figure 6.20 provides the alternative optimal solution with exactly the same objective function value. Note that only the values of some of the shipping variables have changed. Table 6.6 shows this alternative shipping plan. Comparing the optimal solution in Table 6.6 with that in Table 6.5 reveals that the steel mill in Pittsburgh is now shipping its final products to only three countries instead of all four previously. The mill at Youngstown still ships to three countries. Thus, the solution in Table 6.6 may be preferred by management because the mill in Pittsburgh is now responsible for shipping to fewer countries.

TABLE 6.6	*Alternative Shipping Plan for Pittsburgh and Youngstown*			
			TONS SHIPPED FROM	
COUNTRY	STEEL TYPE	DEMAND	PITTSBURGH	YOUNGSTOWN
Japan	High-grade	400	50	350
	Low-grade	200	200	0
Korea	High-grade	200	200	0
	Low-grade	100	100	0
Taiwan	High-grade	200	0	200
	Low-grade	100	0	100
Mexico	High-grade	150	150	0
	Low-grade	50	0	50

Using Special Features of Software Packages

After formulating and solving many different linear programs, you might discover that certain types of constraints appear repeatedly. For example, a **bound constraint** is one in which a single variable is restricted to have a value within a specified range, such as, $5 \leq x_1 \leq 10$, which restricts the value of x_1 between 5 and 10. In contrast, a **range**

Bound constraint
A constraint in which a single variable is restricted to have a value within a specified range.

Range constraint
A constraint that restricts a linear function to have a value within a specified range.

constraint restricts a linear function to have a value within a specified range, such as, $9 \leq 3x_1 + 5x_2 \leq 10$, which restricts the linear function $3x_1 + 5x_2$ between the range 9 and 10. Many computer packages allow you to specify such constraints in a special and simple manner and provide other useful features for representing and/or solving the problem. Consider the linear program in Example 6.1.

EXAMPLE 6.1

$$
\begin{array}{lll}
\text{Maximize} & 3x_1 + 5x_2 & \\
\text{Subject to} & 2x_1 + x_2 \geq 150 & (1) \\
& 2x_1 + x_2 \leq 230 & (2) \\
& x_1 \geq 80 & (3) \\
& x_1 \leq 120 & (4) \\
& x_1, \; x_2 \geq 0 & \blacksquare
\end{array}
$$

```
              American Steel Company's Global Planning
                  OPTIMAL SOLUTION - DETAILED REPORT
         Variable      Value        Cost    Red. cost    Status
  1        IBP       208.3333    140.0000    0.0000       Basic
  2        IBY       220.8333    143.0000    0.0000       Basic
  3        ICP       491.6667    124.0000    0.0000       Basic
  4        ICY       479.1667    127.0000    0.0000       Basic
  5        OBPH      133.3333      0.0000    0.0000       Basic
  6        OBPL       75.0000      0.0000    0.0000       Basic
  7        OCPH      266.6667      0.0000    0.0000       Basic
  8        OCPL      225.0000      0.0000    0.0000       Basic
  9        OBYH      183.3333      0.0000    0.0000       Basic
 10        OBYL       37.5000      0.0000    0.0000       Basic
 11        OCYH      366.6667      0.0000    0.0000       Basic
 12        OCYL      112.5000      0.0000    0.0000       Basic
 13        HP        400.0000     32.0000    0.0000       Basic
 14        LP        300.0000     27.0000    0.0000       Basic
 15        HY        550.0000     39.0000    0.0000       Basic
 16        LY        150.0000     32.0000    0.0000       Basic
 17        SHPJ       50.0000    110.0000    0.0000       Basic
 18        SHPK      200.0000    140.0000    0.0000       Basic
 19        SHPT        0.0000    130.0000    0.0000  Lower bound
 20        SHPM      150.0000     80.0000    0.0000       Basic
 21        SLPJ      200.0000    100.0000    0.0000       Basic
 22        SLPK      100.0000    130.0000    0.0000       Basic
 23        SLPT        0.0000    125.0000    5.0000  Lower bound
 24        SLPM        0.0000     80.0000    2.0000  Lower bound
 25        SHYJ      350.0000    115.0000    0.0000       Basic
 26        SHYK        0.0000    150.0000    5.0000  Lower bound
 27        SHYT      200.0000    135.0000    0.0000       Basic
 28        SHYM        0.0000     90.0000    5.0000  Lower bound
 29        SLYJ        0.0000    110.0000    3.0000  Lower bound
 30        SLYK        0.0000    145.0000    8.0000  Lower bound
 31        SLYT      100.0000    127.0000    0.0000       Basic
 32        SLYM       50.0000     85.0000    0.0000       Basic
```

FIGURE 6.20 An Alternative Optimal Solution from STORM for the Global Planning Problem of ASC.

```
              American Steel Company's Global Planning
                  OPTIMAL SOLUTION - DETAILED REPORT
          Variable        Value       Cost    Red. cost   Status
     Slack Variables
     33  CONSTR   1      570.8333     0.0000     0.0000    Basic
     34  CONSTR   2     1029.1670     0.0000     0.0000    Basic
     35  CONSTR   3        0.0000     0.0000    15.0000 Lower bound
     36  CONSTR   4      800.0000     0.0000     0.0000    Basic
     41  CONSTR   9        0.0000     0.0000   140.0000 Lower bound
     42  CONSTR  10        0.0000     0.0000   124.0000 Lower bound
     43  CONSTR  11        0.0000     0.0000   143.0000 Lower bound
     44  CONSTR  12        0.0000     0.0000   127.0000 Lower bound
     49  CONSTR  17        0.0000     0.0000   176.3333 Lower bound
     50  CONSTR  18        0.0000     0.0000   170.0000 Lower bound
     51  CONSTR  19        0.0000     0.0000   171.3333 Lower bound
     52  CONSTR  20        0.0000     0.0000   163.0000 Lower bound
     53  CONSTR  21        0.0000     0.0000   286.3333 Lower bound
     54  CONSTR  22        0.0000     0.0000   270.0000 Lower bound
     55  CONSTR  23        0.0000     0.0000   316.3333 Lower bound
     56  CONSTR  24        0.0000     0.0000   300.0000 Lower bound
     57  CONSTR  25        0.0000     0.0000   306.3333 Lower bound
     58  CONSTR  26        0.0000     0.0000   290.0000 Lower bound
     59  CONSTR  27        0.0000     0.0000   256.3333 Lower bound
     60  CONSTR  28        0.0000     0.0000   248.0000 Lower bound
     Objective Function Value = 392416.7
```

FIGURE 6.20 (cont.)

BOUND CONSTRAINTS

Observe in Example 6.1 that the two inequality constraints (3) and (4):

$$x_1 \geq 80$$

$$x_1 \leq 120$$

make up a bound constraint on x_1: $80 \leq x_1 \leq 120$. Most computer packages provide an alternative way to enter these constraints. Figure 6.21 illustrates how STORM allows you to do so. The rows labeled "LOWR BOUND" and "UPPR BOUND" allow you to specify both the lower bound (80) and the upper bound (120) associated with each variable without having to write the inequality constraints explicitly.

RANGE CONSTRAINTS

Observe in Example 6.1 that the two inequality constraints (1) and (2):

$$2x_1 + x_2 \geq 150$$

$$2x_1 + x_2 \leq 230$$

are a range constraint on $2x_1 + x_2$: $150 \leq 2x_1 + x_2 \leq 230$. Figure 6.21 illustrates how STORM allows you to compress your inputting efforts. You enter one of the two constraints ($2x_1 + x_2 \geq 150$, in this case) and in the column labeled "RANGE," you specify the difference between the upper and lower rhs values ($230 - 150 = 80$, in this case).

PROVIDING AN INITIAL SOLUTION

It is often necessary to solve a linear program many times, each time changing the data slightly. For example, after formulating and solving a linear programming problem, you learned to ask numerous "What happens if?" questions. Some of these questions can be answered using appropriate sensitivity and parametric analysis, as described in Section 6.5. However, when such questions involve changing more than one value in the formulation, you will need to modify and solve the new model.

Alternatively, if the model is used for making operational decisions, the same model is rerun with different data. Consider a linear programming model whose optimal solution provides a weekly production plan. Each week, new supply data are available at the plants and new demand data from the customers. The model must be changed and resolved. For a large linear programming model, it may be computationally more efficient to use the optimal solution from the previous week as the initial solution for the new linear program (even though it may be infeasible for the new problem) rather than having the simplex algorithm find its own initial solution. This is because finding an initial feasible solution can require substantial computational effort. Furthermore, an arbitrary initial solution found by the simplex algorithm may be "far" from the optimal solution whereas you would expect the previous optimal solution to be "close" to the new one if the coefficients have not changed significantly.

Many computer packages allow you to provide an initial solution from which to begin the search for the optimal solution. Figure 6.21 illustrates this option with STORM. The last row labeled "INIT SOLN" allows you to specify an initial value (100, in this case) for each variable. Alternatively, STORM (and some other packages) allows you to specify that the optimal solution is to be saved as an initial solution for future runs. The simplex algorithm will use those given initial values, even if they are infeasible or do not constitute a basic solution.

These features for handling bound and range constraints and for providing an initial solution are time-saving devices, but there are certain disadvantages to using them. For instance, when using the bound and/or range constraint features, you will not obtain sensitivity and parametric information such as the shadow prices and the sensitivity ranges. If you need this information, enter the constraints in their explicit form. Similarly, if the data to a problem are changed significantly, or if the problem has few variables and constraints, providing an initial solution may be more inefficient than letting the simplex algorithm find its own initial solution.

Title : Example 6.1					
Number of variables	:	2			
Number of constraints	:	1			
Starting solution given	:	YES			
Objective type (MAX/MIN)	:	MAX			
ROW LABEL	X1	X2	CONST TYPE	RHS	RANGE
OBJ COEFF	3.	5.	XXXX	XXXX	XXXX
CONSTR 1	2.	1.	>=	150.	80.
VARBL TYPE	POS	POS	XXXX	XXXX	XXXX
LOWR BOUND	80.	.	XXXX	XXXX	XXXX
UPPR BOUND	120.	.	XXXX	XXXX	XXXX
INIT SOLN	100.	100.	XXXX	XXXX	XXXX

FIGURE 6.21 STORM Input Data for Example 6.1.

Problems of Numerical Stability

Occasionally, when solving a linear programming problem with a computer package you might obtain a solution in which the values of the variables make no sense at all in the context of the problem. If the problem is formulated correctly and the data have been entered accurately into the computer program, the meaningless solution might then arise from the way in which the computer performs computations. A computer cannot work with all digits of real numbers. For example, the computer converts the fraction 1/3 to the real number 0.333 . . . . However, the computer cannot store the infinite number of 3's, so the fraction 1/3 is approximated with a finite number of digits—perhaps 0.33333333—with the rest of the digits dropped. This loss of digits is *truncation error* and leads to inaccuracies when the computer performs numerical operations. If suitable precautions are not taken when writing the computer program, truncation errors can cause meaningless results.

Although most good computerized versions of the simplex algorithm attempt to avoid problems caused by truncation errors, should you obtain an unexpected solution, you might try to solve the problem using the following guidelines:

1. Replace each equality constraint with two inequality constraints in which the rhs value is changed slightly. For example, you might replace the equality constraint:

$$3x_1 + 5x_2 = 10$$

with

$$3x_1 + 5x_2 \leq 10.0001 \qquad \text{and} \qquad 3x_1 + 5x_2 \geq 9.9999$$

As mentioned previously, many computer packages allow you to enter these two inequality constraints as the single range constraint:

$$9.9999 \leq 3x_1 + 5x_2 \leq 10.0001$$

2. Try rewriting some constraints in a different form. For example, the constraint

$$(1/3)x_1 + (2/3)x_2 \leq 7$$

might have been entered into the computer program as:

$$0.3333x_1 + 0.6667x_2 \leq 7$$

Should numerical problems arise in solving this linear program, consider rewriting the original constraint more precisely by multiplying both sides by 3, as follows:

$$x_1 + 2x_2 \leq 21$$

Note, however, that the parametric and sensitivity reports obtained from the computer pertain to the *new* constraint, not the *original* one. For example, increasing the rhs of the original constraint by 1 is equivalent to an increase of 3 in the rhs of the new constraint. Thus, the shadow price of the original constraint is three times that of the new constraint. In a similar way, the range of applicability of the shadow price of the original constraint is one-third that of the new constraint.

3. Read the documentation associated with the specific linear programming package you are using to see if helpful hints are provided for dealing with problems of numerical accuracy.

Summary

In this chapter, you have learned how to use the output obtained from a computer package that solves a linear program. You have seen how to interpret the optimal solution in the context of the specific problem, including the meaning of the values of the slack variables, the shadow prices, and the reduced costs. You have also learned how to use the sensitivity and parametric reports to answer "What happens if?" questions. To do so, first determine what impact the proposed change has on the model. Then, use the appropriate report to evaluate the impact of the change on the current optimal solution and/or objective function value. If you cannot do so, you can always answer the question by changing the appropriate values in the model and solving the new problem.

You now know how to solve linear programming problems that have a single, overall objective. In formulating some problems, however, you may identify more than one objective. How to handle problems with multiple objectives is the topic of Chapter 7.

Exercises

 EXERCISE 6.1   Recall the problem of BlubberMaid, Inc., in Example 3.1, Section 3.1, Chapter 3, in which A is the number of pounds of Airtex, E of Extendex, and R of Resistex to produce to

$$\text{Maximize profit } = 7A + 7E + 6R$$
Subject to

RESOURCE CONSTRAINTS

$$4A + 3E + 6R \leq 8000 \qquad \text{(polymer A in ounces)}$$
$$2A + 2E + 3R \leq 6800 \qquad \text{(polymer B in ounces)}$$
$$4A + 2E + 5R \leq 10400 \qquad \text{(polymer C in ounces)}$$
$$6A + 9E + 2R \leq 17600 \qquad \text{(base in ounces)}$$

DEMAND CONSTRAINTS

$$A \geq 1000 \qquad \text{(Airtex in pounds)}$$
$$E \geq 500 \qquad \text{(Extendex in pounds)}$$
$$R \geq 400 \qquad \text{(Resistex in pounds)}$$

LOGICAL CONSTRAINTS

$$A\,,\ \ E\,,\ \ R \geq 0$$

The following output is from the STORM computer package.

```
        The Product-Mix Problem of BlubberMaid, Inc.
             OPTIMAL SOLUTION - DETAILED REPORT
        Variable        Value        Cost     Red. cost    Status
   1        A       1000.0000      7.0000      0.0000       Basic
   2        E        533.3333      7.0000      0.0000       Basic
   3        R        400.0000      6.0000      0.0000       Basic

Objective Function Value = 13133.33
```

```
              The Product-Mix Problem of BlubberMaid, Inc.
                     OPTIMAL SOLUTION - DETAILED REPORT
          Constraint  Type        RHS         Slack    Shadow price
     1     POLYMER A    <=      8000.0000      0.0000      2.3333
     2     POLYMER B    <=      6800.0000   2533.3330      0.0000
     3     POLYMER C    <=     10400.0000   3333.3330      0.0000
     4          BASE    <=     17600.0000   6000.0000      0.0000
     5       DEMAND-A   >=      1000.0000      0.0000     -2.3333
     6       DEMAND-E   >=       500.0000     33.3333      0.0000
     7       DEMAND-R   >=       400.0000      0.0000     -8.0000


  Objective Function Value = 13133.33


              The Product-Mix Problem of BlubberMaid, Inc.
               SENSITIVITY ANALYSIS OF COST COEFFICIENTS
                            Current    Allowable    Allowable
               Variable     Coeff.      Minimum      Maximum
     1            A         7.0000     -Infinity     9.3333
     2            E         7.0000      5.2500       Infinity
     3            R         6.0000     -Infinity    14.0000


              The Product-Mix Problem of BlubberMaid, Inc.
            SENSITIVITY ANALYSIS OF RIGHT-HAND-SIDE VALUES
                            Current    Allowable    Allowable
          Constraint  Type   Value      Minimum      Maximum
     1     POLYMER A    <=   8000.0000  7900.0000   10000.0000
     2     POLYMER B    <=   6800.0000  4266.6670    Infinity
     3     POLYMER C    <=  10400.0000  7066.6670    Infinity
     4          BASE    <=  17600.0000 11600.0000    Infinity
     5       DEMAND-A   >=   1000.0000     0.0000    1025.0000
     6       DEMAND-E   >=    500.0000  -Infinity     533.3333
     7       DEMAND-R   >=    400.0000    25.0000     416.6667


              The Product-Mix Problem of BlubberMaid, Inc.
         PARAMETRIC ANALYSIS OF RIGHT-HAND-SIDE VALUE - POLYMER A
  COEF = 8000.000    LWR LIMIT = -Infinity    UPR LIMIT = Infinity
         ------- Range -------       Shadow    ---- Variable ----
              From          To        Price     Leave      Enter
  RHS     8000.000    10000.000       2.333    SLACK  4  SLACK  5
  Obj    13133.330    17800.000


  RHS    10000.000    11500.000       1.167    SLACK  3  SLACK  7
  Obj    17800.000    19550.000


  RHS    11500.000    12341.460       0.239    SLACK  5  SLACK  1
  Obj    19550.000    19751.220


  RHS    12341.460     Infinity       0.000    ----  No change  ----
  Obj    19751.220    19751.220


  RHS     8000.000     7900.000       2.333    SLACK  6
  Obj    13133.330    ????.??


  RHS     7900.000     -Infinity   ----  Infeasible in this range  ----
```

Use the foregoing output to answer the following questions:

    a. What is the optimal production plan?
    b. Which of the four resource constraints are binding?
    c. With the current production plan, for which one of the three products can an additional demand of 5% be met? Explain.

EXERCISE 6.2   Use the output in Exercise 6.1 to answer the following: If you could obtain additional quantities of only one of the three polymers, which one would you recommend? Explain.

EXERCISE 6.3   Use the output in Exercise 6.1 to answer the following: Which profit co-efficient(s) could double, while keeping all other coefficients fixed, without affecting the optimal production plan? Explain.

EXERCISE 6.4   Use the output in Exercise 6.1 to answer the following: The profit from Exten-dex has just decreased by 20%. What is the new production plan and total profit? Explain.

EXERCISE 6.5   Use the output in Exercise 6.1 to answer the following. (If unable to do so, obtain the answer by solving an appropriately modified model with your computer pack-age.) The commitment to produce 400 pounds of Resistex has just dropped by 10%. What happens to the optimal profit? Explain.

EXERCISE 6.6   Use the output in Exercise 6.1 to answer the following. (If unable to do so, obtain the answer by solving an appropriately modified model with your computer package.) The company wants to boost its profits to $18,000 by purchasing more of polymer A. How much *additional* polymer A is needed? Explain.

EXERCISE 6.7   Use the output in Exercise 6.1 to answer the following. (If unable to do so, obtain the answer by solving an appropriately modified model with your computer package.) If the demand for Airtex increases by 2%, what is the new optimal production plan? Explain.

EXERCISE 6.8   Recall the problem of MTV Steel in Example 3.2, Section 3.2, Chapter 3, in which you want to determine the values of the variables:

$$AP = \text{the number of tons of steel type A to produce}$$
$$BP = \text{the number of tons of steel type B to produce}$$
$$CP = \text{the number of tons of steel type C to produce}$$
$$AJ = \text{the number of tons of steel type A to buy from Japan}$$
$$BJ = \text{the number of tons of steel type B to buy from Japan}$$
$$CJ = \text{the number of tons of steel type C to buy from Japan}$$

so as to

Maximize profit $= 7AP + 8BP + 5CP + 4AJ + 6BJ + 2CJ$
Subject to

DEMAND CONTRAINTS

AP	$+$	AJ	$=$	2000	(demand A)
	BP	$+ BJ$	$=$	4000	(demand B)
		CP	$+ \quad CJ =$	5000	(demand C)

RESOURCE CONSTRAINTS

$$0.5AP + 0.45BP + 0.6CP \leq 2400 \quad \text{(machine time)}$$
$$AP + BP + CP \leq 5500 \quad \text{(welding material)}$$

LOGICAL CONSTRAINTS

$$AP, \; BP, \; CP, \; AJ, \; BJ, \; CJ \; \geq \; 0$$

The following output is from the STORM computer package.

```
                  The Make or Buy Problem of MTV Steel
                    OPTIMAL SOLUTION - DETAILED REPORT
          Variable        Value        Cost     Red. cost    Status
    1        AP        2000.0000       7.0000      0.0000     Basic
    2        BP           0.0000       8.0000     -0.2500     Lower bound
    3        CP        2333.3330       5.0000      0.0000     Basic
    4        AJ           0.0000       4.0000     -0.5000     Lower bound
    5        BJ        4000.0000       6.0000      0.0000     Basic
    6        CJ        2666.6670       2.0000      0.0000     Basic

  Slack Variables
    10     WELDING     1166.6670       0.0000      0.0000     Basic
    11     HOURS          0.0000       0.0000     -5.0000     Lower bound

         Constraint  Type      RHS         Slack    Shadow price
    1     DEMAND-A    =      2000.0000    0.0000      4.5000
    2     DEMAND-B    =      4000.0000    0.0000      6.0000
    3     DEMAND-C    =      5000.0000    0.0000      2.0000
    4     WELDING     <=     5500.0000 1166.6670      0.0000
    5     HOURS       <=     2400.0000    0.0000      5.0000

  Objective Function Value = 55000
                SENSITIVITY ANALYSIS OF COST COEFFICIENTS
                           Current     Allowable    Allowable
               Variable    Coeff.      Minimum      Maximum
       1         AP        7.0000       6.5000      Infinity
       2         BP        8.0000      -Infinity     8.2500
       3         CP        5.0000       4.6667       5.6000
       4         AJ        4.0000      -Infinity     4.5000
       5         BJ        6.0000       5.7500      Infinity
       6         CJ        2.0000       1.4000       2.3333

              SENSITIVITY ANALYSIS OF RIGHT-HAND-SIDE VALUES
                           Current     Allowable    Allowable
        Constraint  Type    Value      Minimum      Maximum
    1    DEMAND-A    =     2000.0000    0.0000      4800.0000
    2    DEMAND-B    =     4000.0000    0.0000      Infinity
    3    DEMAND-C    =     5000.0000  2333.3330     Infinity
    4    WELDING     <=    5500.0000  4333.3330     Infinity
    5    HOURS       <=    2400.0000  1000.0000     3100.0000
       PARAMETRIC ANALYSIS OF RIGHT-HAND-SIDE VALUE - WELDING
   COEF = 5500.000    LWR LIMIT = -Infinity    UPR LIMIT = Infinity
        -------  Range  -------     Shadow   ----  Variable  ----
             From          To        Price     Leave       Enter
   RHS    5500.000    Infinity       0.000   ----  No change  ----
   Obj   55000.000   55000.000

   RHS    5500.000    4333.333       0.000   SLACK   4          AJ
   Obj   55000.000   55000.000

   RHS    4333.333    4000.000       3.000           AP   SLACK  5
   Obj   55000.000   54000.000

   RHS    4000.000       0.000       3.000                  CP
   Obj   54000.000   42000.000

   RHS       0.000    -Infinity   ----  Infeasible in this range  ----
```

(cont.)

(cont.)

```
              The Make or Buy Problem of MTV Steel
        PARAMETRIC ANALYSIS OF RIGHT-HAND-SIDE VALUE - HOURS
    COEF = 2400.000     LWR LIMIT = -Infinity    UPR LIMIT = Infinity
            ------- Range -------        Shadow   ---- Variable ----
                From          To          Price    Leave      Enter

    RHS      2400.000    3100.000        5.000   SLACK   4          AJ
    Obj     55000.000   58500.000

    RHS      3100.000    3250.000        0.000           CJ  SLACK   5
    Obj     58500.000   58500.000

    RHS      3250.000    Infinity        0.000   ----  No change  ----
    Obj     58500.000   58500.000

    RHS      2400.000    1000.000        5.000           CP         AJ
    Obj     55000.000   48000.000

    RHS      1000.000       0.000        6.000           AP
    Obj     48000.000   42000.000

    RHS         0.000   -Infinity  ----  Infeasible in this range ----
```

Use the foregoing output to answer the following questions:

a. What is the optimal production/purchase plan for MTV Steel?

b. Which of the two resource constraints are binding?

c. If you could obtain either more welding material or more hours of machine time, but not both, which would you choose? Explain.

EXERCISE 6.9   Use the output in Exercise 6.8 to answer the following. (If unable to do so, obtain the answer by solving an appropriately modified model with your computer package.) The Japanese have just increased the price they charge for type C tubing from $7 to $8 per foot. How does the current production/purchase plan change? Explain.

EXERCISE 6.10   Use the output in Exercise 6.8 to answer the following. (If unable to do so, obtain the answer by solving an appropriately modified model with your computer package.) The company wants to increase its profits to $57,500. How many more hours of machine time are needed to accomplish this objective? Explain.

EXERCISE 6.11   Use the output in Exercise 6.8 to answer the following. (If unable to do so, obtain the answer by solving an appropriately modified model with your computer package.) The company can sell its welding material for a profit of $32 per pound. How much should it sell? Explain.

EXERCISE 6.12   Recall the diet problem of Mountain View General Hospital in Example 3.3, Section 3.3, Chapter 3, in which you want to determine the values of the variables:

$$SPAG = \text{the number of 100 grams of spaghetti to include}$$
$$TURK = \text{the number of 100 grams of turkey to include}$$
$$POTA = \text{the number of 100 grams of potatoes to include}$$
$$SPIN = \text{the number of 100 grams of spinach to include}$$
$$APPL = \text{the number of 100 grams of apple strudel to include}$$

so as to

Minimize
$5000SPAG + 5000TURK + 7900POTA + 300SPIN + 14300APPL$
Subject to

NUTRIENT CONSTRAINTS

$$
\begin{array}{llllll}
5000SPAG + & 29300TURK + & 5300POTA + & 3000SPIN + & 4000APPL \geq 63000 & \text{(protein)} \\
1.1SPAG + & 1.8TURK + & 0.5POTA + & 2.2SPIN + & 1.2APPL \geq \quad 10 & \text{(iron)} \\
1.4SPAG + & 5.4TURK + & 0.9POTA + & 0.5SPIN + & 0.6APPL \geq \quad 15 & \text{(niacin)} \\
0.18SPAG + & 0.06TURK + & 0.06POTA + & 0.07SPIN + & 0.15APPL \geq \quad\; 1 & \text{(thiamin)} \\
& & 10POTA + & 28SPIN + & 3APPL \geq \quad 50 & \text{(vitamin C)}
\end{array}
$$

BOUND CONSTRAINTS

$$
\begin{array}{rl}
SPAG \leq & 3 \\
TURK \leq & 3 \\
POTA \leq & 2 \\
SPIN \leq & 1 \\
APPL \leq & 1
\end{array}
$$

LOGICAL CONSTRAINTS

SPAG, TURK, POTA, SPIN, APPL ≥ 0

The following output is from the STORM computer package.

```
          The Diet Problem of Mountain View Hospital
              OPTIMAL SOLUTION - DETAILED REPORT
          Variable      Value       Cost      Red. cost   Status

   1        SPAG        3.0000     5000.0000     0.0000    Basic
   2        TURK        2.8333     5000.0000     0.0000    Basic
   3        POTA        2.0000     7900.0000     0.0000    Basic
   4        SPIN        1.0000      300.0000     0.0000    Basic
   5        APPL        0.6667    14300.0000     0.0000    Basic

   Slack Variables
   6       PROTEIN   51283.3200       0.0000       0.0000    Basic
   7         IRON        2.4000       0.0000       0.0000    Basic
   8        NIACIN       7.2000       0.0000       0.0000    Basic
   9       THIAMIN       0.0000       0.0000   83333.3400 Lower bound
  10      VITAMIN C      0.0000       0.0000     599.9997 Lower bound
  11        SPAG         0.0000       0.0000   10000.0000 Lower bound
  12       TURKEY        0.1667       0.0000       0.0000    Basic
  13      POTATOES       0.0000       0.0000    3099.9970 Lower bound
  14      SPINACH        0.0000       0.0000   22333.3300 Lower bound
  15      STRUDEL        0.3333       0.0000       0.0000    Basic

   Objective Function Value = 54800
```

(cont.)

(cont.)

```
            The Diet Problem of Mountain View Hospital
               OPTIMAL SOLUTION - DETAILED REPORT
         Constraint  Type     RHS          Slack    Shadow price

    1     PROTEIN   >=    63000.0000    51283.3200       0.0000
    2      IRON     >=       10.0000        2.4000       0.0000
    3     NIACIN    >=       15.0000        7.2000       0.0000
    4     THIAMIN   >=        1.0000        0.0000   83333.3400
    5    VITAMIN C  >=       50.0000        0.0000     599.9997
    6      SPAG     <=        3.0000        0.0000  -10000.0000
    7     TURKEY    <=        3.0000        0.1667       0.0000
    8    POTATOES   <=        2.0000        0.0000   -3099.9970
    9    SPINACH    <=        1.0000        0.0000  -22333.3300
   10    STRUDEL    <=        1.0000        0.3333       0.0000
```

```
              SENSITIVITY ANALYSIS OF COST COEFFICIENTS
                         Current     Allowable     Allowable
              Variable   Coeff.      Minimum       Maximum
    1    SPAG         5000.0000     -Infinity     15000.0000
    2    TURK         5000.0000      1666.6670      5422.7270
    3    POTA         7900.0000     -Infinity     11000.0000
    4    SPIN          300.0000     -Infinity     22633.3300
    5    APPL        14300.0000     13370.0000      Infinity
```

```
           SENSITIVITY ANALYSIS OF RIGHT-HAND-SIDE VALUES
                           Current     Allowable    Allowable
         Constraint  Type   Value      Minimum      Maximum
    1     PROTEIN   >=    63000.0000   -Infinity   114283.3000
    2      IRON     >=       10.0000   -Infinity       12.4000
    3     NIACIN    >=       15.0000   -Infinity       22.2000
    4     THIAMIN   >=        1.0000      0.9200        1.0100
    5    VITAMIN C  >=       50.0000     49.8000       51.0000
    6      SPAG     <=        3.0000      2.9444        3.4865
    7     TURKEY    <=        3.0000      2.8333      Infinity
    8    POTATOES   <=        2.0000      1.9000        2.0227
    9    SPINACH    <=        1.0000      0.9643        1.0075
   10    STRUDEL    <=        1.0000      0.6667      Infinity
```

```
       PARAMETRIC ANALYSIS OF RIGHT-HAND-SIDE VALUE - PROTEIN
    COEF = 63000.000   LWR LIMIT = -Infinity   UPR LIMIT = Infinity
            ------- Range -------       Shadow   ---- Variable ----
              From          To          Price    Leave       Enter

    RHS    63000.000    114283.300      0.000    SLACK   1   SLACK   7
    Obj    54800.000     54800.000

    RHS   114283.300    118888.900      0.121    SLACK   8   SLACK   4
    Obj    54800.000     55355.560

    RHS   118888.900    119166.700      1.000    SLACK   7   SLACK   5
    Obj    55355.560     55633.330

    RHS   119166.700    120500.000      3.575    SLACK   6   SLACK  10
    Obj    55633.330     60400.000

    RHS   120500.000    120500.000     14.000    SLACK  11
    Obj    60400.000     60400.000

    RHS   120500.000     Infinity   ---- Infeasible in this range ----

    RHS    63000.000   -2.621E+42      0.000   ---- No change    ----
    Obj    54800.000     54800.000
```

Use the foregoing output to answer the following questions:

a. What is the optimal meal?
b. The proposed meal exceeds the minimum requirements for which of the following nutrients: protein, iron, niacin, thiamin, and vitamin C? Explain.

EXERCISE 6.13 Use the output in Exercise 6.12 to find the total weight of the optimal meal.

EXERCISE 6.14 Use the output in Exercise 6.12 to answer the following. (If unable to do so, obtain the answer by solving an appropriately modified model with your computer package.) It was recently discovered that each 100 grams of apple strudel contains only 13,300 milligrams of fat. How should the proposed meal be changed? Explain.

EXERCISE 6.15 Use the output in Exercise 6.12 to answer the following. (If unable to do so, obtain the answer by solving an appropriately modified model with your computer package.) How much additional fat will the optimal meal have if 51 milligrams of vitamin C are required instead of 50? Explain.

EXERCISE 6.16 Use the output in Exercise 6.12 to answer the following. (If unable to do so, obtain the answer by solving an appropriately modified model with your computer package.) By how much can the protein requirement be increased so that the fat content of the optimal meal remains at 54,800 milligrams? Explain.

EXERCISE 6.17 Fresh Food Farms, Inc., has 50 acres of land on which to plant any amount of corn, soybeans, and lettuce. The following table shows the relevant information pertaining to the yield, net profit, and water requirements of each crop:

CROP	YIELD (kg/acre)	NET PROFIT ($/kg)	REQUIRED WATER (liters/kg)
Corn	640	1.00	8.75
Soybeans	500	0.80	5.00
Lettuce	400	0.60	2.25

Given that 100,000 liters of water are available and that the company has contracted to sell at least 5120 kilograms of corn, the following linear program was developed, in which CN is the number of acres of corn to plant, SB is the number of acres of soybeans to plant, and LT is the number of acres of lettuce to plant:

$$\text{Maximize} \quad 640CN + 400SB + 240LT$$

Subject to

$$
\begin{aligned}
CN + SB + LT &\leq 50 \quad \text{(land)} \\
5600CN + 2500SB + 900LT &\leq 100000 \quad \text{(water)} \\
CN &\geq 8 \quad \text{(corn demand)} \\
CN, \quad SB, \quad LT &\geq 0
\end{aligned}
$$

The following output is from the STORM computer package.

```
                    The Problem of Fresh Food Farms
                    OPTIMAL SOLUTION - DETAILED REPORT
          Variable        Value        Cost    Red. cost   Status
    1        CN          8.0000     640.0000     0.0000     Basic
    2        SB         10.8750     400.0000     0.0000     Basic
    3        LT         31.1250     240.0000     0.0000     Basic


Slack Variables
    4       LAND         0.0000       0.0000  -150.0000  Lower bound
    5       WATER        0.0000       0.0000    -0.1000  Lower bound
    6       CORN         0.0000       0.0000   -70.0000  Lower bound


Objective Function Value = 16940

                    OPTIMAL SOLUTION - DETAILED REPORT
        Constraint Type       RHS          Slack    Shadow price
    1       LAND    <=       50.0000       0.0000      150.0000
    2      WATER    <=   100000.0000       0.0000        0.1000
    3       CORN    >=        8.0000       0.0000      -70.0000


Objective Function Value = 16940

                 SENSITIVITY ANALYSIS OF COST COEFFICIENTS
                           Current      Allowable    Allowable
               Variable     Coeff.       Minimum      Maximum

        1        CN       640.0000      -Infinity     710.0000
        2        SB       400.0000      376.1702      666.6667
        3        LT       240.0000      144.0000      276.1290

              SENSITIVITY ANALYSIS OF RIGHT-HAND-SIDE VALUES
                           Current      Allowable    Allowable
        Constraint  Type    Value        Minimum      Maximum

    1       LAND    <=       50.0000      30.0800      69.3333
    2      WATER    <=   100000.0000   82600.0000  149800.0000
    3       CORN    >=        8.0000       0.0000      11.7021

          PARAMETRIC ANALYSIS OF RIGHT-HAND-SIDE VALUE - LAND
    COEF = 50.000     LWR LIMIT = -Infinity    UPR LIMIT = Infinity
          -------  Range  -------     Shadow   ---- Variable ----
                From          To       Price    Leave      Enter

    RHS      50.000      69.333      150.000           SB   SLACK    1
    Obj   16940.000   19840.000


    RHS      69.333    Infinity        0.000    ---- No change ----
    Obj   19840.000   19840.000


    RHS      50.000      30.080      150.000           LT   SLACK    3
    Obj   16940.000   ?????.???


    RHS      30.080      17.857      206.452           SB   SLACK    2
    Obj   ?????.???   11428.570


    RHS      17.857       ?.???      640.000   SLACK    3
    Obj   11428.570    5120.000


    RHS       ?.???    -Infinity   ---- Infeasible in this range ----
```

```
                     The Problem of Fresh Food Farms
          PARAMETRIC ANALYSIS OF RIGHT-HAND-SIDE VALUE - WATER
       COEF = 100000.000  LWR LIMIT = -Infinity     UPR LIMIT = Infinity
            -------  Range  -------       Shadow   ---- Variable ----
                  From            To       Price    Leave      Enter

       RHS   100000.000   149800.000      0.100         LT SLACK    3
       Obj    16940.000    21920.000

       RHS   149800.000   280000.000    7.742E-02       SB SLACK    2
       Obj    21920.000    32000.000

       RHS   280000.000     Infinity      0.000   ---- No change ----
       Obj    32000.000    32000.000

       RHS   100000.000    82600.000      0.100         SB SLACK    1
       Obj    16940.000    15200.000

       RHS    82600.000    44800.000      ?.???         LT
       Obj    15200.000     5120.000

       RHS    44800.000     -Infinity   ---- Infeasible in this range ----
```

After obtaining this output, the computer went down. As you can see, the printer failed to print the five values in the parametric analysis reports where there is a string of question marks. Complete the output by computing those missing values. Show your work.

EXERCISE 6.18 Use the output in Exercise 6.17 to answer the following questions.

  a. How many kilograms of each crop will be harvested?
  b. In the optimal solution, how much water and land are not utilized? Explain.
  c. By how much would the net profit per kilogram of lettuce have to fall before the current optimal solution changes?

EXERCISE 6.19 Use the output in Exercise 6.17 to answer the following. (If unable to do so, obtain the answer by solving an appropriately modified model with your computer package.) For the same amount of money, management can either lease an additional 10 acres of land for the season or acquire 13,000 liters of water. Which single alternative would you recommend? Explain.

EXERCISE 6.20 Use the output in Exercise 6.17 to answer the following. (If unable to do so, obtain the answer by solving an appropriately modified model with your computer package.) Management wants to obtain a net profit of $25,000. How many liters of water are needed to achieve this goal, assuming the amount of land remains fixed?

EXERCISE 6.21 Use the output in Exercise 6.17 to answer the following. (If unable to do so, obtain the answer by solving an appropriately modified model with your computer package.) Management has just received an offer to lease its land for the season at $200 per acre. How many acres, if any, should it lease? Explain.

EXERCISE 6.22 Consider the linear program in Exercise 2.14 at the end of Chapter 2. The twelve variables in the following STORM output represent the amount of jet fuel to be supplied by each of the three vendors to each of the four airports (for example, the variable V2-A3 represents the amount of fuel supplied from Vendor 2 to Airport 3).

```
                    Jet Refueling (Transportation)
                  OPTIMAL SOLUTION - DETAILED REPORT
          Variable        Value         Cost    Red. cost   Status


   1       V1-A1         0.0000      900.0000    400.0000 Lower bound
   2       V1-A2       170.0000      900.0000      0.0000   Basic
   3       V1-A3         0.0000      800.0000    300.0000 Lower bound
   4       V1-A4       130.0000     1000.0000      0.0000   Basic
   5       V2-A1       150.0000      800.0000      0.0000   Basic
   6       V2-A2        80.0000     1200.0000      0.0000   Basic
   7       V2-A3         0.0000     1300.0000    500.0000 Lower bound
   8       V2-A4         0.0000     1400.0000    100.0000 Lower bound
   9       V3-A1         0.0000      900.0000    400.0000 Lower bound
  10       V3-A2         0.0000     1300.0000    400.0000 Lower bound
  11       V3-A3       350.0000      500.0000      0.0000   Basic
  12       V3-A4       350.0000     1000.0000      0.0000   Basic


Slack Variables
  13     SUPPLY-V1       0.0000        0.0000    300.0000 Lower bound
  14     SUPPLY-V2     370.0000        0.0000      0.0000   Basic
  15     SUPPLY-V3       0.0000        0.0000    300.0000 Lower bound
  16     DEMAND-A1       0.0000        0.0000    800.0000 Lower bound
  17     DEMAND-A2       0.0000        0.0000   1200.0000 Lower bound
  18     DEMAND-A3       0.0000        0.0000    800.0000 Lower bound
  19     DEMAND-A4       0.0000        0.0000   1300.0000 Lower bound

Objective Function Value = 1024000

                    Jet Refueling (Transportation)
                  OPTIMAL SOLUTION - DETAILED REPORT
        Constraint  Type       RHS          Slack    Shadow price


   1     SUPPLY-V1   <=      300.0000       0.0000     -300.0000
   2     SUPPLY-V2   <=      600.0000     370.0000        0.0000
   3     SUPPLY-V3   <=      700.0000       0.0000     -300.0000
   4     DEMAND-A1   >=      150.0000       0.0000      800.0000
   5     DEMAND-A2   >=      250.0000       0.0000     1200.0000
   6     DEMAND-A3   >=      350.0000       0.0000      800.0000
   7     DEMAND-A4   >=      480.0000       0.0000     1300.0000

Objective Function Value = 1024000

                    Jet Refueling (Transportation)
               SENSITIVITY ANALYSIS OF COST COEFFICIENTS
                          Current    Allowable    Allowable
               Variable    Coeff.     Minimum      Maximum


   1       V1-A1       900.0000      500.0000    Infinity
   2       V1-A2       900.0000      800.0000    1200.0000
   3       V1-A3       800.0000      500.0000    Infinity
   4       V1-A4      1000.0000      700.0000    1100.0000
   5       V2-A1       800.0000        0.0000    1200.0000
   6       V2-A2      1200.0000      900.0000    1300.0000
   7       V2-A3      1300.0000      800.0000    Infinity
   8       V2-A4      1400.0000     1300.0000    Infinity
   9       V3-A1       900.0000      500.0000    Infinity
  10       V3-A2      1300.0000      900.0000    Infinity
  11       V3-A3       500.0000     -300.0000     800.0000
  12       V3-A4      1000.0000      700.0000    1300.0000
```

```
                    Jet Refueling (Transportation)
              SENSITIVITY ANALYSIS OF RIGHT-HAND-SIDE VALUES
                             Current    Allowable    Allowable
            Constraint  Type   Value     Minimum      Maximum

      1     SUPPLY-V1   <=    300.0000   130.0000     380.0000
      2     SUPPLY-V2   <=    600.0000   230.0000     Infinity
      3     SUPPLY-V3   <=    700.0000   530.0000     780.0000
      4     DEMAND-A1   >=    150.0000     0.0000     520.0000
      5     DEMAND-A2   >=    250.0000   170.0000     620.0000
      6     DEMAND-A3   >=    350.0000   270.0000     520.0000
      7     DEMAND-A4   >=    480.0000   400.0000     650.0000


                    Jet Refueling (Transportation)
           PARAMETRIC ANALYSIS OF RIGHT-HAND-SIDE VALUE - DEMAND-A4
      COEF = 480.000      LWR LIMIT = -Infinity    UPR LIMIT = Infinity
        -------  Range  -------        Shadow    ---- Variable ----
              From           To         Price     Leave      Enter

      RHS      480.000      650.000    1300.000    V1-A2      V2-A4
      Obj  1024000.000  1245000.000


      RHS      650.000      850.000    1400.000    SLACK    2
      Obj  1245000.000  ???????.???


      RHS      850.000      Infinity  ---- Infeasible in this range ----


      RHS      480.000      ???.???    1300.000    V2-A2  SLACK    1
      Obj  1024000.000   920000.000


      RHS      ???.???      350.000    1000.000    V1-A4  SLACK    3
      Obj   920000.000   870000.000


      RHS      350.000        0.000    ????.???    V3-A4  SLACK    7
      Obj   870000.000   520000.000


      RHS        0.000     -1.024E+40     0.000   ---- No change ----
      Obj   520000.000   520000.000
```

After obtaining this output, the computer went down. As you can see, the printer failed to print the four values in the parametric analysis report where there is a string of question marks. Complete the output by computing those missing values. Show your work.

EXERCISE 6.23 Use the output in Exercise 6.22 to answer the following. (If unable to do so, obtain the answer by solving an appropriately modified model with your computer package.)

a. Prepare a table that shows how much each vendor supplies to each airport and the total cost of doing so.
b. Which vendor(s) have excess supplies of fuel and by how much? Explain.
c. Which cost(s) would have to be changed the least, either up or down, while keeping all other costs the same, in order to change the current shipping plan? Explain.

EXERCISE 6.24 In the output in Exercise 6.22, interpret the reduced cost of 400 for the variable V1-A1 and 300 for the slack variable SUPPLY-V1 in the context of the original problem.

EXERCISE 6.25 Use the output in Exercise 6.22 to answer the following. (If unable to do so, obtain the answer by solving an appropriately modified model with your computer package.) If the demand at Airport 4 increases to 600,000 gallons, explain what happens to the optimal solution and the optimal objective function value.

EXERCISE 6.26 Use the output in Exercise 6.22 to answer the following. (If unable to do so, obtain the answer by solving an appropriately modified model with your computer package.) If the supply of Vendor 2 decreases to 380,000 gallons, explain what happens to the optimal solution and the optimal objective function value.

EXERCISE 6.27 Use the output in Exercise 6.22 to answer the following. (If unable to do so, obtain the answer by solving an appropriately modified model with your computer package.) The company wishes to decrease its total costs to $750,000. To what value should the demand at Airport 4 be decreased? Explain.

EXERCISE 6.28 Use your computer package to verify the optimal solution to the investment problem of Pension Planners, Inc., in Example 3.4, Section 3.4, Chapter 3, and to write a report in which you:

    a. Indicate the highest rate of return that can be achieved if no money is invested in Fund 6.

    b. Discuss the effect that increasing the amount that must be invested in the low-risk investment would have on the optimal rate of return.

    c. Provide the optimal investment strategy if the amount invested in Fund 4 is to be the same as that invested in Fund 5.

EXERCISE 6.29 Use your computer package to verify the optimal solution to the blending problem of Hexxon Oil Company in Example 3.5, Section 3.5, Chapter 3, and to write a report in which you:

    a. Identify which ingredients—sulfur, lead, and phosphorus—are at their allowed limit.

    b. Discuss the effect of individual increases and decreases in the costs of the three crude oils before the current amounts of ingredients in the blend should be changed.

    c. Explain the impact of changes in the maximum sulfur content on the cost of the optimal blend.

    d. Provide the optimal blend and associated cost if the price of Texas crude oil increases by 10%.

    e. Provide the optimal blend and associated cost if the limit on the total amount of additives is decreased from 19% to 15%.

EXERCISE 6.30 Use your computer package to verify the optimal solution to the production-planning problem of the National Steel Corporation in Example 3.6, Section 3.6, Chapter 3, and to write a report in which you:

    a. Discuss the general sensitivity of the optimal production plan to individual changes in each of the monthly production costs.

    b. Explain what happens to the optimal cost as the final inventory requirement is changed.

    c. Provide the optimal production-inventory plan and cost if the inventory costs increase to $150 per ton per month.

    d. Provide the optimal production-inventory plan and cost if the demand in each of the 4 months increases by 100 tons.

CRITICAL-THINKING PROJECT A

Recall Critical-Thinking Project A following the exercises in Chapter 3. Mr. Sam Barton, Production Manager of Hexxon Oil Company, needs to determine the least-cost plan for producing Regular, Unleaded, and Supreme gasoline. To develop the desired production plan, obtain the two formulations from your instructor and prepare a managerial report following these guidelines.

1. Use your computer package to solve the linear programming formulation.
    a. Prepare a table indicating how many barrels of each constituent to blend in making each gasoline. Indicate the total amount of each constituent used, the amount of each type of gasoline produced, and the total daily corporate profits.
    b. In formulating the problem, the minimum for octane rating for Regular is specified as 90, for Unleaded as 96, and Supreme as 110. What is the *actual* octane rating of each gasoline based on the optimal blending plan?
    c. Mr. James Arden, Vice-President of Production, wants to know how sensitive the current production plan is to an increase in the selling price of Supreme gasoline. A recent MBA explained that as long as that selling price does not increase by more than $0.45, the current production plan remains optimal. Explain why that statement is *not* true in this particular model.
    d. By how much must the selling price of Supreme gasoline increase before Hexxon can attain a daily corporate profit of $68,000, assuming all other prices and costs remain fixed? (Hint: Try different values for the selling price of Supreme.)
    e. Suppose the demand for Unleaded gasoline increases to 4100 barrels. What is the new production plan and daily profit? By looking at the new production plan and without referring to the shadow price, explain why the daily corporate profits have decreased, even though the demand for Unleaded gas has increased.

2. Use your linear programming package to solve the second model with the new nonlinear objective function you have been given. Report the solution in the form of your answer to foregoing question 1(a). (Hint: "Guess" a value for the amount of constituent 1 to be blended in making Supreme gasoline [for example, $x_{1s} = 1000$ gallons]. Then determine the objective function coefficient of this variable, which would be 8.00 for this example. Include appropriate lower and upper bounds to force the value of the variable x_{1s} to have the guessed value [1000, in this example] throughout the model. Solve the resulting linear program. Continue guessing new values for this variable x_{1s} in an intelligent way and solving the resulting linear programs.)

CRITICAL-THINKING PROJECT E

Recall Critical Thinking Project E in Chapter 3. You, as Director of Communications of Tele Com, need to determine how to expand the capacity for transmitting data from the office in Los Angeles to the one in Boston, through various intermediate locations. To examine the existing network, obtain the mathematical formulation and diagram from your instructor. Then prepare a managerial report from you, Ms. Amy Jenkins, to the CEO, Ms. Clarissa Bell, that includes the answers to the following questions.

1. Use your computer package to find the maximum number of bits of data per day that can be transmitted from Los Angeles to Boston. Indicate the optimal transmission rates next to each arc of the diagram.

2. The CEO of Tele Com feels that it is necessary to expand the existing system so that at least 25 billion bits of data can be transmitted from Los Angeles to Boston each day. One approach that has been suggested is to increase the maximum transmission rates of certain arcs in the existing system. Considering the time, money, and complexity involved, management wants to know if the desired transmission rate can be achieved by increasing the maximum transmission rate in only one arc.

   In view of the optimal solution in question 1, which arcs would you choose to consider in increasing the maximum transmission rate? Modify the capacity of each such arc, one at a time, to determine the maximum increase you can achieve in the transmission rate from Los Angeles to Boston. Can you reach the target of 25 billion bits per day in this way?

3. A second alternative is to open a new office in Kansas City that could receive incoming data from Denver and/or Albuquerque and retransmit that data to Chicago and/or Atlanta. Again, considering the time, money, and complexity involved, management wants to know if the desired transmission rate can be achieved by having exactly one incoming and one outgoing arc from the new Kansas City office.

   For each combination of one incoming and one outgoing arc at Kansas City, determine the maximum increase you can achieve in the transmission rate from Los Angeles to Boston by setting the maximum transmission rate on the new arcs in Kansas City to any value you desire. Can you reach the target of 25 billion bits per day in this way? If so, how small can you make the maximum transmission rates on the incoming and outgoing arcs to Kansas City and still achieve the desired transmission rate from Los Angeles to Boston?

Video Case

KEEP ON TRUCKING

Yellow Freight is a trucking firm that makes deliveries on goods that take up less than a truck's full capacity. The carrier has 26 breakbulks, which are intermediate points along routes where shipments arrive from several different trucks. At these breakbulks, loads are rearranged by common destination and divided up into smaller shipments that are then trucked out to one of 630 end-of-line (EOL) terminals.

Remember the Pony Express? Riders would carry the mail long distances by changing horses at stations along the route. With a slight variation, Yellow Freight drivers truck their load to breakbulks and detach the trailer. Another driver takes over the load and drives to the next breakbulk. The process continues until the shipment reaches its destination. For example, a shipment may start out from the terminal at Boston, go through breakbulks at Maybrook and Kansas City, and end up at the destination terminal in Des Moines.

On an average day, Yellow Freight makes 60,000 pickups and deliveries; 250,000 separate shipments reach 35,000 communities to 400,000 customers. The network has 630 terminals. To optimize the daily freight routes by balancing service demand with operational costs, Yellow Freight uses SYSNET, the large-scale resource allocation model that runs on their main frame computer.

SYSNET is an advanced, interactive optimization program, a hard-working management tool that offers fast, comprehensive analysis of network conditions to Yellow Freight managers, who can carefully control one of the largest networks in the world and consistently provide high quality service. SYSNET weighs the many trade-offs among variables, including handling costs, capacities, transit time, highway miles, and the number of empty trailers. Operations managers cannot add direct shipments without checking with the SYSNET managers. Why? A small savings that a direct shipment might earn might be more than offset by increased costs in the rest of the system. (Total run-

ning time: 6:00.)

Questions on the Video

1. How many different ways can Yellow Freight ship from Boston to Des Moines?
2. What are the trade-offs between shipping direct and shipping in the regular manner?

Beyond the Video

1. Describe the similarities between Yellow Freight and airlines, with their structured routes. What are the airlines' breakbulks? What problems do they have with "shipping" passengers and handling capacity?
2. Federal Express was one of the pioneers in shipping with a breakbulk, which is its hub in Memphis, Tennessee. Often packages shipped from Atlanta to Miami would go through Memphis. Explain the business rationale for adding extra mileage to these packages.

Practical Considerations

1. What impact does SYSNET have on the authority of a local shipping manager running day-to-day operations at Boston? at Maybrook? Why is centralized authority necessary in a setup such as the one Yellow Freight has?
2. The solution technique for a linear programming problem as large as Yellow Freight's must run faster than the standard simplex technique. Its linear programming model has a special structure that uses only integers. What other algorithms might be faster than the standard simplex?

Source: Yellow Freight, Overland Park, KA, 1991.

MULTIOBJECTIVE OPTIMIZATION USING GOAL PROGRAMMING

. . . .

*M*ountain View General Hospital is committed to excellence in it full-care treatment of patients. Providing patients with the best possible medical care is important, and so is offering them the best in nutrition. Does each meal meet the requirements for protein, iron, niacin, and other important nutrients while keeping fat content down? Can the Nutrition Department prepare such a meal without incurring high costs, which it would then have to pass on to its patients? How does the Nutrition Department come up with a meal that balances the trade-off between nutrition and cost?

The Case Study in this chapter illustrates how the Nutrition Department applies multiobjective goal programming to help answer these important questions.

In all the problems formulated so far, there has been a single overall objective, such as maximizing profits or minimizing costs. In many situations, however, you may have **multiple objectives**—that is, two or more goals to achieve. For example, in an investment problem, you might simultaneously want to maximize the total expected return, maximize the rate of return, minimize the amount of risk involved, and minimize the tax liability.

Multiple objectives
Two or more goals to achieve simultaneously.

Multiple objectives often *conflict* with each other. You can only optimize one objective at the expense of others. For example, to achieve the highest expected return, in general, will result in a portfolio with high risk. Similarly, a portfolio that minimizes risk does so at the expense of expected return. Thus, with multiobjectives, you cannot expect to achieve the best values for all objectives simultaneously. Multiple objectives can occur in linear, integer, and even nonlinear problems, and there are various ways to handle the trade-offs. In this chapter, you will learn one approach to handle these trade-offs in a linear programming model.

■ 7.1 AN EXAMPLE
OF MULTIOBJECTIVE OPTIMIZATION

Recall the make-or-buy decision problem faced by the management of MTV Steel, presented in Example 3.2, Chapter 3.

EXAMPLE 7.1 THE MULTIOBJECTIVE PROBLEM OF MTV STEEL COMPANY MTV Steel Company produces three sizes of tubes: A, which sells for $10 per foot; B, which sells for $12 per foot; and C, which sells for $9 per foot. To manufacture each foot of Tube A requires 0.5 min of processing time on a certain shaping machine. Each foot of Tube B needs 0.45 min, and each foot of Tube C 0.6 min. After production, each foot of tube, regardless of type, requires 1 ounce of welding material. The total production cost is estimated to be $3, $4, and $4 per foot of Tubes A, B, and C, respectively.

For the coming week, MTV Steel has received an exceptionally large order for 2000 feet of Tube A, 4000 feet of Tube B, and 5000 feet of Tube C. As only 40 hours of machine time are available this week and only 5500 ounces of welding material are in inventory, the Production Department will not be able to meet these demands, which require a total of 97 hours of machine time and 11,000 ounces of welding material. Because management does not expect this high level of demand to continue, it does not want to expand production facilities, but it also does not want to lose this business. Therefore, it is considering purchasing some tubes from suppliers in Japan at a delivered cost of $6 per foot of Tube A, $6 per foot of Tube B, and $7 per foot of Tube C. These data are summarized in Table 7.1.

TABLE 7.1	*Data for the Make-or-Buy Problem of MTV Steel*					
TUBE TYPE	SELLING PRICE ($/ft)	DEMAND (ft)	MACHINE TIME (min/ft)	WELDING MATERIAL (oz/ft)	PRODUCTION COST ($/ft)	PURCHASE COST ($/ft)
A	10	2000	0.50	1	3	6
B	12	4000	0.45	1	4	6
C	9	5000	0.60	1	4	7
Amount available			40 hr	5500 oz		

In Example 3.2, Chapter 3, the objective is to determine how much of each tube type to produce and how much to purchase from Japan so as to meet the demands and maximize the company's profits. However, a second objective arises when the CEO informs you that the government has requested a voluntary effort to reduce the amount of money spent on imports. In this make-or-buy problem, in addition to maximizing the total profit, you, as a member of management, also want to *minimize the total cost of the imports.* ■

In Section 3.2, Chapter 3, the problem involving only the profit-maximization objective is formulated using the following six decision variables:

$$AP = \text{the number of feet of Tube A to produce}$$
$$BP = \text{the number of feet of Tube B to produce}$$
$$CP = \text{the number of feet of Tube C to produce}$$
$$AJ = \text{the number of feet of Tube A to buy from Japan}$$
$$BJ = \text{the number of feet of Tube B to buy from Japan}$$
$$CJ = \text{the number of feet of Tube C to buy from Japan}$$

In terms of these decision variables and the problem data, the two objectives are as follows:

1. Maximize profit, as developed in Section 3.2:

    Profit = (profit from production) + (profit from products purchased from Japan)
    $$= (7AP + 8BP + 5CP) + (4AJ + 6BJ + 2CJ)$$

2. Minimize cost of imports, which, using decomposition, is

    Cost of imports = (cost of importing Type A tubes) +

    (cost of importing Type B tubes) + (cost of importing Type C tubes)
    $$= 6AJ + 6BJ + 7CJ$$

Including the demand, resource, and logical constraints identified in Section 3.2, the associated multiobjective linear program—which includes the second objective of minimizing the cost of the imports—is

Maximize	$7AP +$	$8BP +$	$5CP + 4AJ + 6BJ + 2CJ$		(profit)
Minimize			$6AJ + 6BJ + 7CJ$		**(cost of imports)**
Subject to					

DEMAND CONSTRAINTS

	AP			$+ \; AJ$			$= 2000$	(demand for Type A)
		BP			$+ \; BJ$		$= 4000$	(demand for Type B)
			CP			$+ \; CJ$	$= 5000$	(demand for Type C)

RESOURCE CONSTRAINTS

$0.5AP + 0.45BP + 0.6CP$	≤ 2400	(machine time)
$AP + \quad BP + \quad CP$	≤ 5500	(welding material)

LOGICAL CONSTRAINTS

$$AP, \quad BP, \quad CP, \quad AJ, \quad BJ, \quad CJ \geq \quad 0$$

```
LP OPTIMUM FOUND AT STEP        2

        OBJECTIVE FUNCTION VALUE

    1)       55000.000

VARIABLE         VALUE          REDUCED COST
      AP      2000.000000          .000000
      BP         .000000          .250000
      CP      2333.333000          .000000
      AJ         .000000          .500000
      BJ      4000.000000          .000000
      CJ      2666.667000          .000000

    ROW    SLACK OR SURPLUS     DUAL PRICES
     2)          .000000         4.500000
     3)          .000000         6.000000
     4)          .000000         2.000000
     5)          .000000         5.000000
     6)      1166.667000          .000000

NO. ITERATIONS=        2
```

FIGURE 7.1 LINDO Output for the Profit-Maximization Problem of MTV Steel.

The conflict in these two objectives is illustrated by the computer output obtained from LINDO in Figures 7.1 and 7.2. The optimal solution in Figure 7.1 is for the linear program in which the objective is to maximize the profit, ignoring the cost of the imports. That optimal solution is

Linear Program
EX7_1A.DAT

$$AP = 2000.000$$

$$BP = \quad 0.000$$

$$CP = 2333.333$$

$$AJ = \quad 0.000$$

$$BJ = 4000.000$$

$$CJ = 2666.667$$

with a net profit of $55,000. In other words, to maximize profits, MTV Steel should produce 2000 feet of Type A tube and 2333.333 feet of Type C, while importing 4000 feet of Type B tube and 2666.667 feet of Type C from Japan. You can calculate the total cost for importing these amounts of tubes as follows:

$$\text{Cost of imports} = 6AJ + 6BJ + 7CJ$$

$$= (6 * 0) + (6 * 4000) + (7 * 2666.667)$$

$$= \$42,666.67$$

In contrast, the output in Figure 7.2 is the solution to the linear program in which the objective is to minimize the cost of the imports, ignoring profit. That optimal solution is

Linear Program
EX7_1B.DAT

```
LP OPTIMUM FOUND AT STEP        1

        OBJECTIVE FUNCTION VALUE

   1)      39800.000

VARIABLE        VALUE        REDUCED COST
    AJ        799.999900         .000000
    BJ           .000000         .600000
    CJ       5000.000000         .000000
    AP       1200.000000         .000000
    BP       4000.000000         .000000
    CP           .000000         .200000


    ROW    SLACK OR SURPLUS    DUAL PRICES
    2)           .000000        -6.000000
    3)           .000000        -5.400000
    4)           .000000        -7.000000
    5)           .000000        12.000000
    6)        299.999900          .000000

NO. ITERATIONS=         1
```

FIGURE 7.2 LINDO Output for the Cost-Minimization Problem of MTV Steel.

$$AP = 1200.000$$
$$BP = 4000.000$$
$$CP = 0.000$$
$$AJ = 799.999$$
$$BJ = 0.000$$
$$CJ = 5000.000$$

with a net import cost of \$39,800. To minimize the cost of the imports, MTV Steel should produce 1200 feet of Type A tube and 4000 feet of Type B, while importing 800 feet of Type A tube and 5000 feet of Type C from Japan. You can calculate the total profit from these amounts of tubes as follows:

$$\begin{aligned}
\text{Profit} &= 7AP + 8BP + 5CP + 4AJ + 6BJ + 2CJ \\
&= (7 * 1200) + (8 * 4000) + (5 * 0) + (4 * 800) + (6 * 0) + (2 * 5000) \\
&= \$53,600
\end{aligned}$$

As you can see, in an attempt to minimize the cost of the imports, the profit decreases from its maximum value of \$55,000 to \$53,600. Similarly, in an attempt to maximize the profit, the cost of the imports increases from its minimum value of \$39,800 to \$42,666.67. In the next section, you will learn one approach to address the trade-off between such conflicting objectives.

Goal programming
An approach used for solving a multiobjective optimization problem as a linear program that balances trade-offs in conflicting objectives.

◼ 7.2 GOAL PROGRAMMING

How does MTV Steel deal with the conflicting objectives of maximizing profits and minimizing cost of imports? One approach to handle trade-offs in these objectives is **goal programming**, in which, for each objective, you identify goals and penalties.

⟹ **KEY FEATURES**

To apply goal programming in reaching a decision, identify

✔ A **goal** in the form of a specific numerical target value you wish that objective to achieve, and

✔ A **penalty** in the form of a value for each unit the objective is below the goal if the objective is to maximize or above the goal if the objective is to minimize.

Once these goals and penalties are identified, a solution that minimizes the total penalty associated with all objectives is found.

Goal
A specific numerical target value set for an objective in a goal program.

Penalty
A relative value to represent dissatisfaction with each unit an objective is below its goal if the objective is to maximize or above the goal if the objective is to minimize.

7.2.1 Identifying the Goals and Penalties

The goals are the values the decision makers would ideally like to achieve for each objective. For example, in the problem of MTV Steel, the CEO, knowing that the maximum achievable profit is $55,000 from the output in Figure 7.1 may choose to set this value as the target to reflect the goal of achieving the highest possible profit. Knowing that the minimum achievable cost of the imports from the output in Figure 7.2 is $39,800, the CEO may choose this *or some other value* as the goal. For example, the CEO may be equally satisfied if an attempt is made to achieve an import cost of $40,000. This goal of $40,000 can be violated if doing so results in a significant improvement in the profit.

The penalties, in turn, reflect the relative importance to the decision makers of not meeting the goals of each objective. A higher value for a penalty indicates that meeting that goal has a higher priority. In choosing specific values for these penalties, consider the objective of maximizing profits. The goal is $55,000. If this goal is met or exceeded, there is no penalty. If, however, the $55,000 profit goal is not reached, then there *should* be a penalty, and the farther away you are from achieving the goal, the higher the total penalty should be. Penalties can increase either *linearly*, as shown in Figure 7.3(a), or *nonlinearly*, as shown in Figure 7.3(b). In this chapter, only linear penalty functions are considered.

For each objective, you must choose a single numerical value to indicate the penalty *per unit* (a dollar, in this case) for not achieving the goal. This penalty determines the slope of the penalty-function line in Figure 7.3(a). The stiffer the penalty, the steeper the slope. Penalties are chosen to reflect the relative trade-off between the objectives, according to the preference of the decision makers. If the CEO of MTV Steel feels that it is twice as important to meet the target of $55,000 for the profit as it is to meet the target of $40,000 for the cost of the imports, then you can choose these penalties:

Profit penalty = 2 for each dollar of profit below $55,000

Import penalty = 1 for each dollar of import cost above $40,000

In this case, you could alternatively have chosen a profit penalty of 4 and an import penalty of 2 to reflect that the profit goal is twice as important as the cost goal. In general, the penalties have no physical meaning other than to indicate the *relative* importance of meeting the goals. As a general rule, you can arbitrarily set the penalty for not meeting the goal of one of the objectives to 1. For each of the *other* objectives, the penalty is determined by evaluating the importance of not meeting the associated goal in relation to the one whose penalty is set to 1.

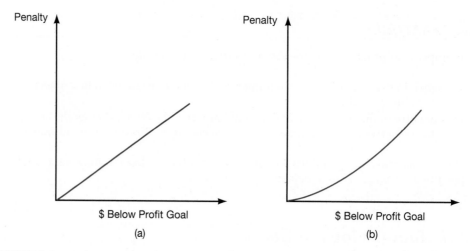

FIGURE 7.3 The Penalties for Not Achieveing a Goal: (a) Linear Penalties, (b) Nonlinear Penalties.

Having identified appropriate values for the goals and for the penalties, you can now formulate a linear programming problem whose solution will provide the best values of the decision variables in terms of minimizing the *total penalty of not meeting the goals*.

7.2.2 The Linear Programming Formulation for a Goal-Programming Problem

To develop an appropriate linear programming model for a goal-programming problem in which you have identified the goals and penalties for each of the objectives, follow the usual steps of identifying variables, a *single* objective function, and constraints.

IDENTIFYING THE DECISION VARIABLES

With the goal-programming approach, in addition to the original decision variables, you will need to define two new variables for each objective: one to represent the amount by which the objective is *over* the specified goal and the other for the amount *under* that goal. For example, for the problem of MTV Steel, the original variables defined in Section 7.1 are

$$AP = \text{the number of feet of Tube A to produce}$$
$$BP = \text{the number of feet of Tube B to produce}$$
$$CP = \text{the number of feet of Tube C to produce}$$
$$AJ = \text{the number of feet of Tube A to buy from Japan}$$
$$BJ = \text{the number of feet of Tube B to buy from Japan}$$
$$CJ = \text{the number of feet of Tube C to buy from Japan}$$

Because there are two objectives, you also need the following *four* decision variables:

$$P^+ = \text{the dollar amount by which the profit exceeds the goal of } \$55{,}000$$
$$P^- = \text{the dollar amount by which the profit falls under the goal of } \$55{,}000$$
$$I^+ = \text{the dollar amount by which the imports exceed the goal of } \$40{,}000$$
$$I^- = \text{the dollar amount by which the imports fall under the goal of } \$40{,}000$$

The final model must ensure that only *one* variable in each pair has a positive value and the other is 0.

IDENTIFYING THE OBJECTIVE FUNCTION

As stated previously, with goal programming, the objective is to

Minimize the total penalty for not meeting the two goals

Applying decomposition results in

Total penalty = (penalty for falling under the profit goal) +
(penalty for exceeding the import goal)

The decision variable P^- is the amount by which the profit goal of \$55,000 is not met. Similarly, I^+ is the amount by which the import goal of \$40,000 is exceeded. Recall that the CEO has assigned a penalty twice as great for each dollar short in profit as the penalty for each dollar exceeding the import goal. Thus, the objective function for this problem is

$$\text{Minimize} \quad 2P^- + 1I^+$$

IDENTIFYING THE CONSTRAINTS

Apply the technique of grouping results in the following four groups of constraints:

1. Demand constraints to satisfy the demands for each type of tube.
2. Resource constraints based on the limited availability of welding material and machine time.
3. Goal constraints to specify the amount by which each goal is or is not met.
4. Logical constraints to ensure that, besides nonnegativity, at least one of P^+ and P^- is 0 and at least one of I^+ and I^- is 0.

The constraints in groups 1 and 2 are precisely those given in the original problem formulation in Section 7.1; namely:

DEMAND CONSTRAINTS

$$AP + AJ = 2000 \quad \text{(demand for Type A)}$$
$$BP + BJ = 4000 \quad \text{(demand for Type B)}$$
$$CP + CJ = 5000 \quad \text{(demand for Type C)}$$

RESOURCE CONSTRAINTS

$$0.5AP + 0.45BP + 0.6CP \leq 2400 \quad \text{(machine time)}$$
$$AP + BP + CP \leq 5500 \quad \text{(welding material)}$$

GOAL CONSTRAINTS

The third group consists of two constraints, one for each of the two goals. Consider the goal of achieving a profit of \$55,000. In terms of the decision variables and other problem data, the profit is

$$\text{Profit} = 7AP + 8BP + 5CP + 4AJ + 6BJ + 2CJ$$

To see how P^+ and P^- represent the amount by which this profit is above or below the target of \$55,000, observe the following:

1. If the profit $7AP + 8BP + 5CP + 4AJ + 6BJ + 2CJ$ exceeds the goal of \$55,000, then the value of P^- should be 0 and that of P^+ should be

$$P^+ = 7AP + 8BP + 5CP + 4AJ + 6BJ + 2CJ - 55000$$

or

$$7AP + 8BP + 5CP + 4AJ + 6BJ + 2CJ - P^+ = 55000$$

2. If the profit $7AP + 8BP + 5CP + 4AJ + 6BJ + 2CJ$ is below the goal of \$55,000, then the value of P^+ should be 0 and that of P^- should be

$$P^- = 55000 - (7AP + 8BP + 5CP + 4AJ + 6BJ + 2CJ)$$

or

$$7AP + 8BP + 5CP + 4AJ + 6BJ + 2CJ + P^- = 55000$$

These two cases can be handled by a *single* constraint:

$$7AP + 8BP + 5CP + 4AJ + 6BJ + 2CJ - P^+ + P^- = 55000 \qquad \text{(profit goal)}$$

with the understanding that at least one of P^+ and P^- is 0.

➡ **KEY FEATURES**

In general, the following goal constraint is included for each original objective:

$$\left\{ \begin{matrix} \text{Value of the} \\ \text{objective} \end{matrix} \right\} - \left\{ \begin{matrix} \text{amount above} \\ \text{the goal} \end{matrix} \right\} + \left\{ \begin{matrix} \text{amount below} \\ \text{the goal} \end{matrix} \right\} = \text{goal}$$

By applying this to the second objective of minimizing the cost $6AJ + 6BJ + 7CJ$ of the imports for which a goal of \$40,000 is set, the second goal constraint is

$$6AJ + 6BJ + 7CJ - I^+ + I^- = 40000 \qquad \text{(import goal)}$$

with the understanding that at least one of I^+ and I^- is 0.

LOGICAL CONSTRAINTS

One group of logical constraints is that all variables are nonnegative. You must also ensure that at least one of P^+ and P^- and one of I^+ and I^- is 0. You could include, for example, the *nonlinear* constraints:

$$P^+ * P^- = 0$$

$$I^+ * I^- = 0$$

However, there is no need to do so as the *objective function* of minimizing the total penalty automatically ensures these conditions. This is because any solution that does not satisfy these conditions cannot be optimal. For example, consider the following feasible solution:

$$AP = 2000 \qquad P^+ = 1000$$
$$AJ = 0 \qquad P^- = 8000$$
$$BP = 3000 \qquad I^+ = 1500$$
$$BJ = 1000 \qquad I^- = 500$$
$$CP = 0$$
$$CJ = 5000 \qquad \text{Objective} = 2P^- + I^+ = 17500$$

Because this solution reflects a net effect of not meeting the profit goal by $P^- - P^+ = \$8000 - \$1000 = \$7000$ and exceeding the import goal by $I^+ - I^- = \$1500 - \$500 = \$1000$, an equivalent feasible solution with a smaller objective function value is obtained by setting $P^+ = 0$, $P^- = 7000$, $I^+ = 1000$, and $I^- = 0$, resulting in the following improved feasible solution:

$$AP = 2000 \qquad P^+ = 0$$
$$AJ = 0 \qquad P^- = 7000$$
$$BP = 3000 \qquad I^+ = 1000$$
$$BJ = 1000 \qquad I^- = 0$$
$$CP = 0$$
$$CJ = 5000 \qquad \text{Objective} = 2P^- + I^+ = 15000$$

Combining all the pieces results in the following linear programming problem.

THE LINEAR GOAL PROGRAM FOR THE MULTIOBJECTIVE PROBLEM OF MTV STEEL

Minimize $\quad 2P^- + I^+$
Subject to

Linear Program
EX7_1C.DAT

DEMAND CONSTRAINTS

$$AP + AJ = 2000 \qquad \text{(demand for Type A)}$$
$$BP + BJ = 4000 \qquad \text{(demand for Type B)}$$
$$CP + CJ = 5000 \qquad \text{(demand for Type C)}$$

RESOURCE CONSTRAINTS

$$0.5AP + 0.45BP + 0.6CP \le 2400 \qquad \text{(machine time)}$$
$$AP + BP + CP \le 5500 \qquad \text{(welding material)}$$

GOAL CONSTRAINTS

$$7AP + 8BP + 5CP + 4AJ + 6BJ + 2CJ - P^+ + P^- = 55000 \quad \text{(profit goal)}$$
$$6AJ + 6BJ + 7CJ - I^+ + I^- = 40000 \quad \text{(import goal)}$$

LOGICAL CONSTRAINTS

$$AP, \ BP, \ CP, \ AJ, \ BJ, \ CJ, \ P^+, \ P^-, \ I^+, \ I^- \ \geq \ 0$$

7.2.3 Computer Solution of the Goal-Programming Problem of MTV Steel

Having formulated a linear program for the problem of MTV Steel, you can apply any linear programming package to obtain the solution. The results of using LINDO are shown in Figure 7.4 in which the variable P^+ is denoted by the symbolic name PPLUS, P^- by PMINUS, I^+ by IPLUS, and I^- by IMINUS. From this report, you can see that the optimal production/import plan is

Produce: 2000 feet of Type A tube and 3111.11 feet of Type B

Import: 888.89 feet of Type B tube and 5000 feet of Type C

In terms of the goals, the value of 777.78 for PMINUS indicates that the profit goal of $55,000 is not met by $777.78. Similarly, the value of IPLUS is 333.33, so the import goal of $40,000 is exceeded by $333.33. In other words, the foregoing production/import plan results in a profit of $54,222.22 and an import cost of $40,333.33.

     This solution is different from the solutions in Figure 7.1 or 7.2, where only one of the two objectives is considered. All three solutions are summarized in Table 7.2. You can see that the goal-programming model achieves a lower import cost at the expense of some of the profit when compared to the profit-maximization model. Similarly, the goal-programming model achieves a larger profit at the expense of increased import costs when compared to the import-minimization model.

TABLE 7.2　*The Optimal Solutions for the Three Models of the Make-or-Buy Problem of MTV Steel*

	SINGLE OBJECTIVE LINEAR PROGRAMS		GOAL PROGRAM
	MAXIMIZE PROFIT	MINIMIZE IMPORTS	MINIMIZE PENALTY
Produce			
Type A	2000.00	1200.00	2000.00
Type B	0.00	4000.00	3111.11
Type C	2333.33	0.00	0.00
Import			
Type A	0.00	800.00	0.00
Type B	4000.00	0.00	888.89
Type C	2666.67	5000.00	5000.00
Profit	55000.00	53600.00	54222.22
Import cost	42666.69	39800.00	40333.33

```
LP OPTIMUM FOUND AT STEP         5

        OBJECTIVE FUNCTION VALUE

    1)      1888.8880

  VARIABLE          VALUE          REDUCED COST
   PMINUS       777.777600          .000000
    IPLUS       333.332800          .000000
       AP      2000.000000          .000000
       AJ          .000000          .888888
       BP      3111.111000          .000000
       BJ       888.888800          .000000
       CP          .000000          .333335
       CJ      5000.000000          .000000
    PPLUS          .000000         2.000000
   IMINUS          .000000         1.000000

      ROW    SLACK OR SURPLUS     DUAL PRICES
       2)          .000000         2.888889
       3)          .000000         6.000000
       4)          .000000        -3.000000
       5)          .000000        22.222220
       6)       388.888800          .000000
       7)          .000000        -2.000000
       8)          .000000         1.000000

  NO. ITERATIONS=        5
```

FIGURE 7.4 LINDO Output for the Goal-Programming Problem of MTV Steel.

CASE STUDY

In this section, you will see how the concept of penalties is used not only to handle trade-offs in different objectives, but also to allow a constraint to be violated with an associated penalty for doing so. Recall the diet problem of Mountain View General Hospital presented in Example 3.3, Chapter 3.

The Original Diet Problem of Mountain View General Hospital

The Nutrition Department of Mountain View General Hospital is preparing a dinner menu for a meal that will be served one day each month. The department has determined that this meal should supply 63,000 milligrams (mg) of protein, 10 mg of iron, 15 mg of niacin, 1 mg of thiamin, and 50 mg of vitamin C. To achieve this objective, the meal is to consist of a certain amount of spaghetti, turkey, scalloped potatoes, spinach, and apple strudel. Each 100 grams of these foods provides the amount of each nutrient indicated in Table 7.3.

TABLE 7.3	*Nutrients Provided by the Various Foods (mg/100grams)*					
	PROTEIN	IRON	NIACIN	THIAMIN	VITAMIN C	FAT
Spaghetti	5000	1.1	1.4	0.18	0.0	5000
Turkey	29300	1.8	5.4	0.06	0.0	5000
Potatoes	5300	0.5	0.9	0.06	10.0	7900
Spinach	3000	2.2	0.5	0.07	28.0	300
Apple Strudel	4000	1.2	0.6	0.15	3.0	14300

The department understands that it has to present a well-balanced meal that a patient enjoys. With this objective in mind, the department will serve no more than 300 grams of spaghetti, 300 grams of turkey, 200 grams of potatoes, 100 grams of spinach, and 100 grams of apple strudel. As Director of the Nutrition Department, you want to determine the composition of a meal that meets the nutritional requirements and that provides the least amount of fat.

The following decision variables are identified in Section 3.3, Chapter 3:

$SPAG$ = the number of 100 grams of spaghetti to include

$TURK$ = the number of 100 grams of turkey to include

$POTA$ = the number of 100 grams of potatoes to include

$SPIN$ = the number of 100 grams of spinach to include

$APPL$ = the number of 100 grams of apple strudel to include

These variables, together with the problem data, result in the following linear program:

Linear Program
DIET_A.DAT

Minimize
$5000SPAG + 5000TURK + 7900POTA + 300SPIN + 14300APPL$
Subject to

NUTRIENT CONSTRAINTS

$$
\begin{array}{llllll}
5000SPAG + & 29300TURK + & 5300POTA + & 3000SPIN + & 4000APPL \geq 63000 & \text{(protein)} \\
1.1SPAG + & 1.8TURK + & 0.5POTA + & 2.2SPIN + & 1.2APPL \geq \quad 10 & \text{(iron)} \\
1.4SPAG + & 5.4TURK + & 0.9POTA + & 0.5SPIN + & 0.6APPL \geq \quad 15 & \text{(niacin)} \\
0.18SPAG + & 0.06TURK + & 0.06POTA + & 0.07SPIN + & 0.15APPL \geq \quad 1 & \text{(thiamin)} \\
& & 10POTA + & 28SPIN + & 3APPL \geq \quad 50 & \text{(vitamin C)}
\end{array}
$$

BOUND CONSTRAINTS

$$
\begin{array}{lllll}
SPAG & & & & \leq \quad 3 \\
& TURK & & & \leq \quad 3 \\
& & POTA & & \leq \quad 2 \\
& & & SPIN & \leq \quad 1 \\
& & & & APPL \leq \quad 1
\end{array}
$$

LOGICAL CONSTRAINTS

$$SPAG, \quad TURK, \quad POTA, \quad SPIN, \quad APPL \geq \quad 0$$

The optimal solution to this problem, which results from using any linear programming software package, is

$$SPAG = 3.000$$

$$TURK = 2.833$$

$$POTA = 2.000$$

$$SPIN = 1.000$$

$$APPL = 0.667$$

The total fat content of this meal is 54,800 milligrams. In other words, the meal should consist of 300 grams of spaghetti, 283.3 grams of turkey, 200 grams of potatoes, 100 grams of spinach, and 66.7 grams of apple strudel.

In discussing this solution, the Hospital Director pointed out that you ignored costs. Also, as Director of the Nutrition Department, you have recently read that the most desirable amount of protein per meal is between 80,000 to 100,000 mg. A new model is needed to address these issues.

The Multiobjective Diet Problem of Mountain View General Hospital

In the new model, there is now a second objective: to minimize the total cost of the meal. Also, the new protein requirement is now a range constraint.

Applying the technique of decomposition to the cost objective function yields:

Minimize cost = (cost of spaghetti used) + (cost of turkey used) +

(cost of potatoes used) + (cost of spinach used) +

(cost of apple strudel used)

To develop a mathematical expression for this objective function, it is necessary to obtain appropriate cost data. Recall that the amounts of food in the meal are expressed in hundreds of grams. As Director of the Nutrition Department, suppose you obtain the following costs per hundred grams for each food item:

FOOD ITEM	COST ($/100 grams)
Spaghetti	0.15
Turkey	0.80
Potatoes	0.12
Spinach	0.20
Apple strudel	0.51

From these data and the decision variables, the cost objective is

Minimize $0.15SPAG + 0.80TURK + 0.12POTA + 0.20SPIN + 0.51APPL$

Including this second objective and adding the range of 80,000 to 100,000 mg for the protein requirement results in the following multiobjective decision problem:

MATHEMATICAL FORMULATION FOR THE MULTIOBJECTIVE DIET PROBLEM OF MOUNTAIN VIEW GENERAL HOSPITAL

Minimize

$$5000SPAG + 5000TURK + 7900POTA + 300SPIN + 14300APPL \qquad \text{(fat)}$$

Minimize

$$0.15SPAG + 0.80TURK + 0.12POTA + 0.20SPIN + 0.51APPL \qquad \text{(cost)}$$

Subject to

NUTRIENT CONSTRAINTS

$$
\begin{array}{llllll}
5000SPAG + 29300TURK + 5300POTA + 3000SPIN + 4000APPL \le 100000 & \text{(maximum-protein)} \\
5000SPAG + 29300TURK + 5300POTA + 3000SPIN + 4000APPL \ge 80000 & \text{(minimum-protein)} \\
1.1SPAG + 1.8TURK + 0.5POTA + 2.2SPIN + 1.2APPL \ge 10 & \text{(iron)} \\
1.4SPAG + 5.4TURK + 0.9POTA + 0.5SPIN + 0.6APPL \ge 15 & \text{(niacin)} \\
0.18SPAG + 0.06TURK + 0.06POTA + 0.07SPIN + 0.15APPL \ge 1 & \text{(thiamin)} \\
10POTA + 28SPIN + 3APPL \ge 50 & \text{(vitamin C)}
\end{array}
$$

BOUND CONSTRAINTS

$$
\begin{array}{ll}
SPAG & \le 3 \\
TURK & \le 3 \\
POTA & \le 2 \\
SPIN & \le 1 \\
APPL & \le 1
\end{array}
$$

LOGICAL CONSTRAINTS

$$SPAG,\quad TURK,\quad POTA,\quad SPIN,\quad APPL \ge 0$$

Linear Program
DIET_A.DAT

You can see that the two objectives conflict by minimizing each objective function individually and then comparing the cost and fat content of the resulting meals. For example, the optimal solution to the linear programming problem obtained from STORM by ignoring temporarily the cost objective function is given in Figure 7.5. The associated meal consists of 300 grams of spaghetti, 232.69 grams of turkey, 193.09 grams of potatoes, 100 grams of spinach, and 89.69 grams of apple strudel, with a total fat content of 55,014.08 mg. Using these values of the variables, you can easily calculate the cost of this meal:

$$
\begin{aligned}
\text{Cost} &= 0.15SPAG + 0.80TURK + 0.12POTA + 0.20SPIN + 0.51APPL \\
&= 0.15(3) + 0.80(2.327) + 0.12(1.931) + 0.20(1) + 0.51(0.897) \\
&= \$3.20
\end{aligned}
$$

Linear Program
DIET_B.DAT

In contrast, the optimal solution to the linear programming problem obtained from STORM by ignoring temporarily the fat objective function is given in Figure 7.6. As you can see, the associated meal is different from the one in Figure 7.5 and now consists of 300 grams of spaghetti, 200 grams each of turkey and potatoes, and 100 grams each of spinach and apple strudel, at a total cost of $3.00. Using these values of the variables, you can easily calculate the fat content of this meal:

$$
\begin{aligned}
\text{Fat} &= 5000SPAG + 5000TURK + 7900POTA + 300SPIN + 14300APPL \\
&= 5000(3) + 5000(2) + 7900(2) + 300(1) + 14300(1) \\
&= 55,400 \text{ mg}
\end{aligned}
$$

```
        The Diet Problem of Mountain View Hospital: Min. Fat
     OPTIMAL SOLUTION - SUMMARY REPORT (NONZERO VARIABLES)
              Variable        Value           Cost
         1       SPAG         3.0000         5000.0000
         2       TURK         2.3269         5000.0000
         3       POTA         1.9309         7900.0000
         4       SPIN         1.0000          300.0000
         5       APPL         0.8969        14300.0000

         Slack Variables
         7    MIN-PROTN    20000.0000            0.0000
         8       IRON          1.7301           0.0000
         9      NIACIN         4.5413           0.0000
        14      TURKEY         0.6731           0.0000
        15    POTATOES         0.0691           0.0000
        17     STRUDEL         0.1031           0.0000

          Objective Function Value = 55014.08
```

FIGURE 7.5 The Meal of Least Fat for the Problem of Mountain View General Hospital.

```
        The Diet Problem of Mountain View Hospital: Min. Cost
     OPTIMAL SOLUTION - SUMMARY REPORT (NONZERO VARIABLES)
              Variable        Value           Cost
         1       SPAG         3.0000          0.1500
         2       TURK         2.0000          0.8000
         3       POTA         2.0000          0.1200
         4       SPIN         1.0000          0.2000
         5       APPL         1.0000          0.5100

         Slack Variables
         6    MAX-PROTN     8800.0110           0.0000
         7    MIN-PROTN    11199.9900           0.0000
         8       IRON          1.3000           0.0000
         9      NIACIN         2.9000           0.0000
        11    VITAMIN C        1.0000           0.0000
        12      WEIGHT         1.0000           0.0000
        14      TURKEY         1.0000           0.0000

          Objective Function Value = 3
```

FIGURE 7.6 The Meal of Least Cost for the Problem of Mountain View General Hospital.

Comparing the two solutions in Figures 7.5 and 7.6 illustrates the conflict in the fat and cost objectives:

	OBJECTIVE	
	MINIMIZE FAT	MINIMIZE COST
Fat of meal (mg)	54,041	55,400
Cost of meal ($)	3.20	3.00

This table shows that minimizing one objective causes the other to increase. One way to handle the trade-off between these conflicts is through the use of goal programming.

The Goal-Programming Approach for the Diet Problem of Mountain View General Hospital

Recall from Section 7.2 that in goal programming you must identify the following for each objective:

1. A goal.
2. A value in the form of a penalty for each unit by which the objective exceeds the goal.
3. A value in the form of a penalty for each unit by which the objective falls below the goal.

Suppose you and the Director of the hospital set a goal of $2.00 per meal. As Director of the Nutrition Department, you might set 55,000 mg as a target for the fat content of the meal. You must now identify appropriate penalties for not meeting each of these goals.

In this case, the objectives are to minimize both the fat content and the cost, so there should be no penalty for achieving values below the goals. In contrast, exceeding either or both of these two goals *should be* penalized. These penalties are meant to reflect the *relative* importance of each objective, so you can arbitrarily set one of these penalties to a value of 1. Assume the penalty for not meeting the cost objective is 1— that is, each dollar by which the actual cost of the meal exceeds the goal of $2.00 incurs a penalty of 1.

To identify the penalty for exceeding the fat content, ask yourself how much you would be willing to allow the cost to increase if you could reduce the fat content by 10 mg. Suppose that answer is $0.90. In that case, the penalty for each milligram of fat over the goal of 55,000 is 0.90/10 = 0.09.

Having identified the goals and the associated penalties, you can create a linear goal-programming model by using the ideas presented in Section 7.2:

1. In addition to the original variables, define two new ones for each objective as follows:

F^+ = the number of milligrams of fat the meal exceeds the goal of 55,000

F^- = the number of milligrams of fat the meal falls below the goal of 55,000

C^+ = the number of dollars by which the cost of the meal exceeds the goal of $2.00

C^- = the number of dollars by which the cost of the meal falls below the goal of $2.00

2. Use the decision variables in step 1 and the associated penalties to formulate a single objective function that minimizes the total penalty. In this case, by decomposition:

$$\text{Total penalty} = (\text{penalty for being above the fat goal}) \ +$$
$$(\text{penalty for being below the fat goal}) \ +$$
$$(\text{penalty for being above the cost goal}) \ +$$
$$(\text{penalty for being below the cost goal})$$
$$= 0.09F^+ + 0F^- + 1C^+ + 0C^-$$

3. In addition to the original constraints, add one new goal constraint for each objective, as described in Section 7.2. In this case,

$$5000SPAG + 5000TURK + 7900POTA + \ 300SPIN + 14300APPL - F^+ + F^- = 55000 \quad \text{(fat)}$$
$$0.15SPAG + \ 0.80TURK + \ 0.12POTA + 0.20SPIN + \quad 0.51APPL - C^+ + C^- = \qquad 2 \quad \text{(cost)}$$

With the new objective in step 2 and the two additional constraints in step 3, the complete goal-programming model for the problem is as follows.

MATHEMATICAL FORMULATION FOR THE GOAL-PROGRAMMING PROBLEM OF MOUNTAIN VIEW GENERAL HOSPITAL

Minimize $\qquad 0.09F^+ + 0F^- + 1C^+ + 0C^-$
Subject to

Linear Program
DIET_C.DAT

GOAL CONSTRAINTS

$$5000SPAG + \ 5000TURK + 7900POTA + \ 300SPIN + 14300APPL - F^+ + F^- = \ 55000 \quad \text{(fat)}$$
$$0.15SPAG + \ 0.80TURK + \ 0.12POTA + 0.20SPIN + \quad 0.51APPL - C^+ + C^- = \qquad 2 \quad \text{(cost)}$$

NUTRIENT CONSTRAINTS

$5000SPAG + 29300TURK + 5300POTA + 3000SPIN + \ 4000APPL$					≤ 100000	(maximum-protein)
$5000SPAG + 29300TURK + 5300POTA + 3000SPIN + \ 4000APPL$					$\geq \ 80000$	(minimum-protein)
$1.1SPAG + \ 1.8TURK + \ 0.5POTA + \ 2.2SPIN + \ 1.2APPL$					$\geq \quad 10$	(iron)
$1.4SPAG + \ 5.4TURK + \ 0.9POTA + \ 0.5SPIN + \ 0.6APPL$					$\geq \quad 15$	(niacin)
$0.18SPAG + \ 0.06TURK + 0.06POTA + 0.07SPIN + \ 0.15APPL$					$\geq \qquad 1$	(thiamin)
$10POTA + \ 28SPIN + \ 3APPL$					$\geq \quad 50$	(vitamin C)

BOUND CONSTRAINTS

$SPAG$	$\leq \quad 3$
$TURK$	$\leq \quad 3$
$POTA$	$\leq \quad 2$
$SPIN$	$\leq \quad 1$
$APPL$	$\leq \quad 1$

LOGICAL CONSTRAINTS

$SPAG, \ TURK, \ POTA, \ SPIN, \ APPL, \ F^+, \ F^-, \ C^+, \ C^- \qquad\qquad \geq \qquad 0$

The solution to this problem obtained from STORM is given in Figure 7.7 and indicates that the optimal meal consists of 300 grams of spaghetti, 232.69 grams of turkey, 193.09 grams of potatoes, 100 grams of spinach, and 89.69 grams of apple strudel. This meal is the same as the one in Figure 7.5 that minimizes the fat content. This indicates that any reduction in the penalty for a small decrease in the cost is *more than negated* by the associated increase in the penalty due to a resulting higher fat content.

On examining the solution more carefully, note that the protein in this meal is at its upper limit of 100,000 mg. This is because the value of the slack variable MIN-PROTN is 20,000, indicating that the minimum protein level of 80,000 mg is exceeded by 20,000 mg. However, suppose you feel that, although it is desirable to have the protein be within the range of 80,000 to 100,000 mg, these bounds can be violated if there is a compensating reduction in the fat and/or cost of the diet. In the next section, you will learn how penalties are used to accomplish this trade-off.

Using Penalties in the Constraints

You have learned how penalties are used to handle the trade-off in two objectives. You can also use penalties in considering whether to allow a constraint to be violated. Consider the constraint that sets the maximum amount of protein in the meal:

$$5000SPAG + 29300TURK + 5300POTA + 3000SPIN + 4000APPL \leq 100000$$

Think of the value 100,000 as a goal. The constraint is of the less-than-or-equal-to type, so there is no penalty for being below this goal. However, there *should be* a penalty for exceeding this goal. Again, this penalty is a subjective value that should reflect the relative importance of exceeding this goal when compared to that of exceeding the fat or cost goals.

```
       The Diet Problem of Mountain View Hospital: Goal Prog.
       OPTIMAL SOLUTION - SUMMARY REPORT (NONZERO VARIABLES)
                Variable          Value            Cost
          1       SPAG           3.0000           0.0000
          2       TURK           2.3269           0.0000
          3       POTA           1.9309           0.0000
          4       SPIN           1.0000           0.0000
          5       APPL           0.8969           0.0000
          6         C+           1.2006           1.0000
          8         F+          14.0754           0.0900


       Slack Variables
         13   MIN-PROTN     20000.0000            0.0000
         14       IRON           1.7301           0.0000
         15      NIACIN           4.5413           0.0000
         20      TURKEY           0.6731           0.0000
         21    POTATOES           0.0691           0.0000
         23     STRUDEL           0.1031           0.0000

           Objective Function Value = 2.467429
```

FIGURE 7.7 The STORM Optimal Solution to the Goal-Programming Problem of Mountain View General Hospital.

To identify this penalty, compare the importance of not meeting this goal to that of not meeting the cost goal of $2.00, for which the penalty is set to 1. You might ask yourself: By how much are you willing to allow the cost to increase if you can decrease the protein in excess of 100,000 mg by 1000 mg? Suppose that the answer is $1.00. In that case, the penalty for each milligram of protein over the goal of 100,000 is 1.00/1000 = 0.001.

Consider now the constraint that restricts the minimum amount of protein in the meal:

$$5000SPAG + 29300TURK + 5300POTA + 3000SPIN + 4000APPL \geq 80000$$

Once again think of the value 80,000 as a goal. Because the constraint is of the greater-than-or-equal-to type, there is no penalty for being above this goal. However, there *should be* a penalty for being below this goal. Again, this penalty is a subjective value that should reflect its importance relative to other goals. Suppose you believe that it is *twice* as important not to be below 80,000 mg of protein as it is to exceed 100,000 mg. In this case, the penalty is twice that of 0.001 established for exceeding the 100,000 maximum goal. So the penalty for falling below 80,000 mg of protein is 0.002 per mg.

The penalties are now identified. The goal-programming model in Section 7.3.3 is modified as follows:

1. Define two new variables for each constraint that may be violated. For violating the maximum allowable amount of protein, define as follows:

$$PU^+ = \text{the number of milligrams by which the protein is above the goal of 100,000}$$

$$PU^- = \text{the number of milligrams by which the protein is below the goal of 100,000}$$

   Similarly, to allow the minimum limit on protein to be violated, define as follows:

$$PD^+ = \text{the number of milligrams by which the protein is above the goal of 80,000}$$

$$PD^- = \text{the number of milligrams by which the protein is below the goal of 80,000}$$

2. Use the decision variables in step 1 and the associated penalties to formulate a single objective function that minimizes the total penalty. In this case, by decomposition:

   Total penalty = (penalty for being above the fat goal) +
   (penalty for being below the fat goal) +
   (penalty for being above the cost goal) +
   (penalty for being below the cost goal) +
   (penalty for being above the upper protein limit) +
   (penalty for being below the upper protein limit) +
   (penalty for being above the lower protein limit) +
   (penalty for being below the lower protein limit)

$$= 0.09F^+ + 0F^- + 1C^+ + 0C^- +$$
$$0.001PU^+ + 0PU^- + 0PD^+ + 0.002PD^-$$

3. Using the approach you applied in writing the goal constraints associated with an objective, replace each constraint that may be violated with one equality constraint. For the upper limit on protein:

$$5000SPAG + 29300TURK + 5300POTA + 3000SPIN + 4000APPL$$
$$-PU^+ + PU^- = 100000$$

Similarly, for the lower limit on protein:

$$5000SPAG + 29300TURK + 5300POTA + 3000SPIN + 4000APPL$$
$$-PD^+ + PD^- = 80000$$

With the new objective in step 2 and the two modified constraints in step 3, the complete goal-programming model for the diet problem is as follows.

Linear Program
DIET_D.DAT

MATHEMATICAL FORMULATION FOR THE FINAL GOAL-PROGRAMMING PROBLEM OF MOUNTAIN VIEW GENERAL HOSPITAL

Minimize $0.09F^+ + 0F^- + 1C^+ + 0C^- + 0.001PU^+ + 0PU^- + 0PD^+ + 0.002PD^-$
Subject to

GOAL CONSTRAINTS

$5000SPAG +$	$5000TURK +$	$7900POTA +$	$300SPIN +$	$14300APPL -$	$F^+ +$	$F^- =$	55000	(fat)
$0.15SPAG +$	$0.80TURK +$	$0.12POTA +$	$0.20SPIN +$	$0.51APPL -$	$C^+ +$	$C^- =$	2	(cost)
$5000SPAG +$	$29300TURK +$	$5300POTA +$	$3000SPIN +$	$4000APPL -$	$PU^+ + PU^- =$		100000	(maximum)
$5000SPAG +$	$29300TURK +$	$5300POTA +$	$3000SPIN +$	$4000APPL -$	$PD^+ + PD^- =$		80000	(minimum)

NUTRIENT CONSTRAINTS

$1.1SPAG +$	$1.8TURK +$	$0.5POTA +$	$2.2SPIN +$	$1.2APPL$	$\geq$	10	(iron)
$1.4SPAG +$	$5.4TURK +$	$0.9POTA +$	$0.5SPIN +$	$0.6APPL$	$\geq$	15	(niacin)
$0.18SPAG +$	$0.06TURK +$	$0.06POTA +$	$0.07SPIN +$	$0.15APPL$	$\geq$	1	(thiamin)
		$10POTA +$	$28SPIN +$	$3APPL$	$\geq$	50	(vitamin C)

BOUND CONSTRAINTS

$SPAG$	$\leq$	3
$TURK$	$\leq$	3
$POTA$	$\leq$	2
$SPIN$	$\leq$	1
$APPL$	$\leq$	1

LOGICAL CONSTRAINTS

$SPAG, TURK, POTA, SPIN, APPL, F^+, F^-, C^+, C^-, PU^+, PU^-, PD^+ \ PD^- \geq 0$

The solution to this problem obtained from STORM is given in Figure 7.8 and indicates that the optimal meal consists of 300 grams of spaghetti, 236.02 grams of turkey, 193.55 grams of potatoes, 100 grams of spinach, and 88.17 grams of apple strudel. The value of $C^+ = 1.2201$ in Figure 7.8 indicates that this meal exceeds the cost goal of $2.00 by $1.22. Because F^+ and F^- are not included in the optimal solution, their values are 0, which means that the fat goal of 55,000 mg is met exactly. Finally, the value of

```
        The Diet Problem of Mountain View Hospital: Goal Prog.
        OPTIMAL SOLUTION - SUMMARY REPORT (NONZERO VARIABLES)
                    Variable        Value          Cost
             1         SPAG         3.0000         0.0000
             2         TURK         2.3602         0.0000
             3         POTA         1.9355         0.0000
             4         SPIN         1.0000         0.0000
             5         APPL         0.8817         0.0000
             6           C+         1.2201         1.0000
            10          PU+       939.1188      1.0000E-03
            12          PD+     20939.1200         0.0000


        Slack Variables
            18         IRON         1.7742         0.0000
            19        NIACIN        4.7161         0.0000
            24        TURKEY        0.6398         0.0000
            25       POTATOES       0.0645         0.0000
            27        STRUDEL       0.1183         0.0000


            Objective Function Value = 2.159224
```

FIGURE 7.8 The STORM Optimal Solution to the Final Goal-Programming Problem of Mountain View General Hospital.

939.1188 for PU^+ in Figure 7.8 indicates that the upper limit of 100,000 mg of protein is exceeded by 939.1188 mg.

➡ KEY FEATURES

You can use goals and penalties to allow constraints to be violated if there is a significant improvement in achieving other goals.

ADDITIONAL MANAGERIAL CONSIDERATIONS

In this chapter, you have learned to use goal programming to address the trade-offs that arise when there are two or more conflicting objectives. In this section, several issues related to this and alternative approaches for handling multiobjective problems are addressed.

Using Two-Sided Penalties

In the problem of MTV Steel in Example 7.1, the two objectives are to maximize the profit and to minimize the cost of the imports. In formulating this problem as a goal program, it is appropriate not to have any penalty—that is, a penalty of 0—for exceeding the profit goal or for being under the import goal. In general, however, positive penalties can be assigned simultaneously for both underachieving as well as overachieving a goal.

Suppose that in manufacturing steel, one objective is to control the level of inventory. Rather than attempting to maximize or minimize the amount of inventory, it may be more appropriate to achieve a specific *level* of inventory. In this case, exceeding this goal is undesirable because idle inventory incurs costs that add no value to the product (the storage cost, the cost of tying up capital that has been spent on acquiring the inventory, and so on). Conversely, having too little inventory may result in shortages when the demand is uncertain. In formulating a goal-programming model for this problem, you should therefore have **two-sided penalties**—that is, penalties both for exceeding the goal and for not meeting the goal. The values for each of these penalties can be different. For example, suppose the penalty for each unit of inventory above the goal is 1 and the penalty for each unit of inventory below this goal is 3. These penalties indicate that underachieving the target inventory level is three times as undesirable as overachieving that goal.

Two-sided penalty
A penalty both for exceeding a goal and for not meeting that goal.

A similar use of two-sided penalties arises when you wish to relax an equality constraint. In the problem of MTV Steel, the original constraints require that demands for each type of tube are met precisely. The use of two-sided penalties allows you to relax this constraint so that you may either exceed or not meet the demand. In both cases, there should be a penalty. For exceeding the demand, the penalty reflects the cost associated with storing each excess foot of tube. For not meeting the demand, the penalty reflects the explicit or implicit cost per foot of tube for being short—costs such as the loss of potential profit from sales not made or the loss of customer goodwill.

Sensitivity Analysis for Goals and Penalties

Recall what you learned in Section 7.2 about formulating a goal program. For each objective, you must identify (1) a desired numerical value for that objective function and (2) a relative penalty for each unit by which the goal in (1) is not met.

The goals are subjective in that they represent values you, or other managers in the organization, would ideally like to achieve. Because the optimal solution to the resulting goal-programming problem depends on the specific values of the goals you set, it is often valuable to perform sensitivity analysis with these values before making final decisions. That is, you should ask questions such as: What happens to the optimal solution and original objective function values when one or more of these goals are changed? Does a slight change in one of these goals cause a significant change in the optimal solution? Does changing one of these goals slightly enable you to obtain more desirable values for some of the other objectives?

Recall that the profit goal of MTV Steel is $55,000 and that its import goal is $40,000. The optimal production/import plan, obtained in Section 7.2, is

Produce:	2000 feet of Type A tube and 3111.11 feet of Type B
Import:	888.89 feet of Type B tube and 5000 feet of Type C

With this plan, MTV Steel falls short of the profit goal of $55,000 by $777.78 and exceeds the import goal of $40,000 by $333.33. That is, this production/import plan results in a profit of $54,222.22 and a total import cost of $40,333.33.

If a goal in the optimal solution is met precisely, then to answer sensitivity questions pertaining to this goal you will need to change the goal and resolve the problem. However, if the optimal solution *does not* achieve the goal, as is the case in this example, sensitivity analysis reports can provide useful information.

For example, you might ask: What happens in the problem of MTV Steel if the profit goal is decreased by $100 from $55,000 to $54,900, all else being the same? The current production and import plan now falls short of this new goal by only $677.78 (instead of the previous $777.78), but is this plan still optimal? By solving the problem with this new profit goal, you will see that only the value of the variable

```
                The Make-or-Buy Problem of MTV Steel
            SENSITIVITY ANALYSIS OF RIGHT-HAND-SIDE VALUES
                             Current      Allowable     Allowable
         Constraint   Type    Value        Minimum       Maximum
    1     DEMAND-A     =     2000.0000    1950.0000     2162.7910
    2     DEMAND-B     =     4000.0000    3944.4450     4129.6300
    3     DEMAND-C     =     5000.0000    4952.3810     5388.8890
    4      WELDING    <=     5500.0000    5111.1110      Infinity
    5        HOURS    <=     2400.0000    1000.0000     2425.0000
    6    GOAL-PROF     =    55000.0000   54222.2200      Infinity
    7     GOAL-IMP     =    40000.0000    -Infinity    40333.3300
```

FIGURE 7.9 STORM Sensitivity Analysis of the Right-Hand Sides for the Goal-Programming Problem of MTV Steel.

P^-—reflecting the amount by which the profit is not achieved—changes, but the actual production/import plan remains the same. In fact, by trial and error, you will discover that as long as the profit goal is not changed too much, the current plan remains optimal, although the amount by which you do not achieve the goal changes. The amount by which you can change this goal without affecting the current production/import plan is precisely the sensitivity range associated with the right-hand side of the profit constraint. In the sensitivity analysis report from STORM in Figure 7.9, the range of 54,222.22 to infinity for the right-hand side of the profit-goal constraint indicates that the current production and import plan remains optimal as long as the goal is above $54,222.22. This information is important because management now knows that setting a profit goal higher than the current goal of $55,000 is futile as doing so will have no affect on the optimal production and import plan.

The penalties for not meeting each objective are subjective values chosen by the decision maker. Before making a final decision, you may want to know how sensitive the optimal solution is to changes in these penalties. For example, in the problem of MTV Steel, the penalty for exceeding the cost of the imports is set to 1 as the basis for determining the other penalties, and therefore sensitivity analysis for this penalty is *not* necessary. In contrast, the penalty of 2 for not meeting the profit goal reflects the belief that this objective is twice as important as that for imports. You might ask how a change in the penalty for not meeting the profit goal affects the optimal production and import plan. Looking at the sensitivity analysis report from STORM for the objective function coefficients in Figure 7.10, you can see that as long as this penalty for P^- is between 0.8571 and 3.0000, the current plan remains optimal. In other words, as long as the relative penalty for not meeting the profit is not more than three times that for exceeding the cost of the imports, the current plan remains optimal.

In the event that the optimal solution is very sensitive to a change in either the goals or the penalties of an objective, increasing your efforts to gather the information to estimate these values more accurately may be worthwhile.

Alternative Approaches for Multiobjective Optimization

When dealing with more than one objective, difficulties arise because these objectives conflict with each other: Improving the value of one objective usually results in worsening one or more of the other objectives. Goal programming, as described in this chapter, is only *one* possible way to evaluate these trade-offs. Other existing methods include the following:

```
              The Make-or-Buy Problem of MTV Steel
              SENSITIVITY ANALYSIS OF COST COEFFICIENTS
                            Current      Allowable     Allowable
                 Variable    Coeff.       Minimum       Maximum
       1            AP       0.0000      -Infinity      0.8889
       2            BP       0.0000      -0.8000        0.2500
       3            CP       0.0000      -0.3333        Infinity
       4            AJ       0.0000      -0.8889        Infinity
       5            BJ       0.0000      -0.2500        0.8000
       6            CJ       0.0000      -Infinity      0.3333
       7            P+       0.0000      -2.0000        Infinity
       8            P-       2.0000       0.8571        3.0000
       9            I+       1.0000       0.6667        2.3333
      10            I-       0.0000      -1.0000        Infinity
```

FIGURE 7.10   STORM Sensitivity Analysis of the Objective Function Coefficients for the Goal-Programming Problem of MTV Steel.

1. The various objectives can be combined into a single, overall objective. For example, for the problem of MTV Steel, you might create the following single maximization objective to express the feeling that an additional $1 of profit is worth $2 of savings in the import costs:

$$(2 * \text{profit}) - (1 * \text{cost of the imports})$$

In general, a *utility function* based on the decision makers' subjective preferences is used to combine multiple objectives into a single overall objective function to be maximized. For example, another utility function that combines the profit and cost of imports for MTV Steel is

$$2 * (\text{profit})^2 - 3 * (\text{cost of the imports})$$

2. The objectives can be ranked in order of importance to the decision maker. You can then obtain the optimal solution for the most important objective, temporarily ignoring the rest. In considering the next most important objective, you do not want the first objective function value to get worse. You can achieve this by incorporating a constraint to ensure that the value of the first objective is equal to its best possible value. The final solution is obtained by repeating this process of optimizing each successive objective and ensuring that no previous objective gets worse. In the problem of MTV Steel, suppose that the profit objective is the most important. Maximizing this objective and temporarily ignoring the import costs result in a maximum profit of $55,000. Now, in attempting to minimize the cost of the imports, you should include the following constraint:

$$\text{Profit} = 7AP + 8BP + 5CP + 4AJ + 6BJ + 2CJ = 55000$$

3. Goal programming and the methods given in 1 and 2 require obtaining subjective values for goals, penalties, utility functions, or rankings of the objectives. In case such values are difficult to obtain explicitly, another approach is to allow the decision makers to select, from the various *feasible* solutions, the one they subjectively prefer, in view of the competing objectives. Decision makers need not consider those feasible solutions that are *dominated* by another feasible solution. Feasible solution A dominates feasible solutions B, C and so on when A is as good as B, C and the others in each objective and better in at least one objective.

Only *nondominated* solutions—in this case, feasible solution A, but there may be others—need be evaluated. Management science techniques are available for systematically generating these nondominated solutions.

SUMMARY

In this chapter, you have learned about multiobjective optimization—that is, how to handle deterministic problems in which there are two or more objectives. In general, objectives conflict with each other. As one objective improves in value, others get worse. The technique of goal programming helps a decision maker arrive at a solution that achieves an acceptable trade-off between objectives.

The idea behind goal programming is to establish a goal for each objective in the form of a specific ideal numerical value (for example, a profit figure or a target output level for production). In general, you will not be able to achieve the goal for each objective, so you must establish penalties for deviating from these goals.

The specific steps in formulating a linear goal-programming model when there are k objectives are as follows:

1. For each objective i, identify a goal G_i and penalties as follows:

$$P_i^+ = \text{the penalty for each unit objective } i \text{ is above } G_i$$
$$P_i^- = \text{the penalty for each unit objective } i \text{ is below } G_i$$

2. In addition to the original variables, define two new nonnegative variables for each objective i as follows:

$$D_i^+ = \text{the amount by which objective } i \text{ is above } G_i$$
$$D_i^- = \text{the amount by which objective } i \text{ is below } G_i$$

3. In addition to the original constraints, create an associated goal constraint for each objective i as follows:

$$(\text{Objective } i) - D_i^+ + D_i^- = G_i$$

4. Create a single objective function of minimizing the total penalty for not meeting the goals:

Minimize the total penalty = (penalty for being above goal 1) +

(penalty for being below goal 1) +

$$\vdots$$

(penalty for being above goal k) +

(penalty for being below goal k)

$$= (P_1^+ * D_1^+ + P_1^- * D_1^-) +$$

$$\vdots$$

$$(P_k^+ * D_k^+ + P_k^- * D_k^-)$$

Solving the resulting single-objective linear program using any available software package provides values for decision variables that satisfy all the original constraints, that represent the amounts by which each goal is not met, and that minimize the total penalty (that is, the sum of the penalties associated with the amount by which each objective differs from its goal).

EXERCISES

EXERCISE 7.1   Philadelphia Paints earns a net profit of $2 per gallon of Regular paint, $3 per gallon of Premium, and $4 per gallon of Supreme. Each gallon of Regular paint requires 1 minute of mixing on a blender, each gallon of Premium 2 minutes, and each gallon of Supreme 3 minutes. The Manager of the Production Department has set a target profit of $100 and aims to use 1 hour of blending time. Maximizing the profit is deemed to be twice as important as minimizing the amount of blending time used. Using the number of gallons of each paint to produce as decision variables, write (a) appropriate goal constraints and (b) a single objective that minimizes the total penalty for not meeting the goals.

EXERCISE 7.2   Chirality Company produces small, medium, and large screws. The Manager of the Production Department wants to produce as many screws as possible, aiming for a total of 17,500. In addition, she has an equal desire to minimize the total weight, hoping to keep that total at around 100 pounds. She knows that 1 pound of each respective type results in 200 small screws, 150 medium screws, and 100 large screws. Using the number of each size screw to produce as decision variables, write (a) appropriate goal constraints and (b) a single objective that minimizes the total penalty for not meeting the goals, assuming that both goals are equally important.

EXERCISE 7.3   Each gallon of Supreme gasoline costs 20% more than Regular to produce and each gallon of Extra costs 10% more than Regular. With a cost of $0.80 per gallon of Regular, the Manager of the Production Department has determined that the minimum production costs to meet the demand for all three types of gasoline for this period is $50,000. In an attempt to maximize the amount of Regular gasoline produced, a target of 40,000 gallons has been set. The Manager also feels that each dollar by which the production costs exceed the goal set at 10% above the minimum possible should be penalized three times as much as each gallon by which the production of Regular falls short of the target. Using the number of gallons of each type of gasoline to produce as decision variables, write (a) appropriate goal constraints and (b) a single objective that minimizes the total penalty for not meeting the goals.

EXERCISE 7.4   Acme Soda Pop Company uses soda water, fruit juice, sugar, and ascorbic acid to produce its LimeLovers drink. The amount of sugar, vitamin C, and the cost associated with each ounce of these ingredients used in producing each bottle of the drink are given in the following table:

	SODA WATER	JUICE	SUGAR	ASCORBIC ACID
Sugar (mg/oz)	0	10	25.5	0
Vitamin C (mg/oz)	0	5		85
Cost ($/oz)	0.01	0.08	0.03	0.05

In addition to minimizing costs, the desired amount of vitamin C in each bottle is between 250 and 300 mg and that of sugar is 200 mg. Each gram by which the amount of vitamin C is outside the acceptable range is twice as unacceptable as each cent by which the target cost of $0.25 is exceeded. Similarly, each gram by which the sugar exceeds the goal is considered three times as unacceptable as each cent by which the cost goal is exceeded.

Using the number of ounces of each ingredient to mix in each bottle as decision variables, write (a) appropriate goal constraints and (b) a single objective that minimizes the total penalty for not meeting the goals.

EXERCISE 7.5 In terms of the x-variables, write all the original objective functions that give rise to the following goal program. Indicate whether those objectives are to be minimized or maximized. (All other variables are those that have been added to formulate the objectives as goals.)

$$\text{Minimize} \qquad 2p^+ \qquad + q^-$$

Subject to

$$
\begin{array}{lll}
x_1 + 2x_2 + 3x_3 - x_4 & \geq 200 & (1) \\
3x_1 + x_2 - x_3 + 2x_4 & \leq 300 & (2) \\
4x_1 + 5x_2 \qquad - p^+ + p^- & = 100 & (3) \\
2x_2 \qquad - 3x_4 \qquad - q^+ + q^- & = 400 & (4) \\
x_1 + x_2 - 2x_3 + 9x_4 & \leq 900 & (5)
\end{array}
$$

$$x_1, \quad x_2, \quad x_3, \quad x_4, \quad p^+, \quad p^-, \quad q^+, \quad q^- \geq 0$$

EXERCISE 7.6 Repeat Exercise 7.5 for the following:

$$\text{Minimize} \qquad 2p^+ \qquad + q^-$$

Subject to

$$
\begin{array}{lll}
5x_1 - x_2 + 9x_3 & \geq 100 & (1) \\
2x_1 + 5x_2 - 2x_3 + x_4 & \leq 150 & (2) \\
x_1 - x_2 + x_3 \qquad - p^+ + p^- & = 400 & (3) \\
2x_1 + 2x_2 + 2x_3 + x_4 & \geq 200 & (4) \\
2x_2 \qquad - 3x_4 \qquad - q^+ + q^- & = 250 & (5)
\end{array}
$$

$$x_1, \quad x_2, \quad x_3, \quad x_4, \quad p^+, \quad p^-, \quad q^+, \quad q^- \geq 0$$

EXERCISE 7.7 For the linear program in Exercise 2.7 at the end of Chapter 2, you want to determine the number of barrels of light crude (L) and of heavy crude oil (H) so as to minimize the total costs—for which management has set a target of $75 million. You must also meet demands for producing gasoline, jet fuel, and kerosene. Because there is less demand in general for kerosene, suppose that a second objective is to minimize the amount of excess kerosene produced and that each barrel in excess of 300,000 is penalized 100 times as much as each dollar of cost overrun.

    a. Formulate an appropriate goal-programming problem.
    b. Use your computer package to prepare a table listing the values of each objective function when each one is used independently as the single overall objective, temporarily ignoring the others, and also when the goal program is solved.

EXERCISE 7.8 For the investment problem of Pension Planners, Inc., in Example 3.4, Section 3.4, Chapter 3, suppose that in addition to maximizing the expected rate of return, you also want to minimize the total risk. In that regard, each dollar invested in a low-risk investment is assigned a risk factor of 1. Each dollar invested in a high-risk investment is three times as risky as that in the low-risk category. Each dollar invested in a medium-risk investment is considered twice as risky as that in the low-risk category. Suppose that each unit by which the return falls short of a goal of 0.168(16.8%) is penalized 25 times more than each unit by which the total risk per dollar invested ($3F_1 + 3F_2 + 3F_3 + 2F_4 + 2F_5 + F_6$) exceeds a target of 1.1.

    a. Formulate an appropriate goal-programming problem.
    b. Use your computer package to prepare a table listing the values of each objective function when each one is used independently as the single overall objective, temporarily ignoring the other, and also when the goal program is solved.

EXERCISE 7.9   For the blending problem in Example 3.5, Section 3.5, Chapter 3, suppose that in addition to minimizing costs, a second objective is to minimize the sulfur content. Assume that each unit by which the sulfur content exceeds the goal of 0.0006 is equivalent to 400 times the value by which the costs exceed (in dollars) the goal of $0.95 per gallon.

    a. Formulate an appropriate goal-programming problem.

    b. Use your computer package to prepare a table listing the values of each objective function when each one is used independently as the single overall objective temporarily ignoring the other, and also when the goal program is solved.

EXERCISE 7.10   Consider the production-planning problem of National Steel Corporation in Example 3.6, Section 3.6, Chapter 3, in which you want to minimize the total costs over a 4-month period—for which management has set a goal of $79 million. In the event of a strike by the steelworkers, a second objective is to maximize the average amount of inventory, for which a target of 3600 tons has been set—that is, the sum of the inventories, $(I_1 + I_2 + I_3 + I_4 + I_5)$ has a goal of 18,000 tons. Assume that the value of each ton by which this sum falls short of the goal is 4000 times that for which each dollar exceeds the targeted budget.

    a. Formulate an appropriate goal-programming problem.

    b. Use your computer package to prepare a table listing the values of each objective function when each one is used independently as the single overall objective, temporarily ignoring the others, and also when the goal program is solved.

EXERCISE 7.11   Case Chemicals produces a compound by mixing two of their products: CS-01 and CS-02. Each liter of CS-01 costs $3 and provides 5 grams of sodium and 2 grams of sulfur to the resulting mixture. Each liter of CS-02 costs $1 and yields 2 grams of sodium and 1 gram of sulfur. The resulting mixture is to contain at least 9 grams of sodium and 4 grams of sulfur. The following goal program is designed to achieve a target cost of $3.50 and produce a goal of 2 liters of mixture, assuming that each dollar of cost overrun has the same penalty as each excess liter of the mixture produced and twice as much as each liter below the target of 2 liters:

$$\text{Minimize} \quad 2C^+ + 2P^+ + P^-$$

Subject to

$5CS - 01 + 2CS - 02$	≥ 9	(sodium)
$2CS - 01 + \quad CS - 02$	≥ 4	(sulfur)
$3CS - 01 + \quad CS - 02 - C^+ + C^- = 3.50$		(cost goal)
$CS - 01 + \quad CS - 02 - P^+ + P^- = 2$		(mixture goal)
All variables ≥ 0		

The following computer output is obtained when solving this problem by STORM:

```
        OPTIMAL SOLUTION - SUMMARY REPORT (NONZERO VARIABLES)
                   Variable           Value              Cost
           1        CS-01            1.0000            0.0000
           2        CS-02            2.0000            0.0000
           3         C+              1.5000            2.0000
           5         P+              1.0000            2.0000


        Objective Function Value = 5


               SENSITIVITY ANALYSIS OF COST COEFFICIENTS
                            Current      Allowable      Allowable
                Variable    Coeff.       Minimum        Maximum
           1     CS-01      0.0000        0.0000         2.0000
           2     CS-02      0.0000       -0.8000         0.0000
           3      C+        2.0000        2.0000         6.0000
           4      C-        0.0000       -2.0000         Infinity
           5      P+        2.0000        0.6667         2.0000
           6      P-        1.0000       -2.0000         Infinity
```

Use the foregoing output to answer the following. A total of how many liters are in the final mixture? How much does the mixture cost to produce?

EXERCISE 7.12   Use the output in Exercise 7.11 or use your computer package to solve an appropriately modified model to answer the following. The CEO feels that cost overruns should be penalized twice as much as they are currently. How does this affect the optimal amounts of CS-01 and CS-02 to use?

EXERCISE 7.13   Pete's Pasta Shop makes two types of noodles: thin and thick. Each pound of thin noodle nets the company a profit of $0.50 and requires 2.5 minutes on its cutting machine. Each pound of thick noodle earns a net profit of $0.40 and needs 1.5 minutes of machine time. The company has 40 hours of machine time available this week and needs to produce at least 400 pounds of thin noodles and 500 pounds of thick noodles. In addition to maximizing profits, for which a goal of $800 has been set, a production target of a total of 1000 pounds of noodles has been set, although more or less can be produced. Using appropriate penalties, the following goal program has been developed:

Minimize $\quad 0.45Q^+ + 0.90Q^- + P^-$

Subject to

THIN			$\geq$	400	(demand for thin noodles)
THICK			$\geq$	500	(demand for thick noodles)
$2.5\,THIN + 1.5\,THICK$			$\leq$	2400	(machine time)
$THIN + \quad THICK -$	$1Q^+ +$	$1Q^-$	$=$	1000	(production goal)
$0.5\,THIN + 0.4\,THICK -$	$1P^+ +$	$1P^-$	$=$	800	(profit goal)

$$\text{All variables} \geq \quad 0$$

The following computer output is obtained when solving this problem by STORM:

```
         OPTIMAL SOLUTION - SUMMARY REPORT (NONZERO VARIABLES)
                  Variable        Value          Cost
             1       THIN        660.0000       0.0000
             2      THICK        500.0000       0.0000
             3        Q+         160.0000       0.4500
             6        P-         270.0000       1.0000


         Slack Variables
             7     DEM-THIN      260.0000       0.0000

    Objective Function Value = 342

              SENSITIVITY ANALYSIS OF COST COEFFICIENTS
                            Current      Allowable     Allowable
                  Variable   Coeff.       Minimum       Maximum
             1      THIN     0.0000       -Infinity      0.0500
             2     THICK     0.0000       -0.0800       Infinity
             3       Q+      0.4500        0.2500        0.5000
             4       Q-      0.9000       -0.4500       Infinity
             5       P+      0.0000       -1.0000       Infinity
             6       P-      1.0000        0.9000        1.8000

              SENSITIVITY ANALYSIS OF RIGHT-HAND-SIDE VALUES
                                Current     Allowable     Allowable
            Constraint  Type     Value       Minimum       Maximum
        1    DEM-THIN    >=     400.0000    -Infinity      660.0000
        2   DEM-THICK    >=     500.0000     100.0000      933.3333
        3      TIME      >=    2400.0000    2000.0000     3750.0000
        4   PROD-GOAL     =    1000.0000    -Infinity     1160.0000
        5   PROFIT-GOA    =     800.0000     530.0000      Infinity

         PARAMETRIC ANALYSIS OF RIGHT-HAND-SIDE VALUE - PROFIT-GOAL
    COEF = 800.000     LWR LIMIT = -Infinity      UPR LIMIT = Infinity
          ------- Range -------      Shadow    ---- Variable  ----
             From          To         Price      Leave       Enter
    RHS    800.000     Infinity       1.000   ----  No change  ----
    Obj    342.000     Infinity


    RHS    800.000     530.000        1.000         P-    SLACK    3
    Obj    342.000      72.000


    RHS    530.000     450.000        0.900         Q+         P+
    Obj     72.000       0.000


    RHS    450.000   -2.048E+40       0.000   ----  No change  ----
    Obj      0.000       0.000
```

Use the foregoing output to answer the following. Is the company exceeding its production goal of 1000 pounds or not? By how much? What profit will the company realize with this optimal solution?

EXERCISE 7.14 Use your computer package to solve an appropriately modified model to answer the following. If the penalty for not meeting the profit goal is doubled from its current value, does the optimal production plan in the output in Exercise 7.13 change? Explain.

EXERCISE 7.15 Use your computer package to solve an appropriately modified model to answer the following. By how much does the profit goal in the goal program in Exercise 7.13 have to decrease before it is optimal to meet the production goal of 1000 pounds exactly? (Hint: Systematically decrease the profit goal by small increments and solve the new problem until the production goal of 1000 pounds is met.)

EXERCISE 7.16 Rich Oil Company has a storage tank in Trenton with a capacity of 100,000 gallons and one in Philadelphia with a capacity of 200,000 gallons. The company would like to ship at least 250,000 gallons to distributors in New York and 100,000 gallons to those in Washington, D.C. In addition, the company wants the total cost to be around $10,000, based on the the following shipping costs ($/gal) between storage tanks and distributors:

	TO	
FROM	NEW YORK	WASHINGTON, D.C.
Trenton	0.05	0.12
Philadelphia	0.07	0.10

The following goal program is designed to handle the trade-off in these three objectives using the fact that each dollar in cost overrun is penalized 11 times as much as each gallon by which a distributor is short:

$$\text{Minimize} \quad N^- + \quad W^- + 11C^+$$

Subject to

$$
\begin{array}{lll}
TN + & TW & \leq 100000 \quad \text{(supply at Trenton)} \\
PN + & PW & \leq 200000 \quad \text{(supply at Philadelphia)} \\
TN + & PN - & N^+ + \quad N^- = 250000 \quad \text{(goal for New York)} \\
TW + & PW - & W^+ + \quad W^- = 150000 \quad \text{(goal for Washington)} \\
0.05TN + 0.12TW + 0.07PN + \\
\qquad 0.1PW - & C^+ + \quad C^- = \quad 10000 \quad \text{(cost goal)}
\end{array}
$$

All variables ≥ 0

The following computer output is obtained when solving this problem by STORM:

```
         OPTIMAL SOLUTION - SUMMARY REPORT (NONZERO VARIABLES)
                  Variable           Value              Cost
            1          TN     100000.0000            0.0000
            3          PN     150000.0000            0.0000
            8          W-     150000.0000            1.0000
            9          C+       5500.0000           11.0000


         Slack Variables
            12        SUP-P     50000.0000            0.0000


             Objective Function Value = 210500

           SENSITIVITY ANALYSIS OF COST COEFFICIENTS
                             Current     Allowable     Allowable
                  Variable    Coeff.      Minimum       Maximum
            1          TN     0.0000     -Infinity       0.2200
            2          TW     0.0000      -0.5400       Infinity
            3          PN     0.0000      -0.2200        0.2300
            4          PW     0.0000      -0.1000       Infinity
            5          N+     0.0000      -0.7700       Infinity
            6          N-     1.0000       0.7700       Infinity
            7          W+     0.0000      -1.0000       Infinity
            8          W-     1.0000       0.0000        1.1000
            9          C+    11.0000      10.0000       14.2857
            10         C-     0.0000     -11.0000       Infinity

           SENSITIVITY ANALYSIS OF RIGHT-HAND-SIDE VALUES
                                Current     Allowable     Allowable
            Constraint   Type    Value       Minimum       Maximum
          1    SUP-T      <=   100000.0000   50000.0000   250000.0000
          2    SUP-P      <=   200000.0000  150000.0000     Infinity
          3    DEM-N      =    250000.0000  171428.6000   300000.0000
          4    DEM-W      =    150000.0000       0.0000     Infinity
          5  COST-GOAL    =     10000.0000    -Infinity    15500.0000

         PARAMETRIC ANALYSIS OF RIGHT-HAND-SIDE VALUE - DEM-N
     COEF = 250000.000  LWR LIMIT = -Infinity    UPR LIMIT = Infinity
            -------- Range --------    Shadow    ---- Variable ----
                  From          To      Price    Leave        Enter
     RHS    250000.000   300000.000    0.770   SLACK    2         N-
     Obj    210500.000   249000.000


     RHS    300000.000     Infinity    1.000   ----  No change  ----
     Obj    249000.000     Infinity


     RHS    250000.000   171428.600    0.770              C+         PW
     Obj    210500.000   150000.000


     RHS    171428.600   100000.000    0.700              PN  SLACK   1
     Obj    150000.000   100000.000


     RHS    100000.000        0.000    0.500              TN         N+
     Obj    100000.000    50000.000


     RHS         0.000  -2.621E+42    0.000   ----  No change  ----
     Obj     50000.000    50000.000
```

Use the foregoing output to answer the following. In the context of this model, what is the meaning of the fact that the values of both N^+ and N^- are 0 in this optimal solution?

EXERCISE 7.17   Use the output in Exercise 7.16 or use your computer package to solve an appropriately modified model to answer the following. How much gasoline do the distributors in Washington, D.C., receive? By how much would the appropriate penalties associated with not meeting the goal for those distributors have to increase before the current solution is no longer optimal?

EXERCISE 7.18   Use the output in Exercise 7.16 or use your computer package to solve an appropriately modified model to answer the following. By how much would the target goal for distributors in New York have to decrease before the total penalty incurred drops to 125,000?

EXERCISE 7.19   The managers of Fresh Food Farms want to decide how many of their 50 acres to plant with corn, how many with soybeans, and how many with lettuce. The farm is limited by the availability of 100,000 gallons of water. Each acre devoted to corn requires 5600 gallons of water and yields a net profit of $640, each acre devoted to soybeans needs 2500 gallons of water and yields a net profit of $400, and each acre of lettuce needs 900 gallons of water and yields a net profit of $240. The following goal program is developed to achieve a target profit of $17,000 while devoting at least 8 acres to growing corn:

Minimize				$C^- + P^-$		
Subject to						
$CN +$	$SB +$	LT		$\leq$	50	(land)
$5600CN +$	$2500SB +$	$900LT$		≤ 100000		(water)
$640CN +$	$400SB +$	$240LT -$	$P^+ + P^- =$	17000		(profit goal)
$CN -$			$C^+ + C^- =$	8		(corn goal)

All variables ≥ 0

The following computer output is obtained when solving this problem by STORM:

```
            OPTIMAL SOLUTION - SUMMARY REPORT (NONZERO VARIABLES)
                    Variable           Value            Cost
            1          CN              7.1429          0.0000
            2          SB             13.3929          0.0000
            3          LT             29.4643          0.0000
            5          C-              0.8571          1.0000

        Objective Function Value = 0.857143
```

```
                SENSITIVITY ANALYSIS OF COST COEFFICIENTS
                               Current      Allowable      Allowable
                Variable        Coeff.       Minimum        Maximum
            1      CN           0.0000       -69.0000        1.0000
            2      SB           0.0000        -0.3125       23.4894
            3      LT           0.0000       -35.6129        0.3750
            4      C+           0.0000        -1.0000       Infinity
            5      C-           1.0000         0.0000       70.0000
            6      P+           0.0000        -0.0143       Infinity
            7      P-           1.0000         0.0143       Infinity
```

```
                SENSITIVITY ANALYSIS OF RIGHT-HAND-SIDE VALUES
                                   Current       Allowable       Allowable
            Constraint  Type        Value         Minimum         Maximum
        1      LAND       <         50.0000       46.6667         50.4000
        2      WATER      <      100000.0000    95000.0000     100600.0000
        3   CORN-GOAL     =          8.0000        7.1429        Infinity
        4     PROFIT      =      17000.0000    16940.0000      17500.0000
```

```
            PARAMETRIC ANALYSIS OF RIGHT-HAND-SIDE VALUE - PROFIT
        COEF = 17000.000   LWR LIMIT = -Infinity      UPR LIMIT = Infinity
        -------  Range  -------          Shadow    ----  Variable  ----
             From           To           Price     Leave       Enter
        RHS  17000.000   17500.000     1.429E-02      CN          P-
        Obj      0.857       8.000

        RHS  17500.000    Infinity        1.000   ----  No change  ----
        Obj      8.000     Infinity

        RHS  17000.000   16940.000     1.429E-02      C-          C+
        Obj      0.857       0.000
```

Use the foregoing output to answer the following.

a. How much of the 50 acres are used under the current plan?
b. Which goals are met?
c. Which goals are not met, and by how much?

EXERCISE 7.20 Use your computer package to solve an appropriately modified problem to answer the following. The management of Fresh Food Farms in Exercise 7.19 feels that the penalty for not devoting enough land to corn is underestimated. How sensitive is the current allocation of land to increases in this value? Explain.

EXERCISE 7.21 Use your computer package to solve an appropriately modified model to answer the following. By how much would the profit goal in the goal program in Exercise 7.19 have to decrease before both the corn and profit objectives can be met? Explain. (Hint: Systematically decrease the profit goal by small increments and solve the new problem until both the corn and profit goals are met.)

CRITICAL-THINKING PROJECT D

Recall Critical-Thinking Project D following the exercises in Chapter 3 in which you, Vice-President of Gasahol, Inc., need to determine the least-cost production and shipping plan for your gasoline–alcohol fuel. To develop the desired production plan, obtain the formulation from your instructor and prepare a managerial report following these guidelines.

1. On the basis of this formulation, explain why you need not consider the four combinations in which $Y = 1$ and $Z = 2$; $Y = 2$ and $Z = 1$; $Y = 2$ and $Z = 2$; and $Y = 2$ and $Z = 0$.

2. Having answered the question posed in the first guideline, list all other possible combinations of assigning values to Y and Z. For each combination, solve the associated problem using your linear programming package. Report the total cost of each combination and identify the one of least cost.

3. Management has decided to use an external supplier, GasMix, to send between 8000 and 15,999 gallons to the customer in San Francisco ($Y = 1$) and up to 7999 gallons to the customer in Los Angeles ($Z = 0$). Replace variables Y and Z with these values, and solve the resulting linear program. Prepare a table indicating the optimal amounts to ship from each plant and from GasMix to each customer. What is the total transportation cost?

4. In reviewing the optimal solution in the third guideline, CEO Tom Barnes noted that all three plants are producing at their capacities. Ideally, he would like these plants to operate at 15% below their capacities but realizes that doing so may increase transportation costs. Formulate a goal-programming problem to achieve these objectives. Use the linear programming formulation in the third guideline by (a) replacing each supply constraint with a corresponding goal constraint in which the target capacities are 15% below their original values; (b) creating one new goal constraint for the transportation costs, in which the target is $40,000; (c) including appropriate bounds on some of the new variables used in (a) and (b) to ensure that no plant exceeds its original capacity and that the cost overrun is at most $2000; and (d) having equal penalties for each gallon by which the capacity goals at each plant are exceeded and for each dollar by which the cost goal is exceeded.

5. Solve the goal-programming problem in the fourth guideline and prepare a table indicating the optimal amounts to ship from each plant and from GasMix to each customer. What is the total transportation cost? Which plant(s) are producing more than their target capacity?

6. By how much can the cost overrun of $2000 in the fourth guideline be decreased before one of the plants produces up to its original capacity? (Hint: Systematically decrease the cost overrun in small increments, and solve the new problem until one of the plants produces up to its original capacity.)

WE ALL SCREAM FOR ICE CREAM—OR YOGURT?

What could be better than some ice cream on a hot summer's day? Well, that's a big question in the frozen desert business where different qualities of ice cream and frozen yogurts are competing for your refreshment dollar. Since 1851, when the first commercial ice cream factory opened in Baltimore, the U.S. has enjoyed a love affair with ice cream, which today is a $9.5 billion-a-year industry. Moreover, the study of ice cream has long been a part of academic study. Penn State University has been holding a two-week course on ice cream since 1890. Students learn about the importance of various ingredients and how to mix, process, flavor, and freeze their creations.

Two illustrious graduates of the correspondence version of the Penn State course are Ben Cohen and Jerry Greenfield. Their Ben & Jerry's Homemade, Inc., is a $58 million business. Their business has capitalized on the yuppie desire for tasty, all-natural premium ice creams. Their products are high in fat, calories, and cholesterol and also more dense—that is, there's less air in them—which differentiates their ice cream from most of the regular ice creams sold in supermarkets.

Frozen yogurt is becoming a strong competitor to ice cream. Jim and Joanne Biltekoff own and run Élan Foods, a fast growing frozen desert business. They aim to offer a product with the rich taste of premium ice cream—without the cream. They use yogurt instead, claiming that their desert has half the calories and 80% less fat and cholesterol than the premium ice creams.

Imagine that you are in the ice cream business, and you want to maximize profits. You also want to hold down your capital costs. Moreover, you're worried about fat content, cholesterol, and calories, but you don't want to sacrifice good taste! You have several objectives in mind, so you need to decide on their relative importance. Do you think you could make ice cream for many different markets? Do you want to expand into the yogurt market, as Ben & Jerry have done? You realize that what you have, in fact, is a goal programming problem. Can you envision the LP blending problem you'd construct to help you answer your questions? (Total running time: 5:40).

Questions on the video

1. What expectations can you identify that customers and owners interviewed in the video have about frozen deserts?

2. Why is it important that desert-store owners offer customers several options?

Beyond the video

1. Consider the diet problem for Mountain View General Hospital in this chapter. What similarities does this hospital problem have to the situation facing frozen desert producers?

2. List at least five goals you might have if you were to make up a goal programming problem focusing on frozen deserts.

Practical considerations

1. Discuss the health and diet concerns about frozen deserts and the impact these concerns have on the product line for a frozen-desert company.

2. Discuss the problem of incorporating taste as one of the programming goals. What might you have to give up to get better taste?

ABC News, "On Business," February 1991

LINEAR INTEGER PROGRAMMING: APPLICATIONS AND ALGORITHMS

• •

*T*he airline industry has been in turmoil. But through all the turbulence of other airlines' bankruptcy and failure, Commuter Airways continues to fly its routes connecting Boston, New York, and Cleveland. To stay airborne, Commuter must keep costs low. How can it keep staffing costs to a minimum while servicing its air routes? How many flight attendants does Commuter need on each flight? How many supervisors? In scheduling its crews, Commuter must also heed Federal Aviation Administration staffing regulations.

The Case Study in this chapter shows how Commuter Airways applies linear integer programming to develop the plan that keeps its business flying while holding staffing costs on the ground.

Integer programming problem
A mathematical model that has a linear objective function and linear constraints but requires that some (or all) variables be restricted to only integer values.

As you learned in Chapter 2, some problems when formulated as mathematical models have a linear objective function and linear constraints, but some (or all) variables are restricted to have integer values. Such models are called **integer programming problems**. In Section 8.1, you will see numerous applications of these models.

The integer requirement on the variables often means that even though the objective function and constraints are linear, the problem cannot be solved by a linear programming algorithm. The reason is that there is no guarantee that the values of the variables in the optimal solution thus obtained are integers. One approach for obtaining an optimal integer solution is to *round* the values in the optimal linear programming solution up or down. Doing so *may* result in an optimal integer solution in some cases. As shown in Section 8.2, however, rounding can result in a feasible solution with a significantly worse objective function value than the optimal solution. Worse, an infeasible solution may arise.

Because of these problems associated with integer programming models, researchers have developed specialized algorithms to obtain an optimal solution in which some variables are required to have integer values. In this chapter, you will learn about formulating and solving these integer programming problems.

■ 8.1 APPLICATIONS OF INTEGER PROGRAMMING PROBLEMS

In this section, you will see several typical applications of integer programming problems in the areas of personnel planning, capital budgeting, work-force scheduling, and warehouse location.

8.1.1 Personnel Planning and Scheduling

All businesses use employees with different skills to perform different tasks. A typical personnel-planning problem managers face is to determine how many of each class of employees are needed to accomplish the needed tasks at the least total cost. Also, given the available personnel, it is often necessary to determine a work schedule that satisfies certain union or governmental requirements as to the mix of workers, length of shift, days off, and so on. Examples include the scheduling of nurses, airline crews, drivers, and the like. In this section, you will see one example of how an integer programming model is used to determine the size and composition of a work-force. Later you will also see a case study involving the scheduling of an airline crew.

EXAMPLE 8.1 A PERSONNEL-PLANNING MODEL FOR BURLINGTON BANK The main branch of Burlington Bank in Vermont requires from 8 to 15 tellers on duty depending on the time of day, as indicated in Table 8.1. Full-time tellers work 8 consecutive hours at $15 per hour starting at 8 A.M. Part-time tellers work 4 consecutive hours at $8 per hour starting at 8 A.M., 10 A.M., or 12 noon. Union regulations require that at all times at least 60% of the tellers be full-time. As Manager of the Personnel Department,

TABLE 8.1 *Teller Requirements for Burlington Bank*

TIME PERIOD		MINIMUM NUMBER OF TELLERS
8–10	A.M.	8
10–12	Noon	10
12–2	P.M.	15
2–4	P.M.	12

make a recommendation as to the number of full-time and part-time employees needed throughout the day to minimize the total daily cost. ∎

Following the steps of problem formulation in Chapter 2, first identify the decision variables. What are you free to choose in this problem? It is clearly the number of full-time and part-time tellers; so define

$$F = \text{the number of full-time tellers to hire}$$

$$P = \text{the number of part-time tellers to hire}$$

However, more precision is necessary. In particular, for part-time tellers, you need to know not only how *many* to hire, but also their *starting times.* One approach is to create three variables, each corresponding to the three starting times:

$$P_8 = \text{the number of part-time tellers starting at 8 A.M. to hire}$$

$$P_{10} = \text{the number of part-time tellers starting at 10 A.M. to hire}$$

$$P_{12} = \text{the number of part-time tellers starting at 12 noon to hire}$$

The next step is to formulate the objective function, which in this case is to minimize the total daily cost. Using the technique of decomposition,

$$\text{Total cost} = (\text{cost of full-time tellers}) +$$

$$(\text{cost of part-time tellers starting at 8 A.M.}) +$$

$$(\text{cost of part-time tellers starting at 10 A.M.}) +$$

$$(\text{cost of part-time tellers starting at 12 noon})$$

Recall that the cost associated with the full-time tellers, who work 8 hours per day, is $15 per hour, which is $120 per day. Part-time tellers work 4 hours per day and earn $8 per hour, or $32 per day. Thus, the objective function is

$$\text{Minimize} \quad 120F + 32P_8 + 32P_{10} + 32P_{12}$$

The final step is to identify the constraints. In this case, Figure 8.1, showing the various time segments and types of tellers, is useful. Using the figure and the technique of grouping, you might identify two groups of constraints: requirement constraints and proportion constraints.

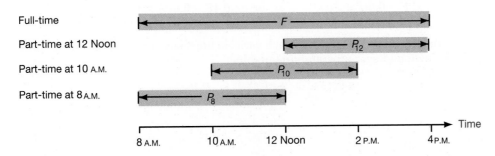

FIGURE 8.1 Schematic Diagram for the Personnel-Planning Problem of Burlington Bank.

REQUIREMENT CONSTRAINTS ON THE TOTAL NUMBER OF TELLERS

In this group, there is one constraint for each time segment, as follows:

1. At least eight tellers are needed from 8 to 10 A.M. Looking at Figure 8.1, you can see that the number of tellers who work during this time segment is composed of the number of the full-time tellers and the number of the part-time tellers who start at 8 A.M. Thus, this constraint is

$$F + P_8 \geq 8$$

2. At least 10 tellers are needed from 10 A.M. to 12 noon. Looking at Figure 8.1, you can see that the number of tellers who work during this time segment are the full-time tellers and the part-time tellers who start at 8 A.M. and at 10 A.M. Thus, this constraint is

$$F + P_8 + P_{10} \geq 10$$

3. At least 15 tellers are needed from 12 noon to 2 P.M. Note that the part-time tellers starting at 8 A.M. have finished their 4-hour shift at 12 noon. The following constraint applies:

$$F + P_{10} + P_{12} \geq 15$$

4. At least 12 tellers are needed from 2 to 4 P.M. Using the same logic as applied in the last step results in the following constraint:

$$F + P_{12} \geq 12$$

PROPORTION CONSTRAINTS

The union regulations require that at least 60% of the tellers must be full-time. Thus, each of the four time segments needs a constraint of the following form:

> Number of full-time tellers should be at least 60% of the total number of tellers

Using the decision variables and Figure 8.1, these four constraints are

$$
\begin{array}{lll}
F \geq 0.6(F + P_8) & \text{or} & 0.4F - 0.6P_8 \geq 0 \\
F \geq 0.6(F + P_8 + P_{10}) & \text{or} & 0.4F - 0.6P_8 - 0.6P_{10} \geq 0 \\
F \geq 0.6(F + P_{10} + P_{12}) & \text{or} & 0.4F - 0.6P_{10} - 0.6P_{12} \geq 0 \\
F \geq 0.6(F + P_{12}) & \text{or} & 0.4F - 0.6P_{12} \geq 0
\end{array}
$$

Adding the logical constraints that each variable must be a nonnegative integer results in the following integer programming problem.

MATHEMATICAL FORMULATION
OF THE PERSONNEL-PLANNING PROBLEM
OF BURLINGTON BANK

Minimize $120F + 32P_8 + 32P_{10} + 32P_{12}$

Subject to:

Integer Program
EX8_1.DAT

REQUIREMENT CONSTRAINTS

$$F + P_8 \geq 8$$
$$F + P_8 + P_{10} \geq 10$$
$$F + P_{10} + P_{12} \geq 15$$
$$F + P_{12} \geq 12$$

PROPORTION CONSTRAINTS

$$0.4F - 0.6P_8 \geq 0$$
$$0.4F - 0.6P_8 - 0.6P_{10} \geq 0$$
$$0.4F - 0.6P_{10} - 0.6P_{12} \geq 0$$
$$0.4F - 0.6P_{12} \geq 0$$

LOGICAL CONSTRAINTS

$$F, \quad P_8, \quad P_{10}, \quad P_{12} \geq 0 \quad \text{and integer}$$

You can now obtain the solution to this model using any software package capable of solving integer programming problems. The results provide the numbers of full-time and part-time tellers to hire, as shown in Section 8.6.

8.1.2 *Capital Budgeting*

A problem many venture-capital and investment companies face is how to allocate a given amount of money to various alternative projects or securities. In some cases, the question is *how much* to invest in each alternative. In other cases, the question is *which* alternatives are to be selected. In the latter case—which involve making a "yes, invest" or "no, do not invest" decision—an appropriate integer programming model is often helpful in choosing among alternatives, as illustrated in the following example.

EXAMPLE 8.2 THE CAPITAL-BUDGETING PROBLEM OF HIGH-TECH High-Tech, a venture-capital investment company, is considering investing up to $1 million in one or more proposals it has received from various entrepreneurs. Each proposal has been screened by the Research Department, and six have a high enough expected rate of return to justify the risk involved. The one-time investment needed and the associated expected rate of return for each project are provided in Table 8.2. As Senior Partner, you have been asked to make recommendations as to which projects should be funded. Your goal is to achieve the highest total expected return on the investment. ■

Following the problem formulation steps in Chapter 2, identify what items you are free to choose. In this case, you can decide whether or not to invest in each of the six projects. As discussed in Section 2.2.2, such "no/yes" decisions are modeled by creating a 0–1 variable for each choice. This leads you to define the following:

TABLE 8.2   *Capital Requirements and Expected Rate of Return for the Projects of High-Tech*

PROJECT	CAPITAL REQUIREMENT ($)	EXPECTED RATE OF RETURN (%)
Bio-Tech	200,000	15.0
Tele-Com	350,000	16.5
Laser-Optics	150,000	13.0
Compu-Ware	125,000	12.5
Medi-Opt	375,000	14.0
Sound-News	70,000	9.0

$$B = \begin{cases} 1 & \text{if High-Tech invests in Bio-Tech} \\ 0 & \text{if High-Tech does not invest in Bio-Tech} \end{cases}$$

$$T = \begin{cases} 1 & \text{if High-Tech invests in Tele-Com} \\ 0 & \text{if High-Tech does not invest in Tele-Com} \end{cases}$$

$$L = \begin{cases} 1 & \text{if High-Tech invests in Laser-Optics} \\ 0 & \text{if High-Tech does not invest in Laser-Optics} \end{cases}$$

$$C = \begin{cases} 1 & \text{if High-Tech invests in Compu-Ware} \\ 0 & \text{if High-Tech does not invest in Compu-Ware} \end{cases}$$

$$M = \begin{cases} 1 & \text{if High-Tech invests in Medi-Opt} \\ 0 & \text{if High-Tech does not invest in Medi-Opt} \end{cases}$$

$$S = \begin{cases} 1 & \text{if High-Tech invests in Sound-News} \\ 0 & \text{if High-Tech does not invest in Sound-News} \end{cases}$$

The next step is to identify the objective function, which is to maximize the total expected return. Using the expected rates of return given in Table 8.2 together with the decision variables and applying the technique of decomposition leads to

Maximize total yearly return

= (return from Bio-Tech)   + (return from Tele-Com)   +
(return from Laser-Optics) + (return from Compu-Ware) +
(return from Medi-Opt)   + (return from Sound-News)

$$\begin{aligned} &= (0.15 * 200{,}000)B && + (0.165 * 350{,}000)T && + \\ &\quad (0.13 * 150{,}000)L && + (0.125 * 125{,}000)C && + \\ &\quad (0.14 * 375{,}000)M && + (0.09 * 70{,}000)S \end{aligned}$$

$$= 30000B + 57750T + 19500L + 15625C + 52500M + 6300S$$

All that remains is to identify the constraints, one of which is not to exceed the budget of $1 million. In terms of the decision variables, this constraint is

$$200000B + 350000T + 150000L + 125000C + 375000M + 70000S \leq 1000000$$

The logical constraints in this problem are that each variable must have a value of 0 or 1. For computational purposes (described in Section 8.4), you write these constraints so that each variable is between 0 and 1 and integer also. For example, the logical constraint for the 0–1 variable B is

$$B \leq 1$$

and

$$B \geq 0 \quad \text{and integer}$$

Adding these logical constraints results in the following integer programming model for the problem of High-Tech.

MATHEMATICAL FORMULATION
OF THE CAPITAL-BUDGETING PROBLEM OF HIGH-TECH

Integer Program
EX8_2.DAT

Maximize $30000B + 57750T + 19500L + 15625C + 52500M + 6300S$

Subject to $200000B + 350000T + 150000L + 125000C + 375000M + 70000S \leq 1000000$ (budget)

$$
\begin{aligned}
B & & \leq 1 \\
T & & \leq 1 \\
L & & \leq 1 \\
C & & \leq 1 \\
M & & \leq 1 \\
S & \leq 1 \\
B, \quad T, \quad L, \quad C, \quad M, \quad S & \geq 0 \quad \text{and integer}
\end{aligned}
$$

You can now use any computer software package capable of solving integer programming problems. The results indicate whether or not to invest in each project, as shown in Section 8.6.

Two other variations of this investment model are given in Section 2.2, Chapter 2. One incorporates the amount of risk associated with each investment; the other considers continued investment over a period of time.

8.1.3 The Cutting-Stock Problem

Many companies face the problem of cutting large-sized products into smaller-sized retail lots. For example, a paper company must cut its large-sized rolls of paper into various smaller-sized rolls to sell to retail customers. In cutting, a company seeks to minimize the total amount of leftover, or *waste*, that must be thrown out or otherwise disposed of while simultaneously meeting known demands for the retail-sized products. An integer programming model can determine how to accomplish this objective.

EXAMPLE 8.3 THE CUTTING-STOCK PROBLEM OF SPIRAL PAPER, INC. Spiral Paper, Inc., sells rolls of paper to various computer and cash-register retailers. Its standard rolls are 20 inches wide. Retailers have placed orders for 1050 rolls of 3-inch width, 2050 rolls of 5-inch width, and 4050 rolls of 8-inch width paper. To produce these smaller rolls, the 20-inch rolls are fed through a cutting machine that has eight different settings, as shown in Table 8.3. Each setting produces a different number of each width of retail-sized roll, leaving a fixed amount of width that is wasted. For example, setting number 6 produces two rolls of 3-inch width, one roll of 5-inch width, and one roll of 8-inch width, leaving a waste of 1 inch from the original 20-inch roll.

These are one-time orders. Any retail-sized rolls left over are sold at discount, resulting in a net loss of $1 for each 3-inch roll, $1.50 for each 5-inch roll, and $2 for each 8-inch roll. The waste is recycled at a net cost of $0.50 per inch. As Manager of the Production Department, you have been asked to determine how to use the different settings of the cutting machine to meet the specified demand for the retail-sized rolls while minimizing the total cost. ■

TABLE 8.3	Rolls of Various Retail Sizes Obtained from the Cutting-Machine Settings			
SETTING	NUMBER OF ROLLS			WASTE
NUMBER	3-in.	5-in.	8-in.	(in.)
1	6	0	0	2
2	0	4	0	0
3	1	0	2	1
4	0	2	1	2
5	4	0	1	0
6	2	1	1	1
7	5	1	0	0
8	1	3	0	2

To determine the variables in this problem, ask what decisions you can make and what constitutes a "cutting plan." You are certainly free to choose the individual settings of the cutting machine and, moreover, you can cut as many 20-inch rolls with that setting as you want. These decisions can be combined into a set of decision variables corresponding to the number of rolls to cut with each fixed setting:

$$x_1 = \text{the number of 20-inch rolls to cut with Setting 1}$$
$$x_2 = \text{the number of 20-inch rolls to cut with Setting 2}$$
$$\vdots$$
$$x_8 = \text{the number of 20-inch rolls to cut with Setting 8}$$

To specify the objective function of minimizing the total cost, apply the technique of decomposition, which leads to

Total cost = (total cost of trim waste from all settings) +
       (total cost from overproducing)

= (cost of trim waste from Setting 1) +
       (cost of trim waste from Setting 2) +

$$\vdots$$

       (cost of trim waste from Setting 8) +

       (cost from overproducing 3-inch rolls) +
       (cost from overproducing 5-inch rolls) +
       (cost from overproducing 8-inch rolls)

For example, each 20-inch roll cut with the first setting produces a trim waste of 2 inches, as seen in Table 8.3. Because x_1 such 20-inch rolls are being cut,

Trim waste from Setting 1 = $2x_1$

By using the decision variables and the trim waste given for each setting in Table 8.3,

Total inches of trim waste = $2x_1 + 0x_2 + 1x_3 + 2x_4 + 0x_5 + 1x_6 + 0x_7 + 2x_8$

Because each inch of waste costs $0.50,

Total cost of trim waste $= 0.50 *$ (total inches of trim waste)

$$= 1x_1 + 0x_2 + 0.5x_3 + 1x_4 + 0x_5 + 0.5x_6 + 0x_7 + 1x_8$$

To specify the waste from overproduction, consider, for example, the number of 3-inch rolls produced. According to Table 8.3, each 20-inch roll cut with the Setting 1 produces six 3-inch rolls. Because x_1 such 20-inch rolls are cut, the total number of 3-inch rolls obtained from this setting is $6x_1$. Similarly, x_2 20-inch rolls cut with Setting 2 produces no 3-inch rolls, and so on. Consequently,

Number of 3-inch rolls produced $= 6x_1 + 0x_2 + 1x_3 + 0x_4 + 4x_5 + 2x_6 + 5x_7 + 1x_8$

Because only 1050 3-inch rolls are needed,

Number of 3-inch rolls overproduced

$$= (6x_1 + 0x_2 + 1x_3 + 0x_4 + 4x_5 + 2x_6 + 5x_7 + 1x_8) - 1050$$

An appropriate demand constraint for 3-inch rolls will ensure that the amount overproduced is nonnegative. Each 3-inch roll overproduced results in a cost of $1; so

Cost from overproducing 3-inch rolls

$$= 1 * \text{(number of 3-inch rolls overproduced)}$$

$$= (6x_1 + 0x_2 + 1x_3 + 0x_4 + 4x_5 + 2x_6 + 5x_7 + 1x_8) - 1050$$

Applying similar logic to the 5-inch and 8-inch rolls overproduced leads to

Cost from overproducing 5-inch rolls

$$= 1.5 * \text{(number of 5-inch rolls overproduced)}$$

$$= (0x_1 + 6x_2 + 0x_3 + 3x_4 + 0x_5 + 1.5x_6 + 1.5x_7 + 4.5x_8) - 3075$$

Cost from overproducing 8-inch rolls

$$= 2 * \text{(number of 8-inch rolls overproduced)}$$

$$= (0x_1 + 0x_2 + 4x_3 + 2x_4 + 2x_5 + 2x_6 + 0x_7 + 0x_8) - 8100$$

In summary, the overall objective function of minimizing the total cost is

$$
\begin{aligned}
\text{Minimize} \quad & (1x_1 + 0x_2 + 0.5x_3 + 1x_4 + 0x_5 + 0.5x_6 + 0x_7 + 1x_8) + \\
& (6x_1 + 0x_2 + 1x_3 + 0x_4 + 4x_5 + 2x_6 + 5x_7 + 1x_8) - 1050 + \\
& (0x_1 + 6x_2 + 0x_3 + 3x_4 + 0x_5 + 1.5x_6 + 1.5x_7 + 4.5x_8) - 3075 + \\
& (0x_1 + 0x_2 + 4x_3 + 2x_4 + 2x_5 + 2x_6 + 0x_7 + 0x_8) - 8100 \\
= \quad & 7x_1 + 6x_2 + 5.5x_3 + 6x_4 + 6x_5 + 6x_6 + 6.5x_7 + 6.5x_8 - 12225
\end{aligned}
$$

The final step in problem formulation is to identify the constraints, which in this case are to meet the specified demand for each retail-sized roll. For example, the number of 3-inch rolls produced must be at least 1050. In determining the objective function, the number of 3-inch rolls produced was already computed. This constraint is

$$\text{Number of 3-inch rolls produced} \geq 1050$$

$$6x_1 + 0x_2 + 1x_3 + 0x_4 + 4x_5 + 2x_6 + 5x_7 + 1x_8 \geq 1050$$

A similar constraint is needed for the 5-inch and 8-inch rolls, resulting in

$$0x_1 + 4x_2 + 0x_3 + 2x_4 + 0x_5 + 1x_6 + 1x_7 + 3x_8 \geq 2050$$
$$0x_1 + 0x_2 + 2x_3 + 1x_4 + 1x_5 + 1x_6 + 0x_7 + 0x_8 \geq 4050$$

Adding the logical constraints that all variables be nonnegative integers—after all, you cannot cut a fraction of a roll—the complete formulation for the problem of Spiral Paper, Inc., is

MATHEMATICAL FORMULATION OF THE CUTTING-STOCK PROBLEM OF SPIRAL PAPER, INC.

Integer Program
EX8_3.DAT

Minimize $7x_1 + 6x_2 + 5.5x_3 + 6x_4 + 6x_5 + 6x_6 + 6.5x_7 + 6.5x_8 - 12225$
Subject to

DEMAND CONSTRAINTS

$6x_1 +$	$0x_2 +$	$1x_3 +$	$0x_4 +$	$4x_5 +$	$2x_6 +$	$5x_7 +$	$1x_8 \geq$	1050	(3-in. rolls)
$0x_1 +$	$4x_2 +$	$0x_3 +$	$2x_4 +$	$0x_5 +$	$1x_6 +$	$1x_7 +$	$3x_8 \geq$	2050	(5-in. rolls)
$0x_1 +$	$0x_2 +$	$2x_3 +$	$1x_4 +$	$1x_5 +$	$1x_6 +$	$0x_7 +$	$0x_8 \geq$	4050	(8-in. rolls)

LOGICAL CONSTRAINTS

$$x_1, \ x_2, \ x_3, \ x_4, \ x_5, \ x_6, \ x_7, \ x_8 \geq 0 \ \text{and integer}$$

You can now use any computer software package capable of solving integer programming problems. The results indicate the number of 20-inch rolls to cut with each of the eight settings, as shown in Section 8.6.

8.1.4 A Location Problem

One class of problems you learned about in Section 2.2, Chapter 2 is the transportation problem, which involves shipping finished goods from supply points, such as plants or warehouses, to demand points, such as retail stores or customers. One strategic decision a manager may have to make is how many plants and/or warehouses to have and where to locate them. By opening more of them, the company can reduce its distribution costs. However, each supply point requires a substantial capital investment and fixed cost. An integer programming model can often help determine which plan results in the least total cost, as illustrated in the next example.

EXAMPLE 8.4 THE PLANT-LOCATION PROBLEM OF THE COSMIC COMPUTER COMPANY The Cosmic Computer Company (CCC) has just gone public and has obtained funds to produce a new microcomputer. The company confidently anticipates monthly demand for 1700 computers from a retail store in San Diego, for 1000 computers from a store in Barstow, for 1500 computers from a store in Tucson, and for 1200 computers from a store in Dallas. To meet this anticipated demand, the management of CCC is considering building assembly plants in San Francisco, Los Angeles, Phoenix, and/or

Denver. The projected monthly production capacities and fixed costs (which include operating the plant, paying the mortgage, and so on) are given in Table 8.4. The cost for shipping a finished microcomputer from each plant to each retail store is given in Table 8.5. As Manager of the Production Division, you have been asked to recommend which plants to build to minimize the total monthly transportation and fixed costs. ■

TABLE 8.4 *Plant Capacities and Fixed Costs*

LOCATION	MONTHLY CAPACITY	MONTHLY FIXED COSTS ($)
San Francisco	1700	70,000
Los Angeles	2000	70,000
Phoenix	1700	65,000
Denver	2000	70,000

TABLE 8.5 *Shipping Costs ($/Computer) from Plants to Retail Stores*

| PLANTS | STORES | | | |
	SAN DIEGO	BARSTOW	TUCSON	DALLAS
San Francisco	5	3	2	6
Los Angeles	4	7	8	10
Phoenix	6	5	3	8
Denver	9	8	6	5

Before formulating this problem, it is useful to draw a diagram to illustrate the four possible locations for the assembly plants and the four retail stores. This, together with the associated supplies and demands, is illustrated in Figure 8.2.

The first step is to realize that this problem requires two decisions: one to determine *which* plants to build, and a second to determine the *number* of microcomputers to ship from each plant actually built to each retail store. For the first decision, you are free to choose which plants in Figure 8.2 to build—that is, to decide whether or not to build a plant at each location. In Section 2.2.2, you learned that each "no/yes" decision is modeled with a separate 0–1 integer variable. In this case, let

$$y_S = \begin{cases} 1 & \text{if a plant is opened in San Francisco} \\ 0 & \text{otherwise} \end{cases}$$

$$y_L = \begin{cases} 1 & \text{if a plant is opened in Los Angeles} \\ 0 & \text{otherwise} \end{cases}$$

$$y_P = \begin{cases} 1 & \text{if a plant is opened in Phoenix} \\ 0 & \text{otherwise} \end{cases}$$

$$y_D = \begin{cases} 1 & \text{if a plant is opened in Denver} \\ 0 & \text{otherwise} \end{cases}$$

The second set of decisions involves how many units to ship from each plant to each retail customer. As seen in Figure 8.2 (and discussed in the transportation problem

Supply Nodes

Demand Nodes

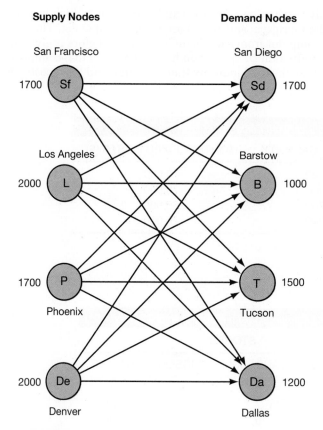

FIGURE 8.2 The Distribution Network of CCC.

of Section 2.2), it is necessary to define the sixteen transportation variables shown in Table 8.6. For example, x_{LB} denotes the number of microcomputers to ship from the plant in Los Angeles to the retail store in Barstow.

The next step is to formulate the objective function of minimizing total costs. Using the technique of decomposition leads to

$$\text{Total costs} = (\text{fixed costs}) + (\text{transportation costs})$$

TABLE 8.6	Symbolic Names for the Shipping Variables for the Plant-Location Problem of CCC			
	STORES			
PLANTS	SAN DIEGO	BARSTOW	TUCSON	DALLAS
San Francisco	x_{SS}	x_{SB}	x_{ST}	x_{SD}
Los Angeles	x_{LS}	x_{LB}	x_{LT}	x_{LD}
Phoenix	x_{PS}	x_{PB}	x_{PT}	x_{PD}
Denver	x_{DS}	x_{DB}	x_{DT}	x_{DD}

where

$$\text{Fixed costs} = \text{(fixed cost of the San Francisco plant)} +$$
$$\text{(fixed cost of the Los Angeles plant)} +$$
$$\text{(fixed cost of the Phoenix plant)} +$$
$$\text{(fixed cost of the Denver plant)}$$

Observe that if the plant in San Francisco is opened, the fixed cost is \$70,000. If the plant is not opened, the fixed cost is 0. In terms of the $0-1$ decision variables, the fixed cost of the plant in San Francisco is $70000y_S$, which results in a cost of \$70,000 if the plant is opened (that is, $y_S = 1$) and \$0 if not ($y_S = 0$). Applying similar logic to each potential plant,

$$\text{Fixed costs} = 70000y_S + 70000y_L + 65000y_P + 70000y_D$$

The total shipping cost is the number of units shipped from each plant to each retail store times the associated shipping cost per unit. Thus,

$$\text{Transportation cost} = (5x_{SS} + 3x_{SB} + 2x_{ST} + 6x_{SD}) +$$
$$(4x_{LS} + 7x_{LB} + 8x_{LT} + 10x_{LD}) +$$
$$(6x_{PS} + 5x_{PB} + 3x_{PT} + 8x_{PD}) +$$
$$(9x_{DS} + 8x_{DB} + 6x_{DT} + 5x_{DD})$$

By combining the fixed and transportation costs, the overall objective is to

$$\text{Minimize} \quad 70000y_S + 70000y_L + 65000y_P + 70000y_D +$$
$$(5x_{SS} + 3x_{SB} + 2x_{ST} + 6x_{SD}) +$$
$$(4x_{LS} + 7x_{LB} + 8x_{LT} + 10x_{LD}) +$$
$$(6x_{PS} + 5x_{PB} + 3x_{PT} + 8x_{PD}) +$$
$$(9x_{DS} + 8x_{DB} + 6x_{DT} + 5x_{DD})$$

The final step is to identify the constraints. Applying the technique of grouping should lead you to the following:

1. Supply constraints to ensure that the number of units shipped from each plant does not exceed capacity.
2. Demand constraints to ensure that each retail store receives *exactly* the number of units requested.
3. Logical constraints.

SUPPLY CONSTRAINTS

Consider the plant in San Francisco. By decomposition,

$$\text{Number of units shipped from SF} = x_{SS} + x_{SB} + x_{ST} + x_{SD}$$

This number should not exceed this plant's capacity. Observe that this plant can produce up to 1700 microcomputers per month *if built*, and 0 units otherwise. Using the $0-1$ decision variable y_S, this capacity is $1700y_S$. Thus, the supply constraint for the plant in San Francisco is

$$x_{SS} + x_{SB} + x_{ST} + x_{SD} \le 1700y_S$$

or

$$x_{SS} + x_{SB} + x_{ST} + x_{SD} - 1700y_S \leq 0 \quad \text{(San Francisco)}$$

Similarly, the supply constraints for the other three assembly plants are

$$
\begin{aligned}
x_{LS} + x_{LB} + x_{LT} + x_{LD} - 2000y_L &\leq 0 \quad \text{(Los Angeles)} \\
x_{PS} + x_{PB} + x_{PT} + x_{PD} - 1700y_P &\leq 0 \quad \text{(Phoenix)} \\
x_{DS} + x_{DB} + x_{DT} + x_{DD} - 2000y_D &\leq 0 \quad \text{(Denver)}
\end{aligned}
$$

DEMAND CONSTRAINTS

Consider the retail store in San Diego. By decomposition,

$$\text{Number of units shipped to SD} = x_{SS} + x_{LS} + x_{PS} + x_{DS}$$

Because this amount must equal the store's demand of 1700 units, the demand constraint at San Diego is:

$$x_{SS} + x_{LS} + x_{PS} + x_{DS} = 1700 \quad \text{(San Diego)}$$

The demand constraints for the other three retail stores are

$$
\begin{aligned}
x_{SB} + x_{LB} + x_{PB} + x_{DB} &= 1000 \quad \text{(Barstow)} \\
x_{ST} + x_{LT} + x_{PT} + x_{DT} &= 1500 \quad \text{(Tucson)} \\
x_{SD} + x_{LD} + x_{PD} + x_{DD} &= 1200 \quad \text{(Dallas)}
\end{aligned}
$$

Finally, add the logical constraints that each shipment variable is nonnegative and integer and that each y-variable have a value of 0 or 1. The final model for the problem of CCC is as follows.

MATHEMATICAL FORMULATION
OF THE PLANT-LOCATION PROBLEM OF CCC

Integer Program
EX8_4.DAT

Minimize
$$
\begin{aligned}
70000y_S + 70000y_L &+ 65000y_P + 70000y_D + \\
(5x_{SS} + \quad 3x_{SB} &+ \quad 2x_{ST} + \quad 6x_{SD}) + \\
(4x_{LS} + \quad 7x_{LB} &+ \quad 8x_{LT} + \quad 10x_{LD}) + \\
(6x_{PS} + \quad 5x_{PB} &+ \quad 3x_{PT} + \quad 8x_{PD}) + \\
(9x_{DS} + \quad 8x_{DB} &+ \quad 6x_{DT} + \quad 5x_{DD})
\end{aligned}
$$

Subject to

SUPPLY CONSTRAINTS

$$
\begin{aligned}
x_{SS} + x_{SB} + x_{ST} + x_{SD} - 1700y_S &\leq 0 \quad \text{(San Francisco)} \\
x_{LS} + x_{LB} + x_{LT} + x_{LD} - 2000y_L &\leq 0 \quad \text{(Los Angeles)} \\
x_{PS} + x_{PB} + x_{PT} + x_{PD} - 1700y_P &\leq 0 \quad \text{(Phoenix)} \\
x_{DS} + x_{DB} + x_{DT} + x_{DD} - 2000y_D &\leq 0 \quad \text{(Denver)}
\end{aligned}
$$

DEMAND CONSTRAINTS

$$x_{SS} + x_{LS} + x_{PS} + x_{DS} = 1700 \qquad \text{(San Diego)}$$
$$x_{SB} + x_{LB} + x_{PB} + x_{DB} = 1000 \qquad \text{(Barstow)}$$
$$x_{ST} + x_{LT} + x_{PT} + x_{DT} = 1500 \qquad \text{(Tucson)}$$
$$x_{SD} + x_{LD} + x_{PD} + x_{DD} = 1200 \qquad \text{(Dallas)}$$

LOGICAL CONSTRAINTS

$$y_S, y_L, y_P, \text{ and } y_D = 0 \text{ or } 1, \text{ and all other variables } \geq 0 \text{ and integer}$$

The results of using a suitable software package indicate which plants to build and how many computers to ship from each plant to each retail store, as shown in Section 8.6.

KEY FEATURES

All examples in this section illustrate the following key features:

✔ Using 0–1 integer variables to model "no/yes" decisions.
✔ Using integer variables to represent quantities that, by their nature, cannot take fractional values but rather must be whole numbers.

In this section, you have seen how integer programming is used to model problems arising in many different business areas including personnel planning, capital budgeting, cutting stock, and location decisions. Once a problem is formulated, the next step is to solve it. Section 8.2 shows how this is done graphically when there are only two integer decision variables.

■ 8.2 LINEAR INTEGER PROGRAMMING: THE GRAPHICAL APPROACH

A graphical approach promotes understanding of the complexities associated with solving linear integer programming problems.

8.2.1 Solving Graphically an Integer Programming Problem with Two Variables

Consider the integer programming problem faced by the Buffalo Urban Development Department (BUDD).

EXAMPLE 8.5 THE INTEGER PROGRAMMING PROBLEM OF BUDD BUDD has obtained a federal grant of $5 million to develop low-income and middle-income apartment buildings on a tract of 180,000 square feet of land. Each type of building requires 20,000 square feet. The estimated cost of each low-income building is $300,000, and the estimated cost of each middle-income building is $600,000. Each low-income building provides 15 units, and each middle-income building provides 12 units. To keep the neighborhood well-balanced, the federal government requires that the ratio of middle-income to low-income apartments be at least 0.80. The director of BUDD wants to determine the greatest number of individual apartments that can be built on the available land with the given budget. ■

PROBLEM FORMULATION

Following the steps of problem formulation given in Chapter 2 and recognizing that you can control the number of each type of apartment building to construct should lead you to identify the following two variables:

$$L = \text{the number of low-income apartment buildings to construct}$$
$$M = \text{the number of middle-income apartment buildings to construct}$$

As specified in the problem description, the objective is to maximize the total number of individual apartments that can be constructed:

$$\text{Maximize} \quad 15L + 12M$$

The budget constraint is that the total construction costs cannot exceed the available grant money. In terms of hundreds of thousands of dollars, that constraint is

$$3L + 6M \leq 50 \quad \text{(budget constraint)}$$

A second constraint is that the land used in the construction cannot exceed the available 180,000 square feet. In terms of thousands of square feet, that constraint is

$$20L + 20M \leq 180 \quad \text{(land constraint)}$$

A third constraint is that the ratio of middle-income to low-income units be at least 0.80:

$$\frac{12M}{15L} \geq 0.80$$

or

$$12M \geq 12L$$

or

$$-L + M \geq 0 \quad \text{(ratio constraint)}$$

By adding the logical constraints that L and M are nonnegative integers, the integer programming problem for BUDD is as follows.

MATHEMATICAL FORMULATION OF THE INTEGER PROGRAMMING PROBLEM FOR BUDD

Integer Program
EX8_5.DAT

$$
\begin{array}{llll}
\text{Maximize} & 15L + 12M & & \\
\text{Subject to} & 3L + 6M \leq 50 & & \text{(budget)} \\
& 20L + 20M \leq 180 & & \text{(land)} \\
& -L + M \geq 0 & & \text{(ratio)} \\
& L, \quad M \geq 0 \text{ and integer} & &
\end{array}
$$

Linear programming relaxation
The linear program obtained by dropping the integer requirements on the variables in an integer programming problem.

SOLVING GRAPHICALLY THE PROBLEM OF BUDD

You might hope to solve this problem by the linear programming techniques discussed in Chapter 4. To do so, you first drop the integer requirement, which yields the **linear programming relaxation** of the original problem. In this example:

LINEAR PROGRAMMING RELAXATION PROBLEM FOR BUDD

$$
\begin{array}{lrll}
\text{Maximize} & 15L + 12M & & \\
\text{Subject to} & 3L + 6M \leq & 50 & \text{(budget)} \\
& 20L + 20M \leq & 180 & \text{(land)} \\
& -L + M \geq & 0 & \text{(ratio)} \\
& L, \quad M \geq & 0 &
\end{array}
$$

The result of solving graphically this linear program is the optimal solution of $L = 4.5$ and $M = 4.5$, with an associated objective function value of 121.5, as illustrated in Figure 8.3(a). Unfortunately, these *fractional solutions* are infeasible with regard to the integer requirement on the variables.

One way to obtain graphically an optimal *integer* solution is to start with the optimal linear programming solution and, on recognizing that the values are fractional, to move the objective function line parallel to itself *toward the feasible integer solutions* until the line goes through the first such point, as shown in Figure 8.3(b). You can see that the optimal integer solution is $L = 4$ and $M = 5$, with an objective function value of 120. Thus, BUDD should contract to build four low-income and five middle-income buildings, providing a total of 120 individual apartments.

The idea of moving the objective function line from the optimal linear programming solution toward the feasible integer solutions is not a viable approach for a computer because there is no practical way to determine when the first *integer* solution is encountered. Another approach is needed. One obvious idea is to examine the neighboring integer values around the optimal linear programming solution. For instance, in this example, the optimal linear programming solution is $L = 4.5$ and $M = 4.5$. The neighboring integer solutions, as seen in Figure 8.3(b), are listed in Table 8.7. In this case, you can see that **rounding** $L = 4.5$ down to 4 and $M = 4.5$ up to 5, yields the optimal integer solution. Unfortunately, this simple idea of rounding does not work in general, as illustrated in Section 8.2.2.

Rounding
Changing a fractional value for a variable to its nearest (larger or smaller) integer value.

TABLE 8.7	*The Neighboring Integer Solutions of the Optimal Linear Programming Solution for the Problem of BUDD*	

L	M	OBJECTIVE FUNCTION VALUE
4	4	108
4	5	120 (optimal)
5	4	Infeasible
5	5	Infeasible

8.2.2 *The Problems with Rounding Noninteger Solutions*

In Section 8.2.1, you saw an example of how an optimal integer solution could be obtained by rounding the optimal linear programming solution appropriately. The results for Example 8.5 are given in Table 8.7. You can see that one of the rounded integer solutions is optimal, but that two of them are actually infeasible. One reason that rounding does not work in general is because for some problems *all* rounded integer solutions are infeasible, as seen in Example 8.6.

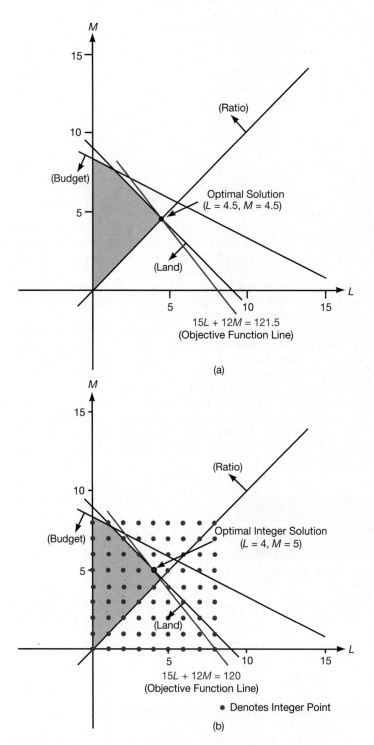

FIGURE 8.3 (a) Optimal Solution to the Linear Programming Relaxation of Example 8.5, (b) Optimal Integer Solution to Example 8.5.

EXAMPLE 8.6 ROUNDING TO INFEASIBLE SOLUTIONS

$$\text{Maximize} \quad 3x_1 + 2x_2$$

$$\begin{aligned}
\text{Subject to} \quad & x_1 + 4x_2 \leq 8 & (1) \\
& -x_1 + 4x_2 \geq 4 & (2) \\
& x_1, \quad x_2 \geq 0 \quad \text{and integer} & \blacksquare
\end{aligned}$$

The graphical solution to Example 8.6 is given in Figure 8.4. The optimal linear programming solution is $x_1 = 2$ and $x_2 = 1.5$, with an objective function value of 9. Looking at Figure 8.4, you can also see that the two neighboring integer solutions obtained by rounding x_2 up to 2 or down to 1 produce integer solutions that are not even feasible, much less equal to the optimal integer solution of $x_1 = 0$ and $x_2 = 2$, whose objective function value is 4.

In contrast to Example 8.6, rounding the optimal linear programming solution to the problem in Example 8.7 *does* provide a feasible integer solution, but not the optimal one.

EXAMPLE 8.7 ROUNDING TO A NONOPTIMAL SOLUTION

$$\text{Maximize} \quad 4x_1 + 5x_2$$

$$\begin{aligned}
\text{Subject to} \quad & 3x_1 + 4x_2 \leq 20 & (1) \\
& 4x_1 + 2x_2 \leq 16 & (2) \\
& x_2 \geq 2 & (3) \\
& x_1, \quad x_2 \geq 0 \quad \text{and integer} & \blacksquare
\end{aligned}$$

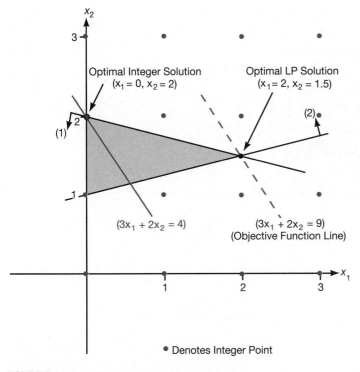

FIGURE 8.4 Optimal Solution to Example 8.6.

In Example 8.7, the optimal solution to the linear programming relaxation is $x_1 = 2.4$ and $x_2 = 3.2$, with an objective function value of 25.6, as seen in Figure 8.5. The results of rounding this solution are given in Table 8.8. You can see that the rounded integer solution in which $x_1 = 2$ and $x_2 = 3$ is feasible with an objective function value of 23. Unfortunately, as seen in Figure 8.5, the optimal integer solution is $x_1 = 0$ and $x_2 = 5$, with an objective function value of 25.

TABLE 8.8	*The Neighboring Integer Solutions of the Optimal Linear Programming Solution for Example 8.7*	
x_1	x_2	OBJECTIVE FUNCTION VALUE
2	3	23
2	4	Infeasible
3	3	Infeasible
3	4	Infeasible

Examples 8.6 and 8.7 show that the approach of obtaining the optimal linear programming solution and then rounding, although simple, may not produce the optimal integer solution or even a feasible one. Another approach is needed. That approach uses the optimal solution of the linear programming relaxation, as described in Section 8.3.

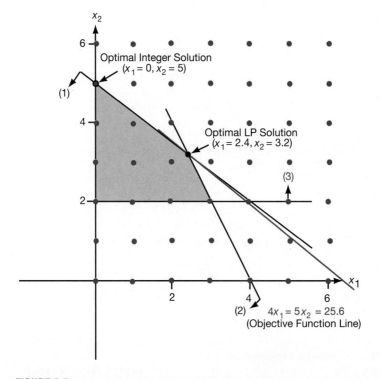

FIGURE 8.5 Optimal Solution to Example 8.7.

■ 8.3 LINEAR INTEGER PROGRAMMING: A CONCEPTUAL APPROACH

In Section 8.2, you learned how to solve graphically an integer programming problem having two variables. This approach cannot be used by computers because they use algebra. In this section, you will learn the conceptual idea behind one method for solving problems having integer variables by computer.

8.3.1 Listing the Possible Integer Solutions

Recall from Chapter 5 the two features of linear programming problems that enable the development of a finite-improvement algorithm:

1. The ability to test a particular feasible solution quickly for optimality.
2. The ability to determine a new feasible solution with a strictly better objective function value when the current solution fails the test.

Unfortunately, no such procedures have yet been found for integer programming problems. The only way currently known to obtain the optimal solution is to evaluate *all* possible integer solutions. Consider the integer programming problem in Example 8.8.

EXAMPLE 8.8 AN INTEGER PROGRAMMING PROBLEM WITH THREE VARIABLES

$$
\begin{array}{lll}
\text{Maximize} & 3x_1 + 2x_2 + x_3 & \\
\text{Subject to} & x_1 + x_2 + x_3 \le 4 & (1) \\
& 2x_1 - x_2 - x_3 \le 0 & (2) \\
& x_1 + x_2 - x_3 \le 0 & (3) \\
& x_1 \quad\quad\quad \le 2 & (4) \\
& \quad x_2 \quad\quad \le 2 & (5) \\
& \quad\quad x_3 \le 2 & (6) \\
& x_1, \ x_2, \ x_3 \ge 0 \quad \text{and integer} & \blacksquare
\end{array}
$$

As described before, one approach to solving this problem includes the following:

1. Make a list of all possible integer solutions.
2. Identify from all feasible integer solutions the one whose objective function value is the best (in this case, the largest).

For this two-step approach to work on a computer, all possible integer solutions in step 1 must be listed in a *systematic* way. In the problem in Example 8.8, observe that constraints (4) to (6) give rise to the three possible integer values of 0, 1, and 2 for each of the three variables. Thus, it is necessary to list all 27 of these combinations of integer values for x_1, x_2, and x_3.

One approach is to list all three values for x_1 and, for each one, list all three values for x_2, which results in nine combinations. For each of these nine, you can then list all three values for x_3, bringing the total number of combinations to 27. This approach is depicted using a **tree**, as illustrated in Figure 8.6, in which

1. each **node**, or circle, in the tree indicates that some variables in the problem have already been given specific integer values
2. from each node, an **arc**, or arrow, leads to a new node to indicate that a new variable is now being given a specific integer value

Tree
A diagram consisting of nodes and arcs used to list all combinations of integer values for variables in an integer programming problem.

Node
A circle in the tree associated with an integer program that indicates that some variables in the problem have been fixed to specific integer values.

Arc
A line with an arrow that connects one node to another node in a tree associated with an integer program to indicate that a new variable is now being fixed to a specific integer value.

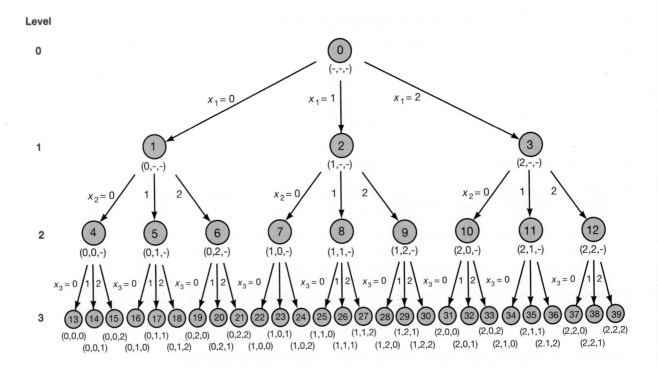

FIGURE 8.6 A Tree Listing All Possible Integer Solutions to Example 8.8.

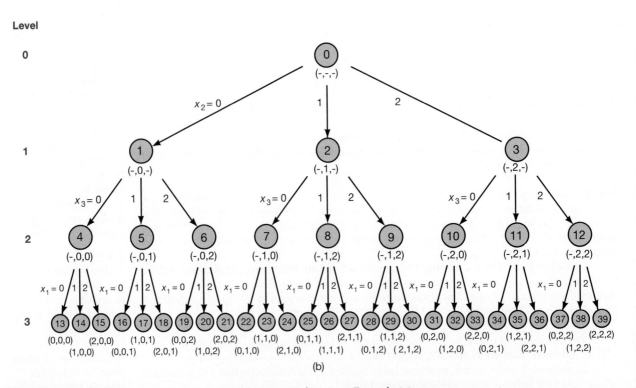

FIGURE 8.7 One Alternative Tree Listing All Possible Integer Solutions to Example 8.8.

In Figure 8.6, the top node 0 labeled $(-,-,-)$ at *level 0* in the tree indicates that no variables have, as yet, been fixed in value. The leftmost arc from that node to node 1, labeled $(0,-,-)$, at level 1 indicates that x_1 is being fixed to the integer value of 0 whereas x_2 and x_3 are not yet fixed. The middle arc from node 0 to node 2, labeled $(1,-,-)$, indicates that x_1 is being fixed to the integer value of 1. The rightmost arc from node 0 to node 3, labeled $(2,-,-)$, indicates that x_1 is being fixed to the integer value of 2.

Consider now node 1, where x_1 is fixed to value 0. The leftmost arc from that node to node 4, labeled $(0,0,-)$, at level 2 indicates that x_2 is being fixed to an integer value of 0 whereas x_3 is not yet fixed. The middle arc from node 1 to node 5, labeled $(0,1,-)$, indicates that x_2 is being fixed to an integer value of 1. The rightmost arc from node 1 to node 6, labeled $(0,2,-)$, indicates that x_2 is being fixed to an integer value of 2. This process is repeated for each node at level 1.

Repeating this process at level 2, where the value of x_3 is being fixed to an integer value, yields 27 **terminal nodes** at level 3, that is, those nodes at which *all* variables have been fixed. In this case, these terminal nodes correspond to the 27 combinations of integer values for x_1, x_2, and x_3. For example, node 15, labeled $(0,0,2)$, corresponds to the integer solution $x_1 = 0$, $x_2 = 0$, and $x_3 = 2$. If there are k integer variables, a tree with k levels gives all the possible combinations of integer values.

In Figure 8.6, at level 1 x_1 is fixed to a specific integer value, at level 2 x_2 is fixed to a specific integer value, and at level 3 x_3 is fixed to a specific integer value. Any other sequence of variables works just as well. For example, in Figure 8.7, at level 1 the value of x_2 is fixed, at level 2 the value of x_3 is fixed, and at level 3 the value of x_1 is fixed. Moreover, from nodes at the same level, you can fix *different* variables. For example, in Figure 8.8 at level 1 x_1 is fixed to specific integer values. However, at level 2 from node 1 x_2 is fixed, and from node 2 x_3 is fixed, and from node 3 x_2 is again fixed. Observe, however, that no matter the sequence, each tree yields the same 27 integer solutions. Only the *order* of these solutions differs. The specific tree to use is determined by computational considerations described in Section 8.4.

Terminal node

A node at the last level in a tree associated with an integer program, corresponding to a specific set of values for the integer variables.

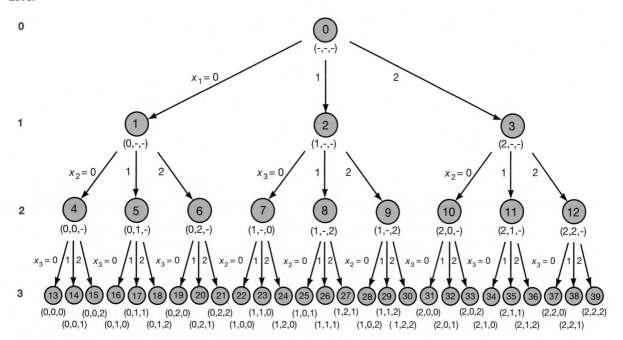

FIGURE 8.8 Another Alternative Tree Listing All Possible Integer Solutions to Example 8.8.

The 27 combinations of values for x_1, x_2, and x_3 in the tree in Figure 8.6 having been listed, the next step, as described in the beginning of this section, is to identify which of the 27 terminal nodes correspond to *feasible* solutions. You would then evaluate the objective function at each feasible solution to find the optimal one.

Although in this example you could easily list and examine all 27 combinations to find the optimal solution, consider an integer programming problem with 10 variables, each of which is restricted to have an integer value—say, between 0 and 9. The number of terminal nodes in the corresponding tree is 10 billion. Even today's fastest computers cannot list and examine this many combinations in a practical amount of time. The answer is to apply some clever methods to eliminate many nodes from consideration. These reducing methods are also effective when the number of integer solutions is infinite, in which case it is not even possible to list them all. The method described in Section 8.3.3 is designed to avoid having to list and to evaluate explicitly all solutions by using the information derived from solving some associated linear programming problems, as discussed in Section 8.3.2.

8.3.2 *Linear Programming Problems Associated with the Nodes of the Tree*

In Section 8.3.1, you saw how a tree is used to list all possible combinations of integer values for the variables in an integer programming problem. At each node in the tree, certain variables in the problem have been fixed to specific integer values. By replacing all those variables in the mathematical model with their assigned values *and temporarily dropping the integer requirements on the remaining variables*, a linear programming problem can be associated with each node in the tree. For example, for node 3 at level 1 in Figure 8.6 the variable x_1 is fixed to a value of 2. By replacing this variable with its assigned value of $x_1 = 2$ in the problem of Example 8.8 and dropping the integer requirements on x_2 and x_3, the linear program associated with node 3 is as follows.

LINEAR PROGRAM AT NODE 3 IN FIGURE 8.6

$$
\begin{aligned}
\text{Maximize} \quad & 6 + 2x_2 + x_3 \\
\text{Subject to} \quad & 2 + \ x_2 + x_3 \le 4 \\
& 4 - \ x_2 - x_3 \le 0 \\
& 2 + \ x_2 - x_3 \le 0 \\
& x_2 \qquad\quad \le 2 \\
& \qquad\quad x_3 \le 2 \\
& x_2 \ , \ x_3 \ge 0
\end{aligned}
$$

To illustrate again, consider node 5 at level 2 in Figure 8.6. At this node, x_1 is fixed to a value of 0 and x_2 is fixed to a value of 1. By replacing those variables with their values in Example 8.8 and dropping the integer requirement on x_3, the linear programming problem associated with node 5 is as follows.

LINEAR PROGRAM AT NODE 5 IN FIGURE 8.6

$$
\begin{aligned}
\text{Maximize} \quad & 0 + 2 + x_3 \\
\text{Subject to} \quad & 0 + 1 + x_3 \le 4 \\
& 0 - 1 - x_3 \le 0 \\
& 0 + 1 - x_3 \le 0 \\
& x_3 \le 2 \\
& x_3 \ge 0
\end{aligned}
$$

> ⇒ **KEY FEATURES**
>
> In summary, associated with each node in the tree is a linear programming problem obtained from the original integer programming problem by
>
> ✔ replacing all the variables that are being fixed with their specific integer values and
> ✔ removing the integer requirements on all remaining variables
>
> The optimal solutions to these linear programming problems are used to reduce the number of terminal nodes in the tree that need to be examined, as described in Section 8.3.3.

8.3.3 The Branch-and-Bound Method: A Conceptual Approach

As mentioned in Section 8.3.1, it is impractical to list and examine all terminal nodes in a tree for integer programming problems having many variables. This is because there are too many terminal nodes at the bottom level of the tree.

> ⇒ **KEY FEATURES**
>
> With the **branch-and-bound method**, rather than looking at the terminal nodes directly, you start at the top level of the tree and proceed from node to node toward the bottom of the tree and the terminal nodes. At each node, the associated linear program is solved. On the basis of this solution, a decision is made as to which nodes in the tree, if any, can be eliminated from further consideration, which reduces the number of terminal nodes that need to be examined.

Branch-and-bound method
A method used to solve an integer programming problem in which the nodes in the associated tree are examined in a systematic way in an attempt to eliminate as many terminal nodes from consideration as possible.

If you can somehow eliminate one of the three nodes at level 1 in the tree in Figure 8.6 (and hence all nodes below the eliminated one) for example, you reduce the number of terminal nodes that must be considered from 27 to 18.

To see how this elimination process is done, begin at the top of the tree in Figure 8.6. At node 0, no variables are fixed in value. Dropping the integer requirements on all three variables in Example 8.8 results in the following linear programming problem at node 0:

LINEAR PROGRAM AT NODE 0

$$
\begin{array}{ll}
\text{Maximize} & 3x_1 + 2x_2 + x_3 \\
\text{Subject to} & x_1 + x_2 + x_3 \le 4 \\
& 2x_1 - x_2 - x_3 \le 0 \\
& x_1 + x_2 - x_3 \le 0 \\
& x_1 \le 2 \\
& x_2 \le 2 \\
& x_3 \le 2 \\
& x_1 , \ x_2 , \ x_3 \ge 0
\end{array}
$$

When solving this linear program by computer, you will discover that the optimal solution is $x_1 = 4/3$, $x_2 = 2/3$, and $x_3 = 2$, with an objective function value of 22/3. Had the values of all three variables been integers, this would be the solution to the integer programming problem. Because there are noninteger values, it is necessary to proceed to level 1 in the tree.

You can now choose *any* one of the nodes at level 1. For illustration purposes, consider node 3, in which x_1 is fixed to a value of 2. The linear programming problem associated with this node is as follows:

LINEAR PROGRAM AT NODE 3

$$\text{Maximize} \quad 6 + 2x_2 + x_3$$
$$\text{Subject to} \quad 2 + \ x_2 + x_3 \le 4$$
$$4 - \ x_2 - x_3 \le 0$$
$$2 + \ x_2 - x_3 \le 0$$
$$x_2 \qquad \le 2$$
$$x_3 \le 2$$
$$x_2 \ , \ x_3 \ge 0$$

When solving this linear program, you will discover that it is infeasible. As a result, this node, *together with all the ones below it* [in particular, nodes labeled (2,0,–), (2,1,–), (2,2,–); (2,0,0), (2,0,1), (2,0,2); (2,1,0), (2,1,1), (2,1,2); (2,2,0), (2,2,1), and (2,2,2)] can be eliminated from further consideration, as illustrated in Figure 8.9(a). As you will learn in Section 8.4, all linear programming problems associated with these eliminated nodes are also infeasible. Returning to level 1 in the tree, consider now node 2, labeled (1,–,–), in which x_1 is fixed to value 1. The corresponding linear programming problem is as follows:

LINEAR PROGRAM AT NODE 2

$$\text{Maximize} \quad 3 + 2x_2 + x_3$$
$$\text{Subject to} \quad 1 + \ x_2 + x_3 \le 4$$
$$2 - \ x_2 - x_3 \le 0$$
$$1 + \ x_2 - x_3 \le 0$$
$$x_2 \qquad \le 2$$
$$x_3 \le 2$$
$$x_2 \ , \ x_3 \ge 0$$

The optimal solution to this linear program is $x_1 = 1$, $x_2 = 1$, and $x_3 = 2$, with an objective function value of 7. In this case, the optimal solution to this linear programming problem happens, by chance, to satisfy the integer requirements. This fortunate occurrence means the following:

1. All nodes below this one can be eliminated from further consideration. As you will learn in Section 8.4, no linear program associated with a node below the current one can produce a better solution [see Figure 8.9(b)].
2. A feasible solution for the original *integer* programming problem has been found.

As a result of condition 2, observe that the objective function value of 7 for the optimal solution of the current linear program, $x_1 = 1$, $x_2 = 1$, and $x_3 = 2$, provides a **lower bound** on the optimal objective function value for the original integer programming problem in Example 8.8. That is, the optimal objective function of the problem in Example 8.8 must be *at least* 7, because you can always use the current integer feasible

Lower bound
A value obtained in the branch-and-bound method; the optimal objective function of an integer program is known to be at least as large as this value.

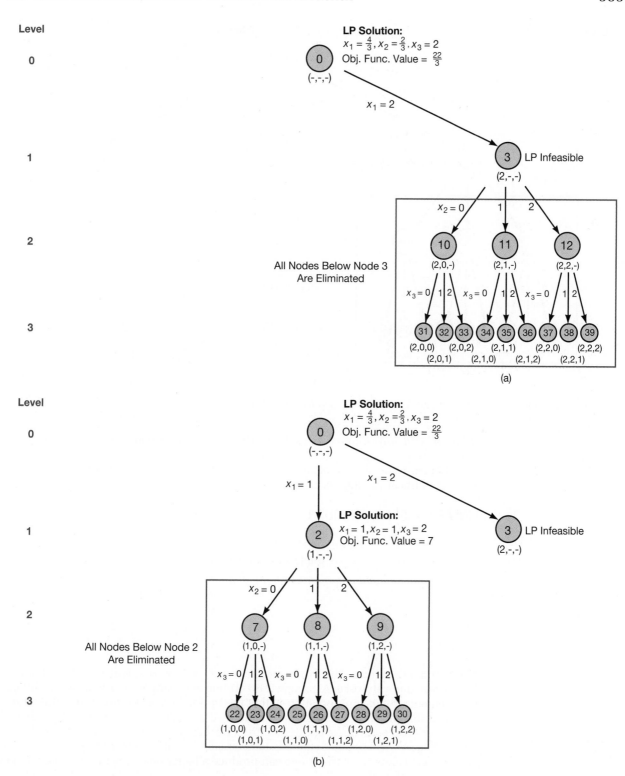

FIGURE 8.9 Using the Branch-and-Bound Method to Solve Example 8.8.

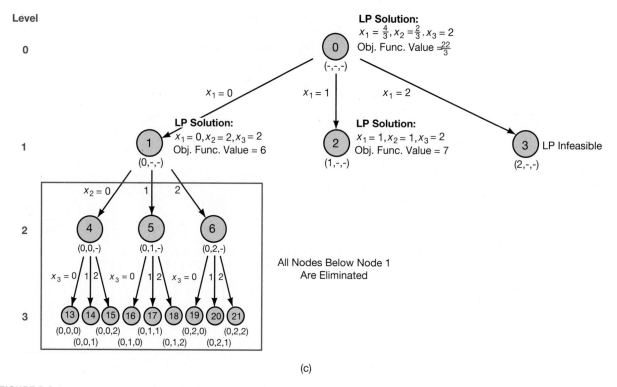

FIGURE 8.9 (*cont.*)   Using the Branch-and-Bound Method to Solve Example 8.8.

solution. This lower bound is useful in dropping further nodes from the tree, as you will now see.

Return to level 1 to examine node 1. At this node, x_1 is fixed to 0, and so the associated linear program is as follows:

LINEAR PROGRAM AT NODE 1

$$
\begin{aligned}
\text{Maximize} \quad & 0 + 2x_2 + x_3 \\
\text{Subject to} \quad & 0 + \ \ x_2 + x_3 \le 4 \\
& 0 - \ \ x_2 - x_3 \le 0 \\
& 0 + \ \ x_2 - x_3 \le 0 \\
& \qquad \ x_2 \qquad \ \le 2 \\
& \qquad \qquad x_3 \le 2 \\
& \qquad x_2 \ , \ \ x_3 \ge 0
\end{aligned}
$$

The optimal solution to this linear program is $x_1 = 0$, $x_2 = 2$, and $x_3 = 2$, with an objective function value of 6. Although this solution also happens to satisfy all the integer requirements, the key observation is that the optimal objective function value of 6 is *less* than that of the lower bound of 7, obtained at node 2. As a result, this node and all the ones below it can be eliminated from further consideration, as shown in Figure 8.9(c). As you will learn in Section 8.4, the reason is that no linear program associated with a node below the current one can produce a better objective function value than the current value of 6.

There are no more nodes in the tree to examine. Therefore, the optimal solution to the integer programming problem is the solution obtained at node 2—namely, $x_1 = 1$, $x_2 = 1$, and $x_3 = 2$, with an optimal objective function value of 7. As a result of the branch-and-bound method, this solution has been obtained after examining only three nodes in the tree. In this example, none of the nodes below level 1 is considered because they were eliminated on the basis of the solutions of linear programs associated with nodes at level 1. However, nodes below level 1 would be examined, by solving the associated linear program, had they *not* been eliminated.

KEY FEATURES

In summary, after solving the linear programming problem associated with the current node, it is possible to eliminate that node and all the ones below it from further consideration when any of the following conditions occur:

✔ The linear program is infeasible.
✔ The optimal solution to the linear programming problem satisfies all the integer requirements. In this case, the current solution is also feasible for the original integer programming problem and thus provides a lower bound.
✔ The optimal objective function value of the linear program is less than or equal to the value of the current lower bound.

Recognizing the importance of having a lower bound, you should also realize that the larger its value, the better. The larger the value of the lower bound, the more likely it is that other nodes can be eliminated by condition 3. You should therefore keep track of the largest lower bound.

The branch-and-bound method ends when all nodes in the tree have been examined or eliminated. The optimal solution to the original integer programming problem is then the feasible integer solution producing the largest lower bound. In the event that no feasible integer solution has been found, the original problem is infeasible.

8.3.4 Solving the Problem of BUDD Using the Branch-and-Bound Method

In Section 8.2, the integer programming model for the planning problem of BUDD is solved graphically. Now that same problem is solved using the branch-and-bound method. Recall the following integer programming problem from Section 8.2:

THE INTEGER PROGRAMMING PROBLEM FOR BUDD

$$
\begin{array}{lll}
\text{Maximize} & 15L + 12M & \\
\text{Subject to} & 3L + 6M \le 50 & \text{(budget)} \\
& 20L + 20M \le 180 & \text{(land)} \\
& -L + M \ge 0 & \text{(ratio)} \\
& L, \quad M \ge 0 \text{ and integer} &
\end{array}
$$

Integer Program
EX8_5.DAT

Begin by drawing a tree to represent all possible integer values of L and M. The land constraint restricts both L and M to a value between 0 and 9. The resulting 100 possible integer solutions are shown as terminal nodes numbered 11 through 110 in the tree given in Figure 8.10.

To apply the branch-and-bound method, solve the relaxed problem at node 0, in which neither L nor M are restricted to be integers. The result is the optimal solution: $L = 4.5$ and $M = 4.5$, with an objective function value of 121.5. Because these values are not integers, proceed to the next level in the tree, in which L is fixed to an integer value.

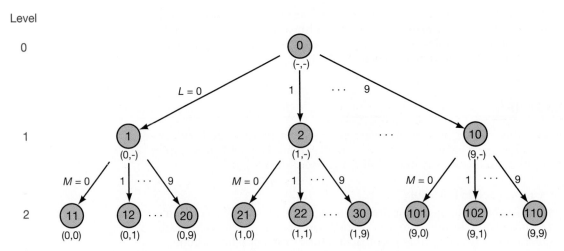

FIGURE 8.10 Listing All Possible Integer Solutions to the Planning Problem of BUDD.

Although you can fix L to any integer value between 0 and 9, because its current value is 4.5, it makes sense to fix L to a value of 5. The associated linear program is

$$
\begin{array}{llll}
\text{Maximize} & 75 + 12M \\
\text{Subject to} & 15 + \ \ 6M \le \ \ 50 & \text{(budget)} \\
& 100 + 20M \le 180 & \text{(land)} \\
& -5 + \ \ \ M \ge \ \ \ 0 & \text{(ratio)} \\
& \ \ \ \ \ \ \ \ \ \ M \ge \ \ \ 0 \ \text{and integer}
\end{array}
$$

This linear programming problem is infeasible, so this node and all the ones below it can be eliminated. In fact, fixing L to any integer value above 5 also results in an infeasible linear program, enabling you to discard all of the nodes at level 1 corresponding to $L = 5, 6, 7, 8,$ and 9, as well as all nodes below these. The elimination of all these nodes is shown in Figure 8.11(a), where the nodes are numbered according to the order in which they are examined.

Proceeding to the remaining nodes at level 1, begin by fixing L to an integer value of 4. The relaxed problem associated with this node is

$$
\begin{array}{llll}
\text{Maximize} & 60 + 12M \\
\text{Subject to} & 12 + \ \ 6M \le \ \ 50 & \text{(budget)} \\
& 80 + 20M \le 180 & \text{(land)} \\
& -4 + \ \ \ M \ge \ \ \ 0 & \text{(ratio)} \\
& \ \ \ \ \ \ \ \ \ \ M \ge \ \ \ 0 \ \text{and integer}
\end{array}
$$

The solution to this relaxed problem is $L = 4$ and $M = 5$, with an objective function value of 120. Because the values of both L and M in this solution are integer:

1. all nodes below this one can be eliminated from further consideration, as shown in Figure 8.11(b) and
2. a feasible solution for the original *integer* programming problem has been found

Observe that the objective function value of 120 for the optimal solution of the current linear program in which $L = 4$ and $M = 5$ provides a *lower bound* on the optimal objective function value for the original integer programming problem of BUDD. That is, the optimal objective function value of the problem of BUDD must be *at least* 120,

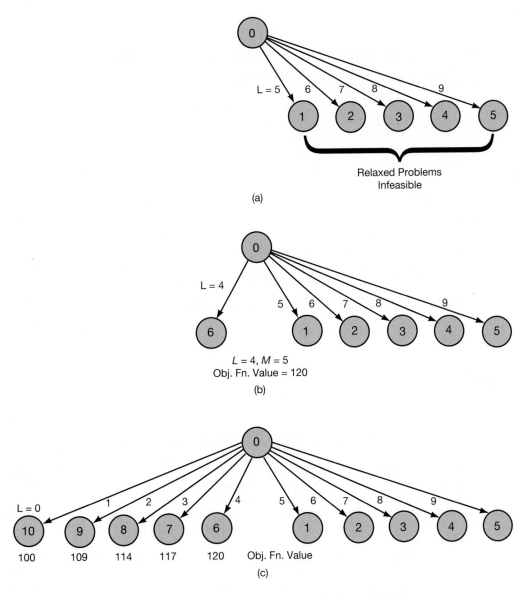

FIGURE 8.11 Using the Branch-and-Bound Approach to Solve the Problem of BUDD.

because you can always use the current feasible integer solution. This lower bound is useful in dropping further nodes from the tree, as you will now see.

Proceeding with the remaining nodes at level 1—in which L is fixed to value 3, 2, 1, and 0—and solving the associated relaxed problems results in optimal objective function values that are *less than* the current lower bound of 120, as summarized in Figure 8.11(c). As a result, all of these nodes, together with the ones below them, can be discarded.

Because there are no more nodes to examine, the solution of $L = 4$ and $M = 5$ associated with the current lower bound of 120 is the optimal solution for BUDD. This means that BUDD should construct four low-income buildings and five middle-income buildings, resulting in a total of 120 individual apartments.

In Section 8.4, you will learn some of the mathematical details of the branch-and-bound method and how even more nodes in the tree can be eliminated from further consideration.

■ 8.4 THE BRANCH-AND-BOUND METHOD: A MATHEMATICAL APPROACH

In Section 8.3, you learned the conceptual ideas of how the branch-and-bound method is used to reduce the number of integer solutions that need to be examined to solve an integer programming problem. In this section, some mathematical justification as to why this technique works is presented. You will also learn other conditions under which even more solutions can be eliminated from consideration.

8.4.1 Properties of Linear Programming Relaxation Problems

Recall from Section 8.3 that the first step in solving an integer programming problem is to use a tree to list all possible combinations of integer values for the variables. Consider the integer programming problem in Example 8.9.

EXAMPLE 8.9 AN INTEGER PROGRAMMING PROBLEM WITH THREE VARIABLES

$$
\begin{array}{lll}
\text{Maximize} & 2x_1 + 3x_2 + x_3 & \\
\text{Subject to} & x_1 + x_2 + x_3 \leq 5 & (1) \\
& -x_1 + 2x_2 - x_3 \leq 1 & (2) \\
& x_1 + x_2 - x_3 \leq 0 & (3) \\
& x_1, \quad x_2, \quad x_3 \geq 0 \quad \text{and integer} & \blacksquare
\end{array}
$$

The tree in which the terminal nodes at the bottom level correspond to all possible integer values for the three variables in Example 8.9 is shown in Figure 8.12. Keep in mind that with the branch-and-bound method, you work from the top of the tree down. The more nodes at or near the top that are eliminated, the more lower nodes—including the terminal nodes—are eliminated without investigation.

Recall that each node in the tree corresponds to certain variables being fixed to specific integer values. Thus, it is possible to associate with each node in the tree:

1. an integer programming problem obtained by replacing all fixed variables with their specific integer values and
2. a linear programming problem obtained by temporarily dropping the integer requirement on all remaining variables

For example, consider node 1 at level 1 in Figure 8.12. This node corresponds to x_1 being fixed to value 0, so the associated integer and linear programming problems for this node are as follows:

INTEGER PROGRAM AT NODE 1

$$
\begin{array}{ll}
\text{Maximize} & 0 + 3x_2 + x_3 \\
\text{Subject to} & 0 + x_2 + x_3 \leq 5 \\
& 0 + 2x_2 - x_3 \leq 1 \\
& 0 + x_2 - x_3 \leq 0 \\
& x_2, \quad x_3 \geq 0 \text{ and integer}
\end{array}
$$

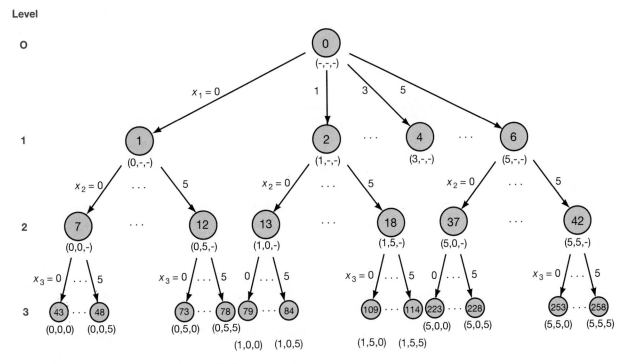

FIGURE 8.12 Listing All Possible Integer Solutions to Example 8.9

LINEAR PROGRAM AT NODE 1

Maximize $0 + 3x_2 + x_3$
Subject to $0 + \ \ x_2 + x_3 \le 5$
$0 + 2x_2 - x_3 \le 1$
$0 + \ \ x_2 - x_3 \le 0$
$x_2 \ , \ x_3 \ge 0$

The branch-and-bound method is designed to use the solution to the linear programs at each node to determine which nodes, if any, can be dropped from the tree. As you learned in Chapter 4, *any* linear program is infeasible, optimal, or unbounded. The implications of each of these three cases for the linear programs at each node are discussed in what follows.

A LINEAR PROGRAM AT A NODE IS INFEASIBLE

In the event that a linear program at a node is infeasible,

1. the associated integer programming problem at that node is also infeasible and
2. all linear programming problems (and hence corresponding integer programs) associated with nodes *below* this node are also infeasible

The observation in condition 1 is true because the associated integer problem has all the constraints of the linear programming problem together with the *additional* constraints that some of the variables be integer. Similarly, any linear programming problem associated with a node below the current one has all the constraints in the current linear program, and more. If it is not possible to satisfy the constraints of the current linear program, it will not be possible to satisfy a program with *additional* constraints.

 KEY FEATURES

Fact 1: If a linear programming problem at a node is infeasible, then so is the integer problem at that node, as well as all problems associated with nodes below the current one.

Consider node 4, labeled $(3,-,-)$ at level 1 in the tree of Figure 8.12. You can verify that the associated linear program is infeasible. Fact 1 indicates that all integer and linear programs associated with nodes below this one [that is, nodes labeled $(3,0,-),\ldots,(3,5,-);(3,0,1),\ldots,(3,0,5);\ldots;(3,5,0),\ldots,(3,5,5)$] are also infeasible.

A LINEAR PROGRAM AT A NODE IS OPTIMAL

When the linear program associated with a node has an optimal solution, such a solution provides the best possible value of the objective function with the given constraints. Any linear program with *additional* constraints cannot have a better optimal objective function value. In particular:

1. the optimal objective function value of the associated integer program at a node cannot exceed that of the corresponding linear program
2. the optimal objective function value of any linear program, and hence the corresponding integer program, associated with a node *below* the current one cannot exceed that of the current linear program

KEY FEATURES

Fact 2: If the current linear program has an optimal solution, then the optimal objective function value of the corresponding integer problem, as well as any linear or integer problem associated with a node below the current one, cannot exceed that of the current one.

Consider node 2 in the tree in Figure 8.12. The optimal solution to the linear program associated with this node is $x_1 = 1$, $x_2 = 3/2$, and $x_3 = 5/2$, with an optimal objective function value of 9. As a result, the optimal objective function value of the integer program at this node cannot exceed 9. In fact, that optimal solution is $x_1 = 1$, $x_2 = 1$, and $x_3 = 3$, with an objective function value of 8. Also, for example, the linear program associated with node 13 below node 2—in which x_1 is fixed to 1 and x_2 to 0—has an optimal objective function value of 6, which of course does not exceed 9. This worse objective function value results because the linear problem associated with node 13 has all the constraints of the linear problem associated with node 2 and also the constraint that x_2 be 0. Similarly, the optimal objective function value of any linear problem associated with a node below node 2 will not exceed 9.

As a consequence of Fact 2, Fact 3 arises.

KEY FEATURES

Fact 3: If, at any node, the optimal solution to the linear problem happens to satisfy all the *integer* requirements, then that solution is also optimal for the integer programming problem associated with that node. Moreover, because the best integer solution to all integer and linear programs below this node has been found, there is no need to examine any node below this one.

Consider node 1, labeled $(0,-,-)$, in Figure 8.12, at which x_1 is fixed to 0. The optimal solution to the linear program is $x_1 = 0$, $x_2 = 2$, and $x_3 = 3$, with an objective function value of 9. Because this solution satisfies the integer requirements for both x_2 and x_3, it is also an optimal solution to the corresponding integer problem. Moreover, all nodes below node 1 can be eliminated.

Facts 1 to 3 help to eliminate nodes *below* the current one. The next group of ideas helps eliminate nodes to *either side* of the current one, as well as all nodes below them.

To illustrate, consider the optimal solution to the linear program associated with the top node in Figure 8.12, which is $x_1 = 0.5$, $x_2 = 2$, and $x_3 = 2.5$, with an objective function value of 9.5. Because x_1 and x_3 have *fractional values*, you must examine additional nodes below this one. What happens when x_1, for example, is fixed to a particular integer value between 0 and 5, as illustrated by the six nodes at level 1 in the tree in Figure 8.12? By setting the value of x_1 to 2, for example, the optimal solution to the linear programming problem is $x_1 = 2$, $x_2 = 0.5$, and $x_3 = 2.5$, with an objective function value of 8.

The results of solving all six linear programming problems in which x_1 is fixed to a different integer value between 0 and 5 are summarized in Table 8.9. The key observations are as follows:

1. The farther the value of x_1 from 0.5 [the value of x_1 in the optimal solution to the linear program at the current node $(-,-,-)$], the worse the optimal value of the objective function for the associated linear program.
2. Once the linear programming problem is infeasible for a particular integer value of x_1 larger (smaller) than 0.5, *all* integer values of this variable larger (smaller) than this one also produce an infeasible linear program.

TABLE 8.9 Optimal Solutions and Objective Function Values for Fixed Integer Values of x_1

x_1	x_2	x_3	OPTIMAL OBJECTIVE FUNCTION VALUE
0	2.0	3.0	9.0
0.5	2.0	2.5	9.5 (optimal linear program solution)
1	1.5	2.5	9.0
2	0.5	2.5	8.0
3	—	—	Infeasible
4	—	—	Infeasible
5	—	—	Infeasible

➡️ **KEY FEATURES**

Fact 4: The farther the value of a variable is fixed from its value in the optimal solution of a linear program, the worse the value of the optimal objective function of the associated linear program.

Fact 5: Once a linear programming problem is infeasible for a fixed integer value of a variable larger (smaller) than its optimal value in the linear problem, all larger (smaller) values of this variable result in infeasible linear programming problems.

These two facts are used to help eliminate nodes at either side of the current one, as described in Section 8.4.2.

A LINEAR PROGRAM AT A NODE IS UNBOUNDED

When a linear program at a node is unbounded, you might think that the integer programming problem is also unbounded. However, this is not always the case. It may be that the integer programming problem is infeasible, as illustrated graphically by the example in Figure 8.13.

➡️ **KEY FEATURES**

Fact 6: If the linear program at a node is unbounded, the integer programming problem is either unbounded or infeasible.

These six facts pertaining to the linear programming problems at the nodes are used in Section 8.4.2 to describe a branch-and-bound approach for solving integer programming problems.

8.4.2   The Branch-and-Bound Algorithm

Branching
The process of systematically working from the top of a tree toward the terminal nodes.

As mentioned in Section 8.4.1, the approach to solving the integer program in Example 8.9 requires examining all 216 possible integer solutions corresponding to the 216 terminal nodes numbered 43 through 258 in the tree in Figure 8.12. The branch-and-bound method described conceptually in Section 8.3 is designed to avoid this lengthy process. You begin at the top of the tree and systematically work down, or **branch**, toward the terminal nodes, eliminating some from consideration. In this section, you will learn how Facts 1 to 6 in Section 8.4.1 are used to eliminate nodes both to the sides and below the current node. The optimal solution is found once all nodes have been examined or eliminated. Example 8.9 illustrates this process.

ITERATION 0: EXAMINE NODE 0

First, examine node 0 of the tree in Figure 8.12, where none of the variables has been fixed. The associated linear program at this node is

$$
\begin{array}{llr}
\text{Maximize} & 2x_1 + 3x_2 + x_3 & \\
\text{Subject to} & x_1 + x_2 + x_3 \leq 5 & (1) \\
& -x_1 + 2x_2 - x_3 \leq 1 & (2) \\
& x_1 + x_2 - x_3 \leq 0 & (3) \\
& x_1 , x_2 , x_3 \geq 0 &
\end{array}
$$

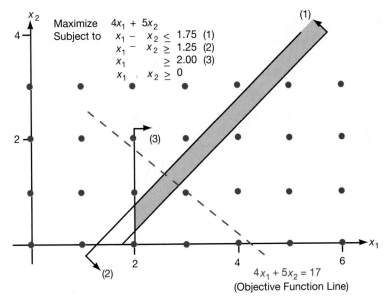

(a) Infeasible Integer Program

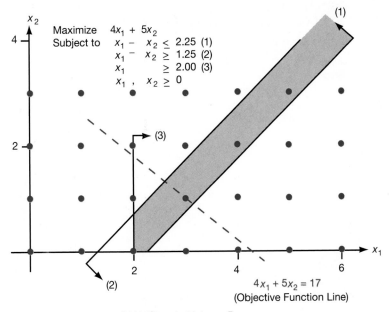

(b) Unbounded Integer Program

FIGURE 8.13 Solution of an Integer Program with an Associated Unbounded
Linear Problem.

Using a computer to solve this problem results in the optimal solution of $x_1 = 0.5$, $x_2 = 2$, and $x_3 = 2.5$, with an objective function value of 9.5, as shown in Figure 8.14(a). Neither x_1 nor x_3 satisfies the integer requirements, so more nodes need to be examined.

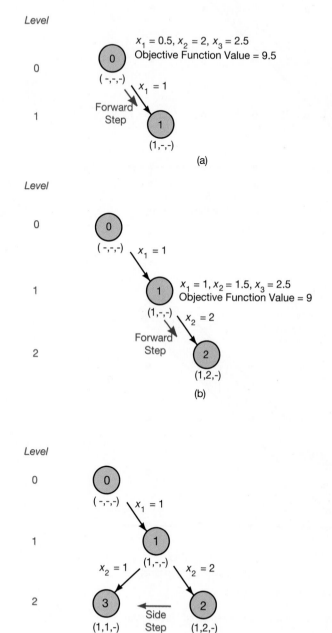

FIGURE 8.14 Using the Branch-and-Bound Approach to Solve Example 8.9.

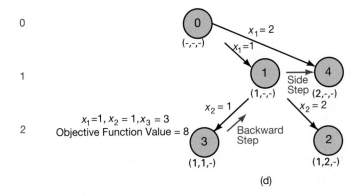

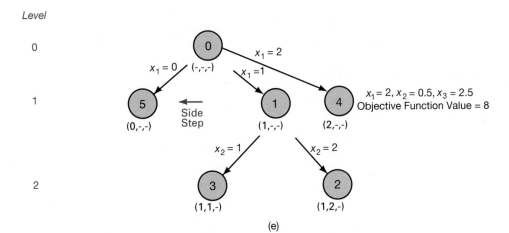

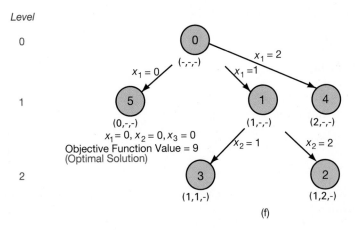

FIGURE 8.14 (*cont.*)   Using the Branch-and-Bound Approach to Solve Example 8.9.

1. Choose which variable with a fractional value to fix (either x_1 or x_3 in this case).
2. Then determine which integer value the variable chosen in 1 should be fixed to.

Branching rule
Any specific rule used in the branch-and-bound method to determine the new node to examine at the next level in the tree.

Many choices can be made. A **branching rule** is any specific rule that you (or the computer) can follow to determine a new node to examine at the next level in the tree. A branching rule is used to select a particular variable that does not satisfy the integer requirement and to fix it to a specific integer value. Because this step involves moving down a level in the tree and brings you closer to a solution, it is called a **forward step**. One commonly used branching rule that has proven to be computationally efficient in practice is the following.

Forward step
In the branch-and-bound method, moving down one level in the tree to the next node.

KEY FEATURES

Branching Rule for the Forward Step. Select a variable whose fractional value is farthest from an integer value and fix it to the first integer value larger than its fractional value.

In this example, $x_1 = 0.5$ and $x_3 = 2.5$ are equally distant from integer values, so x_1 is arbitrarily selected for branching. As seen in Figure 8.14(a), its value is fixed to 1, which is the first integer larger than 0.5.

ITERATION 1: EXAMINE NODE (1,–,–)

The linear program at this node is

$$
\begin{array}{lll}
\text{Maximize} & 2 + 3x_2 + x_3 & \\
\text{Subject to} & 1 + x_2 + x_3 \leq 5 & (1) \\
& -1 + 2x_2 - x_3 \leq 1 & (2) \\
& 1 + x_2 - x_3 \leq 0 & (3) \\
& x_2\,,\ x_3 \geq 0 &
\end{array}
$$

Using a computer to solve this problem results in the optimal solution of $x_1 = 1$, $x_2 = 1.5$, and $x_3 = 2.5$, with an objective function value of 9. Because x_2 and x_3 do not satisfy the integer requirements, the same branching rule is used again to move down the tree. Now x_2 is selected and fixed to value 2, as shown in Figure 8.14(b).

ITERATION 2: EXAMINE NODE (1,2,–)

The linear program at this node is

$$
\begin{array}{lll}
\text{Maximize} & 2 + 6 + x_3 & \\
\text{Subject to} & 1 + 2 + x_3 \leq 5 & (1) \\
& -1 + 4 - x_3 \leq 1 & (2) \\
& 1 + 2 - x_3 \leq 0 & (3) \\
& x_3 \geq 0 &
\end{array}
$$

This problem is infeasible. According to Facts 1 and 5, the following nodes are eliminated from further consideration:

1. All the nodes below node (1,2,–) because of Fact 1.
2. All nodes at level 2 to the right of node (1,2,–) below node (1,–,–) because of Fact 5.

You need not take another forward step because Fact 1 has eliminated all the nodes below the current node (1,2,–). The branch-and-bound method now directs you to examine all nodes at the *same* level as the current node (1,2,–)—that is, the other nodes that stem from node (1,–,–). To do so in a systematic way, take a **side step** to the nearest node to the right of the current node (1,2,–) that has not yet been examined. If there is none, take a side step to the nearest node to the left that has not yet been examined. This rule is summarized as follows.

Side step
In the branch-and-bound method, examining another node at the same level as the current node in the tree.

KEY FEATURES

Side Step. When no forward step is necessary, use a side step to examine sequentially each node to the right of the current one, the closest one first; then return to the current node and examine each node to the left, the closest one first.

In this case, by condition 2, all nodes to the right of the current one have already been eliminated. You should therefore take a side step to the nearest node on the left to examine node (1,1,–), as shown in Figure 8.14(c).

ITERATION 3: EXAMINE NODE (1,1,–)

The linear program at this node is

$$\text{Maximize} \quad 2 + 3 + x_3$$
$$\text{Subject to} \quad 1 + 1 + x_3 \leq 5 \tag{1}$$
$$-1 + 2 - x_3 \leq 1 \tag{2}$$
$$1 + 1 - x_3 \leq 0 \tag{3}$$
$$x_3 \geq 0$$

The optimal solution to this problem is $x_1 = 1$, $x_2 = 1$, and $x_3 = 3$, with an objective function value of 8. Because this solution satisfies all integer requirements, the following conditions hold:

1. This solution is feasible for the original integer program in Example 8.9. As a result, the optimal objective function value for the original integer problem must be at least that of this feasible solution, namely, 8. This value of 8 is now a lower bound for the original integer program.
2. By Fact 3, all nodes below the current one can be eliminated.
3. By Fact 4, the optimal objective function value of the linear program associated with all nodes to the left of the current one cannot exceed that of the current one, which is 8. Therefore, none of these nodes can produce an integer solution with a better objective function value than the lower bound of 8.

At this point, all nodes at level 2, below node (1,–,–), have been examined or eliminated, and the current lower bound is 8. There are no more nodes below node (1,–,–) to examine, so a **backward step** is used to select the next node. Move *back* to the previous level—that is, to node (1,–,–)—and apply a side step, first to the right, and then to the left of node (1,–,–).

Backward step
In the branch-and-bound method, moving up to a node in the previous level of the tree.

KEY FEATURES

Backward Step. When no side step can be taken at the current level, move back up to the node at the previous level and then perform side steps.

In this case, moving back to node $(1,-,-)$ and applying a side step to the right results in examining node $(2,-,-)$, as seen in Figure 8.14(d).

ITERATION 4: EXAMINE NODE $(2,-,-)$

The linear program at this node is

$$
\begin{aligned}
\text{Maximize} \quad & 4 + 3x_2 + x_3 \\
\text{Subject to} \quad & 2 + \;\; x_2 + x_3 \le 5 & (1) \\
& -2 + 2x_2 - x_3 \le 1 & (2) \\
& 2 + \;\; x_2 - x_3 \le 0 & (3) \\
& x_2 \;,\; x_3 \ge 0
\end{aligned}
$$

Using a computer to solve this problem results in an optimal solution of $x_1 = 2$, $x_2 = 0.5$, and $x_3 = 2.5$, with an objective function value of 8. According to Fact 2, no node below this one can provide a feasible integer solution with an objective function value better than the current lower bound of 8 [associated with the integer solution $x_1 = 1$, $x_2 = 1$, $x_3 = 3$ obtained at node $(1,1,-)$]. So all nodes below node $(2,-,-)$ are eliminated.

From Facts 4 and 5, you know that the linear program associated with all nodes to the right of the current node $(2,-,-)$ will either be infeasible or have an optimal objective function value of at most 8, the optimal value at node $(2,-,-)$. None of these nodes can produce a better feasible integer solution, and so you can eliminate them.

A forward step is not required, and so a side step is used. All nodes to the right of node $(2,-,-)$ have now been examined or eliminated. A side step to the left is used to examine node $(0,-,-)$, as seen in Figure 8.14(e).

ITERATION 5: EXAMINE NODE $(0,-,-)$

The linear program at this node is

$$
\begin{aligned}
\text{Maximize} \quad & 0 + 3x_2 + x_3 \\
\text{Subject to} \quad & 0 + \;\; x_2 + x_3 \le 5 & (1) \\
& -0 + 2x_2 - x_3 \le 1 & (2) \\
& 0 + \;\; x_2 - x_3 \le 0 & (3) \\
& x_2 \;,\; x_3 \ge 0
\end{aligned}
$$

Using a computer to solve this problem results in the optimal solution of $x_1 = 0$, $x_2 = 2$, and $x_3 = 3$, with an associated objective function value of 9. As seen in Figure 8.14(f), because this solution satisfies all the integer requirements:

1. This is another feasible solution to the original integer problem. Moreover, its objective function value is better than the previous lower bound of 8. This latest solution provides a new lower bound of 9.

2. By Fact 2, all nodes below the current node $(0,-,-)$ can be eliminated.

All nodes at level 1, below node $(-,-,-)$, have been examined or eliminated. A backward step is used next to move to node 0. But node 0 has already been examined, and so *all* nodes in the tree have now been examined or eliminated. This in turn means that the solution to the original integer programming problem has been attained—namely, the feasible integer solution associated with the current lower bound. In this case, that solution is $x_1 = 0$, $x_2 = 2$, and $x_3 = 3$, with an objective function value of 9.

Observe that even though the entire tree in this example has 216 terminal nodes, the branch-and-bound algorithm enabled you to find the optimal solution by examining only six nodes. The savings in time and effort are even more significant for larger problems. In particular, observe how the lower bound is used to eliminate many nodes. The larger the lower bound, the more likely it is that nodes can be eliminated. It is therefore important to obtain quickly as large a lower bound as possible.

For example, if you know a feasible integer solution to the original problem, or if one can be obtained by rounding down the solution to the associated linear program, you should use that integer solution as a lower bound immediately. This same idea can be applied at any node. For example, at iteration 0, corresponding to node 0, rounding down the solution to the associated linear program does *not* result in a feasible integer solution. However, rounding down the solution at iteration 1, corresponding to node $(1,-,-)$, *does* result in a feasible solution of $x_1 = 1$, $x_2 = 1$, and $x_3 = 2$, with an objective function value—and hence a lower bound—of 7.

KEY FEATURES

Summary of the Branch-and-Bound Algorithm

For a given integer programming problem, an optimal solution can be found with the branch-and-bound method by applying the following steps:

Step 0. *Initialization*: Solve the linear program associated with node 0.
a. If this problem is infeasible, stop. The integer problem is also infeasible.
b. If this problem has an optimal solution that satisfies all the integer requirements, stop. This solution is also optimal for the integer problem.
c. If this problem has an optimal solution that does not satisfy all the integer requirements, see if rounding down this solution provides a feasible integer solution and hence a lower bound. In any case, call node 0 the *current node* and go to Step 1.

Step 1. *Take a Forward Step*: Move down a level in the tree by (1) selecting a variable whose current fractional value is farthest from an integer and (2) fixing it to the smallest integer value higher than its fractional value. Call this the current node and go to Step 2 to examine it.

Step 2. *Examine a Node*: Solve the linear program associated with the current node.
a. If this linear program is infeasible, eliminate this and all nodes below and to the same side as this one, and go to Step 3.
b. If this linear program has an optimal solution that satisfies all the integer requirements, then determine whether this feasible integer solution provides a larger lower bound than the current lower bound. In any case, eliminate all nodes below and to the same side as this one, and go to Step 3.
c. If this linear program has an optimal solution that does not satisfy all the integer requirements, then determine whether the objective function value is less than the current lower bound. If so, eliminate all nodes below and to the same side as this one, and go to Step 3. Otherwise, see if rounding down the current solution results in a feasible integer solution with a better lower bound than the current one. In either case, call this node the current one and go to Step 1 to take another forward step.

Step 3. *Take a Side Step*: Move to the closest unexamined node at the same level and to the right of the current one and go to Step 2. If no such node exists, move to the closest unexamined node to the left and go to Step 2. If no such node exists, go to Step 4.

Step 4. *Take a Backward Step*: Move back a level from the current node to the new current node. If the new current node is node 0, stop. The integer solution associated with the best lower bound is the optimal solution to the original integer problem. If no feasible integer solution has been found, the original integer problem is infeasible. If the new current node is *not* node 0, go to Step 3.

■ 8.5 SOLVING MIXED LINEAR INTEGER PROGRAMMING PROBLEMS

In all the examples presented in Section 8.1, *all* variables are required to be integers. In some problems, however, only *some* variables need to have integer values whereas others may be continuous. Such problems are called **mixed integer programming problems**. These problems, once formulated, are solved in precisely the same way as those in which all variables are restricted to be integers.

Mixed integer programming problem A problem in which some variables are restricted to have integer values but other variables can be continuous.

Recall the problem of Case Chemicals in Section 4.1, Chapter 4. Two solvents, CS-01 and CS-02, are produced at the Cleveland plant. The Blending Department of the plant currently has five full-time employees each working 40 hours per week and two part-time employees each working 15 hours per week. These employees handle machines that blend certain chemicals to produce each solvent. The products, once blended, are refined in the Purification Department, which currently employs six full-time workers at 40 hours per week each and one part-time worker who puts in 10 hours per week. The hours required in the Blending and Purification Departments needed to produce each of the products are provided in Table 8.10.

TABLE 8.10 *Blending and Purification Requirements (hr/1000 gal)*		
	CS-01	CS-02
Blending	2	1
Purification	1	2

Case Chemicals has an almost unlimited supply of raw materials needed to produce the two solvents and can sell any amount of CS-01. The demand for the more specialized product, CS-02, is limited to at most 120 thousand gallons per week. The Accounting Department of the company estimates a net profit of $0.30 per gallon for CS-01 and $0.50 per gallon for CS-02.

The following formulation, presented in Section 4.1, Chapter 4, helps you determine x_1 and x_2, the number of thousands of gallons of CS-01 and CS-02 to produce so as to maximize weekly profits (in hundreds of dollars):

$$
\begin{array}{lll}
\text{Maximize} & 3x_1 + 5x_2 & \\
\text{Subject to} & 2x_1 + x_2 \leq 230 & \text{(blending)} \quad (1) \\
& x_1 + 2x_2 \leq 250 & \text{(purification)} \quad (2) \\
& x_2 \leq 120 & (3) \\
& x_1 \geq 0 & (4) \\
& x_2 \geq 0 & (5)
\end{array}
$$

The optimal production plan, as determined graphically in Section 4.2, is $x_1 = 70$ and $x_2 = 90$, with a weekly profit of \$66,000.

To increase profits, the President is considering an expansion, as described in Example 8.10.

EXAMPLE 8.10 THE EXPANSION PROBLEM OF CASE CHEMICALS With the current facilities, up to three more full-time workers can be hired in *each* of the Blending and Purification Departments at a weekly cost of \$800 per employee. Management can also consider expanding productions facilities at an estimated cost of \$20,000 per week. This expansion would allow the company to hire up to eight additional workers in each department, which is five more than what could be hired in each department without the expansion. As Manager of the Production Department, you have been asked to make appropriate hiring and expansion recommendations. ∎

8.5.1 Formulating the Expansion Problem of Case Chemicals

You are free to determine the number of additional employees to hire in each department. Two new decision variables (in addition to the production variables x_1 and x_2) arise:

$$NB = \text{the number of new employees to hire in the Blending Department}$$

$$NP = \text{the number of new employees to hire in the Purification Department}$$

Another decision you need to make is whether or not the expansion should be undertaken. To model this "no/yes" decision, define the following 0–1 variable:

$$
EXP = \begin{cases} 1 & \text{if expansion is undertaken} \\ 0 & \text{otherwise} \end{cases}
$$

Turning to the objective function, the new hiring and expansion decisions reduce the overall weekly profits. The weekly cost of the employees is $800(NB + NP) = 8(NB + NP)$ hundreds of dollars and that of the expansion is $20000EXP = 200EXP$ hundreds of dollars. So the new objective function, expressed in hundreds of dollars, is to maximize

$$
\begin{aligned}
\text{Net weekly profit} &= (\text{profit from production}) - \\
&\quad (\text{cost of new hires}) - \\
&\quad (\text{cost of expansion}) \\
&= (3x_1 + 5x_2) - 8(NB + NP) - 200EXP \\
&= 3x_1 + 5x_2 - 8NB - 8NP - 200EXP
\end{aligned}
$$

The new hires increase the number of hours of labor available in both departments. Recall that without new hires 230 hours are available in the Blending Department. Each new hire in this department results in an additional 40 hours. Because NB such people are hired, the new constraint for the Blending Department is

$$2x_1 + x_2 \leq 230 + 40NB$$

or

$$2x_1 + x_2 - 40NB \leq 230 \qquad \text{(blending)}$$

Similarly, for the Purification Department, the new constraint is

$$x_1 + 2x_2 \leq 250 + 40NP$$

or

$$x_1 + 2x_2 - 40NP \leq 250 \qquad \text{(purification)}$$

A new group of constraints, however, is the limit on the number of new hires. That limit depends on whether expansion is undertaken. For example, for the Blending Department:

$$NB \leq \begin{cases} 3 & \text{if no expansion is undertaken (that is, } EXP = 0) \\ 8 & \text{if expansion is undertaken (that is, } EXP = 1) \end{cases}$$

Because the expansion allows an additional five workers to be hired, the two foregoing conditions can be written in terms of the variable EXP as the following *single* constraint:

$$NB \leq 3 + 5EXP$$

or

$$NB - 5EXP \leq 3 \qquad \text{(new hires in Blending)}$$

Similarly, for new hires in the Purification Department:

$$NP \leq 3 + 5EXP$$

or

$$NP - 5EXP \leq 3 \qquad \text{(new hires in Purification)}$$

Finally, add the constraint that no more than 120 thousand gallons of CS-02 can be produced and the logical constraints that NB and NP are nonnegative integers, that EXP is a 0–1 variable, and that x_1 and x_2 are nonnegative variables. The complete mixed integer programming formulation for the expansion problem of Case Chemicals follows:

THE MIXED INTEGER FORMULATION
FOR THE EXPANSION PROBLEM OF CASE CHEMICALS

Integer Program
EX8_10.DAT

$$
\begin{array}{llr}
\text{Maximize} & 3x_1 + 5x_2 - 8NB - 8NP - 200EXP & \\
\text{Subject to} & 2x_1 + x_2 - 40NB \leq 230 & (1) \\
& x_1 + 2x_2 - 40NP \leq 250 & (2) \\
& x_2 \leq 120 & (3) \\
& NB - 5EXP \leq 3 & (4) \\
& NP - 5EXP \leq 3 & (5) \\
& EXP \leq 1 & (6) \\
& x_1 , \; x_2 \geq 0 & \\
& NB , \quad NP , \quad EXP \geq 0 \quad \text{and integer} &
\end{array}
$$

Recall from Section 8.1 that constraint (6) together with the requirement that EXP be a nonnegative integer ensure that the value of EXP is either 0 or 1.

8.5.2 Solution to the Mixed Integer Problem of Case Chemicals

ITERATION 0

Following the branch-and-bound procedure, first solve the linear program associated with the original problem, in which all integer requirements are dropped. The following optimal solution and objective function value result:

OPTIMAL SOLUTION TO THE LINEAR PROGRAM AT NODE 0

$x_1 = 215$; $x_2 = 120$; $NB = 8$; $NP = 5.125$; $EXP = 1$ objective value $= 940$

This solution corresponds to node 0 in the tree of Figure 8.15(a). Subsequent nodes are numbered in the order in which they are examined.

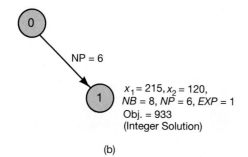

$x_1 = 215$, $x_2 = 120$, $NB = 8$, $NP = 5.125$,
$EXP = 1$; Obj. $= 940$

(a)

$NP = 6$

$x_1 = 215$, $x_2 = 120$,
$NB = 8$, $NP = 6$, $EXP = 1$
Obj. $= 933$
(Integer Solution)

(b)

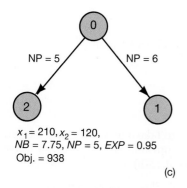

$NP = 5$ $NP = 6$

$x_1 = 210$, $x_2 = 120$,
$NB = 7.75$, $NP = 5$, $EXP = 0.95$
Obj. $= 938$

(c)

FIGURE 8.15 Using the Branch-and-Bound Approach to Solve the Mixed Integer Problem of Case Chemicals.

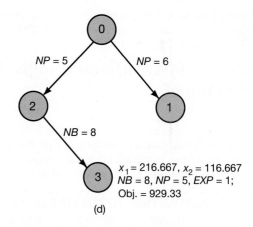

$x_1 = 216.667$, $x_2 = 116.667$
$NB = 8$, $NP = 5$, $EXP = 1$;
Obj. $= 929.33$

(d)

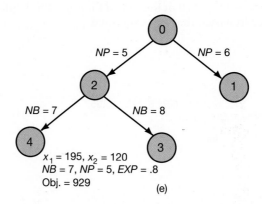

$x_1 = 195$, $x_2 = 120$
$NB = 7$, $NP = 5$, $EXP = .8$
Obj. $= 929$

(e)

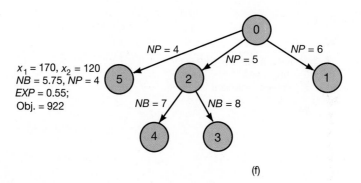

$x_1 = 170$, $x_2 = 120$
$NB = 5.75$, $NP = 4$
$EXP = 0.55$;
Obj. $= 922$

(f)

FIGURE 8.15 (*cont.*)   Using the Branch-and-Bound Approach to Solve the Mixed
Integer Problem of Case Chemicals.

ITERATION 1

Because *NP* is fractional at value 5.125, it is necessary to take a forward step by fixing
NP to 6, the first integer value larger than 5.125. The optimal solution to the linear
program associated with this node, labeled 1 in Figure 8.15(b), is

OPTIMAL SOLUTION TO THE LINEAR PROGRAM AT NODE 1

$x_1 = 215$; $x_2 = 120$; $NB = 8$; $NP = 6$; $EXP = 1$ objective value $= 933$

Because this solution satisfies *all* integer requirements, the following hold:

1. A lower bound of 933 is now available.
2. All nodes below node 1 can be dropped, as stated by Fact 3 in Section 8.4.
3. All nodes to the right of node 1 (corresponding to larger values of NP) can be dropped, as stated by Facts 4 and 5 in Section 8.4.

ITERATION 2

Proceeding with a side step to the left of node 1 in Figure 8.15(b) results in fixing NP to 5 at node 2 in Figure 8.15(c). Solving the associated linear program results in

OPTIMAL SOLUTION TO THE LINEAR PROGRAM AT NODE 2

$x_1 = 210$; $x_2 = 120$; $NB = 7.75$; $NP = 5$; $EXP = 0.95$; objective value = 938

Because the optimal objective function value of 938 is larger than the current lower bound of 933, Fact 2 in Section 8.4 *cannot* be used to drop any nodes. Furthermore, the current solution does not satisfy all the integer requirements. Thus, a forward step is necessary.

ITERATION 3

By using the branching rule in a forward step, NB is selected and fixed to value 8 at node 3 in Figure 8.15(d). Solving the associated linear program in which $NP = 5$ and $NB = 8$ results in the following optimal solution:

OPTIMAL SOLUTION TO THE LINEAR PROGRAM AT NODE 3

$x_1 = 216.667$; $x_2 = 116.667$; $NB = 8$; $NP = 5$; $EXP = 1$; objective value = 929.33

Observe that x_1 and x_2 have fractional values. However, these variables are not restricted to have integer values in the original mixed integer programming formulation, so no forward step is taken to fix these variables to integer values. Moreover, because the optimal objective function value of 929.33 is less than the current lower bound of 933 the following holds:

1. All nodes below node 3 can be dropped, as stated by Fact 2 in section 8.4.
2. All nodes to the right of node 3 (corresponding to larger values of NB) can be dropped, as stated by Fact 4 and 5 in section 8.4.

ITERATION 4

A side step is now taken from node 3 by fixing NB to 7 at node 4 in Figure 8.15(e). The optimal solution to the associated linear program in which $NP = 5$ and $NB = 7$ is

OPTIMAL SOLUTION TO THE LINEAR PROGRAM AT NODE 4

$x_1 = 195$; $x_2 = 120$; $NB = 7$; $NP = 5$; $EXP = 0.8$; objective value = 929

Because this optimal objective function value of 929 is less than the current lower bound of 933 the following hold:

1. All nodes below node 4 can be dropped, as stated by Fact 2 in Section 8.4.
2. All nodes to the left of node 4 (corresponding to smaller values of NB) can be dropped, as stated by Facts 4 and 5 in Section 8.4.

ITERATION 5

All integer values of *NB* associated with nodes below node 2 have been examined or discarded. A backward step fixes *NP* to 4 at node 5 in Figure 8.15(f). The optimal solution to the associated linear program in which $NP = 4$ is

OPTIMAL SOLUTION TO THE LINEAR PROGRAM AT NODE 5

$x_1 = 170$; $x_2 = 120$; $NB = 5.75$; $NP = 4$; $EXP = 0.55$;   objective value $= 922$

This optimal objective function value of 922 is less than the current lower bound of 933, so:

1. All nodes below node 5 can be dropped by Fact 2 in Section 8.4.
2. All nodes to the left of node 5 (corresponding to smaller values of *NP*) can be dropped by Facts 4 and 5 in Section 8.4.

All nodes have now been examined or discarded. The optimal solution to the problem of Case Chemicals is the solution associated with the current lower bound of 933:

$$x_1 = 215$$
$$x_2 = 120$$
$$NB = 8$$
$$NP = 6$$
$$EXP = 1$$

Objective function value $= 933$

This means that you should make the following recommendations to the President of Case Chemicals:

1. Expand the production facilities (because $EXP = 1$).
2. Hire eight additional employees in the Blending Department (because $NB = 8$).
3. Hire six additional employees in the Purification Department (because $NP = 6$).
4. Produce 215,000 gallons of CS-01 and 120,000 gallons of CS-02 (because $x_1 = 215$ and $x_2 = 120$).

These decisions result in a net weekly profit of $93,300, which is larger than the $66,000 earned before the expansion and new hiring.

■ 8.6 LINEAR INTEGER PROGRAMMING: USING THE COMPUTER

In Sections 8.3 and 8.4, you learned how to use the branch-and-bound method to solve integer programming problems. For any but the smallest such problems, it is necessary to use a computer to obtain the solution. In this section, you will learn to handle integer programming problems with the computer.

8.6.1 Computer Analysis of the Personnel-Planning Model for Burlington Bank

Recall the personnel-planning problem in which the management of Burlington Bank needs to determine F (the number of full-time tellers) and P_8, P_{10}, and P_{12} (the number of part-time tellers to hire starting at 8 A.M., 10 A.M., and 12 noon, respectively) to meet staffing requirements and satisfy union regulations at the least total cost. In Section 8.1.1, the following integer programming model was developed:

Minimize $120F + 32P_8 + 32P_{10} + 32P_{12}$
Subject to

REQUIREMENT CONSTRAINTS

$$
\begin{array}{llll}
F + P_8 & & \geq 8 & \text{(TIME 8-10)} \\
F + P_8 + P_{10} & & \geq 10 & \text{(TIME 10-12)} \\
F + P_{10} + P_{12} & \geq 15 & \text{(TIME 12-2)} \\
F + P_{12} & \geq 12 & \text{(TIME 2-4)}
\end{array}
$$

PROPORTION CONSTRAINTS

$$
\begin{array}{lll}
0.4F - 0.6P_8 & \geq 0 & \text{(RATIO 8-10)} \\
0.4F - 0.6P_8 - 0.6P_{10} & \geq 0 & \text{(RATIO 10-12)} \\
0.4F - 0.6P_{10} - 0.6P_{12} \geq 0 & \text{(RATIO 12-2)} \\
0.4F - 0.6P_{12} \geq 0 & \text{(RATIO 2-4)}
\end{array}
$$

LOGICAL CONSTRAINTS

$$F, \quad P_8, \quad P_{10}, \quad P_{12} \geq 0 \quad \text{and integer}$$

Integer Program
EX8_1.DAT

The solution to this problem can now be obtained by entering the data for this problem to any integer programming package. The results of using STORM are given in Figure 8.16. From the first part of this report, you can see that the management of Burlington Bank should hire nine full-time tellers, no part-time tellers starting at 8 A.M., one part-time teller to work from 10 A.M. until 2 P.M., and five from 12 noon until 4 P.M., at a total daily cost of $1272.

The second part of the report in Figure 8.16 addresses the constraints. As in linear programming, the values of the slack variables in integer programming indicate how binding are the associated constraints. For example, the value of 1 for the slack variable associated with the constraint labeled TIME 8-10 indicates that the optimal staffing results in having one additional teller above the minimum requirement of eight between the hours of 8 and 10 A.M. The value of 0 for the slack variable associated with the constraint labeled TIME 10-12 means that no extra tellers—beyond the 10 required between 10 A.M. and 12 noon—are staffed. Observe that any increase in the number of tellers needed during any time interval above the value of the associated slack variable requires a change in the optimal staffing policy and the related costs.

Recall that union regulations require that, at all times, at least 60% of the work force be full-time workers. The value of 0 for the slack variable associated with the constraint labeled RATIO 12-2 indicates that *precisely* 60% of the work force consists of full-time tellers, as required. The nonzero values of the slack variables associated with the remaining three RATIO constraints indicate that during the associated time intervals *more than* 60% of the work force consists of full-time tellers.

```
          The Personnel-Planning Problem of the Burlington Bank
                OPTIMAL SOLUTION - SUMMARY REPORT
        Variable          Value         Cost  Lower bound  Upper bound

        F                     9      120.0000            0     Infinity
        P8                    0       32.0000            0     Infinity
        P10                   1       32.0000            0     Infinity
        P12                   5       32.0000            0     Infinity

    Objective Function Value = 1272


          The Personnel-Planning Problem of the Burlington Bank
                OPTIMAL SOLUTION - SUMMARY REPORT
            Constraint  Type       RHS          Slack

            TIME 8-10    >=      8.0000        1.0000
            TIME 10-12   >=     10.0000        0.0000
            TIME 12-2    >=     15.0000        0.0000
            TIME 2-4     >=     12.0000        2.0000
            RATIO 8-10   >=      0.0000        3.6000
            RATIO10-12   >=      0.0000        3.0000
            RATIO 12-2   >=      0.0000        0.0000
            RATIO 2-4    >=      0.0000        0.6000

          Objective Function Value = 1272
```

FIGURE 8.16 STORM Output Report to the Personnel-Planning Problem of Burlington Bank.

8.6.2 *Computer Solution to the Capital-Budgeting Problem of High-Tech*

Recall Example 8.2. The management of High-Tech needs to determine in which of six alternative projects to invest. That problem is modeled in Section 8.1 by the following integer programming problem in which B, T, L, C, M, and S are 0–1 variables whose values indicate whether to invest in the associated venture:

Integer Program
EX8_2.DAT

Maximize
$$30000B + 57750T + 19500L + 15625C + 52500M + 6300S$$
Subject to
$$200000B + 350000T + 150000L + 125000C + 375000M + 70000S \leq 1000000 \quad \text{(budget)}$$
$$B \leq 1$$
$$T \leq 1$$
$$L \leq 1$$
$$C \leq 1$$
$$M \leq 1$$
$$S \leq 1$$
$$B, \quad T, \quad L, \quad C, \quad M, \quad S \geq 0 \quad \text{and integer}$$

The solution to this problem obtained from the LINDO software package, illustrated in Figure 8.17, indicates that High-Tech should invest in four of the six ventures:

Bio-Tech, Tele-Com, Medi-Opt, and Sound-News. This is because the values of these associated decision variables in the optimal solution are 1. The value of 0 for the remaining two variables indicates that High-Tech should *not* invest in Laser-Optics and Compu-Ware. The total expected yearly return for these investments is $146,550.

The value of 5000 for the slack variable associated with the budget constraint, labeled ROW 2), indicates that all but $5000 of the $1 million budget needs to be invested.

```
        OBJECTIVE FUNCTION VALUE

   1)        146550.00

 VARIABLE        VALUE          REDUCED COST
      B         1.000000        -30000.000000
      T         1.000000        -57750.000000
      L          .000000        -19500.000000
      C          .000000        -15625.000000
      M         1.000000        -52500.000000
      S         1.000000         -6300.000000


   ROW    SLACK OR SURPLUS      DUAL PRICES
    2)       5000.000000            .000000

 NO. ITERATIONS=       25
 BRANCHES=      6 DETERM.=   1.000E   0
```

FIGURE 8.17 The LINDO Output Report to the Capital-Budgeting Problem of High-Tech.

8.6.3 Computer Solution to the Cutting-Stock Problem of Spiral Paper, Inc.

In Example 8.3, the management of Spiral Paper, Inc., must determine how to cut 20-inch rolls of paper into smaller rolls of 3, 5, and 8 inches to minimize the cost of waste and overproduction. The following integer programming model is developed in Section 8.1, in which $x_1, x_2, \ldots, x_8$ are the number of 20-inch rolls to cut according to each of the eight settings of the cutting machine:

Minimize $\quad 7x_1 + 6x_2 + 5.5x_3 + 6x_4 + 6x_5 + 6x_6 + 6.5x_7 + 6.5x_8 - 12225$

Subject to

Integer Program
EX8_3.DAT

DEMAND CONSTRAINTS

$$6x_1 + 0x_2 + 1x_3 + 0x_4 + 4x_5 + 2x_6 + 5x_7 + 1x_8 \geq 1050 \quad \text{(demand 3 in.)}$$
$$0x_1 + 4x_2 + 0x_3 + 2x_4 + 0x_5 + 1x_6 + 1x_7 + 3x_8 \geq 2050 \quad \text{(demand 5 in.)}$$
$$0x_1 + 0x_2 + 2x_3 + 1x_4 + 1x_5 + 1x_6 + 0x_7 + 0x_8 \geq 4050 \quad \text{(demand 8 in.)}$$

LOGICAL CONSTRAINTS

$$x_1, \quad x_2, \quad x_3, \quad x_4, \quad x_5, \quad x_6, \quad x_7, \quad x_8 \geq 0 \quad \text{and integer}$$

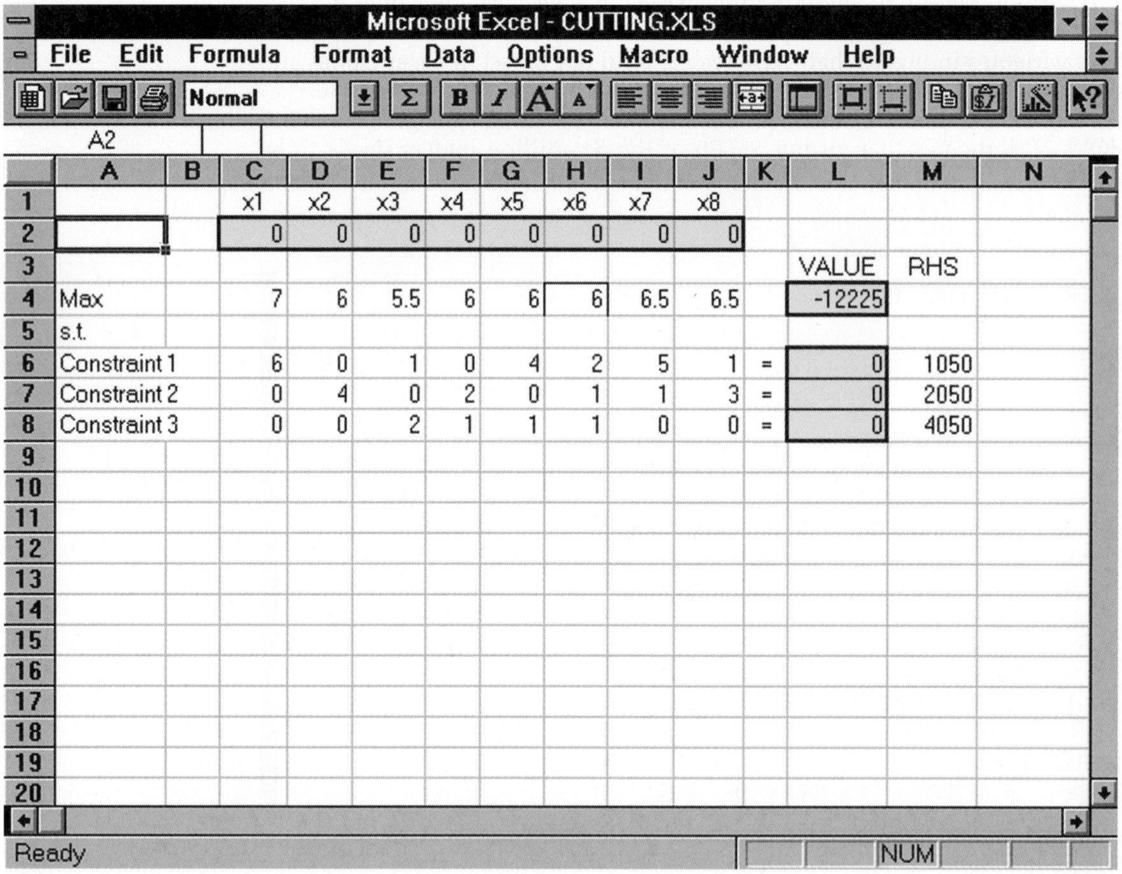

FIGURE 8.18 EXCEL Input Screen for the Cutting-Stock Problem of Spiral Paper, Inc.

Observe that one of the terms in the objective function of this problem is the constant −12225. Because fixed numbers in the objective function are not affected by the values of the variables, fixed numbers are generally not entered into computer packages. Rather, they are left off, and when the optimal objective function value is obtained from the computer, the constant value is added on. However, with a spreadsheet-based linear programming package such as EXCEL, this constant is easily included in the cell that evaluates the objective function.

The spreadsheet containing the data for this problem in a format EXCEL can solve is shown in Figure 8.18. The layout and format of this spreadsheet are the same as those used in Section 6.6 for solving a linear programming problem. Observe again that the nonnegativity and integer constraints on the variables and the types of the constraints ($\leq, \geq, =$) are not part of the spreadsheet. This information is provided when you use the SOLVER command to solve the problem.

The optimal solution obtained from the EXCEL software package is given in Figure 8.19. The values of 513 for x_2 and 2025 for x_3 indicate that these numbers of 20-inch rolls are to be cut using the second and third settings, respectively. Recall the settings of the cutting machine listed in Table 8.3 in Section 8.1.3. The second setting cuts each of the 513 20-inch rolls into four 5-inch rolls (with no waste). The third setting cuts each of the 2025 20-inch rolls into one 3-inch and two 8-inch rolls (with a waste of 1 inch

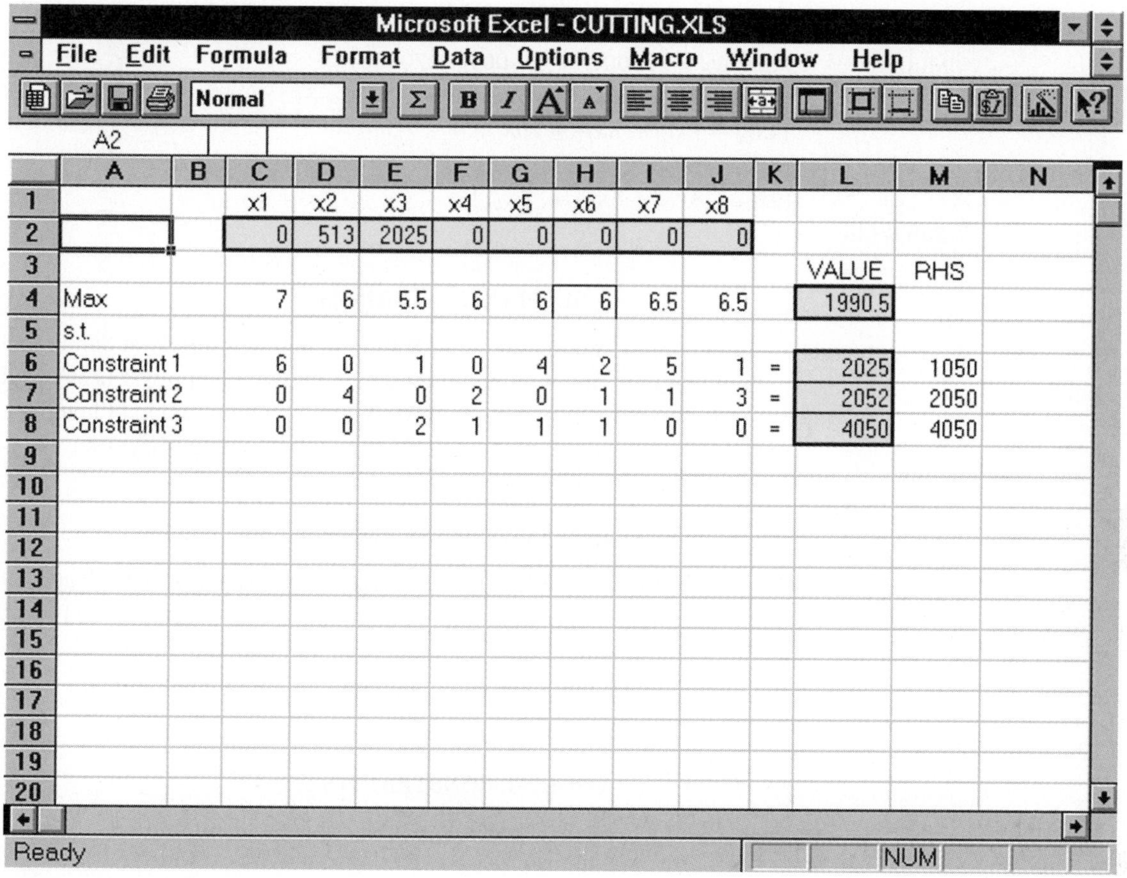

	A	B	C	D	E	F	G	H	I	J	K	L	M	N
1			x1	x2	x3	x4	x5	x6	x7	x8				
2			0	513	2025	0	0	0	0	0				
3												VALUE	RHS	
4	Max		7	6	5.5	6	6	6	6.5	6.5		1990.5		
5	s.t.													
6	Constraint 1		6	0	1	0	4	2	5	1	=	2025	1050	
7	Constraint 2		0	4	0	2	0	1	1	3	=	2052	2050	
8	Constraint 3		0	0	2	1	1	1	0	0	=	4050	4050	

FIGURE 8.19 EXCEL Output Report for the Cutting-Stock Problem of Spiral Paper, Inc.

per roll). The total cost of the waste and overproduction from the optimal objective function value given in the cell in row 4 and column L in Figure 8.19 is \$1990.50.

The left-hand-side values for the three constraints in column L of Figure 8.19 indicate that the optimal cutting plan produces 2025 3-inch rolls, which is 975 rolls *more* than the 1050 rolls required. In contrast, the value in row 8 indicates that the optimal plan produces exactly 4050 8-inch rolls, as required.

8.6.4 Computer Solution to the Location Problem of Cosmic Computer Company

Recall the problem in Example 8.4. The management of CCC needs to determine where to locate computer assembly plants with known production capacities so as to satisfy demands at retail stores while minimizing total transportation and operating costs. That problem is formulated in Section 8.1, with the following integer programming model in which the 0–1 variables y_S, y_L, y_P, and y_D are used to indicate whether or not a plant should be opened in the associated location. The remaining x variables indicate the number of computers to ship from each plant to each retail store:

**Integer Program
EX8_4.DAT**

Minimize
$$70000y_S + 70000y_L + 65000y_P + 70000y_D +$$
$$(5x_{SS} + 3x_{SB} + 2x_{ST} + 6x_{SD}) +$$
$$(4x_{LS} + 7x_{LB} + 8x_{LT} + 10x_{LD}) +$$
$$(6x_{PS} + 5x_{PB} + 3x_{PT} + 8x_{PD}) +$$
$$(9x_{DS} + 8x_{DB} + 6x_{DT} + 5x_{DD})$$

Subject to

SUPPLY CONSTRAINTS

$$x_{SS} + x_{SB} + x_{ST} + x_{SD} - 1700y_S \leq 0 \quad \text{(supply at San Francisco)}$$
$$x_{LS} + x_{LB} + x_{LT} + x_{LD} - 2000y_L \leq 0 \quad \text{(supply at Los Angeles)}$$
$$x_{PS} + x_{PB} + x_{PT} + x_{PD} - 1700y_P \leq 0 \quad \text{(supply at Phoenix)}$$
$$x_{DS} + x_{DB} + x_{DT} + x_{DD} - 2000y_D \leq 0 \quad \text{(supply at Denver)}$$

DEMAND CONSTRAINTS

$$x_{SS} + x_{LS} + x_{PS} + x_{DS} = 1700 \quad \text{(demand at San Diego)}$$
$$x_{SB} + x_{LB} + x_{PB} + x_{DB} = 1000 \quad \text{(demand at Barstow)}$$
$$x_{ST} + x_{LT} + x_{PT} + x_{DT} = 1500 \quad \text{(demand at Tucson)}$$
$$x_{SD} + x_{LD} + x_{PD} + x_{DD} = 1200 \quad \text{(demand at Dallas)}$$

LOGICAL CONSTRAINTS

$y_S, y_L, y_P,$ and $y_D = 0$ or 1, and all other variables ≥ 0 and integer

The optimal solution obtained from the STORM software package is given in Figure 8.20. The value of 1 for the three variables y_S, y_L, and y_P and the value of 0 for y_D indicate that plants should be built in San Francisco, Los Angeles, and Phoenix, but not in Denver. The values of the remaining x-variables indicate the number of computers to ship from these three plants to each of the four retail stores, as summarized in Table 8.11. The associated total monthly cost for this plan is \$228,100, which includes \$205,000 in operating expenses for the three plants and \$23,100 in total transportation costs.

In the second part of the report in Figure 8.20, all slack variables are 0. This indicates that each plant produces *precisely* its capacity and that each retail store receives *precisely* its demand.

In this section, you have learned how to interpret the results obtained by solving integer programming problems using a computer package. A case study on this topic is presented next.

TABLE 8.11 *Optimal Shipping Plan for the Location Problem of CCC*

PLANTS	STORES			
	SAN DIEGO	BARSTOW	TUCSON	DALLAS
San Francisco	0	500	0	1200
Los Angeles	1700	300	0	0
Phoenix	0	200	1500	0

```
                    The Location Problem of CCC
                OPTIMAL SOLUTION - SUMMARY REPORT
      Variable        Value         Cost  Lower bound  Upper bound
      YS                  1    70000.0000           0            1
      YL                  1    70000.0000           0            1
      YP                  1    65000.0000           0            1
      YD                  0    70000.0000           0            1
      XSS                 0        5.0000           0     Infinity
      XSB               500        3.0000           0     Infinity
      XST                 0        2.0000           0     Infinity
      XSD              1200        6.0000           0     Infinity
      XLS              1700        4.0000           0     Infinity
      XLB               300        7.0000           0     Infinity
      XLT                 0        8.0000           0     Infinity
      XLD                 0       10.0000           0     Infinity
      XPS                 0        6.0000           0     Infinity
      XPB               200        5.0000           0     Infinity
      XPT              1500        3.0000           0     Infinity
      XPD                 0        8.0000           0     Infinity
      XDS                 0        9.0000           0     Infinity
      XDB                 0        8.0000           0     Infinity
      XDT                 0        6.0000           0     Infinity
      XDD                 0        5.0000           0     Infinity


   Objective Function Value = 228100

                  The Location Problem of CCC
              OPTIMAL SOLUTION - SUMMARY REPORT
      Constraint  Type        RHS          Slack
      SUPPLY SF    <=       0.0000        0.0000
      SUPPLY LA    <=       0.0000        0.0000
      SUPPLY P     <=       0.0000        0.0000
      SUPPLY D     <=       0.0000        0.0000
      DEMAND SD     =    1700.0000        0.0000
      DEMAND B      =    1000.0000        0.0000
      DEMAND T      =    1500.0000        0.0000
      DEMAND D      =    1200.0000        0.0000


   Objective Function Value = 228100
```

FIGURE 8.20 STORM Output Report to the Location Problem of Cosmic Computer Company.

CASE STUDY

In this section, your knowledge of integer programming is brought together through a case study involving problem formulation, solution by computer, and interpretation of the results. Consider the crew-scheduling problem faced by the management of Commuter Airways.

The Problem of Scheduling Crews for Commuter Airways

Commuter Airways is a regional airline with a hub in Cleveland and regular commuter flights to Boston and New York, as shown in Figure 8.21. Each node in the figure represents a city. Each arc, or arrow, represents a flight between the connected cities (the flight number is shown next to that arc). Management requires that each of the six flights has at least one supervisor and the minimum number of cabin attendants indicated in Table 8.12. The airline has only eight cabin attendants and four supervisors currently working for them. In addition, FAA regulations require that there be at least one supervisor for every two cabin attendants on each flight. Based on the estimated arrival and departure times, crew members can be assigned to more than one flight. However, management wants to ensure that all crew members start and return to Cleveland. This avoids overnight stays because all personnel live in the hub city of Cleveland. Five flight plans meeting these and other requirements (such as total flight time per day) have been identified in Table 8.13. For example, Plan D consists of Flights 2, 4, and 6, which is a trip from Cleveland to Boston to New York and back to Cleveland, as seen in Figure 8.21. Table 8.13 also provides the cost of assigning each type of crew member to the corresponding flight plan. As Manager of the Personnel Department, you have been asked to determine the number of each type of crew member to assign to each flight plan to satisfy the given staffing and FAA requirements with least total cost.

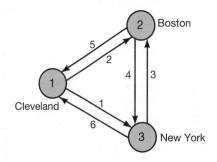

FIGURE 8.21 The Flight Network of Commuter Airways.

TABLE 8.12	*Management Requirements for Crew Members Needed on Each Flight*			
			MINIMUM NUMBER OF	
FLIGHT	FROM	TO	SUPERVISORS	CABIN ATTENDANTS
1	Cleveland	New York	1	3
2	Cleveland	Boston	1	4
3	New York	Boston	1	3
4	Boston	New York	1	2
5	Boston	Cleveland	1	5
6	New York	Cleveland	1	2

TABLE 8.13 *Cost of Each Crew Member on Each Flight Plan*

		COST PER	
FLIGHT PLAN	FLIGHT SEQUENCE	SUPERVISOR	CABIN ATTENDANT
A	1–6	300	200
B	2–5	300	200
C	1–3–5	500	400
D	2–4–6	500	400
E	1–3–4–6	800	640

Problem Formulation

At first glance you might consider as the variables the number of supervisors and cabin attendants to assign to each *flight*. However, with these variables, you will find that it is difficult to ensure that all crew members start and return to Cleveland. Because the five plans in Table 8.13 are designed to accomplish this goal, a better approach is to determine the number of supervisors and cabin attendants to assign to each *plan*. This gives rise to the following 10 variables:

$$SA = \text{the number of supervisors assigned to Plan A}$$
$$SB = \text{the number of supervisors assigned to Plan B}$$
$$SC = \text{the number of supervisors assigned to Plan C}$$
$$SD = \text{the number of supervisors assigned to Plan D}$$
$$SE = \text{the number of supervisors assigned to Plan E}$$

$$CA = \text{the number of cabin attendants assigned to Plan A}$$
$$CB = \text{the number of cabin attendants assigned to Plan B}$$
$$CC = \text{the number of cabin attendants assigned to Plan C}$$
$$CD = \text{the number of cabin attendants assigned to Plan D}$$
$$CE = \text{the number of cabin attendants assigned to Plan E}$$

To create the objective function of minimizing total cost, use decomposition and the costs in Table 8.13, which results in the following:

$$\text{Total cost} = (\text{cost of supervisors}) + (\text{cost of cabin attendants})$$

$$= (\text{cost of supervisors on Plan A}) +$$

$$\vdots$$

$$(\text{cost of supervisors on Plan E}) +$$
$$(\text{cost of cabin attendants on Plan A}) +$$

$$\vdots$$

$$(\text{cost of cabin attendants on Plan E})$$

$$= 300SA + 300SB + 500SC + 500SD + 800SE +$$
$$200CA + 200CB + 400CC + 400CD + 640CE$$

To identify the constraints, apply the technique of grouping, which leads to four groups of constraints:

1. Minimum requirement on the number of supervisors on each flight.
2. Minimum requirement on the number of cabin attendants on each flight.
3. Availability of supervisors and cabin attendants.
4. FAA requirement on the ratio of supervisors to cabin attendants.

MINIMUM REQUIREMENT ON THE NUMBER OF SUPERVISORS ON EACH FLIGHT

This group consists of six constraints, one for each flight. For example, for Flight 1, there must be at least one supervisor, as indicated in Table 8.12. Because Flight 1 is on Plans A, C, and E (from Table 8.13), the total number of supervisors assigned to Flight 1 is

$$\text{Supervisors on Flight 1} = SA + SC + SE$$

Thus, the supervisor constraint for Flight 1 is

$$SA + SC + SE \geq 1 \qquad \text{(S-ON-FT 1)}$$

Applying the same reasoning for the remaining five flights gives rise to the following constraints:

$$
\begin{aligned}
SB + SD &\geq 1 \qquad \text{(S-ON-FT 2)}\\
SC + SE &\geq 1 \qquad \text{(S-ON-FT 3)}\\
SD + SE &\geq 1 \qquad \text{(S-ON-FT 4)}\\
SB + SC &\geq 1 \qquad \text{(S-ON-FT 5)}\\
SA + SD + SE &\geq 1 \qquad \text{(S-ON-FT 6)}
\end{aligned}
$$

MINIMUM REQUIREMENT ON THE NUMBER OF CABIN ATTENDANTS ON EACH FLIGHT

This group also consists of six constraints, one for each flight. For example, for Flight 1, there must be at least three cabin attendants, as indicated in Table 8.12. Because Flight 1 is on Plans A, C, and E (from Table 8.13), the total number of cabin attendants assigned to Flight 1 is

$$\text{Cabin attendants on Flight 1} = CA + CC + CE$$

Thus, the cabin-attendant constraint for Flight 1 is

$$CA + CC + CE \geq 3 \qquad \text{(C-ON-FT 1)}$$

The same reasoning for the remaining five flights results in the following constraints:

$$
\begin{aligned}
CB + CD &\geq 4 \qquad \text{(C-ON-FT 2)}\\
CC + CE &\geq 3 \qquad \text{(C-ON-FT 3)}\\
CD + CE &\geq 2 \qquad \text{(C-ON-FT 4)}\\
CB + CC &\geq 5 \qquad \text{(C-ON-FT 5)}\\
CA + CD + CE &\geq 2 \qquad \text{(C-ON-FT 6)}
\end{aligned}
$$

AVAILABILITY CONSTRAINTS

The total number of supervisors assigned to all plans cannot exceed the four that are available. To convert this constraint into a mathematical form, use decomposition:

Total number of supervisors = (number of supervisors on Plan A) +

$$\vdots$$

(number of supervisors on Plan E)

$$= SA + SB + SC + SD + SE$$

Thus, the availability constraint for the supervisors is

$$SA + SB + SC + SD + SE \leq 4 \qquad \text{(TOTAL S)}$$

Similarly, the availability constraint for the cabin attendants is

$$CA + CB + CC + CD + CE \leq 8 \qquad \text{(TOTAL C)}$$

RATIO CONSTRAINTS

Per FAA regulations, there must be at least one supervisor for every two cabin attendants on each flight. Six ratio constraints result. For example, the number of supervisors and the number of cabin attendants assigned to Flight 1 are given in the foregoing constraints labeled S-ON-FT 1 and C-ON-FT 1:

$$\text{Supervisors on Flight 1} = SA + SC + SE$$

$$\text{Cabin attendants on Flight 1} = CA + CC + CE$$

Thus, the ratio constraint for Flight 1 is

$$\text{Supervisors on Flight 1} \geq \tfrac{1}{2}(\text{cabin attendants on Flight 1})$$

$$SA + SC + SE \geq \tfrac{1}{2}(CA + CC + CE)$$

Multiplying both sides by 2 and bringing all S-variables to the other side results in

$$-2SA - 2SC - 2SE + CA + CC + CE \leq 0 \qquad \text{(RATIO-ON-1)}$$

Applying the same reasoning for the remaining five flights gives rise to the following ratio constraints:

$$
\begin{array}{lll}
-2SB - 2SD + \ \ CB + CD & \leq 0 & \text{(RATIO-ON-2)} \\
-2SC - 2SE + \ \ CC + CE & \leq 0 & \text{(RATIO-ON-3)} \\
-2SD - 2SE + \ \ CD + CE & \leq 0 & \text{(RATIO-ON-4)} \\
-2SB - 2SC + \ \ CB + CC & \leq 0 & \text{(RATIO-ON-5)} \\
-2SA - 2SD - 2SE + CA + CD + CE \leq 0 & & \text{(RATIO-ON-6)}
\end{array}
$$

Adding the logical constraints that all variables be nonnegative integers results in the following complete integer programming problem.

MATHEMATICAL FORMULATION OF THE CREW-SCHEDULING PROBLEM OF COMMUTER AIRWAYS

Integer Program
CREW.DAT

Minimize

$$300SA + 300SB + 500SC + 500SD + 800SE +$$
$$200CA + 200CB + 400CC + 400CD + 640CE$$

Subject to

SUPERVISOR CONSTRAINTS ON EACH FLIGHT

$SA + SC + SE \geq 1$	(S-ON-FT 1)
$SB + SD \geq 1$	(S-ON-FT 2)
$SC + SE \geq 1$	(S-ON-FT 3)
$SD + SE \geq 1$	(S-ON-FT 4)
$SB + SC \geq 1$	(S-ON-FT 5)
$SA + SD + SE \geq 1$	(S-ON-FT 6)

CABIN-ATTENDANT CONSTRAINTS ON EACH FLIGHT

$CA + CC + CE \geq 3$	(C-ON-FT 1)
$CB + CD \geq 4$	(C-ON-FT 2)
$CC + CE \geq 3$	(C-ON-FT 3)
$CD + CE \geq 2$	(C-ON-FT 4)
$CB + CC \geq 5$	(C-ON-FT 5)
$CA + CD + CE \geq 2$	(C-ON-FT 6)

AVAILABILITY CONSTRAINTS

$$SA + SB + SC + SD + SE \leq 4 \quad \text{(TOTAL S)}$$
$$CA + CB + CC + CD + CE \leq 8 \quad \text{(TOTAL C)}$$

RATIO CONSTRAINTS ON EACH FLIGHT

$-2SA - 2SC - 2SE + CA + CC + CE \leq 0$	(RATIO-ON-1)
$-2SB - 2SD + CB + CD \leq 0$	(RATIO-ON-2)
$-2SC - 2SE + CC + CE \leq 0$	(RATIO-ON-3)
$-2SD - 2SE + CD + CE \leq 0$	(RATIO-ON-4)
$-2SB - 2SC + CB + CC \leq 0$	(RATIO-ON-5)
$-2SA - 2SD - 2SE + CA + CD + CE \leq 0$	(RATIO-ON-6)

LOGICAL CONSTRAINTS

All variables ≥ 0 and integer

Computer Solution

With the problem now formulated, any appropriate computer package can solve it. It is interesting to note that if you were to drop the integer requirements on the variables and solve the resulting linear program, the values of some of the variables in the optimal solution will have fractional values (try this on your computer package). Thus, to obtain the optimal *integer* solution, it is necessary to use an integer programming package. The results of using STORM are given in Figure 8.22.

```
                    Airline Crew Scheduling Problem
                  OPTIMAL SOLUTION - SUMMARY REPORT
     Variable         Value        Cost  Lower bound  Upper bound

     SA                  0      300.0000          0     Infinity
     SB                  1      300.0000          0     Infinity
     SC                  2      500.0000          0     Infinity
     SD                  1      500.0000          0     Infinity
     SE                  0      800.0000          0     Infinity
     CA                  0      200.0000          0     Infinity
     CB                  2      200.0000          0     Infinity
     CC                  3      400.0000          0     Infinity
     CD                  2      400.0000          0     Infinity
     CE                  0      640.0000          0     Infinity


  Objective Function Value = 4200



                  OPTIMAL SOLUTION - SUMMARY REPORT
           Constraint  Type       RHS          Slack

           S-ON-FT 1    >=      1.0000        1.0000
           S-ON-FT 2    >=      1.0000        1.0000
           S-ON-FT 3    >=      1.0000        1.0000
           S-ON-FT 4    >=      1.0000        0.0000
           S-ON-FT 5    >=      1.0000        2.0000
           S-ON-FT 6    >=      1.0000        0.0000
           C-ON-FT 1    >=      3.0000        0.0000
           C-ON-FT 2    >=      4.0000        0.0000
           C-ON-FT 3    >=      3.0000        0.0000
           C-ON-FT 4    >=      2.0000        0.0000
           C-ON-FT 5    >=      5.0000        0.0000
           C-ON-FT 6    >=      2.0000        0.0000
           TOTAL S      <=      4.0000        0.0000
           TOTAL C      <=      8.0000        1.0000
           RATIO-ON-1   <=      0.0000        1.0000
           RATIO-ON-2   <=      0.0000        0.0000
           RATIO-ON-3   <=      0.0000        1.0000
           RATIO-ON-4   <=      0.0000        0.0000
           RATIO-ON-5   <=      0.0000        1.0000
           RATIO-ON-6   <=      0.0000        0.0000
```

FIGURE 8.22 STORM Output Report for the Integer Programming Problem of Commuter Airways.

From the first part of the report in Figure 8.22, you can see that it is optimal to assign one supervisor and two cabin attendants to Plans B and D, and two supervisors and three cabin attendants to Plan C. Plans A and E are not used. The total cost for this assignment is $4200.

Turning to the second part of the report, which deals with the constraints, you can see that the values of all slack variables associated with minimum cabin-attendant requirements are 0. This means that each flight has met its minimum requirements precisely. In contrast, the values of the slack variables for the associated supervisor constraints on Flights 1, 2, 3, and 5 are positive, which indicates that those flights have more supervisors than the minimum of one that management requires. Recall the FAA regulations on the ratio of the number of supervisors to cabin attendants.

Finally, the values of 0 and 1 for the slack variables associated, respectively, with the supervisor and cabin-attendant availability constraints (labeled TOTAL S and TOTAL C) indicate that all four supervisors are assigned and that seven of the eight available cabin attendants are assigned.

ADDITIONAL MANAGERIAL CONSIDERATIONS

In this chapter, you have learned to solve problems in which some (or all) of the variables are restricted to have integer values. To solve these integer programming problems requires listing and examining, either implicitly or explicitly, all combinations of integer values for these variables. In general, solving integer programming problems requires substantial computational effort (significantly more than comparably sized linear programming problems demand). As a manager, you need to be aware of this fact and may need to take some of the following precautions and measures to ensure that an acceptable solution is obtained in a reasonable amount of time.

Care When Formulating an Integer Programming Problem

Because the amount of time needed to obtain a solution to an integer programming problem depends directly on the number of integer variables, care should be taken during the formulation phase to minimize the number of such variables. For example, as you learned in Chapter 2, there are often different ways to formulate the same problem. Suppose you need to determine how many and which of five comparably skilled employees should be assigned to a particular shift. One approach is to define five 0–1 variables, one for each employee. The value of each variable indicates whether or not that person is assigned to the given shift. But note that the employees have the same skills, and so it does not matter which particular employees are assigned, only *how many* of them are assigned. You could, therefore define a single variable whose value represents the number of employees to assign to the shift. By cutting down on the number of variables, the amount of computing time—and its cost—are reduced. This approach was used in the case study.

When formulating problems, you may at first believe that certain variables need to have integer values—for example, in determining the number of dollars to invest in a portfolio or the number of gallons of paint to produce and sell in 1-gallon containers. If the values of these variables are expected to be relatively large (for example, tens of thousands), very little is lost if the integer requirement is omitted. For example, if the optimal linear programming solution indicates that you should invest $59,225.253 or produce 15,880.7 gallons of paint, little harm, if any, is done if you actually invest $59,225 or produce 15,880 gallons of paint.

Another way to reduce the number of integer variables in a model is to be aware that, in certain cases, even though the integer requirement on some variables must be included with the formulation, *there is no need to treat them as integers when solving the problem*. This is because researchers have determined that the constraints of certain problems ensure that the solution obtained will automatically satisfy the integer constraints even though the integer requirement is excluded. One such class of problems, as you will learn in Chapter 9, is the transportation problem, which you have already seen in Section 2.2, Chapter 2. As another example, consider the plant-location problem of CCC, presented in Section 8.1, in which the integer x-variables represent the number of computers to ship, and the y-variables are 0–1 variables whose values indicate whether to build an assembly plant at a specific location. For fixed integer values of the y-variables, the resulting problem in the x-variables is a transportation problem whose optimal solution will automatically have integer values. The integer requirement on the x-variables can therefore be omitted when solving the problem. This is because requiring the y-variables to be integer will ensure an optimal solution in which the x-variables are integers.

Care When Solving an Integer Programming Problem

As you learned in Section 8.4, the branch-and-bound method is designed to reduce the number of integer solutions that need to be examined in an integer programming problem. However, in problems of even moderate size (typically, 100 or more integer variables), the number of such solutions to be examined is so large that computers may not be able to handle the task in any reasonable amount of time. When using a computer package to solve such problems, you may need to use some of the following guidelines:

1. If possible, provide a known feasible integer solution when you run the program. This solution then can be used immediately as a lower bound, thus potentially eliminating many solutions in the branch-and-bound procedure.
2. Provide special *stopping rules* that permit the program to terminate when it reaches a solution that, while perhaps not optimal, is acceptable. Consider any of the following stopping rules, after which the program will terminate and report the best feasible integer solution found up to that point:
   a. A limit on the amount of time the computer program is allowed to run (for example, 30 minutes).
   b. A maximum number of nodes that the branch-and-bound procedure is allowed to examine (for example, 100).
   c. An acceptable quality of solution expressed as a percent. (For example, an acceptable quality of 1% indicates that the program should stop when the objective function value of the current integer solution is within 1% of the optimal value.)

The specific choice depends on which of these options is available on the computer package you are using. Furthermore, some packages may allow you to continue processing if you are not satisfied with the solution provided at the point the stopping rule halts the program.

Using Specialized Algorithms

As discussed above, you learned that certain integer programming problems, such as the transportation problem, have special features that allow you to drop the integer requirement on the variables altogether. There are other problems that, while you must keep the integer requirement, have special types of constraints that have allowed researchers to develop associated specialized algorithms. These specialized algorithms are substantially more efficient than the general branch-and-bound method presented in Section 8.4. Thus, if the general integer programming package you have is unable to obtain an acceptable solution in a reasonable amount of time, see if your problem can be solved by one of these more specialized algorithms. For example, the crew-scheduling problem of Commuter Airways presented in the case study is small enough that a solution with the branch-and-bound procedure is easily obtained. But many scheduling problems can have thousands of integer variables, making it impossible to solve with standard software. However, specialized branch-and-bound procedures are available for solving these large scheduling problems.

Using Heuristic Algorithms

Some integer programming problems are so large that even specialized algorithms cannot reach acceptable solutions in reasonable amounts of time, even using the foregoing stopping rules. For such problems, researchers have developed *heuristic algorithms*. These are algorithms designed specifically to obtain approximate solutions that, while not guaranteed to be optimal, can be found quickly. As one example, recall the cutting-stock problem of Spiral Paper, Inc., presented in Section 8.1. A problem like this in practice may require thousands of variables corresponding to the different settings on the cutting machine. One heuristic that performs well and is commonly used in practice is to solve the relaxed linear programming problem and simply round off all fractional values in the optimal solution to their next highest integer value.

In some problems, specialized heuristics take advantage of the structure in the constraints of large integer programming problems. For example, recall the portfolio problem of High-Tech presented in Section 8.1, which resulted in the following formulation used to determine which projects to invest in with a budget of $1 million:

Maximize
$$30000B + 57750T + 19500L + 15625C + 52500M + 6300S$$

Subject to
$$200000B + 350000T + 150000L + 125000C + 375000M + 70000S \leq 1000000$$
$$B \leq 1$$
$$T \leq 1$$
$$L \leq 1$$
$$C \leq 1$$
$$M \leq 1$$
$$S \leq 1$$
$$B, \quad T, \quad L, \quad C, \quad M, \quad S \geq 0 \quad \text{and integer}$$

One intuitive heuristic is as follows:

1. Order all the investments in terms of the highest rate of return.
2. Select as many of these investments in the order obtained in step 1 as long as funds are available.

Applying the first step of this heuristic to the High-Tech problem results in ordering the projects as shown in Table 8.14.

Applying the second step of the heuristic results in investing in Tele-Com, Bio-Tech, Medi-Opt, and Sound-News, with an annual expected return of $146,550 on an investment of $995,000 of the $1 million budget. By chance, this heuristic solution is precisely the same as the optimal one obtained in Section 8.6 with the branch-and-bound procedure. In general, the heuristic solution will not produce the optimal solution but should provide an acceptable solution quickly. Note also that a heuristic solution can be used to provide an initial lower bound for the branch-and-bound procedure.

TABLE 8.14	*Projects for High-Tech in Descending Order of Rate of Return*
PROJECT	RATE OF RETURN
Tele-Com	0.165
Bio-Tech	0.150
Medi-Opt	0.140
Laser-Optics	0.130
Compu-Ware	0.125
Sound-News	0.090

SUMMARY

In this chapter, you have learned to formulate and to solve problems in which some (or all) of the variables are restricted to have integer values. Such variables arise not only when the items they represent must be whole numbers, but also when "no/yes" decisions must be made. In the latter case, 0–1 integer variables are used. Because of the substantial amount of computer time required to solve integer programming problems with many integer variables, care should be used when formulating these problems, as discussed in the section on Additional Managerial Considerations.

Once the problem has been formulated, you would like to obtain an optimal solution. Although the graphical method in Section 8.2 provides insight, computers cannot work with geometry but instead must work with algebra. Because of the integer requirement, one computational approach is to list and examine, either implicitly or explicitly, all possible combinations of integer solutions through the use of a tree. The number of such combinations at times can be extremely large. The branch-and-bound procedure is designed to avoid having to examine a large fraction of these possible solutions. This method requires solving many linear programming problems. Therefore, obtaining optimal solutions to integer programming problems requires significantly more computer time than for comparably sized linear programming problems. As a result, it may be necessary to limit the amount of time a computer package is allowed to take in producing a solution. As described in the section on Additional Managerial Considerations, a manager may have to settle for an acceptable solution that may not be the optimal solution.

EXERCISES

EXERCISE 8.1 Suppose that P_1, P_2, and P_3 are variables whose values are 1 if a particular plant is to be opened and 0 otherwise. Write a *separate* linear constraint for each of the following word constraints.

    a. If Plant 1 is opened, then Plant 2 should not be opened.
    b. If Plant 1 is opened, then Plant 2 should also be opened.
    c. At least one of the three plants must be opened.

EXERCISE 8.2 Suppose that P_1, P_2, and P_3 are variables whose values are 1 if a particular plant is to be opened and 0 otherwise. Write a *single* linear constraint that reflects each of the following word constraints.

    a. Not more than two of the three plants should be opened.
    b. If neither Plant 2 nor Plant 3 is opened, then Plant 1 should not be opened.
    c. If Plant 1 is opened or Plant 3 is not opened, then Plant 2 must be opened.

EXERCISE 8.3   Toys Unlimited makes small and large SuperDuper balls by mixing different amounts of a base and a special resiliency compound. Small balls sell for $0.59 and require a ratio of 2:1 for the mixture of base to compound. Large balls sell for $0.79 and require a ratio of 4:3. Current inventories are 1000 pounds of the base and 500 pounds of the compound. Each small ball requires 1.5 ounces of compound and each large ball 2 ounces. Formulate a model to determine the optimal production quantities.

EXERCISE 8.4   The city of Wobegone is planning the purchase of new police cruisers that cost $15,000 each, ambulances that cost $25,000 each, and fire trucks that cost $48,000. City regulations require at least one ambulance for every two fire trucks. Also, the total amount spent on police vehicles must be at least twice that spent on fire trucks. Each of the three fire stations must have at least one fire truck but not more than two. Formulate a model to determine the maximum number of fire trucks to purchase with a total budget of $700,000.

EXERCISE 8.5   Hardware Unlimited has four machines that can each produce three types of screws: small, medium, and large at the following rates (in lb of screws/min):

MACHINE	SCREW SIZE		
	SMALL	MEDIUM	LARGE
1	10	8	6
2	20	14	10
3	15	12	8
4	16	14	12

Each machine requires a different amount of time for being tooled to produce the various screws, as given in the following table (in minutes):

MACHINE	SCREW SIZE		
	SMALL	MEDIUM	LARGE
1	20	30	40
2	30	40	50
3	15	20	30
4	45	45	45

Each machine is to be tooled to produce only one size of screw per day. If the profit margin per pound for small screws is $1.25, for medium screws $1.75, and for large screws $2.00, formulate a model to determine which machine should be tooled to produce which type of screw so as to maximize the net profit obtainable in an 8-hour day (that must include setup times).

EXERCISE 8.6   The Euclid School Board is formulating a plan to desegregate its two elementary schools, which can handle up to 1100 and 700 students each. Black and white students can be transported in buses from any of three housing districts to either of the two schools. The following data have been collected:

DISTRICT	NUMBER OF WHITES	NUMBER OF BLACKS	TOTAL	MILES TO	
				SCHOOL 1	SCHOOL 2
1	350	150	500	3	7
2	250	100	350	4	4
3	900	50	950	6	4

Formulate a model that minimizes the total student-miles traveled while assuring the following:

a. All students go to school.
b. No school has more students than its capacity.
c. Each school has between 40% and 60% white students in its population.

For each of the following exercises, determine graphically whether (a) the associated linear programming problem is infeasible, optimal, or unbounded, and (b) the integer programming problem is infeasible, optimal, or unbounded (indicate all feasible integer solutions with heavy black dots, and label each constraint). For those in which both problems in (a) and (b) are optimal, find the optimal solutions and indicate whether the integer solution can be obtained by rounding the linear programming one.

EXERCISE 8.7   (See the foregoing instructions.)

$$\begin{aligned}
\text{Maximize} \quad & 6x_1 + 5x_2 \\
\text{Subject to} \quad & 5x_1 + x_2 \le 15 & \text{(a)} \\
& 2x_1 + 4x_2 \le 19 & \text{(b)} \\
& x_1, \ x_2 \ge 0 \quad \text{and integer}
\end{aligned}$$

EXERCISE 8.8   (See the instructions preceding Exercise 8.7.)

$$\begin{aligned}
\text{Minimize} \quad & -2x_1 - 3x_2 \\
\text{Subject to} \quad & x_1 - 2x_2 \le 2 & \text{(a)} \\
& 2x_1 - x_2 \ge 0 & \text{(b)} \\
& x_1, \ x_2 \ge 0 \quad \text{and integer}
\end{aligned}$$

EXERCISE 8.9   (See the instructions preceding Exercise 8.7.)

$$\begin{aligned}
\text{Minimize} \quad & -2x_1 - 3x_2 \\
\text{Subject to} \quad & 7x_1 + 24x_2 \le 45 & \text{(a)} \\
& -x_1 + 4x_2 \ge 5 & \text{(b)} \\
& x_1, \ x_2 \ge 0 \quad \text{and integer}
\end{aligned}$$

EXERCISE 8.10   (See the instructions preceding Exercise 8.7.)

$$\begin{aligned}
\text{Maximize} \quad & 12x_1 + 4x_2 \\
\text{Subject to} \quad & 30x_1 + 8x_2 \le 105 & \text{(a)} \\
& 4x_1 + 4x_2 \le 21 & \text{(b)} \\
& 4x_2 \le 17 & \text{(c)} \\
& x_1, \ x_2 \ge 0 \quad \text{and integer}
\end{aligned}$$

EXERCISE 8.11   (See the instructions preceding Exercise 8.7.)

$$\begin{aligned}
\text{Minimize} \quad & -2x_1 - 5x_2 \\
\text{Subject to} \quad & 4x_1 - 2x_2 \ge 10 & \text{(a)} \\
& 3x_1 + x_2 \le 5 & \text{(b)} \\
& x_1, \ x_2 \ge 0 \quad \text{and integer}
\end{aligned}$$

EXERCISE 8.12   (See the instructions preceding Exercise 8.7.)

$$\begin{array}{ll}
\text{Maximize} & x_1 + x_2 \\
\text{Subject to} & 2x_1 - 2x_2 \leq 1 \qquad \text{(a)} \\
& -4x_1 + 4x_2 \leq -1 \qquad \text{(b)} \\
& x_1, \quad x_2 \geq 0 \quad \text{and integer}
\end{array}$$

EXERCISE 8.13   Draw a tree to represent all possible integer solutions to the following integer program:

$$\begin{array}{ll}
\text{Maximize} & x_1 + x_2 \\
\text{Subject to} & 5x_1 + x_2 \leq 10 \\
& 2x_1 + 4x_2 \leq 8 \\
& x_1 = 0, 1, \text{ or } 2; \quad x_2 = 0 \text{ or } 1
\end{array}$$

EXERCISE 8.14   Draw a tree to represent all possible integer solutions to the following integer program:

$$\begin{array}{ll}
\text{Minimize} & x_1 - 2x_2 + 3x_3 \\
\text{Subject to} & x_1 + x_2 + x_3 \leq 2 \\
& 2x_1 - x_2 - x_3 \leq 0 \\
& -x_1 - 2x_2 + 2x_3 \geq 0 \\
& \text{All variables are 0 or 1}
\end{array}$$

EXERCISE 8.15   In the following integer program, consider a tree in which the variables are fixed from left to right with their next largest integer value. Use the given information consisting of the current node in the tree, the solution to the associated linear program, and the current lower bound to indicate which nodes, if any, can be dropped from further consideration.

$$\begin{array}{ll}
\text{Maximize} & 2x_1 + 3x_2 \\
\text{Subject to} & -x_1 + x_2 \leq 1 \\
& -x_1 + x_2 \geq 0 \\
& 2x_1 + x_2 \leq 3 \\
& x_1 = 0 \text{ or } 1; \quad x_2 = 0, 1, \text{ or } 2
\end{array}$$

Current lower bound: none.
Current node: the one in which neither x_1 nor x_2 is fixed.
Solution to the associated linear program: $x_1 = 0.667$, $x_2 = 1.667$.

EXERCISE 8.16   Repeat Exercise 8.15 using the following information at the current node:

Current lower bound: none.
Current node: the one in which x_1 is fixed to 1.
Solution to the associated linear program: $x_1 = 1$, $x_2 = 1$.

EXERCISE 8.17 Repeat Exercise 8.15 for the following:

$$\begin{array}{ll}
\text{Maximize} & 3x_1 + 2x_2 \\
\text{Subject to} & x_1 - x_2 \leq 1 \\
& x_1 - x_2 \geq 0 \\
& x_1 + 2x_2 \leq 3 \\
& x_1 = 0, 1, \text{ or } 2; \ x_2 = 0 \text{ or } 1
\end{array}$$

Current lower bound: none.
Current node: the one in which x_1 is fixed to 2.
Solution to the associated linear program: infeasible.

EXERCISE 8.18 Repeat Exercise 8.17 using the following information at the current node:

Current lower bound: 5.
Current node: the one in which x_1 is fixed to 0.
Solution to the associated linear program: $x_1 = 0$, $x_2 = 0$.

EXERCISE 8.19 Consider the following integer program and partial tree:

$$\begin{array}{ll}
\text{Maximize} & 5x_1 + 3x_2 + x_3 \\
\text{Subject to} & x_1 + x_2 + x_3 \leq 3 \\
& 5x_1 \quad\quad - 2x_3 \leq 2 \\
& x_1, \ x_2, \ x_3 \geq 0 \quad \text{and integer}
\end{array}$$

Partial tree: node 0 and the three nodes obtained by fixing x_2 to 1, 2, and 3.

a. Write the linear program associated with node 0.
b. Solve the problem in part (a) using your computer package.
c. Use the solution from part (b) to indicate the new lower bound. Which nodes, if any, can be dropped? Explain.
d. Indicate which node is selected next in the partial tree.
Repeat the process until all nodes in the partial tree have been examined or eliminated. When done, indicate if additional nodes need to be examined. If not, provide the solution to the original integer programming problem.

EXERCISE 8.20 Repeat Exercise 8.19 for the following integer program and partial tree:

$$\begin{array}{ll}
\text{Minimize} & 2x_1 + 5x_2 - 4x_3 \\
\text{Subject to} & x_1 + 2x_2 - 3x_3 \geq 5 \\
& x_1 - 3x_2 + x_3 \geq 8 \\
& x_2 + x_3 \geq 7 \\
& x_1, \ x_2, \ x_3 \geq 0 \quad \text{and integer}
\end{array}$$

Partial tree: node 0, the three nodes obtained by fixing x_2 to 2, 3, and 4, and with x_2 fixed to 3, the two nodes in which x_3 is fixed to 4 and 5. (Observe that the objective function is to be minimized.)

EXERCISE 8.21 Universal Tent Company makes large and small tents. Large tents require 10 square meters of material, 15 minutes of time on the stitching machine, and net the company a profit of $90. Small tents use 6 square meters of material, 7.5 minutes of machine time, and yield a profit of $70. In this quarter, there are 15,000 square meters of material and 25,000 minutes of machine time available. Given that the number of large tents should be at least half the number of small tents, the following integer program was developed to determine how many large tents (L) and small tents (S) to make this quarter:

$$\text{Maximize} \quad 90L + 70S$$
$$\text{Subject to}$$
$$10L + 6.0S \leq 15000 \quad \text{(material)}$$
$$15L + 7.5S \leq 25000 \quad \text{(machine time)}$$
$$2L - S \geq 0$$
$$L, \quad S \geq 0 \quad \text{and integer}$$

Use your computer package to solve this integer program. Interpret the values of the variables in the context of the problem. Which constraints are binding—that is, hold with equality at optimality? What does this mean in the context of the problem?

EXERCISE 8.22   With a budget of $1 million, RV World needs to reorder its stock of standard vans, which cost $20,000 each, deluxe vans, which cost $28,000 each, and customized vans, which cost $40,000 each. The Manager wants to ensure that there are at least twice as many standard vans as deluxe vans and at least three times as many deluxe vans as customized vans. Given that there should be at least three customized vans, the following integer programming problem was developed to determine the number of standard vans (S), deluxe vans (D), and customized vans (C) to order to have the most number of vans possible in stock:

$$\text{Maximize} \quad S + D + C$$
$$\text{Subject to}$$
$$20000S + 28000D + 40000C \leq 1000000$$
$$S - 2D \geq 0$$
$$D - 3C \geq 0$$
$$C \geq 3$$
$$S, \quad D, \quad C \geq 0 \quad \text{and integer}$$

Use your computer package to solve this integer program. Interpret the values of the variables in the context of the problem. Which constraints are binding—that is, hold with equality at optimality? What does this mean in the context of the problem?

EXERCISE 8.23   Hacker Company makes electronic circuit boards for PCs. Each fax-modem, data-compression, and sound-synthesizer board requires a certain number of minutes of machine time for chip insertion, soldering, assembly, and testing. These data (in minutes) together with the number of minutes of machine time available for each operation, the minimum number of each board, and the net profits are summarized in the following table:

| | \multicolumn{3}{c}{BOARD} | |
	FAX-MODEM	DATA-COMPRESSION	SOUND SYNTHESIZER	AVAILABLE
Chip insertion	0.3333	0.25	0.5	500
Soldering	0.5	0.5	0.5	600
Assembly	2.0	2.0	1.0	2000
Testing	1.5	2.0	3.5	2400
Profit ($)	10	10	8	
Minimum production	500	300	250	

The following integer programming problem was developed to determine the number of fax-modems (F), data-compression (D), and synthesizer (S) boards to produce:

Maximize $\quad 10F + 10D + 8M$

Subject to

$$0.3333F + 0.25D + 0.5M \le 500 \quad \text{(chip insertion)}$$
$$0.5F + 0.5D + 0.5M \le 600 \quad \text{(soldering)}$$
$$2F + 2D + M \le 2000 \quad \text{(assembly)}$$
$$1.5F + 2D + 3.5M \le 2400 \quad \text{(testing)}$$
$$F \ge 500 \quad \text{(minimum F)}$$
$$D \ge 300 \quad \text{(minimum D)}$$
$$M \ge 250 \quad \text{(minimum M)}$$
$$F, \quad D, \quad M \ge 0 \quad \text{and integer}$$

The following output was obtained from the STORM software package:

```
              OPTIMAL SOLUTION - DETAILED REPORT
        Variable      Value       Cost    Red. cost    Status
 1          F       564.0000    10.0000    10.0000 Lower bound
 2          D       300.0000    10.0000    10.0000 Lower bound
 3          M       272.0000     8.0000     8.0000 Upper bound

Slack Variables
 4       CHIP INS   101.0188     0.0000     0.0000    Basic
 5       SOLDERING   32.0000     0.0000     0.0000    Basic
 6       ASSEMBLY     0.0000     0.0000     0.0000    Basic
 7       TESTING      2.0000     0.0000     0.0000    Basic
 8         MIN F     64.0000     0.0000     0.0000    Basic
 9         MIN D      0.0000     0.0000     0.0000 Lower bound
10         MIN M     22.0000     0.0000     0.0000    Basic

Objective Function Value = 10816

              OPTIMAL SOLUTION - DETAILED REPORT
     Constraint  Type      RHS        Slack   Shadow price
 1    CHIP INS   <=     500.0000   101.0188     0.0000
 2    SOLDERING  <=     600.0000    32.0000     0.0000
 3    ASSEMBLY   <=    2000.0000     0.0000     0.0000
 4    TESTING    <=    2400.0000     2.0000     0.0000
 5      MIN F    >=     500.0000    64.0000     0.0000
 6      MIN D    >=     300.0000     0.0000     0.0000
 7      MIN M    >=     250.0000    22.0000     0.0000
```

Use the foregoing output to answer the following. How many of each board should the company make? What is the total profit?

EXERCISE 8.24 Use your computer package to find the new solution for Exercise 8.23 if all four operations have 10% more time available.

EXERCISE 8.25 Use your computer package to determine what happens to the optimal solution and profit in Exercise 8.23 if a minimum of 550 fax-modems must be produced?

EXERCISE 8.26 Use your computer package to determine what happens to the optimal solution and profit in Exercise 8.23 if an additional 400 minutes of machine time are available for assembly?

EXERCISE 8.27   The management of High Tech is considering investing in six projects, each requiring a certain amount of initial capital. These data together with an associated risk factor (between 0 and 1) and the expected annual return are given in the following table:

PROJECT	CAPITAL	RISK	RETURN
P1	100,000	0.50	0.20
P2	200,000	0.40	0.15
P3	170,000	0.70	0.30
P4	250,000	0.65	0.25
P5	400,000	0.45	0.17
P6	250,000	0.75	0.40

The general partners have agreed that the total risk, obtained by adding the risk factors for each project undertaken, should not exceed 3.0. Also, at most two projects can have a risk factor exceeding 0.6. The following integer programming problem was developed to determine in which projects to invest with a $1 million budget to achieve the highest expected annual return:

Maximize

$20000P1 + 30000P2 + 51000P3 + 62500P4 + 68000P5 + 100000P6$
Subject to

$$0.5P1 + \quad 0.4P2 + \quad 0.7P3 + \quad 0.65P4 + \quad 0.45P5 + \quad 0.75P6 \leq \quad 3 \quad \text{(risk)}$$

$$P3 + \quad P4 + \quad \quad + \quad P6 \leq \quad 2 \quad \text{(maximum risk)}$$

$$100P1 + \quad 200P2 + \quad 170P3 + \quad 250P4 + \quad 400P5 + \quad 250P6 \leq 1000 \quad \text{(budget)}$$

All variables must be 0 or 1

The following output was obtained from the STORM software package:

```
                OPTIMAL SOLUTION - DETAILED REPORT
        Variable        Value         Cost     Red. cost   Status
   1       P1         1.0000   20000.0000   20000.0000 Lower bound
   2       P2         0.0000   30000.0000   30000.0000 Upper bound
   3       P3         0.0000   51000.0000   51000.0000 Upper bound
   4       P4         1.0000   62500.0000   62500.0000 Lower bound
   5       P5         1.0000   68000.0000   68000.0000 Lower bound
   6       P6         1.0000  100000.0000  100000.0000 Lower bound

Slack Variables
   7      RISK        0.6500       0.0000       0.0000    Basic
   8    MAXRISK       0.0000       0.0000       0.0000    Basic
   9     BUDGET       0.0000       0.0000       0.0000    Basic

Objective Function Value = 250500

                OPTIMAL SOLUTION - DETAILED REPORT
        Constraint Type      RHS         Slack   Shadow price
   1      RISK      <=      3.0000       0.6500       0.0000
   2    MAXRISK     <=      2.0000       0.0000       0.0000
   3     BUDGET     <=   1000.0000       0.0000       0.0000
```

Use the foregoing output to answer the following.
a. In which projects should High Tech invest? What is the expected annual return for doing so?
b. What is the total risk associated with these investments?
c. How much of the available budget is not invested?

EXERCISE 8.28   In Exercise 8.27, suppose the general partners add the requirement that project P_1 can be funded only if P_2 is funded. Modify the formulation and use your computer package to determine the new investment plan.

CRITICAL-THINKING PROJECT B

Recall Critical-Thinking Project B following the exercises in Chapter 3, in which you, Vice-President of Production for ASA Steel, need to determine the least-cost plan for producing iron plates at the eight factories and for buying from outside suppliers. To develop the desired plan, obtain the formulation from your instructor and prepare a managerial report following these guidelines.

1. Use your computer package to solve the problem. Prepare a table to show how many tons of each iron plate are produced at each factory and how many tons are purchased from each outside supplier. Indicate which factories have not used their entire budgets.

Management has decided to purchase the entire supply of all five types of iron plates from subcontractor 3 only. Modify the formulation to purchase only from subcontractor 3 and solve the associated *linear* program. Use the solution to address each of the following questions (assume that each question pertains to the original linear programming problem in which only subcontractor 3 is used):

2. Management has decided to give to one factory 8% of the total surplus monies from the production budgets of those factories that have not used their entire budget. To which single factory would you recommend giving the money? Explain.
3. Management has ordered a 2% decrease in the combined budgets of the eight factories. To cause the least disruption to current plans, the budget of only one factory is to be changed. Factories 1, 3, and 7 are exempt from budget cuts. Which one of the remaining factories would you recommend have its budget reduced? What happens to the total cost of the plan after making the cut at this factory? Explain.
4. The CEO of ASA would like to reduce the total production costs to $8.4 million by increasing the budget of a single factory. The budget at which factory would have to be increased the least to achieve the stated production costs? Explain.
5. A Vice-President of ASA asked the meaning of the sensitivity range of the objective function coefficients. A recent MBA explained that as long as a coefficient remains within the range and no other objective function coefficients change, the current production plan remains optimal. Explain why that statement is not true in this particular model.

TYRANNY OF CHOICES

Bell Communications Research, Inc. (Bellcore) was formed on January 1, 1984, when the regional Bell Operating Companies, now the Bellcore Client Companies (BCCs) were divested from AT&T. Bellcore provides applied research, engineering services, and software systems to the BCCs and its other industry clients. While working on the problem of minimizing the cost of procuring equipment and supplies from many different vendors, Bellcore researchers realized that they had developed an application that could be generalized for use by any purchasing organization including those of BCCs.

How important is this application? Consider that a purchasing organization is faced with a multitude of products from several vendors, where not all vendors offer all the products. Moreover, volume discounts can vary considerably. One particular BCC can choose from among 284 products and four suppliers, which results in about 10^{300} possible solutions—a "tyranny of choices." Even the fastest computer would take millions of years to look at all these possibilities and find the best.

The Bellcore application is called PDSS—Procurement Decision Support System. It helps each company in finding the optimal procurement decision. What makes procurement decisions so complex are the discounts that suppliers offer for volume business. Traditionally, a supplier gives a discount based on how many units of a particular item a business orders. Some suppliers take discounts a step further and base them on dollar volume of items ordered from the same family of products. With this approach, it might be worthwhile for a company to pay a higher price for one item from Supplier A—and thereby qualify for a higher discount rate applied to several products—than to choose a cheaper price for the item from Supplier B.

PDSS expresses procurement alternatives as integer programming problems. It uses the branch and bound strategy to narrow down the choices quickly and efficiently. The system also shows the costs of alternative buying strategies. Potential savings from PDSS could be substantial. (Total running time: 9:52.)

Questions on the Video

1. Which branches can never be part of the possible feasible solution set?

2. What is meant by a "tyranny of choices"?

Beyond the Video

1. How else could PDSS be applied?

2. How important is a user-friendly interface for this application?

Practical Considerations

1. How is a procurement decision simplified if only unit-volume discounts are available?

2. How do business volume discounts change a company's relationships with its suppliers? What information might a procuring company need in negotiating prices?

Source: Bell Communications Research, Red Bank, NJ.

DISTRIBUTION NETWORK PROBLEMS: TRANSPORTATION, TRANSSHIPMENT, AND ASSIGNMENT PROBLEMS

....

Much of the country moves on tires, but who moves the tires to the customers? Good Tire, an Ohio-based tire manufacturer, needs to know how to minimize its shipping costs while continuing to satisfy regional demand for its products. Might using warehouses reduce overall shipping costs? If so, how many warehouses should be maintained, and where should they be located? Top management understands that establishing warehouses would likely reduce shipping charges, but then the warehouses themselves take a bite out of profits. What strategic plan makes the most financial sense to Good Tire?

The Case Study in this chapter examines how Good Tire uses distribution methods to determine the setup that nets them the most profit.

Many problems, when formulated, exhibit a special structure in their constraints or in their objective function. By designing solution procedures (algorithms) to take advantage of the special structure, it is possible to solve problems more efficiently than would otherwise be possible. This chapter presents one such class of problems—*distribution network problems*—and the algorithms for obtaining the solution to the corresponding mathematical models.

■ 9.1 WHAT IS A DISTRIBUTION NETWORK?

One class of problem that has a special structure in its constraints when formulated mathematically deals with the distribution of goods. Generally, these goods must be shipped from known *supply points* (factories, plants, and the like) to known *demand points* (customers, retail outlets, and so on), possibly through *intermediate points* (regional and/or field warehouses, for example). The overall objective is to find the best distribution plan—that is, the amount to ship along each route from the supply points, through the intermediate points, to the demand points. By "best" is meant a plan that minimizes the total shipping costs, yields the largest profit, or optimizes some other corporate objective specified by management. It is also necessary to satisfy certain constraints:

1. Not shipping more than the specified capacity from each supply point.
2. Shipping goods only along valid routes.
3. Meeting (or exceeding) known demand at the demand points.

A problem of this type is a distribution network problem. One favorable feature of such a problem is that many aspects can be represented concisely by a diagram called a **distribution network**. A distribution network consists of a finite collection of circles, called **nodes,** each of which represents a plant, warehouse, or retail outlet. Nodes from which goods are to be shipped (such as factories or plants) are **supply nodes.** Nodes that are to receive goods to meet known demands (such as retail outlets) are **demand nodes.** Nodes that receive goods from other nodes for redistribution (such as warehouses) are **transshipment nodes,** or **intermediate nodes.**

Selected pairs of nodes in a network are connected with an arrow, called an **arc,** to represent a valid shipping route from the originating node to the destination node as indicated by the direction of the arrow (see Figure 9.1). The network picture may contain various problem data. For example, the number next to each supply node in Figure 9.1 represents the *capacity* of that supply node—that is, the maximum number of units that can be shipped from that node. For instance, the plant represented by node 1 in Figure 9.1 can ship up to 1000 units. Similarly, the number next to each demand node in Figure 9.1 represents the *demand* at that node—that is, the minimum number of units that node needs to receive to meet demand there. For instance, the demand at the retail outlet designated node 6 is 700 units. Each arc may also have a number associated with it. For example, the numbers above the arcs in Figure 9.1 represent the cost of shipping one unit between the two nodes connected by that arc. The cost of shipping one unit from node 1 to node 4 is 4 (which may be $4, $400, or even $4000). Other problem information, such as the maximum number of units that can be shipped along a given arc, can also be included with the network.

9.1.1 *An Example of a Distribution Network Problem*

The first step in formulating a distribution network problem is to draw the corresponding network by identifying the nodes and arcs in the problem under consideration. You then write the appropriate problem data next to each node and/or arc. Consider the following problem of Medical Technologies, Inc.

Distribution network
A finite collection of nodes (each of which represents a plant, warehouse, or retail outlet); an arc indicates the ability to ship goods between the two nodes connected by the arc.

Node
A circle in a distribution network used to represent a plant, warehouse, or retail outlet.

Supply node
A node from which goods are to be shipped.

Demand node
A node that is to receive goods to meet known demands.

Transshipment, or intermediate node
A node that receives goods from other nodes for redistribution.

Arc
A line in a distribution network connecting a pair of nodes that is used to represent a valid shipping route from the originating node to the destination node.

Supply Nodes **Transshipment Nodes** **Demand Nodes**

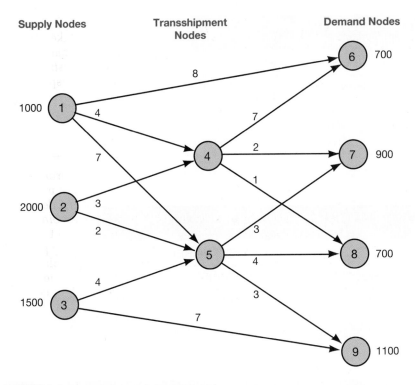

FIGURE 9.1 A General Distribution Network.

EXAMPLE 9.1 THE DISTRIBUTION PROBLEM OF MEDICAL TECHNOLOGIES, INC.

Medical Technologies, Inc. (MTI), is a manufacturer and international distributor of high-resolution X-ray equipment used in hospitals. The plant in Paris, Texas, can produce up to 100 machines per year; the one in Davenport, Iowa, 200 machines; and the plant in Springfield, Oregon, 150 machines. For the coming year, customers in Japan have ordered 120 machines, those in South Korea 80, those in New Zealand 70, and those in Australia 110 machines.

The machines produced in Texas and Iowa can be shipped to the regional warehouses in Hungary and/or Hawaii. Those produced in Oregon must be shipped to the one in Hawaii. The regional warehouses, in turn, can ship to either the field warehouse in Fiji or to the one in the Philippines. All regional and field warehouses do not store machines in inventory and thus should ship out exactly as many machines as they receive. Customers in South Korea and New Zealand can receive machines from either of the field warehouses. However, due to international trade agreements, customers in Japan must obtain their machines exclusively from the Philippines, and those in Australia must receive theirs only from Fiji. The shipping costs per machine from plants to the regional warehouses, to field warehouses, and finally to customers are given in Tables 9.1, 9.2, and 9.3, respectively. As Distribution Manager, you have been asked to determine the shipping plan of least total cost. ∎

9.1.2 Network Representation of a Distribution Problem

The first step in formulating this problem mathematically is to draw a network picture that represents the flow of products from plants through warehouses to customers. The network should contain 11 nodes, one for each of the three plants, the two regional

TABLE 9.1	Shipping Costs ($/Machine) from Plants to Regional Warehouses

	REGIONAL WAREHOUSES	
PLANTS	HUNGARY	HAWAII
Texas	200	400
Iowa	300	400
Oregon	N/A	500

TABLE 9.2	Shipping Costs ($/Machine) from Regional to Field Warehouses

	FIELD WAREHOUSES	
REGIONAL WAREHOUSES	PHILIPPINES	FIJI
Hungary	800	600
Hawaii	700	400

TABLE 9.3	Shipping Costs ($/Machine) from Field Warehouses to Customers

	CUSTOMERS			
FIELD WAREHOUSES	JAPAN	SOUTH KOREA	NEW ZEALAND	AUSTRALIA
Philippines	700	600	800	N/A
Fiji	N/A	700	500	600

warehouses, the two field warehouses, and the four customers, as illustrated in Figure 9.2. An arc should connect a pair of these nodes if it is possible to ship machines directly from the originating node to the destination node, as specified in the problem description. For example, because the plant in Oregon can ship only to the regional warehouse in Hawaii, there *should* be an arc from the node corresponding to the plant in Oregon to the node corresponding to the regional warehouse in Hawaii but *not* to the one corresponding to Hungary. The arcs are also shown in Figure 9.2 together with the corresponding unit shipping costs. The network in the figure also includes the plant capacities and the customer demands next to the corresponding supply and demand nodes, respectively.

9.1.3 Mathematical Formulation of a Distribution Network Problem

Following the steps of problem formulation as presented in Chapter 2, the first step is to identify the variables. In this case, it is necessary to determine the number of machines to ship along each direct route: from plants, through warehouses, to customers. That is, there should be one variable for each of the 15 arcs shown in Figure 9.2. Here, the first subscript of the symbolic name of each variable is the number of the originating node and the second subscript is that of the destination node. For example, $x_{7,10}$ represents the number of machines to ship from node 7 (Fiji) to node 10 (New Zealand).

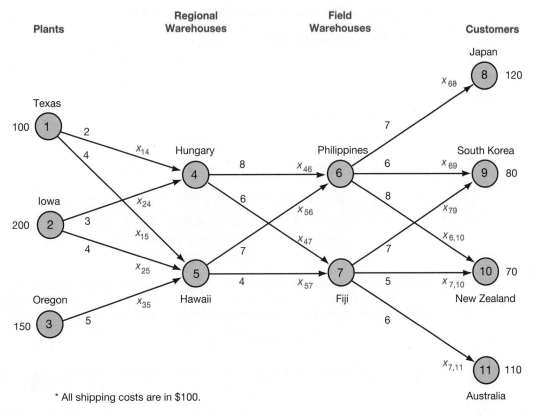

FIGURE 9.2 The Distribution Network of the Problem of MTI.

The next step is to identify the objective function, which is to minimize the total shipping costs. By using the variables, the data in Tables 9.1 to 9.3, and the technique of decomposition, the objective function in hundreds of dollars is

Minimize total shipping cost =

     (shipping cost from plants to regional warehouses) +

     (shipping cost from regional to field warehouses) +

     (shipping cost from field warehouses to customers)

$$= 2x_{14} + 4x_{15} + 3x_{24} + 4x_{25} + 5x_{35} +$$
$$8x_{46} + 6x_{47} + 7x_{56} + 4x_{57} +$$
$$7x_{68} + 6x_{69} + 8x_{6,10} + 7x_{79} + 5x_{7,10} + 6x_{7,11}$$

The final step in formulating this problem mathematically is to identify the constraints. Using the technique of grouping leads to the following four classes of constraints:

1. Supply constraints specifying that each plant must not ship more than its production capacity. For example, from the information given in Figure 9.2:

     Units shipped from Paris, Texas ≤ 100

By using the technique of decomposition and Figure 9.2,

Units shipped from Paris, Texas = (units shipped to Hungary) +

(units shipped to Hawaii)

$$= x_{14} + x_{15}$$

Thus, the supply constraint for Paris, Texas, is

$$x_{14} + x_{15} \leq 100$$

Each supply constraint in this group is derived in the same way;

SUPPLY CONSTRAINTS

$x_{14} + x_{15} \leq 100$	(capacity at Paris, Texas)	(1)
$x_{24} + x_{25} \leq 200$	(capacity at Davenport, Iowa)	(2)
$x_{35} \leq 150$	(capacity at Springfield, Oregon)	(3)

2. Regional warehouse constraints specifying that the number of units shipped from each regional warehouse should be equal to the number of units received by each of those warehouses. This is because, as stated in the problem description, regional warehouses do not store machines. For example, for the regional warehouse located in Hungary, from the network in Figure 9.2:

Units shipped from Hungary = units shipped to Hungary

$$x_{46} + x_{47} = x_{14} + x_{24}$$

Similarly, for the regional warehouse in Hawaii:

Units shipped from Hawaii = units shipped to Hawaii

$$x_{56} + x_{57} = x_{15} + x_{25} + x_{35}$$

Putting all variables on the left-hand side of these two constraints, one has

REGIONAL-WAREHOUSE CONSTRAINTS

$x_{46} + x_{47} - x_{14} - x_{24}$	$= 0$ (balance at Hungary)	(4)
$x_{56} + x_{57} - x_{15} - x_{25} - x_{35} = 0$	(balance at Hawaii)	(5)

3. Field-warehouse constraints specifying that the number of units shipped from each field warehouse should be equal to the number of units received by each of those warehouses, just like with the regional warehouses. Following the same logic used to develop the regional-warehouse constraints and using information in Figure 9.2 leads to the following two constraints for the field warehouses in the Philippines and Fiji:

FIELD-WAREHOUSE CONSTRAINTS

$x_{68} + x_{69} + x_{6,10} - x_{46} - x_{56} = 0$	(balance at Philippines)	(6)
$x_{79} + x_{7,10} + x_{7,11} - x_{47} - x_{57} = 0$	(balance at Fiji)	(7)

4. Demand constraints specifying that each customer must receive its demand. For example, for South Korea, the network in Figure 9.2 indicates

Units shipped to South Korea = 80

By using the technique of decomposition and Figure 9.2,

Units shipped to South Korea = (units shipped from Philippines) +

(units shipped from Fiji)

$$= x_{69} + x_{79}$$

Thus, the demand constraint for South Korea is

$$x_{69} + x_{79} = 80$$

Each demand constraint in this group is derived in the same way:

DEMAND CONSTRAINTS

x_{68}	$= 120$	(demand in Japan)	(8)
$x_{69} + x_{79}$	$= 80$	(demand in South Korea)	(9)
$x_{6,10} + x_{7,10}$	$= 70$	(demand in New Zealand)	(10)
$x_{7,11}$	$= 110$	(demand in Australia)	(11)

The final set of constraints is the logical constraints. They specify that each variable is a nonnegative integer:

LOGICAL CONSTRAINTS

All variables ≥ 0 and integer   (12)

By putting together all the pieces, the following mathematical formulation of the distribution problem of MTI is obtained.

MATHEMATICAL FORMULATION OF THE DISTRIBUTION PROBLEM OF MTI

Minimize $2x_{14} + 4x_{15} + 3x_{24} + 4x_{25} + 5x_{35} +$

$8x_{46} + 6x_{47} + 7x_{56} + 4x_{57} +$

$7x_{68} + 6x_{69} + 8x_{6,10} + 7x_{79} + 5x_{7,10} + 6x_{7,11}$

Subject to

Transshipment
MTI_1.DAT

SUPPLY CONSTRAINTS

$x_{14} + x_{15} \leq 100$	(capacity at Paris, Texas)	(1)
$x_{24} + x_{25} \leq 200$	(capacity at Davenport, Iowa)	(2)
$x_{35} \leq 150$	(capacity at Springfield, Oregon)	(3)

REGIONAL-WAREHOUSE CONSTRAINTS

$x_{46} + x_{47} - x_{14} - x_{24} = 0$	(balance at Hungary)	(4)
$x_{56} + x_{57} - x_{15} - x_{25} - x_{35} = 0$	(balance at Hawaii)	(5)

FIELD-WAREHOUSE CONSTRAINTS

$$x_{68} + x_{69} + x_{6,10} - x_{46} - x_{56} = 0 \quad \text{(balance at Philippines)} \tag{6}$$
$$x_{79} + x_{7,10} + x_{7,11} - x_{47} - x_{57} = 0 \quad \text{(balance at Fiji)} \tag{7}$$

DEMAND CONSTRAINTS

$$
\begin{aligned}
x_{68} &= 120 && \text{(demand in Japan)} & (8)\\
x_{69} + x_{79} &= 80 && \text{(demand in South Korea)} & (9)\\
x_{6,10} + x_{7,10} &= 70 && \text{(demand in New Zealand)} & (10)\\
x_{7,11} &= 110 && \text{(demand in Australia)} & (11)
\end{aligned}
$$

LOGICAL CONSTRAINTS

$$\text{All variables} \geq 0 \text{ and integer} \tag{12}$$

As you learned in Chapters 1 and 2, once a problem has been formulated mathematically, the next step is to select an appropriate solution procedure, as discussed in Section 9.1.4.

9.1.4   Solving Distribution Network Problems

Recall that after formulating a problem mathematically, the next step is to classify the resulting model, as described in Section 2.3, so as to select an appropriate solution procedure. For the distribution model of MTI presented in Section 9.1.3, that classification is all linear constraints, linear objective function, and integer variables.

Because of the integer variables, a network distribution problem is *not* a linear program. Researchers in the field of management science have recognized that many problems require some (or all) of the variables to be integers. They have developed solution procedures to solve such problems, collectively called *integer programming algorithms*, some of which are described in Chapter 8. Although these procedures do in fact yield optimal solutions, even a moderate number of variables or constraints in an integer programming problem can demand too much computational time, sometimes up to 1000 times as much computer time as a linear programming problem of similar size.

➡ ### KEY FEATURES

Because of the special structure of the constraints that arise in a distribution network problem, researchers have been able to show that by dropping the integer requirement on all variables and solving the resulting linear program, all variables in the optimal solution will *automatically* have integer values.

You can verify this by solving the problem of MTI using your linear programming package. Consequently, in the mathematical model of the distribution problem, the constraint that "all variables are integer" need not be included when solving the problem. This in turn means that the distribution network model can be solved as a linear program by the simplex algorithm discussed in Chapters 4 to 6, for example, rather than by an integer programming algorithm.

Even as a linear program, practical distribution network problems have large numbers of variables and constraints. Moreover, for most companies, the distribution network problem is an *operational* problem that needs to be solved periodically—each time with new supply, demand, or cost figures—on a weekly, monthly, or quarterly basis. Consider a moderate-sized problem having 10 plants, 5 regional warehouses, 20 field warehouses, and 500 customers. Assuming goods can be shipped from each plant to each regional warehouse, from each regional to each field warehouse, and from each field warehouse to each customer, the resulting network model has $(10 * 5) + (5 * 20) + (20 * 500) = 10,150$ variables and $10 + 5 + 20 + 500 = 535$ constraints. Solving such large linear programs, if possible at all on the software available to you, may require so much computer time as to be impractical on an operational basis.

Because of the need to solve these large network problems, researchers have developed specialized algorithms that are much more efficient than the simplex algorithm. In particular, they have identified three *classes* of distribution network problems: *transportation, transshipment*, and *assignment problems*. Each of these classes has its own special structure and its own solution procedure that takes advantage of that structure, as described in Sections 9.2, 9.7, and 9.8. (The problem of MTI is a transshipment problem whose computer solution is presented in Section 9.7.) Not all network problems can be solved efficiently. In Appendix 9C you will see one example of a network problem—the traveling salesperson problem—for which there is no known efficient algorithm.

■ 9.2 THE TRANSPORTATION PROBLEM

In this section, you will learn about one specific class of distribution problem common to many companies: how to ship finished goods in the least-cost manner, directly from the plants to the retail outlets, without intermediate warehouses. Such a distribution problem is called a *transportation problem*. The problem of Cosmic Computer Company (CCC) presented in Section 2.2 is an example of the transportation problem. What follows is a restatement of that problem.

EXAMPLE 9.2 THE TRANSPORTATION PROBLEM OF CCC CCC has three microcomputer assembly plants. The one located in San Francisco has a monthly production capacity of 1700 units, the one located in Los Angeles 2000 units, and the one in Phoenix 1700 units. The microcomputers are sold through four retail stores. The one located in San Diego has placed an order of 1700 units for the coming month, the one in Barstow 1000 units, the one in Tucson 1500 units, and the one in Dallas 1200 units. The cost of shipping one microcomputer from each assembly plant to each of the different retail stores is given in Table 9.4. As a Distribution Manager, you want to formulate a mathematical model for finding the least-cost shipping schedule. ■

The network diagram for CCC is illustrated in Figure 9.3. The 12 variables indicating how many computers to ship from each plant to each retail outlet are identified in Table 9.5. The associated mathematical model developed in Section 2.2, Chapter 2, is presented in what follows:

TABLE 9.4 *Shipping Costs ($/Computer) from Plants to Stores*

	STORES			
PLANTS	SAN DIEGO	BARSTOW	TUCSON	DALLAS
San Francisco	5	3	2	6
Los Angeles	4	7	8	10
Phoenix	6	5	3	8

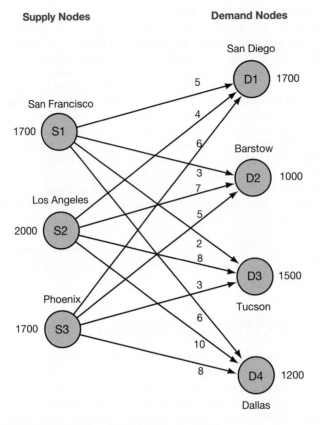

FIGURE 9.3 The Distribution Network of CCC.

TABLE 9.5 *Decision Variables for the Transportation Problem of CCC*

	STORES			
PLANTS	SAN DIEGO	BARSTOW	TUCSON	DALLAS
San Francisco	x_{SS}	x_{SB}	x_{ST}	x_{SD}
Los Angeles	x_{LS}	x_{LB}	x_{LT}	x_{LD}
Phoenix	x_{PS}	x_{PB}	x_{PT}	x_{PD}

MATHEMATICAL FORMULATION OF THE TRANSPORTATION PROBLEM OF CCC

Transportation
CCCTR.DAT

Minimize
$$(5x_{SS} + 3x_{SB} + 2x_{ST} + 6x_{SD}) +$$
$$(4x_{LS} + 7x_{LB} + 8x_{LT} + 10x_{LD}) +$$
$$(6x_{PS} + 5x_{PB} + 3x_{PT} + 8x_{PD})$$

Subject to

CAPACITY CONSTRAINTS

$$x_{SS} + x_{SB} + x_{ST} + x_{SD} \le 1700 \quad \text{(San Francisco)}$$
$$x_{LS} + x_{LB} + x_{LT} + x_{LD} \le 2000 \quad \text{(Los Angeles)}$$
$$x_{PS} + x_{PB} + x_{PT} + x_{PD} \le 1700 \quad \text{(Phoenix)}$$

DEMAND CONSTRAINTS

$$x_{SS} + x_{LS} + x_{PS} = 1700 \quad \text{(San Diego)}$$
$$x_{SB} + x_{LB} + x_{PB} = 1000 \quad \text{(Barstow)}$$
$$x_{ST} + x_{LT} + x_{PT} = 1500 \quad \text{(Tucson)}$$
$$x_{SD} + x_{LD} + x_{PD} = 1200 \quad \text{(Dallas)}$$

LOGICAL CONSTRAINTS

$$x_{SS}, \ x_{SB}, \ x_{ST}, \ x_{SD}, \ x_{LS}, \ x_{LB}, \ x_{LT}, \ x_{LD},$$
$$x_{PS}, \ x_{PB}, \ x_{PT}, \ x_{PD} \geq 0 \text{ and integer}$$

As you learned in Section 9.1.4, one approach to solving this problem is to drop the integer requirement in the previous logical constraints. You can verify with your computer package that by solving the resulting linear program, the optimal solution automatically satisfies the integer requirements. However, a more efficient method for obtaining an optimal solution is available. The conceptual ideas behind that algorithm are presented in the next section.

■ 9.3 THE TRANSPORTATION ALGORITHM: A CONCEPTUAL APPROACH

In Section 9.2, you saw an example of a transportation problem formulated as a mathematical model based on the network. In this section, you will learn the conceptual ideas of an efficient specialized algorithm for solving *all* transportation problems. This algorithm requires that *the total amount of supplies be precisely equal to the total amount of demand.* Such a problem is called a **balanced transportation problem** because the supplies and demands are in balance. Example 9.2, the CCC transportation problem, is an example of a balanced transportation problem because of the following:

Balanced transportation problem
A transportation problem in which the total supply is equal to the total demand.

$$\text{Total supply} = 1700 + 2000 + 1700$$
$$= 5400$$
$$\text{Total demand} = 1700 + 1000 + 1500 + 1200$$
$$= 5400$$

In most practical situations, the total supply is not equal to the total demand, which results in what is called an **unbalanced transportation problem.** In Section 9.3.1, you will learn how to convert unbalanced problems into equivalent balanced problems.

9.3.1 Converting a Transportation Problem from Unbalanced to Balanced

A transportation problem can be unbalanced in one of two ways. Either there is too much demand and not enough supply or there is too much supply and not enough demand.

EXCESS SUPPLY

Consider the transportation problem of Magazines, Inc., publisher of *News Monthly* magazine.

TABLE 9.6   *Shipping Costs ($/Magazine) for Magazines, Inc.*

	REGIONAL DISTRIBUTORS		
PRINT SHOPS	CHICAGO	SEATTLE	WASHINGTON, D.C.
Los Angeles	0.07	0.05	0.10
New York	0.03	0.11	0.04

EXAMPLE 9.3 THE TRANSPORTATION PROBLEM OF MAGAZINES, INC. Each month, 5000 copies of *News Monthly* are printed at each of two shops: one in Los Angeles and one in New York. From there, the magazines are shipped to three regional distributors. For this month, the distributor in Chicago has ordered 4000 copies, the one in Seattle 2000 copies, and the one in Washington, D.C., 2500 copies. The shipping cost per magazine from each print shop to each distributor is given in Table 9.6. As Distribution Manager, you are to determine the least-cost shipping plan. ∎

Dummy customer
An artificial demand node added to an unbalanced transportation problem; it is used to receive the excess supply of goods and thus lead to a balanced problem.

Dummy arc
An artificially created arc that connects a dummy node to another node in a transportation problem.

Transportation
MAG_1.DAT

Observe that the total supply of 10,000 magazines exceeds the total demand of 8500. To solve this problem by the transportation algorithm described later in this section, it is first necessary to convert this unbalanced problem into a balanced one. This is accomplished by introducing a new demand node—called a **dummy customer**—to receive the excess supply of 1500 magazines (10,000 − 8500). This new dummy customer node is connected by a **dummy arc** to each of the supply nodes, as illustrated in Figure 9.4.

The next question is: How much does it cost to ship a magazine from each supply node to this dummy customer? To answer this question, first consider what it means to ship 500 magazines, for example, from Los Angeles to this dummy customer. Of the 5000 magazines available at the print shop in Los Angeles, 4500 are shipped to the three existing customers, and thus the amount of 500 shipped to a dummy customer represents the surplus at Los Angeles.

Now you must determine the cost of this surplus. What does Magazines, Inc., do with its surplus? In cases where these surplus units are not produced, there is no shipping cost associated with each unit. However, in this case, the company donates excess copies to libraries, for which it receives a tax credit of $0.05 per copy in Los Angeles and $0.08 per copy in New York. These tax benefits translate to a "shipping" cost of − $0.05 per surplus magazine in Los Angeles and − $0.08 for each magazine in New York. The data pertaining to this new, balanced transportation problem are summarized in Table 9.7.

The solution to this balanced problem can be obtained now using the specialized transportation algorithm developed later in this section. The result is given in Section 9.4.

TABLE 9.7   *Data for the Balanced Transportation Problem of Magazines, Inc.*

PRINT SHOPS	SHIPPING COST ($/MAGAZINE) FOR REGIONAL DISTRIBUTORS (AND DUMMY CUSTOMER)				
	CHICAGO	SEATTLE	WASHINGTON, D.C.	DUMMY	SUPPLIES
Los Angeles	0.07	0.05	0.10	-0.05	5000
New York	0.03	0.11	0.04	-0.08	5000
Demands	4000	2000	2500	1500	

Supply Nodes

Demand Nodes

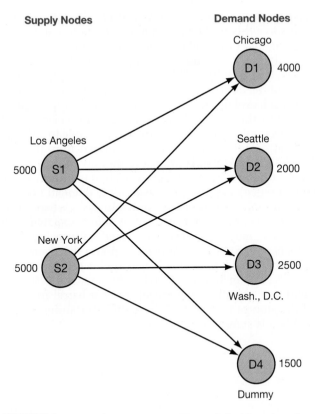

FIGURE 9.4 Balanced Transportation Network for Magazines, Inc.

EXCESS DEMAND

An unbalanced transportation problem might also arise when there is more demand than available supplies. Consider the problem of Rich Oil Company, which ships gasoline from its refineries to various storage tanks.

EXAMPLE 9.4 THE TRANSPORTATION PROBLEM OF RICH OIL COMPANY Rich Oil Company has a gasoline refinery located in New Orleans with a production capacity of 300,000 barrels per week and one in Newark with a capacity of 500,000 barrels per week. The gasoline from these refineries is shipped to four regional storage tanks. The tank in Washington, D.C., needs 200,000 barrels for the next week, the one in Tampa 100,000, the one in Atlanta 400,000, and the one in Cincinnati 300,000 barrels. The shipping cost per barrel from each refinery to the storage tanks is given in Table 9.8. As Distribution Manager, you are to determine the least-cost shipping plan. ■

TABLE 9.8 *Shipping Costs ($/Barrel) for Rich Oil Company*

	STORAGE TANKS			
REFINERIES	WASHINGTON, D.C.	TAMPA	ATLANTA	CINCINNATI
New Orleans	0.10	0.05	0.07	0.09
Newark	0.05	0.11	0.08	0.07

Dummy supply node
An artificial supply
node added to
an unbalanced
transportation
problem; it provides
the supply needed
to meet the excess
demand and thus leads
to a balanced problem.

Transportation
RICH_1.DAT

In this problem, the total demand of 1 million barrels exceeds the total supply of 800,000 barrels. Once again, to solve this problem by the transportation algorithm described later in this section, first convert this unbalanced problem into a balanced one. This is accomplished by introducing a new **dummy supply node** to "produce" the excess demand of 200,000 barrels of gasoline. This new dummy supply node is connected by a *dummy arc* to each of the demand nodes, as illustrated in Figure 9.5.

How much does it cost to ship a barrel of gasoline from the dummy supply node to each of the storage tanks? To answer this question, first understand precisely what it means to ship 50,000 barrels, for example, from the dummy supply node to Atlanta. Of the 400,000 barrels demanded at Atlanta, 350,000 will be shipped from the two refineries and the shortage of 50,000 barrels comes from the dummy supply node. Thus, the amount shipped along a dummy arc represents the shortage (that is, the number of units of demand that cannot be met) at the corresponding demand node.

Now, you can determine the cost of these "shortage" units. In cases where these shortages can be ignored without penalty, there is no cost (a cost of 0) associated with each shortage unit. In other cases, there may be a "cost" associated with each unit of demand that cannot be met. In the case of Rich Oil Company, suppose that each such shortage unit must be purchased from the spot market (a local supplier) at a per barrel cost of $21.00 in Washington, D.C., $19.00 in Tampa, $22.00 in Atlanta, and $20.00 in Cincinnati. These prices represent the "shipping" (shortage) cost per barrel from the dummy supply node to each of the storage tanks. The information pertaining to this now balanced transportation problem is summarized in Table 9.9.

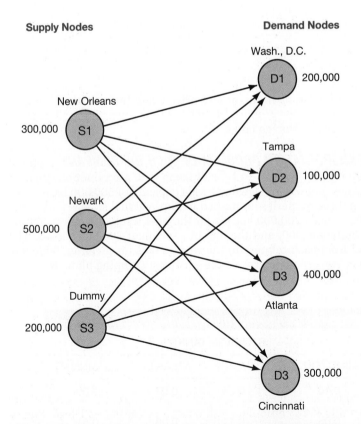

FIGURE 9.5 Balanced Transportation Network for Rich Oil Company.

TABLE 9.9 *Data for the Balanced Transportation Problem of Rich Oil Company*

	SHIPPING COST ($/BARREL) FOR STORAGE TANKS				
REFINERIES	WASHINGTON, D.C.	TAMPA	ATLANTA	CINCINNATI	SUPPLIES
New Orleans	0.10	0.05	0.07	0.09	300,000
Newark	0.05	0.11	0.08	0.07	500,000
Dummy	21.00	19.00	22.00	20.00	200,000
Demands	200,000	100,000	400,000	300,000	

KEY FEATURES

Examples 9.3 and 9.4 illustrate the following key features:

✔ In case there is excess supply, use a dummy customer to absorb this excess supply and to balance the problem.
✔ In case there is excess demand, use a dummy supply to provide this excess demand and to balance the problem.

Now that you know how to convert an unbalanced transportation problem into an equivalent balanced one, it is time to learn how these problems are solved efficiently with a specialized algorithm.

9.3.2 The Transportation Tableau

For balanced transportation problems, all of the relevant data can be represented in a rectangular table called a **transportation tableau**. Recall the example of Cosmic Computer Company presented in Example 9.3 in Section 9.1. The data for that balanced problem is given in the transportation tableau of Figure 9.6. In this tableau, each row corresponds to one of the supply nodes and each column corresponds to a demand node. Each square at the intersection of a row and a column is called a **cell,** and the number in the upper-left corner of each cell is the cost for shipping one unit from the associated supply node to the demand node. For example, the number 8 in the cell in row 2 and column 3 of the tableau in Figure 9.6 is the cost for shipping one computer from supply node 2 (Los Angeles) to demand node 3 (Tucson). The value to the right of each row represents the number of units at that supply node and the value under each column represents the number of units demanded at that node.

Recall that the objective of the transportation problem is to determine the optimal shipping plan—that is, the number of units to ship from each supply node to each demand node to minimize the total transportation cost. One possible shipping plan for CCC is given in Figure 9.7, where the circled number in the middle of each cell represents the number of computers to ship from the associated supply node to the demand node. For example, the value of 1500 in row 1 and column 1 means that the plant in San Francisco ships 1500 computers to the retail outlet in San Diego. Empty cells mean that no units are shipped between these points. Note that each number is

Transportation tableau
A rectangular table containing all of the relevant data for a balanced transportation problem.

Cell
A square at the intersection of a row and a column in a transportation tableau.

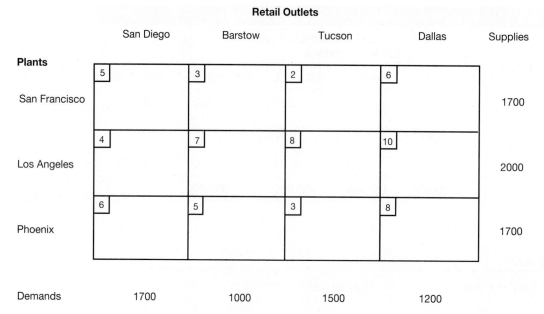

FIGURE 9.6 The Transportation Tableau for CCC.

nonnegative. The total cost of $34,600 for this shipping plan appears in the bottom-right corner of the transportation tableau, as seen in Figure 9.7.

Because the problem is balanced, the total number of units shipped from each supply node must equal the available supplies at that node, and the total number of units received by each demand node must equal the demand at that node.

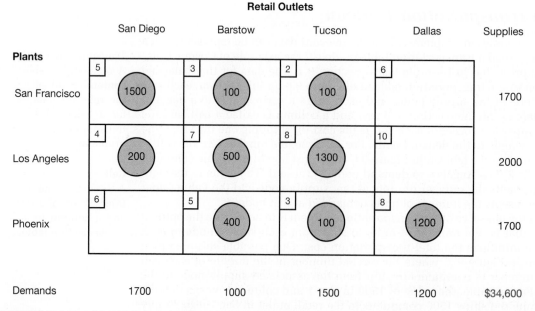

FIGURE 9.7 A Feasible Shipping Plan for CCC.

➡ **KEY FEATURES**

A **feasible shipping plan** consists of numbers in each cell of the transportation tableau such that the following hold:

✔ Each number is a nonnegative integer.
✔ The numbers in each row add up to the supply figure at the right of that row.
✔ The numbers in each column add up to the demand figure at the bottom of that column.

Feasible shipping plan
A set of nonnegative integer values for the cells in a transportation tableau that indicate the number of units to ship along the corresponding arc and that collectively satisfy the supply and demand constraints at each node.

9.3.3 The Properties of an Optimal Shipping Plan

Unfortunately, the number of feasible shipping plans for CCC, such as the one in Figure 9.7, is very large. The goal of this section is to identify properties of an optimal shipping plan that reduce the number of feasible shipping plans that need to be examined.

To limit the number of solutions that need to be considered, observe that the shipping plan in Figure 9.7 cannot be an optimal one for CCC. The reason is that this shipping plan contains a *cycle*, as indicated in Figure 9.8(a). A cycle in the transportation tableau is a path that starts with one given nonempty cell, moves along that row to another nonempty cell (possibly skipping some empty or nonempty cells), moves up or down in that column to another nonempty cell (possibly skipping some empty and nonempty cells), and, by alternating between nonempty cells in rows and columns, returns to the starting cell. Only the nonempty cells where you change direction are included in the cycle. For example, the cycle in Figure 9.8(b) consists of the six cells in (row 1, column 1), (row 1, column 3), (row 3, column 3), (row 3, column 2), (row 2, column 2), and (row 2, column 1).

When a shipping plan contains a cycle, it is always possible to produce a new plan *having no cycle* whose total shipping cost is less than or equal to the current one. For example, by using the cycle in Figure 9.8(b), a better shipping plan is obtained as follows.

1. Evaluate the following two alternatives.

   a. Starting in any cell in the cycle (for example, in row 1 and column 1), calculate the effect on the shipping cost of alternately adding and subtracting 1 unit to the amount shipped in each cell in the cycle in Figure 9.8(b). The result is illustrated in Figure 9.9(a). These changes yield a new feasible shipping plan because each increase in the number of units shipped somewhere is offset by a corresponding decrease in the same row and column. Each cell containing a +1 increases the total cost by the associated unit shipping cost in that cell, and each cell containing a −1 decreases the total cost by the unit shipping cost. This new shipping plan costs $4 *more* than the original one because

$$\text{Change in the shipping cost} = 5 - 2 + 3 - 5 + 7 - 4$$
$$= 4$$

   b. Starting in any cell in the cycle (for example, in row 1 and column 1), calculate the effect on the shipping cost of alternately subtracting and adding 1 unit to the amount shipped in each cell in the cycle in Figure 9.8(b). The result is illustrated in Figure 9.9(b). These changes yield a new feasible shipping plan because each decrease in the number of units shipped somewhere is offset by

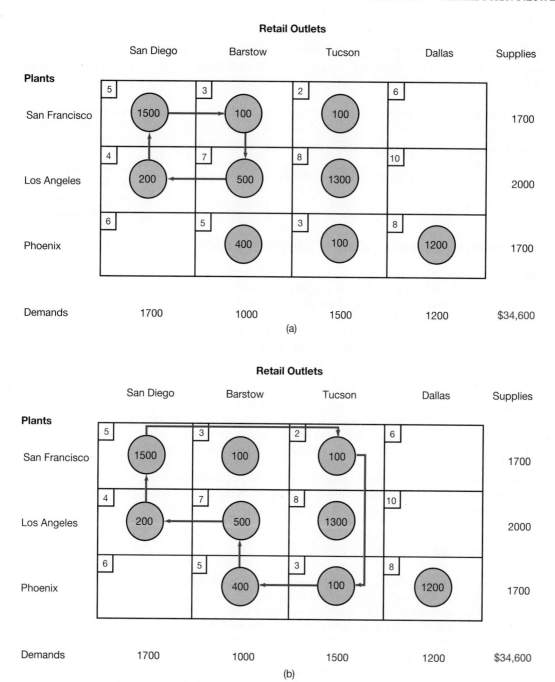

FIGURE 9.8 Illustration of Cycles in the Shipping Plan of Figure 9.7.

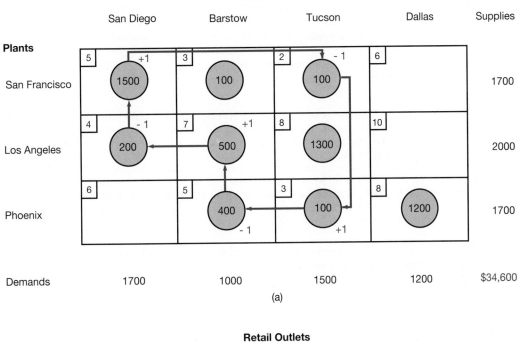

(a)

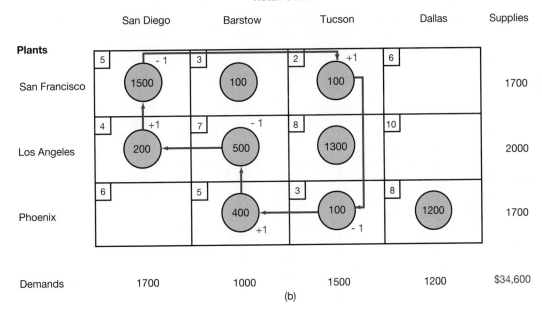

(b)

FIGURE 9.9 Using a Cycle to Find a Better Shipping Plan.

a corresponding increase in the same row and column. Each cell containing a -1 decreases the total cost by the associated unit shipping cost in that cell, and each cell containing a $+1$ increases the total cost by the unit shipping cost. This new shipping plan costs \$4 *less* than the original one because

$$\text{Change in the shipping cost} = -5 + 2 - 3 + 5 - 7 + 4$$
$$= -4$$

2. Identify whichever of step 1(a) or 1(b) results in a *decrease* in the total shipping cost. In this case, step 1(b) results in a decrease of \$4 in the total shipping cost. In fact, by alternately subtracting and adding as much as 100 units (the minimum shipment in those cells in the cycle with a -1) to each cell in the cycle, all the shipping amounts remain nonnegative. Doing so decreases the total shipping cost by $\$4 \times 100 = \$400$, and makes the cell in row 3 and column 3 empty. You can easily verify that this new shipping plan given in Figure 9.10 is feasible and costs \$400 less than that of the previous shipping plan. Also, this plan has one less nonempty cell, and the cycle used to obtain this plan has been eliminated.

In conclusion, whenever a shipping plan has a cycle, you can apply the foregoing process repeatedly to eliminate each cycle and eventually create a new shipping plan of the same or lower cost having no cycle at all.

KEY FEATURES

To find an optimal shipping plan, you need consider only those plans that contain no cycles. Furthermore, for a problem having m supply nodes and n demand nodes, researchers have determined that each such shipping plan should contain at most $m + n - 1$ nonempty cells.

Retail Outlets

Plants	San Diego	Barstow	Tucson	Dallas	Supplies
San Francisco	5 / 1400	3 / 100	2 / 200	6	1700
Los Angeles	4 / 300	7 / 400	8 / 1300	10	2000
Phoenix	6	5 / 500	3 / Now Empty Cell	8 / 1200	1700
Demands	1700	1000	1500	1200	\$34,200 New Shipping Cost

FIGURE 9.10 An Improved Shipping Plan for CCC.

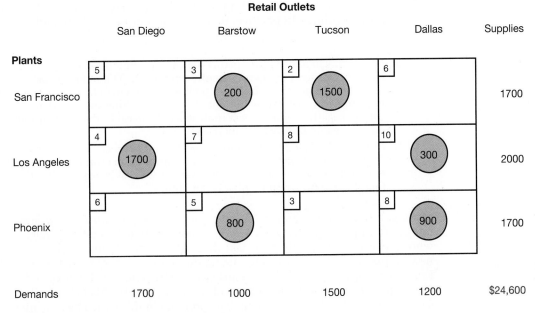

FIGURE 9.11 A Shipping Plan for CCC That Contains No Cycles.

For example, for CCC, the number of rows is $m = 3$, corresponding to the three plants, and the number of columns is $n = 4$, corresponding to the four retail outlets. Thus, a shipping plan for CCC with no cycles will have at most $m + n - 1 = 3 + 4 - 1 = 6$ nonempty cells. An example of such a shipping plan is illustrated in Figure 9.11. The conceptual idea of the transportation algorithm is presented in Section 9.3.4.

9.3.4 A Finite-Improvement Algorithm for the Transportation Problem: A Conceptual Approach

Built on the properties of an optimal solution discussed in Section 9.3.3, the following is a conceptual *finite-improvement algorithm* for obtaining an optimal shipping plan to a transportation problem in which there are m supply points and n demand points.

CONCEPTUAL STEPS OF THE STEPPING STONE ALGORITHM

Step 0. *Initialization*: Find an initial feasible integer shipping plan that has $m + n - 1$ nonempty cells and no cycles, and go to Step 1. (There are many different ways to find this initial shipping plan. The mathematical details of one method are given in Section 9.6.)

Step 1. *Test for Optimality*: Check if the current shipping plan has the least total cost. If so, stop with an optimal shipping plan; otherwise, go to Step 2. To understand how this test for optimality is performed, recall that many cells of the transportation tableau are empty. Each indicates that in the current plan 0 units are shipped between the corresponding supply and demand points. The test for optimality consists of asking the following question: Is it possible to create a new shipping plan by shipping one unit in a currently empty cell and incur less total cost than the current shipping plan? If the answer is no, then the current plan is optimal. In practice, this test is accomplished in the following two steps:

    a. *Computing Reduced Costs*: In this step, a single number called the *reduced cost*, is computed for each currently empty cell. The reduced cost represents the amount by which the total shipping cost changes if one unit is shipped in that cell while not shipping anything in any other empty cell. A negative reduced cost indicates a decrease in the total cost and a positive value indicates an increase.

    b. *Checking Reduced Costs*: In the event that all reduced costs computed in Step 1(a) are nonnegative, the current shipping plan is optimal; otherwise, there is at least one empty cell whose reduced cost is negative, indicating that the current shipping plan is not optimal.

Step 2. *Moving*: If the current shipping plan is not optimal, construct a new feasible integer shipping plan that has $m + n - 1$ nonempty cells and no cycles and whose total cost is strictly less than the current one. Return to Step 1. The new shipping plan is constructed using the information obtained in Step 1. From Step 1(b), it is possible to identify a currently empty cell whose reduced cost is the *most* negative. Because each unit shipped in this cell results in a savings, it is natural to ship as much as possible in this cell. The new plan is therefore obtained by shipping the *maximum* number of units possible in this cell (and changing the amounts shipped in some of the nonempty cells to satisfy the supply-and-demand constraints). Doing so results in a new shipping plan having $m + n - 1$ nonempty cells with no cycles. The mathematical details are given in Section 9.5.

Stepping stone algorithm
A finite-improvement algorithm for solving balanced transportation problems that is a specialized version of the simplex algorithm.

    The algorithm described in this section is called the **stepping stone algorithm**. You may recognize a similarity between these steps and those of the simplex algorithm presented in Chapter 5. In fact, the stepping stone algorithm is a specialization of the simplex algorithm for transportation problems.

9.3.5 *Comparing the Stepping Stone and Simplex Algorithms*

In Chapter 5, you learned that the simplex algorithm moves from one basic feasible solution to another. Correspondingly, the stepping stone algorithm moves from one shipping plan having $m + n - 1$ nonempty cells and no cycles to another. Researchers have proved that each such shipping plan corresponds to a basic feasible solution of the linear programming formulation of the transportation problem presented in Section 9.2. In fact, each nonempty cell in the transportation tableau corresponds to a basic variable, and each empty cell is a nonbasic variable.

    In Chapter 5, you learned that testing a basic feasible solution requires computing a reduced cost for each nonbasic variable. Correspondingly, testing a shipping plan also involves computing a reduced cost for each empty cell (that is, each nonbasic variable). In either case, the values of these reduced costs indicate the change in the objective function per unit of increase in the nonbasic variable (empty cell).

    In the simplex algorithm, when the current basic feasible solution is not optimal, you learned to move to a new basic feasible solution with a strictly better objective function value. This movement is accomplished by increasing, as much as possible, the value of the nonbasic variable that leads to the greatest rate of improvement in the objective function, as indicated by the reduced cost. Correspondingly, when a shipping plan is not optimal, you move to a new one with a strictly better objective function value (see Step 2 in Section 9.3.4). This movement is accomplished by shipping as is the supply number. The supply at San Francisco is now depleted and so this row is crossed off.

Repeating this process $m + n - 1$ times results in an integer feasible shipping plan having no cycles. For the example of CCC, these 6 $(3 + 4 - 1)$ steps are illustrated in Figures 9.18 to 9.23.

In summary, an initial shipping plan using the matrix minimum method is obtained as follows.

KEY FEATURES

The Matrix Minimum Method for Finding an Initial Shipping Plan

✔ Identify an uncrossed cell whose cost is the smallest. (In case of ties, choose any such cell.)

✔ For the identified cell, determine the smaller of the remaining supply in that row and the remaining demand in that column.

✔   **i.** Put the amount just determined in the identified cell.

    ii. Reduce the remaining supply in the row by the amount shipped in this cell.

    iii. Reduce the remaining demand in the column by the amount shipped in this cell.

    iv. Cross out the row or column whose remaining supply or demand has now been reduced to 0.

Repeating these steps exactly $m + n - 1$ times results in an integer feasible shipping plan having no cycles.

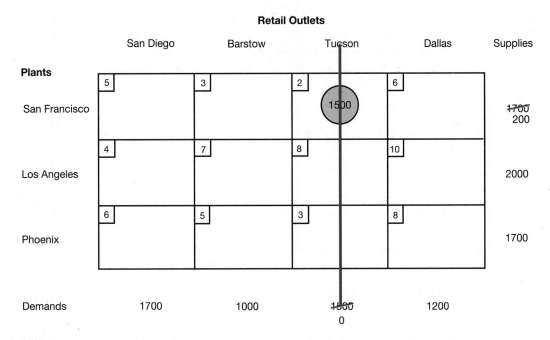

FIGURE 9.18 Iteration 1 of the Matrix Minimum Method for the Transportation Problem of CCC.

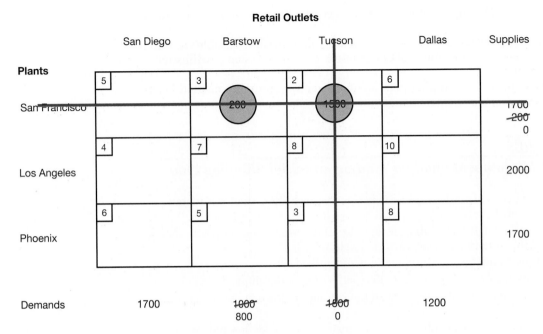

FIGURE 9.19 Iteration 2 of the Matrix Minimum Method for the Transportation Problem of CCC.

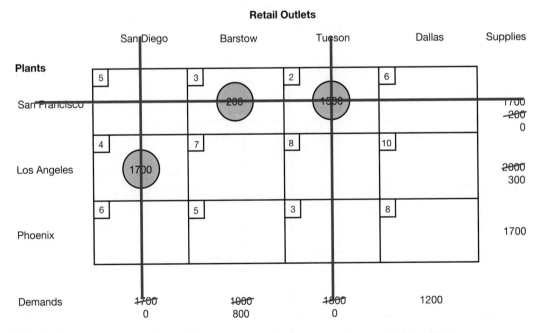

FIGURE 9.20 Iteration 3 of the Matrix Minimum Method for the Transportation Problem of CCC.

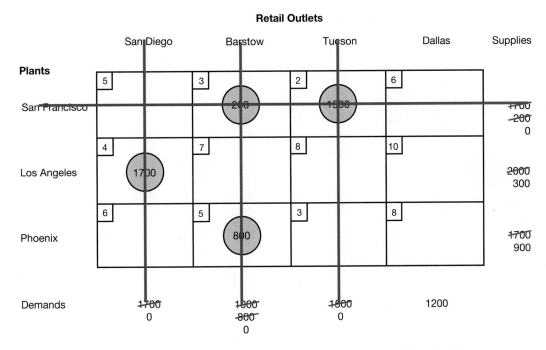

FIGURE 9.21 Iteration 4 of the Matrix Minimum Method for the Transportation Problem of CCC.

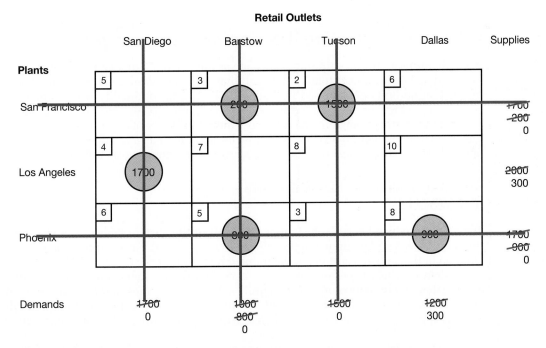

FIGURE 9.22 Iteration 5 of the Matrix Minimum Method for the Transportation Problem of CCC.

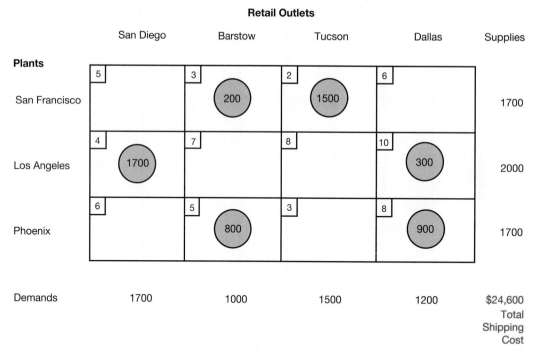

FIGURE 9.23 The Initial Shipping Plan Obtained by the Matrix Minimum Method for the New Line Transportation Problem of CCC.

9.5.2 Step 1: Testing A Shipping Plan for Optimality

After obtaining an initial shipping plan, such as the one in Figure 9.23, you next determine if it is the one of least total cost. Recall that each empty cell in the current tableau means that no units are shipped in that cell. The test for optimality is performed by computing a single number, called the *reduced cost*, for *each* empty cell. The reduced cost represents the change in the total cost that would be obtained by shipping one unit in that empty cell. If a reduced cost is negative, the current shipping plan is not optimal. The mathematical details for computing the reduced costs follow.

STEP 1(A): COMPUTING REDUCED COSTS USING CYCLES

To compute reduced costs, select any empty cell in the current tableau (for example, the cell in row 1 and column 1 of the tableau in Figure 9.23). Now, suppose one unit is shipped in that cell at a cost of $5, the number boxed off in the upper left-hand corner. A problem now arises because you have exceeded the available supply in that row and the demand in that column by one unit each. To restore these supply-and-demand constraints, you must alter the current shipping plan to accommodate the new unit being shipped. *This must be accomplished without using any of the remaining empty cells.*

   Consider how to restore the supply constraint corresponding to row 1 in Figure 9.23. Because one additional unit is being shipped in the cell in row 1 and column 1, one *less* unit must be shipped in some other cell in row 1. You could choose to reduce the amount shipped in column 2 or column 3 in row 1. For example, suppose the amount shipped in column 3 is reduced to 1499. Making this change means that the demand in column 3 is not satisfied by one unit. The other cells in column 3 are empty, so there is no way to supply the additional unit of demand in that column.

Therefore, altering the amount shipped in column 3 of row 1 is not a feasible course of action.

To restore the supply constraint in row 1, consider instead reducing the amount shipped in column 2 by one unit to 199. Making this change means that the demand in column 2 is not satisfied by one unit. That unit of demand can be restored by shipping one *additional* unit in row 3 and column 2. Of course, this means that the supply in row 3 will be exceeded by one unit. The only possible place to reduce this supply is in column 4 of row 3.

The process of keeping supply and demand in balance continues until the column of the starting cell is finally balanced. The sequence of cells in which shipping amounts must change when one unit is shipped in the empty cell from San Francisco to San Diego (row 1 and column 1) is shown in Figure 9.24. This collection of cells forms a *cycle*. The +1 or −1 in each cell of the cycle indicates whether one unit more or less is shipped in that cell to maintain the balance of supply and demand.

With supply and demand now balanced, it is possible to compute the change in the total shipping costs—that is, the reduced cost for the cell in row 1 and column 1. For each cell in the cycle requiring an additional shipment of one unit (indicated by +1 above the current shipping amount), an additional cost equal to the unit shipping cost in that cell is incurred. Similarly, for each cell requiring a decreased shipment of one unit (indicated by a −1 located above the current shipping amount), there is a savings equal to the unit shipping cost in that cell. Adding and subtracting the additional costs and savings in the cells in the cycle yields the net change in the total shipping costs if one unit is shipped in the selected empty cell. For the cell in row 1 and column 1, this net change is

$$\text{Reduced cost} = (5) - (3) + (5) - (8) + (10) - (4)$$

$$= +5$$

This reduced cost of +5 indicates that for each unit shipped in the empty cell in row 1 and column 1, the total shipping cost increases by $5. Hence, it is not profitable for CCC to use this cell to create a better shipping plan.

Now it is necessary to compute a reduced cost for *each* empty cell. Doing so requires finding the appropriate cycle each time. To a certain extent, this is a trial-and-error process, but there is always *one and only one* such cycle. To find this unique cycle, think of each row and column of the tableau as a street and each nonempty cell as a traffic light. Given the starting cell whose reduced cost is being computed, start "driving" along the row and select a traffic light at which to turn. "Driving" in that column, select another traffic light at which to turn, and so on, with the ultimate objective of returning to the starting cell. (The same cycle is obtained if you start in the empty cell and proceed along the column first.)

Having found the desired cycle, begin by putting a +1 in the starting empty cell and alternately putting a −1 and +1 in each cell in the cycle where a turn occurs. The reduced cost of the starting cell is computed by adding and subtracting the per-unit costs of the cells in the cycle, as indicated by the +1 and −1 numbers. This process is illustrated in Figures 9.25 to 9.29 for each of the remaining five empty cells and the results are summarized in the empty cells in Figure 9.30.

You have learned to compute the reduced cost of each empty cell by finding an appropriate cycle of cells in the tableau. Another method for computing these reduced costs that is computationally faster but less intuitive is the *MODI method*, described in Appendix 9A at the end of the chapter.

STEP 1(B): CHECKING REDUCED COSTS

A reduced cost has been computed and written in each nonempty cell in the tableau of Figure 9.30. The test for optimality is performed by seeing if *all* reduced costs are

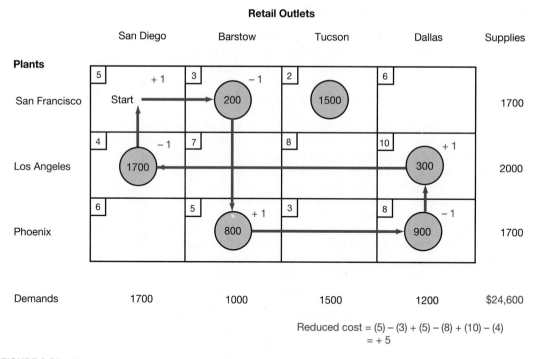

Reduced cost = (5) − (3) + (5) − (8) + (10) − (4)
          = + 5

FIGURE 9.24 The Cycle for Finding the Reduced Cost of the Cell in Row 1 and Column 1.

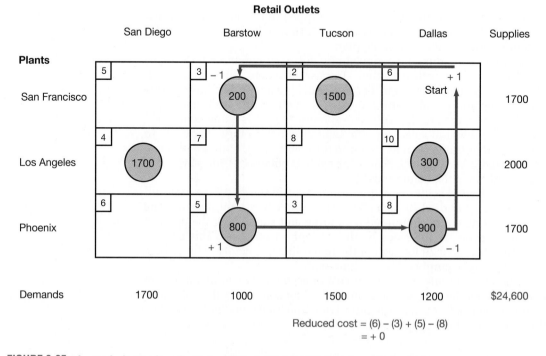

Reduced cost = (6) − (3) + (5) − (8)
          = + 0

FIGURE 9.25 The Cycle for Finding the Reduced Cost of the Cell in Row 1 and Column 4.

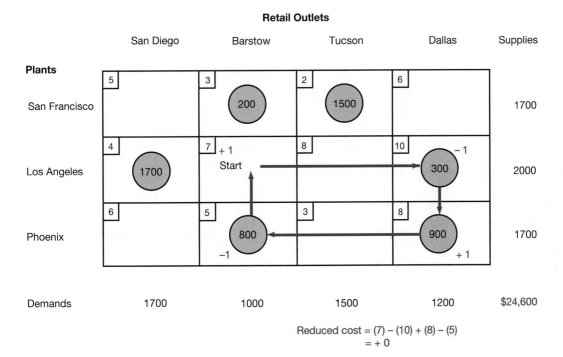

FIGURE 9.26 The Cycle for Finding the Reduced Cost of the Cell in Row 2 and Column 2.

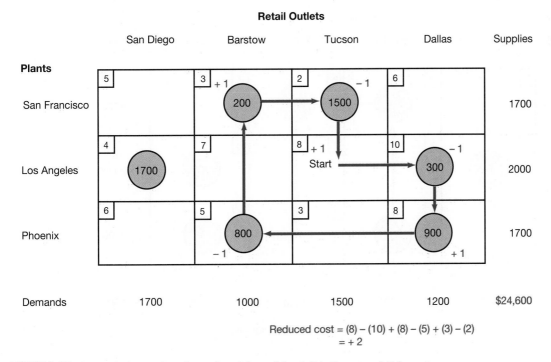

FIGURE 9.27 The Cycle for Finding the Reduced Cost of the Cell in Row 2 and Column 3.

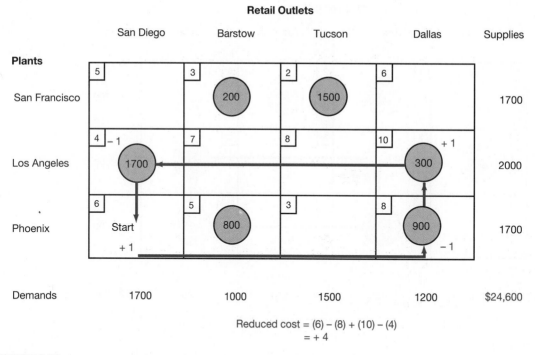

FIGURE 9.28 The Cycle for Finding the Reduced Cost of the Cell in Row 3 and Column 1.

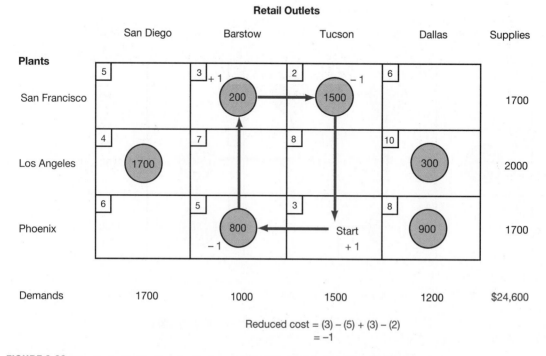

FIGURE 9.29 The Cycle for Finding the Reduced Cost of the Cell in Row 3 and Column 3.

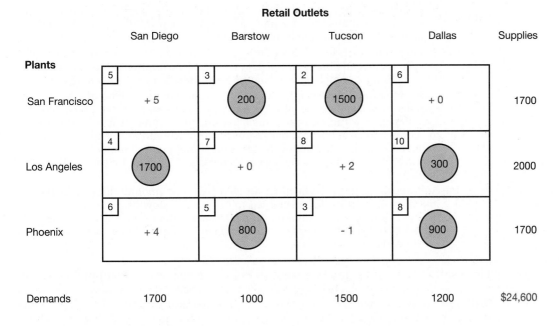

FIGURE 9.30 The Reduced Costs of the empty Cells for the Shipping Plan in Figure 9.23.

nonnegative. If so, the current shipping plan is optimal; otherwise, it is not. The reduced cost of -1 in row 3 and column 3 of the tableau in Figure 9.30 indicates that the current shipping plan is not optimal.

9.5.3 Step 2: Moving to an Improved Shipping Plan

Having determined in Step 1(b) that the current shipping plan is not optimal, you can now construct a new feasible integer plan whose total shipping cost is less than that of the current one. The information obtained in Step 1(b) enables you to do so, as follows:

a. Choose the empty cell whose reduced cost is most negative (in this case, the cell in row 3 and column 3 in Figure 9.30).

b. Determine the maximum number of units that can be shipped in the cell identified in (a), recalling that each unit shipped in that cell reduces the total shipping costs by the value of the reduced cost.

To accomplish (b), look again at the cycle obtained in Step 1(a) when computing the reduced cost of the chosen cell (see Figure 9.29). Recall that when one unit is shipped in this chosen cell, it is necessary to change the amounts shipped in all other cells in the cycle. The amount shipped in each such cell is either increased or decreased by one unit to maintain the supply-and-demand constraints. Correspondingly, if *two* units are shipped in the chosen cell instead of one unit, the amount shipped in each cell in the cycle must be increased or decreased by *two* units in order to maintain the supply-and-demand constraints. So what prevents you from shipping an arbitrarily large number of units in the chosen cell?

The answer is that a change in one of the other cells in the cycle might result in shipping a *negative* number of units in that cell, which cannot be permitted. To determine the maximum number of units that can be shipped in the chosen cell:

i. Locate all cells in the cycle where a *decrease* in the number of units shipped is necessary to maintain the supply-and-demand constraints. This would be the cells in row 1, column 3 and in row 3, column 2 in Figure 9.29.

ii. Among all the cells identified in step (i), find the one where the minimum number of units is currently being shipped. In this case, the minimum is 800 units in row 3 and column 2, which is less than the 1500 units in row 1 and column 3.

iii. Ship the amount identified in step (ii) in the chosen cell and modify the amounts shipped in each cell of the cycle accordingly. In this example, shipping 800 units from Phoenix to Tucson results in decreasing the shipments from San Francisco to Tucson and from Phoenix to Barstow by 800 units and increasing the shipment from San Francisco to Barstow by 800 units. These new shipments are shown in Figure 9.31 and indicate a savings in total costs of $800, $1 for each unit shipped in the new cell.

iv. As a result of the modifications in step (iii), the amount shipped in the cell identified in step (ii) has decreased to 0. This cell now becomes an empty cell. (In the event that the amount shipped in more than one cell in the cycle decreases to 0, *degeneracy* has occurred and requires special handling, as described in Appendix 9B.)

The result of performing previous steps (i) to (iv) is a new feasible shipping plan with $m + n - 1$ nonempty cells having no cycles and whose total shipping cost is less than that of the previous one. Compare the total shipping cost of $24,600 for the original shipping plan in Figure 9.30 with that of $23,800 for the new plan in Figure 9.31.

Steps 1 and 2 of the stepping stone algorithm can now be repeated, starting with the latest shipping plan, until a shipping plan is obtained in which *all* reduced costs of the empty cells are nonnegative. The results of doing so for Example 9.2 are illustrated in Figures 9.32 to 9.35. You can see that the solution in Figure 9.35 is an optimal shipping plan for CCC, with a total cost of $23,100.

It is interesting to observe that for this optimal solution there are two empty cells with reduced costs of 0. This indicates that by selecting one of these cells and using Step 2 of the algorithm, a new shipping plan with the same cost can be obtained—that is, there are alternative optimal solutions.

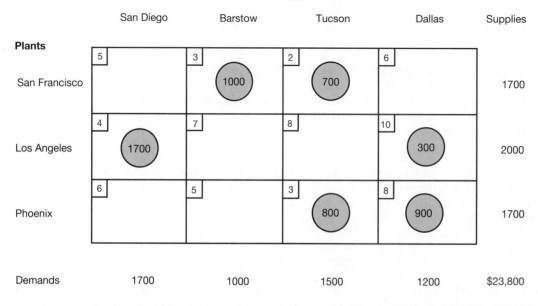

FIGURE 9.31 The New Shipping Plan for CCC.

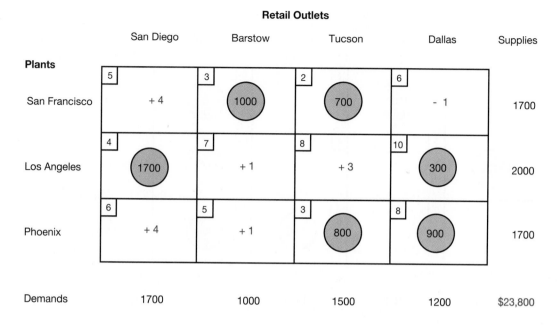

FIGURE 9.32 Step 1: Computing Reduced Costs and Testing for Optimality.

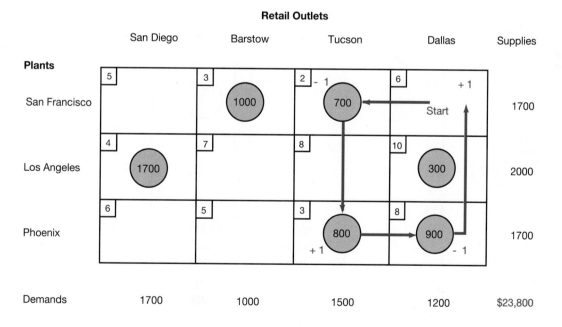

FIGURE 9.33 Step 2(a): Identifying an Empty Cell to Find an Improved Shipping Plan.

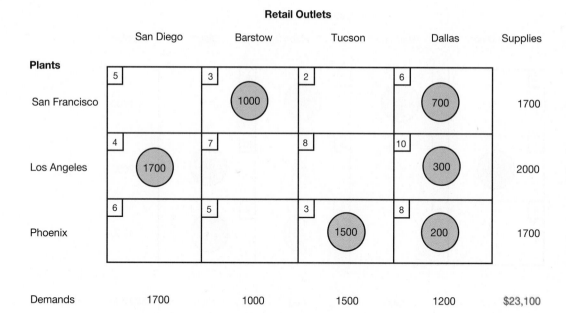

FIGURE 9.34 Step 2(b): Finding an Improved Shipping Plan.

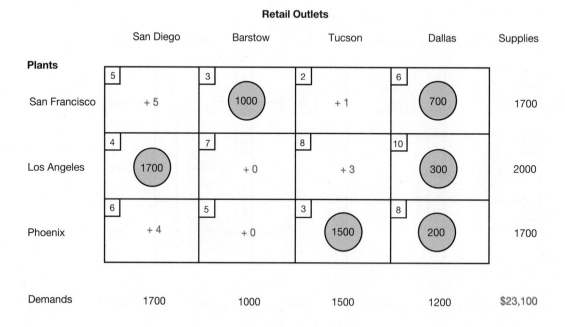

FIGURE 9.35 Computing Reduced Costs and Testing for Optimality.

→ **KEY FEATURES**

Summary of the Stepping Stone Algorithm

In summary, the stepping stone algorithm for solving a transportation problem having m supply nodes and n demand nodes consists of the following steps.

THE STEPPING STONE ALGORITHM

Step 0. *Initialization*: Find an initial feasible integer shipping plan that has $m + n - 1$ nonempty cells and no cycles. To do so, use the matrix minimum method by repeating the following three steps $m + n - 1$ times:

   a. Identify an uncrossed cell whose cost is the smallest. (In case of ties, choose any such cell.)

   b. For the cell identified in Step 0(a), determine the smaller of the remaining supply in that row and the remaining demand in that column.

   c. Now perform the following four steps:
      i. Put the amount determined in Step 0(b) in the identified cell.
      ii. Reduce the remaining supply in the row by the amount shipped in this cell.
      iii. Reduce the remaining demand in the column by the amount shipped in this cell.
      iv. Cross out the row or column whose remaining supply or demand has now been reduced to 0.

Step 1. *Test for Optimality*: Determine if the current shipping plan has the least total shipping cost as follows:

   a. *Computing Reduced Costs*: For each empty cell, find the unique cycle that starts and ends in that cell. Using this cycle, compute the reduced cost for this cell.

   b. *Checking Reduced Costs*: If all the reduced costs computed in Step 1(a) are nonnegative, stop—the current shipping plan is optimal. Otherwise, go to Step 2.

Step 2. *Moving*: Having determined in Step 1(b) that the current shipping plan is not optimal, construct a new feasible integer shipping plan whose total cost is less than that of the current one using the information obtained in Step 1(b) as follows:

   a. Choose the empty cell whose reduced cost is most negative.

   b. Determine the maximum number of units that can be shipped in the cell identified in Step 2(a).

   c. Modify the amounts shipped in each cell of the cycle. Go to Step 1.

In this section, you have learned the mathematical details of the stepping stone algorithm. A problem arises in Step 0(c) when both the supplies and demands are simultaneously reduced to 0. A similar type of problem arises in Step 2(c) when more than one amount shipped in the current plan is reduced to 0. These problems of *degeneracy* are resolved in Appendix 9B. In the next section, you will see several extensions to the basic transportation problem and learn how the resulting model can be solved using the stepping stone algorithm or a modification of it.

■ 9.6 VARIATIONS OF THE TRANSPORTATION PROBLEM

So far in this chapter, you have learned to formulate and solve the basic transportation problem: to minimize the total shipping cost from the supply to the demand nodes, given the per-unit shipping cost and the supplies and demands. In this section, you will learn how some additional constraints and modifications to this basic problem are formulated and solved using the same (or a slightly modified) stepping stone algorithm.

9.6.1 Incorporating Additional Costs and/or Profits

Until now, the primary focus has been on minimizing the total shipping cost. In some transportation problems, however, additional costs or revenues need to be considered.

INCORPORATING UNEQUAL MANUFACTURING COSTS

To illustrate the need to include additional costs, consider a slight modification to the problem of Magazines, Inc., presented in Example 9.3, Section 9.3.1. Rather than having *already* printed 10,000 copies of the magazine to be shipped, suppose you can *determine* the number of magazines to print based on known fixed orders from customers.

EXAMPLE 9.8 THE MODIFIED TRANSPORTATION PROBLEM OF MAGAZINES, INC.
Each month, *up to* 5000 copies of a magazine can be printed at each of two print shops: one in Los Angeles and one in New York. From there, the magazines are shipped to three regional distributors located in Chicago, Seattle, and Washington, D.C. For this month, these three distributors have ordered 4000, 2000, and 2500 copies, respectively. Table 9.13 provides the shipping cost per magazine from each of the print shops to each of the distributors. As Distribution Manager, you are to determine the least-cost shipping plan. ■

Observe that you need print only 8500 copies, which is the total demand. The question is how many copies to print and ship at each print shop. An appropriate transportation model can be used to answer this question. To formulate this problem, it is first necessary to convert this unbalanced problem into a balanced one. As you learned in Section 9.3, this is accomplished by introducing a new dummy demand node (Dumcus) to receive the excess supply of 1500 magazines (10,000 − 8,500). This new node is connected by a dummy arc to each of the supply nodes.

How much does it cost to ship a magazine from each supply node to this dummy customer? To answer this question, first understand precisely what it means to ship 500 magazines, for example, from Los Angeles to this dummy customer. What this means is that, of the 5000 magazines that *can* be printed in Los Angeles, only 4500 *need be* printed and shipped to the three customers; the remaining 500magazines *need not be*

TABLE 9.13 *Shipping Costs ($/Magazine) for Magazines, Inc.*

	REGIONAL DISTRIBUTORS		
PRINT SHOPS	CHICAGO	SEATTLE	WASHINGTON, D.C.
Los Angeles	0.07	0.05	0.10
New York	0.03	0.11	0.04

TABLE 9.14	Shipping Costs, Supplies, and Demands for the Balanced Transportation Problem of Magazines, Inc.				
	SHIPPING COST ($/MAGAZINE) FOR REGIONAL DISTRIBUTORS (AND DUMMY CUSTOMER)				
PRINT SHOPS	CHICAGO	SEATTLE	WASHINGTON, D.C.	DUMCUS	SUPPLIES
Los Angeles	0.07	0.05	0.10	0.0	5000
New York	0.03	0.11	0.04	0.0	5000
Demands	4000	2000	2500	1500	

printed at all. That is, the amount shipped along a dummy arc represents the number of magazines that need not be printed or shipped from that print shop. The cost along this arc is 0 because no units are actually printed and shipped from this print shop. These shipping costs and other data are summarized in Table 9.14.

The results obtained by solving this problem with the stepping stone algorithm using STORM appear in Figure 9.36. You can see that the shop in Los Angeles will print only 3500 of its 5000-copy capability. The total cost for this optimal shipping plan is $380.00.

Transportation
MAG_2.DAT

The optimal shipping plan given in Figure 9.36 is obtained by minimizing the total *shipping cost*. With this objective function, it makes no difference whether the print run in Los Angeles or in New York is 1500 below its capacity. However, what if the publication costs are higher in New York, say $0.40 in New York and $0.30 in Los Angeles? In this case, it may be more cost effective to print fewer copies in New York than under the current shipping plan. The actual number depends on the trade-off between the production and shipping costs. How can the model be changed to incorporate this consideration?

One way to handle this case is to assign to each cell a *new* unit cost, which is the sum of the production and shipping costs. Table 9.15 shows the new costs obtained. For example, the cost of $0.37 in the cell corresponding to Los Angeles to Chicago is the cost of $0.30 for printing a copy in Los Angeles plus the cost of $0.07 for shipping a copy from Los Angeles to Chicago. Note that the cost associated with each dummy arc remains at 0 because no magazines are printed or shipped along that arc.

Figure 9.37 shows the optimal shipping plan obtained for this new problem. The previous solution, in Figure 9.36, indicates that it was optimal to reduce the Los Angeles print run by 1500 magazines. Now, however, when considering the difference in the production costs, it is optimal to reduce the New York print run by 1500 copies instead.

Transportation
MAG_3.DAT

Compare the difference in the total costs under the two different plans. First, include the production costs in the plan in Figure 9.36, in which the shorter run occurs in Los Angeles:

TABLE 9.15	Shipping and Production Costs ($/Magazine) for the Balanced Transportation Problem of Magazines, Inc.				
PRINT SHOPS	CHICAGO	SEATTLE	WASHINGTON, D.C.	DUMCUS	SUPPLIES
Los Angeles	0.37	0.35	0.40	0.0	5000
New York	0.43	0.51	0.44	0.0	5000
Demands	4000	2000	2500	1500	

```
      TRANSPORTATION - OPTIMAL SOLUTION - DETAILED REPORT
   ------- Cell  ------                Unit      Cell    Reduced
   Row            Column    Amount     Cost      Cost     Cost

   LA             CHICAGO    1500      0.0700   105.0000   0.0000*
   LA             SEATTLE    2000      0.0500   100.0000   0.0000*
   LA         WASH. D.C.        0      0.1000     0.0000   0.0200
   LA              DUMCUS    1500      0.0000     0.0000   0.0000*
   LA Subtotal = 205.0000

   NEW YORK       CHICAGO    2500      0.0300    75.0000   0.0000*
   NEW YORK       SEATTLE       0      0.1100     0.0000   0.1000
   NEW YORK    WASH. D.C.    2500      0.0400   100.0000   0.0000*
   NEW YORK        DUMCUS       0      0.0000     0.0000   0.0400
   NEW YORK Subtotal = 175.0000

   Total Cost = 380.0000                        * Basic cells
   Number of iterations = 2
```

FIGURE 9.36 STORM Output for the Modified Transportation Problem of Magazines, Inc.

$$\text{Total previous costs} = (\text{production costs}) + (\text{shipping costs})$$
$$= (\text{production cost in Los Angeles}) +$$
$$(\text{production cost in New York}) +$$
$$(\text{total shipping costs})$$
$$= (3500 * 0.30 + 5000 * 0.40) + 380$$
$$= \$3430$$

This cost of $3430 is $90 more than that of $3340 for the shipping plan in Figure 9.37.

INCORPORATING UNEQUAL REVENUES

In Example 9.8, you saw the need to include production as well as shipping costs to formulate a correct transportation model. In some cases, additional *revenues* need to be considered. For example, consider an unbalanced problem in which there is more demand for a manufactured product at the company-owned retail outlets than can be supplied. Modeling such a problem in the way you have studied so far results in an optimal solution in which the shortage at each demand node is determined solely on the unit shipping costs. However, suppose that the finished goods, once received by the retail outlet, are sold at different prices. Intuitively, this means that the demand at those retail outlets selling the finished goods at a higher price should be met first. The actual amounts, however, are determined by the trade-off in shipping costs and selling prices. How can you incorporate this consideration into the transportation model?

In this situation, the overall objective is to *maximize* the total profit—that is, the total revenues less the total shipping costs. This is achieved by assigning to each cell in the transportation tableau a unit *profit* of the selling price at the corresponding retail outlet minus the shipping cost for that cell.

To solve the resulting model, it is necessary to *maximize* rather than *minimize* the objective function. Exercise 9.8 shows how the stepping stone algorithm is modified to achieve this goal.

```
                        Magazines, Inc.
           TRANSPORTATION - OPTIMAL SOLUTION - DETAILED REPORT
    ------- Cell ------              Unit       Cell    Reduced
    Row              Column   Amount  Cost       Cost    Cost

    LA              CHICAGO    3000   0.3700   1110.0000  0.0000*
    LA              SEATTLE    2000   0.3500    700.0000  0.0000*
    LA           WASH. D.C.       0   0.4000      0.0000  0.0200
    LA               DUMCUS       0   0.0000      0.0000  0.0600*
    LA Subtotal = 1810.0000


    NEW YORK        CHICAGO    1000   0.4300    430.0000  0.0000*
    NEW YORK        SEATTLE       0   0.5100      0.0000  0.1000
    NEW YORK     WASH. D.C.    2500   0.4400   1100.0000  0.0000*
    NEW YORK         DUMCUS    1500   0.0000      0.0000  0.0000*
    NEW YORK Subtotal = 1530.0000


    Total Cost = 3340.0000                    * Basic cells
    Number of iterations = 4
```

FIGURE 9.37 STORM Output for Magazines, Inc., When the Production Costs Are Included.

9.6.2 The Capacitated Transportation Problem

In all the transportation problems so far, you have been able to ship as many units as desired from each supply node to each demand node. However, in some cases, there may be restrictions on the number of units that can be shipped along a particular arc. For example, recall the problem of Rich Oil Company in Example 9.4, Section 9.3.1, where it is necessary to determine how best to ship gasoline from refineries in New Orleans and Newark to storage tanks in Washington, D.C., Atlanta, Tampa, and Cincinnati. For this problem, the optimal solution in Figure 9.15 in Section 9.4 indicates that 300,000 barrels are to be shipped from New Orleans to Atlanta. Suppose the gasoline between these two cities is shipped by a pipeline in which the maximum number of barrels that can be transported during that week is 200,000. In this case, the current shipping plan is *infeasible*—that is, it cannot be implemented.

    This new problem is called a **capacitated transportation problem** because there are capacities associated with one or more of the arcs. Researchers have modified the stepping stone algorithm to incorporate bounds on the amounts shipped from supply to demand nodes. Many computer packages allow you to include these capacities. For instance, the optimal shipping plan obtained by STORM for Rich Oil Company in which there is a capacity of 200,000 in the cell from New Orleans to Atlanta is shown in Figure 9.38.

    Previously, it was optimal to ship 300,000 barrels from New Orleans to Atlanta. In the new shipping plan in Figure 9.38, it is optimal to ship only 200,000 barrels. The remaining 100,000 barrels at New Orleans are shipped to Cincinnati. Because of the new restriction, the total cost has increased by $3000 ($3,956,000 − $3,953,000).

Capacitated transportation problem
A transportation problem in which the amounts shipped along certain arcs have limited capacities.

9.6.3 Prohibited Routes

In all the transportation problems so far, it has been possible to ship from every supply node to every demand node. In many applications, however, some of these shipping routes might be "prohibited." For example, if oil is being shipped between refineries

Transportation
RICH_2.DAT

```
                    The Rich Oil Company (Capacitated) Problem
                TRANSPORTATION - OPTIMAL SOLUTION - DETAILED REPORT
        -------  CELL  ------                 Unit        Cell      Reduced
        Row             Column    Amount      Cost        Cost       Cost
        NEW ORLEAN    WASH D.C.        0      0.1000      0.0000     0.0300
        NEW ORLEAN       TAMPA        0      0.0500      0.0000     0.9600
        NEW ORLEAN     ATLANTA   200000      0.0700  14000.0000    -0.0300
        NEW ORLEAN     CINCIN.   100000      0.9000   9000.0000     0.0000*
        NEW ORLEAN Subtotal = 23000.000

        NEWARK        WASH D.C.   200000      0.0500  10000.0000     0.0000*
        NEWARK           TAMPA        0      0.1100      0.0000     1.0400
        NEWARK         ATLANTA   100000      0.0800   8000.0000     0.0000*
        NEWARK         CINCIN.   200000      0.0700  14000.0000     0.0000*
        NEWARK Subtotal = 32000.0000

        DUMSUP        WASH D.C.        0     21.0000      0.0000     1.0200
        DUMSUP           TAMPA   100000     19.0000  1.9000E+06     0.0000*
        DUMSUP         ATLANTA        0     22.0000      0.0000     1.9900
        DUMSUP         CINCIN.   100000     20.0000  2.0000E+06     0.0000*
        DUMSUP Subtotal = 3900000.0000

        Total Cost = 3956000.000                      *Basic cells
        Number of iterations = 3
```

FIGURE 9.38 STORM Output for the Capacitated Transportation Problem of Rich Oil Company.

and storage tanks via a pipeline, the current network may not have a direct link between each refinery and each storage tank. As another example, suppose a company is shipping its finished goods from production plants to retail outlets by railroad. Once again, it may happen that this railroad network does not connect all plants to all retail outlets.

The question is how to model situations that contain one or more prohibited routes and obtain solutions. There are two basic approaches. For each cell of the transportation tableau that corresponds to a supply node and a demand node that have no direct link, follow either approach:

1. Make the unit cost of that cell a "prohibitively large" value relative to other costs in the tableau. Because this route is so expensive, the stepping stone algorithm is not likely to select this cell for shipping any units.
2. Assign a capacity of 0 and any unit cost to that cell. The capacity of 0 ensures that no units are shipped in this cell, irrespective of the cost. Now solve the resulting problem as a capacitated transportation problem.

The advantage of the first approach is that the resulting problem can be solved directly by the stepping stone algorithm presented in Section 9.5. The disadvantage, however, is that it is not clear how large to make the unit cost of the prohibited cells. Too small a cost may result in a solution in which some units are shipped along the prohibited route. Too large a cost may result in computational problems for the computer.

The advantage of the second approach is that the capacity of 0 for a prohibited cell makes the choice of the unit cost irrelevant. However, the resulting capacitated model requires a special extension to the stepping stone algorithm in order to obtain a solution. The details are beyond the scope of this book. If the software you have available has the capability to solve a capacitated transportation problem, then you should use the second approach; otherwise, you will have to use the first approach.

9.6.4 Lower Bounds on Supplies and/or Demands

In an unbalanced transportation problem in which there is more supply than demand, the stepping stone algorithm determines the surplus at each supply node through the use of a dummy demand node based solely on the unit costs. In many applications, however, other managerial considerations may govern the decision of how to determine the surplus amounts. For instance, recall from Example 9.8 that Magazines, Inc., can print up to 5000 copies of a magazine at each of its two print shops to meet a known demand of 8500 copies from its three distributors. Based on the shipping and printing costs, it is optimal to have a surplus of 1500 copies in New York and none in Los Angeles. However, suppose that due to overhead and fixed costs, the print shop in New York *must* produce at least 75% of its capacity (that is, 3750 copies) and that the one in Los Angeles *must* produce at least 80% (that is, 4000 copies) to be profitable. How can these *lower bounds on supplies* be incorporated in the transportation model?

Having a lower bound of 3750 copies for the print shop in New York, with a capacity of 5000, means that the surplus there cannot exceed 1250 (5000 − 3750). Similarly, the lower bound of 4000 copies in Los Angeles, with a capacity of 5000, means that the surplus there cannot exceed 1000 (5000 − 4000). The lower-bound constraints on the supplies are handled by placing a capacity of 1250 and 1000 on the dummy arcs from New York and Los Angeles to the dummy customer, respectively, and solving the resulting capacitated transportation problem. The results for Magazines, Inc., are shown in Figure 9.39. You can see that in the new model, it is optimal to have 500 surplus magazines in New York and 1000 surplus magazines in Los Angeles.

What happens when an unbalanced transportation problem has more demand than supply? To incorporate a lower bound on one or more demand nodes—that is, it is necessary to meet *at least* a certain amount of the demand at a node—assign appropriate capacities to the dummy arcs from the dummy supply node to each such

Transportation
MAG_4.DAT

```
              Magazines, Inc. (with lower bounds)
          TRANSPORTATION - OPTIMAL SOLUTION - DETAILED REPORT
------- Cell  ------             Unit      Cell      Reduced
Row            Column   Amount    Cost      Cost       Cost

LA            CHICAGO    2000    0.0700   140.0000   0.0000*
LA            SEATTLE    2000    0.0500   100.0000   0.0000*
LA         WASH. D.C.       0    0.1000     0.0000   0.0200
LA            DUMCUS     1000   -0.0500   -50.0000  -0.0100
LA Subtotal = 190.0000


NEW YORK      CHICAGO    2000    0.0300    60.0000   0.0000*
NEW YORK      SEATTLE       0    0.1100     0.0000   0.1000
NEW YORK   WASH. D.C.    2500    0.0400   100.0000   0.0000*
NEW YORK      DUMCUS      500   -0.0800   -40.0000   0.0000*
NEW YORK Subtotal = 120.0000


Total Cost = 310.0000                      * Basic cells
Number of iterations = 2
```

FIGURE 9.39 STORM Output With Lower Bounds for Magazines, Inc.

customer. Here, these "appropriate" capacities are the differences between the actual demand and the minimum amount that must be shipped there.

In this section, you have learned how certain managerial considerations can be incorporated into a modified transportation problem, and how to obtain an optimal solution to the resulting model. In the next section, you will learn how to solve the more general distribution problem presented in Section 9.1.

■ 9.7 THE GENERAL NETWORK DISTRIBUTION PROBLEM: THE TRANSSHIPMENT PROBLEM

In Section 9.1, the general network distribution problem is introduced for solving problems involving the transportation and distribution of goods from suppliers to customers directly and/or through intermediate warehouses.

KEY FEATURES

Network distribution problems are represented by a network having the following features:

✔ A finite collection of *nodes*, each of which represents a plant, warehouse, or retail outlet. The three kinds of nodes are as follows:
   a. The *supply nodes* from which goods are shipped (such as factories or plants).
   b. The *demand nodes* where goods are received to meet known demands (such as retail outlets).
   c. The intermediate or *transshipment nodes* where goods are received from other nodes for redistribution (such as warehouses).
✔ Arrows or *arcs* connecting pairs of nodes to represent a valid shipping route from the originating node to the destination node as indicated by the direction of the arrow.
✔ Various data associated with the problem, such as the following:
   a. The available supplies at each supply node.
   b. The known demands at each demand node.
   c. The cost of shipping one unit along each arc.
   d. The *capacities*—that is, the minimum and maximum number of units that can be shipped along each arc.

When there are no transshipment nodes, the problem is called a *transportation problem*, and you learned to solve such problems in Sections 9.3 to 9.6. In this section, you will learn how to solve the more general *transshipment problem* by computer.

9.7.1 The Transshipment Algorithm: A Conceptual Approach

Recall from Example 9.1 in Section 9.1 that a transshipment problem is, in fact, a linear programming problem. Although you could therefore solve such problems with any linear programming package, for a moderate-sized distribution network—having, for example, 5 plants, 20 warehouses, and 200 customers—the associated linear program has 4100 variables and 225 constraints. To solve such large problems efficiently requires a specialized algorithm that takes advantage of the particular structure arising in the constraints of transshipment problems.

The method for solving a transshipment problem is similar to that of the transportation problem. It is, in fact, a finite-improvement algorithm consisting of the following basic steps.

KEY FEATURES
Conceptual Steps of the Transshipment Algorithm

Step 0. *Initialization:* Find an initial feasible shipping plan that satisfies all supply-and-demand constraints while maintaining balance at all transshipment nodes.

Step 1. *Test for Optimality:* Test the current shipping plan to see if it is optimal— that is, if it is the plan incurring the least total costs. If so, stop with the optimal solution; if not, go to Step 2.

Step 2. *Moving:* Use the fact that the current shipping plan is not optimal to create a new feasible shipping plan with less total cost than the current one. Go to Step 1.

These steps are analogous to those of the stepping stone algorithm for the transportation problem, with certain modifications to handle the transshipment nodes and the capacities on each arc. The details are beyond the scope of this book. However, in Section 9.7.2, you will learn how to interpret the output from using such an algorithm on a computer.

9.7.2 The Transshipment Algorithm: Using The Computer

To illustrate how the transshipment algorithm is used, recall the distribution problem of Medical Technologies, Inc. (MTI), presented in Section 9.1 and whose network diagram is repeated in Figure 9.40. Recall that the objective is to determine the least-cost plan to ship X-ray machines from plants in Texas, Iowa, and Oregon through two regional warehouses in Hungary and Hawaii, through two field warehouses in the Philippines and Fiji, and ultimately to four customers in Japan, South Korea, New Zealand, and Australia.

In addition to the supply, demand, and balance constraints discussed in Section 9.1, MTI has realized that due to the current staffing at various field warehouses, a maximum of 200 machines can be shipped through field warehouses in the Philippines and Fiji—that is, there is a capacity of 200 associated with nodes 6 and 7 in Figure 9.40. Computer packages allow capacities *only* on the arcs. A modification in the network is needed to transform the capacities on the *nodes* to capacities on (some new) *arcs*.

Consider the capacity of 200 on node 6—that is, on the field warehouse in the Philippines. To transform this capacity on a node to a capacity on an arc:

1. Split node 6 into two nodes, 6A and 6B, in the modified network.
2. Adjust the arcs. All the arcs that originate at node 6 in the original network originate at node 6B in the modified network. All the arcs that terminate at node 6 in the original network terminate at node 6A in the modified network.
3. Add an arc from node 6A to node 6B in the modified network and assign it a unit shipping cost of 0.

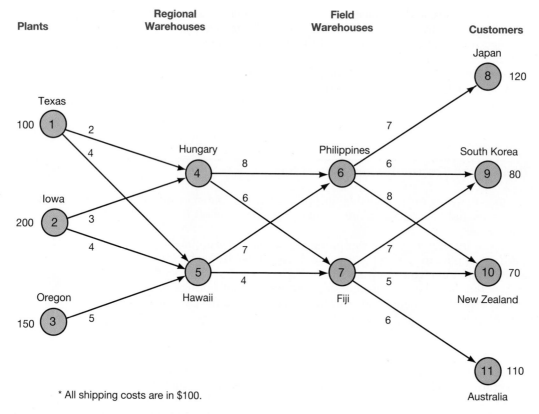

FIGURE 9.40 The Distribution Network of the Problem of MTI.

Transportation
MTI_2.DAT

Because shipment along the new arc connecting nodes 6A and 6B is precisely the shipment through the field warehouse in the Philippines, a capacity of 200 on this arc represents the maximum shipment that can be made through this field warehouse. Repeating this process for node 7 representing the field warehouse in Fiji, results in the modified network in Figure 9.41.

With the modified network in Figure 9.41, it is now possible to solve the transshipment problem by entering the data into any applicable computer software. Doing so with STORM and applying the transshipment algorithm results in the solution in Figure 9.42.

The first three lines in this report correspond to the three plants in Texas, Iowa, and Oregon, which are entered in STORM as having their "From" node as "." and "To" node as the corresponding node number in the network of Figure 9.41. The flows of 100, 200, and 80 indicate the number of X-ray machines shipped from the plants in Texas, Iowa, and Oregon, respectively.

To see where those machines are shipped to, consider the plant at Texas and look at the corresponding node 1 in Figure 9.41. Because machines are shipped from Texas to the regional warehouses in Hungary (node 4) and Hawaii (node 5), identify the rows in Figure 9.42 corresponding to shipments from node 1 to nodes 4 and 5. In this case, that is rows 4 and 5. The values in row 4 indicate a shipment of 100 machines from Texas to Hungary (as shown in the column labeled "Flow") at a unit cost of 2 hundred dollars (as shown in the column labeled "Unit Cost"), resulting in a total shipping cost of 100 machines * ($200/machine) = $20,000 (as shown by the number 200 in the column labeled "Shipping Cost"). Similarly, the values in row 5 indicate that no machines are shipped from Texas to Hawaii. The shipments detailed in the report are summarized in Tables 9.16 to 9.18. The total cost is $591,000.

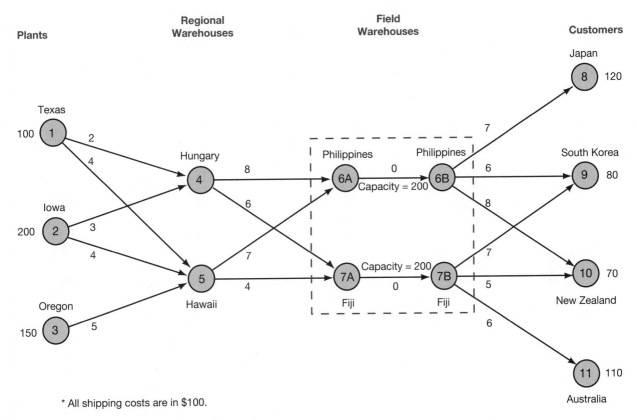

* All shipping costs are in $100.

FIGURE 9.41 Modified Distribution Network of the Problem of MTI.

The final column, labeled "Reduced Cost" in Figure 9.42 provides additional information analogous to reduced costs in the simplex algorithm in Chapters 5 and 6 and the transportation algorithm in Section 9.5. For the transshipment problem of MTI, the reduced costs carry the following information:

1. The reduced cost associated with a supply node indicates the change in the transportation costs for each additional unit available at that node, *up to a certain limit*, assuming all else remains the same. For example, the reduced cost of −2 in the first row of the report in Figure 9.42 indicates that each additional machine available at the plant in Texas, *up to a certain limit*, reduces the total shipping cost by $200.

2. The reduced cost associated with a demand node indicates the change in the transportation costs for each additional unit of demand at that node, *up to a certain limit*, assuming all else remains the same. For example, the reduced cost of 17 in the last row of the report in Figure 9.42 indicates that each additional machine

TABLE 9.16	*Shipping Plan from Plants to Regional Warehouses*	
	REGIONAL WAREHOUSES	
PLANTS	HUNGARY	HAWAII
Texas	100	0
Iowa	80	120
Oregon	N/A	80

```
          The Transshipment Problem of Medical Technologies, Inc.
                    TRANSSHIPMENT - DETAILED REPORT
                                          Unit      Shipping    Reduced
Arc         From    To      Flow          Cost        Cost       Cost

S-TEXAS      .      1        100           0           0          -2
S-IOWA       .      2        200           0           0          -1
S-OREGON     .      3         80           0           0           0
TEX-HUN      1      4        100           2         200           0
TEX-HAW      1      5          0           4           0           1
IOW-HUN      2      4         80           3         240           0
IOW-HAW      2      5        120           4         480           0
ORE-HAW      3      5         80           5         400           0
HUN-PHI      4      6A       180           8        1440           0
HUN-FIJ      4      7A         0           6           0           1
HAW-PHI      5      6A         0           7           0           0
HAW-FIJ      5      7A       200           4         800           0
6A-6B        6A     6B       180           0           0           0
7A-7B        7A     7B       200           0           0          -2
PHI-JAP      6B     8        120           7         840           0
PHI-KOR      6B     9         60           6         360           0
PHI-N.Z.     6B     10         0           8           0           4
FIJ-KOR      7B     9         20           7         140           0
FIJ-N.Z.     7B     10        70           5         350           0
FIJ-AUST.    7B     11       110           6         660           0
D-JAPAN      8      .        120           0           0          19
D-KOREA      9      .         80           0           0          18
D-N.Z.       10     .         70           0           0          16
D-AUST.      11     .        110           0           0          17

Total cost = 5910
```

FIGURE 9.42 STORM Report for the Transshipment Problem of MTI.

TABLE 9.17 *Shipping Plan From Regional to Field Warehouses*

	FIELD WAREHOUSES	
REGIONAL WAREHOUSES	PHILIPPINES	FIJI
Hungary	180	0
Hawaii	0	200

TABLE 9.18 *Shipping Plan From Field Warehouses to Customers*

	CUSTOMERS			
FIELD WAREHOUSES	JAPAN	SOUTH KOREA	NEW ZEALAND	AUSTRALIA
Philippines	120	60	0	N/A
Fiji	N/A	20	70	110

required by the customer in Australia, *up to a certain limit*, increases the total shipping cost by $1700.

3. The reduced cost associated with each other arc indicates the change in the transportation costs for each additional unit shipped along that arc, *up to a certain limit*. For example, the reduced cost of 1 in row 5 of the report in Figure 9.42 indicates that one additional machine shipped from Texas to Hawaii increases the total shipping cost by $100.

Even though further analysis is needed to determine the limits up to which these reduced costs are valid, this information can be used to understand how increased supplies or demands affect the total transportation costs.

9.7.3 *Summary of the Transshipment Problem*

The transshipment problem is a distribution network problem involving supply, transshipment, and demand nodes. Arcs connecting pairs of these nodes may have capacities in the form of lower and upper bounds on the amounts shipped along those arcs. When *nodes* have capacities, however, it is necessary to create a modified network that a computer program can solve. The capacities on the nodes in the original network are transformed into capacities on arcs in the modified network.

In this section, you have learned how to use a transshipment algorithm to solve an associated problem and how to interpret the results thus obtained. Just as the transportation problem is a special type of transshipment problem that merits its own algorithm, so the *assignment problem* is a special type of transportation problem that merits its own algorithm. The assignment problem and its associated algorithm are presented in the next section.

■ 9.8 THE ASSIGNMENT PROBLEM

In many decision problems it is necessary to *assign* an item from one group (such as a machine, an employee, and the like) to an item in a second group (such as a task, a project, and so on). Consider for example, assigning jobs to machines in a manufacturing plant, assigning sales representatives to territories, or assigning researchers to projects.

➡ **KEY FEATURES**

In making an assignment, two conditions often must be met:

✔ Each item in the first group must be assigned to exactly one item in the second group.
✔ Each item in the second group must be assigned to exactly one item in the first group.

Balanced assignment problem
An assignment problem in which the number of items in each of two groups is the same.

Because for each assigned pair there is an associated "cost"—for example, the amount of time it takes to accomplish a task assigned to a particular machine—the objective is to choose assignments that minimize total cost.

To satisfy these two assignment conditions, the number of items in each group must be the same. Such a problem is called a **balanced assignment problem.** As you will see in Example 9.9 in Section 9.8.1, for an **unbalanced assignment problem,** it is possible to create an equivalent balanced problem whose solution provides the optimal solution to the original problem.

Unbalanced assignment problem
An assignment problem in which the number of items in each of two groups is not the same.

9.8.1 Network and Mathematical Representation of an Assignment Problem

To illustrate an example of the assignment problem, consider the problem faced by the management of Containers, Inc.

EXAMPLE 9.9 THE ASSIGNMENT PROBLEM OF CONTAINERS, INC. Containers, Inc., makes containers of many sizes and shapes. It has recently received orders to produce various amounts of five different sizes of kitchen containers. Each container size can be produced on any one of four machines. Due to different technologies and setup times, the total number of hours, including the setup time, needed to process each container size on each machine varies, as shown in Table 9.19. In the table, the container size is indicated in the first column by its height and diameter in inches.

Setting up a machine to switch from making one size container to another takes a long time, so management has decided that each machine will produce containers of only one size. Therefore, only four of the five sizes will be produced on the four available machines within the allotted deadline. Because the revenue on each size of container is approximately the same, the management of Containers, Inc., is indifferent as to which of the five orders is not met. As Manager of the Production Department, you have been asked to determine which four of the five orders to accept and to develop a production plan that minimizes the total processing time for satisfying those orders. ∎

In this problem, you can recognize the features of an assignment problem. You have to assign an item from one group—that is, an order for one of the five sizes—to an item in a second group—that is, the machines. In this case, the problem is unbalanced because there are five orders and only four machines. To resolve this problem, an approach similar to handling the unbalanced transportation problem in Section 9.3 is used. That is, you can do the following:

1. Add as many dummy items to one of the groups as needed to make the two groups equal in size.
2. For each dummy item added, identify an appropriate cost associated with assigning each item in the *other* group to this dummy item.

For the problem of Containers, Inc., this requires adding one dummy machine. There are now five orders and five machines, resulting in a balanced assignment problem. Keep in mind that Machine 5 does not, in fact, exist. Containers assigned to this machine are not produced and therefore contribute nothing to the total processing time. The data for the balanced assignment problem are shown in Table 9.20.

TABLE 9.19 *Total Processing Time (hr) for Producing Each Size of Container on Each Machine*

CONTAINER SIZE	MACHINE			
	1	2	3	4
3 × 4	25	20	28	30
4 × 6	24	22	25	23
6 × 8	30	30	28	25
8 × 12	38	32	30	30
12 × 18	40	40	28	30

TABLE 9.20 *Total Processing Time (hr) for Producing Each Size of Container on Each Machine, Including Dummy Machine 5*

CONTAINER SIZE	MACHINE				
	1	2	3	4	5
3 × 4	25	20	28	30	0
4 × 6	24	22	25	23	0
6 × 8	30	30	28	25	0
8 × 12	38	32	30	30	0
12 × 18	40	40	28	30	0

To formulate this problem as a network, create one node for each order and a separate node for each machine, as shown in Figure 9.43. Connect each node corresponding to an order to each node corresponding to a machine with an arc to indicate the *possibility* of assigning that order to the associated machine. Above each arc, write the number of hours of processing time associated with that assignment, as given in Table 9.20. This has been done in the network diagram of Figure 9.43. (Due to lack of space, the processing times for only a few arcs are shown.)

In the context of this network, the assignment problem is to select five arcs (that is, assignments) that have no nodes in common (that is, each order is assigned to exactly one machine, and vice versa) in such a way that the total processing time of these five arcs is as small as possible. For example, the assignment in Figure 9.44 is one possible assignment and has a total processing time of 105 hours. Because this assignment may not be optimal, mathematical tools are needed to identify the optimal assignment. The first step is to create a mathematical model.

To formulate this problem mathematically, use the techniques presented in Chapter 2. That is, first identify the decision variables. In this case, you are free to choose which order to assign to which machine. Another way of saying this is that for each order, you are free to assign, or not to assign, the order to a particular machine. This "no/yes" decision should lead you to identify a collection of 0–1 variables. For example, for the first order and the second machine, define

$$x_{12} = \begin{cases} 1 & \text{if Order 1 is assigned to Machine 2} \\ 0 & \text{if Order 1 is not assigned to Machine 2} \end{cases}$$

A similar variable is needed for each combination of the five orders and five machines, resulting in the 25 0–1 decision variables shown in Table 9.21.

TABLE 9.21 *Symbolic Names of the Variables for the Assignment Problem of Containers, Inc.*

ORDER	MACHINE				
	1	2	3	4	5
1	x_{11}	x_{12}	x_{13}	x_{14}	x_{15}
2	x_{21}	x_{22}	x_{23}	x_{24}	x_{25}
3	x_{31}	x_{32}	x_{33}	x_{34}	x_{35}
4	x_{41}	x_{42}	x_{43}	x_{44}	x_{45}
5	x_{51}	x_{52}	x_{53}	x_{54}	x_{55}

Orders   **Machines**

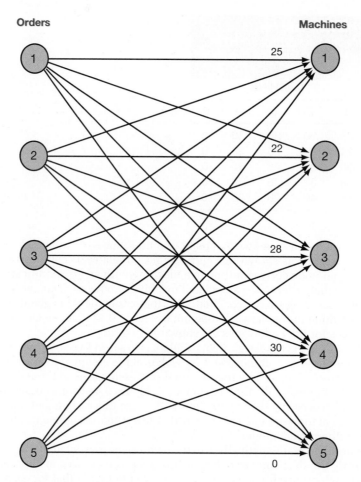

FIGURE 9.43 Network Representation of the Assignment Problem of
Containers, Inc.

The objective is to find an assignment of least total processing time. Applying decomposition results in

$$
\begin{aligned}
\text{Total processing time} = \ &(\text{processing time for Order 1}) + \\
&(\text{processing time for Order 2}) + \\
&(\text{processing time for Order 3}) + \\
&(\text{processing time for Order 4}) + \\
&(\text{processing time for Order 5})
\end{aligned}
$$

For the first order, the processing time depends on the machine to which the order is assigned. For example, if the order is assigned to the first machine, the processing time, from Table 9.20, is 25 hours, *but only if this order is assigned to the first machine.* By using the decision variable x_{11}, then, this processing time is $25x_{11}$. Similarly, if the first order is assigned to the second machine, the processing time is 20 hours, so using x_{12}, this portion is $20x_{12}$. Considering each of the five machines, then

$$\text{Processing time for Order 1} = 25x_{11} + 20x_{12} + 28x_{13} + 30x_{14} + 0x_{15}$$

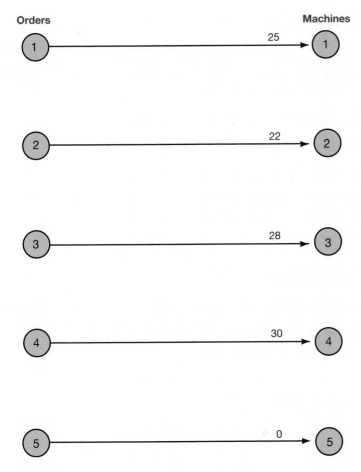

FIGURE 9.44 A Feasible Solution to the Assignment Problem of
Containers, Inc.

Using the data in the remaining four rows of Table 9.20 results in the following objective function:

$$
\begin{aligned}
\text{Minimize} \quad & 25x_{11} + 20x_{12} + 28x_{13} + 30x_{14} + 0x_{15} + \\
& 24x_{21} + 22x_{22} + 25x_{23} + 23x_{24} + 0x_{25} + \\
& 30x_{31} + 30x_{32} + 28x_{33} + 25x_{34} + 0x_{35} + \\
& 38x_{41} + 32x_{42} + 30x_{43} + 30x_{44} + 0x_{45} + \\
& 40x_{51} + 40x_{52} + 28x_{53} + 30x_{54} + 0x_{55}
\end{aligned}
$$

For the constraints, the technique of grouping should lead you to identify the following groups:

1. Order-assignment constraints to ensure that each order is assigned to exactly one machine.
2. Machine-assignment constraints to ensure that each machine is to process exactly one order.
3. Logical constraints.

ORDER-ASSIGNMENT CONSTRAINTS

This group consists of five constraints, one for each order. For example, the first order must be assigned to exactly one machine. This means that of the five variables, x_{11}, x_{12}, x_{13}, x_{14}, and x_{15}, exactly one of them must have a value of 1 and the others must all have a value of 0. Mathematically, this constraint is

$$x_{11} + x_{12} + x_{13} + x_{14} + x_{15} = 1 \qquad \text{(Order 1)}$$

This same logic leads to the remaining four constraints in this group:

$$x_{21} + x_{22} + x_{23} + x_{24} + x_{25} = 1 \qquad \text{(Order 2)}$$
$$x_{31} + x_{32} + x_{33} + x_{34} + x_{35} = 1 \qquad \text{(Order 3)}$$
$$x_{41} + x_{42} + x_{43} + x_{44} + x_{45} = 1 \qquad \text{(Order 4)}$$
$$x_{51} + x_{52} + x_{53} + x_{54} + x_{55} = 1 \qquad \text{(Order 5)}$$

MACHINE-ASSIGNMENT CONSTRAINTS

This group consists of five constraints, one for each machine. For example, the first machine must process exactly one order. This means that of the five variables, x_{11}, x_{21}, x_{31}, x_{41}, and x_{51}, exactly one of them must have a value of 1 and the others must all have a value of 0. Mathematically, this constraint is

$$x_{11} + x_{21} + x_{31} + x_{41} + x_{51} = 1 \qquad \text{(Machine 1)}$$

The remaining four constraints in this group are

$$x_{12} + x_{22} + x_{32} + x_{42} + x_{52} = 1 \qquad \text{(Machine 2)}$$
$$x_{13} + x_{23} + x_{33} + x_{43} + x_{53} = 1 \qquad \text{(Machine 3)}$$
$$x_{14} + x_{24} + x_{34} + x_{44} + x_{54} = 1 \qquad \text{(Machine 4)}$$
$$x_{15} + x_{25} + x_{35} + x_{45} + x_{55} = 1 \qquad \text{(Machine 5)}$$

LOGICAL CONSTRAINTS

The only logical constraints are that each decision variable have a value of 0 or 1.

Putting together all the pieces results in the following complete mathematical formulation of the assignment problem of Containers, Inc.

COMPLETE FORMULATION OF THE ASSIGNMENT PROBLEM OF CONTAINERS, INC.

Assignment
EX9_6.DAT

$$\begin{aligned}
\text{Minimize} \quad & 25x_{11} + 20x_{12} + 28x_{13} + 30x_{14} + 0x_{15} + \\
& 24x_{21} + 22x_{22} + 25x_{23} + 23x_{24} + 0x_{25} + \\
& 30x_{31} + 30x_{32} + 28x_{33} + 25x_{34} + 0x_{35} + \\
& 38x_{41} + 32x_{42} + 30x_{43} + 30x_{44} + 0x_{45} + \\
& 40x_{51} + 40x_{52} + 28x_{53} + 30x_{54} + 0x_{55}
\end{aligned}$$

Subject to

ORDER-ASSIGNMENT CONSTRAINTS

$$x_{11} + x_{12} + x_{13} + x_{14} + x_{15} = 1 \qquad \text{(Order 1)}$$
$$x_{21} + x_{22} + x_{23} + x_{24} + x_{25} = 1 \qquad \text{(Order 2)}$$
$$x_{31} + x_{32} + x_{33} + x_{34} + x_{35} = 1 \qquad \text{(Order 3)}$$
$$x_{41} + x_{42} + x_{43} + x_{44} + x_{45} = 1 \qquad \text{(Order 4)}$$
$$x_{51} + x_{52} + x_{53} + x_{54} + x_{55} = 1 \qquad \text{(Order 5)}$$

MACHINE-ASSIGNMENT CONSTRAINTS

$$x_{11} + x_{21} + x_{31} + x_{41} + x_{51} = 1 \qquad \text{(Machine 1)}$$
$$x_{12} + x_{22} + x_{32} + x_{42} + x_{52} = 1 \qquad \text{(Machine 2)}$$
$$x_{13} + x_{23} + x_{33} + x_{43} + x_{53} = 1 \qquad \text{(Machine 3)}$$
$$x_{14} + x_{24} + x_{34} + x_{44} + x_{54} = 1 \qquad \text{(Machine 4)}$$
$$x_{15} + x_{25} + x_{35} + x_{45} + x_{55} = 1 \qquad \text{(Machine 5)}$$

LOGICAL CONSTRAINTS

All variables must be 0–1 integer variables

Look carefully at the network in Figure 9.43 and at the foregoing mathematical formulation.

KEY FEATURES

This balanced assignment problem is in fact a transportation problem. Note these points:

- ✔ Each of the five orders for containers can be thought of as a supply node with a supply of one unit (corresponding to the one order).
- ✔ Each of the five machines can be thought of as a demand node with a demand of one unit (corresponding to processing one order).
- ✔ The transportation cost from each supply node to each demand node is the time for processing the associated order on the corresponding machine.

As a result, it is possible to solve an assignment problem not only by the stepping stone algorithm in Section 9.2, but also by the simplex algorithm in Chapter 6 (because the resulting solution will always have integer values for a transportation problem). However, because of the wide applications discussed at the beginning of this section, it is desirable to have a more efficient algorithm for solving large assignment problems. It is possible to develop such an algorithm because of the particularly simple form of the constraints, as described in Section 9.8.2.

9.8.2 The Assignment Algorithm

The solution procedure described in this section is designed to solve a balanced assignment problem in which the numbers of items in the two groups are the same. As discussed in Section 9.8.1, any unbalanced assignment problem can be converted to an equivalent balanced problem by adding the appropriate number of dummy items to the group with fewer items and carefully determining the costs associated with assigning these dummy items to each of the items in the other group.

Assignment matrix
A table that contains all the relevant data for a balanced assignment problem.

The relevant data for a balanced assignment problem are summarized in an **assignment matrix** that has the same number of rows as columns. Each number in a cell is the cost of assigning the item in the associated row to the item in the associated column. For the problem of Containers, Inc., the assignment matrix is

	1	2	3	4	5
1	25	20	28	30	0
2	24	22	25	23	0
3	30	30	28	25	0
4	38	32	30	30	0
5	40	40	28	30	0

A feasible solution to this assignment problem involves five assignments—that is, selecting five cells in the assignment matrix with the following properties:

1. Exactly one cell in each row is selected (as an order can be assigned to only one machine).
2. Exactly one cell in each column is selected (as a machine can process only one order).

For example, the assignment in Figure 9.44 is shown by the five circled cells in Figure 9.45, with a total processing time of 105 hours.

The objective is to find an *optimal assignment*—that is, a feasible assignment with the least total processing time. The assignment algorithm that achieves this objective is based on the observation that if in the assignment matrix either:

1. the same number is added to or subtracted from every cell in one row, or
2. the same number is added to or subtracted from every cell in one column,

then, the optimal assignment *remains the same.* For example, consider subtracting 10 from every cell in the first column in the previous assignment matrix. The objective

	1	2	3	4	5
1	(25)	20	28	30	0
2	24	(22)	25	23	0
3	30	30	(28)	25	0
4	38	32	30	(30)	0
5	40	40	28	30	(0)

FIGURE 9.45 A Feasible Solution to the Assignment Problem of Containers, Inc.

function in the mathematical formulation of Section 9.8.1 correspondingly changes from

$$25x_{11} + 20x_{12} + 28x_{13} + 30x_{14} + 0x_{15} +$$
$$24x_{21} + 22x_{22} + 25x_{23} + 23x_{24} + 0x_{25} +$$
$$30x_{31} + 30x_{32} + 28x_{33} + 25x_{34} + 0x_{35} +$$
$$38x_{41} + 32x_{42} + 30x_{43} + 30x_{44} + 0x_{45} +$$
$$40x_{51} + 40x_{52} + 28x_{53} + 30x_{54} + 0x_{55}$$

to

$$(25 - 10)x_{11} + 20x_{12} + 28x_{13} + 30x_{14} + 0x_{15} +$$
$$(24 - 10)x_{21} + 22x_{22} + 25x_{23} + 23x_{24} + 0x_{25} +$$
$$(30 - 10)x_{31} + 30x_{32} + 28x_{33} + 25x_{34} + 0x_{35} +$$
$$(38 - 10)x_{41} + 32x_{42} + 30x_{43} + 30x_{44} + 0x_{45} +$$
$$(40 - 10)x_{51} + 40x_{52} + 28x_{53} + 30x_{54} + 0x_{55}$$

In other words,

New objective function = (old objective function) −

$$10(x_{11} + x_{21} + x_{31} + x_{41} + x_{51})$$

The constraints are unchanged. Recall the constraint labeled Machine 1 in the formulation in Section 9.8.1:

$$x_{11} + x_{21} + x_{31} + x_{41} + x_{51} = 1 \qquad \text{(Machine 1)}$$

Substituting this constraint into the foregoing equation for the new objective function yields

New objective function = (old objective function) − 10

Adding or subtracting the same number from every cell in a column (or row) reduces the objective function by this number *but does not change the optimal solution.*

The objective now is to create a sequence of assignment matrices systematically, each obtained from the previous one by adding and/or subtracting a constant value from each row and/or column. The goal is to reach a final assignment matrix in which you can easily identify the optimal assignment. For example, if all the values in the final assignment matrix are nonnegative and a feasible assignment can be found in which each selected cell has a value of 0, then that assignment, with a total processing time of 0, is optimal. This is because any other feasible assignment must have a nonnegative total processing time.

KEY FEATURES

To obtain the optimal assignment, each new assignment matrix will satisfy:

✔ **Property 1.** All numbers are nonnegative.
✔ **Property 2.** Each row and each column has at least one cell with a value of 0.

Whenever, in any such matrix, you find an assignment in which each selected cell has a value of 0, you have, in fact, found the optimal assignment.

In summary, the conceptual steps of the assignment algorithm are as follows:

CONCEPTUAL STEPS OF THE ASSIGNMENT ALGORITHM

Step 0. *Initialization*: By subtracting appropriate numbers from the rows and/or columns of the original assignment matrix, create a new assignment matrix having Properties 1 and 2.

Step 1. *Test for Optimality*: If it is possible to find a feasible assignment in the current matrix in which each selected cell has value 0, stop with an optimal assignment; otherwise, go to Step 2.

Step 2. *Moving*: By adding and/or subtracting appropriate numbers from the rows and/or columns of the current assignment matrix, create a new assignment matrix having Properties 1 and 2 and go to Step 1.

The details of these steps are developed using the problem of Containers, Inc.

STEP 0 (INITIALIZATION)

To create the initial matrix having Properties 1 and 2, begin with the original assignment matrix and perform the following:

1. For each row, identify the smallest number and subtract that value for every cell in this row. This step results in a matrix with all numbers nonnegative and at least one zero value in each row.

2. After completing the row subtractions, for each column, identify the smallest number and subtract that value for every cell in this column. This step results in a matrix with all numbers nonnegative and at least one zero value in each column.

In the example of Containers, Inc., observe that the smallest value in each row is 0. Subtracting this number has no effect on the values in each row. However, the smallest value in the five columns are 24, 20, 25, 23, and 0, respectively. From every number in column 1 subtract 24, from every number in column 2 subtract 20, and so on. The matrix in Figure 9.46(a) results. This matrix satisfies Properties 1 and 2. Every number is nonnegative, and at least one cell in each column and row is 0.

ITERATION 1: STEP 1 (TEST FOR OPTIMALITY)

In this step, attempt to identify a feasible assignment in the current matrix in which each selected cell has the value 0. If such an assignment cannot be found, then find the maximum number of cells having a value of 0 that creates a *partial* assignment—that is, an assignment that includes *at most* one cell in each row and column. In the matrix in Figure 9.46(a), the partial assignment having the maximum number of cells with a value of 0 includes the three cells in row 1 and column 2, row 2 and column 1, and row 3 and column 5. These three cells are circled in Figure 9.46(a). Because not all five orders have been assigned, it is necessary to go to Step 2.

ITERATION 1: STEP 2 (MOVING)

In this step, it is necessary to add and/or subtract appropriate numbers from the rows and/or columns of the current assignment matrix to obtain a new assignment matrix with Properties 1 and 2. Proceed as follows:

a. Cover all cells containing zero values by drawing a line through the fewest number of rows and columns as possible. (This requires the same number of lines as cells identified in Step 1.) If there are several ways to do so, arbitrarily select one.

b. Among all uncrossed cells, identify the one with smallest value and do the following:

   i Subtract this number from all uncrossed rows.
   ii Add this number to all crossed columns.

The net result of performing the computations in steps (i) and (ii) is that the value in each uncrossed cell is reduced by this value, and each value in a cell in both a crossed row and column is increased by this value.

Applying Step 2 to the matrix in Figure 9.46(a) results in crossing out rows 1 and 2, and column 5, as shown in Figure 9.46(b).

From the remaining uncrossed cell, the one in row 3 and column 4 has the smallest value, which is 2. This value is subtracted from all uncrossed cells, and added to the cells in row 1 and column 5, and row 2 and column 5, because these two cells are both in crossed rows and columns. The result is the new assignment matrix in Figure 9.46(c). By using this new matrix, Step 1 is performed again.

	1	2	3	4	5
1	1	0	3	7	0
2	0	2	0	0	0
3	6	10	3	2	0
4	14	12	5	7	0
5	16	20	3	7	0

(a)

	1	2	3	4	5
1	1	0	3	7	0
2	0	2	0	0	0
3	6	10	3	2	0
4	14	12	5	7	0
5	16	20	3	7	0

(b)

FIGURE 9.46 Applying the Assignment Algorithm to the Problem of Containers, Inc.

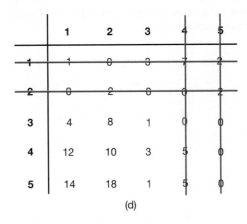

	1	2	3	4	5
1	1	(0)	3	7	2
2	(0)	2	0	0	2
3	4	8	1	(0)	0
4	12	10	3	5	(0)
5	14	18	1	5	0

(c)

	1	2	3	4	5
1	1	0	3	7	2
2	0	2	0	0	2
3	4	8	1	0	0
4	12	10	3	5	0
5	14	18	1	5	0

(d)

	1	2	3	4	5
1	1	(0)	3	8	3
2	(0)	2	0	1	3
3	3	7	0	(0)	0
4	11	9	2	5	(0)
5	13	17	(0)	5	0

(e)

FIGURE 9.46 (cont.)

ITERATION 2: STEP 1 (TEST FOR OPTIMALITY)

Again, try to identify a feasible assignment in which the selected cells all have the value 0. In this case, there is no such assignment. However, a partial assignment having four cells with a value of 0 is indicated by the circled cells in Figure 9.46(c). The partial assignment in Figure 9.46(c) has one more cell of value 0 than the partial assignment in Figure 9.46(a); however, such improvement may not always occur in each iteration.

ITERATION 2: STEP 2 (MOVING)

In this step, appropriate numbers are again added to and/or subtracted from the rows and/or columns of the current assignment matrix to obtain a new assignment matrix with Properties 1 and 2. Proceed by crossing out rows 1 and 2, and columns 4 and 5, as shown in Figure 9.46(d).

From the remaining uncrossed cells, the one in row 3 and column 3 has the smallest value, which is 1. This value of 1 is then subtracted from all uncrossed cells and added to the cells in which both the row and column have been crossed. The result is the new assignment matrix in Figure 9.46(e). By using this new matrix, Step 1 is performed again.

ITERATION 3: STEP 1 (TEST FOR OPTIMALITY)

Again test for optimality by attempting to identify a feasible assignment in which all the selected cells have value 0. Such an assignment *is* possible, as shown by the circled cells in Figure 9.46(e). By using the original processing times in Table 9.20 for the problem of Containers, Inc., this optimal solution results in the assignment shown in Table 9.22.

COMPUTER SOLUTION

The solution of the problem of Containers, Inc., obtained from the STORM software package is shown in Figure 9.47. This assignment, which is the same as the one in Figure 9.46(e), results in a total processing time of 97 hours. Observe that Order 4 is not filled because it has been assigned to the dummy Machine 5. Finally, note that the same solution is obtained when using the computer package QSB, as shown in Figure 9.48.

Assignment
EX9_6.DAT

TABLE 9.22	Optimal Assignment for the Problem of Containers, Inc.	
CONTAINER SIZE	MACHINE	TIME
3 × 4	Machine 2	20
4 × 6	Machine 1	24
6 × 8	Machine 4	25
8 × 12	Dummy	0
12 × 18	Machine 3	28
	Total Cost =	97

```
     The Assignment Problem of Containers, Inc.
               OPTIMAL SOLUTION
     Row                  Column           Cost


     3 X 4                MACHINE 2          20
     4 X 6                MACHINE 1          24
     6 X 8                MACHINE 4          25
     8 X 12               DUMMY               0
     12 X 18              MACHINE 3          28


     Total Cost = 97
     Number of Iterations = 3
```

FIGURE 9.47 STORM Output for the Assignment Problem of Containers, Inc.

```
|--------------------------------------------------------------------|
|      Summary of Assignments for Containers Inc.     Page: 1        |
|--------------------------------------------------------------------|
|  Object  |  Task  |Cost/Prof.| Object  |  Task  |Cost/Prof.|
|----------+--------+----------+---------+--------+----------|
|   3x4    |   M2   |  +20.00  |  8x12   | Dummy  |       0  |
|   4x6    |   M1   |  +24.00  |  12x18  |  M3    |  +28.00  |
|   6x8    |   M4   |  +25.00  |         |        |          |
|--------------------------------------------------------------------|
|   Minimum OBJ = 97   Iteration = 3   CPU second = .1640625        |
|--------------------------------------------------------------------|
```

FIGURE 9.48 QSB Output for the Assignment Problem of Containers, Inc.

➡ **KEY FEATURES**

Summary of the Steps of the Assignment Algorithm

To solve a balanced assignment problem, follow these steps.

THE ASSIGNMENT ALGORITHM

Step 0. *Initialization*: Create the initial matrix having Properties 1 and 2 by modifying the original assignment matrix as follows:

1. For each row, identify the smallest number and subtract that value from every cell in this row.
2. For each column, identify the smallest number and subtract that value from every cell in this column.

> **Step 1.** *Test for Optimality*: Attempt to identify a feasible assignment in the current matrix in which each selected cell has the value 0. If such an assignment is found, stop—this is the optimal solution; otherwise, find the maximum number of assignments that *do have* a value of zero and go to Step 2.
>
> **Step 2.** *Moving*: Create a new assignment matrix having Properties 1 and 2 by performing the following:
>
> > **1.** Cover all cells containing zero values by drawing a line through the fewest number of rows and columns possible.
> >
> > **2.** Identify, among all uncrossed cells, the one with the smallest value and
> > **a.** subtract this number from all uncrossed cells and
> > **b.** add this number to all cells in both a crossed row and column
>
> Now go to Step 1.

In this section, you have learned the assignment algorithm, which is an efficient method for solving a balanced assignment problem. Having learned the applications and algorithms associated with the transportation, transshipment, and assignment problems, you can now bring this knowledge together with a case study.

CASE STUDY

In this section, you can apply your knowledge of distribution network problems in formulating and solving a complex problem. Consider the problem facing the management of Good Tire, Inc.

The Warehouse-Location Problem of Good Tire, Inc.

Good Tire, Inc., is a manufacturer and distributor of automobile tires. The plant located in Akron, Ohio, ships tires directly to 10 wholesale customers. Due to the large travel distances involved, the company has decided to open several regional warehouses closer to their customers. Doing so will allow tires to be delivered on a more timely basis. The Planning Division has identified five suitable locations: Cleveland, Harrisburg, Chicago, Trenton, and Louisville. For a warehouse built at each location, Table 9.23 provides the capacity in thousands of tires per month together with the associated shipping cost per tire from the plant in Akron to each potential warehouse and the monthly overhead costs for operating the warehouse.

Good Tire, Inc., has steady long-term relationships with the 10 wholesale customers. The Sales Department has observed that the demand remains fairly constant from one month to the next. The Accounting and Sales Departments have put together data pertaining to the 10 wholesale customers of Good Tire, Inc. Table 9.24 contains the monthly demands in thousands of tires and the projected transportation cost per tire from each of the five proposed warehouses to the 10 wholesalers.

As Manager of the Corporate Planning Department, you have been asked to make a recommendation as to which warehouse locations should be selected to meet all monthly demands while minimizing total monthly costs.

TABLE 9.23 *Costs Associated with Opening a Warehouse*

LOCATION	CAPACITY (000/MONTH)	SHIPPING COST ($/TIRE) FROM THE PLANT	OVERHEAD COST ($/MONTH)
Cleveland	80	0.25	40,000
Harrisburg	60	0.50	20,000
Chicago	60	0.75	30,000
Trenton	60	0.75	25,000
Louisville	60	0.75	20,000

Identifying an Approach to Solving the Warehouse-Location Problem of Good Tire, Inc.

At first glance, you might think of formulating a single transportation problem in which the supply nodes correspond to the five warehouses and the demand nodes correspond to the 10 wholesale customers. The problem with this approach, however, is that the warehouses do not yet exist; one of your tasks is to *decide* which ones to build. If you decide to build and use all five warehouses, then that transportation model is appropriate, but what about the possibility of building and using only four (or fewer) of the five warehouses?

You might consider creating 32 transportation models, one for each possible combination of one warehouse, two warehouses, three warehouses, and so on. Although this is possible, you can save much time and effort by looking carefully at the data and using common sense. The total demand of the 10 wholesalers is 248,000 tires. Looking at the capacities of the five proposed warehouses will lead you to realize that to meet this total demand at least four of the five warehouses *must* be built. Therefore, *only* the following combinations need be considered:

1. All five warehouses.
2. All five except for the one at Harrisburg.
3. All five except for the one at Chicago.

TABLE 9.24 *Transportation Costs and Demands for Wholesale Customers*

CUSTOMERS	CLEVE.	HARRIS.	CHICAGO	TRENTON	LOUISVILLE	DEMAND
Cleveland	0.25	0.63	1.75	2.13	1.75	30
Cincinnati	1.25	1.50	1.50	2.75	0.50	20
Dayton	0.75	1.38	1.38	2.38	1.00	18
Indianapolis	1.63	1.75	1.00	3.50	0.50	16
Chicago	1.75	2.38	0.25	3.88	1.50	38
Buffalo	1.00	1.13	2.75	1.88	2.75	22
Pittsburgh	0.63	0.88	2.38	1.75	2.00	27
Philadelphia	2.13	0.63	3.88	0.50	3.50	32
Nashville	2.63	2.88	2.38	4.25	0.88	19
Boston	3.25	2.75	5.00	1.25	4.88	26

SHIPPING COST($/TIRE) FROM REGIONAL WAREHOUSE

Total Demand = 248

4. All five except for the one at Trenton.

5. All five except for the one at Louisville.

Observe that the combination of "all five except for the one at Cleveland" is not included. This is because the total capacity of the remaining four warehouses is only 240,000 tires, which is not enough to meet the total demand of 248,000.

Now follow this approach:

1. Create a transportation problem associated with each of the five foregoing combinations.

2. Determine the least-cost shipping plan and associated total monthly transportation cost for each combination.

3. Add the monthly overhead costs of each selected warehouse to the amount obtained in step 2 for each combination.

4. Find the one combination that provides the least total (transportation plus overhead) monthly cost.

Solving the Warehouse-Location Problem of Good Tire, Inc.

Now formulate the appropriate transportation model for each of the five combinations of warehouse locations identified previously. For example, if all five warehouses are built, the associated transportation problem has one supply node for each of these warehouses and one demand node for each of the 10 wholesale customers. This problem is not balanced because the total capacity of 320,000 tires at the five warehouses exceeds the total demand of 248,000 tires by the wholesalers, so a dummy customer is added to absorb the excess capacity of 72,000 tires.

To complete the formulation, you must now specify a "shipping cost" from each warehouse to each customer, including the dummy customer. In so doing, observe that the cost of shipping a tire from a warehouse to a particular customer must first include the cost of getting the tire from the plant in Akron to the warehouse and then shipping that tire to the customer. For example, by using the information in Tables 9.23 and 9.24, the total shipping cost from the warehouse in Cleveland to the wholesaler in Buffalo is

$$
\begin{aligned}
\text{Total shipping cost} \quad &= \quad \text{(cost from Akron)} + \text{(cost from Cleveland to Buffalo)} \\
&= \quad 0.25 + 1.00 \\
&= \quad 1.25
\end{aligned}
$$

Performing similar computations for each warehouse-to-customer combination results in the total transportation costs in Table 9.25. Observe from the table that the cost to the dummy customer from each warehouse is 0 because the surplus at each warehouse need not be shipped from the plant in Akron.

The solution to this transportation problem obtained from an appropriate computer package is provided in Table 9.26. The total transportation cost is $292,850. By adding the overhead cost of $135,000 for the five warehouses, as given in Table 9.23, the total monthly cost for this combination is $427,850.

This process of formulating the appropriate transportation model, obtaining the solution from a computer, and adding the monthly overhead costs of all warehouses in the combination must be done for each of the remaining four combinations. To save time and effort, note that each of the remaining four combinations excludes exactly one of the warehouses. One way to solve the associated transportation problem is to modify the information in Table 9.25 by deleting the column corresponding to the excluded warehouse or, more simply, by setting the capacity of that warehouse to 0

Transportation
GDTIRE.DAT

TABLE 9.25 *Total Transportation Costs and Demands for Wholesale Customers*

CUSTOMERS	TOTAL SHIPPING COST ($/TIRE) FROM REGIONAL WAREHOUSE					DEMAND
	CLEVE.	HARRIS.	CHICAGO	TRENTON	LOUISVILLE	
Cleveland	0.50	1.13	2.50	2.88	2.50	30
Cincinnati	1.50	2.00	2.25	3.50	1.25	20
Dayton	1.00	1.88	2.13	3.13	1.75	18
Indianapolis	1.88	2.25	1.75	4.25	1.25	16
Chicago	2.00	2.88	1.00	4.63	2.25	38
Buffalo	1.25	1.63	3.50	2.63	3.50	22
Pittsburgh	0.88	1.38	3.13	2.50	2.75	27
Philadelphia	2.38	1.13	4.63	1.25	4.25	32
Nashville	2.88	3.38	3.13	5.00	1.63	19
Boston	3.50	3.25	5.75	2.00	5.63	26
Dummy Customer	0.00	0.00	0.00	0.00	0.00	72
Capacities	80	60	60	60	60	

TABLE 9.26 *Optimal Shipments from Regional Warehouses to Wholesale Customers*

CUSTOMERS	TOTAL SHIPMENT (THOUSANDS) from Regional Warehouse					DEMAND
	CLEVE.	HARRIS.	CHICAGO	TRENTON	LOUISVILLE	
Cleveland	30					30
Cincinnati					20	20
Dayton	18					18
Indianapolis					16	16
Chicago			38			38
Buffalo	5	17				22
Pittsburgh	27					27
Philadelphia		32				32
Nashville					19	19
Boston				26		26
Dummy Customer		11	22	34	5	72
Capacities	80	60	60	60	60	

Total transportation costs = $292,850

and adjusting the demand of the dummy customer to obtain a balanced problem. The results of doing this are summarized in Table 9.27.

From Table 9.27, you can see that the combination having the least total monthly cost—$422,540—includes all warehouses except the one in Harrisburg. You should therefore recommend opening the four warehouses in Cleveland, Chicago, Trenton, and Louisville. However, it is worth noting that the next best alternative of opening all five warehouses has an additional monthly cost of only $5310. If future demand is likely to increase, perhaps in the longer run Good Tire, Inc., would be better off building all five warehouses now. After all, the additional $5310 that would be necessary is quite small compared to the total costs, which are on the order of $400,000. You might therefore want to present this alternative to management also.

TABLE 9.27	Total Monthly Costs for Each Combination in the Warehouse-Location Problem of Good Tire, Inc.		
COMBINATION	SHIPPING COST	MONTHLY OVERHEAD	TOTAL
All five	292,850	135,000	427,850
All except Harrisburg	307,540	115,000	422,540
All except Chicago	350,770	105,000	455,770
All except Trenton	334,700	110,000	444,700
All except Louisville	349,640	115,000	464,640

ADDITIONAL MANAGERIAL CONSIDERATIONS

In this chapter, you have learned that a distribution network problem, when formulated mathematically, results in a linear program with the additional constraints that all variables must be integers. You also learned that there are specialized algorithms for solving such problems efficiently. However, software using these specialized algorithms may not be available in your organization. If anticipated usage does not justify the cost of acquiring such software, you can always solve the resulting problem as a linear program (by ignoring the integer requirement on the variables) using linear programming software packages which are more commonly available.

Solving distribution network problems as linear programs is not as efficient as using the specialized algorithms, but there is an additional advantage to doing so. Most linear programming software packages provide much information pertaining to sensitivity and parametric analysis (see Sections 6.3 and 6.4). This information is used to answer numerous questions of the form "What happens if ?" In case this information is needed and your specialized package does not provide these reports, you should solve the problem as a linear program.

In Section 9.3, you learned to convert an unbalanced transportation problem into an equivalent balanced one by adding an appropriate dummy supply or demand node together with dummy arcs. Most computer packages will do so automatically. However, they also assign a cost of 0 to each dummy arc. As you learned in Examples 9.3 and 9.4 in Section 9.3, these costs of 0 for the dummy arcs may *not* be appropriate. In these cases, you must explicitly include the dummy node, arcs, and associated costs when you enter the information into the computer package.

In Section 9.6, you saw how to include various additional constraints to the basic transportation problem. In some cases, the resulting problem could be solved using the standard stepping stone algorithm; in other cases, more specialized algorithms are necessary, for example, to solve the capacitated transportation problem. If your distribution network problem involves these additional constraints, you will need to determine if the software you have available is capable of solving this variation. If not, attempt to formulate an "equivalent" problem that your software *is* capable of handling.

SUMMARY

In this chapter, you learned to formulate and solve distribution network problems, including transportation, transshipment, and assignment problems. All of these problems can be represented pictorially by a network containing appropriate supply, demand, and transshipment nodes together with arcs that connect certain pairs of these nodes. The overall objective is to determine how best to ship (or transport, or assign) the goods (be they machines, people, or whatever) from the supply nodes, through the transshipment nodes, to the demand nodes to minimize the total costs (or maximize the total profits) while meeting specified demands and not exceeding available supplies. You also learned to convert an unbalanced problem in which the total supply is not equal to the total demand into an equivalent balanced problem by adding a dummy supply or dummy demand node together with dummy arcs. In so doing, you learned of the care that must be taken in assigning appropriate costs to the dummy arcs that correspond to surplus supply or demand.

The mathematical formulation of these network distribution problems results in a linear program with the additional constraint that the values of the variables must be integers. Specialized algorithms, such as the stepping stone algorithm, are available to solve these problems efficiently. You learned that these algorithms start with an initial shipping plan and then move to a better one (in terms of cost or profit), until an optimal shipping plan is obtained. You also learned how to solve distribution network problems by computer and how to interpret the results thus obtained.

APPENDIX 9A
COMPUTING REDUCED COSTS
BY THE MODI METHOD

Modified distribution method (MODI)
A method for computing the reduced costs of the empty cells in a transportation tableau.

In this appendix, you will learn another method for computing reduced costs of the empty cells in a transportation tableau (see Section 9.5). This method is called the **modified distribution method** (MODI). Recall the transportation problem of CCC discussed in Section 9.5. The initial shipping plan for this problem using the matrix minimum method was derived in Section 9.5 and is reproduced here as Figure 9.49. MODI method requires computing a value u_i for each row and a value v_j for each column of the tableau. These values are chosen so that for each *nonempty* cell in row i and column j, the unit shipping cost c_{ij} is equal to the row value u_i plus the column value v_j. For example, for the nonempty cell in row 1 and column 2 in Figure 9.49, whose unit cost is 3:

$$u_1 + v_2 = \ 3 \quad \text{(row 1, column 2)}$$

Similarly, for the remaining nonempty cells in Figure 9.49:

$$u_1 + v_3 = \ 2 \quad \text{(row 1, column 3)}$$

$$u_2 + v_1 = \ 4 \quad \text{(row 2, column 1)}$$

$$u_2 + v_4 = 10 \quad \text{(row 2, column 4)}$$

$$u_3 + v_2 = \ 5 \quad \text{(row 3, column 2)}$$

$$u_3 + v_4 = \ 8 \quad \text{(row 3, column 4)}$$

In this case, there are seven unknowns (u_1, u_2, u_3, v_1, v_2, v_3, and v_4) but only six equations. One set of values for these seven variables can be found by arbitrarily setting one of the variables to 0—say, u_1—and then using the list of equations to find the remaining values. On setting u_1 to 0, solve all equations for the nonempty cells in row 1.

EQUATIONS FROM ROW 1 ($u_1 = 0$)

$$u_1 + v_2 = 3, \qquad \text{so } v_2 = 3$$

Retail Outlets

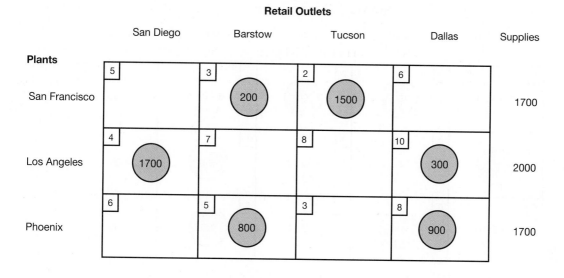

FIGURE 9.49 Initial Shipping Plan Obtained by the Matrix Minimum Method for the Transportation Problem of CCC.

$$u_1 + v_3 = 2, \quad \text{so } v_3 = 2$$

Having found the values of v_2 and v_3 for columns 2 and 3, now solve the equations corresponding to the remaining nonempty cells in those columns.

REMAINING EQUATIONS FROM COLUMNS 2 AND 3 $(v_2 = 3, v_3 = 2)$

$$u_3 + v_2 = 5, \quad \text{so } u_3 = 2$$

Having found the value of u_3 for row 3, now solve the equations corresponding to the remaining nonempty cells in that row.

REMAINING EQUATIONS FROM ROW 3 $(u_3 = 2)$

$$u_3 + v_4 = 8, \quad \text{so } v_4 = 6$$

Continuing the process of alternating between rows and columns results in the following complete list of values:

$$u_1 = 0, \quad u_2 = 4, \quad u_3 = 2$$

$$v_1 = 0, \quad v_2 = 3, \quad v_3 = 2, \quad v_4 = 6$$

These values are shown next to the appropriate rows and columns of the tableau in Figure 9.50.

Once these row and column values are obtained, the reduced cost of each *empty* cell in row i and column j with a unit shipping cost of c_{ij} is computed as follows:

$$\text{Reduced cost of empty cell } (i, j) = c_{ij} - u_i - v_j$$

Retail Outlets

Plants	San Diego $v_1 = 0$	Barstow $v_2 = 3$	Tucson $v_3 = 2$	Dallas $v_4 = 6$	Supplies
San Francisco $u_1 = 0$	[5] 5 - 0 - 0 = +5	[3] 200	[2] 1500	[6] 6 - 0 - 6 = + 0	1700
Los Angeles $u_2 = 4$	[4] 1700	[7] 7 - 4 - 3 = + 0	[8] 8 - 4 - 2 = + 2	[10] 300	2000
Phoenix $u_3 = 2$	[6] 6 - 2 - 0 = + 4	[5] 800	[3] 3 - 2 - 2 = - 1	[8] 900	1700
Demands	1700	1000	1500	1200	$24,600

FIGURE 9.50 Using the MODI Method to Compute the Reduced Costs of the Empty Cells for the Shipping Plan in Figure 9.49.

For example, the reduced cost of the empty cell in row 1 and column 4 whose unit shipping cost is 6 is

$$\text{Reduced cost of empty cell } (1, 4) = 6 - u_1 - v_4$$
$$= 6 - 0 - 6$$
$$= 0$$

The computation of these reduced costs is shown in Figure 9.50. As you can see, these reduced costs are identical to the values obtained in Figure 9.30 in Section 9.5.

APPENDIX 9B
RESOLVING DEGENERACY IN THE TRANSPORTATION ALGORITHM

Section 9.5 describes the steps of the stepping stone algorithm for solving the transportation problem. In some cases, special care is needed to handle unusual conditions that can arise.

■ 9B.1 RESOLVING DEGENERACY IN THE MATRIX MINIMUM METHOD

As you learned in Section 9.5, the first step in solving a balanced transportation problem with m supply nodes and n demand nodes is to find an initial shipping plan using $m + n - 1$ cells and having no cycles. The matrix minimum method requires the following steps:

1. Identify an uncrossed cell whose cost is the smallest. (In case of ties, choose any such cell.)
2. For the cell identified in (1), determine the smaller of the remaining supply in that row and the remaining demand in that column.
3.
    i. Put the amount determined in (2) in the identified cell.
    ii. Reduce the remaining supply in the row by the amount shipped in this cell.
    iii. Reduce the remaining demand in the column by the amount shipped in this cell.
    iv. Cross out the row or column whose remaining supply or demand has now been reduced to 0.

A problem arises in (iv) when *both* the supply and the demand are reduced simultaneously to 0. This situation is referred to as **degeneracy**. In this case, you should do the following:

1. Cross out the row.
2. Arbitrarily choose any uncrossed cell in this column.
3. Assign a shipment of 0 to this cell and consider it as a *nonempty* cell.
4. Cross out this column.

Degeneracy
A problem that arises in solving some transportation problems when both the supply and the demand are reduced simultaneously to 0 during an iteration of the matrix minimum method.

Consider the transportation tableau in Figure 9.51 involving three supply nodes (Plant 1, Plant 2, and Plant 3) and three demand nodes (Customer 1, Customer 2, and Customer 3).

Follow the steps of the matrix minimum method. The cell of least cost occurs in row 1 and column 1. Assigning a shipment of 2 to this cell (which is the minimum of the available supply of 4 and the demand of 2) reduces the corresponding supply and demand by 2. Crossing out column 1 results in the tableau of Figure 9.52.

Now the least-cost cell that is uncrossed is in row 1 and column 3. Assigning a shipment of 2 to this cell (which is the minimum of the remaining supply of 2 and the demand of 2) reduces the corresponding supply and demand by 2. Both the supply in row 1 and the demand in column 3 are now 0. To resolve this degeneracy, follow these additional steps:

	Customer 1	Customer 2	Customer 3	Supplies
Plant 1	2	4	3	4
Plant 2	5	5	7	4
Plant 3	3	9	6	2
Demands	2	6	2	

FIGURE 9.51 Transportation Tableau.

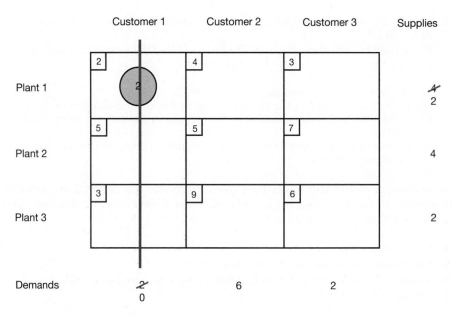

FIGURE 9.52 First Step of the Matrix Minimum Method.

1. Cross out row 1.
2. Arbitrarily choose any uncrossed cell in column 3 (say, in row 3).
3. Assign a shipment of 0 to the cell in row 3 and column 3, and consider that cell to be nonempty.
4. Cross out column 3.

Performing these steps results in the tableau of Figure 9.53.

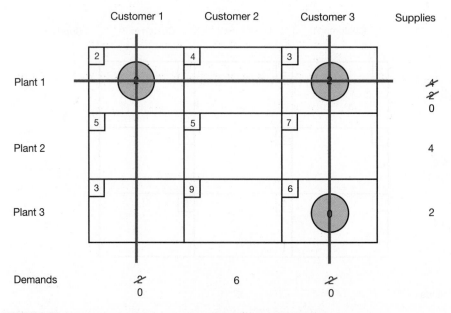

FIGURE 9.53 Resolving Degeneracy in the Matrix Minimum Method.

Continuing with the matrix minimum method for two more iterations, you will discover that no other degeneracies occur, and you should obtain the initial shipping plan of Figure 9.54.

It is important to realize that although the value of 0 in row 3 and column 3 means that no units are shipped from supply node 3 to demand node 3, this cell is *different* from an empty cell. Recall that reduced costs are computed for each *empty* cell. Because the cell in row 3 and column 3 is *not* empty, no reduced cost is computed for this cell. Moreover, this cell, with a value of 0, can be used in finding the cycle for computing the reduced costs of empty cells.

Consider computing the reduced cost of the cell in row 3 and column 1. The appropriate cycle contains the four corner cells of the tableau of Figure 9.54—including the cell containing the value of 0—as indicated by the values of $+1$ and -1 in the tableau of Figure 9.55.

From the cycle in the tableau of Figure 9.55, you can see that the reduced cost for the cell in row 3 and column 1 is $+3 - 6 + 3 - 2 = -2$. This negative value indicates that the current shipping plan is not optimal. The total shipping cost of $48 will be reduced by $2 for each unit that can be shipped in this cell. You can also verify that this empty cell has the most negative reduced cost.

According to the stepping stone algorithm, to determine the *maximum* number of units that can be shipped in this cell, you must look at the cells in the cycle containing a value of -1 (the cells in row 3, column 3 and in row 1, column 1). Note that the minimum of these shipping numbers is 0, as determined by the value of 0 in the cell in row 3 and column 3. In other words, *zero* units can be shipped along the arc corresponding to the cell in row 3 and column 1.

In spite of this problem, it is still possible to proceed with the stepping stone algorithm, just as you would normally do. Put a value of 0 in the cell in row 3 and column 1, and consider it to be nonempty. Erase the value of 0 in the cell in row 3 and column 3, and consider it to be empty. Observe that the values in the other cells in the cycle need not be changed in this case because no units are being shipped in the new cell. The tableau of Figure 9.56 results and includes the new reduced costs.

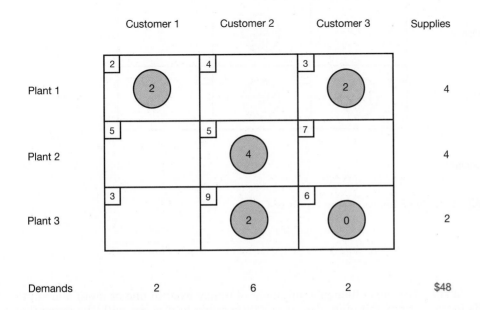

FIGURE 9.54 Initial Shipping Plan.

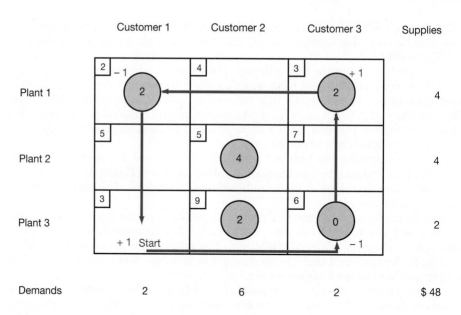

FIGURE 9.55 Computing the Reduced Cost of the Cell in Row 3 and Column 1.

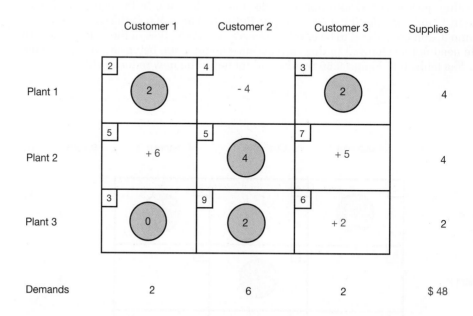

FIGURE 9.56 New Shipping Plan and Reduced Costs.

In summary, even though a shipment of 0 may exist in one or more nonempty cells in the current shipping plan, it is still possible to proceed with the remaining steps of the stepping stone algorithm.

■ 9B.2 RESOLVING DEGENERACY IN THE STEPPING STONE ALGORITHM

Degeneracy can also arise in the stepping stone algorithm when a new shipping plan is being determined. Observe that the tableau of Figure 9.56 indicates that the current shipping plan is not optimal because of the reduced cost of −4 in the cell in row 1 and column 2. As you proceed with the stepping stone algorithm, it is necessary to determine the maximum number of units that can be shipped in this cell using the cycle in Figure 9.57.

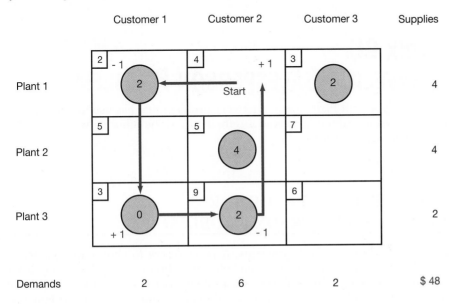

FIGURE 9.57 Resolving Degeneracy in the Stepping Stone Algorithm.

	Customer 1	Customer 2	Customer 3	Supplies
Plant 1	2 0	4 2	3 2	4
Plant 2	5 + 2	5 4	7 + 2	4
Plant 3	3 2	9 + 3	6 + 1	2
Demands	2	6	2	$ 40

FIGURE 9.58 The Optimal Shipping Plan.

Identify the cells in the cycle with a value of −1. The maximum number of units that can be shipped in this cell in row 1 and column 2 is two units. In making the appropriate adjustments to the nonempty cells in the cycle, observe that the amounts shipped in the cells in row 1, column 1 and in row 3, column 2 are simultaneously reduced to 0. When this type of degeneracy occurs, choose one and only one of these cells to become empty. All other such cells remain nonempty with a shipment of 0. For example, arbitrarily choosing to make the cell in row 3 and column 2 empty results in the new shipping plan, with the new reduced costs, shown in Figure 9.58.

The fact that all reduced costs are nonnegative now indicates that the current shipping plan is optimal.

APPENDIX 9C
THE TRAVELING-SALESPERSON PROBLEM

In this appendix you will learn about a network problem that has useful applications but that unfortunately cannot be solved as efficiently as the other network problems you have learned in this chapter.

■ 9C.1 APPLICATIONS OF THE TRAVELING-SALESPERSON PROBLEM

Traveling-salesperson problem
The problem of determining the least-cost sequence of nodes to visit so that each node in the network is visited exactly once and the trip ends at the starting node.

In many applications of network problems, it is necessary to choose a *sequence* of nodes to visit so as to accomplish a specified objective. In this appendix, you will see two applications of the **traveling-salesperson problem**: Given a network and a cost (or distance) associated with each arc, it is necessary to start from a specified originating node, visit each and every other node exactly once, and return to the starting node in the least-cost manner. For example, a bus that leaves the school yard must stop at various locations once to pick up students and ultimately return to the school yard in the shortest possible time. As another example, consider the weekly delivery problem faced by the management of Good Tire, Inc.

EXAMPLE 9.10 THE TRAVELING-SALESPERSON PROBLEM OF GOOD TIRE, INC.
Good Tire, Inc., manufactures tires at its plant in Akron and has regional warehouses throughout the country, one of which is located in St. Louis. From this regional warehouse, weekly deliveries are made to five local retail stores by one truck. The driving times in minutes between any two stores and between the regional warehouse and any store are given in Table 9.28.

TABLE 9.28 *Driving Time (min) for the Problem of Good Tire, Inc.*

	WAREHOUSE	STORE 1	2	3	4	5
Warehouse	—	40	55	45	60	65
Store 1		—	60	55	60	50
Store 2			—	55	70	90
Store 3				—	50	70
Store 4					—	70

As Manager of the Distribution Department, you are to determine if the truck driver can make all deliveries and return to the warehouse within 8 hours, allowing 30 minutes for unloading at each store. ■

To formulate this problem as a network, identify one node for the regional warehouse and five additional nodes for each of the five retail stores. An arc between two nodes represents the road connection between the associated locations. This network is illustrated in Figure 9.59. Note that each arc has arrows on both ends, which indicate that travel is possible in both directions. The number next to each arc is the travel time between the associated nodes in either direction, as given in Table 9.28. (If the travel times were different in each direction, you would use two arcs, one in each direction, together with the associated travel times.)

The next step is to specify an overall objective and describe the problem in terms of the network. In this case, the overall objective is to determine if the driver can visit each store exactly once, unload the tires, and return to the warehouse within 8 hours. Of these 8 hours (480 minutes), only 330 minutes are available for driving because the total unloading time at the five stores is $5 * 30 = 150$ minutes. Is 330 minutes enough driving time? One way to find out is to determine the *delivery schedule*—that is, the sequence of stores to visit—that requires the least total driving time and to see if this sequence takes less than the 330 available minutes. That is, the objective is to determine a sequence of nodes to visit so that

1. The warehouse is the starting and ending node.
2. Each and every node is visited exactly once.
3. The total driving time is as small as possible.

For instance, consider the following schedule:

Warehouse → Store 1 → Store 2 → Store 3 → Store 4 → Store 5 → Warehouse

with a total driving time of

$$\text{Total driving time} = 40 + 60 + 55 + 50 + 70 + 65 = 340$$

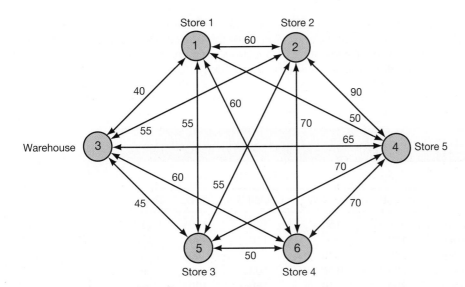

FIGURE 9.59 Network Representation of the Traveling-Salesperson Problem of Good Tire, Inc.

Observe that a schedule is a "cycle" that contains every node exactly once. Unfortunately, this particular cycle does not allow the driver to make all the deliveries and return to the warehouse within the 330 minutes of available driving time. You could try other cycles in the hope of finding one for which the total driving time *is* below 330 minutes. A better approach, however, is to determine the cycle with the *least* total driving time and see if it is less than 330 minutes.

KEY FEATURES
The Traveling-Salesperson Problem

Given a network and a cost (or distance, or time, and so on) associated with each arc, find a cycle of least *total* cost (or distance, or time, and so on) that includes each and every node exactly once.

This problem is called the traveling-salesperson problem because it reflects the task of a salesperson who needs to start in his or her home city, visit customers in various other cities exactly once, and eventually return to his or her own city so as to minimize the total cost of the effort.

In the traveling-salesperson problem of Good Tire, Inc., the nodes represent certain physical locations. However, there are many other types of decision problems that can be formulated as traveling-salesperson problems in which the nodes do *not* represent physical locations, but rather other aspects of the problem, as you will see in the next example.

EXAMPLE 9.11 THE TRAVELING-SALESPERSON PROBLEM OF PHILADELPHIA PAINT
COMPANY   Philadelphia Paint Company produces five colors of paint each month. When switching from one color to the next, the blending machine must be cleaned and prepared for the next color. This setup time depends on which color was just produced and which color is to be produced next. The setup times when switching between all pairs of colors are given in Table 9.29. As Manager of the Production Department, you are to determine the sequence in which to produce the five colors so as to minimize the total setup time. ■

The first step in creating a network problem is to identify the nodes and arcs. In this case, create five nodes, one for each of the five colors. An arc connecting one node to another indicates switching from producing one color (corresponding to the first node) to another color (that of the other node).

TABLE 9.29	*Setup Times (minutes) When Switching from One Color to Another*				
			TO		
FROM	WHITE	YELLOW	ORANGE	RED	BLACK
White	—	150	120	100	110
Yellow	170	—	110	90	100
Orange	200	170	—	80	100
Red	220	190	100	—	90
Black	300	210	180	130	—

The next step is to identify data associated with the nodes and/or arcs. In this case, the setup times in Table 9.29 are associated with each arc in the network.

Now it is necessary to describe the problem and objective in terms of the network. As stated, the objective is to determine the sequence in which to produce the five colors every month so that the total setup time is as small as possible. For example, the setup time for the following sequence is 730 minutes.

$$150 \; + \; 110 \; + \; 80 \; + \; 90 \; + \; 300 \; = \; 730$$
$$\text{White} \rightarrow \text{Yellow} \rightarrow \text{Orange} \rightarrow \text{Red} \rightarrow \text{Black} \rightarrow \text{White}$$

Observe that after producing Black, it is necessary to prepare the machine for producing White for the *next* production cycle, thus incurring the final setup time of 300 minutes. In the context of the network, the objective is achieved by finding a cycle that includes all the nodes so that the sum of the times of the arcs in the cycle is as small as possible. That is, this problem is a traveling-salesperson problem.

You will now learn some of the current methods available for solving traveling-salesperson problems.

■ 9C.2 THE TRAVELING-SALESPERSON PROBLEM: SOME HEURISTICS

At first glance, you might think that the travel-salesperson problem can be solved by finding the shortest path from the starting node back to itself. Unfortunately, this is not the case because that path most likely will not contain *all* the nodes in the network, as required.

KEY FEATURES

Unlike other network problems for which it is possible to develop efficient, specialized algorithms, *no efficient procedure currently exists for the traveling-salesperson problem,* despite persistent and continuing efforts of researchers in the field.

Although it is possible to obtain the optimal solution for the traveling-salesperson problem, handling large problems (even more than 20 nodes) can be computationally impractical because of the amount of time required to do so. To overcome this obstacle, researchers have developed numerous *heuristics* that are designed to obtain a "good" solution relatively quickly, though that solution may not be optimal. These heuristics fall into two basic categories:

1. **Tour-construction heuristics,** which build a cycle by including sequentially one node at a time until all nodes are used.
2. **Tour-improvement heuristics,** which, starting with an initial cycle, attempt to construct new cycles with progressively less total cost.

One commonly used heuristic in each category is now presented. You will also learn to interpret the results of using heuristics on a computer.

Tour-construction heuristic An approach to solving a traveling-salesperson problem that builds a cycle by including sequentially one node at a time until all nodes are used.

Tour-improvement heuristic An approach to solving a traveling-salesperson problem that starts with an initial cycle on all the nodes and attempts to construct new cycles on all the nodes with progressively less total cost.

A TOUR-CONSTRUCTION HEURISTIC FOR THE TRAVELING-SALESPERSON PROBLEM

With tour-construction heuristics, the basic idea is to start with a cycle of two nodes and create sequentially larger cycles by

1. Selecting a new node to be included.
2. Determining where to insert that selected node in the current cycle.

There are many different ways to choose the initial two nodes and many rules for selecting and inserting a new node. One such strategy called the cheapest-insertion algorithm is presented here.

To find the first cycle, select the two nodes that result in the least-cost cycle. For Example 9.11, trying all different cycles with two nodes and computing the setup time of the cycle results in choosing nodes O and R—that is, producing Orange, then Red, and then Orange—with a total setup time of 180 minutes, as shown in Figure 9.60(a).

ITERATION 1

To choose the next node to include in the current cycle, look at each remaining node. For example, consider node W. If you *were* to choose this node next, the first question is *where*, in the existing cycle, to insert it. In this case, you could insert node W either between nodes O and R or between nodes R and O.

1. Inserting node W between nodes O and R results in a total setup time of

$$200 \;+\; 100 + 100 \qquad = 400$$
$$\text{Orange} \rightarrow \text{White} \rightarrow \text{Red} \rightarrow \text{Orange}$$

2. Inserting node W between nodes R and O results in a total setup time of

$$80 \;+\; 220 \;+\; 120 \qquad = 420$$
$$\text{Orange} \rightarrow \text{Red} \rightarrow \text{White} \rightarrow \text{Orange}$$

The first total setup time is less than the second, so the first sequence is preferable, *if node W were selected next.* However, you can also select node Y or B. In each case, you can choose the best way to insert that node into the current cycle. That is, is the chosen node better between nodes O and R or between nodes R and O? The results of the various possibilities are summarized in Table 9.30.

TABLE 9.30	*Effect of Inserting a New Node in the Cycle O → R → O*		
NODE SELECTED	INSERTED BEWTEEN	NEW CYCLE	TOTAL SETUP TIME (MIN)
W	O and R	O → W → R → O	400
	R and O	O → R → W → O	420
Y	O and R	O → Y → R → O	360
	R and O	O → R → Y → O	380
B	O and R	O → B → R → O	330
	R and O	O → R → B → O	350

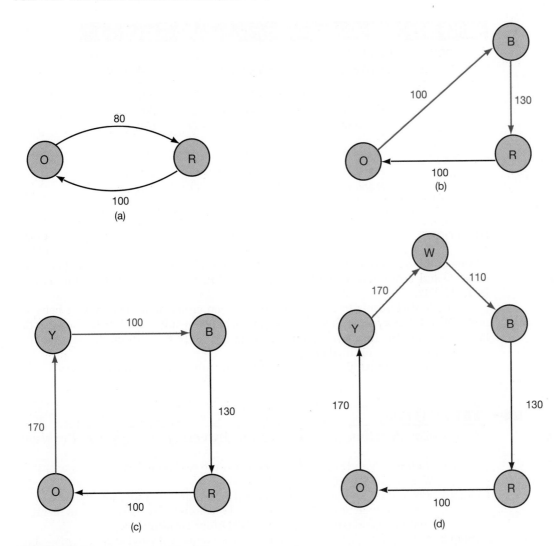

FIGURE 9.60 Tour-Construction Heuristic.

From the table, you can see that the best option is to insert node B between nodes O and R, resulting in a new cycle with a total setup time of 330, as shown in Figure 9.60.

ITERATION 2

The next step is to choose another node to insert, either node W or Y. For each choice, you can determine the best place to insert that node in the current cycle of Figure 9.60(b)—that is, the place that results in the least total setup time. For example, the selected node can be inserted between nodes O and B, nodes B and R, or nodes R and O. The total setup time for doing so in each case is given in Table 9.31.

From the table, you can see that the best choice is to insert node Y either between nodes O and B or between nodes B and R, which yields a cycle with a total setup time of 500. Arbitrarily choosing the former results in the new cycle shown in Figure 9.60(c).

TABLE 9.31   *Effect of Inserting a New Node in the Cycle* $O \to B \to R \to O$

NODE SELECTED	INSERTED BETWEEN	NEW CYCLE	TOTAL SETUP TIME (MIN)
W	O and B	$O \to W \to B \to R \to O$	540
	B and R	$O \to B \to W \to R \to O$	600
	R and O	$O \to B \to R \to W \to O$	570
Y	O and B	$O \to Y \to B \to R \to O$	500
	B and R	$O \to B \to Y \to R \to O$	500
	R and O	$O \to B \to R \to Y \to O$	530

ITERATION 3

At this point, only node W remains to be included. This node can be inserted between nodes O and Y, or nodes Y and B, or nodes B and R, or nodes R and O, as summarized in Table 9.32.

The best choice is to insert node W between either nodes O and Y or between nodes Y and B. A cycle with a total setup time of 680 results. Arbitrarily choosing the latter results in the final cycle shown in Figure 9.60(d). Keep in mind that this final cycle may not be the optimal one.

The steps of this tour-construction heuristic are summarized as follows:

➡ **KEY FEATURES**

A Tour-Construction Heuristic for the Traveling-Salesperson Problem

Step 0. *Initialization*: Create a cycle between the two nodes whose total cost is as small as possible.
Step 1. *Evaluation*: If all nodes are included in the current cycle, stop. Otherwise, for each node not in the current cycle, determine the best place to insert that node and compute the total cost of the resulting cycle.
Step 2. *Selection and Insertion*: Among all the nodes evaluated in Step 1, choose one that yields a new cycle of least total cost when inserted in its best location. Insert that node into its best location to create the new cycle. Go back to Step 1.

It seems that many computations are needed to perform this heuristic just to find a good, but not necessarily optimal, solution. However, the effort involved is *substantially* less than that needed to obtain the *optimal* solution.

TABLE 9.32   *Effect of Inserting a New Node in the Cycle* $O \to Y \to B \to R \to O$

NODE SELECTED	INSERTED BETWEEN	NEW CYCLE	TOTAL SETUP TIME (MIN)
W	O and Y	$O \to W \to Y \to B \to R \to O$	680
	Y and B	$O \to Y \to W \to B \to R \to O$	680
	B and R	$O \to Y \to B \to W \to R \to O$	720
	R and O	$O \to Y \to B \to R \to W \to O$	740

A TOUR-IMPROVEMENT HEURISTIC
FOR THE TRAVELING-SALESPERSON PROBLEM

As stated at the beginning of this section, a tour-improvement heuristic is one that starts with an initial complete cycle (such as the one found by a tour-construction heuristic) and attempts to find new complete cycles whose total cost is progressively smaller. The various heuristics in this class differ in the specific manner in which the new complete cycles are found.

One tour-improvement heuristic is called the **two-arc interchange method**. The basic idea is to remove two arcs from the current cycle and then replace them with two new arcs to create a new cycle. To illustrate with the problem of Example 9.11, consider, as the initial cycle, the one obtained in Figure 9.60(d), with a total setup time of 680 minutes. Now remove any two *nonadjacent arcs*, such as the arc from node O to node Y and the arc from node W to node B. Doing so results in breaking the cycle into two pieces, A and B, as shown in Figure 9.61(a).

A new complete cycle can be constructed in one of two ways:

1. Reverse the direction of all the arcs in piece A; then add two appropriate arcs to reconnect the two pieces into a cycle.
2. Reverse the direction of all the arcs in piece B; then add two appropriate arcs to reconnect the two pieces into a cycle.

For example, reversing the arcs in piece A in Figure 9.61(a) results in an arc from node W to node Y, as shown in Figure 9.61(b). Trying various ways, you will quickly discover that the *only* way to connect the two pieces in Figure 9.61(b) to form a complete cycle is to add the arcs from node Y to node B and from node O to node W, as shown by the dashed-line arcs in Figure 9.61(b). As you can easily compute, the setup time of the resulting cycle is 680 minutes.

Similarly, reversing the arcs in piece B in Figure 9.61(a) results in arcs from node O to node R and node R to node B, as shown in Figure 9.61(c). The only way to connect the two pieces in Figure 9.61(c) to form a complete cycle is to add the arcs from node B to node Y and from node W to node O, as shown by the dashed-line arcs. The setup time of the resulting cycle is 670 minutes.

Because the total setup time of 670 minutes for the cycle in Figure 9.61(c) is less than that of 680 minutes for the original cycle in Figure 9.60(d), a new improved cycle is found. This process of removing and adding two arcs can be done for all possible combinations of two nonadjacent arcs to remove from the original cycle to find the "best" improved cycle, if there is one. If no such improved cycle can be found, the procedure stops with the current cycle. Otherwise, the procedure is repeated with the improved cycle made the current one. The cycle in Figure 9.61(c) is in fact the best one that can be found by this two-arc interchange procedure.

Two-arc interchange method
A heuristic for obtaining an improved cycle by removing two arcs from the current cycle and inserting two appropriate new arcs.

9C.2.1 *The Traveling-Salesperson Problem:*
Using the Computer

To illustrate how to interpret the results of using a heuristic on the computer, recall the traveling-salesperson problem in Example 9.10. The Manager of Good Tire, Inc., is to determine if it is possible for a truck driver to make all deliveries from a warehouse to five retail stores and return to the warehouse within 8 hours, given the traveling time between each pair of stores and/or the warehouse and allowing 30 minutes for each delivery. The answer requires solving a traveling-salesperson problem to determine the truck route requiring the least travel time.

The result of applying the two-arc interchange heuristic in STORM to this problem is shown in Figure 9.62. You can see that the best cycle found by that heuristic is to make the following sequence of deliveries:

Traveling Salesperson
SGEX_8.DAT

Traveling Salesperson
SGEX11_4.DAT

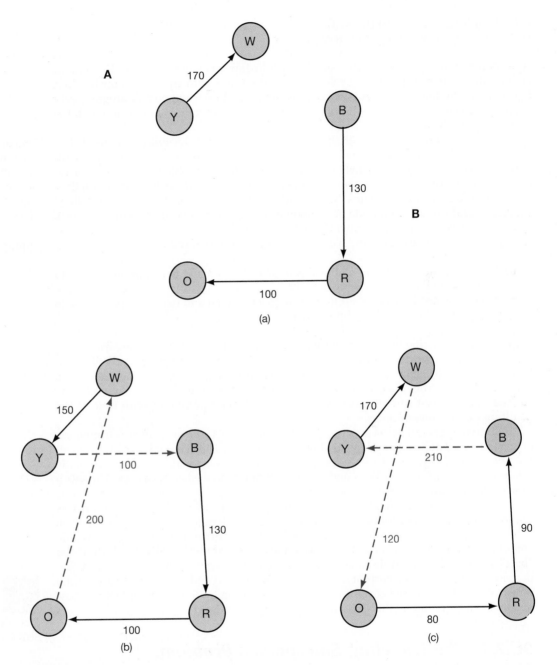

FIGURE 9.61 Two-Arc Interchange Method for Tour Improvement.

Warehouse → Store 2 → Store 3 → Store 4 → Store 5 → Store 1 → Warehouse

with a total travel time of 320 minutes. Adding 30 minutes for each of the five deliveries results in a total time of 470 minutes. This is less than the allowable 8 hours (480 minutes), which means that the daily delivery management wants can be achieved.

The solution obtained from the QSB software package for the problem of Good Tire, Inc., is shown in Figure 9.63. The first line on the left-hand side of that report indicates that it is optimal to go first from the Warehouse to Store 1. The second line on

```
The Traveling-Salesperson Problem of Good Tire, Inc.
    BEST TRAVELING SALESPERSON'S TOUR FOUND

         -------- Arc -------
      From Node      To Node      Arc Length

      WAREHOUSE      STORE 2       55.0000
      STORE 2        STORE 3       55.0000
      STORE 3        STORE 4       50.0000
      STORE 4        STORE 5       70.0000
      STORE 5        STORE 1       50.0000
      STORE 1        WAREHOUSE     40.0000

         Length of tour = 320.0000
```

FIGURE 9.62 STORM Output for the Traveling-Salesperson Problem of Good Tire, Inc.

```
|--------------------------------------------------------------|
|      Summarized Traveling for Good Tire Inc.    Page: 1      |
|--------------------------------------------------------------|
| City    | To City | Distance | City   | To City | Distance  |
|---------+---------+----------+--------+---------+-----------|
| Ware    | Store1  | +40.00   | Store3 | Store2  | +55.00    |
| Store1  | Store5  | +50.00   | Store4 | Store3  | +50.00    |
| Store2  | Ware    | +55.00   | Store5 | Store4  | +70.00    |
|--------------------------------------------------------------|
|     Minimum OBJ = 320  Iteration = 3  CPU second = .9882813  |
|--------------------------------------------------------------|

Optimal Traveling Route:

Ware -- Store1 -- Store5 -- Store4 -- Store3 -- Store2 -- Ware
```

FIGURE 9.63 QSB Output for the Traveling-Salesperson Problem of Good Tire, Inc.

the left-hand side says to travel then from Store 1 to Store 5. To see where to go next, locate Store 5 in the third row under the column labeled "City" on the right-hand side of the report. The next store to travel to is Store 4, as indicated in the column labeled "To City." You can thus construct the optimal order in which to drive to the stores. Alternatively, you can read that sequence from the bottom of the report:

Warehouse → Store 1 → Store 5 → Store 4 → Store 3 → Store 2 → Warehouse

At first glance, you might think that this solution is different from the one in Figure 9.62. However, careful examination reveals that the sequence of cities is the same in both cases, but they are listed in *reverse* order. In this problem, the travel time between stores is the same in either direction, so it does not matter whether the driver goes from the Warehouse to Store 2 to Store 3 to Store 4 to Store 5 to Store 1 and then back to the Warehouse (as in the solution in Figure 9.62), or from the Warehouse to Store 1 to Store 5 to Store 4 to Store 3 to Store 2 and then back to the Warehouse (as in the solution in Figure 9.63). In both cases, the total travel time is 320 minutes.

Finally, observe that the solution provided by QSB in Figure 9.63 is stated to be the "Optimal Traveling Route," but the solution from STORM in Figure 9.62 is only the "Best Traveling-Salesperson Tour Found." In other words, the solution obtained from QSB is optimal, but the solution obtained from STORM may not be. This is because STORM uses the two-arc interchange heuristic. In the problem of Good Tire, Inc., however, that heuristic just *happened* to produce the optimal solution, which is the one shown in Figure 9.63.

In this appendix, you have seen several applications of the traveling-salesperson problem. Unlike the other network problems you saw in Chapter 9, there is no efficient algorithm for solving a large traveling-salesperson problem. In such cases, heuristics (like the tour-construction and two-interchange heuristics) can obtain good, but not optimal, solutions.

EXERCISES

EXERCISE 9.1   Mediscan, Inc., leases specialized X-ray equipment to hospitals. There are currently three machines located in New York, two in Chicago, and three in Los Angeles. Hospitals in Dallas require four machines. Those in Denver and Phoenix each need two machines. The cost of shipping (in dollars) one machine from each city to each hospital is given in the following table:

	TO		
FROM	DALLAS	DENVER	PHOENIX
New York	1600	1800	2500
Chicago	900	1000	1800
Los Angeles	1400	1000	400

    a. Draw a distribution network indicating the appropriate supplies, demands, and other relevant data (where appropriate, add dummy nodes and dummy arcs to obtain a balanced problem).
    b. Formulate a mathematical model to determine how many machines should be shipped from each city to each hospital so as to incur the least cost.

EXERCISE 9.2   For the problem of MediScan, Inc., in Exercise 9.1:
    a. Draw the initial transportation tableau.
    b. Find a starting solution using the matrix minimum method.
    c. Perform the stepping stone algorithm to obtain the optimal solution.
    d. Use your computer package to obtain the optimal solution.

EXERCISE 9.3   Mediscan, Inc., has just received an additional request for two of its machines in Miami. It costs $1300 to ship one machine to Miami from New York, $1400 from Chicago, and $2700 from Los Angeles. Use your computer package to solve the modified problem, assuming that any demand that cannot be met incurs no penalty. How does this change affect the optimal solution in Exercise 9.2? Who should receive machines and who should not?

EXERCISE 9.4   American Motors, Inc., can send a total of up to 200 automobiles by truck and 600 by railroad from its factory in Detroit to its dealers in Chicago, Cleveland, Washington, D.C., and Philadelphia. The cost (in dollars) for sending one car to each of the dealers by truck and by train and the dealer demands are given in the following table:

BY	SHIPPING COST ($/CAR) TO			
	CHICAGO	CLEVELAND	WASHINGTON, D.C.	PHILADELPHIA
Truck	30	20	50	60
Train	45	30	75	90
Demand (cars)	300	100	250	150

a. Draw a distribution network indicating the appropriate supplies, demands, and other relevant data (where appropriate, add dummy nodes and dummy arcs to obtain a balanced problem).
b. As Manager of the Logistics Department, formulate a mathematical model to determine how to send the cars to the dealers to minimize the total transportation costs.

EXERCISE 9.5 Interpret the optimal solution and objective function value from the following computer output for the problem of American Motors, Inc., in Exercise 9.4. Write your answer as a memo from you, as Manager of the Distribution Department, to Mr. Allen Jones, Vice-President of Operations.

```
                    (American Motors, Inc.)
        TRANSPORTATION - OPTIMAL SOLUTION - SUMMARY REPORT
        -------  Cell  ------              Unit        Cell
        Row          Column     Amount     Cost        Cost
        TRUCK        WASH. D.C.     50     50.0000   2500.0000
        TRUCK        PHILADEL.     150     60.0000   9000.0000
        TRUCK Subtotal = 11500.0000


        TRAIN        CHICAGO       300     45.0000  13500.0000
        TRAIN        CLEVELAND     100     30.0000   3000.0000
        TRAIN        WASH. D.C.    200     75.0000  15000.0000
        TRAIN Subtotal = 31500.0000

        Total Cost = 43000.0000
```

EXERCISE 9.6 For the problem of American Motors, Inc., in Exercise 9.4:

a. Draw the initial transportation tableau.
b. Find a starting solution using the matrix minimum method.
c. Perform the stepping stone algorithm to obtain the optimal solution.
d. Use your computer package to obtain the optimal solution.

EXERCISE 9.7 The management of American Motors, Inc., has just received an additional order of 75 automobiles from its dealer in Cincinnati. The shipping rate per car to this dealer is $28 by truck and $42 by train. Use your computer package to solve the modified problem, assuming that any demand that cannot be met incurs no penalty. How does this change affect the optimal solution in Exercise 9.5? Who receives their full orders and who does not?

EXERCISE 9.8 Consider a balanced transportation problem in which the objective function is to be *maximized* rather than minimized.

a. Develop a *matrix maximum method* for finding an initial shipping plan by modifying the steps of the matrix minimum method.

b. What modifications are needed in the stepping stone algorithm to obtain a shipping plan that maximizes rather than minimizes the objective function?

EXERCISE 9.9   Pine Trees, Inc., has harvested 400 tons of lumber from pine forests located outside of Vancouver, 200 tons from forests near Seattle, and 150 tons outside of Portland. Japan has placed an order for 200 tons at a price of $1200 per ton, Taiwan needs 300 tons and will pay $1100 per ton, and Singapore wants 250 tons at $1000 per ton. It costs Pine Trees, Inc., $500 to get each ton from the lumber fields to the port in Vancouver, $400 per ton to the port in Seattle, and $300 per ton to Portland. The following table provides the cost for shipping each ton by sea from these ports to the respective countries:

| FROM | SHIPPING COST ($/TON) OF LUMBER BY SEA TO | | |
	JAPAN	TAIWAN	SINGAPORE
Vancouver	250	250	200
Seattle	250	200	200
Portland	200	150	150

a. Draw a distribution network indicating the appropriate supplies, demands, and other relevant data (where appropriate, add dummy nodes and dummy arcs to obtain a balanced problem).
b. Formulate a mathematical model to determine a distribution plan that maximizes corporate profits.

EXERCISE 9.10   For the problem of Pine Trees, Inc., in Exercise 9.9:

a. Draw the initial transportation tableau.
b. Find a starting solution using the matrix maximum method (see Exercise 9.8).
c. Perform the stepping stone algorithm for a maximization problem (see Exercise 9.8) to obtain the optimal solution.
d. Use your computer package to obtain the optimal solution.

EXERCISE 9.11   After harvesting all of the lumber in its fields, Pine Trees, Inc., has been told that Singapore must cancel its order. All the harvested lumber must still be trucked from the fields to the ports in Vancouver, Seattle, and Portland at the costs given in Exercise 9.9. Lumber not shipped from those ports must be stored at a cost of $25, $20, and $15 per ton, respectively. Use your computer package to solve the modified problem. What is the optimal plan?

EXERCISE 9.12   Hexxon Oil Company has six international oil consultants, three of whom are currently located in the United States, two in Russia, and one in Nigeria. Saudi Arabia has requested two consultants for 1 week at a rate of $4200 each. Venezuela has requested one consultant for 1 week at a rate of $4000. Indonesia has requested three consultants for a week at a weekly rate of $4000 each. Weekly expenses per consultant are $1400 in Saudi Arabia, $1000 in Venezuela, and $700 in Indonesia. The following table shows the round-trip air fares (in dollars) for flying the consultants:

| FROM | TO | | |
	SAUDI ARABIA	VENEZUELA	INDONESIA
United States	1800	800	2000
Russia	1600	1800	1700
Nigeria	1300	1200	1500

a. Draw a distribution network indicating the appropriate supplies, demands, and other relevant data (where appropriate, add dummy nodes and dummy arcs to obtain a balanced problem).

b. Formulate a mathematical model to determine how to get the requested number of consultants to each country so as to maximize the net profit (total revenues minus total costs, including round-trip air fare) of Hexxon Oil.

EXERCISE 9.13 For the problem of Hexxon Oil Company in Exercise 9.12:

a. Draw the initial transportation tableau.

b. Find a starting solution using the matrix maximum method (see Exercise 9.8).

c. Perform the stepping stone algorithm for a maximization problem (see Exercise 9.8) to obtain the optimal solution.

d. Use your computer package to obtain the optimal solution.

EXERCISE 9.14 Saudi Arabia has just canceled its request for one of the consultants. The management of Hexxon Oil knows that a consultant residing in Russia for a week earns a net profit of $1000, a consultant in Nigeria earns $800, and a consultant in the United States earns nothing. Use your computer package to solve the modified problem. How does this information change the optimal solution obtained for Exercise 9.13?

EXERCISE 9.15 World Oil receives crude oil from the Middle East at its facilities in Marseille and Venice. The oil is then shipped via a pipeline with pumping stations in Dijon, Bern, Reims, and Luxembourg to storage tanks in Paris, Cologne, and Brussels. The approximate distances in kilometers between points connected by a pipeline segment are given in the following tables:

FROM	TO	
	DIJON	BERN
Marseille	475	450
Venice	—	425

FROM	TO	
	REIMS	LUXEMBOURG
Dijon	240	275
Bern	375	325

FROM	TO		
	PARIS	BRUSSELS	COLOGNE
Reims	130	175	—
Luxembourg	—	150	140

This month, 250,000 barrels of oil are available in Marseille and 150,000 barrels are in Venice. The storage tank facility in Paris needs to receive 200,000 barrels, and the facilities in Brussel and Cologne each need to receive 100,000 barrels.

a. Draw a distribution network indicating the appropriate supplies, demands, and other relevant data (where appropriate, add dummy nodes and dummy arcs to obtain a network having a single source and a single sink).

b. Formulate a mathematical model to determine how the oil should be shipped from these facilities to minimize the total kilometers the oil travels (that is, the sum of the number of barrels of oil times the number of kilometers it travels).

EXERCISE 9.16   Interpret the optimal solution and objective function value from the following output for the problem of World Oil in Exercise 9.15. A dummy node called SOURCE has been added and connected with dummy arcs to the nodes corresponding to Marseille and Venice. Likewise, a dummy node called DEST has been added and connected by dummy arcs to the nodes corresponding to Paris, Brussels, and Cologne. In the following computer output, each single letter in the column labeled "Arc" is the first letter of the corresponding city. For example, the letters M-D in the third row of the report correspond to the arc from Marseille to Dijon. Write your answer as a memo from you, Vice-President of Operations, to Mr. Etienne Lute, Manager of Operations in Marseille, and to Mr. Giorgio Marconi, Manager of Operations in Venice.

```
                              World Oil
                  TRANSSHIPMENT - SUMMARY REPORT
                                           Unit      Shipping
        Arc         From   To    Flow      Cost        Cost
        SOURCE-M     .      1      250        0           0
        SOURCE-V     .      2      150        0           0
        M-D          1      3      250      475      118750
        V-B          2      4      150      425       63750
        D-R          3      5      250      240       60000
        B-L          4      6      150      325       48750
        R-P          5      7      200      130       26000
        R-B          5      8       50      175        8750
        L-B          6      8       50      150        7500
        L-C          6      9      100      140       14000
        P-DEST       7      .      200        0           0
        B-DEST       8      .      100        0           0
        C-DEST       9      .      100        0           0


        Total cost = 347500
```

EXERCISE 9.17   Fresh Fruits imports bananas from plantations in Honduras and Costa Rica to both Miami and San Diego. The company sells bananas in both cities. The rest are redistributed to Denver, Kansas City, and Ft. Worth. This month, 200,000 pounds of bananas have been harvested in Honduras and 100,000 pounds in Costa Rica. The demand for resale is 75,000 pounds in Miami, and 60,000 pounds in San Diego. Denver needs 60,000 pounds, Kansas City is expecting 40,000 pounds, and Ft. Worth wants 65,000 pounds. The following distances (in miles) are known:

	TO	
FROM	MIAMI	SAN DIEGO
Honduras	900	2400
Costa Rica	1200	2700

	TO		
FROM	DENVER	KANSAS CITY	FT. WORTH
Miami	2107	1226	1343
San Diego	1095	1833	1348

a. Draw a distribution network indicating the appropriate supplies, demands, and other relevant data (where appropriate, add dummy nodes and dummy arcs to obtain a network having a single source and a single sink).

b. Formulate a mathematical model to determine how the bananas should be transported to minimize the total number of miles the bananas travel, (that is, the sum of the number of bananas times the number of miles they travel).

EXERCISE 9.18 Interpret the optimal solution and objective function value from the following output for the problem of Fresh Fruits in Exercise 9.17. A dummy node called SOURCE has been added and connected with dummy arcs to the nodes corresponding to Honduras and Costa Rica. Likewise, a dummy node called DEST has been added and connected by dummy arcs to the nodes corresponding to Denver, Kansas City, Ft. Worth, Miami, and San Diego. In the following computer output, each single letter in the column labeled "Arc" is the first letter of the corresponding city or country. For example, the letters H-M in the third row of the report correspond to the arc from Honduras to Miami. Write you answer as a memo from you, Manager of Distribution, to Mr. José Rodrigez, Manager of Operations in Honduras, and to Sra. Christina Bolanos, Manager of Operations in Costa Rica.

```
                        Fresh Fruits
              TRANSSHIPMENT - SUMMARY REPORT
                                       Unit      Shipping
    Arc        From  To     Flow       Cost        Cost
    SOURCE-H    .     1      200         0           0
    SOURCE-C    .     2      100         0           0
    H-M         1     4      200        900       180000
    C-M         2     4       40       1200        48000
    C-S         2     3       60       2700       162000
    M-D         4     5       60       2107       126420
    M-K         4     6       40       1226        49040
    M-F         4     7       65       1343        87295
    M-DEST      4     .       75         0           0
    S-DEST      3     .       60         0           0
    D-DEST      5     .       60         0           0
    K-DEST      6     .       40         0           0
    F-DEST      7     .       65         0           0

        Total cost = 652755
```

EXERCISE 9.19 For the problem of Fresh Fruits in Exercise 9.17, management has decided to minimize the total cost of transportation rather than the number of miles the bananas travel. In that regard, the cost per mile for shipping 1000 pounds of bananas is $0.10. Also, each 1000 pounds of bananas shipped through Miami incurs an additional $50 in special port taxes. Use your computer package to solve the modified problem. What shipping plan minimizes the total transportation costs?

EXERCISE 9.20 Arthur J. Big and Company is an accounting firm that has one tax specialist at each of its offices in Washington, D.C., Cleveland, Louisville, and Atlanta. The head office has received a request for one tax specialists from each of its clients in Columbus, Nashville, Charleston, and Pittsburgh. The travel costs are proportional to the distances, which are given (in miles) in the following table:

	To			
From	**Columbus**	**Nashville**	**Charleston**	**Pittsburgh**
Washington	431	659	342	247
Cleveland	140	533	248	129
Louisville	214	174	259	393
Atlanta	585	246	501	683

    a. Draw a distribution network indicating the appropriate supplies, demands, and other relevant data (where appropriate, add dummy nodes and dummy arcs to obtain a balanced problem).

    b. As a general partner of the firm, formulate a mathematical model to determine how to send one specialist to each city to minimize the total travel costs.

EXERCISE 9.21   For the problem of Arthur J. Big and Company in Exercise 9.20:

    a. Draw the initial assignment matrix.
    b. Perform the assignment algorithm to obtain the optimal solution.
    c. Use your computer package to obtain the optimal solution.

EXERCISE 9.22   As a general partner of Arthur J. Big and Company, you have just learned that the client in Nashville has cancelled the request for a tax specialist. Use your computer package to solve the modified problem. How does this change affect the optimal solution in Exercise 9.21?

EXERCISE 9.23   Consider a balanced assignment problem in which the objective function is to be *maximized* rather than minimized.

    a. How can you convert the maximization objective function into an equivalent minimization objective function? (Hint: Consider the approach of converting the objective function of a linear programming problem to standard form, as presented in Section 5.4.)

    b. In converting a maximization objective function to a minimization objective function by the technique in part (a), some of the resulting coefficients may have negative values. After performing Step 0 of the assignment algorithm, explain why all values in the matrix become nonnegative.

EXERCISE 9.24   One-To-One runs a dating service in which men and women fill out a questionnaire regarding their preferences in a mate. From these questionnaires, a computer program determines which men are "compatible" with which women. The following list results:

NAMES OF MEN	NAMES OF COMPATIBLE WOMEN
Adams	Berk, Heart
Clark	Heart
Gifford	Berk, Heart
Patton	Heart, Delroy, Macy, Thomas

    a. Draw a distribution network indicating relevant data (where appropriate, add dummy nodes and dummy arcs to obtain a balanced problem).

    b. As Manager of One-To-One, formulate a mathematical model to determine the maximum number of compatible couples that can be arranged. (Hint: What is an appropriate cost or profit for each man-woman pair?)

EXERCISE 9.25   Interpret the optimal solution and objective function value from the following computer output for the problem of One-To-One in Exercise 9.24. This output was obtained by applying a maximization assignment algorithm in which the objective function coefficient is 1 for a variable corresponding to a man and a woman who are compatible and 0 otherwise.

```
                          One-To-One
                       OPTIMAL SOLUTION
            Row              Column          Cost
            ADAMS            THOMAS            0
            CLARK            HEART             1
            GIFFORD          BERK              1
            PATTON           DELROY            1


                     Total Cost = 3
```

EXERCISE 9.26   For the problem of One-To-One in Exercise 9.24:

   a. Draw the initial assignment matrix after converting the maximization objective function to a minimization objective function (see Exercise 9.23).
   b. Perform the assignment algorithm to obtain the optimal solution.
   c. Use your computer package to obtain the optimal solution.

EXERCISE 9.27   As the manager of One-To-One, you have just learned that Ms. Berk has moved to another city and is no longer available. Also, it was discovered that Mr. Adams is compatible with Ms. Delroy. Use your computer package to solve the modified problem. How do these changes affect the optimal solution in Exercise 9.26?

EXERCISE 9.28   Cosmic Computer Company manufactures integrated-circuit (IC) boards using an automated programmable IC insertion machine. One particular type of board requires the placement of five different ICs. The distance in millimeters between any two ICs is given in the following table:

	IC-A	IC-B	IC-C	IC-D	IC-E
IC-A	—	35	35	60	45
IC-B		—	22	30	50
IC-C			—	48	55
IC-D				—	50

Keeping in mind that the machine can move from one chip location to any other at a constant velocity, you want to determine how the machine should be programmed to insert these five chips on a board to maximize the number of completed boards that can be produced in a given time interval.

   a. Draw an appropriate network with all relevant data.
   b. What is the objective of this problem?

EXERCISE 9.29   Cole Chemicals makes six different compounds. Due to economies of scale, each compound is produced once during a 24-hour day. The profit obtained depends not only on which compound is produced, but also on the next compound produced. This occurs because each compound leaves some impurities that affect the quality of the next compound produced. Profits (in dollars) are indicated in the following table:

COMPOUND	FOLLOWED BY					
	A	B	C	D	E	F
A	—	250	300	100	—	170
B	250	—	160	—	270	150
C	300	160	—	230	—	140
D	100	—	230	—	220	—
E	—	270	—	220	—	100
F	170	150	140	—	100	—

a. Draw an appropriate network with all relevant data.
b. What is the objective of this problem?

EXERCISE 9.30   Consider the following distances between nodes in a traveling-salesperson problem:

FROM	TO			
	1	2	3	4
1	—	9	4	12
2	9	—	7	10
3	4	7	—	6
4	12	10	6	—

a. Use the tour-construction heuristic (cheapest-insertion algorithm) to find an initial traveling-salesperson tour.
b. Starting with the tour 1–4–3–2–1, perform the two-interchange algorithm until further improvement is no longer possible. Report the final tour obtained.

EXERCISE 9.31   Consider the following distances between nodes in a traveling-salesperson problem:

FROM	TO				
	A	B	C	D	E
A	—	15	12	20	—
B	15	—	8	22	13
C	12	8	—	15	16
D	20	22	15	—	18
E	—	13	16	18	—

a. Use the cheapest-insertion algorithm to find an initial traveling-salesperson tour.
b. Starting with the tour A–C–E–B–D–A, perform the two-interchange algorithm until further improvement is no longer possible. Report the final tour obtained.

EXERCISE 9.32   Modify the tour-construction heuristic (cheapest-insertion algorithm) for the traveling-salesperson problem so that you can solve a maximization problem. That is, given a nonnegative value associated with each arc in a network, you want a modified insertion algorithm to find a tour of maximum total value.

EXERCISE 9.33   Interpet the following computer output for the production problem of Cole Chemicals in Exercise 9.29.

```
The Production Problem of Cole Chemicals
From Node    To Node    Arc Length
COMP A       COMP C      300.0000
COMP C       COMP D      230.0000
COMP D       COMP E      220.0000
COMP E       COMP B      270.0000
COMP B       COMP F      150.0000
COMP F       COMP A      170.0000

Optimal Objective Function Value = 1340.0000
```

EXERCISE 9.34   For the problem in Exercise 9.29, the Manager of Cole Chemicals has been told that she also needs to produce a new compound, G, each day. This new compound cannot be produced immediately before or after A. The profits associated with compounds following G are the same as when those compounds follow A. Appropriately modify the problem and use your computer package to determine the new sequence in which to produce the compounds that maximize the daily profit.

CRITICAL-THINKING PROJECT C

Recall Critical-Thinking Project C in Chapter 3, in which Mr. John Porter, Production Manager of Hexxon Oil Company, is trying to determine an optimal plan for transporting oil from Mexico by tanker and from Alaska by pipeline to each of three refineries. Obtain the formulation from your instructor. Then prepare a managerial report following these guidelines.

1. Explain why you need consider only those combinations in which all three tankers are assigned to refineries and why you can ignore those combinations that assign only one or two tankers. Also explain why you need never consider sending more than one tanker to a refinery.

2. On the basis of guideline 1, list the six possible combinations that assign all three tankers to transport oil from the port in Mexico to each of the three refineries. For each combination, solve the associated problem using the transportation module of your computer package. Report the total cost for each assignment, including the fixed costs, and indicate the one of least total cost.

3. The management of Hexxon has decided to lease Tanker A for transporting oil to Refinery 1, Tanker B for Refinery 3, and Tanker C for Refinery 2.
   a. For this assignment, prepare a table indicating how much oil is received at each refinery and from where.
   b. By how much would the cost of pumping 1000 barrels of oil from Alaska have to decrease before it is profitable to pump oil to Refinery 2?
   c. Management wants to decrease the total cost of transporting all the oil to $3.5 million by reducing the amount received at one of the refineries. The company can reduce the amount received by which refinery the least to accomplish the stated goal? What is that amount? (Hint: Repeatedly solve appropriately modified transportation problems to find the desired reduction for each refinery.)

Video Case

PACKING THEM IN

UPS is the world's largest package distribution company, operating a global network that handles 11 million packages a day. The public sees a reliable, efficient company with friendly drivers in those familiar brown vans arriving on time, but more goes on at UPS than meets the eye.

UPS maintains one of the largest jet cargo airline fleets in the world, with more than 60 customized Boeing 757 planes. The company also keeps a full range of ground transportation vehicles, from the brown vans to trailers and even to bicycles. All its vehicles have been designed to increase fuel and operating efficiency and to reduce pollution and noise.

The technical heart of the UPS information system is a sophisticated computer network that spans the globe, keeping UPS in constant touch with its packages and customers. In connection with management science techniques, this information system continually solves many transportation, transshipment, and assignment problems.

The video features a huge map room, where 49,000 maps, each a 7 mile by 9 mile section of the United States, are kept. These maps are electronically stored in the mainframe computer so that UPS can access any address. Through advanced tracking devices, the computer system can quickly assign the nearest available driver for an immediate package pickup. Each driver has a state-of-the-art portable computerized clip board that stores the account numbers, delivery times, and even the customer's signature for that day's route. At the end of the day the clipboard is docked into a terminal and all data downloaded to the mainframe system. This information is vital to the efficient operation of this complex delivery system.

UPS has been pioneering "intelligent packaging," using bar coding, scanning, and sorting equipment for tracking, tracing, and billing quickly and efficiently while continuing the tradition of on-time delivery. (Total running time: 6:03.)

QUESTIONS ON THE VIDEO

1. What are some of the statistics that point to UPS as the largest package delivery company in the United States and the world?

2. What are some of the flexible services that UPS can offer?

BEYOND THE VIDEO

3. Describe how you could apply the transshipment problem for handling pickups and deliveries within a major city.

4. What are some of the data needed on a daily basis for assigning drivers to trucks and to routes?

PRACTICAL CONSIDERATIONS

5. Why is it cheaper for UPS to send a package from Miami to Atlanta through its hub in Louisville than shipping directly from Miami to Atlanta?

6. Discuss the similarities between UPS and Yellow Freight (the company described in the video for Chapter 6).

Source: United Parcel Service (UPS), Atlanta, GA, 1991.

CHAPTER 1

PROJECT MANAGEMENT: CPM AND PERT

So you have a great idea for an animated film. You go to Prisney Productions with your proposal. The company believes in your vision and signs you to a contract. Prisney knows the business inside and out and realizes that getting the film to market quickly is essential to making this the box office smash it could be. But coordinating the various activities that go into making an animated film—the animation itself, scoring and recording the music, editing, distributing, and so on—takes time. How soon can this film be ready for release? Can you beat the clock and get it to market sooner if you can coax additional money from the executive offices?

The Case Study in this chapter looks at how Prisney applies project management techniques to handle this most important project.

In this chapter, a management science technique that helps monitor and control a project involving numerous interrelated tasks is presented. Supervising these projects requires many management skills, one of which is to keep the project on schedule. Management science can help do so by providing answers to such questions as:

1. What is the earliest time at which the entire project can be completed?
2. To meet this completion time, which tasks are *critical*, in the sense that a delay in any of those tasks results in a delay in the completion of the entire project?
3. Is it possible to expedite certain tasks so as to finish the entire project earlier? If so, which tasks, and at what additional cost?

When a project involves few tasks, the answers to these questions can often be found with little effort. However, when planning a project involving hundreds or thousands of interrelated tasks to be performed by different people, the management science tools presented in this chapter provide a systematic way not only to answer these questions, but also to monitor the project throughout its duration.

Critical Path Method (CPM)
A method used to manage projects in which the times needed to complete the individual tasks are known with relative certainty.

The techniques for managing projects presented in this chapter were developed independently by two teams of researchers in the mid-1950s. The Dupont Company created the first technique, called the **Critical Path Method (CPM),** to manage projects in which the time needed to complete the individual tasks was known with relative certainty. The U.S. Navy developed the second technique, called the **Project Evaluation and Review Technique (PERT),** to manage the Polaris Missile Project, which involved about 5000 tasks and several thousand subcontractors. The time required to complete many of those tasks was uncertain. These two techniques are similar except that CPM is used for managing projects involving deterministic task times and PERT is used for those involving probabilistic task times. The former technique is discussed in Sections 10.1 through 10.4 and the latter in Section 10.5.

Project Evaluation and Review Technique (PERT)
A method used to manage projects in which some of the times needed to complete the individual tasks are uncertain.

■ 10.1 DEVELOPING THE PROJECT NETWORK

To illustrate how project management techniques are applied to monitor a project, consider the one faced by the management of Period Publishing Company.

EXAMPLE 10.1 THE PROJECT OF PERIOD PUBLISHING COMPANY Period Publishing Company has just signed a contract with an author to publish and market a new textbook. As the Vice President, you want to know the earliest possible completion date for this project. ■

You can determine the completion time using project-management techniques by following these four steps:

1. Identify the individual tasks that make up the project.
2. Obtain a time estimate for the completion of each task.
3. Identify the time relationships between the tasks. Which tasks must be completed before others can begin?
4. Draw a *project-network diagram* to reflect the information in steps 1 to 3.

Each of these steps is described in more detail in what follows.

10.1.1 Identifying Individual Tasks

Complete projects consist of various individual tasks. To monitor projects, you must first identify those tasks. They can vary both in the time required to complete them and in their complexity. Complex tasks can be viewed as projects that themselves need monitoring by being further divided into subtasks. For example, in designing the space shuttle, one task is to develop onboard computer systems. Because this task is itself a major project, you might further divide it into subtasks consisting of developing computer systems for life support, engine control, and collecting and transmitting data. Although there is no unique way of deciding how small or large an individual task should be, here are some guidelines to follow:

1. Each task should have a distinct beginning and end in the context of the project. For example, in the case of Period Publishing Company, preparing the manuscript of the book *does* have a specific beginning with the signing of the contract and a specific end when the manuscript is delivered to the publisher. In contrast, selling the finished text is *not* a task because it has no distinct end, though it does have a distinct beginning.

2. The completion of each task should be necessary to the completion of the project and should represent a milestone in the progress of the project. For example, developing promotional materials is necessary for the successful marketing of the book and represents a major accomplishment in terms of the overall project.

3. The size of a task should be roughly at the level of your control. For example, as Vice President, your main concern is when the *entire* manuscript is finished, not when the individual chapters are finished. In contrast, if you are the Editor in charge of this book, then you *should* be concerned with the progress of the individual chapters.

4. There should be some person(s) responsible for the completion of each individual task. For example, the Legal Department would be responsible for obtaining all copyright agreements and other legal contracts before the book is published.

On the basis of these guidelines you, as Vice President of Period Publishing Company, might identify eight tasks that are under your control and that must be completed for the project to be successful. These tasks for Period Publishing Company are listed in Table 10.1. Though the order of the tasks in this table is immaterial, it is important to include *all* relevant tasks right from the start. If unexpected tasks arise in the course of the project, delays may occur in the rush to accomplish them. For example, suppose you omitted the legal tasks (G in Table 10.1) and suddenly discover that this task must be completed before the book can be produced. You might even have to recall the book if this task is forgotten and legal problems arise.

TABLE 10.1	The List of Tasks for the Period Publishing Company Project
LABEL	**DESCRIPTION**
A	Author preparation of manuscript
B	Design promotional materials
C	Produce promotional materials
D	Copy edit the manuscript
E	Proofread and correct the page proofs
F	Produce the final book
G	Obtain all legal permissions and copyrights
H	Conduct a sales training meeting

10.1.2 Obtaining Time Estimates for Each Task

It should be clear that the total amount of time it takes to complete the entire project depends, in some way, on how long it takes to perform each individual task. It therefore becomes necessary to obtain some estimate of the amount of time required for completing each task. An estimate might be developed by the following:

1. Relying on past experience on similar projects.
2. Consulting with the people in charge of each individual task.
3. Using historical data.

Suppose you have obtained the time estimates in Table 10.2 for the tasks of this particular project after consulting with appropriate members of each department.

For this project, you may feel that the time needed to complete each task is fairly well known with no significant variability. Other projects involve tasks whose completion time is uncertain or must be estimated with a significant amount of uncertainty. How to handle projects of this nature is discussed in Section 10.5.

TABLE 10.2   *Time Estimates for the Tasks of the Period Publishing Company Project*

LABEL	DESCRIPTION	TIME ESTIMATE (weeks)
A	Author preparation of manuscript	30
B	Design promotional materials	6
C	Produce promotional materials	4
D	Copy edit the manuscript	5
E	Proofread and correct the page proofs	10
F	Produce the final book	8
G	Obtain all legal permissions and copyrights	14
H	Conduct a sales training meeting	2

10.1.3 Creating the Precedence Table for the Project

As noted previously, the amount of time it takes to complete an entire project is based on the completion times of the individual tasks. However, that total completion time is *not* equal to the sum of the individual task times because some tasks can be performed simultaneously. Other tasks, though, cannot begin until certain prior tasks are completed. To determine the minimum amount of time required to complete the entire project, you must first understand how the individual tasks are related to each other. You must identify which task(s) must be completed before another task can begin.

Consider Task F: producing the final book for Period Publishing Company. Looking at *all* the other tasks in Table 10.2, using your knowledge of this business, and understanding the company's policy, you identify the following list of tasks that must be completed before the final book can be produced:

LABEL	DESCRIPTION
A	The author has submitted the final manuscript
D	The manuscript has been copy edited
E	The page proofs have been proofread and corrected
G	The legal permissions and copyrights have been obtained

Even in this list, there are some tasks that depend on others. For example, copy editing the manuscript (Task D) cannot begin until the manuscript is received (Task A); proofreading and correcting (Task E) cannot begin until the manuscript has been received (Task A) and copy edited (Task D). Finally, the legal work (Task G) cannot begin until the manuscript is received (Task A). Careful examination of these relationships indicates that when Tasks E and G are finished, Tasks A and D will already have been completed. In other words, the production of the book (Task F) can begin as soon as the following two tasks are completed:

LABEL	DESCRIPTION
E	The page proofs have been proofread and corrected
G	The legal permissions and copyrights have been obtained

This shortened list of tasks make up the list of **immediate-predecessor tasks** for producing the final book (Task F).

KEY FEATURES

The list of immediate predecessors of a particular task of interest include those tasks that

- ✔ must be completed before the task of interest can begin, and
- ✔ do not depend for their start on the completion of any other immediate-predecessor task in this list.

Of all the tasks that must be completed before a given task can start, you need identify only the immediate-predecessor tasks. Doing so requires knowledge of the particular project and how the tasks are related to each other in terms of sequence. As Vice President, you have prepared the **precedence table** in Table 10.3, which lists the immediate predecessors for each task together with their time estimates, obtained in Section 10.1.2.

Immediate-predecessor task
A task that must be completed before the task of interest can begin and that does not depend for its start on the completion of any other immediate-predecessor task in this list.

Precedence table
A table that lists the immediate predecessors for each task.

10.1.4 Drawing the Project Network

Recall that one of the main objectives of project management is to determine the minimum amount of time needed to complete the entire project. Identifying the precedence relationships among the individual tasks, as in Table 10.3, is a first step in that direction. An even better understanding of these relationships can be obtained by converting

TABLE 10.3   *Precedence Table for the Tasks of the Period Publishing Company Project*

LABEL	DESCRIPTION	TIME ESTIMATE (weeks)	IMMEDIATE PREDECESSORS
A	Author preparation of manuscript	30	None
B	Design promotional materials	6	A
C	Produce promotional materials	4	B, G
D	Copy edit the manuscript	5	A
E	Proofread and correct the page proofs	10	D
F	Produce the final book	8	E, G
G	Obtain all legal permissions and copyrights	14	A
H	Conduct a sales training meeting	2	C, F

Project network
A network diagram that consists of a finite collection of nodes and arcs used to represent the tasks and their precedence relationships in a project.

Activity-on-Arc Representation
A convention used in a project network diagram in which each arc corresponds to one of the activities and the two nodes connected by that arc represent the beginning and end of that activity.

Activity-on-Node Representation
A convention used in a project network diagram in which each node represents a task and an arc connects two nodes if one node corresponds to an immediate-predecessor task of the other node.

the precedence information into a **project network.** A network consists of a finite collection of *nodes* and *arcs*. An arc is an arrow that connects one node to another.

In project management, the nodes and arcs in the project network have a special meaning in the context of the specific problem, depending on which of the following two standard approaches is used:

1. **Activity-on-Arc Representation:** In this approach, each arc corresponds to one of the activities; the nodes that are connected by that arc represent the beginning and end of that activity.
2. **Activity-on-Node Representation:** In this approach, each node represents one of the tasks (or activity); an arc connects two nodes if one node corresponds to an immediate-predecessor task of the other node.

Either approach can be adopted for drawing the project network. The solution procedure that follows depends on which one is chosen. Just be sure that the computer package available for project management can handle the approach chosen for drawing the project network. Because there is no universal agreement as to which of these approaches is better, the activity-on-arc representation is used throughout this chapter. The activity-on-node representation is described in Appendix 10A. Before the project network for the Period Publishing Company project in Example 10.1 is drawn, several smaller examples are presented to illustrate in general how project networks are drawn.

Consider first a project consisting of three tasks whose precedence relationships are given in Example 10.2.

EXAMPLE 10.2   REPRESENTING THE PRECEDENCE RELATIONSHIPS

TASK	IMMEDIATE PREDECESSORS
A	None
B	A
C	B

■

To build the corresponding project network, begin by drawing a node numbered 0 to represent the beginning of the entire project. Starting from that node, draw one arc for each activity that has no immediate predecessor—that is, that can begin immediately because it depends on no other activities. Label each such arc with the corresponding task symbol. In this example, Task A has no immediate predecessor, so draw one arc from node 0. This arc is labeled A, corresponding to Task A, as seen in Figure 10.1(a). Each arc must have a terminal node with a distinct number to represent the end of that

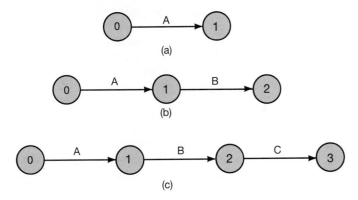

FIGURE 10.1 The Project Network for Example 10.2.

activity. In this case, the terminal node for arc A is node 1, as shown in Figure 10.1(a). In general, there may be several arcs from node 0, but in any case there will *always* be at least one such arc.

In Figure 10.1(a), node 1 represents the point *in time* at which Task A is completed. Ask yourself which activities can now begin, given that Task A has been completed. The easiest way to determine that is to check the precedence table and identify those tasks that have *only* A as their immediate predecessor. In this example, Task B is the only such task. To represent this fact, draw an arc out of node 1. Label this arc B, corresponding to Task B, and label its terminal node with the number 2; see Figure 10.1(b). Node 2 represents that point *in time* at which Task B is completed.

Continuing with this scheme from node 2, ask what tasks can begin now that Task B has been completed. From the precedence relationships, the answer is Task C. Draw the corresponding arc labeled C from node 2 and a terminal node numbered 3. The project network of Figure 10.1(c) is now complete.

KEY FEATURES

The arcs *entering* a given node represent the immediate-predecessor tasks of all the activities corresponding to the arcs *leaving* the node. In fact, one way to verify that the project network is correct is to create a precedence table from the project network and to check that this table is identical to the precedence table used to build the network.

Some other guidelines in drawing a correct project network are now illustrated. Consider a project consisting of five tasks with the precedence relationships given in Example 10.3.

EXAMPLE 10.3 USING DUMMY ACTIVITIES AND/OR DUMMY NODES

TASK	IMMEDIATE PREDECESSORS
A	None
B	None
C	A
D	B
E	C, D

As before, begin by drawing a node numbered 0 to represent the beginning of the entire project. Both Tasks A and B have no immediate predecessors, so they can begin immediately. Note the two arcs labeled A and B and the two terminal nodes numbered 1 and 2 in Figure 10.2(a). Now consider node 1, which represents the point in time at which Task A is completed. Asking which tasks can now begin, you should identify Task C. You are led to draw a new arc labeled C and a corresponding terminal node numbered 3, as in Figure 10.2(b).

In Figure 10.2(b), node 2 represents the time at which Task B is completed; node 3 represents the time at which Task C is completed. Choosing node 3—an arbitrary selection because the order of nodes considered does not matter—ask which tasks can begin now that Task C is completed. The answer is none, because Task E requires the completion of not only Task C, but also Task D, as indicated in the foregoing precedence table.

Turning to node 2, ask which tasks can begin now that Task B is completed. In this case, from the precedence table the answer is Task D. This fact is represented by a new arc labeled D and a corresponding terminal node numbered 4 in Figure 10.2(c).

By looking at nodes 3 and 4, representing the times at which Tasks C and D are completed, respectively, it would appear that no other activity can be started. To start the remaining Task E requires that *both* Tasks C and D are completed, as indicated in the foregoing precedence table. Unfortunately, there is no single node in Figure 10.2(c) to represent the fact that both Tasks C and D are completed. Three different approaches to resolving this problem follow:

1. *Combining Nodes:* In this approach, replace the two terminal nodes 3 and 4 with a single node that represents that point in time at which *both* Tasks C and D are completed. This new node, now numbered 3, is illustrated in Figure 10.2(d).

2. *Creating Dummy Activities:* In this approach, create a **dummy activity**—that is, an artificial activity that is not part of the project and that requires no time to complete. The dummy activity is used only to reflect the proper precedence relationships. In this example, that dummy activity is represented by a dotted arrow connecting node 4 to node 3 in Figure 10.2(e). Now, node 3 represents the time at which Task C as well as the dummy activity—and so Task D—are *both* completed. (Note that if the dotted arrow were to point from node 3 to node 4, then node 4 would represent the time at which Task C and the dummy activity are both completed.)

3. *Creating Dummy Nodes:* In this approach, a **dummy node** numbered 5 is created. To reflect that this dummy node represents that point in time at which both Tasks C and D are completed, connect both Nodes 3 and 4 in Figure 10.2(c) to the dummy node with two dummy activities, as illustrated in Figure 10.2(f).

Dummy activity
An artificial activity requiring no time that is included in a project network to ensure the correct precedence relationship between certain tasks.

Dummy node
An artificial node included in a project network to represent a point in time at which certain activities are completed and to ensure the correct precedence relationship between certain tasks.

Assume the method of combining nodes is used. As shown in Figure 10.2(d), node 3 represents the time at which both Tasks C and D are completed. A final arc, labeled E, is drawn from this node to represent Task E. This arc ends at node 4, which is the point in time at which Task E ends, as shown in Figure 10.2(g).

What if you use the method of creating dummy activities? As indicated in Figure 10.2(e), node 3 represents the time at which Tasks C and D are completed. Extend an arc, labeled E, from node 3 to node 5, as shown in Figure 10.2(h). This arc stands for Task E, which is completed at node 5.

If you choose the method of creating dummy nodes, refer to Figure 10.2(f). In this figure, node 5 represents the point in time at which both Tasks C and D are completed. Extend an arc, labeled E, from node 5 and add a terminal node numbered 6. The network in Figure 10.2(i) results.

The next example illustrates the *necessity* of having to add dummy nodes as well as dummy activities. To that end, consider a project consisting of five activities with the precedence relationships given in Example 10.4.

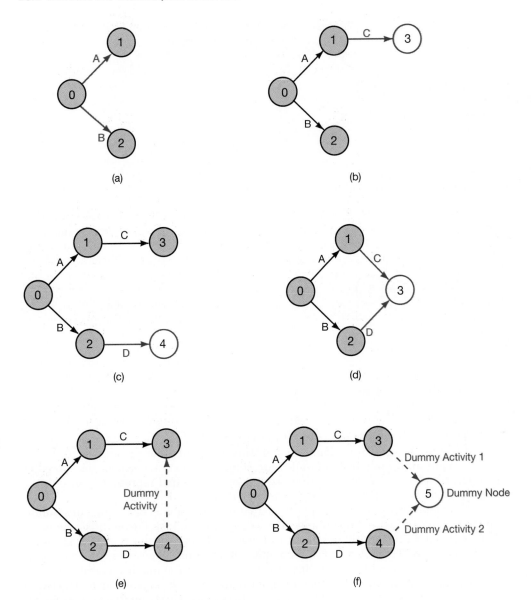

FIGURE 10.2 The Project Network for Example 10.3.

EXAMPLE 10.4 USING DUMMY NODES AND DUMMY ACTIVITIES

TASK	IMMEDIATE PREDECESSORS
A	None
B	None
C	A
D	B
E	A, B

The project is completed when Tasks C, D, and E are all completed. ∎

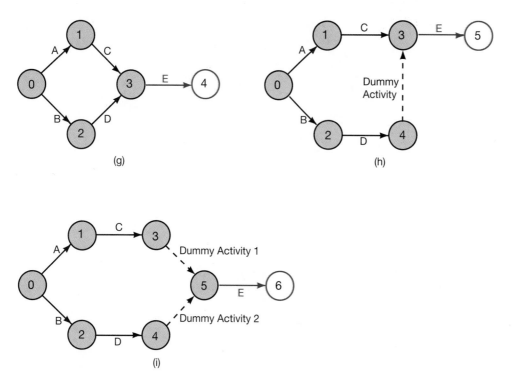

FIGURE 10.2 (*cont.*)   Alternative Project Network for Example 10.3.

The result of building the project network for the first four tasks (A to D) in the ususal way is illustrated in Figure 10.3(a). However, note that the remaining Task E cannot begin until both Tasks A and B are completed, as indicated in the foregoing precedence table. Unfortunately, there is no single node that represents that point in time at which both Tasks A and B are completed.

To resolve this problem, first observe that *in this case* it is not correct to combine nodes 1 and 2 in Figure 10.3(a) and then add an arc for Task E from this new node. This is because the resulting network in Figure 10.3(b) indicates that Task C cannot begin until both Tasks A and B are completed, and this is not correct according to the precedence table in Example 10.4. Furthermore, observe that by creating this new node, there are now two arcs connecting node 0 to node 1, thus creating a *loop* between two nodes. Because most computer packages for solving CPM and PERT problems do not allow such loops, they must be avoided when constructing the project network.

Another approach for resolving the problem of adding Task E is to add a dummy activity, as discussed before. You might think of adding a dummy activity connecting node 1 to 2, for example. The result of doing so and then adding an arc from node 2 to represent Task E is shown in Figure 10.3(c). Once again, however, the precedence relationships of that project network are no longer correct. The project network in Figure 10.3(c) indicates that Task D cannot begin until both Tasks A and B are completed, and this is not correct according to the foregoing precedence table.

The *only* correct way to include Task E is to add a dummy node and two dummy activities that connect nodes 1 and 2 to the dummy node. This dummy node represents that point in time at which both Tasks A and B are completed. An arc from this dummy node, as drawn in Figure 10.3(d), indicates that Task E can now begin.

Although the project network in Figure 10.3(d) correctly reflects the precedence relationships, observe that there are three *terminal* nodes with no arcs from them—namely, nodes 3, 4, and 6. Just as there is a single node to indicate the beginning of the entire project, it is easier to identify the end of the project if there is a single node

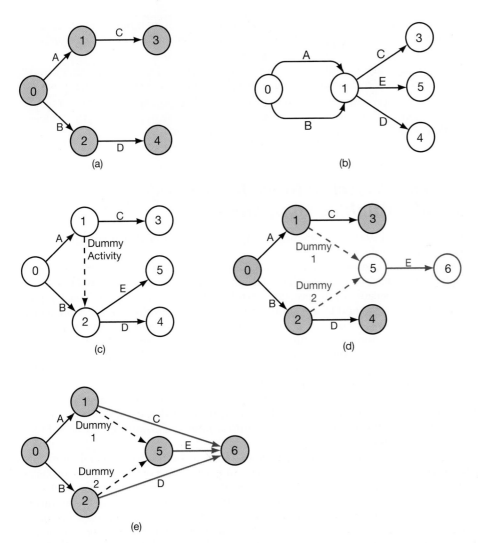

FIGURE 10.3 A Project Network for Example 10.4.

representing that event. One way to bring this about is to combine all terminal nodes into a single node, as shown for Example 10.4 in Figure 10.3(e).

KEY FEATURES

In summary, to draw a project network that correctly reflects the precedence relationships using the activity-on-arc representation, keep the following guidelines in mind:

✔ Build the network sequentially, adding one arc corresponding to one activity at a time, by choosing a terminal node and asking what task(s) can now begin. Recall that this node represents the point in time when all activities corresponding to arcs entering that node are completed.
✔ Avoid loops in which more than one arc connects the same two nodes.

✔ When there is no node representing the completion of *all* immediate predecessors of the new task to be added, consider combining nodes, adding dummy activities, or adding dummy nodes (and activities).

✔ When completed, combine all terminal nodes with no arcs leaving them into a single node to represent the time at which the entire project is completed.

✔ Use the final project network to list the immediate predecessors of each task; then verify that those relationships are correct, as specified in the precedence table.

10.1.5 The Project Network for the Project of Period Publishing Company

Recall the project of Period Publishing Company in Example 10.1 whose precedence table is shown in Table 10.4.

Figure 10.4(a) shows the result of building the network corresponding to Tasks A, B, D, E, and G. Observe that no other task can be added to any of terminal nodes 2, 4, and 5 in the figure because of the precedence relationships. In particular, Task C cannot begin until both Tasks B and G are completed, and there is no single node representing the completion of those two tasks. By using the technique of adding a dummy activity to connect node 4 to node 2, it is now possible to add an arc from node 2 for Task C, as shown in Figure 10.4(b). Similarly, for Task F, which requires the completion of Tasks E and G, a dummy activity is added to connect node 4 to node 5. The result of adding an arc from node 5 for Task F is shown in Figure 10.4(c).

Finally, Task H requires the completion of both Tasks C and F. There is no single node in Figure 10.4(c) representing that point in time. In this case, the difficulty can be resolved by combining nodes 6 and 7 into a new node—numbered 6 in Figure 10.4(d)—and then adding an arc for Task H.

Because of the manner in which dummy nodes and activities are used, there is no unique way of constructing a project network. Another correct network for the project of Period Publishing Company is shown in Figure 10.5. As a general rule, project networks containing fewer nodes and/or arcs are preferable because subsequent computations can be performed more quickly on smaller networks. However, *the most important property is that the project network correctly reflect the relationships specified in the precedence table.* Thus, you should be more concerned with this aspect rather than minimizing the number of dummy nodes and/or arcs needed to create the network.

Having identified the individual tasks involved in a project, obtained their time estimates, created the precedence table, and drawn the project network, you are now prepared to learn how to use this information to determine the earliest time at which

TABLE 10.4	*Precedence Table for the Tasks of the Period Publishing Company Project*		
LABEL	DESCRIPTION	TIME ESTIMATE (weeks)	IMMEDIATE PREDECESSORS
A	Author preparation of manuscript	30	None
B	Design promotional materials	6	A
C	Produce promotional materials	4	B, G
D	Copy edit the manuscript	5	A
E	Proofread and correct the page proofs	10	D
F	Produce the final book	8	E, G
G	Obtain all legal permissions and copyrights	14	A
H	Conduct a sales training meeting	2	C, F

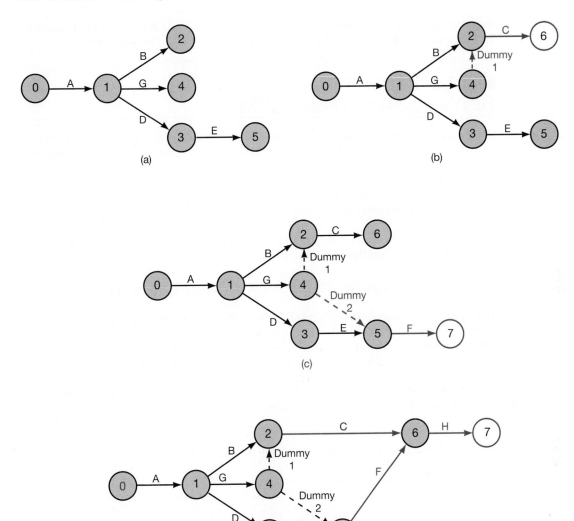

FIGURE 10.4 A Project Network for Period Publishing Company.

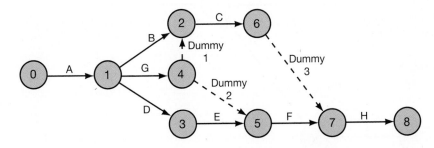

FIGURE 10.5 An Alternative Project Network for Period Publishing Company.

the entire project can be finished and to identify which tasks must be kept on schedule for the project to be completed on time. This is the topic of the next section.

■ 10.2 PROJECT MANAGEMENT USING DETERMINISTIC TIMES (CPM)

In this section, you will learn how to use the project network together with deterministic task-completion times to manage projects by answering the following questions:

1. What is the earliest time at which the entire project can be completed?
2. To meet this completion time, which tasks are critical, in the sense that a delay in any of those tasks results in a delay in the completion of the entire project?

The technique used to answer the first question is presented in Section 10.2.1. The method for identifying the critical tasks is developed in Section 10.2.2.

10.2.1 Computing The Project-Completion Time

The systematic computations needed to determine the earliest completion time are illustrated for the project of Period Publishing Company in Example 10.1 in Section 10.1. Although there are several different project networks corresponding to this project, the network in Figure 10.6 is used. Note that the deterministic completion time of each task is written next to the arc corresponding to that task in the figure.

To find the earliest completion time of the entire project, proceed systematically from the beginning, determining the following for each task:

Earliest start time
The earliest time at which a task can possibly begin.

1. The **earliest start time**—that is, the earliest time at which that task can begin.
2. The **earliest finish time**—that is, the earliest time at which that task can end.

The earliest finish time of the final task is the earliest time at which the entire project can be completed. (In the event that there is more than one terminal task, the earliest completion time of the entire project is the maximum of the earliest finish times of all such tasks.)

Earliest finish time
The earliest time at which a task can possibly end.

To compute the earliest start time for a particular task, recall the concept of the immediate-predecessor tasks—that is, those tasks that must be completed before the current task can begin. It is necessary to know when *each* of these predecessor tasks is finished:

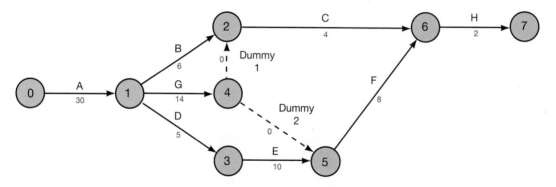

FIGURE 10.6 A Project Network with Task Times for Period Publishing Company.

Rule 1. To compute the earliest start time of a particular task, you must know the earliest finish times of each immediate-predecessor task.

Consider a Task Z that has Tasks W, X, and Y as immediate predecessors, as shown in Figure 10.7. Suppose you already know that Task W ends earliest at time 8, Task X ends at time 10, and Task Y ends at time 15. Because Task Z cannot begin until *all three* of these predecessor tasks are completed, it is clear that the earliest Task Z can begin is time 15. In general, the following rule is used to compute the earliest start time of a task:

Rule 2. The earliest start time of a task for which the earliest finish times of all its immediate-predecessor tasks are known is the *maximum* of those earliest finish times.

For any task whose earliest start time has been found by Rule 2, the earliest finish time of that task is obtained by the following rule:

Rule 3. Earliest finish time = (earliest start time) + (task time)

If Task Z in Figure 10.7 requires 7 units of time to complete, its earliest finish time is

$$\text{Earliest finish time} = (\text{earliest start time}) + (\text{task time})$$
$$= 15 + 7$$
$$= 22$$

Applying Rules 1 to 3 in a systematic way results in the earliest start and finish times for each task and hence for the entire project. Recall that each arc corresponds to a task in the project, including the dummy arcs that correspond to dummy activities requiring no time. Each node in the project network represents a point in time at which all entering arcs correspond to tasks that are completed. With this in mind, it is possible to compute the earliest start and finish times of each task using the project network by performing Step 0, which follows, and then repeating Steps 1 and 2, which follow, until all tasks have been assigned their earliest start and finish times.

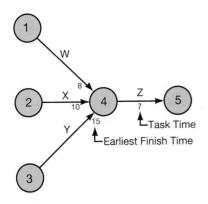

FIGURE 10.7 Using Precedence Relationships to Find the Earliest Start Time.

KEY FEATURES

Steps for Computing the Earliest Start and Finish Times

Step 0. Identify the node corresponding to the beginning of the entire project. Compute and write the following next to each leaving arc:
- **a.** The earliest start time—that is, 0 (because the corresponding task can begin immediately).
- **b.** The earliest finish time according to Rule 3—that is

$$\text{Earliest finish time} = (\text{earliest start time}) + (\text{task time})$$
$$= 0 + (\text{task time})$$
$$= \text{task time}$$

Step 1. Select any node where all entering arcs have been labeled with their earliest start and finish times.

Step 2. For the node selected in Step 1, compute and write the following next to each leaving arc:
- **a.** The earliest start time according to Rule 2—that is

$$\text{Earliest start time} = \text{maximum of the earliest finish times of all entering arcs}$$

- **b.** The earliest finish time according to Rule 3—that is

$$\text{Earliest finish time} = (\text{earliest start time}) + (\text{task time})$$

ITERATION 1

Look now at the project network of Period Publishing Company in Figure 10.6. To apply Step 0 to that network, note that Task A begins the entire project. Assign it, then, the earliest start time of 0 and earliest finish time of 30, which is its task time. Adding this information to the project network results in Figure 10.8(a).

Applying Step 1, select node 1 in the figure because all arcs entering that node—in this case, the arc corresponding to Task A—have already been labeled.

Applying Step 2, label the arcs leaving node 1—which correspond to Tasks B, G, and D—with their earliest start and finish times. Observe that the maximum of the earliest finish times of all arcs entering node 1 is 30. According to Step 2(a), the earliest start time of Tasks B, G, and D is 30. The earliest finish times for these tasks, computed using Step 2(b), follows:

(Earliest start time)	+	(task time)	=	earliest finish time	
30	+	6	=	36	(Task B)
30	+	14	=	44	(Task G)
30	+	5	=	35	(Task D)

These times are written as labels next to the corresponding arcs in Figure 10.8(b).

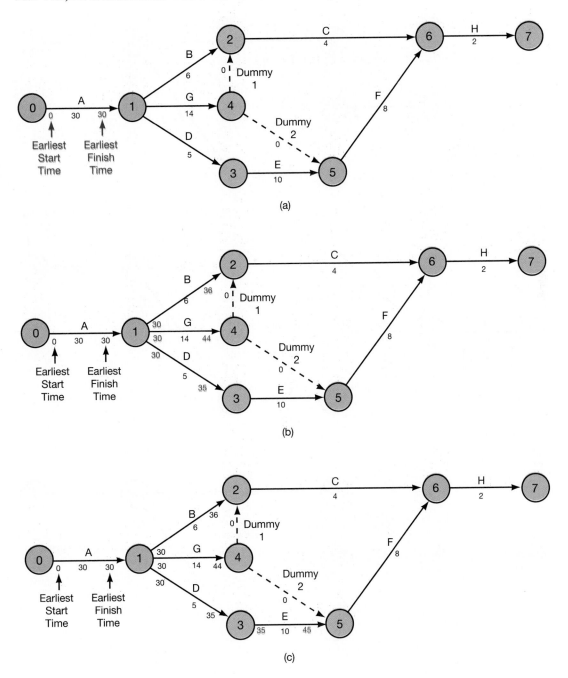

FIGURE 10.8 Computing the Earliest Start and Finish Times for the Project Network for Period Publishing Company.

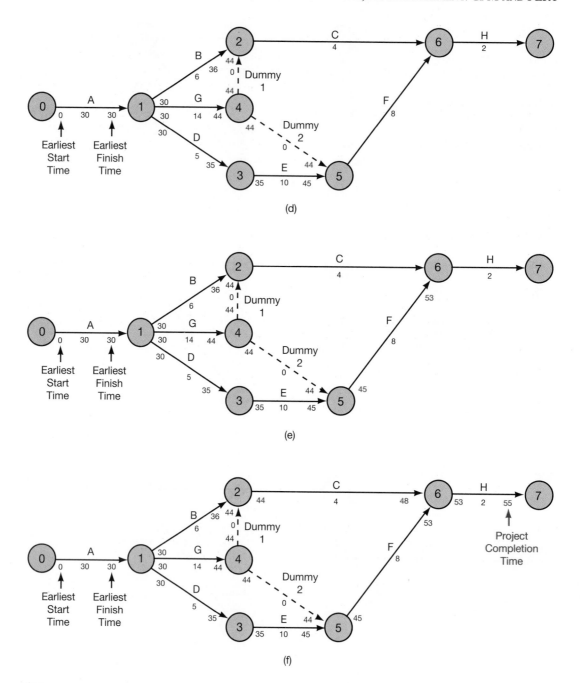

FIGURE 10.8 (*cont.*)   Computing the Earliest Start and Finish Times for the Project Network for Period Publishing Company.

ITERATION 2

In applying Step 1 again, observe that it is not possible to select node 2 because the arc entering from node 4, corresponding to the dummy activity, has not yet been labeled. However, node 3 *can* be selected because *all* its entering arcs—namely, the arc corresponding to Task D—have been labeled.

Apply Step 2(a) to the single arc leaving node 3, which corresponds to Task E. The earliest start time of this task is the earliest finish time of 35 for the single arc entering node 3, corresponding to Task D. The earliest finish time of Task E, according to Step 2(b), is as follows:

(Earliest start time) + (task time) = earliest finish time
    35   +   10   =   45   (Task E)

These times are written next to the arc corresponding to Task E in Figure 10.8(c).

ITERATION 3

Applying Step 1 again leads you to select node 4 because its only entering arc, corresponding to Task G, is labeled.

Applying the now familiar steps and rules, you can see that the earliest finish time of Task G is 44. Thus, 44 becomes the earliest start time for the two arcs leaving node 4, which represent Dummy Activities 1 and 2. The earliest finish times for these dummy activities are computed as follows:

(Earliest start time) + (task time) = earliest finish time
    44   +   0   =   44   (Dummy 1)
    44   +   0   =   44   (Dummy 2)

These times are written next to the arcs corresponding to the dummy activities in Figure 10.8(d).

ITERATION 4

At this point, all arcs entering nodes 2 and 5 are labeled, so you can apply Step 1 to them. Arbitrarily choosing node 5 first, apply Step 2(a) to the one arc leaving that node, which corresponds to Task F. According to Rule 2, the earliest start time is

Earliest start time = maximum of the earliest finish times of
                      all arcs entering node 5

= maximum {earliest finish time of Task E,
                earliest finish time of Dummy 2}

= maximum {45, 44}

= 45

According to Step 2(b), the earliest finish time of Task F is computed as follows:

(Earliest start time) + (task time) = earliest finish time
    45   +   8   =   53   (Task F)

These times are written next to the arc corresponding to Task F in Figure 10.8(e).

Repeating Steps 1 and 2 for nodes 2 and 6 results in the completed project network in Figure 10.8(f). The earliest finish time for the final task—the 55 for the completion of Task H—is the earliest completion time for the entire project. As Vice President of Period Publishing Company, you know now that the project will take 55 weeks. You could use this information and the start and finish time for each activity to make up budgets and to schedule personnel, as necessary.

This section has provided a systematic sequence of computations that, when performed on the project network, results in the earliest completion time and schedule of the entire project. You will learn in the next section how to determine which tasks are critical in the sense that the slightest delay in those tasks results in a delay in the completion of the project.

10.2.2 Identifying Critical Tasks

In this section, you will learn how to use the project network together with the individual task completion times and the earliest start and finish times computed in Section 10.2.1 to determine which tasks are critical. *Critical* means that a delay in any one of those tasks results in a delay in the entire project. Project delays can result in additional costs, lost revenues, and/or not meeting contractual obligations. For example, failure to publish the textbook of Period Publishing Company on time may result in a substantial loss in sales because schools will not be able to adopt the book for the targeted semester or term. Therefore, as a manager, you will need to monitor these critical tasks closely to see that they are completed on time so that the entire project is kept on schedule.

Consider identifying the critical tasks in the problem of Period Publishing Company. Refer to Figure 10.8(f). Is Task G—obtaining legal permissions—critical, or can this task be delayed without affecting the completion of the project? The answer to this question is not obvious because this task is in the "middle" of the network. In contrast, it is quite apparent that Task H—conducting the sales training meeting, at the "end" of the network—*is* critical because any delay in this activity results in a corresponding delay of the project. You can see from the network in Figure 10.8(f) that for Task H to be kept on time—that is, to begin in week 53—it is important that Task F—producing the final book—is not delayed. Hence, Task F is also critical.

You can see now that the easiest way to identify the critical tasks is to start at the end of the network and proceed backward toward the beginning of the project, examining each task. To determine which ones are critical, then, requires computing the following for each task:

Latest finish time
The latest time a task can end while still allowing the project to be completed at its earliest possible time.

1. The **latest finish time**—that is, the latest a task can end while still allowing the project to be completed at its earliest possible time, as determined in Section 10.2.1 (55 weeks for the project of Period Publishing Company).
2. The **latest start time**—that is, the latest time the task can begin so that it will end by its latest finish time.

Any activity whose latest start time is the same as that task's earliest start time computed in Section 10.2.1 is critical. This is because the only way to keep the project on schedule is to start this task *exactly* by this common time.

Latest start time
The latest time a task can begin and still end by its latest finish time.

To compute the latest finish time for a particular task, observe that a delay in this particular task affects all **successor tasks**—that is, those tasks for which this one task is a predecessor—because those successor tasks cannot begin until this one is finished. This observation gives rise to the following rule, which are added to the three rules presented in Section 10.2.1:

Successor task
A task for which the task of interest is a predecessor.

> **Rule 4.** To compute the latest finish time of a particular task, you must know the latest start times of each immediate-successor task.

Consider a Task K that has Tasks L, M, and N as successors, as shown in Figure 10.9. Suppose you already know that the latest start times of Tasks L, M, and N are 10, 7, and 12, respectively. Because these tasks cannot begin until Task K is completed, it is

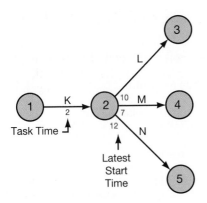

FIGURE 10.9 Using the Precedence Relationship to Find the Latest Finish Time.

clear that the latest Task K can *finish* and keep Tasks L, M, and N on schedule is 7. Otherwise Task M cannot start by its latest start time of 7. In general, the following rule is used to compute the latest finish time of a task:

> **Rule 5.** For a task for which the latest start times of all its immediate-successor tasks are known, the latest finish time of that task is the *minimum* of the latest start times of all the immediate-successor tasks.

For any task whose latest finish time has been found by Rule 5, the latest *start* time of that task is obtained by the following rule:

> **Rule 6.** Latest start time = (latest finish time) − (task time)

Thus, if Task K in Figure 10.9 requires two units of time to complete, its latest start time is

$$\text{Latest start time} = (\text{latest finish time}) - (\text{task time})$$
$$= 7 - 2$$
$$= 5$$

Applying Rules 4 to 6 in a systematic way results in the latest start and finish times for each task. First, perform Step 0, which follows, and then repeat Steps 1 and 2, which follow until all tasks have been assigned their latest start and finish times.

KEY FEATURES

Steps for Computing the Latest Start and Finish Times

Step 0. Identify the node corresponding to the end of the entire project. Compute and write the following next to each entering arc:
  a. The latest finish time, which is the earliest project completion time as determined in Section 10.2.1 (because any further delay in these tasks will delay the entire project).
  b. The latest start time according to Rule 6—that is

$$\text{Latest start time} = (\text{latest finish time}) - (\text{task time})$$
$$= (\text{project-completion time}) - (\text{task time})$$

Step 1. Select a node, all of whose leaving arcs have already been labeled with their latest start and finish times.

Step 2. For the node selected in Step 1, compute and write the following next to each entering arc:

    a. The latest finish time according to Rule 5—that is

$$\text{Latest finish time} = \text{minimum of the latest start} \\ \text{times of all leaving arcs}$$

    b. The latest start time according to Rule 6—that is

$$\text{Latest start time} = (\text{latest finish time}) - (\text{task time})$$

ITERATION 1

For the project of Period Publishing Company, apply Step 0 to the project network in Figure 10.8(f). The arc corresponding to Task H is assigned its latest finish time of 55 and latest start time of 53, corresponding to 55 minus its task time of 2. These start and finish times are shown in Figure 10.10(a).

Applying Step 1, select node 6 in the figure because all arcs leaving from that node—namely, the arc corresponding to Task H—have already been labeled.

Applying Step 2 to node 6, label the entering arcs corresponding to Tasks C and F according to Steps 2(a) and 2(b). Observe that the latest finish time of all arcs entering node 6 is 53 because there is only *one* leaving arc with a latest start time of 53. Thus, the latest finish time of Tasks C and F is 53, and the latest start times are computed according to Step 2(b) as follows:

$$(\text{Latest finish time}) - (\text{task time}) = \text{latest start time}$$

| 53 | − | 4 | = | 49 | (Task C) |
| 53 | − | 8 | = | 45 | (Task F) |

These times are written as labels next to the corresponding arcs in Figure 10.10(b).

ITERATION 2

In applying Step 1 again, observe that it is not possible to select node 4 because the arcs leaving node 4 corresponding to the two dummy activities have not yet been labeled. However, node 2 *can* be selected because *all* its leaving arcs—namely, the arc corresponding to Task C—have been labeled.

Apply Step 2(a) to the two arcs entering node 2 that correspond to Tasks B and the dummy activity. The latest finish time is the latest start time of the single arc leaving node 2 corresponding to Task C—namely 49—as seen in Figure 10.10(b). Thus, the latest start times of Task B and the dummy activity according to Step 2(b) are

$$(\text{Latest finish time}) - (\text{task time}) = \text{latest start time}$$

| 49 | − | 6 | = | 43 | (Task B) |
| 49 | − | 0 | = | 49 | (Dummy 1) |

These times are written next to the arcs corresponding to Task B and the dummy activity in Figure 10.10(c).

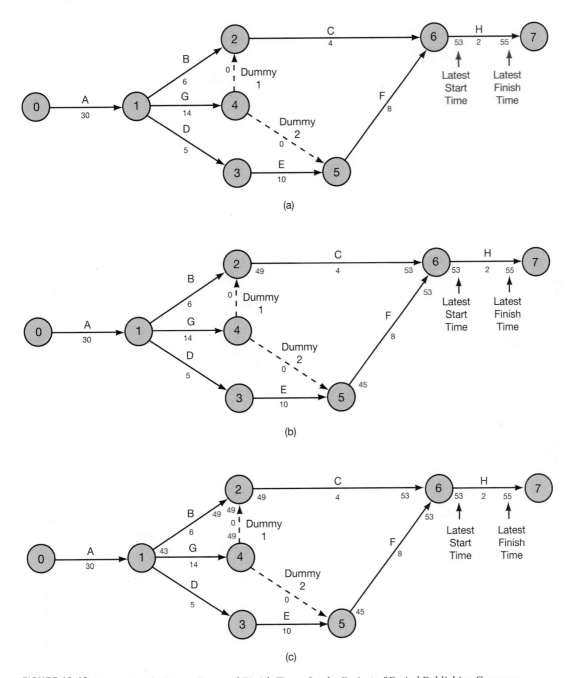

FIGURE 10.10 Computing the Latest Start and Finish Times for the Project of Period Publishing Company.

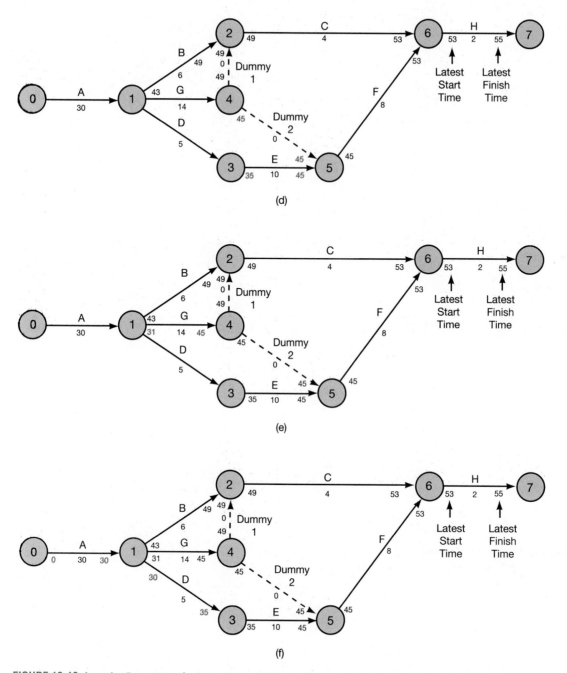

FIGURE 10.10 (*cont.*)   Computing the Latest Start and Finish Times for the Project of Period Publishing
Company.

ITERATION 3

Applying Step 1 again leads you to select node 5 because its one leaving arc, corresponding to Task F, is labeled.

Apply Step 2(a) to the two arcs entering node 5, which correspond to Task E and the dummy activity. The latest finish time is the latest start time of the single arc leaving node 5 corresponding to Task F—namely, 45—as seen in Figure 10.10(c). Thus, the latest start times of Task E and the dummy activity according to Step 2(b) are

(Latest finish time) − (task time) = latest start time

| 45 | − | 10 | = | 35 | (Task E) |
| 45 | − | 0 | = | 45 | (Dummy 2) |

These times are written as labels next to the corresponding arcs in Figure 10.10(d).

ITERATION 4

Step 1 now allows you to select either node 3 or node 4 because all arcs leaving these nodes have been labeled.

Arbitrarily choose node 4 and apply Step 2(a) to the single entering arc, corresponding to Task G. The latest finish time for Task G according to Rule 5 is

Latest finish time = minimum of the latest start times of all
arcs leaving node 4

= minimum {latest start time of Dummy 1,
latest start time of Dummy 2}

= minimum {49, 45}

= 45

Thus, according to Step 2(b), the latest start time of Task G is computed as follows:

(Latest finish time) − (task time) = latest start time

| 45 | − | 14 | = | 31 | (Task G) |

These times are written next to the arc corresponding to Task G in Figure 10.10(e).

Repeating Steps 1 and 2 twice results in the latest start and finish times for all tasks, as shown in Figure 10.10(f).

Having made these computations, you can now identify the critical and noncritical tasks. For each task, first compute the **slack time,** which is the difference between the latest and earliest start times:

Slack time = (latest start time) − (earliest start time)

Using the computations in Figures 10.8(f) and 10.10(f) and computing the slack times results in the **activity schedule** shown in Table 10.5.

The slack times in this table represent the amount of time by which the corresponding task can be delayed without delaying the entire project, *assuming that all other tasks are performed on time.* For example, the slack time of 5 for Task C means that if all other tasks are completed on time, Task C can begin up to 5 weeks late without delaying the project. *Thus, any task whose slack time is 0 is critical because that task cannot be delayed at all without affecting the completion time of the entire project.* So, Tasks A, D, E, F, and H are **critical tasks,** as indicated by the asterisk (∗) in the last column of the activity schedule in the table. As the Vice President, you should monitor these critical tasks carefully to keep the project on schedule.

Slack time
The difference between the latest and earliest start times; it is the amount of time a task can be delayed without affecting the earliest completion of the project.

Activity schedule A table that summarizes the earliest and latest start and finish times and slack times of each task in a project.

Critical task A task whose slack time is 0, indicating that any delay in this task will cause a delay in the completion of the entire project.

TABLE 10.5	Activity Schedule and Critical Tasks for the Project of the Period Publishing Company				
TASK	EARLIEST START (ES)	EARLIEST FINISH (EF)	LATEST START (LS)	LATEST FINISH (LF)	SLACK (LS − ES)
A	0	30	0	30	0*
B	30	36	43	49	13
C	44	48	49	53	5
D	30	35	30	35	0*
E	35	45	35	45	0*
F	45	53	45	53	0*
G	30	44	31	45	1
H	53	55	53	55	0*
Dummy 1	44	44	49	49	5
Dummy 2	44	44	45	45	1

Critical path

A sequence of critical tasks in a project that connect the beginning of the project to the end.

Figure 10.11 includes the slack time for each task. The colored arcs correspond to the critical tasks for the project of Period Publishing Company. As you can see, these tasks collectively form a **critical path** from the beginning to the end of the project. In general, there may be several critical paths. Adding the task times of all the activities along any such path results in the earliest completion time of the project; in this case, the time is 55 weeks.

Section 10.2 has provided a systematic sequence of computations that, when performed on the project network, enables you to identify the earliest completion time of the project and the associated critical tasks. The following section shows how to use a computer package to obtain this information and interpret the results to form an associated activity schedule.

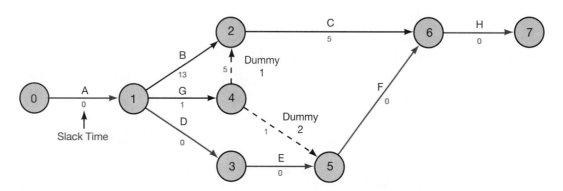

FIGURE 10.11 The Critical Tasks for the Project of Period Publishing Company.

■ 10.3 Project Management with Deterministic Task Times: Using the Computer

For the project of Period Publishing Company, you have already identified the individual tasks and their precedence relationships, drawn the project network, and collected the individual task times. With this information, any project-management computer package can be used to compute the earliest and latest start and finish times and the amount of slack time for each task. You can then determine the earliest time the project can be completed and which tasks are critical. To use such a package, you will need to enter the list of activities, their precedence relationship, and the individual task times. How to do so depends on the specific package being used. In some cases, you can enter the precedence table directly. In other cases, you have to enter the project network by specifying which nodes are connected by the arc corresponding to each task.

The results obtained from STORM appear in Figure 10.12. There, the 10 tasks, including the two dummy activities, are listed. The report contains one column for each of the following:

Project Management
PERPUB.DAT

```
           The Project of the Period Publishing Company
                ACTIVITIES IN THE ORDER AS ENTERED

   Activity            Activity   Earliest    Latest
     Name     Symb       Time    Start/Fin   Start/Fin      Slack

   TASK A      A       30.0000     0.0000      0.0000      0.0000 c
                                  30.0000     30.0000
   TASK B      B        6.0000    30.0000     43.0000     13.0000
                                  36.0000     49.0000
   TASK C      C        4.0000    44.0000     49.0000      5.0000
                                  48.0000     53.0000
   TASK D      D        5.0000    30.0000     30.0000      0.0000 c
                                  35.0000     35.0000
   TASK E      E       10.0000    35.0000     35.0000      0.0000 c
                                  45.0000     45.0000
   TASK F      F        8.0000    45.0000     45.0000      0.0000 c
                                  53.0000     53.0000
   TASK G      G       14.0000    30.0000     31.0000      1.0000
                                  44.0000     45.0000
   TASK H      H        2.0000    53.0000     53.0000      0.0000 c
                                  55.0000     55.0000
   DUMMY (1)  DUM1      0.0000    44.0000     49.0000      5.0000
                                  44.0000     49.0000
   DUMMY (2)  DUM2      0.0000    44.0000     45.0000      1.0000
                                  44.0000     45.0000


   The computations were based on 10 activities
   Earliest project completion time = 55.0000
```

FIGURE 10.12 STORM Results for the Project of Period Publishing Company.

1. The earliest start and finish times. For example, for Task B, the earliest start time is 30 and the earliest finish time is 36.
2. The latest start and finish times. For example, for Task B, the latest start time is 43 and the latest finish time is 49.
3. The slack time. For example, Task B has 13 weeks of slack time, indicating that Task B can be delayed for up to 13 weeks without affecting the completion of the project.

As described in Section 10.2.2, each task with a slack time of 0 is critical and is indicated by the letter "c" in the last column of Figure 10.12. The report indicates that the entire project can be completed in 55 weeks, with Tasks A, D, E, F, and H being critical, which coincides with the results obtained by hand in Section 10.2.2.

These results are further confirmed by the output from the computer package QSB shown in Figure 10.13. The completion time of 55 weeks, the earliest start and finish times for each task, the slack times, and the critical tasks and path are all the same.

To monitor the project properly, you need to know not only the earliest completion time and the critical tasks, but also *when* each individual task should be scheduled to start and when it must be completed so that the project remains on time. That information is contained in both the reports in Figures 10.12 and 10.13 as the earliest start and finish times of each task. With STORM, it is possible to display this information in a manner that is easier to see and understand, as shown in the bar chart in Figure 10.14. There is one row for each task. The 60 columns correspond to the 55-week completion time. Therefore, each column represents 55/60 of a week. The string of characters in each row indicates when the corresponding task must begin and end. The critical tasks are those whose string of characters is made up of the letter "c." The

```
|----------------------------------------------------------------------------|
|               CPM Analysis for Period Publishing Co      Page   1          |
|----------------------------------------------------------------------------|
|Activity|     Activity       |Earliest| Latest |Earliest| Latest | Slack  |
|No. Name|Exp.Time  Variance| Start  | Start  | Finish | Finish | LS-ES  |
|----------------------------------------------------------------------------|
| A       |+30.0000  0        |0       |0       |+30.0000|+30.0000|Critical|
| B       |+6.00000  0        |+30.0000|+43.0000|+36.0000|+49.0000|+13.0000|
| C       |+4.00000  0        |+44.0000|+49.0000|+48.0000|+53.0000|+5.00000|
| D       |+5.00000  0        |+30.0000|+30.0000|+35.0000|+35.0000|Critical|
| E       |+10.0000  0        |+35.0000|+35.0000|+45.0000|+45.0000|Critical|
| F       |+8.00000  0        |+45.0000|+45.0000|+53.0000|+53.0000|Critical|
| G       |+14.0000  0        |+30.0000|+31.0000|+44.0000|+45.0000|+1.00000|
| H       |+2.00000  0        |+53.0000|+53.0000|+55.0000|+55.0000|Critical|
| Dummy1  |0         0        |+44.0000|+49.0000|+44.0000|+49.0000|+5.00000|
| Dummy2  |0         0        |+44.0000|+45.0000|+44.0000|+45.0000|+1.00000|
|----------------------------------------------------------------------------|
|          Expected completion time = 55    Total cost = 0                   |
|----------------------------------------------------------------------------|

  Critical paths for Period Publishing Co  with completion time =   55
    Total cost = 0

  CP # 1 : A - D - E - F - H
```

FIGURE 10.13 QSB Results for the Project of Period Publishing Company.

```
The Project of the Period Publishing Company
BAR CHART: NONCRITICAL ACTIVITIES SORTED BY EARLIEST START

    0                                                 55
----+-----+-----+-----+-----+-----+-----+-----+-----+-----+-----+
A   |ccccccccccccccccccccccccccccccccccc                  |
D   |                              ccccc                   |
E   |                                ccccccccccc           |
F   |                                      ccccccccc |
H   |                                              cc
B   |                         xxxxxx.............          |
G   |                         xxxxxxxxxxxxxxx.             |
DUM1|                                    x....             |
DUM2|                                    x.               |
C   |                                    xxxx......        |
----+-----+-----+-----+-----+-----+-----+-----+-----+-----+-----+
```

FIGURE 10.14 Bar Chart for the Project of Period Publishing Company.

string of characters for all other tasks consists of the letter "x" followed by a sequence of periods (.) indicating the approximate amount of slack, based on the time scale. For example, the periods in the row corresponding to Task C indicate that that task can be delayed without delaying the completion of the project. Recall that each column represents 55/60 week. The six periods in this row indicate a slack of approximately $6 * (55/60) = 5.5$, or about 5 weeks.

In this section, you have learned to interpret the computer output to determine the project-completion time, the critical tasks, and the activity schedule. In the next section, you will learn how additional resources can be used to expedite the completion of the project.

■ 10.4 EXPEDITING A PROJECT USING CRASHING TECHNIQUES

In many projects, management may decide that the earliest completion time is not acceptable. In such cases, additional resources can often be used to expedite—to speed up—certain tasks, resulting in an earlier completion of the project. In this section, you will learn how a linear programming model can be formulated to determine which tasks should be expedited to achieve a specific desired completion time, and at what cost.

In the example of Period Publishing Company, suppose that the President decides that a completion time of 55 weeks, as calculated in Section 10.2.1, is too long. You have been asked to make recommendations on how the project can be shortened by 2 months, to 47 weeks.

10.4.1 Obtaining Additional Cost Data for the Tasks

What tasks in the project can be shortened and by how much? Of course, shortening tasks clearly requires additional resources—such as paying for overtime, additional staff, and/or subcontracting. Thus, the first steps are to list, for each task:

Crashing time
The minimum possible time in which a task can realistically be completed using additional resources.

1. The **crashing time**—that is, the minimum possible time in which the task can realistically be completed using additional resources.
2. The cost of the additional resources needed to shorten the task time to any value between its normal and crashing times.

To obtain the crashing time, you can consult with people involved in the task. For example, consider the task of designing promotional materials in the project for Period Publishing Company. This task is originally estimated to require 6 weeks. However, after discussions with the Manager of the Design Department, you discovered that by hiring some part-time help and/or using overtime, the needed materials could be designed in as little as 4 weeks, but not less. Thus, with additional resources, the completion time of this task can be shortened by 2 weeks to a crashing time of 4 weeks.

Time costs money. To establish how much the time costs, begin by obtaining two cost estimates for completing the task in (a) its normal time and (b) its crashing time. In the project of Period Publishing Company, suppose that designing the promotional materials is estimated to cost $6000 if completed in its normal time of 6 weeks and $9000 if completed in its crashing time of 4 weeks. In fact, for an appropriate amount between $6000 and $9000, you can complete this task in any time between 6 and 4 weeks. However, obtaining cost estimates for *each* possible time between the 4 and 6 weeks can be difficult, expensive, and time-consuming. One commonly used approximation is to assume that the costs behave *linearly* within the given time range, as shown in Figure 10.15. Based on this assumption, an approximate *cost per unit of time* can be computed using the following formula:

$$\text{Per-unit cost} = \frac{(\text{cost at crashing time}) - (\text{cost at normal time})}{(\text{normal time}) - (\text{crash time})}$$

For the task of designing the promotional materials,

$$\text{Per-unit cost} = \frac{9000 - 6000}{6 - 4}$$
$$= \frac{3000}{2}$$
$$= 1500$$

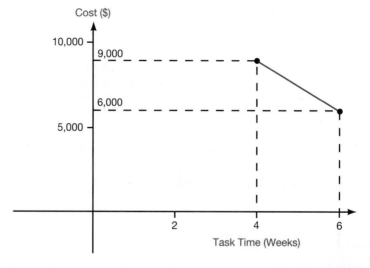

FIGURE 10.15 Linear Time-Cost Trade-off for Designing Promotional Materials.

In other words, it will cost an additional $1500 for each week this task is shortened.

These data and computations for each task of the project of Period Publishing Company are shown in Table 10.6. Note that the per-unit cost for Task H, the sales training meeting, has not been computed. That task cannot be shortened at all.

10.4.2 Developing the Crashing Model

With the data in Table 10.6 and the project network, it is now possible to develop a linear programming model to determine which tasks to shorten, and by how much, to achieve a given target completion time for the entire project in the least-cost manner. To do so, follow the problem formulation steps in Chapter 2.

IDENTIFYING THE DECISION VARIABLES

Asking what you can control and/or need to determine in this problem should lead you to identify as the decision variables the amount of time by which to shorten each task. Thus, for the example of Period Publishing Company, define

$$Y_A = \text{the number of weeks by which to shorten Task A}$$

$$Y_B = \text{the number of weeks by which to shorten Task B}$$

$$\vdots$$

$$Y_H = \text{the number of weeks by which to shorten Task H}$$

The values of these decision variables reduce the task completion times to the amounts shown next to each arc in Figure 10.16. For example, the new completion time of Task C is $4 - Y_C$—that is, the normal time of 4 weeks less the number of weeks, Y_C, by which that task is shortened.

IDENTIFYING THE OBJECTIVE FUNCTION

The overall objective is to minimize the total additional resources needed to meet the target completion time for the project. Having computed the per-unit costs listed in Table 10.6 associated with shortening each task, and noting that the cost of the variable Y_H is irrelevant because its value will be restricted to 0, the objective function in mathematical terms is

$$\text{Minimize} \quad 1000Y_A + 1500Y_B + 500Y_C + 750Y_D + 600Y_E +$$
$$1250Y_F + 2500Y_G + 0Y_H$$

TABLE 10.6 *Crashing Costs for the Tasks of Period Publishing Company*

TASK	NORMAL TIME	NORMAL COST	CRASH TIME	CRASH COST	MAXIMUM REDUCTION	COST PER WEEK
A	30	5000	26	9000	4	1000
B	6	6000	4	9000	2	1500
C	4	10000	3	10500	1	500
D	5	5000	3	6500	2	750
E	10	4500	7	6300	3	600
F	8	20000	6	22500	2	1250
G	14	10000	12	15000	2	2500
H	2	25000	2	25000	0	—

IDENTIFYING THE CONSTRAINTS

Using the technique of grouping, you might identify two groups of constraints:

1. The maximum amount of time by which each task can be shortened.
2. The targeted project completion time (in this case, 47 weeks).

For the constraints in group 1, all that are needed are the upper bounds on the decision variables $Y_A, \ldots, Y_H$. The maximum values of these variables are given in the column labeled "Maximum Reduction" in Table 10.6. Combining these values with the implicit nonnegativities of these variables gives rise to the following constraints:

BOUND CONSTRAINTS

$$0 \le Y_A \le 4 \quad \text{(Bound A)}$$
$$0 \le Y_B \le 2 \quad \text{(Bound B)}$$
$$0 \le Y_C \le 1 \quad \text{(Bound C)}$$
$$0 \le Y_D \le 2 \quad \text{(Bound D)}$$
$$0 \le Y_E \le 3 \quad \text{(Bound E)}$$
$$0 \le Y_F \le 2 \quad \text{(Bound F)}$$
$$0 \le Y_G \le 2 \quad \text{(Bound G)}$$
$$0 \le Y_H \le 0 \quad \text{(Bound H)}$$

Specifying the constraint in group 2 requires care. Looking at the project network in Figure 10.16, it is necessary to know when Task H is completed to determine when the entire project is finished. This in turn requires knowing when all the immediate predecessors of Task H are completed—that is, when Tasks C and F are completed. In fact, to specify that the project be completed by its target time, it is necessary to know when each individual task can begin. Because these values are as yet unknown and depend on the values of $Y_A, \ldots, Y_H$, it is advisable to define additional variables for each *node* in the project network as follows:

$X_0 =$ the time at which all tasks stemming from node 0 can begin

$X_1 =$ the time at which all tasks stemming from node 1 can begin

$$\vdots$$

$X_7 =$ the time at which all tasks stemming from node 7 can begin

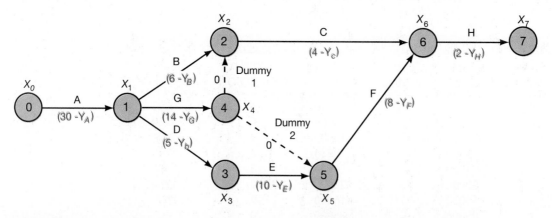

FIGURE 10.16 Decision Variables for Expediting the Project of Period Publishing Company.

With these variables, it is now possible to specify that the project must begin at time 0 and end within 47 weeks with the following two constraints:

$$X_0 = 0 \quad \text{(start)}$$
$$X_7 \leq 47 \quad \text{(finish)}$$

All that remains are the constraints that specify that a task can begin only after all its immediate-predecessor tasks are completed. For example, looking at node 1 in Figure 10.16, Tasks B, G, and D can begin only after Task A is completed. Because X_1 is that time at which these three tasks can begin, this node constraint follows:

NODE 1 CONSTRAINT

Beginning time of tasks stemming from node 1 ≥ finishing times of all tasks entering node 1
Beginning time of Tasks B, G, D ≥ finishing time of Task A
Beginning time of Tasks B, G, D ≥ (beginning time of Task A) +
(shortened time for Task A)
$$X_1 \geq X_0 + (30 - Y_A) \quad \text{(Task A)}$$

Look now at node 2 in Figure 10.16. A constraint is needed to specify that Task C can begin only after Tasks B and the dummy activity are completed. In particular, this node constraint follows:

NODE 2 CONSTRAINT

Beginning time of tasks stemming from node 2 ≥ finishing times of all tasks entering node 2

In this case, because there are two arcs entering Node 2, Task C can begin only after *both* those tasks are completed, thus giving rise to the following *two* constraints.

TASK B CONSTRAINT

Beginning time of Task C ≥ finishing time of Task B
Beginning time of Task C ≥ (beginning time of Task B) +
(shortened time for Task B)
$$X_2 \geq X_1 + (6 - Y_B) \quad \text{(Task B)}$$

DUMMY (1) CONSTRAINT

Beginning time of Task C ≥ finishing time of dummy activity
Beginning time of Task C ≥ (beginning time of dummy activity) +
(time for dummy activity)
$$X_2 \geq X_4 + 0 \quad \text{(Dummy 1)}$$

Proceeding systematically to each node and writing a constraint for each entering activity results in the following constraints for nodes 3 through 7.

NODE 3 CONSTRAINT

$$X_3 \geq X_1 + (5 - Y_D) \quad \text{(Task D)}$$

NODE 4 CONSTRAINT

$$X_4 \geq X_1 + (14 - Y_G) \quad \text{(Task G)}$$

NODE 5 CONSTRAINTS

$$X_5 \geq X_4 + 0 \qquad \text{(Dummy 2)}$$
$$X_5 \geq X_3 + (10 - Y_E) \qquad \text{(Task E)}$$

NODE 6 CONSTRAINTS

$$X_6 \geq X_2 + (4 - Y_C) \qquad \text{(Task C)}$$
$$X_6 \geq X_5 + (8 - Y_F) \qquad \text{(Task F)}$$

NODE 7 CONSTRAINTS

$$X_7 \geq X_6 + (2 - Y_H) \qquad \text{(Task H)}$$

By adding the implicit nonnegativity on the X-variables, the complete crashing model is as follows.

CRASHING MODEL FOR THE PROJECT OF PERIOD PUBLISHING COMPANY

Linear Program
PERPUBLP.DAT

$$\text{Minimize} \quad 1000Y_A + 1500Y_B + 500Y_C + 750Y_D +$$
$$600Y_E + 1250Y_F + 2500Y_G + 0Y_H$$

Subject to

BOUND CONSTRAINTS

$$0 \leq Y_A \leq 4 \qquad \text{(Bound A)}$$
$$0 \leq Y_B \leq 2 \qquad \text{(Bound B)}$$
$$0 \leq Y_C \leq 1 \qquad \text{(Bound C)}$$
$$0 \leq Y_D \leq 2 \qquad \text{(Bound D)}$$
$$0 \leq Y_E \leq 3 \qquad \text{(Bound E)}$$
$$0 \leq Y_F \leq 2 \qquad \text{(Bound F)}$$
$$0 \leq Y_G \leq 2 \qquad \text{(Bound G)}$$
$$0 \leq Y_H \leq 0 \qquad \text{(Bound H)}$$

PROJECT-COMPLETION CONSTRAINTS

$$X_0 = 0 \qquad \text{(start)}$$
$$X_7 \leq 47 \qquad \text{(finish)}$$

NETWORK CONSTRAINTS

NODE 1 CONSTRAINT
$$X_1 \geq X_0 + (30 - Y_A) \qquad \text{(Task A)}$$

NODE 2 CONSTRAINTS
$$X_2 \geq X_1 + (6 - Y_B) \qquad \text{(Task B)}$$
$$X_2 \geq X_4 + 0 \qquad \text{(Dummy 1)}$$

NODE 3 CONSTRAINT
$$X_3 \geq X_1 + (5 - Y_D) \qquad \text{(Task D)}$$

NODE 4 CONSTRAINT

$$X_4 \geq X_1 + (14 - Y_G) \qquad \text{(Task G)}$$

NODE 5 CONSTRAINTS

$$X_5 \geq X_4 + 0 \qquad \text{(Dummy 2)}$$
$$X_5 \geq X_3 + (10 - Y_E) \qquad \text{(Task E)}$$

NODE 6 CONSTRAINTS

$$X_6 \geq X_2 + (4 - Y_C) \qquad \text{(Task C)}$$
$$X_6 \geq X_5 + (8 - Y_F) \qquad \text{(Task F)}$$

NODE 7 CONSTRAINTS

$$X_7 \geq X_6 + (2 - Y_H) \qquad \text{(Task H)}$$

$$\text{and} \quad X_0, \ldots, X_7 \geq 0$$

10.4.3 Solving the Crashing Model

Having formulated the appropriate crashing model, you can now use any linear programming package to obtain the solution. For example, Figure 10.17 shows the results of using LINDO. From the values of the Y-variables in that output, you can see that to complete the project by the target time of 47 weeks, it is necessary to shorten the times of Task A by 4 weeks, Task E by 2 weeks, Task F by 2 weeks, and Task G by 1 week. The total cost for doing this is an additional \$10,200, as indicated in the line labeled "1)" near the top of the report in Figure 10.17.

Linear Problem
PERPUBL.DAT

```
LP OPTIMUM FOUND AT STEP      2

       OBJECTIVE FUNCTION VALUE

     1)      10200.000

  VARIABLE        VALUE          REDUCED COST
      YA         4.000000            .000000
      YB          .000000        1500.000000
      YC          .000000         500.000000
      YD          .000000         150.000000
      YE         2.000000            .000000
      YF         2.000000            .000000
      YG         1.000000            .000000
      YH          .000000            .000000
      X0          .000000        3100.000000
      X7        47.000000            .000000
      X1        26.000000            .000000
      X2        41.000000            .000000
      X4        39.000000            .000000
      X3        31.000000            .000000
      X5        39.000000            .000000
      X6        45.000000            .000000
```

FIGURE 10.17 LINDO Solution to the Crashing Model for Project of Period Publishing Company.

You might think that to reduce the project-completion time from 55 to 47 weeks would require shortening one or more activities by an equivalent total of 55 − 47 = 8 weeks. However, in this case, it is necessary to shorten four tasks—Tasks A, E, F, and G—by a total of 9 weeks to achieve the goal.

You present these results, and the President is very satisfied. But she wishes to know how much more it would cost to reduce the completion time of the project by an additional 4 weeks. You are prepared for such a question. You have obtained the parametric analysis report, as described in Chapter 6, on the right-hand-side value of the constraint labeled "finish", which pertains to the project completion time in the formulation. This report, obtained from LINDO, is given in Figure 10.18.

The first line in the report in Figure 10.18 deals with the original value of 47 weeks for the completion of the project and is not of particular interest. The next row, however, contains information for finishing the project *between* 46 weeks (as indicated by the number 46.0000 in the column labeled "RHS VAL" in this row) and 47 weeks (as indicated by the number 47.0000 in the column labeled RHS VAL in the *previous* row). The project can be finished in 46 weeks at an additional cost of $3100 over the $10,200 obtained from the optimal solution to the crashing model, as indicated by the dual price (shadow price) in the second row. The final value of 13,300 in the last column of the second row indicates that it will cost $13,300 to achieve a completion time of 46 weeks for the project. The President must weigh this additional cost against the potential benefits of having the book come out 1 week earlier.

The third row of the report in Figure 10.18 contains information for finishing the project *between* 46 weeks (as indicated by the number 46.0000 in the column labeled "RHS VAL" in this row) and 46 weeks (as indicated by the number 46.0000 in the column labeled "RHS VAL" in the *previous* row). Because these two values—46—are the same, the information in the third row is not useful.

```
          Crashing Model for Period Publishing Company

      PARAMETRIC ANALYSIS OF RIGHT-HAND SIDE VALUE - FINISH

      VAR        VAR     PIVOT    RHS       DUAL PRICE     OBJ
      OUT        IN      ROW      VAL       BEFORE PIVOT   VAL
                                  47.0000   3100.00        10200.0
   SLK   6        YD      18      46.0000   3100.00        13300.0
   SLK   8   ART           7      46.0000   3250.00        13300.0
                                  40.0000   +INFINITY      INFEASIBLE

      VAR        VAR     PIVOT    RHS       DUAL PRICE     OBJ
      OUT        IN      ROW      VAL       BEFORE PIVOT   VAL
                                  47.0000   3100.00        10200.0
         YG    SLK   7     8      48.0000   3100.00        7100.00
         YF    SLK   2    12      50.0000   1250.00        4600.00
         YA    SLK  16     2      54.0000   1000.00        600.000
         YE         X0     6      55.0000   600.000        .000000
   ART         SLK   9    10      55.0000   .000000        .000000
         YH    SLK  11     9      55.0000   .000000        .000000
                                  60.0000   .000000        .000000
```

FIGURE 10.18 LINDO Parametric Analysis on the Completion Time of the Project of Period Publishing Company.

the project between 40 weeks (as indicated by the number 40.0000 in the column labeled "RHS VAL" in this row) and 46 weeks (as indicated by the number 46.0000 in the column labeled "RHS VAL" in the *previous* row). As indicated by the word "INFEASIBLE" in the column labeled "OBJ VAL" in the fourth row, you can tell the President that it is not possible to shorten the project by another 4 weeks. In fact, the project cannot be shortened below 46 weeks.

The next part of the report in Figure 10.18 pertains to *increasing* the completion time of the project beyond the 47 weeks. For example, you might wish to advise the President that an additional $3100 can be *saved* if the project can be completed in 48 instead of 47 weeks. This time–cost trade-off information for each range in the parametric report in Figure 10.18 is shown in Figure 10.19.

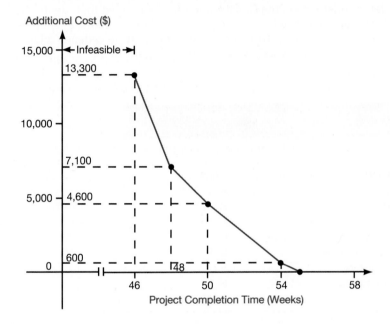

FIGURE 10.19 The Time-Cost Trade-off for the Project of Period Publishing Company.

In this section, you have learned how to create a linear programming model to determine which tasks to shorten so as to meet a given target completion time for a project. In Sections 10.1 through 10.4, you have learned how to schedule a complex project consisting of a collection of individual tasks. In so doing, the completion times of the individual tasks were assumed to be known with relative certainty. Many projects, however, have task times that can vary significantly depending on uncontrollable factors. It is necessary to take this variability into account. You will learn how this is done in the next section.

■ 10.5 PROJECT MANAGEMENT USING PROBABILISTIC TASK TIMES (PERT)

In monitoring projects, a manager often encounters unanticipated delays in completing various tasks, resulting in a corresponding delay in the entire project. One way to handle such problems is to take this variability into account when estimating the individual task-completion times. Rather than assuming that the task times are known with certainty—as was the case in the example of the project of Period Publishing Company in Sections 10.1 to 10.4—it may be more appropriate to estimate the task times, acknowledging the uncertainty. Monitoring such projects requires *probabilistic analysis,* as described in this section. Throughout this section, it is assumed that the reader is familiar with the basic notions of probability and statistics.

10.5.1 Listing the Tasks, Identifying the Precedence Relationships, and Drawing the Project Network

Consider the problem of Home Construction, Inc., a company that builds single-family homes. As in the deterministic case, the Construction Manager must first identify the major tasks (and their immediate predecessors) required to build a home, as shown in Table 10.7. As you learned in Section 10.1, these tasks and their precedence relationships can be drawn in a project network, as illustrated in Figure 10.20.

TABLE 10.7	*Immediate Predecessors for the Project of Home Construction, Inc.*	
TASK	DESCRIPTION	IMMEDIATE PREDECESSORS
A	Foundation	None
B	Frame	A
C	Roofing	B
D	Plumbing	A
E	Electrical wiring	C
F	Doors and windows	D, E
G	Interior finishing	F
H	Exterior finishing	F
I	Inspection	G, H

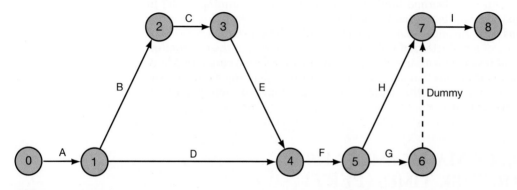

FIGURE 10.20 A Project Network for the Project of Home Construction, Inc.

10.5.2 *Estimating Task-Completion Times*

The completion times of these tasks are quite variable because of uncertainty in weather conditions, obtaining supplies, maintaining labor relations, and so on. Thus, a single time estimate is inappropriate. To incorporate this variability requires knowing the *probability distribution* for the completion times of each task. This, in turn, requires knowing the parameters of the distribution, among them the *mean* and *variance*. Obtaining the distribution and its parameters is often difficult and time consuming. However, one approach that has proved reliable in practice is to approximate these unknown distributions with a *beta distribution*. The analysis in this section does not require the exact form of the distribution, but requires only the knowledge of three parameters: the minimum value, the maximum value, and the most likely value, as shown in Figure 10.21.

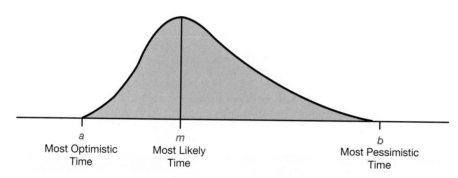

FIGURE 10.21 Beta Distribution of a Task Time.

KEY FEATURES

In the context of the tasks of a project, obtain three time estimates for each task:

✔ Most optimistic time *a*—that is, the shortest time in which the task can be completed.

✔ Most pessimistic time *b*—that is, the longest time a task might take within reason.

✔ Most likely time *m*—that is, the time this task requires most frequently under normal circumstances.

For a beta distribution, these three time estimates are then combined to give the expected value (mean) and standard deviation of the completion time of a task according to the following formulas:

$$\text{Expected task time} = \frac{a + 4m + b}{6}$$

$$\text{Standard deviation} = \frac{b - a}{6}$$

Suppose that for Task C, putting on the roof, the three time estimates obtained from the roofing subcontractors are

$$a = \text{most optimistic} = 3 \quad \text{weeks}$$
$$b = \text{most pessimistic} = 11 \quad \text{weeks}$$
$$m = \text{most likely} \quad = 5.5 \text{ weeks}$$

By using these estimates, the expected task time and the standard deviation are computed as follows:

$$\text{Expected task time} = \frac{a + 4m + b}{6}$$
$$= \frac{3 + 4(5.5) + 11}{6}$$
$$= 6$$
$$\text{Standard deviation} = \frac{b - a}{6}$$
$$= \frac{11 - 3}{6}$$
$$= 1.333$$

The Construction Manager has obtained these estimates and made the appropriate computations for each of the remaining tasks, as summarized in Table 10.8.

TABLE 10.8 *Estimates of the Completion Times for the Tasks of Home Construction, Inc.*

		TIME ESTIMATES (WEEKS)			TIME COMPUTATIONS (WEEKS)	
TASK	DESCRIPTION	a	m	b	MEAN	STD. DEV.
A	Foundation	2	3	4	3	0.333
B	Frame	4	7.5	8	7	0.667
C	Roofing	3	5.5	11	6	1.333
D	Plumbing	2.5	4	5.5	4	0.500
E	Electrical wiring	2	3	4	3	0.333
F	Doors and windows	3	5	7	5	0.667
G	Interior finishing	3	3.5	7	4	0.667
H	Exterior finishing	2	5	8	5	1.000
I	Inspection	1	1	1	1	0.000

10.5.3 *Computing the Expected Project-Completion Time*

Project Management
HOMECON.DAT

Using the mean completion times for the tasks in Table 10.8 together with the project network in Figure 10.20, you can compute the earliest *expected* completion time for the entire project in exactly the same way as for projects with deterministic task times, as described in Section 10.2.1. Similarly, the latest start and finish times are computed as described in Section 10.2.2. The results appear in Figure 10.22. The STORM software package provides the information given in Figure 10.23. As you can see, the expected completion time of this project is 30 weeks with a standard deviation of 1.9720, given in the last line of the report. The calculation of this standard deviation is discussed in Section 10.5.4. You will also notice from this report that all tasks are critical except for D, G, and the dummy activity. Task D can be delayed by up to 12 weeks without affecting the expected completion time of the entire project, assuming all other tasks are completed within their expected times. Similarly, Task G can be delayed for up to 1 week.

10.5.4 Probabilistic Analysis of the Project-Completion Time

Recall that the project-completion time computed in Section 10.5.3 is the *expected* completion. The *actual* completion time can vary because the completion times of the tasks themselves are variable. Because the expected completion time of 30 weeks is, to

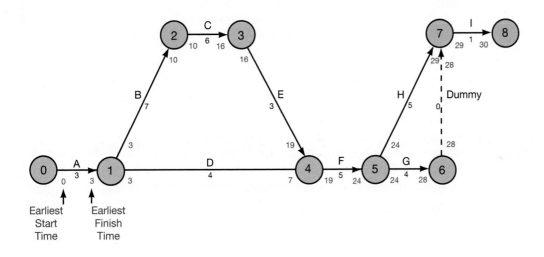

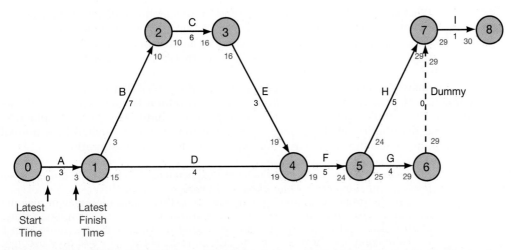

FIGURE 10.22 (a) Computing the Earliest Start and Finish Times and (b) Computing the Latest Start and Finish Times for the Project Network for Home Construction, Inc.

```
                    Home Construction, Inc.
            ACTIVITIES IN THE ORDER AS ENTERED
  Activity          Mean Time   Earliest    Latest
   Name      Symb   /Std Dev   Start/Fin   Start/Fin      Slack
 FOUNDATION  A        3.0000     0.0000      0.0000     0.0000 c
                      0.3333     3.0000      3.0000
 FRAME       B        7.0000     3.0000      3.0000     0.0000 c
                      0.6667    10.0000     10.0000
 ROOFING     C        6.0000    10.0000     10.0000     0.0000 c
                      1.3333    16.0000     16.0000
 PLUMBING    D        4.0000     3.0000     15.0000    12.0000
                      0.5000     7.0000     19.0000
 ELECTRICAL  E        3.0000    16.0000     16.0000     0.0000 c
                      0.3333    19.0000     19.0000
 DOORS/WIND  F        5.0000    19.0000     19.0000     0.0000 c
                      0.6667    24.0000     24.0000
 INTERIOR    G        4.0000    24.0000     25.0000     1.0000
                      0.6667    28.0000     29.0000
 EXTERIOR    H        5.0000    24.0000     24.0000     0.0000 c
                      1.0000    29.0000     29.0000
 INSPECTION  I        1.0000    29.0000     29.0000     0.0000 c
                      0.0000    30.0000     30.0000
 DUMMY       DUM      0.0000    28.0000     29.0000     1.0000
                      0.0000    28.0000     29.0000
 The computations were based on 10 activities
 Expected project completion time   = 30.0000
 Activity std dev = (pessimistic - optimistic) / 6.0
 Std dev of project completion time = 1.9720
```

FIGURE 10.23 STORM Output for the Project of Home Construction, Inc.

some degree, unreliable, the Construction Manager should ask questions such as the following:

> **a.** What is the probability of meeting a specific completion date for the project? For example, what is the probability of constructing the house within 32 weeks?
>
> **b.** What completion date can be met with a given level of confidence? For example, what is the latest completion date that you are 95% confident of meeting.

To answer probabilistic questions, you need the probability distribution for the completion time of the project. Obtaining that distribution is usually impossible because of the complex precedence relationships of the individual tasks. In practice, the actual distribution of the project completion time is approximated by a normal distribution. To use this approximation requires the following assumptions:

> **1.** The tasks determined as critical using the expected task times remain critical, *even if the actual completion times of the tasks vary.*
>
> For the project of Home Construction, Inc., this assumption may or may not be true. For example, this assumption is not true if the actual completion times of all tasks equal their expected values except for G, which takes more than 5 weeks to complete. In this case, the critical tasks change. Task G now becomes critical, whereas Task H is no longer critical. However, if this assumption is true, the completion time of the project is the sum of the completion times of the individual

critical tasks *along a critical path*. In this example, there is only one critical path, so

$$
\begin{aligned}
\text{Project-completion time} = {} &\text{(completion time of Task A)} + \\
&\text{(completion time of Task B)} + \\
&\text{(completion time of Task C)} + \\
&\text{(completion time of Task E)} + \\
&\text{(completion time of Task F)} + \\
&\text{(completion time of Task H)} + \\
&\text{(completion time of Task I)}
\end{aligned}
$$

2. The completion time of each task is *independent* of the completion time of any other task—that is, the amount of time it takes to complete a task does not depend on the time it takes to complete any other task.

For the project of Home Construction, Inc., this assumption, too, may or may not be true. For instance, suppose the same machine is used for both finishing the interior and the exterior (Tasks G and H). If a breakdown of the machine causes a delay in finishing the interior (Task G), then it is very likely that a similar delay will occur in finishing the exterior (Task H). In this case, Tasks G and H are *dependent*. However, if two different machines are used for these tasks, the assumption of independence is probably valid. This assumption of independence, together with assumption 1, enables you to conclude that for any critical path:

Expected project-completion time   = sum of the expected completion times of all tasks along that critical path

Variance of the project-completion time = sum of the variances of the completion times of the tasks along that critical path

For the project of Home Construction, Inc.,

Expected project-completion time = sum of the expected completion times of all tasks along that critical path

$$= 3 + 7 + 6 + 3 + 5 + 5 + 1$$

$$= 30$$

Variance of the project-completion time = sum of the variances of the completion times of the tasks along that critical path

$$
\begin{aligned}
= {} &\text{(variance of the completion time of Task A)} + \\
&\text{(variance of the completion time of Task B)} + \\
&\text{(variance of the completion time of Task C)} + \\
&\text{(variance of the completion time of Task E)} + \\
&\text{(variance of the completion time of Task F)} + \\
&\text{(variance of the completion time of Task H)} + \\
&\text{(variance of the completion time of Task I)}
\end{aligned}
$$

$$
\begin{aligned}
= {} &(0.333)^2 + (0.667)^2 + (1.333)^2 + (0.333)^2 + \\
&(0.667)^2 + (1.000)^2 + (0.000)^2
\end{aligned}
$$

$$= 3.889$$

In the event that a project network has more than one critical path, compute the expected value and the variance of the project-completion time along each critical path. Then, for subsequent computations, choose the one whose variance is the *largest*. (All these critical paths will provide the same expected completion time.)

3. The completion time of the project follows the *normal distribution* with a mean and variance as computed in assumption 2.

   This assumption is valid for projects having a large number of individual tasks along a critical path because of the *central limit theorem*.

With these three assumptions, the project-completion time of Home Construction, Inc., has a normal distribution with a mean of 30 weeks and a variance of 3.889 (that is, a standard deviation of $\sqrt{3.889} = 1.972$). Using this information, you can now answer the questions posed earlier:

a. What is the probability of constructing the house within 32 weeks?

   From your knowledge of the normal distribution, the answer to this question is equivalent to finding the area to the left of 32 under a normal distribution with a mean of 30 and a standard deviation of 1.972, as illustrated in Figure 10.24. To do so, compute

$$z = \frac{32 - \text{mean}}{\text{std. dev.}}$$

$$= \frac{32 - 30}{1.972}$$

$$= 1.014$$

Now look up this value in the standard-normal table in Appendix B to obtain the desired probability of $0.5 + 0.3447 = 0.8447$. In other words, the probability of constructing the house within 32 weeks is 84.47%.

b. What completion date should be given so that 95% of the time, the house will be finished within this time?

   To answer this question, you need to determine that point x where the area under the normal distribution to the left of x is 0.95, as shown in Figure 10.25. The normal table in Appendix B yields the z-value of 1.645 for which the area to the left is 0.95. You can now compute the value of x from the definition of z as follows:

$$z = 1.645 = \frac{x - \text{mean}}{\text{std. dev.}}$$

$$= \frac{x - 30}{1.972}$$

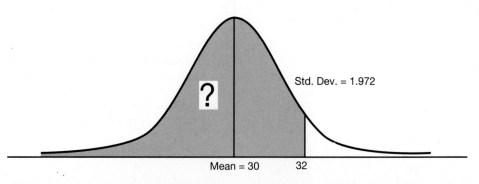

FIGURE 10.24 Computing the Probability of Meeting a Target-Completion Date.

Solving for x yields

$$x = (1.972 * 1.645) + 30$$

$$= 33.24$$

In other words, you can be 95% confident of meeting a target date with a completion time of 33.24 weeks.

In general, it is useful to know the probability of meeting any specific target-completion time for the project. Table 10.9 contains such a list for the project of Home Construction, Inc. The table is obtained using the same technique applied in answering previous question (a). The information in Table 10.9 shows the trade-off between the target-completion time and the probability of meeting that target. That is, as the target time is shortened, there is a smaller and smaller likelihood of meeting that target. As manager of this project, you can use the information in Table 10.9 to determine what completion time to promise to your customers and have some degree of confidence in being able to meet that schedule.

In this section, you have learned to analyze projects in which the individual task times are uncertain. By obtaining estimates of the optimistic, most likely, and pessimistic completion times for each task, it is possible to compute an expected completion time for the entire project. Due to the uncertainty in the task-completion times, you learned to ask questions pertaining to the probability of meeting various target-completion times. Answering these probabilistic questions requires making various assumptions. In case these assumptions are not satisfied in your project, the method discussed here may still provide a good approximation. However, more accurate answers can often be obtained to these probabilistic questions using the technique of computer simulation described in Chapters 14 and 15. In the next section, a case study in project management is presented.

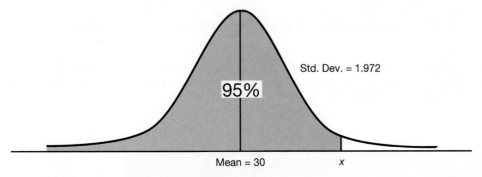

FIGURE 10.25 Computing a Target-Completion Date with a Given Confidence Level.

TABLE 10.9	Probability of Project Completion for Different Target Times
TARGET TIME	PROBABILITY (%)
27.0000	6.4095
28.0000	15.5247
29.0000	30.6045
30.0000	50.0000
31.0000	69.3955
32.0000	84.4753
33.0000	93.5905
34.0000	97.8739
35.0000	99.4385

CASE STUDY

In this section, your knowledge of project management is brought together through a case study. Consider the project faced by the management of Prisney Productions.

Problem Description and Formulation

Prisney Productions makes animated films and has recently contracted to produce a new feature animation that includes an opening short cartoon. As Executive Producer, you have identified the tasks that need to be handled. They appear in Table 10.10, which also includes your estimate of their completion times.

With your years of experience in the film industry, you know the following:

1. The music cannot be recorded until it is scored.
2. To mix the music with the animation—that is, to superimpose the music over the animation—it is necessary to have the animation, the recorded music, and the credits.
3. After the mixing is done, the preview can be obtained.
4. Once the mixing and cartoon are prepared, the editing can take place to produce the finished film.
5. Copies are made after the finished film and the preview are obtained.

These precedence relationships in the form of immediate predecessors are summarized in Table 10.11. Based on these precedence relationships, you have created the project network shown in Figure 10.26.

TABLE 10.10 Tasks and Completion Times for the Project of Prisney Productions

TASK	DESCRIPTION	TASK TIME (WEEKS)
A	Do the animation	12
B	Prepare the credits	2
C	Score the music	8
D	Record the music	2
E	Mix the music and animation	1
F	Prepare the opening cartoon	8
G	Prepare the preview	1
H	Edit	2
I	Make the copies	1

TABLE 10.11	Precedence Relationships for the Project of Prisney Productions	
TASK	DESCRIPTION	IMMEDIATE PREDECESSORS
A	Do the animation	None
B	Prepare the credits	None
C	Score the music	None
D	Record the music	C
E	Mix the music and animation	A, B, D
F	Prepare the opening cartoon	None
G	Prepare the preview	E
H	Edit	E, F
I	Make the copies	G, H

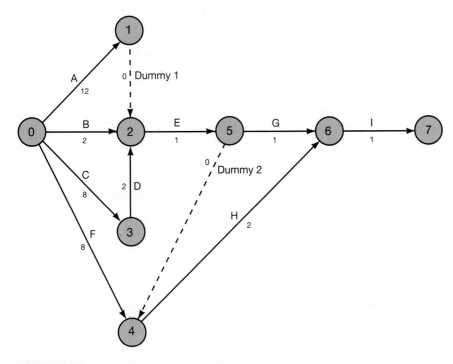

FIGURE 10.26 Project Network for Prisney Productions.

Solution Procedure

With the data in Figure 10.26 you can now use any computer package to obtain the activity schedule. STORM results are shown in Figure 10.27. As you can see, the earliest the project can be completed is in 16 weeks. Tasks A (doing the animation), E (mixing the music and the animation), H (editing the film), and I (making copies) are critical. The slightest delay in any one of these tasks will delay the completion of the project, so you should monitor them closely. You might also want to watch Task G (preparing the preview) because its slack time of only 1 means that a delay of more than 1 week will delay the entire project.

Project Management
PRIS_1.DAT

```
              The Project of Prisney Productions
              ACTIVITIES IN THE ORDER AS ENTERED
 Activity              Activity   Earliest      Latest
  Name      Symb        Time     Start/Fin    Start/Fin      Slack
 ACT   1    A         12.0000     0.0000       0.0000      0.0000 c
                                 12.0000      12.0000
 ACT   2    B          2.0000     0.0000      10.0000     10.0000
                                  2.0000      12.0000
 ACT   3    C          8.0000     0.0000       2.0000      2.0000
                                  8.0000      10.0000
 ACT   4    D          2.0000     8.0000      10.0000      2.0000
                                 10.0000      12.0000
 ACT   5    E          1.0000    12.0000      12.0000      0.0000 c
                                 13.0000      13.0000
 ACT   6    F          8.0000     0.0000       5.0000      5.0000
                                  8.0000      13.0000
 ACT   7    G          1.0000    13.0000      14.0000      1.0000
                                 14.0000      15.0000
 ACT   8    H          2.0000    13.0000      13.0000      0.0000 c
                                 15.0000      15.0000
 ACT   9    I          1.0000    15.0000      15.0000      0.0000 c
                                 16.0000      16.0000
 ACT  10    DUM1       0.0000    12.0000      12.0000      0.0000 c
                                 12.0000      12.0000
 ACT  11    DUM2       0.0000    13.0000      13.0000      0.0000 c
                                 13.0000      13.0000
 The computations were based on 11 activities
 Earliest project completion time = 16.0000
```

FIGURE 10.27 STORM Activity Schedule for the Project of Prisney Productions.

Managerial Questions and Analysis

You presented these results to the CEO, who decided to allocate up to $7500 additional funds to shorten the completion time as much as possible. You have been asked to determine the new completion time as well as the new activity schedule.

TABLE 10.12	Crashing Costs for the Tasks of the Project of Prisney Productions			
		TASK TIME (WEEKS)		CRASHING COST
TASK	DESCRIPTION	NORMAL	CRASH	($/WEEK)
A	Do the animation	12	10	5000
B	Prepare the credits	2	1	1000
C	Score the music	8	6	1500
D	Record the music	2	1	1000
E	Mix the music and animation	1	1	—
F	Prepare the cartoon	8	4	2000
G	Prepare the preview	1	1	—
H	Edit	2	1	500
I	Make the copies	1	1	—

Realizing the need for a crashing model, as described in Section 10.4, you must first collect additional data relating the cost–time trade-off for each activity. Those data are used to compute the cost of shortening each task by 1 week, as summarized in Table 10.12. You might attempt to answer the question by formulating a standard crashing model as discussed in Section 10.4. However, that model was designed to minimize additional costs to meet a given completion time. In this case, you have a given *budget* and wish to determine the associated earliest completion time that can be achieved while staying within that budget. To do so requires careful analysis. Two different approaches are presented.

METHOD 1: USING PARAMETRIC ANALYSIS ON THE CRASHING MODEL

One approach to determine the new completion time is as follows:

1. Formulate the usual crashing model, as described in Section 10.4, with the current completion time of 16 weeks. This model is shown in Figure 10.28.
2. Solve this model using any linear programming package. The summary report produced by STORM is shown in Figure 10.29 and lists only those variables with nonzero values. Observe that with the target-completion time of 16 weeks, no tasks need be shortened. This completion time can be achieved with the normal times.

Linear Program
PRISLP_1.DAT

3. Obtain the parametric analysis report on the completion-time constraint, as shown in Figure 10.30.
4. Use the parametric analysis report in step 3 to create the cost–time trade-off diagram. To find the completion time t that can be achieved with an additional cost of $7500, observe from Figure 10.30 that t is somewhere between 13 weeks (which costs an additional $10,500) and 15 weeks (which costs $500). Note that the shadow price in the range of 13 to 15 is -5000. The additional cost for any time t in this range is

$$\text{Additional cost} = 10,500 + (t - 13) * (-5,000)$$
$$= 75,500 - 5,000 * t$$

Because you know that the additional cost you have in your budget is $7500, you can solve this equation for t to obtain

$$t = \frac{75,500 - \text{additional cost}}{5,000}$$
$$= \frac{75,500 - 7,500}{5,000}$$
$$= 13.6$$

These four steps lead you to conclude that with an additional budget of $7500, you can shorten the project-completion time to 13.6 weeks. The information in Figure 10.31 does not indicate *which* tasks need to be shortened. One way to obtain this information is to change the right-hand-side value in the completion-time constraint (labeled "finish") in the crashing model in Figure 10.28 from 16 to 13.6 and solve the new linear program. The result from STORM is given in Figure 10.32. You can see that Task A (do the animation) and Task H (editing) need to be shortened by 1.4 and 1 week, respectively.

Linear Program
PRISLP_2.DAT

Minimize $5000Y_A + 1000Y_B + 1500Y_C + 1000Y_D + 0Y_E +$
$2000Y_F + 0Y_G + 500Y_H + 0Y_I$

Subject to

BOUND CONSTRAINTS

$$0 \leq Y_A \leq 2 \qquad \text{(Bound A)}$$
$$0 \leq Y_B \leq 1 \qquad \text{(Bound B)}$$
$$0 \leq Y_C \leq 2 \qquad \text{(Bound C)}$$
$$0 \leq Y_D \leq 1 \qquad \text{(Bound D)}$$
$$0 \leq Y_E \leq 0 \qquad \text{(Bound E)}$$
$$0 \leq Y_F \leq 4 \qquad \text{(Bound F)}$$
$$0 \leq Y_G \leq 0 \qquad \text{(Bound G)}$$
$$0 \leq Y_H \leq 1 \qquad \text{(Bound H)}$$
$$0 \leq Y_I \leq 0 \qquad \text{(Bound I)}$$

PROJECT COMPLETION CONSTRAINTS

$$X_0 = 0 \qquad \text{(start)}$$
$$X_7 \leq 16 \qquad \text{(finish)}$$

NETWORK CONSTRAINTS

Node 1 Constraint
$$X_1 \geq X_0 + (12 - Y_A) \qquad \text{(Task A)}$$

Node 2 Constraints
$$X_2 \geq X_0 + (2 - Y_B) \qquad \text{(Task B)}$$
$$X_2 \geq X_3 + (2 - Y_D) \qquad \text{(Task D)}$$
$$X_2 \geq X_1 + 0 \qquad \text{(Dummy 1)}$$

Node 3 Constraint
$$X_3 \geq X_0 + (8 - Y_C) \qquad \text{(Task C)}$$

Node 4 Constraints
$$X_4 \geq X_0 + (8 - Y_F) \qquad \text{(Task F)}$$
$$X_4 \geq X_5 + 0 \qquad \text{(Dummy 2)}$$

Node 5 Constraint
$$X_5 \geq X_2 + (1 - Y_E) \qquad \text{(Task E)}$$

Node 6 Constraints
$$X_6 \geq X_5 + (1 - Y_G) \qquad \text{(Task G)}$$
$$X_6 \geq X_4 + (2 - Y_H) \qquad \text{(Task H)}$$

Node 7 Constraints
$$X_7 \geq X_6 + (1 - Y_I) \qquad \text{(Task I)}$$

and $X_0, \ldots, X_7 \geq 0$

FIGURE 10.28 The Crashing Model for the Project of Prisney Productions.

```
The Crashing Model for the Project of Prisney Productions
 OPTIMAL SOLUTION - SUMMARY REPORT (NONZERO VARIABLES)
           Variable        Value        Cost
      2       X1          12.0000      0.0000
      3       X2          12.0000      0.0000
      4       X3           8.0000      0.0000
      5       X4          13.0000      0.0000
      6       X5          13.0000      0.0000
      7       X6          15.0000      0.0000
      8       X7          16.0000      0.0000
      Slack Variables
     21     TASK B        10.0000      0.0000
     22     TASK D         2.0000      0.0000
     25     TASK F         5.0000      0.0000
     28     TASK G         1.0000      0.0000
 Objective Function Value = 0
```

FIGURE 10.29 STORM Output for the Crashing Model for the Project of Prisney Productions.

```
      The Crashing Model for the Project of Prisney Productions
       PARAMETRIC ANALYSIS OF RIGHT-HAND SIDE VALUE - FINISH
  COEF = 16.000        LWR LIMIT = -Infinity     UPR LIMIT = Infinity
         -------  Range  -------      Shadow    ----  Variable  ----
             From          To         Price      Leave        Enter
  RHS      16.000      16.000     -500.000       YH   SLACK     2
  Obj       0.000       0.000
  RHS      16.000    Infinity        0.000  ----  No change  ----
  Obj       0.000       0.000
  RHS      16.000      15.000     -500.000       YH           YE
  Obj       0.000     500.000
  RHS      15.000      15.000        0.000       YE           YI
  Obj     500.000     500.000
  RHS      15.000      15.000        0.000       YI           YA
  Obj     500.000     500.000
  RHS      15.000      13.000    -5000.000  SLACK   5          YD
  Obj     500.000   10500.000
  RHS      13.000      13.000    -6000.000       YA
  Obj   10500.000   10500.000
  RHS      13.000    -Infinity  ---- Infeasible in this range  ----
```

FIGURE 10.30 STORM Parametric Analysis for the Completion-Time Constraint of the Crashing Model in Figure 10.28.

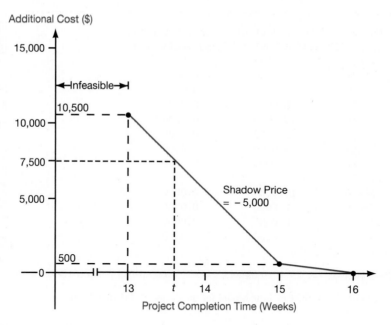

FIGURE 10.31 The Time–Cost Trade-Off for the Project of Prisney Productions.

METHOD 2: MODIFYING THE CRASHING MODEL

A second approach to determine the new completion time with the additional budgeted $7500 is to create a modified crashing model in which

1. The objective is to minimize the project-completion time—that is, from Figure 10.28:

$$\text{Minimize} \quad X_7$$

```
       The Crashing Model for the Project of Prisney Productions
         OPTIMAL SOLUTION - SUMMARY REPORT (NONZERO VARIABLES)
                    Variable          Value            Cost
            2          X1            10.6000          0.0000
            3          X2            10.6000          0.0000
            4          X3             8.0000          0.0000
            5          X4            11.6000          0.0000
            6          X5            11.6000          0.0000
            7          X6            12.6000          0.0000
            8          X7            13.6000          0.0000
            9          YA             1.4000       5000.0000
           16          YH             1.0000        500.0000
           Slack Variables
           22       TASK B            8.6000          0.0000
           23       TASK D            0.6000          0.0000
           26       TASK F            3.6000          0.0000
         Objective Function Value = 7499.998
```

FIGURE 10.32 STORM Report for the Crashing Model with Completion Time of 13.6.

Minimize $\quad X_7$

Subject to

BUDGET CONSTRAINT

$\quad\quad\quad 5000Y_A + 1000Y_B + 1500Y_C + 1000Y_D +$

$\quad\quad\quad 0Y_E + 2000Y_F + 0Y_G + 500Y_H + 0Y_I \leq 7500 \quad\quad$ (budget)

BOUND CONSTRAINTS

$\quad\quad\quad\quad 0 \leq Y_A \leq 2 \quad\quad\quad\quad$ (Bound A)

$\quad\quad\quad\quad 0 \leq Y_B \leq 1 \quad\quad\quad\quad$ (Bound B)

$\quad\quad\quad\quad 0 \leq Y_C \leq 2 \quad\quad\quad\quad$ (Bound C)

$\quad\quad\quad\quad 0 \leq Y_D \leq 1 \quad\quad\quad\quad$ (Bound D)

$\quad\quad\quad\quad 0 \leq Y_E \leq 0 \quad\quad\quad\quad$ (Bound E)

$\quad\quad\quad\quad 0 \leq Y_F \leq 4 \quad\quad\quad\quad$ (Bound F)

$\quad\quad\quad\quad 0 \leq Y_G \leq 0 \quad\quad\quad\quad$ (Bound G)

$\quad\quad\quad\quad 0 \leq Y_H \leq 1 \quad\quad\quad\quad$ (Bound H)

$\quad\quad\quad\quad 0 \leq Y_I \leq 0 \quad\quad\quad\quad$ (Bound I)

PROJECT BEGINNING CONSTRAINT

$\quad\quad\quad X_0 = \quad 0 \quad\quad\quad\quad$ (start)

NETWORK CONSTRAINTS

$\quad$ Node 1 Constraint

$\quad\quad\quad X_1 \geq X_0 \; + (12 - Y_A) \quad\quad\quad\quad$ (Task A)

$\quad$ Node 2 Constraints

$\quad\quad\quad X_2 \geq X_0 \; + (2 - Y_B) \quad\quad\quad\quad$ (Task B)

$\quad\quad\quad X_2 \geq X_3 \; + (2 - Y_D) \quad\quad\quad\quad$ (Task D)

$\quad\quad\quad X_2 \geq X_1 \; + 0 \quad\quad\quad\quad$ (Dummy 1)

$\quad$ Node 3 Constraint

$\quad\quad\quad X_3 \geq X_0 \; + (8 - Y_C) \quad\quad\quad\quad$ (Task C)

$\quad$ Node 4 Constraints

$\quad\quad\quad X_4 \geq X_0 \; + (8 - Y_F) \quad\quad\quad\quad$ (Task F)

$\quad\quad\quad X_4 \geq X_5 \; + 0 \quad\quad\quad\quad$ (Dummy 2)

$\quad$ Node 5 Constraint

$\quad\quad\quad X_5 \geq X_2 \; + (1 - Y_E) \quad\quad\quad\quad$ (Task E)

$\quad$ Node 6 Constraints

$\quad\quad\quad X_6 \geq X_5 \; + (1 - Y_G) \quad\quad\quad\quad$ (Task G)

$\quad\quad\quad X_6 \geq X_4 \; + (2 - Y_H) \quad\quad\quad\quad$ (Task H)

$\quad$ Node 7 Constraints

$\quad\quad\quad X_7 \geq X_6 \; + (1 - Y_I) \quad\quad\quad\quad$ (Task I)

and $\quad X_0, \ldots, X_7 \geq 0$

FIGURE 10.33 The Modified Crashing Model for the Project of Prisney Productions.

```
          The Crashing Model for the Project of Prisney Productions
            OPTIMAL SOLUTION - SUMMARY REPORT (NONZERO VARIABLES)
                      Variable            Value              Cost
              2          X1             10.6000            0.0000
              3          X2             10.6000            0.0000
              4          X3              8.0000            0.0000
              5          X4             11.6000            0.0000
              6          X5             11.6000            0.0000
              7          X6             12.6000            0.0000
              8          X7             13.6000            1.0000
              9          YA              1.4000            0.0000
             16          YH              1.0000            0.0000
          Slack Variables
             22        TASK B            8.6000            0.0000
             23        TASK D            0.6000            0.0000
             26        TASK F            3.6000            0.0000
          Objective Function Value = 13.6
```

FIGURE 10.34 STORM Output for the Modified Crashing Model in Figure 10.33.

2. A new budget constraint is added to ensure that the total crashing costs do not exceed $7500:

$$5000Y_A + 1000Y_B + 1500Y_C + 1000Y_D + 0Y_E$$
$$+ 2000Y_F + \quad 0Y_G + \ 500Y_H + 0Y_I \leq 7500$$

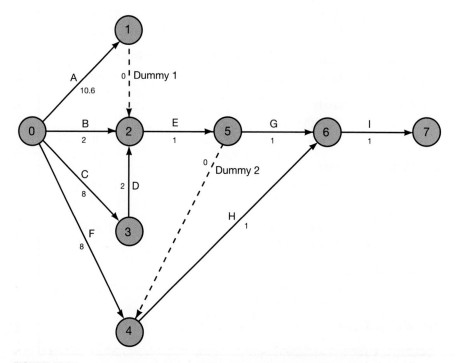

FIGURE 10.35 Project Network with New Task Times for Prisney Productions.

The complete model is shown in Figure 10.33, and the associated solution obtained from STORM is given in Figure 10.34. From the solution, you can see that it is optimal to shorten Task A (animation) by 1.4 weeks and Task H (editing) by 1 week, at a total cost of $7500. These results match the solution achieved using the first method.

Linear Program
PRISLIP_3.DAT

FINDING THE NEW ACTIVITY SCHEDULE

You have determined that with an additional $7500 the project can be competed in 13.6 weeks by shortening Tasks A and H by 1.4 and 1 week, respectively. The project network with these two new task times is shown in Figure 10.35. All that remains is to set the new activity schedule.

One way to do this is to use the values of the X-variables in Figures 10.32 or 10.34. This is possible because each X-variable represents the time at which all tasks stemming from the associated node can begin. For example, the value of 11.6 weeks for X_4 means that, according to Figure 10.35, Task H can begin at this time and, because its new task time is 1 week, can finish at 12.6 weeks.

Alternatively, the new activity schedule can be obtained by using a PERT/CPM computer package to solve the network in Figure 10.35. The STORM results are given in Figure 10.36. From this activity schedule, you can see that Tasks A, E, G, H, and I now need to be monitored closely to achieve the completion time of 13.6 weeks because they are all critical.

Project Management
PRIS_2.DAT

```
                 The Project of Prisney Productions
              ACTIVITIES IN THE ORDER AS ENTERED
  Activity            Activity   Earliest    Latest
   Name     Symb       Time     Start/Fin  Start/Fin    Slack
  ACT  1    A        10.6000     0.0000     0.0000     0.0000 c
                                10.6000    10.6000
  ACT  2    B         2.0000     0.0000     8.6000     8.6000
                                 2.0000    10.6000
  ACT  3    C         8.0000     0.0000     0.6000     0.6000
                                 8.0000     8.6000
  ACT  4    D         2.0000     8.0000     8.6000     0.6000
                                10.0000    10.6000
  ACT  5    E         1.0000    10.6000    10.6000     0.0000 c
                                11.6000    11.6000
  ACT  6    F         8.0000     0.0000     3.6000     3.6000
                                 8.0000    11.6000
  ACT  7    G         1.0000    11.6000    11.6000     0.0000 c
                                12.6000    12.6000
  ACT  8    H         1.0000    11.6000    11.6000     0.0000 c
                                12.6000    12.6000
  ACT  9    I         1.0000    12.6000    12.6000     0.0000 c
                                13.6000    13.6000
  ACT 10    DUM1      0.0000    10.6000    10.6000     0.0000 c
                                10.6000    10.6000
  ACT 11    DUM2      0.0000    11.6000    11.6000     0.0000 c
                                11.6000    11.6000
  The computations were based on 11 activities
  Earliest project completion time = 13.6000
```

FIGURE 10.36 New STORM Activity Schedule for the Project of Prisney Productions.

ADDITIONAL MANAGERIAL CONSIDERATIONS

In Sections 10.1 to 10.5, you learned how CPM and PERT techniques are used to plan and schedule a project in which the task times are deterministic or probabilistic. In this section, other managerial issues pertaining to project management are presented.

Using CPM and PERT to Monitor a Project

Managers use CPM and PERT techniques as a planning tool to schedule a project, as discussed in Sections 10.1 to 10.5. Once the project is underway, unanticipated events may prevent certain tasks from being completed as scheduled. Therefore, managers must not only *plan* projects, but also *monitor* them throughout to evaluate progress and replan the schedule if necessary. After the project has started, you should obtain a progress report periodically and update the project network by doing the following:

1. Assign a completion time of 0 for each task already completed.
2. Change the completion times of the remaining tasks in progress to the amount of time still needed to finish those tasks.
3. Apply CPM and PERT techniques to obtain the completion time and the new critical activities for that part of the project that remains.

Consider the project of Period Publishing Company in Example 10.1 in Section 10.1. Suppose that as the Vice President, you have called a progress meeting 40 weeks after the start of the project. The status of the various tasks at that time is reported in Table 10.13.

To monitor the remaining tasks in the project, observe that Tasks A, B, and D are completed. Their completion times are thus set to 0. Tasks E and G are 50% completed, so their *remaining* completion times are 5 and 7 weeks, respectively. All other tasks remain unchanged because they have not yet been started. The network with these new task times—together with the earliest and latest start and finish times as well as the new critical path—are shown in Figure 10.37. You can see that the remaining completion time for the project is 17 weeks and the new critical activities are Tasks G, F, and H.

First, observe that the total completion time for the project is the 40 weeks spent so far plus another 17 weeks needed to finish the remaining tasks, as shown in Figure 10.37(a). This new completion time of $40 + 17 = 57$ is 2 weeks more than the original completion time of 55 weeks computed in Section 10.2. This is because, according

TABLE 10.13	*Progress Report for the Project of Period Publishing Company*		
LABEL	DESCRIPTION	TIME ESTIMATE (WEEKS)	PERCENT COMPLETED
A	Author preparation of manuscript	30	100
B	Design promotional materials	6	100
C	Produce promotional materials	4	0
D	Copy edit the manuscript	5	100
E	Proofread and correct the copy-edited manuscript	10	50
F	Produce the final book	8	0
G	Obtain all legal permissions and copyrights	14	50
H	Conduct a sales training meeting	2	0

to the *original plan*, Task G should have started at the end of 30 weeks. Thus, at the end of 40 weeks, 10 of the 14 weeks required for Task G should have been completed. However, the progress report in Table 10.13 shows that only 50% (that is, 7 of the 14 weeks required for this task) has *actually* been completed. There is a delay of 3 weeks in this task. Because this delay of 3 weeks is 2 weeks more than the slack of 1 week for this task computed in Section 10.2.2, there is now a delay of 2 weeks for the entire project.

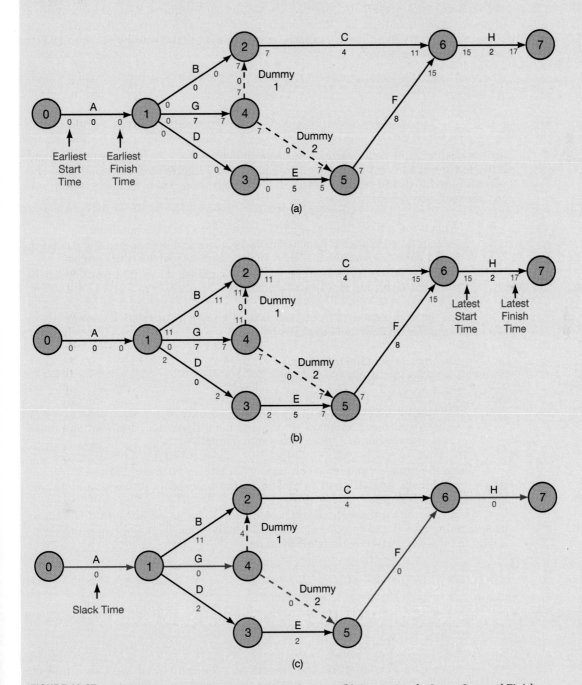

FIGURE 10.37 (a) Computing the Earliest Start and Finish Times, (b) Computing the Latest Start and Finish Times, and (c) the Critical Tasks for the Remaining Project of Period Publishing Company.

Relying on Assumptions

In the development in Sections 10.4 and 10.5, several assumption are made in order to proceed with the mathematical analysis. Care must be taken in acting upon the result of the analysis in the event that the assumptions are not valid for your project. For example, in developing the crashing model to determine which tasks to expedite, it was assumed that for each task, the time–cost relationship is linear, as illustrated in Figure 10.15. This assumption may or may not be valid for a particular project. In a similar way, the probabilistic analysis in Section 10.5 requires several assumptions to answer such questions as "What is the probability of meeting a particular target completion time?" In either case, place only as much reliance on the solution as you have in the assumptions.

SUMMARY

In this chapter, you have learned the management science techniques of CPM and PERT to control and monitor projects involving many interrelated tasks performed by various individuals internal or external to the organization. These techniques help you answer such questions as:

1. What is the earliest time at which the entire project can be completed?
2. To meet this completion time, which tasks are critical in the sense that a delay in any of those tasks results in a delay in the completion of the entire project?
3. Is it possible to expedite certain tasks so as to finish the entire project earlier? If so, which tasks, and at what additional cost?

When the completion time of each task is known with relative certainty, you learned to answer the first two questions by

a. Identifying the individual tasks.
b. Obtaining time estimates for each task.
c. Creating the precedence table for the project.
d. Drawing the project network.
e. Using a systematic approach to compute the earliest and latest start and finish times of each task, and hence of the entire project.

When the time to complete each task is not known with certainty, you learned to use probabilistic analysis and to determine the probability of meeting a specific target-completion time.

To answer the third question, you learned how to formulate an appropriate linear programming model and to obtain parametric analysis on the completion-time constraint to form the cost–time trade-off diagram.

APPENDIX 10A
THE ACTIVITY-ON-NODE REPRESENTATION
OF A PROJECT NETWORK

As you learned in Section 10.1, after identifying the individual tasks in a project, obtaining their time estimates, and creating the precedence table, it is necessary to convert this information into a project network that consists of a finite collection of *nodes* and *arcs*. You learned how to draw a project network using the activity-on-arc representation, in which each arc represents an activity and each node represents a point in time at which certain tasks are completed and others can then begin. In this appendix, an alternative approach to drawing a project network—namely, the *activity-on-node representation*—is presented.

■ 10A.1 DRAWING THE PROJECT NETWORK

With the activity-on-node representation, each node represents one of the activities. An arc connects two nodes if one node corresponds to an immediate-predecessor task of the other node, as specified in the precedence table. Recall Example 10.3, which is repeated here as Example 10.5.

EXAMPLE 10.5 THE ACTIVITY-ON-NODE REPRESENTATION

ACTIVITY (TASK)	IMMEDIATE PREDECESSORS
A	None
B	None
C	A
D	B
E	C, D

The project is completed when Task E is completed. ■

To create the project network, do the following:

1. Draw one node for each of the tasks. Label each node with the corresponding task symbol. The five nodes and their labels for this example are shown in Figure 10.38(a).
2. For each task in the precedence table, draw an arc from each node corresponding to an immediate predecessor of that task to the node corresponding to the task. These arcs for the example are shown in Figure 10.38(b).

As explained in Section 10.1, it is desirable to be able to identify the beginning of the entire project in the network. When there is only one task with no immediate predecessor, the node corresponding to that task represents the beginning of the project. However, when there is more than one such task, no single node represents the beginning of the project. To overcome this problem, create a *dummy activity* whose corresponding node is labeled "Start," which requires no time. An arc is drawn from the Start node to each node corresponding to tasks having no immediate predecessors. This is done for Tasks A and B in Example 10.5, as shown in Figure 10.38(c).

In a similar manner, when there is only one task that is not the immediate predecessor of any other task, the node corresponding to this task represents the end of the project. (In Example 10.5, node E, corresponding to Task E, represents the end of the project.) However, when there is more than one such task (and therefore more than one corresponding terminal node having no arc leaving it), it is desirable to create a dummy activity and corresponding "Finish" node to represent the end of the project. An arc is drawn from each terminal node to the Finish node. In contrast to the activity-on-arc representation, with the activity-on-node representation no other dummy nodes and/or arcs are needed.

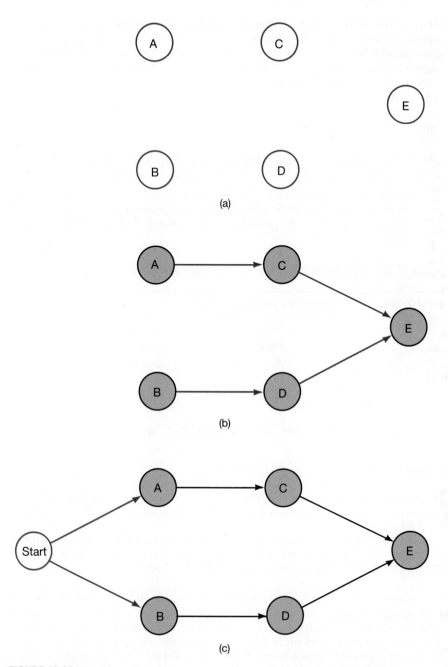

FIGURE 10.38 The Project Network for Example 10A.1 Using the Activity-on-Node Representation.

To illustrate the activity-on-node representation once again, consider the project of Period Publishing Company, presented in Example 10.1. The precedence table for that project is repeated here as Table 10.14.

By following the two steps for drawing the associated activity-on-node representation, Figure 10.39 illustrates the project network. Each node also includes the corresponding task time.

Using the activity-on-node representation, it is also possible to compute the earliest completion time for the project by performing the same systematic sequence of computations as discussed in Section 10.2. In this case, however, those computations are performed at each node instead of at each arc. After computing the earliest and latest start and finish times for each node, you can identify the critical tasks (those whose slack time is 0) and the associated critical path.

As with any project, you may be able to use additional resources to shorten the time it takes to complete the project by applying the *crashing techniques* described in Section 10.4. After collecting the necessary cost information for shortening each task, you formulate a linear programming model to determine the amount of time by which to shorten each task to meet a target-completion time in a least-cost way. With the activity-on-node representation, you define two variables for each *node*: one to represent the amount of time by which to shorten the corresponding task and one to represent the earliest time at which that task can begin. You then use the project network and the precedence table to develop constraints to ensure that each task can begin only after all its immediate-predecessor tasks are completed.

When the task times are uncertain, you should use the probabilistic approach of CPM, described in Section 10.5, appropriately modified for the activity-on-node representation.

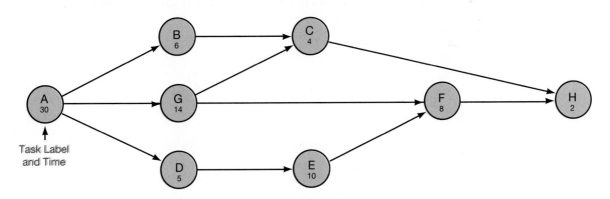

FIGURE 10.39 A Project Network with Task Times for Period Publishing Company.

TABLE 10.14	*Precedence Table for the Tasks of the Period Publishing Company Project*		
LABEL	DESCRIPTION	TIME ESTIMATE (WEEKS)	IMMEDIATE PREDECESSORS
A	Author preparation of manuscript	30	None
B	Design promotional materials	6	A
C	Produce promotional materials	4	B, G
D	Copy edit the manuscript	5	A
E	Proofread and correct the page proofs	10	D
F	Produce the final book	8	E, G
G	Obtain all legal permissions and copyrights	14	A
H	Conduct a sales training meeting	2	C, F

EXERCISES

EXERCISE 10.1 Consider a project whose tasks and immediate predecessors are given in the following table along with the nodes in the project network connected by the arc corresponding to the task.

TASK	FROM NODE	TO NODE	IMMEDIATE PREDECESSOR
A	0	1	—
B	0	2	—
C	1	3	A
D	?	4	B, C

On the basis of this table, draw a complete project network that includes an arc for Task D ending at node 4 in the manner specified by each of the following. You may need to combine nodes or add dummy nodes and/or dummy arcs to ensure the correct precedence relationships.

    a. Have the arc for Task D start at node 3.
    b. Have the arc for Task D start at node 2.
    c. Include Task D *without using any dummy arcs.*
    d. Have the arc for Task D start at a dummy node.

EXERCISE 10.2 The following table lists the seven tasks needed to assemble a barbeque. Use the given list of *all* predecessors to prepare a list of only the *immediate* predecessors for each task.

TASK	PREDECESSORS
A	—
B	—
C	A
D	B
E	A, C
F	B, D
G	A, B, C, D, E

EXERCISE 10.3 Use the given list of *all* predecessors to prepare a list of only the *immediate* predecessors for each task.

TASK	PREDECESSORS
A	—
B	A
C	A
D	—
E	A, B
F	A, B, C, E

EXERCISE 10.4 Use the immediate predecessors to draw the network for each of the projects in Exercises 10.2 and 10.3.

EXERCISE 10.5 Consider the following project information.

TASK	TIME (WEEKS)	FROM NODE	TO NODE
A	3	0	1
B	2	0	2
C	4	1	3
D	6	2	3
E	5	2	4
F	1	3	4

    a. Draw the project network on the basis of the given information.
    b. Prepare a list of immediate predecessors for each task.

EXERCISE 10.6 Consider the following project information.

TASK	TIME (MONTHS)	FROM NODE	TO NODE
A	5	0	1
B	3	0	2
C	2	1	4
Dummy 1	0	1	3
Dummy 2	0	2	3
D	6	3	5
E	6	2	5
F	4	4	5
G	1	5	6

    a. Draw the project network on the basis of the given information.
    b. Prepare a list of immediate predecessors for each task (except the dummy tasks).

EXERCISE 10.7 Use the following computer output for the project in Exercise 10.5 to write a brief managerial report that indicates the earliest completion time of the project and the amount of time by which each task can (or cannot) be delayed without affecting the completion time of the project.

```
                ACTIVITIES IN THE ORDER AS ENTERED
    Activity              Activity   Earliest    Latest
     Name      Symb         Time    Start/Fin  Start/Fin      Slack
    ACT   1    A          3.0000     0.0000     1.0000       1.0000
                                     3.0000     4.0000
    ACT   2    B          2.0000     0.0000     0.0000       0.0000
                                     2.0000     2.0000
    ACT   3    C          4.0000     3.0000     4.0000       1.0000
                                     7.0000     8.0000
    ACT   4    D          6.0000     2.0000     2.0000       0.0000
                                     8.0000     8.0000
    ACT   5    E          5.0000     2.0000     4.0000       2.0000
                                     7.0000     9.0000
    ACT   6    F          1.0000     8.0000     8.0000       0.0000
                                     9.0000     9.0000
    The computations were based on 6 activities
    Earliest project completion time = 9.0000
```

EXERCISE 10.8   Use the following computer output for the project in Exercise 10.6 to write a brief managerial report that indicates the earliest completion time of the project and the amount of time by which each task can (or cannot) be delayed without affecting the completion time of the project.

```
                ACTIVITIES IN THE ORDER AS ENTERED
    Activity              Activity   Earliest    Latest
     Name      Symb         Time    Start/Fin  Start/Fin      Slack
    ACT   1    A          5.0000     0.0000     0.0000       0.0000
                                     5.0000     5.0000
    ACT   2    B          3.0000     0.0000     2.0000       2.0000
                                     3.0000     5.0000
    ACT   3    C          2.0000     5.0000     5.0000       0.0000
                                     7.0000     7.0000
    DUMMY 1    D1         0.0000     5.0000     5.0000       0.0000
                                     5.0000     5.0000
    DUMMY 2    D2         0.0000     3.0000     5.0000       2.0000
                                     3.0000     5.0000
    ACT   4    D          6.0000     5.0000     5.0000       0.0000
                                    11.0000    11.0000
    ACT   5    E          5.0000     3.0000     6.0000       3.0000
                                     8.0000    11.0000
    ACT   6    F          4.0000     7.0000     7.0000       0.0000
                                    11.0000    11.0000
    ACT   7    G          1.0000    11.0000    11.0000       0.0000
                                    12.0000    12.0000
    The computations were based on 9 activities
    Earliest project completion time = 12.0000
```

EXERCISE 10.9   The management of World Airways wants to determine the minimum amount of time needed to turn around a plane from the moment it reaches the gate until it is ready to leave the gate. To that end, the Flight Manager has identified the following tasks that need to be accomplished between arrival and departure:

TASK	DESCRIPTION	TASK TIME (MIN.)
A	Unload the passengers	15
B	Unload the luggage	25
C	Refuel the engines	30
D	Clean the interior	15
E	Load the meals	15
F	Load the luggage	20
G	Board the passengers	20
H	Perform the safety check	10

The meals cannot be loaded nor the interior cleaned until the passengers are unloaded. The departing luggage cannot be loaded until the arriving luggage has been unloaded. The passengers cannot board until the interior is cleaned. The safety check can be performed only after the engines have been fueled and the meals, luggage, and passengers have been loaded.

a. Identify the immediate predecessors of each task.
b. Draw the project network.

EXERCISE 10.10 Home Sellers, Inc., helps individuals sell their homes. To make a sale, the following tasks must be completed:

TASK	DESCRIPTION	TASK TIME (DAYS)
A	Inspect the house	4
B	Appraise the house	3
C	Do the title search	4
D	Get the tax clearance	5
E	Get the sales permit	2
F	Find a buyer	21
G	Get a mortgage	14
H	Get the legal documents	10
I	File the legal documents	1
J	Final closing	1

The appraisal is done after the inspection. To get the sales permit, you must first obtain the tax clearance. A buyer cannot be found until the house is inspected and appraised, the title search is complete, and the sales permit is obtained. After a buyer is found, the legal documents can be prepared and the buyer can obtain a mortgage. Once the legal documents are obtained, they can be filed with the county. The final closing can take place once the mortgage is obtained and the legal documents are filed.

a. Identify the immediate predecessors of each task.
b. Draw the project network.

EXERCISE 10.11 Cabinets Unlimited is a company where all types of cabinets are manufactured and assembled. A new model is to be manufactured, which requires the following tasks:

TASK	DESCRIPTION	TASK TIME (MIN)
A	Prepare the wheels	10
B	Mount the wheels	5
C	Assemble the sides	15
D	Attach the top	11
E	Attach the base	10
F	Insert the brackets	5
G	Insert the shelves	5
H	Attach the doors	10
I	Attach the back panel	10
J	Paint the unit	15

The wheels are mounted after they are prepared. The base cannot be attached until the sides are assembled and the wheels mounted. The top cannot be attached nor the brackets inserted until the sides are assembled. The shelves are inserted after the brackets are installed. The back panel is attached after the base and top are attached. The doors are attached after the shelves are inserted and the top and base are attached. The unit is painted after the back and doors are attached.

    a. Identify the immediate predecessors of each task.
    b. Draw the project network.

EXERCISE 10.12 Broadway Productions is a company that puts together musicals for Broadway. A new musical has just been signed, and the producer has identified the following tasks that need to be accomplished before the show can open:

TASK	DESCRIPTION	TASK TIME (WEEKS)
A	Prepare each part	5
B	Score the music	3
C	Hire the cast	4
D	Design the choreography	3
E	Dance rehearsal	4
F	Prepare the scenery	6
G	Prepare the costumes	5
H	Dress rehearsal	6
I	Full rehearsal	4
J	Final rehearsal	2

The choreography is done after the music is scored. The dance rehearsal cannot begin until each part is prepared, the cast is hired, and the choreography completed. The scenery is designed and built after the dance rehearsal. Costumes are prepared once the cast is hired. The dress rehearsal is done after the dance rehearsal and after the costumes are ready. The dress rehearsal is followed by the full rehearsal, which also requires the scenery. The final rehearsal follows the full rehearsal.

    a Identify the immediate predecessors of each task.
    b Draw the project network.

EXERCISE 10.13 For the project in Exercise 10.5, (a) compute by hand the earliest and latest start and finish times for each task, (b) prepare an activity schedule, and (c) identify all critical tasks and paths.

EXERCISE 10.14 Repeat Exercise 10.13 for the project in Exercise 10.6.

EXERCISE 10.15 Repeat Exercise 10.13 for the project in Exercise 10.9.

EXERCISE 10.16 Repeat Exercise 10.13 for the project in Exercise 10.10.

EXERCISE 10.17 Repeat Exercise 10.13 for the project in Exercise 10.11.

EXERCISE 10.18 Repeat Exercise 10.13 for the project in Exercise 10.12.

EXERCISE 10.19 For the project in Exercise 10.11, the additional cost in dollars (normal cost − crash cost) to obtain the crashing times for each of the tasks follow:

TASK	DESCRIPTION	TIME (MIN) NORMAL	CRASH	COST
A	Prepare the wheels	10	5	5
B	Mount the wheels	5	4	2
C	Assemble the sides	15	10	5
D	Attach the top	11	6	5
E	Attach the base	10	7	3
F	Insert the brackets	5	4	2
G	Insert the shelves	5	4	2
H	Attach the doors	10	8	6
I	Attach the back panel	10	8	6
J	Paint the unit	15	10	20

a. Formulate an appropriate crashing model to achieve a completion time of 48 minutes using this information.
b. Solve the model in part (a) using your computer package.
c. How much will it cost to achieve an assembly time of 48 minutes? Which task should be shortened to achieve this goal? By how much?
d. What is the shortest assembly time that can be achieved with an additional expenditure of $19?

EXERCISE 10.20 For the project in Exercise 10.12, the additional cost in dollars (normal cost − crash cost) to obtain the crashing times for each of the tasks follow:

TASK	DESCRIPTION	TIME (WEEKS) NORMAL	CRASH	COST
A	Prepare each part	5	3	1000
B	Score the music	3	2	1000
C	Hire the cast	4	3	500
D	Design the choreography	3	3	—
E	Dance rehearsal	4	3	2500
F	Prepare the scenery	6	4	1000
G	Prepare the costumes	5	3	1000
H	Dress rehearsal	6	4	5000
I	Full rehearsal	4	3	2500
J	Final rehearsal	2	2	—

a. Formulate an appropriate crashing model to achieve a completion time of 18 weeks using this information.

b. Solve the model in part (a) using your computer package.

c. Prepare a table showing the additional cost needed to open the musical for each week prior to the earliest possible opening time.

d. How can an opening date of 18 weeks be achieved—that is, which tasks must be shortened, and by how much?

 EXERCISE 10.21   For the project in Exercise 10.9, assume the task times are variable, with the optimistic, most likely, and pessimistic task times as follows:

TASK	DESCRIPTION	TASK TIME (MIN)		
		OPTIMISTIC	MOST LIKELY	PESSIMISTIC
A	Unload the passengers	12	15	20
B	Unload the luggage	20	25	35
C	Refuel the engines	27	30	40
D	Clean the interior	12	15	20
E	Load the meals	12	15	20
F	Load the luggage	15	20	30
G	Board the passengers	15	20	30
H	Perform the safety check	10	10	10

a. Compute by hand the earliest expected completion time, identify the critical tasks and path, and determine the variance of the project-completion time.

b. Use your computer package to verify your computations in part (a).

c. What is the probability of being able to depart in 1 hour?

d. Management wants 95% of its flights to depart on time, assuming they arrive on time. What is the least amount time (to the nearest minute) management should plan for between arrival at the gate and departure?

EXERCISE 10.22   For the project in Exercise 10.10, assume the task times are variable, with the optimistic, most likely, and pessimistic task times as follows:

TASK	DESCRIPTION	TIME (DAYS)		
		OPTIMISTIC	MOST LIKELY	PESSIMISTIC
A	Inspect the house	2	4	5
B	Appraise the house	1	3	5
C	Do the title search	3	4	6
D	Get the tax clearance	3	5	10
E	Get the sales permit	1	2	2
F	Find a buyer	7	21	42
G	Get a mortgage	7	14	30
H	Get the legal documents	5	10	14
I	File the legal documents	1	1	1
J	Final closing	1	1	1

a. Use your computer package to find the earliest expected completion time, the critical tasks and path, and the variance of the project-completion time.

b. A homeowner wants to know how much time to allow to have a 95% chance of selling her home.

c. What is the probability of selling a house within 7 weeks? Within 8 weeks? Within 9 weeks?

EXERCISE 10.23 For the project in Exercise 10.11, assume the task times are variable, with the optimistic, most likely, and pessimistic task times as follows:

TASK	DESCRIPTION	TIME (MIN)		
		OPTIMISTIC	MOST LIKELY	PESSIMISTIC
A	Prepare the wheels	5	10	18
B	Mount the wheels	4	5	8
C	Assemble the sides	10	15	32
D	Attach the top	6	11	25
E	Attach the base	7	10	15
F	Insert the brackets	4	5	8
G	Insert the shelves	4	5	8
H	Attach the doors	8	10	25
I	Attach the back panel	8	10	25
J	Paint the unit	10	15	40

a. Use your computer package to find the earliest expected completion time, the critical tasks and path, and the variance of the project-completion time.
b. What is the probability of completing a cabinet within 65 minutes?
c. What is the probability of completing two cabinets within 130 minutes? (Hint: The completion time for two cabinets is the sum of two normal random variables with the same mean and variance.)

EXERCISE 10.24 For the project in Exercise 10.12, assume the task times are variable, with the optimistic, most likely, and pessimistic task times as follows:

TASK	DESCRIPTION	TIME (WEEKS)		
		OPTIMISTIC	MOST LIKELY	PESSIMISTIC
A	Prepare each part	3	5	8
B	Score the music	2	3	5
C	Hire the cast	2	4	5
D	Design the choreography	2	3	6
E	Dance rehearsal	2	4	8
F	Prepare the scenery	3	6	9
G	Prepare the costumes	2	5	8
H	Dress rehearsal	4	6	9
I	Full rehearsal	3	4	8
J	Final rehearsal	1	2	6

a. Use your computer package to find the earliest expected completion time, the critical tasks and path, and the variance of the project-completion time.
b. What is the probability of being ready for opening within half a year?
c. Each week beyond half a year that the production does not open costs management $10,000. Because new musicals always open on a Saturday, a delay by a fraction of a week effectively results in an additional week delay. Thus, for example, if the completion is delayed by 1.4 weeks, it effectively costs $20,000. How much should management budget for these additional expenses? (Hint: The probability of opening after 26 weeks but before 27 weeks equals the probability of opening any time up to 27 weeks minus the probability of opening any time up to 26 weeks.)

CRITICAL-THINKING PROJECT F

Intelligent Systems, Inc., designs and manufactures robots for use in various industries. Top-level management is considering the development of a new robot for the automobile industry. The primary selling feature of this robot is its own internal self-diagnostic and maintenance software programs. However, the company will undertake this project only if the prototype can be ready for demonstration purposes at the next Robotics Convention to be held in Tokyo exactly 1 year from now. As Senior Vice-President, Ms. Cathy Barnett has been asked to determine the feasibility of preparing a prototype by that time.

Following good project-management techniques, she has broken down this complex project into nine individual tasks and a dummy task provided in the table that follows. After consulting with heads of each department, she has also obtained estimates for the number of weeks needed to complete each task. These task times are also given in the table. Ms. Barnett has identified eight nodes (numbered 0 through 7) in the project network to represent the points in time at which certain tasks are completed and other tasks can begin. The arcs in the project network connect the pair of nodes listed in the last two columns of the table.

TASK LABEL	DESCRIPTION	WEEKS	FROM NODE	TO NODE
A	Design phase	10	0	1
B	Develop the operating software	18	1	2
C	Develop the diagnostic software	24	2	5
D	Develop the hardware	20	1	3
E	Develop the first prototype using the hardware and operating software	4	3	4
F	Test and modify the first prototype	8	4	5
G	Include the diagnostic software; test and modify the prototype	8	5	6
H	Develop marketing materials	16	4	6
I	Conduct the training meeting for the convention	2	6	7
Dummy	—	0	2	3

Prepare a managerial report from Ms. Barnett to the CEO, Mr. Arnold Kopeck, following these guidelines.

1. Draw the network diagram based on the information in the table (include the node numbers). Next to each arc, include both the task label associated with that arc and the number of weeks needed to complete that task.
2. Use your network diagram in guideline 1 to identify the immediate predecessors of each task (other than the dummy task).
3. Use your project-management software package to determine by how many weeks the project will have to be shortened if the robot is to be developed within 1 year. Identify the critical tasks.
4. On the basis of the critical tasks in guideline 3, you call a meeting with Mr. Carlos Rodriguez, Director of Software Development. In view of the 18 weeks needed to develop the operating software (Task B) and the subsequent 24 weeks for the diagnostic software (Task C), you ask Mr. Rodriguez if he can reduce these times somehow. He answers that he could take two programmers off the operating software task and use them for developing the diagnostics. Doing so, he says, will

increase the time it takes to develop the operating software from 18 to 22 weeks but decrease the time for developing the diagnostic software from 24 to 18 weeks. By how much does this change affect the completion time of the project?

5. After realizing that the proposed changes in guideline 4 shorten the completion time—but not by enough—you call another meeting with Mr. Rodriguez. In that meeting, you ask him by how many weeks he can further reduce the times for developing the operating and diagnostic software in guideline 4 if additional part-time programmers are hired. He says that at most each task can be shortened by 2 weeks. What impact does this change have on the completion time?

6. As a last attempt to complete the project within 1 year, you ask Mr. Rodriguez why the development of the diagnostic software could not begin immediately after the design meeting instead of waiting until the operating software is finished. He says that the company would have to hire a new systems analyst to oversee the development of the diagnostic software. In that case, he recommends allowing 30 weeks for that task because the employee would be new to the company. Developing the operating software would take 18 weeks. Draw the new project network that reflects these changes. Can the project now be completed in 1 year? Prepare an activity schedule and indicate the critical tasks.

PREPARE FOR DEPARTURE

How do the airlines manage the task of getting airplanes ready for their passengers? Bill Rodenhizer, of the now-defunct Eastern Airlines, explains the basic tasks involved in preparing a commercial airplane that arrives in Boston for its next take-off 45 to 60 minutes later. The following simplified chart shows the tasks that must be done inside and outside the plane, along with the time it takes to complete them.

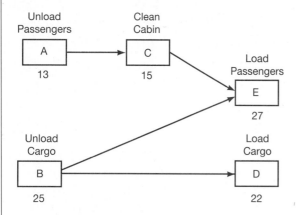

The graph demonstrates that certain tasks must be done first—that is, the graph indicates precedence relationships. In an obvious example, the arriving passengers must be unloaded and the cabin cleaned before the new passengers can be boarded. Likewise, the old cargo has to be carted off to make room for the next flight's cargo. The constraints for the model are defined by maintaining the required precedence relationships and completing all tasks by the deadlines.

The critical path is the longest (in terms of time) sequence of tasks, and the time it takes to complete this sequence is the earliest finish time for the whole project. Of the three paths through the system—A-C-E (55 minutes), B-E (52 minutes), and B-D (47 minutes)—the longest lasts 55 minutes.

Can the airline use the critical path method (CPM) to save money? Turn to the critical path, and consider the implications of shortening a particular task along the critical path. If activity A (unloading passengers) is reduced 6 minutes, the critical path is indeed shortened—but only by 3

minutes, not 6. Why? The path A-C-E is no longer the critical path. It now lasts only 48 minutes. The new critical path is B-E, which still takes 52 minutes to complete. Should the airline, then, spend the money necessary to shorten the A-C-E path by 6 minutes? Reducing this activity will not reduce the time needed to complete the entire project as much as one might have first suspected.

A second example of an important application of CPM looks at the thousands of activities required in constructing a building.

Contractors use CPM to estimate just how long a project will take and thereby develop a construction schedule.

Questions on the video

1. Give two realistic reasons why the old cargo needs to be unloaded before the new passengers are boarded.

2. What are some of the major tasks that must be done in constructing a building? How might they be sequenced in a CPM diagram?

Beyond the video

1. What are some ways to speed up some of the tasks in preparing the airplane? What might some of the costs be in implementing your suggestions?

2. How can CPM be applied to writing a research or term paper for one of your courses? How could this technique help you?

Practical considerations

1. If there are thousands of tasks to be done in constructing a building, how does CPM help the project manager to "manage by exception"?

2. How likely do you think that the times given for completing the tasks in getting the airplane ready are exact? What impact might a variation in a task's time have on the CPM model?

Source: "For All Practical Purposes," from *The Consortium for Mathematics and its Applications* (Arlington, MA: 1986), Programs 1 and 4.

CHAPTER 11

DECISION ANALYSIS

••••••••••••••••••••••••

*S*tar Productions turns out television series. To fill an open slot in its prime-time schedule, the studio has contracted with a rising young director to handle its new concept, "New York Life," and has opened negotiations with several well-known actors. But Star Productions faces some tough questions. How much should it invest in this untried product? The answer to this question depends in part on how much confidence Star has that the series will succeed. Will "New York Life" enrich Star's earnings or be a black hole soaking up dollars with no return?

The Case Study in this chapter shows you how Star Productions applies decision analysis to come up with the answers it needs.

The management science techniques in the previous chapters help managers make decisions on *deterministic problems*. In these problems, all the relevant information is assumed to be known with relative certainty. There are, however, many situations in which a manager must make a decision today whose results depend on uncertain future events. For example, consider the Vice-President of Manufacturing for a sports shoe business. If he knew exactly how many pairs of shoes the business will sell next month, he would put into production just that amount. In actuality, of course, future demand is at least in part unknown. He will not know what sales will be until well after he must decide how large the production run will be.

A person starting up a new service station faces a similar problem. How many pumps should she put in? How many islands? How many garages? The resulting success of her business depends on how many customers she will have to serve, but that information is uncertain at the time these building decisions must be made.

Probabilistic problem
A problem in which some (or all) of the relevant information is not known with certainty at the time the decision must be made.

Management science provides numerous techniques for helping people reach decisions to these **probabilistic problems,** in which some (or all) of the relevant information is not known with certainty at the time the decision must be made. In this chapter, a technique is presented for analyzing one class of probabilistic problems with the following characteristics.

1. There are one or more points in time at which decisions have to be made.

For example, Compu-Ware has just developed a new laser-storage device for computers. Following corporate policy for new products, management must make a decision now on how much to invest in production and promotion with the understanding that the results will be evaluated after 2 years. A second decision then must be made on the company's commitment to this product for the next 3 years. In this case, there are *two* points in time at which decisions must be made: the initial investment decision and the evaluation after 2 years.

Decision alternative
Any one of a finite number of decisions a manager can select in a decision problem.

2. At each point in time when a decision must be made, there is a finite number of **decision alternatives** available. The number and types of alternatives can depend on the previous decisions made and on what has happened subsequent to those decisions.

For instance, for the problem of Compu-Ware, the first decision is to determine the amount of the initial investment, which might range from a low of $2 million to a high of $6 million, with any amount in between a possibility. From a *strategic* point of view, the difference between investing $2 million or $2.005 million is insignificant. Rather, what is important is the *level* of commitment, which the management of Compu-Ware has identified as low ($2 million), moderate ($4 million), and high ($6 million). These, then, become the first three decision alternatives: low investment, moderate investment, and high investment.

A second decision is needed after 2 years. The decision alternatives at that time depend on the initial decision and on how successful the product is during the first 2 years. For example, if the initial decision is moderate investment and after 2 years the product is considered a failure, the alternatives might be to abandon production or to continue production at a low level. If the product is deemed to be moderately successful after 2 years, the decision alternatives might include the previous two as well as the third alternative of increasing production.

State, or outcome
A possible future condition resulting from a decision.

3. Which decision alternative you select depends on costs and/or profits associated with each decision and on an unknown future. The future can be described by a finite number of possible **states,** or **outcomes.**

With Compu-Ware, consider the initial decision. The revenues during the first 2 years depend on how successful the product is. This "success" might be described by the following three *outcomes*: failure, moderate success, or high success. The likelihood of each of these states depends on the initial decision taken. For example, the lower the initial investment, the more likely it is for the product to fail. The higher the initial investment, the more likely the product is to succeed.

4. A sequence of decisions must be made that satisfies an overall *criterion* for the organization.

For the example of Compu-Ware, it is necesary to make two decisions: one now and one in 2 years. To do so, you first need to identify the overall goal of the organization. For example, the criterion might be to maximize the probability of achieving a targeted revenue or to protect the company from the worst possible outcome.

Decision analysis is the technique used to help managers choose the "best" sequence of decisions in these problems. Section 11.1 describes how decision analysis is used to make **single-level decisions**—that is, one decision that must be made at a single point in time. These techniques are then generalized in Section 11.5 for making **multilevel decisions**—that is, decisions at various sequential points in times.

Decision analysis
A technique used to help managers choose the "best" sequence of decisions in certain problems.

■ 11.1 SINGLE-LEVEL DECISION MAKING

How does decision analysis help a manager make a single-level decision? Consider the problem faced by the management of Star Productions.

Single-level decision
A decision that must be made at a single point in time.

EXAMPLE 11.1 THE SINGLE-LEVEL DECISION PROBLEM OF STAR PRODUCTIONS
Star Productions, a producer of television series, has just contracted to produce a new prime-time show, *New York Life*. The President has asked you to determine an appropriate initial investment for the 2-hour pilot and the subsequent eight 1-hour episodes in the series. ■

Multi-level decisions
A set of decisions that must be made at various sequential points in time.

11.1.1 Problem Formulation

The first step in using decision analysis is to identify a finite number of decision alternatives. Although the ultimate objective is to determine the *amount* to invest, the strategic decision *you* have to make is the *level* of investment. The board of directors breaks investment for new programs into three broad levels, which then become the decision alternatives:

1. Low level (L): none of the actors has substantial name recognition.
2. Moderate level (M): the lead actor has name recognition, but none of the supporting actors do.
3. High level (H): more than one of the actors have name recognition.

The financial implications of these decisions depend on the future, unknown success of this series. The next step is to characterize those future states by identifying a finite number of possible outcomes. In this case, you might identify the following possibilities:

1. Failure (F): less than 10% of the viewing audience tunes in.
2. Success (S): 10% to 20% of the audience tunes in.
3. Great success (G): more than 20% of the audience tunes in.

Your job is to evaluate each investment alternative on the basis of profits. The profit is based not only on the initial investment decision, but also on the resulting success of the program. To use the technique of decision analysis, it is necessary to collect the appropriate data *for each decision-outcome pair*. For the problem of Star Productions, this is done by listing each pair and estimating the associated profit. Common sense tells you that the higher the level of commitment (whatever the dollar amount), the greater the amount the studio may lose. If you decide to invest at the high level and the show is a failure, the studio will lose a lot. This is because poor ratings will result in lower advertising revenues from sponsors and, at the same time, production costs, stars' salaries, and other expenses must still be met. At the other extreme, if you decide to invest at a low level and the show is a great success, this allows the studio to charge higher advertising rates. In this case, the studio can expect to do very well because the initial investment is low and the advertising revenues will be high.

You use your experience, industry information, and the studio's Accounting Department to gather the profits likely to result from each decision-outcome pair. These profit estimates appear in Table 11.1, which is called a **payoff table.**

Payoff table
A table that summarizes the expected payoff (reward, cost, and so on) for each possible decision-outcome pair.

TABLE 11.1   *Payoff Table ($ Millions) for the Decision Problem of Star Productions*

DECISIONS	OUTCOMES		
	FAILURE (F)	SUCCESS (S)	GREAT SUCCESS (G)
Low (L)	−2	5	8
Moderate (M)	−5	10	12
High (H)	−8	6	15

11.1.2   Making the Decision

The payoff table indicates that if you decide to make a high initial investment, the studio may earn a profit of $15 million in the event that the show is a great success. But the studio may lose $8 million if the show is a failure. In contrast, if you decide to make a low initial investment, the studio may earn a profit of only $8 million if the show is a great success. However, it will lose only $2 million if the show is a failure. What decision should you recommend?

The choice of the "best" investment alternative (L, M, or H) depends on the criterion of the management of Star Productions. Different criteria can lead to different decisions. In this section, several criteria are discussed.

OPTIMISTIC (MAXIMAX) CRITERION

One criterion used to make decisions is to choose the alternative that has the potential of producing the largest possible profit based on the payoff table. To use this criterion, identify the maximum possible profit for each decision alternative. In this case, from Table 11.1,

ALTERNATIVE	MAXIMUM PROFIT
Low	8
Moderate	12
High	15

Of these alternatives, the one able to produce the largest profit is the high investment, with a maximum possible revenue of $15 million. This criterion *maximizes* the *maximum* possible profit—thus its name, **maximax.**

Maximax
A decision-making criterion that maximizes the maximum possible profit.

Do you follow the optimistic criterion and decide to make the high investment? The advantage of this criterion is that it has the potential of returning the maximum possible profit. However, be advised that this optimistic choice carries a high risk. If the show fails, the company will lose $8 million, a fact that is ignored when the optimistic criterion is applied. To consider this loss possibility, another more conservative decision criterion is available.

THE PESSIMISTIC (MAXIMIN) CRITERION

The objective here is to select the alternative that *maximizes* the *minimum* possible profit, and hence the name **maximin**. For each alternative, identify the profit generated under the worst possible outcome. From Table 11.1, these amounts for the problem of Star Productions are

Maximin
A decision-making criterion that maximizes the minimum possible profit.

ALTERNATIVE	MINIMUM PROFIT
Low	−2
Moderate	−5
High	−8

The alternative that maximizes these minimum profits is a low investment, leading to a profit of −$2 million, which ensures the minimum possible loss.

This is a pessimistic criterion because it guards against the worst possible outcome. The optimistic criterion, in contrast, considers only the best possible outcome. The next criterion attempts to combine these two extremes.

HURWICZ'S CRITERION

With this criterion, the idea is to combine the optimistic and pessimistic criteria by deciding *how* optimistic or pessimistic you want to be, as follows:

1. Choose a **coefficient of optimism**, α (alpha), which is a value between 0 and 1 (the closer α is to 1, the more optimistic you are).

2. Compute for each alternative:

   Weighted profit $= \alpha * (\text{maximum profit}) + (1 - \alpha) * (\text{minimum profit})$

3. Select the alternative having the largest weighted profit.

Coefficient of optimism
A value between 0 and 1 that reflects the decision maker's degree of optimism when using Hurwicz's criterion.

To illustrate with the example of Star Productions, assume that $\alpha = 0.7$. This value means that you are more optimistic than pessimistic. Using the preceding formula, compute the weighted profit for the three alternatives. For example, for the alternative of low investment:

$$\text{Weighted profit} = \alpha * (\text{maximum profit}) + (1 - \alpha) * (\text{minimum profit})$$
$$= 0.7 * (8) + (1 - 0.7) * (-2)$$
$$= 5.0$$

The results of similar computations for the other two investment alternatives are summarized in Table 11.2. On the basis of these results, the alternative of high investment is selected because its weighted profit of 8.1 is the largest of the three alternatives.

TABLE 11.2 *Maximum, Minimum, and Weighted Profits with $\alpha = 0.7$ for the Problem of Star Productions*

ALTERNATIVE	MAXIMUM PROFIT	MINIMUM PROFIT	WEIGHTED PROFIT
Low	8	−2	5.0
Moderate	12	−5	6.9
High	15	−8	8.1

Observe that if α is chosen to be 1, then this criterion is precisely the optimistic criterion because the weighted profit becomes equal to the maximum profit. Similarly, when α is chosen to be 0, this criterion is the pessimistic one. Thus, the closer you choose a value of α to 1, the more optimistic a criterion you are using to make the decision; likewise, the closer you choose α to 0, the more pessimistic a criterion you are using. Figure 11.1 illustrates how the choice of alternatives varies as α varies between 0 and 1 for the problem of Star Productions. From this figure, you can see that for all values of α between 0 and 3/7, the alternative of low investment is selected; for values of α between 3/7 and 1/2, the alternative of moderate investment is selected; and for all values of α between 1/2 and 1, the alternative of high investment is selected.

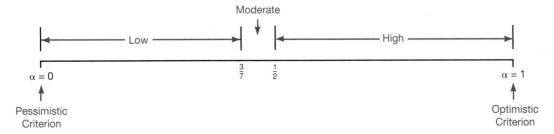

FIGURE 11.1 Hurwicz's Criterion for Different Values of α.

MINIMAX-REGRET CRITERION

Suppose you choose the alternative of low investment for the problem of Star Productions. In the event that the series is a great success (that is, the outcome is G), the studio will earn an estimated $8 million. However, if you had *known* that the outcome was going to be a great success, you could have earned $15 million for the studio had you chosen the alternative of high investment. In this case, having chosen low investment, you have a "regret" of 15 − 8 = $7 million. The objective of this new criterion is to choose the alternative that minimizes the "regret" for not having chosen the best one, based on the outcome.

In general, for each *outcome*, first identify the optimal decision that *could* have been made. Any other alternative, therefore, results in a regret because it was not the best one. This regret for a nonoptimal alternative can be quantified as

Regret = (profit from the best decision) − (profit from the nonoptimal decision)

For example, for the outcome of failure for the problem of Star Productions, the optimal decision is low investment, resulting in a loss of only $2 million. The regret associated with choosing moderate investment, therefore, is

$$\text{Regret} = -2 - (-5) = +3$$

Minimax regret
A decision-making criterion that minimizes the maximum regret associated with not having made the best possible decision.

The values in Table 11.3 summarize the regret for each outcome and each decision. The values of 0 indicate that there is no regret because those alternatives are the best decisions for the associated outcomes.

The regret table is then used to select the decision that *minimizes* the *maximum* regret, hence the name **minimax regret,** as follows:

1. Compute the maximum regret for each alternative.
2. Select the decision having the smallest value in step 1.

From the regret table for the problem of Star Productions, the maximum regret for each decision is:

TABLE 11.3 Regret Table for the Problem of Star Productions

	OUTCOMES		
DECISIONS	FAILURE (F)	SUCCESS (S)	GREAT SUCCESS (G)
Low (L)	0	5	7
Moderate (M)	3	0	3
High (H)	6	4	0

DECISION	MAXIMUM REGRET
Low	7
Moderate	3
High	6

With this criterion, the alternative of moderate investment is chosen because its maximum regret of $3 million is the smallest of the three alternatives. In other words, you can tell management that by selecting moderate investment, no matter what outcome results, the studio will at worst earn $3 million less than had it known what the future outcome was going to be.

In all of the previous criteria, no attempt is made to incorporate the *probability* of each of the outcomes occurring. One way to do so is through the use of probabilistic analysis, as described in the next criterion.

PROBABILISTIC CRITERION

The probabilistic criterion allows you to incorporate your knowledge (or beliefs) about the *relative* likelihood of each outcome. For instance, for the decision problem of Star Productions, you might believe, based on experience, that there is an equal chance that the series will be a success or a failure, but a smaller chance of it being a great success. To incorporate these beliefs about the likelihoods of the various outcomes you must

1. Estimate the probability of each outcome.
2. Use these probabilities to compute an *expected profit* (see the Student Resource Manual) for each alternative.
3. Choose the alternative having the largest expected profit (sometimes called the *expected monetary value*).

Suppose you estimate the probability for each of the possible outcomes in the problem of Star Productions as shown in Table 11.4. These probabilities are then used to compute an expected profit for each decision alternative, as follows:

ALTERNATIVE	EXPECTED PROFIT
Low	$0.4(-2) + 0.4(\ 5) + 0.2(\ 8) = 2.8$
Moderate	$0.4(-5) + 0.4(10) + 0.2(12) = 4.4$
High	$0.4(-8) + 0.4(\ 6) + 0.2(15) = 2.2$

TABLE 11.4   *Estimated Probabilities of Outcomes for the Problem of Star Productions*

	OUTCOMES		
	FAILURE (F)	SUCCESSFUL (S)	GREAT SUCCESS (G)
Probability	0.4	0.4	0.2

With this criterion, the alternative of moderate investment is selected because the expected profit of $4.4 million is the largest of the three alternatives. This means that with the decision of moderate investment, if you produced this series *many times*, on average, you would expect the studio to earn $4.4 million in profit (sometimes more and sometimes less). Although you are not going to produce this *particular* series many times, the studio will produce many other series. By using the probabilistic criterion in all these decisions, you would expect that the average profit realized from all the series produced is maximized. In summary, the probabilistic criterion is applicable when you are going to make these types of decisions for many other similar projects.

KEY FEATURES

In this section, you have learned to use various criteria to select one of a finite number of decisions for a problem in which there are also a finite number of possible future outcomes. To do so, you must

✔ Build the payoff table by estimating the profit associated with each decision-outcome pair.
✔ Select one of the following criteria: optimistic, pessimistic, Hurwicz's, minimax regret, or probabilistic, on the basis of management investment philosophy.
✔ Select the alternative that achieves the goals of the chosen criterion.

It is extremely important to realize that the choice of criterion determines the selection of the decision. This is the case for the example of Star Productions, as summarized in Table 11.5.

In this section, you have learned to use decision analysis to make one decision in which the future outcome is unknown. Observe that if you *knew* what the future outcome would be, you could make the correct decision easily. How much is it worth to have this information about the future? The answer is provided in Section 11.2.

TABLE 11.5   *Summary of Decisions for Each Criterion for the Problem of Star Productions*

CRITERIA	OPTIMAL INVESTMENT DECISION
Optimistic	High
Pessimistic	Low
Hurwicz's ($\alpha = 0.7$)	High
Minimax regret	Moderate
Probabilistic (0.4, 0.4, 0.2)	Moderate

■ 11.2 EXPECTED VALUE OF PERFECT INFORMATION

In Section 11.1 you learned how decision analysis is used to select one of several alternative decisions when faced with an uncertain future. The choice hinges on the decision maker's criterion. If you *knew* what the future would be—that is, if you had **perfect information**—you could easily choose the best alternative. Although it is not possible to know the future precisely, it may be possible to use market research to gain additional knowledge about the future. You would certainly not pay more for this research than you would to know the future exactly—that is, to obtain perfect information. In this section, you will learn how to determine the value of having perfect information.

Perfect information Information about the future that, in hindsight, would allow you to have chosen the best alternative.

Recall that the probabilistic criterion described in Section 11.1 indicates that moderate investment is the best alternative for the decision problem of Star Productions. By using the probabilities for the outcomes given in Section 11.1, the alternative of moderate investment results in the following expected profit:

$$\text{Expected profit} = 0.4(-5) + 0.4(10) + 0.2(12)$$

$$= 4.4$$

To determine the expected value of perfect information, it is necessary to compute the *additional* expected profit that could be obtained by having this perfect information. That is:

$$\begin{pmatrix} \text{Expected value} \\ \text{of perfect infor-} \\ \text{mation} \end{pmatrix} = \begin{pmatrix} \text{expected profit} \\ \text{with perfect} \\ \text{information} \end{pmatrix} - \begin{pmatrix} \text{expected profit} \\ \text{without perfect} \\ \text{information} \end{pmatrix}$$

The expected profit without perfect information is calculated as $4.4 million. To compute the expected profit *with* perfect information, consider each future outcome. Suppose that the series *will* be a failure. In this case, the best decision is low investment, with a return of −$2 million. Similarly, for each future outcome, you can easily identify the best decision. For this example, this leads to Table 11.6. The probabilities of 40% for failure, 40% for success, and 20% for great success must be considered. That is, 40% of the time the outcome *will* be a failure, and your decision of low investment will result in a loss of $2 million. The other two outcomes must be considered in the same way. Hence, the expected profit with perfect information is

$$\begin{pmatrix} \text{Expected profit} \\ \text{with perfect} \\ \text{information} \end{pmatrix} = 0.4(-2) + 0.4(10) + 0.2(15)$$

$$= 6.2$$

TABLE 11.6	Best Decision and Profit for Each Outcome in the Problem of Star Productions	
FUTURE OUTCOME	BEST INVESTMENT DECISION	PROFIT
Failure	Low	−2
Success	Moderate	10
Great success	High	15

Thus, the expected value of this perfect information—that is, the *additional* expected profit that could be obtained with this information—is:

$$
\begin{pmatrix} \text{Expected value of} \\ \text{perfect} \\ \text{information} \end{pmatrix} = \begin{pmatrix} \text{expected profit} \\ \text{with perfect} \\ \text{information} \end{pmatrix} - \begin{pmatrix} \text{expected profit} \\ \text{without perfect} \\ \text{information} \end{pmatrix}
$$

$$
= 6.2 - 4.4
$$

$$
= 1.8
$$

In other words, having perfect information is worth $1.8 million to Star Productions because knowing this information increases its expected profit from $4.4 to $6.2 million.

KEY FEATURES

In summary, the expected value of perfect information is obtained by

✔ Estimating the probability of each future outcome.
✔ Using these probabilities to find the expected return without perfect information by applying the probabilistic criterion, as described in Section 11.1.
✔ Calculating the expected value with perfect information by

    a. Identifying the best decision and the corresponding profit for each future outcome.
    b. Multiplying the profit for each future outcome by the corresponding probability of that outcome and summing the results.

✔ Computing the difference of the expected profit with perfect information and the expected profit without perfect information, as determined in the previous two steps.

This expected value of perfect information provides an estimate of how valuable it is to know the future. Although in most cases you cannot know the future precisely, it may still be worthwhile to conduct market research—for example, a survey of television viewers—to gain some additional information about the future. But to gain this information costs money. You should never pay more than what it is worth to have perfect information, which is $1.8 million for the problem of Star Productions. So, how much *should* you pay? The answer depends on the reliability of the market survey, as described in Section 11.3.

■ 11.3 EXPECTED VALUE OF SAMPLE INFORMATION

By conducting a market survey, it is often possible to obtain better knowledge about the future outcomes. For example, for the decision problem of Star Productions, management first used its previous experience to estimate the following probabilities for the three possible outcomes of the new TV series: 0.4 for failure, 0.4 for success, and 0.2 for great success. Applying the probabilistic criterion discussed in Section 11.1, to these estimates leads to a decision of moderate investment.

If these probabilities are changed, a different decision may be more appropriate. Suppose the probabilities of these future outcomes are 0.7 for failure, 0.25 for success, and 0.05 for great success. In this case, applying the probabilistic criterion leads to a decision of low investment, with an expected return of $0.25 million. The change in probabilities has brought about a change in the optimal decision and in the expected profit. The importance of accurate estimates of the probabilities of the outcomes is quite clear. The objective of market research is to help the manager make more accurate probability estimates. In this section, you will learn how this is done and how much you should be willing to invest in this kind of research.

KEY FEATURES

Using market research to modify probabilities involves the following steps:

✔ Design and conduct the market survey.
✔ Revise the probabilities of the various outcomes based on the result of the market survey.
✔ Identify the optimal decision based on the revised probabilities.

Each of these steps is described in greater detail in what follows. To follow this development, you may want to review the concepts of conditional probabilities, probability trees, and joint probability tables, as given in the Student Resource Manual.

11.3.1 Designing and Conducting the Market Research

The purpose of market research is to design and to conduct a survey that results in a descriptive *indicator*, or rating, for the proposed project. The indicator might be a numeric rating—between, say, 1 and 10—measuring the desirability of the project. Alternatively, for the new TV series of Star Productions, suppose the indicator is an "unfavorable" (I1) or a "favorable" (I2) recommendation for the project. That is:

INDICATOR	DESCRIPTION
I1	Less than 10% of the target audience is expected to watch the series on a regular basis.
I2	More than 10% of the target audience is expected to watch the series on a regular basis.

Ultimately, the result of the market survey—one of these two indicators—is used to reevaluate the probabilities of the various outcomes so that an appropriate investment decision can then be made. However, these results may not be correct because the survey is not based on the *entire* targeted audience, but rather on a smaller, random sample. The particular sample surveyed may respond differently from the broader audience that includes all viewers. The question then becomes: How reliable are the market-research results?

Suppose the series will be a great success. The survey, however, may indicate otherwise by returning indicator I1. You would consider the survey to be reliable if the chance of obtaining the wrong information from the survey is small. To determine the reliability of the survey, you need to evaluate, for each outcome, the probability that each indicator will result from the survey. These probabilities are based on your belief from past experience with similar surveys and the track record of the marketing organization conducting this research. Suppose the management of Star Productions has evaluated the proposed survey with the results in Table 11.7. For instance, the value of 0.9 in the table indicates that if the series will be a great success, management

TABLE 11.7 *Conditional Probabilities of Indicators Given the Outcome for the Problem of Star Productions*

	OUTCOME		
INDICATOR	F	S	G
I1	0.8	0.3	0.1
I2	0.2	0.7	0.9

believes that 90% of the time the market survey will correctly result in indicator I2 as opposed to I1. That is:

$$P(I2 \mid G) = \text{the conditional probability of the indicator being}$$
$$\text{I2 given that the series is a great success}$$
$$= 0.90$$

Similarly, the conditional probability that the survey results in indicator I1 if the series will be a failure is 0.8.

These conditional probabilities and the original probability estimates of the various outcomes can be summarized in a **probability tree,** as shown in Figure 11.2. The first set of three arcs from node 1 are the three possible outcomes F, S, and G, with their respective prior probabilities of 0.4, 0.4, and 0.2 written next to each arc. The two arcs from node 2 refer to the two indicators I1 and I2, assuming the outcome F, with the corresponding conditional probabilities of 0.8 and 0.2 from Table 11.7. Similarly, the two arcs from nodes 3 and 4 refer to the two indicators I1 and I2, assuming the outcomes S and G, respectively, with their associated conditional probabilities.

These conditional probabilities are then used to obtain revised estimates of the probabilities of the various outcomes, depending on which indicator results from the survey, as described next.

Probability tree
A tool for visualizing and performing decision analysis consisting of nodes and arcs that summarize decision alternatives and probabilities of the outcomes.

11.3.2 Revising the Probabilities Based on the Market Research

Consider what will happen *if* the market research for Star Productions is performed. The survey will be analyzed and will result in either the conclusion that less than 10% of the target audience is expected to watch the new series (I1) or more than 10% will watch (I2). How will you use this conclusion to compute new estimates of the probabilities of the various outcomes? If the survey results in indicator I1, what is the new probability that the show will be a failure—that is, what is the conditional probability $P(F \mid I1)$? The conditional probability that it is a success—that is, $P(S \mid I1)$? The conditional probability that it is a great success—that is, $P(G \mid I1)$? Similarly, what are these probabilities if the survey results in indicator I2? These conditional probabilities, also called **posterior probabilities**, are computed according to the following formulas (see the Student Resource Manual):

Posterior probabilities
Revised probabilities of outcomes obtained on the basis of indicators from a market survey.

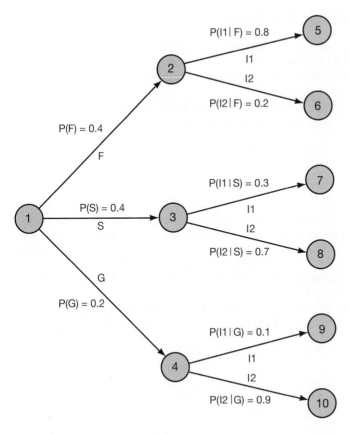

FIGURE 11.2 The Conditional Probability Tree for the Problem of Star Productions.

WHEN THE MARKET RESEARCH INDICATES I 1

$$P(F \mid I1) = \frac{P(F \text{ and } I1)}{P(I1)}$$

$$P(S \mid I1) = \frac{P(S \text{ and } I1)}{P(I1)}$$

$$P(G \mid I1) = \frac{P(G \text{ and } I1)}{P(I1)}$$

WHEN THE MARKET RESEARCH INDICATES I 2

$$P(F \mid I2) = \frac{P(F \text{ and } I2)}{P(I2)}$$

$$P(S \mid I2) = \frac{P(S \text{ and } I2)}{P(I2)}$$

$$P(G \mid I2) = \frac{P(G \text{ and } I2)}{P(I2)}$$

These computations require the following:

Joint Probabilities
The probability of two events both occurring.

1. The **joint probabilities** in the numerators—that is, the probability that a particular pair of outcome and indicator will occur.
2. The **marginal probabilities** in the denominator of each indicator occurring.

Marginal Probabilities
The probability that one particular event occurs.

The joint probabilities can be obtained from the probabilities in Table 11.7. For example, the joint probability of outcome F and indicator I1 is

$$P(F \text{ and } I1) = P(I1 \mid F) * P(F)$$
$$= 0.8 * 0.4$$
$$= 0.32$$

That is, there is a 32% chance that the market research results in indicator I1 *and*, in fact, the show is a failure. Observe that this probability of F and I1 is the product of the arc probabilities in Figure 11.2 corresponding to the outcome F and indicator I1 leading to node 5. Similar computations using Figure 11.2 result in the joint probabilities in Table 11.8. This table includes all combinations of outcomes and indicators, so all these joint probabilities sum to 1.

The sum of the values in each row of Table 11.8 provides the marginal probabilities of the corresponding indicators. That is:

$$P(I1) = 0.32 + 0.12 + 0.02$$
$$= 0.46$$
$$P(I2) = 0.08 + 0.28 + 0.18$$
$$= 0.54$$

These marginal probabilities and the joint probabilities in Table 11.8 yield the revised probabilities of the outcomes based on the results of the market research.

TABLE 11.8   *Joint Probabilities of Outcomes and Indicators for the Problem of Star Productions*

	OUTCOME		
INDICATOR	F	S	G
I1	0.32	0.12	0.02
I2	0.08	0.28	0.18

IF THE MARKET RESEARCH RESULTS IN INDICATOR I1

$$P(F|I1) = \frac{P(F \text{ and } I1)}{P(I1)} = \frac{0.32}{0.46} = 0.69565$$

$$P(S|I1) = \frac{P(S \text{ and } I1)}{P(I1)} = \frac{0.12}{0.46} = 0.26087$$

$$P(G|I1) = \frac{P(G \text{ and } I1)}{P(I1)} = \frac{0.02}{0.46} = 0.04348$$

IF THE MARKET RESEARCH RESULTS IN INDICATOR I 2

$$P(F|I2) = \frac{P(F \text{ and } I2)}{P(I2)} = \frac{0.08}{0.54} = 0.14815$$

$$P(S|I2) = \frac{P(S \text{ and } I2)}{P(I2)} = \frac{0.28}{0.54} = 0.51852$$

$$P(G|I2) = \frac{P(G \text{ and } I2)}{P(I2)} = \frac{0.18}{0.54} = 0.33333$$

Now these revised estimates of the probabilities of the various outcomes can be used to determine the best decision, as described next.

11.3.3 Identifying The Optimal Decision Based on the Revised Probabilities

You have obtained a new estimate of the probability of each outcome depending on the indicator resulting from the market research. You can now identify the best decision alternative as the one that maximizes the expected profit, as determined by the probabilistic criterion.

IF THE MARKET RESEARCH RESULTS IN INDICATOR I 1

DECISION	EXPECTED PROFIT
Low	0.69565 (−2) + 0.26087 (5) + 0.04348 (8) = 0.26089
Moderate	0.69565 (−5) + 0.26087 (10) + 0.04348 (12) = −0.34779
High	0.69565 (−8) + 0.26087 (6) + 0.04348 (15) = −3.34778

In this case, the optimal decision is low investment because the corresponding expected profit of $260,890 is the largest of the three alternatives.

IF THE MARKET RESEARCH RESULTS IN INDICATOR I 2

DECISION	EXPECTED PROFIT
Low	0.14815 (−2) + 0.51852 (5) + 0.33333 (8) = 4.96294
Moderate	0.14815 (−5) + 0.51852 (10) + 0.33333 (12) = 8.44441
High	0.14815 (−8) + 0.51852 (6) + 0.33333 (15) = 6.92587

In this case, the optimal decision is moderate investment because the corresponding expected profit of $8,444,410 is the largest of the three alternatives.

Performing the market research will help management choose the investment decision, as summarized in Table 11.9.

TABLE 11.9	Optimal Decisions and Expected Profits for the Two Indicators in the Problem of Star Productions	
INDICATOR	OPTIMAL DECISION	EXPECTED PROFIT
I 1	Low	0.26089
I 2	Moderate	8.44441

11.3.4 Computing the Expected Value of the Sample Information

In Section 11.3.3, you learned how your profits would improve *if* the market research is conducted. How much, then, should you be willing to pay for this market research—that is, what is the expected value of obtaining this sample information?

KEY FEATURES

The expected value of the sample information is the difference between the profit you can expect to earn with this information and without this information:

$$\begin{pmatrix} \text{Expected value of} \\ \text{sample information} \end{pmatrix} = \begin{pmatrix} \text{expected profit} \\ \text{with sample} \\ \text{information} \end{pmatrix} - \begin{pmatrix} \text{expected profit} \\ \text{without sample} \\ \text{information} \end{pmatrix}$$

From the probabilistic criterion in Section 11.1, the expected profit without sample information, using the original probability estimates of 0.4, 0.4, and 0.2 for the three outcomes, is

Expected profit without sample information = 4.4

To compute the expected profit *with* the sample information, recall that the expected profit depends on the results of the market research. Thus,

$$\begin{pmatrix} \text{Expected} \\ \text{profit} \\ \text{with sample} \\ \text{information} \end{pmatrix} = \begin{pmatrix} \text{expected} \\ \text{profit} \\ \text{when the} \\ \text{indicator} \\ \text{is I1} \end{pmatrix} * P(I1) + \begin{pmatrix} \text{expected} \\ \text{profit} \\ \text{when the} \\ \text{indicator} \\ \text{is I2} \end{pmatrix} * P(I2)$$

Using the expected profits in Table 11.9 together with the probabilities of 0.46 for P(I1) and 0.54 for P(I2), as computed in Section 11.3.2, you have

$$\begin{pmatrix} \text{Expected profit} \\ \text{with sample} \\ \text{information} \end{pmatrix} = (0.26089 * 0.46) + (8.44441 * 0.54)$$

$$= 4.67999$$

Finally, the expected value of the sample information is

$$\begin{pmatrix} \text{Expected value} \\ \text{of sample} \\ \text{information} \end{pmatrix} = \begin{pmatrix} \text{expected profit} \\ \text{with sample} \\ \text{information} \end{pmatrix} - \begin{pmatrix} \text{expected profit} \\ \text{without sample} \\ \text{information} \end{pmatrix}$$

$$= 4.67982 - 4.40000$$

$$= 0.27999$$

This means that the expected profit for Star Productions will increase by \$279,990 if the results of the market research are used. In other words, the management of Star Productions should not spend more than \$279,990 to conduct this market research.

Recall from Section 11.2 that the additional expected profit for obtaining *perfect* information is \$1.8 million. One measure of the value of the market research, called the

efficiency of the sample information, is the percent of this additional expected profit that is obtainable from the sample information. That is:

$$\begin{pmatrix} \text{Efficiency of} \\ \text{sample} \\ \text{information} \end{pmatrix} = \left(\frac{\text{expected value of sample information}}{\text{expected value of perfect information}} \right) * 100$$

$$= \left(\frac{0.27999}{1.8} \right) * 100$$

$$= 15.56\%$$

In other words, this sample information provides about 16% of the value that would be obtained from having perfect information. In general, the larger this value, the more useful the market research.

In this section, you have learned how market research is used to help make the best decision. You have also learned to determine how much this added information is worth. In Section 11.4, you will learn how to interpret the results of performing the decision analysis presented in Sections 11.1 to 11.3 by computer.

■ 11.4 SINGLE-LEVEL DECISION PROBLEMS: USING THE COMPUTER

In Sections 11.1 to 11.3, you learned to use different decision criteria to select one of several alternative actions when the future outcomes are uncertain. In this section, you will see how to interpret the results when these computations are performed by computer. When you use a decision-analysis package on a computer, you must provide:

1. The payoff data.
2. The list of criteria, as described in Section 11.1, you wish to evaluate.
3. The probabilities of each outcome, if probabilistic analysis is desired.
4. The conditional probabilities of each sample information indicator, if you want to determine the expected value of the sample information.

Return to the problem of Star Productions. The payoffs for its new television series are given in Table 11.1. On entering these data into the STORM software package—together with the probabilistic data as described in steps 3 and 4—and requesting that all available criteria be evaluated, the results in Figure 11.3 are obtained.

Decision Analysis
EX11_1.DAT

The reports in Figures 11.3(a) to 11.3(e) provide the results of using the optimistic (MAXIMAX), pessimistic (MAXIMIN), minimax-regret (MINIMAX REGRET), equally likely (EQUALLY LIKELY), and Hurwicz's (HURWICZ) with $\alpha = 0.7$ criteria. The equally likely criterion is the probabilistic criterion in which each outcome is assumed to be equally likely to occur. Because this assumption is not realistic, this criterion is not generally used in practice. The payoffs in each row of each table are the values of the associated alternatives as computed according to the criterion applied to that table. The optimal alternative for each criterion is indicated by an * to the right of the associated row. For example, the values of 8, 12, and 15 in the payoff column of the table in Figure 11.3(a) are the maximum possible payoffs for the three alternatives of low, moderate, and high investment, respectively. The * in the last row indicates that, with the optimistic criterion (MAXIMAX) of maximizing the maximum possible return, the high-investment alternative is the one to choose. Its payoff of 15 is the largest of the three alternatives. The results in Figure 11.3 (f) provide a summary of which alternative to select for each of the five criteria listed previously.

```
            The Decision Problem of Star Productions
            DETERMINISTIC ANALYSIS - DETAILED REPORT
                    MAXIMAX CRITERION
               Alternative            Payoff
               LOW                      8.00
               MODERATE                12.00
               HIGH                    15.00 *
                          (a)


            The Decision Problem of Star Productions
            DETERMINISTIC ANALYSIS - DETAILED REPORT
                    MAXIMIN CRITERION
               Alternative            Payoff
               LOW                     -2.00 *
               MODERATE                -5.00
               HIGH                    -8.00
                          (b)


            The Decision Problem of Star Productions
            DETERMINISTIC ANALYSIS - DETAILED REPORT
                    MINIMAX REGRET CRITERION
               Alternative       Payoff Regret
               LOW                      7.00
               MODERATE                 3.00 *
               HIGH                     6.00
                          (c)


            The Decision Problem of Star Productions
            DETERMINISTIC ANALYSIS - DETAILED REPORT
                  EQUALLY LIKELY CRITERION
               Alternative          Mean Payoff
               LOW                      3.67
               MODERATE                 5.67 *
               HIGH                     4.33
                          (d)


            The Decision Problem of Star Productions
            DETERMINISTIC ANALYSIS - DETAILED REPORT
                    HURWICZ CRITERION
             OPTIMISM PARAMTER  (ALPHA) :0.70
               Alternative    Hurwicz Payoff
               LOW                      5.00
               MODERATE                 6.90
               HIGH                     8.10 *
                          (e)


            The Decision Problem of Star Productions
            DETERMINISTIC ANALYSIS - SUMMARY REPORT
                  Criterion            Decision
                  MAXIMAX                HIGH
                  MAXIMIN                 LOW
                  MINIMAX REGRET       MODERATE
                  EQUALLY LIKELY       MODERATE
                  HURWICZ                HIGH
                          (f)
```

FIGURE 11.3 STORM Output for the Decision Problem of Star Productions.

```
              The Decision Problem of Star Productions
                     PROBABILISTIC ANALYSIS
                 EXPECTED VALUE - SUMMARY REPORT
                 Decision      Expected Payoff
                 LOW                   2.80
                 MODERATE              4.40 *
                 HIGH                  2.20
                          (g)


              The Decision Problem of Star Productions
                     PROBABILISTIC ANALYSIS
                 EXPECTED VALUE OF PERFECT INFORMATION
       State       Prob  Decision       Payoff   Prob*Payoff
       FAILURE     0.4000 LOW           -2.00    -8.00E-01
       SUCCESSFUL  0.4000 MODERATE      10.00     4.00
       V. SUCC.    0.2000 HIGH          15.00     3.00
       Expected Payoff with Perfect Information...      6.20
       Expected Payoff Without Perfect Information      4.40
       Expected Value of Perfect Information......      1.80
                          (h)


              The Decision Problem of Star Productions
                     PROBABILISTIC ANALYSIS
         EXPECTED VALUE OF SAMPLE INFORMATION - SUMMARY REPORT
       Indicator    Prob  Decision        Payoff   Prob*Payoff
       INDICTR  1 0.4600  LOW            2.61E-01   1.20E-01
       INDICTR  2 0.5400  MODERATE           8.44   4.56
       Expected Payoff...........................      4.68
       Expected Payoff Without Sample Information..    4.40
       Expected Value of Sample Information.......  2.80E-01
       Efficiency of Sample Information (%)........    15.56
       Expected Net Gain from Sampling............  2.80E-01
                          (i)
```

FIGURE 11.3 (cont.) STORM Output for the Decision Problem of Star Productions.

The remaining three reports in Figures 11.3(g) to 11.3(i) pertain to probabilistic analysis. The results in Figure 11.3(g) are the expected payoffs for the three investment alternatives on the basis of the probabilities of 0.4 for failure, 0.4 for success, and 0.2 for great success. As indicated by the $*$, the alternative of moderate investment provides the maximum expected payoff of $4.4 million.

Figure 11.3(h) provides the expected value of obtaining perfect information. The last three rows of that report indicate that the expected payoff with perfect information is $6.2 million, that without perfect information is $4.4 million, and the value of having perfect information is $1.8 million, which is the difference between these two. That is, management should not spend more than $1.8 million on a market survey capable of providing perfect information.

The expected value of obtaining sample information for the problem of Star Productions is provided in the report of Figure 11.3(i). You can compare the expected payoff of $4.40 million without sample information to the expected payoff of $4.68 million with sample information. The expected value of this sample information is the difference of these two values, $280,000, which is displayed in the report as 2.80E-01 ($0.28 million). This sample information has an efficiency of 15.56% because its

```
                    Decision criterion : Maximax
       Experiment outcome: 1    Decision: A3    Maximax =   15
                              (a)
                    Decision criterion : Maximin
       Experiment outcome: 1    Decision: A1    Maximin = -2
                              (b)
                  Decision criterion : Minimax regret
     Experiment outcome: 1    Decision: A2    Minimax regret =   3
                              (c)
                 Decision criterion : Expected value
     Experiment outcome: 1    Decision: A2    Expected value =   4.4
                              (d)
                 Decision criterion : Expected value
    Experiment outcome: 1    Decision: A1    Expected value =   .2608695
    Experiment outcome: 2    Decision: A2    Expected value =   8.444444
              EVPI = 1.8    EVSI = .2799997
        Efficiency of Sample Information = .1555554
                              (e)
```

FIGURE 11.4 QSB Output for the Desision Problem of Star Productions.

expected value of $280,000 represents 15.56% of the expected value of $1.8 million associated with having perfect information.

Comparable results are obtained from the software package QSB, as shown in Figures 11.4(a) to 11.4(e), in which the three decision alternatives are labeled A1 for low investment, A2 for moderate investment, and A3 for high investment. The output in Figures 11.4(a) to 11.4(c) provides the optimal decision for the problem of Star Productions using the optimistic (maximax), pessimistic (maximin), and minimax-regret criteria, respectively. Those optimal decisions (and associated payoffs) are the same as reported by STORM in Figures 11.3(a) to 11.3(c). Observe, however, that QSB reports payoffs *only* for the optimal decision.

QSB provides no reports comparable to those in Figures 11.3 (d) to 11.3(f). However, the QSB report in Figure 11.4(d) provides the same optimal decision using the probabilistic criterion as does STORM in Figure 11.3(g). With the probabilities of 0.4 for the series being a failure, 0.4 for a success, and 0.2 for a great success, the optimal decision in Figure 11.4(d) is A2—moderate investment—with an expected payoff of $4.4 million.

The final QSB report in Figure 11.4(e) pertains to the sample information. The first line of that report shows that if the outcome of the survey is indicator I1 (Experiment Outcome: 1), then the optimal decision is A1—low investment—with an expected profit of $0.260895 million. Similarly, if the outcome of the survey is indicator I2 (Experiment Outcome: 2), then the optimal decision is A2—moderate investment—with an expected profit of $8.444444 million. These optimal decisions and expected profits are the same as those computed in Section 11.3.3. The third line of the QSB report in Figure 11.4(e) provides the expected value of perfect information (EVPI = 1.8), which is the same as that reported by STORM in Figure 11.3(h). From the third and fourth lines of the QSB report in Figure 11.4(e), the expected value of the sample information (EVSI = 0.2799997) and the efficiency of the sample information (0.1555554) are approximately the same as those in the STORM report in Figure 11.3(i).

In this section, you have learned to interpret the results of performing single-level decision analysis on a computer. Probabilistic techniques are used to take into account the probabilities of the various future outcomes. Those probabilities were assumed to be independent of your decision. In some cases, however, your decision may affect the *likelihood* of the outcomes. For example, the TV series of Star Productions is more likely to be a great success if your decision is high investment as compared to low investment. This is because with high investment, you will be able to use actors with name recognition, which in turn may result in a more successful series. In Section 11.5, you will learn how the techniques you have seen so far are extended to handle the case when the probabilities of the outcomes depend on your decisions. You will also learn how single-level decision-analysis techniques are extended when you must make successive decisions at different points in time.

■ 11.5 DECISION TREES AND MULTILEVEL DECISION MAKING

In this section, you will learn how decision analysis is used when you are faced with having to make successive decisions or when the probabilities of the outcomes depend on your decisions. In these cases, a *decision tree* is a useful tool.

11.5.1 *The Decision Tree*

A **decision tree** is a graphical representation of the alternatives, outcomes, probabilities, and payoffs associated with a decision problem. Return to the decision problem of Star Productions. The associated payoffs and probabilities for the three investment alternatives are repeated in Table 11.10. These data can be represented by a decision tree. To draw this tree, begin with a node numbered 0 to represent that point in time at which a decision must be made. At this decision point, one of three investment alternatives must be chosen (low, moderate, or high). Draw one node for each possible alternative and connect node 0 to each of these nodes with an arc, as illustrated in Figure 11.5.

Now consider node 1, which represents choosing the alternative of low investment. There are three possible outcomes: failure, success, and great success. These outcomes are denoted by the nodes numbered 4, 5, and 6, respectively, which are connected to node 1. Node 4 represents the outcome of failure in the event of low investment. In this case, the expected payoff, according to Table 11.10, is −$2 million, as written next to node 4. Similarly, the expected payoffs of 5 and 8 are written next to nodes 5 and 6, respectively.

The arc connecting node 1 to node 4 represents the outcome of failure, if the alternative of low investment is selected. You can therefore associate with this arc the conditional probability of such an outcome occurring. As given in Table 11.10:

$$\text{Prob(failure | low investment)} = P(F \mid L) = 0.4$$

This value is written next to that arc in Figure 11.5. Similarly, the conditional proba-

Decision tree
A graphical representation of the alternatives, outcomes, probabilities, and payoffs associated with a decision problem.

TABLE 11.10 *Payoff Table ($ Millions) for the Decision Problem of Star Productions*

| DECISIONS | PAYOFF OF OUTCOMES | | |
	FAILURE (F)	SUCCESS (S)	GREAT SUCCESS (G)
Low (L)	−2	5	8
Moderate (M)	−5	10	12
High (H)	−8	6	15
Probabilities	0.4	0.4	0.2

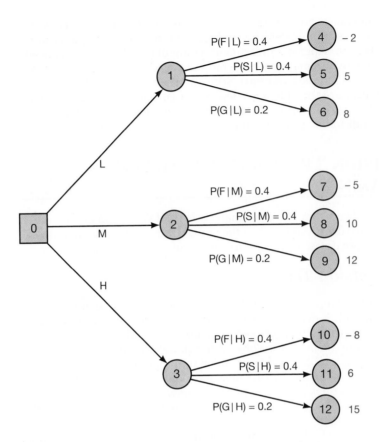

FIGURE 11.5 The Decision Tree for the Problem of Star Productions.

bilities of 0.4 and 0.2 are written next to the two arcs from node 1 to nodes 5 and 6, respectively.

Likewise, Figure 11.5 shows the corresponding information for nodes 7, 8, and 9 and the arcs connecting them to node 2, and for nodes 10, 11, and 12 and the arcs connecting them to node 3. Finally, observe that node 0 is represented by a square. This indicates that node 0 is a **decision node,** corresponding to a point in time at which a decision must be made. In contrast, the **probabilistic nodes**—nodes 1, 2, and 3, from which the uncertain outcomes stem—and the **terminal nodes**—nodes 4 through 12—are represented by circles.

The decision tree helps you see the interrelationships among all the elements of the problem. How can you use the tree to select the best alternative? You must first compute the expected payoff associated with each alternative that corresponds to nodes 1, 2, and 3. The expected payoff for node 1 is obtained by adding the results of multiplying each payoff associated with a terminal node connected to node 1 (that is, nodes 4, 5, and 6) with the corresponding branch probability. That is:

$$
\begin{pmatrix} \text{Expected payoff} \\ \text{for node 1} \end{pmatrix} = \begin{pmatrix} \text{expected payoff} \\ \text{for node 4} \end{pmatrix} * \begin{pmatrix} \text{Prob. associated} \\ \text{with arc 1–4} \end{pmatrix} +
$$
$$
\begin{pmatrix} \text{expected payoff} \\ \text{for node 5} \end{pmatrix} * \begin{pmatrix} \text{prob. associated} \\ \text{with arc 1–5} \end{pmatrix} +
$$
$$
\begin{pmatrix} \text{expected payoff} \\ \text{for node 6} \end{pmatrix} * \begin{pmatrix} \text{prob. associated} \\ \text{with arc 1–6} \end{pmatrix} +
$$
$$
= (-2 * 0.4) + (5 * 0.4) + (8 * 0.2)
$$
$$
= 2.8
$$

You write this value next to node 1. Similar computations identify the expected pay-offs for nodes 2 and 3. The resulting information is summarized in Figure 11.6. Now it is easy to identify the best alternative. It is that of moderate investment because its expected payoff of $4.4 million at node 2 is the largest of the three alternatives, as seen in Figure 11.6. This optimal decision is the same as the one obtained in Section 11.1 because the computations are the same. However, a decision tree provides the ability to handle more complex decision problems—for example, a problem in which the investment decision influences the probabilities of the outcomes. Consider the following modification to the problem of Star Productions.

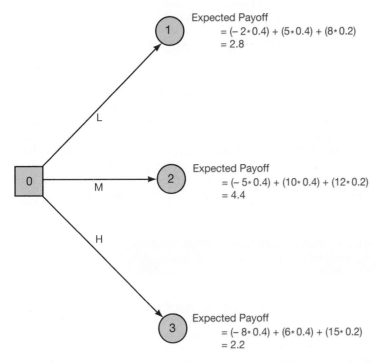

Expected Payoff
$= (-2*0.4) + (5*0.4) + (8*0.2)$
$= 2.8$

Expected Payoff
$= (-5*0.4) + (10*0.4) + (12*0.2)$
$= 4.4$

Expected Payoff
$= (-8*0.4) + (6*0.4) + (15*0.2)$
$= 2.2$

FIGURE 11.6 Computing the Expected Payoff Associated with Each Decision for the Problem of Star Productions.

EXAMPLE 11.2 THE PROBLEM OF STAR PRODUCTIONS WITH PROBABILITIES DEPENDENT ON THE ALTERNATIVES

In further discussion on the results obtained so far, the Vice-President in charge expressed concern about the assumption that the probability of 0.4 for a failure, 0.4 for a success, and 0.2 for a great success remains the same regardless of how large an investment is made. In fact, she believes that the likelihood of the new series being a failure, a success, or a great success depends on the level of investment. The more invested, the higher the probability of the series doing well. She quantifies these beliefs by estimating probabilities for each decision-outcome pair, as given in Table 11.11. For example, the value of 0.5 in the row associated with high investment (H) and the column associated with being a success (S) reflects her belief that there is a 50% chance that the new series will be a success if a high investment is made—that is:

$$P(S \mid H) = 0.5$$

On the basis of the conditional probabilities in Table 11.11 and the previous profit table, what investment alternative should be recommended to maximize the expected profit? ■

To answer this question, you can again draw the decision tree, which is the same as the one in Figure 11.5. In this case, however, the probabilities associated with the arcs from nodes 1, 2, and 3 are those in Table 11.11, as shown in Figure 11.7. Now, the same computations can be made to determine the expected payoff for each alternative. For example, the expected payoff for node 1, corresponding to low investment, is

$$\binom{\text{Expected payoff}}{\text{for node 1}} = \binom{\text{expected payoff}}{\text{for node 4}} * \binom{\text{prob. associated}}{\text{with arc 1-4}} +$$

$$\binom{\text{expected payoff}}{\text{for node 5}} * \binom{\text{prob. associated}}{\text{with arc 1-5}} +$$

$$\binom{\text{expected payoff}}{\text{for node 6}} * \binom{\text{prob. associated}}{\text{with arc 1-6}} +$$

$$= (-2 * 0.6) + (5 * 0.3) + (8 * 0.1)$$

$$= 1.1$$

The results of making these computations for nodes 1, 2, and 3 are written next to these nodes in Figure 11.8. Now it is easy to identify the best alternative—namely, that of high investment. Its expected payoff of \$5.9 million is the highest of the three alternatives. By using the probabilities in Table 11.11 that depend on the alternatives, as opposed to the probabilities in Table 11.10 which are independent of the decision, the optimal decision has changed from moderate to high investment.

Now that you know what a decision tree is, in Section 11.5.2 you will learn how this concept is used to make multilevel decisions at different points in time.

TABLE 11.11   *Conditional Probabilities of the Outcomes Given a Decision for the Problem of Star Productions*

	OUTCOMES		
DECISIONS	FAILURE (F)	SUCCESS (S)	GREAT SUCCESS (G)
Low (L)	0.6	0.3	0.1
Moderate (M)	0.4	0.4	0.2
High (H)	0.2	0.5	0.3

11.5.2 Multilevel Decision Making Using Decision Trees

In this section, decision trees are expanded to enable you to make decisions at several points in time. These decisions cannot be made independently of each other because the decision you make at the first point in time can affect significantly the decision at the next point in time. Consider a modification to the problem of Star Productions in which the only possible outcomes are that the new series is a failure or a success. This simplification is made to keep the subsequent computations and discussion more manageable. The associated profit estimates are given in Table 11.12, and the conditional probabilities of the outcomes given the decision are shown in Table 11.13. The corresponding decision tree is illustrated in Figure 11.9. Now, suppose that after running the series for 8 weeks, a second decision is to be made on the funding level for the remaining season.

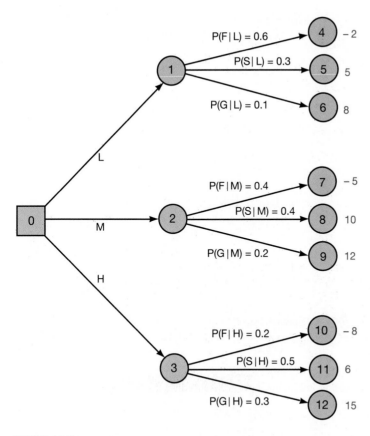

FIGURE 11.7 The Decision Tree for the Problem of Star Productions with Probabilities Depending on the Alternatives.

DEVELOPING THE MULTILEVEL DECISION TREE

The choice of alternatives for the second decision depends on what the first decision is (low, moderate, or high investment) and what outcome is realized after 8 weeks (failure or success). For example, the alternatives in Table 11.14 might be available for the second decision if the first decision is to make a high investment. Of course, the list of combinations grows when you consider the other two initial investment possibilities and the two outcomes—failure and success—that could stem from them. It is helpful to organize two-level decision problems by first listing all combinations of decisions

TABLE 11.12	Payoff Table ($ Millions) for the Modified Decision Problem of Star Productions	
	PAYOFF OF OUTCOMES	
	FAILURE	SUCCESS
DECISIONS	(F)	(S)
Low (L)	−2	5
Moderate (M)	−5	8
High (H)	−8	10

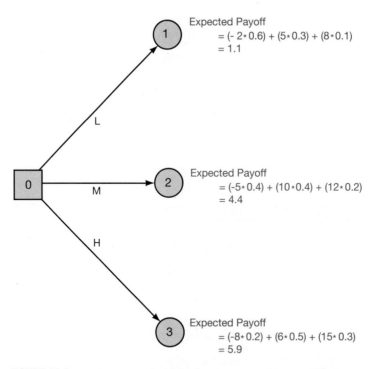

FIGURE 11.8 Computing the Expected Payoff Associated with Each Decision for the Problem of Star Productions with Probabilities Depending on the Alternatives.

TABLE 11.13	*Conditional Probabilities of the Outcomes Given a Decision for the Modified Problem of Star Productions*

	OUTCOMES	
DECISIONS	FAILURE (F)	SUCCESS (S)
Low (L)	0.7	0.3
Moderate (M)	0.6	0.4
High (H)	0.3	0.7

TABLE 11.14	*Second-Level Decision Alternatives for High Initial Investment in the Multilevel Decision Problem of Star Productions*

FIRST-LEVEL		SECOND-LEVEL
DECISION	OUTCOME	DECISION ALTERNATIVES
High	Failure	Abandon the series
High	Success	Continue with moderate promotional budget or Continue with high promotional budget

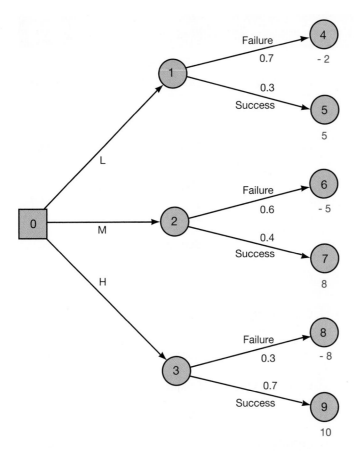

FIGURE 11.9 The First-Level Decision Tree for the Modified Problem of Star Productions.

and possible outcomes from the first level. For the problem of Star Productions, these various combinations are represented in the first-level decision tree by the terminal nodes numbered 4 through 9 in Figure 11.9. For each such combination, you must identify the available decision alternatives at the second decision point, as done before for the combination of high initial investment and the two possible outcomes. The complete list for the second-level decision for the problem of Star Productions is given in Table 11.15 under the column labeled "Second-Level Decision."

The list of alternatives for the second decision point can be added to the first-level decision tree in Figure 11.9. Each terminal node in that tree now becomes a decision node for the second level. From each of these second-level decision nodes is an arc and corresponding node representing a possible second-level decision alternative. This extended tree for Star Productions is illustrated in Figure 11.10.

As with the alternatives at the first level, it is necessary to identify a second-level payoff for each second-level alternative. This later payoff depends on what the outcome is as a result of the decision made at the second point. You must first identify for each possible second-level alternative—corresponding to the nodes numbered 10 through 9 in Figure 11.10—the possible outcomes as a result of making these decisions. For example, consider node 18, corresponding to a first-level decision of high investment with an outcome of the series being a success, and a second-level decision of continuing with a moderate promotional budget. The outcomes then might be as follows:

TABLE 11.15	*Second-Level Decisions, Outcomes, Probabilities, and Profits for the Multilevel Decision Problem of Star Productions*				

FIRST-LEVEL		SECOND-LEVEL			
DECISION	OUTCOME	DECISION	OUTCOME	PROB.	PROFIT
Low	Failure	Abandon the series	—	—	−1
Low	Success	Continue at moderate funding	Failure	0.4	−2.5
			Success	0.6	8
		Continue at high funding	Failure	0.2	−4
			Success	0.8	7
Moderate	Failure	Abandon the series	—	—	−2
Moderate	Success	Continue at moderate funding	Failure	0.3	−4
			Success	0.7	4
		Continue at high funding	Failure	0.1	−5
			Success	0.9	4
High	Failure	Abandon the series	—	—	−3
High	Success	Continue at moderate funding	Failure	0.2	−5
			Success	0.8	3
		Continue at high funding	Failure	0.1	−6
			Success	0.9	2

1. The series is considered to be a failure for the season.
2. The series is considered to be a success for the season.

Observe that the possible outcomes can vary from one node to another. For example, if a second-level alternative is to abandon the series, then there are no outcomes at all for this node.

It is now necessary to estimate the *conditional* probability for each second level outcome and an associated second-level payoff, over and above those of the first level. For example, consider the case in which the initial decision is high investment, the series is a success, and the second-level decision is to commit to a moderate promotional budget, leading to node 17. Under these conditions, you might estimate that there is a probability of 0.8 that the series will be a success at the end of the season, in which case there is an expected profit of $3 million above the first-level profits. These probability and profit estimates and those for the other second-level outcome of failure

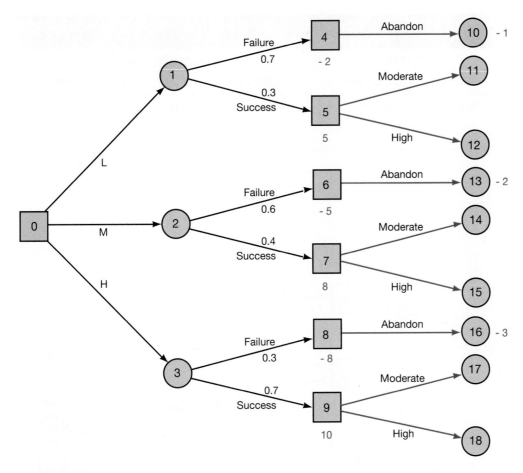

FIGURE 11.10 The Decision Tree with Second-Level Decisions for the Problem of Star Productions.

from node 17 are summarized as follows in Table 11.16. These estimated second-level probabilities and profits in millions of dollars for the remaining combinations of first- and second-level decisions and outcomes are also given in Table 11.15.

These various second-level data are then added to the decision tree. Stemming from each terminal node numbered 10 through 18 in Figure 11.10 is an arc and corresponding node to represent a possible second-level outcome. Next to each such arc is the associated conditional probability of that outcome occurring. Next to each new terminal node is the associated second-level profit. For the problem of Star Productions, this extended tree is illustrated in Figure 11.11.

DETERMINING THE OPTIMAL DECISIONS

Now it is possible to use the decision tree with the conditional probabilities and profits to arrive at the best decision at each decision point. To do so, work backward in the tree starting from the terminal nodes and proceed toward node 0. At each node, the objective is to compute the optimal expected profit for all future events—that is, the profit at that node plus the best expected future profit from then on. For example, working backward, first consider all nodes connected only to the terminal nodes in the

TABLE 11.16	*Second-Level Conditional Probabilities and Payoffs for the Outcomes After Node 17 in Figure 11.10*				
FIRST-LEVEL		SECOND-LEVEL			
DECISION	OUTCOME	DECISION	OUTCOME	PROB.	PROFIT
High	Success	Moderate	Failure (F)	0.2	−5
			Success (S)	0.8	3

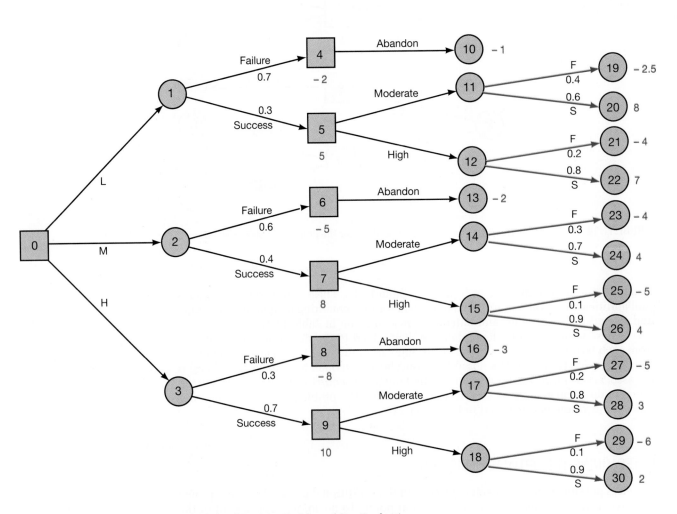

FIGURE 11.11 Decision Tree for the Multilevel Decision Problem of Star Productions.

final tree, nodes 11 and 12, 14 and 15, and 17 and 18 in Figure 11.11. For node 11, the profit at node 11 is 0, so the expected total profit is

$$\begin{pmatrix} \text{Expected total profit} \\ \text{at node 11} \end{pmatrix} = \begin{pmatrix} \text{payoff at} \\ \text{node 11} \end{pmatrix} + \begin{pmatrix} \text{expected future profit} \\ \text{from node 11} \end{pmatrix}$$

$$= 0 + (\text{prob. of arc 11–19} * \text{payoff at node 19}) +$$

$$(\text{prob. of arc 11–20} * \text{payoff at node 20})$$

$$= 0 + (0.4) * (-2.5) + (0.6) * (8)$$

$$= 3.8$$

Performing a similar computation for each of the nodes connected to the terminal nodes results in the values written next to these nodes in the tree of Figure 11.12.

Proceeding backward, it is now necessary to compute the total expected profits for nodes 4 through 9. You need only use the expected profits at nodes 10 through 18 that were just computed. For example, consider node 5, representing a second-level decision point at which an initial low investment is made and the seriesis considered

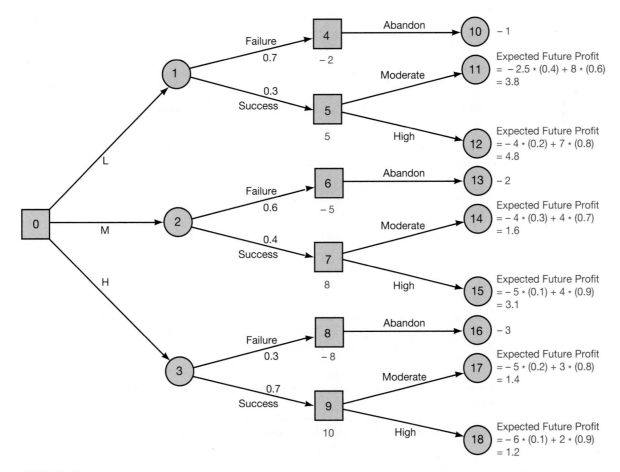

FIGURE 11.12 Computing Expected Future Profits at Nodes 11, 12, 14, 15, 17, and 18 for the Decision Problem of Star Productions.

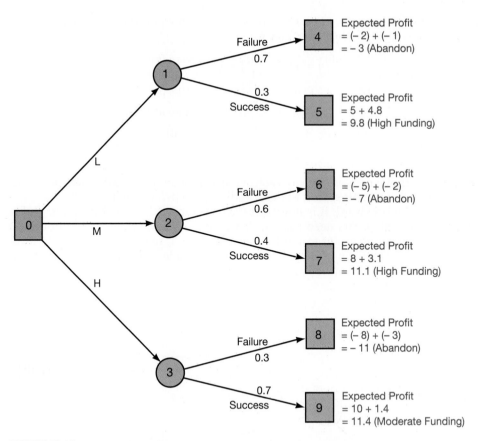

FIGURE 11.13 Expected Future Profits at Nodes 4 Through 9 for the Decision Problem of Star Productions.

a success. At this decision point, you can select either of the following:

1. Moderate promotional budget, leading to node 11, with an expected future profit of $3.8 million.
2. High promotional budget, leading to node 12, with an expected future profit of $4.8 million.

Thus, at node 5, the optimal decision is to choose a high promotional budget, resulting in an expected future profit of $4.8 million. Adding this to the profit of 5 at node 5 results in the expected total profit of $9.8 million.

For each of the remaining decision nodes 4 through 9, the best decision alternative is the one leading to a node having the maximum expected future profit. These values for nodes 4 through 9 are added to the profits for these nodes. The results are given in Figure 11.13.

Working backward again, consider nodes 1, 2, and 3. These are probabilistic nodes, and computations similar to those performed for node 11 are needed. For example, for node 1, the expected total future profit is

$$\begin{pmatrix} \text{Expected total profit} \\ \text{at node 1} \end{pmatrix} = \begin{pmatrix} \text{payoff at} \\ \text{node 1} \end{pmatrix} + \begin{pmatrix} \text{expected future profit} \\ \text{from node 1} \end{pmatrix}$$

$$= 0 + (\text{prob. of arc 1–4} * \text{payoff at node 4}) +$$
$$(\text{prob. of arc 1–5} * \text{payoff at node 5})$$

$$= 0 + (0.7) * (-3) + (0.3) * (9.8)$$

$$= 0.84$$

Performing corresponding computations for nodes 2 and 3 results in the values written next to these nodes in the tree of Figure 11.14.

Finally, to compute the total expected profits for node 0, you need only use the values of nodes 1, 2, and 3 that were just computed. At this decision point, you can select

1. Low initial investment, leading to node 1, with an expected future profit of $0.84 million,
2. Moderate initial investment, leading to node 2, with an expected future profit of $0.24 million,
3. High initial investment, leading to node 3, with an expected future profit of $4.68 million.

Thus, at node 0, the optimal decision is to choose a high initial investment, resulting in a total expected future profit of $4.68 million.

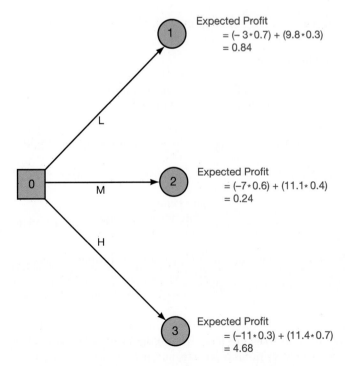

FIGURE 11.14 Computing the Expected Future Profit Associated with Each First-Level Decision for the Problem of Star Productions.

From these computations, the optimal decision at the first level is high initial investment, leading to node 3. The optimal decision at the second level depends on the resulting outcome at node 3, leading to node 8 or 9. The associated optimal decisions are the ones that produce the optimal total expected profits for these nodes, as shown in Figure 11.13, leading to the following decisions:

OUTCOME	NODE	OPTIMAL SECOND-LEVEL DECISION
Failure	8	Abandon the series
Success	9	Moderate promotional budget

KEY FEATURES

Although the example of Star Productions involved only two decision points, the ideas discussed here can be used for multilevel decision making involving any number of sequential decisions. Follow these steps:

✔ Draw a decision tree with as many levels as there are decision points. For each level:

    a. At each decision node, identify the available decision alternatives and draw an associated arc and probability node.

    b. At each probability node in (a), identify the possible outcomes and draw an associated arc and decision node. Then write the corresponding conditional arc probabilities and node profits.

✔ Working backward from the terminal nodes to node 0, compute the total expected profit as follows:

    a. For a probability node, compute

$$\begin{pmatrix}\text{Total expected}\\\text{profit}\end{pmatrix} = \begin{pmatrix}\text{payoff at}\\\text{this node}\end{pmatrix} + \begin{pmatrix}\text{expected future profit}\\\text{from this node}\end{pmatrix}$$

    where the expected future profit is computed by adding the products of the conditional probability of each leaving arc and the associated profit of the connected node.

    b. For a decision node, compute

$$\begin{pmatrix}\text{Total expected}\\\text{profit}\end{pmatrix} = \begin{pmatrix}\text{payoff at}\\\text{this node}\end{pmatrix} + \begin{pmatrix}\text{maximum of the expected}\\\text{future profits of the}\\\text{connected nodes}\end{pmatrix}$$

✔ Identify the optimal decisions by starting at node 0, where the optimal decision is known. For each possible outcome, identify the decision that results in the optimal values for the associated node.

You have learned how decision trees are used in making multilevel sequential decisions. Because these trees grow very quickly in size, computers are typically used to perform the necessary computations.

■ 11.6 Decision Analysis: Using the Computer

In this section, you will learn to interpret the output obtained from solving a decision problem on the computer. You have already seen the computer output for solving the problem of Star Productions when the probabilities assigned to the various outcomes do not depend on the decision alternative selected. When those probabilities *do* depend on the decision, as described in Section 11.5, results are obtained by drawing an appropriate decision tree and using a computer to make the necessary computations, as you will see in Section 11.6.1. Decision trees and computer packages are also used to obtain optimal decisions for a multilevel problem involving sequential decisions, as shown in Section 11.6.2.

11.6.1 Single-Level Decisions Using the Computer

Recall the modified problem of Star Productions in which the probabilities of the three outcomes depend on the decisions summarized in Tables 11.17 and 11.18. The corresponding decision tree is shown again in Figure 11.15.

These data must now be entered into a computer package. How this is done depends on the particular package. STORM requires that for each arc (or branch), you provide the two nodes connected by this arc. If the arc corresponds to an outcome, you must also provide the associated probability. In Section 11.5, the resulting payoff is asssociated with the terminal node of the arc; in STORM, however, that payoff is entered with the arc leading to the terminal node.

Decision Analysis
EX11_2.DAT

The results of entering the data from the decision tree in Figure 11.15 into the STORM computer package are shown in Figure 11.16. The optimal decision for this problem is associated with node 0 and can be found in the first three lines of the output in Figure 11.16. Reading across that portion of the report, you can see that node 0 is a decision node ("Dec") with an expected total payoff of $5.9 million. The decision that provides this payoff is that of high investment, as indicated by the ∗ to the right of line 3. This decision is selected as the best one because its total expected payoff, consisting

TABLE 11.17	Payoff Table ($ Millions) for the Decision Problem of Star Productions		
	PAYOFF OF OUTCOMES		
DECISIONS	FAILURE (F)	SUCCESS (S)	GREAT SUCCESS (G)
Low (L)	−2	5	8
Moderate (M)	−5	10	12
High (H)	−8	6	15

TABLE 11.18	Conditional Probabilities of Outcomes Given a Decision for the Problem of Star Productions		
	OUTCOMES		
DECISIONS	FAILURE (F)	SUCCESS (S)	GREAT SUCCESS (G)
Low (L)	0.6	0.3	0.1
Moderate (M)	0.4	0.4	0.2
High (H)	0.2	0.5	0.3

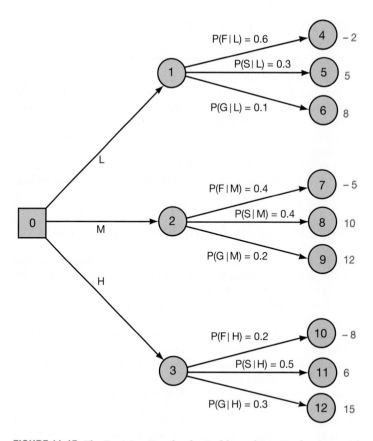

FIGURE 11.15 The Decision Tree for the Problem of Star Productions with
Probabilities that Depend on the Alternatives.

of the branch payoff (0.0) and the expected payoff of the terminal node 3 (5.9), is larger
than that of the other two branches (namely, 0.0 + 1.1 and 0.0 + 4.4).

To see how this value of 5.9 is obtained for node 3, proceed to the portion of
the report in Figure 11.16 corresponding to this node, which is the last three lines
of the report. Reading across that portion, you can see that node 3 is a probability
node ("Prob"). It has three outcome branches with associated probabilities of 0.2, 0.5,
and 0.3 and payoffs of −8, 6, and 15. These payoffs are entered in STORM with the
branches rather than with the terminal nodes, so the expected payoff of 5.9 at node 3
is computed as follows:

$$\begin{pmatrix} \text{Expected pay-} \\ \text{off at node 3} \end{pmatrix}$$

$= (\text{prob. of branch H-FAILURE}) * (\text{branch payoff} + \text{payoff from terminal node 10 on}) +$

$\quad (\text{prob. of branch H-SUCCESS}) * (\text{branch payoff} + \text{payoff from terminal node 11 on}) +$

$\quad (\text{prob. of branch H-G SUCC}) * (\text{branch payoff} + \text{payoff from terminal node 12 on})$

$= 0.2 * (-8 + 0) + 0.5 * (6 + 0) + 0.3 * (15 + 0)$

$= 5.9$

Similar information is available for the two probability nodes 1 and 2.

```
                 The Problem of Star Productions, Inc.
                      DETAILED DECISIONS REPORT
      ---- From Node ----     ---- Emanating Branch ----     --- To Node --
   Name Type  Exp Payoff  Name        Prob       Payoff  Name  Exp Payoff
   0    Dec      5.900    LOW          .           0.000  1         1.100
                          MODERATE     .           0.000  2         4.400
                          HIGH         .           0.000  3         5.900*
   1    Prob     1.100    L-FAILURE   0.600       -2.000  4         0.000
                          L-SUCCESS   0.300        5.000  5         0.000
                          L-G SUCC.   0.100        8.000  6         0.000
   2    Prob     4.400    M-FAILURE   0.400       -5.000  7         0.000
                          M-SUCCESS   0.400       10.000  8         0.000
                          M-G SUCC.   0.200       12.000  9         0.000
   3    Prob     5.900    H-FAILURE   0.200       -8.000  10        0.000
                          H-SUCCESS   0.500        6.000  11        0.000
                          H-G SUCC.   0.300       15.000  12        0.000
```

FIGURE 11.16 STORM Output for the Single-Level Problem of Star Productions with Probabilities that Depend on the Alternatives.

```
              Decision-Tree Analysis
    Node      Type of node     Expected value    Decision
     1          decision            5.9             High
     2          chance              1.1
     3          chance              4.4
     4          chance              5.9
```

FIGURE 11.17 QSB Output for the Single-Level Problem of Star Productions with Probabilities that Depend on the Alternatives.

Comparable results are obtained from the QSB software package, as shown in Figure 11.17. However, when you enter the decision tree into that package, node numbers must begin at 1 (instead of 0). From the first line of that report, you can see that the optimal decision at the decision node 1 is high investment, with an expected profit of $5.9 million. This is the same as reported by STORM for node 0 in Figure 11.16. The remaining three lines of the report in Figure 11.17 provide the expected profits at the three probability ("chance") nodes 2, 3, and 4, which are, respectively, $1.1, $4.4, and $5.9 million. Once again, these values coincide with those obtained from STORM in Figure 11.16 for nodes 1, 2, and 3.

11.6.2 Multilevel Decisions Using the Computer

How are computers used to determine the optimal decisions in multilevel sequential decision problems? Revisit the multilevel decision problem of Star Productions in Section 11.5.2, where management must make an initial investment decision and, 8 weeks later, a promotional-budget decision for the rest of the season.

To solve this problem, the decision tree in Figure 11.11 in Section 11.5.2 is drawn, and all needed conditional probabilities and payoffs are assigned. Once again, these data must be entered into the computer. By using STORM, the output shown in Figure 11.18 results. Keep in mind that in STORM, the node payoff is entered with the branch leading to this node.

Decision Analysis
SPTREE.DAT

```
                    The Problem of Star Productions, Inc.
                          OPTIMAL DECISIONS REPORT
        ---- From Node ----     ---- Emanating Branch ----     --- To Node --
     Name Type  Exp Payoff  Name          Prob      Payoff  Name  Exp Payoff
     0    Dec        4.680   HIGH            .        0.000  3         4.680
     3    Prob       4.680   H-FAILURE     0.300     -8.000  8        -3.000
                             H-SUCCESS     0.700     10.000  9         1.400
     8    Dec       -3.000   H-F-A           .       -3.000  16        0.000
     9    Dec        1.400   H-S-M           .        0.000  17        1.400
     16   End        0.000
     17   Prob       1.400   H-S-M-F       0.200     -5.000  27        0.000
                             H-S-M-S       0.800      3.000  28        0.000

     27   End        0.000
     28   End        0.000
```

FIGURE 11.18 STORM Output for the Multilevel Decision Problem of Star Productions.

To interpret the output, recall that the first decision occurs at node 0. From the first line of the report associated with that node, you can see that the total expected payoff for the entire season is $4.68 million. This value is achieved by making the best possible decision at *each* level. For the first level, the optimal decision is HIGH initial investment, leading to node 3 in the decision tree, as indicated in the first line of the report in Figure 11.18.

To see what the optimal decision is at the second level (pertaining to the size of the promotional budget), proceed to that portion of the report on node 3, which is the next two lines of the report. You can see that node 3 is a probability node with two outcome branches. The associated probabilities are 0.3 and 0.7, and the payoffs are -8 and 10. (Recall that these payoffs are entered into STORM with the branches.) The expected payoff of 4.68 at node 3 is computed as follows:

$$\begin{pmatrix} \text{Expected pay-} \\ \text{off at node 3} \end{pmatrix}$$

$$= (\text{prob. of branch H-FAILURE}) * (\text{branch payoff} + \text{payoff from node 8 on}) +$$

$$(\text{prob. of branch H-SUCCESS}) * (\text{branch payoff} + \text{payoff from node 9 on})$$

$$= 0.3 * (-8 - 3) + 0.7 * (10 + 1.4)$$

$$= 4.68$$

The optimal decision at the second level depends on the specific outcome after the first-level decision. For example, if that outcome is a failure, you are led from node 3 to node 8 in the decision tree, where the second-level decision must now be made. To determine the optimal decision, locate that portion of the report corresponding to node 8. Reading across that line, you see that the optimal decision is to follow the branch H-F-A (under the column labeled "Name" under the "Emanating Branch"). The symbol H-F-A was entered into STORM with the data for the branch in the decision tree in Figure 11.11 connecting nodes 8 and 16 and signifies that this branch is reached by a first-level decision of high investment (H), followed by the outcome of a failure (F), followed by the second-level decision to abandon the series (A). In other words, the second-level decision in this case is to abandon the series, with an expected future payoff of $-$3 million.

In contrast, suppose the outcome after the first-level decision is a success, leading you from node 3 to node 9 in the decision tree. To determine the optimal second-level decision in this case, locate that portion of the report on node 9. You can see that the optimal decision is to follow the branch H-S-M, indicating that the second-level decision is a moderate promotional budget, with an expected future payoff of $1.4 million. This value is obtained using the information on node 17 in the report.

The optimal first-level decision for the management of Star Productions is high initial investment at node 0. The optimal second-level decisions are as follows:

Abandon the series if the outcome as a result of high initial investment is a failure.

Proceed with a moderate promotional budget if the outcome as a result of high initial investment is a success.

In this section, you have learned how to interpret the results of using a computer for determining the optimal decision in a single-level or multilevel decision problem. In all these problems, the choice of the decision is based on the desire to maximize the expected payoff. In Section 11.7, you will learn another criterion that is often used in choosing the decisions.

■ 11.7 DECISION MAKING USING UTILITY THEORY

In the probabilistic analysis so far, the optimal choice for the decision alternative is the one that maximizes the expected *payoff*, using the values in the payoff table. In many cases, maximizing the expected payoff may be reasonable, but in some cases, it may not be appropriate. For example, everyone knows that the expected payoff from any lottery is a negative value (otherwise the state would not make money). Therefore, if people were to make the decision to play or not to play the lottery on the basis of maximizing expected payoff, no one would play the lottery. However, many people *do* play the lottery. This is because many people are willing to take a high risk of losing a small amount of money for a negligible chance of winning a large amount. These people are obviously using a criterion other than maximizing expected payoff.

As another example, consider buying health insurance. Again, the expected payoff is negative (otherwise insurance companies would not make money). Yet, people *do* buy health insurance. In this case, people are willing to pay money to insure against a small probability of spending a lot of money in medical expenses. These people are also using a criterion other than maximizing expected payoff.

Why is it, therefore, that in the *same* decision situation, some people choose one alternative (buying a lottery ticket) and others do not? The answer is that people have different *monetary values*. To some people, the "value" of losing $1 in the lottery is relatively very small compared to the "value" of possibly winning. To others, the "value" of losing the $1 is relatively much more than the "value" of possibly winning. This difference indicates that people value money differently, based on their *personal* preferences. The objective of this section is to present a systematic approach for quantifying a decision maker's relative value for money, called **utility**. These utilities are then used to select a decision alternative. Consider the example of Home Appliances.

Utility
A numerical way to represent a decision maker's relative value for money.

11.7.1 *Problem Description*

Home Appliances has been selling refrigerators, stoves, and other large home appliances for decades. At a recent board meeting, the members decided to enter the electronics business by purchasing a television dealership for the next 5 years. After some review, the following alternatives were suggested.

1. Buy a dealership from a company that has standard, well-known products with substantial brand-name recognition. This alternative, denoted by B, offers the highest probability of gaining a significant market share, but the cost is relatively high due to the name of the company.

2. Buy a dealership from a company that has standard products but that does not have name recognition. This alternative, denoted by N, offers a smaller chance of gaining market share, but it costs less.

3. Buy a dealership from a new company that has developed an innovative television set with the capability of internal digital recording. This company's philosophy is to continue developing products that other companies do not have. This alternative, denoted by I, is risky, but it offers the possibility of a large payoff if the product is accepted in the marketplace.

The Accounting Department has compiled the expected profits for each alternative associated with the outcomes of low market share (L), average market share (A), and high market share (H). These profits, in millions of dollars, are given in Table 11.19. The Research Department has used a market survey to determine that the probability of capturing market share depends on which type of dealership is purchased. These conditional probabilities are given in Table 11.20. As Vice-President of Strategic Planning, which of the three dealerships would you recommend to the board of Home Appliances to purchase?

TABLE 11.19   *Payoff Table ($ Millions) for the Decision Problem of Home Appliances*

	OUTCOMES		
DECISIONS	LOW (L)	AVERAGE (A)	HIGH (H)
B	−5	4	7
N	−1	2	5
I	−1	3	15

TABLE 11.20   *Conditional Probabilities of Outcomes Given a Decision for the Problem of Home Appliances*

	OUTCOMES		
DECISIONS	LOW (L)	AVERAGE (A)	HIGH (H)
B	0.3	0.5	0.2
N	0.4	0.4	0.2
I	0.6	0.3	0.1

11.7.2 Selecting the Decision Using the Expected Profit

To determine the best alternative, you know that you must first select a decision criterion. Suppose you decide to use the criterion of maximizing the expected profit. You must now compute the expected profit for each decision alternative, as you learned in Section 11.5.1. The results of these computations are summarized in Table 11.21.

Decision Analysis
HOME_EP.DAT

TABLE 11.21	Computing the Expected Profit for Each Decision in the Problem of Home Appliances
DECISION	EXPECTED PROFIT
B	$-5 * (0.3) + 4 * (0.5) + \ 7 * (0.2) = 1.9$
N	$-1 * (0.4) + 2 * (0.4) + \ 5 * (0.2) = 1.4$
I	$-1 * (0.6) + 3 * (0.3) + 15 * (0.1) = 1.8$

On the basis of these results, your recommendation to the board would be alternative B—that is, to buy the dealership having name recognition, with an expected profit of $1.9 million. However, you know that most members of the board are more aggressive and willing to take risks. The possibility of larger rewards may be worth the associated risk of losing some amount of money. One way to capture how the board members value money is to use utility theory, as described next.

11.7.3 Making the Decision Using Utility Theory

To use this approach, you must first associate with each profit in Table 11.19, a utility in the form of a numeric value that reflects the board's relative preferences. This is accomplished by working with the board and taking the following steps.

ORDERING ALL THE PROFITS

Begin by arranging all profits in descending order. In this case, these nine decreasing profits are 15, 7, 5, 4, 3, 2, −1, −1, −5. Because the utilities of these profits are *relative*, you can arbitrarily assign a utility of, say, 100 to the highest profit ($15 million in this case) and 0 to the lowest profit (−$5 million in this case).

CONVERTING PROFITS INTO UTILITIES

To determine the utility of the remaining profits relative to the two foregoing extreme profits, you need to conduct an interview with the decision makers. Consider the profit of $7 million. To determine the associated utility, you need to know how the board values $7 million *relative to* the highest profit of $15 million and *relative to* the lowest profit of −$5 million. You obtain this value in a systematic way by presenting the members with a sequence of fictitious lottery games. For example, you may start by asking them to consider a lottery that offers them the potential of winning $15 million (the highest profit in the profit table) with a probability 0.05 and winning −$5 million (the lowest profit) with a probability of $1 - 0.05 = 0.95$. Would they prefer this lottery to a guaranteed profit of $7 million (the profit for which the utility is sought)? In this case, most likely the board will prefer the guaranteed profit of $7 million. In contrast, if the probabilities in the lottery were reversed (and the probability of winning $15 million was 0.95), the members would probably prefer playing the lottery.

Your goal is to determine the probability, p, in the lottery for winning $15 million (and so $1 - p$ for winning −$5 million) so that the members are indifferent to playing the lottery or taking the guaranteed profit of $7 million. You find this value of p by systematically offering the board members this lottery with different probabilities each time and asking them whether the majority prefers the lottery or the guaranteed profit. For this example, suppose the result of this interview process is the value of $p = 0.40$. That is, the board is indifferent between taking the guaranteed profit of $7 million and playing a lottery that offers $15 million with a probability of $p = 0.40$ and −$5 million with a probability of $1 - p = 0.60$. In this case, the sought-after utility of $7 million is $100 * p = 100 * 0.40 = 40$. It is interesting to note that this means the members are indifferent between the profit of $7 million and the *expected profit* of the lottery, which is $(15 * p) + [-5 * (1 - p)] = \$3$ million. This indicates that the members are willing to pay $7 million to play a lottery whose expected profit is *only* $3 million. This is because they value the opportunity of making $15 million relatively more.

You must now repeat this interview process to find the utilities for each of the remaining profits. Suppose you have done so and have obtained the results shown in Table 11.22. Of course, you would expect the utilities to decrease as the profit decreases from its highest value to its lowest value.

Utility table
A table obtained by replacing each value in a payoff table by the associated utility.

After you obtain the utilities for each profit, you create a **utility table** by replacing each value in the payoff table (Table 11.19) by the associated utility. Table 11.23 is the utility table for the problem of Home Appliances.

TABLE 11.22	Utilities Associated with the Profits for the Decision Problem of Home Appliances	
PROFIT	p	UTILITY ($100 * p$)
15	—	100
7	0.40	40
5	0.30	30
4	0.25	25
3	0.20	20
2	0.16	16
−1	0.10	10
−1	0.10	10
−5	—	0

TABLE 11.23	Utility Table for the Decision Problem of Home Appliances		
	OUTCOMES		
DECISIONS	LOW (L)	AVERAGE (A)	HIGH (H)
B	0	25	40
N	10	16	30
I	10	20	100

MAKING THE DECISION USING THE UTILITY TABLE

After converting the profits into utilities, the final step is to use those utilities to select the decision alternative that *maximizes the expected utility*. By using the probabilities of the outcomes previously identified in Table 11.20, the expected utility for each decision alternative is shown in Table 11.24.

On the basis of these results, your recommendation to the board would be the third alternative, I, which is to buy the dealership having the innovative products, with an expected utility of 22.0. Observe that this decision is different from the optimal alternative of B when maximizing the expected profit is used as the criterion. This change is consistent with the more aggressive investment philosophy of the board, reflected by its utilities.

Decision Analysis
HOME_EU.DAT

TABLE 11.24	**Computing the Expected Utility for Each Decision in the Problem of Home Appliances**
DECISION	EXPECTED UTILITY
B	$0*(0.3) + 25*(0.5) + 40*(0.2) = 20.5$
N	$10*(0.4) + 16*(0.4) + 30*(0.2) = 16.4$
I	$10*(0.6) + 20*(0.3) + 100*(0.1) = 22.0$

11.7.4 Utility Functions

Further insight into the meaning of utilities can be gained by drawing a graph of the utilities versus the profits. This is done in Figure 11.19 for the nine utilities and profits in the problem of Home Appliances. By interpolating between these points, you can create an underlying **utility function** that converts any profit to an associated utility. In this case, that utility function lies below the straight line connecting the two extreme points, marked A and B in Figure 11.19. In general, a utility function that lies below this line indicates a decision maker who is **risk-seeking**, which means that the person prefers a relatively aggressive investment philosophy.

In contrast, suppose your interview with the members of the board of Home Appliances has resulted in the utilities for the profits shown in Table 11.25. In this case,

Utility function
A formula or method for converting any profit of a decision maker to an associated utility.

Risk-seeking
A decision maker whose utility function indicates a preference for taking risks.

TABLE 11.25	**A Conservative Set of Utilities Associated with the Profits for the Decision Problem of Home Appliances**	
PROFIT	p	UTILITY $(100*pp)$
15	—	100
7	0.75	75
5	0.70	70
4	0.65	65
3	0.55	55
2	0.50	50
−1	0.35	35
−1	0.35	35
−5	—	0

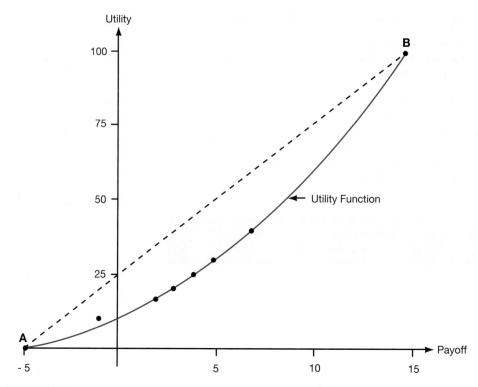

FIGURE 11.19 The Risk-Seeking Utility Function for Home Appliances.

these utilities indicate a more conservative investment philosophy. For example, the value of $p = 0.75$ associated with a profit of $7 million indicates that the members are indifferent between the guaranteed profit of $7 million and the lottery, even though its expected profit is $(15 * 0.75) + [(-5) * 0.25] = \$10$ million. That is, the board members are not willing to pay $7 million to play a lottery whose expected profit is *actually* $10 million. This indicates that the board members are conservative with regard to taking risk.

If these "conservative" utilities are used, the decision that now maximizes the expected utility is that of N, as you are asked to verify in the exercises at the end of the chapter. That is, with these utilities, it is now optimal to acquire the dealership that has standard products but no significant brand-name recognition.

Risk-averse
A decision maker whose utility function indicates a preference for avoiding risks.

These profits and utilities are plotted in Figure 11.20. In this case, the underlying utility function lies *above* the straight line. In general, a utility function that is above the straight line indicates a decision maker who is **risk-averse**, which means that the person prefers a conservative investment philosophy. A decision maker who is satisfied with maximizing the expected profit is **risk-neutral**, and this person's utility function *is* the straight line.

Risk-neutral
A decision maker who is satisfied with maximizing the expected profit.

You have learned how the concept of utilities is used in decision analysis to capture the investment philosophy of decision makers. Once the profits are converted to associated utilities, the computations used to find expected utilities are the same as those discussed in Section 11.4 used to find the expected profits.

KEY FEATURES

You can therefore use utilities in multi level decision making by doing the following:

✔ Converting all profits to utilities by the interview process described in this section.

✔ Drawing a decision tree, as described in Section 11.4.

✔ Performing identical computations, as described in Section 11.4, using the utilities in place of profits, to select the optimal sequence of decisions that maximizes the total expected utility.

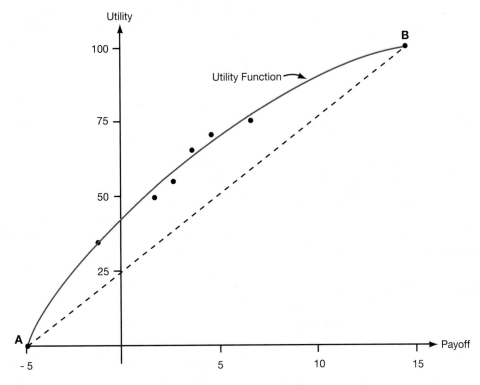

FIGURE 11.20 The Risk-Averse Utility Function for Home Appliances.

CASE STUDY

As a manager, you have learned the importance of asking questions of the form: "What happens if?" For example, for the single-level decision problem of Star Productions given in Section 11.5.1 you might ask: What happens to the optimal decision if the condition probabilities in Table 11.11, repeated here as Table 11.26, change? Another way of asking this question is: How sensitive is the optimal decision of high investment to changes in these probabilities? Such questions are important in decision theory because the probabilities used in the calculations are only *estimates*. If the optimal decision is determined to be very sensitive, you may want to spend additional time and effort to obtain more reliable estimates. The objective of this section is to determine the sensitivity ranges of some of the conditional probabilities in Table 11.26.

Determining the Sensitivity Ranges of the Conditional Probabilities for High Investment

Assume in this study that the probabilities of the three possible outcomes resulting from both a low and a moderate initial investment remain as shown in Table 11.26. By how much can the probabilities of the three possible outcomes resulting from a high initial investment change and yet the optimal decision remain high investment?

To answer this question, think of the three probabilities in the last row of Table 11.26 as the variables p_1, p_2, and p_3, whose values can change. You know that

$$p_1 + p_2 + p_3 = 1$$

or

$$p_3 = 1 - p_1 - p_2$$

The objective is to determine the values for p_1 and p_2 so that the optimal decision is still high initial investment.

One approach to solving this problem is to choose specific values for p_1 and p_2 and use a computer package to see if high investment remains the optimal decision. The problem with doing so is that there is an *infinite* number of possible values for p_1 and p_2. A more systematic approach is needed.

To understand that approach, recall the decision tree shown in Figure 11.21, in which the probabilities associated with the three outcomes for high investment are p_1, p_2, and $p_3 = 1 - p_1 - p_2$. To determine the optimal decision, it is necessary to obtain the expected profits for nodes 1, 2, and 3.

EXPECTED PROFIT FOR NODE 1

$$\begin{aligned}
\text{Expected profit for node 1} &= (0.6 * \text{profit from node 4}) + \\
&\quad (0.3 * \text{profit from node 5}) + \\
&\quad (0.1 * \text{profit from node 6}) \\
&= [0.6 * (-2)] + [0.3 * 5] + \\
&\quad [0.1 * 8] \\
&= 1.1
\end{aligned}$$

TABLE 11.26 *Conditional Probabilities of Outcomes Given a Decision for the Problem of Star Productions*

| | OUTCOMES | | |
DECISIONS	FAILURE (F)	SUCCESS (S)	GREAT SUCCESS (G)
Low (L)	0.6	0.3	0.1
Moderate (M)	0.4	0.4	0.2
High (H)	0.2	0.5	0.3

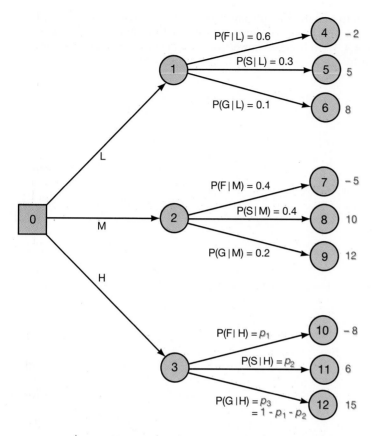

| The Decision Tree for the Problem of Star Productions.

Observe that these computations *do not* depend on p_1, p_2, and p_3.

EXPECTED PROFIT FOR NODE 2

$$\text{Expected profit for node 2} = (0.4 * \text{profit from node 7}) +$$
$$(0.4 * \text{profit from node 8}) +$$
$$(0.2 * \text{profit from node 9})$$
$$= [0.4 * (-5)] + [0.4 * 10] +$$
$$[0.2 * 12]$$
$$= 4.4$$

Observe again that these computations also *do not* depend on p_1, p_2, and p_3.

EXPECTED PROFIT FOR NODE 3

$$\text{Expected profit for node 3} = [p_1 * \text{profit from node 10}] +$$
$$[p_2 * \text{profit from node 11}] +$$
$$[p_3 * \text{profit from node 12}]$$
$$= [p_1 * (-8)] + [p_2 * 6] +$$
$$[(1 - p_1 - p_2) * 15]$$
$$= 15 - 23p_1 - 9p_2$$

For high investment to remain the optimal decision, its associated expected profit of $15 - 23p_1 - 9p_2$ should be at least as large as that of low investment at 1.1 and moderate investment at 4.4. Both of these conditions are ensured provided that p_1 and p_2 satisfy the single condition:

$$15 - 23p_1 - 9p_2 \geq 4.4$$

or

$$23p_1 + 9p_2 \leq 10.6 \tag{1}$$

Also, p_1 and p_2 are probabilities, so

$$0 \leq p_1 \leq 1 \tag{2}$$

$$0 \leq p_2 \leq 1 \tag{3}$$

Finally, to ensure that $p_3 = 1 - p_1 - p_2$ is also a probability, p_1 and p_2 must satisfy $p_3 = 1 - p_1 - p_2 \geq 0$:

$$p_1 + p_2 \leq 1 \tag{4}$$

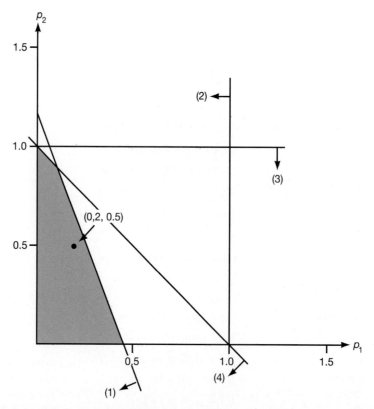

FIGURE 11.22 Sensitivity Analysis for the Outcome Probabilities with High Investment for the Problem of Star Productions.

Use the graphical procedure for drawing inequality constraints having two variables (as described in Chapter 4). The values of p_1 and p_2 that satisfy (1) through (4) are indicated by the shaded region in Figure 11.22. In other words, as long as p_1 and p_2 have values inside the shaded region, the optimal decision remains at high investment.

The original values of $p_1 = 0.2$ and $p_2 = 0.5$ indeed lie inside the shaded region. Their "distances" from the boundary provide a measure of how sensitive the current optimal decision is to changes in their values. In this case, if both p_1 and p_2 increase by 0.05, the decision of high investment is no longer optimal; instead, moderate investment is optimal. If you believe that your initial estimates of $p_1 = 0.2$ and $p_2 = 0.5$ are not accurate to within 0.05, then you should spend additional effort in obtaining more accurate probability estimates. For example, you may consider conducting a focus group with industry experts to obtain estimates of these probabilities.

Determining the Sensitivity Ranges of the Conditional Probabilities for Moderate and Low Investment

You can perform a similar analysis to determine how sensitive the current decision of high investment is with regard to changes in the conditional probabilities associated with moderate investment, assuming those of low and high investment remain unchanged. Think of the three probabilities in the second row of Table 11.26 as the variables p_1, p_2, and p_3, whose values can change. The objective is to determine the values for p_1 and p_2 so that the optimal decision is still high investment. This occurs when the expected profit for high investment exceeds that of low and moderate investment—that is, when p_1 and p_2 satisfy:

$$17p_1 + 2p_2 \geq 6.1 \qquad (1)$$
$$0 \leq \quad p_1 \qquad \leq 1 \qquad (2)$$
$$0 \leq \qquad p_2 \leq 1 \qquad (3)$$
$$p_1 + \quad p_2 \leq 1 \qquad (4)$$

The shaded region in Figure 11.23 depicts the values of p_1 and p_2 that satisfy (1) through (4). As long as p_1 and p_2 have values inside the shaded region, the optimal decision remains at high investment.

The original values of $p_1 = 0.4$ and $p_2 = 0.4$ lie inside the shaded region. Again, their "distances" from the boundary provide a measure of how sensitive the current optimal decision is to changes in their values.

Finally, for low investment, think of the conditional probabilities associated with low investment in the first row of Table 11.26 as the variables p_1, p_2, and $p_3 = 1 - p_1 - p_2$. The four appropriate conditions needed to ensure that high investment remains optimal are

$$10p_1 + 3p_2 \geq 2.1 \qquad (1)$$
$$0 \leq \quad p_1 \qquad \leq 1 \qquad (2)$$
$$0 \leq \qquad p_2 \leq 1 \qquad (3)$$
$$p_1 + \quad p_2 \leq 1 \qquad (4)$$

The shaded region in Figure 11.24 depicts the values of p_1 and p_2 that satisfy (1) through (4). As long as p_1 and p_2 have values inside the shaded region, the optimal decision remains at high investment.

The original values of $p_1 = 0.6$ and $p_2 = 0.3$ lie inside the shaded region. Once again, their "distances" from the boundary provide a measure of how sensitive the current optimal decision is to changes in their values.

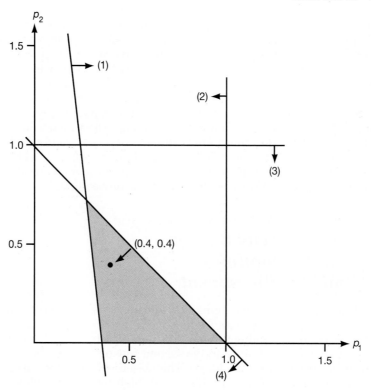

FIGURE 11.23 Sensitivity Analysis for the Outcome Probabilities with
Moderate Investment for the Problem of Star Productions.

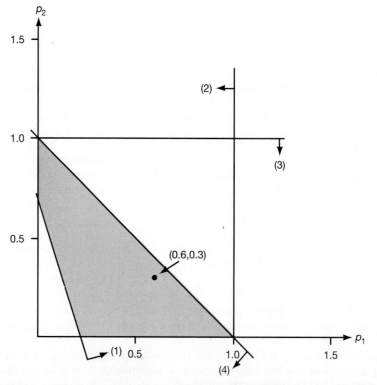

FIGURE 11.24 Sensitivity Analysis for the Outcome Probabilities with Low
Investment for the Problem of Star Productions.

In this section, you have learned to apply your knowledge of decision trees to determine how sensitive the optimal decision is to some of the probability estimates. Next, additional issues pertaining to the use of decision theory are discussed from a managerial point of view.

ADDITIONAL MANAGERIAL CONSIDERATIONS

As a manager, there are several issues you should be aware of pertaining to the use of decision analysis as described in Sections 11.1 through 11.7.

Issues Related to the Problem Formulation

To use decision analysis, you must first identify a finite number of decision alternatives. In some problems, however, the number of alternatives is very large, or even infinite. For example, consider an investment problem in which you need to decide *how much to invest* rather than the *level of investment*. The former gives rise to a very large number of alternatives, one for each possible amount of investment, making it impractical to solve such a problem by the techniques discussed in this chapter.

More advanced techniques are available for solving these problems with many alternatives. But you can still use the techniques of this chapter if you group the alternatives into a few different levels of investment, as was done for the problem of Star Productions. The company could have listed its investment alternatives as $100,000; $100,001; and so on, from its minimum up to its maximum possible commitment. Would such a long list of alternatives be meaningful? Probably not. To the people running Star Productions, there likely is little difference between an investment of, say, $100,000 and $200,000. Managers would deem any amount within this range about equal in terms of risk and rewards. Thus, the groupings used by Star Productions make sense and ease the technical aspects of solving the problem.

After identifying the collection of decision alternatives, you must decide whether to use probabilities in selecting the best one. The choice depends on the following:

1. The availability of data. For example, to use probabilistic analysis, you will need to obtain estimates of the likelihood of each outcome, and this information may simply be unavailable.
2. The risk preference. The probabilistic analysis identifies the decision that maximizes the expected payoff. However, if you are a conservative investor, you may prefer maximizing the minimum possible payoff by using the pessimistic criterion in Section 11.1 or maximizing the expected utility, as discussed in Section 11.7.

Another issue is the *size* of the problem. Even in a single-level problem, the number of decision alternative-and-outcome combinations can be so large that collecting the payoff data may be too difficult and expensive to be worthwhile. This difficulty is compounded in multilevel decision problems because the size of the decision tree grows very rapidly with each level. You should therefore choose the number of decision levels based on your ability to estimate all the needed payoff and probability information. Even if you *can* obtain all the data, be sure your computer package can handle the size of the resulting decision tree.

Issues Related to the Computer Software

There are numerous software packages for performing decision analysis on a computer. The appropriate choice depends on the characteristics of your problem and the type of analysis desired. In choosing software, ask these questions: Does the package perform analysis with and/or without the use of probabilities? Does it perform single-level and/or multilevel analysis? Does it handle the size of the decision tree in your problem (in terms of the number of nodes and branches)? Can you obtain graphical output and/or tabular reports of the results?

You may also want to see if the software package indicates *alternative optimal decisions*. In some problems, at a given decision point, two or more different decisions may result in the same (expected) payoff. In this case, you would like to list these various alternatives and select the one that is easiest to implement or the one that achieves some secondary objective for the organization. For example, if two decision alternatives have the same expected payoff, you may prefer the one that is less likely to result in a significant loss.

Sensitivity Analysis

After identifying the optimal decision, a manager should realize that this choice is based on the accuracy of the estimated data and the choice of the decision criterion. Slight changes in the data may lead to completely different decisions. You should learn to ask the following "What happens if?" questions: (1) What happens to the optimal decision and payoff if one or more payoffs and/or probabilites change? (2) By how much can one particular payoff or probability change without affecting the optimal decision? Both of these questions can be answered using a computer package. For question (1), change the appropriate data to their new values and resolve the problem.

To answer question (2), however, requires a systematic trial-and-error process. First, increase the datum of interest from its current value by a small amount and re-solve the problem. Continue to do so until the optimal decision changes for the first time. This datum can increase from its original value to approximately this final value without affecting the optimal decision. Then, perform a similar analysis by decreasing the datum from its initial value in small increments. The interval around the original value thus obtained is the *sensitivity range* for this datum. If this range is large, then the optimal decision is not overly sensitive to this value. However, a small range indicates that the optimal decision is quite sensitive to this value. You may wish to spend additional time and effort to obtain a more accurate estimate of the data.

As mentioned, to use decision analysis, you must select one specific decision criterion. What is the right criterion? Try several alternative criteria that are close to your investment goals. If the optimal decision in all (or most) cases remains the same, you can be more confident that this optimal decision fits with your investment philosophy. However, if different criteria result in many different decisions, then the optimal decision depends very heavily on the choice of the criterion. In this case, you may wish to consult colleagues as to the trade-off between the benefits and risks of using the various criteria in making a final decision.

SUMMARY

Decision analysis is a technique for helping managers make decisions to problems whose future outcomes are uncertain. Your problem must have the following characteristics:

1. There is a sequence of points in time at which certain decisions have to be made.
2. At each such decision point, there is a finite number of alternatives available, depending on the previous decisions made, and what has resulted from those decisions.

3. The costs and/or profits associated with each decision depend on an unknown future that can be described by a finite number of possible outcomes after each decision.

4. A sequence of decisions that satisfy an overall organization criterion must be selected.

To determine the optimal decision in a single-level problem, you need to do the following:

1. Select a decision criterion that matches your investment philosophy. The criteria include: optimistic, pessimistic, Hurwicz's, minimax regret, probabilistic, and expected utility.

2. Obtain estimates of the data needed, such as payoffs, and in the probabilistic case, the likelihood of the various outcomes.

3. Perform computations on the basis of the choice in step 1 and the data in step 2.

For multilevel problems, the decisions cannot be made independently of each other because a decision at one point in time can affect significantly the decision at future points in time. To identify the sequence of optimal decisions, you need to do the following:

1. Draw a decision tree representing the alternatives and possible outcomes at each level.

2. Estimate the conditional probabilities of each outcome and the associated additional payoffs.

3. Work backward from the terminal nodes to node 0 in the tree, performing appropriate computations to determine the maximum expected future payoff from the current node (assuming you make the optimal decision at each subsequent decision point).

4. Identify the optimal decisions by starting at node 0, where the optimal decision is known, and for each possible outcome, identify the decision used in obtaining the optimal values in step 3 for the associated node.

EXERCISES

EXERCISE 11.1 Fireworks Unlimited recently suffered a severe loss due to an explosion. Its insurance coverage allows the company a choice of settling for a fixed amount of money—which, after months of negotiation, is $800,000—or rebuilding the factory. In either case, the company is planning to sell out. If the factory is not rebuilt, it must be demolished at a cost of $100,000. After that, the land can be sold as undeveloped commercial real estate. Management believes that the amount of money the company will receive for the real estate depends on the state of the economy at the time of the sale, as listed in the second column of the table that follows. Alternatively, if the factory is rebuilt, the business can be sold directly. The value for the business also depends on the state of the economy at the time of the sale, as listed in the third column of the table.

ECONOMIC CONDITION	ESTIMATED REAL-ESTATE VALUE	ESTIMATED BUSINESS VALUE
Poor	$400,000	$900,000
Average	$700,000	$1,200,000
Good	$1,100,000	$2,000,000

   a. Identify the decision alternatives.
   b. Identify the possible states/outcomes.
   c. Determine the payoff matrix for each alternative-outcome pair—that is, build the payoff matrix.
   d. Construct a decision tree, as described in Section 11.5.

EXERCISE 11.2   The management of California Gas and Electric is in the process of deciding whether to replace its aging fleet of vehicles by purchasing new cars at a cost of $18,000 each or used ones for $10,000 each. Alternatively, it can lease cars for 5 years at a cost per year of $2,500 for new cars and $1,500 for old cars. After 5 years, the company buys the cars that were new for $10,000 and those that were used for $5,000. From past experience, company management knows that the resale value of these new and used cars depends on their condition at the end of the 5 years:

CONDITION	ESTIMATED USED-CAR RESALE VALUE	ESTIMATED NEW-CAR RESALE VALUE
Poor	$2000	$8,000
Fair	$4000	$10,500
Good	$6000	$13,000

   a. Identify the decision alternatives.
   b. Identify the possible states/outcomes.
   c. Build the payoff matrix for each alternative-outcome pair ignoring the time-value of money.
   d. Construct a decision tree, as described in Section 11.5.
   e. Discuss how you can incorporate the time-value of money in building the payoff matrix in part (c). (You need not perform any computations.)

EXERCISE 11.3   The directors of Pension Planners, Inc., must choose one of three comparable mutual funds in which to invest $1 million. The staff of the Research Department has estimated the expected return in 1 year for each of the three mutual funds on the basis of poor, moderate, or excellent performance of the Dow Jones average, as follows:

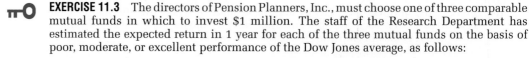

DOW JONES PERFORMANCE	LIKELIHOOD	FUND 1	FUND 2	FUND 3
Poor	0.2	$50,000	$25,000	$40,000
Moderate	0.6	$75,000	$50,000	$60,000
Excellent	0.2	$100,000	$150,000	$175,000

   Use the payoff matrix to compute by hand the optimal decision and associated payoff using each of the following criteria:

   a. Optimistic.
   b. Pessimistic.
   c. Hurwicz's (with $\alpha = 0.6$).
   d. Minimax regret.
   e. Probabilistic with the given values.
   f. Prepare a summary table with your results.

EXERCISE 11.4   Use your computer or otherwise determine what happens to the optimal decision for each criterion in Exercise 11.3 if the projected returns on the three funds are overestimated by 10% if the Dow Jones average performs poorly.

EXERCISE 11.5 For the case in which the Dow Jones average performs moderately, use your computer to determine by how much the estimated return for Fund 2 can increase or decrease (to the nearest thousand dollars) without affecting the optimal decision for each criterion in Exercise 11.3.

EXERCISE 11.6 Suppose that the probability estimate that the Dow Jones average performs poorly is fixed at 0.20 in Exercise 11.3. Use your computer (or otherwise) to determine by how much the remaining probabilities can change without affecting the optimal decision using the probabilistic criterion.

EXERCISE 11.7 Use your computer or otherwise determine the range of values for α for which the optimal decision using Hurwicz's criterion remains the same as computed in Exercise 11.3.

EXERCISE 11.8 For the problem of Pension Planners in Exercise 11.3, compute the following:

- **a.** The optimal decision and payoff for each outcome.
- **b.** The expected payoff without perfect information.
- **c.** The expected payoff with perfect information.
- **d.** The expected value of perfect information using the results of parts (a) to (c).

EXERCISE 11.9 The general partners of Pension Planners in Exercise 11.3 want to conduct a survey of independent money managers to find out if the managers believe the economic climate in the upcoming year will be favorable (I_1) or unfavorable (I_2). The staff of the Research Department estimates that the survey would cost $5000. The staff also believes that if the Dow Jones performance will be poor, the likelihood of the survey resulting in I_1 is 5% and that the likelihood of it resulting in I_2 is 95%. If the Dow Jones performance will be moderate, indicator I_1 is likely to occur 40% of the time and I_2 will happen 60% of the time. If the Dow Jones performance will be excellent, the probability of getting indicator I_1 is 75% and that of I_2 is 25%.

- **a.** Draw an appropriate probability tree.
- **b.** Compute tables with the appropriate joint, marginal, and revised probabilities associated with the market survey.
- **c.** For each indicator, use the revised probabilities of the outcomes to compute the expected payoff for each decision and to determine the optimal decision.
- **d.** Compute the expected payoff without the sample information.
- **e.** Compute the expected payoff with the sample information.
- **f.** Compute the expected value of the sample information.
- **g.** Combine your results in parts (a) to (f) to determine whether or not the survey should be conducted.

EXERCISE 11.10 Combine your results from Exercises 11.8 and 11.9 to compute the efficiency of the sample information.

EXERCISE 11.11 The owners of FastFoods, Inc., are trying to decide whether to build a new outlet at a strip mall, at an indoor mall, or at a remote location that analysts believe has a large growth potential. In addition to a building cost of $100,000 regardless of location, the annual rent on a 5-year lease at the strip mall is $30,000, at the indoor mall is $50,000, and at the remote location is $10,000. The probability that the 5-year sales will be below average is estimated at 0.3. The probability for average 5-year sales is 0.5 and that of above-average 5-year sales is 0.2. The staff of the Marketing Department has prepared the following total 5-year revenue projections for each possible outcome:

30,000 Per YEAR

SALES	STRIP MALL	INDOOR MALL	REMOTE LOCATION
Below average	$100,000	$200,000	$50,000
Average	$200,000	$400,000	$100,000
Above average	$400,000	$600,000	$300,000

Use the payoff matrix to compute by hand the optimal decision and associated payoff using each of the following criteria, ignoring any cash flow after 5 years:

　　a. Optimistic.
　　b. Pessimistic.
　　c. Hurwicz's (with $\alpha = 0.6$).
　　d. Minimax regret.
　　e. Probabilistic with the given values.
　　f. Prepare a summary table with your results.

EXERCISE 11.12　Use your computer or otherwise determine what happens to the optimal decision for each criterion in Exercise 11.11 if the projected below-average revenues are all reduced by 10%.

EXERCISE 11.13　Use your computer or otherwise determine by how much the estimated 5-year revenue at the indoor mall can increase or decrease (to the nearest thousand dollars) under the average projection of sales without affecting the optimal decision for each criterion in Exercise 11.11.

EXERCISE 11.14　Suppose that the probability for an average projection is fixed at 0.50 in Exercise 11.11. Use your computer (or otherwise) determine by how much the remaining probabilities can change without affecting the optimal decision using the probabilistic criterion.

EXERCISE 11.15　Use your computer or otherwise determine the range of values for α for which the optimal decision using Hurwicz's criterion remains the same as computed in Exercise 11.11.

EXERCISE 11.16　For the problem of FastFoods, Inc., in Exercise 11.11, compute the following:

　　a. The optimal decision and payoff for each outcome.
　　b. The expected payoff without perfect information.
　　c. The expected payoff with perfect information.
　　d. The expected value of perfect information using the results of parts (a) to (c).

EXERCISE 11.17　The management of FastFoods, Inc., in Exercise 11.11 is considering hiring Prediction Sciences to conduct a survey to determine whether a significant number of people will (I_1) or will not (I_2) eat at the restaurant on a regular basis. The Marketing Department of Prediction Sciences, in conjunction with FastFoods, Inc., believes that if the sales outcome will be above average, 85% of the time the survey should result in I_1 and 15% of the time in I_2. For the outcome of average sales, both indicators are equally likely. If the sales outcome will be below average, I_1 is 25% likely and I_2 is 75% likely to occur.

　　a. Draw an appropriate probability tree.
　　b. Compute tables with the appropriate joint, marginal, and revised probabilities associated with the market survey.
　　c. For each indicator, use the revised probabilities of the outcomes to compute the expected payoff for each decision and to determine the optimal decision.
　　d. Compute the expected payoff without the sample information.
　　e. Compute the expected payoff with the sample information.

f. Compute the expected value of the sample information.
g. Combine your results in parts (a) to (f) to determine whether or not the survey should be conducted.

EXERCISE 11.18 Combine your results from Exercises 11.16 and 11.17 to compute the efficiency of the sample information.

EXERCISE 11.19 Mr. Joe Williams, an entrepreneur, is considering buying one of the following retail businesses: a camera store, a hardware store, or an electronics store, for approximately the same initial investment. For the camera store, he estimates that there is a 20% chance that the sales performance will be average, resulting in an annual return of $20,000. These values and similar information for the hardware and electronic stores are summarized in the following payoff and probability tables:

PAYOFF TABLE

| STORE | SALES PERFORMANCE | | |
	AVERAGE	GOOD	EXCELLENT
Camera	$20,000	$75,000	$100,000
Hardware	$30,000	$60,000	$100,000
Electronics	$25,000	$75,000	$150,000

PROBABILITY TABLE

| STORE | SALES PERFORMANCE | | |
	AVERAGE	GOOD	EXCELLENT
Camera	0.20	0.60	0.20
Hardware	0.15	0.70	0.15
Electronics	0.05	0.60	0.35

a. Draw an appropriate decision tree identifying the probability and decision nodes.
b. Compute the expected payoff at each probability node.
c. Identify the optimal decision.

EXERCISE 11.20 For the problem of FastFoods, Inc., described in Exercise 11.11, management feels that the probabilities of the sales outcome depend on where the restaurant is located. These probabilities and expected annual revenues for each location are given in the following tables:

STRIP MALL

SALES	PROBABILITY	REVENUE
Below average	0.15	$100,000
Average	0.60	$200,000
Above average	0.25	$400,000

INDOOR MALL

SALES	PROBABILITY	REVENUE
Below average	0.35	$200,000
Average	0.50	$400,000
Above average	0.15	$600,000

REMOTE LOCATION

SALES	PROBABILITY	REVENUE
Below average	0.20	$50,000
Average	0.40	$100,000
Above average	0.20	$300,000

    a. Draw an appropriate decision tree identifying the probability and decision nodes.
    b. Compute the expected payoff at each probability node.
    c. Identify the optimal decision.

EXERCISE 11.21   Larry Litigant has just received a phone call from his attorney, Bernie, informing him that the doctor he sued is willing to settle the case for $25,000. Larry must decide whether to accept this offer. If he rejects it, the attorney estimates a 20% chance that the other side will retract its offer altogether and force a trial, a 60% chance it will leave the offer unchanged, and a 20% chance that it will increase the offer to $35,000. If the other side leaves the offer unchanged or increases it, Larry can again decide to accept the offer or to go to trial. His attorney has indicated that although the case has merit, there are also some weaknesses. How will the judge rule? The attorney estimates a 40% chance that the ruling will favor the doctor, in which case Larry will incur about $10,000 in legal fees; a 50% chance that the ruling will be in favor of Larry for $25,000 in addition to legal fees; and a 10% chance that the ruling will be in favor of Larry for $100,000 in addition to legal fees.

    a. Draw an appropriate decision tree identifying the probability and decision nodes.
    b. Compute by hand the payoff associated with each probability and decision node. Identify the optimal decision at each decision node. Should Larry accept or reject the initial offer?
    c. Use your computer package to verify your results in part (b).

EXERCISE 11.22   Use your computer or otherwise determine by how much the legal expenses of $10,000 can increase (to the nearest thousand dollars) in Exercise 11.21 before the optimal decision is to accept the current settlement offer of $25,000.

EXERCISE 11.23   Use your computer or otherwise determine by how much the amount of a "big judgment" in Exercise 11.21 would have to increase over the current level of $100,000 for Larry to prefer going to trial rather than agreeing to any of the possible settlement offers.

EXERCISE 11.24   For the problem of Home Appliances in Section 11.7, use the utilities in the following table to show that the optimal decision is to buy the dealership having no significant name recognition:

PAYOFF	p	UTILITY ($100 * p$)
15	—	100
7	0.75	75
5	0.70	70
4	0.65	65
3	0.55	55
2	0.50	50
−1	0.35	35
−1	0.35	35
−5	—	0

EXERCISE 11.25 For the problem of FastFoods, Inc., in Exercise 11.11, the utility of the smallest payoff of $-\$150,000$ is set to 0 and that of the largest payoff of $\$250,000$ is set to 100. An interview process with the management, as described in Section 11.7, has resulted in utilities for the remaining payoffs that can be approximated by the following utility function:

$$\text{Utility of } x \text{ thousand dollars } = 18.75 + 0.2x + 0.0005x^2$$

a. Use this function to compute the utilities of all the remaining payoffs.
b. Identify the decision that maximizes the expected utility.

CRITICAL-THINKING PROJECT G
THE EXPANSION PROBLEM OF FASTFOODS, INC.

Mr. Charles Emory, owner of FastFoods, Inc., is considering the 5-year consequences of expanding his restaurant business in one of two ways. The first alternative is to build one large restaurant at a cost of $175,000. The second alternative is to build a small restaurant now, at a cost of $100,000, and then to consider building a second small restaurant at the same cost 1 year from now. As Vice-President of Sales, he has asked you, Mr. Alex Bailey, to analyze the possibilities and to make appropriate recommendations.

Your first step is to estimate the annual profit associated with having a large restaurant, which you feel depends on whether the sales are below average, average, or above average. On the basis of your knowledge of many other large restaurants the company owns in similar locations, you have estimated the following probabilities of these outcomes and the resulting profits in each of the 5 years:

SALES	PROBABILITY	ANNUAL PROFIT
Below average	0.20	−$50,000
Average	0.60	$100,000
Above average	0.20	$140,000

If a small restaurant is built, the outcome at the end of the first year will be either a strong cash flow of $100,000, with a probability you estimate to be 0.6, or a weak cash flow, resulting in a loss of $30,000. Regardless of the cash-flow situation at the end of the first year, you can then choose to build another small restaurant or just keep the existing small restaurant. The annual profit from *each* small restaurant for each of the remaining 4 years of the 5-year planning period depends on whether the sales are below average, average, or above average. The probabilities of these sales outcomes, in turn, are influenced by how successful the first small restaurant is during its first year of operation. Specifically, if the cash-flow status at the end of the first year is strong, then there is a much higher likelihood that the sales from then on will be average or above average, as summarized by your analysis in the following table:

SALES	PROBABILITY	ANNUAL PROFIT
Below average	0.10	−$30,000
Average	0.65	$75,000
Above average	0.25	$100,000

If the outcome after the first year with the first small restaurant is a weak cash flow, there is a much higher likelihood that sales from then on will be below average, as your analysis reveals in the following table:

SALES	PROBABILITY	ANNUAL PROFIT
Below average	0.60	−$30,000
Average	0.30	$75,000
Above average	0.10	$100,000

Ignoring the cash flow after 5 years, write a managerial report for Mr. Emory covering the 5-year planning period of FastFoods, Inc., which should include the following items.

1. Draw an appropriate decision tree that shows the payoff associated with each probability and decision node.

2. Use your computer or otherwise answer the following questions *on the basis of the decision tree you obtain from your instructor:*
   a. Is it better to build a large or a small restaurant initially? What is the expected 5-year return associated with the optimal decision?
   b. Suppose the small restaurant is built first. What decision should be made a year from now? Should you build another small restaurant or not? Does the decision depend on the cash-flow status at the end of the first year? Explain.
   c. After presenting your results, Mr. Emory said that although the company has built many large restaurants and is quite certain of the estimated construction cost of $175,000, the cost for building a small restaurant is much more uncertain. By how much could this cost of $100,000 increase (to the nearest thousand dollars) before the initial decision changes.
   d. Assume the initial construction-cost estimates are correct. Mr. Emory noticed you estimated that after 1 year there is a 60% chance of having a strong cash flow if a small restaurant is built initially. He feels that this probability is only 50%. How does this change affect the initial decision? By how much could this probability decrease from 60% before the initial decision changes?

DECISIONS "ON THE BUBBLE"

As head of a research institute, how do you decide which of 500 to 700 proposed projects to fund? How do you decide the level of funding for those projects you choose to pursue? How do you compare and rank projects that may be as different as apples and oranges? How do you satisfy many different interest groups, each with its favorite project? Ron Edelstein, director of planning and appraisal at the Gas Research Institute (GRI), faces these questions yearly. GRI has an annual $200 million budget to allocate to research projects, so the answers he develops to these questions carry tremendous importance.

GRI is the collective research and development arm of the U.S. natural gas industry, with members drawn from the three segments of the natural gas business—producers, pipelines, and local distribution companies and services. Since 1980, the GRI planning department has used PAM (Project Appraisal Methodology) to help in the initial rankings of projects. PAM makes the first cuts in GRI's search for which projects to fund for the upcoming fiscal year. PAM combines rigorous, single-level decision analysis with the subjective analysis of highly trained, experienced personnel.

Research and development projects may be new products, technologies, processes, or basic research investigations. Projects are evaluated as to potential funding over a five-year horizon and, because they take longer than a year to develop and complete, they are reevaluated annually. Each project is examined using five appraisal criteria—three quantitative and two subjective—for a 30-year payback period. The resulting "scores" are multiplied by the probability of technical and commercial success. Projects are then ranked and assigned a funding level.

Those projects that just make or miss funding are considered "on the bubble." They receive special scrutiny from four groups made up of various specialists within and outside the natural gas industry. Their opinions are passed on to the board of directors, which makes the final funding decisions.

PAM has helped GRI become a successful part of the natural gas industry. Funded projects have yielded 240 products, processes, and techniques that have so far saved the consumer about $10 billion. (Total running time: 12:00.)

Questions on the video

1. What are the five appraisal criteria (three objective, two subjective) that PAM uses in its evaluations?

2. What is the time frame for the projected costs and the time frame for projected benefits?

Beyond the video

1. What are some of the environmental and safety concerns that different energy industries might face?

2. How does PAM take into consideration alternative projects within GRI and competing projects from outside the natural gas industry?

Practical considerations

1. How does GRI introduce the element of risk into the PAM analysis? How, specifically, is risk assessed?

2. How can a tool like PAM help any company use management-by-exception in determining which of its proposed R&D projects to fund each year?

Source: Gas Research Institute, Chicago, Illinois.

CHAPTER 2

INVENTORY MODELS

· ·

Do Not Feed the Animals, the sign warns. So you decide to enjoy the peanuts yourself, but what do the zoo animals eat? The Director at the Metropolitan Zoo must ensure that the animals' meals include the correct blend of protein, vitamins, and bulk. But there is no free lunch in the animal world either. Getting the food on the table (or in the cage) entails costs. There are purchasing costs, ordering costs, and inventory costs. How does the Director strike the proper balance in meeting demand by keeping enough of the proper foods on hand while minimizing the zoo's total costs?

The Case Study in this chapter illustrates how the tools of inventory management help the zoo director formulate the best plan at the best price.

Inventories are those items on hand to be used by or sold to a customer. You are familiar with inventories of, say, an electronics store. The VCRs, tape decks, and so on are the items in inventory. The consumer is the customer. However, the notion of *items* and *customers* can be greatly expanded to many different kinds of businesses.

In a manufacturing setting, the inventories are the raw materials used to produce finished goods. The lumber, nails, varnish, and other materials necessary to build a bookcase are the inventory items. The production facility is the customer.

Consider the surgical unit of a hospital. One aspect of managing this unit is to ensure that there are enough surgical supplies on hand so that there is never a shortage during operations. Here, the surgical supplies are the items. The patients are the customers.

Almost every business has operating expenses—rent, postage, electricity, supplies, and a myriad of other outlays. These expenses are the "customers" and the inventory "item" these customers use is cash.

You can see that the concepts of items in inventory and customers can have many different meanings. The techniques of this chapter apply equally well to them all, regardless of what the specific "items" and "customers" are. Before examining the details of inventory management, first consider the advantages of having large inventories:

1. To avoid shortages. When the future demand for an item is known and timely deliveries from a supplier can be relied on, you can always place orders so that all the demand is met without the need for inventory. However, uncertainty in the demand or delivery times can result in shortages if not enough inventory is maintained. For example, without enough inventory, a hardware store might lose a sale because it runs out of paint due to a higher-than-expected demand. A hospital patient might lose much more if the hospital runs out of surgical supplies when a delay in a shipment occurs. The possibility of a shortage when the demand or the delivery time is uncertain is an argument in favor of maintaining large inventories.

2. To take advantage of economies of scale. By ordering in larger quantities, a business may obtain its supplies at a lower cost. Also, the business would place fewer orders, which saves administrative efforts and costs.

3. To maintain a smooth work flow in a multistage production facility. For example, consider a company that produces athletic shoes. Beginning inventory may be material—the canvas, the rubber for the soles, and so on—that the Cutting Department needs. The cutout shapes are the **work-in-process inventory,** which the Assembly Department glues and stitches together. If a breakdown causes production in the Cutting Department to halt, the Assembly Department can continue operating only by tapping existing work-in-process inventories. More generally, when production rates vary at different stages, a company that maintains work-in-process inventories can keep operations running smoothly. That is, each department can function more independently when it has access to work-in-process inventories.

Each of these reasons argues in favor of having large inventories on hand. But items sitting idly in inventory tie up funds that could be otherwise used or invested to earn profits. Moreover, some items are *perishable*—that is, they have a limited shelf life. For example, the glue that the Assembly Department uses may last only so long. If inventories are too large, some of the old glue may have to be thrown out, at a significant cost.

You can see that there are some reasons to have high inventories and other reasons to have low inventories. **Inventory management** is a technique to help managers evaluate these trade-offs and obtain the answer to the following questions:

1. When should current inventories be replenished?
2. How much should be ordered?

Inventories
Items that are on hand to be used by or sold to a customer.

Work-in-process inventory
Items completed in one stage in a manufacturing process that are used as inventory for the next stage.

Inventory management
The techniques used to help managers determine when current inventories should be replenished and how much should be ordered.

In this chapter, you will learn about several common inventory models and how to use a computer to help manage inventory levels in various settings.

■ 12.1 CHARACTERISTICS OF INVENTORY MODELS

In this section, you will learn about the different characteristics that make up inventory models. These characteristics influence the mathematical analysis used in determining the best way to manage the inventories. When you want to apply inventory management to your business setting, you will need to identify which of these characteristics your model has so that you can use an appropriate computer package to perform the correct analysis.

12.1.1 Independent vs. Dependent Demand

When considering managing the inventory of several different items, you must first determine whether the items are related to each other or not. For example, the demands for most of the individual items in a grocery store are *independent* of each other. The demand for milk this week does not affect the demand for fruit. In contrast, consider an inventory of disk drives, hard disks, and other components for assembling microcomputers. Here, the demand is *dependent* because the demand for the final product—that is, assembled computers—determines the demand for the individual components. A demand for 500 microcomputers each having two disk drives and a hard disk requires 1000 disk drives and 500 hard disks. These demands in turn drive the demands for the components used in making the disk drives and the hard disks, and so on. In these cases, the demand for components and subassemblies is created by the demand for a higher-level product. The models in this chapter are based on the assumption of **independent demand.** The management of inventories involving **dependent demand** requires the technique of *materials requirement planning (MRP)* and is beyond the scope of this book.

Independent demand
Two or more items in which the demand for one item does not affect the demand for any of the other items.

Dependent demand
Two or more items in which the demand for one item determines or affects the demand for one or more of the other items.

12.1.2 Deterministic vs. Probabilistic Demand

The next feature of an inventory system pertains to the type of (independent) demand for the item. There are two basic categories: deterministic demand and probabilistic demand.

Deterministic demand
Demand for an item that is known with certainty.

Probabilistic demand
Demand for an item that is subject to a significant amount of uncertainty and variability.

KEY FEATURES

✔ **Deterministic demand:** the demand for the item per time period is known with certainty. For example, in an automated manufacturing process, you might know that a machine inserts precisely 20 chips per minute on an integrated-circuit board. Here, the chips are the items to be kept in inventory; the machine is the customer; and the deterministic demand is 20 chips per minute.

✔ **Probabilistic demand:** the demand for the item per time period is subject to a significant amount of uncertainty and variability. For example, in a hospital, you do not know how many and what type of patients you will have next week, which results in an uncertain demand for medical supplies.

12.1.3 Shortages

In determining how to maintain inventory levels, a critical issue is whether **shortages,** sometimes called **stockouts,** are allowed. That is, is it acceptable to run out of an item? In a retail store, running out of an item may not be desirable, but management can allow it to happen because the consequences are not critical. In contrast, a hospital should never run out of operating supplies.

When shortages are allowed, another issue is how they are handled. For example, if an item is not currently available in a retail store, the customer may go elsewhere, resulting in a *lost sale*. In contrast, if raw materials are not available in a manufacturing facility, the demand for the raw material remains and is met when the next shipment arrives. In this case, the demand is not lost, but rather is met in subsequent periods. This shortage is said to be handled as a *backorder*.

Shortage, or stockout
A circumstance in which available inventory is insufficient to meet demand.

12.1.4 Lead Times

When an order is placed to replenish inventories, there is a delay, called a **lead time,** in receiving those goods from the supplier. Like demands, lead times are *deterministic* if you know precisely how long it takes to receive the goods, or *probabilistic* if the time of delivery is uncertain. Managers must consider lead times in deciding when to order inventories because customer demand for items continues during this lead time. That is, you must have enough inventory on hand to meet the demand during this period.

Lead time
The time between placing an order for goods and the arrival of those goods from the supplier.

12.1.5 Quantity Discounts

When inventories are replenished from outside suppliers, the amount paid per item may depend on the size of the order. In other words, there may be *quantity discounts*: the more items ordered, the less each item costs. This affects the ordering policy. It may be beneficial to order in larger amounts less frequently if the savings in the purchase costs offset the additional costs of carrying the larger inventory.

12.1.6 Ordering Policy

There are two basic strategies, called **ordering policies,** used in determining when and how much to order.

Ordering policy
An approach for determining how and when to replenish inventories.

➡ **KEY FEATURES**

✔ Order items at fixed time intervals. The amount to order is determined by the inventory level at the time the order is placed. The amount ordered each time varies. For example, consider restocking milk in a grocery store. Every Tuesday the dairy manager orders the milk, and the quantity depends on how many gallons are on the shelf when she places the order. This policy is also called **periodic review** as it requires reviewing the inventory level at fixed points in time to determine how much to order.

✔ Order a fixed number of items when the inventory on hand reaches a certain prespecified level, called the **reorder point.** In this case, the amount ordered is always the same, but the time between orders may vary. For example, a bar manager may reorder beer when the current supply falls below three kegs. This level may be reached in 4 weeks when business is slow or in 1 week when business is brisk, say, during Super Bowl week. This policy is

Periodic review
An ordering policy that requires reviewing the inventory level at fixed points in time to determine how much to order on the basis of the amount of inventory on hand at that time.

Reorder point
The inventory level at which a new order should be placed.

Continuous review
An ordering policy that requires reviewing the inventory continuously to determine when the reorder point is reached.

also called **continuous review** as it requires continuous monitoring of the inventory to determine when the reorder point is reached.

You have seen the characteristics that make up an inventory system. The subsequent mathematical analysis is based on these features and on the costs associated with the system. These cost components are identified in Section 12.2.

■ 12.2 COST COMPONENTS OF AN INVENTORY SYSTEM

Identifying the individual characteristics of the inventory system, as described in Section 12.1, is the first step in determining the optimal inventory policy. Ideally, you want an inventory policy that incurs the least total expected cost per time period. The next step, therefore, is to understand and estimate the various cost components of such a system, as described in this section.

12.2.1 The Ordering, or Setup, Cost (K)

Ordering, or setup cost
(K) The cost for placing an order to replenish inventories that is independent of the number of units ordered.

The cost associated with replenishing an inventory is an **ordering cost** or **setup cost**—denoted by K. This is a fixed cost, independent of the number of units ordered or produced. This cost is incurred each time an order is placed or a machine is set up for a production run.

When placing an order, the cost K may include the clerical and managerial times needed to prepare the order, a charge for transmitting the order by fax, for example, and a fixed charge by the supplier for processing and/or delivering the order. For example, each time a sporting-goods store orders tennis rackets from a wholesaler, it may incur a fixed cost of $50, independent of the number ordered.

When a machine is prepared for a production run to resupply an inventory of finished goods, the fixed setup cost may include the labor and overhead required to prepare the machine and the opportunity cost of the time the machine is not used productively. For example, preparing a machine to produce blue paint after producing red paint may require 2 hours of labor for cleaning the machine and loading the raw materials for the production run. The cost K in this case includes the cost of the labor and the opportunity cost of losing the machine's productivity for 2 hours.

12.2.2 The Purchase Cost (C)

Purchase cost
(C) The cost per item ordered.

Each unit ordered incurs a **purchase cost**—denoted by C—which is a direct cost per unit. For example, when a sporting-goods store orders tennis rackets from a wholesaler, it incurs a cost for each racket ordered (in addition to the fixed cost of the order). If Q rackets—say, 8—each costing $75 are ordered, then

$$\text{Total purchase cost} = (\text{cost per unit}) * (\text{number of units})$$
$$= C * Q$$
$$= 75 * 8$$
$$= \$600$$

As discussed in Section 12.1, the purchase cost per unit may depend on the number of units ordered because of quantity discounts. For example, tennis rackets may cost

$75 each if fewer than 20 are ordered and $70 per racket if 20 or more are ordered. In this case, if Q rackets are ordered, the associated cost is

$$\text{Total purchase cost} = \begin{cases} 75 * Q, & \text{if } Q < 20 \\ 70 * Q, & \text{if } Q \geq 20 \end{cases}$$

12.2.3 The Holding Cost (H)

As mentioned in Section 12.1, there may be a significant **holding cost**—denoted by H. This is a cost per time period for each item in inventory. A holding cost may include the following:

Holding cost (H)
The cost per time period for each item held in inventory.

1. The storage costs made up of warehouse overhead, insurance, special handling requirements (such as refrigeration), pilferage, breakage, and the like. When a warehouse is used for many different products, it is difficult to determine how much of the total storage costs pertain to each individual product. A common accounting practice, therefore, is to estimate the storage cost of an individual item as a fraction of its unit cost. For example, the cost for storing a motor home for 1 year might be estimated at $1000, which is the fraction 0.05 of its $20,000 value.

2. The opportunity cost of the money tied up in inventory that could otherwise have been used or invested. For example, consider a business that maintains an inventory of 100 motor homes, each costing $20,000. This inventory costs $2 million. Had this money been invested at, say, a rate of 6% per year, it would have earned $120,000 for the year. This $120,000 is the opportunity cost per year of the inventory. This opportunity cost is a fraction (0.06) of the cost of the item.

The total storage and opportunity costs that make up the holding costs are computed as a fraction i of the unit cost C described in Section 12.2.2. The fraction i is called the **carrying rate** and is the sum of the fractions used in computing the storage and opportunity costs. For example, the carrying rate for the motor home is $i = 0.05 + 0.06 = 0.11$ per year. In general, the total holding cost per time period for each unit of the item in inventory is

Carrying rate (i)
The fraction of the purchase cost of an item often used to compute the holding cost.

$$H = (\text{carrying rate per period}) * (\text{cost of the unit})$$
$$= i * C$$

For example, for the motor home valued at $20,000 with a carrying rate of 0.11, the holding cost per year for each unit is

$$H = i * C$$
$$= 0.11 * 20000$$
$$= \$2200$$

12.2.4 The Shortage Cost (B)

The **shortage cost** is the cost of not meeting demand. That is, it is the cost of running out of the item. Recall that when demand cannot be met, the sale is lost or the item is backordered. For example, if a steel manufacturer is unable to meet a demand of 15 tons, this amount is a lost sale if the customer goes elsewhere or is backordered if the customer is willing to wait.

Shortage cost (B)
The cost associated with not meeting demand.

The shortage costs often consist of two components:

1. An *explicit cost* associated with each unit of shortage. The company that cannot meet the order may give its customer a discount on the amount backordered. For

example, the steel company may have to offer a discount of $500 on each of the 15 tons of shortage. Alternatively, the company may obtain the amount needed to fulfill the order from an outside supplier. Obviously this cost cuts into the company's profits. Of course, the loss of potential profit is also an explicit cost if the customer goes elsewhere.

2. An *implicit cost* associated with lost customer satisfaction. For example, the fact that a customer is unable to obtain your product on time may result in the loss of goodwill, thus affecting subsequent orders.

The explicit costs can often be obtained from actual data, but the implicit costs are estimated subjectively. In any event, to perform the subsequent economic analysis, you need to identify a shortage cost B for each unit of unsatisfied demand. This cost is the amount that you feel is an accurate penalty for not meeting demand. For example, when estimating this cost for critical surgical supplies in a hospital, this cost should be set at infinity to indicate that such shortages are infinitely expensive and must not occur.

When items are backordered, in addition to these fixed costs, the shortage costs may include a time-dependent component in the form of explicit and implicit costs *for each unit of time* an item remains backordered. For example, in addition to a $500 discount for each ton of steel short, a company may also have to pay a further discount of $50 per ton for each week the order is late.

■ 12.3 THE ECONOMIC-ORDER-QUANTITY (EOQ) INVENTORY MODEL

As discussed in Section 12.1, the mathematical analysis for an inventory system depends on the specific characteristics of the model.

Economic-order-quantity (EOQ) model
A mathematical model used as the basis for inventory management in which the demand and lead time are deterministic, shortages are not allowed, and inventory is replaced in batches all at once.

KEY FEATURES

In this section, such an analysis is performed for one commonly occurring model—the **economic-order-quantity (EOQ) model**—in which the following characteristics are assumed to hold:

✔ The inventory pertains to one and only one item.

✔ The inventory is replenished in batches rather than being replaced continuously over time.

✔ The demand is deterministic and occurs at a known constant rate of D units per time period.

✔ The lead time L is deterministic and known (for example, $L = 2$ weeks means that an order placed today arrives in inventory 2 weeks later).

✔ Shortages are not allowed. That is, there must always be enough inventory on hand to meet the demand. (This can be accomplished because the demand is deterministic.)

✔ Ordering occurs in a fixed quantity Q^* when the inventory reaches a certain reorder point R. Implementing this reorder policy therefore requires monitoring the inventory regularly to determine when level R is reached. The appropriate values of both Q^* and R are chosen to achieve an overall minimum total cost based on the following components:

a. A fixed ordering cost of K per order.

b. A purchase cost of C per unit regardless of the number of the units ordered (that is, there is no quantity discount).

  c. A carrying rate of i (that is, the holding cost is $H = i * C$ for each unit in inventory per time period).
  d. Shortage costs are irrelevant because shortages are not allowed.

12.3.1 An Example of an EOQ Problem

To illustrate the EOQ model, consider the problem you face as Manager of Supplies for Suburban Hospital.

EXAMPLE 12.1 THE EOQ INVENTORY PROBLEM OF SUBURBAN HOSPITAL Suburban Hospital serves a small community. One supply used frequently is X-ray film, which is ordered from an out-of-town supplier. As Manager of Supplies, you are to determine how and when to place orders to ensure that the hospital never runs out of this critical item and, at the same time, keep the total cost as low as possible. ∎

Inventory
EX12_1.DAT

To perform the analysis, you must first identify the characteristic of the system. In this case:

1. Only one item is being considered: X-ray film.
2. This film is replaced in batches ordered from the out-of-town supplier.
3. Past records indicate that demand has been relatively constant at 1500 films per month and so can be considered deterministic.
4. The supplier has committed to meet orders in 1 week (that is, the lead time is $L = 1$ week).
5. Shortages are not allowed, as specified by hospital management.

Having identified these characteristics, you have as your objective to determine the optimal order quantity, denoted by Q^*, and associated reorder point, R. To do so, you must first obtain estimates of the relevant cost components listed. Suppose the Accounting Department of the hospital has provided the following values:

1. A fixed ordering cost of $100 to cover the costs of placing each order, paying delivery charges, and so on.
2. A purchase cost of $20 per film with no quantity discount.
3. A carrying rate of 30% per year (that is, $i = 0.30$) to reflect the cost of storing the film in a special area as well as the opportunity cost of the money invested in the idle inventory.

12.3.2 Computing the Optimal Order Quantity

You will notice that the various data values provided by the Accounting Department have different time units. For example, the carrying rate is 30% per *year*, the demand is 1500 films per *month*, and the lead time is 1 *week*. The first step, therefore, is to express all these quantities in terms of a common time period. Although you are free to choose the time period, you must use that value consistently throughout the analysis. In this case, suppose a year is chosen as the common time period. The hospital operates all 52 weeks during the year, so this choice of time period results in the following values:

1. Annual demand $D = (1500 \text{ films/month}) * (12 \text{ months/year}) = 18,000$ films per year
2. Lead time $L = 1$ week $= 1/52$ of a year
3. Annual carrying rate of $i = 0.30$

4. Ordering cost $K = \$100$ per order
5. Purchase cost $C = \$20$ per film
6. Annual holding cost $H = i * C = 0.30 * 20 = \$6$ per film per year

To understand how the order quantity Q impacts the inventory level over time, suppose that you are ordering in batches of $Q = 4500$ films and that you are starting with precisely this many films in stock, as indicated in Figure 12.1. The horizontal axis represents the time in years; the vertical axis represents the inventory level—that is, the number of X-ray films on hand. The demand is deterministic, so these original 4500 films diminish at the constant rate of $D = 18,000$ per year. Thus, it is easy to see that in 1/4 year, this original inventory decreases to 0. As shown in Figure 12.1, the straight line connecting the original inventory level of 4500 at time 0 to the final inventory of 0 at time 0.25 (which is Q/D) year indicates how the inventory decreases continuously over that time interval.

Shortages are not allowed, so the first order of $Q = 4500$ films should be placed to ensure that it arrives not later than 0.25 year. However, if the order arrives too soon, you will incur unnecessary holding costs. Thus, given the lead time of 1/52 year—that is, 1 week—this order should be placed at precisely 1/52 year before the current inventory is scheduled to run out. Doing so replenishes the inventory at time 0.25 year from 0 to its starting level of $Q = 4500$ films, and the process is repeated, as shown in Figure 12.1.

To evaluate the policy of ordering $Q = 4500$ films, you can compute the associated annual cost as follows:

$$\begin{Bmatrix} \text{Total} \\ \text{annual cost} \end{Bmatrix} = \begin{Bmatrix} \text{annual} \\ \text{ordering cost} \end{Bmatrix} + \begin{Bmatrix} \text{annual} \\ \text{purchase cost} \end{Bmatrix} + \begin{Bmatrix} \text{annual} \\ \text{holding cost} \end{Bmatrix}$$

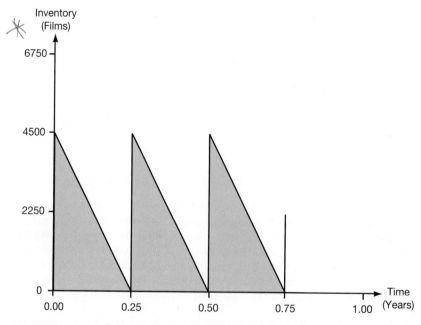

FIGURE 12.1 Inventory Behavior of X-Ray Film for Suburban Hospital with $Q = 4500$.

The annual ordering cost is the cost per order times the number of orders per year. Because the annual demand is $D = 18,000$ films and orders are placed in quantities of $Q = 4500$, there are four orders $(18000/4500 = D/Q)$ placed each year. Thus,

$$\text{Annual ordering cost} = (\text{cost per order}) * (\text{number of orders})$$
$$= K * (D/Q)$$
$$= 100 * (18000/4500)$$
$$= 400$$

The total annual purchase cost is simply the cost per film times the number of films ordered in a year:

$$\text{Annual purchase cost} = (\text{cost per unit}) * (\text{demand})$$
$$= C * D$$
$$= 20 * 18000$$
$$= 360,000$$

The holding cost depends on the number of units in inventory. In each order cycle, this number varies from a maximum value of 4500 down to 0 at a constant rate. On average, there are $Q/2 = 2250$ films in storage throughout the year. The annual holding cost is the average number of units in inventory times the cost of holding each unit for a year. The carrying rate of $i = 0.30$, so the annual holding cost is:

$$\left\{ \begin{array}{l} \text{Annual} \\ \text{holding cost} \end{array} \right\} = \left\{ \begin{array}{l} \text{average} \\ \text{inventory} \end{array} \right\} * \left\{ \begin{array}{l} \text{annual} \\ \text{holding cost} \\ \text{per unit} \end{array} \right\}$$
$$= (Q/2) * H$$
$$= (Q/2) * (i * C)$$
$$= 2250 * (0.30 * 20)$$
$$= 13,500$$

Combining the three components results in the following total annual cost when ordering in quantities of size $Q = 4500$:

$$\left\{ \begin{array}{l} \text{Total} \\ \text{annual cost} \end{array} \right\} = \left\{ \begin{array}{l} \text{annual} \\ \text{ordering cost} \end{array} \right\} + \left\{ \begin{array}{l} \text{annual} \\ \text{purchase cost} \end{array} \right\} + \left\{ \begin{array}{l} \text{annual} \\ \text{holding cost} \end{array} \right\}$$
$$= 400 + 360000 + 13500$$
$$= 373,900$$

The idea now is to perform a similar economic analysis for different order quantities Q and then to identify the one incurring the least total annual cost. Although you could do this on a trial-and-error basis, it is possible to write an expression for this total annual cost in terms of the *unknown* order quantity Q and the other *known* problem data. Figure 12.2 illustrates how the inventory changes over time when a general unknown order quantity Q is used. From the economic analysis, the associated total annual cost in terms of Q, K, D, i, and C is

$$\left\{ \begin{array}{l} \text{Total} \\ \text{annual cost} \end{array} \right\} = \left\{ \begin{array}{l} \text{annual} \\ \text{ordering cost} \end{array} \right\} + \left\{ \begin{array}{l} \text{annual} \\ \text{purchase cost} \end{array} \right\} + \left\{ \begin{array}{l} \text{annual} \\ \text{holding cost} \end{array} \right\}$$
$$= (K * D/Q) + (C * D) + (\tfrac{1}{2} Q * i * C)$$

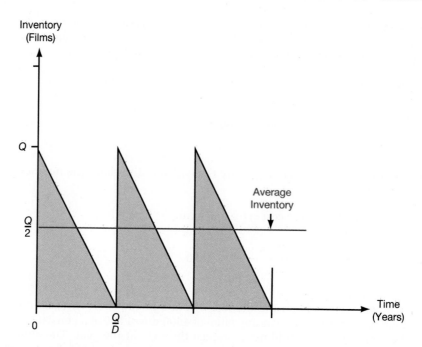

FIGURE 12.2 Inventory Behavior of X-Ray Film for Suburban Hospital with Order Quantity Q.

From this expression you can see that as Q increases:

1. The annual ordering cost of $(K * D/Q)$ decreases, as shown in Figure 12.3(a).
2. The annual purchase cost of $(C * D)$ remains unchanged, as shown in Figure 12.3(b).
3. The annual holding cost of $(\frac{1}{2}Q) * i * C$ increases linearly, as shown in Figure 12.3(c).

Economic order quantity
The amount to order in an EOQ model that achieves the minimum total cost.

Because the annual purchase cost of $(C * D)$ does not depend on Q, this component remains constant as Q changes. In contrast, the annual ordering and holding costs *do* depend on Q, and thus these components vary in value as Q changes. Observe that a large value of Q reduces the ordering costs and a small value of Q reduces the holding costs. The objective is to find the **economic order quantity,** Q^*, that achieves the minimum *total* cost consisting of these three components, as seen in Figure 12.3(d). As shown in Appendix 12A, researchers have used calculus to determine that the economic order quantity is

$$Q^* = \sqrt{\frac{2 * D * K}{H}}$$

$$= \sqrt{\frac{2 * D * K}{i * C}}$$

For the problem of Suburban Hospital, $D = 18,000$, $K = 100$, $i = 0.30$, and $C = 20$, so the economic order quantity is

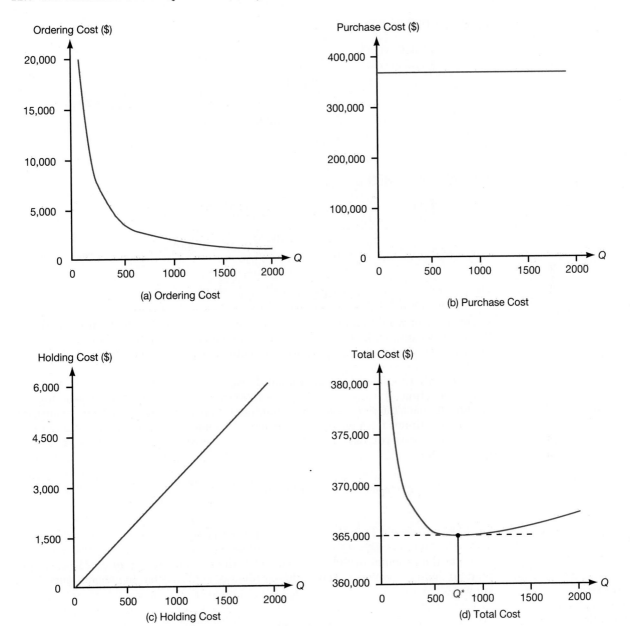

FIGURE 12.3 Costs as a Function of the Order Quantity Q.

$$Q^* = \sqrt{\frac{2 * D * K}{i * C}}$$

$$= \sqrt{\frac{2 * 18000 * 100}{0.30 * 20}}$$

$$= 774.60$$

Because it is not possible to order fractions of X-ray films, the order quantity should be either 774 or 775. To determine which one, compute the total annual cost associated with each of these values as follows:

ANNUAL COST WHEN $Q = 774$

$$\left\{\begin{matrix} \text{Total} \\ \text{annual cost} \end{matrix}\right\} = (K * D/Q) + (C * D) + (\tfrac{1}{2}Q * i * C)$$

$$= \left(\frac{100 * 18000}{774}\right) + (20 * 18000) + \left(\frac{774}{2 * 0.30 * 20}\right)$$

$$= 2325.58 + 360000 + 2322$$

$$= 364{,}647.58$$

ANNUAL COST WHEN $Q = 775$

$$\left\{\begin{matrix} \text{Total} \\ \text{annual cost} \end{matrix}\right\} = (K * D/Q) + (C * D) + (\tfrac{1}{2}Q * i * C)$$

$$= \left(\frac{100 * 18000}{775}\right) + (20 * 18000) + \left(\frac{775}{2 * 0.30 * 20}\right)$$

$$= 2322.58 + 360000 + 2325$$

$$= 364{,}647.58$$

In general you would choose the order quantity that provides the least total cost. In this case, because both costs are the same, you can choose to order either 774 or 775 films each time, at a total annual cost of $364,647.58. Suppose you decide to order 775 films.

Note that to meet the total annual demand of 18,000 films when 775 films are ordered at a time, it is necessary to place $18000/775 = 23.23$ orders each year. It is not possible to place fractions of an order, but there is no need to do so. This is because the demand continues from one year to the next. In some years you may place 23 orders, and in other years you may place 24 in such a way as to average 23.23. In general, once Q^* is known,

$$\text{Average number of orders per period} = \frac{\text{demand per period}}{\text{order quantity}}$$

$$= \frac{D}{Q^*}$$

For the problem of Suburban Hospital, there is an average of 23.23 orders per year. So the time between each of these orders is $1/23.23$ year. In general, once Q^* is known,

$$\text{Time between orders} = \frac{\text{order quantity}}{\text{demand per period}}$$

$$= \frac{Q^*}{D}$$

12.3.3 Determining the Reorder Point

You have seen that it is optimal to order 775 films an average of 23.23 times per year. The next step is to determine *when* to place those orders. That is, it is necessary to identify the *reorder point*—the inventory level at which to place an order so that the current inventory level just reaches 0 when the new order arrives. Recall that the lead time for receiving an order for the problem of Suburban Hospital is $1/52$ year. The question, therefore, is how many films are needed in inventory to cover the demand during this lead time while the order is being filled?

Because 18,000 films are demanded each year, $18,000 * (1/52) = 346.15$ films are needed during this lead time. In other words, when the inventory of X-ray films reaches a level of 346 films, a new order for 775 films should be placed, as shown in Figure 12.4. When that order is received 1 week later, the current inventory of 346 films will have just reached 0.

In general, given the lead time L and the demand D, the reorder point R is computed as follows:

$$\text{Reorder point } (R) = \text{ demand during the lead time}$$
$$= D * L$$

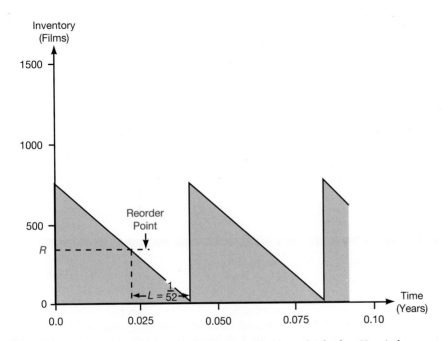

FIGURE 12.4 Determining the Reorder Point for the Problem of Suburban Hospital.

12.3.4 *The EOQ Model: Using the Computer*

Now that you know the idea behind obtaining the optimal inventory policy for an EOQ model, you can use the computer to perform the computations. The results of solving the EOQ problem of Suburban Hospital on STORM are shown in Figure 12.5. The first portion of the report confirms the optimal order quantity of $Q^* = 775$ films and the reorder point of $R = 346$. Note, too, that the number of orders is confirmed at 23.2 per year. The final column of the report in Figure 12.5 indicates that at any point in time, at most one order is waiting to be received. In general, however, when the lead time is large, more than one order might be outstanding. For example, if the lead time is 0.10 of a year, then, from Figure 12.4, you can see that at the beginning of the third cycle, the two previous orders have not yet arrived. In this case, there are *two* outstanding orders.

The second part of the report in Figure 12.5 (AGGREGATE INVENTORY VALUES) pertains to the annual costs associated with this inventory policy. This optimal policy incurs a total cost of $4,647.58 per year. Observe that this value does *not* include the constant cost of $360,000 for purchasing the 18,000 films per year at $20 each. Thus, the *total* cost is $360,000 + \$4,647.58 = \$364,647.58$, which is the same as the amount obtained in Section 12.3.2. As discussed there, the cost of $4,647.58 consists

Inventory
EX12_1.DAT

```
              The EOQ Model of the Suburban Hospital
                        ORDERING INFORMATION
       Item           Item    Orders /    Order     Reorder  Max Orders
       Name           ID      Setups      Size      Point    Outstanding

       X-RAY FILM      1        23.2        775       346        1




              The EOQ Model of the Suburban Hospital
                  AGGREGATE INVENTORY VALUES
               Inventory carrying charge = 30.00%
                      Service level = 95.00%


     Total number of items . . . . . . . . . . . .          1


     Average working stock investment ($) . . . . . . .     7750.00

     Cost to order EOQ items ($/yr) . . . . . . . . .       2322.58
     Average working stock carrying cost ($/yr) . . . .     2325.00
     Total cost ($/yr) . . . . . . . . . . . . .            4647.58

     Number of orders of EOQ item . . . . . . . . . .       23
```

FIGURE 12.5 STORM Results for the EOQ Problem of Suburban Hospital.

of an annual ordering cost of $2,322.58 and an annual carrying cost of $2,325.00, as indicated in the report in Figure 12.5. In fact, these two costs are always equal for the optimal order quantity in an EOQ model. In this case, these two costs are slightly different because the order quantity, Q^*, was rounded to an integer value.

Recall from Section 12.3.2 that the average inventory during a cycle is one-half of the maximum inventory level, which is $775/2 = 387.5$ films. The associated value is 387.5 films $* \$20$ per film $= \$7,750.00$. This value tells the manager that an average of $7,750.00 is tied up in inventory throughout the year and is reported as the "average working stock investment" in Figure 12.5.

These results are confirmed by the output obtained from the QSB software package in Figure 12.6. The first portion of the report shows the data that were entered; the second portion shows the results. The first line of the EOQ Output section indicates an optimal order quantity of 774.597 X-ray films, which is also the maximum inventory level during a cycle. The row labeled "Maximum backorder" is not relevant because backorders are not allowed in this problem. The value of 0.043 in the row labeled "Order interval" is the time between placing orders. That is, an order is placed every 0.043 year. In other words, there are $1/0.043 = 23.2$ orders placed each year. This value matches that obtained from STORM in Figure 12.5.

The remaining lines of the report in Figure 12.6 pertain to the costs of the EOQ policy. The annual order and holding costs are both $2323.79, which is about the same as the corresponding values obtained from STORM in Figure 12.5. The difference occurs because in STORM the order quantity has been rounded up to 775 X-ray films. The value of 360000.000 in the row labeled "Material cost per year" is the total annual cost of ordering the 18,000 films at $20 per film. Finally, note that the total annual cost of $364,647.59 in the last line of the report in Figure 12.6 is the same (except for one penny) as what was computed in Section 12.3.2.

```
              EOQ Results for Suburban Hospital

Input Data:
     Demand per year (D) =  18000
     Order or setup cost per order (Co) =  100
     Holding cost per unit per year (Ch) =  6
     Shortage cost per unit per year (Cs) =  1
     Shortage cost per unit, independent of time (c) =  0
     Replenishment or production rate per year (P) =  1
     Lead time for a new order in year (LT) =  .0192307
     Unit cost (C) =  20
EOQ Output:
     EOQ                 =        774.597
     Maximum inventory =          774.597
     Maximum backorder =            0.000
     Order interval    =            0.043 year
     Reorder point     =          346.153
          Ordering cost =         2323.790
          Holding cost  =         2323.790
          Shortage cost =            0.000
     Subtotal of inventory cost per year    =        4647.580
     Material cost per year                 =      360000.000
     Total cost per year                    =      364647.590
```

FIGURE 12.6 QSB Results for the EOQ Problem of Suburban Hospital.

➡ ## KEY FEATURES

In summary, to determine the optimal inventory policy for a problem satisfying the six assumptions listed at the beginning of Section 12.3, you must first estimate the following data:

$$D = \text{the demand per period}$$

$$L = \text{the lead time for receiving an order}$$

$$i = \text{the carrying rate per period}$$

$$K = \text{the fixed cost of placing an order}$$

$$C = \text{the purchase cost of ordering each unit}$$

$$H = i * C = \text{the holding cost per unit per period}$$

You can then calculate the economic order quantity (Q^*), the average number of orders per period, the time between orders, and the reorder point (R) as follows:

$$Q^* = \sqrt{\frac{2 * D * K}{H}}$$

$$= \sqrt{\frac{2 * D * K}{i * C}}$$

$$\text{Average number of orders } = D/Q^*$$
$$\text{Time between orders } = Q^*/D$$
$$\text{Reorder point } R = D * L$$

In determining these values, it is assumed that each unit is ordered at a purchase cost of $C. In many problems, however, discounts are given for large orders. The analysis in the next section looks at this situation.

■ 12.4 THE ECONOMIC-ORDER-QUANTITY MODEL WITH QUANTITY DISCOUNTS

As presented in Section 12.3, you can determine the economic order quantity and reorder point for an EOQ model in which the unit purchase cost does not depend on the quantity ordered. In many practical situations, however, suppliers offer significant discounts for placing larger orders. Determining the optimal inventory policy when quantity discounts are available in an EOQ model is the objective of this section.

12.4.1 An Example of an EOQ Problem with Quantity Discounts

Consider the following modification to the problem of Suburban Hospital.

Inventory
EX12_2.DAT

EXAMPLE 12.2 THE INVENTORY PROBLEM OF THE SUBURBAN HOSPITAL WITH QUANTITY DISCOUNTS As described in Section 12.3, you as Manager of Supplies determined an optimal inventory policy based on a purchase cost of $20 per film. Just recently, however, you have received a new price list from the supplier that offers a quantity discount for placing large orders. This is given in what follows, together with the other original problem data:

1. An annual demand of $D = 18,000$ films per year.
2. A lead time of 1 week, that is, $L = 1/52$ year.
3. An annual carrying rate of $i = 0.30$ per year.
4. A fixed ordering cost of $K = \$100$ per order.
5. A purchase cost C based on the number of films ordered as follows:

NUMBER ORDERED	COST PER UNIT ($)
1–499	20
500–999	18
1000 and over	16

For example, if 700 films are ordered, each one costs $18. A total purchase cost of $12,600 results.

6. An annual holding cost of $H = i * C$ that now depends on the number of films ordered and the associated unit cost (C).

How do these quantity discounts affect the optimal order policy? ■

12.4.2 Computing the Optimal Order Quantity

One way to handle quantity discounts is to take the following three steps:

Step 1. For each unit cost C in the table in Section 12.4.1, determine the optimal order quantity in the associated range. For example, for $C = \$16$, determine the order quantity above 1000 units that incurs the least total cost.

Step 2. For each unit cost C, compute the total annual cost based on the optimal order quantity determined in Step 1.

Step 3. Select the unit cost and associated order quantity that result in the least total annual cost, as calculated in Step 2.

To determine the optimal order quantities for each unit cost C as required in Step 1, you might first try using the EOQ formula from Section 12.3, as follows:

PURCHASE COST, C ($/UNIT)	$Q^* = \sqrt{\frac{2*D*K}{i*C}}$
20	775
18	816
16	866

However, the EOQ formula does not ensure that the resulting order quantities are within the ranges over which the unit prices are valid. For example, look at the EOQ order quantity of 866 associated with the cost of $16 per film. This value is below the minimum of 1000 that the supplier requires before dropping the cost to $16 per film. Similarly, the order quantity of 775 associated with the cost of $20 per film is outside the required range of 1–499.

From these computations you can see that the EOQ formula may not result in an order quantity that lies *within the associated range over which that unit cost is applicable*. To find that quantity, look at Figures 12.7(a) to 12.7(c), which show how the total annual cost varies with the order quantity for each of the three different unit costs. Observe the following:

1. When the cost is $20 per film, the order quantity of 775 obtained from the EOQ formula in Section 12.3 exceeds the upper limit of 499. As you can see in Figure 12.7(a), the total annual cost in the range of 1–499 is minimized when 499 films are ordered.
2. When the cost is $18 per film, the order quantity of 816 obtained from the EOQ formula lies in the associated range of 500–999. As seen in Figure 12.7(b), this is precisely where the total annual cost is minimized.
3. When the cost is $16 per film, the order quantity of 866 obtained from the EOQ formula is below the lower limit of 1000. As you can see in Figure 12.7(c), the total annual cost in the range of 1000 and above is minimized when 1000 films are ordered.

KEY FEATURES

It is possible to compute the optimal order quantity for each unit cost according to the following general rules:

✔ If the order quantity Q determined by the EOQ model is above the upper limit of the range associated with the unit cost, then the upper limit of the range is the best order quantity for this unit cost. This is the case when you consider the purchase price of $C = \$20$ per film.

✔ If the order quantity Q determined by the EOQ model is within the range associated with the unit cost, then Q is the best order quantity for this unit cost. This is the case when you consider the purchase price of $C = \$18$ per film.

✔ If the order quantity Q determined by the EOQ model is below the lower limit of the range associated with the unit cost, then the lower limit of the range is the best order quantity for this unit cost. This is the case when you consider the purchase price of $C = \$16$ per film.

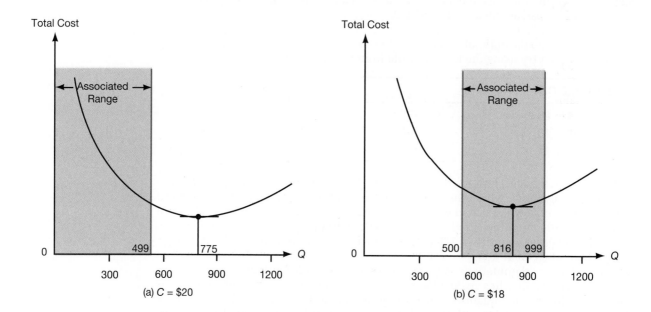

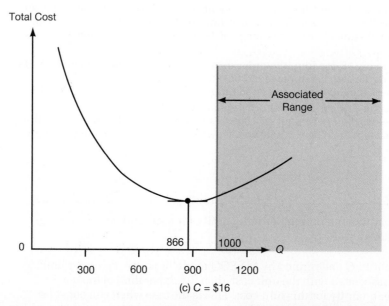

FIGURE 12.7 Total Annual Cost as a Function of Q for Each Value of C for the Problem of Suburban Hospital.

Once the best order quantity within each range is found, it is possible to compute the associated total cost, as required in step 2. This is done using the following formula from Section 12.3:

$$\left\{\begin{matrix}\text{Total} \\ \text{annual cost}\end{matrix}\right\} = \left\{\begin{matrix}\text{annual} \\ \text{ordering cost}\end{matrix}\right\} + \left\{\begin{matrix}\text{annual} \\ \text{purchase cost}\end{matrix}\right\} + \left\{\begin{matrix}\text{annual} \\ \text{holding cost}\end{matrix}\right\}$$

$$= (K * D/Q) + (C * D) + (\tfrac{1}{2}Q * i * C)$$

Using this formula for this example results in the following information for each range:

NUMBER ORDERED	COST PER UNIT (C)	BEST Q	TOTAL COST ($)
1–499	20	499	365,104.21
500–999	18	816	328,409.08
1000 and over	16	1000	292,200.00

From this table, you can easily identify the optimal order quantity of 1000, as required in step 3. Its associated total cost of $292,200 is the least of the three alternatives.

You can now determine the average number of orders and the reorder point, as follows:

$$\text{Average number of orders} = D/Q^*$$
$$= 18000/1000$$
$$= 18$$

$$\text{Reorder point } (R) = D * L$$
$$= 18000 * (1/52)$$
$$= 346.15$$

KEY FEATURES

In summary, when quantity discounts are available for an EOQ model in the form of different unit costs depending on the number of units ordered, as specified by a range of values, the optimal inventory policy is determined as follows:

Step 1. For each unit cost C, determine the best order quantity in the associated range, as follows:

    a. For each range and associated unit cost, compute the order quantity Q by the standard EOQ formula:

$$Q = \sqrt{\frac{2 * D * K}{H}}$$
$$= \sqrt{\frac{2 * D * K}{i * C}}$$

b. For each range, use the value of Q computed in (a) to determine the best order quantity, Q', whose value *is* within the range, as follows:

$$Q' = \begin{cases} \text{lower limit} & \text{if } Q < \text{lower limit} \\ Q & \text{if } Q \text{ is in the range} \\ \text{upper limit} & \text{if } Q > \text{upper limit} \end{cases}$$

That is, the best order quantity Q' is Q if Q is within the range, and the nearest limit to Q otherwise.

Step 2. For each range, use the best order quantity computed in Step 1(b) together with the associated unit cost to determine the total cost per period using the formula:

$$\begin{Bmatrix} \text{Total} \\ \text{annual cost} \end{Bmatrix} = \begin{Bmatrix} \text{annual} \\ \text{ordering cost} \end{Bmatrix} + \begin{Bmatrix} \text{annual} \\ \text{purchase cost} \end{Bmatrix} + \begin{Bmatrix} \text{annual} \\ \text{holding cost} \end{Bmatrix}$$

$$= (K * D/Q') + (C * D) + (\tfrac{1}{2}Q' * i * C)$$

Step 3. Identify the order quantity, Q^*, in Step 2 that incurs the least total cost.

Using the value of Q^* from Step 3, compute the average number of orders per period and the reorder point R as follows:

$$\text{Average number of orders } = D/Q^*$$

$$\text{Reorder point } R = D * L$$

■ 12.5 THE PRODUCTION-ORDER-QUANTITY (POQ) INVENTORY MODEL

The mathematical analysis for an inventory system in which an order is replenished all at once at a fixed point in time is presented in Section 12.3. However, in many production settings, such as when a car manufacturer stocks parts to meet the demand for the assembly plants, the inventory is replenished continuously over time as the production proceeds. For such inventory problems, a manager needs to determine the following:

Production-order-quantity (POQ) model
A mathematical model used as the basis for inventory management in which the demand and lead time are deterministic, shortages are not allowed, and inventory is replaced continuously over time through a production process.

1. When to issue a production order.
2. How many units of the item to produce.

KEY FEATURES

In this section, the mathematical analysis is performed for a **production-order-quantity (POQ) model,** in which the following characteristics are assumed to hold:

✔ The inventory pertains to one and only one item.
✔ The demand for the item is deterministic and occurs at a known rate of D units per time period. For example, $D = 6000$ parts per year.

> ✔ The lead time L is deterministic and known. For example, $L = 2$ weeks means that a production order, once placed, requires 2 weeks of setup time, tooling, and so on before production can begin to replenish the inventory.
> ✔ The order is produced at a known *production rate* of P units per time period. For example, $P = 10,000$ parts per year.
> ✔ The cost of producing each unit is fixed and does not depend on the number of units in the production run.
> ✔ Shortages are not allowed—that is, there must always be enough inventory on hand to meet the demand. This goal can be achieved because the demand is deterministic.
> ✔ When the inventory reaches a level R, a production order for Q^* units is issued. The appropriate values for both Q^* and R are chosen to achieve an overall minimum total cost based on the following components:
>   a. A fixed production-setup cost of $\$K$ per order.
>   b. A holding cost H per unit per period in the form of $i * C$, where C is the value of one unit, and i is the carrying rate per period. Note that C may include the production cost, the value of the materials used, overhead, and so on.
>   c. Shortage costs are irrelevant because shortages are not allowed.

12.5.1 An Example of a POQ Problem

Consider the problem faced by Home Appliances.

EXAMPLE 12.3 THE POQ INVENTORY PROBLEM OF HOME APPLIANCES Home Appliances is a manufacturer of refrigerators, stoves, and other large appliances that are supplied to retail stores throughout the country. Because of the high costs of producing refrigerators, you, as Production Manager, want to determine how many and when to produce them to meet an anticipated demand of 6000 per year. Of course, you want to incur the least total cost of doing so. ∎

Inventory
EX12_3.DAT

To perform the analysis, you must first identify the characteristic and data of the system. In this case:

1. Only one item is being considered—the refrigerators.
2. The demand is relatively constant at a rate of $D = 6000$ refrigerators per year.
3. To start a production run requires a setup time of 1 week—that is, lead time $L = 1$ week.
4. During the run, refrigerators are produced at a rate of $P = 800$ per month.
5. The production cost per refrigerator does not depend on the number produced. In this case, the production cost does not affect the inventory policy. On average, 6000 refrigerators are produced to meet the demand every year. The annual production cost is the same (6000 * production cost per refrigerator), regardless of the inventory policy. As a result, there is no need to know the production cost per unit because this information will not affect the inventory policy.
6. Shortages are not allowed.

Having identified these characteristics and data, you want to determine the reorder point, R, at which to issue a production order, and the optimal production quantity, Q^*. To do so, you must first obtain estimates of the relevant cost components listed above. Suppose the Accounting Department of Home Appliances has provided you with the following values:

1. A fixed setup cost of $1000 per run to cover the cost of preparing the equipment, the workers' schedules, and so on.
2. A value of $C = \$250$ per refrigerator.
3. A carrying rate of $i = 0.24$ per year to reflect the cost of storing and the opportunity cost of the money invested in the idle inventory.

12.5.2 *Computing the Optimal Order Quantity*

As in Example 12.1 in Section 12.3, you will notice that the various data values provided by the Accounting Department use different time units. For example, the production rate is 800 refrigerators per *month*, the demand is 6000 per *year*, and the lead time is 1 *week*. The first step is to express all these quantities in a common unit of time. You are free to choose any time unit, but you must use that unit consistently throughout the analysis. In this case, suppose that a month is chosen as the common time period. The plant operates all 12 months, so this choice of time unit results in the following values:

1. Production rate of $P = 800$ refrigerators per month
2. Annual demand of $D = (6000/\text{year})/(12 \text{ months/year}) = 500$ refrigerators per month
3. Lead time of $L = 1$ week $= 1/52$ year $= 12/52$ month
4. Setup cost of $K = \$1000$ per production run
5. Value of each refrigerator is $C = \$250$
6. Carrying rate of $i = 0.24$ per year $= 0.24/12$ per month $= 0.02$
7. Monthly holding cost of $H = i * C = 0.02 * 250 = \$5$ per refrigerator per month

Before conducting the analysis, observe that because shortages are not allowed, the production rate P must be at least the demand rate D—as is the case in this example—otherwise it will not be possible to meet the demand, even if the entire plant is used exclusively to produce refrigerators year round.

To understand how the order quantity Q and reorder point R are related and how they affect the inventory level over time, suppose there is no inventory and that you have just started a production run of $Q = 400$ refrigerators. The inventory level over time is illustrated in Figure 12.8. The horizontal axis represents the time in months and the vertical axis represents the number of refrigerators in inventory. The inventory level at a point in time is based on the following observations:

1. The 400 refrigerators are produced at the rate of $P = 800$ per month. This run, then, requires $Q/P = 400/800 = 1/2$ month to fill.
2. During this 1/2 month, refrigerators are sold at the rate of 500 per month. Thus, inventory is building up at a net rate of $P - D = 800 - 500 = 300$ per month. During the production period of 1/2 month, the inventory level increases from its beginning value of 0 to a final value of $(P - D) * Q/P = 300 * (1/2) = 150$, as illustrated in Figure 12.8 by the straight line from time 0 to 0.5 months.
3. After the production run is completed, the inventory of 150 refrigerators is sold at the rate of $D = 500$ per month. Thus, this inventory runs out in $150/500 = 0.3$ month, as illustrated in Figure 12.8 by the straight line from time 0.5 to 0.8.

To ensure no shortages and also to avoid unnecessarily high inventory levels, the next order should be issued so that production starts at time 0.8 month. The span of time of 0.8 month, during which the inventory starts at 0, builds up to its maximum value of 150, and decreases back to 0, is called the **cycle time**, denoted by T. In general, the cycle time is the amount of time needed to use up Q refrigerators. That is,

Cycle time
The time during which inventory starts at 0, builds up to its maximum value, and decreases back to 0.

$$\text{Cycle time, } T = Q/D$$

$$= 400/500$$

$$= 0.8 \text{ month}$$

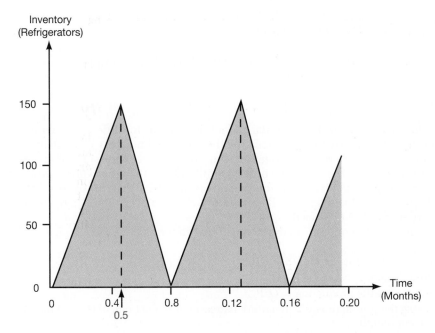

FIGURE 12.8 Inventory Behavior of Refrigerators for Home Appliances with $Q = 400$.

Recall that the lead time is $L = 12/52 = 0.231$ month, so the next production order should be placed at time $T - L = 0.8 - 0.231 = 0.569$ month. When the inventory level reaches 0 at time 0.8, the entire *inventory cycle* begins again, as shown in Figure 12.8.

To evaluate the policy of producing $Q = 400$ refrigerators every $T = 0.8$ month, you can compute the associated monthly cost as follows:

$$\text{Total monthly cost} = (\text{monthly setup cost}) + (\text{monthly holding cost})$$

Recall that the production cost is independent of Q and is therefore not included. The monthly setup cost is the cost per setup times the number of setups per month. Because the monthly demand is $D = 500$ refrigerators and the production quantity is $Q = 400$, there is an average of $D/Q = 500/400 = 1.25$ setups per month. Thus,

$$\begin{aligned} \text{Monthly setup cost} &= (\text{cost per setup}) * (\text{number of setups}) \\ &= K * (D/Q) \\ &= 1000 * (500/400) \\ &= 1250 \end{aligned}$$

The holding cost depends on the number of units in inventory, which varies over time from 0 to 150 and back to 0. Thus, on average, there are $150/2 = 75$ refrigerators in inventory throughout the month. The monthly holding cost is the average number of units in inventory times the cost of holding each unit for a month. The carrying rate is 0.02, so the monthly holding cost is

$$\begin{aligned} \text{Monthly holding cost} &= (\text{average inventory}) * (\text{monthly holding cost per unit}) \\ &= 75 * H \\ &= 75 * (i * C) \\ &= 75 * (0.02 * 250) \\ &= 375 \end{aligned}$$

Combining the two components results in the following total monthly cost when producing in quantities of size $Q = 400$ every $T = 0.8$ month:

$$\text{Total monthly cost} = (\text{monthly setup cost}) + (\text{monthly holding cost})$$
$$= 1250 + 375$$
$$= 1625$$

The idea now is to perform a similar economic analysis for different order quantities Q and then to identify the one incurring the least total monthly cost. To avoid a time-consuming trial-and-error investigation, you can write an expression for this total monthly cost in terms of the *unknown* order quantity Q and the other *known* problem data and then use mathematical techniques to determine the Q that minimizes that expression. Figure 12.9 illustrates how the inventory changes over time when a general unknown order quantity Q is used.

From the earlier economic analysis, recall that in terms of $Q, P, D, K, i,$ and C:

1. Number of setups per month $= D/Q$
2. Monthly setup cost $= K * (D/Q)$
3. Duration of the production $= Q/P$
4. During the production, the inventory increases at the net rate of $(P - D)$ refrigerators per month
5. From steps 3 and 4, the maximum inventory level is $(P - D) * (Q/P)$
6. From step 5,

$$\text{Average inventory} = (1/2) * \text{maximum inventory}$$
$$= (1/2) * (P - D) * (Q/P)$$

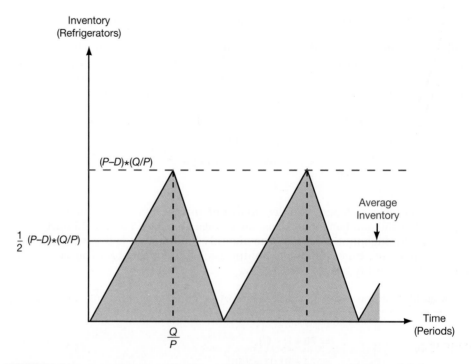

FIGURE 12.9 Inventory Behavior of Refrigerators for Home Appliances with General Order
Quantity Q.

※ **7.** From step 6,

$$\text{Monthly inventory cost} = (\text{average inventory}) * H$$
$$= (1/2) * (P - D) * (Q/P) * H$$
$$= (1/2) * (P - D) * (Q/P) * i * C$$

By using steps 2 and 7, the total monthly cost is computed as follows:

$$\text{Total monthly cost} = (\text{monthly setup cost}) + (\text{monthly holding cost})$$
$$= K * (D/Q) + (1/2) * (P - D) * (Q/P) * i * C$$

From this expression, and as you can see in Figure 12.10, as Q increases:

1. The monthly setup cost of $(K * D/Q)$ decreases.
2. The monthly holding cost of $[(1/2) * (P - D) * (Q/P) * i * C]$ increases linearly.

By combining these two components, the total monthly cost varies as shown in Figure 12.10. The objective is to find the **production order quantity, Q^***, that achieves the minimum total cost. As shown in Appendix 12A, researchers have used calculus to determine that this production order quantity is

$$Q^* = \sqrt{\frac{2 * D * K}{H * \left(\frac{P-D}{P}\right)}}$$

Production order quantity
The amount to order in a POQ model that achieves the minimum total cost.

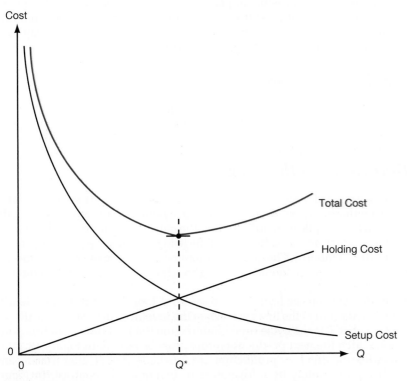

FIGURE 12.10 Total Cost as a Function of the Order Quantity Q.

$$= \sqrt{\frac{2 * D * K}{i * C * \left(\frac{P-D}{P}\right)}}$$

For the problem of Home Appliances, $P = 800$, $D = 500$, $K = 1000$, $i = 0.02$, and $C = 250$, so the optimal order quantity is

$$Q^* = \sqrt{\frac{2 * D * K}{i * C * \left(\frac{P-D}{P}\right)}}$$

$$= \sqrt{\frac{2 * 500 * 1000}{0.02 * 250 * \left(\frac{800-500}{800}\right)}}$$

$$= \sqrt{\frac{1000000}{1.875}}$$

$$= 730.3$$

It is not possible to manufacture fractions of refrigerators, so the production order quantity should be either 730 or 731, whichever incurs the least total inventory cost. In this case, both order quantities result in the same monthly cost of $1369.31, so either can be used. For this analysis, a POQ of 730 refrigerators is chosen.

To meet the total monthly demand of 500 refrigerators when 730 are produced at a time, an order is placed every 500/730 month. That is, 0.685 order of 730 refrigerators is placed each month. It is not possible to place fractions of an order, and there is no need to do so. The demand continues from one month to the next. In some months, you may place no orders and in others you may place one order in such a way as to average 0.685 per month. In general, once Q^* is known,

$$\text{Average number of orders per period} = \frac{\text{demand per period}}{\text{order quantity}}$$

$$= \frac{D}{Q^*}$$

12.5.3 Determining the Reorder Point

The optimal production order quantity is 730 refrigerators. The next step is to determine *when* to place these orders. What is the *reorder point*? The reorder point is the inventory level at which to place an order so that the current inventory level reaches 0 just when the new production starts. Recall that the lead time for setting up the production run is 1 week (0.231 month). The question, therefore, is how many refrigerators are needed in inventory to cover the demand during this lead time before the production begins.

The answer depends on the lead time. To see why, look at Figure 12.11. Identify the point in time T at the end of the first cycle when the inventory decreases to 0. (Recall from Section 12.5.2 that T is the cycle time.) Subtracting the lead time from this point yields the time at which the next production order must be issued. In Figure 12.11(a), this time occurs *after* the previous production has finished—that is, after time t—and the demand is being met solely by refrigerators in inventory. In contrast, in Figure 12.11(b), the reorder point occurs *during* the previous production run prior to time t. Computing the reorder point depends on which of these two cases is applicable.

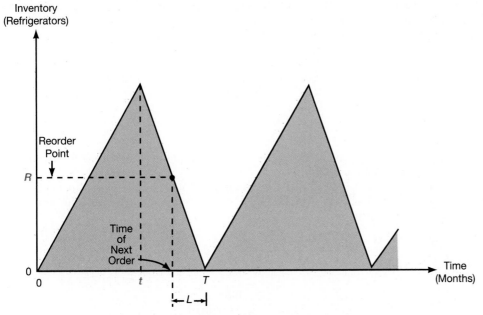

(a) Next Order Occurs After Production Is Finished

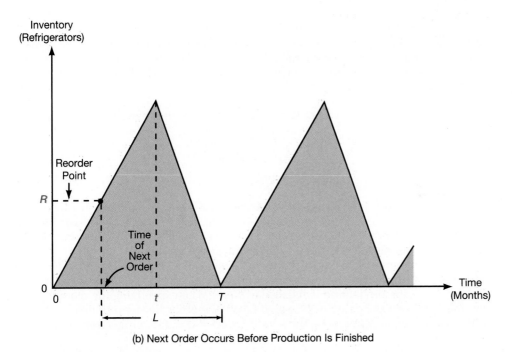

(b) Next Order Occurs Before Production Is Finished

FIGURE 12.11 How the Reorder Point Depends on the Lead Time.

For the problem of Home Appliances, the cycle time T is the time at which the number of units from the production run (730 refrigerators, in this example), is used up. Because the demand occurs at a rate of 500 per month:

$$T = \frac{Q^*}{D}$$
$$= \frac{730}{500}$$
$$= 1.46$$

This means that each inventory cycle—from the time the inventory is 0 until it again reaches 0—lasts 1.46 months.

To find t—that is, the time at which the previous production is finished—notice that it is the time needed to produce $Q^* = 730$ refrigerators. Because the production rate is 800 per month,

$$t = \frac{Q^*}{P}$$
$$= \frac{730}{800}$$
$$= 0.9125$$

Subtracting the lead time of $L = 0.231$ month from $T = 1.46$ months results in placing the next production order at time $1.46 - 0.231 = 1.229$. As shown in Figure 12.12(a), this reorder time occurs after t.

The reorder point is the inventory level at time 1.229. In this case, because there is no production during the lead time (because the time of reorder is after t), the demand is met only from inventory at the rate of $D = 500$ per month. The reorder point is the number of refrigerators needed to meet the demand during the lead time of $L = 0.231$ month. That is:

$$\text{Reorder point } R = \text{demand during the lead time}$$
$$= L * D$$
$$= 0.231 * 500$$
$$= 115.5$$

In other words, after production from the previous order is finished, just before the inventory decreases to 115.5—when $R = 116$ refrigerators—it is time to issue the next production order for $Q^* = 730$ refrigerators. Doing so ensures that this new order begins when the remaining 116 refrigerators in inventory are used up.

It is important to note that the inventory level reaches the reorder point of $R = 116$ refrigerators *twice* during the inventory cycle: once during the production—*before t*— and once after the production is finished—*after t*. When specifying the reorder point, you must indicate the value of R and whether to reorder *during* production or *after*. In the case of Home Appliances, the reorder point of $R = 116$ refrigerators occurs *after* production.

In contrast, if the lead time is 3 weeks—that is, $L = 0.693$ of a month instead of 0.231—then the reorder time is $1.46 - 0.693 = 0.767$ and occurs during the previous production, as shown in Figure 12.12(b). To compute the reorder point, notice that it is precisely the amount of inventory accumulated during the production time of 0.767 month. Recall that during the production period, the inventory accumulates at the rate of $P - D = 800 - 500 = 300$ refrigerators per month, so the reorder point R is $300 * 0.767 = 230.1$. During a production run, just before the inventory builds up to 230.1—when $R = 231$ refrigerators—it is time to issue the next production order

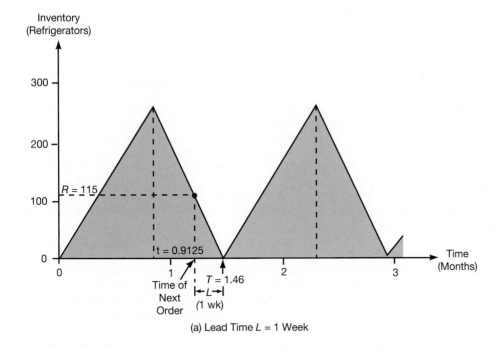

(a) Lead Time L = 1 Week

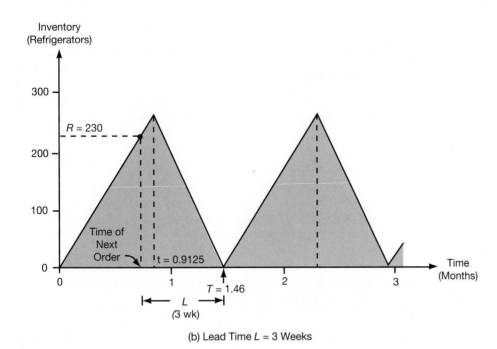

(b) Lead Time L = 3 Weeks

FIGURE 12.12 Reorder Point for the Problem of Home Appliances.

of $Q^* = 730$ refrigerators. Doing so ensures that this new production begins when the current production is over and all inventory decreases to 0.

12.5.4 *The POQ Model: Using the Computer*

Inventory
EX12_3.DAT

Now that you know how to obtain the optimal inventory policy for a POQ model, you can allow the computer to perform those computations. The results of solving the POQ problem of Home Appliances on STORM is shown in Figure 12.13. The first portion of the report confirms the optimal order quantity of $Q^* = 730$ refrigerators and the reorder point of 116. However, observe that the report does *not* indicate whether the reorder point occurs during production or after. From the analysis in Section 12.5.3, you know that this particular reorder point occurs *after* production. Finally, note that the number of setups is 8.2 per *year*, which is equivalent to $8.2/12 = 0.683$ setup per month. This value is approximately the same as the value of 0.685 calculated in Section 12.5.3.

The second part of the report in Figure 12.13 shows the annual costs associated with this inventory policy. This optimal policy incurs a total setup and inventory cost of $16,431.68 per year. You can see that this value is about 12 times the monthly cost of $1369.31 computed in Section 12.5.2. As discussed there, this total consists of annual setup costs of $8,219.18 and annual carrying costs of $8,212.50. Finally, observe that the report in Figure 12.13 provides an "Average working stock investment" of $34,218.75. This amount is the dollar value of the average inventory throughout the year. Recall from Section 12.5.2 that the average inventory during a cycle is one-half of the maximum inventory level that occurs at time t. In this example $t = 0.9125$, and the

```
           Production Order Quantity for Home Appliances
                      ORDERING INFORMATION
     Item              Item    Orders /     Order    Reorder  Max Orders
     Name               ID      Setups       Size     Point   Outstanding

     REFRIDGE            1        8.2         730       116        1




           Production Order Quantity for Home Appliances, Inc.
                   AGGREGATE INVENTORY VALUES
                 Inventory carrying charge = 24.00%



     Total number of items . . . . . . . . . . . . . .         1
     Average working stock investment ($) . . . . . . .    34218.75

     Cost to order POQ items ($/yr) . . . . . . . . . .     8219.18
     Average working stock carrying cost ($/yr) . . . .     8212.50
     Total cost ($/yr) . . . . . . . . . . . . . . . .     16431.68

     Number of setups for POQ items . . . . . . . . . .        8
```

FIGURE 12.13 STORM Results for the POQ Problem of Home Appliances.

maximum inventory level is $(P - D) * t = (800 - 500) * 0.9125 = 273.75$ refrigerators. Thus, the average inventory is $273.75/2 = 136.875$, and the associated value is 136.875 refrigerators $* \$250$ per refrigerator $= \$34,218.75$. This value tells the manager that an average of $34,218.75 is tied up in inventory throughout the year.

These results are confirmed by the output from the QSB software package, as given in Figure 12.14. The first portion of the report shows the data that were entered into QSB; the second portion provides the results of solving the problem. The first line of the results confirms the optimal production quantity of 730.297 refrigerators per order. The value of 273.861 in the next line is the maximum number of refrigerators in inventory during a cycle. The next row of the report is not relevant because backorders are not allowed in this problem. The value of 1.461 in the next row, labeled "Order interval," is the time between orders. That is, a new order for refrigerators is placed every 1.461 months, or, equivalently, there are $(1/1.461)) * 12 = 8.2$ orders per year, which is the same value obtained from STORM in Figure 12.13. The next value of 115.385 confirms the reorder point of 116 refrigerators.

The remaining rows of the report pertain to the costs of this inventory policy. For example, the monthly ordering and holding costs are both equal to $684.65, or $12 * 684.65 = \$8215.80$ per year, which is approximately the same as the corresponding values obtained from STORM in Figure 12.13. The only reason these values are slightly different is because in STORM the order quantity is rounded up to 730. Finally, the value of 125000 in the row labeled "Material cost per month" is the value of the 500 refrigerators demanded each month at $250 each.

```
              EOQ Results for Home Appliances


 Input Data:
      Demand per month (D) =  500
      Order or setup cost per order (Co) =  1000
      Holding cost per unit per month (Ch) =  5
      Shortage cost per unit per month (Cs) =  1
      Shortage cost per unit, independent of time (c) =  0
      Replenishment or production rate per month (P) =  800
      Lead time for a new order in month (LT) =  .2307692
      Unit cost (C) =  250
 EOQ Output:
      EOQ              =         730.297
      Maximum inventory =        273.861
      Maximum backorder =          0.000
      Order interval   =           1.461 month
      Reorder point    =         115.385
          Ordering cost =        684.653
          Holding cost  =        684.653
          Shortage cost =          0.000
      Subtotal of inventory cost per month    =      1369.306
      Material cost per month                 =    125000.000
      Total cost per month                    =    126369.305
```

FIGURE 12.14 QSB Results for the POQ Problem of Home Appliances.

➡ **KEY FEATURES**

In summary, to determine the optimal inventory policy for a production problem satisfying the assumptions listed at the beginning of Section 12.5, you must first estimate or know the following data:

$$P = \text{the production rate per period}$$
$$D = \text{the demand per period}$$
$$L = \text{the lead time for setting up an order}$$
$$i = \text{the carrying rate per period}$$
$$K = \text{the fixed cost of setting up the production run}$$
$$C = \text{the value of each unit}$$
$$H = i * C = \text{the holding cost per unit per period}$$

You can then calculate the production order quantity (Q^*), the average number of orders per period, and the reorder point (R) as follows:

$$Q^* = \sqrt{\frac{2 * D * K}{H * \left(\frac{P-D}{P}\right)}}$$

$$= \sqrt{\frac{2 * D * K}{i * C * \left(\frac{P-D}{P}\right)}}$$

Average number of orders $= D/Q^*$

$$R = \begin{cases} D * L, & \text{if } T - L \geq t \\ (P - D) * (T - L), & \text{if } T - L < t \end{cases}$$

where $T = Q^*/D$ and $t = Q^*/P$.

■ 12.6 INVENTORY SYSTEMS WITH PROBABILISTIC DEMAND: THE CONTINUOUS-REVIEW MODEL

Continuous-review model
A model in which inventory levels are monitored continuously to determine the reorder point.

In Section 12.3, the optimal inventory policy is determined for an EOQ model in which the demand is assumed to be deterministic. In some applications, this may be a valid assumption, but in many situations, the demand is known only with a great deal of uncertainty. Probabilistic techniques are needed to analyze and determine the optimal inventory policy for such problems. A review of the necessary probability concepts is provided in the Student Resource Manual. Appropriate analysis then depends on which of the following two ordering policies you wish to use:

Periodic-review model
A model in which the inventory is reviewed at fixed points in time and the amount to order is determined by the inventory level at that time.

1. A **continuous-review model**, in which inventory levels are monitored continuously and when the reorder point is reached Q^* units are ordered.
2. A **periodic-review model**, in which the inventory is reviewed periodically, say, every T time periods, and the size of the order is determined by the inventory level at that time.

The first of these two policies is analyzed in this section. The second is addressed in Section 12.7.

To illustrate the continuous-review policy, recall the EOQ problem of ordering X-ray films for Suburban Hospital in Section 12.3. In determining the optimal inventory policy, the demand D of 18,000 films per year is used. Although it may be fairly true that on *average* 18,000 films are used per year, most likely there are fluctuations in the demand from week to week, month to month, and even year to year. As Manager of Supplies, how do you deal with this uncertainty?

12.6.1 Computing the Order Quantity (Q*) and the Reorder Point (R)

To analyze a problem involving probabilistic demand, you must ideally know the associated *probability distribution*: For any value of the demand, you should know the probability of that demand occurring. Even if you were able to obtain such a probability distribution, which in practice can be quite difficult, deriving the optimal inventory policy using this distribution is mathematically complex and, in many cases, not possible.

One commonly used approach to overcome these difficulties in an EOQ model where the demand is probabilistic is to do the following:

1. Obtain an estimate of the *average* demand D' per time period.
2. Compute the order quantity Q^* and the reorder point R using the EOQ formula in Section 12.3 by replacing the deterministic demand D by the average demand D'.

This approach, though not optimal, is easy to implement and has worked well in practice. To illustrate with the problem of Suburban Hospital, suppose the demand is probabilistic, but that the *average* annual demand D' is 18,000 films. Applying the formulas in Section 12.3 and using the appropriate data for this problem resulted in the following inventory policy:

Inventory
EX12_1P.DAT

$$Q^* = \sqrt{\frac{2 * D' * K}{i * C}}$$

$$= \sqrt{\frac{2 * 18000 * 100}{0.30 * 20}}$$

$$= 774.60 \qquad \text{(rounded up to 775)}$$

$$R = D' * L$$

$$= 18000 * (1/52)$$

$$= 346$$

In other words, the policy is to order 775 films whenever the current inventory level drops to 346 films.

In the event that the demand is probabilistic, however, this policy has serious drawbacks. For example, the foregoing reorder point R is based on the assumption that *precisely* 346 films are used during the lead time of 1 week. However, should 350 films be needed during this time, the hospital will run out, as seen in the second inventory cycle in Figure 12.15. In fact, with probabilistic demand, the inventory level varies unpredictably over time, as shown in the figure. In general, this variability in demand raises two important points:

1. The time between orders varies in the probabilistic case. This is because the amount of time it takes for the inventory level to reach the reorder point R depends on the unknown, probabilistic demand.
2. If the demand during the lead time should exceed the inventory level of the reorder point, a shortage occurs.

With the policy of reordering when there are 346 films in inventory, Suburban Hospital will run out of X-ray film approximately 50% of the time. Clearly, this is unacceptable. Although it may not be possible, or economical, to ensure that the hospital *never* runs out, the objective is to control the likelihood of such an event, as described in Section 12.6.2.

12.6.2 Computing the Amount of Safety Stock to Meet a Service Level

Service level
(α) A fraction representing the probability that the decision maker chooses of being able to meet demand during the lead time when the demand is probabilistic.

One approach to controlling shortages when the demand is probabilistic is to specify a **service level**, α, in the form of a minimum desired probability of meeting the demand:

$$\text{Service level of } \alpha = \text{Prob\{meeting the demand during an inventory cycle\}}$$

$$= \text{Prob\{demand during the lead time} \leq R\}$$

For example, specifying a service level of $\alpha = 0.95$ for Suburban Hospital means that management wants to meet the demand for X-ray films in at least 95% of the inventory cycles or, equivalently, that shortages occur in at most 5% of the inventory cycles.

One way to achieve the goal of a specified service level is to have **safety stock** (S), which is additional inventory available to cover fluctuations in demand during the lead time. To determine *how much* safety stock to have, you want to choose S together with R so that the probability of not running out with a total $(R + S)$ units in inventory during the lead time is at least the service level α. That is:

Safety stock
(S) Additional inventory used to cover fluctuations in demand during the lead time.

$$\text{Prob\{demand during the lead time } L \leq R + S\} \geq \alpha$$

It is clear that if the amount of safety stock S is very large, you will be easily able to meet the service level. However, as shown in Figure 12.16, having this safety stock raises the average inventory level by that amount, and thus additional holding costs arise. The

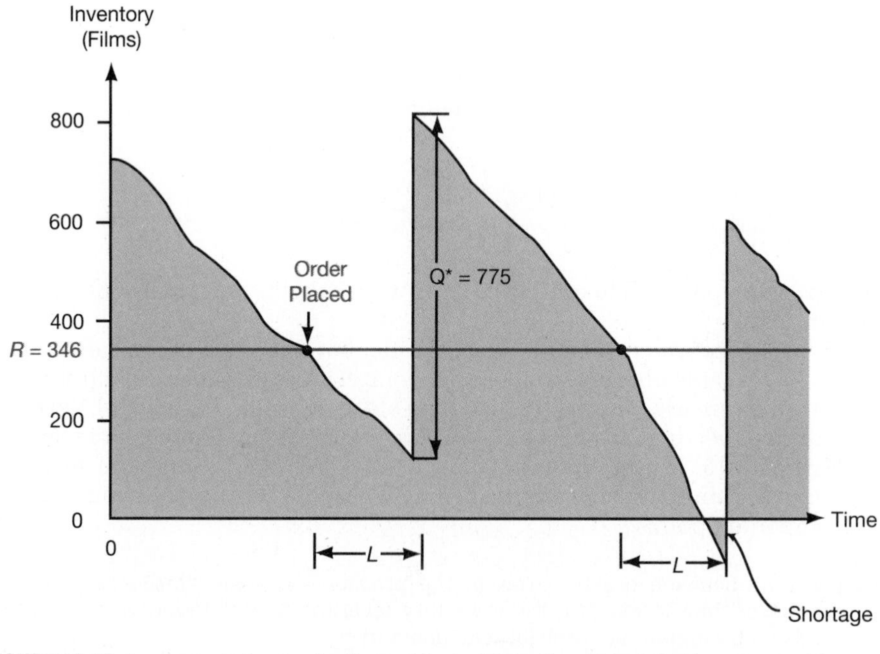

FIGURE 12.15 Inventory Behavior for the Problem of Suburban Hospital When Demand is Probabilistic.

objective, therefore, is to determine the *minimum* amount of safety stock needed to meet the specified service level. To do so requires knowing the probability distribution of the demand. As mentioned previously, obtaining the probability distribution can be difficult and putting it to use can be mathematically too complicated. In practice, using the *normal distribution* for the demand has proven reliable.

KEY FEATURES

To use a normal distribution to determine the amount of safety stock needed during the lead time, you must estimate:

✔ The mean, μ_L, which is the average demand during the lead time L, that is, $\mu_L = R$.
✔ The standard deviation, σ_L, of the demand during the lead time.

Returning to the example of Suburban Hospital, recall that the average demand D' is assumed to be 18,000 films per year. After performing statistical analysis on previous records, suppose management estimates the standard deviation, σ, of this annual demand to be 1000 films per year. These data are converted from their given time periods (1 year, in this case) into the mean and standard deviation during the lead time (that is, 1/52 year). One practical way to do this is to use the assumption that the mean and the variance during the fraction of a year that corresponds to the lead time is equal to that same fraction of the yearly mean and variance. For example, if the yearly demand has a mean of 18,000 with a standard deviation of 1000 (that is, a variance of 1,000,000), then the demand during 1/4 year has a mean of $(1/4)(18,000) = 4500$ and

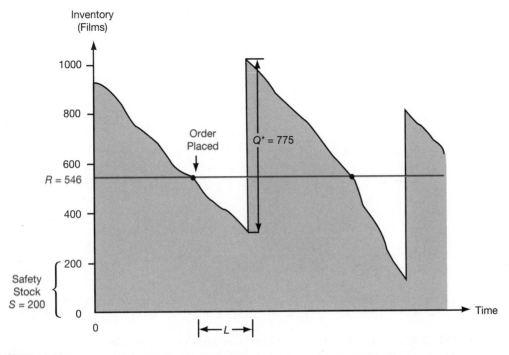

FIGURE 12.16 Effect of Safety Stock on the Inventory Level.

a variance of $(1/4)(1,000,000) = 250,000$. With this assumption, the values of μ_L and σ_L are computed as follows:

$$\mu_L = R = D' * L$$

$$\sigma_L^2 = \sigma^2 * L, \text{ that is, } \sigma_L = \sigma * \sqrt{L}$$

For the problem of Suburban Hospital,

$$\mu_L = D' * L$$
$$= 18000 * (1/52)$$
$$= 346$$
$$\sigma_L = \sigma * \sqrt{L}$$
$$= 1000 * \sqrt{1/52}$$
$$= 138.67$$

With these values for μ_L and σ_L, the amount of safety stock is determined using the normal distribution. Specifically, the safety stock S is chosen so that

$$\text{Prob\{demand during the lead time} \leq R + S\} = \alpha$$

See Figure 12.17. You must identify the value of $(R + S)$ so that the area under the normal curve to the left of this point is equal to α. To do so, as described in the Student Resource Manual:

1. Find the z-value so that the area under the standard normal distribution to the left of z is α. For the problem of Suburban Hospital in which $R = 346$ and $\alpha = 0.95$, the z-value from the table in Appendix B is 1.645.

2. From the Student Resource Manual,

$$z = \frac{(R + S) - \mu_L}{\sigma_L}$$
$$= \frac{(R + S) - R}{\sigma_L}$$
$$= \frac{S}{\sigma_L}$$

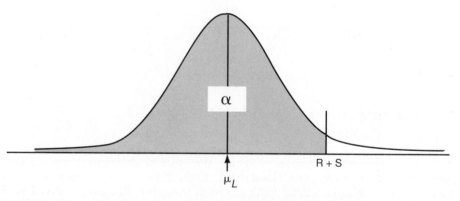

FIGURE 12.17 Using the Normal Distribution to Determine the Safety Stock.

Solving for S results in

$$S = z * \sigma_L$$

For the example of Suburban Hospital in which $z = 1.645$, as determined in step 1, and $\sigma_L = 138.67$, you can compute the safety stock S by

$$S = z * \sigma_L$$
$$= 1.645 * 138.67$$
$$= 228.12 \qquad \text{(rounded up to 229)}$$

The hospital should maintain a safety stock of 229 films. In other words, to ensure the service level of 0.95, the hospital should order 775 films whenever the inventory level decreases to $R + S = 346 + 229 = 575$. Unlike the deterministic case, in which this order of 775 films occurs *every* 0.0435 year, in the probabilistic case, the point in time when the inventory decreases to 575 films is not known with certainty. The inventory therefore must be monitored continuously to determine when the level drops below 575 films.

Finally, note that the safety stock increases the average inventory level by S units, thus increasing the average annual cost. By using the formula in Section 12.3 and the relevant data:

$$\left\{\begin{array}{l}\text{Total annual}\\\text{cost}\end{array}\right\} = \left\{\begin{array}{l}\text{annual order-}\\\text{ing cost}\end{array}\right\} + \left\{\begin{array}{l}\text{annual}\\\text{purchase cost}\end{array}\right\} + \left\{\begin{array}{l}\text{annual hold-}\\\text{ing cost}\end{array}\right\}$$

$$= \left(K * \frac{D'}{Q}\right) + (C * D') + \left[\left(\frac{Q}{2} + S\right) * i * C\right]$$

$$= \left(100 * \frac{18000}{775}\right) + (20 * 18000) + \left[\left(\frac{775}{2} + 229\right) * 0.30 * 20\right]$$

$$= 2322.58 + 360000 + 3699$$

$$= 366021.58$$

Thus, the average annual cost has increased by $S * H = S * i * C = \$1374$ over the previous cost of \$364,647.58.

In this section, you have learned how to determine the amount of safety stock to meet a specified service level α. You can also see that as α increases, so do the following values:

1. The associated z-value for the normal distribution.
2. The safety stock $S = z * \sigma_L$.
3. The holding cost $S * H$ of the safety stock.

There is a trade-off: The higher the desired service level, the higher the cost needed to meet that level.

12.6.3 *The Probabilistic EOQ Model: Using the Computer*

Now that you know how to determine the amount of safety stock to achieve a specified service level, you can turn to a computer to perform those calculations, as is done in this section. The probabilistic EOQ model of Suburban Hospital is solved by the STORM software package, and the results are given in Figure 12.18.

Inventory
EX12_1P.DAT

```
                    ORDERING INFORMATION
Item            Item    Orders /    Order     Reorder   Max Orders
Name            ID      Setups       Size     Point    Outstanding

X-RAY FILM       1       23.2        775       575         1

             (a)   The Optimal Policy Report




                  ANNUAL COST INFORMATION
Item            Item      Order    Working    Safety        Total
Name            ID        Cost   Stock Cost  Stock Cost      Cost

X-RAY FILM       1      2322.58   2325.00    1374.00      6021.58

             (b)   The Annual Cost Report



              SAFETY STOCK EXCHANGE TABLE
                CARRYING RATE = 30.00 %
         Service           Safety           Annual
         Level, %         Stock, $        Stockouts

          90.00            3560.00           2.32
          92.50            4000.00           1.74
          95.00            4580.00           1.16
          97.50            5440.00          5.81E-01
          99.99           10320.00          2.32E-03

(c)   The Amount of Safety Stock for Different Service Levels
```

FIGURE 12.18 STORM Report for the Probabilistic EOQ Problem of Suburban Hospital.

The report in Figure 12.18(a) indicates that the order quantity Q^* is 775 X-ray films. This report also confirms the reorder point of 575 films. Note also from the report that on average there are 23.2 orders per year. However, due to the variability in demand, in years when the demand is below the average of 18,000 films, there will be fewer orders; in years when the demand exceeds the average, there will be more orders.

The cost information associated with this inventory policy is given in the output in Figure 12.18(b). The cost of $360,000 for purchasing an average of 18,000 films per year is not included. The ordering cost of $2322.58 indicated in the report is obtained by multiplying the average number of orders per year (23.2) by the ordering cost of $100 per order. Recall that the use of safety stock increases the average inventory from $Q^*/2$ to $Q^*/2 + S$. As shown in the report in Figure 12.18(b), the holding cost associated with the *working stock* of $Q^*/2$ used to meet the average demand is $(Q^*/2) * H = (775/2) * 6 = \$2325$. The holding cost of the safety stock S used to handle variability in the demand is $S * H = 229 * 6 = \$1374$. Thus, the total average ordering and holding cost is $6021.58, as shown in the report in Figure 12.18(b).

As mentioned previously, there is a trade-off between the service level α and the cost of having enough safety stock S to meet this service level. The STORM report in

Figure 12.18(c) shows the purchasing cost of the safety stock needed to meet different service levels. For example, to ensure that demand is met in 95% of the inventory cycles—that is, $\alpha = 0.95$—it is necessary to have a safety stock of $S = 229$ films. The cost for purchasing these 229 films is $229 * 20 = \$4580$, as shown in the third line of the report in Figure 12.18(c). This safety stock incurs additional holding costs at the rate of 30% per year. This trade-off between the service level α and the value of the safety stock S is shown in the graph of Figure 12.19. There you can see that as α approaches 1.00, which is a service level of 100%, the value of the safety stock needed increases at a faster and faster rate. As a manager, you should evaluate these trade-offs to determine an appropriate service level.

On average there are 23.2 orders placed per year. When α is 0.95, this means that 5% of these 23.2 inventory cycles will have shortages. Equivalently, there will be an average of $0.05 * 23.2 = 1.16$ *stockouts* per year, as shown in the last column of the report in Figure 12.18(c) corresponding to $\alpha = 0.95$.

12.6.4 *Summary*

In this section, you have seen how variability in demand affects the average inventory level and how it may result in shortages. You have learned that one way to control these shortages is to have safety stock. The amount of safety stock is determined by specifying a service level α corresponding to the desired probability of not running out of stock. To find the optimal policy requires knowing the probability distribution of the demand and using complex mathematical analysis.

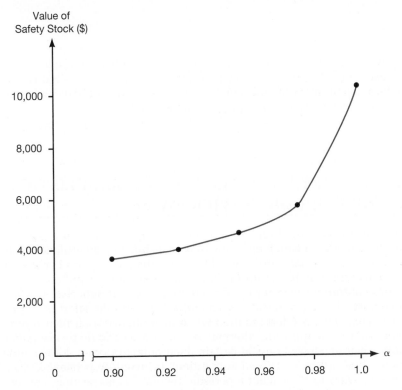

FIGURE 12.19 Trade-Off Between the Service Level and the Value of the Safety
Stock.

➡️ ***KEY FEATURES***

To implement an approach that has worked well in practice, follow these steps:

✔ Use the EOQ formula from Section 12.3 to compute

$$Q^* = \sqrt{\frac{2 * D' * K}{i * C}}$$
$$R = D' * L$$

✔ Given the average demand D' and the standard deviation σ of the demand per period, compute the mean and standard deviation of the demand over the lead time L as follows:

$$\mu_L = R = D' * L$$
$$\sigma_L = \sigma * \sqrt{L}$$

✔ Use the service level α to compute the safety stock S by
  a. Finding the z-value so that the area under the standard-normal distribution to the left of z is α.
  b. Compute $S = z * \sigma_L$.

✔ Compute the reorder point as $R + S$.
✔ Compute the average cost per period as

$$\left(K * \frac{D'}{Q} \right) + (C * D') + \left[\left(\frac{Q}{2} + S \right) * i * C \right]$$

Carrying the safety stock S requires an investment of $(C * S)$ dollars and incurs additional holding costs of $(i * C * S)$ dollars. These costs increase as the desired service level increases. Implementing this policy requires a continuous review of the inventory to determine when the level reaches the appropriate reorder point.

■ 12.7 INVENTORY SYSTEMS WITH PROBABILISTIC DEMAND: THE PERIODIC-REVIEW MODEL

In Section 12.6, you learned how to modify the EOQ formulas to obtain a practical inventory policy for a model in which the demand is probabilistic. Ordering when the inventory reaches the reorder point is designed to save costs but requires continuous monitoring of the inventory. This monitoring comes at a cost in time and money. If a company conducts continuous monitoring of many items—say, if Suburban Hospital monitors its inventory of linen, surgical equipment, and so on—the effort may grow out of hand. Also, consider the effort required when many items reach their reorder points at different times. An appealing alternative is to use a *periodic-review policy*, in which inventories are reviewed only at certain fixed points in time—for example, once every month—and orders are placed at that time, if inventory is needed. There are many alternative ways to implement a periodic review. In this section, you will learn the details of one such policy, as illustrated in the next example, where you will see how much to order to meet a specified service level.

12.7.1 The Periodic-Review Problem of Suburban Hospital

Recall the problem of ordering X-ray films for Suburban Hospital, in which the relevant data are as follows:

1. The annual demand is normally distributed with a mean of $D' = 18,000$ films per year and a standard deviation of $\sigma = 1000$ films.
2. Lead time of $L = 1$ week $= 1/52$ year.
3. Annual carrying rate of $i = 0.30$ per year.
4. Ordering cost of $K = \$100$ per order.
5. Purchase cost of $C = \$20$ per film.
6. Annual holding cost of $H = i * C = 0.30 * 20 = \$6$ per film per year.
7. The desired service level is $\alpha = 0.95$.

The hospital currently lacks the funds to keep a full staff, and the inventory-management system has not yet been computerized. The director of the hospital therefore has decided to make all inventory decisions every 4 weeks. What is the appropriate inventory policy under these conditions?

12.7.2 Determining the Periodic-Review Policy

The ultimate objective is to determine how many films to order after observing the number in inventory at the end of a 4-week period so as to meet a specified service level. To achieve this goal, it is first necessary to understand how the inventory level changes over time. Assume that you have just taken inventory at the end of a 4-week period and have found I_1 films to be in stock. Based on this number, you place an order for (some as-yet unknown number) q_1 films. Those q_1 films will arrive only after the lead time of $L = 1$ week, during which the probabilistic demand is met from the existing inventory of I_1 films, as shown in Figure 12.20.

At time $L = 1$ week, the inventory level increases instantaneously when the order of q_1 films arrives. From this point on, the inventory again decreases based on the probabilistic demand. At the next review point of $T = 4$ weeks (that is, 3 weeks after the first order arrives), the inventory is reviewed and a new order of q_2 films is placed based on the observed inventory level of I_2. This process is repeated every $T = 4$ weeks.

In general, if I films are in stock at the time of the review and q films are then ordered, the total of $I + q$ films must last until the next order arrives. As seen in Figure 12.20, this next order arrives after time $T + L$. As an example, suppose that $I = 500$ films are in stock at the time of the review. The expected demand during the next $T + L = 5$ weeks is $18000 * (5/52) = 1731$ films. To meet this demand, you might consider ordering an additional $q = 1731 - 500 = 1231$ films. However, the demand is probabilistic, so there is approximately a 50% chance that the actual demand will exceed the available inventory during these five weeks. This is clearly unacceptable. The amount ordered should exceed 1231 films, but by how much?

To answer this question, recall that the Director has specified a service level of $\alpha = 0.95$. Thus, the amount q should be chosen so that 95% of the time the demand is met during the time $T + L$ of 5 weeks. To determine this amount q, recall that the annual demand is assumed to be normally distributed with mean $D' = 18,000$ and standard deviation $\sigma = 1000$. Thus, with the assumptions on the demand as discussed in Section 12.6, the demand during the time $T + L = 5$ weeks $= 5/52$ year is normally distributed with:

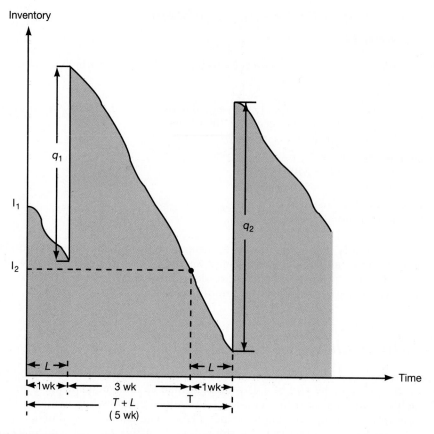

FIGURE 12.20 Inventory Behavior for the Periodic-Review Problem of Suburban Hospital.

$$\text{Mean } \mu_{T+L} = D' * (T + L)$$
$$= 18000 * (5/52)$$
$$= 1730.77$$

$$\text{Standard deviation } \sigma_{T+L} = \sqrt{(T + L)} * \sigma$$
$$= \sqrt{5/52} * 1000$$
$$= 310.09$$

As shown in Figure 12.21, the amount q should be chosen so that the area under the normal curve with a mean of 1730.77 and a standard deviation of 310.09 to the left of $I + q$ should be equal to the service level of $\alpha = 0.95$. To find such a q:

1. Use the standard-normal table in Appendix B to find the z-value associated with 0.95, which is 1.645.

2. Use the z-value in step 1 and the following formula to compute q:

$$z = \frac{(I + q) - \mu_{T+L}}{\sigma_{T+L}}$$

That is:

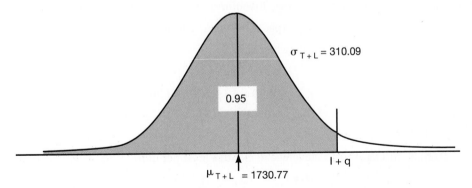

FIGURE 12.21 Using the Normal Distribution to Find the Order Amount for a Periodic-Review Policy.

$$q = \mu_{T+L} + (z * \sigma_{T+L}) - I$$

$$= 1730.77 + (1.645 * 310.09) - 500$$

$$= 1740.87$$

In other words, if there are 500 films in inventory at the time of review, then to meet the service level of $\alpha = 0.95$, an order should be placed for 1741 films. Doing so will ensure that there is a 95% chance of meeting the demand during the 5 weeks before the next order arrives. This order of 1741 films together with the 500 currently in stock provides for a safety stock of $z * \sigma_{T+L} = 510$ films above the expected demand of 1731. Observe that as the review period T increases, so does σ_{T+L} and hence the safety stock. In other words, the less frequently you choose to review, the more safety stock (and associated cost) is needed.

To use this policy every 4 weeks, it is *not* necessary to perform the previous computations each time based on the observed inventory level. This is because the amount $I + q$ (the amount needed to meet the demand during the time $T + L$ at the specified service level) must always be the same. That is:

$$I + q = \mu_{T+L} + (z * \sigma_{T+L})$$

$$= 1730.77 + (1.645 * 310.09)$$

$$= 2240.87 \text{ (rounded up to 2241)}$$

In summary, the periodic-review policy for the director of Suburban Hospital is to check the inventory every 4 weeks. If the amount in stock is I films, then an order is placed for $(2241 - I)$ films.

12.7.3 Computing the Cost of the Periodic-Review Policy

In terms of the data and the order frequency $T = 4$ weeks $= 4/52$ year, the annual costs associated with using this policy are

$$\text{Annual ordering cost} = (\text{cost per order}) * (\text{average number of orders})$$

$$= K * (1/T)$$

$$= 100 * (52/4)$$

$$= \$1,300$$

$$\text{Annual holding cost} = \text{(average inventory)} * \text{(holding cost per unit)}$$
$$= [(\tfrac{1}{2})\text{expected demand during period } T +$$
$$\text{safety stock}] * H$$
$$= [(\tfrac{1}{2}D' * T) + S] * i * C$$
$$= [(\tfrac{1}{2} * 18000 * \tfrac{4}{52}) + 510] * 0.30 * 20$$
$$= \$7,213.85$$

$$\text{Annual purchase cost} = \text{(average demand)} * \text{(cost per unit)}$$
$$= D' * C$$
$$= 18000 * 20$$
$$= \$360,000$$

$$\text{Total annual cost} = \text{(annual ordering cost)} + \text{(annual holding cost)} +$$
$$\text{(annual purchase cost)}$$
$$= 1300 + 7213.85 + 360000$$
$$= \$368,513.85$$

These total annual costs of \$368,513.85 are \$2,492.27 more than the cost of \$366,021.58 associated with the continuous-review policy for the same problem as discussed in Section 12.6.2. This additional cost reflects the trade-off between the convenience of performing periodic inventory reviews and having to monitor the inventory continuously.

12.7.4 Periodic-Review Policy When the Lead Time (L) Exceeds the Review Period (T)

In performing the computations in Sections 12.7.2 and 12.7.3, it was assumed that an order placed at the beginning of the review period arrives before the next review occurs—that is, that the lead time L is less than the review period T. If this is not the case, care is needed when determining the amount to order. This is because the amount I observed in inventory *does not* include the amount on order that has not yet arrived. To account for this *unobserved* inventory when review is done, let

$$I = \left\{ \begin{matrix} \text{number of} \\ \text{units on hand} \end{matrix} \right\} + \left\{ \begin{matrix} \text{total number of units of} \\ \text{outstanding orders} \end{matrix} \right\}$$

That is, I is the sum of the inventory on hand and the total number of units being shipped. All other calculations are the same as those in Section 12.7.2.

➡ **KEY FEATURES**

In summary, in this section you have seen how to obtain an inventory policy when periodic instead of continuous review of inventory is desired. To do so, obtain estimates of:

✔ The average D' and the standard deviation σ of the demand per period.
✔ The review period T.

✔ The lead time L.

✔ The service level α.

✔ The costs components consisting of:

   a. The ordering cost of $\$K$ per order.

   b. The purchase cost of $\$C$ per unit.

   c. The carrying rate i per period.

Using these values, compute the amount $I + q$ to meet the demand during the time $T + L$ at the desired service level of α as follows:

✔ Compute the mean and standard deviation of the demand during the time $T + L$ by

$$\mu_{T+L} = D' * (T + L)$$
$$\sigma_{T+L} = \sqrt{(T + L)} * \sigma$$

✔ Find the z-value in the standard-normal table associated with the service level α.

✔ Compute the "order-up-to" amount $I + q$ as

$$I + q = \mu_{T+L} + (z * \sigma_{T+L})$$

To implement the periodic review policy:

✔ Review the inventory every T time units to observe its level of I units.

✔ Order q units so that $I + q$ is precisely equal to the "order-up-to" amount.

The cost associated with this policy is

$$\text{Total cost} = (\text{ordering cost}) + (\text{holding cost}) + (\text{purchase cost})$$
$$= \left(K * \frac{1}{T}\right) + \left\{ \left[\left(\frac{1}{2}D' * T\right) + S \right] * i * C \right\} + (D' * C)$$

In Sections 12.1 through 12.7, you have learned how to derive inventory policies for several different models and ordering policies. Your knowledge of this material is brought together with the following case study.

CASE STUDY

Consider the inventory problem you face as Director of the Metropolitan Zoo.

Problem Description

The Metropolitan Zoo has a large number of animals that require feeds with various nutritional components. These requirements are met by mixing three different feeds: a Vitamin Feed (V), a Protein Feed (P), and Bulk (B). On the basis of the current mix and number of animals, the zoo uses approximately 20,000 pounds of V at 60 cents per pound, 40,000 pounds of P at 45 cents a pound, and 60,000 pounds of the B at 26 cents a pound each month. These demands are expected to remain the same for the next few years.

The supplier of these feeds can make a delivery in 3 days. The fixed delivery cost charged by the supplier, together with other processing costs, amounts to $200 per order. As Director, you want to determine the optimal inventory policy for the three feeds, assuming a carrying rate of 0.30 per year.

Problem Analysis

You should first recognize that the individual inventory problems associated with each of the three feeds satisfy the assumptions of an EOQ model with deterministic demand. You therefore can obtain the optimal inventory policy for each feed independently using the following data:

FEED	DEMAND, D (LB/MONTH)	PURCHASE COST, C ($/LB)	ORDERING COST, K ($/ORDER)	LEAD TIME, L (MONTHS)	CARRYING RATE, i (PER YEAR)
V	20,000	0.60	200	0.1	0.30
P	40,000	0.45	200	0.1	0.30
B	60,000	0.26	200	0.1	0.30

Inventory
ZOO_1.DAT
ZOO_2.DAT
ZOO_3.DAT
ZOO_4.DAT

The three optimal inventory policies can be obtained by applying the formulas in Section 12.3. Doing so with the STORM computer package results in the output in Figures 12.22(a) and 12.22(b). The first line of the report in Figure 12.22(a) indicates that whenever the inventory level of the Vitamin Feed drops to 2000 pounds, a new order for 23,094 pounds of the feed should be placed. This policy results in an average of 10.4 orders per year. Similarly, when the inventory levels of the Protein and Bulk reach 4000 and 6000 pounds, respectively, orders should be placed for 37,712 and 60,764 pounds, respectively, of those feeds. Doing so results in an average of 12.7 orders for Protein Feed and 11.8 orders for Bulk per year.

The annual costs, excluding the fixed purchasing costs, associated with these policies is given in the report of Figure 12.22(b). Adding the value in the last column of that report for each of the three feeds results in a total annual variable cost of $13,987.71.

Turning to the issue of implementation, you will notice that this policy requires continuously monitoring the level of the three feeds to determine when each one drops below its reorder point, and placing *separate* orders for each of the three feeds when the appropriate reorder points are reached.

To simplify the handling of this inventory, you might consider a policy in which *all three feeds are ordered at the same time*. The Accounting Department gives you the information that the fixed cost of ordering all three feeds together is $300 per order. This cost seems more attractive than the $600 total for placing three separate orders. However, ordering all three feeds together may result in larger inventories, thus offsetting the savings in the ordering costs. The analysis that follows is used to determine whether it is cost effective to order all three feeds at the same time.

Analysis of the Combined Ordering Policy

To develop an inventory policy for ordering all three feeds at the same time, think of the three feeds collectively as a "single" item to which the EOQ formulas can then be applied. You must first obtain appropriate data values for this single item, which will

```
        The Feed-Supply Problem of the Metropolitan Zoo
                  ORDERING INFORMATION
  Item          Item   Orders /     Order    Reorder  Max Orders
  Name           ID    Setups       Size     Point    Outstanding
  VITAMIN         1     10.4        23094     2000         1
  PROTEIN         2     12.7        37712     4000         1
  BULK            3     11.8        60764     6000         1


                          (a)



        The Feed-Supply Problem of the Metropolitan Zoo
                  ANNUAL COST INFORMATION
  Item          Item     Order   Working    Safety        Total
  Name           ID       Cost  Stock Cost Stock Cost      Cost
  VITAMIN         1     2078.46   2078.46     0.00        4156.92
  PROTEIN         2     2545.61   2545.56     0.00        5091.17
  BULK            3     2369.82   2369.80     0.00        4739.62

                          (b)
```

FIGURE 12.22 STORM Report for the Three Feeds of the Metropolitan Zoo: (a) Optimal Order Quantity and Reorder Point, and (b) Annual Costs for the Policy in (a).

be called the Mix. For example, what is the annual demand for this Mix? The annual demand for the three feeds are 20,000, 40,000, and 60,000 pounds. The annual demand for the Mix is the total of these three, which is 120,000 pounds.

The next needed data value is the purchase cost per pound of this Mix. The three feeds are purchased in the ratio of 2 to 4 to 6, so each pound of the Mix consists of $2/12 = 1/6$ pound of Vitamin Feed, $4/12 = 1/3$ pound of Protein Feed, and $6/12 = 1/2$ pound of Bulk. Use the purchase costs of the individual feeds given earlier to compute the cost per pound of the Mix:

$$\text{Purchase cost of the Mix} = (\text{cost of } 1/6 \text{ pound of Vitamin Feed}) +$$
$$(\text{cost of } 1/3 \text{ pound of Protein Feed}) +$$
$$(\text{cost of } 1/2 \text{ pound of Bulk})$$
$$= (1/6)(0.60) + (1/3)(0.45) + (1/2)(0.26)$$
$$= \$0.38$$

With the fixed ordering cost of \$300, the same lead time of 0.1 month and the carrying rate of $i = 0.30$, the EOQ formulas now can be used to obtain the optimal inventory policy for the Mix. The result using the STORM package is shown in Figures 12.23(a) and 12.23(b). The report in Figure 12.23(a) indicates that whenever the *combined* inventory of the three feeds drops to 12,000 pounds, an order of 87,057 pounds of the Mix is placed. This policy results in an average of 16.5 orders per year. Recall the ratio of 2 to 4 to 6 of the three feeds in the Mix. This policy results in the following quantities for the three individual feeds in each order of the 87,057 pounds of the Mix:

$$\text{Vitamin Feed} = (1/6)(87057) = 14509.5 \text{ pounds}$$
$$\text{Protein Feed} = (1/3)(87057) = 29019.0 \text{ pounds}$$
$$\text{Bulk} = (1/2)(87057) = 43528.5 \text{ pounds}$$

The annual cost of $9,924.52 for this policy appears in the report in Figure 12.23(b). This cost excludes the total purchase cost of the three feeds. Comparing this annual cost with that of $13,987.71 when the three feeds are ordered individually, you can see an annual saving of $4,063.19, or about 29%, over the previous policy. This savings is due primarily to the reduced cost of ordering all three feeds together.

Postoptimality Analysis

Before implementing a policy, as a manager you should first consider other aspects of the problem that were not included in the model. For example, to implement this policy, on average, how much cash is tied up in the inventory?

To answer this question, recall from Section 12.3 that in an EOQ model, the average amount of inventory is $Q^*/2$. Thus, the average value of this inventory is $C * (Q^*/2)$. For the Mix, this value is

$$\text{Value of average inventory} = C * (Q^*/2)$$
$$= 0.38 * (87,057/2)$$
$$= \$16,540.83$$

Suppose the Zoo's accountant has recommended that this amount be lowered to $15,000 for cash-flow reasons. One way to achieve this goal is to reduce the average inventory level. The appropriate amount is obtained from the foregoing formula, that is:

$$C * (Q/2) = 15000$$

Solving for Q gives

$$Q = (2 * 15000)/0.38$$
$$= 78,947.37$$

The reorder point remains unchanged at 12,000 pounds. The annual cost for this new policy is larger than when the order quantity is $Q^* = 87,057$ pounds because this value

---

The Feed-Supply Problem of the Metropolitan Zoo
ORDERING INFORMATION

Item Name	Item ID	Orders / Setups	Order Size	Reorder Point	Max Orders Outstanding
MIX	4	16.5	87057	12000	1

(a)

The Feed-Supply Problem of the Metropolitan Zoo
ANNUAL COST INFORMATION

Item Name	Item ID	Order Cost	Working Stock Cost	Safety Stock Cost	Total Cost
MIX	4	4962.27	4962.25	0.00	9924.52

(b)

FIGURE 12.23 STORM Report for the Mix of Metropolitan Zoo: (a) Optimal Order Quantity and Reorder Point for the Mix, and (b) Annual Costs for the Policy in (a).

of Q^* is the one that minimizes the total annual costs. Compared to Q^*, the new order quantity of 78,947 pounds results in lower average inventory and, hence, lower holding cost. However, the costs associated with having to reorder more frequently more than offset these savings.

Another way to view this cash-flow problem is to realize that at the current carrying rate of 0.30, an average of $16,540.38 is tied up in inventory. The desire to lower the amount of money invested in inventory indicates that there is now a greater "value" associated with these monies than originally estimated by the carrying rate of 0.30. To determine by how much to increase the carrying rate, observe that as the carrying rate i increases, Q^* decreases. You therefore can try different values of the carrying rate i until finding the one that results in an average inventory value of $15,000. For example, the report in Figure 12.24 obtained from STORM shows the trade-off in the working stock—the value of the average inventory level ($C * Q/2$)—for different carrying rates. To achieve the desired goal of $15,000, the carrying rate needs to be about 0.365. In other words, a higher carrying rate of 0.365 should be used to obtain the optimal inventory policy, which is shown in Figure 12.25. You can see that the optimal policy is to order 78,926 pounds of the Mix whenever the combined inventory of the three feeds drops to 12,000 pounds. The value of the average inventory for this policy is within the $15,000 requested by the acountant because

$$\text{Value of average inventory} = C * (Q^*/2)$$
$$= 0.38 * (78,926/2)$$
$$= \$14,995.94$$

```
The Feed-Supply Problem of the Metropolitan Zoo
       WORKING STOCK EXCHANGE TABLE
   Carrying          Working          Cost   of
   Charge,%          Stock, $        Orders, $
     35.00           15313.81          5359.87
     36.00           15099.68          5435.88
     36.50           14995.94          5473.48
     37.00           14894.29          5510.84
     37.50           14794.54          5547.99
```

FIGURE 12.24 The Trade-off Between the Carrying Rate and the Value of the Average Inventory for the Feed-Supply Problem of the Metropolitan Zoo.

```
       The Feed-Supply Problem of the Metropolitan Zoo
                   ORDERING INFORMATION
  Item          Item   Orders /     Order    Reorder  Max Orders
  Name          ID     Setups       Size     Point    Outstanding

  MIX            4       8.2         78926    12000        1
```

FIGURE 12.25 The Optimal Inventory Policy from STORM for the Feed-Supply Problem of the Metropolitan Zoo with $i = 0.365$.

ADDITIONAL MANAGERIAL CONSIDERATIONS

In Sections 12.1 through 12.7, you have seen how to determine inventory policies for models satisfying certain assumptions. In this section, other managerial issues you should be aware of relating to inventory systems are discussed.

Sensitivity Analysis

As with any of the techniques in management science, the optimal policy for an inventory model depends on the data used in performing the computations. Most of the time these data are estimated. As a result, when you obtain the solution, you should learn to ask questions like: "What happens to the optimal solution if one or more data values change?" "How sensitive is the optimal solution to changes in one of these data values?" For an EOQ inventory model, you might ask any of the following questions:

1. How does a change in the holding cost per unit affect the annual cost? (As the holding cost increases, it becomes more cost effective to maintain lower inventory levels, which in turn increases the number of orders.)

2. How does a change in the lead time affect the order quantity and the reorder point? For example, if the lead time is cut in half, you may discover that the amount of safety stock needed decreases significantly. In this case, you might consider negotiating with the supplier to reduce the lead time.

3. What are the financial consequences of using the optimal policy based on one set of cost estimates when, in reality, those costs are different? For instance, for the example of Suburban Hospital, recall that the order quantity of 775 X-ray films is based on an ordering cost of $100 per order. What is the impact of ordering 775 films if the ordering cost is actually $125? The annual cost associated with ordering 775 films when the actual ordering cost of $125 is

$$\text{Total annual cost} = (K * \frac{D}{Q}) + (C * D) + (\frac{Q}{2} * i * C)$$
$$= (125 * \frac{18000}{775}) + (20 * 18000) + (\frac{775}{2} * 0.30 * 20)$$
$$= 2903.23 + 360000 + 2325$$
$$= 365,228.23$$

In contrast, the optimal order quantity $Q^* = 866$ obtained from the EOQ formula in Section 12.3 when the ordering cost is $K = \$125$ results in the following annual cost:

$$\text{Total annual cost} = (K * \frac{D}{Q}) + (C * D) + (\frac{Q}{2} * i * C)$$
$$= (125 * \frac{18000}{866}) + (20 * 18000) + (\frac{866}{2} * 0.30 * 20)$$
$$= 2598.15 + 360000 + 2598$$
$$= 365,196.15$$

As you can see, if the actual ordering cost is $125, then ordering 775 films instead of 866 results in an additional cost of about $32. However, this is insignificant compared with the total cost, so there is no need to be overly concerned about how accurate the estimate of the ordering cost is in this case.

In general, the answers to sensitivity questions are obtained by changing the value of the parameter of interest and rerunning the model to obtain the new optimal solution and associated costs. If you discover that the optimal solution is particularly sensitive to one or more of these data values, then care should be taken to obtain as accurate an estimate of these values as possible.

The ABC Classification

In all the inventory models in this chapter, ordering has been done for only one item, independent of other items. In general, however, organizations often need to be concerned with the inventory of hundreds or even thousands of different items, such as the numerous drugs in a drug store or the various supplies in a hospital. Regardless of the specific inventory model used to derive an optimal policy, it will be necessary to monitor the level of each individual item to determine when to reorder. Tracking thousands of items can often require excessive resources in terms of time, effort, and staff. The **ABC classification** is commonly used in such situations to identify which of the various items are the most important to monitor from a cost point of view.

Consider two drugs that have the same demand. The first one costs $100 per bottle, and the second costs $5 per bottle. If you were able to monitor and control the inventory level of only one of these drugs carefully, you would surely choose the more expensive one because of its greater cost. The ABC classification therefore has you rank items according to their total dollar value—the annual demand times the value of that item—and then put each one into one of the following three categories:

ABC Classification
A method for grouping items into three classes on the basis of their total dollar value so as to identify those items having the greatest impact on inventory costs.

1. *Class A items* are those few items that account for the most significant proportion of the overall total dollar value. The inventories of these items should be monitored accurately and the optimal policy followed carefully to control the total cost. Typically, only the top 10–20% of the items in terms of their total dollar value are put into this category.
2. *Class C items* are the majority of items whose overall total dollar value, when compared to those in Class A, is very small, to the point of being almost insignificant. The inventory levels of these items need not be monitored closely. To cut down on the expense of tracking, these items can be ordered in bulk. Even if ordering in bulk is not the optimal policy, the low dollar value of these items means that overall costs are not significantly affected. Typically, the bottom 40–60% of the items in terms of their total dollar value are put into this category.
3. *Class B items* are the remaining ones that are not as important as those in Class A but are more significant than those in Class C.

Other Inventory Models

In addition to the EOQ and POQ models presented in Sections 12.3 through 12.6, researchers have obtained ordering policies for many other inventory models, for example:

1. Models in which the demand is deterministic but may be different from one period to the next.
2. Models in which the lead time is probabilistic rather than deterministic.
3. EOQ models in which several different items must be stocked. When the ordering and holding costs for each item are known and independent of how many and which items are ordered, then the optimal inventory policy for each item can be found separately using the models in this chapter. However, if savings can be achieved by ordering groups of items, a different inventory policy is available and can be found in the literature.
4. In the examples in this chapter, no consideration is given to the time value of money. A cost of $1000 incurred this year is not the same as a cost of $1000 incurred 5 years from now. Optimal inventory policies have been obtained for models that include the time value of money.

In summary, though the standard EOQ and POQ models are applicable in many situations, many other models exist in the inventory literature.

The inventory systems discussed in this chapter are motivated by the desire to have enough supplies on hand to meet anticipated demands. As you have learned, doing so involves a significant holding cost. To reduce these costs, the Japanese have developed a philosophy referred to as *just-in-time* (JIT) inventory, as discussed in the next section.

Just-in-Time Inventory Management

Just-in-time
A system in which inventories are made available only at those times when they are needed.

The objective of the **just-in-time (JIT)** system is to eliminate or greatly reduce the inventory needed in a production process. This is accomplished by obtaining parts only when they are just about to be used in the production process, thus giving rise to the name "just-in-time." Auto companies such as Toyota and Honda are successfully using this JIT system.

The JIT approach can eliminate the need for safety stock and unnecessary inventories, thus reducing costs and increasing profits. However, there are little or no inventories available as backup, and so for the JIT system to be successful requires certain conditions.

1. A repetitive production process in which (a) the same product is produced over and over again and (b) the demand is relatively stable—that is, large fluctuations do not occur.
2. A physical production layout designed to reduce the amount of work-in-process inventories while maintaining a balanced work flow at the various work stations.
3. The ability to receive small orders from suppliers frequently rather than fewer and larger batches less often. The supplier must be extremely reliable and able to deliver with little or no lead time.
4. Total quality management so that parts arriving from suppliers and moving from one work station to another function as specified. There is little or no inventory to replace faulty parts.

With JIT systems, the idea is to begin at the *end* of the production process, where the final product is completed. The demand for that final product is used to trigger the demands for its constituent parts in the preceding production step. The demands for those parts, in turn, trigger the demands for *their* constituent parts, and so on. Thus, the demand for the final finished product is said to *pull* the demands for all the other parts. In contrast, when individual parts build up as work-in-process inventories, those inventories trigger the production at the subsequent step and are thus said to *push* the production process.

When properly implemented, JIT systems have proven cost effective. They can also lead to increased quality and identification of bottlenecks in the production process. For these reasons, more and more companies are investigating the possibility of using the JIT philosophy or appropriate aspects of it.

Dependent Demand: Materials Requirement Planning (MRP)

The models in this chapter provide inventory policies for a *single* item. When more than one item is involved, these models can be applied to the individual items if their demands are *independent*—that is, not related to each other. In many production processes, however, the demands for the individual items are dependent on the demand of the final product in which they are used as subcomponents. An example is shown in Figure 12.26 where each complete unit of a final product FP consists of the following:

1. One unit of each of subassemblies SA-1 and SA-2. It takes one time period, say, 1 week, to assemble the final product.
2. Each unit of SA-1 requires one unit of raw material RM-1 and two units of subassembly SA-2. It takes 2 weeks to perform this assembly.
3. Each unit of SA-2 requires two units of raw material RM-1 and three units of raw material RM-2. It takes 1 week to perform this assembly.

In this case, the demands for the raw materials RM-1 and RM-2 depend on the demand for the subassemblies SA-1 and SA-2, which in turn depend on the demand for the final product. One unit of the final product generates a total demand of seven units of RM-1 and nine units of RM-2.

These dependencies affect not only all the demands, but also their distribution over time. For example, the timing of the nine units of RM-2 needed to produce one unit of the final product by the end of week 6 is critical, as seen in Table 12.1. This is because six of those nine units of RM-2 must be available by the end of week 2 so that they can be used to produce two units of SA-2, which in turn are used in making SA-1. The remaining three units of RM-2 are not needed until the end of week 4, when they are used to produce another unit of SA-2 required for the final product. From a timing point of view, it is possible to obtain six units of RM-2 by the end of week 2 and the remaining three units by the end of week 4, resulting in two production (or supply) orders. However, it may be less expensive to place a single order for all nine units of RM-2 to arrive by the end of week 2 and to hold three of those units in inventory for 2 weeks until they are needed.

Materials requirement planning (MRP) is a technique that, given an external demand for a final product and/or for some individual components:

1. Determines the demands of the dependent items.

Materials requirement planning An inventory management technique that provides not only the order quantities and reorder points but also a schedule of when each item is needed, and in what quantities, during a production process.

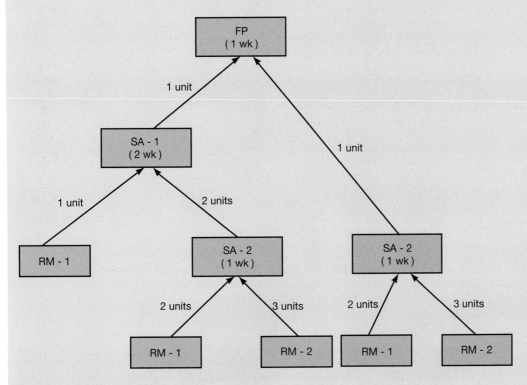

FIGURE 12.26 Product Tree for the Final Product FP.

2. Creates a schedule of when each item is needed, and in what quantities.
3. Creates a production schedule for each item based on the setup and holding costs involved.

TABLE 12.1	*Timing Requirements for the Items Used in the One Unit of the Final Product in Week 6*

	WEEK						
	1	2	3	4	5	6	7
FP						1	
SA-1					1		
SA-2			2		1		
RM-1		4	1	2			
RM-2		6		3			

Identifying the Appropriate Inventory Model

Whatever model is selected for determining the inventory policy, certain assumptions must be met. If your application satisfies all of these assumptions, then you can expect the policy to produce good results. However, if one or more of the assumptions are not met, take care. For example, in an EOQ model with deterministic demand, it is assumed that the demand occurs continuously over time. If the demand for a particular toy is 1200 per year, then the assumption in an EOQ model is that 100 toys are needed each month, or about 23 each week. If, however, the demand for these 1200 toys is *seasonal*, with 1000 of them demanded during the Christmas season of November and December and the remaining 200 sold continuously through the rest of the year, then the inventory policy obtained from an EOQ model is *not* valid.

When your model does not satisfy the assumptions of one of the models presented in this chapter, you can try one of the following approaches:

1. Determine if there is an optimal policy for your model by checking the inventory literature or contacting a consultant.
2. Determine if your problem can be *reasonably* approximated by one of the existing models through which an optimal inventory policy can be found. In such a case, you should monitor the implementation carefully because the policy, though optimal for the approximating model, may have some unexpected results in your system.
3. If no existing model can be used, the technique of *simulation* described in Chapters 14 and 15 can often be applied.

You may also want to see if the JIT philosophy is appropriate and appplicable to your business. Consider the MRP approach when the demand for items depend on each other.

Information Systems for Inventory Control

As you have learned, implementing inventory policies requires periodic or continuous monitoring of inventory levels to determine when the next order must be placed and how many units to order. When only one item is involved, this task is easily handled, but monitoring inventories of hundreds or thousands of items is time-consuming and expensive. Computerized *information systems* are available or can be designed to track the inventories of the numerous items. These systems also issue purchase orders automatically to an appropriate supplier when the inventory reaches the reorder point.

SUMMARY

In this chapter, you have learned to develop models for monitoring and controlling inventories of a single item. Although having large inventories helps meet customer demands, they can incur significant costs. Optimal inventory policies are designed to address this trade-off by determining when and how many units to order. Such policies may involve ordering different amounts at fixed time intervals or the same amount at different time intervals. In any case, the type of policy depends on the particular characteristics of the system, some of which are

1. Dependent vs. independent demand for items.
2. Deterministic vs. probabilistic demand.
3. How shortages are handled, or if they are allowed at all.
4. Lead time.
5. Cost components including ordering/setup costs, purchase costs and quantity discounts, and holding costs.

In Section 12.3, you learned about the optimal inventory policy for an EOQ model in which Q^* units of a single item are ordered when the inventory level reaches the reorder point R, computed as follows:

$$Q^* = \sqrt{\frac{2 * D * K}{H}}$$

$$= \sqrt{\frac{2 * D * K}{(i * C)}}$$

$$R = D * L$$

where

D = the deterministic demand rate in units per time period

L = the known lead time

K = the fixed processing cost per order

C = the purchase cost for each unit ordered

i = the carrying rate as a fraction of the purchase cost C

$H = i * C$ = the holding cost per unit per time period

In Section 12.4, you learned how to use these formulas appropriately when quantity discounts are available.

The EOQ model is appropriate when orders are filled in a single batch. However, in many production settings, the orders are filled continuously during the production run at a given rate. In such situations, when the inventory level of the item reaches a reorder point R, a production order for Q^* units is issued. Use the production rate P, together with the same data from the EOQ model, to compute the values of Q^* and R as follows:

$$Q^* = \sqrt{\frac{2*D*K}{H*\left(\frac{P-D}{P}\right)}}$$

$$= \sqrt{\frac{2*D*K}{i*C*\left(\frac{P-D}{P}\right)}}$$

$$R = \begin{cases} D*L & \text{if } T-L \geq t \\ (P-D)*(T-L) & \text{if } T-L < t \end{cases}$$

where $T = Q^*/D$ and $t = Q^*/P$.

When the demand for an EOQ model is probabilistic instead of deterministic, a safety stock of S units can be used to handle the variability in the demand during the lead time. Management must specify a service level α in the form of a value representing the fraction of inventory cycles in which the demand should be met with no shortages. Use this value, together with the average demand D' and the standard deviation σ of the demand per time period, to compute the order quantity Q^* and the amount of safety stock S as follows:

$$Q^* = \sqrt{\frac{2*D*K}{i*C}}$$

$$R = D'*L$$

$$S = z*\sigma_L$$

where z is obtained from the standard-normal table associated with the service level of α, and $\sigma_L = \sigma * \sqrt{L}$. For such a model, the reorder point is then $R + S$.

When implementing an inventory policy, keep the following points in mind:

1. The ABC classification scheme can be used to identify which of a large number of different items needs to be monitored most closely.
2. It is desirable to ask sensitivity questions, such as:
   a. How does a change in the holding cost per unit affect the annual cost?
   b. How does a change in the lead time affect the order quantity and the reorder point?
   c. What are the financial consequences of using the optimal policy based on a set of cost estimates that may not be accurate?

3. It is important to monitor the results carefully, especially if the inventory policy is obtained from a model that only approximates the situation you actually face.
4. The need for appropriate information systems to keep track of inventory levels, to identify the appropriate reorder points, and to issue the actual order.
5. The possibility of using materials requirement planning (MRP) systems or the just-in-time (JIT) system if appropriate for your production setting.

APPENDIX 12A
DERIVATION OF THE OPTIMAL EOQ AND POQ FORMULAS

In Sections 12.3 and 12.5, you learned that the optimal order quantities Q^* for both the EOQ and POQ models are chosen as those values that minimize the total cost per period. In this appendix, you will see how these values are determined. In terms of the as-yet unknown order quantity Q, those total costs, $TC(Q)$, have the following general mathematical form:

$$TC(Q) = a + bQ + \frac{c}{Q} \tag{1}$$

where a, b and c are positive known values. According to the results in calculus, the value of Q that minimizes $TC(Q)$ is the one that makes the derivative of $TC(Q)$ equal to 0. By using calculus to obtain the derivative, the desired Q must satisfy

$$\frac{dTC(Q)}{dQ} = b - \frac{c}{Q^2} = 0$$

Solving for Q yields

$$Q^* = \sqrt{\frac{c}{b}} \tag{2}$$

This Q^* minimizes $TC(Q)$ because the second derivative

$$\frac{d^2 TC(Q)}{dQ^2} = 2\frac{c}{Q^3}$$

is nonnegative for positive Q and c. This result in Equation (2) is now applied to the specific cost functions for the EOQ and POQ models.

■ 12A.1 THE ORDER QUANTITY FOR THE EOQ MODEL

Recall from Section 12.3 that the total cost per period in an EOQ inventory model is

$$\begin{aligned}
\text{Total cost} = {}& TC(Q) \\
= {}& (\text{ordering cost}) + (\text{purchase cost}) + (\text{holding cost}) \\
= {}& \left(K * \frac{D}{Q} \right) + (C * D) + (\tfrac{1}{2} * Q * i * C)
\end{aligned}$$

where, as described in Section 12.2,

$$K = \text{the known ordering cost}$$
$$D = \text{the known demand per period}$$
$$C = \text{the known cost per unit}$$
$$i = \text{the known carrying rate}$$

Comparing this cost function to the one in Equation (1), you can see that

$$a = C * D$$
$$b = \tfrac{1}{2} * C * i$$
$$c = K * D$$

Substituting these values into Equation (2) yields the order quantity for the EOQ model, that is:

$$Q^* = \sqrt{\frac{c}{b}}$$

$$= \sqrt{\frac{2 * K * D}{i * C}}$$

■ 12A.2 THE ORDER QUANTITY FOR THE POQ MODEL

Recall from Section 12.5 that the total cost per period in a POQ inventory model is

$$\text{Total cost} = TC(Q)$$
$$= (\text{setup cost}) + (\text{holding cost})$$
$$= \left(K * \frac{D}{Q} \right) + \tfrac{1}{2} * (P - D) * \left(\tfrac{Q}{P} \right) * i * C$$

where, as described in Section 12.5,

$$K = \text{the known setup cost}$$
$$D = \text{the known demand per period}$$
$$P = \text{the known production rate per period}$$
$$C = \text{the known value of each unit}$$
$$i = \text{the known carrying rate}$$

Comparing this cost function to the one in Equation (1), you can see that

$$a = 0$$
$$b = \frac{1}{2} * \left(\frac{P - D}{P} \right) * i * C$$
$$c = K * D$$

Substituting these values into Equation (2) yields the order quantity for the POQ model, that is:

$$Q^* = \sqrt{\frac{c}{b}}$$

$$= \sqrt{\frac{2 * K * D}{\left(\frac{P-D}{P} \right) * i * C}}$$

EXERCISES

In Exercises 12.1 to 12.6, determine (a) if the demand is deterministic or probabilistic; (b) whether or not shortages can occur and, if so, whether they lead to backorders or lost sales; (c) whether the lead time is deterministic or probabilistic; (d) all appropriate costs (ordering, purchase, holding, and shortage) expressed in terms of the same time units; (e) whether or not there are quantity discounts; and (f) whether the desired inventory policy requires periodic or continuous review.

EXERCISE 12.1 (See the preceding instructions.) The management of FastFoods, Inc., has developed a new low-fat quarter-pound burger. Demand at the company's one outlet is estimated to average 10,000 burgers per week and follows a normal distribution with a standard deviation of 750. To meet anticipated customer demands and to maintain the meat's freshness, the store manager will place an order for 1000 pounds of meat at $0.50 per pound with the supplier whenever the freezer contains less than 500 pounds. The supplier will deliver the meat in 2 days and charge $75 for shipping. The Accounting Department estimates that an additional $35 covers all other ordering costs and that the annual carrying rate will be 0.25.

EXERCISE 12.2 (See the instructions preceding Exercise 12.1.) New England Electric Company produces electricity from a coal-fired generator. The company has contracted to supply power at a constant rate all year round, which requires 5000 tons of coal annually. The coal is obtained by railroad from Pennsylvania Mining Company at a cost of $750 per ton, and an order is filled 10 days after it is placed. The Accounting Department estimates an annual holding cost of $15 per ton of coal in inventory and knows from historical records that an order costs $250 to process.

EXERCISE 12.3 (See the instructions preceding Exercise 12.1.) The *Daily News* plans to print 100,000 copies of its new afternoon newspaper each weekday. Management estimates that this volume will require 1000 rolls of paper a year. The *Daily News* has reached an agreement with its supplier to place orders of the same amount at regular time intervals. The fixed cost is $175 for delivery of the rolls after two weeks at a per-unit cost based on the number of rolls ordered as follows: $425 per roll if fewer than 100 rolls are ordered; $400 per roll if the order is between 100 and 200 rolls; and $375 per roll for any larger order. The Accounting Department estimates an additional $45 in clerical costs for placing and handling the order and suggests a carrying rate of 30% per year.

EXERCISE 12.4 (See the instructions preceding Exercise 12.1.) Toys Unlimited carries so many different toys that they are reordered collectively on a regular basis once every 4 weeks. The amount depends on inventory levels at the time of order. Management is particularly concerned with this policy as it applies to their most popular electronic toy, the Dragon-Slayer Video System, whose annual demand is normally distributed with a mean of 500 units and a standard deviation of 100. If the store runs out of stock of this system, the customer is given a 5% discount from the regular price of $150 and picks the unit up when the next order arrives. The supplier in Taiwan charges $105 per delivered unit and requires 2 weeks notice. The Accounting Department allocates $75 per order and estimates an annual cost of $30 for each unit in inventory.

EXERCISE 12.5 (See the instructions preceding Exercise 12.1.) Hexxon Oil Company has a large facility in New Jersey that refines crude oil into various petroleum products at a constant rate. The refining process therefore requires continuous operation. The crude oil is fed from storage tanks to the processing plant at a rate of 100 barrels per hour, 24 hours a day, all year long. An electronic monitoring device continuously measures the amount of crude in the tank so that the Manager of Operations can place an order when the level falls below a certain amount. The crude oil itself costs $20 per barrel under the current long-term contract and is received from the Middle East by a tanker that arrives anywhere from 18 to 22 days after the order is placed, with equal probability. Placing and receiving an order costs $1000, and the carrying rate is currently set at 0.30 per year.

EXERCISE 12.6 (See the instructions preceding Exercise 12.1.) Passion Soda Bottling Company sells its soda in 16-ounce bottles and 12-ounce aluminum cans. The bottles are recycled and new ones ordered only once a year. Sensitive to environmental issues, management is changing its policy on aluminun cans so that the cans, too, will now be recycled. Passion's new can supplier cannot commit to a fixed delivery time. It has, however, been agreed that the cans will be provided any time after 1 week but before 2 weeks of receiving an order. An order costs $125 in delivery and administrative processing charges and is to be placed whenever there are fewer than 30,000 cans. Review of historical data indicates that the monthly demand for soda averages 3,000,000 ounces and follows a normal distribution with a standard deviation of 500,000 ounces. One-third of this amount is sold in bottles and the rest in cans. If the company runs out of cans, leftover orders can be filled when the new supply arrives. The Accounting Department recommends a cost of $0.05 in lost goodwill for each can the company cannot fill on time. The accountants also suggest a carrying rate of 0.25 per year.

EXERCISE 12.7   Good Tire Distributors buys about 48,000 tires over the course of a year at a cost of $20 each from its parent company, Good Tire, Inc., for resale to local retailers. Each order incurs a fixed cost of $75 for processing and delivery charges and arrives 1 week after the order is placed. Assuming an annual carrying rate of $i = 0.25$ per year, use the EOQ formulas to determine the following:

    a. The optimal order quantity Q^*.
    b. The reorder point R.
    c. The number of orders per year.
    d. The total annual cost.

EXERCISE 12.8   The demand for Good Tire tires in Exercise 12.7 is anticipated to increase by 9% next year. How does this affect the optimal order quantity, the reorder point, and the total annual cost?

EXERCISE 12.9   By how much would the cost of a tire in Exercise 12.7 have to increase for the order quantity to decrease by 5%?

EXERCISE 12.10   Management has learned that the ordering cost of $75 in Exercise 12.7 was underestimated by $50. When you order according to the optimal policy in Exercise 12.7, what is the total annual cost if the ordering cost is $125 instead of $75? How does this compare with the annual cost of the optimal policy derived on the basis of an ordering cost of $125 instead of $75?

EXERCISE 12.11   Good Tire, Inc., in Exercise 12.7 has recently proposed quantity discounts for their distributors based on the number, Q, of tires ordered according to the following cost per tire:

$$C = \begin{cases} \$20 & \text{if } Q < 1200 \\ \$18 & \text{if } 1200 \leq Q < 1500 \\ \$16 & \text{if } 1500 \leq Q \end{cases}$$

    a. Apply the EOQ formula to determine the order quantity associated with each price, using the data from Exercise 12.7. Is that order quantity within the allowable range for that price?
    b. Find the optimal order quantity and total annual cost for each range.
    c. Use your answer in part (b) to determine the optimal order quantity, reorder point, and total annual cost for this problem.

EXERCISE 12.12   Assume now that the demand for the problem of Good Tire Distributors in Exercise 12.7 is probabilistic with an expected value of 48,000 tires per year and a standard deviation of 721.11 tires. Compute the following by hand:

    a. The optimal order quantity.
    b. The mean and standard deviation of the demand during the lead time.
    c. The amount of safety stock needed to ensure no more than two stockouts during a year.
    d. The total annual cost of the optimal continuous-review inventory policy.

EXERCISE 12.13   How often should management of Good Tire Distributors in Exercise 12.12 expect stockouts if the amount of safety stock is 150 tires?

EXERCISE 12.14   Assume the management of Good Tire Distributors in Exercise 12.12 has budgeted $750 for annual holding cost for safety stock. Using the same order quantity as computed in Exercise 12.12, answer these questions:

a. What level of safety stock can management afford?

b. What frequency of stockouts can be expected per year?

EXERCISE 12.15 Management of Good Tire Distributors in Exercise 12.12 wants to maintain a service level of 90% but cannot store a safety stock in excess of 110 tires. One way to achieve this goal is to negotiate a shorter lead time with the supplier (Good Tire, Inc.). Use your computer to determine by how much the lead time needs to decrease from its current value of 1 week.

EXERCISE 12.16 In Exercise 12.12, assume the management of Good Tire Distributors wants to achieve a service level of 95% with a periodic review policy every 4 weeks. Compute the following by hand:

a. The mean and standard deviation of the demand during the review period of $T = 4$ weeks plus the lead time of $L = 1$ week.

b. The amount of safety stock and the ordering policy to achieve the given service level.

c. On the basis of your ordering policy in part (b), how many tires should you order if there are only 600 tires in inventory at the time of review?

d. The total annual cost of the optimal inventory policy in part (b).

EXERCISE 12.17 For the problem in Exercise 12.16, answer these questions:

a. What service level can management achieve if it orders up to 4800 tires every 4 weeks?

b. If management has allocated $10,000 for inventory holding costs, how many tires can Good Tire Distributors afford in safety stock? What is the highest service level achievable?

EXERCISE 12.18 Creative Coffees sells about 100 tons of roasted coffee beans each year to supermarkets. The company's importer charges $1 per pound plus $300 per order. Once an order is placed, it takes 4 weeks for Creative's South American partner to roast the beans, clear them through customs, and get them to Creative's plant. An additional $50 covers the clerical and other costs associated with placing an order. Assuming an annual carrying rate of $i = 0.25$ per year, use the EOQ formulas to determine the following:

a. The optimal order quantity Q^*.

b. The reorder point R.

c. The number of orders per year.

d. The total annual cost.

EXERCISE 12.19 The importer in Exercise 12.18 has told Creative Coffees that for an additional $200 per order, she can reduce the lead time to 2 weeks. Should the company pay the additional money? Explain.

EXERCISE 12.20 Prior to obtaining the results in Exercise 12.18, Creative Coffees had been ordering 10 tons of beans each time. What would the carrying rate have to be for this order quantity to be optimal according to the EOQ formula? Explain.

EXERCISE 12.21 If the carrying rate is $i = 0.25$ per year how much money is saved each year using the optimal order quantity in Exercise 12.18 instead of 10 tons of beans per order?

EXERCISE 12.22 The importer in Exercise 12.18 has just offered quantity discounts to Creative Coffees based on the number, Q, of pounds of coffee ordered, according to the following cost per pound:

$$C = \begin{cases} \$1.00 & \text{if } Q < 24,000 \\ \$0.80 & \text{if } 24,000 \le Q < 26,000 \\ \$0.75 & \text{if } 26,000 \le Q \end{cases}$$

a. Apply the EOQ formula to determine the order quantity associated with each price using the data from Exercise 12.18. Is that order quantity within the allowable range for that price?
b. Find the optimal order quantity and total annual cost for each range.
c. Use your answer in part (b) to determine the optimal order quantity, reorder point, and total annual cost for this problem.

EXERCISE 12.23   Assume now that the demand for the problem of Creative Coffees in Exercise 12.18 is probabilistic, with an expected value of 100 tons of beans per year and a standard deviation of 25,238.85 pounds. Compute the following by hand:

a. The optimal order quantity.
b. The mean and standard deviation of the demand during the lead time.
c. The amount of safety stock needed to ensure no more than two stockouts during a year.
d. The total annual cost of the optimal continuous-review inventory policy.

EXERCISE 12.24   How often should the management of Creative Coffees in Exercise 12.23 expect stockouts if the safety stock is 6500 pounds of beans?

EXERCISE 12.25   Assume the management of Creative Coffees has budgeted $1500 for annual holding costs for safety stock.

a. What level of safety stock can management afford?
b. What frequency of stockouts can be expected per year?

EXERCISE 12.26   Management of Creative Coffees in Exercise 12.23 wants to maintain a service level of 80% but cannot store a safety stock in excess of 5000 pounds. One way to achieve this goal is to negotiate a shorter lead time with the supplier. Use your computer to determine by how much the lead time needs to decrease from its current value of 4 weeks.

EXERCISE 12.27   The importer in Exercise 12.23 has told Creative Coffees that for an additional $200 per order, she can reduce the lead time to 2 weeks. Should the company pay the additional money? Explain. Why is your answer here different from the one in Exercise 12.19?

EXERCISE 12.28   Assume now that a periodic-review policy is used for the probabilistic version of the problem of Creative Coffees in Exercise 12.23. Management wants to achieve a service level of 90% with a periodic review policy every 2 weeks. Compute the following by hand:

a. The mean and standard deviation of the demand during the review period of $T = 2$ weeks plus the lead time of $L = 4$ weeks.
b. The amount of safety stock and the ordering policy to achieve the given service level.
c. On the basis of your policy in part (b), how many pounds of coffee beans should you order if there are only 10,000 pounds in inventory at the time of review?
d. The total annual cost of the optimal inventory policy in part (b).

EXERCISE 12.29   For the problem in Exercise 12.28, answer these questions:

a. What service level can management achieve if the current inventory plus the amount ordered adds up to 16,000 pounds of beans every 2 weeks?
b. If management has allocated $3000 for inventory holding costs, how many pounds of beans can Creative Coffees afford in safety stock? What is the highest service level achievable?

EXERCISE 12.30 Soundly Speaking manufactures loudspeakers of all kinds for stereo systems. The annual demand for its most popular model, which sells for $30 per speaker, is 10,400 units. The plant can produce about 300 of these speakers each week, but half a week is needed to set up the equipment for making this particular model. The Accounting Department estimates $500 for each setup to cover the administrative costs and recommends a carrying rate of 30%. Use the POQ formulas to determine the following:

a. The optimal production order quantity Q^*.
b. The reorder point R and whether this point occurs before or after the production is finished.
c. The number of orders per year.
d. The total annual cost.

EXERCISE 12.31 Case Chemicals uses a process that requires a constant flow of 20 liters per hour of a highly toxic chemical, each liter of which costs $10. Its supplier needs three full days to prepare an order and get its truck to Case Chemicals. Due to the hazardous nature of the chemical, the truck can fill the storage tank at a rate of only 100 liters per hour. The Accounting Department estimates $200 ordering and setup cost to cover the delivery and other labor charges. Because of extremely high insurance costs for keeping this hazardous material in a storage tank, the annual carrying rate is 1040%. Use the POQ formulas to determine the following:

a. The optimal production order quantity Q^*.
b. The reorder point R and whether this point occurs before or after the filling process is finished.
c. The number of orders per year.
d. The total annual cost.

CRITICAL-THINKING PROJECT H
THE INVENTORY PROBLEM OF TENNIS, ANYONE?

At a recent meeting of the management of Tennis, Anyone?, management decided to sell tennis balls carrying the company logo at their 20 retail stores throughout California. As Manager of Supplies, you, Ms. Andrea Kapel, have been asked to find an appropriate supplier and to develop an inventory policy for stocking and reordering 52,000 cans a year, which is the estimated (deterministic) demand.

After a great deal of research, you located two reliable suppliers, one in Texas and one in Taiwan. In preliminary discussions, the American supplier told you that it could supply the balls at a cost of $1.38 per can and that each order would carry an additional $150 fixed charge and require 4 weeks to fill. The supplier in Taiwan can do the job for $1.25 per can because of cheaper labor. However, this company requires 12 weeks to prepare and deliver the order by sea. The associated fixed cost for each order is $1000, which includes the cost of the shipping container, customs expenses, and so on. To determine the inventory policy for each supplier, you have spoken with Ms. Suni Amoto in the Accounting Department, who advised you to include an additional $50 to cover the administrative costs for processing an order with the American supplier and $150 if you use the supplier in Taiwan. She also informed you that the current policy is to use a carrying rate of 26% per year. On the basis of this information, write a managerial report along the following lines.

1. Prepare a table showing the total annual costs (purchase, ordering, and holding) for the optimal inventory policy using each of the two suppliers. Which supplier would you recommend?

2. On presenting your results, the president, Ms. Karen Van Horn, said that she would prefer using the American supplier because that firm is more accessible and also because its lead time is much shorter. She wants to negotiate with them on the cost per can. By how much will she need to have the American supplier reduce its cost of $1.38 per can in order for the total costs (purchase, ordering, and holding) to be the same as those for the Taiwanese supplier?

3. After hard negotiations, Ms. Van Horn was able to reach a price agreement of $1.30 per can with the American supplier. For the associated optimal inventory policy, prepare a table that shows how many cans to order each time, when and how often those orders are placed, and the costs (purchase, ordering, and holding) for this policy. One of the conditions of the contract is that *orders must always be in multiples of 15 cans*, because each carton the supplier produces contains 15 cans of balls. Will you need to modify your ordering quantity to meet this condition? If so, how?

4. As a result of your efforts, Ms. Van Horn has decided to work with the American supplier under the terms in guideline 3. However, during your meeting with her, she wants to plan for future increases in ordering costs. She also was concerned with the assumption that the demand is deterministic and that the supplier may have underestimated the lead time. To address these issues, Ms. Van Horn has asked you to prepare a report that answers the following questions:

   a. By how much can the fixed ordering cost of $200 increase (to the nearest dollar) before it is less expensive to use the Taiwanese supplier?

   b. Assuming the demand is *probabilistic* (with a standard deviation of 100 cans per week), how much will the company have to allocate to annual holding costs to cover a safety stock sufficient to ensure a 99% service level?

   c. The company wishes to achieve a 98% service level and is willing to allocate $160 per year to annual holding costs for safety stock. By how much can the lead time increase from 4 weeks?

JUST IN TIME

NCR Corporation, a successful American manufacturer of computer equipment, has a niche in the banking industry and point-of-sales terminals (computerized sales registers). C. Neil Jorgensen, vice-president of manufacturing, stresses the importance of controlling the cost of inventory.

NCR works closely with its suppliers to form cooperative bonds. NCR demands from its suppliers top performance, competitive pricing, and reliable, frequent deliveries of the components NCR needs. In turn, suppliers are rewarded with large-volume contracts.

The JIT vision extends beyond the relationship between supplier and manufacturer. In the manufacturing area itself, JIT promotes close cooperation between management and production people. The video looks at three JIT techniques.

1. *Kanban* is the Japanese word for "card." When workers run out of parts, they mark a *kanban* card to signal their need for more. The *kanban* card "pulls" parts out of inventory and into the manufacturing area. The *kanban* technique contrasts with the traditional "push" system, which produces more and more parts regardless of demand, leading to needless stockpiling of material and needless costs.

2. *Group technology* combines all the specialized production lines. This technique leads NCR to larger, more efficient production lines. Workers can handle any of several parts, which means they can switch from one task to another rather than producing one part endlessly.

3. In traditional manufacturing settings, defects are detected when final assemblies are inspected. With *statistical process control*, each production line is monitored carefully and statistical measurements are used to prevent defects from occurring in the first place.

NCR employees are empowered to invent their own *kanban* signals, decide which jobs take top priority, inspect their own work, and talk with other workers to solve any problems that arise. In one plant JIT results were dramatic. A nine-step process was reduced to four steps, large inventories were eliminated, production space was cut in half, and the average daily production per line for the highest volume product was doubled. (Total running time: 6:38.)

Questions on the video

1. Which of the nine process steps did JIT eliminate? What is the next goal?

2. Why can JIT work in either manual or automated manufacturing settings?

Beyond the video

1. Traditional American manufacturers have been accused of practicing "just in case" inventory methods. What do you think are some of the differences in the philosophy between traditional "push" systems and the JIT "pull" system?

2. How must employees be trained to implement JIT in the manufacturing area?

Practical Considerations

1. What demands does JIT make on setup times and costs to achieve consistency with the EOQ model presented in this chapter?

2. What are the benefits to the employee of being able to perform several tasks instead of just one?

Source: National Cash Register (NCR), Dayton, OH, 1987.

QUEUEING MODELS

. . . .

*N*ational Public TV is conducting another fund-raising telethon. Corporate support has nearly dried up, and the network needs to open up a wider revenue stream from private viewers. The network has commitments from volunteers to handle the phone lines for this five-day effort, but management must still decide what phone system is the best choice. How many phone lines should the network rent? Management doesn't want to spend the money it so desperately needs for programming on an unnecessary number of phone lines. Still, the network cannot afford to have the people who call up to pledge money get a busy signal or be put on hold for so long that they hang up.

This chapter provides you with the tools you need to analyze National Public TV's situation, which belongs to a category of problems addressed by queueing models.

Many production and service industries have a **queueing system**, in which "items" (or customers) arrive at a "station," wait in a "line" (or queue), obtain some kind of "service," and then leave the system. Consider the following examples:

- Customers arrive at a bank, wait in a line for service from one of the tellers, and then leave the bank.
- Parts in a production process arrive at one particular work station from various other stations, wait in a holding bin for processing on a machine, and then proceed to another work station.
- After finishing their grocery shopping, customers select a check-out line, wait for a cashier to total their bill, and then leave the store.
- Phone calls arrive at an airline reservation center, hold for the next available sales agent, are processed by that agent, and leave the system when the customer hangs up.

✳Managerial problems related to queueing systems are classified into two basic groups:

✳1. *Analysis problems.* You might be interested in knowing if a *given* system is performing satisfactorily. You need to answer one or more of the following questions:

   a. What is the average time a customer or item has to wait in line before being served?
   b. What fraction of the time are the servers busy processing items?
   c. What is the average and maximum numbers of customers that wait in line?

   On the basis of these answers, managers will make decisions such as whether to employ more people or to add an additional work station to improve the level of service, or whether it is necessary to increase the size of the waiting area.

✳2. *Design problems.* You want to design the features of a system to accomplish an overall objective. This may involve asking such questions as the following:

   a. How many people or stations should be employed to provide acceptable service? For example, how many tellers should you hire at a bank during the lunch hour?
   b. Should customers wait in a single line (as is the case in many banks) or in multiple lines (as is done in supermarkets)?
   c. Should there be a separate work station to handle "special" items (such as a first-class check-in at an airline counter)?
   d. How large a space is needed in which items are to wait? For example, in a phone reservation system, how large a holding capacity should there be? That is, how many phone calls should be held before the next calling customer receives a busy signal?

   These design decisions are made by evaluating the merits of various alternative systems through answering the analysis questions posed in group 1 and then selecting the alternative that meets management objectives.

This chapter provides techniques for analyzing a given queueing system. However, the specific mathematical techniques depend on the *class* of systems to which your queueing problem belongs. These classes are based on characteristics of the different components of the system, as presented in Section 13.1. In Section 13.2, various measures used to evaluate the performance of these systems are described.

✗Queueing system
A system in which items (or customers) arrive at a station, wait in a line (or queue), obtain some kind of service, and then leave the system.

■ 13.1 CHARACTERISTICS OF A QUEUEING SYSTEM

Customer population
The collection of all possible customers in a queueing system.

Arrival process
The way in which customers from the population arrive for service.

Queueing process
The way in which the customers wait for service.

Queueing discipline
The way customers are selected for service.

Service process
The way and rate at which the customers are served.

Departure process
The way items leave a queueing system.

One-step queueing system
A system in which items leave after being served at a single work station.

Network of queues
A system in which an item may proceed from one work station to another before leaving the system.

To discuss a queueing system, it is best to identify the important characteristics that appear in the following key features section and are also shown in Figure 13.1.

KEY FEATURES

The following characteristics apply to queueing systems:

✔ A **customer population,** which is the collection of all possible customers.

✔ An **arrival process,** which is how the customers from this population arrive.

✔ A **queueing process,** which consists of (a) the way in which the customers wait for service and (b) the **queueing discipline,** which is how they are then selected for service.

✔ A **service process,** which is the way and rate at which the customers are served.

✔ **Departure processes,** which are of the following two types:

   a. Items leave the system completely after being served, resulting in a **one-step queueing system.** For example, as shown in Figure 13.2(a), customers at a bank wait in a single line, are served by one of three tellers, and, once served, leave the system.

   b. Items, once finished at a station, proceed to some other work station to receive further service, resulting in a **network of queues.** For example, the items shown in Figure 13.2(b) are first processed at work station A and then routed either to station B or C. The finished items at both stations B and C must then be processed at station D before leaving the system.

Different mathematical analyses are needed for each of these two types of departure processes. In this chapter, only one-step systems are considered.

Analyzing a one-step queueing system depends on the precise features of the first four components, as discussed in detail in what follows.

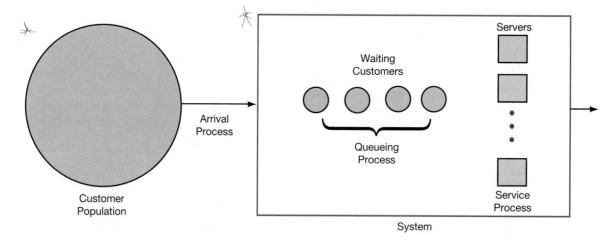

FIGURE 13.1 Components of a Queueing System.

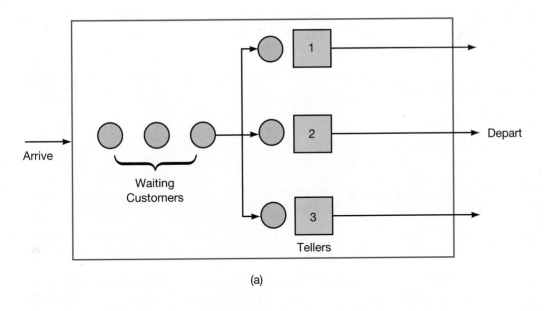

(a)

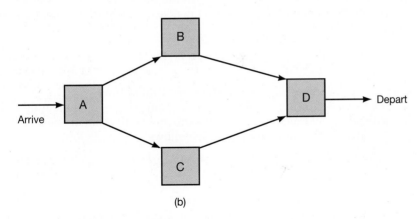

(b)

FIGURE 13.2 Departure Process of a Queueing System.

13.1.1 The Customer Population

In considering the customer base, the primary concern is the *size* of the population. For problems such as those of a bank or supermarket, where the number of potential customers is quite large (hundreds or thousands), the size of the population is considered, for all practical purposes, to be *infinite*.

In contrast, consider a factory having four machines, which often break down and require repair service at a machine shop. In this case, the machines are the customers and the machine shop is the server. The size of this customer population is only 4. Analysis of *finite* (that is, limited-size) populations is more complicated than that in which the population base is considered to be infinite.

13.1.2 The Arrival Process

The arrival process is the way in which customers arrive for service. The most important characteristic of the arrival process is the **interarrival time**, which is the amount of time between two successive arrivals. This quantity is important because the smaller

Interarrival time
The amount of time between two successive arrivals of customers in a queueing system.

the interarrival time, the more frequently customers arrive, which increases demands on the available servers.

➡ KEY FEATURES

There are two basic classes of interarrival times:

- ✔ *Deterministic*, in which each successive customer arrives after the same fixed and known amount of time. A classic example is an assembly line, where the jobs arrive at a station at unvarying time intervals (called the *cycle time*).
- ✔ *Probabilistic*, in which the time between successive arrivals is uncertain and varies. Probabilistic interarrival times are described by a probability distribution.

In the probabilistic case, determining the actual distribution is often difficult. However, one distribution—the *exponential distribution*—has proved to be reliable in many practical situations. As reviewed in the Student Resource Manual, the density function for an exponential distribution depends on one parameter—say, λ (the Greek letter lambda)—and is given by

$$f(t) = (1/\lambda)e^{-\lambda * T}$$

where λ is the average number of arrivals per unit of time.

As discussed in the Student Resource Manual, given an amount of time T, you can use this density function to compute the probability that the next customer arrives within T units of the previous arrival, as follows:

$$P(\text{interarrival time} \leq T) = 1 - e^{-\lambda * t}$$

For instance, if customers arrive at a bank at an average rate of $\lambda = 20$ per hour and if a customer has just arrived, then the probability that the next customer arrives within 10 minutes (that is, $T = 1/6$ hour) is

$$P(\text{interarrival time} \leq 1/6 \text{ hour}) = 1 - e^{-20*(1/6)}$$
$$= 1 - e^{-3.3333}$$
$$= 1 - 0.036$$
$$= 0.964$$

Poisson distribution
A distribution that describes the probability of a given number of arrivals occurring in a given interval of time when the interarrival time follows an exponential distribution.

Another equally valid approach to describe the arrival process is to use the probability distribution of the *number of arrivals*. For example, you might be interested in the probability that two customers arrive within the next 10 minutes. When the interarrival-time distribution is exponential with parameter λ, the probability distribution for the number of arrivals is called a **Poisson distribution** and is given by

$$P(\text{number of arrivals in time } T = k) = \frac{e^{-\lambda * T}(\lambda * T)^k}{k!}$$

where $k! = k(k - 1) \ . \ . \ . \ (2)(1)$.

For example, when $\lambda = 20$ customers per hour and $T = 1/6$ hour, the probability of $k = 2$ customers arriving within the next 10 minutes is

$$P(\text{number of arrivals in 10 minutes} = 2) = \frac{e^{-(20)(1/6)}(20/6)^2}{2!}$$
$$= \frac{0.036 * 11.111}{2}$$
$$= 0.20$$

In this case, the arrival process is called a **Poisson process,** but in general, an arrival process may follow any other distribution.

Poisson process
A random process in which the time between successive arrivals follows an exponential distribution.

13.1.3 The Queueing Process

Part of the queueing process deals with the way in which customers wait for service. The customers may wait in a single line for the next available server, as in a bank; see Figure 13.3(a). This is a **single-line queueing system.** In contrast, customers may select one of several lines in which to wait for service, as in a supermarket; see Figure 13.3(b). This is a **multiple-line queueing system.**

Another characteristic of the queueing process is the number of waiting spaces available in each line—that is, the number of customers that can (or will) wait for service in that line. In some cases, such as a bank, that number is quite large and poses no practical problems, so for analysis purposes the amount of waiting space is considered *infinite*. In contrast, a phone system can hold only a *finite* (that is, limited) number of calls, after which subsequent calls are denied access to the system. The infinite and finite waiting-space conditions require different mathematical analyses.

Single-line queueing system
A queueing system in which the customers wait in a single line for the next available server.

Multiple-line queueing system
A queueing system in which arriving customers may select one of several lines in which to wait for service.

> ### KEY FEATURES
>
> Another feature of the queueing process is the *queueing discipline*, which is the way the waiting customers are selected for service. Some of the common ways follows
>
> ✔ **First-In-First-Out (FIFO).** The customers are served in the order of their arrival in the line. The customers in a bank and supermarket, for example, are selected in this way.
> ✔ **Last-In-First-Out (LIFO).** The customer who has arrived most recently is processed first. An example arises in a production process where the items arrive at a work station and are stacked one on top of the other. The worker selects the item on top of the stack for processing, which is the last one to have arrived, for service.
> ✔ **Priority selection.** Each arriving customer is given a priority and selected for service accordingly. One example is patients arriving at an emergency room of a hospital. The more severe the case, the higher the "customer's" priority.

First-in-first-out (FIFO)
A queueing discipline in which customers are served in the order of their arrival in the line.

Last-in-first-out (LIFO)
A queueing discipline in which the customer who has arrived most recently is served first.

Priority selection
An arrival process in which each arriving customer is given a priority and selected for service accordingly.

In this chapter, only FIFO selection is discussed, which is the most commonly used queue discipline.

13.1.4 The Service Process

The service process defines how waiting customers are served. In some cases, there may be more than one station in the system that can provide the needed service. Banks and

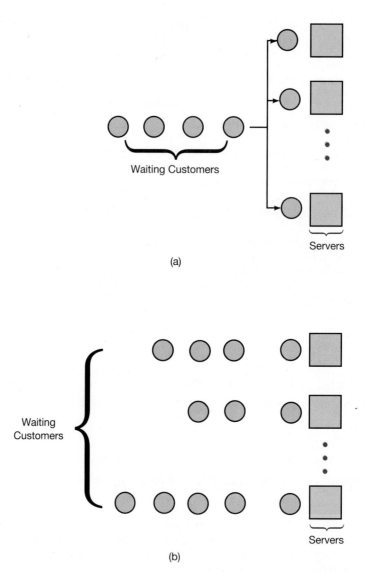

FIGURE 13.3 (a) Single-Line and (b) Multiple-Line Queueing Systems.

Multiple-channel queueing system
A system is which arriving customers may go through one of several possible work stations.

supermarkets, once again, are good examples. Each teller and each check-out person is a station that provides the same service. Such setups are called **multiple-channel queueing systems.** In these systems, servers may be *identical*, in that each provides the same *rate* of service, or *nonidentical*. For example, if all tellers at a bank are equally experienced, they may be considered to be identical. In this chapter, only identical servers are considered.

In contrast to a multiple-channel system, consider a production process with one work station that provides the needed service. All items must go through that one station. This is a **single-channel queueing system.** It is important to note that even in a single-channel system there may be multiple servers who *together* perform the needed task. For example, a hand car-wash business, which is a single station, may have two employees who work on your car simultaneously.

Single-channel queueing system
A system in which arriving customers go through one work station.

Another characteristic of the service process is the number of customers served at one time by one station. In banks and supermarkets (multiple-channel systems) and in a car wash (a single-channel system), only one customer is served at a time. In contrast, waiting passengers at a bus stop are served as a group, up to the capacity of the arriving bus. In this chapter, only one-at-a-time service is considered.

Yet another characteristic of a service process is whether **preemption** is allowed— that is, can a server stop processing its current customer to accommodate a newly arriving customer? For example, in an emergency room, preemption occurs when a doctor working on a noncritical case is called to handle a more critical injury. In this chapter, the models discussed do not allow preemption.

Preemption
A service process in which a server can stop processing its current customer to accomodate a new arriving customer.

Whatever the service process, it is necessary to have an understanding of how much time is required to perform the service. This quantity is important because the longer the service time, the longer arriving customers will have to wait for service. As in the case of the arrival process, this time can be *deterministic* or *probabilistic*. With a deterministic service time, each customer requires precisely the same known amount of time to be served. With a probabilistic service time, each customer requires a different and uncertain amount of service time.

Probabilistic service times are described mathematically by a probability distribution. In practice, determining the actual distribution is difficult. However, one distribution that has proved reliable in many applications, such as when dealing with banks and supermarkets, is the *exponential distribution*. In this case, its density function depends on one parameter—say, μ (the Greek letter mu)—and is given by

$$s(t) = (1/\mu)e^{-\mu * t}$$

where

μ = average number of customers served per unit of time, so

$1/\mu$ = average time spent serving a customer

In general, the service time can follow any distribution, but before you can analyze the system, you will need to identify that distribution.

13.1.5 *Classifications of Queueing Models*

As mentioned at the beginning of this chapter, to apply appropriate mathematical techniques, you must identify the characteristics of your queueing system based on the customer population and on the arrival, queueing, and service processes. The classification method presented here pertains to a queueing system in which the customer population size is infinite, the arriving customers wait in a single line, and the waiting space in each line is effectively infinite.

KEY FEATURES

In this method symbols describe the system's characteristics.

✔ The *arrival process*. This symbol describes the interarrival time distribution, which is one of the following:
  a. **D** to denote that the interarrival time is deterministic.
  b. **M** to denote that the interarrival times are probabilistic and follow an exponential distribution.
  c. **G** to denote that the interarrival times are probabilistic and follow a general distribution other than the exponential.

✔ The *service process*. This symbol describes the service-time distribution, which is one of the following:

a. **D** to describe a deterministic service time.
b. **M** to denote that the service times are probabilistic and follow an exponential distribution.
c. **G** to denote that the service times are probabilistic and follow a general distribution other than the exponential.

✔ *The queueing process.* This number *c* denotes how many parallel stations or channels are in the system. (Recall that the servers are assumed to be identical in their rate of service.)

Consider a system labeled M/M/3. The first M indicates that the interarrival time is probabilistic and follows an exponential distribution. The second M denotes that the service time is also probabilistic and follows an exponential distribution. The 3 means that the system has three parallel stations, each providing service at an identical rate.

KEY FEATURES

When the waiting space and/or customer population size is finite, the following two additional symbols are included to indicate these limitations:

✔ A number **K** representing the maximum number of customers that can be in the system at any one time (that is, in service or waiting in line). This number is equal to the number of parallel stations plus the total number of customers that can wait for service.
✔ A number **L** representing the total number of customers in the population.

When either of the symbols is omitted, it is assumed that the corresponding values are infinite. For example, M/M/3//10 indicates that the system has room for an infinite number of customers—the number for K has been left off—but that only 10 possible customers exist.

In this section, you have learned that the basic features of a queueing system include the number of available customers, and the arrival, queueing, and service processes. These characteristics are used to classify a system so that appropriate mathematical analysis then can be applied to evaluate the performance of the system on the basis of the measures presented in Section 13.2.

■ 13.2 PERFORMANCE MEASURES FOR EVALUATING A QUEUEING SYSTEM

The ultimate objective of queueing theory is to answer managerial questions pertaining to the design and operation of a queueing system. The manager of a bank may want to decide whether to schedule three or four tellers during the lunch hour. In a production setting, the manager may want to evaluate the impact of buying a new machine that can process items at a faster rate.

Any queueing system goes through two basic phases. For example, consider the amount of time the customers have to wait at a bank over the course of a day, as shown in Figure 13.4. When the bank first opens in the morning, there is no one in the system, so the first few customers are served immediately. As more customers arrive, the queue slowly builds up and the amount of time they have to wait starts to increase. As the

Waiting Time

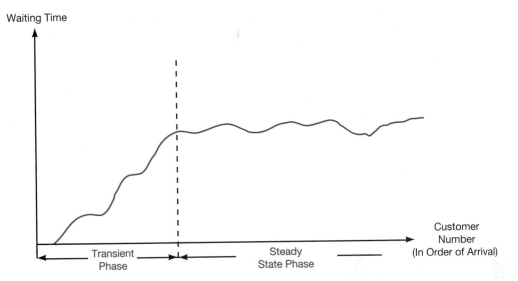

FIGURE 13.4 The Transient and Steady-State Phases.

day progresses, the system settles into a condition in which the effect of the initial lack of customers has worn off and the waiting time for customers has reached a fairly stable level. As indicated in Figure 13.4, the beginning phase, which retains the effects of the initial conditions, is called the **transient phase.** After the effects of the initial conditions are worn off the system enters a **steady state.** Although questions pertaining to both phases are important, this section deals *only* with steady-state behavior.

13.2.1 Some Common Performance Measures

There are many different **performance measures** used to evaluate a queueing system in steady state, some of which are described in this section. To design and operate a queueing system, managers are generally concerned with the level of service a customer receives as well as the proper utilization of the business's service facilities. Some of the measures for evaluating performance arise from asking the following questions.

1. Time-related questions focusing on the customer, such as:
   a. What is the average time an arriving customer has to wait in the queue before being served? The associated performance measure is the **average waiting time,** denoted by W_q.
   b. What is the average time a customer spends in the entire system, including waiting and service? The associated performance measure is the **average time in the system,** denoted by W.

2. Quantitative questions pertaining to the number of customers, such as:
   a. On average, how many customers are waiting in the queue for service? The associated performance measure is the **mean queue length,** denoted by L_q.
   b. What is the average number of customers in the system? The associated performance measure is the **mean number in the system,** denoted by L.

3. Probabilistic questions involving both the customers and the servers, such as:
   a. What is the probability that an arriving customer has to wait for service? The associated performance measure is the **blocking probability,** denoted by p_w.
   b. At any particular time, what is the probability that a server is busy? The associated performance measure is the **utilization,** denoted by U. This performance measure also indicates the fraction of time a server is busy.

Transient phase
The beginning time period of a queueing system which retains the effects of the initial conditions.

Steady state
The condition of the system after the initial conditions have worn off.

Performance measure
A numerical value used to evaluate the merits of a queueing system in steady state.

Average waiting time
(W_q) The average time an arriving customer has to wait in the queue before being served.

Average time in the system (W) The average time a customer spends from arrival to departure in a queueing system.

Mean queue length (L_q) The average number of customers that are waiting in line for service.

**Mean number
in the system** (L)
The average number
of customers in the
system at any given
time.

Blocking probability
(p_w) The probability
that an arriving
customer has to wait
for service.

Utilization (U) The
fraction of time a server
is busy on average.

**State-probability
distribution**
The probability of n
customers being in the
queueing system when
it is in steady-state.

**Probability of service
denial** (p_d) The
probability that an
arriving customer
cannot enter the system
because the queue is
full.

c. What is the probability that there are n customers in the system? The associated performance measure is obtained by computing the probability P_0 that there is no customer in the system, the probability P_1 that there is one customer in the system, and so on. This results in the **state-probability distribution**, denoted by P_n, $n = 0, 1, \ldots$.
d. If the waiting space is finite, what is the probability that the queue is full and an arriving customer is turned away? The associated performance measure is the **probability of service denial**, denoted by p_d.

4. Cost-related questions such as:
   a. What is the average cost per unit of time to operate the system?
   b. How many work stations are needed to achieve the greatest cost-effectiveness?

The specific calculation of these performance measures depends on the class of queueing systems, as identified in Section 13.1. Some of these measures are related to each other. Knowing the value of one measure allows you to find the value of a related measure. These general relationships are described first in Section 13.2.2 before the methods used to compute these performance measures for a given queueing system are presented.

13.2.2   *Relationships Among Performance Measures*

The computation of many performance measures depends on the arrival and service processes of the specific queueing system. Recall from Section 13.1 that in the probabilistic case, these processes are described mathematically by arrival and service distributions. Even without knowing the specific distribution, relationships between some of the performance measures can be obtained for certain queuing systems using only the following parameters of the arrival and service processes:

$$\lambda = \text{the average number of arrivals per unit of time}$$

$$\mu = \text{the average number of customers served per unit of time at a station}$$

Assume an infinite customer population and an unlimited amount of waiting space in the line. The total time a customer spends in the system is the amount of time spent waiting in line plus the amount of time being served:

$$\left\{\begin{array}{l}\text{Average time} \\ \text{in the system}\end{array}\right\} = \left\{\begin{array}{l}\text{average} \\ \text{waiting time}\end{array}\right\} + \left\{\begin{array}{l}\text{average} \\ \text{service time}\end{array}\right\}$$

The average time in the system and the average waiting time are represented by the quantities W and W_q, respectively. The average service time can be expressed in terms of the parameter μ. For example, if μ is four customers per hour, then, on the average, each customer requires 1/4 hour of service. In general, the average service time is $1/\mu$, thus leading to the following relationship:

$$W = W_q + \frac{1}{\mu} \tag{1}$$

Now consider the relationship between the average number of customers in the system and the average time each customer spends in the system. Imagine that a customer just arrived and is expected to stay in the system on average 1/2 hour. During this half hour, other customers are arriving at the rate of λ—say, 12 per hour. When this customer leaves the system after half an hour, he leaves behind an average of $(1/2) * 12 = 6$

new customers. That is, on average, there are six customers in the system at any given time. In terms of λ and the performance measures, then

$$\begin{Bmatrix} \text{Average number} \\ \text{of customers} \\ \text{in the system} \end{Bmatrix} = \begin{Bmatrix} \text{average number} \\ \text{of arrivals} \\ \text{per unit of time} \end{Bmatrix} * \begin{Bmatrix} \text{average time} \\ \text{in the system} \end{Bmatrix}$$

so

$$L = \lambda * W \qquad (2)$$

Using similar logic results in the following relationship between the average number of customers waiting in the queue and the average waiting time in the queue:

$$\begin{Bmatrix} \text{Average number} \\ \text{of customers} \\ \text{in the queue} \end{Bmatrix} = \begin{Bmatrix} \text{average number} \\ \text{of arrivals} \\ \text{per unit of time} \end{Bmatrix} * \begin{Bmatrix} \text{average time} \\ \text{in the queue} \end{Bmatrix}$$

so

$$L_q = \lambda * W_q \qquad (3)$$

Assuming you know the values of λ and μ, the values for the four measures, W, W_q, L, and L_q, can be found from Equations (1) to (3) once the value for any *one* of them is determined. For example, suppose that λ is 12 and μ is 4 and that you have determined that L_q, the average number of customers waiting in the queue, is 3:

$$W_q = \frac{L_q}{\lambda} \quad \text{[from (3)]}$$

$$= \frac{3}{12}$$

$$= \frac{1}{4}$$

$$W = W_q + \frac{1}{\mu} \quad \text{[from (1)]}$$

$$= \frac{1}{4} + \frac{1}{4}$$

$$= \frac{1}{2}$$

$$L = \lambda * W \quad \text{[from (2)]}$$

$$= 12 * \frac{1}{2}$$

$$= 6$$

KEY FEATURES

In summary, knowing λ and μ, the following relationships hold:

$$W = W_q + \frac{1}{\mu}$$

$$L = \lambda * W$$

$$L_q = \lambda * W_q$$

In this section, you have learned the performance measures used in evaluating a queueing system and the various relationships among them. Finding the values for these measures depends on the specific class of queueing model you have. Sections 13.3 through 13.6 show how to find these values for some commonly occurring classes of queueing models and how to interpret these measures when they are obtained from a computer package.

■ 13.3 ANALYZING A SINGLE-LINE SINGLE-CHANNEL QUEUEING SYSTEM WITH EXPONENTIAL ARRIVAL AND SERVICE PROCESSES (M/M/1)

In this section, you will see how to compute the various performance measures described in Section 13.2 and to interpret associated computer output for analyzing an M/M/1 queueing system consisting of the following:

1. A customer population that is infinite.
2. An arrival process in which customers show up according to a Poisson process at an average rate of λ customers per unit of time.
3. A queueing process consisting of a single infinite-capacity waiting line with a queue discipline of first-in-first-out.
4. A service process consisting of a single server processing customers according to an exponential distribution with an average of μ customers per unit of time.

For this system to reach a steady-state condition, *the average service rate, μ, must be greater than the average arrival rate, λ.* If this were not the case, the queue in the system would continue to grow in size because, on average, more customers arrive than can be processed per unit of time. Consider the problem of the Ohio Turnpike Commission.

EXAMPLE 13.1 THE QUEUEING PROBLEM OF THE OHIO TURNPIKE COMMISSION

The Ohio Turnpike Commission (OTC) has a number of stations for weighing trucks along the Ohio Turnpike to see that their weight is within federal regulations. One such station is illustrated in Figure 13.5. The management of OTC is considering upgrading the service at these weigh stations, and it has selected one facility as a model

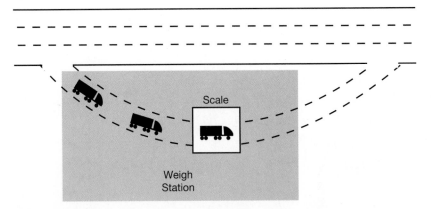

FIGURE 13.5 Queuing System for the Weigh Station Along the Ohio Turnpike.

to study before implementing changes. Management wants to analyze and understand the performance of the current system during peak hours, when the maximum number of trucks arrive, figuring that if the system can perform well during this period, service at all other times will be even better. ■

Queueing
EX13_1A.DAT

The Manager of Operations feels that the current system in Figure 13.5 meets the four conditions presented earlier. Her next step is to estimate the average arrival and service rates at this station. From the available data, suppose she determines these values to be

λ = the average number of trucks arriving per hour = 60

μ = the average number of trucks that can be weighed per hour = 66

The value of $\mu = 66$ is more than that of $\lambda = 60$, so steady-state analysis of this system is possible.

13.3.1 Computing the Performance Measures

In terms of the parameters μ and λ, researchers have derived formulas for computing the various performance measures described in Section 13.2 for an M/M/1 queueing system. These formulas are often expressed in terms of the **traffic intensity,** ρ (the Greek letter rho), which is the ratio of λ over μ. For the problem of OTC, this traffic intensity is

Traffic intensity (ρ)
The ratio of the arrival rate λ to the service rate μ.

$$\rho = \frac{\lambda}{\mu}$$
$$= \frac{60}{66}$$
$$= 0.9091$$

The closer ρ is to 1, the more heavily loaded the system is, resulting in longer lines and associated waiting times.

In terms of ρ, λ, and μ, the performance measures for the problem of OTC are computed as follows:

1. Probability that no customers are in the system (P_0):

$$P_0 = 1 - \rho$$
$$= 1 - 0.9091$$
$$= 0.0909$$

This value indicates that about 9% of the time an arriving truck does not have to wait for service because the weigh station is empty. Equivalently stated, about 91% of the time an arriving truck has to wait.

2. Average number in the line (L_q):

$$L_q = \frac{\rho^2}{1 - \rho}$$

$$= \frac{(0.9091)^2}{1 - 0.9091}$$

$$= 9.0909$$

In other words, in steady state, on the average, the weigh station can expect to have approximately nine trucks waiting for service (not including the one being weighed).

Having just determined a value for L_q, you can compute the values of W_q, W, and L using the relationships derived in Section 13.2, as follows.

3. Average waiting time in the queue (W_q):

$$W_q = \frac{L_q}{\lambda}$$

$$= \frac{9.0909}{60}$$

$$= 0.1515$$

This value indicates that, on the average, a truck has to wait 0.1515 hour—about 9 minutes—in line before the weighing process begins.

4. Average waiting time in the system (W):

$$W = W_q + \frac{1}{\mu}$$

$$= 0.1515 + \frac{1}{66}$$

$$= 0.1667$$

This value indicates that, on average, a truck spends 0.1667 hour—10 minutes—from start to finish.

5. Average number in the system (L):

$$L = \lambda * W$$

$$= 60 * 0.1667$$

$$= 10$$

This value indicates that, on the average, there are a total of 10 trucks at the weigh station, either being weighed or waiting for that service.

6. Probability that an arriving customer has to wait (p_w):

$$p_w = 1 - P_0 = \rho$$

$$= 0.9091$$

This value, as stated in step 1, indicates that about 91% of the time an arriving truck has to wait.

7. Probability of n customers in the system (P_n):

$$P_n = \rho^n * P_0$$

By using this formula, the following probabilities are obtained:

n	P_n
0	0.0909
1	0.0826
2	0.0751
3	0.0683
⋮	⋮

This table provides the probability distribution for the number of trucks in the system. The numbers in this table can be used to answer a question such as: What is the probability that there will be no more than three trucks in the system? In this case, the answer of 0.3169 is obtained by adding the first four probabilities in the table for $n = 0, 1, 2$, and 3.

8. Utilization (U):

$$U = \rho$$

$$= 0.9091$$

This value indicates that about 91% of the time the weighing facility is in use (a truck is being weighed). Equivalently, about 9% of the time the station is idle, with no trucks being weighed.

The general formulas for computing these various performance measures for an M/M/1 queueing system with an infinite customer population and an unlimited-capacity waiting area are summarized in Table 13.1 in terms of the parameters λ, μ, and ρ. Now that you know the formulas for the various performance measures, you can let the computer perform those computations and turn your attention to managerial issues, as described in Section 13.3.2.

13.3.2 Interpreting the Performance Measures

In evaluating the current system, the management of OTC finds that many performance measures are within acceptable ranges. For example, an expected time of $W = 10$ minutes for a driver to get through the weighing process is not unreasonable. Also, an average of $L_q = 9$ trucks waiting to be weighed is tolerable because the off ramp has a capacity of 15 trucks, but management is concerned that the line sometimes may back up into the turnpike.

TABLE 13.1	**Formulas for Computing Performance Measures of an M/M/1 Queueing System**
PERFORMANCE MEASURE	GENERAL FORMULA
Average number in the line	$L_q = \dfrac{\rho^2}{1 - \rho}$
Average waiting time in the queue	$W_q = L_q / \lambda$
Average waiting time in the system	$W = W_q + \dfrac{1}{\mu}$
Average number in the system	$L = \lambda * W$
Probability that no customers are in the system	$P_0 = 1 - \rho$
Probability that an arriving customer has to wait	$p_w = 1 - P_0 = \rho$
Probability of n customers in the system	$P_n = \rho^n * P_0$
Utilization	$U = \rho$

To calculate the likelihood of this happening, you must compute the probability that the number of trucks in the system is 17 or more (one being served and 16 or more waiting on the ramp). This number is obtained by adding up the probabilities, P_n, of n trucks being in the system, for $n = 17, 18, \ldots$. This results in a value of 0.20—that is, about 20% of the time trucks will be backed up over the entire exit ramp and into the turnpike. As this is not an acceptable level of performance, management wants to improve the overall efficiency of the system—not only for this reason, but also because it anticipates increased truck traffic on the turnpike in the near future. A recent report indicates that OTC should plan for a peak arrival rate of about 70 trucks per hour instead of the current 60.

To address these issues, OTC management has proposed hiring an additional worker that will result in an increase in efficiency of about 10%. That is, with this extra person, about 73 trucks per hour can be weighed instead of the original 66. As Manager of Operations, you have been asked to evaluate the impact of this proposal.

This analysis can be accomplished using the formulas in Section 13.3.1. Only the service and arrival rates change. The results of using the queueing module of STORM to compute the various performance measures for the new system in which the arrival and the service rate of μ is 73 are given in Figure 13.6.

The first three lines in the report in Figure 13.6 show the input data. Specifically, this system consists of one server, with an arrival rate of 70 trucks per hour and a service rate of 73 trucks per hour.

The remaining part of that report lists the values of the various performance measures. Management is particularly concerned with both the average time a truck driver spends in the system and the expected number of trucks waiting on the ramp. From the results in Figure 13.6, you can report that on average a truck driver spends 0.3333 hour (20 minutes) from start to finish. Also, the average number of trucks waiting on the ramp is about 22.

These performance measures are confirmed by the output from QSB shown in Figure 13.7. The first line of the report shows the arrival and service rates. The average time a truck driver spends in the system (W) is 0.332712 hour, which is slightly different from that in Figure 13.6 due to roundoff error. Also, from the QSB report in Figure 13.7, the average number of trucks waiting on the ramp (L_q) is 22.3308, which is also slightly different from the value of 22.3744 reported in Figure 13.6 because of roundoff error.

On the basis of these results, the management of OTC finds this level of performance unacceptable, not only because drivers will complain about spending an average of 20 minutes in the system, but also because the expected queue length of 22

<table>
<tr><td>Queueing
EX13_1B.DAT</td></tr>
</table>

```
                The Problem of the Ohio Turnpike Commission
                           OTC : M / M / C
                   Q U E U E    S T A T I S T I C S


        Number of identical servers . . . . . . . . .         1
        Mean arrival rate . . . . . . . . . . . . .      70.0000
        Mean service rate per server  . . . . . . . .    73.0000

        Mean server utilization (%) . . . . . . . . .    95.8904
        Expected number of customers in queue . . . .    22.3744
        Expected number of customers in system  . . .    23.3333
        Probability that a customer must wait . . . .     0.9589
        Expected time in the queue  . . . . . . . . .     0.3196
        Expected time in the system . . . . . . . . .     0.3333
```

FIGURE 13.6 STORM Output for the M/M/1 Queueing Problem of OTC with $\lambda = 70$ and $\mu = 73$.

```
              Final Solution for the Problem of the OTC
                             M/M/1
   With lambda = 70 customers per hour   and f = 73 customers per hour
              Overall system effective arrival rate =  69.9994 per hour
              Overall system effective service rate =  69.9994 per hour
       Overall system effective utilization factor = 0.958904
    Average number of customers in the system (L) =   23.2897
    Average number of customers in the queue (Lq) =   22.3308
       Average time a customer in the system (W) = 0.332712 hour
       Average time a customer in the queue (Wq) = 0.319014 hour
   The probability that all servers are idle (Po) = 0.041105
   The probability an arriving customer waits(Pw) = 0.958895
              Probability of n Customers in the System
        P(0)  = 0.04110    P(1)   = 0.03942
```

FIGURE 13.7 QSB Output for the M/M/1 Queuing Problem of OTC with $\lambda = 70$ and $\mu = 73$.

far exceeds the available capacity of 15, thus posing a possible traffic hazard on the turnpike.

To obtain acceptable performance levels, another alternative has been proposed—namely, building a second scale on the other side of the weigh station. Using the current personnel to operate both scales, management estimates, will result in the ability to weigh about 40 trucks per hour on each scale.

Once again, you have been asked to evaluate this proposal. In this case, however, you *cannot* use the results in Section 13.3.1. This is because the proposed system now has *two* servers, and the analysis in Section 13.3.1 applies to a system with only *one* server. The appropriate analysis is presented in Section 13.4.

■ 13.4 ANALYZING A SINGLE-LINE MULTIPLE-CHANNEL QUEUEING SYSTEM WITH EXPONENTIAL ARRIVAL AND SERVICE PROCESSES (M/M/C)

In this section, you will see how to compute the various performance measures described in Section 13.2 and to interpret associated computer output for analyzing an M/M/c queueing system consisting of the following:

1. A customer population that is infinite.
2. An arrival process in which customers show up according to a Poisson process at an average rate of λ customers per unit of time.
3. A queueing process consisting of a single infinite-capacity waiting line with a queue discipline of first-in-first-out.
4. A service process consisting of c identical servers, each processing customers according to an exponential distribution with an average of μ customers per unit of time.

This system differs from the M/M/1 system in Section 13.3 only in step 4, which allows c servers instead of just 1. For an M/M/c system to reach a steady-state condition, *the average total service rate of $c * \mu$ must be strictly greater than the average arrival rate,* λ. If this were not the case, the queue in the system would continue to grow in size because, on average, more customers arrive than can be processed per unit of time.

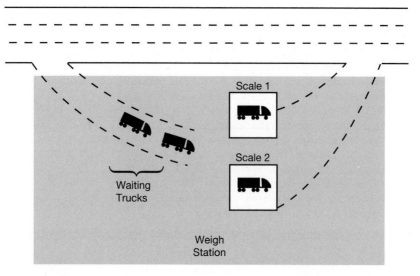

FIGURE 13.8 Queueing System with Two Scales for the Problem of OTC.

Queueing
OTC_MM2.DAT

Recall the last proposal of OTC for building a second scale in the weighing station, as described in Section 13.3.2 and illustrated in Figure 13.8. This proposal results in a system with two servers—two scales—and the following estimated arrival using the current personnel:

$$c = 2 \text{ servers}$$

$$\lambda = 70 \text{ trucks per hour}$$

$$\mu = 40 \text{ trucks per hour on each scale}$$

The value of $c * \mu = 2 * 40 = 80$ is more than that of $\lambda = 70$, so steady-state analysis of this system can be performed.

13.4.1 Computing the Performance Measures

Researchers have derived formulas for computing the various performance measures for an M/M/c queueing system in terms of parameters μ and λ. These formulas are once again expressed in terms ρ, which is the ratio of λ over μ. For the problem of OTC:

$$\rho = \frac{\lambda}{\mu}$$

$$= \frac{70}{40}$$

$$= 1.75$$

In terms of ρ, λ, and μ, the performance measures for the problem of OTC are computed as follows:

1. Probability that no customers are in the system (P_0):

$$P_0 = \frac{1}{\left(\displaystyle\sum_{n=0}^{c-1} \frac{\rho^n}{n!}\right) + \left(\frac{\rho^c}{c!}\right) * \left(\frac{c}{c - \rho}\right)}$$

where

$$\sum_{n=0}^{c-1} \frac{\rho^n}{n!} = \frac{\rho^0}{0!} + \frac{\rho^1}{1!} + \ldots + \frac{\rho^{c-1}}{(c-1)!}$$

and $k! = k(k-1)\ldots 1$ (and $0! = 1$). For the problem of OTC in which $\rho = 1.75$ and $c = 2$,

$$\sum_{n=0}^{c-1} \frac{\rho^n}{n!} = \frac{(1.75)^0}{0!} + \frac{(1.75)^1}{1!}$$

$$= 1 + 1.75$$

$$= 2.75$$

$$\frac{\rho^c}{c!} * \frac{c}{c-\rho} = \frac{(1.75)^2}{2!} * \frac{2}{2-1.75}$$

$$= 1.53125 * 8$$

$$= 12.25$$

$$P_0 = \frac{1}{2.75 + 12.25}$$

$$= \frac{1}{15}$$

$$= 0.06667$$

This value of P_0 indicates that about 7% of the time the weigh station is empty.

2. Average number in the line (L_q):

$$L_q = \frac{\rho^{c+1}}{(c-1)!} * \frac{1}{(c-\rho)^2} * P_0$$

$$= \frac{(1.75)^3}{1!} * \frac{1}{(2-1.75)^2} * 0.06667$$

$$= 5.359375 * 16 * 0.06667$$

$$= 5.7167$$

In words, on average, the weigh station can expect to have approximately six trucks waiting for service (not including any being weighed).

Now that a value for L_q has been determined, the values of W_q, W, and L can be computed using the relationships derived in Section 13.2:

3. Average waiting time in the queue (W_q):

$$W_q = \frac{L_q}{\lambda}$$

$$= \frac{5.7167}{70}$$

$$= 0.081667$$

This value indicates that on average, a truck has to wait 0.0817 hour—about 5 minutes—in line before the weighing process begins.

4. Average waiting time in the system (W):

$$W = W_q + \frac{1}{\mu}$$

$$= 0.081667 + \frac{1}{40}$$

$$= 0.081667 + 0.025$$

$$= 0.10667$$

This value indicates that on average, a truck has to spend 0.10667 hour—about 7 minutes—from start to finish.

5. Average number in the system (L):

$$L = \lambda * W$$

$$= 70 * 0.10667$$

$$= 7.4667$$

This value indicates that on average, there are between seven and eight trucks in the weigh station, either being weighed or waiting for that service.

6. Probability that an arriving customer has to wait (p_w):

$$p_w = \frac{1}{c!} * \rho^c * \frac{c}{c - \rho} * P_0$$

$$= \frac{1}{2!} * (1.75)^2 * \frac{2}{2 - 1.75} * 0.06667$$

$$= 0.5 * 3.0625 * 8 * 0.06667$$

$$= 0.81667$$

This value indicates that about 82% of the time an arriving truck has to wait, or, equivalently, about 18% of the time an arriving truck is weighed without having to wait.

7. Probability of n customers in the system (P_n):
If $n \le c$:

$$P_n = \frac{\rho^n}{n!} * P_0$$

By using this formula, the following probabilities are obtained:

n	P_n
0	0.06667
1	0.11667
2	0.10210

If $n > c$:

$$P_n = \frac{\rho^n}{(c!)c^{n-c}} * P_0$$

By using this formula, the following probabilities are obtained:

n	P_n
3	0.08932
4	0.07816
$\vdots$	$\vdots$

These tables provide the probability distribution for the number of trucks in the system. The numbers in these tables can be used to answer such a question as: What is the probability that at least one scale is not being used? This probability is the same as the probability that there are less than two trucks in the system. Adding the first two probabilities in the table for $n = 0$ and 1 provides the answer of 0.18334.

8. Utilization (U):

$$U = 1 - \left[P_0 + \left(\frac{c-1}{c} \right) P_1 + \left(\frac{c-2}{c} \right) P_2 + \ldots + \left(\frac{1}{c} \right) P_{c-1} \right]$$

$$= 1 - \left[P_0 + \left(\frac{1}{2} \right) P_1 \right]$$

$$= 1 - [0.06667 + (0.5 * 0.11667)]$$

$$= 1 - 0.125$$

$$= 0.875$$

This value indicates that each scale is occupied about 87.5% of the time.

Table 13.2 summarizes these formulas for an M/M/c queueing system with an infinite customer population and an unlimited-capacity waiting area, in terms of parameters λ, μ, and ρ. Observe that when $c = 1$, these formulas result in the same values of the performance measures of an M/M/1 system derived in Section 13.3. You can now let the computer perform those computations and turn your attention to managerial issues.

TABLE 13.2 *Formulas for Computing Performance Measures of an M/M/c Queueing System*

PERFORMANCE MEASURE	GENERAL FORMULA
Probability that no customers are in the system	$P_0 = \dfrac{1}{\left(\sum\limits_{n=0}^{c-1} \dfrac{\rho^n}{n!} \right) + \left(\dfrac{\rho^c}{c!} \right) * \left(\dfrac{c}{c - \rho} \right)}$
Average number in the line	$L_q = \dfrac{\rho^{c+1}}{(c-1)!} * \dfrac{1}{(c - \rho)^2} * P_0$
Average waiting time in the queue	$W_q = \dfrac{L_q}{\lambda}$
Average waiting time in the system	$W = W_q + \dfrac{1}{\mu}$
Average number in the system	$L = \lambda * W$
Probability that an arriving customer has to wait	$p_w = \dfrac{1}{c!} * \rho^c * \dfrac{c}{c - \rho} * P_0$
Probability of n customers ($n \leq c$) in the system	$P_n = \dfrac{\rho^n}{n!} * P_0$
Probability of n customers ($n > c$) in the system	$P_n = \dfrac{\rho^n}{(c!)c^{n-c}} * P_0$
Utilization	$U = 1 - \left[P_0 + \left(\dfrac{c-1}{c} \right) P_1 + \left(\dfrac{c-2}{c} \right) P_2 + \ldots + \left(\dfrac{1}{c} \right) P_{c-1} \right]$

13.4.2 *Interpreting the Performance Measures*

The results of evaluating the formulas in Table 13.2 with the STORM package for the proposed queueing system of OTC are shown in Figure 13.9. The first three lines in the report in the figure are the input data. This system has an arrival rate of 70 trucks per hour and two servers, with an average service rate of 40 trucks per hour each.

The report in Figure 13.9 also lists the values of the performance measures. You can report to management on both the average time a truck driver spends in the system and the expected number of trucks waiting on the ramp. From the last line of the report in Figure 13.9, you can note that on average, a truck driver spends 0.1067 hour (about 7 minutes) from start to finish. Also, the average number of trucks waiting on the ramp is about 5.7167.

OTC management finds this level of performance acceptable. However, management again asks whether trucks will be backed up onto the turnpike. This event occurs when there are two trucks being weighed and more than 15 trucks waiting on the ramp. What is the likelihood that more than 17 trucks will be in the system at any one time?

You can use the STORM report in Figure 13.10 to answer this question. Specifically, the likelihood of this event is obtained by adding the probabilities in the figure for each value of $n = 18, 19, \ldots$. The probability turns out to be 9.6%. If this is not acceptable, alternative models must be suggested. For example, hiring an additional person to increase the service rate or increasing the capacity of the waiting area by having two separate waiting lines rather than the one may be appropriate.

The performance measures for this problem are confirmed by the output from QSB shown in Figure 13.11. The first line of that report shows the arrival rate of 70 trucks per hour and the service rate of 40 trucks per hour for each of the scales. The average amount of time a truck driver spends in the system (W) is 0.106667, the same as in Figure 13.9. The average number of trucks on the ramp waiting to be weighed (L_q) is 5.716664, which is also the same as shown in Figure 13.9.

You have seen how to compute and interpret performance measures for an M/M/c queueing system both by hand and by computer. When there are only one or two alternative systems to analyze, an acceptable choice can often be made based on the performance measures. However, when many alternatives are available, additional cost information must sometimes be used in selecting the best one, as described in Section 13.5.

```
              The Problem of the Ohio Turnpike Commission
                        OTC : M / M / C
                   Q U E U E    S T A T I S T I C S


    Number of identical servers . . . . . . . . .         2
    Mean arrival rate . . . . . . . . . . . . . .    70.0000
    Mean service rate per server  . . . . . . . .    40.0000

    Mean server utilization (%) . . . . . . . . .    87.5000
    Expected number of customers in queue . . . .     5.7167
    Expected number of customers in system  . . .     7.4667
    Probability that a customer must wait . . . .     0.8167
    Expected time in the queue  . . . . . . . . .     0.0817
    Expected time in the system . . . . . . . . .     0.1067
```

FIGURE 13.9 STORM Performance Measures for the Two-Server Problem of OTC.

```
                The Problem of the Ohio Turnpike Commission
                           OTC : M / M / C
                PROBABILITY DISTRIBUTION OF NUMBER IN SYSTEM
    Number  Prob  0    0.1  0.2  0.3  0.4  0.5  0.6  0.7  0.8  0.9   1
                  +----+----+----+----+----+----+----+----+----+----+
         0  0.0667|***+                                             |
         1  0.1167|******---                                        |
         2  0.1021|*****+--------                                   |
         3  0.0893|****+--------------                              |
         4  0.0782|****-------------------                          |
         5  0.0684|***+---------------------                        |
         6  0.0598|***------------------------                      |
         7  0.0524|***-----------------------------                 |
         8  0.0458|**+--------------------------------              |
         9  0.0401|**+-----------------------------------           |
        10  0.0351|**-------------------------------------          |
        11  0.0307|**---------------------------------------        |
        12  0.0269|*+-----------------------------------------      |
        13  0.0235|*+-------------------------------------------    |
        14  0.0206|*+---------------------------------------------  |
        15  0.0180|*---------------------------------------------   |
        16  0.0157|*----------------------------------------------  |
        17  0.0138|*----------------------------------------------- |
        18  0.0121|*----------------------------------------------- |
        19  0.0105|*------------------------------------------------ |
        20  0.0092|+------------------------------------------------ |
        21  0.0081|+------------------------------------------------ |
        22  0.0071|+-------------------------------------------------|
        23  0.0062|+-------------------------------------------------|
        24  0.0054|+-------------------------------------------------|
     OVER   0.0376|**-----------------------------------------------|
                  +----+----+----+----+----+----+----+----+----+----+
```

FIGURE 13.10 STORM Probability of n Trucks in the Two-Server System of OTC.

```
              Final Solution for the Problem of the OTC
                             M/M/2
  With lambda = 70 customers per hour   and f = 40 customers per hour
            Overall system effective arrival rate =  70.0000 per hour
            Overall system effective service rate =  70.0000 per hour
     Overall system effective utilization factor = 0.875001
  Average number of customers in the system (L) = 7.466666
  Average number of customers in the queue (Lq) = 5.716664
      Average time a customer in the system (W) = 0.106667 hour
      Average time a customer in the queue (Wq) = 0.081667 hour
  The probability that all servers are idle (Po)= 0.066667
  The probability an arriving customer waits(Pw)= 0.816667
            Probability of n Customers in the System
  P(0)   = 0.06667    P(1)   = 0.11667
```

FIGURE 13.11 QSB Performance Measures for the Two-Server Problem of OTC.

■ 13.5 ECONOMIC ANALYSIS OF QUEUEING SYSTEMS

In Section 13.4, you saw the advantage of having more than one server—namely, to reduce both the waiting time and the number of customers waiting for service. Clearly, the more servers, the better the customer service. However, each server incurs operating costs. How do you evaluate this trade-off between service level and cost?

In the example of the Ohio Turnpike Commission in Section 13.4, the decision to build two scales—that is, to have two servers—is based solely on achieving an acceptable service level, which in this case means to ensure reasonable waiting times and queue lengths. In some problems, it is possible to use cost information to perform an economic analysis of the trade-off between the number of servers and the level of customer service. Consider the example of American Weavers, Inc.

Queueing
EX13_2A.DAT

EXAMPLE 13.2 THE QUEUEING PROBLEM OF AMERICAN WEAVERS, INC. American Weavers, Inc., owns a cloth manufacturing plant in Georgia. The plant has a large number of weaving machines that jam frequently. These machines are repaired on a first-come-first-serve basis by one of seven available repair persons. During several tours, the Production Manager has observed that on average about 10 to 12 machines are out of operation at any one time due to jams. She knows that hiring additional repair personnel will lower this number, thus leading to increased production, but she does not know how many more to hire. As a management consultant, you have been brought in to help determine this number. ■

13.5.1 *Modeling and Analyzing the Current Queueing System*

Your first step is to analyze current operating conditions. You should recognize that the weaving machines make up a queueing model. The customers are the machines that jam from time to time. There is a large number of such machines, so you might reasonably assume an infinite customer population. There are seven independent and identical servers who repair these machines on a first-come-first-serve basis. You can think of these machines as forming a single line waiting for the next available repair person.

To model this operation, your next step is to collect and analyze data pertaining to the arrival and service processes. Assume you find that:

1. The occurrence of jammed machines can be approximated by a Poisson arrival process with an average rate of 25 per hour.
2. Each jammed machine requires a random amount of time for repair that can be approximated by an exponential distribution with an average service time of 15 minutes, which, for each server, is an average rate of four machines per hour.

With these observations, the current system can be modeled as an M/M/7 queueing system with $\lambda = 25$, $\mu = 4$, and an infinite population and waiting space.

The results of obtaining the associated performance measures by STORM are given in Figure 13.12. As you can see, the Production Manager was quite accurate in her estimate that 10 to 12 machines are jammed on average at any point in time. In fact, that number in the report is 12.09. The last line of the report indicates that these jammed machines are out of operation for an average of 0.4839 hour, about 29 minutes.

As the consultant, you have been asked to recommend the number of additional repair personnel to hire. You now know the performance measures for a crew of seven people. How do these performance measures change with additional repair persons?

```
              M/M/7 : M / M / C
         QUEUE    STATISTICS

Number of identical servers . . . . . . . .         7
Mean arrival rate . . . . . . . . . . . .      25.0000
Mean service rate per server  . . . . . . .     4.0000

Mean server utilization (%) . . . . . . . .    89.2857
Expected number of customers in queue . . . .   5.8473
Expected number of customers in system  . . .  12.0973
Probability that a customer must wait . . . .   0.7017
Expected time in the queue  . . . . . . . . .   0.2339
Expected time in the system . . . . . . . . .   0.4839
```

FIGURE 13.12 STORM Performance Measures for the Problem of American Weavers, Inc., with Seven Repair Persons.

The associated performance measures for crews of 7 through 11 repair persons are summarized in Table 13.3.

As the crew size increases from 7 to 11, the average number of machines out of operation decreases from about 12 to 6.333. Similarly, the average length of time a machine is out of operation decreases from 0.4839 hour (about 29 minutes) to 0.2533 hour (about 15 minutes). You now need cost information to determine how many—if any—additional repair persons to hire.

13.5.2 Cost Analysis of the Queueing System

In analyzing the merits of hiring additional repair persons at American Weavers, Inc., you might identify two important cost components:

1. A cost per hour based on the size of the crew:

$$\left\{\begin{array}{l}\text{Total crew cost} \\ \text{per hour}\end{array}\right\} = \left\{\begin{array}{l}\text{cost per hour for} \\ \text{each repair person}\end{array}\right\} * \left\{\begin{array}{l}\text{number of} \\ \text{repair persons}\end{array}\right\}$$

TABLE 13.3 *Performance Measures for the Problem of American Weavers, Inc., with Different Crew Sizes*

	NUMBER OF REPAIR PERSONS				
	7	8	9	10	11
Utilization (%)	89.2857	78.1250	69.4444	62.5000	56.8182
Expected number in queue	5.8473	1.4936	0.5363	0.2094	0.0830
Expected number in system	12.0973	7.7436	6.7863	6.4594	6.3330
Probability that a customer must wait	0.7017	0.4182	0.2360	0.1257	0.0630
Expected time in queue	0.2339	0.0597	0.0215	0.0084	0.0033
Expected time in system	0.4839	0.3097	0.2715	0.2584	0.2533

2. A cost per hour based on the number of machines out of operation:

$$\left\{\begin{array}{l}\text{Total cost}\\\text{of waiting}\end{array}\right\} = \left\{\begin{array}{l}\text{cost per hour for}\\\text{each machine}\\\text{out of operation}\end{array}\right\} * \left\{\begin{array}{l}\text{average number}\\\text{of machines}\\\text{out of operation}\end{array}\right\}$$

To proceed, you need to know the cost per hour of each repair person (denoted by c_s) and the cost per hour of a machine out of operation (denoted by c_w), which is the cost of an hour of lost production. Suppose the Accounting Department tells you that each repair person costs the company $50 per hour, including taxes, benefits, and so on. The cost of an hour of lost production should include explicit costs, such as the amount of lost profit, and implicit costs, such as loss of customer goodwill if the supply deadline is missed. These implicit costs are difficult to estimate. However, suppose the Accounting Department estimates that the company loses $100 for each hour a machine is out of operation. You can now compute a total cost for each of the different crew sizes. For a crew of size 7, the expected number of machines in the system is 12.0973 (see Table 13.3), so

$$\begin{aligned}\text{Total cost} &= (\text{cost of crew}) + (\text{cost of waiting})\\[4pt]
&= \left\{\left(\begin{array}{l}\text{cost per hour}\\\text{per person}\end{array}\right) * \left(\begin{array}{l}\text{number of}\\\text{repair persons}\end{array}\right)\right\} +\\[4pt]
&\quad\ \left\{\left(\begin{array}{l}\text{cost per hour}\\\text{for each machine}\\\text{out of operation}\end{array}\right) * \left(\begin{array}{l}\text{expected number}\\\text{of machines}\\\text{out of operation}\end{array}\right)\right\}\\[4pt]
&= (50 * 7) + (100 * 12.0973)\\[4pt]
&= \$1559.73 \text{ per hour}\end{aligned}$$

Performing similar computations for each of the remaining crew sizes results in the hourly costs for each alternative presented in Table 13.4.

From the results, you can see that the alternative incurring the least cost per hour, $1128.63, is to have a total of nine repair persons. Hence, your recommendation to the Production Manager of American Weavers, Inc., is to hire two additional repair persons. These two new employees will cost $100 per hour, but this additional cost is more than offset by savings due to the fewer number of machines out of operation. Your recommendation will reduce the hourly cost from $1559.73 to $1128.63, a savings of about $430 per hour, more than covering your consulting fees.

TABLE 13.4   *Hourly Cost for Different Crew Sizes for the Problem of American Weavers, Inc.*

CREW SIZE	EXPECTED NUMBER IN THE SYSTEM	HOURLY COST ($)				
7	12.0973	(50 * 7)	+	(100 * 12.0973)	=	1559.73
8	7.7436	(50 * 8)	+	(100 * 7.7436)	=	1174.36
9	6.7863	(50 * 9)	+	(100 * 6.7863)	=	1128.63
10	6.4594	(50 * 10)	+	(100 * 6.4594)	=	1145.94
11	6.3330	(50 * 11)	+	(100 * 6.3330)	=	1183.30

KEY FEATURES

In summary, to evaluate a queuing system in which you control the number of servers or their rate of service, you need the following cost estimates and performance measure:

✔ The cost per server per unit of time (c_s).
✔ The cost per unit of time for a customer waiting in the system (c_w).
✔ The average number of customers in the system (L).

For each alternative involving c servers, compute the following total cost per unit of time:

$$\begin{Bmatrix}\text{Total cost per unit} \\ \text{time with } c \text{ servers}\end{Bmatrix} = (\text{cost of servers}) + (\text{cost of waiting})$$

$$= \left\{ \begin{pmatrix}\text{cost per server} \\ \text{per unit of time}\end{pmatrix} * \begin{pmatrix}\text{number of} \\ \text{servers}\end{pmatrix} \right\} +$$

$$\left\{ \begin{pmatrix}\text{cost per customer} \\ \text{per unit of time}\end{pmatrix} * \begin{pmatrix}\text{expected number} \\ \text{of customers} \\ \text{in the system}\end{pmatrix} \right\}$$

$$= (c_s * c) + (c_w * L)$$

Finally, select the alternative that provides the least total cost per unit of time.

13.6 ANALYSIS OF OTHER QUEUEING MODELS USING THE COMPUTER

In Section 13.1, you learned that there are different queueing models based on the characteristics of the system. You know that the population of possible customers may be finite or infinite, the waiting area may be limited or unlimited in capacity, and the service process may or may not follow an exponential distribution.

The M/M/c models and examples presented in Sections 13.2 through 13.5 all assume an infinite customer population, an unlimited waiting area, and a Poisson arrival and exponential service distribution. On the basis of these assumptions, you compute the performance measures using the formulas in Section 13.4. What happens when one or more of these assumptions does not fit the queueing system under investigation? In some cases, it is still possible to compute the performance measures. However, the formulas grow quite complex, and a computer package is needed to perform the calculations. In this section, you will see how to interpret the results of such computations for a variety of commonly encountered queueing models in which arriving customers wait in a single line.

13.6.1 An M/M/c System with a Finite Customer Population (M/M/c//K)

In the queueing models you have seen so far, it has been assumed that there is an infinite population of customers. Although this is never true in reality, for many practical situations the assumption is reasonable. For example, when the actual population is very large—such as customers arriving at a supermarket or a bank—this assumption is quite justifiable. In some models, however, the assumption of an infinite population is not appropriate. For example:

1. A maintenance staff provides repair service for a computer lab consisting of 50 microcomputers. Here the 50 computers are customers; the repair-staff members are the servers.

2. A company services elevators in 30 office buildings. Here the 30 buildings are customers; the repair-staff members are the servers.

3. A fleet of company cars is available for 20 senior executives. Here the 20 executives are the customers; the cars in the fleet are the servers.

In each of these examples, the customer population is quite limited in size. Obtaining performance measures using the assumption of an infinite customer population can produce invalid results. Recall the problem faced by the Production Manager of American Weavers, Inc., where weaving machines jam from time to time and require service. In performing the analysis, you, as the consultant, were led to believe that there was a sufficient number of weaving machines—customers—so that the assumption of an infinite population was valid. The results you developed in Section 13.5 on the basis of this assumption led to the recommendation to hire two additional repair persons to supplement the current crew of seven.

On further discussion with the Production Manager, however, you have learned that there are only 100 weaving machines. Before writing your final report, you need to see if treating the customer population as finite has any significant impact on your recommendation.

In general, the assumption of a finite population affects the arrival process. With an infinite population, the arrival rate remains the same, no matter how many customers have arrived. This is *not* the case with a finite population. Suppose you estimate that customers from an infinite population arrive at a grocery store at a rate of, say, 20 per hour. Even if there are already 60 customers in the store, it is reasonable to assume that new customers will continue to arrive at the rate of 20 per hour because there is an "infinite" number of them still out there. However, suppose this store has a base of only 100 customers and 60 are already in the store. It is no longer reasonable to assume that the remaining 40 will arrive at the rate of 20 per hour because there are too few of them left out there.

KEY FEATURES

In general, with a finite number of customers, the arrival rate decreases as the number of customers in the system increases, because there are fewer remaining customers left to arrive.

The arrival process for a finite population cannot be described mathematically by a *fixed* arrival rate because the rate changes on the basis of the number of customers in the system. The more customers in the system, the lower the rate of customer arrivals. Consider the extremes. If the system has no customers, the arrival rate will be at its highest level. If all of the customers are in the system at a given time, the arrival rate will drop to zero. How, then, do you specify the arrival rate?

The arrival process is described by considering the *arrival rate of each individual customer*. That is, you must identify how frequently one particular customer arrives. In the problem of American Weavers, with 100 machines, you must determine the rate at which each machine requires repair. Suppose that frequency is once every 4 hours. This frequency is converted into a rate per hour:

$$\lambda = 1/4 = 0.25 \text{ jam per hour per machine}$$

```
            M/M/7/K : M / M / C / K / K
            Q U E U E   S T A T I S T I C S

Number of identical servers . . . . . . . . .        7
Mean arrival rate per customer  . . . . . . .     0.2500
Mean service rate per customer  . . . . . . .     4.0000
Size of the source population . . . . . . .        100

Mean server utilization (%)  . . . . . . . .     82.5102
Expected number of customers in queue . . . .     1.8128
Expected number of customers in system  . . .     7.5885
Probability that a customer must wait . . . .     0.5254
Expected time in the queue  . . . . . . . . .     0.0785
Expected time in the system . . . . . . . . .     0.3285
```

FIGURE 13.13 STORM Performance Measures for the Problem of American Weavers, Inc., with a Finite Population.

Recall that there is currently a crew of seven persons, each capable of repairing a machine in an average of 15 minutes. The service rate per server is $\mu = 4$ machines per hour. Remember, also, that the hourly cost of each repair person is $50 and that the hourly cost of lost production when a machine is jammed is $100. Entering these data into the STORM software package—together with the fact that the population size is 100—yields the values of the performance measures given in Figure 13.13.

Queueing
EX13_2B.DAT

Compare the performance measures in Figure 13.13 with those in Figure 13.12 in Section 13.5 corresponding to an infinite population. You can see that there are some differences. For example, with an infinite population, the expected number of machines out of operation is 12.0973. With a finite population of 100, that same statistic is 7.5885. What causes this significant difference? With an infinite population, the arrival rate is fixed at 25 machines per hour, regardless of how many machines are under repair at any point in time. But consider the finite population of 100 machines. If all 100 machines are working, the rate of jamming is also 25 per hour (0.25 jam per machine * 100 machines). But what happens when, say, 10 machines are jammed? There are

```
            M/M/7/K : M / M / C / K / K
            COST ANALYSIS PER UNIT TIME

                             Current System      Optimal System *
Number of servers      |          7         |          8         |
Cost per server        |      50.0000       |      50.0000       |
Cost of service        |            350.0000|            400.0000|
Mean number in system  |       7.5885       |       6.5145       |
Waiting cost/customer  |     100.0000       |     100.0000       |
Cost of waiting        |            758.8500|            651.4500|
                                 ----------          ----------
TOTAL COST                       1108.8500           1051.4500
              * Optimization is over number of servers
```

FIGURE 13.14 STORM Economic Analysis for the Problem of American Weavers, Inc., with a Finite Population.

only 90 machines operating, so the rate goes down to 22.5 (0.25 jam per machine $*$ 90 machines) jammed machines per hour. These fewer arrivals result in a smaller number of jammed machines needing repair.

The STORM economic analysis for this example, with its finite population, is shown in Figure 13.14. The costs for each server and for waiting are the same here as before. The last line of that report provides the total cost of $1108.85 per hour for the current system with seven repair persons. STORM performs a similar economic analysis with different numbers of repair persons and reports the crew size of least total hourly cost in the last column, labeled "Optimal System," of the report in Figure 13.14. As you can see, the optimal crew size is only eight with a finite population of 100. This crew size is less than the optimal nine when an infinite population is assumed because fewer machines are jammed. You should therefore modify your recommendation and suggest that only one additional repair person be hired.

13.6.2 An M/M/c System with Limited Waiting Capacity (M/M/c/K)

Is the assumption of an unlimited waiting area for customers valid? The queueing models so far have used this assumption. In many practical situations, this assumption is in fact reasonable. In a bank, the waiting area is limited, but the customers waiting never need more than this space. Even when the line becomes very long, the waiting space can be extended into the aisles. Thus, for all practical purposes, the waiting area can be assumed to be unlimited. In some models, however, this assumption is not appropriate.

1. A phone reservation system can hold only a limited number of calls. Here the arriving calls are the customers; the reservation agents are the servers.
2. In a production facility, parts arriving from a previous production stage to a machine for further processing wait on a conveyor belt with limited capacity. If the waiting parts fill the conveyor belt to capacity, the production at the previous stage must come to a halt. Here the parts arriving from the previous stage are the customers; the machine is the server.
3. A parking lot, once filled to capacity, must turn away arriving cars. Here the arriving cars are the customers; each parking space is a server, and there is no waiting space.

In each of these examples, there is no waiting area or the capacity of the area is limited. Once the waiting area is full, arriving customers are turned away and may, or may not, return. In these cases, the performance measures obtained using the assumption of an unlimited waiting area may be invalid. By modifying the formulas for computing the performance measures to take into account the limited waiting space, valid results can be obtained.

➡ **KEY FEATURES**

These systems give rise to additional issues:

✔ What is the probability that an arriving customer is turned away and denied service because the waiting area is full? This performance measure is called the *probability of service denial*, denoted by p_d.

✔ When performing economic analysis, a third cost component—a cost associated with losing a customer—must be considered along with the cost per server and the cost of waiting.

Consider the problem faced by National Public TV (NPTV).

EXAMPLE 13.3 THE LIMITED WAITING-CAPACITY PROBLEM OF NATIONAL PUBLIC TV The Manager of the local station of NPTV, a nonprofit television network, is planning a special 5-day fund-raising telethon and is trying to determine the type of phone system to rent for receiving pledges. The local phone company provides systems of 15 or 20 lines. With each system, an option of holding 0, 5, or 10 calls is available with a total daily cost as follows:

SYSTEM	NUMBER OF PHONES	CALLS HELD	TOTAL COST ($/DAY)
1	15	0	150
2	20	0	220
3	15	5	180
4	20	5	264
5	15	10	225
6	20	10	330

As Manager of the station, you want to determine the most economical system to use. ∎

As with any queueing system, your first task is to identify appropriate arrival and service processes. In this case, a Poisson arrival process and an exponential service rate have historically proved reasonable for phone systems. Assume that your research reveals these data:

1. Arrival rate = λ = 150 calls per hour.
2. Service rate per phone line = μ = 12 calls per hour.

To analyze the performance of one of these six different systems, you must enter these data into a computer package capable of providing measures for M/M/c models with limited waiting capacity. The STORM results for the first system, with 15 lines and no calls held, are shown in Figure 13.15. Except for the last line of the report, all performance measures are interpreted as in any M/M/c model. Note the performance measure of the probability of service denial (p_d), a new and important statistic, in the last line of the report. The value of 0.1005 indicates that with this system there is a

Queueing
EX13_3.DAT

```
            M/M/15/0 : M / M / C / K
         Q U E U E   S T A T I S T I C S

Number of identical servers . . . . . . . . .        15
Mean arrival rate . . . . . . . . . . . . .    150.0000
Mean service rate per server  . . . . . . . .   12.0000
Waiting room capacity . . . . . . . . . . .         0

Mean server utilization (%) . . . . . . . . .   74.9592
Expected number of customers in queue . . . .    0.0000
Expected number of customers in system  . . .   11.2439
Probability that a customer must wait . . . .    0.1005
Probability of service denial . . . . . . . .    0.1005
```

FIGURE 13.15 STORM Performance Measures for the M/M/15/0 Problem of National Public TV.

10% chance that a caller receives a busy signal because all 15 lines are in use. This customer may or may not call back. In the latter case, revenues are lost.

To perform an economic analysis for such systems, you need to know the cost of the servers and the cost of waiting. You also need to estimate the cost of losing a customer when the waiting space is filled. For the problem of NPTV, these three cost components are estimated as follows:

1. *Cost per server*: Each server corresponds to one phone line. The total cost to NPTV can be converted to a cost per phone line per hour. Assume the telethon is conducted for 8 hours each day. The associated cost for the first system is

$$c_s = (\$150/\text{day})/(8 \text{ hours/day})/(15 \text{ phone lines})$$

$$= 1.25$$

Thus, with this system of 15 servers (phone lines), this hourly cost is

$$\text{Total cost of servers} = (\text{cost per server}) * (\text{number of servers})$$

$$= c_s * c$$

$$= 1.25 * 15$$

$$= \$18.75 \text{ per hour}$$

2. *Cost of waiting*: In this case, there is no direct cost of a contributor spending time on the line to make a pledge, so

$$c_w = 0$$

Thus, the cost per hour of customers in the system is

$$\left\{ \begin{matrix} \text{Total cost} \\ \text{of waiting} \end{matrix} \right\} = \left\{ \begin{matrix} \text{cost of} \\ \text{waiting} \end{matrix} \right\} * \left\{ \begin{matrix} \text{number of} \\ \text{customers} \\ \text{in the system} \end{matrix} \right\}$$

$$= c_w * L$$

$$= 0 * 11.2439$$

$$= \$0 \text{ per hour}$$

3. *Cost of a lost customer*: Here it is necessary to estimate how much money is lost when a person gets a busy signal and is unable to make a contribution. The management of NPTV knows from past experience that the average donation per call is $50. However, this amount is not always lost when a contributor cannot get through because 80% will continue calling. The cost of a lost customer in this case is then

$$c_d = (\$50 \text{ per call}) * (\text{probability of losing the call})$$

$$= 50 * 0.20$$

$$= \$10.00 \text{ per denial}$$

This figure is a cost for *each customer* denied service. To compute this total cost per hour, it is necessary to know *how many* customers are denied service each hour. Recall that the arrival rate is $\lambda = 150$ calls per hour and that the probability of a customer being denied service is $p_d = 0.1005$ (see Figure 13.15). On average, then,

$150 * 0.1005 = 15.075$ customers are denied service each hour. Thus, the hourly cost of lost customers is

$$\begin{Bmatrix} \text{Total cost} \\ \text{of denial} \end{Bmatrix} = \begin{Bmatrix} \text{cost per} \\ \text{denial} \end{Bmatrix} * \begin{Bmatrix} \text{number of} \\ \text{arrivals} \end{Bmatrix} * \begin{Bmatrix} \text{probability of} \\ \text{service denial} \end{Bmatrix}$$

$$= c_d * \lambda * p_d$$

$$= 10 * 150 * 0.1005$$

$$= \$150.75 \text{ per hour}$$

These three cost components are added to give the total hourly cost for the first system with 15 lines and no waiting:

$$\text{Total cost} = (\text{cost of servers}) + (\text{cost of waiting}) + (\text{cost of service denial})$$

$$= (c_s * c) + (c_w * L) + (c_d * \lambda * p_d)$$

$$= (1.25 * 15) + (0 * 11.2439) + (10.00 * 150 * 0.1005)$$

$$= 18.75 + 0 + 150.75$$

$$= \$169.50 \text{ per hour}$$

A similar analysis can now be performed on each of the remaining five phone systems. The results are summarized in Table 13.5. Look at the total hourly cost of each system in the final line of that table. The costs indicate that it is most economical to have a system with 20 phone lines and the capability of holding up to five calls, at a total hourly cost of $34.90 (System 4).

TABLE 13.5 *Economic Analysis of the Six Phone Systems for the Problem of NPTV*

	SYSTEM					
	1	2	3	4	5	6
Number of lines	15	20	15	20	15	20
Waiting capacity	0	0	5	5	10	10
c_s	1.25	1.375	1.50	1.65	1.875	2.0625
c_w	0.00	0.00	0.00	0.00	0.00	0.00
c_d	10.00	10.00	10.00	10.00	10.00	10.00
L	11.235	12.331	12.722	12.527	13.565	12.555
p_d	0.1005	0.0135	0.0311	0.0013	0.0114	0.0001
Total cost ($/hr)	169.50	47.78	69.08	34.90	45.26	41.43

13.6.3 A Queuing System with a General Service-Time Distribution (M/G/c)

In all the queuing systems discussed so far, the service time is assumed to follow an exponential distribution with a known mean service rate of μ. In some models, however, this assumption may not be valid. One extreme example is when the service time is deterministic—that is, each customer requires the same known amount of service time (as in an assembly line with a fixed cycle time). Even when the service time is probabilistic, you may not know its distribution or it may not be exponential. In such cases, you can use appropriate queuing analysis by identifying the service process as being "general" (G).

KEY FEATURES

To obtain performance measures for such systems, in addition to the average arrival rate of λ, you must estimate:

✔ The average amount of time per service.
✔ The standard deviation of the service time, which yields a measure of its variability. (Note that a standard deviation of 0 corresponds to a deterministic service time.)

Consider the problem of the Los Alamos branch of the Texas Bureau of Motor Vehicles.

Queueing
EX13_4.DAT

EXAMPLE 13.4 THE QUEUEING PROBLEM OF THE TEXAS BUREAU OF MOTOR VEHICLES The Los Alamos branch office currently has three clerks processing auto registrations. Recently, they have received complaints from customers having to wait too long during the lunch-hour period, from 11:30 A.M. to 1:30 P.M. To ease the problem, you, as Office Manager, are trying to determine how many additional employees to hire for this 2-hour period so that the waiting time is less than 10 minutes. ∎

The arrival of customers might reasonably be assumed to follow a Poisson process. On the basis of historical data, you estimate the average arrival rate during the lunch hours to be $\lambda = 46$ customers per hour. Although you are uncertain of the service time distribution, a time study has revealed that each clerk needs an average of 5 minutes (0.08333 hour) to handle a customer, with a standard deviation of 2 minutes (0.0333 hour).

These data indicate that each clerk can process an average of $\mu = 12$ customers per hour. Thus, to handle the peak estimate of 46 customers per hour—that is, to ensure that the total service rate of $c * \mu$ exceeds the total arrival rate of λ—it is necessary to have at least four clerks on duty. Entering these data into the STORM software package using an M/G/4 model (to indicate that the service time distribution is not exponential) yields the performance measures given in Figure 13.16. You can see that there is an average of 12 customers in the queue, and each of them has to wait an average of

```
             M/G/4 : M / G / C
          Q U E U E   S T A T I S T I C S


Number of identical servers . . . . . . . . .        4
Mean arrival rate . . . . . . . . . . . . .    46.0000
Mean service rate per server   . . . . . . .   12.0000
Standard deviation of service time  . . . . .   0.0333

Mean server utilization (%) . . . . . . . . .   95.8330
Expected number of customers in queue . . . .   12.1272
Expected number of customers in system  . . .   15.9605
Probability that a customer must wait . . . .    0.9092
Expected time in the queue  . . . . . . . . .    0.2636
Expected time in the system . . . . . . . . .    0.3470
```

FIGURE 13.16 STORM Performance Measures for the M/G/4 Problem of Texas BMV.

```
               M/G/5 : M / G / C
              QUEUE   STATISTICS

Number of identical servers . . . . . . . .        5
Mean arrival rate . . . . . . . . . . . . .   46.0000
Mean service rate per server   . . . . . . .  12.0000
Standard deviation of service time  . . . . .  0.0333

Mean server utilization (%) . . . . . . . . .  76.6664
Expected number of customers in queue . . . .   0.9369
Expected number of customers in system  . . .   4.7702
Probability that a customer must wait . . . .   0.4916
Expected time in the queue  . . . . . . . . .   0.0204
Expected time in the system . . . . . . . . .   0.1037
```

FIGURE 13.17 STORM Performance Measures for the M/G/5 Problem of Texas BMV.

0.2636 hour (about 16 minutes) before being served. In total, each customer spends 0.3470 hour (about 21 minutes) at the bureau.

This level of service is not acceptable because the average waiting time of 16 minutes exceeds the target of 10 minutes. It is therefore necessary to have at least five clerks on duty. Changing the number of servers from 4 to 5 and solving the new M/G/5 model yields the results shown in Figure 13.17. You can see that with five clerks on duty, the average waiting time in the queue has decreased to 0.0204 hour, a little over 1 minute. This is well within the target of 10 minutes, so you decide to increase the number of clerks from 3 to 5 during the lunch hour.

In this section, you have seen how the computer obtains performance measures for some commonly occurring queueing systems other than the M/M/c system. These other models include an M/M/c system with a finite population, an M/M/c system with a limited waiting capacity, and an M/G/c system in which the service time follows a general distribution whose mean and standard deviation must be estimated. Other issues a manager should be concerned with when analyzing or designing queueing systems are discussed next.

ADDITIONAL MANAGERIAL CONSIDERATIONS

You have learned to design and analyze some typical queueing systems by evaluating various performance measures and by conducting appropriate economic analysis. In this section, several important issues relevant to this analysis are discussed from a managerial point of view.

Choosing an Appropriate Model

Although the ultimate objective of a queueing model is to evaluate various performance measures, the ability to compute those measures is restricted to a limited number of different models (such as the M/M/c or M/G/c systems). Your particular queueing problem may not fit the models that your computer package is capable of handling. In these cases, you must do one of the following:

1. Obtain a computer package that *is* capable of analyzing your model.

2. Locate appropriate formulas from a specialized queueing-theory book for computing the needed performance measures, and this may not always be possible.

3. Make some assumptions about your problem that allow you to approximate it with one of the queueing models for which the formulas for the performance measures are available.

Consider a soft-drink bottling machine. Empty bottles arrive one at a time and are filled in groups of 24 at once. Unlike the previous models, in which each customer in the queue is served individually, here the machine processes a group of 24 bottles simultaneously. If there are fewer than 24 bottles in the queue, the machine must wait.

One way to approximate this system is to identify each group of 24 bottles as one "customer." This is done by modifying the arrival process to express an arrival rate associated with each *batch*. For example, if the original bottles arrive at an average rate of 48 bottles per minute, then each group of 24 bottles arrives at an approximate rate of two batches per minute. Similarly, the service time must be expressed as the amount of time needed for the machine to fill all 24 bottles, not each one individually. The associated performance measures must be interpreted accordingly. For example, if the average number of customers in the queue is, say, 5, this means that on average there are approximately $5 * 24 = 120$ bottles waiting to be filled.

When using an approximating model, be aware that the performance measures you obtain may *not* be what you see in practice. Before implementing decisions based on modeled results, you should attempt to validate them. To validate the approximation used in the bottling example, suppose the model results in an average of five customers in the system. If this approximation is valid, you should indeed observe an average of about 120 bottles waiting to be filled in practice. Only if you determine that the approximating model is valid should you consider implementing decisions on the basis of performance measures obtained from it.

Additional Queueing Systems

As you have learned, a queueing system has many individual components and characteristics, including an arrival and service process, a queue discipline, and so on. The specific results in this chapter apply *only* to a system with the following characteristics:

1. Customers arrive and will continue to wait in a single queue until they are served, one at a time.

2. The queue discipline is first-in-first-out—that is, the first customer to arrive is the first one to be served.

3. Once customers are served, they leave the system forever—that is, there is only one work station.

In many applications, however, these characteristics may vary, for example:

1. Customers may *arrive in batches* and/or wait in *multiple lines*. In the latter case, an arriving customer probably joins the shortest queue but may later *jockey* between lines, as their lengths change.

2. Waiting customers may be *served in groups* rather than individually. The group may be fixed in size, as is the case in the previous bottling example, or may vary in size, as when a bus picks up waiting passengers.

3. The choice of which customer to serve may be other than first-in-first-out, such as in an emergency room of a hospital.

4. Arriving customers, on seeing the length of the queue, may choose not to wait and thus *balk*. Alternatively, they may wait in line for some time and then decide to leave, thus *reneging*.

5. Some customers after being served *may not leave the system*, but rather proceed to another work station for further processing. They may even return to the first station a second time. This results in a system with a *network* of work stations rather than a single work station.

These varying characteristics result in more-complex systems that in many cases cannot be analyzed directly because mathematical formulas cannot be derived. For such situations, the management science technique of *simulation*, presented in Chapters 14 and 15, can often be used for design and analysis.

Sensitivity Analysis

Your computer package may be able to handle your model and provide you with exact performance measures. Still, you should keep in mind that results you obtain depend on estimates of the arrival and service rates. These estimates may or may not be accurate, so you should learn to ask "What happens if?" questions. For example, in an M/M/c queueing system, you might have estimated that 50 customers arrive for service each hour. On the basis of this information and other cost data, suppose you have determined that the system of least cost requires five servers. Before implementing this decision, you should ask some of the following questions:

1. How many servers should be hired if the arrival rate is 52, 55, or 60 customers per hour?
2. By how much would the arrival rate have to increase or decrease, keeping all other data the same, before it is no longer optimal to have five servers?
3. By how much would the service rate have to increase or decrease, keeping all other data the same, before it is no longer optimal to have five servers?
4. By how much can the cost of each server increase or decrease before it is no longer optimal to have five servers?

These questions are answered by repeatedly computing the performance measures and economic analysis for the model, each time changing the data of interest. If the results are sensitive to a particular data value, that value should receive particular attention. Your time might be well spent focusing on this value to obtain a more accurate estimate.

Sensitivity analysis can be performed on virtually all performance measures, depending on which one(s) you are most concerned with. For example, even with an M/M/1 queue, you can ask (and answer) each of the following types of questions:

1. By how much would the arrival rate have to increase before the average length and/or waiting time in the queue exceeds some acceptable limit?
2. By how much could the service rate have to decrease before the probability that there are more than 10 customers in the system exceeds an acceptable level?

Only after careful analysis of these sensitivity questions should a solution be implemented. Even then, the implementation should be monitored closely to see that the results obtained in practice are what was expected from the model.

Trade-Off Analysis

In trying to determine the "best" queueing system, you may focus on one particular performance measure. For example, you may want a system that has a high utilization—that is, the fraction of time each server is busy should be close to 1. You might achieve such a result by having fewer servers, so that those you do have are busy more of the time or you might try to increase the arrival rate so that the queue is almost never empty. For example, in a production environment, you might release more jobs more quickly to the system.

In most cases, however, you will typically find that there is a trade-off: As one performance measure improves, others deteriorate. For example, Table 13.6 shows the contrast of utilization versus waiting time when changing the arrival rate λ in an M/M/1 system with a service rate of $\mu = 20$ customers per hour. As the arrival rate of λ increases from 10 to 18, the utilization increases from 50% to 90%—a desirable change. However, at the same time the waiting time for a customer in the queue increases from 0.05 hour (3 minutes) to 0.45 hour (27 minutes). As Manager, you must choose a value of λ that produces an acceptable utilization of your servers and an acceptable waiting time for your customers.

TABLE 13.6	*Trade-Off Between Utilization and Average Waiting Time for an M/M/1 Queue with $\mu = 20$ per Hour*		
λ	ρ	UTILIZATION	AVERAGE TIME IN QUEUE (HR)
10	0.5	0.50	0.050
12	0.6	0.60	0.075
14	0.7	0.70	0.116
16	0.8	0.80	0.200
18	0.9	0.90	0.450

SUMMARY

In this chapter, you have seen how to apply queueing theory in designing and analyzing systems in which items arrive at a station, wait in a line, obtain some kind of service, and then leave. You also learned that to analyze such queueing models involves computing some of the following performance measures:

1. The average waiting time that an arriving customer has to spend in line before being served (W_q).
2. The average time a customer spends in the system (W).
3. The average queue length (L_q).
4. The average number of customers in the system (L).
5. The probability that an arriving customer has to wait for service (p_w).
6. The average server utilization (U).
7. The probability that there are n customers in the system (P_n).

The formulas needed to compute these measures depend on the specific characteristics of the following four components:

1. The customer population.
2. The arrival process.
3. The queueing process and discipline.
4. The service process.

You have also seen how to use the computer to obtain these measures for many commonly occurring models and how to interpret and use the results to make managerial decisions. Doing so often involves evaluating alternative systems. The choice can be based on achieving a desired performance level or on an economic analysis that associates an overall cost to each alternative, which allows you to choose the one of least cost.

The formulas for computing the various performance measures are available only for certain simple models, such as the M/M/c and M/G/c systems. If your system is too complex to be approximated by one of the models for which the mathematical formulas are available, the technique of simulation, presented in Chapters 14 and 15, can often be used.

EXERCISES

In Exercises 13.1 to 13.6, identify and briefly describe the following aspects of the queueing scenario: (a) the customers and the servers, (b) the customer population and size, (c) the arrival process and appropriate parameters for the arrival distribution, (d) the queueing process and discipline, and (e) the service process and appropriate parameters for the service-time distribution.

EXERCISE 13.1 (See the preceding instructions.) Due to recent complaints, the Maintenance Division of California Gas and Electric is trying to decide how many repair persons they need to have to provide an acceptable level of service to their customers. Complaints come into a service center according to an exponential distribution with an average rate of 20 calls per day. The time for a repair person to reach the site, handle the problem, and return also follows an exponential distribution, with an average time of 3 hours and 30 minutes.

EXERCISE 13.2 (See the instructions preceding Exercise 13.1.) The aircraft carrier *U.S.S. Enterprise* has a complement of 80 jet fighters. After routine operations, the planes are brought from the flight deck to below deck, two at a time. The elevator trip from one deck to the other takes 20 seconds, and 10 seconds are needed to load and to unload aircraft on the elevator. Planes arrive at the elevator from the flight deck every 30 seconds.

EXERCISE 13.3 (See the instructions preceding Exercise 13.1.) The Manager of the American Savings Bank wants to determine the minimum number of tellers needed to handle lunchtime customers. The average time between two customers arriving is 2 minutes but the actual time follows an exponential distribution. Each teller can handle an average of 12 customers an hour, but the time for each customer varies according to an exponential distribution.

EXERCISE 13.4 (See the instructions preceding Exercise 13.1.) The plant at American Auto has a continuously operating machine that stamps pieces of sheet metal into fenders for cars. The sheet metal is transported by a conveyor belt at a continuous rate of two per minute. Each arriving piece is stacked on top of the previous ones, up to a maximum of 20, at which time the conveyor belt stops. The belt restarts when the number of pieces in the stack drops below 20. Every 42 seconds, a robot arm picks up the piece on top of the stack and places it in the stamping machine, which then produces the fender.

EXERCISE 13.5 (See the instructions preceding Exercise 13.1.) The owner of FastFoods, Inc., wants to determine the impact of converting the one drive-through window into two windows. At the first window, the customers would order and pay for the food. At the second window, they would pick up the food. Cars arrive according to an exponential distribution at the average rate of 90 per hour during the lunch period, from 11:45 A.M. to 1:15 P.M. If, however, the driveway in front of the first window is full (with up to 10 cars), the arriving customer leaves. The driveway of the second window can hold only three cars. The time to place an order, pay, and receive change follows an exponential distribution with an average of 20 seconds. The amount of time it takes to receive the food varies according to a normal distribution. On average, an order is filled in 30 seconds, with a variance of 9.

EXERCISE 13.6   (See the instructions preceding Exercise 13.1.) The city of Tokyo has just opened a small domestic airport on landfill in Tokyo Bay. Two runways are available for arriving aircraft, which land in the order in which they arrive (unless, of course, an emergency arises). For safety reasons, the Tokyo Air Traffic Commission has determined that at most 12 aircraft can be in a holding pattern waiting to land at any point in time. If more arrive, they are diverted to Haneda Airport. During the peak periods, aircraft are projected to arrive according to an exponential distribution at an average rate of 30 per hour and depart at a rate of about 20 per hour. The landing phase of an aircraft begins when controllers in the tower give permission to a pilot for the final approach. Data from other airports having a similar runway configuration indicate that the time required for landing and exiting the runway follows a normal distribution with a mean of 80 seconds and a standard deviation of 30 seconds. Departing aircraft use the runway for an average of 30 seconds, with a standard deviation of 10 seconds.

EXERCISE 13.7   California Gas and Electric Company has one representative at a service center to handle customer questions. The number of phone calls coming into the center follows a Poisson distribution with an average rate of approximately 10 per hour. The time needed to answer each call follows an exponential distribution with an average of 4 minutes. Use the relationship between the Poisson and exponential distributions to answer the following questions:

    a. What is the average time between arriving calls?
    b. What is the average number of calls a representative can handle in 1 hour?
    c. What is the probability that there are exactly five calls in 1 hour?
    d. What is the probability that a second call comes in within 3 minutes of the previous call?

EXERCISE 13.8   The SootheSayer Brokerage Firm manages portfolios of common stocks. Its computers monitor stock prices and, when certain conditions arise, they issue buy or sell signals. These signals follow a Poisson process with an average of one every 15 minutes. Before acting on the computers' recommendation, a financial analyst evaluates the scenario and makes a final decision on the number of shares to trade, if any. The time for this evaluation follows an exponential distribution with an average of 12 minutes. Use the relationship between the Poisson and exponential distributions to answer the following questions:

    a. What is the probability that exactly four buy/sell signals are generated in 1 hour?
    b. If the computers just issued a buy/sell signal, what is the probability that the next one is issued within 10 minutes?
    c. What is the average number of buy/sell signals an analyst can handle in a 3-hour period?
    d. If a buy/sell signal arrives, what is the probability that the analyst finishes the evaluation within 15 minutes? What is the probability that it takes more than 20 minutes?

EXERCISE 13.9   For the queueing problem of American Savings Bank in Exercise 13.3, suppose there is only one teller. Each hour he can handle an average of 12 customers, who arrive at a rate of one about every 7.5 minutes. For this system, customers will have to wait an average of 10 minutes before reaching the teller. Use the relationships in Section 13.2.2 and the given information to find the values of W, W_q, L, and L_q.

EXERCISE 13.10   For the queueing problem of American Savings Bank in Exercise 13.3, suppose there is only one teller. Each hour he can handle an average of six customers, who arrive at a rate of one about every 12 minutes. Management has observed that there seems to be an average of five customers in the bank at any given time. Use the relationships in Section 13.2.2 and the given information to find the values of W, W_q, L, and L_q.

EXERCISE 13.11 For the queueing problem of California Gas and Electric Company in Exercise 13.7, compute all the performance measures listed in Table 13.1 in Section 13.3.1 by hand and interpret those values in the context of the problem. (Compute only the probabilities of 0, 1, and 2 customers being in the system.)

EXERCISE 13.12 For the queueing problem of the SootheSayer Brokerage Firm in Exercise 13.8, assume that on average a buy/sell signal is generated every 8 minutes and that there are two financial analysts. Each analyst is capable of making an evaluation in about 12 minutes. Compute all the performance measures listed in Table 13.2 in Section 13.4.1 by hand, and interpret those values in the context of the problem. (Compute only the probabilities of 0, 1, and 2 customers being in the system.)

EXERCISE 13.13 Use your computer to answer the following sensitivity questions for the problem of California Gas and Electric Company in Exercise 13.7:

a. How many incoming calls per hour can there be before the average time a customer spends on the phone exceeds 20 minutes?
b. How much time could the average call take for answering before there is an average of two calls on hold waiting to be answered?
c. How many more calls would need to be answered each hour before the probability that there are two calls in the system drops to 0.125?

EXERCISE 13.14 Use your computer to answer the following sensitivity questions for the problem of the SootheSayer Brokerage Firm in Exercise 13.12:

a. On average, how much additional time can each analyst take before more than 1 hour elapses on average from the time a buy/sell signal is generated until he or she makes a final decision?
b. On average, how many signals per hour can arrive before there is an average of three of them waiting to be analyzed?
c. How many analysts are needed to ensure that, on average, no more than 15 minutes elapse from the time a buy/sell signal is generated until an analyst makes a final decision?

EXERCISE 13.15 New York Taxi Cab Company maintains a service facility for major repairs and maintenance of its vehicles. Historical data show that (a) taxis have major breakdowns according to a Poisson process at an average rate of 2 every 24 hours, including weekends, and (b) the amount of time required by a mechanic to fix a taxi follows an exponential distribution with an average of 16.8 hours. However, management can rely on mechanics showing up only 80% of the time because of illness and vacation time. The Accounting Department has indicated that (i) the total cost per hour of a mechanic, including salary, benefits, and taxes, is $24, and (ii) the average taxi cab earns a net profit of $100 in a 24-hour period. Use your computer to determine whether the company should have two or three mechanics on duty at all times. For each of the two systems you evaluate, specify the values of c, λ, μ, c_w, c_s, and the total cost per unit of time. (Note: To approximate this scenario by an M/M/c queueing system, increase the average service time appropriately to account for absence of mechanics.)

EXERCISE 13.16 The PayFast supermarket currently has four cashiers. The company wants to upgrade its service either by hiring an additional cashier or by putting in bar-code scanners at each checkout. Historical data indicate that (a) customers arrive according to a Poisson process at the average rate of 45 per hour and (b) the amount of time a cashier needs to handle a customer follows an exponential distribution with an average rate of 15 customers per hour. Consultants estimate that modernizing with bar-code equipment would increase efficiency by 20%. The Accounting Department suggests that the "cost" of a waiting customer should be valued at $30 per hour and that the hourly cost of a cashier is $15, including benefits. However, to cover the cost of the bar-code equipment, the hourly rate of the cashier should be increased to $18. Use your computer to determine whether the company should hire an additional cashier or install the bar-code equipment at the existing check-outs. (Assume that customers form a single queue when checking out.) For each of the two systems you evaluate, specify the values of c, λ, μ, c_w, c_s, and the total cost per unit of time.

EXERCISE 13.17   Recall the queueing problem of the Ohio Turnpike Commission in Section 13.4, in which there are two scales at a weigh station, trucks arrive at the rate of 70 per hour, and each scale can process 40 trucks per hour. Use your computer to determine how many trucks (to the nearest whole number) can arrive on average per hour before a driver can expect to spend an average of more than 10 minutes at the weigh station.

EXERCISE 13.18   Recall again the queueing problem of the Ohio Turnpike Commission in Section 13.4, in which there are two scales at a weigh station, trucks arrive at the rate of 70 per hour, and each scale can process 40 trucks per hour. If hiring part-time help increases the service rate for each scale from 40 to 44 trucks per hour, use your computer to determine how many trucks (to the nearest whole number) can arrive on average per hour before a driver can expect to spend the same amount of time at the weigh station as in the current system.

EXERCISE 13.19   Recall once again the queueing problem of the Ohio Turnpike Commission in Section 13.4, in which there are two scales at a weigh station, trucks arrive at the rate of 70 per hour, and each scale can process 40 trucks per hour. Management is considering modernizing the weighing equipment to improve the service rate. Use your computer package to determine on average how many more trucks per hour each scale would need to weigh to ensure that there is less than a 5% chance that the number of trucks waiting in line will exceed the capacity of 15 on the off ramp.

EXERCISE 13.20   Recall the problem of American Weavers, Inc., in Section 13.5. When the population is considered infinite, the optimal number of repair persons is 9, there are an average of 25 jammed machines per hour, each repair person costs the company a total of $50 per hour and needs 15 minutes to fix a jammed machine, and the opportunity cost of a jammed machine is $100 per hour. Use your computer package to determine on average how many jams per hour (to the nearest whole number) the system could have before it is more economical to have 10 repair persons.

EXERCISE 13.21   For the conditions of Exercise 13.20, use your computer package to determine how sensitive the optimal crew size of nine repair persons is to the average number of minutes needed to fix a jammed machine. Explain.

EXERCISE 13.22   For the conditions of Exercise 13.20, the Accounting Department is not very confident of the estimate of $100 per hour for the opportunity cost of a jammed machine. In fact, the Department Head says that the estimate may be off by as much as $25 in either direction. Use your computer package to determine if management needs to be concerned about this estimate in deciding the number of repair persons that should be hired. Discuss.

EXERCISE 13.23   For the queueing problem of California Gas and Electric Company in Exercise 13.7, the average number of incoming calls has increased to 80 per hour. The company currently has a staff of six representatives, each of whom can handle about 15 calls per hour. Management is considering dividing the representatives into two equal groups: one to handle calls on gas-related problems and the other to focus on electricity questions. Consultants estimate that this approach would enable representatives in each group to increase efficiency by 20%. Assume that incoming calls are equally likely to be about gas-related problems as about electricity-related problems. To approximate this proposal as two M/M/c queues, what is a reasonable arrival rate for calls coming into each of the two groups?

EXERCISE 13.24   For Exercise 13.23, compare the average amount of time a customer spends on the phone (a) if the six representatives are not split up and (b) if they are split into two equal groups. On the basis of this criterion, should management create these two groups?

EXERCISE 13.25　Is your answer to Exercise 13.24 the same if splitting the representatives does not improve the service rate? Explain.

EXERCISE 13.26　Recall the queueing problem of the PayFast supermarket in Exercise 13.16 that is modeled as an M/M/4 queueing system in which an average of 45 customers per hour arrive at the check-out lines and each of the four cashiers can handle an average of 18 customers per hour when the bar-code scanners are installed. Consider modeling this same problem as four separate M/M/1 queueing systems, one for each cashier. Assume that customers are equally likely to choose any one of the four lines and do not switch lines. What is an appropriate arrival rate for each of the M/M/1 systems?

EXERCISE 13.27　For Exercise 13.26, compare the average number of customers in the entire checkout area using both the M/M/4 and the four M/M/1 systems. How do you explain the difference?

CRITICAL-THINKING PROJECT I
THE QUEUEING PROBLEM OF TEXAS AIRWAYS

As Vice-President of Operations for Texas Airways, you, Ms. Kimberly Brown, have been asked to look into complaints that passengers in Dallas are spending too much time at the check-in counter and that the line is too long. To learn more about this problem, you developed a queueing model to study the existing system, which currently consists of one waiting line and four ticket agents.

After preliminary data analysis, you discovered that passengers arrive during the busiest hours according to a Poisson process at a rate of 132 per hour. Each ticket agent requires an average of 1.75 minutes to process a passenger, but the time for a customer is random and follows an exponential distribution. Prepare a managerial report along the following lines:

1. For the busy hours, determine the average number of passengers waiting in line and how much time (in minutes) they spend both in line waiting for service and for the complete check-in process.
2. In view of the results in guideline 1, you decided to discuss the problem with the ticket agents to find out what is causing the delays. Some customers, the agents said, need only to check-in, and they move quickly. Other customers take longer, purchasing tickets, checking flight schedules, and so on. On the basis of these discussions, it was suggested that service could be improved by having two separate lines: one line (and one ticket agent) devoted to passengers with time-consuming special problems and the other line (and three ticket agents) for check-in passengers only. To examine this idea, further data analysis was performed to determine that an average of 12 of the 132 passengers arriving each hour require special handling. Their random service time is not exponential but instead takes an average of 3 minutes with a standard deviation of 1 minute. The remaining 120 passengers that arrive each hour require an average of 80 seconds for check-in, and this time is random and follows an exponential distribution. For these two queues, report the same statistics as you did in guideline 1 for passengers requiring special handling and for those needing only to check-in. Assuming that arrivals for each queue still follow a Poisson process with appropriate arrival rates.
3. Mr. Carlos Moreno, Manager of the Dallas Airport check-in counter for Texas Airways, suggested that further improvements might be possible because many check-in passengers are daily commuters with no baggage. Perhaps, he suggested, it might be advisable to split the newly proposed check-in line into two lines: one for passengers with baggage and one for passengers without baggage. Data analysis

revealed that of the average 120 passengers arriving for check-in per hour, 45% of them had baggage and required an average of 96 seconds each for check-in; this time is random and follows an exponential distribution. The remaining 55% had no baggage and so could be processed in an average of 48 seconds; this time is also random and follows an exponential distribution. Assuming that arrivals in both queues follow a Poisson process with appropriate arrival rates, explain why in this scenario, you *should not* consider having one ticket agent for passengers with baggage and two agents for passengers without baggage if you have two separate lines for check-in passengers. Instead, you *should* consider having two ticket agents for passengers with baggage and one ticket agent for passengers with no baggage.

4. What are the waiting-time statistics for passengers with and without baggage in the system proposed in guideline 3? Who waits longer in line, on average: passengers with baggage or passengers without baggage?

5. Assume that the President of the company wants check-in passengers to spend an average of less than 5 minutes waiting in line for check-in service. Which system would you choose, the one in guideline 2 or the one in guideline 3? Explain.

Video Case

A VISIT TO DISNEY

How popular is Disney World in Orlando, Florida? Since it opened in 1971, 200 million people have visited Disney World, waiting in lines for its many attractions. Disney management pays a lot of attention to how it handles its customers as they wait in these lines.

In management science, lines are often called queues, and queueing theory applies in many different settings. At Disney World, for example, visitors form a line to gain access to the Captain Nemo ride while the Captain Nemo submarines themselves form lines as they drop off and pick up passengers. How well Disney handles lines and crowds is critical to its business.

Norm Doerges, the director of Epcot (which is a part of Disney World), discusses how Epcot was designed. First, Disney researchers collected hard data by observing how people spend their time at the park. How long do they wait in line? How long do they actually spend at the attractions? How much time do they spend eating? How long does it take them to make up their minds about what to do next? Second, Disney asked customers their opinions about how long they would wait for various attractions and services. Epcot designers then constructed a model to simulate events and traffic flow at the park with an eye toward eliminating long waits. Keeping customer needs in mind at the design stage meant that Epcot could avoid making large-scale, expensive changes to the park after it was built. (Total running time: 4:45.)

Questions on the video

1. How long were people willing to wait at Disney World for popular attractions? What factors influenced their decisions?
2. Comment on how Disney monitors its queues and how often it does so.
3. What kinds of objective and subjective data does Disney collect for its simulation model?

Beyond the video

1. Why don't supermarkets use the single queue system seen in most banks?
2. What cost savings may result from using a queueing model to decide how many servers (checkers, tellers, and so forth) to have on duty?

Practical applications

1. Give three advantages of a multiple-queue system (as seen, say, at a supermarket) over a single-queue system.
2. Give three advantages of a single-queue system (as seen, for example, at a bank) over a multiple-queue system.

Source: "For All Practical Purposes," from *The Consortium for Mathematics and Its Applications* (Arlington, MA: 1986), Program 1.

COMPUTER SIMULATION: THE GENERAL METHODOLOGY

*T*he complaints from the people riding your bus service—the Regional Transit Authority—are growing. These rush-hour customers are tired of waiting for the bus in the morning. Moreover, the longer between buses, the more crowded the bus shelter becomes. Your customers are becoming all the more upset as winter rolls in and more and more people have no protected place to sit. Clearly, it's time to consider increasing bus service. Suppose you increased service from one bus every 20 minutes to one bus every 15 minutes? Would your customers be satisfied?

This chapter investigates how computer simulations can model possible outcomes and thereby offer insights to the people responsible for making decisions, including the Manager of Operations at Regional Transit Authority.

In all the examples throughout this book, it has been possible to obtain solutions through mathematical techniques. When dealing with some real-world problems, however, the resulting model may be so complex or large that it is not possible or practical to develop a solution methodology based on mathematical analysis. Alternatively, to apply an existing mathematical technique may require additional assumptions that are not applicable or realistic.

In such cases, an alternative approach is to use the management science technique of **computer simulation.** As the term indicates, with this technique, you design and build a computer model that mimics the actual problem scenario. You then use the model to learn how the system behaves—asking managerial "What happens if?" questions. For example, you might build a computer model to simulate the following:

Computer simulation
A computer model that mimics an actual problem scenario.

1. The daily operation of a bank or hospital, to understand the impact of adding more tellers or nurses.
2. The operation of a harbor or airport, to understand the flow of traffic and its associated congestion.
3. The production process in a manufacturing plant, to identify bottlenecks in the production line.
4. The traffic flow on a freeway or in a complicated communication system, to determine whether expansion is necessary.

The basic concepts used in designing a computer simulation model are presented in Section 14.1.

■ 14.1 THE BASIC CONCEPT OF COMPUTER SIMULATION

In this section, two examples illustrate the basic steps involved in building a simulation model.

14.1.1 A First Example Of Computer Simulation

Consider the problem faced by the New York Lottery Commission.

EXAMPLE 14.1 THE COMPUTER SIMULATION PROBLEM OF THE NEW YORK LOTTERY COMMISSION The staff of the New York Lottery Commission has just designed a new instant lottery. As shown in Figure 14.1, each lottery card contains three rows. In each row, there are two boxes, one of which has a hidden value of $1 and the other $5. The player scratches any one box from each row to discover the associated dollar value. If all three uncovered numbers are the same, the player wins that amount. Before committing the state to this game and printing a large number of cards, you, as director of the Lottery Commission, want to evaluate the economic feasibility of the game. Among the questions you must answer is: What is the lowest amount that the state can charge for each card and still expect to make a profit? ■

Due to the simple nature of this problem, it is possible to apply probability theory to obtain the desired answer: The amount to charge should be at least equal to the expected payoff for the card. The expected payoff, based on the two possible winnings of $1 and $5, is computed as follows:

$$\text{Expected payoff} = \$1 * \left\{ \begin{array}{l} \text{probability of} \\ \text{winning } \$1 \end{array} \right\} + \$5 * \left\{ \begin{array}{l} \text{probability of} \\ \text{winning } \$5 \end{array} \right\}$$

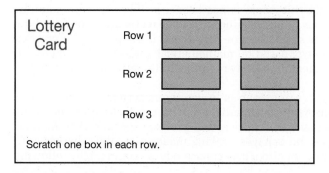

FIGURE 14.1 Instant Lottery Card for the New York Lottery
Commission.

It is now necessary to determine the probability of winning each of $1 and $5. Observe that there is an even chance of scratching either value in each row, and recall the rules of the game:

$$
\begin{aligned}
\text{Probability of winning \$1} &= \text{probability that the scratched box} \\
&\qquad \text{in all three rows has \$1} \\
&= (\text{probability that the scratched box in row 1 has \$1}) \ast \\
&\qquad (\text{probability that the scratched box in row 2 has \$1}) \ast \\
&\qquad (\text{probability that the scratched box in row 3 has \$1}) \\
&= (1/2) \ast (1/2) \ast (1/2) \\
&= 1/8
\end{aligned}
$$

Similarly,

$$
\begin{aligned}
\text{Probability of winning \$5} &= \text{probability that the scratched box} \\
&\qquad \text{in all three rows has \$5} \\
&= (\text{probability that the scratched box in row 1 has \$5}) \ast \\
&\qquad (\text{probability that the scratched box in row 2 has \$5}) \ast \\
&\qquad (\text{probability that the scratched box in row 3 has \$5}) \\
&= (1/2) \ast (1/2) \ast (1/2) \\
&= 1/8
\end{aligned}
$$

By using these two probabilities:

$$
\begin{aligned}
\text{Expected payoff} &= \$1 \ast \left\{ \begin{array}{l} \text{probability of} \\ \text{winning \$1} \end{array} \right\} + \$5 \ast \left\{ \begin{array}{l} \text{probability of} \\ \text{winning \$5} \end{array} \right\} \\
&= \$1 \ast (1/8) + \$5 \ast (1/8) \\
&= \$0.75
\end{aligned}
$$

In other words, by charging $0.75, the Commission can expect to break even in the long run.

In this problem, it is possible to obtain the desired result directly by mathematical analysis. However, this example is now used to illustrate how the methodology of computer simulation is applied to obtain a similar result.

The idea of simulation is to mimic the actual situation in which a large number of people is expected to play the new lottery game. Three different ways to conduct this simulation are now described.

PHYSICAL SIMULATION

You might simulate the game *physically* as follows. Print a large number of cards (say, 100), have someone scratch the boxes on each card, tabulate the payoff for each card ($0, $1, or $5), and use the payoffs from all the cards to compute the average payoff. This process provides an *estimate* of the expected payoff, and that can be used as the basis for making a decision. To obtain an accurate estimate would require printing a large number of cards just for this experiment, but this is both costly and time-consuming. The next alternative avoids some of these problems.

SIMULATION BY ANALOGY

Rather than simulate this game physically, you might simulate the game by *analogy*. For example, consider the analogy between scratching a box in one row of the card and flipping a coin. The value of the box scratched in each row is either $1 or $5, with equal probability. Similarly, the value of a coin flip is either "heads" or "tails," with equal probability. Here, "heads" by analogy is $1 and "tails" by analogy is $5. You can simulate the lottery results by following these steps a large number of times (say, 100):

1. Flip a coin three times, once to determine the outcome for each row.
2. Record the associated "payoff" for the outcome in step 1: $1 if all three flips are "heads," $5 if all three flips are "tails," and $0 otherwise.

Adding up the payoffs of these 100 trials and dividing by 100 provides an estimate of the expected payoff for the game.

This approach has eliminated the need to print the 100 cards, but it requires significant manual effort to flip the coins, tabulate the results, and perform the final computations. The repetitive nature of these tasks makes them ideally suited for the computer.

SIMULATION BY COMPUTER

How can you use a computer to "flip" the coin, tabulate the results, and perform the needed computations? The answer is to write a computer program in which the flipping of the coin is simulated using random numbers to represent the result of the flip. For instance, all computer languages include the capability of generating a random number uniformly distributed between 0 and 1 (see the Student Study Resource Manual). You can then associate a value between 0.0 and 0.5 as corresponding to the outcome of a "head" and a value exceeding 0.5 and less than or equal to 1.0 corresponding to a "tail," as shown in Figure 14.2. Because the random numbers are uniformly distributed, the outcome of a "head" and a "tail" is equally likely.

With this capability, the computer simulation consists of repeating the following steps a large number of times (say, 100):

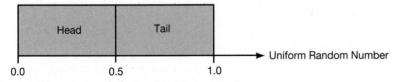

FIGURE 14.2 Simulating the Flip of a Coin Using a Uniform 0–1 Random Number.

1. Generate three uniformly distributed random numbers between 0 and 1 corresponding to the outcomes of the three coin flips.
2. Record the "payoff" of $1 if all three numbers are less than or equal to 0.5 (all three "heads"), $5 if all three numbers are greater than 0.5 (all three "tails"), and $0 otherwise.

Finally, the computer can be programmed to add up these 100 payoffs and divide the total by 100 to obtain an estimate of the expected payoff.

Normally, you would write a computer program to generate the random numbers in this simulation. For illustration purposes, however, the random numbers in the table in Appendix A are used instead. (These random numbers were in fact generated by a computer.)

To begin the simulation, arbitrarily start with any number in the table and choose successive numbers, by row, as needed. For example, to simulate one trial of the new lottery card, choose any three consecutive numbers in a row of the table—say, row 2—leading to the following results:

	OUTCOMES		
FLIP NUMBER	RANDOM NUMBER	FLIP RESULT	$ AMOUNT
1	0.995255	Tails	5
2	0.577849	Tails	5
3	0.980588	Tails	5

This trial corresponds to scratching a $5 value in each of the three rows and therefore results in a payoff of $5.

For the second trial, use the *next* three random numbers in row 2 of the table in Appendix A:

	OUTCOMES		
FLIP NUMBER	RANDOM NUMBER	FLIP RESULT	$ AMOUNT
1	0.894205	Tails	5
2	0.332668	Heads	1
3	0.355729	Heads	1

This trial corresponds to scratching a $5 value in the first row of the card and a $1 value in the second and third rows, resulting in a payoff of $0.

The first five trials thus obtained are shown in Table 14.1. Continuing this process for a total of 100 trials results in a total payoff of $82.00, which provides an estimate of the expected payoff of 82/100 = $0.82 per card. This value is higher than the actual expected payoff of $0.75 obtained using probability theory. To obtain a more accurate estimate of the expected payoff, you will need to perform many more trials—that is, **replications** of the simulation—than the 100 performed in this example. The details of determining *how many* more trials are necessary are discussed in Chapter 15.

Observe that the approach of computer simulation has overcome the drawbacks of the previous two methods by eliminating the cost associated with printing cards in the physical simulation and the time and manual effort needed to flip coins and tabulate the results in the simulation by analogy. Moreover, once the computer program is written and tested, it is a simple matter to perform the experiment 100,000 times instead of 100 times to obtain a better estimate of the expected payoff.

Replication
One complete performance of a simulation.

TABLE 14.1 *Results of Simulating the First Five Cards for the Problem of the New York Lottery Commission*

| | ROW 1 | | | ROW 2 | | | ROW 3 | | | |
| | RANDOM | | $ | RANDOM | | $ | RANDOM | | $ | $ |
TRIAL	NUMBER	H/T	AMT.	NUMBER	H/T	AMT.	NUMBER	H/T	AMT.	PAYOFF
1	0.995255	T	5	0.577849	T	5	0.980588	T	5	5.00
2	0.894206	T	5	0.332668	H	1	0.355729	H	1	0.00
3	0.937265	T	5	0.520743	T	5	0.449925	H	1	0.00
4	0.524444	T	5	0.540955	T	5	0.802009	T	5	5.00
5	0.287153	H	1	0.639474	T	5	0.535043	T	5	0.00

14.1.2 A Second Example of Computer Simulation

Consider the problem faced by the manager of First-Run Videos, Inc.

EXAMPLE 14.2 THE COMPUTER SIMULATION OF THE PROBLEM OF FIRST-RUN VIDEOS, INC. First-Run Videos, Inc., is a store that purchases first-run videos for $25 a copy, rents them for $3 per day, and after 1 month sells them to another store for $5 a copy. Based on historical data, the store has estimated the following probabilities of daily demand for each movie:

NUMBER OF COPIES	PROBABILITY
0	0.15
1	0.25
2	0.45
3	0.10
4	0.05

As Manager of First-Run Videos, you want to decide how many copies of each new movie to order: 0, 1, 2, 3, or 4. ∎

It is again possible to apply probability theory to obtain the desired answer. The optimal decision is the one that results in the largest expected profit over the life of the video, which is 1 month (30 days). To illustrate, suppose that three copies are ordered. In this case:

$$\text{Expected profit} = (\text{expected revenue for 1 month}) +$$
$$(\text{selling price of the 3 copies}) -$$
$$(\text{purchase cost of the 3 copies})$$
$$= (\text{expected revenue per day} * 30 \text{ days}) +$$
$$(\$5 * 3) - (\$25 * 3)$$
$$= (\text{Expected revenue per day} * 30) - \$60$$

In computing the expected revenue on a given day, keep in mind that there are only three copies of the tape available for rental. A fourth demand for a particular movie during any 1 day cannot be met and thus generates no additional income. Therefore, the expected daily revenue is computed as follows:

$$
\begin{aligned}
\text{Expected revenue per day} = {}& \$0 * (\text{probability of 0 request}) + \\
& \$3 * (\text{probability of 1 request}) + \\
& \$6 * (\text{probability of 2 requests}) + \\
& \$9 * (\text{probability of 3 requests}) + \\
& \$9 * (\text{probability of 4 requests}) \\
= {}& (0 * 0.15) + (3 * 0.25) + \\
& (6 * 0.45) + (9 * 0.10) + (9 * 0.05) \\
= {}& \$4.80
\end{aligned}
$$

Therefore,

$$
\begin{aligned}
\text{Expected profit} &= (\text{expected revenue per day} * 30) - \$60 \\
&= (\$4.80 * 30) - \$60 \\
&= \$84
\end{aligned}
$$

In other words, purchasing three copies of the video is expected to result in a profit of $84 at the end of the month. The results of performing similar computations for ordering 0, 1, 2, 3, and 4 tapes are given in Table 14.2. You can see that ordering two copies of the video is optimal because it results in the largest profit, $90.50.

For this problem also it has been possible to obtain the desired results by direct mathematical analysis. The methodology of computer simulation is now used to achieve a similar result. Suppose you decide to order two copies of the tape at a cost of $50. To estimate the expected revenues using simulation, it is necessary to mimic the process of customers requesting copies of the video tape over a 30-day period and then perform the computations to determine the associated revenues and, ultimately, the total profit. The following steps are performed for each of the 30 days in the month:

1. Generate the daily demand, that is, the number of requests for this tape on the given day according to the probability distribution given in the problem description.
2. Compute the associated rental revenue based on the fact that you have two copies of the tape available.

TABLE 14.2   *Expected Profits for the Problem of First-Run Videos, Inc.*

NUMBER OF COPIES	PURCHASE COST ($)	EXPECTED REVENUE $/DAY	EXPECTED REVENUE $/MONTH	RESALE VALUE ($)	NET PROFIT ($)
0	0	0.00	0.00	0	0.00
1	25	2.55	76.50	5	56.50
2	50	4.35	130.50	10	90.50
3	75	4.80	144.00	15	84.00
4	100	4.95	148.50	20	68.50

Subsequently, the total expected profit is computed by

$$\text{Total expected profit} = \text{(total rental revenue)} +$$
$$\text{(resale revenue)} - \text{(purchase cost)}$$
$$= \text{(total rental revenue)} +$$
$$(2 * 5) - (2 * 25)$$
$$= \text{(total rental revenue)} - 40$$

To obtain the total rental revenue, as described in previous steps 1 and 2, it is necessary to generate the daily demand according to the following table:

NUMBER OF COPIES	PROBABILITY
0	0.15
1	0.25
2	0.45
3	0.10
4	0.05

Once again, uniformly distributed random numbers between 0 and 1 can be used to do so. The idea is to use the capability of the computer language to generate such a random number and use its value to determine an associated daily demand in such a way that there is a 15% chance that the resulting demand is 0, a 25% chance that it is 1, and so on. This can be accomplished as shown in Figure 14.3. That is, generate a uniform random number between 0 and 1 and determine the associated daily demand according to the following table:

RANGE OF UNIFORM NUMBER*	ASSOCIATED DAILY DEMAND
0.00–0.15	0
0.15–0.40	1
0.40–0.85	2
0.85–0.95	3
0.95–1.00	4

*Each interval is meant to include the smaller value but not the larger one.

For example, if the uniform random number generated is 0.333, the corresponding daily demand is 1 because the value of 0.333 falls in the range of 0.15–0.40.

Normally, you would write a computer program to generate these random numbers. For illustration purposes, however, uniform random numbers from the table in

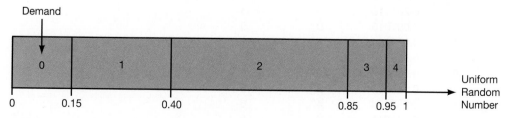

FIGURE 14.3 Generating the Daily Demand Using a Uniform 0–1 Random Number.

Appendix A are used. For example, to simulate the first day, choose any number in the table—say, the value of 0.856269 in row 16 and column 2. This random number corresponds to a daily demand of three copies. Because only two copies of the tape are available for rental, the associated revenue is

$$\text{Revenue for Day 1} = 2 \text{ copies} * (\$3 \text{ per copy}) = \$6$$

To simulate the second day, select the *next* random number by row in the table, which is 0.201616, in row 16 and column 3. This value in turn corresponds to a demand of one copy, and the associated revenue is

$$\text{Revenue for Day 2} = 1 \text{ copy} * (\$3 \text{ per copy}) = \$3$$

The rest of the simulation consists of the following:

1. Selecting the next random number by row.
2. Determining the associated daily demand.
3. Computing the daily revenue based on two copies of the tape being available.

These computations are summarized for the first 10 days in Table 14.3. Continuing the simulation for a total of 30 days and adding up the daily revenues results in a total rental revenue of $135 from this simulation. The 30-day profit is

$$\text{Total profit} = (\text{total revenue}) - 40$$
$$= 135 - 40$$
$$= \$95$$

To determine the optimal number of copies to purchase, it is necessary to repeat the previous simulation for each of the remaining choices of buying one, three, or four copies. However, rather than generating new daily demands in each case, you can reuse the *same* demands in Table 14.3 and simply compute the rental revenue associated with the number of copies available. The results of doing so for 30 days and computing the profits are summarized in Table 14.4. On the basis of *this simulation*, you can see that it is optimal to order three copies because its associated profit of $99

TABLE 14.3	*Simulating Ten Days of Demand for the Problem of First-Run Videos, Inc.*		
DAY	UNIFORM RANDOM NUMBER	DEMAND	REVENUE
1	0.856269	3	6
2	0.201616	1	3
3	0.091010	0	0
4	0.990284	4	6
5	0.926374	3	6
6	0.090610	0	0
7	0.519490	2	6
8	0.988134	4	6
9	0.516041	2	6
10	0.629143	2	6

∘TABLE 14.4	*Profits for the Simulation Results of the Problem of First-Run Videos, Inc.*			
NUMBER OF COPIES	PURCHASE COST ($)	REVENUE ($/MONTH)	RESALE VALUE ($)	PROFIT ($)
0	0.00	0.00	0.00	0.00
1	25.00	78.00	5.00	58.00
2	50.00	135.00	10.00	95.00
3	75.00	159.00	15.00	99.00
4	100.00	165.00	20.00	85.00

is the highest. Observe that the conclusion to order three copies, based on the result of this one simulation, is *different* from the analytical results in Table 14.2, in which it is optimal to order only two copies. This is because the simulation methodology provides only an *estimate*. To obtain a more accurate estimate, you will need to repeat this 30-day simulation many more times, as you will learn in Chapter 15.

You have seen the basic concepts used in simulating a problem scenario. The idea is to build a computer model to understand, in a *statistical* sense, how the system performs. This is accomplished by repeating the simulation many times, each time using different random numbers to obtain different results from the simulation. The results of these repetitions are then used to provide an *estimate* of the system's true performance. The larger the number of repetitions, the more reliable are the resulting estimates.

■ 14.2 ADVANTAGES AND DISADVANTAGES OF COMPUTER SIMULATION

From the examples presented in Sections 14.1.1 and 14.1.2, you can identify the following disadvantages of using a computer simulation:

1. The numerical results obtained are based on the *specific* set of random numbers used in the simulation, the values of which correspond to only one of many possible outcomes. Thus, the final values reported in a simulation are only *estimates* of the true values for which you are looking. For instance, the computer simulation of the New York Lottery Commission in Example 14.1 resulted in overestimating the expected payoff per card. The simulation of the problem of First-Run Videos in Example 14.2 indicated that three copies of the video tape should be purchased, but the mathematical analysis showed that it is best to buy only two copies.

   Making wrong decisions based on the results of a simulation may have serious financial consequences. For example, if the simulation in Example 14.1 underestimates the expected payoff of a lottery card, the New York Lottery Commission may not charge enough for that card and might lose significant amounts of money.

2. To obtain more accurate estimates and to minimize the likelihood of making a wrong decision, you should (a) use a large number of trials in each simulation and/or (b) repeat the entire simulation a large number of times. For instance, in Example 14.1, you might have the computer simulate 10,000 cards instead of 100; in Example 14.2, you might simulate the profit from 1 month 20 different times rather than just once. In these examples running extra simulations can easily be done with a reasonable amount of computational effort. For more complex problems, however, a large number of repetitions can require significant amounts of computer time.

3. Each simulation requires its own special design to mimic the actual scenario under investigation and its own associated computer program. Although it is possible to

learn and use specialized software packages, the development effort in designing and programming real-world simulations is extremely time-consuming.

As a result of these disadvantages, you should attempt to solve your problem using analytical techniques whenever possible. Doing so generally requires less effort and results in exact answers rather than estimates. Therefore, the problems in Examples 14.1 and 14.2 should be solved analytically rather than with a computer simulation. Nonetheless, in spite of the disadvantages, computer simulation is one of the more commonly used techniques because it offers the following advantages:

1. Simulation allows you to analyze large, complex problems for which analytical results are *not* available. In fact, most real-world problems fit in this category. Consider the problem of First-Run Videos. Analytical results were obtained assuming that the demand distribution is the same on each day and that each tape is returned after 1 day. However, in a more realistic scenario, the demand distribution depends on the day of the week. Friday and Saturday would have higher demands. Also, a rented tape may be returned after 1, 2, or even 3 days. Even if the return distribution were known, obtaining analytical results in this case would be quite difficult. Simulation provides a practical alternative.

2. As with any form of simulation, computer simulation allows the decision maker to experiment with many different policies and scenarios without actually changing or experimenting with the actual existing system. For example, with computer simulation, you can study the impact of adding a new work station to a production line without having to set up the work station physically.

3. Computer simulation allows you to compress time. For example, you can study the long-range impact of a policy for a bank for an entire year in a computer simulation lasting just a few minutes. The alternative of actually implementing the policy and observing its results over a year may not be practical.

4. Some analytical techniques require a sophisticated mathematical background both to use and to understand. A computer simulation may require little or no complex mathematics and so may be intuitively more understandable. As a result, it may be easier to convince others in the organization that your proposal or policy is sound when it is backed up by a simulation model rather than by an analytical model. For this reason, computer simulation may be used *even though* the problem can be analyzed using mathematical techniques.

In Section 14.1, you learned the basic concepts of how a computer simulation is used to obtain estimates of certain values on which a decision is based. In Section 14.3, the details of the steps involved in designing a simulation are presented.

■ 14.3 THE COMPUTER-SIMULATION METHODOLOGY

Designing and implementing a computer simulation depends on the system being modeled and also on the specific computer language or package you have available. However, certain general steps are performed in each simulation, as described in this section.

14.3.1 Classifying the System

The design of a simulation model depends on classifying the system as one of two types:

Discrete-event system
A system whose state changes only at certain points in time.

1. A **discrete-event system,** in which the state of the system changes only at certain points in time. For example, in modeling the operation of a bank, the state of the system is described by the number of customers in line and which of the tellers are currently busy. The state of this system changes only at those points in time

when either (a) a new customer arrives or (b) a customer finishes being served and leaves the bank.

2. A **continuous system,** in which the state of the system changes continuously over time—that is, at each moment in time. For example, in simulating the flight of the space shuttle, the state of the system is described by its position, speed, acceleration, and so on. These characteristics are changing constantly.

Continuous system
A system whose state changes continuously at each moment in time.

In this text, only discrete-event systems are modeled. A discrete-event system can be further classified as one of the following two types:

1. A **terminating system,** in which there are precise and known starting and ending points. For instance, the problems of the New York Lottery Commission and of First-Run Videos in Section 14.1 are terminating. In the first example, the starting point is the purchase of the lottery card and the ending point is when the three boxes are scratched to reveal the payoff. In the second example, the starting point is when the new videos arrive and the ending point is 30 days later, when these videos are sold.

Terminating system
A system in which there are precise and known starting and ending points.

2. A **nonterminating system** is one that is on-going, one without precise known starting and ending points. Consider simulating a manufacturing facility. The production process continues on and on. The conditions at the end of one day are the starting conditions for the next day. There is no clear beginning and ending point for the process.

Nonterminating system
A system that is ongoing and without precise known starting and ending points.

When a system is terminating, the **length of the simulation**—that is, the amount of time over which to conduct the simulation for purposes of analysis—is from its beginning point to its ending point. To obtain reliable results for a terminating system, you need to determine how many *times* to repeat the simulation. In contrast, for a nonterminating system, you need to choose not only the number of times to repeat the simulation, but also an appropriate *length* of each simulation. For example, you might choose to simulate the production process for a length of 1 day and repeat the simulation 50 times. Alternatively, you might choose a length of 50 days and perform the simulation only once. Details on the length and number of simulation runs are given in Chapter 15.

Length of the simulation
The amount of time over which to conduct the simulation.

14.3.2 Identifying the Components of a Computer Simulation

Before designing the details of a computer simulation, it is critical to have a clear understanding of the *objectives* of the study in the form of specific numerical **outputs**. For instance, in Example 14.1, the objective is to determine a price for the new lottery card, which creates the need to obtain an output value of the expected payoff of the card. Examples of possible outputs for other simulations are as follows:

Output
An objective of a simulation study in the form of a specific numerical value.

1. To evaluate the performance of a bank: (a) the average time a customer spends waiting in line, (b) the fraction of time the tellers are busy serving customers, and (c) the average and maximum length of the waiting line.
2. To evaluate an inventory policy: (a) the average inventory level over a period of time, (b) the number of times and the amount by which you are unable to meet the demand, and (c) the total associated cost.
3. To evaluate the anticipated cash flow of a business based on future probabilistic sales: (a) the expected net-present value of the cash flow and (b) the expected rate of return.

Input
A numerical value that is needed to determine the outputs of a simulation.

Initial condition
A value that expresses the state of the system at the beginning of a simulation.

Deterministic data
Known values needed to calculate the outputs of a simulation.

Probabilistic data
Numerical quantities whose values are uncertain but needed to obtain the outputs of the simulation.

With the outputs identified, the next step is to identify the **inputs**. These are the numerical values that, once determined, allow you to start the simulation and to calculate all the desired outputs. These inputs fall into three general categories.

1. **Initial conditions**—that is, initial values that express the state of the system at the beginning of the simulation. For example, in simulating the daily operation of a bank, the initial conditions correspond to opening the bank in the morning when there are no customers and all the tellers are available. In simulating the monthly operation of a steel plant, the initial conditions might include such items as the amount of iron ore in inventory, the initial work-in-process inventory, the amount of finished steel in inventory, and the number of furnaces in operation at the beginning of the month.

2. **Deterministic data**—that is, known values that are needed to perform the calculations that yield the outputs. For example, in simulating the daily operation of a bank, deterministic data values are the number of tellers available and the number of hours each works. For the simulation of steel production, these deterministic values might include the cost of producing steel, the selling price, the number of shifts, the number of workers on each shift, and so on. In addition, deterministic data for both of these problems include the length of the simulation. In the case of the bank—a terminating system—the length of the simulation is one 8-hour day. For the steel production—a nonterminating system—you must determine an appropriate length of the simulation.

3. **Probabilistic data**—that is, quantities whose values are uncertain but needed to obtain the outputs of the simulation. In simulating the daily operation of a bank, the arrival times of the customers and the amount of time needed to serve each of them are two probabilistic data values. In simulating the steel plant, the demands for the finished goods as well as the amount of time needed at each stage in the production process might constitute probabilistic data. Although the *specific values* of these probabilistic data are uncertain, their general behavior must be known through a probability distribution or a density function depending, respectively, on whether the value is discrete or continuous (see the Student Resource Manual).

To illustrate the design of a simulation for the problem of First-Run Videos, recall that the desired output is the expected 30-day profit associated with purchasing a given number of copies of a video tape. To obtain this value requires the following inputs:

1. Initial conditions stating that all the purchased tapes are in the store and available for rental at the beginning of the simulation.

2. The deterministic data consisting of:

   a. The number of copies purchased.
   b. The purchase price of a new tape.
   c. The rental cost per day for each tape.
   d. The sales price after 30 days.
   e. The length of the simulation—30 days.

3. Probabilistic data consisting of the number of tapes demanded on each of the 30 days in the month.

In this example, the initial conditions that all purchased tapes are available for rent every day makes the process of initialization straightforward. However, in many simulations, defining the initial conditions is not so trivial. Furthermore, the choice of the initial conditions can affect the output values of the simulation. One commonly used approach is to choose what you consider to be likely or reasonable starting conditions, and then to run the simulation for a long enough period of time so that the effect of the initial conditions is not significant.

KEY FEATURES

In summary, to develop a simulation for a discrete-event system, you will need to identify the following:

✔ The *outputs* whose values you want to obtain as the objectives of the simulation.

✔ The *inputs*—whose values are used to compute the outputs—consisting of the following:

1. *Initial conditions*, which express the state of the system at the beginning of the simulation.
2. *Deterministic data*, whose values are known and used to compute the outputs.
3. *Probabilistic data*, whose values are uncertain (but whose probability distribution is known) but are needed for computing the outputs.

14.3.3 Designing the Computer Simulation

Once you have identified the outputs and the inputs needed to compute them, the actual simulation consists of generating random numbers and bookkeeping.

KEY FEATURES

The two steps in computer simulation are:

Step 1. *Generating Random Numbers*:   Obtain the probabilistic inputs for the model by generating random numbers according to the associated known distributions.

Step 2. *Bookkeeping*:   Design a systematic method for storing and processing all the input values and for performing the computations needed to obtain the output values.

For First-Run Videos, recall that the desired output is the expected 30-day profit associated with a given number of purchased tapes, say, 2. The inputs for that simulation are

    i. Two copies purchased.
    ii. The daily demands whose distribution is

NUMBER OF COPIES	PROBABILITY
0	0.15
1	0.25
2	0.45
3	0.10
4	0.05

    iii. A purchase price of $25 per tape.

    iv. A rental revenue of $3 per day.

    v. The resale value of $5 per tape after 30 days.

In Section 14.1.2, you saw how Step 1 is performed using uniform random numbers between 0 and 1 to generate daily demands with the distribution in (ii) (see Figure 14.3 in Section 14.1).

    The bookkeeping for Step 2 is accomplished by

a. Storing the known data values in (i), (iii), (iv), and (v).

b. Using the daily demands generated in Step 1 together with the data values in (a) to compute the associated daily revenue as

$$\text{Daily revenue} = \begin{cases} (\text{demand} * 3), & \text{if demand} \leq \text{copies purchased} \\ (\text{copies purchased} * 3), & \text{if demand} > \text{copies purchased} \end{cases}$$

c. Computing the total rental revenue as the sum of the revenue for each of the 30 days.

d. Computing the total profit by

$$\text{Total profit} = (\text{total rental revenue}) -$$
$$(\text{total purchase cost}) +$$
$$(\text{total resale revenue})$$
$$= (\text{total rental revenue}) -$$
$$(25 * \text{number of copies}) +$$
$$(5 * \text{number of copies})$$

    The bookkeeping scheme depends on the specific system being modeled. Once the probabilistic inputs are generated, the scheme is usually straightforward. As you have seen in Examples 14.1 and 14.2, it is necessary to use random numbers to compute the probabilistic inputs for a simulation. Some insight into how this is done in general is given in Section 14.3.4.

14.3.4   *Generating Random Numbers*

In the examples in Section 14.1, you saw how random numbers between 0 and 1 are used to obtain values for random variables that have a known *discrete* probability distribution in which the random variable of interest can assume one of a *finite* number of different values. In some applications, however, the random variables are *continuous* that is, they can assume any real value according to a *continuous* probability distribution. For example, in simulating the operation of a bank, the amount of time a teller spends with a customer is such a random variable, which might follow an exponential distribution (see the Student Resource Manual). This is defined by the density function:

$$f(t) = \lambda * e^{-\lambda * t}$$

where $1/\lambda$ is the average time of service (that is, λ is the average number of customers served per unit of time). In this section, you will learn how to generate random numbers having an exponential distribution with a known value of λ as well as those from any other type of probability distribution.

GENERATING UNIFORM 0–1 RANDOM NUMBERS

One of the most commonly used methods to generate random numbers following a known distribution relies on using uniformly distributed random numbers between 0 and 1. As discussed in the Student Resource Manual and illustrated in Figure 14.4,

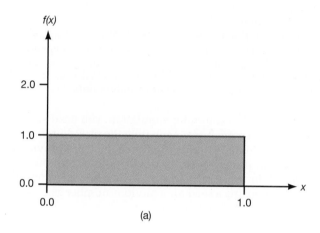

(a)

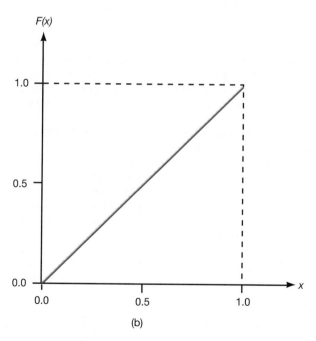

(b)

FIGURE 14.4 (a) Density Function $f(x)$ and (b) Cumulative Distribution Function $F(x)$ for Uniform 0–1 Random Numbers.

such numbers have the following density function, $f(x)$, and cumulative distribution function, $F(x)$:

$$f(x) = 1$$
$$F(x) = x$$

The computer languages used for developing simulations all have a built-in capability for generating a sequence of random numbers between 0 and 1 in which the following holds:

Seed

A user-supplied initial value that determines the specific sequence of numbers obtained from a random-number generator.

Pseudo-random number

A number that is created by a random-number generator; collectively, pseudo-random numbers obey the desired statistical properties of 0–1 random numbers.

1. The approach is based on numerical methods.
2. The specific sequence depends on a user-supplied initial value called the **seed.** For a particular seed, the sequence is then determined. Each time that same seed is used, the same sequence of random numbers is generated.
3. The generated numbers satisfy the following properties: (a) they are uniformly distributed between 0 and 1, and (b) successive numbers are statistically independent of each other. As a result, even though the seed determines the precise sequence of numbers, collectively these numbers obey the desired statistical properties of 0–1 random numbers. They are therefore called **pseudo-random numbers**.

To use pseudo-random-number generators in a computer simulation, you need supply only an initial arbitrary integer number as a seed. Then, each time the pseudo-random-number generator is used, the next 0–1 "random" number in the sequence is provided. The numbers in Appendix A are, in fact, pseudo-random numbers from the uniform random-number generator in @RISK. Arbitrarily choosing a starting row and column in this table is analogous to arbitrarily choosing a seed for a random-number generator.

USING 0–1 RANDOM NUMBERS TO GENERATE A CONTINUOUS DISTRIBUTION

To generate a random number following a distribution *other* than the uniform distribution, start with a uniform random number between 0 and 1 and appropriately transform that number into the desired value. This approach is used in Examples 14.1 and 14.2. For instance, in Example 14.2, a random number between 0 and 1 is transformed to generate a demand between 0 and 4 according to the known discrete distribution given in that problem description.

You will now see how 0–1 random numbers are used to generate random values for continuous variables following a known probability distribution. Suppose that T is such a variable representing the amount of time a teller spends with a customer in a bank. From historical records, suppose that this teller serves an average of 12 customers an hour. Suppose that statistical analysis of historical data also indicates that the associated random variable T closely follows an exponential distribution in which $\lambda = 12$. As discussed in the Student Resource Manual, the associated density function, $f(t)$, and cumulative distribution function, $F(t)$, are

$$f(t) = \lambda * e^{-\lambda * t}$$
$$= 12 * e^{-12 * t}$$
$$F(t) = P(T \le t)$$
$$= 1 - e^{-\lambda * t}$$
$$= 1 - e^{-12 * t}$$

These functions are graphed in Figure 14.5.

Suppose that in developing a simulation you need to know how much time the teller spends with one specific customer.

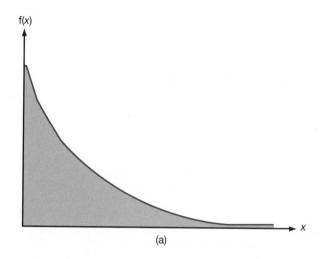

(a)

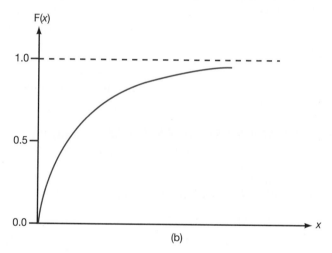

(b)

FIGURE 14.5 (a) Density Function and (b) Cumulative Distribution Function for Random Numbers with an Exponential Distribution.

KEY FEATURES

That is, you need to generate a random number following the previous exponential distribution. To do so using 0–1 random numbers, follow these steps—that work for any general distribution—whose justification is given in Appendix 14A:

✔ Generate a uniform random number between 0 and 1—say, U.
✔ For the given value of U, use the cumulative distribution $F(t)$ to determine the value of t as shown in Figure 14.6. That is, use the value of U to find the value of t for which

$$F(t) = U$$

✔ Use the value of t as the random number.

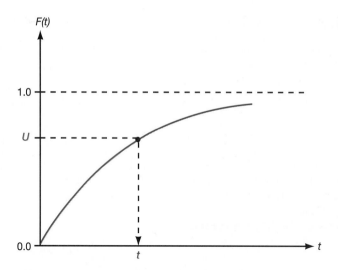

FIGURE 14.6 Generating a Random Number Using a Cumulative
Distribution Function and a Uniform 0–1 Random
Number.

The next two examples show how these steps are used to generate random numbers
following an exponential and normal distribution.

EXAMPLE 14.3 *GENERATING EXPONENTIAL RANDOM NUMBERS* To apply this general approach to generate random numbers following an exponential distribution with
a known value of λ, you would do the following:
a. Generate a uniform 0–1 random number U.
b. Use the value of U to solve the following equation for t:

$$F(t) = U$$

or

$$1 - e^{-\lambda * t} = U$$

or

$$e^{-\lambda * t} = 1 - U$$

Doing so requires using the logarithm function, ln, to obtain

$$t = -(1/\lambda) * \ln(1 - U) \qquad \blacksquare$$

For the specific example involving the bank teller, in which $\lambda = 12$ and a uniform
random number of, say, $U = 0.3329$ is generated, the amount of time needed to serve
one particular customer is

$$t = -(1/\lambda) * \ln(1 - U)$$
$$= -(1/12) * \ln(1 - 0.3329)$$
$$= -(1/12) * (-0.4048)$$
$$= 0.3373 \text{ hour}$$

EXAMPLE 14.4 GENERATING NORMAL RANDOM NUMBERS As a second example, suppose you need to generate the demand D for milk that follows a normal distribution with a mean of 750 gallons per day and a standard deviation of 100 gallons. To do so for a normally distributed random variable having a mean of μ and a standard deviation of σ, do the following:

a. Generate a uniform 0–1 random number—say, U.

b. Use this value of U to find a value of t for which

$$F(t) = P(D \leq t) = U$$

That is, find the value of t for which the area under the normal distribution to the left of t in Figure 14.7 is U. To do so, use the standard-normal table in Appendix B to find the associated z-value; then compute t, as follows:

$$z = \frac{t - \mu}{\sigma}$$

so

$$t = \mu + (\sigma * z) \qquad \blacksquare$$

For the specific milk example in which $U = 0.1515$, $\mu = 750$, and $\sigma = 100$, the z-value from Appendix B is about -1.03, and so

$$t = \mu + (\sigma * z)$$
$$= 750 + [100 * (-1.03)]$$
$$= 647 \text{ gallons}$$

Using 0–1 random numbers to generate probabilistic inputs is often called *Monte Carlo* simulation. The method got its name during World War II when scientists used random numbers to estimate, in a statistical sense, the solutions to complex mathematical problems.

The methods described here are not the most efficient ones available but are used in this book because they are conceptually easy to understand. You will now see how these ideas are used in designing a computer simulation.

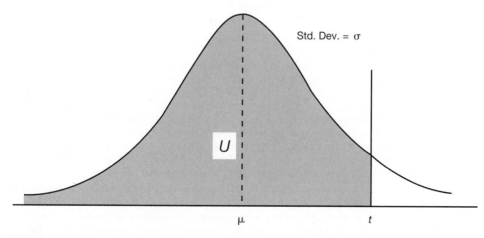

FIGURE 14.7 Generating Normal Random Numbers.

■ 14.4 A SIMULATION OF A BUS STOP

In this section, you will see an example of how simulation methodology is used to analyze a more challenging decision problem. Consider the problem faced by the Regional Transit Authority of Cleveland.

14.4.1 Problem Description

The Regional Transit Authority (RTA) has bus service from various suburbs to downtown. Management has received a number of complaints that customers at one of the suburban stops are having to wait too long during the morning rush hours of 7 to 9 A.M. The riders are also complaining that there are not enough seats in the shelter for all the passengers to wait comfortably in the winter months. To respond to these complaints, management is considering increasing the frequency on that route from the current service of one bus every 20 minutes to one bus every 15 minutes. As Manager of Operations, you have been asked to investigate the impact of this new policy on customer service by measuring the average amount of time a customer has to wait for a bus, the average number of customers waiting at the stop, and the maximum number of customers waiting.

Through data studies, the RTA has determined that about 30 customers arrive per hour at this stop during the rush hour (that is, at a rate of about 0.5 per minute). The data also show that the time between two arriving customers can be approximated by an exponential distribution with an average rate of $\lambda = 0.5$ per minute. A time study also reveals that buses typically arrive late at their scheduled stops by an amount of time that follows a normal distribution with a mean of 4 minutes and a standard deviation of 1 minute.

To evaluate the proposed bus schedule, you should realize that the models described in Chapter 13 are *not* directly applicable to this queueing problem. The main reason is that the customers are not served one at a time, but rather as a group. Simulation is a reasonable way to evaluate this system.

14.4.2 Designing the Simulation

As discussed in Section 14.3.1, before designing the details of a computer simulation, it is critical to have a clear understanding of the objectives of the study in the form of specific numerical *outputs*. For the RTA, the appropriate outputs are the three given in the problem description in Section 14.4.1.

The next step is to identify the inputs for this simulation whose values, once determined, allow you to calculate these outputs. Recall, from Section 14.3, that the inputs fall into the following three categories:

1. The *initial conditions*, which here are the number of customers already at the stop at the time corresponding to the beginning of the simulation and the time when the next bus is scheduled to arrive. These values should represent the most likely starting conditions at the beginning of the rush-hour period and should be estimated based on experience. For the purposes of illustration, assume that you are starting the simulation at a point in time when a bus has just left. In this case, there is no one waiting at the stop, and the next bus is scheduled to arrive in 15 minutes. If the simulation is performed for a long enough period of time, the effect of these initial conditions on the output should be minimal.

2. The *deterministic data*, consisting of the length of time over which to perform this simulation. In this case, suppose you decide to simulate the bus stop for 1 hour.

3. The *probabilistic data*, generated when needed, consisting of the following:
   a. The arrivals of the customers, whose interarrival times are assumed to follow an exponential distribution with a mean rate of $\lambda = 0.5$ per minute.

b. The arrival time of each bus. The buses are *scheduled* to arrive every 15 minutes. However, they are late by an amount of time that follows a normal distribution with a mean of $\mu = 4$ minutes and a standard deviation of $\sigma = 1$ minute.

With these outputs and inputs, the actual simulation consists of generating appropriate random numbers and an associated bookkeeping scheme.

14.4.3 *Generating Random Numbers*

As discussed earlier, there are two probabilistic inputs. Each needs to be generated using random numbers according to their underlying probability distribution.

GENERATING ARRIVING CUSTOMERS

One of the probabilistic inputs for this simulation is the arrival of customers at the stop, whose interarrival times follow an exponential distribution with a mean of $\lambda = 0.5$ per minute. That time—t_a, in *minutes*—between successive arrivals is obtained by

a. Generating a uniform 0–1 random number U.
b. Computing

$$t_a = -(1/0.5) * \ln (1 - U)$$

GENERATING THE ARRIVAL OF A BUS

The buses are scheduled to arrive every 15 minutes. If the simulation is started at time $T = 0$, then the first bus should arrive at time $T = 15$, the second bus at time $T = 30$, and so on. However, these buses are late by an amount of time that follows a normal distribution with a mean of $\mu = 4$ minutes and a standard deviation of $\sigma = 1$. This random time—t_l, by which a bus is late—is generated using the following steps:

a. Generate a uniform 0–1 random number U.
b. Find a z-value from the standard-normal table in Appendix B so that the area to the left of z is U.
c. Compute t_l as follows:

$$t_l = \mu + (\sigma * z)$$
$$= 4 + (1 * z)$$

14.4.4 *Designing the Bookkeeping Scheme*

One of the best ways to approach the bookkeeping scheme is to use the technique of *working through a specific example*. Take specific values for the given inputs, and perform the needed computations by hand to determine the desired output. Recall the values for the initial conditions at time $T = 0$ for this problem: The stop is empty and the next bus is scheduled to arrive in 15 minutes.

To compute the outputs, you need to know the status of the system (number of customers in the system) *at every point in time*. However, observe that the status of the system changes *only* when either:

1. a new customer arrives, or when
2. a bus arrives.

It is necessary to record the status of the system only at these points in time. You must know which of these events occurs next and when. To begin, consider the initial state of the system at time $T = 0$.

BOOKKEEPING AT TIME $T = 0$

At time $T = 0$, there is no one waiting at the stop and a bus has just left. To determine when the status of this system changes, you need to know the following:

1. The time at which the next customer arrives.
2. The time at which the next bus arrives.

These values need to be generated randomly according to their distributions.

Determining When the Next Customer Arrives

Use 0–1 random numbers to determine the arrival time of the next customer, as follows:

1. Arbitrarily start by choosing a uniform 0–1 random number—say, $U = 0.894206$ in row 2 and column 4 of the table in Appendix A.
2. Compute the interarrival time, t_a, as follows:

$$t_a = -(1/0.5) * \ln(1 - U)$$
$$= -2 * \ln(1 - 0.894206)$$
$$= 4.49 \text{ minutes}$$

In other words, the next customer arrives 4.49 minutes from now, at time $T = 0 + 4.49 = 4.49$.

Determining When the Next Bus Arrives

The next bus is *scheduled* to arrive at time $T = 15$ minutes, but it will *actually* arrive late by a random amount of time, t_l. To determine t_l, use the next 0–1 random number in the table, $U = 0.332668$ in row 2 and column 5. From the standard-normal table in Appendix B, the z-value for which the area to the left of z is U is about -0.43. Using this z-value, compute:

$$t_l = \mu + (z * \sigma)$$
$$= 4 + (-0.43 * 1)$$
$$= 3.57 \text{ minutes}$$

In other words, the next bus is 3.57 minutes late. It therefore arrives at time $T = 15 + 3.57 = 18.57$. See Table 14.5.

TABLE 14.5 *Status of the System at Time $T = 0$*

TIME	EVENT	NUMBER OF CUSTOMERS	ARRIVAL TIME OF NEXT CUSTOMER	NEXT BUS
0.00	—	0	4.49	18.57

Moving the Clock Time T

From Table 14.5, you can see that the status of the system remains the same until the first customer arrives at time $T = 4.49$. This is because this customer arrives before the next bus.

BOOKKEEPING AT TIME $T = 4.49$

When this first customer arrives at time $T = 4.49$, you must perform the following steps:

1. *Change the Status of the System*: The customer joins the others waiting at the stop, so increase the number of waiting customers by 1 (0 + 1 = 1).
2. *Schedule the Next Arriving Customer*: A new customer will arrive. To determine when, generate an interarrival time, t_a, according to an exponential distribution. Use the next 0–1 random number, $U = 0.355729$ from row 3 and column 1, and compute

$$t_a = -(1/0.5) * \ln(1 - U)$$
$$= -2 * \ln(1 - 0.355729)$$
$$= 0.88 \text{ minutes}$$

The next customer arrives 0.88 minute from now, at time $T = 4.49 + 0.88 = 5.37$.

These changes are summarized in Table 14.6 in the row corresponding to time $T = 4.49$. Note that the first customer has arrived, as indicated by the word "Customer" in the column labeled "Event."

Moving the Clock Time T

From the second row of Table 14.6, you can see that the status of the system remains the same until the next customer arrives at time $T = 5.37$. (The bus is still not there.)

BOOKKEEPING AT TIME $T = 5.37$

When this customer arrives, perform the following steps:

TABLE 14.6 *Status of the System Up to Time T = 4.49*

TIME	EVENT	NUMBER OF CUSTOMERS	ARRIVAL TIME OF	
			NEXT CUSTOMER	NEXT BUS
0.00	—	0	4.49	18.57
4.49	Customer	1	5.37	18.57

TABLE 14.7 *Status of the System Up to Time T = 5.37*

TIME	EVENT	NUMBER OF CUSTOMERS	ARRIVAL TIME OF	
			NEXT CUSTOMER	NEXT BUS
0.00	—	0	4.49	18.57
4.49	Customer	1	5.37	18.57
5.37	Customer	2	10.91	18.57

1. *Change the Status of the System*: The customer joins the others waiting at the stop, so increase the number of waiting customers from 1 to 2.
2. *Schedule the Next Arriving Customer*: A new customer will arrive. To determine when, generate an interarrival time, t_a, according to an exponential distribution. Use the next 0–1 random number, $U = 0.937265$ from row 3 and column 2, and compute

$$t_a = -(1/0.5) * \ln(1 - U)$$
$$= -2 * \ln(1 - 0.937265)$$
$$= 5.54 \text{ minutes}$$

The next customer arrives 5.54 minutes from now, at time $T = 5.37 + 5.54 = 10.91$.

These changes are summarized in Table 14.7 in the row corresponding to time $T = 5.37$, at which time a new customer arrives.

Repeating this process reveals that customers continue to arrive, as summarized in Table 14.8. Note customer 7, who arrives at 16.62. This is the last person to arrive before the first bus arrives at 18.57. On the basis of the information in the last row of Table 14.8, you can see that the next event is the arrival of the first bus at time $T = 18.57$.

TABLE 14.8   *Status of the System Up to Time T = 16.62*

TIME	EVENT	NUMBER OF CUSTOMERS	ARRIVAL TIME OF	
			NEXT CUSTOMER	NEXT BUS
0.00	—	0	4.49	18.57
4.49	Customer	1	5.37	18.57
5.37	Customer	2	10.91	18.57
10.91	Customer	3	12.38	18.57
12.38	Customer	4	13.58	18.57
13.58	Customer	5	15.06	18.57
15.06	Customer	6	16.62	18.57
16.62	Customer	7	19.86	18.57

BOOKKEEPING AT TIME $T = 18.57$

When this bus arrives, perform the following bookkeeping steps:

1. *Change the Status of the System*: All customers board the bus, so reduce the number of waiting customers to 0.
2. *Determine the Arrival Time of the Next Bus*: The next bus is *scheduled* to arrive at time $T = 30$ minutes, but it will *actually* arrive late by a random amount of time, t_l. To determine t_l, use the next 0–1 random number in the table, $U = 0.287153$ in row 4 and column 3. From the standard-normal table in Appendix B, the corresponding z-value is about -0.565. Using this z-value, compute

$$t_l = \mu + (z * \sigma)$$
$$= 4 + (-0.565 * 1)$$
$$= 3.44 \text{ minutes}$$

In other words, the next bus is 3.44 minutes late. It therefore arrives at time $T = 30 + 3.44 = 33.44$.

This arrival and the status of the system at $T = 18.57$ are given in the last row of Table 14.9.

TABLE 14.9 *Status of the System Up to Time T = 18.57*

| | | NUMBER OF | ARRIVAL TIME OF | |
| | | | --- | --- |
TIME	EVENT	CUSTOMERS	NEXT CUSTOMER	NEXT BUS
0.00	—	0	4.49	18.57
4.49	Customer	1	5.37	18.57
5.37	Customer	2	10.91	18.57
10.91	Customer	3	12.38	18.57
12.38	Customer	4	13.58	18.57
13.58	Customer	5	15.06	18.57
15.06	Customer	6	16.62	18.57
16.62	Customer	7	19.86	18.57
18.57	Bus	0	19.86	33.44

From these sample events, you can see that the status of the system changes only when one of two events occurs: (a) a new customer arrives or (b) a bus arrives. Depending on which event occurs first, the clock is moved to that point in time and the following associated bookkeeping operations are performed.

BOOKKEEPING WHEN A NEW CUSTOMER ARRIVES

1. *Change the Status of the System*: Increase the number of waiting customers by 1.
2. *Schedule the Arrival Time of the Next Customer*: Determine when the next customer arrives by generating a random interarrival time from the exponential distribution.
3. Add this information as the next row in the table.

BOOKKEEPING WHEN A BUS ARRIVES

1. *Change the Status of the System*: Decrease the number of waiting customers to 0 because all these customers board the bus. Assume that the bus always has enough space for all waiting customers.
2. *Determine the Arrival Time of the Next Bus*: Determine when the *next* bus arrives by adding to its *scheduled* arrival time a random amount of time generated from a normal distribution.
3. Add this information as the next row in the table.

These steps are repeated over and over again until the clock time exceeds the duration established at the start of the problem, which in this case is 1 hour. These data up to time $T = 60$ minutes are provided in Table 14.10.

14.4.5 *Obtaining The Final Statistics*

Recall from Section 14.4.1 that the sought-after objectives—that is, the outputs—of this simulation are as follows:

TABLE 14.10 *Status of the System Up to Time T = 60.0*

| | | NUMBER OF | ARRIVAL TIME OF | |
| | | | | |
TIME	EVENT	CUSTOMERS	NEXT CUSTOMER	NEXT BUS
0.00	—	0	4.49	18.57
4.49	Customer	1	5.37	18.57
5.37	Customer	2	10.91	18.57
10.91	Customer	3	12.38	18.57
12.38	Customer	4	13.58	18.57
13.58	Customer	5	15.06	18.57
15.06	Customer	6	16.62	18.57
16.62	Customer	7	19.86	18.57
18.57	Bus	0	19.86	33.44
19.86	Customer	1	21.90	33.44
21.90	Customer	2	23.43	33.44
23.43	Customer	3	26.42	33.44
26.42	Customer	4	30.49	33.44
30.49	Customer	5	32.00	33.44
32.00	Customer	6	36.35	33.44
33.44	Bus	0	36.35	50.83
36.35	Customer	1	39.29	50.83
39.29	Customer	2	40.92	50.83
40.92	Customer	3	40.98	50.83
40.98	Customer	4	41.14	50.83
41.14	Customer	5	42.45	50.83
42.45	Customer	6	43.29	50.83
43.29	Customer	7	45.95	50.83
45.95	Customer	8	49.68	50.83
49.68	Customer	9	51.82	50.83
50.83	Bus	0	51.82	64.23
51.82	Customer	1	52.16	64.23
52.16	Customer	2	52.22	64.23
52.22	Customer	3	56.21	64.23
56.21	Customer	4	58.06	64.23
58.06	Customer	5	63.55	64.23

1. The expected waiting time for a customer at the stop.
2. The average number of customers waiting.
3. The maximum number of customers waiting.

The last step is to use the information in Table 14.10 to obtain these statistics.

COMPUTING THE EXPECTED WAITING TIME

The average waiting time at the stop is computed using the following formula:

$$\text{Average waiting time} = \frac{\text{total waiting time of all customers}}{\text{total number of customers}}$$

From the data in Table 14.10, a total of 27 customers have arrived at the stop.

To obtain the value in the numerator requires knowing how the number of waiting customers varied over time. That information is also available in Table 14.10 and has

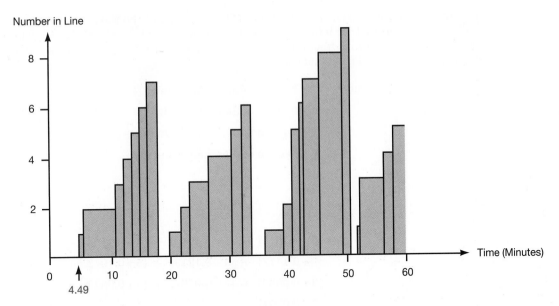

FIGURE 14.8 Number in Line at the Bus Stop Over Time.

been transferred to Figure 14.8. From time $T = 0$ to $T = 4.49$, there are no customers at the stop. From time $T = 4.49$ to $T = 5.37$, that one customer waits for a period of 0.88 minutes;

$$\text{Waiting time from } T = 4.49 \text{ to } T = 5.37 = 1 * (5.37 - 4.49)$$

$$= 0.88 \text{ minutes}$$

Then, from time $T = 5.37$ to $T = 10.91$, there are two customers waiting, and their combined waiting time during that period is

$$\text{Waiting time from } T = 5.37 \text{ to } T = 10.91 = 2 * (10.91 - 5.37)$$

$$= 11.08 \text{ minutes}$$

Performing this computation for each time interval in Figure 14.8 and adding these waiting times together provides the total waiting time of

$$\text{Total waiting time} = 205.03 \text{ minutes}$$

and so the average waiting time is

$$\text{Average waiting time} = \frac{\text{total waiting time}}{\text{number of customers}}$$

$$= \frac{205.03}{27}$$

$$= 7.5938 \text{ minutes}$$

On average, a customer can expect to wait about 7.6 minutes before the next bus arrives.

COMPUTING THE AVERAGE NUMBER OF CUSTOMERS AT THE STOP

As shown in Figure 14.8, during a total of 60 minutes the number of customers at the stop varies from 0 up to a maximum of 9. The number of waiting customers is 0 for a total of 9.69 minutes, which is 9.69/60 = 0.1615 fraction of the time. The number of waiting customers is 1 for a total of 6.20 minutes, which is 6.20/60 = 0.1034 fraction of the time. These various fractions are summarized in Table 14.11. With these values, the average number of customers is

$$
\begin{aligned}
\text{Average number} = {} & (0 * \text{fraction of time 0 is waiting}) \; + \\
& (1 * \text{fraction of time 1 is waiting}) \; + \\
& (2 * \text{fraction of time 2 are waiting}) \; + \\
& (3 * \text{fraction of time 3 are waiting}) \; + \\
& \;\;\vdots \\
& (9 * \text{fraction of time 9 are waiting})
\end{aligned}
$$

$$
\begin{aligned}
= {} & (0 * 0.1615) \; + \; (1 * 0.1043) \; + \; (2 * 0.1460) \; + \\
& (3 * 0.1417) \; + \; (4 * 0.1213) \; + \; (5 * 0.1042) \; + \\
& (6 * 0.0639) \; + \; (7 * 0.0767) \; + \; (8 * 0.0623) \; + \\
& (9 * 0.0191)
\end{aligned}
$$

$$
= 3.4172
$$

In other words, on average three to four customers are waiting at the stop during the 60 minutes.

TABLE 14.11 *Fractions of Time Different Number of People are Waiting*

NUMBER WAITING	TOTAL TIME	FRACTION OF TIME (TOTAL TIME / 60.0)
0	9.69	0.1615
1	6.20	0.1034
2	8.76	0.1460
3	8.50	0.1417
4	7.28	0.1213
5	6.25	0.1042
6	3.83	0.0639
7	4.60	0.0767
8	3.74	0.0623
9	1.15	0.0191

COMPUTING THE MAXIMUM NUMBER OF CUSTOMERS WAITING

From Table 14.10, you can see that during this simulation of 60 minutes, there is a maximum of nine customers waiting at the stop.

ADDITIONAL CONSIDERATIONS

It is important to realize that the specific statistics obtained in this section are based on the following:

1. The given initial conditions, in which there is no one waiting at the stop.
2. The data generated during a rush hour for *one* day, which are based on the specific random numbers used.

When the computation of the statistics is based on the relatively short period of 60 minutes, the initial conditions can have a significant effect on the final values. However, if the simulation is performed over a longer period of time—say, over a 2-hour period—you can assume that the effects of the initial conditions are relatively insignificant. In general, the longer the period you simulate, the less the impact of the initial conditions.

Another way to become more certain of the values of the estimates of the performance measures is to repeat the previous simulation and computations for many different days, and then take the average of each statistic. In Chapter 15, you will learn more about how many days you need to repeat the simulation to become reasonably confident of the estimates.

Once you present the final statistics to the management, RTA can determine if this schedule will provide an acceptable level of service. For example, management will implement this schedule if it feels that customers will not mind waiting an average of 7.5 minutes. The management can use the average number of waiting customers and the maximum number of customers waiting to decide how big a shelter is needed.

ADDITIONAL MANAGERIAL CONSIDERATIONS

You have seen how and when to use simulation to analyze complex systems. Doing so involves building an appropriate computer model to calculate desired outputs using relevant inputs. Decisions are then made based on the results of the simulation. In this section, several issues related to using simulation and implementing the results are discussed.

Data Collection

Although the probabilistic inputs are eventually generated by the computer using random numbers, their *distribution* must first be determined. In addition, the deterministic inputs and the initial conditions must also be specified when the simulation model is built. Keep in mind that obtaining all three types of inputs can be costly and time-consuming because it involves collecting and analyzing appropriate data.

For example, in using a computer simulation to determine how long a traffic light should remain green and how long it should remain red at a busy intersection, the interarrival times between cars constitute a probabilistic input. From historical experience there is reason to believe that the underlying distribution is exponential for intersections in general, but you should verify this assumption for the traffic flow at this particular intersection. Even if this assumption is valid, you must still estimate the mean of the distribution. You may have to hire an individual or purchase a mechanical device to record the arrival times of cars at the light over a certain period of time. Statistical analysis is then needed to determine the appropriate mean and to validate the assumption that the interarrival times follow an exponential distribution. If the exponential assumption is not valid, you can still use whatever distribution is appropriate in the simulation.

Because the output of a simulation is based entirely on the values of the inputs, the reliability of the output is only as good as the accuracy of the inputs. Therefore, sufficient time and effort should be devoted to collecting and analyzing data.

Statistical Aspects of Simulation

As you learned in Section 14.3, one set of input values to a simulation model is the set of initial conditions, which describe the state of the system at the time the simulation begins. In many cases, these values are fixed and easily determined due to the nature of the system. For example, in simulating the daily operation of a bank, the initial values describing the beginning of the simulation (that is, the start of the day) are that no customers are yet in the system and, consequently, that all available tellers are idle. In contrast, in some problems the initial conditions are not so readily available or, in fact, are not known. For example, in simulating the rush-hour operation of the bus stop for the problem of the Regional Transit Authority in Section 14.4, the initial conditions consist of the number of customers at the stop and the scheduled arrival of the next bus. These values vary from day to day and cannot be known with certainty. In these cases, initial values are generally chosen in one of the following ways:

1. By assigning values on the basis of your knowledge of how the system works and what you would most likely expect at the time corresponding to the beginning of the simulation.

2. By assigning *any* reasonable initial values and running the simulation long enough to minimize the influence of the initial conditions. For example, whether you start with no customers or three customers at the stop will have little impact on the final statistics if the simulation is run for a period of 2 hours.

3. By assigning *any* reasonable initial values and running the simulation for some initial time period, say T'. Then discard all statistics accumulated during this period except the final conditions. Use these final conditions as the initial conditions for running another simulation. A second set of statistics is then compiled and recorded.

Statistical analysis is used to determine the appropriate length of the simulation run in step 2 and the initial time period T' in step 3. These analyses are beyond the scope of this book, but they can be found in any standard book on computer simulation.

Obtaining the output value from a single simulation run is statistically analogous to drawing a single sample from a population. This is because the sequence of random numbers used in the simulation run is based on the initial uniform random number chosen and is only one of many possible outcomes. In Chapter 15, you will learn how to determine the number of simulation runs needed to achieve a specified level of confidence in estimating the average of the output value.

SUMMARY

In this chapter, you have learned that the management science technique of computer simulation is a useful tool for studying complex systems that cannot be analyzed mathematically because of the following:

1. It is not possible or practical to develop a solution methodology based on mathematical analysis.

2. To apply mathematical analysis requires additional assumptions about the model that are not applicable or realistic.

The design and analysis of a simulation model depends on first classifying the system as either a discrete-event system, in which the state of the system changes only at certain points in time, or a continuous system, in which the state of the system changes at every moment in time, continuously. Only discrete-event systems are discussed in this chapter. These discrete systems are further classified as terminating, in which there are precise and known starting and ending conditions, or nonterminating, in which the system is on-going. In the former case, it is necessary to determine only the *number* of simulation runs; in the latter case, you must also determine the *length* of each simulation run.

Designing the details of a computer simulation involves specifying the objectives of the study in the form of specific numerical outputs. Then you must identify the needed inputs, which fall into one of the following three categories:

1. Initial conditions, which describe the beginning state of the system.
2. Deterministic data, consisting of known values needed to perform the calculations in obtaining the outputs.
3. Probabilistic data, consisting of those quantities whose values are needed to obtain the outputs of the simulation, but are uncertain. Although the specific values of these probabilistic data are unknown, their general behavior must be known through a probability distribution or a density function depending, respectively, on whether the values are discrete or continuous.

The actual simulation consists of using a computer simulation package or other computer language to write a model to perform the following two steps:

Step 1. *Generating Random Numbers*: Obtain the probabilistic inputs for the model by generating random numbers according to the associated distributions.
Step 2. *Bookkeeping*: Design a systematic method for storing and processing all the input values and for performing the computations needed to obtain the output values.

The output obtained from one simulation run is only one of many possible values. Therefore, in general you cannot have confidence in the output value from a single simulation run. Rather, you need to repeat the simulation run many times—each time using a different initial uniform random number—thereby obtaining different output values.

APPENDIX 14A
USING 0–1 RANDOM NUMBERS TO OBTAIN RANDOM NUMBERS FROM A GIVEN DISTRIBUTION

In Section 14.2, you learned how to transform a 0–1 random number into one that follows a given density function, $f(t)$, and its associated cumulative distribution function, $F(t)$, by performing the following steps:

1. Generate a uniform random number between 0 and 1—say, U.
2. For the given value of U in Step 1, use the cumulative distribution $F(t)$ to determine the value of t for which

$$F(t) = U$$

3. Use the value of t computed in Step 2 as the desired random number.

These three steps are justified by the following mathematical theorem.

Theorem 14.1 *Let $f(t)$ be a given density function with cumulative distribution function $F(t)$. If R is a uniformly distributed random variable whose value is between 0 and 1, then the value T that satisfies $R = F(T)$ is a random variable whose cumulative distribution is $F(t)$.*

Proof: From the definition of a cumulative probability distribution as reviewed in the Student Resource Manual, to prove that T has cumulative distribution $F(t)$ requires showing that

$$P(T \le t) = F(t)$$

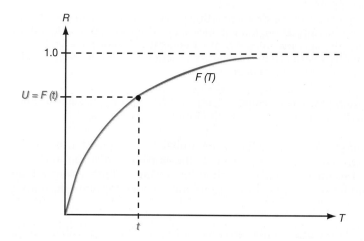

FIGURE 14.9　Generating a Random Number Using a Cumulative Distribution Function and a Uniform 0–1 Random Number.

To show this is true for the random variable T for which $R = F(T)$, from Figure 14.9, observe that $T \le t$ whenever $R \le U$ (where $U = F(t)$). Thus,

$$P(T \le t) = P(R \le U)$$
$$= U \qquad \text{(because R is uniform 0–1)}$$
$$= F(t) \qquad \text{(because $U = F(t)$)} \qquad ■$$

As a result of Theorem 14.1, if you know a value U for the uniform 0–1 random variable R, then you can generate a corresponding value for the random variable T with a cumulative distribution $F(t)$ by determining that value of t for which

$$F(t) = U$$

EXERCISES

In Exercises 14.1 to 14.6, show how to use a uniform random number U between 0 and 1 to obtain a corresponding value for a random variable X having the given discrete or continuous probability distribution. Illustrate by computing the value of the random variable X corresponding to each of the following 0–1 random numbers: (a) 0.1, (b) 0.6, (c) 0.8, and (d) 0.9.

EXERCISE 14.1   (See the preceding instructions.) A discrete random variable X whose value can be 1, 2, or 3 with respective probabilities of 1/2, 1/3, and 1/6.

EXERCISE 14.2   (See the instructions preceding Exercise 14.1.) A discrete random variable X that has a 75% chance of having a value of 1, a 20% chance of having a value of 2, and a 5% chance of having a value of 3.

EXERCISE 14.3   (See the instructions preceding Exercise 14.1.) An exponential random variable X with rate $\lambda = 10$.

EXERCISE 14.4   (See the instructions preceding Exercise 14.1.) A normal random variable X with mean $\mu = 100$ and standard deviation $\sigma = 10$.

EXERCISE 14.5   (See the instructions preceding Exercise 14.1.) A continuous random variable X that is uniformly distributed between 2 and 5. (Hint: The cumulative distribution function is $F(x) = (x - 2)/3$.)

EXERCISE 14.6   (See the instructions preceding Exercise 14.1.) A continuous random variable X whose cumulative distribution function is

$$F(x) = \begin{cases} 0.2x & \text{if } 0 \le x < 1 \\ 0.5x - 0.3 & \text{if } 1 \le x < 2 \\ 0.3x + 0.1 & \text{if } 2 \le x < 3 \end{cases}$$

EXERCISE 14.7   The New York Lottery Commission is considering a modification to the game proposed in Section 14.1 in which each game card has three rows of six boxes each. In each row, one of those six boxes covers a picture of a pineapple, three boxes cover cherries, and two boxes cover lemons. The player scratches one box in each row, but only until one of the following conditions occurs: (a) a lemon appears (in which the player loses), or (b) two cherries appear (in which case the player wins $1), or (c) two pineapples appear (in which case the player wins $5). Apply probability theory to determine the expected payoff of the lottery card.

EXERCISE 14.8   For the problem in Exercise 14.7, perform six simulations to compute the expected payoff of a lottery card. Use the 0–1 random numbers starting in row 3 and column 1 in the table in Appendix A and the result in Exercise 14.1.

EXERCISE 14.9   Explain how the result in Exercise 14.8 can be made a more accurate estimate of the true expected profit computed in Exercise 14.7.

EXERCISE 14.10   The management of Hexxon Oil Company has identified 10 promising sites for drilling oil wells in one area of the North Slope of Alaska. Through extensive studies, geologists estimate a 20% chance that over its lifetime such a well produces between 0 and 1 million barrels of oil, a 50% chance of its yielding between 1 million and 2 million barrels, and a 30% chance of its generating between 2 million and 3 million barrels. Because the geologists cannot be more precise, management assumes that the actual yield within each interval is equally likely. Assume that a well costs $1.4 million to drill and to operate over its lifetime and that the average selling price of each barrel is $20. Use probability theory to compute the expected profit from each well and the total profit from the 10 wells. (Hint: The expected number of barrels from a well is computed by adding the results of multiplying the average number of barrels in each of the three intervals by the respective probabilities of 0.2, 0.5, and 0.3.)

EXERCISE 14.11   For the problem in Exercise 14.10, perform 10 simulations to compute the expected profit from one well. Use the 0–1 random numbers starting in row 3 and column 1 in the table in Appendix A and the result in Exercise 14.6. What is your estimate of the expected profit from all 10 wells?

EXERCISE 14.12   Explain how the result in Exercise 14.11 can be made a more accurate estimate of the true expected profit computed in Exercise 14.10.

EXERCISE 14.13   After seeing the simulation presented in Section 14.1, the Manager of First-Run Videos wants to make the model more realistic by incorporating a higher demand on weekends and by including the fact that some videos are not returned the next day. The demand for tapes on weekdays is given in Section 14.1 as 0–4 copies, but demand for Friday and Saturday rentals is different. These demand probabilities and the probability of a rented tape being returned after 1, 2, or 3 days are given in the following tables:

WEEKEND DEMAND DISTRIBUTION	
NUMBER OF TAPES	PROBABILITY
0	0.05
1	0.10
2	0.20
3	0.40
4	0.25

RETURN DISTRIBUTION	
NUMBER OF DAYS	PROBABILITY
1	0.75
2	0.15
3	0.10

Any tape not returned after 1 day is charged an additional $2 per day. Assume that the store purchases three copies of the tape and that all other data for the problem are as given in Section 14.1.

    a. Identify the outputs.
    b. Identify the inputs consisting of (i) what data you would need to obtain in order to specify the initial conditions, (ii) the deterministic data, and (iii) the probabilistic data.
    c. What does the bookkeeping scheme consist of? (You need *not* perform the simulation.)

EXERCISE 14.14   Perform the simulation in Exercise 14.13 to compute the daily revenue for a period of 10 days starting on a Friday. Use the 0–1 random numbers in the table in Appendix A, starting in column 1 of the indicated rows, as follows:

    a. Row 1 for determining the number of copies demanded on a Friday or Saturday.
    b. Row 10 for determining the number of copies demanded on a day other than a Friday or Saturday.
    c. Row 20 for determining when each rented video is returned.

EXERCISE 14.15   The Manager of American Dairy Foods needs to replace the refrigeration unit for storing butter. She must choose either a unit capable of storing 1000 pounds or a unit capable of storing 1100 pounds. To decide whether the larger unit is necessary, the Manager wants to know, for each size, how often the company would not have enough butter to meet demand. Statistical analysis has revealed that the demand for butter follows a normal distribution with a mean of 100 pounds per day and a standard deviation of 10 pounds. Each Monday morning, the Manager plans to place an order for whatever amount is needed to fill the unit. That order is then filled on Wednesday morning. For example, suppose there are 250 pounds of butter in the freezer on Monday morning. With the 1000-pound freezer, an order is placed for 750 pounds. In contrast, with the 1100-pound freezer, an order is placed for 850 pounds.

    a. Identify the outputs.
    b. Identify the inputs consisting of (i) what data you would need to obtain in order to specify the initial conditions, (ii) the deterministic data, and (iii) the probabilistic data.
    c. What does the bookkeeping scheme consist of? (You need *not* perform the simulation.)

EXERCISE 14.16   Perform the simulation in Exercise 14.15 for a period of 2 weeks. Begin on a Monday morning with 250 pounds of butter in inventory. Report the daily inventory level and how often a shortage occurs for each of the two freezers. For both simulations, use uniform 0–1 random numbers starting in column 1 of row 15 in the table in Appendix A to generate the daily demands for butter.

CRITICAL-THINKING PROJECT J
THE SATELLITE COMMUNICATION PROBLEM
OF TELE COMM: PART I

The management of Tele Comm wants to improve its satellite communication service from Tokyo to New York. In the current network, messages can be sent from Tokyo to New York through either one of two different satellite paths, as shown in Figure 14.10.

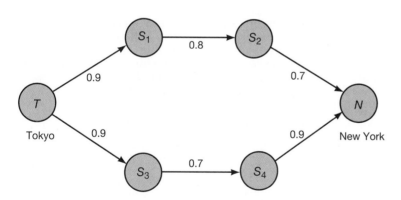

FIGURE 14.10 Communication Network for Telecom.

       The top path involves sending a message from Tokyo to New York via Satellite 1 (S_1) and then Satellite 2 (S_2). The second alternative is to send the message from Tokyo to New York via Satellite 3 (S_3) and then Satellite 4 (S_4). Due to their current orbits, these satellites can communicate with each other and with the cities only a *fraction* of the time. Those fractions are written next to each arc in the network. For example, the value of 0.9 next to the arc connecting Tokyo to Satellite 1 indicates that there is a 90% probability that a message from Tokyo can be received by Satellite 1. Similarly, the value of 0.8 next to the arc from Satellite 1 to Satellite 2 indicates that 80% of the time a message from Satellite 1 can be received by Satellite 2. All these probabilities are independent of each other. The Vice-President of Operations, Mr. Carry Fisher, has been asked to propose a way to ensure that messages can be sent successfully from Tokyo to New York 90% of the time.

His first step is to determine the probability that a message can be sent from Tokyo to New York with the current system. From your knowledge of conditional probability (see the Student Resource Manual), you compute this as the probability that the message can be sent by the top path (T–S_1–S_2–NY) plus the probability that the message can be sent by the bottom path (T–S_3–S_4–NY) *given that the message cannot be sent by the top path*:

$$P(T - N) = P(T - S_1) * P(S_1 - S_2) * P(S_2 - N) + [1 - P(T - S_1) *$$
$$P(S_1 - S_2) * P(S_2 - N)] * P(T - S_3) * P(S_3 - S_4) * P(S_4 - N)$$
$$= 0.9 * 0.8 * 0.7 + [1 - 0.9 * 0.8 * 0.7] * 0.9 * 0.7 * 0.9$$
$$= 0.504 + [1 - 0.504] * 0.567$$
$$= 0.785232$$

That is, with the current system there is only a 78.5% chance that a message can be sent from Tokyo to New York.

To improve this performance, Mr. Fisher has called his Manager of Operations, Mr. Henry James, to make recommendations. You, Mr. Henry James, have then called together your technical staff for discussions. Your technical staff proposed the following two alternatives:

1. Alter the orbit of Satellite 2 slightly, resulting in an 80% probability that a message sent from Satellite 2 can then reach New York, without affecting any of the other probabilities. Also, alter the orbit of Satellite 3 to increase the probability to 80% that a message sent from Satellite 3 is received by Satellite 4. If both these orbital changes are made, what is the probability that a message from Tokyo can reach New York?

2. With substantially more effort, the orbit of Satellite 1 can be changed so that Satellite 1 and Satellite 3 can now communicate *back and forth* with each other 80% of the time, without affecting any of the other probabilities. Design a simulation to determine the probability of a message from Tokyo reaching New York in the new system. Include a description of the inputs and outputs and how you would use random numbers. What does the bookkeeping scheme consist of? Illustrate your design by performing five simulations.

CHRYSLER TAKES A NEW STEP

Faced with declining U.S. car sales and increased competition in producing quality cars from Japanese manufacturers, Chrysler Corporation made a bold move when it opened its new Chrysler Technology Center (CTC) outside Detroit, Michigan.

CTC cost $1 billion and features 3.3 million square feet of work space, equivalent in size to seven Rose Bowls. CTC has under one roof all that is necessary to bring a car from an idea to a working pilot model in three years. According to Lee Iacocca, then chairman of Chrysler Corporation, CTC is an "idea factory," where Chrysler can improve on the efforts of the Japanese to build quality cars. With its long-range perspective, CTC serves as a monument to the end of short-term planning that has plagued U.S. manufacturing.

During the brief tour of the facilities, it is shown that CTC has the ability to perform many types of simulation, from computer-aided design to physical simulation of weather, altitude, and road conditions. Chrysler can determine, for example, how a car would perform at a 12,000-foot altitude at 100% humidity. Engineers can test how easily proposed engines start at −30° and at 135°, and they can evaluate emission levels as well. Simulation is expensive, but the alternative—making design changes after production has begun—is even more expensive.

Don Sherman, editor at large of *Motor Trend* magazine, comments that CTC is an expensive gamble, but he goes on to say that there is really no other choice and that Chrysler is very aggressive with this move. The first Chrysler employees to tour the facility were enthusiastic about Chrysler's commitment to leadership in the industry and to their own future as employees of a forward-looking company. (Total running time: 3:05.)

Questions on the video

1. What elements of CTC seem to make this a people-centered environment and not just a technological marvel?
2. Why do people believe that CTC is a gamble?

Beyond the video

1. Burger King uses simulation to test potential new products and to experiment in how it lays out its kitchens. What are the advantages of this approach?
2. Aircraft manufacturers have been using wind tunnels for decades to test designs. What do they hope to learn from these simulations?

Practical considerations

1. Why use computer simulations on automobile designs before building prototypes of parts or entire models?
2. What are the advantages to Chrysler of having all its facilities under one roof at the CTC? Would other companies do well to follow Chrysler's lead?

Source: Chrysler Corporation, Dearborn, MI, 1992.

CHAPTER 5

COMPUTER SIMULATION: APPLICATIONS AND STATISTICAL ANALYSIS

*F*ixed-rate or variable-rate mortgage? Buying a house is likely the largest investment you will ever make, and a difference of even a fraction of a percentage point in your mortgage rate can have an immense impact on your finances. The variable rate you're considering is tied to the overall economy. The task at hand, then, is to project the variable-rate course of the economy over the life of your 15-year mortgage and compare the resulting variable rate against the fixed rate. Would the variable-rate mortgage be the better choice? You can't wait for the future to happen. You must make your decision now.

This chapter looks at how you might find the answer to your mortgage question by running repeated simulations through your computer and using the resulting information to evaluate the variable-rate alternative.

In Chapter 14, you learned the basic concepts of simulation. Several simple examples illustrated the general methodology. Recall, however, that the primary advantage of simulation is to study large and complex systems that cannot be analyzed easily by direct mathematical analysis. In this chapter, you will see how simulation applies to problems in diverse areas, including a problem from finance, one from inventory management, and one from a queueing system. You will also learn how to use statistical analysis to determine the number of simulation runs or replications to perform so that you can achieve a desired level of confidence in the output value.

■ 15.1 A FINANCIAL SIMULATION

One area in which decision makers commonly apply simulation is in financial problems. Decisions in financial problems depend on various future economic conditions that are uncertain at the time the decision must be made. An appropriate simulation model allows you to evaluate the likely results of these decisions, as illustrated in the following mortgage problem.

15.1.1 *Problem Description*

Suppose you are about to buy a home and must decide how to finance your purchase. You have two options. One option is a 15-year fixed mortgage at 8% with no points (one point is 1% of the mortgage amount). The other option is a 15-year variable-rate mortgage with an initial rate of 7%. This rate is adjusted every 3 years by the amount of change in the prime rate (a key rate that banks charge their best customers) that has occurred over that period of time. The maximum rate is 10%. The merits of the two mortgages are analyzed on the basis of 15 annual payments made at the *end* of each year, although the analysis could be done equally well using 180 monthly payments. The future prime rates are of course unknown, but suppose a respected economist has told you that she believes the likelihood that this rate will change in any 3-year period is as follows:

AMOUNT OF CHANGE	PROBABILITY
+2.0	0.05
+1.5	0.05
+1.0	0.15
+0.5	0.15
+0.0	0.20
−0.5	0.15
−1.0	0.15
−1.5	0.05
−2.0	0.05

15.1.2 *Designing the Simulation*

As discussed in Section 14.3.1, Chapter 14, before designing the details of a computer simulation, it is critical to have a clear understanding of the objectives of the study in the form of specific numerical *outputs*. For the mortgage problem, it is necessary to compare the annual payments of the fixed- and variable-rate mortgages. For the purposes of simplifying the illustration, the tax implications of the two mortgages are not taken into account, but they could be included with additional bookkeeping. The total principal amount of the mortgage is the same in both cases, so the comparison can be performed on a "per $1000" basis.

One common approach to comparing two streams of payments is a cash-flow analysis based on the *net present value*, which takes the time value of money into account. For example, would you prefer $1 today or $1.10 one year from now? The answer depends on the discount (interest) rate. If you can earn more than 10% interest, you will prefer $1 now because its value will be more than $1.10 a year from now. In general, the **net present value (NPV)** of an amount $A at some future time t is the amount $P that would have to be invested today, at a known discount rate, so that the $P will be worth $A at time t. For example, if A is $100, t is 3, and the discount rate is 8% per year, then the net present value is $P = $79.38. That is, $P = $79.38 invested today at an interest rate of 8% per year will grow to A = $100 at the end of t = 3 years. The specific mathematical formulas needed to obtain the net present value are presented when needed in this section. To use the concept of net present value to compare the two mortgages, compute the following:

Net present value (NPV)
An amount of money $P that would have to be invested today, at a known discount rate, so that the $P will be worth $A at some future time t.

1. The annual payments based on the fixed mortgage rate.
2. The annual payments based on the variable mortgage rate.
3. The amount by which the variable payment exceeds the fixed payment for each year.
4. The net present value of these differences using an appropriate discount rate. It is up to you to choose the discount rate that is appropriate based on your other investment opportunities. For example, if you believe that over the next 15 years you can earn an average of 6% in a bond fund, then your discount rate is 6%. For the purpose of illustration, the discount rate used here is the average of the five variable rates applicable during each of the five 3-year periods.

A positive net present value for these differences indicates that the fixed-rate mortgage is preferable because it is expected to cost less in terms of today's dollars. In summary, then, the net present value of the differences in the 15 annual payments of the two mortgages constitutes the output of this simulation.

The next step is to identify the inputs for this simulation. These values, once determined, allow you to calculate the net present value. Recall from Section 14.3, Chapter 14, that the inputs fall into the following three categories:

1. The initial conditions, which in this case express the starting interest rate of 7% for the variable-rate mortgage.
2. The deterministic data consisting of the following:
   a. The interest rate of 8% for the fixed-rate mortgage.
   b. The principal amount of $1000.
   c. The term of the loan, which is 15 years.
3. The probabilistic data that are generated when needed, consisting of the interest rates that are applicable for the variable-rate mortgage during each of the four remaining 3-year periods.

Having identified the outputs and the inputs needed to compute them, you next need to generate appropriate random numbers and develop an associated bookkeeping scheme.

15.1.3 Generating Random Numbers

The probabilistic inputs for this simulation are the four interest rates at the beginning of years 4, 7, 10, and 13 for the variable-rate mortgage. The amount by which each successive rate differs from its predecessor should follow the distribution given in the problem description. To generate a random number from this discrete distribution, use the procedure presented in Section 14.3, Chapter 14. That is:

1. Generate a uniform 0–1 random number—say, U.
2. Determine the change in the interest rate based on where this value of U lies in Table 15.1.

TABLE 15.1	Using Uniform Random Numbers to Determine the Change in Interest Rate
RANGE OF U	CHANGE IN INTEREST RATE
0.00–0.05	+2.0
0.05–0.10	+1.5
0.10–0.25	+1.0
0.25–0.40	+0.5
0.40–0.60	+0.0
0.60–0.75	−0.5
0.75–0.90	−1.0
0.90–0.95	−1.5
0.95–1.00	−2.0

For example, recall that the variable-rate interest for Years 1–3 is 7%. To generate the interest rate for Years 4–6, arbitrarily select a uniform 0–1 random number—say, $U = 0.703888$, from row 16 and column 1 in the table in Appendix A. According to Table 15.1, the interest rate *decreases* by 0.5% because this value of U falls in the range of 0.60 to 0.75. Thus, the interest rate for Years 4–6 is

$$\text{Interest in Years 4–6} = (\text{interest in Years 1–3}) + (\text{change})$$
$$= 7.0 - 0.5$$
$$= 6.5\%$$

Keep in mind, however, that whenever this interest rate exceeds 10%, the terms of the mortgage dictate that only 10% be charged.

15.1.4 Designing the Bookkeeping Scheme

One of the best ways to approach the bookkeeping scheme is to use the technique of *working through a specific example*. Take specific values for the inputs and perform the needed computations by hand to determine the output. In this case, you need to compute the annual payments for each of the two mortgage options.

Recall the following data from the problem description in Section 15.1.1:

$$\text{Principal} = P = 1000$$
$$\text{Fixed interest rate} = i = 0.08$$
$$\text{Present-worth factor} = r = \frac{1}{1+i} = \frac{1}{1.08} = 0.92593$$
$$\text{Number of years remaining} = n = 15$$

The annual payment at the end of the year for the fixed mortgage is computed by the formula

$$\text{Payment} = P * \frac{i}{1 - r^n}$$

$$= 1000 * \frac{0.08}{1 - (0.92593)^{15}}$$

$$= \$116.83$$

In contrast, the annual payment for the variable-rate mortgage changes every 3 years, based on the applicable interest rate, the remaining principal, and the number of years left.

BOOKKEEPING FOR YEARS 1–3

For the first 3 years, the variable-rate interest is 7% (so $i = 0.07$ and $r = 1/(1 + i) = 1/1.07 = 0.93458$). The remaining principal is $P = 1000$, so the payment in each of those years is

$$\text{Payment} = P * \frac{i}{1 - r^n}$$

$$= 1000 * \frac{0.07}{1 - (0.93458)^{15}}$$

$$= \$109.79$$

To compute the payment for each of the next 3 years—that is, for Years 4, 5, and 6—it is first necessary to know how much principal remains to be paid. In other words, a portion of each of the annual payments of $109.79 is for interest and the remainder goes to pay off the principal. In particular, for Year 1:

$$\text{Beginning principal} = 1000$$

$$\text{Payment} = 109.79$$

$$\text{Interest at } 7\% = 0.07 * 1000$$

$$= 70.00$$

$$\text{Principal payment} = (\text{payment}) - (\text{interest})$$

$$= 109.79 - 70.00$$

$$= 39.79$$

$$\text{Remaining principal} = (\text{beginning principal}) - (\text{principal payment})$$

$$= 1000 - 39.79$$

$$= 960.21$$

Thus, at the beginning of Year 2, the remaining principal is $960.21. Similar computations for Years 2 and 3 result in the following:

	YEAR 1	YEAR 2	YEAR 3
Beginning principal	1000.00	960.21	917.63
Payment	109.79	109.79	109.79
Interest	70.00	67.21	64.23
Principal payment	39.79	42.58	45.56
Remaining principal	960.21	917.63	872.07

BOOKKEEPING FOR YEARS 4–6

To determine the annual payment for each of the next 3 years on the unpaid principal of \$872.07 and 12 remaining years, it is necessary to use random numbers to generate the applicable interest rate. Arbitrarily select a starting uniform 0–1 random number from the table in Appendix A, say, $U = 0.703888$ in row 16 and column 1. According to Table 15.1, the interest rate *decreases* by 0.5% because this value of U falls in the range of 0.60 to 0.75. Thus, the interest rate for Years 4–6 is

$$\text{Interest in Years 4–6} = (\text{interest in Years 1–3}) + (\text{change})$$
$$= 7.0 - 0.5$$
$$= 6.5\%$$

Accordingly, for these 3 years:

$$\text{Principal} = P = 872.07$$
$$\text{Interest rate} = i = 0.065$$
$$\text{Present-worth factor} = r = \frac{1}{1+i} = \frac{1}{1.065} = 0.93897$$
$$\text{Number of years remaining} = n = 12$$

and so the annual payment for this period is

$$\text{Payment} = P * \frac{i}{1 - r^n}$$
$$= 872.07 * \frac{0.065}{1 - (0.93897)^{12}}$$
$$= \$106.89$$

To compute the payment for each of the next 3 years—that is, for Years 7, 8, and 9—it is first necessary to know how much principal remains to be paid. In other words, a portion of each of the annual payments of \$106.89 is for interest and the remainder goes to pay off the principal. In particular, for Year 4:

$$\text{Beginning principal} = 872.07$$
$$\text{Payment} = 106.89$$
$$\text{Interest at 6.5\%} = 0.065 * 872.07$$
$$= 56.68$$
$$\text{Principal payment} = (\text{payment}) - (\text{interest})$$
$$= 106.89 - 56.68$$
$$= 50.21$$
$$\text{Remaining principal} = (\text{beginning principal}) - (\text{principal payment})$$
$$= 872.07 - 50.21$$
$$= 821.86$$

Thus, at the beginning of Year 5, the remaining principal is \$821.86. Similar computations for Years 5 and 6 result in the following:

	YEAR 4	YEAR 5	YEAR 6
Beginning principal	827.07	821.86	768.39
Payment	106.89	106.89	106.89
Interest	56.68	53.42	49.95
Principal payment	50.21	53.47	56.94
Remaining principal	821.86	768.39	711.45

BOOKKEEPING FOR YEARS 7–9

To determine the annual payment for each of the next 3 years on the unpaid principal of $711.45 and 9 remaining years, it is necessary to use random numbers to generate the applicable interest rate. Select the next uniform 0–1 random number of $U = 0.856269$, from row 16 and column 2 in the table in Appendix A. According to Table 15.1, the interest rate *decreases* by 1.0% because this value of U falls in the range of 0.75 to 0.90. Thus, the interest rate for Years 7–9 is

$$\text{Interest in Years 7–9} = (\text{interest in Years 4–6}) + (\text{change})$$
$$= 6.5 - 1.0$$
$$= 5.5\%$$

SUMMARY OF BOOKKEEPING IN YEARS 1–15

Lotus Spreadsheet
MTGAGE_1.WK1

Performing similar computations for all the remaining years results in the information presented in Table 15.2. This table represents the bookkeeping scheme necessary to keep track of the 15 annual payments used to compare this variable-rate mortgage with that of the fixed-rate mortgage. The final step is to compare these two payment streams by computing the net present value of the difference in annual payments.

BOOKKEEPING TO COMPARE ANNUAL PAYMENTS

Recall that to compare the two mortgages, it is necessary to compute the following:

TABLE 15.2 *Annual Payments for the Variable-Rate Mortgage*

YEAR	1	2	3	4	5	6	7
Beginning Balance	1000.00	960.21	917.63	872.07	821.86	768.39	711.45
Variable Payment	109.79	109.79	109.79	106.89	106.89	106.89	102.34
Interest	70.00	67.21	64.23	56.68	53.42	49.95	39.13
Principal	39.79	42.58	45.56	50.21	53.47	56.94	63.21
Remaining Balance	960.21	917.63	872.07	821.86	768.39	711.45	648.24

YEAR	8	9	10	11	12	13	14	15
Beginning Balance	648.24	581.56	511.21	438.84	361.76	279.67	193.52	100.48
Variable Payment	102.34	102.34	105.60	105.60	105.60	108.53	108.53	108.53
Interest	35.66	31.99	33.23	28.52	23.51	22.38	15.49	8.05
Principal	66.68	70.35	72.37	77.08	82.09	86.15	93.04	100.48
Remaining Balance	581.56	511.21	438.84	361.76	279.67	193.52	100.48	0.00

1. The annual payments based on the fixed-rate mortgage.
2. The annual payments based on the variable-rate mortgage.
3. The amount by which the variable payment exceeds the fixed payment for each year.
4. The net present value of these differences using a discount rate that is the average of the five variable rates applicable during each of the five 3-year periods.

The values for steps 1 to 3 are summarized in the first four columns in Table 15.3. To find the net present values of these differences, it is necessary to compute the discount rate. Use the five interest rates for the variable-rate mortgage in Table 15.3 to compute the discount rate:

$$\text{Discount rate} = \text{average interest rate}$$

$$= [(\text{rate in Years 1–3}) + (\text{rate in Years 4–6}) +$$

$$(\text{rate in Years 7–9}) + (\text{rate in Years 10–12}) +$$

$$(\text{rate in Years 13–15})] / 5$$

$$= (7.0 + 6.5 + 5.5 + 6.5 + 8.0)/5$$

$$= 6.7\%$$

By using the following data, then

$$\text{Discount rate} = d = 0.067$$

$$\text{Present-worth factor} = r = \frac{1}{1 + d} = \frac{1}{1.067} = 0.93721$$

The net present value of any amount A at the end of year m is computed by the formula:

$$\text{Net present value} = A * r^m$$

TABLE 15.3 *Comparing the Annual Payments of the Two Mortgages*

YEAR	INTEREST RATE	ANNUAL PAYMENT VARIABLE	FIXED	DIFFERENCE	NPV
1	7.0	109.79	116.83	− 7.04	− 6.60
2	7.0	109.79	116.83	− 7.04	− 6.18
3	7.0	109.79	116.83	− 7.04	− 5.79
4	6.5	106.89	116.83	− 9.94	− 7.67
5	6.5	106.89	116.83	− 9.94	− 7.19
6	6.5	106.89	116.83	− 9.94	− 6.74
7	5.5	102.34	116.83	−14.49	− 9.20
8	5.5	102.34	116.83	−14.49	− 8.62
9	5.5	102.34	116.83	−14.49	− 8.08
10	6.5	105.60	116.83	−11.23	− 5.87
11	6.5	105.60	116.83	−11.23	− 5.50
12	6.5	105.60	116.83	−11.23	− 5.16
13	8.0	108.53	116.83	− 8.30	− 3.57
14	8.0	108.53	116.83	− 8.30	− 3.35
15	8.0	108.53	116.83	− 8.30	− 3.14
				Total	−92.66

TABLE 15.4 *Summary of 35 Simulations of the Mortgage Problem*

RUN	YEARS 4–6 U	RATE	YEARS 7–9 U	RATE	YEARS 10–12 U	RATE	YEARS 13–15 U	RATE	NPV
1	0.7039	0.065	0.8563	0.055	0.2016	0.065	0.0910	0.080	−92.6696
2	0.9264	0.055	0.0906	0.07	0.5195	0.07	0.9881	0.05	−99.5531
3	0.6291	0.065	0.3583	0.07	0.8872	0.06	0.5361	0.06	−84.4378
4	0.1817	0.08	0.4278	0.08	0.8364	0.07	0.7327	0.065	−35.2746
5	0.2918	0.075	0.7908	0.065	0.8926	0.055	0.3613	0.06	−75.6462
6	0.7968	0.06	0.6121	0.055	0.2075	0.065	0.8680	0.055	−112.0810
7	0.1110	0.08	0.0214	0.1	0.0251	0.1	0.2183	0.1	11.0926
8	0.6176	0.065	0.9565	0.045	0.9301	0.03	0.6861	0.025	−163.9220
9	0.5377	0.07	0.8779	0.06	0.3469	0.065	0.1557	0.075	−78.6119
10	0.9222	0.055	0.0827	0.07	0.2408	0.08	0.1072	0.09	−78.0904
11	0.5212	0.07	0.1299	0.08	0.9839	0.06	0.4256	0.06	−62.1982
12	0.2665	0.075	0.8311	0.065	0.4113	0.065	0.9249	0.05	−71.3720
13	0.9698	0.05	0.1605	0.06	0.7804	0.05	0.0815	0.065	−133.9300
14	0.7512	0.06	0.2824	0.065	0.7315	0.06	0.7074	0.055	−102.6880
15	0.0990	0.085	0.1870	0.095	0.9442	0.08	0.6581	0.075	−1.0827
16	0.1619	0.08	0.8069	0.07	0.4670	0.07	0.6909	0.065	−47.2256
17	0.0367	0.09	0.0348	0.1	0.8657	0.1	0.4953	0.1	−33.6953
18	0.7265	0.065	0.7430	0.06	0.9437	0.045	0.2400	0.055	−112.3160
19	0.9032	0.055	0.2250	0.065	0.2227	0.075	0.2680	0.08	−91.1629
20	0.3507	0.075	0.9338	0.06	0.9857	0.04	0.8743	0.03	−107.2170
21	0.1153	0.08	0.6157	0.075	0.5498	0.075	0.0238	0.095	−30.0901
22	0.4864	0.07	0.2642	0.075	0.4886	0.075	0.2486	0.085	−50.1687
23	0.9705	0.05	0.1145	0.06	0.3374	0.065	0.5099	0.065	−120.9700
24	0.7448	0.065	0.0618	0.08	0.0484	0.1	0.2738	0.1	−33.6953
25	0.8175	0.06	0.7287	0.055	0.8572	0.045	0.0406	0.065	−125.0850
26	0.4833	0.07	0.6371	0.065	0.0804	0.08	0.4372	0.08	−59.9688
27	0.8976	0.06	0.3183	0.065	0.7154	0.06	0.7471	0.055	−102.6880
28	0.0782	0.085	0.6974	0.08	0.6217	0.075	0.9688	0.055	−25.5896
29	0.7887	0.06	0.1926	0.07	0.6699	0.065	0.3783	0.07	−86.5302
30	0.1745	0.08	0.3678	0.085	0.1821	0.095	0.8932	0.085	−9.4039
31	0.2856	0.075	0.9864	0.055	0.4365	0.055	0.0793	0.07	−85.0627
32	0.7970	0.06	0.9002	0.045	0.1997	0.055	0.1809	0.065	−130.3140
33	0.7890	0.06	0.9085	0.045	0.4628	0.045	0.8225	0.035	−154.2220
34	0.8329	0.06	0.2176	0.07	0.7250	0.065	0.9125	0.05	−93.8383
35	0.3770	0.075	0.7558	0.065	0.8162	0.055	0.9494	0.04	−83.0496

Mean = −78.9361
Std. Dev. = 42.1812

For example, for the first year, the difference in the annual payments is $A = \$109.79 - \$116.83 = -\$7.04$, and so the net present value of this amount is

$$\text{Net present value} = A * r^m$$

$$= -7.04 * (0.93721)^1$$

$$= -6.60$$

Similarly, for the second year, in which $m = 2$ and the difference in annual payments is also $A = -7.04$,

$$\text{Net present value} = A * r^m$$
$$= -7.04 * (0.93721)^2$$
$$= -6.18$$

The result of performing these computations for each of the remaining 13 years is summarized in the last column of Table 15.3. Adding up the 15 numbers in this column provides the result that the net present value of the differences in the annual payments of the two mortgages is -92.66. This means that, *in this simulation*, the variable-rate mortgage is preferable to the fixed-rate mortgage due to the negative net present value of the differences.

It is important to realize that this conclusion is based on only *one* possible outcome. In order to achieve a higher degree of reliability, this simulation should be performed a large number of times. In Section 15.5, you will learn how to determine an appropriate number of repetitions to perform. The results of performing 35 repetitions are summarized in Table 15.4. The average of -78.9361 for the 35 net present values in this table is a reliable estimate of the expected differences in the two mortgages. Keep in mind that this figure of -78.9361 is the expected difference for each $1000 dollars borrowed. If you borrow $200,000, the expected difference between the two mortgages will be $-78.9361 * 200 = -\$15,787.22$. On the basis of these results, you should prefer the variable-rate mortgage, if other factors, such as taxes, are not considered.

In this section, you have seen how a simulation is used to perform a financial analysis. In Section 15.2, you will see an application of simulation to evaluate an inventory system.

■ 15.2 A SIMULATION OF AN INVENTORY PROBLEM

Another common area in which simulation is useful is in analyzing inventory systems for which the analytical methods discussed in Chapter 12 are not applicable. Consider the problem faced by the management of American Dairy Foods, Inc.

15.2.1 *Problem Description*

Among many other products, American Dairy Foods, Inc. (ADF), supplies milk to various convenience stores in a suburb of Madison. ADF orders milk directly from a local farm co-op at $1.50 per gallon and stores it at a central ADF facility. From there, the milk is distributed to the stores on an "as-needed" basis at a price of $2.00 per gallon. Statistical analysis of historical sales has revealed that the daily demand arising at the central facility can be approximated quite accurately with a normal distribution having a mean of 750 gallons and a standard deviation of 100.

The Accounting Department of ADF has negotiated with the farm co-op a fixed cost of $100 per order to cover the delivery and processing charges. ADF's experience with the co-op reveals that 80% of the time the order for milk ADF placed at the beginning of a day is delivered by the co-op the following morning. However, 20% of the time that order is delivered the morning of the second day after the order is placed.

As Manager of Operations for ADF, you want to determine an inventory policy that maximizes the expected daily profit based on an inventory holding cost of $H = \$0.02$ per gallon per day. In determining this policy, you need to take into account that milk is perishable. In that regard, corporate policy dictates that any milk in the central facility over 7 days old cannot be distributed to the stores. Instead, it is sold to local food banks for $0.50 per gallon.

In determining the optimal policy, you should realize that the models described in Chapter 12 are *not* directly applicable. One reason is that the lead time in this problem is *uncertain*, whereas the results in Chapter 12 are based on a *known* lead time. Also, the perishable aspect of this problem renders the mathematical analysis in Chapter 12 invalid. For these reasons, a simulation is a reasonable way to evaluate different policies, as described in Section 15.2.2.

15.2.2 *Identifying the Class of Inventory Policies*

As discussed in Chapter 12, there are two basic classes of inventory policies.

> 1. With a *continuous-review policy*, a fixed amount is ordered whenever the inventory level drops below a certain *reorder point*.
> 2. With a *periodic-review policy*, different amounts are ordered based on the observed inventory level at fixed points in time.

For the problem of ADF, the latter policy is more appropriate because that company needs to satisfy demand on a daily basis and will order based on its inventory level at the beginning of each day. ADF has decided to implement this policy in two steps:

> 1. Obtain the inventory level of sellable milk, I, at the beginning of each day and add the number of gallons of milk, B, already ordered from the co-op but not yet received.
> 2. Place a new order only if $I + B$ is below some minimum level—say, s gallons. In this event, order an amount so as to have a total of S gallons of milk in inventory and on order—that is, the order amount is $S - (I + B)$ gallons.

For example, if $s = 500$ and $S = 2000$, then the policy is to order milk only if the inventory on hand and on order is below 500 gallons. In this event, ADF places an order to bring the inventory on hand and on order up to a total of 2000 gallons.

The objective is to determine the values of s and S that maximize the expected daily profit. Although it would be desirable to use mathematical analysis to obtain the best values for s and S, doing so in this case is not straightforward because of the complexity caused by the uncertain lead time and the perishability of the milk. A viable approach is to use simulation to evaluate the expected daily profit associated with different values of s and S and then select the pair of values that provides the largest expected daily profit. To illustrate how simulation is used to evaluate one particular choice, suppose that $s = 900$ and $S = 4000$.

15.2.3 *Designing the Simulation*

As discussed in Section 14.3.1, Chapter 14, before designing the details of a computer simulation, it is critical to have a clear understanding of the objectives of the study in the form of specific numerical outputs. For the problem of American Dairy Foods, that output is the expected daily profit.

The next step is to identify the inputs for this simulation. You need these values to calculate the expected daily profit. Recall, from Section 14.3, Chapter 14, that the inputs fall into the following three categories.

> 1. The initial conditions in this case express the amount of 1-day-old milk in stock, 2-day-old milk in stock, and so on at the beginning of the simulation. Another initial condition is whether an order has been placed prior to the first day of the simulation and, if so, the amount ordered and its expected arrival day. These initial values should reflect the most likely starting conditions on any given day and should be obtained by estimation based on your experience. For the purposes of this

illustration, assume that no orders are outstanding and that the initial inventories are as follows:

DAYS OLD	SYMBOL	INITIAL INVENTORY (GALLONS)
0	I_0	0
1	I_1	500
2	I_2	300
3	I_3	0
4	I_4	0
5	I_5	100
6	I_6	100

2. The deterministic data consist of:
   a. The following cost and revenue data, as described in Section 15.2.1:
      i. Purchase cost = C = $1.50 per gallon
      ii. Ordering cost = K = $100
      iii. Holding cost per day = H = $0.02 per gallon per day
      iv. Resale value = R = $0.50 per gallon
   b. The values of $s = 900$ gallons and $S = 4000$ gallons to be evaluated by this simulation. (That is, on any day that starts off with less than $s = 900$ gallons of milk at the central facility or on order, ADF must order more. The current inventory plus the total amount ordered, including previously ordered milk not yet received, must be equal to $S = 4000$ gallons.)
   c. The number of days to simulate—say, $n = 100$.
3. The probabilistic data, generated when needed, consist of:
   a. A demand for milk on each of the days in the simulation, which is assumed to follow a normal distribution with a mean of 750 gallons and a standard deviation of 100 gallons.
   b. A lead time of 1 or 2 days, with probabilities of 0.8 and 0.2, respectively, whenever an order is placed.

The actual simulation consists of generating appropriate random numbers and an associated bookkeeping scheme.

15.2.4 *Generating Random Numbers*

One of the probabilistic inputs for this simulation is the daily demand, which follows a normal distribution, with a mean $\mu = 750$ gallons per day and a standard deviation of $\sigma = 100$. To generate such a random number recall, from Section 14.3, Chapter 14, the following general steps:

1. Generate a uniform 0–1 random number U.
2. Find a z-value from the standard-normal table in Appendix B so that the area to the left of z is U.
3. Obtain the random demand, d, by computing:

$$d = \mu + (\sigma * z)$$
$$= 750 + (100 * z)$$

In addition, whenever an order is placed, the random lead time needs to be generated according to the following discrete distribution:

DAYS	PROBABILITY
1	0.8
2	0.2

As discussed in Section 14.3, this can be accomplished by the following:

1. Generating a uniform 0–1 random number U.
2. Determining the lead time by

$$\text{Lead time} = \begin{cases} 1 & \text{if } U < 0.8 \\ 2 & \text{if } U \geq 0.8 \end{cases}$$

15.2.5   *Designing the Bookkeeping Scheme*

Again, use the technique of *working through a specific example*. Take specific values for the inputs and perform the needed computations by hand to determine the output. Recall the values for the initial conditions and other deterministic inputs for the problem of American Dairy Foods, Inc. The appropriate computations for each day are shown in what follows.

BOOKKEEPING FOR DAY 1

Step 1. *Receiving Orders*: To begin with, no orders are outstanding, so no milk is received at the beginning of this day. Hence, the initial inventories remain unchanged at

I_0	I_1	I_2	I_3	I_4	I_5	I_6
0	500	300	0	0	100	100

Step 2. *Ordering*: By observing that the total inventory of $I = I_0 + I_1 + \ldots + I_6 = 1000$ is above the minimum reorder point of $s = 900$, no order is placed on Day 1.

Step 3. *Generating the Demand*: The demand for this day must be generated according to a normal distribution, with a mean of 750 and a standard deviation of 100. As discussed earlier, this is done using a 0–1 random number as follows:

1. Randomly select a 0–1 random number from the table in Appendix A—say, $U = 0.770145$, from row 6 and column 1.
2. Obtain the associated z-value of about 0.73 from the table in Appendix B so that the area to the left of z is $U = 0.770145$.
3. Compute the demand as

$$\begin{aligned} d = &\ \mu + (\sigma * z) \\ = &\ 750 + (100 * z) \\ = &\ 750 + (100 * 0.73) \\ = &\ 823 \text{ gallons} \end{aligned}$$

Step 4. *Updating the Inventory*: It is first necessary to determine if the demand generated in Step 3 can be met with the existing inventory. In this case, the answer is yes because the demand of $d = 823$ gallons is less than the total available inventory of 1000 gallons. In general,

$$\text{Amount sold} = \begin{cases} d & \text{if } d \leq \text{total inventory} \\ \text{total inventory} & \text{otherwise} \end{cases}$$

The inventory amounts classified by age must be updated to account for sales. Because milk is perishable, ADF sells its oldest milk first. ADF meets the demand for 823 gallons by selling all 100 gallons of its 6-day-old milk, all 100 gallons of its 5-day-old milk, all 300 gallons of its 2-day-old milk, and 323 gallons of its 1-day-old milk. Also, at the end of the first day—which is the beginning of the second day—the milk remaining in inventory ages by 1 day. To reflect this change, the amount in inventory for each age group becomes that of the next-oldest age group, as follows:

		INVENTORY		
DAYS OLD	SYMBOL	BEGINNING OF DAY 1	DEMAND MET	BEGINNING OF DAY 2
0	I_0	0	—	0
1	I_1	500	323	0
2	I_2	300	300	$500 - 323 = 177$
3	I_3	0	—	$300 - 300 = 0$
4	I_4	0	—	0
5	I_5	100	100	0
6	I_6	100	100	$100 - 100 = 0$
7	I_7	0	0	$100 - 100 = 0$

Step 5. *Computing the Daily Profit*: To compute the net daily profit, recall that each gallon of milk costs $1.50 and is sold to stores at $2.00 and to food banks for $0.50. This results in a profit of $0.50 for each gallon sold to stores and a loss of $1.00 for each gallon sold to food banks. This information, the other relevant cost data, and the sales yield the net profit:

$$\text{Net profit} = (\text{profit from milk sold to stores}) -$$
$$(\text{loss from milk sold to food banks}) -$$
$$(\text{cost of ordering that day}) -$$
$$(\text{cost of holding that day's inventory})$$

where

$$\text{Profit from stores} = (\text{gallons sold to stores}) * (\text{profit per gallon})$$
$$= 823 * 0.50$$
$$= 411.50$$

$$\text{Loss from food banks} = \begin{cases} \text{gallons sold to} \\ \text{food banks} \end{cases} * (\text{loss per gallon})$$
$$= \begin{cases} \text{gallons of 7-day-old milk} \\ \text{at the end of Day 1} \end{cases} * 1.00$$
$$= 0.00$$

$$\text{Cost of ordering} = \begin{cases} 0 & \text{if no order is placed} \\ 100 & \text{if an order is placed} \end{cases}$$

$$= 0 \text{ (because no order is placed on Day 1)}$$

$$\left\{\begin{array}{l}\text{Inventory}\\\text{holding cost}\end{array}\right\} = \left\{\begin{array}{l}\text{number of gallons}\\\text{of milk in inventory}\\\text{less than 7 days}\\\text{old at the end of}\\\text{Day 1}\end{array}\right\} * \left\{\begin{array}{l}\text{holding}\\\text{cost per}\\\text{gallon per}\\\text{day}\end{array}\right\}$$

$$= 177 * 0.02$$

$$= 3.54$$

The net profit for the first day is

$$\begin{aligned}\text{Net profit} =\ & \text{(profit from milk sold to stores)} -\\ & \text{(loss from milk sold to food banks)} -\\ & \text{(cost of ordering that day)} -\\ & \text{(cost of holding that day's inventory)}\\ =\ & 411.50 - 0 - 0 - 3.54\\ =\ & \$407.96\end{aligned}$$

BOOKKEEPING FOR DAY 2

Step 1. *Receiving Orders*: No orders have as yet been placed, so no milk is received at the beginning of this day. The initial inventories remain unchanged at

I_0	I_1	I_2	I_3	I_4	I_5	I_6
0	0	177	0	0	0	0

Step 2. *Ordering*: Observe that the total inventory of $I = I_0 + I_1 + \ldots + I_6 = 177$ is *below* the minimum reorder point of $s = 900$. An order therefore is placed to bring the inventory up to $S = 4000$. This order is for $4000 - 177 = 3823$ gallons of milk. As discussed in the problem description, this milk arrives either on Day 3 (with probability 0.80) or on Day 4 (with probability 0.20). To generate this random lead time, select the next random number, 0.556772, from row 6 and column 2 of the table in Appendix A. Because this number is less than 0.80, the lead time is 1 day, so this order arrives at the beginning of Day 3.

Step 3. *Generating the Demand*: The demand for this day must be generated according to a normal distribution, with a mean of 750 and a standard deviation of 100:

    a. Select the next random number, 0.028899, from row 6 and column 3 of the table in Appendix A.

    b. Obtain the associated z-value of about -1.9 from the table in Appendix B so that the area to the left of z is $U = 0.028899$.

    c. Compute the demand as

$$\begin{aligned}d =\ & \mu + (\sigma * z)\\ =\ & 750 + (100 * z)\\ =\ & 750 + [100 * (-1.9)]\\ =\ & 560 \text{ gallons}\end{aligned}$$

Step 4. *Updating the Inventory*: It is first necessary to determine if the demand generated in Step 3 can be met with the existing inventory. In this case, the answer is no because the demand of 560 gallons is more than the total available inventory of 177 gallons. Thus, the actual amount sold is only 177 gallons. The inventory must be updated to show the effect of these sales. In this case, the entire inventory is sold, and all inventory values become 0:

I_0	I_1	I_2	I_3	I_4	I_5	I_6
0	0	0	0	0	0	0

Step 5. *Computing the Daily Profit*: As before, the net profit is

$$\text{Net profit} = (\text{profit from milk sold to stores}) -$$
$$(\text{loss from milk sold to food banks}) -$$
$$(\text{cost of ordering that day}) -$$
$$(\text{cost of holding that day's inventory})$$
$$= (177 * 0.50) - (0 * 1.00) - 100 - 0$$
$$= -\$11.50$$

BOOKKEEPING FOR DAY 3

Step 1. *Receiving Orders*: Because the order of 3823 gallons placed on Day 2 has a lead time of 1 day (see Step 2 on Bookkeeping for Day 2), that order arrives at the beginning of this day. Add this amount to I_0, the current inventory level of 0-day-old milk:

I_0	I_1	I_2	I_3	I_4	I_5	I_6
3823	0	0	0	0	0	0

Step 2. *Ordering*: The total inventory of $I = I_0 + I_1 + \ldots + I_6 = 3823$ is above the minimum reorder point of $s = 900$, so no order is placed on Day 3.

Step 3. *Generating the Demand*: The demand for this day must be generated according to a normal distribution, with a mean of 750 and a standard deviation of 100:

1. Select the next random number, 0.076490, from row 6 and column 4 of the table in Appendix A.
2. Obtain the associated z-value of about -1.43 from the table in Appendix B so that the area to the left of z is $U = 0.076490$.
3. Compute the demand as

$$d = \mu + (\sigma * z)$$
$$= 750 + (100 * z)$$
$$= 750 + [100 * (-1.43)]$$
$$= 607 \text{ gallons}$$

Step 4. *Updating the Inventory*: It is first necessary to determine if the demand generated in Step 3 can be met with the existing inventory. In this case, the answer is yes because the demand of 607 gallons is less than the total available inventory of 3823 gallons. Now the inventory must be updated to reflect these sales. The entire amount of 893 gallons is met from the 3823 gallons of 0-day-old milk, so that value becomes $3823 - 607 = 3216$. Furthermore, this remaining 0-day-old milk becomes 1-day-old at the end of this day. Thus, the new inventory levels are

I_0	I_1	I_2	I_3	I_4	I_5	I_6
0	3216	0	0	0	0	0

Step 5. *Computing the Daily Profit*: As before, the net profit is:

$$\text{Net profit} = (\text{profit from milk sold to stores}) -$$
$$(\text{loss from milk sold to food banks}) -$$
$$(\text{cost of ordering that day}) -$$
$$(\text{cost of holding that day's inventory})$$
$$= (607 * 0.50) - (0 * 1.00) - 0 - (3216 * 0.02)$$
$$= \$239.18$$

The results of repeating this process for the first 20 days are summarized in Table 15.5. If the process is continued for 100 days, you will obtain a total profit of $30,517.62. Dividing this total by 100 results in an estimated expected daily profit of $305.18.

Recall that this value is only an *estimate* based on one particular simulation. The estimate can be made more reliable by increasing the number of days in this one simulation or repeating the 100-day simulation many more times. In Section 15.5, you will learn how to determine an appropriate number of times to repeat this simulation so that the resulting estimate is within a prespecified accuracy.

TABLE 15.5   *Results of Simulating the First 20 Days of the Problem of American Dairy Foods, Inc.*

	INVENTORY (AFTER RECEIVING TODAY'S ORDER)								PLACE ORDER			DEMAND		NET
DAY	I_0	I_1	I_2	I_3	I_4	I_5	I_6	TOTAL	YES/NO	U	LEAD TIME	U	GAL	PROFIT
1	0	500	300	0	0	100	100	1000	No			0.7701	823	407.96
2	0	0	177	0	0	0	0	177	Yes	0.5568	1	0.0289	560	−11.50
3	3823	0	0	0	0	0	0	3823	No			0.0765	607	239.18
4	0	3216	0	0	0	0	0	3216	No			0.4815	746	323.60
5	0	0	2470	0	0	0	0	2470	No			0.3435	710	319.80
6	0	0	0	1760	0	0	0	1760	No			0.7348	812	387.04
7	0	0	0	0	948	0	0	948	No			0.8455	851	423.56
8	0	0	0	0	0	97	0	97	Yes	0.6565	1	0.5894	772	−51.50
9	3903	0	0	0	0	0	0	3903	No			0.1570	650	259.94
10	0	3253	0	0	0	0	0	3253	No			0.0298	562	227.18
11	0	0	2691	0	0	0	0	2691	No			0.8635	859	392.86
12	0	0	0	1832	0	0	0	1832	No			0.6041	776	366.88
13	0	0	0	0	1056	0	0	1056	No			0.9359	902	447.92
14	0	0	0	0	0	154	0	154	Yes	0.2122	1	0.6427	786	−23.00
15	3846	0	0	0	0	0	0	3846	No			0.9619	927	405.12
16	0	2919	0	0	0	0	0	2919	No			0.9187	889	403.90
17	0	0	2030	0	0	0	0	2030	No			0.4228	731	339.52
18	0	0	0	1299	0	0	0	1299	No			0.6531	789	384.30
19	0	0	0	0	510	0	0	510	Yes	0.4077	1	0.8816	868	155.00
20	3490	0	0	0	0	0	0	3490	No			0.8583	857	375.84

Remember that the goal is to determine the values for the reorder point s and the amount S—which is the value that inventory should be brought up to—that maximize the expected daily profit. The simulation presented here evaluates the merits of the policy in which $s = 900$ and $S = 4000$. On the basis of your knowledge of this business, you should choose numerous other values for s and S and perform similar simulations. Then choose the values of s and S that produce the largest expected daily profit according to the simulation.

Before implementing the policy obtained from this simulation, as Manager you should consider other aspects of the problem. For example, you may want to take into account how often the inventory policy results in shortages—that is, not being able to supply milk to your stores. Also, you may want to know the impact of reviewing the inventory every other day instead of every day. All of these "What-happens-if?" questions can be explored by making appropriate changes to the design and bookkeeping of this simulation.

■ 15.3 A Simulation of a Queueing Problem

In this section, you will see an example of how simulation is used to evaluate a queueing system in which arriving items wait in lines for service. Consider the problem of the New Jersey Turnpike Commission.

15.3.1 Problem Description

The New Jersey Turnpike Commission wants to improve the traffic flow through its toll booths. One manager has suggested that car pooling be encouraged by having special booths only for cars with two or more passengers, with the rest of the booths for other traffic. These special booths are called express lanes. The Commission has selected one toll plaza to use as a pilot in developing and evaluating the impact of this proposal before extending this idea to other plazas. As Manager of Operations, you want to determine the impact on the current traffic flow of converting one of the three current booths at this toll plaza to an express booth, as shown in Figure 15.1.

Through data studies, the Commission has determined that the selected toll plaza currently serves about 20 vehicles per minute during the rush hour. Of these cars, only about 1/3 have two or more passengers. The data also show that the time between two arriving vehicles can be approximated by an exponential distribution, with an average rate of $\lambda = 20$ vehicles per minute.

Historical data indicate that booths handling general traffic require a processing time per vehicle that obeys the following distribution:

TIME (SECONDS)	PROBABILITY
3–8	0.6
8–13	0.3
13–18	0.1

No such data are available for the proposed express booth. The service time at the express booth is not expected to follow the previous distribution because that distribution pertains to cars, trucks, and all other vehicles, whereas the express booth is only for cars. From experience with express booths at other locations, you believe the service time can be approximated closely by an exponential distribution, with a mean rate of 10 cars per minute.

You should realize that the models described in Chapter 13 are *not* directly applicable. One reason is that the service times of the booths follow different distributions,

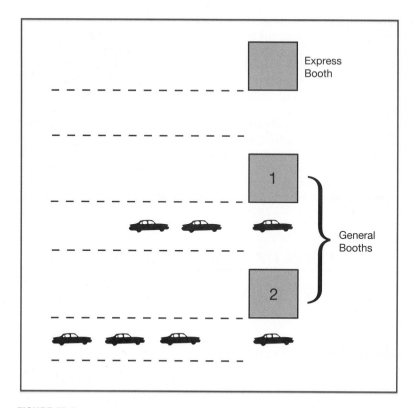

FIGURE 15.1 Proposed Toll Plaza for the New Jersey Turnpike Commission.

one of which is not exponential. A second reason is that cars with two or more passengers are free to join *any* of the three queues, whereas all other traffic must join one of the two queues for the general booths. Moreover, among the allowed booths, each vehicle chooses to join the shortest queue. For these reasons, you cannot apply the models of Chapter 13 here. A simulation offers a reasonable means for evaluating this system.

15.3.2 Designing the Simulation

What are the objectives of the study in the form of specific numerical *outputs*? For the problem of the New Jersey Turnpike Commission, the appropriate outputs are identified as follows:

1. The expected waiting time for a vehicle at each booth.
2. The average number of vehicles in each line.
3. The average utilization of each booth—that is, the fraction of time the booth is serving a vehicle.

The next step is to identify the inputs for this simulation. As always, the inputs fall into the following three categories.

1. The initial conditions here are the number of vehicles either being served or in line at each booth at the time the simulation begins. These values should reflect the most likely conditions during the rush hour. As Manager of Operations, you should estimate them on the basis of your experience. For the purpose of this example, assume that the express line is empty and that at each of the general

booths, a car has just pulled up to begin service. Also, there are two cars waiting in line for one of the general booths and three cars waiting in line for the other general booth. Recall that if the simulation is conducted for a long enough period of time, the initial conditions should have little effect on the final results.

2. The deterministic data consist of the length of time over which to perform this simulation—say, 2 hours—and the fact that there are one express and two general booths.

3. The probabilistic data, generated when needed, consist of the following:
   a. The arrivals of the vehicles, whose interarrival times are assumed to follow an exponential distribution, with a mean rate of $\lambda = 20$ vehicles per minute.
   b. The type of each arriving vehicle, which is either an *express vehicle* (a car with at least two people) or a *general vehicle* (all other vehicles). The probability is 0.3333 that an arriving vehicle qualifies for the express lane and 0.6667 that it does not qualify, as given in the problem description.
   c. The service time for a vehicle at a general booth, which is assumed to follow the given historical distribution.
   d. The service time for a car at the express booth, which is assumed to follow an exponential distribution with a mean rate of 10 cars per minute.

The actual simulation consists of generating appropriate random numbers and an associated bookkeeping scheme, which are now described.

15.3.3 *Generating Random Numbers*

Each of the four probabilistic inputs needs to be generated using random numbers according to their underlying probability distributions.

GENERATING ARRIVING VEHICLES

One of the probabilistic inputs for this simulation is the arrival of vehicles. The interarrival time follows an exponential distribution with a mean of $\lambda = 20$ vehicles per minute. Recall, from Section 14.3, Chapter 14, that the time, t_a, in *seconds* between successive arrivals is obtained by:

- Generating a uniform 0–1 random number U.
- Computing

$$t_a = -(1/20) * 60 * \ln (1 - U)$$

GENERATING THE TYPE OF AN ARRIVING VEHICLE

An arriving vehicle is either an express vehicle (probability 0.3333) or a general vehicle (probability 0.6667). Determining the type of an arriving vehicle, therefore, can be accomplished by:

- Generating a uniform 0–1 random number U.
- Determining the vehicle type by

$$\text{Type} = \begin{cases} \text{express} & \text{if } U < 0.3333 \\ \text{general} & \text{if } U \geq 0.3333 \end{cases}$$

GENERATING THE SERVICE TIME AT A GENERAL BOOTH

The amount of time needed to process a vehicle at a general booth follows this historical distribution:

TIME (SECONDS)	PROBABILITY
3–8	0.6
8–13	0.3
13–18	0.1

To generate this continuous distribution based on these empirical values, first obtain its cumulative distribution function, $F(x)$, as shown in Figure 15.2 (see the Student Resource Manual). To generate a random number from this particular cumulative distribution function, recall the general approach, described in Section 14.3, Chapter 14:

- Generate a uniform 0–1 random number U.
- Find the service time, t_s, which is the value of x for which

$$F(x) = U$$

Finding the desired value for t_s depends on whether U is between 0.0 and 0.6, between 0.6 and 0.9, or between 0.9 and 1.0, as shown in Figure 15.3. Specifically, the service time t_s is computed as follows:

$$t_s = \begin{cases} 3 + 5 * \dfrac{U}{0.6} & \text{if } 0.0 \leq U < 0.6 \\[2ex] 8 + 5 * \dfrac{U - 0.6}{0.3} & \text{if } 0.6 \leq U < 0.9 \\[2ex] 13 + 5 * \dfrac{U - 0.9}{0.1} & \text{if } 0.9 \leq U < 1.0 \end{cases}$$

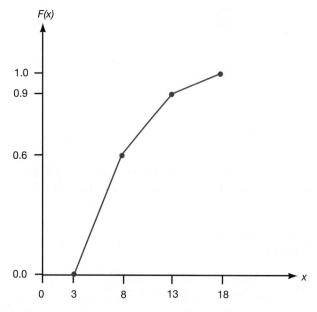

FIGURE 15.2 Cumulative Distribution Function for the Time Required to Process a Vehicle at a General Booth.

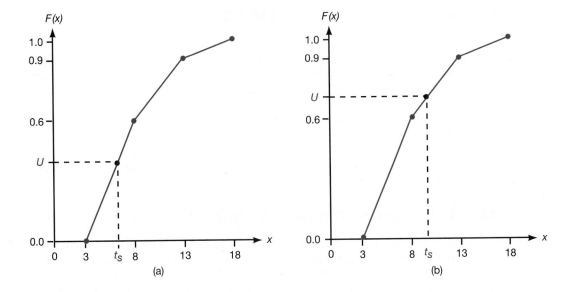

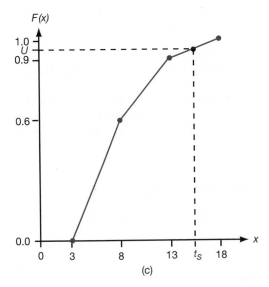

FIGURE 15.3 Generating a Random Number with the Cumulative Distribution Function Given in Figure 15.2: (a) U between 0.0 and 0.6, (b) U between 0.6 and 0.9, and (c) U between 0.9 and 1.0.

For example, if $U = 0.7424$, then

$$t_s = 8 + 5 * \frac{U - 0.6}{0.3}$$

$$= 8 + 5 * \frac{0.7424 - 0.6}{0.3}$$

$$= 10.3733 \text{ seconds}$$

GENERATING THE SERVICE TIME AT AN EXPRESS BOOTH

The amount of time needed to process a car at an express booth is assumed to follow an exponential distribution, with a mean of $\lambda = 10$ cars per minute. This service time, t_s, in *seconds* is obtained by:

1. Generating a uniform 0–1 random number U.
2. Computing

$$t_s = -(1/10) * 60 * \ln(1 - U)$$

15.3.4 *Designing the Bookkeeping Scheme*

Recall the values for the initial conditions for this problem: The express booth is empty, there is one car starting service at each of the other two booths, and there are two cars waiting at the first general booth and three cars waiting at the other general booth.

To achieve the desired outputs, you need to know the status of the system *at every point in time*. How many cars are in line at each booth? Is each booth busy or not? How long does each vehicle take for service? In the previous examples in this chapter, the status of the system changed only at *regular* time intervals—for example, every year in the mortgage problem in Section 15.1 and every day for the inventory problem in Section 15.2. In this problem, however, the status changes at *different* time intervals. In fact, the status changes when either

1. a new vehicle arrives, or when
2. a vehicle finishes service at a booth and leaves the system

It is necessary to record the status of the system *only at these points in time*. You must know which of these events occurs next and when. To begin with, consider the initial state of the system at time $T = 0$. The two general booths have just begun serving a vehicle.

BOOKKEEPING AT TIME $T = 0$

At time $T = 0$, the system is described by the following initial conditions:

1. The express line is empty, and the server there is idle.
2. The line at the first general booth has two vehicles, and the server is busy just starting service on a third vehicle.
3. The line at the second general booth has three vehicles, and the server is busy just starting service on a fourth vehicle.

To determine when the status of this system changes, you need to know the times at which the vehicles at the two general booths are finished and when the next vehicle arrives at the toll plaza. These values need to be generated randomly according to their distributions.

DETERMINING WHEN THE NEXT VEHICLE LEAVES THE TOLL PLAZA

Use random numbers to determine when the two vehicles currently being served at each of the two general booths are finished.

1. For the first vehicle: Arbitrarily start by choosing a uniform 0–1 random number—say, $U = 0.689315$, from row 1 and column 2 of the table in Appendix A. Then compute the length of service, t_s, as

$$t_s = 8 + 5 * \frac{U - 0.6}{0.3}$$

$$= 8 + 5 * \frac{0.689315 - 0.6}{0.3}$$

$$= 9.49 \text{ seconds}$$

2. For the second vehicle: Choose the next uniform 0–1 random number, $U = 0.122662$, from row 1 and column 3 of the table in Appendix A. Then compute the length of service, t_s, as

$$t_s = 3 + 5 * \frac{U}{0.6}$$

$$= 3 + 5 * \frac{0.122662}{0.6}$$

$$= 4.02 \text{ seconds}$$

The vehicle at the first general booth leaves the system 9.49 seconds from now, at time $T = 0 + 9.49 = 9.49$. The vehicle at the second general booth leaves at time $T = 0 + 4.02 = 4.02$.

DETERMINING WHEN THE NEXT VEHICLE ARRIVES

To determine when the next vehicle arrives, use the next 0–1 random number in the table, $U = 0.151792$, from row 1 and column 4. Accordingly, the interarrival time is

$$t_a = -(1/20) * 60 * \ln(1 - U)$$

$$= -3 * \ln(1 - 0.151792)$$

$$= 0.49 \text{ seconds}$$

That is, the next vehicle arrives 0.49 second from now, at time $T = 0 + 0.49 = 0.49$.

To determine the type of the arriving vehicle, use the next 0–1 random number, $U = 0.245387$ from row 1 and column 5, which means that the car is an express vehicle (because $U < 0.3333$).

These arrival and departure times and the status of the system are summarized in Table 15.6, which describes the initial conditions, at time $T = 0$.

1. *Event*: This column indicates which event (a new arriving vehicle or a departing vehicle) has resulted in a change in the status of the system at this time. In general, this column will contain "Arr." for an arrival or "Dep." for a departure. At the current time, $T = 0$, a "—" is used to indicate the initial conditions.

TABLE 15.6   *Status of the System at Time $T = 0$*

		STATUS[a]/UNTIL TIME . . .			NUMBER IN LINE			NEXT ARRIVAL	
TIME	EVENT[b]	EXP.	GEN. 1	GEN. 2	EXP.	GEN. 1	GEN. 2	TIME	TYPE
0.00	—	I—	B 9.49	B 4.02	0	2	3	0.49	E

[a]Status of the booth is I for idle or B for busy.
[b]Arr./Dep. means that the event at the current time is an arrival/departure.

2. *Status/Until Time*: These columns provide the status of the three booths:
   a. The express booth is idle, indicated by the letter I.
   b. The first general booth is busy, indicated by the letter B, and the vehicle currently being served finishes at time 9.49, the value generated before.
   c. The second general booth is busy (B), and the vehicle being served finishes at time 4.02.
3. *Number in Line*: These columns provide the number of vehicles waiting in line at each booth. There are 0 vehicles in line at the express booth, and 2 and 3 vehicles in line at the two general booths.
4. *Next Arrival*: These columns provide the time at which the next vehicle arrives and whether that vehicle qualifies for the express booth or not. As generated before, the next vehicle arrives at time 0.49 and is an express vehicle, indicated by the letter E.

MOVING THE CLOCK TIME T

On the basis of the information in Table 15.6, you can see that the status of the system remains the same until the new express vehicle arrives at time $T = 0.49$. This arrival occurs before either of the two vehicles currently being served at the general booths is finished.

BOOKKEEPING AT TIME $T = 0.49$

When this express vehicle arrives at time $T = 0.49$, you need to perform the following two steps:

1. Change the status of the system as follows:
   a. Decide which line the arriving vehicle chooses to enter—in this case, the express booth line.
   b. Determine if the arriving vehicle can begin service at the chosen booth. In this case, the vehicle can begin service because the express booth is idle. Thus, the server at the express booth becomes busy. To determine for how long, generate a random number for this service time. Using the next 0–1 random number of $U = 0.995255$, from row 2 and column 1 of the table, results in:

$$t_s = -(1/10) * 60 * 1n(1 - U)$$
$$= -6 * 1n(1 - 0.995255)$$
$$= -6 * (-5.3517)$$
$$= 32.11 \text{ seconds}$$

In other words, this vehicle finishes its service 32.11 seconds from now, at time $T = 0.49 + 32.11 = 32.60$.

2. Determine the time of the next arriving vehicle. Again generate a random interarrival time using the next 0–1 random number, $U = 0.577849$, from row 2 and column 2, as follows:

$$t_a = -(1/20) * 60 * 1n(1 - U)$$
$$= -3 * 1n(1 - 0.577849)$$
$$= -3 * (-0.8633)$$
$$= 2.59 \text{ seconds}$$

The next vehicle arrives 2.59 seconds from now, at time $T = 0.49 + 2.59 = 3.08$.
   To determine the type of this arriving vehicle, use the next 0–1 random number, $U = 0.980588$, from row 2 and column 3, to conclude that this is a general vehicle (because $U > 0.3333$).

TABLE 15.7 *Status of the System Up to Time T = 0.49*

TIME	EVENT	STATUS/UNTIL TIME … EXP.	GEN. 1	GEN. 2	NUMBER IN LINE EXP.	GEN. 1	GEN. 2	NEXT ARRIVAL TIME	TYPE
0.00	—	I—	B 9.49	B 4.02	0	2	3	0.49	E
0.49	Arr.	B 32.60	B 9.49	B 4.02	0	2	3	3.08	G

These changes are summarized in Table 15.7, in the row corresponding to time $T = 0.49$, at which time a new vehicle arrives.

MOVING THE CLOCK TIME T

On the basis of the information in the second row of Table 15.7, you can see that the status of the system remains the same until the new general vehicle arrives at time $T = 3.08$. This arrival occurs before any of the vehicles currently being served is finished.

BOOKKEEPING AT TIME $T = 3.08$

When this general vehicle arrives at time $T = 3.08$, you need to perform the following two steps:

1. Change the status of the system as follows:
   a. Decide which line the arriving vehicle chooses to enter. In this case, the vehicle enters the line for the first general booth because there are only two cars waiting there, compared to three waiting at the second general booth.
   b. Determine if the arriving vehicle can begin service at the chosen booth. In this case, the vehicle cannot begin service because the chosen booth is busy. This vehicle increases the line length from 2 to 3.

2. Determine the time of the next arriving vehicle. Again generate a random inter-arrival time using the next 0–1 random number, $U = 0.894206$, from row 2 and column 4, as follows:

$$t_a = -(1/20) * 60 * 1n(1 - U)$$

$$= -3 * 1n(1 - 0.894206)$$

$$= -3 * (-2.2467)$$

$$= 6.74 \text{ seconds}$$

The next vehicle arrives 6.74 seconds from now, at time $T = 3.08 + 6.74 = 9.82$.
To determine the type of this arriving vehicle, use the next 0–1 random number, $U = 0.332668$, from row 2 and column 5, to conclude that this is an express vehicle.

These changes are summarized in Table 15.8 in the row corresponding to time $T = 3.08$, at which time a new vehicle arrives.

MOVING THE CLOCK TIME T

From Table 15.8, you can see that the status of the system remains the same until the vehicle in the second general booth is finished service at time $T = 4.02$. This event occurs before either the vehicle being served at the express booth or the vehicle being served at the first general booth is finished and before the next arrival of a vehicle, scheduled at time 9.82.

TABLE 15.8 *Status of the System Up to Time T = 3.08*

		STATUS/UNTIL TIME ...			NUMBER IN LINE			NEXT ARRIVAL	
TIME	EVENT	Exp.	GEN. 1	GEN. 2	EXP.	GEN. 1	GEN. 2	TIME	TYPE
0.00	—	I—	B 9.49	B 4.02	0	2	3	0.49	E
0.49	Arr.	B 32.60	B 9.49	B 4.02	0	2	3	3.08	G
3.08	Arr.	B 32.60	B 9.49	B 4.02	0	3	3	9.82	E

BOOKKEEPING AT TIME $T = 4.02$

When this vehicle finishes service at the second general booth at time $T = 4.02$, the following changes take place:

1. The vehicle leaves the second general booth and the entire system.
2. Because the line at this booth is not empty, the first vehicle in the line enters this booth for service.
   a. The length of this line decreases from 3 to 2.
   b. The server at this booth remains busy.
   c. To determine for how long the server will be busy with this vehicle requires generating a random service time. Use the next random number, $U = 0.355729$, from row 3 and column 1, and compute

$$t_s = 3 + 5 * \frac{U}{0.6}$$
$$= 3 + 5 * \frac{0.355729}{0.6}$$
$$= 5.97 \text{ seconds}$$

This vehicle finishes service 5.97 seconds from now, at time $T = 5.97 + 4.02 = 9.99$ seconds.

These changes are summarized in Table 15.9 in the row corresponding to time $T = 4.02$, when a vehicle finishes its service at the second general booth.

From these sample events, you can see that the status of the system changes only when one of two events occurs: (a) a new vehicle arrives or (b) a vehicle completes its service at a booth. Depending on which event occurs first, the clock is moved to that point in time and the following associated bookkeeping operations are performed.

BOOKKEEPING WHEN A NEW VEHICLE ARRIVES

1. Change the status of the system, as follows:
   a. Decide which line the arriving vehicle chooses to enter.

TABLE 15.9 *Status of the System Up to Time T = 4.02*

		STATUS/UNTIL TIME ...			NUMBER IN LINE			NEXT ARRIVAL	
TIME	EVENT	Exp.	GEN. 1	GEN. 2	EXP.	GEN. 1	GEN. 2	TIME	TYPE
0.00	—	I—	B 9.49	B 4.02	0	2	3	0.49	E
0.49	Arr.	B 32.60	B 9.49	B 4.02	0	2	3	3.08	G
3.08	Arr.	B 32.60	B 9.49	B 4.02	0	3	3	9.82	E
4.02	Dep.	B 32.60	B 9.49	B 9.99	0	3	2	9.82	E

    b. Determine if the arriving vehicle can begin service at the chosen booth.

      i. If the chosen booth is idle, then the vehicle immediately enters for service. In this case, a random service time from the appropriate distribution is generated to determine when the vehicle finishes service.

      ii. If the chosen booth is currently busy, then the vehicle enters the waiting line. The number of vehicles in that line is increased by 1.

2. Determine when the *next* vehicle arrives by generating a random interarrival time from the exponential distribution. Also, determine whether that vehicle qualifies for the express booth by generating a 0–1 random number.

3. Add this information as the next row in the table.

BOOKKEEPING WHEN A VEHICLE FINISHES SERVICE

1. The vehicle leaves the booth and the entire system.

2. If the line at that booth is not empty, the next car moves up for service, and:

    a. The length of that line is reduced by 1.

    b. The server at that booth remains busy.

    c. A random number is generated from the appropriate distribution to determine how long that car will require service and at what time it will be finished.

3. If the line at that booth is empty, the server becomes idle.

4. This information is added as the next row in the table.

These steps are repeated over and over again until the clock time exceeds the duration established at the start of the problem, which in this case is 2 hours. These data up to time $T = 60$ seconds are provided in Table 15.10.

15.3.5 *Obtaining the Final Statistics*

Recall from Section 15.3.1 that the sought-after objectives—that is, the outputs—of this simulation are the following:

1. The expected waiting time for a vehicle at each booth.

2. The average number of vehicles in each line.

3. The average utilization of each booth—that is, the fraction of time the booth is serving a vehicle.

The last step is to use the information in the final table to obtain these statistics. Although the table you use will contain data spanning the full 2 hours of the simulation, for illustration purposes, the appropriate computations are now performed with the data in Table 15.10, which go to time $T = 60$ seconds.

COMPUTING THE EXPECTED WAITING TIME AT EACH BOOTH

Consider the flow of vehicles at the first general booth. The average waiting time at this booth is computed using the following formula:

$$\text{Average waiting time} = \frac{\left\{\begin{array}{l}\text{total waiting time of all vehicles in}\\ \text{that line}\end{array}\right\}}{\left\{\begin{array}{l}\text{total number of vehicles served by}\\ \text{that booth}\end{array}\right\}}$$

These two quantities can be obtained from the data in Table 15.10. From the table, up to time $T = 60$, you can count that seven vehicles have been served in the first general booth (the first one finishing at time 9.49, the second one at 24.35, and so on).

TABLE 15.10 *Status of the System Up to Time T = 60*

TIME	EVENT	STATUS/UNTIL TIME ...			NUMBER IN LINE			NEXT ARRIVAL	
		Exp.	Gen. 1	Gen. 2	EXP.	GEN. 1	GEN. 2	TIME	TYPE
0.00	—	I —	B 9.49	B 4.02	0	2	3	0.49	E
0.49	Arr.	B 32.60	B 9.49	B 4.02	0	2	3	3.08	G
3.08	Arr.	B 32.60	B 9.49	B 4.02	0	3	3	9.82	E
4.02	Dep.	B 32.60	B 9.49	B 9.99	0	3	2	9.82	E
9.49	Dep.	B 32.60	B 24.35	B 9.99	0	2	2	9.82	E
9.82	Arr.	B 32.60	B 24.35	B 9.99	1	2	2	12.03	G
9.99	Dep.	B 32.60	B 24.35	B 17.36	1	2	1	12.03	G
12.03	Arr.	B 32.60	B 24.35	B 17.36	1	2	2	14.36	G
14.36	Arr.	B 32.60	B 24.35	B 17.36	1	3	2	15.38	G
15.38	Arr.	B 32.60	B 24.35	B 17.36	1	3	3	17.68	G
17.36	Dep.	B 32.60	B 24.35	B 29.85	1	3	2	17.68	G
17.68	Arr.	B 32.60	B 24.35	B 29.85	1	3	3	19.94	G
19.94	Arr.	B 32.60	B 24.35	B 29.85	1	4	3	30.09	G
24.35	Dep.	B 32.60	B 31.99	B 29.85	1	3	3	30.09	G
29.85	Dep.	B 32.60	B 31.99	B 33.09	1	3	2	30.09	G
30.09	Arr.	B 32.60	B 31.99	B 33.09	1	3	3	30.33	G
30.33	Arr.	B 32.60	B 31.99	B 33.09	1	4	3	31.60	G
31.60	Arr.	B 32.60	B 31.99	B 33.09	1	4	4	37.20	G
31.99	Dep.	B 32.60	B 39.90	B 33.09	1	3	4	37.20	G
32.60	Dep.	B 33.62	B 39.90	B 33.09	0	3	4	37.20	G
33.09	Dep.	B 33.62	B 39.90	B 36.34	0	3	3	37.20	G
33.62	Dep.	I —	B 39.90	B 36.34	0	3	3	37.20	G
36.34	Dep.	I —	B 39.90	B 48.73	0	3	2	37.20	G
37.20	Arr.	I —	B 39.90	B 48.73	0	3	3	39.98	G
39.90	Dep.	I —	B 44.67	B 48.73	0	2	3	39.98	G
39.98	Arr.	I —	B 44.67	B 48.73	0	3	3	43.07	G
43.07	Arr.	I —	B 44.67	B 48.73	0	4	3	50.59	G
44.67	Dep.	I —	B 53.56	B 48.73	0	3	3	50.59	G
48.73	Dep.	I —	B 53.56	B 55.13	0	3	2	50.59	G
50.59	Arr.	I —	B 53.56	B 55.13	0	3	3	56.99	G
53.56	Dep.	I —	B 61.31	B 55.13	0	2	3	56.99	G
55.13	Dep.	I —	B 61.31	B 72.01	0	2	2	56.99	G
56.99	Arr.	I —	B 61.31	B 72.01	0	3	2	59.00	E
59.00	Arr.	B 60.81	B 61.31	B 72.01	0	3	2	63.76	G

To obtain the value in the numerator requires knowing how the length of the line in front of the first general booth varied over time. That information is also available in Table 15.10 and has been transferred to Figure 15.4. From time $T = 0$ to $T = 3.08$, there are two vehicles in the line at the first general booth. Their combined waiting time up to that point is

$$\text{Waiting time from } T = 0 \text{ to } T = 3.08 = 2 * 3.08$$

$$= 6.16 \text{ seconds}$$

Then, from time $T = 3.08$ to $T = 9.49$ there are three vehicles in line:

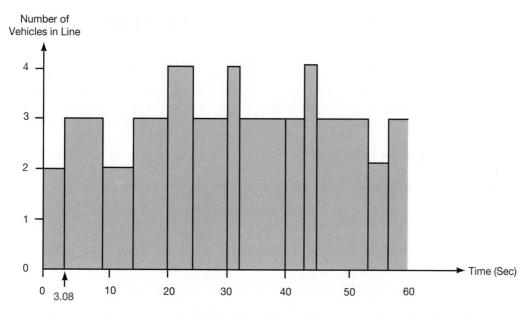

FIGURE 15.4 Number in Line at General Booth 1 Over Time.

$$\text{Waiting time from } T = 3.08 \text{ to } T = 9.49 = 3 * (9.49 - 3.08)$$

$$= 19.23 \text{ seconds}$$

Performing this computation for each time interval in Figure 15.4 and adding these waiting times together provide the total waiting time of

$$\text{Total waiting time } = 176.22 \text{ seconds}$$

and so the average waiting time is

$$\text{Average waiting time} = \frac{\text{total waiting time}}{\text{number of vehicles served}}$$

$$= \frac{176.22}{7}$$

$$= 25.17 \text{ seconds}$$

On average, a vehicle at the first general booth can expect to wait about 29 seconds before entering the toll booth.

Performing similar computations for the other two booths results in the following expected waiting times:

BOOTH	EXPECTED WAITING TIME (SECONDS)
Express	7.59
General 1	25.17
General 2	19.99

COMPUTING THE AVERAGE NUMBER OF VEHICLES AT EACH BOOTH

Once again, consider the first general booth. As shown in Figure 15.4, during a total of 60 seconds the number of vehicles in the line varies from 2 up to a maximum of 4. The length of the line is 2 for a total of 11.4684 seconds, which is $11.4684/60 = 0.1911$ fraction of the time. The length of the line is 3 for a total of 40.8563 seconds, which is $40.8563/60 = 0.6809$ fraction of the time. These various fractions are summarized as follows:

NUMBER IN LINE	TOTAL TIME	FRACTION OF TIME (TOTAL TIME/60.0)
0	0.0000	0.0000
1	0.0000	0.0000
2	11.4684	0.1911
3	40.8563	0.6809
4	7.6753	0.1279

With these values, the average length of the line is

$$
\begin{aligned}
\text{Average length} = {} & 0 * (\text{fraction of time the length is } 0) + \\
& 1 * (\text{fraction of time the length is } 1) + \\
& 2 * (\text{fraction of time the length is } 2) + \\
& 3 * (\text{fraction of time the length is } 3) + \\
& 4 * (\text{fraction of time the length is } 4) \\
= {} & (0 * 0.0000) + (1 * 0.0000) + (2 * 0.1911) + \\
& (3 * 0.6809) + (4 * 0.1279) \\
= {} & 2.9365
\end{aligned}
$$

At the first general booth, the average number of vehicles waiting in the line during the 60 seconds is about 3.

Performing a similar computation for each of the lines at the other two booths results in the following information for the time period covered by the data in Table 15.10:

BOOTH	AVERAGE NUMBER OF VEHICLES
Express	0.3796
General 1	2.9365
General 2	2.6656

COMPUTING THE AVERAGE UTILIZATION OF EACH BOOTH

Consider the express booth. The utilization of this booth is the fraction of time that the booth is busy. Thus:

$$
\text{Utilization} = \frac{\text{amount of time the booth is busy}}{\text{total time}}
$$

The value for the numerator is obtained from the data in Table 15.10 by identifying the time intervals during which that booth is busy, as shown in Figure 15.5. As you can see, from time $T = 0$ up to $T = 0.49$, the booth is idle. From time $T = 0.49$ to $T = 33.62$, the booth is busy for a total of $33.62 - 0.49 = 33.13$ seconds. The only other time the express booth is busy is from time $T = 59$ to $T = 60$ for a period of 1 second. Adding these two amounts of busy time results in

$$\text{Amount of time the express booth is busy} = 34.13 \text{ seconds}$$

Thus, the utilization for this booth is

$$\text{Utilization} = \frac{\text{amount of time the booth is busy}}{\text{total time}}$$

$$= \frac{34.13}{60}$$

$$= 0.5688$$

In other words, the express booth is busy about 57% of the time.

Performing a similar computation for the other two booths results in the following utilizations:

BOOTH	UTILIZATION
Express	0.5688
General 1	1.0000
General 2	1.0000

ADDITIONAL CONSIDERATIONS

It is important to realize that the specific statistics obtained in Section 15.3.5 are based on the given initial conditions, in which the express booth is idle and the two general booths are both busy and have vehicles waiting in line. Also, the data generated are during a rush hour for 1 day.

When the computation of the statistics is based on the relatively short period of 60 seconds, the initial conditions can have a significant effect on the final values. However, if the simulation is performed over a "long" period of time—say, over a 2-hour period—the effects of the initial conditions are relatively insignificant.

Another way to become more certain of the values of the estimates of the performance measures is to repeat the earlier simulation and computations for many different

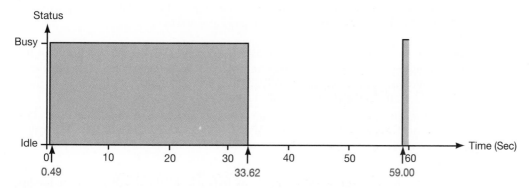

FIGURE 15.5 Status of the Express Booth Over Time.

days and then take the average of each statistic. In Section 15.5, you will learn more about how many days you need to repeat the simulation to become reasonably confident of the performance measures.

Once the final statistics are obtained, the Manager can evaluate the merits of having an express booth at a toll plaza. By examining the average waiting times, the Manager can decide if the three booths provide an acceptable level of service. If not, construction of another booth might be considered. Moreover, the Manager can try to determine if reduced waiting time at the express booth is sufficient incentive to encourage car pooling.

From the average queue lengths, the Manager can determine if the waiting vehicles will back up too much and cause a traffic hazard. If so, the Commission might again want to consider opening another booth.

The average utilizations at the booths provide the Manager with a measure of the work load at each booth. For example, based on the data collected for a period of 60 seconds, the express lane is busy less than 60% of the time, but both general booths are busy all the time. This information may be used to schedule the workers at these booths. For example, workers might rotate between the general and express booths to balance their work loads.

■ 15.4 Simulation Software

In Chapter 14 and Sections 15.1 through 15.3, you have learned the basic methodology and seen how to design and perform a simulation. Because the bookkeeping scheme involves significant and repetitive computations that are impractical to perform manually for large problems, a computer is a practical alternative.

> ### KEY FEATURES
>
> It is possible to write your own specialized program in an appropriate language, such as C or Pascal, but you would need detailed knowledge of the specific programming language and significant amounts of time to develop, debug, and test the program. Although the resulting program can be computationally efficient, the development time and effort may not be justified unless the model is used repeatedly over a long period of time to make on-going operational decisions. Alternatively, if the simulation is used as a one-time strategic planning tool, it may be worthwhile developing the model with one of the various available simulation software packages. Using a software package eliminates the development time, but the computational time it takes to perform the simulation may be significantly greater than the time a custom-built program would need.
>
> Simulation software packages provide the common *building blocks* that you must put together in the proper sequence to construct a model of your particular system. These packages fall into two basic categories:
>
> ✔ *Specialized* software packages, which are designed to simulate a problem belonging to a special class. For example, @RISK is used to simulate problems involving risk analysis; SIMFACTORY® is used to simulate the operations of a manufacturing process; and so on.
> ✔ *General-purpose* software packages, which are flexible enough to simulate almost any system. GPSS, SIMAN, SLAM®, and SIMSCRIPT are examples.

Although it is beyond the scope of this book to teach the details of a specific language, in this section you will get a brief introduction on using one software package from each category to develop a simulation model. The objective is to give you an appreciation of how software packages can help you develop a simulation.

15.4.1 An Example of Simulating with the Software Package @RISK

In this section, you will see how the software package @RISK is used to simulate the variable-vs-fixed-rate mortgage problem introduced in Section 15.1. Recall that the objective of that problem is to determine whether a 15-year fixed-rate mortgage at 8% is better than a 15-year variable-rate mortgage. The variable-rate mortgage has an initial rate of 7% and is adjusted every 3 years by the amount of change in the prime rate at that time. The maximum rate is 10%. The merits of the two mortgages are compared using the net present value of the differences in the 15 annual payments made at the *end* of each year using a discount rate equal to the average of the five variable interest rates. The future prime rates are unknown, of course, but recall that you obtained the following probabilities of change in this rate in any period of 3 years:

AMOUNT OF CHANGE	PROBABILITY
+2.0	0.05
+1.5	0.05
+1.0	0.15
+0.5	0.15
+0.0	0.20
−0.5	0.15
−1.0	0.15
−1.5	0.05
−2.0	0.05

The package @RISK works with LOTUS. The LOTUS spreadsheet for this problem is shown in Figures 15.6 and 15.7. These spreadsheets contain the results of computing the net present value of the differences between the variable- and fixed-rate payments in which the changes in the prime rate in Years 4, 7, 10, and 13 are, respectively, −0.5%, −1.0%, 1%, and 1.5%. As you can see at the top of Figure 15.6, these compu-tations are based on the following:

@RISK Spreadsheet
MTGAGE_2.Wk1

1. A principal amount of $1000.
2. A fixed rate of 8%, resulting in 15 annual payments of $116.83 each. (This value is obtained using the built-in LOTUS function @PMT with an interest rate of 8%, a principal of $1000, and a length of 15 years.)
3. An initial variable rate of 7%.

To perform this simulation, it is first necessary to determine the remaining vari-able interest rates. This information is given in the next portion of the spreadsheet in Figure 15.6. For example, the change in Years 4–6 is −0.005, corresponding to −0.5%. Adding this change to the initial rate of 0.07 results in the applicable interest rate of 0.065. The row labeled "Payment" indicates the annual payment that would be made on a principal of $1000 at the associated interest rate for the remaining number of years. For example, for Years 1–3, at the interest rate of 0.07, the 15 annual payments on a principal of $1000 are $109.79. For Years 4–6, at the interest rate of 0.065, the remaining 12 annual payments on a principal of $1000 are $122.57. These payments are obtained from the function @PMT and are used in the subsequent computations.

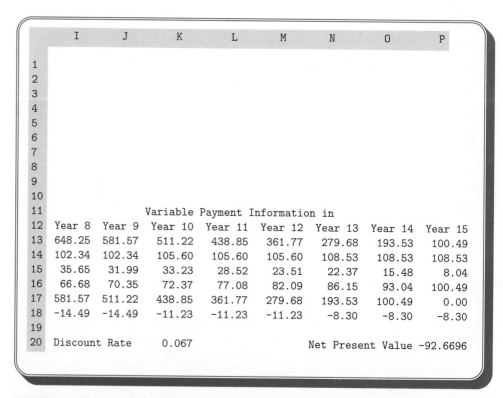

	A	B	C	D	E	F	G	H
1			The Variable-Versus-Fixed-Rate Mortgage Problem					
2								
3	Principal	1000	Fixed Int. Rate		0.08	Fixed Payment		116.83
4			Var. Int. Rate		0.07			
5								
6		Yr. 1-3	Yr. 4-6	Yr. 7-9	Yr.10-12	Yr.13-15		
7	Change	0.000	-0.005	-0.010	0.010	0.015		
8	Interest	0.07	0.065	0.055	0.065	0.08		
9	Payment	109.79	122.57	143.84	206.57	388.03		
10								
11				Variable Payment Information in				
12		Year 1	Year 2	Year 3	Year 4	Year 5	Year 6	Year 7
13	Beg. Bal.	1000.00	960.21	917.63	872.06	821.86	768.39	711.45
14	Var. Pay.	109.79	109.79	109.79	106.89	106.89	106.89	102.34
15	Interest	70.00	67.21	64.23	56.68	53.42	49.95	39.13
16	Principal	39.79	42.58	45.56	50.20	53.47	56.94	63.21
17	Rem. Bal.	960.21	917.63	872.06	821.86	768.39	711.45	648.25
18	Difference	-7.03	-7.03	-7.03	-9.94	-9.94	-9.94	-14.49

FIGURE 15.6 @RISK Computations for the Payments in Years 1–7 for the Variable- vs. Fixed-Rate Mortgage Problem.

	I	J	K	L	M	N	O	P
1								
2								
3								
4								
5								
6								
7								
8								
9								
10								
11			Variable Payment Information in					
12	Year 8	Year 9	Year 10	Year 11	Year 12	Year 13	Year 14	Year 15
13	648.25	581.57	511.22	438.85	361.77	279.68	193.53	100.49
14	102.34	102.34	105.60	105.60	105.60	108.53	108.53	108.53
15	35.65	31.99	33.23	28.52	23.51	22.37	15.48	8.04
16	66.68	70.35	72.37	77.08	82.09	86.15	93.04	100.49
17	581.57	511.22	438.85	361.77	279.68	193.53	100.49	0.00
18	-14.49	-14.49	-11.23	-11.23	-11.23	-8.30	-8.30	-8.30
19								
20	Discount Rate		0.067			Net Present Value		-92.6696

FIGURE 15.7 @RISK Computations for the Payments in Years 8–15 for the Variable- vs. Fixed-Rate Mortgage Problem.

The remaining information in Figure 15.6 is the computation of the payments for the variable-rate mortgage in each of Years 1–7, including the annual payment, the amount of interest and principal, and the remaining balance of the $1000 original principal. For example, in Year 1, the beginning balance ("Beg. Bal.") is the original $1000. The variable payment ("Var. Pay.") at the end of that year is $109.79, as shown in the row labeled "Payment" and column labeled "Yr. 1–3" in Figure 15.6. Of this amount, $70.00 is interest ("Interest") calculated by multiplying the $1000 principal by the applicable rate of 0.07, and the difference of $39.79 ("Principal") is payment toward the $1000 principal, which results in a remaining balance ("Rem. Bal.") of $960.21.

Similarly, for Year 4, the beginning balance ("Beg. Bal.") is $872.06, which is the remaining balance at the end of Year 3. The applicable rate for Years 4–6 is 0.065 and so the three annual payments for each of those years is

$$\text{Annual payment} = \left\{ \begin{array}{l} \text{annual payment based} \\ \text{on \$1000 of principal} \\ \text{with an interest rate of} \\ \text{0.065 and 12 remaining} \\ \text{years} \end{array} \right\} * \left\{ \begin{array}{c} \text{Principal at the be-} \\ \text{ginning of Year 4} \\ \hline 1000 \end{array} \right\}$$

$$= 122.57 * \left(\frac{872.06}{1000} \right)$$

$$= \$106.89$$

The annual payment ("Var. Pay.") at the end of Year 4 is $106.89, of which $56.68 is interest ("Interest") calculated by multiplying the $872.06 principal by the applicable rate of 0.065. The difference of $50.20 ("Principal") is payment toward the $872.06 principal. The remaining balance ("Rem. Bal.") is $821.86.

These computations are performed sequentially for each of the 15 years, and the results are given in Figures 15.6 and 15.7. The final line in each spreadsheet is the difference between the variable-rate payment and the fixed-rate payment of $116.83. By using these differences and the discount rate of 0.067, which is the average of the five applicable variable interest rates of 0.07, 0.065, 0.055, 0.065, and 0.08, the built-in LOTUS function @NPV provides the net present value of −92.66, as shown in Figure 15.7. Observe that these values are the same as the ones obtained from the single simulation performed in Section 15.1.

The spreadsheets in Figures 15.6 and 15.7 are based on *one set of specific changes* in the applicable variable rate. This simulation needs to be performed many times, each time with changes in the rate randomly generated according to the given distribution. The package @RISK allows you to do precisely this by specifying those cells in the spreadsheet whose values are to be generated randomly. This is accomplished by associating the desired distribution with each such cell. (The details of doing so are beyond the scope of this book.)

Repeating the simulation 100 times using @RISK results in the output in Figures 15.8 and 15.9. The output in Figure 15.8 is a histogram showing the percentage of the 100 simulation runs that resulted in a net present value in a given range. The most important observation from this figure is that about 5% (corresponding to the rightmost vertical bar) of the 100 simulation runs resulted in a positive net present value. This means that there is about a 5% chance that the fixed-rate mortgage will be better. In the upper-right corner, you can also see that the average net present value for these 100 simulation runs is −67.97734. This means that on average the variable-rate mortgage is better.

The output in Figure 15.9 provides detailed statistics for the 100 simulation runs. The first line of that report confirms the mean net present value of −67.97734. You can also verify that only 5% of these runs resulted in a positive net present value, as shown in line 5 of the report (labeled "Probability of Positive Result"). The second portion of

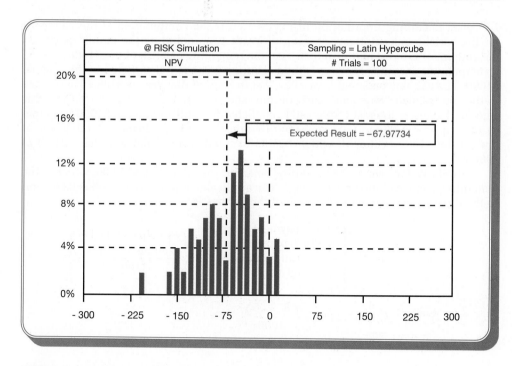

FIGURE 15.8 Output from 100 Simulations with @RISK for the Variable- vs. Fixed-Rate
Mortgage Problem.

the report (labeled "Percentile Probabilities") provides the cumulative frequencies. For
example, from line 6 of that portion, you can see that 25% of the 100 simulation runs
resulted in a net present value less than −101.9098. This means that there is about a
25% chance that on a loan of $1000, the net present value of the variable-rate mortgage
will be better than the fixed-rate mortgage by about 102.

15.4.2 An Example of Simulating with the Software Package SIMAN

In this section, you will see how the general-purpose software package SIMAN is used
to simulate the queueing problem of the New Jersey Turnpike Commission presented
in Section 15.2. Recall that the objective is to study the impact of converting one of
three booths at a toll plaza to an express booth exclusively for cars having two or more
passengers. The outputs consist of the following statistics for each booth:

1. The expected waiting time for a vehicle.
2. The average number of vehicles in each line.
3. The average utilization—that is, the fraction of time the booth is serving a vehicle.

The inputs are based on the following data applicable to the arrival and service of
vehicles at the plaza:

1. The interarrival time of the vehicles follows an exponential distribution with a
   mean arrival rate of 20 per minute, and 1/3 of those vehicles are cars with at least
   two passengers.
2. The amount of time needed for service at each of the two general booths is given
   by the following distribution based on historical data:

```
        NPV (in Cell P20)
        @RISK Risk Analysis    24-Dec-1992
        ================================
        Expected/Mean Result = -67.97734
        Maximum Result = 17.54548
        Minimum Result = -212.0394
        Range of Possible Results = 229.5849
        Probability of Positive Result = 5.0000001%
        Probability of Negative Result = 95%
        Standard Deviation = 48.62752
        Skewness = -.514432
        Kurtosis = 3.013305
        Variance = 2364.635
        ERRs Calculated = 0
        Values Filtered = 0
        Simulations Executed = 1
        Iterations = 100
        Percentile Probabilities:
        (Chance of Result <= Shown Value)
        (Actual Values)
        ================================
                              <=-212.0394= 0%
                              <=-153.827= 5%
                              <=-134.3389= 10%
                              <=-121.5886= 15%
                              <=-111.6461= 20%
                              <=-101.9098= 25%
                              <=-94.6683= 30%
                              <=-90.0167= 35%
                              <=-78.4055= 40%
                              <=-70.5165= 45%
                              <=-59.083 = 50%
                              <=-55.0015= 55%
                              <=-48.4792= 60%
                              <=-42.9457= 65%
                              <=-40.747 = 70%
                              <=-33.5565= 75%
                              <=-25.0567= 80%
                              <=-17.2515= 85%
                              <=-7.99   = 90%
                              <=-1.4548 = 95%
                              <= 17.5455= 100%
```

FIGURE 15.9 Statistical Report from 100 Simulations with @RISK for the Variable- vs. Fixed-Rate Mortgage Problem.

TIME (SECONDS)	PROBABILITY
3–8	0.6
8–13	0.3
13–18	0.1

3. The service time at the express booth is assumed to follow an exponential distribution with a mean rate of 10 cars per minute—that is, a mean service time of 6 seconds per car.

4. The simulation is started with no vehicles in the system. These initial conditions should have little impact as the length of the simulation run of 2 hours is sufficiently long.

A program written in SIMAN requires two separate portions:

1. The *experimental framework*, in which the input and output data are described.
2. The *model*, which describes the logical sequence of events in the system.

These portions for the problem of the New Jersey Turnpike Commission are shown in Figures 15.10 and 15.11. To understand these two portions, recall that vehicles flow through this system. In general, the objects that flow through the system in a simulation are referred to as *transactions*. In this problem, the transactions (vehicles) flow through the system by arriving at the toll plaza, selecting an appropriate queue to wait in, receiving service at that booth, and exiting the system. In this context, the express booth, whose symbol is EXPB, is referred to as resource number 1; the two general booths, whose symbols are GENB1 and GENB2, are referred to as resource numbers 2 and 3. Each booth has a queue. The queue at the express booth is numbered 1 and the others are numbered 2 and 3. With these notations, the two portions of the SIMAN program for this problem are described in more detail in what follows.

```
BEGIN;                                                           <1>
PROJECT,TOLL BOOTH SIMULATION,MARK FLEISCHER, 10/01/94;          <2>
DISCRETE,200,3;                                                  <3>
RESOURCES: 1, EXPB:
           2, GENB1:
           3, GENB2;                                             <4>
PARAMETERS: 1,3:
            2,6:
            3,0,3,.6,8,.9,13,1.0,18;                             <5>
DSTAT: 1, NQ(1), EXP Q:
       2, NQ(2), GEN1 Q:
       3, NQ(3), GEN2 Q:
       4, NR(1), EXP BOOTH:
       5, NR(2), GBOOTH 1:
       6, NR(3), GBOOTH 2;                                       <6>
TALLIES: 1, WAIT IN EXP Q:
         2, WAIT IN GEN1 Q:
         3, WAIT IN GEN2 Q;                                      <7>
REPLICATE,1,0,7200;                                              <8>
END;                                                             <9>
```

FIGURE 15.10 Experimental Framework for the SIMAN Program for the Problem of the New Jersey Turnpike Commission.

```
BEGIN;                                                           < 1>
;                                          Section 1: Arrival
        CREATE:EX(1,1):MARK(1);                                  < 2>
        BRANCH,1: WITH,0.33,EXPRESS:
              ELSE,GENERAL;                                      < 3>
;                         Section 2: Choose Q for Express Vehicles
EXPRESS FINDJ,1,3:MIN(NQ(J)+NR(J));                              < 4>
        BRANCH,1:
              IF,J.EQ.1,EXP:
              IF,J.EQ.2,GEN1:
              ELSE,GEN2;                                         < 5>
;                         Section 3: Choose Q for General Vehicles
GENERAL FINDJ,2,3:MIN(NQ(J)+NR(J));                              < 6>
        BRANCH,1:
              IF,J.EQ.2,GEN1:
              ELSE,GEN2;                                         < 7>
;                               Section 4: Logic for Express Q
EXP     QUEUE,1;                                                 < 8>
        SEIZE:EXPB;                                              < 9>
        TALLY:1,INT(1);                                          <10>
        DELAY:EX(2,2);                                           <11>
        RELEASE:EXPB:DISPOSE;                                    <12>
;                               Section 5: Logic for General Q1
GEN1    QUEUE,2;                                                 <13>
        SEIZE:GENB1;                                             <14>
        TALLY:2,INT(1);                                          <15>
        DELAY:CP(3,3);                                           <16>
        RELEASE:GENB1:DISPOSE;                                   <17>
;                               Section 6: Logic for General Q2
GEN2    QUEUE,3;                                                 <18>
        SEIZE:GENB2;                                             <19>
        TALLY:3,INT(1);                                          <20>
        DELAY:CP(3,3);                                           <21>
        RELEASE:GENB2:DISPOSE;                                   <22>
;
END;                                                            <23>
```

FIGURE 15.11 Model for the SIMAN Program for the Problem of the New Jersey Turnpike Commission.

THE EXPERIMENTAL FRAMEWORK FOR THE PROBLEM OF THE NEW JERSEY TURNPIKE COMMISSION

The statements comprising the experimental framework of the SIMAN program used to describe the size of the system and its associated input parameters and the output values are shown in Figure 15.10. The statements numbered < 1 > and < 9 > indicate the beginning and end of the experimental framework. Each of the remaining statements, whose numbers are shown in angle brackets, are described briefly in what follows.

SIMAN Program
TPIKE.EXP

STATEMENT NUMBER	DESCRIPTION
< 2 >	Provides the title, author, and date of this program. This information appears at the top of all outputs produced by SIMAN.
< 3 >	Indicates that this is a DISCRETE event simulation that allows for at most 200 transactions (vehicles) simultaneously in the system, with at most three queues.
< 4 >	Indicates that there are three RESOURCES numbered 1, 2, and 3 and named EXPB, GENB1, and GENB2, corresponding to the three toll booths.
< 5 >	Provides numerical values for the deterministic and probabilistic data. In this case, the first line indicates an average arrival rate of one vehicle every 3 seconds; the second line indicates an average service time of 6 seconds at the express booth; and the third line is the cumulative distribution of the service time for the general booths, which, as shown in Figure 15.12, is 0 up to 3 seconds, increases linearly to 0.6 at 8 seconds, to 0.9 at 13 seconds, and to 1.0 at 18 seconds.
< 6 >	Identifies the standard output values to be reported in this simulation: the three queue-length statistics denoted by NQ(1), NQ(2), and NQ(3), and the statistics, including utilization, for the three resources (servers) denoted by NR(1), NR(2), and NR(3).
< 7 >	Indicates that in addition to the standard output values in < 6 >, three other output statistics are to be TALLIED, as described later in the model.
< 8 >	Indicates that this simulation is to be performed one time, starting at time 0 and ending after 7200 seconds (2 hours).

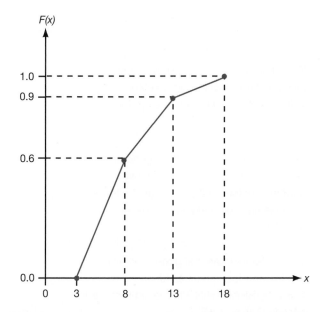

FIGURE 15.12 Cumulative Distribution Function for the Time
Required to Process a Vehicle at a General Booth.

THE MODEL FOR THE PROBLEM OF THE NEW JERSEY TURNPIKE COMMISSION

The statements that make up the model of the SIMAN program shown in Figure 15.11 are used to describe how the system works. Consider how a transaction (vehicle) flows through the system. The following events take place:

SIMAN Program
TPIKE.MOD

SECTION NUMBER	STATEMENT NUMBER	DESCRIPTION
1	< 2 >	A vehicle arrives (CREATE) with an exponential interarrival time whose average value is given by the first PARAMETER in the experimental framework (that is, 3 seconds). The arrival time of each vehicle is MARKed—that is, recorded for each such transaction.
	< 3 >	This vehicle is an EXPRESS vehicle with a 0.33 probability and a GENERAL one otherwise. BRANCH to the corresponding section of the model.
2	< 4 >	This statement for an arriving express vehicle determines which of the three queues has the fewest vehicles (including the vehicle being served).

SECTION NUMBER	STATEMENT NUMBER	DESCRIPTION
	< 5 >	This statement has that express vehicle join the shortest queue as identified in < 4 > by BRANCHING to the appropriate section of the model.
3	< 6 >	This statement for an arriving general vehicle determines which of the two queues, numbered 2 and 3, has the fewer vehicles (including the vehicle being served).
	< 7 >	This statement has that general vehicle join the shortest queue as identified in < 6 > by BRANCHING to the appropriate section of the model.
4	< 8 >	The vehicle entering the express line joins the QUEUE numbered 1.
	< 9 >	This vehicle waits in line until it can SEIZE (that is, obtain service from) the express booth EXPB.
	< 10 >	This statement TALLIES the waiting time in the queue numbered 1.
	< 11 >	This statement indicates that this vehicle requires a service time that is exponentially distributed with a mean given by the PARAMETER numbered 2 in the experimental framework (that is, 6 seconds).
	< 12 >	Having finished service, the vehicle RELEASES the express booth EXPB and is DISPOSED from the system.
5		This section corresponds to the queue numbered 2 at general booth 1 and is analogous to Section 4.
6		This section corresponds to the queue numbered 3 at general booth 2 and is analogous to Section 4.

OUTPUT OF THE SIMAN PROGRAM FOR THE PROBLEM OF THE NEW JERSEY TURNPIKE COMMISSION

On running the program in Figures 15.10 and 15.11, the output in Figure 15.13 is obtained. The first portion is the information provided in Statement < 2 > from the experimental framework in Figure 15.10.

The next portion of the output shows the statistics for the waiting times in the three queues, as requested in Statement < 7 > of the experimental framework and tabulated in Statements < 10 >, < 15 >, and < 20 > of the model. For example, the average waiting time for the 736 cars that joined the express queue is 7.7884 seconds with a standard deviation of 1.5673 seconds. The maximum amount of time a car had to wait in this line is 80.561 seconds. Similar statistics are provided for the other two general queues.

The final portion of the output in Figure 15.13 provides statistics on the lengths of the three queues and the utilization of the booths. For example, there is an average of 0.79615 car waiting in line at the express booth with a standard deviation of 1.7369. The minimum and maximum numbers of vehicles in this line are 0 and 9, respectively. At the end of the 2 hours of simulation, there is no car waiting in this line. Similar statistics are reported for the queues in front of the two general booths. The last three lines provide the statistics pertaining to the utilization of the three booths. For example, the average utilization of the express booth is 0.61686, with a standard deviation of 0.78811. This booth is busy about 62% of the time. Similar statistics are given for the utilization of the two general booths.

In this section, you have seen how specialized and general-purpose software packages are used to perform a simulation. As you might expect, such packages generally shorten the time required to develop a simulation model when compared to writing your own program in a standard computer language such as C or Pascal. Regardless of

```
                 Summary for Replication 1 of 1

  Project: TOLL BOOTH SIMULATION        Run execution date : 10/1/1994
  Analyst: MARK FLEISCHER               Model revision date: 10/1/1994
  Replication ended at time     : 7200.0

                         TALLY VARIABLES
  Identifier       Average  Variation  Minimum   Maximum   Observations
  --------------------------------------------------------------------
  WAIT IN EXP Q     7.7884   1.5673    .00000    80.561      736
  WAIT IN GEN1 Q    34.042   .81961    .00000    122.16      847
  WAIT IN GEN2 Q    29.943   .86853    .00000    116.42      849

                     DISCRETE-CHANGE VARIABLES
  Identifier       Average  Variation  Minimum   Maximum   Final Value
  --------------------------------------------------------------------
  EXP Q             .79615   1.7369    .00000    9.0000      .00000
  GEN1 Q            4.0047   .81246    .00000    14.000      .00000
  GEN2 Q            3.5308   .90444    .00000    13.000      .00000
  EXP BOOTH         .61686   .78811    .00000    1.0000      1.0000
  GBOOTH 1          .96795   .18197    .00000    1.0000      .00000
  GBOOTH 2          .94784   .23459    .00000    1.0000      1.0000
```

FIGURE 15.13 Output from the SIMAN Program for the Problem of the New Jersey Turnpike Commission.

which language you use, you need to determine how long each simulation run should be and how many runs to perform so as to be confident of the output statistics obtained. These issues are addressed in the next section.

■ 15.5 STATISTICAL ANALYSIS OF SIMULATION OUTPUT

From the examples in Sections 15.1 to 15.3, you have seen that simulation is a useful tool for studying complex problems that cannot be analyzed directly by mathematical techniques. By designing an associated simulation in which appropriate random numbers are generated, and by using other inputs, you can obtain an estimate of the desired output. It is important to realize, however, that a single simulation provides only *one* of many possible values for the output. This is because all random numbers used in performing the calculations, in fact, are based on the first one selected from the uniform random-number table or generator. Choosing a different initial uniform random number and performing *the same calculations* will result in a different value for the output.

Recall the variable- vs. fixed-rate mortgage problem in Section 15.1 in which you want to determine the expected net present value of the differences in the two mortgage payments. Although the "true" value of this output is not known, simulation helps you estimate this output. By using the initial uniform random number from row 16 and column 1 of the table in Appendix A, the first simulation run estimates this number to be −92.6696, as shown in the first row of Table 15.4. Based on this estimate, you would conclude that the variable-rate mortgage is better. However, if the initial uniform random number is chosen from row 22 and column 1, these same computations result in an estimate of +11.09258, as seen in row 7 of Table 15.4. In this case, you would conclude that the fixed-rate mortgage is better.

In other words, the result of a single simulation can lead to different estimates, and hence conclusions, depending on which initial uniform random number is chosen. Therefore, in general, you cannot have confidence in the output value obtained from a *single* simulation run. Rather, you need to repeat the simulation run many times— each time using a different initial uniform random number—thereby obtaining different output values. Then, by taking an average, you can obtain a more reliable estimate of the "true" mean of the output value.

To draw an analogy, the output value obtained from a single simulation run is the same as obtaining an estimate for an entire population based on one specific observation. For example, in manufacturing light bulbs, you are interested in estimating their average life, which is the number of hours until they burn out. To estimate this output value, you can randomly sample one single bulb and observe how long it lasts. However, suppose that bulb lasts only 15 hours. Would you believe that the average life of *all* bulbs in the production run is only 15 hours? Probably not. In other words, you cannot determine the average life for the entire (light-bulb) population based on a single observation. Rather, you would sample many bulbs and determine the average life of these bulbs. If the sample size is large enough, then you would have a reliable estimate of the average life of the bulbs in the entire production.

The objective of this section is to help you determine how many simulation runs are needed to achieve a desired level of confidence in the output value. After all, some important decisions may be influenced by the results of your simulation, so you ought to be confident that the numbers behind your decisions are accurate. The number of runs to perform depends on what types of output values are being estimated. In this section, such an analysis is conducted for the following two types of output values.

1. Estimating the *mean of an output value*. For example, for the variable- vs. fixed-rate mortgage problem in Section 15.1, the output is the net present value of the

differences in the 15 annual payments. The objective of the simulation study is to estimate the expected net present value.

2. Estimating a *proportion*. For example, suppose that the objective of the problem of the variable- vs. fixed-rate mortgage in Section 15.1 was to estimate the probability that the variable-rate mortgage is *significantly* better than the fixed-rate mortgage. If you believe that a difference in the net present value of the 15 annual payments of less than -50 is significant, then this probability is estimated by the proportion of simulation runs that result in the difference being less than -50.

In both cases, you want to determine how many times to run the simulation so that the results obtained are within a specified accuracy.

15.5.1 Determining the Sample Size for Estimating a Mean Value

To understand how many times to repeat a simulation run when the objective is to estimate the mean of an output value, it is best to begin by choosing a specific number of simulation runs and asking how accurate is the estimate of the resulting output value. To answer this question requires creating a confidence interval around the estimate (see the Student Resource Manual).

CREATING A CONFIDENCE INTERVAL FOR THE TRUE MEAN OF AN OUTPUT VALUE

Recall again the variable- vs. fixed-rate mortgage problem, in which the output value is the expected net present value—say, μ—of the differences between the variable- and fixed-rate annual payments over 15 years. In Section 15.1, the average of 35 simulation runs is used to obtain an estimate of $\bar{x} = -78.9361$ for μ. The question now is: How close is this estimated value to the true value of μ?

To answer this question, recall your knowledge of statistical estimation (see the Student Resource Manual). The objective is to determine a value for e and create an interval of the form

$$\bar{x} \pm e$$

so that, with a certain degree of confidence, you can say that the true mean, μ, is in this interval. You select the "degree of confidence" in the form of a value for α between 0 and 1 so that with $(1 - \alpha) * 100\%$ confidence you can say that μ is in this interval. For example, to be 95% confident, you would choose a value of $\alpha = 0.05$.

KEY FEATURES

Having chosen an appropriate value for α, you compute the associated confidence interval by

$$\bar{x} \pm t_{(n-1),\alpha/2} * \frac{s}{\sqrt{n}}$$

where

n	= the sample size (that is, the number of simulation runs)
$\bar{x}$	= the sample average
s	= the sample standard deviation
$t_{(n-1),\alpha/2}$	= the value from the t-distribution with $n - 1$ degrees of freedom so that the area to the right of this value is $\alpha/2$.

To illustrate with the mortgage example, in which

$$
\begin{aligned}
\alpha &= 0.05 \\
n &= 35 \\
\overline{x} &= -78.9361 \\
s &= 42.18124 \text{ (see the bottom of Table 15.4 in Section 15.1)} \\
t_{(n-1),\alpha/2} &= 2.03 \text{ (see the } t\text{-table in Appendix B)}
\end{aligned}
$$

the associated confidence interval is

$$
\begin{aligned}
\overline{x} &\pm \left(t_{(n-1),\alpha/2} * \frac{s}{\sqrt{n}} \right) \\
&= -78.9361 \pm \left(2.03 * \frac{42.18124}{\sqrt{35}} \right) \\
&= -78.9361 \pm 14.47
\end{aligned}
$$

Accuracy of the estimate

A numerical measure of how reliable a simulation output is.

In other words, you can be 95% confident that the true expected net present value of the differences in the variable and fixed annual payments over the 15 years is within 14.47 of the estimated value of -78.9361 obtained from the 35 simulation runs. This value of $e = 14.47$ is therefore called the **accuracy of the estimate** and offers a measure of how reliable is the simulation output.

For a fixed value of α, the accuracy of the estimate can be improved only by increasing the sample size, n, which means increasing the number of simulation runs. You will now learn how to determine that value to achieve a desired accuracy of the estimate.

DETERMINING THE SAMPLE SIZE TO ACHIEVE A GIVEN CONFIDENCE LEVEL AND ACCURACY

Suppose you feel that the level of accuracy of 14.47 calculated earlier associated with a 95% confidence interval should be reduced to $e = 10$. That is, you would like to know that the true expected net present value of the differences in the mortgage payments is within 10 of the value estimated by the simulation. This goal can be accomplished by increasing the number of simulation runs from $n = 35$ to a new value, n^*, such that

$$
\text{Accuracy } e = t_{(n^*-1),\alpha/2} * \frac{s}{\sqrt{n^*}}
$$

Solving for n^* gives

$$
n^* = \left(\frac{t_{(n^*-1),\alpha/2} * s}{e} \right)^2
$$

Although the value of e is known to be 10, that of $t_{(n^*-1),\alpha/2}$ depends on n^*. Moreover, the value of the sample standard deviation s cannot be determined until performing the n^* simulation runs (and n^* is not yet known).

For large values of n, the t-distribution can be approximated closely by that of the standard-normal distribution, so one approach to overcoming the problem that $t_{(n^*-1),\alpha/2}$ depends on n^* is to replace $t_{(n^*-1),\alpha/2}$ with the corresponding value of the standard normal. Specifically, $t_{(n^*-1),\alpha/2}$ is replaced with $z_{\alpha/2}$ so that the area under the standard-normal distribution to the right of this value is $\alpha/2$. That is:

$$
n^* = \left(\frac{z_{\alpha/2} * s}{e} \right)^2
$$

> ### KEY FEATURES
>
> An iterative approach is used to overcome the fact that the value of s is not known:
>
> **Step 0.** Select an initial value for n.
> **Step 1.** Perform n simulation runs.
> **Step 2.** On the basis of the results of all simulation runs, compute $\bar{x}, s$, and
>
> $$n^* = \left(\frac{z_{\alpha/2} * s}{e} \right)^2$$
>
> **Step 3.** If $n \geq n^*$, stop. Enough simulation runs have been performed. Otherwise, perform $n^* - n$ more simulation runs. You have now performed a total of n^* simulations, so set the sample size $n = n^*$ and go back to Step 2.

Perform the steps given as key features with the mortgage example, in which

$$
\begin{aligned}
\alpha &= 0.05 \\
e &= 10 \\
z_{\alpha/2} &= 1.96
\end{aligned}
$$

Step 0. Select an initial value for n—say, $n = 35$.
Step 1. Perform n simulation runs.
Step 2. Based on the results of all simulation runs, as shown in Table 15.4 in Section 15.1, compute:

$$
\begin{aligned}
\bar{x} &= -78.9361 \\
s &= 42.18124 \\
n^* &= \left(\frac{z_{\alpha/2} * s}{e} \right)^2 \\
&= \left(\frac{1.96 * 42.18124}{10} \right)^2 \\
&= 70.413 \text{ (rounded up to 71)}
\end{aligned}
$$

Step 3. Because $n = 35 < n^* = 71$, it is necessary to perform $n^* - n = 71 - 35 = 36$ more simulation runs before returning to Step 2.

Observe that Steps 2 and 3 are repeated until n exceeds n^*. From the formula for n^*, you can see that as the value of e decreases (that is, you desire a more accurate estimate), the value of n^* increases. For example, if e is reduced by a factor of 2, from 10 to 5, n^* increases by a factor of 4, from 71 to about 282.

Here you have learned how to determine an appropriate number of simulation runs to estimate the mean of an output value to achieve a desired level of accuracy. A similar analysis is needed when the objective is to estimate a proportion.

15.5.2 Determining the Sample Size for Estimating a Proportion

To understand how many times to repeat a simulation run when the objective is to estimate a proportion, it is best to begin by choosing a specific number of simulation runs and asking how accurate is the estimate obtained. Answering this question requires creating a confidence interval around the estimate of the proportion.

CREATING A CONFIDENCE INTERVAL FOR A PROPORTION

To illustrate, recall again the variable- vs. fixed-rate mortgage problem in Section 15.1 in which the objective now is to determine the probability (π) that the net present value of the differences in the 15 annual payments is less than $-\$50$. This is estimated by computing the proportion (p) of runs in which this event occurs. For example, from the results of the 35 runs in Table 15.4 in Section 15.1, 26 resulted in the net present value of the differences being less than -50. Thus the estimate of the probability π is

$$p = \frac{26}{35} = 0.743$$

The question, now, is: How close is this estimated value p to the true value of π?

To answer this question, turn to statistical estimation (see the Student Resource Manual). The objective is to determine a value for e and to create an interval in the form:

$$p \pm e$$

so that, with a certain degree of confidence, you can say that the true proportion π is in this interval. You choose the "degree of confidence" in the form of a value for α between 0 and 1 so that with $(1 - \alpha) * 100\%$ confidence you can say that π is in this interval. To be 95% confident, you would choose a value of $\alpha = 0.05$.

➡ KEY FEATURES

Both $n * p = 35 * 0.743 = 26$ and $n * (1 - p) = 35 * 0.257 = 9$ are greater than 5, so the associated confidence interval using the normal approximation (see the Student Resource Manual) is given by

$$p \pm \left[z_{\alpha/2} * \sqrt{\frac{p(1-p)}{n}} \right]$$

where

n = the sample size (that is, the number of simulation runs)
p = the sample proportion
$z_{\alpha/2}$ = the z-value from the standard-normal distribution so that the area to the right of z is $\alpha/2$.

In the mortgage example:

α = 0.05
n = 35
p = 0.743
$z_{\alpha/2}$ = 1.96 (see the standard-normal table in Appendix B)

so the associated confidence interval is

$$p \pm \left[z_{\alpha/2} * \sqrt{\frac{p(1-p)}{n}} \right]$$

$$0.743 \pm \left[1.96 * \sqrt{\frac{0.743 * 0.257}{35}} \right]$$

$$0.743 \pm 0.145$$

In other words, you would like to know the true probability that the net present value of the differences in the variable and fixed annual payments over the 15 years is less than -50. From the preceding computations you can be 95% confident that this value is within 0.145 of the estimate of 0.743 obtained from the 35 simulation runs. This accuracy of the estimate, 0.145, offers a measure of how reliable is the simulation output.

For a fixed value of α, the accuracy of the estimate can be improved only by increasing the sample size n, the number of simulation runs.

DETERMINING THE SAMPLE SIZE TO ACHIEVE A GIVEN CONFIDENCE LEVEL AND ACCURACY

Suppose you feel that the level of accuracy of 0.145 calculated earlier associated with a 95% confidence interval should be reduced to $e = 0.10$. This goal can be accomplished by increasing the number of simulation runs from $n = 35$ to a new value n^* so that:

$$\text{Accuracy } e = z_{\alpha/2} * \sqrt{\frac{p(1-p)}{n^*}}$$

Solving for n^* gives

$$n^* = p * (1-p) * \left(\frac{z_{\alpha/2}}{e} \right)^2$$

The value of e is known to be 0.10 and that of $z_{\alpha/2}$ is 1.96 from the standard-normal table in Appendix B. However, the value of the sample proportion p cannot be determined until performing the n^* simulation runs (and n^* is not yet known).

KEY FEATURES

An iterative approach is used to overcome the fact that the value of p is not known:

Step 0. Select an initial value for n.

Step 1. Perform n simulation runs.

Step 2. On the basis of the results of all simulation runs, compute p and

$$n^* = p * (1-p) * \left(\frac{z_{\alpha/2}}{e} \right)^2$$

Step 3. If $n \geq n^*$, stop. Enough simulation runs have been performed. Otherwise perform $n^* - n$ more simulation runs. Now you have performed a total of n^* simulations, so set the sample size $n = n^*$ and go back to Step 2.

With the mortgage example:

$$\alpha = 0.05$$
$$e = 0.10$$
$$z_{\alpha/2} = 1.96$$

perform these steps.

Step 0. Select an initial value for n—say, $n = 35$.
Step 1. Perform n simulation runs.
Step 2. Based on the results of all simulation runs, as shown in Table 15.4 in Section 15.1, compute:

$$p = 0.743$$

$$n^* = p * (1 - p) * \left(\frac{z_{\alpha/2}}{e}\right)^2$$

$$= (0.743 * 0.257) * \left(\frac{1.96}{0.10}\right)^2$$

$$= 73.36 \text{ (rounded up to 74)}$$

Step 3. Because $n = 35 < n^* = 74$, it is necessary to perform $n^* - n = 74 - 35 = 39$ more simulation runs before returning to Step 2.

Observe that Steps 2 and 3 are repeated until n exceeds n^*.

In this section, you have seen how the output from a single simulation run is just one of many values that could have been obtained, depending on the specific initial uniform random number that is chosen. To obtain a more accurate estimate of the output value, many simulation runs must be performed, each using a different initial uniform random number. You have also learned how to determine the number of such runs to perform so as to achieve a specified accuracy. Next, additional issues pertaining to simulation are discussed from a managerial point of view.

ADDITIONAL MANAGERIAL CONSIDERATIONS

You have seen how and when managers use simulation to analyze complex systems. Managers then make decisions based on the results of the simulation. In the Managerial Considerations of Chapter 14, you learned about the importance of obtaining reliable data. In this section, several other issues related to using simulation and implementing the results are discussed.

Validation

Recall that the primary advantage of computer simulation is to study complex systems that cannot directly be analyzed mathematically. The computer model is meant to mimic the system, but the output may not be accurate because of two reasons:

1. *Inaccuracy in building the model.* Your model may not accurately mimic the true system because:
   a. The system is so complex that you consciously (or unconsciously) exclude certain aspects.

    b. In developing the model, you may have made certain assumptions that may not mirror reality. You may have been forced to make these assumptions because you lacked information or because you wanted to simplify building the model. For example, in simulating the queueing system of the New Jersey Turnpike Commission, you assumed that once a vehicle chooses the shortest allowable line to join at the toll plaza, the vehicle remains in that line. In practice, however, a vehicle may switch to another allowable line that becomes shorter or seems to be moving faster.

2. *Inaccuracy in the values of the data.* You may have estimated some input values inaccurately.

Because of these two reasons, you want to *validate* your computer model before relying on its outputs. That is, you want to make sure that the model contains no major oversights or numerical errors and provides an *adequate* representation of the system being simulated.

A computer model is validated in any of the following ways:

1. Before using a simulation model to study changes to an existing system, model the current system first. For the problem of the New Jersey Turnpike Commission, you should first simulate the existing system with three general booths to see if the average waiting times, queue lengths, and utilizations that the model produces conform with current operating conditions. Only then should you model the proposed system, in which one general booth is changed to an express booth to handle cars with two or more passengers.

2. Make sure that the results of the computer simulation are consistent with your expectations based on your knowledge of the system.

3. Before implementing any change, conduct a small-scale pilot study based on the results of the simulation model to see that the actual results conform to those predicted by the model. For example, the New Jersey Turnpike Commission should create an express toll booth at only one plaza and compare the results to those predicted by the simulation model. Once satisfied, management can consider making similar changes at other toll plazas.

Statistical Aspects of Simulation

As you learned in Chapter 14, one set of input values to a simulation model is the set of initial conditions that describes the state of the system at the time the simulation begins. In many cases, these values are fixed and easily determined due to the nature of the system. For example, in simulating the daily operation of a bank, the initial values that describe the conditions at the beginning of the simulation (that is, the day) are that no customers are yet in the system and, consequently, that all available tellers are idle. In contrast, in some problems, the initial conditions are not so readily available or, in fact, are not known. For example, in simulating the rush-hour operation of the toll plaza for the problem of the New Jersey Turnpike Commission, the initial conditions consist of the number of vehicles at each of the three toll booths and the idle/busy status of each booth. These values vary from day to day and cannot be known with certainty. In such cases, initial values are generally chosen in one of the following ways:

1. By assigning values on the basis of your knowledge of how the system works and what you would most likely expect at the time corresponding to the beginning of the simulation.

2. By assigning *any* reasonable initial values and running the simulation long enough to minimize the influence of the initial conditions. For example, whether you assign one vehicle or 10 vehicles to each of the three toll booths will have little impact on the final statistics if the simulation is run for a period of 2 hours.

3. By assigning *any* reasonable initial values and running the simulation for some initial time period, say, T'. Then discard all statistics accumulated during this period except the final conditions. Use the final conditions as the initial conditions for running another simulation. This second set of statistics is then compiled and recorded.

Statistical analysis is used to determine the appropriate length of the simulation run in step 2 and the initial time period T' in step 3. These analyses are beyond the scope of this book, but they can be found in any standard book on computer simulation.

As discussed in Section 15.5, obtaining the output value from a single simulation run is statistically analogous to drawing a single sample from a population. In Section 15.5, you learned how to determine the number of simulation runs needed to achieve a specified level of confidence in estimating the average of the output value. Another important aspect involved in designing a model to simulate a nonterminating system is the *length* of each simulation run. In the problem of the New Jersey Turnpike Commission, the *length* of the simulation was chosen to be 2 hours because the typical rush-hour period is 2 hours. However, it might be possible to obtain reliable estimates of the output value by simulating for a period of only 30 minutes. Determining the appropriate length requires a type of statistical analysis that is beyond the scope of this book, but it can be found in standard books on computer simulation.

Computational Concerns

Performing any simulation requires writing a computer program to mimic the actual system and to collect the appropriate statistics. You can either use an available package, as discussed in Section 15.4, or write a program specially tailored for your system and needs in an appropriate computer language. As a manager, it is important to realize that both approaches require significant programming skills. Furthermore, once the computer models are developed, running them to obtain the output values often requires substantial amounts of computer time (sometimes many hours) because of the length of each run and the number of runs needed to obtain reliable estimates.

Using a simulation package saves time in developing the model, but the software may run fairly slowly. Conversely, writing your own program takes more time to develop, but the customized program generally uses less computer time because it has been tailored to the particular problem at hand. There is, then, a trade-off between developmental time and computational effort. As a general guideline, if you intend to use the simulation model repeatedly, perhaps every week or every month, it might be worthwhile to spend extra effort in developing your own simulation program to save significant subsequent computer time.

SUMMARY

In this chapter, you have seen applications of using computer simulation to make decisions in such diverse areas as finance, inventory management, and queueing systems. The output obtained from one simulation run is only one of many possible values. Therefore, in general, you cannot have confidence in the output value obtained from only one run. Rather, you need to repeat the simulation run many times—each time using a different initial uniform random number—thereby obtaining different output values. The actual number, n, of runs to perform is based on whether you are estimating the mean of an output value or a proportion and also on the degree of confidence and accuracy desired in the form of a value for α and e, respectively.

Keep in mind that even though simulation requires significant amounts of developmental and computational expertise and effort, the technique is the only one that can provide useful and reliable information for most real-world systems that are large and complex.

EXERCISES

EXERCISE 15.1 The city of Tokyo is considering building a small domestic airport with one runway on landfill in Tokyo Bay. The runway will operate between the hours of 6 A.M. and midnight. Aircraft are expected to arrive for landing during this time according to a Poisson process at an average rate of 30 per hour. The time between departing aircraft is assumed to follow an exponential distribution, with a mean of 1 minute. Data analysis from similar operations indicates that the time required for landing or taking off and exiting the runway is normally distributed, with a mean of 90 seconds and a standard deviation of 30 seconds. The Manager of the Air Traffic Commission wants to know the average amount of time an arriving plane spends waiting for the runway and the same statistic for a departing flight. Assume that aircraft use the runway on a first-come-first-serve basis, regardless of whether the aircraft is landing or departing. Assume also that the simulation begins with no aircraft in the system. Complete the following table by using the three random numbers beginning in column 3 of row 1 of the table in Appendix A to determine the times at which the next three planes (A_3, A_4, A_5) enter the system for landing. Then use the three random numbers beginning in column 3 of row 10 to determine the amount of time each of the planes A_3, A_4, and A_5 will require for using the runway to land. Observe that all times in the table are in *minutes*.

AIRCRAFT NUMBER	ARRIVAL TIME			LANDING TIME		
	RANDOM NUMBER	INTERARRIVAL TIME	TIME OF ENTRY	RANDOM NUMBER	z-VALUE	AMOUNT OF LANDING TIME
A_1	0.710621	2.48	2.48	0.653071	0.39	1.70
A_2	0.689315	2.34	4.82	0.407682	0.26	1.63
A_3						
A_4						
A_5						

EXERCISE 15.2 Continue the simulation in Exercise 15.1. Complete the following table using the three random numbers beginning in column 3 of row 20 of the table in Appendix A to determine the times at which the next three planes (D_3, D_4, D_5) enter the system for departing. Then use the three random numbers beginning in column 3 of row 30 to determine the amount of time each of the planes, D_3, D_4, and D_5, will require for using the runway to takeoff. Observe that all times in the table are in *minutes*.

AIRCRAFT NUMBER	DEPARTURE TIME			TAKEOFF TIME		
	RANDOM NUMBER	INTERARRIVAL TIME	TIME OF ENTRY	RANDOM NUMBER	z-VALUE	AMOUNT OF TAKEOFF TIME
D_1	0.291777	0.34	0.34	0.098975	−1.29	0.86
D_2	0.790803	1.56	1.91	0.186970	−0.90	1.05
D_3						
D_4						
D_5						

EXERCISE 15.3   Continue the simulation in Exercise 15.1. Complete the following table by combining the results from Exercises 15.1 and 15.2 to determine the *sequence* in which the 10 planes use the runway, assuming that no other arrivals or departures occur. For each of these 10 planes:

  a. Indicate the time at which it enters the system.
  b. Determine the times at which the plane both starts and finishes using the runway.
  c. Compute the amount of time the plane has to wait before it starts using the runway.

Observe that all times in the table are in *minutes*.

AIRCRAFT NUMBER	TIME OF ENTRY	RUNWAY START TIME	RUNWAY USAGE TIME	RUNWAY FINISH TIME	AMOUNT OF WAITING TIME
D_1	0.34	0.34	0.86	1.20	0.00
D_2	1.91	1.91	1.05	2.96	0.00
A_1	2.48	2.96	1.70	4.66	0.48
			$\vdots$		

EXERCISE 15.4   Continue the simulation in Exercise 15.1. From the table in Exercise 15.3, compute the average amount of time (in minutes) an arriving plane has to wait in the system before the runway is available for the plane to start its landing and the average amount of time a departing plane has to wait before the runway is available for the plane to start its takeoff.

EXERCISE 15.5   At the Emergency Room of Mountain View General Hospital, victims in need of immediate operative care are currently divided into two groups. Class 1 patients are those who, in general, require less surgical time but must be tended to as soon as possible and are given top priority for an operating room (OR). Class 2 patients are expected to make a full recovery as long as they receive an operation within a reasonable amount of time and are thus given a lower priority. Data analysis has revealed that on the busiest evenings, Friday and Saturday, patients requiring operations arrive according to a Poisson process at the rate of about two every hour. There are about three times as many Class 2 patients as Class 1 patients. Historical data also indicate that the amount of time needed to operate on these patients and prepare the OR for the next patient follows an exponential distribution with an average of 30 minutes for Class 1 and 60 minutes for Class 2. The Director of the hospital is concerned with the level of service and wants to estimate the average amount of time Class 1 and 2 patients have to wait before entering an OR. Assume that the OR is empty and that no patients are waiting.

  Complete the following table by using the 10 random numbers in the table in Appendix A beginning in column 4 of row 21 to determine the times at which the next 10 patients (P_6 through P_{15}) requiring operations arrive at the Emergency Room. Then use the 10 random numbers beginning in column 4 of row 61 to determine the class of patients $P_6,\ldots,P_{15}$. Finally, use the 10 random numbers beginning in column 4 of row 41 to determine the amount of time that will be required to operate on patients $P_6,\ldots,P_{15}$. Observe that all times reported in the table are in *hours*.

PATIENT NUMBER	RANDOM NUMBER	INTERARRIVAL TIME	ARRIVAL TIME	RANDOM NUMBER	CLASS	RANDOM NUMBER	OR TIME
P_1	0.361285	0.22	0.22	0.119091	1	0.046130	0.02
P_2	0.134913	0.07	0.29	0.412597	2	0.838763	1.82
P_3	0.796802	0.80	1.09	0.787108	2	0.483300	0.66
P_4	0.612066	0.47	1.56	0.162120	1	0.637125	0.51
P_5	0.207541	0.12	1.68	0.303749	2	0.804000	0.08
			$\vdots$				

EXERCISE 15.6   Continue the simulation in Exercise 15.5. Complete the following table by using the results from Exercise 15.5 to determine the *sequence* in which the first 15 patients use the operating room, assuming that no other patients arrive. For each one:

a. Indicate the patient number and the time that the patient arrives at the Emergency Room.

b. Determine the times at which the patient starts and finishes using the OR.

c. Compute the amount of time the patient has to wait before the operation starts.

Observe that all times in the table are in *hours*.

PATIENT		ARRIVAL	OR TIMES			WAITING
NUMBER	CLASS	TIME	START	OPERATING	FINISH	TIME
P_1	1	0.22	0.22	0.02	0.24	0.00
P_2	2	0.29	0.29	1.82	2.11	0.00
P_4	1	1.57	2.11	0.51	2.62	0.54
			⋮			

EXERCISE 15.7   From the table in Exercise 15.6, compute the average amount of time (in hours) a Class 1 patient has to wait before the OR is available for starting the operation and the same statistic for Class 2 patients.

EXERCISE 15.8   The owner of FastFoods wants to determine the impact of converting its drive-through window into two sections: an ordering window, where the customers request food and pay for it, and a pickup window, where customers are given the food. The driveway for the ordering window is designed to hold a maximum of 10 cars, after which, new arriving cars leave. Cars arrive according to a Poisson process at the average rate of 180 per hour during the lunch period, from 11:45 A.M. to 1:15 P.M. The driveway for the pickup window can hold three cars. The average time to place an order, pay, and receive change follows a normal distribution with a mean of 25 seconds and a standard deviation of 12 seconds. The amount of time it takes to receive the food also varies according to a normal distribution. On average, an order is filled in 30 seconds with a standard deviation of 15 seconds. The owner is interested in the amount of time a person spends at this drive-through restaurant. Given the following list of arrival times, ordering times (time needed to place an order), and fill times (time needed to fill an order) in seconds, use an appropriate bookkeeping scheme to fill in all remaining values in each row of the following table. Compute, in seconds:

a. The start-order time.
b. The finish-order time.
c. The time of leaving Window 1.
d. The time filling an order begins.
e. The time of leaving Window 2.

CAR NO.	ARRIVAL TIME	START ORDER	ORDER TIME	FINISH ORDER	LEAVE WINDOW 1	START FILL	FILL TIME	LEAVE WINDOW 2
1	10.00	10.00	12.40	22.40	22.40	22.40	38.40	60.80
2	12.30	22.40	10.20	32.60	32.60	60.80	36.60	97.40
3	14.00		12.60				24.50	
4	16.70		12.30				18.90	
5	21.20		12.60				22.50	
6	24.10		11.10				13.70	
7	36.70		10.20				14.00	
8	45.80		23.40				12.30	
9	67.60		15.20				15.00	
10	76.40		28.40				16.10	

EXERCISE 15.9   From the table in Exercise 15.8, compute the amount of time (in seconds) each car spends at the restaurant. What is the average waiting time for these 10 cars?

EXERCISE 15.10   The Traffic-Control Division of Dallas is planning to put in a light at an intersection of 2 one-way streets. Data analysis has revealed that rush-hour traffic arrives according to a Poisson process at an average rate of one car every 5 seconds in the North–South direction and one car every 10 seconds in the East–West direction. Previous experience also indicates that the *maximum* number of cars that can get through the intersection in the North–South direction can be approximated accurately by a normal distribution with an average of 15 cars and a standard deviation of 5 cars. The Manager of Operations wants to evaluate the effect of setting a length of 30 seconds for the green light in the North–South direction and 15 seconds in the East–West direction. Specifically, the Manager wants to know, for the North–South direction, the average time a car must wait to get through the intersection. To perform this simulation, begin by using the three 0–1 random numbers starting in column 1 and row 22 of the table in Appendix A to determine the maximum number of cars (to the next largest whole number) that can get through the first, second, and third green lights, respectively.

EXERCISE 15.11   Continue the simulation in Exercise 15.10. Next to each car in the following table, write the number of the green light (first, second, or third) in which that car gets through the intersection. Assume the initial conditions that at time 0, the light has just turned green in the North–South direction and there is no car waiting.

CAR NO.	ARRIVAL TIME (SECONDS)	GREEN LIGHT NUMBER	WAITING TIME (SECONDS)
1	3.50		
2	6.75		
3	10.20		
4	12.50		
5	16.10		
6	25.25		
7	28.80		
8	33.30		
9	38.50		
10	40.25		
11	44.40		
12	50.00		
13	54.40		
14	59.60		
15	68.10		
16	75.50		
17	80.10		
18	82.20		
19	88.80		
20	89.90		

EXERCISE 15.12   On the basis of the results in Exercise 15.11, fill in the last column of that table by computing the amount of time each car has to wait, if at all, from the time of its arrival until the *beginning* of the green light during which it gets through the intersection.

EXERCISE 15.13 On the basis of the results in Exercise 15.12, compute the average amount of time a car has to wait before seeing the green light during which it gets through the intersection.

EXERCISE 15.14 An assembly line at a factory consists of 10 serial work stations. Every 2 minutes, a frame for the product enters the first work station and must then go through all 10 work stations, each of which adds one component. Prior to the assembly operation at each work station, an inspection is performed that requires a random amount of time that, based on historical data, is uniformly distributed between 0.25 and 0.5 minute. Generally, about 5% of the frames are rejected at each station. A rejected frame at any work station is sent back to the previous station for rework. The frames rejected at Station 1, however, are discarded. Historical data show that the assembly time at each station is normally distributed with a mean of 1.5 minutes and a standard deviation of 0.3 minute. Also, it takes 2 minutes to transfer the frame from one station to another.

    To estimate the average time an assembly takes from beginning to end, 30 simulations of 8 hours each resulted in an average of 50 minutes and a standard deviation of 10 minutes.
    a. Create a 95% confidence interval for the estimate of the average time for the frame to go through all 10 work stations. Interpret the meaning of this interval.
    b. If you want to estimate the average time within an accuracy of 2 minutes, how many more simulations will you need to perform?

EXERCISE 15.15 Every Monday morning, a drug store receives 115 gallons of a drug that has a limited shelf life of 1 week. Any amount not sold by the following Sunday is returned to the supplier for disposal. The Store Manager has noticed a loss of customers. They purchase the drug elsewhere because of a shortage at the store. To estimate how frequently such shortages occur, the weekly operation of the store is simulated with the following empirical distribution of daily demand in gallons:

DEMAND	PROBABILITY
10–12	0.1
12–14	0.2
14–16	0.3
16–18	0.2
18–20	0.2

The output of 50 independent simulations (1 week each) indicated that in 6 weeks, there was a shortage. On the basis of these results, answer the following questions:
    a. What proportion of weeks can the store expect a shortage?
    b. Create a 95% confidence interval for the estimate in part (a). Interpret the meaning of this interval.
    c. If you want to estimate the proportion within an accuracy of 0.02, how many more simulations will you need to perform?

CRITICAL-THINKING PROJECT K

THE SATELLITE COMMUNICATION PROBLEM OF TELECOMM: PART II

Recall the Satellite Communication Problem of TeleComm presented in the Critical-Thinking Project following the exercises in Chapter 14. TeleComm wants to improve its satellite communication service from Tokyo to New York. With the current network, messages can be sent from Tokyo to New York through either one of two different satellite paths, as shown in Figure 15.14.

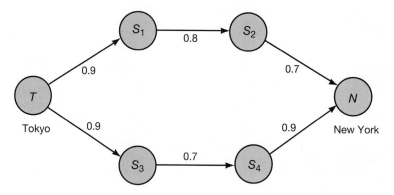

FIGURE 15.14

The top path involves sending a message from Tokyo to New York via Satellite 1 (S_1) and then Satellite 2 (S_2). The second alternative is to send the message from Tokyo to New York via Satellite 3 (S_3) and Satellite 4 (S_4). Due to their current orbits, these satellites can communicate with each other and with the cities only a *fraction* of the time. Those fractions are written next to each arc in the network shown. For example, the value of 0.9 next to the arc connecting Tokyo to Satellite 1 indicates that there is a 90% probability that a message from Tokyo can be received by Satellite 1. Similarly, the value of 0.8 next to the arc from Satellite 1 to Satellite 2 indicates that 80% of the time a message from Satellite 1 can be received by Satellite 2. All these probabilities are independent of each other.

Recall from the project description in Chapter 14 that with this system, there is only a 78.5% chance that a message can be sent from Tokyo to New York. The Vice-President of Operations, Mr. Carry Fisher, has been asked to propose a way to ensure that 90% of the time, messages can be sent from Tokyo to New York. In meeting with his technical staff, two alternatives were proposed:

    a. Alter the orbit of Satellite 1 so that 80% of the time it can communicate back and forth with Satellite 3 without affecting any of the other probabilities; see Figure 15.15.

    b. Alter the orbit of Satellite 2 so that 80% of the time it can communicate back and forth with Satellite 4 without affecting any of the other probabilities; see Figure 15.16.

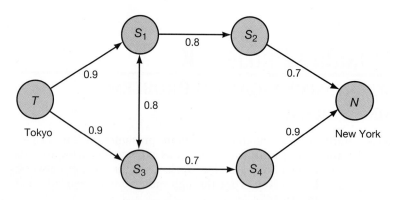

FIGURE 15.15

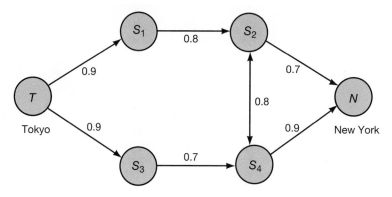

FIGURE 15.16

Mr. John Black on your technical staff used the package @RISK to perform 1000 simulations for each proposed system. He found that for the first alternative, 810 of the 1000 simulations resulted in a successful link from Tokyo to New York. For the second alternative, 840 simulations resulted in a successful link. On the basis of these results, prepare a managerial report for Mr. Carry Fisher that includes a discussion of the following issues:

1. Estimate the probability that at any given time there is a communication link from Tokyo to New York in each of the two proposed systems.
2. Create a 95% confidence interval for each of your estimates in step 1. Can you conclude that one of these systems is better? Explain. If not, what do you propose doing?
3. If you want the accuracy of each of the probability estimates in step 1 to be within 0.01, how many more simulations will you need to perform for each system?

Video Case

VIRTUAL REALITIES

Want to tour a house that hasn't been built yet? How about walking on Mars or strolling through a prehistoric forest? Computer-generated worlds exist that you can see, feel, and hear. Many people believe that the technology of virtual reality (VR) will soon revolutionize the way we live.

VR is a computer-driven simulation of sight, sound, and touch. Motion sensors inside a helmet and on gloves allow the user to experience different worlds without ever leaving the room. The goal of VR is to submerge the user into different experiences. But does VR have any application beyond the computer game arcade? Consider the following possibilities.

1. One simulation takes you inside a car's engine and lets you move the parts around to develop an understanding of how the engine works.
2. Scientists at NASA's Ames Research Center have taken two-dimensional electronic pictures from the *Viking* Mars orbiter and built a three-dimensional model of that planet's surface. Through virtual reality, you can hike across the Martian landscape, shrinking and enlarging yourself to explore features of different sizes.
3. Detailed models of city landscapes allow urban planners to redesign Main Street without lifting a stone or a pencil.
4. Architects can show you around your new home before it is built. You might discover that the kitchen, though it appears to work well for cooking, isn't laid out well for handling parties.

The applications of VR will likely grow as the technology becomes more widely available. Inventive managers, both in the service industry and in manufacturing, will learn how to apply VR to more and more aspects of running their businesses and may save a tremendous amount in costs that might otherwise be unwisely committed. (Total running time: 12:17.)

Questions on the Video

1. What was the original application that started VR?
2. What kind of video arcade games illustrate some of the early work in VR?
3. How much do VR systems currently cost?

Beyond the Video

1. Architects have used VR in designing hospitals, trying to "see" the building through the eyes of someone in a wheel chair. What are some of the benefits of using VR as a planning tool?
2. Assume that in the near future VR becomes reasonably affordable for even small businesses. How might VR benefit managers in a small service business?

Practical considerations

1. How long do you think it would take to write a computer program for VR?
2. What kind of computer power is necessary for VR programs?

Source: ABC News, "Primetime Live," September 9, 1991

FORECASTING

. . . .

*Y*ou are a representative on the city council for Maple Heights, and the mayor has asked you to project medical costs for the city's employees. Over the last few years, the budget has been inaccurate, and Maple Heights has had to tap resources that had been earmarked for recreation centers to meet the medical costs of its employees. The mayor has said that your prediction need not be perfect—no one has a crystal ball—but the forecast for the next year must be more accurate than past forecasts.

This chapter provides various techniques for using historical data to make future predictions.

Forecast
A prediction about the future.

The success of a business often depends on the ability to **forecast**—that is, to make predictions about the future. These predictions are used for making two broad types of decisions: on-going operating decisions and long-term strategic decisions. Consider on-going operating decisions, such as allocating scarce resources, buying raw materials, determining work schedules, and so on. Failure to predict the future accurately can result in excessive costs. For example, overestimating the demand for a product can result in buying too much raw material, hiring too many employees, and/or having too many finished goods lying idle in inventory. Underestimating demand can be equally detrimental, resulting in not having enough supplies or available cash, being unable to satisfy customer demands, and so on.

Long-term strategic decisions likewise depend on accurate predictions. A company might open a new plant if the demand for a product is expected to increase substantially for a sustained period of time, or it might discontinue the product altogether if the demand is forecasted to decrease and remain unprofitable.

The need to forecast demand for making intelligent operating and strategic decisions arises in service businesses also. For example

- A hospital must predict demand in the form of the number of patients. This information is used to make operating decisions, such as the scheduling of medical staff, and strategic decisions, such as whether to add a new wing to increase capacity.

- A school system must predict the demand in the form of the number of students. This information is used to make operating decisions, such as the scheduling of teachers, classrooms, and other existing facilities, and to make strategic decisions, such as whether to build more schools.

- The airline industry must predict the demand in the form of the number of passengers on each route. This information is used to make operating decisions, such as determining the size of the plane and crew to use and adjusting fares, and strategic decisions, such as whether to increase the number of flights on the route.

Management science provides several quantitative approaches for forecasting that involve *building* an appropriate mathematical model using historical data and *using* the model to forecast future unknown demands. Because these approaches, or models, are built on historical data, they are applicable *only* to predicting demand for items for which a substantial amount of historical information is available and not for new products.

Time-series model
A forecasting model in which future demand is predicted on the basis of the past behavior of the demand over a period of time.

Causal model
A forecasting model in which the future demand is predicted on the basis of known and quantifiable factors that affect the demand.

➡ *KEY FEATURES*

In this chapter, two commonly used classes of forecasting models are described:

✔ The class of **time-series models,** in which future demand is predicted on the basis of historical behavior of demand over a period of time.
✔ The class of **causal models,** in which future demand is predicted on the basis of other known and quantifiable factors that affect the demand.

■ 16.1 CLASSIFICATION OF TIME-SERIES MODELS

Time series
Demand data that are recorded sequentially over time.

As already mentioned, the forecasting models discussed here apply to a demand in which a significant amount of historical data is available. These data, recorded sequentially over time, collectively form a **time series.** In this chapter, it is assumed that these values are recorded at equally spaced time intervals—such as every week, every month, every quarter, or every year. Throughout this chapter, the variable t represents the number of time periods *from some initial base point*. For example, for yearly data starting from the base year 1980, a value of $t = 13$ refers to the year 1993. The demand in period t is represented by the symbol D_t.

To use a time series for building a forecasting model, you must first understand the various general patterns and possible behavior of the demand over time. These different types of time-series models are described in the remainder of this section.

16.1.1 Level Models

One type of model—the **level model**—is applicable when the demand per period is relatively constant over time around a fixed but unknown value A, as shown by the horizontal line in Figure 16.1. Because the data vary from one year to the next, one does not know the *exact* value for A. What value should be used? For example, the annual sales of all-season tires for Good Tire, Inc., of Akron, may follow this level pattern. The company has been in business for many years and has reached a stable size, so the demand is relatively constant from one year to the next. How does it best estimate its yearly sales figure? In Section 16.3, you will learn how past historical data of the demand are used to obtain an estimate of the value for the *parameter A*.

Whatever the value for A, the *actual demand*, D_t, in a particular period t may vary above or below A, as shown by the individual dots in Figure 16.1. These variations in demand from the value A in a level model are assumed to have no underlying causal explanation and are therefore called **random error,** denoted by the symbol e_t in period t. For example, in some years, the actual sales of tires for Good Tire are above the value A (e_t is positive), and in other years, sales are below the value A (e_t is negative) for no identifiable reason. These random errors are assumed to average to zero.

Level model
A forecasting model that is applicable when the demand per period is relatively constant over time around a fixed but unknown value A.

Random error
A variation in demand that is assumed to have no underlying causal explanation.

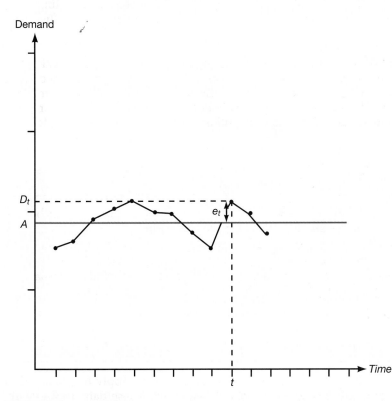

FIGURE 16.1 Level Model.

⮕   ***KEY FEATURES***

A level model of the demand D_t in a period t is described mathematically in terms of the unknown quantities A and the random error e_t in period t by

$$D_t = A + e_t$$

Because e_t is random unexplainable error with an average value of 0, the forecast, F_t, for the future unknown demand D_t in period t is

$$F_t = A$$

Suppose, for example, that the historical data for Good Tire result in an estimate of $A = 96,000$. Your best forecast for sales next year is 96,000 tires.

16.1.2 *Trend Models*

Trend model
A forecasting model that is applicable when the demand per period shows a generally increasing or decreasing pattern over time.

Another type of model—the **trend model**—is applicable when the demand per period shows a generally increasing or decreasing pattern over time. For example, the annual amount spent on health care per employee in the city of Maple Heights follows this pattern. Those costs have been increasing continuously over the past 20 years. As shown in Figures 16.2(a) and 16.2(b), this trend can be either *linear* or *nonlinear*. In this chapter, only linear-trend models are discussed. The *actual demand*, D_t, in a particular period t, however, may vary above or below this trend line, as shown by the individual dots in Figure 16.2(a). These variations from the line in a trend model are again random errors that are assumed to have no underlying causal explanation.

⮕   ***KEY FEATURES***

A linear-trend model of the demand D_t in a period t is described mathematically by

$$D_t = A + Bt + e_t$$

where

$$A = \text{the intercept of the trend line}$$
$$= \text{the expected demand at time } t = 0$$
$$= \text{the expected demand in the base period}$$
$$B = \text{the slope of the trend line}$$
$$= \text{the expected increase in the demand per period}$$

Here again e_t is random unexplainable error with an average value of 0, so the best forecast, F_t, for the demand D_t at some future time t is

$$F_t = A + Bt$$

In Section 16.4, you will learn how historical data of the demand are used to obtain estimates of the values for the *parameters* A and B. Suppose, for example, that the

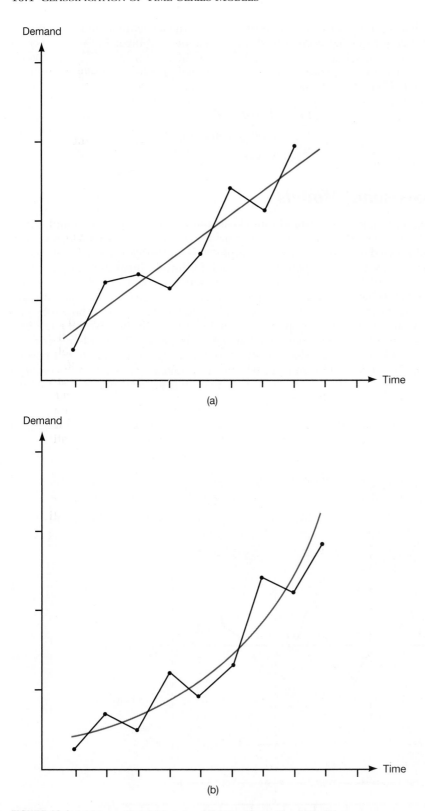

FIGURE 16.2 (a) Linear-Trend Model and (b) Nonlinear-Trend Model.

health-cost data starting in the base year of 1980 provide an estimate of $A = 1000$ and $B = 200$. That is, the average annual health-care cost per employee in the base year of 1980 is \$1000 and, on average, these costs have been increasing at the rate of \$200 per year. Using these estimates, your forecast for the annual health-care cost per employee in the year 1995 (that is, $t = 15$) is

$$F_{15} = A + (B * 15)$$
$$= 1000 + (200 * 15)$$
$$= \$4000$$

16.1.3 Seasonal Models

Seasonal model

A forecasting model that is applicable when the demand per period within a year has a definite seasonal pattern that repeats every year.

A third type of model—the **seasonal model**—is applicable when the demand within a certain time framework—for example, a year—has a definite seasonal pattern that repeats, as illustrated in Figure 16.3. For example, the monthly gasoline sales of Hexxon Oil Company follow a seasonal pattern. Here, and for future illustration purposes, the time framework will be one year. Each year, there is a recognizable increase in the months of June, July, and August—when people drive more on vacations—as compared to the rest of the year. The *actual demand*, D_t, in a particular period t, however, may vary above or below this seasonal pattern, as shown by the individual dots in Figure 16.3. These variations in a seasonal model are again assumed to be random error.

To describe a seasonal model, you must first identify m, the number of periods within a year. For Hexxon Oil, m is 12 because the time series is based on *monthly* data. If the data are collected quarterly, the value of m is 4, corresponding to the four quarters of a year.

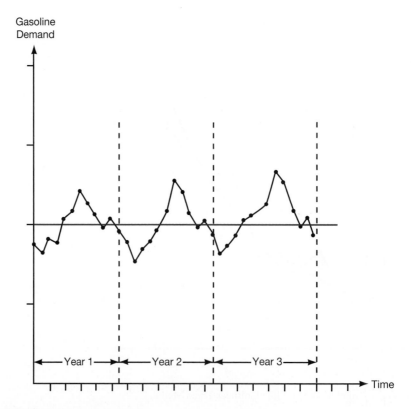

FIGURE 16.3 Seasonal Model.

For m periods, the seasonal model is described in terms of **seasonality indices** $S_1, S_2, \ldots, S_m$, which indicate whether the demand is above or below a base value, A, in each period $1, 2, \ldots, m$ of a year. One commonly used approach is the **multiplicative seasonal model,** in which the expected demand in any season k within the year is $A * S_k$. Thus, a value for S_k above 1 means that the expected demand in that period exceeds the base value A, and a value below 1 indicates that the demand is below A. In Section 16.5, you will learn how historical data describing the demand are used to obtain estimates of the values for the *parameters* A and the seasonality indices $S_1, S_2, \ldots, S_m$.

A multiplicative seasonal model for predicting the demand D_t in an *arbitrary* period t is described mathematically in terms of A and $S_1, S_2, \ldots, S_m$ and the random error e_t in period t by determining the period k within the year where t falls and then computing

$$D_t = (A * S_k) + e_t$$

Again, e_t is random unexplainable error with an average value of 0. The best forecast, F_t, for the future demand D_t in period t is

$$F_t = A * S_k$$

where t corresponds to season k.

For example, monthly data for Hexxon Oil starting in January 1990 give rise to a value of $m = 12$. Suppose that historical data yield an estimate of $A = 600,000$ gallons per month and the following estimates of the twelve seasonality indices:

JAN.	FEB.	MAR.	APR.	MAY	JUN.	JUL.	AUG.	SEP.	OCT.	NOV.	DEC.
S_1	S_2	S_3	S_4	S_5	S_6	S_7	S_8	S_9	S_{10}	S_{11}	S_{12}
0.8	0.8	0.9	0.9	1.0	1.1	1.3	1.2	1.1	1.0	1.0	0.9

Those indices whose values exceed 1 (in June through September) indicate that the expected demand in those months is higher than the base value of $A = 600,000$ gallons.

Suppose you decided to use this multiplicative seasonal model to forecast the demand for Hexxon Oil gasoline at time $t = 54$—that is, in July 1994, which is 54 months from the base month of January 1990 (when $t = 0$). For July, $k = 7$ (corresponding to the month of July) and so

$$F_{54} = A * S_7 = 600,000 * 1.3 = 780,000 \text{ gallons}$$

16.1.4 Trend-Seasonal Models

A final type of model is a **trend-seasonal model,** in which the demand exhibits both a linear trend as well as a seasonal effect, as shown in Figure 16.4. For example, the monthly demand for electricity at South Florida Power Company has shown a linearly increasing trend over the past 10 years due to an increase in the number of retired people moving to the area and a seasonal component due to the extensive use of air conditioning from May through September.

A **multiplicative trend-seasonal model** of the demand is described in terms of the intercept A and the slope B of the trend line together with seasonality indices $S_1, S_2, \ldots, S_m$, which indicate whether the expected demand is above or below the trend line in each period $1, 2, \ldots, m$ of a year. In Section 16.6, you will learn how to

Seasonality index
A numerical value that indicates whether the demand in a season is above or below a base value.

Multiplicative seasonal model
A forecasting model in which the demand during a season is obtained by multiplying the level by the associated seasonality index.

Trend-seasonal model
A forecasting model in which the demand exhibits both a linear trend as well as a seasonal effect.

Multiplicative trend-seasonal model
A trend-seasonal forecasting model in which the demand during a season is obtained by multiplying the amount on the trend line by the associated seasonality index.

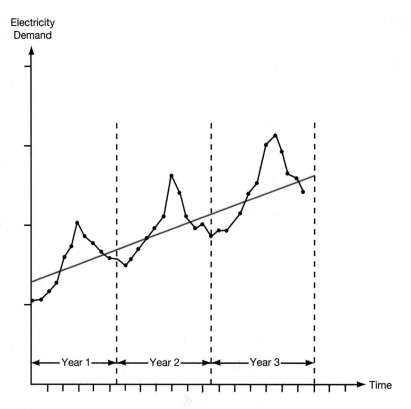

FIGURE 16.4 Trend-Seasonal Model.

use historical data of the demand to obtain estimates of the values for the *parameters* consisting of A and B and the seasonality indices $S_1, \ldots, S_m$.

KEY FEATURES

The trend-seasonal model for predicting the demand D_t in an *arbitrary* period t is described mathematically in terms of the unknown quantities A, B, and $S_1, S_2, \ldots, S_m$ and the random error e_t in period t by determining the period k within the year where t falls and then computing

$$D_t = (A + Bt) * S_k + e_t$$

Once again, e_t is random unexplainable error with an average value of 0. The forecast, F_t, for the future demand in period t is

$$F_t = (A + Bt) * S_k$$

where t corresponds to season k.

You have read about several different types of time-series models. How you measure the forecast accuracy of these models for comparative purposes is the topic of Section 16.2.

■ 16.2 Performance Measures for Evaluating Forecasting Models

As you learned in Section 16.1, there are many different forecasting models you can use for your specific problem. Even if you know which *form* of model to use, there are various methods for using historical data to obtain estimates of the *parameters* of the selected model (such as the value of A in a level model or the values of A and B in a trend model). You will ultimately want to choose the model and the method for estimating the parameters that result in the most "accurate" forecasts. How, then, do you measure the accuracy of a specific forecasting model? In this section, three of the most common measures are presented.

Suppose that you have developed a forecasting model for predicting the monthly sales of a particular model of car based on the following data from the previous six months:

MONTH	SALES VOLUME
1	50
2	66
3	75
4	70
5	68
6	72

Before using a forecasting model to predict *future unknown* demands, you can first obtain a measure of the accuracy of your model by *examining its performance on the already existing data*. For example, you can use your model to predict car sales in Month 1 and then compare this forecast with the actual sales that occurred in Month 1. This prediction and comparison with actual sales also can be done for each of the remaining five months of the foregoing data. Suppose your model results in the following forecasts for the sales in those same 6 months:

MONTH (t)	ACTUAL SALES (D_t)	FORECASTED SALES (F_t)
1	50	54
2	66	61
3	75	74
4	70	68
5	68	73
6	72	71

Forecast error
The amount by which the actual demand differs from the forecasted demand.

Ideally, you would like the forecasted sales to be precisely equal to the actual sales, but, as you can see, they are not. You can easily compute the **forecast error** for each month as the amount by which the actual demand exceeds the forecast—that is, $(D_t - F_t)$—as shown in the following table:

t	D_t	F_t	ERROR $(D_t - F_t)$
1	50	54	−4
2	66	61	5
3	75	74	1
4	70	68	2
5	68	73	−5
6	72	71	1

As you can see, positive forecast errors indicate that the actual demand exceeds the forecast, and negative errors mean that the demand is below the forecast.

A different forecasting model for this problem likely will produce a different set of forecast errors. What you need is a method for comparing two (or more) models to determine which one is more accurate. Because one model may not consistently outperform another in *all* time periods, a measure in the form of a *single* numerical value that reflects overall performance is used to compare models.

At first, you might consider using a simple *average* of all the forecast errors as such a measure. The problem with this measure is that it does not reveal the magnitude of the individual errors. Consider two forecasting models. The first model leads to two errors between the actual and forecasted demands: 1 and −1, which average to 0. The second model also leads to two errors: 5 and −5, which also average to 0. Comparing the two models using these averages reveals no difference—they are both 0—but certainly the first model is the more accurate one. Three measures that overcome this problem are described in this section.

16.2.1   Root Mean Square Error (RMSE)

Root mean square error (RMSE)
The performance measure of a forecasting model obtained by computing the square root of the average of the squares of the forecast errors.

One approach that avoids the problem of having positive forecast errors cancel negative forecast errors is to compute the **root mean square error (RMSE)**, which is the square root of the average of the *squares* of the forecast errors. That is, with n periods of data:

$$\text{RMSE} = \sqrt{\frac{(D_1 - F_1)^2 + (D_2 - F_2)^2 + \ldots + (D_n - F_n)^2}{n}}$$

$$= \sqrt{\frac{\sum_{t=1}^{n}(D_t - F_t)^2}{n}}$$

Doing so for the $n = 6$ periods in the foregoing car-sales example results in the following RMSE:

t	D_t	F_t	ERROR $(D_t - F_t)$	SQUARE ERROR $[(D_t - F_t)^2]$
1	50	54	−4	16
2	66	61	5	25
3	75	74	1	1
4	70	68	2	4
5	68	73	−5	25
6	72	71	1	1

$$\text{Total} = 72$$
$$\text{RMSE} = \sqrt{\frac{72}{6}} = 3.464$$

Ideally, you would like the value of RMSE to be 0, indicating a perfect forecast. In general, the smaller the value of RMSE, the better the forecasting model.

16.2.2 Mean Absolute Error (MAE)

Another approach to evaluating a forecasting model based on a collection of forecast errors is to compute the **mean absolute error (MAE),** which is the average of the absolute value of the forecast errors. For the car-sales example, MAE is computed as follows:

t	D_t	F_t	ERROR $(D_t - F_t)$	ABSOLUTE ERROR $(|D_t - F_t|)$
1	50	54	−4	4
2	66	61	5	5
3	75	74	1	1
4	70	68	2	2
5	68	73	−5	5
6	72	71	1	1

$$\text{Total} = 18$$
$$\text{MAE} = \frac{18}{6} = 3$$

Mean absolute error (MAE) The performance measure of a forecasting model obtained by computing the average of the absolute value of the forecast errors.

Intuitively, the MAE value of 3 in this example indicates that this model forecasts sales that, on average, are expected to be within three cars above or below the actual sales. The lower the MAE, the more accurate the forecasting model.

16.2.3 Mean Absolute Percent Error (MAPE)

The MAE measure in Section 16.2.2 is based on the absolute value of the forecast errors. However, this measure does not distinguish between a forecast error of 5 in period 1 when the actual demand is 100 and the same error of 5 in period 2 when the actual demand is 1000. In the former case, the error represents a deviation of 5% from the actual demand; in the latter case, the deviation is only 0.5%.

When the actual demand fluctuates substantially in value from one period to the next, a more appropriate measure of a forecasting method is the **mean absolute percent error (MAPE),** which is the average of the absolute forecast errors as a percentage of the actual demand. For the foregoing car-sales example, this measure is computed in the following table:

Mean absolute percent error (MAPE) The performance measure of a forecasting model obtained by computing the average of the absolute forecast errors as a percentage of the actual demand.

t	D_t	F_t	ERROR $(D_t - F_t)$	ABSOLUTE ERROR $(|D_t - F_t|)$	% ABSOLUTE ERROR $\left[\left(\dfrac{|D_t - F_t|}{D_t}\right) * 100\right]$
1	50	54	−4	4	8.00
2	66	61	5	5	7.58
3	75	74	1	1	1.43
4	70	68	2	2	2.86
5	68	73	−5	5	7.35
6	72	71	1	1	1.39
				Total =	28.61
				MAPE =	$\dfrac{28.61}{6} = 4.77$

Intuitively, the MAPE value of 4.77 in this example indicates that this model forecasts sales that, on average, are expected to be within 4.77% above or below the actual sales.

16.2.4 Using the RMSE to Create a Confidence Interval for Future Demands

The most popular performance measure for evaluating a forecasting model is the root mean square error. Assuming that the error in each period (e_t) is a normally-distributed random variable with a mean of 0 and that these errors are independent of each other, the value of the RMSE is an estimate of the standard deviation of the forecast error. This estimate then can be used to measure the accuracy of forecasts for future predicted demands.

KEY FEATURES

Having selected a forecasting model and calculated its RMSE based on the historical data, you can create a *confidence interval* (see the Student Resource Manual) for future predicted demands as follows:

✔ Choose a desired *level of confidence* in the form of a percentage. Then determine the associated value for α between 0 and 1 so that $100 * (1 - \alpha)$ is your selected level of confidence. For example, to build a 95% confidence interval, choose α as 0.05.
✔ Use your model to obtain the future forecast, F_t, in period t.
✔ The associated confidence interval is

$$F_t \pm (z * \text{RMSE})$$

where z is the value so that the area to the left of z, under the standard-normal curve, is $(1 - \alpha/2)$.

In the car-sales example, suppose your model results in a sales forecast for Month 7 of $F_7 = 72$ cars. Recall that the value of RMSE = 3.464. For a confidence level of 95%, the value of α is 0.05 and the corresponding z-value from the table in Appendix B is $z = 1.96$. Thus, the 95% confidence interval is

$$F_t \pm (z * \text{RMSE}) = 72 \pm (1.96 * 3.464) = 72 \pm 6.789.$$

In other words, you can be 95% confident that the *actual* car sales in Month 7 will be within 6.789 (say, 7) of the forecasted value of 72, that is, between 65 and 79.

In general, the value of $z * \text{RMSE}$ indicates the accuracy of the forecast in that the actual demand is expected to be within this amount above or below the forecasted value $(1 - \alpha)$ % of the time. Thus, the the smaller the *size* of the confidence interval—$2 * z * \text{RMSE}$— the more accurate and hence reliable is the forecast.

16.2.5 Bias of a Forecasting Model

The three indicators—MAE, MAPE, and RMSE—are used to measure how close the forecasts of a model are to the actual demands, regardless of whether those forecasts are above or below the actual demand. In contrast, the **bias of a forecasting model**—that is, the tendency of the model, on average, to overpredict or underpredict—is another useful way to measure the reliability of the model. The forecast errors can sometimes indicate bias in a model. For example, in the extreme case, if all the forecast errors are positive $(D_t - F_t > 0)$, then the model consistently underestimates the actual demand (because $F_t < D_t$). One numerical measure of the bias of a forecasting model is the average of all the forecast errors:

> **Bias of a forecasting model** The tendency of a model, on average, to overpredict or underpredict the actual demand.

$$\text{Average error} = \sum_{t=0}^{n-1} (D_t - F_t) / n$$

When this value is positive, the model, on average, underpredicts the actual demand. When the average error is negative, the model has a tendency to overpredict.

How can bias arise? Suppose a level model is selected. A statistically large positive bias may result if, in fact, there is an increasing trend in the demand. As a general guideline, if a model has significant positive or negative bias (as determined in a statistical sense), you may want to investigate the reason for this bias and determine a more appropriate model. The specific statistical method for determining if there is a significant amount of bias in a forecasting model is beyond the scope of this text but can be found in any standard book on statistical methods.

◀ **KEY FEATURES**

In summary, you can use any one of the following three performance measures to evaluate a forecasting model in which D_t is the actual demand in period t and F_t is the forecasted demand in period t:

$$\text{RMSE} = \sqrt{\frac{\sum_{t=1}^{n} (D_t - F_t)^2}{n}}$$

$$\text{MAE} = \frac{\sum_{t=1}^{n} |D_t - F_t|}{n}$$

$$\text{MAPE} = \frac{\sum_{t=1}^{n} \left(\frac{|D_t - F_t|}{D_t} \right) * 100}{n}$$

The average of the forecast errors is a measure of the bias of a forecasting model.

You now need to know the methods for building the models themselves. You will ultimately choose the model and method in which the value of the selected measure of forecast error you select is smallest.

■ 16.3 DEVELOPING AND USING A LEVEL MODEL FOR FORECASTING

As you learned in Section 16.1, a level model is applicable when the demand per period is relatively constant over time around an unknown value A. For example, the annual sales of all-season tires for Good Tire may follow this pattern. The historical data in Table 16.1 and corresponding plot in Figure 16.5 indicate the relatively constant annual demand over the past 13 years.

Recall from Section 16.1 that for a level model with a random error e_t in period t, the demand D_t in period t is given by

$$D_t = A + e_t$$

As you learned, the forecasting process requires:

1. Building a model by using historical data to estimate the value of A.
2. Then using the model to make forecasts of the demand in future periods, in this case:

$$F_t = \text{forecast of demand in period t} = A$$

TABLE 16.1	Historical Tire Sales for Good Tire from 1980 to 1992	
YEAR	t	TIRE SALES (D_t)
1980	0	76,900
1981	1	81,200
1982	2	95,500
1983	3	91,800
1984	4	102,100
1985	5	106,000
1986	6	99,800
1987	7	98,300
1988	8	86,000
1989	9	76,900
1990	10	106,800
1991	11	98,500
1992	12	85,000
	Total =	1,204,800
	Average =	92,677

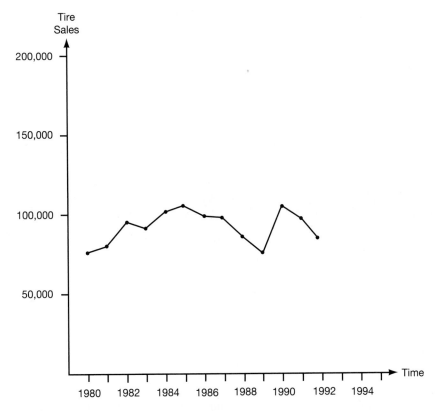

FIGURE 16.5 Sales of Good Tire from 1980 to 1992.

By looking at the historical data for Good Tire in Table 16.1, perhaps the most obvious choice you can think of for estimating A is the *average* of these 13 values—namely, $A = 92,677$ tires (approximately). This value of A is then used as a forecast of the demand, F_{13}, for tires in 1993.

At the end of 1993, you will again want to use this model to forecast the demand F_{14} for tires in period 14—that is, 1994. At that time, you will have the *actual* sales data for 1993, so you can compute a new average that now includes this one additional data point. For example, if 94,400 tires are actually sold in 1993, then the new average of 92,800 for the 14 years of data would serve as the revised estimate of A and hence the forecast for 1994.

The main drawback to this approach is that *all* historical values are used in computing the new average, so the estimate of A changes very slowly from one period to the next. Suppose that sales change abruptly. Perhaps Good Tire has driven a major competitor out of business and has acquired many new customers. Even with this new level of higher sales from year to year, the estimated value of A will change only slowly. That is, this method of averaging all available data is very slow in reacting to a shift in the value of A. Forecasts based on this value of A therefore will not be as accurate as they should be. Two alternative methods that account for shifts in the value of A more quickly are discussed next .

Moving average
A method for developing a forecasting model in which you calculate the average of the historical data from the k most-recent periods.

16.3.1 *The Method of Moving Averages*

The method of **moving averages** uses the average of the data from only the k most recent periods as an estimate of A. For example, with $k = 5$ for the model of Good Tire,

Forecasting
GDTR_MA.DAT

the value for A used in forecasting the 1993 sales is the average of the number of tires sold in the previous 5 years. By using the data in Table 16.1,

$$A = [(\text{sales in } 1988) + (\text{sales in } 1989) + (\text{sales in } 1990) +$$
$$(\text{sales in } 1991) + (\text{sales in } 1992)]/5$$
$$= (86{,}000 + 76{,}900 + 106{,}800 + 98{,}500 + 85{,}000)/5$$
$$= 90{,}640$$

Thus, the forecast, F_{13}, for tire sales in 1993 is

$$F_{13} = A = 90{,}640 \text{ tires}$$

Again, suppose that the actual sales at the end of 1993 are 94,400 tires. The new estimate of A used to forecast sales in 1994 is obtained by dropping the sales in 1988 and adding those in 1993, as follows:

$$A = [(\text{sales in } 1989) + (\text{sales in } 1990) +$$
$$(\text{sales in } 1991) + (\text{sales in } 1992) + (\text{sales in } 1993)]/5$$
$$= (76{,}900 + 106{,}800 + 98{,}500 + 85{,}000 + 94{,}400)/5$$
$$= 92{,}320$$

Hence, the forecast, F_{14}, for tire sales in 1994 is

$$F_{14} = A = 92{,}320 \text{ tires}$$

With this approach, each time a new *actual* value becomes available, a new estimate of A is obtained using this new value in place of the kth oldest one, thus giving rise to the term "moving average."

You might realize at this point that there is nothing special about using a moving average of five periods to estimate the value of A. Why not use $k = 4$ or $k = 6$ periods? One way to decide on an appropriate value for k is to evaluate the performance of each possible k as applied to all the available historical data using one of the measures described in Section 16.2.

For example, to evaluate the 5-year moving average for Good Tire, you need 5 years of historical data to compute the first average. Therefore, start at the end of 1984, at which point the 5-year data from 1980 through 1984 are available to provide the following forecast, F_5, for 1985:

$$F_5 = A$$
$$= [(\text{sales in } 1980) + (\text{sales in } 1981) + (\text{sales in } 1982) +$$
$$(\text{sales in } 1983) + (\text{sales in } 1984)]/5$$
$$= (76{,}900 + 81{,}200 + 95{,}500 + 91{,}800 + 102{,}100)/5$$
$$= 89{,}500 \text{ tires}$$

Comparing this forecasted value of $F_5 = 89{,}500$ with the actual demand of $D_5 = 106{,}000$ tires in 1985 reveals a forecast error of

$$\text{Forecast error} = D_5 - F_5 = 106000 - 89500 = 16{,}500 \text{ tires}$$

A similar error is obtained for each of the years 1986 through 1992 by

1. Using the previous 5-year average as the forecast F_t in period t:

$$F_t = \frac{D_{t-5} + D_{t-4} + D_{t-3} + D_{t-2} + D_{t-1}}{5}$$

2. Computing the forecast error as the difference between the actual demand D_t and the forecast F_t:

$$\text{Forecast error} = D_t - F_t$$

These forecasts and corresponding errors are shown both in Figure 16.6 and in the columns labeled "Forecast" and "Error" in Table 16.2.

Having obtained the forecast errors, you can compute each of the three performance measures—RMSE, MAE, and MAPE. On the basis of the averages in the last row of Table 16.2, the three measures are

$$\text{RMSE} = \sqrt{151{,}831{,}650} = 12{,}322$$

$$\text{MAE} = 10{,}437.5$$

$$\text{MAPE} = 11.5000$$

The RMSE of 12,322 is an estimate of the standard deviation of the forecast errors. Intuitively, the value of 10,437.5 for the MAE indicates that the 5-year moving-average method results in an expected forecast error of about 10,438 tires above or below the actual annual demand. Similarly, the MAPE of 11.5 means that this forecasting method results in an error that is expected to be 11.5% above or below the actual demand.

Similar measures now can be computed for each moving average of size k. The corresponding RMSE, MAE, and MAPE are summarized in Table 16.3 for $k = 3, 4, 5,$ and 6. As you can see, regardless of which performance measure (RMSE, MAE, or MAPE) you choose, the 6-year moving average provides the smallest value. In general,

TABLE 16.2 *Forecast Errors for Good Tire Based on 5-Year Moving Averages*

YEAR	t	DEMAND (D_t)	FORECAST (F_t)	ERROR $(D_t - F_t)$	SQUARE ERROR $[(D_t - F_t)^2]$	ABSOLUTE ERROR $(\lvert D_t - F_t \rvert)$	% ABSOLUTE ERROR $\left[\left(\frac{\lvert D_t - F_t \rvert}{D_t}\right) * 100\right]$
1980	0	76,900					
1981	1	81,200					
1982	2	95,500					
1983	3	91,800					
1984	4	102,100					
1985	5	106,000	89,500	16,500	272,250,000	16,500	15.5660
1986	6	99,800	95,320	4,480	20,070,400	4,480	4.4890
1987	7	98,300	99,040	−740	547,600	740	0.7528
1988	8	86,000	99,600	−13,600	184,960,000	13,600	15.8139
1989	9	76,900	98,440	−21,540	463,971,600	21,540	28.0104
1990	10	106,800	93,400	13,400	179,560,000	13,400	12.5468
1991	11	98,500	93,560	4,940	24,403,600	4,940	5.0152
1992	12	85,000	93,300	−8,300	68,890,000	8,300	9.7647
			Total		1,214,653,200	83,500	91.9588
			Average		151,831,650	10,437.5	11.4949

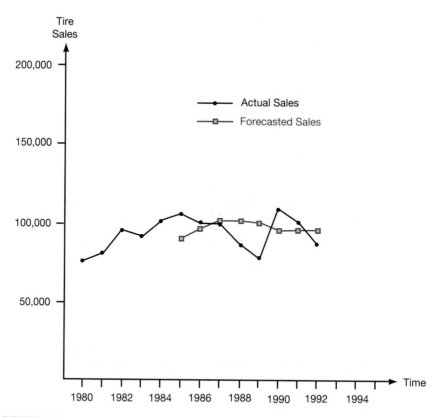

FIGURE 16.6 Forecasting the Sales of Good Tire Using 5-Year Moving Averages.

however, for each performance measure, you may find that a different value for k produces the smallest value of that measure. In this event, you should choose the measure that most appropriately reflects how you want to evaluate the accuracy of a forecast.

One of the primary advantages of the method of moving averages is that it is easy to understand and implement, even by hand. The disadvantage is that it does not always react reliably to changes in the actual value of the parameter A. For example, if k is large, then the new data values slowly change the value of the moving averages, as shown in Figure 16.7, where the level A shifts up in value in Period 12. You can see that a long period of time is required for the values of this moving average to catch up to and reveal a shift in the level A. Alternatively, if k is small, then random errors leading to one-time changes in the data can significantly change the value of the moving average,

TABLE 16.3	Measures of 3-, 4-, 5-, and 6-Year Moving Averages for the Problem of Good Tire		
k	RMSE	MAE	MAPE
3	11,916	10,447	11.27
4	12,749	10,833	11.77
5	12,322	10,437	11.49
6	11,246	9,619	10.94

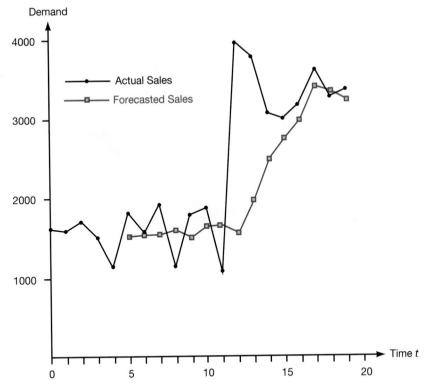

FIGURE 16.7 Forecasting a Time Series with a Shift in Level Using 5-Year Moving Averages.

thus reflecting a false shift in the level A. The method in Section 16.3.2 is designed to overcome some of these problems.

16.3.2 Exponential Smoothing

The method of **exponential smoothing** is designed to use the forecast error in one period to correct and improve the forecast for the next period. Again, consider the level time-series model of Good Tire in Table 16.1 in Section 16.3.1. Suppose you have already used these historical data to obtain an estimate of $A = 94,000$, which you then use as the forecast for the tire sales in 1993. Assume that the actual demand in that year is 94,400 tires. Thus, your forecast error is $94,400 - 94,000 = 400$.

This error may arise from random, unexplainable causes or from a true increase in the level A of the time series. You would want to adjust your estimate of A for the 1994 forecast to accommodate the true increase, ignoring any random fluctuation. Your next forecast therefore should increase by the *fraction* of the 1993 forecast error of 400 tires you attribute to an *actual* shift in the value of A. Mathematically, you specify this fraction in the form of a value for α between 0 and 1, called the **smoothing constant**. For example, when α is 0.1, you are attributing 10% of the current forecast error to an actual shift in the value of A and 90% to randomness.

In general, the closer α is to 1, the larger the fraction of the forecast error you attribute to an actual shift. Similarly, the closer α is to 0, the more you are ignoring the forecast error. Thus, the more you believe that the demand is relatively stable—that is, the error results from a one-time random occurrence—the smaller you should choose the value for α. Although your own judgment, experience, and knowledge of the market are important in determining an appropriate value for α, empirical experience has shown that a value between 0.10 and 0.30 often results in reliable forecasts. You

Exponential smoothing
A method for developing a forecasting model in which you use the forecast error in one period to correct and improve the forecast for the next period.

Smoothing constant
A fraction you specify that determines the degree by which the forecast in the next period is influenced by the current forecast error.

may choose, however, a larger value of α for a short period of time in the event that you expect the level A of demand to change permanently in the immediate future because of special circumstances (for example, as a result of an aggressive promotional campaign). Once the computed level of the forecasting model has changed in accordance with these special circumstances, you may then revert back to a smaller value of α.

KEY FEATURES

For a specific value of α, you use exponential smoothing to modify your previous estimate of A from period $(t-1)$, which is the forecast F_{t-1}, to create a new estimate of A and hence the forecast F_t for the next period t:

$$\left\{\begin{array}{l}\text{Forecast for} \\ \text{period } t\end{array}\right\} = \left\{\begin{array}{l}\text{previous forecast} \\ \text{for period } (t-1)\end{array}\right\} + \alpha * \left\{\begin{array}{l}\text{forecast error} \\ \text{in period } (t-1)\end{array}\right\}$$

That is:

$$F_t = F_{t-1} + \alpha * (D_{t-1} - F_{t-1})$$

To apply this method to the problem of Good Tire and to forecast tire sales F_{13} in 1993, first select an appropriate value of α—say, 0.10. According to the formula,

$$F_{13} = F_{12} + 0.10 * (D_{12} - F_{12})$$

Thus, you also need the forecast F_{12}, which was made for 1992. This, in turn, requires the forecast for 1991, and so on. These forecasts are obtained sequentially by starting at the *beginning* of the time series data (1980 in this case) and applying exponential smoothing, year by year, through 1992. To do this, an initial forecast for 1980 is needed.

There are various methods used to obtain this initial forecast. If there are enough historical data, the forecast you use to start the process will have little impact after a few periods. One simple approach, for example, is to use the actual sales of $D_0 = 76,900$ tires in 1980 as the initial forecast, F_0, for 1980, and consequently there is no forecast error for 1980. With this starting point, exponential smoothing generates forecasts in each year from 1981 through 1993. For 1981,

$$F_1 = F_0 + \alpha * (D_0 - F_0)$$
$$= 76,900 + 0.10 * (76,900 - 76,900)$$
$$= 76,900 \text{ tires}$$

Because the actual demand in 1981 is $D_1 = 81,200$, you can compute the accuracy of this forecast as follows:

$$\begin{array}{lll}
\text{Forecast error} & = D_1 - F_1 & = 81,200 - 76,900 = 4,300 \\
\text{Squared error} & = (D_1 - F_1)^2 & = (4,300)^2 \qquad = 18,490,000 \\
\text{Absolute error} & = |D_1 - F_1| & = |4,300| \qquad = 4,300
\end{array}$$

$$\text{\% absolute error} = \left(\frac{|D_1 - F_1|}{D_1}\right) * 100 = \left(\frac{4,300}{81,200}\right) * 100 = 5.30$$

Similarly, for 1982,

$$F_2 = F_1 + \alpha * (D_1 - F_1)$$
$$= 76{,}900 + 0.10 * (81{,}200 - 76{,}900)$$
$$= 76{,}900 + 430$$
$$= 77{,}330$$

Forecast error $= D_2 - F_2$ $= 95{,}500 - 77{,}330 = 18{,}170$

Squared error $= (D_2 - F_2)^2$ $= (18{,}170)^2$ $= 330{,}148{,}900$

Absolute error $= |D_2 - F_2|$ $= |18{,}170|$ $= 18{,}170$

% Absolute error $= \left(\dfrac{|D_2 - F_2|}{D_2}\right) * 100 = \left(\dfrac{18{,}170}{95{,}500}\right) * 100 = 19.03$

The forecasts and errors are summarized in Figure 16.8 and in Table 16.4 for 1980 through 1992. The desired forecast, F_{13}, for 1993 based on this exponential smoothing approach is

$$F_{13} = F_{12} + \alpha * (D_{12} - F_{12})$$
$$= 89434 + 0.10 * (-4434)$$
$$= 88{,}991 \text{ tires}$$

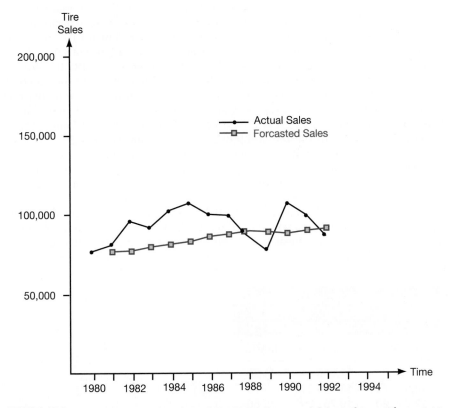

FIGURE 16.8 Forecasting the Sales of Good Tire Using Exponential Smoothing with $\alpha = 0.10$.

TABLE 16.4 *Exponential Smoothing for the Problem of Good Tire with* $\alpha = 0.10$

YEAR	t	DEMAND (D_t)	FORECAST (F_t)	ERROR $(D_t - F_t)$	SQUARE ERROR $[(D_t - F_t)^2]$	ABSOLUTE ERROR $(|D_t - F_t|)$	% ABSOLUTE ERROR $\left[\left(\dfrac{|D_t - F_t|}{D_t}\right) * 100\right]$
1980	0	76,900	76,900				
1981	1	81,200	76,900	4,300	18,490,000	4,300	5.30
1982	2	95,500	77,330	18,170	330,148,900	18,170	19.03
1983	3	91,800	79,147	12,653	160,098,400	12,653	13.78
1984	4	102,100	80,412	21,688	470,356,300	21,688	21.24
1985	5	106,000	82,581	23,419	548,446,300	23,419	22.09
1986	6	99,800	84,923	14,877	221,326,200	14,877	14.91
1987	7	98,300	86,411	11,889	141,356,200	11,889	12.09
1988	8	86,000	87,600	−1,600	2,558,700	1,600	1.86
1989	9	76,900	87,440	−10,540	111,084,000	10,540	13.71
1990	10	106,800	86,386	20,414	416,744,600	20,414	19.11
1991	11	98,500	88,427	10,073	101,463,100	10,073	10.23
1992	12	85,000	89,434	−4,434	19,663,900	4,434	5.22
				Average	211,811,380	12,839	13.22
				RMSE	14,554		

Forecasting
GDTR_ES.DAT

Any value of α between 0 and 1 could have been used. As mentioned previously, empirical experience has shown that for a stable time series, a value for α between 0.10 and 0.30 often results in reliable forecasts. Even within this range, there are many values of α you could choose. You might decide to have the computer evaluate the performance of numerous choices of α within this range on all the available historical data. For example, the results of using STORM with $\alpha = 0.10$ are shown in Figures 16.9 to 16.11. In Figure 16.11 you can see that for $\alpha = 0.10$, the RMSE measure is 12189.92. Why is this value different from the value of 14554 computed in Table 16.4? As indicated in Figure 16.9, the STORM software package uses the demand in the first four periods (that is, $t = 0, 1, 2, 3$) to obtain the initial estimates rather than just the one period used in the calculations in Table 16.4. STORM computes the performance measures based only on the forecast errors in the remaining nine periods (that is $t = 4, 5, \ldots, 12$), as shown in Figure 16.10. Finally, note the value of 5311.6670 ("Mean Err") in Figure 16.11. This value is the average of the forecast errors and indicates a positive bias—that is, on average, this model tends to underpredict the actual demand. Statistical tests need to be performed to determine if this bias is significant.

The results of using STORM for $\alpha = 0.10, 0.20$, and 0.30 are summarized in Table 16.5. On the basis of these results, you should prefer the value of $\alpha = 0.20$ if you select the RMSE as your performance measure. However, either of the other two measures leads you to prefer $\alpha = 0.30$.

TABLE 16.5 *Performance Measures with $\alpha = 0.10, 0.20$, and 0.30 for the Problem of Good Tire*

α	RMSE	MAE	MAPE
0.10	12,189.92	11,305.44	11.78
0.20	12,092.79	11,045.33	11.70
0.30	12,230.90	10,761.89	11.50

```
Exponential Smoothing for the Problem of Good Tire
        INITIAL CONDITIONS FOR SERIES    1
                                 Level
            Component            Model

            Level            86612.4500
            Trend                  N/A
            Seasonal  1            N/A
            Seasonal  2            N/A

    Above values are based on the first 4 periods of data
```

FIGURE 16.9 Initial Level from STORM for the Problem of Good Tire Using Exponential Smoothing with $\alpha = 0.10$.

```
Exponential Smoothing for the Problem of Good Tire
     LEVEL MODEL-FITTING STATISTICS FOR SERIES    1
         SMOOTHING CONSTANTS USED : 0.10(LEVEL)
Period          Actual   Forecast    Error     Level
PERIOD    4     102100     86612     15488 88161.2000
PERIOD    5     106000     88161     17839 89945.0800
PERIOD    6      99800     89945      9855 90930.5700
PERIOD    7      98300     90931      7369 91667.5200
PERIOD    8      86000     91668     -5668 91100.7600
PERIOD    9      76900     91101    -14201 89680.6900
PERIOD   10     106800     89681     17119 91392.6200
PERIOD   11      98500     91393      7107 92103.3600
PERIOD   12      85000     92103     -7103 91393.0200
```

FIGURE 16.10 STORM Output for the Problem of Good Tire Using Exponential Smoothing with $\alpha = 0.10$.

```
      Exponential Smoothing for the Problem of Good Tire
    MODEL-FITTING / VALIDATION-ERROR STATISTICS FOR SERIES    1

                        Level
    Statistic           Model

    Model Fitting Error Statistics for 9 periods from PERIOD    4
    Mean Err            5311.6670
    Mean % Err             4.3556
    Mean Absolute Err  11305.4400
    Mean Abs % Err        11.7809
    Root Mean Sq Err   12189.9200
```

FIGURE 16.11 Performance Measures from STORM for the Problem of Good Tire Using Exponential Smoothing with $\alpha = 0.10$.

Of course, you can try other values for α. In fact, STORM has the capability of finding the value of α that leads to the smallest value of RMSE. For this problem, that value of 0.17 is obtained automatically by the search technique in STORM. The associated output is shown in Figures 16.12 to 16.14.

```
Exponential Smoothing for the Problem of Good Tire
          INITIAL CONDITIONS FOR SERIES     1
                                        Level
                   Component            Model

                   Level             86612.4500
                   Trend                 N/A
                   Seasonal  1           N/A
                   Seasonal  2           N/A
          Above values are based on the first 4 periods of data
```

FIGURE 16.12 Initial Level from STORM for the Problem of Good Tire Using Exponential Smoothing with $\alpha = 0.17$.

```
Exponential Smoothing for the Problem of Good Tire
     LEVEL MODEL-FITTING STATISTICS FOR SERIES     1
          SMOOTHING CONSTANTS USED : 0.17(LEVEL)
Period             Actual   Forecast     Error     Level
PERIOD   4         102100     86612      15488 89245.3300
PERIOD   5         106000     89245      16755 92093.6200
PERIOD   6          99800     92094       7706 93403.7100
PERIOD   7          98300     93404       4896 94236.0800
PERIOD   8          86000     94236      -8236 92835.9400
PERIOD   9          76900     92836     -15936 90126.8300
PERIOD  10         106800     90127      16673 92961.2700
PERIOD  11          98500     92961       5539 93902.8600
PERIOD  12          85000     93903      -8903 92389.3700
```

FIGURE 16.13 STORM Output for the Problem of Good Tire Using Exponential Smoothing with $\alpha = 0.17$.

```
    Exponential Smoothing for the Problem of Good Tire
   MODEL-FITTING / VALIDATION ERROR STATISTICS FOR SERIES    1
                            Level
Statistic                   Model

Model-Fitting Error Statistics for 9 periods from PERIOD    4

Mean Err               3775.7780
Mean % Err                2.6821
Mean Absolute Err     11125.7800
Mean Abs % Err           11.7430
Root Mean Sq Err      12081.5800
```

FIGURE 16.14 Performance Measures from STORM for the Problem of Good Tire Using Exponential Smoothing with $\alpha = 0.17$.

16.3.3 Comparing Moving Averages and Exponential Smoothing

An informative relationship exists between the methods of exponential smoothing and moving averages. If a moving average of the past k data values is used, each such value is multiplied by $1/k$ and then added together to obtain the forecast. For example, when $k = 3$, the forecast for period t is

$$F_t = \frac{D_{t-3} + D_{t-2} + D_{t-1}}{3}$$

$$= \tfrac{1}{3}D_{t-3} + \tfrac{1}{3}D_{t-2} + \tfrac{1}{3}D_{t-1}$$

In contrast, with exponential smoothing, each of these k data values is given a *different* weight. This is because the forecast for period t is

$$F_t = F_{t-1} + \alpha * (D_{t-1} - F_{t-1})$$

$$= \alpha * D_{t-1} + (1 - \alpha) * F_{t-1}$$

However, F_{t-1} is obtained from F_{t-2} and D_{t-2} by the formula

$$F_{t-1} = \alpha * D_{t-2} + (1 - \alpha) * F_{t-2}$$

Substituting this expression for F_{t-1} in the formula for F_t yields

$$F_t = \alpha * D_{t-1} + (1 - \alpha) * F_{t-1}$$

$$= \alpha * D_{t-1} + (1 - \alpha) * [\alpha * D_{t-2} + (1 - \alpha) * F_{t-2}]$$

$$= \alpha * D_{t-1} + \alpha * (1 - \alpha) * D_{t-2} + (1 - \alpha)^2 * F_{t-2}$$

Repeating this process for F_{t-2}, F_{t-3}, and so on results in the following expression for computing F_t in terms of $D_{t-1}, D_{t-2}, \ldots, D_0$, assuming that $F_1 = D_0$:

$$F_t = \alpha * D_{t-1} + \alpha * (1 - \alpha) * D_{t-2} + \alpha * (1 - \alpha)^2 * D_{t-3} + \cdots + \alpha * (1 - \alpha)^{t-1} * D_0$$

For example, when $\alpha = 0.10$,

$$F_t = 0.10 * D_{t-1} + 0.09 * D_{t-2} + 0.081 * D_{t-3} + \cdots$$

You can see that the forecast F_t is a *weighted* sum of all the previous historical demands in which larger weights are given to the more recent data. In other words, the forecast is obtained by "smoothing" the past data using weights that involve exponents of $(1 - \alpha)$, thus giving rise to the name "exponential smoothing."

16.3.4 Forecasting with a Level Model

In Sections 16.3.1 and 16.3.2, you learned two methods for using historical data to *develop* a level model. You can use either the method of moving averages or that of exponential smoothing to obtain an estimate of the value for A at the end of period t. By using this estimate of A, the forecast for the next period $(t + 1)$ is

$$F_{t+1} = \text{current estimate of A}$$

For instance, in the example of Good Tire, suppose you have built a model based on exponential smoothing using the historical data through 1992 and the best value of $\alpha = 0.17$, as obtained by STORM in Section 16.3.2. You can then use that model to forecast demands in the next period. For example, by using the actual demand, $D_{12} = 85,000$, and the forecast, $F_{12} = 93,903$ for 1992 in Figure 16.13, the forecast F_{13} for tire sales in 1993 is

$$F_{13} = \text{current estimate of } A$$
$$= F_{12} + \alpha * (D_{12} - F_{12})$$
$$= 93,903 + 0.17 * (85,000 - 93,903)$$
$$= 92,389 \text{ tires (approximately)}$$

Note that this value is the same as the current estimate of A at the end of 1992 reported by STORM under the column labeled "Level" in Figure 16.13.

As described in Section 16.2.4, if the random errors e_t are normally distributed, you can determine a confidence interval around this forecast. Suppose you want a 95% confidence interval, for which the associated z-value from the standard-normal table in Appendix B is 1.96. Note that the value for the RMSE from Figure 16.14 is 12,081.58. The associated confidence interval is

$$92,389 \pm 1.96 * 12,081.58 = 92,389 \pm 23,680$$

That is, with 95% confidence, you can believe that the actual sales for tires in 1993 will be within 23,680 of the forecasted value of 92,389.

You can also use the model—that is, the current estimate of A—to make longer-range forecasts over a *sequence* of periods. For example, the forecasts for each of the next 4 years of tire sales for Good Tire are

$$F_{13} = F_{14} = F_{15} = F_{16} = \text{current estimate of } A = 92,389 \text{ tires}$$

All these forecasts are the same because you do not yet have the actual demand in 1993 with which to improve your current estimate of A. At the end of 1993, when those sales become available, however, you will want to change your current estimate of A, and hence your forecasts for 1994 through 1996, and beyond.

You have learned to use the methods of moving averages and exponential smoothing to obtain forecasts when the underlying model is assumed to be level. However, when the data show a trend and/or seasonal behavior, other methods that take these aspects into account are needed to develop reliable forecasts. In Section 16.4, forecasting procedures for trend models are discussed.

■ 16.4 DEVELOPING AND USING A TREND MODEL FOR FORECASTING

In this section, you will learn how historical data are used to estimate the parameters of a trend model for obtaining reliable forecasts. Consider the problem of trying to predict the 1993 average annual medical costs for an employee of the city of Maple Heights. Historical data from 1980 through 1992, given in Table 16.6 and illustrated in Figure 16.15, clearly show an increasing trend. As seen in Figure 16.15, using either the method of moving averages or exponential smoothing discussed in Section 16.3 results in forecasts that, in this case, consistently underestimate the actual costs.

TABLE 16.6	Average Annual Medical Costs per Employee for the City of Maple Heights from 1980 through 1992	
YEAR	t	COST ($/YR/EMPLOYEE)
1980	0	996
1981	1	1150
1982	2	1352
1983	3	1661
1984	4	1941
1985	5	2075
1986	6	2193
1987	7	2411
1988	8	2500
1989	9	2931
1990	10	3041
1991	11	3175
1992	12	3523

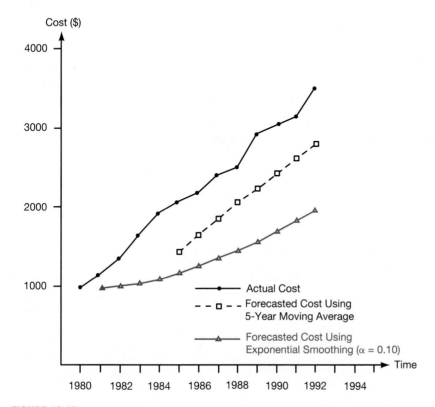

FIGURE 16.15 Forecasting the Average Annual Medical Cost per Employee for the City of Maple Heights Using Level Models.

You can develop a more accurate forecasting model based on the belief that *there is* an underlying trend. By assuming a linear trend, an appropriate model for obtaining a forecast F_t in period t is

$$F_t = A + Bt$$

where

> $A =$ the intercept of the trend line (in this case, the medical costs when $t = 0$—that is, in the base year 1980)

> $B =$ the slope of the trend line (in this case, the rate at which medical costs are increasing each year)

In this section, you will learn several ways in which historical data are used to obtain estimates for parameters A and B and how to use those estimates to make future forecasts.

16.4.1   *The Method of Linear Regression*

Observe that different values for A and B result in different trend models—that is, in different straight lines. One approach, therefore, is to determine values for A and B so that the resulting line "fits" the historical data as accurately as possible.

➡ KEY FEATURES

Statisticians have determined that in terms of n historical demands $D_0, \ldots, D_{n-1}$, the values of A and B that provide the best line are

$$B = \frac{\displaystyle\sum_{t=0}^{n-1} t * D_t - n * \bar{t} * \bar{D}}{\displaystyle\sum_{t=0}^{n-1} t^2 - n * \bar{t}^2}$$

$$A = \bar{D} - B * \bar{t}$$

where

$$\bar{D} = \text{the average demand} \;=\; \frac{\displaystyle\sum_{t=0}^{n-1} D_t}{n}$$

$$\bar{t} = \text{the average value of } t = \frac{\displaystyle\sum_{t=0}^{n-1} t}{n} = \frac{n-1}{2}$$

TABLE 16.7		*Regression Calculations for the Problem of Maple Heights*		
YEAR	t	D_t	t^2	$t * D_t$
1980	0	996	0	0
1981	1	1150	1	1150
1982	2	1352	4	2704
1983	3	1661	9	4983
1984	4	1941	16	7764
1985	5	2075	25	10375
1986	6	2193	36	13158
1987	7	2411	49	16877
1988	8	2500	64	20000
1989	9	2931	81	26379
1990	10	3041	100	30410
1991	11	3175	121	34925
1992	12	3523	144	42276
Sum	78	28949	650	211001
Average	6	2226.85		

For the example of Maple Heights, the necessary computations are shown in Table 16.7. On the basis of these values, the estimates of parameters A and B are

$$B = \frac{\sum_{t=0}^{n-1} t * D_t - n * \bar{t} * \bar{D}}{\sum_{t=0}^{n-1} t^2 - n * \bar{t}^2}$$

$$= \frac{211,001 - 13 * 6 * 2,226.85}{650 - 13 * (6)^2}$$

$$= 204.98$$

$$A = \bar{D} - B * \bar{t}$$

$$= 2,226.85 - (204.98 * 6)$$

$$= 996.97$$

In other words, the method of regression applied to the historical data in Table 16.6 results in the following trend model:

$$F_t = A + Bt = 996.97 + 204.98t$$

The value of $B = 204.98$ indicates that, on average, the medical costs are increasing at the rate of \$204.98 per year for each employee.

Having built the model—and assuming you expect this trend to continue—you can forecast the annual medical costs F_{13} in 1993 (that is, $t = 13$) as follows:

$$F_{13} = A + B * 13$$

$$= 996.97 + 204.98 * 13$$

$$= \$3661.71$$

The *actual* medical costs in 1993, however, will likely differ from this predicted value. Thus, to forecast for 1994, you will want to use the new data from 1993 together with the previous data in Table 16.6 to obtain new estimates of A and B.

The method of regression gives equal weight to all the historical data. As you saw earlier, this means that the estimates of A and B change only slightly with each new data value. If there is an abrupt change in the values of A and/or B, many periods must pass before the estimates reflect the true extent of the new values. When you anticipate an abrupt shift in the true values of A and B, better forecasting methods are available. These methods are the moving-average and exponential-smoothing approaches (discussed for the level model) which are modified to take the trend into account. The latter method is described in Section 16.4.2.

16.4.2   *The Method of Exponential Smoothing in Trend Models*

To understand how the method of exponential smoothing applies to a trend model, suppose that, based on historical data, you have obtained estimates A_{t-1} of A and B_{t-1} of B up through period $(t-1)$, resulting in the following forecast, F_t, for period t:

$$F_t = A_{t-1} + B_{t-1} * t$$

If you were also to use this model to forecast the demand in the next period—that is, in period $(t+1)$—you would obtain:

$$
\begin{aligned}
F_{t+1} &= A_{t-1} + B_{t-1} * (t+1) \\
&= A_{t-1} + B_{t-1} * t + B_{t-1} \\
&= (A_{t-1} + B_{t-1} * t) + B_{t-1} \\
&= F_t + B_{t-1}
\end{aligned}
$$

In other words, using the current model, your forecast for demand in period $(t+1)$ is the expectation for the demand in period t (estimated as F_t) plus the amount B_{t-1}, which accounts for the trend.

The idea behind exponential smoothing is to use the *actual* demand D_t that occurs in period t to correct your estimates of the expected demand in period t and also of the value of B_{t-1}. You can then obtain a new forecast for F_{t+1}. These corrections are accomplished in the following two steps:

1. Because the actual demand, D_t, that occurred in period t is different from the forecasted demand, F_t, there is a forecast error of $(D_t - F_t)$. As with exponential smoothing, described in Section 16.3, you can use this forecast error to correct the estimate of the expected demand in period t from its previous value of F_t. Choose an appropriate smoothing constant in the form of a value for α between 0 and 1, and then compute the modified estimate of the expected demand, L_t, in period t as follows:

$$L_t = F_t + \alpha * (D_t - F_t)$$

2. The modified value L_t is now used to obtain a corrected value for the slope B_{t-1}. The estimates L_t of the expected demand in period t and L_{t-1} of the expected demand in period $t-1$ provide a new slope of $(L_t - L_{t-1})$. This value may be different from the previous value of B_{t-1}. Some of this difference of $[(L_t - L_{t-1}) - B_{t-1}]$ is due to a change in the trend (and some may be random error). Represent the fraction of this difference that you believe *is* attributable to a "real" change with β, another

smoothing constant. You now can correct the previous estimate of the slope, B_{t-1}, to obtain the new estimate, B_t, as follows:

$$B_t = B_{t-1} + \beta * [(L_t - L_{t-1}) - B_{t-1}]$$

You have obtained the correction L_t for the expected demand in period t as well as the new slope B_t, so the forecast for period $t + 1$ is

$$F_{t+1} = L_t + B_t$$

KEY FEATURES

In summary, in a given period t, you have the forecasted value F_t based on the estimate L_{t-1} of the expected demand in period $t - 1$ and the slope B_{t-1}. After observing the actual demand, D_t, in this period, you forecast F_{t+1}, for period $(t + 1)$, by computing

✔ $L_t = F_t + \alpha * (D_t - F_t)$
✔ $B_t = B_{t-1} + \beta * [(L_t - L_{t-1}) - B_{t-1}]$
✔ $F_{t+1} = L_t + B_t$

These computations are illustrated for the problem of Maple Heights using the smoothing constants $\alpha = 0.1$ and $\beta = 0.2$. However, you will need initial estimates for A and B. There are various methods for obtaining these estimates. One way is to use regression analysis on the data from the first few periods. For instance, using the data in the first 5 years, from 1980 through 1984, in the problem of Maple Heights (see Table 16.8) results in the following initial estimates of A and B:

$$B = \frac{\sum_{t=0}^{n-1} t * D_t - n * \bar{t} * \bar{D}}{\sum_{t=0}^{n-1} t^2 - n * \bar{t}^2}$$

$$= \frac{16{,}601 - (5 * 2 * 1420)}{30 - [5 * (2)^2]}$$

$$= 240.10$$

TABLE 16.8	Regression Calculations for 1980 through 1984 for the Problem of Maple Heights			
YEAR	t	D_t	t^2	$t * D_t$
1980	0	996	0	0
1981	1	1150	1	1150
1982	2	1352	4	2704
1983	3	1661	9	4983
1984	4	1941	16	7764
Sum	10	7100	30	16,601
Average	2	1420		

$$A = \bar{D} - B * \bar{t}$$
$$= 1420 - (240.1 * 2)$$
$$= 939.80$$

Exponential smoothing is now applied to obtain forecasts in years 1985, 1986, and so on. To obtain the forecast for 1985—that is, $t = 5$—you need L_4 and the estimate of the slope B_4 for 1984. The latter is $B_4 = B = 240.10$, as computed in the foregoing initial regression. The value for L_4 is computed by using the regression model to find the forecast F_4 and then modifying this value using the smoothing formula. That is:

$$F_4 = A + B * 4$$
$$= 939.80 + 240.10 * 4$$
$$= 1900.20$$
$$L_4 = F_4 + \alpha * (D_4 - F_4)$$
$$= 1900.20 + 0.1 * (1941 - 1900.20)$$
$$= 1904.28$$

With these initial values, the forecast, F_5, for 1985 is

$$F_5 = L_4 + B_4$$
$$= 1904.28 + 240.10$$
$$= 2144.38$$

Exponential smoothing for this trend model now can be performed for each subsequent year starting from 1985.

COMPUTATIONS FOR 1985 ($t =5$)

1. $L_5 = F_5 + \alpha * (D_5 - F_5)$
   $= 2144.38 + 0.10 * (2075 - 2144.38)$
   $= 2137.44$

2. $B_5 = B_4 + \beta * [(L_5 - L_4) - B_4]$
   $= 240.10 + 0.20 * [(2137.44 - 1904.28) - 240.10]$
   $= 238.71$

3. $F_6 = L_5 + B_5$
   $= 2137.44 + 238.71$
   $= 2376.15$

The rounded values for L_5 and B_5 are summarized in Table 16.9 in the row corresponding to $t = 5$ (1985), and the value of the forecast F_6 is shown in the row for $t = 6$ (1986).

COMPUTATIONS FOR 1986 ($t =6$)

1. $L_6 = F_6 + \alpha * (D_6 - F_6)$
   $= 2376.15 + 0.10 * (2193 - 2376.15)$
   $= 2357.84$

2. $B_6 = B_5 + \beta * [(L_6 - L_5) - B_5]$
   $= 238.71 + 0.20 * [(2357.84 - 2137.44) - 238.71]$
   $= 235.05$

YEAR	t	D_t	F_t	$D_t - F_t$	L_t	B_t	$(D_t - F_t)^2$
TABLE 16.9 *Exponential Smoothing for the Problem of Maple Heights*							
1980	0	996					
1981	1	1150					
1982	2	1352					
1983	3	1661					
1984	4	1941					
1985	5	2075	2144	−69	2137	238.71	4,761
1986	6	2193	2376	−183	2358	235.05	33,489
1987	7	2411	2593	−182	2575	231.41	33,124
1988	8	2500	2806	−306	2775	225.29	93,636
1989	9	2931	3001	−70	2994	223.89	4,900
1990	10	3041	3218	−177	3200	220.36	31,329
1991	11	3175	3420	−245	3396	215.45	60,025
1992	12	3523	3611	−88	3602	213.69	7,744

Total = 269,008

RMSE = 183.37

3. $F_7 = L_6 + B_6$
$$= 2357.84 + 235.05$$
$$= 2592.89$$

The rounded values for L_6 and B_6 are summarized in Table 16.9 in the row corresponding to $t = 6$ (1986), and the value of the forecast F_7 is shown in the row for $t = 7$ (1987).

Similar computations for each of the remaining years through 1992 provide the forecasts and associated errors shown in Figure 16.16 and Table 16.9. Observe that in computing the performance measures, the first five periods—$t = 0, 1, \ldots, 4$, which were used to compute the initial values—are not included.

Other values of α and β between 0 and 1 could have been used. Your own opinion is important in determining appropriate values for α and β, but empirical experience indicates that values between 0.10 and 0.30 often result in good forecasts.

As before, you can use the computer to evaluate a performance measure on all the available historical data for several different choices of α and β within this range. For example, the result of using STORM with $\alpha = 0.10$ and $\beta = 0.20$ is shown in Figures 16.17 to 16.19. The column labeled "Level" shows the values of L_t and not the current estimates of A. In Figure 16.19, you can see that the RMSE measure of 100.5281 is different from the value of 183.37 computed in Table 16.9. This is because the STORM software package uses its own method to obtain the initial estimates based on the demand in the first four periods (see Figure 16.17) rather than the regression method used in the calculations in Table 16.9. STORM computes the performance measures based on the forecast errors in the remaining nine periods, as shown in Figure 16.18.

The results of using STORM to evaluate all nine combinations of $\alpha = 0.1, 0.2$, and 0.3 and $\beta = 0.1, 0.2$, and 0.3 are summarized in Table 16.10. On the basis of these results, you should prefer the values of $\alpha = 0.30$ and $\beta = 0.10$ if you select the RMSE as your performance measure. However, the other two measures lead you to prefer $\alpha = 0.10$ and $\beta = 0.10$. Suppose you use the RMSE measure and hence select $\alpha = 0.30$ and $\beta = 0.10$. You now use these smoothing constants to build the model shown in Figure 16.20 and Figure 16.21, where the column labeled "Level" in Figure 16.21 provides the values of L_t and that labeled "Trend" shows the estimates, B_t, of the slope. How do you use the model in Figures 16.20 and 16.21 to forecast medical costs for 1993?

Forecasting
MHMED.DAT

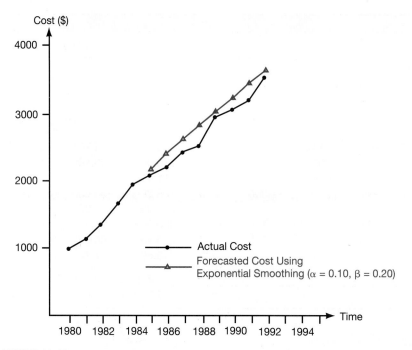

FIGURE 16.16 Forecasting the Average Annual Medical Cost per Employee for the City of Maple 'Heights Using Exponential Smoothing with $\alpha = 0.10$ and $\beta = 0.20$.

```
            INITIAL CONDITIONS FOR SERIES    1
                              Trend
            Level              1614.8370
            Trend               216.7678
            Seasonal  1            N/A
            Seasonal  2            N/A
      Above values are based on the first 4 periods of data
```

FIGURE 16.17 Initial Estimates from STORM for the Problem of Maple Heights with $\alpha = 0.10$ and $\beta = 0.20$.

```
            TREND MODEL-FITTING STATISTICS FOR SERIES    1
            SMOOTHING CONSTANTS USED : 0.10(LEVEL), 0.20(TREND)
```

Period		Actual	Forecast	Error	Level	Trend
PERIOD	4	1941	1832	109	1842.5450	218.9557
PERIOD	5	2075	2062	13	2062.8500	219.2257
PERIOD	6	2193	2282	-89	2273.1680	217.4442
PERIOD	7	2411	2491	-80	2482.6510	215.8519
PERIOD	8	2500	2699	-199	2678.6530	211.8819
PERIOD	9	2931	2891	40	2894.5810	212.6912
PERIOD	10	3041	3107	-66	3100.6450	211.3657
PERIOD	11	3175	3312	-137	3298.3100	208.6255
PERIOD	12	3523	3507	16	3508.5420	208.9468

FIGURE 16.18 Using Exponential Smoothing with $\alpha = 0.10$ and $\beta = 0.20$ for the Problem of Maple Heights.

```
      MODEL-FITTING / VALIDATION-ERROR STATISTICS FOR SERIES    1
                          Trend
Statistic                 Model

Model-Fitting Error Statistics for 9 periods from PERIOD    4

Mean Err              -43.6667
Mean % Err             -1.5290
Mean Absolute Err      83.2222
Mean Abs % Err          3.3203
Root Mean Sq Err      100.5281
```

FIGURE 16.19 Performance Measures from STORM for the Problem of Maple Heights Using Exponential Smoothing with $\alpha = 0.10$ and $\beta = 0.20$.

```
         INITIAL CONDITIONS FOR SERIES    1
                          Trend
         Component        Model
         Level          1614.8370
         Trend           216.7678
         Seasonal  1        N/A
         Seasonal  2        N/A

Above values are based on the first 4 periods of data
```

FIGURE 16.20 Initial Esimates from STORM with $\alpha = 0.30$ and $\beta = 0.10$ for the Problem of Maple Heights.

```
        TREND MODEL-FITTING STATISTICS FOR SERIES    1
        SMOOTHING CONSTANTS USED : 0.30(LEVEL), 0.10(TREND)
Period        Actual   Forecast     Error     Level      Trend
PERIOD   4     1941      1832         109   1864.4240   220.0497
PERIOD   5     2075      2084          -9   2081.6310   219.7655
PERIOD   6     2193      2301        -108   2268.8780   216.5136
PERIOD   7     2411      2485         -74   2463.0740   214.2818
PERIOD   8     2500      2677        -177   2624.1490   208.9612
PERIOD   9     2931      2833          98   2862.4770   211.8978
PERIOD  10     3041      3074         -33   3064.3620   210.8966
PERIOD  11     3175      3275        -100   3245.1810   207.8888
PERIOD  12     3523      3453          70   3474.0490   209.9867
```

FIGURE 16.21 Using Exponential Smoothing with $\alpha = 0.30$ and $\beta = 0.10$ for the Problem of Maple Heights.

TABLE 16.10   *Performance Measures from STORM for Various Combinations of α and β for the Problem of Maple Heights*

α	β	MEAN ERROR	MEAN % ERROR	MAE	MAPE	RMSE
0.1	0.1	−44.7778	−1.5495	82.5556	3.2980	100.6606
0.1	0.2	−43.6667	−1.5290	83.2222	3.3203	100.5281
0.1	0.3	−42.1111	−1.4902	83.8889	3.3428	100.3045
0.2	0.1	−34.1111	−1.2498	84.1111	3.3293	97.8860
0.2	0.2	−31.0000	−1.1704	84.7778	3.3503	98.3175
0.2	0.3	−27.4444	−1.0738	85.8889	3.3938	99.1099
0.3	0.1	−24.8889	−0.9774	86.4444	3.4099	97.7662
0.3	0.2	−20.5556	−0.8601	87.8889	3.4680	99.3283
0.3	0.3	−15.8889	−0.7266	88.7778	3.5063	101.2582

16.4.3 *Forecasting with a Trend Model*

In Section 16.4.1, you learned how to use historical data to develop a trend model using exponential smoothing. Working through the end of period t results in the current estimate, L_t, of the expected demand in period t together with a slope, B_t, of the trend line. You can then forecast the demand in period $(t+1)$ as

$$F_{t+1} = (\text{current estimate of demand in period } t) + (\text{estimate of slope})$$

$$= L_t + B_t$$

For instance, from the last line of the model in Figure 16.21, you can see that the current estimate of expected medical costs in 1992 is $L_{12} = \$3474.0490$ and that of the slope of the trend line is $B_{12} = \$209.9867$ per year. You can use that model to forecast medical costs, F_{13}, in 1993 (that is, $t = 13$), as follows:

$$F_{13} = (\text{current estimate of demand in period 12}) + (\text{estimate of slope})$$

$$= L_{12} + B_{12}$$

$$= 3474.0490 + 209.9867$$

$$= \$3684.03$$

As described in Section 16.2.4, you can determine a confidence interval around this forecast. Suppose you want a 95% confidence interval, for which the associated z-value from the standard-normal table in Appendix B is 1.96. Noting that the value for the RMSE from Table 16.10 is 97.7662, the associated confidence interval is

$$3684.03 \pm (1.96 * 97.7662) = 3684.03 \pm 191.62$$

That is, with 95% confidence, you can believe that the actual medical costs per employee in 1993 will be within \$191.62 above or below the forecasted value of \$3684.03. You can also use the model—that is, the current estimate of L_{12} and B_{12}—to make longer-range forecasts over a *sequence* of periods. For example, the forecast, F_{14}, for the medical costs in 1994 is

$$F_{14} = (\text{current estimate of demand in period 13}) + (\text{estimate of slope})$$

Because actual medical costs for 1993 are not yet available, you cannot compute the value of L_{13}, so the best estimate of the demand for 1993 is the value of $F_{13} = \$3684.03$

forecasted earlier. Similarly, the best estimate of the slope is $B_{12} = 209.9867$, resulting in the following forecast for 1994:

$$F_{14} = \text{(current estimate of demand in period 13)} + \text{(estimate of slope)}$$
$$= F_{13} + B_{12}$$
$$= 3684.03 + 209.9867$$
$$= \$3894.02$$

When actual cost data become available for 1993, you may want to use that information to modify your estimates of the expected demand in period 13 and the slope. These new estimates will then provide a new forecast for 1994.

KEY FEATURES

In general, after building a trend model using the data through period t to obtain estimates of L_t and B_t, you can forecast for any future period $t + k$ by computing

$$F_{t+k} = L_t + (k * B_t)$$

However, be advised that forecasting too far in the future may not be too reliable.

You have now learned how to use exponential smoothing on historical data to build and forecast with a trend model. However, when the data show a seasonal behavior, other methods are needed to develop reliable forecasts. In Section 16.5, forecasting procedures for seasonal models are discussed.

◼ 16.5 DEVELOPING AND USING A SEASONAL MODEL FOR FORECASTING

As you learned in Section 16.1, a seasonal model is applicable when the demand shows a consistent increase or decrease in certain specific seasons within the year. For example, a toy manufacturer generally observes increased sales in the fourth quarter of each year due to the Christmas season.

To describe a seasonal model, you must first identify m, the number of periods within a year. The toy manufacturer collects data quarterly, so $m = 4$. The multiplicative seasonal model is then described in terms of *seasonality indices*, $S_1, S_2, \ldots, S_m$, that indicate whether the demand is above ($S_k > 1$) or below ($S_k < 1$) a base value A in each period $k = 1, 2, \ldots, m$ of a year. The specific seasonal model is

$$D_t = (A * S_k) + e_t$$

Here again, e_t is random unexplainable error with an average value of 0. The best forecast, F_t, for the future demand in period t is

$$F_t = A * S_k$$

where period t falls in season k.

Modifications of the methods of moving averages and exponential smoothing described in Sections 16.3 and 16.4 are applied to historical data to obtain estimates of the unknown values for the parameters A and the seasonality indices $S_1, S_2, \ldots, S_m$. In

TABLE 16.11	*Quarterly Sales Data for Al's Gas 'n' Go Station from 1987 Through 1993*			
YEAR	QUARTER 1	QUARTER 2	QUARTER 3	QUARTER 4
1988	80,120	91,660	115,840	71,940
1989	86,760	92,920	125,960	75,920
1990	90,880	96,540	130,460	80,750
1991	94,260	104,680	134,840	86,960
1992	97,240	108,680	140,550	85,280
1993	101,560	111,200	144,770	89,520

this section, you will see how a computer package accomplishes these tasks and how these values are changed and updated as new data become available.

16.5.1 An Example of a Seasonal Model

Forecasting
GASNGO_1.DAT

Consider the problem faced by the Manager of Al's Gas 'n' Go Station, an independent gas station. How many gallons of gasoline should be ordered in each of the four quarters for 1994? The Manager has historical data on the sales figures for each quarter from 1988 through 1993, as given in Table 16.11 and plotted in Figure 16.22.

These data indicate a clear seasonal pattern in which the demand for gasoline in the third quarter, corresponding to the heavy driving months of July, August, and

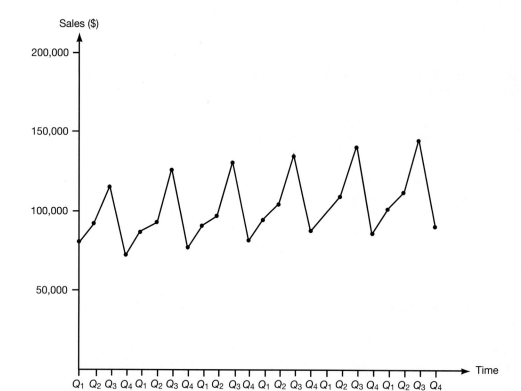

FIGURE 16.22 Quarterly Sales for Al's Gas 'n' Go Station.

September, is higher than in the other quarters. To arrive at an accurate forecast for future gasoline demand, you should develop, analyze, and use a seasonal model.

16.5.2 Using the Computer to Develop a Seasonal Model

There are numerous computer packages for developing seasonal models based either on the method of moving averages or on exponential smoothing. Similar to the methods described in Sections 16.3 and 16.4, seasonal models using the method of exponential smoothing are developed by applying the following steps.

KEY FEATURES
Developing a Seasonal Model

Step 1. Use some portion of the available data (for example, the first eight periods) to obtain initial estimates of the base value A and the seasonality indices S_i for each season, which results in the initial forecasting model. Computer packages generally decide the appropriate number of periods to use for these initial estimates, depending on the number of seasonality indices that must be estimated.

Step 2. For each of the remaining periods of data not used in Step 1, sequentially:
   a. Use the current estimates of the parameters to forecast the demand, F_t, for the next period in which data are available.
   b. Modify the estimates of A and of the seasonality indices S_i after comparing the forecast, F_t, in Step 2(a) with the actual demand, D_t, in that period. This is done using smoothing constants α for A and γ (the Greek letter gamma) for the seasonality indices S_i. The specific formulas, however, are beyond the scope of this book and are not given here.

Step 3. Evaluate the merits of the final model obtained from Step 2 by computing the performance measures described in Section 16.2.

When using such a computer package, you will need to provide:

1. The specific historical data (such as those given in Table 16.11).
2. The number of periods in a year (4, in this case, corresponding to the four quarters).
3. The value of the two smoothing constants α and γ used in Step 2(b) to modify the estimates of A and S_i.

STORM is now used to build a seasonal model using exponential smoothing in which both smoothing constants have the value 0.10. These smoothing constants and the data from the first eight quarters (from the first quarter of 1988 through the fourth quarter of 1989) in Table 16.11 result in the initial model whose parameters are given in Figure 16.23. This is Step 1. You can see that this initial model has determined a base of $A = 94{,}333.61$ gallons and the four seasonality indices $S_1 = 0.90537$ (rounded up to 0.9054 in the report), $S_2 = 0.9751$, $S_3 = 1.3143$, and $S_4 = 0.7944$.

Forecasting
GASNGO_1.DAT

```
The Seasonal Gasoline Model for Al's Gas 'n' Go
        INITIAL CONDITIONS FOR SERIES    1
                                Seasonal
             Component            Model
             Level            94333.6100
             Trend                   N/A
             Seasonal  1         0.9054
             Seasonal  2         0.9751
             Seasonal  3         1.3143
             Seasonal  4         0.7944
    Above values are based on the first 8 periods of data
```

FIGURE 16.23 STORM Initial Seasonal Model for the Problem of Al's Gas 'n' Go Station.

According to Step 2(a), these initial estimates are then used to forecast the demand, F_9, for gasoline in period $t = 9$. Because $t = 9$ corresponds to the first quarter of the year, the values of A and the seasonality index S_1 (for the first quarter of a year) yield the forecast

$$F_9 = A * S_1 = 94{,}333.61 * 0.90537 = 85{,}407 \text{ gallons}$$

This forecast of $F_9 = 85{,}407$ gallons is then compared to the actual demand of $D_9 = 90{,}880$ gallons. The forecast error of $D_9 - F_9 = 5473$ gallons is used to modify the estimates of A and S_1. STORM uses appropriate smoothing formulas to obtain the new estimates of $A = 94{,}938.06$ and $S_1 = 0.9106$ shown in Figure 16.24 in the columns labeled "Level" and "Seasonal" of the first row, labeled "PERIOD 9."

This new model is now used to forecast the demand F_{10} for gasoline in period $t = 10$ (the periods are numbered starting with 1 for the first quarter of 1988)—that is, in the second quarter of 1990:

$$F_{10} = A * S_2 = 94{,}938.06 * 0.9751 = 92{,}574 \text{ gallons}$$

This forecast of $F_{10} = 92{,}574$ gallons is then compared to the actual demand of $D_{10} = 96{,}540$ gallons. The forecast error of $D_{10} - F_{10} = 3966$ gallons is used to modify the estimates of A and S_2. These new estimates of $A = 95{,}344.75$ and $S_2 = 0.9788$ are shown in Figure 16.24 in the columns labeled "Level" and "Seasonal" of the second row, labeled "PERIOD 10."

Such forecasts and modifications for each subsequent quarter of available data through the fourth quarter of 1993 are given in the corresponding rows of Figure 16.24. The rows labeled "PERIOD 9," "PERIOD 13," "PERIOD 17," and "PERIOD 21" all pertain to forecasts in the first season of a year and hence result in modifications to the seasonality index S_1. Similarly, the rows labeled "PERIOD 10," "PERIOD 14," "PERIOD 18," and "PERIOD 22" all pertain to forecasts in the second season of a year and so result in modifications to the seasonality index S_2, and so on. From the last four rows in this figure, the model obtained from all the available data is the one in which $A = 1.0489\text{E}+5 = 104{,}890$ (the value in the column labeled "Level" in the last row) and $S_1 = 0.9286$, $S_2 = 1.004$, $S_3 = 1.3359$, and $S_4 = 0.8136$.

According to Step 3, you should now evaluate the merits of this model using any of the measures described in Section 16.2. These measures, as computed by STORM for this problem, are reported in Figure 16.25. For example, you can see that this final model provides a root mean square error of 6713.715. Rather than trying other values for the smoothing constants in order to reduce the RMSE further, suppose you believe,

```
             The Seasonal Gasoline Model for Al's Gas 'n' Go
            SEASONAL MODEL-FITTING STATISTICS FOR SERIES    1
         SMOOTHING CONSTANTS USED : 0.10(LEVEL), 0.10(SEASONAL)
  Period          Actual   Forecast     Error     Level    Seasonal
  PERIOD    9      90880     85407       5473 94938.0600     0.9106
  PERIOD   10      96540     92574       3966 95344.7500     0.9788
  PERIOD   11     130460    125315       5145 95736.1900     1.3192
  PERIOD   12      80750     76048       4702 96328.0900     0.7987
  PERIOD   13      94260     87713       6547 97047.1000     0.9166
  PERIOD   14     104680     94994       9686 98036.6100     0.9877
  PERIOD   15     134840    129327       5513 98454.5000     1.3242
  PERIOD   16      86960     78640       8320 99496.1300     0.8063
  PERIOD   17      97240     91202       6038 1.0015E+05     0.9221
  PERIOD   18     108680     98927       9753 1.0114E+05     0.9964
  PERIOD   19     140550    133934       6616 1.0164E+05     1.3301
  PERIOD   20      85280     81951       3329 1.0205E+05     0.8092
  PERIOD   21     101560     94101       7459 1.0286E+05     0.9286
  PERIOD   22     111200    102495       8705 1.0374E+05     1.0040
  PERIOD   23     144770    137978       6792 1.0425E+05     1.3359
  PERIOD   24      89520     84358       5162 1.0489E+05     0.8136
```

FIGURE 16.24 Using Historical Data and Exponential Smoothing to Develop a Seasonal Model from STORM for Al's Gas 'n' Go Station.

```
             The Seasonal Gasoline Model for Al's Gas 'n' Go
        MODEL-FITTING / VALIDATION-ERROR STATISTICS FOR SERIES    1
                            Seasonal
  Statistic                  Model
  Model-Fitting Error Statistics for 16 periods from PERIOD    9
  Mean Err               6450.3750
  Mean % Err                6.1985
  Mean Absolute Err      6450.3750
  Mean Abs % Err            6.1985
  Root Mean Sq Err       6713.7150
```

FIGURE 16.25 Performance Measures for the Final STORM Seasonal Model of Al's Gas 'n' Go.

based on experience and knowledge of the market, that the current values of $\alpha = 0.10$ and $\gamma = 0.10$ are appropriate. Should you use this model? Can you be confident of the resulting forecasts for future demands?

16.5.3 Using a Seasonal Model for Forecasting

For the forecasting problem of Al's Gas 'n' Go Station, use the final estimate of $A = 1.0489E+05 = 104{,}890$ and $S_1 = 0.9286$, $S_2 = 1.0040$, $S_3 = 1.3359$, and $S_4 = 0.8136$ given in the last four rows and the last two columns in Figure 16.24. The forecast, F_{25}, for the next quarter (that is, the first quarter of 1994) is

$$F_{25} = \text{(current estimate of } A) * \text{(current estimate of } S_1)$$

$$= 104{,}890 * 0.9286$$

$$= 97{,}401 \text{ gallons}$$

As described in Section 16.2.4, you can determine a confidence interval around this forecast. Suppose you want a 95% confidence interval, for which the associated z-value from the standard-normal table in Appendix B is 1.96. The value for the RMSE from Figure 16.25 is 6713.7150, so the associated confidence interval is

$$97,401 \pm (1.96 * 6713.715) = 97,401 \pm 13,159$$

That is, with 95% confidence, you can believe that the actual sales for gasoline in the first quarter of 1994 will be within 13,159 gallons of the forecasted value of 97,401 gallons. As Manager, you must decide if this amount of error is acceptable.

If you are planning how to order for the entire year of 1994, the forecasts F_{26}, F_{27}, and F_{28} for the remaining three quarters are estimated as follows:

$$F_{26} = \text{(current estimate of } A) * \text{(current estimate of } S_2)$$
$$= 104,890 * 1.0040$$
$$= 105,310 \text{ gallons}$$
$$F_{27} = \text{(current estimate of } A) * \text{(current estimate of } S_3)$$
$$= 104,890 * 1.3359$$
$$= 140,123 \text{ gallons}$$
$$F_{28} = \text{(current estimate of } A) * \text{(current estimate of } S_4)$$
$$= 104,890 * 0.8136$$
$$= 85,339 \text{ gallons}$$

When the actual demand for gasoline in each quarter of 1994 becomes known, you may want to revise your estimates of the parameter A and the seasonality indices S_1, S_2, S_3, and S_4 before forecasting demand in 1995 and beyond.

◼ 16.6 Developing and Using a Trend-Seasonal Model for Forecasting

Forecasting
GASNGO_2.DAT

In some cases, the historical demand shows not only a seasonality, but also an overall trend. You can identify this combination in the data for Al's Gas 'n' Go Station by looking at Figure 16.26, where you can see that the forecast based on the seasonal model developed in Section 16.5.2 *consistently underestimates* the actual demand. You can develop and evaluate another forecasting model that incorporates this trend component together with the seasonal aspect.

As you learned in Section 16.1.4, one way to describe a combined multiplicative trend-seasonal model is in terms of a trend line having an intercept A and a slope B together with seasonality indices $S_1, S_2, \ldots, S_m$, which indicate whether the expected demand is above or below the trend line in each season $1, 2, \ldots, m$ of a year. The model for the demand, D_t, in an arbitrary period t requires determining the period k within the year where t falls, and is given by

$$D_t = (A + B * t) * S_k + e_t$$

Again, e_t is a random unexplainable error with an average value of 0. The forecast, F_t, for the future demand in period t is

$$F_t = (A + B * t) * S_k \qquad \text{(where } t \text{ corresponds to season } k)$$
$$= [A + B * (t - 1) + B] * S_k$$

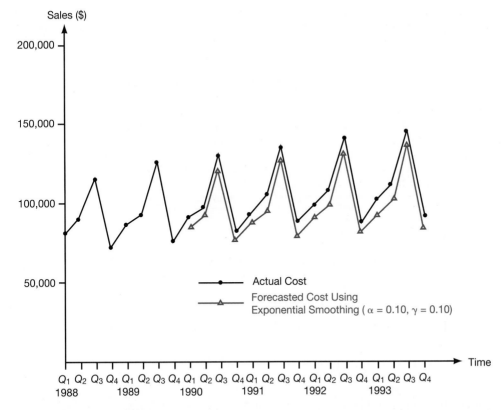

FIGURE 16.26 Forecasting Quarterly Sales for Al's Gas 'n' Go Station Using Exponential Smoothing for a Seasonal Model with $\alpha = 0.10$ and $\gamma = 0.10$.

Here, $A + B * (t - 1)$ is the value on the trend line in period $(t - 1)$, as seen in Figure 16.27. This value, denoted by L_{t-1}, has not been adjusted by the seasonality index for period $(t - 1)$ and therefore is called the **expected deseasonalized demand** in period $(t - 1)$. In terms of L_{t-1}, the trend-seasonal model is

$$F_t = [A + B * (t - 1) + B] * S_k$$
$$= (L_{t-1} + B) * S_k$$

Expected deseasonalized demand
An estimate of demand in the previous period that has not been adjusted by the seasonality index.

In the next section, you will see how to use the computer to obtain estimates of these parameters.

16.6.1 Using the Computer to Develop a Trend-Seasonal Model

In a manner similar to the methods described in Sections 16.5.2, trend-seasonal models are developed by applying a multistep procedure.

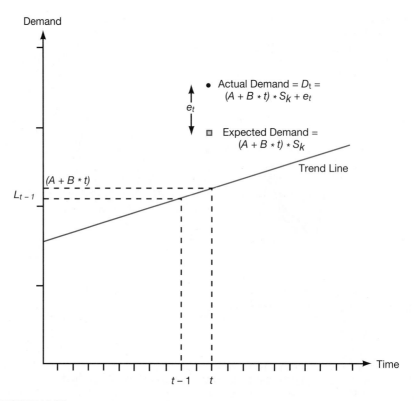

FIGURE 16.27 Expected Deseasonalized Demand in a Trend-Seasonal Model.

⟹   **KEY FEATURES**

Developing a Trend-Seasonal Forecasting Model

Step 1. Use a portion of the available data through some period $(t - 1)$ to obtain initial estimates of the expected deseasonalized demand L_{t-1} and of the slope of the trend line B_{t-1}. You must also estimate the seasonality indices S_i for each season. The computer package determines the appropriate number of periods to use for these initial estimates.

Step 2. For each of the remaining periods of data not used in Step 1, sequentially:
    a. Apply the current estimates to forecast the demand, F_t, for the next period in which data are available by computing

$$F_t = (L_{t-1} + B_{t-1}) * S_k$$

    where k corresponds to the season associated with period t.
    b. On the basis of comparing the forecast, F_t, in Step 2(a) with the actual demand, D_t, in that period, compute new estimates for L_t, B_t, and the seasonality indices S_i. This is done using smoothing constants α for L, β for B, and γ for the seasonality indices S_i.

Step 3. Evaluate the merits of the final model from Step 2 by computing the performance measures described in Section 16.2.

Forecasting
GASNGO_2.DAT

In this section, STORM is used to build a trend-seasonal model for the forecasting problem of Al's Gas 'n' Go Station applying exponential smoothing. All three smoothing constants are given the value 0.10. After entering these values and the data from Table 16.11 in Section 16.5, STORM uses the first eight quarters of data (from the first quarter of 1988 through the fourth quarter of 1989) to obtain the initial model whose parameters are given in Figure 16.28. This is Step 1. You can see that this initial model has determined that $L_8 = 97,510.29$ gallons, $B_8 = 1377.61$ gallons per quarter, and the four seasonality indices are $S_1 = 0.92813$ (rounded down to 0.9281 in the report), $S_2 = 0.9850$, $S_3 = 1.3080$, and $S_4 = 0.7792$. Note that in this and all other reports pertaining to trend-seasonal models, STORM refers to the expected deseasonalized demand, L_t, as the "Level" component.

According to Step 2(a), these values of L_8, B_8, and S_1 are then used to forecast the demand for gasoline in period $t = 9$—that is, in the first quarter of 1990—as follows:

$$F_9 = (L_8 + B_8) * S_1$$
$$= (97,510.29 + 1377.61) * 0.92813$$
$$= 91,781 \text{ gallons}$$

This forecast of $F_9 = 91,781$ gallons is then compared to the actual demand of $D_9 = 90,880$ gallons. STORM then uses the forecast error of $D_9 - F_9 = -901$ gallons and applies smoothing formulas (which are not included in this book) to estimate L_9 and to modify the estimates of B and S_1. These new values of $L_9 = 98,790.83$, $B_9 = 1367.9020$, and $S_1 = 0.927$ are shown in Figure 16.29 in the columns labeled "Level," "Trend," and "Seasonal" of the first row, labeled "PERIOD 9."

Forecasts and modifications for each subsequent quarter of available data through the fourth quarter of 1993 are given in the corresponding rows of Figure 16.29. From the last four rows in this figure, the model obtained from all the available data is the one in which $L_{24} = 1.1586E+05 = 115,860$ (the value in the column labeled "Level" in the last row) and $B_{24} = 1140.5640$ (the value in the column labeled "Trend" in the last row). From the last four rows in the report, $S_1 = 0.91997$ (rounded up to 0.920), $S_2 = 0.98364$ (rounded up to 0.984), $S_3 = 1.295$, and $S_4 = 0.77971$ (rounded up to 0.780).

According to Step 3, you should now evaluate the merits of this model using any of the measures described in Section 16.2. These measures, as computed by STORM for this problem, are reported in Figure 16.30. For example, you can see that this model provides a root-mean-square error of 2763.0770. Contrast this value to the RMSE of 6713.7150 for the seasonal model in Section 16.5.2. On the basis of this criterion and your subjective choices of 0.10 for all of the three smoothing constants, you should

```
The Seasonal Gasoline Model for Al's Gas 'n' Go
      INITIAL CONDITIONS FOR SERIES   1
                      Trend-Seas
      Component           Model
      Level           97510.2900
      Trend            1377.6100
      Seasonal  1         0.9281
      Seasonal  2         0.9850
      Seasonal  3         1.3080
      Seasonal  4         0.7792

 Above values are based on the first 8 periods of data
```

FIGURE 16.28 Initial Trend-Seasonal Model from STORM for the Problem of Al's Gas 'n' Go Station.

prefer using the trend-seasonal model over the seasonal one in Section 16.5.2. As always, you can use the computer to search for values of the smoothing constants that provide the smallest RMSE. The process of forecasting the future unknown demands for gasoline using this trend-seasonal model is described in Section 16.6.2.

```
               The Seasonal Gasoline Model for Al's Gas 'n' Go
                TREND-SEAS MODEL-FITTING STATISTICS FOR SERIES    1
           SMOOTHING CONSTANTS USED : 0.10(LEVEL), 0.10(TREND), 0.10(SEASONAL)
     Period          Actual   Forecast     Error      Level       Trend Seasonal
     PERIOD    9      90880      91781      -901  98790.8300   1367.9020    0.927
     PERIOD   10      96540      98660     -2120  99943.4800   1346.3780    0.983
     PERIOD   11     130460     132487     -2027  1.0113E+05   1330.8790    1.306
     PERIOD   12      80750      79846       904  1.0258E+05   1342.4850    0.780
     PERIOD   13      94260      96370     -2110  1.0370E+05   1319.7300    0.925
     PERIOD   14     104680     103245      1435  1.0516E+05   1334.3280    0.984
     PERIOD   15     134840     139106     -4266  1.0617E+05   1301.6700    1.303
     PERIOD   16      86960      83832      3128  1.0787E+05   1341.7730    0.783
     PERIOD   17      97240     101076     -3836  1.0880E+05   1300.3250    0.922
     PERIOD   18     108680     108378       302  1.1013E+05   1303.3890    0.985
     PERIOD   19     140550     145153     -4603  1.1108E+05   1268.0560    1.299
     PERIOD   20      85280      87930     -2650  1.1201E+05   1234.2010    0.781
     PERIOD   21     101560     104446     -2886  1.1293E+05   1202.9040    0.920
     PERIOD   22     111200     112378     -1178  1.1402E+05   1190.9430    0.984
     PERIOD   23     144770     149636     -4866  1.1483E+05   1153.4810    1.295
     PERIOD   24      89520      90528     -1008  1.1586E+05   1140.5640    0.780
```

FIGURE 16.29 Using Historical Data and Exponential Smoothing to Develop a Trend-Seasonal Model with STORM for the Problem of Al's Gas 'n' Go Station.

```
               The Seasonal Gasoline Model for Al's Gas 'n' Go
            MODEL-FITTING / VALIDATION-ERROR STATISTICS FOR SERIES    1
                              Trend-Seas
     Statistic                   Model
     Model-Fitting Error Statistics for 16 periods from PERIOD    9
     Mean Err          -1667.6250
     Mean % Err           -1.4058
     Mean Absolute Err  2388.7500
     Mean Abs % Err        2.2015
     Root Mean Sq Err   2763.0770
```

FIGURE 16.30 Performance Measures for the Final STORM Trend-Seasonal Model of Al's Gas 'n' Go Station.

16.6.2   Using a Trend-Seasonal Model for Forecasting

The final trend-seasonal model obtained in Section 16.6.1 for Al's Gas 'n' Go Station is now used to make forecasts for future unknown demands. For example, the forecast, F_{25}, for the next quarter (that is, the first quarter of 1994) is

$$F_{25} = (L_{24} + B_{24}) * S_1$$
$$= (115{,}860 + 1140.5640) * 0.91997$$
$$= 107{,}637 \text{ gallons}$$

You can determine a confidence interval around this forecast. Assume you want a 95% confidence interval. The associated z-value from the standard-normal table in Appendix B is 1.96. The value for the RMSE from Figure 16.30 is 2763.0770, so the associated confidence interval is

$$107{,}637 \pm (1.96 * 2763.077) = 107{,}637 \pm 5416$$

That is, with 95% confidence, you can believe that the actual sales of gasoline for the first quarter of 1994 will be within 5416 of the forecasted value of 107,637 gallons. Observe that this accuracy of 5416 is significantly better than the accuracy of 13,159 for the seasonal model developed in Section 16.5.

If you are planning for the entire year of 1993, the forecasts F_{26}, F_{27}, and F_{28} for the remaining three quarters are estimated as follows:

$$F_{26} = (L_{24} + B_{24} * 2) * S_2$$
$$= (115{,}860 + 1140.5640 * 2) * 0.98364$$
$$= 116{,}208 \text{ gallons}$$
$$F_{27} = (L_{24} + B_{24} * 3) * S_3$$
$$= (115{,}860 + 1140.5640 * 3) * 1.2950$$
$$= 154{,}470 \text{ gallons}$$
$$F_{28} = (L_{24} + B_{24} * 4) * S_4$$
$$= (115{,}860 + 1140.5640 * 4) * 0.77971$$
$$= 93{,}894 \text{ gallons}$$

As the actual demand for gasoline in each quarter of 1994 becomes known, you may want to revise your estimates of parameters L and B, and the seasonality indices S_1, S_2, S_3, and S_4 before forecasting demand in 1995 and beyond.

In this section, you have learned how the computer is used with historical data to develop and evaluate a trend-seasonal forecasting model. To build these models, you can use your knowledge of the business to select appropriate values of the smoothing constants. Another possible approach is to try several different sets of values for these smoothing constants and to select the one that provides the best model in terms of one of the performance measures described in Section 16.2. The computer is ideally suited for this trial-and-error approach.

The forecasting models in Sections 16.3 through 16.6 are based on a time series. In some problems, however, the demand depends not only on time, but also on other identifiable and measurable quantities that are easy to obtain and/or to forecast.

■ 16.7 FORECASTING USING CAUSAL FACTORS

In all the models discussed so far, forecasts for future demands are based on the assumption that the demand fluctuations follow a natural trend and/or seasonal behavior over time and will continue to do so in the future. Through the use of a time series, these forecasting methods attempt to model demand as a function of time. In many cases, however, demand depends not only on time but also on other measurable and predictable factors. For example, new housing sales depend on economic factors such as mortgage rates, unemployment statistics, and so on. Overseas car sales depend on foreign-exchange rates, prevailing interest rates in those countries, and so on. The need for medical supplies at a hospital depends on the occupancy rate. Gasoline tax revenues depend on the price of gasoline and indicators that reflect the general status of the economy, such as the unemployment rate, GDP, and so on. *Causal models* that capture the cause-and-effect relationship between demand and these nontime factors can provide more accurate forecasts.

Consider the problem faced by the management of Sun Resorts International. It has a resort located in Hawaii that specializes in conventions, but also has regular tourist business. Management wishes to obtain accurate quarterly revenue forecasts for determining budget and staffing needs. The Accounting Department has provided the quarterly revenue for the past 5 years, as shown in Table 16.12.

You might first consider using these data to build a time-series model. Using STORM to evaluate level, trend, seasonal, and trend-seasonal models and to search for the best possible smoothing constants results in the performance measures given in Table 16.13. For the root-mean-square error, the best model is a level one with an RMSE of 2.3786. Assume a confidence level of 95% and apply this model to predict next quarter's revenue. The resulting forecast is accurate only to within approximately $1.96 * RMSE$, which comes to $4.662 million. This error is quite large compared to the size of the revenues in Table 16.12, so you should consider building a better forecasting model.

Forecasting
SUN_1.DAT

TABLE 16.12	*Quarterly Revenue Data from 1989 through 1993 at Sun Resorts International*			
	REVENUE ($ MILLIONS)			
YEAR	QUARTER 1	QUARTER 2	QUARTER 3	QUARTER 4
1989	9.45	4.92	4.36	8.81
1990	10.63	9.09	5.65	9.65
1991	9.66	11.25	7.80	9.92
1992	9.00	3.83	4.80	3.70
1993	6.75	2.37	4.63	5.37

TABLE 16.13	*Performance Measures for Time-Series Models for the Problem of Sun Resorts International*			
	LEVEL MODEL	TREND MODEL	SEASONAL MODEL	TREND-SEASONAL MODEL
Best smoothing constants found				
α	0.50	0.60	0.70	0.70
β		0.20		0.10
γ			1.00	1.00
Model-fitting error statistics for 12 periods from Period 9				
Mean error	− 0.5078	− 0.4551	− 0.4891	−0.8612
Mean % error	−24.1890	−17.2674	−17.2547	−20.7971
MAE	1.9969	1.9386	2.2073	2.6180
MAPE	43.0220	41.0519	43.2812	48.4292
RMSE	2.3786	2.4848	2.5142	2.9164

16.7.1 *Building and Using a Causal Forecasting Model*

In developing a *causal* model, identify one or more predictable characteristics that influence the quarterly revenue. The Manager of Sun Resorts International believes that one of the most reliable factors in predicting the next quarter's total revenue is the *number of convention bookings made by the beginning of that quarter*. A larger number of bookings signals not only greater convention revenue, but also greater non-convention revenue. This is because larger convention bookings indicate an overall better economy, which generally leads to more vacation business. These convention bookings are made well in advance, so this information is available to forecast next quarter's sales.

As a first step, you will want to use regression analysis to develop a model that relates quarterly revenue to the convention bookings. The Accounting Department has provided you with the booking data at the beginning of each quarter from 1989 through 1993, shown in Table 16.14. The plot of quarterly revenue as a function of the number of bookings is shown in Figure 16.31 and indicates a linear relationship between these two values. This relationship is described by a straight line of the form

$$\text{Quarterly revenue} = A + B * (\text{number of bookings})$$

You can apply the regression formulas in Section 16.4 to estimate the values of the intercept A and the slope B that make the resulting straight line best fit the data in Table 16.14. STORM, for example, produces the estimate of $A = -0.298079$ and $B = 0.833907$, resulting in the following causal forecasting model:

Forecasting
SUN_2.DAT

$$\text{Quarterly revenue} = -0.298079 + 0.833907 * (\text{number of bookings})$$

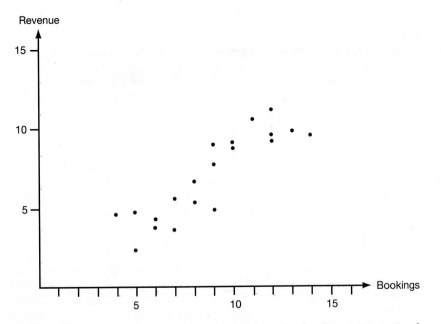

FIGURE 16.31 Quarterly Revenue vs. Number of Bookings for Sun Resorts International.

TABLE 16.14	Quarterly Revenue and Convention Booking Data from 1989 through 1993 at Sun Resorts International		
YEAR	QUARTER	REVENUE	NUMBER OF BOOKINGS
1989	1	9.45	12
1989	2	4.92	9
1989	3	4.36	6
1989	4	8.81	10
1990	1	10.63	11
1990	2	9.09	10
1990	3	5.65	7
1990	4	9.65	12
1991	1	9.66	14
1991	2	11.25	12
1991	3	7.80	9
1991	4	9.92	13
1992	1	9.00	9
1992	2	3.83	6
1992	3	4.80	5
1992	4	3.70	7
1993	1	6.75	8
1993	2	2.37	5
1993	3	4.63	4
1993	4	5.37	8

STORM also provides the "standard error of the estimate" for this regression model, which is analogous to the RMSE. This value of 1.300232 is a significant improvement over the RMSE value of 2.3786 for the best time-series model in Table 16.13.

How do you use this model to forecast the revenue in the next quarter? Assume that there are 10 convention bookings at the beginning of the first quarter of 1994. Then:

$$\text{Quarterly revenue} = -0.298079 + 0.833907 * (\text{number of bookings})$$

$$= -0.298079 + 0.833907 * 10$$

$$= \$8.04 \text{ million}$$

Management can now use this projected revenue of $8.04 million to make operational and strategic decisions. For example, management may allocate a certain percentage of these revenues as a budget for supplies, salaries, and other functional areas. If this forecasted revenue is expected to result in a significant surplus of dollars, management may consider undertaking an expansion or some other investment opportunity.

You can achieve further improvements to this causal forecasting model by identifying other factors that affect the quarterly revenues—for example, the expected long-range weather forecast, the amount of money spent on advertising in the past six months, and so on. You can use "time" as one of these variables if the revenues show some time-dependent behavior. These additional factors are considered in a **multiple-regression model.** Although this topic is beyond the scope of this book, STORM or other statistical software packages can be used to build and analyze multiple-regression models.

Multiple-regression model
A causal forecasting model in which more than one factor is used to predict future demand.

ADDITIONAL MANAGERIAL CONSIDERATIONS

In this chapter, you have learned several methods for forecasting future demands. The reliability of these forecasts depends on numerous factors which a manager should consider.

All forecasting methods discussed in this chapter are used to make predictions about the future on the basis of historical data. Implicit in these models, therefore, is the underlying assumption that the past behavior of the demand is a reliable predictor of the future demand. When might this assumption be invalid? Consider predicting prices in the stock market or the demand for products with short life-spans. In the first case, historical data do not necessarily reveal future behavior. In the second case, there are not enough historical data— if any at all—to be meaningful.

When the past behavior *can* be projected realistically into the future, the reliability of such forecasts depends on the following:

1. The correct choice of a forecasting model.
2. The availability of sufficient and accurate historical data to estimate the parameters of the model.
3. Validating the model before using it.
4. The specific way in which the final model is used for forecasting.
5. Monitoring and reestimating the parameters of the model.

Choice of a Forecasting Model

You should select the type of model on the basis of your knowledge of the underlying nature of the product and the result of evaluating different models through the use of appropriate performance measures.

All the models discussed in this chapter are based on the assumption of an underlying *linear* trend. In some cases, this assumption may not be valid because there is a *nonlinear* trend. For example, the demand for a product may show higher growth in earlier years with a gradual decrease in later years. Some computer packages allow you to forecast such behavior with an appropriate nonlinear model.

In addition to trend and seasonal components, some businesses exhibit *cyclical behavior* over the years. This behavior is due to general multiyear economic cycles, such as periods of high interest rates followed by periods of low interest rates, periods of high and then low inflation, and periods of high and then low unemployment. Forecasting methods and computer packages are available for incorporating these business cycles in the model.

Availability of Historical Data

All the models described in this chapter require that you use historical data to obtain estimates of parameters in the model. To get accurate estimates, you need sufficient and reliable data. The reliance on historical data makes these methods unusable or unreliable for new products, which have no significant demand history. For such cases, alternative methods—such as market surveys or qualitative techniques that rely on the experience of individuals—are more appropriate.

Model Validation

The choice of the model and its parameters—such as the smoothing constants in exponential smoothing—is generally based on how accurately the resulting model fits the historical data in terms of some performance measure. The *future* forecasts, however, may not be as accurate as those for historical data. Therefore, before relying heavily on future predictions, you should attempt to *validate* the model. That is, you would like to establish confidence in the model's accuracy when forecasting demands in *new* periods.

One way to gain confidence is to monitor the performance of the model for some number of future periods—but this means waiting for the actual demands to occur. An alternative approach is to use only a *portion* of the historical data in developing and testing different models and their parameters. The best model—selected on the basis of your choice of a performance measure—is then validated by comparing its forecasts with the actual demands *in the remaining unused portion of the data*. The closer the model's forecasts are to what the actual demand was, the more confident you can be in the model's ability to forecast future demands.

Short-Range Versus Long-Range Forecasts

Once you have selected an appropriate model and estimated its parameters, the model is used to make short-range or long-range forecasts. Short-range forecasts focus on operational issues. For example, what is the appropriate amount of raw materials to order for next month's production? Long-range forecasts center on strategic decisions. For example, will growth continue long enough into the future to warrant opening another manufacturing plant?

The methods discussed in this chapter generally work well for short-range forecasts because you often expect the historical behavior of the demand to continue into the *immediate* future. You should be careful, however, in using these methods for long-range forecasts that may lead to significant financial commitments. For such forecasts, causal models that incorporate various significant factors (including economic indicators, product cycles, and so on) or qualitative models that rely on market surveys or the judgment of "experts" may be more appropriate. As an analogy, yesterday's weather may provide a reasonable forecast of tomorrow's weather, but not for the weather a month from now.

Monitoring and Updating the Model

After developing and validating a model to establish confidence, you will use that model to make future short-range forecasts. You should monitor the performance of the model by continuously comparing the forecasts with what actually occurs. If you consider the forecast errors to be too large, you should rebuild the model by applying the techniques of this chapter using *all* available data. Resulting changes in the parameters may provide a new model that performs more accurately.

SUMMARY

In this chapter, you have learned about two classes of methods for forecasting future demands:

1. With *time-series models*, the assumption is that future demand will follow the same pattern of behavior over time as it has in the past, through a level, trend, seasonal, or trend-seasonal model.
2. With *causal models*, the assumption is that the future demand will depend in a linear way on one or more predictable and measurable factors.

Whichever method is chosen, the final forecast is obtained by a two-part process:

1. Building and testing various forecasting models using historical data to estimate parameters through moving averages, exponential smoothing, or regression analysis. Generally, you will select the model having the smallest value of a selected performance measure, such as the mean absolute error, the mean absolute percent error, or the root mean square error.
2. Using the best model from part 1 to make forecasts of unknown demands in future periods.

You will want to monitor the performance of the selected model and use the forecast errors in future periods to revise your estimates of the parameters or to create a new model altogether.

EXERCISES

For the scenarios in Exercises 16.1 to 16.8: (a) Use your general knowledge of the type of business to indicate whether you feel that a level, trend, seasonal, or trend-seasonal model is most appropriate for forecasting future demands. Give your reasons. (b) Plot the given historical demand data to verify that this graph supports your choice of models in part (a).

EXERCISE 16.1 (See the previous instructions.) Cable Com established its office in Maple Heights 3 years ago and has experienced steady growth in the number of households subscribing to its Cable TV service. The Manager needs to forecast the future number of subscribers to determine when to increase the number of repair persons and other staff members. The company has the following records on the number of subscribers in each of the past 12 months.

JAN.	FEB.	MAR.	APR.	MAY	JUN.	JUL.	AUG.	SEP.	OCT.	NOV.	DEC.
1704	1712	1752	1764	1805	1835	1831	1866	1884	1930	1919	1951

EXERCISE 16.2 (See the instructions preceding Exercise 16.1.) Jolly Donuts has been in business for 10 years. The Manager needs to forecast weekly sales of donuts to determine how much flour, sugar, oil, and other ingredients to purchase. The company has the following records on the number of dozens of donuts sold in each of the previous 16 weeks:

WEEK	0	1	2	3	4	5	6	7	8	9	10	11	12	13	14	15
SALES	386	379	408	405	403	395	399	418	381	389	410	393	378	399	390	408

EXERCISE 16.3 (See the instructions preceding Exercise 16.1.) RV World has been selling recreational vehicles of various kinds in a stable, well-to-do suburb of Chicago for the past 10 years. The Manager needs to forecast quarterly demands to place orders for their best-selling deluxe van. The number of these deluxe vans sold in each quarter of the past 4 years is

YEAR	JAN.-MAR.	APR.-JUN.	JUL.-SEP.	OCT.-DEC.
1990	21	39	35	21
1991	23	38	31	23
1992	25	34	38	20
1993	24	43	40	20

EXERCISE 16.4 (See the instructions preceding Exercise 16.1). The Nature Company in Bangor, Maine, orders a 4-month supply of wild birdseed in January, May, and September of each year for resale to local residents. Company records show the following history in terms of the number of pounds of wild birdseed sold to its customers in each of the past 4 years:

YEAR	JAN.-APR.	MAY-AUG.	SEP.-DEC.
1990	4010	2670	3070
1991	4010	2680	3330
1992	4040	2570	3210
1993	3880	2690	3360

EXERCISE 16.5 (See the instructions preceding Exercise 16.1.) South Florida Power provides electricity to customers in a part of southern Florida where retirement communities have been growing steadily over the past 10 years. Management needs to forecast quarterly demand for electricity (in terms of the number of kilowatt-hours) to plan for peak loads, ordering supplies of fuel for the generators, and so on. The company files show the following record of the number of kilowatt-hours used in each quarter of the past 4 years:

YEAR	JAN.-MAR.	APR.-JUN.	JUL.-SEP.	OCT.-DEC.
1990	5,290	7,733	11,246	7,470
1991	6,011	8,780	12,606	8,369
1992	6,743	9,699	14,077	9,215
1993	7,353	10,638	15,320	10,109

EXERCISE 16.6 (See the instructions preceding Exercise 16.1.) The Surgeon General's office has continually increased its advertising campaign over the years to warn the public about the dangers of tobacco. To help estimate medical expenditures on lung cancer and tobacco-related diseases, the Surgeon General wants to predict the number of tobacco users in the United States on an annual basis. The Surgeon General estimates that each tobacco user pays an average of about $125 per year in tobacco sales tax. Note the following record of the tobacco sales-tax revenues (in $ millions) for the past 10 years:

YEAR	1984	1985	1986	1987	1988	1989	1990	1991	1992	1993
TAXES	4630	4630	4412	4092	3943	3534	3509	3141	3097	3030

EXERCISE 16.7 (See the instructions preceding Exercise 16.1.) United Dairy Wholesalers supplies local area stores with many dairy products, including milk, on a daily basis. Management needs to determine how many gallons of milk to order from its supplier, Fresh Dairy Farms, each week. The company has sold the following number of gallons in each of the past 10 weeks:

WEEK	0	1	2	3	4	5	6	7	8	9
GALLONS	15074	14554	14046	15364	16344	15500	15938	14177	16094	17037

EXERCISE 16.8 (See the instructions preceding Exercise 16.1.) Due primarily to the generosity of the public over the past 10 years, National Public TV has gradually expanded its operations. At the beginning of each year, the Manager needs to forecast the amount of money that the organization can expect to raise in tax-deductible donations from the public during each of two annual fund drives, one in June and one in December. She will use these forecasts to prepare budgets for salaries, to develop new TV programs, and so on. The results of the fund drives (in $ thousands) for each of the previous 6 years follows:

	1988	1989	1990	1991	1992	1993
June	738	862	893	994	1114	1503
December	1245	1645	1646	1957	2108	2407

EXERCISE 16.9 Suppose you believe that a level model is appropriate for the problem of United Dairy Wholesalers in Exercise 16.7. Assuming a parameter of $A = 16,125$ gallons of milk per week, forecast the demand for milk in each of the next 2 weeks.

EXERCISE 16.10 Suppose you believe that a trend model is appropriate for the problem of Cable Com in Exercise 16.1. Using $t = 0$ for the first period of data, assume that management estimated parameters of $A = 1650$ subscribers and $B = 30$ subscribers per month. Forecast the number of subscribers in each of the next 3 months.

EXERCISE 16.11 Consider a seasonal model appropriate for the problem of RV World in Exercise 16.3. Using $t = 0$ for the first period of data, assume that management estimated a parameter of $A = 30$ deluxe vans per quarter and seasonality indices of 0.8 for January through March, 1.3 for April through June, 1.2 for July through September, and 0.7 for October through December. Forecast the expected revenue in each of the next four quarters, given that each deluxe van sells for $35,000.

EXERCISE 16.12 Research indicates that a trend-seasonal model is appropriate for the problem of South Florida Power in Exercise 16.5. Using $t = 0$ for the first period of data, assume parameters of $A = 7500$ kilowatt-hours and $B = 250$ kilowatt-hours per quarter, and seasonality indices of 0.7 for January through March, 1.0 for April through June, 1.4 for July through September, and 0.9 for October through December. Forecast the expected number of kilowatt-hours of demand for electricity in each of the next four quarters.

EXERCISE 16.13 For the problem of Cable Com in Exercise 16.1, suppose your model, when applied to the available historical data, results in the following forecasts:

JAN.	FEB.	MAR.	APR.	MAY	JUN.	JUL.	AUG.	SEP.	OCT.	NOV.	DEC.
1702	1725	1749	1772	1795	1818	1841	1864	1887	1910	1933	1956

    a. Compute and interpret the MAE performance measure.
    b. Compute and interpret the MAPE performance measure.
    c. Compute and interpret the RMSE performance measure.
    d. Find a 98% confidence interval for the December forecast. Is the *actual* number of subscribers within this interval?

EXERCISE 16.14 For the problem of Jolly Donuts, suppose the forecast from a level model is 400 dozen donuts for each of the same 10 weeks as in Exercise 16.2.

    a. Compute and interpret the MAE performance measure.
    b. Compute and interpret the MAPE performance measure.
    c. Compute and interpret the RMSE performance measure.
    d. Find a 98% confidence interval for the final forecast. Is the *actual* sale of donuts within this interval?

EXERCISE 16.15 Develop a level model for the problem of United Dairy Wholesalers in Exercise 16.7 using the method of moving averages with $k = 4$. Compute the RMSE when this method is applied to all historical data.

EXERCISE 16.16 Repeat Exercise 16.15 for $k = 5$.

EXERCISE 16.17 Develop a level model for the problem of United Dairy Wholesalers in Exercise 16.7 using exponential smoothing with $\alpha = 0.10$. Use the historical sales in the first week as the initial forecast. What is the RMSE for this model?

EXERCISE 16.18 Use exponential smoothing and your computer to develop the best level model you can for the problem of United Dairy Wholesalers in Exercise 16.7. That is, find the value of α that results in the smallest value of the RMSE.

EXERCISE 16.19   Develop a trend model for the problem of Cable Com in Exercise 16.1. Use $\alpha = 0.10$, $\beta = 0.10$, and the first 4 months of data for the initial regression.

EXERCISE 16.20   Consider building a trend model for the problem of Cable Com in Exercise 16.1 using exponential smoothing in which the value of β is fixed to 0.10. Use your computer to find the value of α that results in the smallest value of the RMSE.

EXERCISE 16.21   Use your computer package to develop the best seasonal model you can for the problem of RV World in Exercise 16.3. Use trial and error, if necessary, to find the values of the smoothing constants that result in the smallest value of the RMSE based on all historical data. What is the final value of the RMSE you obtain?

EXERCISE 16.22   Use your computer package to develop the best trend-seasonal model you can for the problem of South Florida Power in Exercise 16.5. Use trial and error, if necessary, to find the values of the smoothing constants that result in the smallest value of the RMSE based on all the historical data. What is the final value of the RMSE you obtain?

EXERCISE 16.23   Use the level model you obtained in Exercise 16.18 to do the following:

    a. Forecast demand for each of the next 4 weeks.
    b. Find a 90% confidence interval for the forecast of the fourth week in part (a).

EXERCISE 16.24   Use the trend model you obtained in Exercise 16.20 to do the following:

    a. Forecast demand for each of the next 4 months.
    b. Find a 90% confidence interval for the forecast of the fourth month in part (a).

EXERCISE 16.25   Use the seasonal model you obtained in Exercise 16.21 to do the following:

    a. Forecast demand for each of the next four quarters.
    b. Find a 90% confidence interval for the forecast of the fourth quarter in part (a).

EXERCISE 16.26   Use the trend-seasonal model you obtained in Exercise 16.22 to do the following:

    a. Forecast demand for each of the next four quarters.
    b. Find a 90% confidence interval for the forecast of the fourth quarter in part (a).

EXERCISE 16.27   For the problem of Jolly Donuts in Exercise 16.2, use your computer together with all of the historical data to develop the best level and trend models you can with the method of exponential smoothing. Which of these two models would you select to use for future forecasts? Explain.

EXERCISE 16.28   For the problem of the Surgeon General in Exercise 16.6, use your computer together with all of the historical data to develop the best level and trend models you can with the method of exponential smoothing. Which of these two models would you select to use for future forecasts? Explain.

EXERCISE 16.29   For the problem of the Nature Company in Exercise 16.4, use your computer together with all of the historical data to develop the best level, trend, seasonal, and trend-seasonal models you can with the method of exponential smoothing. (Use three seasons in the seasonal models.) Which of these four models would you select to use for future forecasts? Explain.

EXERCISE 16.30   For the problem of National Public TV in Exercise 16.8, use your computer together with all of the historical data to develop the best level, trend, seasonal, and trend-seasonal models you can with the method of exponential smoothing. (Use two seasons in the seasonal models.) Which of these four models would you select to use for future forecasts? Explain.

EXERCISE 16.31   The city of Maple Heights needs to forecast their quarterly tax revenues to plan the city's operating budgets. The city's accountant feels that there is a strong linear correlation between the unemployment rate and tax revenues. To test his hypothesis, he has collected the following data for the past 12 quarters:

TAX REVENUE ($ MILLIONS)	UNEMPLOYMENT RATE (%)
14.5	8.5
15.2	8.0
15.0	7.5
12.0	7.0
10.5	7.0
10.8	7.5
8.5	8.5
9.0	9.0
10.1	8.5
10.3	8.5
10.8	8.0
11.2	7.0

a. Use your computer or otherwise develop a causal model to forecast the quarterly tax revenue as a function of the unemployment rate.

b. From your model in part (a), what tax revenue can the city expect next quarter if the unemployment rate is projected to be 7.5%?

EXERCISE 16.32   The management of Fresh Food Farms needs to forecast the yield of winter wheat to develop strategic plans for sales and marketing. The Manager of their farm in Kansas knows that the yield depends heavily on the amount of rainfall during the previous summer. To establish this relationship, the following historical data for the past 10 years have been collected:

YEAR	YIELD (THOUSAND BUSHELS)	RAINFALL (INCHES)
1984	110	6.5
1985	120	7.2
1986	105	7.5
1987	115	9.0
1988	125	8.3
1989	75	2.2
1990	95	5.0
1991	110	6.6
1992	110	7.5
1993	120	8.1

a. Use your computer or otherwise develop a causal model to forecast the yield of winter wheat as a function of the rainfall.

b. From your model in part (a), how many bushels of wheat can Fresh Food Farms expect next winter if the rainfall during the previous summer was 7.0 inches?

CRITICAL-THINKING PROJECT L
THE FORECASTING PROBLEM OF AMERICAN AUTO PARTS

The management of American Auto Parts is having a meeting to plan the operating budgets for next year. The Senior Vice-President of Sales, Mr. Tom Tremellon, knows that a large portion of the company's income is derived from sales of their 1-year, 3-year, and lifetime batteries. He has asked you, Manager of Production, to prepare an estimate of the revenues the company can expect in each of the four quarters of next year from 1-year, 3-year, and lifetime batteries, as well as the total revenue from all these batteries.

To prepare your forecast, you have contacted Mr. Beasley in the Accounting Department, who has provided you with the following sales figures (in $ thousands) in each quarter of the previous 4 years:

YEAR	QUARTER	TOTAL	1-YEAR	3-YEAR	LIFETIME
1990	1	1050	205	325	520
	2	600	123	180	297
	3	575	150	155	270
	4	982	190	285	507
1991	1	1010	206	310	494
	2	652	115	190	347
	3	537	150	160	227
	4	990	210	300	480
1992	1	998	200	300	498
	2	650	138	205	307
	3	550	101	150	299
	4	932	175	275	482
1993	1	1070	200	315	555
	2	632	125	191	316
	3	525	110	160	255
	4	980	200	288	492

Use these data and your computer to prepare a managerial report along these guidelines:

1. Use exponential smoothing to develop the best (level, trend, seasonal, or trend-seasonal) model you can for forecasting the quarterly revenue from 1-year batteries. Do the same for 3-year and lifetime batteries, and also for the total revenue. Use the RMSE performance measure for selecting the best model in each case.
2. Use the four models you obtained in guideline 1 to forecast revenues from each individual type of battery and for the total revenue in each quarter of 1994. Create 98% confidence intervals for each forecast.

When you showed these results to Mr. Tremellon, he pointed out that the sum of the forecasts for sales from the three batteries is *not* equal to the forecast of the total revenue. To achieve consistency in these forecasts, your staff proposed the following approaches.

    a. Use the best models you obtained in guideline 1 for forecasting the revenues from each of the three types of batteries. Then, forecast the total revenue as the sum of these three forecasts. With this method, what forecast would you obtain for the total revenue in each of the eight quarters from 1992 through 1993? Compare these forecasts to the actual total revenues, and compute the resulting RMSE measure.

    b. Ms. Inez Sanchez from your staff noted that, on the basis of the historical data, the average percentage of total revenue contributed by 1-year batteries is about 20%, that from 3-year batteries averages 30%, and that from lifetime batteries is 50%. Ms. Sanchez proposed forecasting the *total* revenue according to the best model in guideline 1, and then forecasting the individual battery sales by multiplying the forecast of the total revenue by the percentage contributed by that type of battery. With this method, what forecast would you obtain for the revenue from each of the three individual types of batteries in each of the eight quarters from 1992 through 1993? Compare these forecasts to the actual revenues, and compute the resulting RMSE measure for each type of battery.

    c. Compare the two approaches in parts (a) and (b) by preparing a summary table of the RMSE measures for forecasting the revenues from the three types of batteries and the total revenue. Discuss the advantages and disadvantages of each method.

GOING UP? GOING DOWN?

This news report looks at the trend in house prices—falling. But is this a short-term trend or the beginning of a long-term trend? Experts disagree on what the duration of the trend will be, but they all concur that selling a house is much more difficult now than in the recent past. This is true not only in California, but also in New York and the New England states, where a ten-year economic boom has disappeared and also in the energy belt—Texas, Oklahoma, and Colorado.

Some observers believe that the downward trend in house prices is a sign of an overall slowing economy. Others see the trend stemming from the market's regrouping after huge increases, at least in California. Two Harvard University economists go so far as to challenge the long-held belief that housing prices will recover at all. They are predicting a drop in inflation-adjusted prices of 47% from 1987 to 2007! One factor causing the reduction in price is the end of the Baby Boom. Less demand means lower prices. Their report shows that the annual rate of increase in demand for houses was 1.85% from 1940 to 1950, 1.66% from 1970 to 1980, 1.33% from 1980 to 1990, and, they predict, a mere 0.62% from 1990 to 2010.

David Gribin, President of the National Association of Realtors, disagrees. He contends that the study does not take into account the demand by more single people and by more unmarried people living together. Moreover, people are living longer, which also expands demand. Gribin sees increased housing demand continuing indefinitely.

David Seiders, of the National Association of Home Builders, says the number of households is growing but at a slow rate. He disagrees about house prices falling over the long term and expects to find pockets of rising demand.

So how do you predict house prices for the next year? for the next twenty years? Which eco-nomic indicators are independent variables, and which have nothing to do with house prices? Who is right and who is wrong? Perhaps the old adage is true: "Forecasting is difficult, especially in regards to the future!" (Total running time: 6:03)

Questions on the Video

1. According to the banker in this video, why can't the housing boom in prices continue to rocket upward?

2. What factors in the California housing market offer hope for continued increasing prices?

Beyond the Video

1. What factors would you want to include in forecasting housing prices for the next few years? How could you know that they are independent variables?

2. What if the current gross national product is a good predictor of housing prices. Why isn't it an independent (causal) variable?

Practical Considerations

1. What are the advantages and disadvantages of using exponential smoothing with time series data as a forecasting device for housing prices?

2. What are the advantages and disadvantages of using regression analysis as a forecasting device for housing prices? What are some possible independent (casual) variables?

Source: ABC News, "Business World," November 12, 1989

UNIFORM 0–1 RANDOM NUMBERS

. . . .

ROW	COLUMN 1	COLUMN 2	COLUMN 3	COLUMN 4	COLUMN 5
1	0.710621	0.689315	0.122662	0.151792	0.245387
2	0.995255	0.577849	0.980588	0.894206	0.332668
3	0.355729	0.937265	0.520743	0.449925	0.524444
4	0.540955	0.802009	0.287153	0.639474	0.535043
5	0.775780	0.869542	0.529965	0.886293	0.966121
6	0.770145	0.556772	0.028899	0.076490	0.481478
7	0.343473	0.734783	0.845545	0.656500	0.589383
8	0.157032	0.029818	0.863518	0.604055	0.935888
9	0.212234	0.642681	0.961934	0.918677	0.422801
10	0.653071	0.407682	0.881552	0.858275	0.570146
11	0.977652	0.487892	0.013273	0.260349	0.795282
12	0.975838	0.843771	0.466162	0.562409	0.088356
13	0.965437	0.714330	0.376533	0.958318	0.120434
14	0.713048	0.024331	0.602066	0.027124	0.871373
15	0.133274	0.920458	0.851877	0.069328	0.557392
16	0.703888	0.856269	0.201616	0.091010	0.990284
17	0.926374	0.090610	0.519490	0.988134	0.516041
18	0.629143	0.358251	0.887227	0.536066	0.876335
19	0.181700	0.427751	0.836395	0.732682	0.194614
20	0.291777	0.790803	0.892606	0.361285	0.134913
21	0.796802	0.612066	0.207541	0.867992	0.643772
22	0.111042	0.021402	0.025139	0.218308	0.166139
23	0.617587	0.956544	0.930096	0.686074	0.906655
24	0.537686	0.877935	0.346850	0.155703	0.828657
25	0.922245	0.082725	0.240781	0.107211	0.074571
26	0.521208	0.129917	0.983885	0.425556	0.670349
27	0.266486	0.831130	0.411308	0.924871	0.372697
28	0.969831	0.160541	0.780415	0.081479	0.978355
29	0.751207	0.282401	0.731524	0.707410	0.954090
30	0.098975	0.186970	0.944184	0.658111	0.281406
31	0.161860	0.806918	0.467050	0.690936	0.868426
32	0.036671	0.034758	0.865670	0.495294	0.673941
33	0.726528	0.742987	0.943660	0.239953	0.414932
34	0.903186	0.225020	0.222686	0.267985	0.807680
35	0.350716	0.933751	0.985739	0.874297	0.666797
36	0.115327	0.615675	0.549845	0.023784	0.108900
37	0.486450	0.264246	0.488591	0.248616	0.055821
38	0.970500	0.114470	0.337354	0.509939	0.469512
39	0.744811	0.061828	0.048431	0.273799	0.627639
40	0.817456	0.728662	0.857226	0.040613	0.838763

ROW	COLUMN 1	COLUMN 2	COLUMN 3	COLUMN 4	COLUMN 5
41	0.483300	0.637125	0.080400	0.437212	0.794956
42	0.897614	0.318327	0.715434	0.747114	0.842927
43	0.078201	0.697404	0.621731	0.968783	0.929130
44	0.788700	0.192556	0.669860	0.378314	0.597476
45	0.174524	0.367794	0.182073	0.893222	0.324380
46	0.285591	0.986351	0.436527	0.079341	0.769183
47	0.797000	0.900241	0.199731	0.180857	0.030699
48	0.789047	0.908515	0.462808	0.822485	0.818121
49	0.832943	0.217610	0.725040	0.912463	0.294987
50	0.377017	0.755755	0.816209	0.949419	0.914049
51	0.804105	0.292134	0.777885	0.271430	0.041762
52	0.583059	0.834394	0.739542	0.518513	0.005909
53	0.989099	0.855518	0.110949	0.591993	0.009983
54	0.860591	0.972363	0.443269	0.730795	0.552113
55	0.032945	0.037347	0.720441	0.698265	0.793371
56	0.882390	0.392908	0.910643	0.150460	0.741321
57	0.879197	0.682809	0.086015	0.073432	0.223084
58	0.941482	0.007292	0.210738	0.170874	0.791108
59	0.189683	0.465246	0.269013	0.270372	0.847177
60	0.209596	0.497169	0.026775	0.119091	0.412597
61	0.787108	0.162112	0.303749	0.208099	0.955852
62	0.530295	0.374119	0.704453	0.491346	0.100280
63	0.575767	0.623656	0.568668	0.348405	0.772226
64	0.523853	0.123505	0.622577	0.502817	0.214387
65	0.363422	0.945588	0.641177	0.647198	0.765005
66	0.187833	0.733598	0.512342	0.663414	0.263076
67	0.508270	0.885455	0.419297	0.250179	0.165553
68	0.255540	0.705141	0.569610	0.884206	0.256231
69	0.184977	0.384714	0.740921	0.047487	0.197686
70	0.135095	0.141069	0.413815	0.505367	0.934344
71	0.925998	0.984827	0.601362	0.146015	0.904327
72	0.901653	0.545815	0.428570	0.042546	0.779311
73	0.825154	0.202509	0.820247	0.235114	0.676303
74	0.191053	0.121735	0.380181	0.541718	0.645131
75	0.382784	0.709690	0.117210	0.444473	0.152389
76	0.588595	0.582226	0.468163	0.558871	0.139352
77	0.762018	0.782028	0.498796	0.116102	0.533921
78	0.302761	0.065208	0.781183	0.500876	0.974500
79	0.595805	0.092959	0.964891	0.566075	0.873448
80	0.862287	0.688504	0.205448	0.204097	0.542091

B

STATISTICAL TABLES

....

B.1 THE STANDARD-NORMAL DISTRIBUTION

Entries in the table give the area under the standard-normal curve between 0 and the given z-value. For example, for $z = 1.25$, the area under the curve between 0 and $z = 1.25$ is 0.3944.

z	0.00	0.01	0.02	0.03	0.04	0.05	0.06	0.07	0.08	0.09
0.0	0.0000	0.0040	0.0080	0.0120	0.0160	0.0199	0.0239	0.0279	0.0319	0.0359
0.1	0.0398	0.0438	0.0478	0.0517	0.0557	0.0596	0.0636	0.0675	0.0714	0.0753
0.2	0.0793	0.0832	0.0871	0.0910	0.0948	0.0987	0.1026	0.1064	0.1103	0.1141
0.3	0.1179	0.1217	0.1255	0.1293	0.1331	0.1368	0.1406	0.1443	0.1480	0.1517
0.4	0.1554	0.1591	0.1628	0.1664	0.1700	0.1736	0.1772	0.1808	0.1844	0.1879
0.5	0.1915	0.1950	0.1985	0.2019	0.2054	0.2088	0.2123	0.2157	0.2190	0.2224
0.6	0.2257	0.2291	0.2324	0.2357	0.2389	0.2422	0.2454	0.2486	0.2518	0.2549
0.7	0.2580	0.2612	0.2642	0.2673	0.2704	0.2734	0.2764	0.2794	0.2823	0.2852
0.8	0.2881	0.2910	0.2939	0.2967	0.2995	0.3023	0.3051	0.3078	0.3106	0.3133
0.9	0.3159	0.3186	0.3212	0.3238	0.3264	0.3289	0.3315	0.3340	0.3365	0.3389
1.0	0.3413	0.3438	0.3461	0.3485	0.3508	0.3531	0.3554	0.3577	0.3599	0.3621
1.1	0.3643	0.3665	0.3686	0.3708	0.3729	0.3749	0.3770	0.3790	0.3810	0.3830
1.2	0.3849	0.3869	0.3888	0.3907	0.3925	0.3944	0.3962	0.3980	0.3997	0.4015
1.3	0.4032	0.4049	0.4066	0.4082	0.4099	0.4115	0.4131	0.4147	0.4162	0.4177
1.4	0.4192	0.4207	0.4222	0.4236	0.4251	0.4265	0.4279	0.4292	0.4306	0.4319
1.5	0.4332	0.4345	0.4357	0.4370	0.4382	0.4394	0.4406	0.4418	0.4429	0.4441
1.6	0.4452	0.4463	0.4474	0.4484	0.4495	0.4505	0.4515	0.4525	0.4535	0.4545
1.7	0.4554	0.4564	0.4573	0.4582	0.4591	0.4599	0.4608	0.4616	0.4625	0.4633
1.8	0.4641	0.4649	0.4656	0.4664	0.4671	0.4678	0.4686	0.4693	0.4699	0.4706
1.9	0.4713	0.4719	0.4726	0.4732	0.4738	0.4744	0.4750	0.4756	0.4761	0.4767
2.0	0.4772	0.4778	0.4783	0.4788	0.4793	0.4798	0.4803	0.4808	0.4812	0.4817
2.1	0.4821	0.4826	0.4830	0.4834	0.4838	0.4842	0.4846	0.4850	0.4854	0.4857
2.2	0.4861	0.4864	0.4868	0.4871	0.4875	0.4878	0.4881	0.4884	0.4887	0.4890
2.3	0.4893	0.4896	0.4898	0.4901	0.4904	0.4906	0.4909	0.4911	0.4913	0.4916
2.4	0.4918	0.4920	0.4922	0.4925	0.4927	0.4929	0.4931	0.4932	0.4934	0.4936
2.5	0.4938	0.4940	0.4941	0.4943	0.4945	0.4946	0.4948	0.4949	0.4951	0.4952
2.6	0.4953	0.4955	0.4956	0.4957	0.4959	0.4960	0.4961	0.4962	0.4963	0.4964
2.7	0.4965	0.4966	0.4967	0.4968	0.4969	0.4970	0.4971	0.4972	0.4973	0.4974
2.8	0.4974	0.4975	0.4976	0.4977	0.4977	0.4978	0.4979	0.4979	0.4980	0.4981
2.9	0.4981	0.4982	0.4982	0.4983	0.4984	0.4984	0.4985	0.4985	0.4986	0.4986
3.0	0.4986	0.4987	0.4987	0.4988	0.4988	0.4989	0.4989	0.4989	0.4990	0.4990

B.2 THE *t*-DISTRIBUTION

Entries in the table give t values for an area or probability in the upper tail of the t-distribution. For example, with 10 degrees of freedom and a 0.05 area in the upper tail, $t = 1.812$.

DEGREES	AREA IN UPPER TAIL				
OF FREEDOM	0.10	0.05	0.025	0.01	0.005
1	3.078	6.314	12.706	31.821	63.657
2	1.886	2.920	4.303	6.965	9.925
3	1.638	2.353	3.182	4.541	5.841
4	1.533	2.132	2.776	3.747	4.604
5	1.476	2.015	2.571	3.365	4.032
6	1.440	1.943	2.447	3.143	3.707
7	1.415	1.895	2.365	2.998	3.499
8	1.397	1.860	2.306	2.896	3.355
9	1.383	1.833	2.262	2.821	3.250
10	1.372	1.812	2.228	2.764	3.169
11	1.363	1.796	2.201	2.718	3.106
12	1.356	1.782	2.179	2.681	3.055
13	1.350	1.771	2.160	2.650	3.012
14	1.345	1.761	2.145	2.624	2.977
15	1.341	1.753	2.131	2.602	2.947
16	1.337	1.746	2.120	2.583	2.921
17	1.333	1.740	2.110	2.567	2.898
18	1.330	1.734	2.101	2.552	2.878
19	1.328	1.729	2.093	2.539	2.861
20	1.325	1.725	2.086	2.528	2.845
21	1.323	1.721	2.080	2.518	2.831
22	1.321	1.717	2.074	2.508	2.819
23	1.319	1.714	2.069	2.500	2.807
24	1.318	1.711	2.064	2.492	2.797
25	1.316	1.708	2.060	2.485	2.787
26	1.315	1.706	2.056	2.479	2.779
27	1.314	1.703	2.052	2.473	2.771
28	1.313	1.701	2.048	2.467	2.763
29	1.311	1.699	2.045	2.462	2.756
30	1.310	1.697	2.042	2.457	2.750
40	1.303	1.684	2.021	2.423	2.704
60	1.296	1.671	2.000	2.390	2.660
120	1.289	1.658	1.980	2.358	2.617
∞	1.282	1.645	1.960	2.326	2.576

ANSWERS TO SELECTED EXERCISES

CHAPTER 2

2.1 Let x_{OT} = the number of pounds of oranges to ship from Orlando to Tampa,
  x_{OM} = the number of pounds of oranges to ship from Orlando to Miami,
  x_{OJ} = the number of pounds of oranges to ship from Orlando to Jacksonville,
  x_{GT} = the number of pounds of oranges to ship from Gainesville to Tampa,
  x_{GM} = the number of pounds of oranges to ship from Gainesville to Miami,
  x_{GJ} = the number of pounds of oranges to ship from Gainesville to Jacksonville.

2.3 1. Two supply constraints.
  2. Three demand constraints.
  3. One logical constraint (nonnegativity) for each variable.

2.5 Max $0.25x_{OT} + 0.3375x_{OM} + 0.27x_{OJ} + 0.245x_{GT} + 0.33x_{GM} + 0.2775x_{GJ}$

2.7 Min $25L + 22H$
  s.t. $0.45L + 0.35H \geq 1{,}260{,}000$ (Gasoline)
  $0.18L + 0.36H \geq 900{,}000$ (Jet fuel)
  $0.30L + 0.20H \geq 300{,}000$ (Kerosene)
  $L , H \geq 0$

2.9 Max $6{,}740C + 5{,}100S$
  s.t. $200C + 150S \leq 80{,}000$ (Material constraint)
  $18C + 20S \leq 9{,}000$ (Labor constraint)
  $C \leq 1{,}500$ (Maximum number of compacts)
  $S \leq 200$ (Maximum number of subcompacts)
  $C , S \geq 0$ and integer.

2.11 Min $2.15M + 2.25C + 1.25A$
  s.t. $40M + 30C + 10A \geq 80$ (Protein)
  $5M + 50C + 30A \geq 60$ (Vitamin A)
  $20M + 30C + 40A \geq 50$ (Vitamin B)
  $30M + 50C + 60A \geq 30$ (Vitamin C)
  $M \geq 0.5$ (Min. milk)
  $C \geq 0.5$ (Min. cheese)
  $A \geq 0.5$ (Min. apples)
  $M , C , A \geq 0$

2.13 Let x_1 = number of type 1 trucks to buy,
  x_2 = number of type 2 trucks to buy,
  x_3 = number of type 3 trucks to buy.

  Min $800x_1 + 650x_2 + 500x_3$
  s.t. $50{,}000x_1 + 40{,}000x_2 + 25{,}000x_3 \leq 500{,}000$ (Budget)
  $120{,}000x_1 + 75{,}000x_2 + 60{,}000x_3 \geq 800{,}000$ (Demand)
  $x_1 + x_2 + x_3 \leq 10$ (Fleet size)
  $x_3 \geq 3$ (At least three type 3)
  $x_1 - x_2 - x_3 \leq 0$ (Ratio)
  $x_1 , x_2 , x_3 \geq 0$ and integer

2.15

Frequency	100.0	100.1	100.3	100.7	101.0	101.1	101.4	101.8
Variable	x_1	x_2	x_3	x_4	x_5	x_6	x_7	x_8

  Max $x_1 + x_2 + x_3 + x_4 + x_5 + x_6 + x_7 + x_8$
  s.t. $x_1 + x_2 + x_3 \leq 1$
  $x_3 + x_4 \leq 1$
  $x_4 + x_5 + x_6 \leq 1$
  $x_5 + x_6 + x_7 \leq 1$
  $x_6 + x_7 \leq 1$
  $x_7 + x_8 \leq 1$
  $0 \leq x_i \leq 1$ and integer, $i = 1, 2, \ldots, 8$.

2.17 Let R_1 = number of runs in Division 1,
R_2 = number of runs in Division 2,
R_3 = number of runs in Division 3,
A = number of Component A,
B = number of Component B,
C = number of completed units.

Max $\quad C$
s.t.

$$8R_1 + 5R_2 + 3R_3 \quad\quad \le 100 \quad \text{(Raw material 1)}$$
$$6R_1 + 9R_2 + 8R_3 \quad\quad \le 200 \quad \text{(Raw material 2)}$$
$$7R_1 + 6R_2 + 8R_3 - A = \quad 0 \quad \text{(Component A)}$$
$$5R_1 + 9R_2 + 4R_3 \quad\;\; - B = \quad 0 \quad \text{(Component B)}$$
$$C - \frac{1}{4}A \quad\quad\quad \le \quad 0$$
$$C - \frac{1}{3}B \quad\quad\quad \le \quad 0$$
$$R_1, R_2, R_3, A, B, C \ge 0 \quad \text{and integer}$$

2.19 Max $\quad 3.5S + 0.0001S^2 + 4.5Q + 0.0002Q^2 + 6.0P + 0.0003P^2$
s.t.

$$S + Q + P \le 25{,}000$$
$$10{,}000 \le S \le 18{,}000$$
$$6{,}000 \le Q \le 10{,}000$$
$$2{,}500 \le P \le 5{,}000$$

2.21 Min $\quad 6\pi RH + 7.64\pi R^2$
s.t.

$$\pi R^2 H \ge 10$$
$$R, \quad\quad H \ge 0$$

2.23 Min $\quad (9.4a + b - 280)^2 + (10.4a + b - 281.5)^2 +$
$(14.5a + b - 337.4)^2 + (15.8a + b - 404.2)^2 +$
$(16.8a + b - 402.1)^2 + (17.4a + b - 452.0)^2$

2.25 a. Let A = the number of grams of air-popped popcorn,
N = the number of grams of natural peanut butter.

b. Let P_A = the number of grams of protein per gram of A,
P_N = the number of grams of protein per gram of N,
C_A = the number of grams of carbohydrates per gram of A,
C_N = the number of grams of carbohydrates per gram of N,
F_A = the number of grams of fat per gram of A,
F_N = the number of grams of fat per gram of N,
D_A = the cost in \$ per gram of A,
D_N = the cost in \$ per gram of N.

c. Min $\quad D_A A + D_N N$
s.t.

$$P_A A + P_N N \ge 4 \quad \text{(Protein)}$$
$$C_A A + C_N N \le 10 \quad \text{(Carbohydrates)}$$
$$F_A A + F_N N \le 2 \quad \text{(Fat)}$$
$$A, \quad N \ge 0$$

2.27 Max $\quad 21.25S_1 + 19.50S_2 + 24.75L_1 + 23.25L_2$

$$S_1 + S_2 \quad\quad\quad\quad \ge 600$$
$$L_1 + L_2 \ge 400$$
$$0.41667S_1 \quad\quad + 0.729L_1 \quad\quad \le 160$$
$$+ 0.2777S_2 \quad\quad + 0.5208L_2 \le 160$$
$$S_1, \quad S_2, \quad L_1, \quad L_2 \ge 0$$

CHAPTER 3

3.1 Let Fr-FFF = the number of gallons to ship from Fresno to Fresh Food Farms
Fr-AG = the number of gallons ot ship from Fresno to American Growers
B-FFF = the number of gallons to ship from Bakersfield to Fresh Food Farms
B-AG = the number of gallons to ship from Bakersfield to American Growers

This leads to the following problem formulation:

Min $0.04\text{Fr-FFF} + 0.06\text{Fr-AG} + 0.05\text{B-FFF} + 0.03\text{B-AG}$
$s.t.$

$$
\begin{array}{llllll}
\text{Fr-FFF} + & \text{Fr-AG} & & & \leq 14{,}000 & \text{(Fresno supply)}\\
& & \text{B-FFF} + & \text{B-AG} \leq 16{,}000 & & \text{(Bakersfield supply)}\\
\text{Fr-FFF} & & + \quad \text{B-FFF} & = 10{,}000 & & \text{(FFF demand)}\\
& \text{Fr-AG} & + \quad \text{B-AG} & = 20{,}000 & & \text{(AG demand)}\\
\text{Fr-FFF} \;, & \text{Fr-AG} \;, & \text{B-FFF} \;, \text{B-AG} \geq & 0 & &
\end{array}
$$

3.3   Let Ip_i = the pounds of peanut butter in inventory at the beginning of month i; $i = 1, 2, 3, 4$
        Is_i = the pounds of pysyllium seed in inventory at the beginning of month i; $i = 1, 2, 3, 4$
        Pp_i = the production in pounds of peanut butter during month i; $i = 1, 2, 3$
        Ps_i = the production in pounds of pysyllium seed during month i; $i = 1, 2, 3$

Min $0.05Is_1 + 0.05Is_2 + 0.05Is_3$
$s.t.$

Inventory Balance Constraints

$$
\begin{array}{lll}
Ip_1 & = 0 & \text{(initial inventory PB)}\\
Is_1 & = 0 & \text{(initial inventory psyllium)}\\
Ip_4 & = 0 & \text{(final inventory PB)}\\
Is_4 & = 0 & \text{(final inventory Psyllium)}\\
-Ip_1 + Ip_2 - Pp_1 + 400 = 0 & & \text{(inventory PB in June)}\\
-Is_1 + Is_2 - Ps_1 + 600 = 0 & & \text{(inventory psyllium in June)}\\
-Ip_2 + Ip_3 - Pp_2 + 450 = 0 & & \text{(inventory PB in July)}\\
-Is_2 + Is_3 - Ps_2 + 700 = 0 & & \text{(inventory psyllium in July)}\\
-Ip_3 + Ip_4 - Pp_3 + 500 = 0 & & \text{(inventory PB in August)}\\
-Is_3 + Is_4 - Ps_3 + 650 = 0 & & \text{(inventory psyllium in August)}
\end{array}
$$

Production/Time Constraints

$$
\begin{array}{ll}
0.01667Pp_1 + 0.0333Ps_1 \leq 20 & \text{(production May)}\\
0.01667Pp_2 + 0.0333Ps_2 \leq 20 & \text{(production June)}\\
0.01667Pp_3 + 0.0333Ps_3 \leq 20 & \text{(production July)}
\end{array}
$$

Inventory Capacity Constraints

$$
\begin{array}{l}
Ip_1 \leq \;\; 500\\
Ip_2 \leq \;\; 500\\
Ip_3 \leq \;\; 500\\
Ip_4 \leq \;\; 500\\
Is_1 \leq 1000\\
Is_2 \leq 1000\\
Is_3 \leq 1000\\
Is_4 \leq 1000
\end{array}
$$

Logical Constraints,
        $Ip_i, Is_i, Pp_i, Ps_i \geq 0$ for $i = 1, 2, 3, 4$

3.5 Max $1800S$
        $s.t.$

$$
\begin{array}{lll}
1800S - 1400L = 0 & \text{(Equal production amounts)}\\
S + \quad L = 1 & \text{(Fractions add to 1)}\\
S \;, \quad L \geq 0
\end{array}
$$

3.7 Min S
        $s.t.$

$$
\begin{array}{lll}
C & \leq 0.20 & \text{(Max. charcoal)}\\
C & \geq 0.10 & \text{(Min. charcoal)}\\
-0.5C + \quad P \leq 0.00 & & \text{(Saltpeter/charcoal ratio)}\\
0.5S + 0.6C + 0.3P \leq 0.35 & & \text{(Component amounts)}\\
S + \quad C + \quad P = 1.00 & & \text{(Balance)}\\
S \;, \quad C \;, \quad P \geq \quad 0
\end{array}
$$

3.9 Let B = the number of pounds of the base to produce,

       B' = the number of pounds of the base to purchase,

   GP1 = the number of pounds of Gum Product 1 to produce,

  GP1$'$ = the number of pounds of Gum Product 1 to purchase,

   GP2 = the number of pounds of Gum Product 2 to produce,

  GP2$'$ = the number of pounds of Gum Product 2 to purchase.

This leads to the following formulation:

Min. $1.75B + 3B' + 2\text{GP1} + 3.25\text{GP1}' + 2.25\text{GP2} + 3.75\text{GP2}'$

s.t.

$$
\begin{array}{rcrcrcrcl}
B & + & B' & & & & & = & 400 \\
& & & & \text{GP1} & + & \text{GP1}' & = & 400 \\
& & & & & & \text{GP2} + \text{GP2}' & = & 400 \\
B & + & \text{GP1} & & + & \text{GP2} & & \leq & 800 \\
B\,, & & B'\,, \quad \text{GP1}\,, & & \text{GP1}'\,, & & \text{GP2}\,, \quad \text{GP2}' & \geq & 0
\end{array}
$$

3.11 Max $3.86OC + 5.33GC$

s.t.

$$
\begin{array}{rcl}
OC & \leq & 1000 \\
GC & \leq & 1000 \\
0.057OC + 0.067GC & \leq & 150 \\
OC, \quad GC & \geq & 0
\end{array}
$$

3.13 Let $F1O$ = the number of barrels to ship from Field 1 to Oklahoma City,

   $F1T$ = the number of barrels to ship from Field 1 to Tulsa,

   $F2O$ = the number of barrels to ship from Field 2 to Oklahoma City,

   $F2T$ = the number of barrels to ship from Field 2 to Tulsa,

   $F3O$ = the number of barrels to ship from Field 3 to Oklahoma City,

   $F3T$ = the number of barrels to ship from Field 3 to Tulsa.

Min. $4.5F1O + 5.1F2O + 5.7F3O + 2F1T + 2.3F2T + 2.6F3T$

s.t.

$$
\begin{array}{rcl}
F1T + F2T + F3T \leq 150{,}000 & & \text{(Pipeline)} \\
F1O \quad\quad\quad + F1T = 100{,}000 & & \text{(Field 1)} \\
F2O \quad\quad + F2T = 100{,}000 & & \text{(Field 2)} \\
F3O \quad\quad + F3T = 100{,}000 & & \text{(Field 3)} \\
F1O\,, \quad F2O\,, \quad F3O\,, \quad F1T\,, \quad F2T\,, \quad F3T \geq 0 & &
\end{array}
$$

3.15 Let R = the number of gallons of red ink produced,

     B = the number of gallons of blue ink produced,

     G = the number of gallons of green ink produced,

   R_{A1} = the number of gallons of additive A1 used in red ink,

   R_{A2} = the number of gallons of additive A2 used in red ink,

   R_{A3} = the number of gallons of additive A3 used in red ink,

   B_{A1} = the number of gallons of additive A1 used in blue ink,

   B_{A2} = the number of gallons of additive A2 used in blue ink,

   B_{A3} = the number of gallons of additive A3 used in blue ink,

   G_{A1} = the number of gallons of additive A1 used in green ink,

   G_{A2} = the number of gallons of additive A2 used in green ink,

   G_{A3} = the number of gallons of additive A3 used in green ink.

   R_B = the number of gallons of base used in red ink,

   B_B = the number of gallons of base used in blue ink,

   G_B = the number of gallons of base used in green ink.

Max $R + B + G$

s.t.

Resource Constraints

$$
\begin{array}{rclcl}
R_{A1} + B_{A1} + G_{A1} & \leq & 1000 & & \text{(Total A1)} \\
R_{A2} + B_{A2} + G_{A2} & \leq & 1500 & & \text{(Total A2)} \\
R_{A3} + B_{A3} + G_{A3} & \leq & 2000 & & \text{(Total A3)} \\
R_B + B_B + G_B & \leq & 4000 & & \text{(Total base)}
\end{array}
$$

Balance for Red Ink

$$
\begin{array}{rcl}
R_{A1} - 3R_{A2} & = & 0 \\
2R_{A2} - R_{A3} & = & 0 \\
R_{A1} + R_{A2} + R_{A3} - R_B & = & 0 \\
R_{A1} + R_{A2} + R_{A3} + R_B - R & = & 0
\end{array}
$$

Balance for Blue Ink

$$3B_{A1} - 2B_{A2} \qquad\qquad\qquad = \quad 0$$
$$4B_{A2} \qquad - 3B_{A3} \qquad\qquad = \quad 0$$
$$B_{A1} + \ B_{A2} + \ B_{A3} - B_B \qquad\quad = \quad 0$$
$$B_{A1} + \ B_{A2} + \ B_{A3} + B_B - B = \quad 0$$

Balance for Green Ink

$$2G_{A1} - \ G_{A2} \qquad\qquad\qquad = \quad 0$$
$$3G_{A2} - 2G_{A3} \qquad\qquad = \quad 0$$
$$G_{A1} + \ G_{A2} + \ G_{A3} - G_B \qquad\quad = \quad 0$$
$$G_{A1} + \ G_{A2} + \ G_{A3} - G_B - G = \quad 0$$

Logical Constraints

$$R, \qquad B, \qquad G \qquad\qquad \geq \quad 0$$
$$R_{A1}, \quad B_{A1}, \quad G_{A1} \qquad\qquad \geq \quad 0$$
$$R_{A2}, \quad B_{A2}, \quad G_{A2}, \qquad\qquad \geq \quad 0$$
$$R_{A3}, \quad B_{A3}, \quad G_{A3} \qquad\qquad \geq \quad 0$$
$$R_B, \qquad B_B, \qquad G_B \qquad\qquad \geq \quad 0$$

3.17   Let C = the number of acres allotted to growing corn,
S = the number of acres allotted to growing soy beans,
L = the number of acres allotted to growing lettuce,
N = the number of acres allotted to growing cotton,
B = the number of acres allotted to growing broccoli.

Max $448C + \ 400S + 240L + \ 225N + \ 245B$
s.t.

$$C + \qquad S + \quad L + \qquad N + \qquad B \leq \qquad 50 \qquad \text{(Acreage)}$$
$$5600C + 2500S + 900L + 1275N + 1225B \leq 100000 \qquad \text{(Water)}$$
$$640C \qquad\qquad\qquad\qquad\qquad\qquad \geq \quad 5120 \qquad \text{(Min. corn)}$$
$$C \ , \qquad S \ , \qquad L \ , \qquad N \ , \qquad B \geq \qquad 0$$

3.19   Max $(13.5F1 + 15.2F2 + 16.5F3 + 2.04F4 + 2.3F5 + 1.54F6)/1,000,000$
s.t.

Investment-Limitation Constraints

$$45F1 + \ 76F2 + 110F3 \qquad\qquad\qquad\qquad\qquad \geq \quad 500000$$
$$45F1 + \ 76F2 + 110F3 \qquad\qquad\qquad\qquad\qquad \leq \quad 750000$$
$$17F4 + \ 23F5 \qquad\qquad\qquad \geq \quad 200000$$
$$17F4 + \ 23F5 \qquad\qquad\qquad \leq \quad 300000$$
$$22F6 \geq \quad 50000$$

Diversification Constraints

$$90F1 - \ 76F2 \qquad\qquad\qquad\qquad\qquad\qquad\qquad = \qquad 0$$
$$135F1 \qquad\qquad - 110F3 \qquad\qquad\qquad\qquad\qquad = \qquad 0$$
$$34F4 - \ 23F5 \qquad\qquad\qquad = \qquad 0$$

Logical Constraints

$$45F1 + \ 76F2 + 110F3 + \ 17F4 + \ 23F5 + \ 22F6 = 1000000$$
$$F1 \ , \qquad F2 \ , \qquad F3 \ , \qquad F4 \ , \qquad F5 \ , \qquad F6 \geq \qquad 0$$

3.21   Max $0.191667H + 0.106667M + 0.07L$
s.t.

Investment-Limitation Constraints

$$H \qquad\qquad\qquad\qquad\qquad \geq 0.50$$
$$H \qquad\qquad\qquad\qquad\qquad \leq 0.75$$
$$M \qquad\qquad\qquad \geq 0.20$$
$$M \qquad\qquad\qquad \leq 0.30$$
$$L \geq 0.05$$

Logical Constraints

$$H + \qquad\quad M + \qquad L = 1.00$$
$$H \ , \qquad\qquad M \ , \qquad L \geq \quad 0$$

CHAPTER 4

4.1   This problem has the optimal solution at $x_1 = 0.6$, $x_2 = 2.4$ with an objective function value of 4.2.

4.3   This problem is *unbounded*.

4.5   This problem is *infeasible* because not *all* of the constraints can be satisfied simultaneously.

4.7   This problem has alternative optima at $x_1 = 0$, $x_2 = 2$, and $x_1 = \frac{3}{5}$, $x_2 = \frac{12}{5}$ with an objective function value of 12.

4.9   This problem has an optimal solution at $x_1 = 2$, $x_2 = 1$ with an objective function value of 4. Here, three constraints go through a single point at the optimal solution.

4.11   This problem has an optimal solution at $x_1 = 1$, $x_2 = 3$ with an objective function value of 5. However, the objective function is parallel to constraint (c), so there are an infinite number of alternative optimal solutions.

4.13   a. The optimal purchase plan is to buy $L = 1{,}400{,}000$ barrels of light crude oil and $H = 1{,}800{,}000$ barrels of heavy crude oil at a total cost of \$74,600,000.
     b. The plan in (a) results in 1,260,000 barrels of gasoline, 900,000 barrels of jet fuel, and 780,000 barrels of kerosene.

4.15   This problem has an optimal solution at $C = 250$, $S = 200$ with an objective function value of 2,705,000. This means that it is optimal to produce 250 compacts and 200 subcompacts.

4.17   As long as the cost of light crude oil is between 11 and 28.2857 dollars per barrel (and that of heavy crude is held constant), the purchase plan in Exercise 4.13 remains optimal. As long as the cost of heavy crude oil is between 19.4444 and 50.0 dollars per barrel (and that of light crude is held constant), the purchase plan in Exercise 4.13 remains optimal.

4.19   As long as the profit for a compact car is between 0 and 6800 (and that of a subcompact car is held constant), the production plan in Exercise 4.15 remains optimal. As long as the profit for a subcompact car is between 5055 and infinity (and that of a compact car is held constant), the production plan in Exercise 4.15 remains optimal.

4.21   a. For constraint (a), the demand for gasoline can range from 875,000 to 2,250,000 without changing the value of its shadow price. For constraint (b), the demand for jet-fuel can vary from 504,000 to 1,296,000 without changing the value of its shadow price.
     b. For constraints (a) and (b), the shadow prices are 50.9091 and 11.6162, respectively.

4.23   a. For constraint (a), the availability of raw materials can range from 30,000 to 85,555.56 and for constraint (d), the upper bound on the number of subcompacts to produce can range from 0 to 276.9231 without changing the value of the shadow prices associated with these constraints.
     b. For constraints (a) and (d), the shadow prices are 33.7 and 45.0, respectively.

4.25   a. The objective function value, that is, the cost of the oil would, however, increase from \$74,600,000 to \$87,200,000, but the optimal values for L and H would remain the same because the new cost of \$29 for heavy crude oil is within the sensitivity range calculated in Exercise 4.17.
     b. The purchase plan and optimal objective function value change because \$29 falls outside the range for L indicated in the solution to Exercise 4.17.

4.27   The profit margin of compacts can increase by \$60 without affecting the optimal production plan while the profit margin of subcompacts can decrease by only \$45 without affecting the optimal production plan.

CHAPTER 5

5.1
$$\begin{aligned}
\text{Max} \quad & -x_1 + 2x_2 \\
\text{s.t.} \quad & 6x_1 - 2x_2 + s_1 && = 3 \\
& -2x_1 + 3x_2 && + s_2 && = 6 \\
& x_1 + x_2 && + s_3 = 3 \\
& x_1, \ x_2, \ s_1, \ s_2, \ s_3 \geq 0
\end{aligned}$$

5.3
$$\begin{aligned}
\text{Max} \quad & -2x_1 + x'_2 + 3x'_3 - 3x''_3 \\
\text{s.t.} \quad & x_1 - 2x'_2 - x'_3 + x''_3 + s_1 && = 11 \\
& -x_1 - x'_2 - x'_3 + x''_3 && = 1 \\
& -2x_1 + 3x'_2 + 4x'_3 - 4x''_3 && - s_2 = 8 \\
& x_1, \ x'_2, \ x'_3, \ x''_3, \ s_1, \ s_2 \geq 0
\end{aligned}$$

5.5
$$\begin{aligned}
\text{Max} \quad & -25L - 22H \\
\text{s.t.} \quad & 0.45L + 0.35H - s_1 && = 1{,}260{,}000 \\
& 0.18L + 0.36H - s_2 && = 900{,}000 \\
& 0.30L + 0.20H - s_3 && = 300{,}000 \\
& L, \ H, \ s_1, \ s_2, \ s_3 \geq 0
\end{aligned}$$

5.7   The reduced cost of 6 for the nonbasic variable x_2 indicates that the objective function value will *increase* by 6 for every unit increase in x_2, if all other nonbasic variables remain at value 0.

     The reduced cost of 1 for the nonbasic variable s_2 indicates that the objective function value will *increase* by 1 for every unit increase in s_2, if all other nonbasic variables remain at value 0.

     The solution is *not* optimal.

5.9   The optimal solution to the standard-form linear program is $x_1 = 0$, $x_2 = 4$, $x_3 = 6$, $s_1 = -5 + 2x_1 - x_2 + 3x_3 = 9$, $s_2 = 8 - x_1 - 2x_2 = 0$, with an objective function value of 18.

5.11 a. The values are $x_1 = 10$, $x_2 = 6$, $x_3 = 0$, and $x_4 = 0$, with an objective function value of 0.

b. The values are $x_1 = 0$, $x_2 = 16$, $x_3 = 5$, and $x_4 = 0$, with an objective function value of 5.

c. The reduced cost of x_3 was positive in the initial bfs in part (a). This is because when x_3 becomes basic in part (b), the objective function value increases from 0 to 5.

5.13 a.

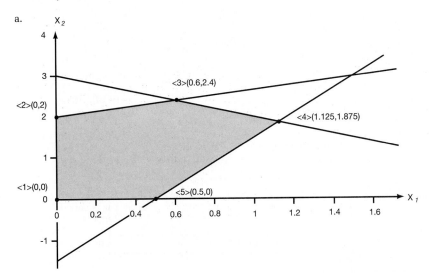

b. and c.

Max $-x_1 + 2x_2$
s.t. $6x_1 - 2x_2 + s_1 \qquad\qquad = 3$
$\qquad -2x_1 + 3x_2 \quad\; + s_2 \qquad = 6$
$\qquad x_1 + x_2 \qquad\quad + s_3 = 3$
$\qquad x_1 \; , \quad x_2 \; , \; s_1 \; , \; s_2 \; , \; s_3 \geq 0$

The following are all basic feasible solutions and their corresponding extreme points:

x_1	x_2	s_1	s_2	s_3	Extreme point
0	0	3	6	3	<1>
0	2	7	0	1	<2>
0.6	2.4	4.2	0	0	<3>
1.125	1.1875	0	2.625	0	<4>
0.5	0	0	7	2.5	<5>

d.

Extreme pt.	x_1	x_2	Obj. func.
< 1 >	0	0	0
< 2 >	0	2	4
< 3 >	0.6	2.4	4.2* optimal

5.15 a.

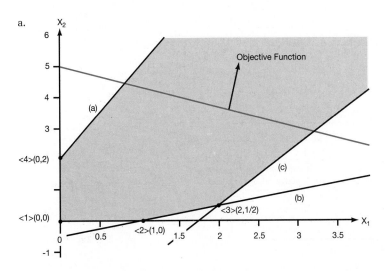

b. and c.

Max $\quad 2x_1 + 3x_2$

s.t. $\quad -3x_1 + x_2 + s_1 \qquad\qquad = 2$

$\qquad\quad x_1 - 2x_2 \qquad + s_2 \qquad = 1$

$\qquad\quad 4x_1 - 2x_2 \qquad\qquad + s_3 = 7$

$\qquad\quad x_1, \quad x_2, \quad s_1, \quad s_2, \quad s_3 \geq 0$

The following are all basic feasible solutions and their corresponding extreme points:

x_1	x_2	s_1	s_2	s_3	Extreme point
0	0	2	1	7	<1>
1	0	5	0	3	<2>
2	0.5	7.5	0	0	<3>
0	2	0	5	11	<4>

d.

Extreme pt.	x_1	x_2	Obj. func.
< 1 >	0	0	0
< 2 >	1	0	2
< 3 >	2	0.5	5.5
Unbounded			

or

Extreme pt.	x_1	x_2	Obj. func.
< 1 >	0	0	0
< 4 >	0	2	6
Unbounded			

5.17 The following are adjacent to the bfs (0, 5, 0, 0, 1):

a. The bfs (3, 0, 0, 0, 4) is obtained by making x_2 nonbasic and x_1 basic.

d. The bfs (0, 2, 1, 0, 0) is obtained by making x_5 nonbasic and x_3 basic.

5.19 Solution (d) is visited next.

Solution (d): In this bfs, x_5 has the most positive reduced cost and becomes basic. Therefore, solution (b) is visited next.

Solution (b): In this bfs, the reduced cost of all nonbasic variables are ≤ 0, indicating that the current bfs is optimal.

5.21 a. and b.

Basic Variables	x_1, x_2, x_3, x_4	Obj. func.	
x_1, x_2	(2, 3, 0, 0)	9	bfs
x_1, x_3	(−1, 0, 3, 0)	Infeasible	
x_1, x_4	(−4, 0, 0, 3)	Infeasible	
x_2, x_3	(0, 1, 2, 0)	−1	bfs
x_2, x_4	(0, 2, 0, 1)	4	bfs
x_3, x_4	(0, 0, 4, −1)	Infeasible	

c.   BFS Number 1

Basic Variables	Nonbasic Variables	Exchange	
x_1, x_2	x_3, x_4		
adjacent to			
x_3, x_2	x_1, x_4	x_1 and x_3	x_3 has neg. reduced cost
and			
x_4, x_2	x_1, x_3	x_1 and x_4	x_4 has neg. reduced cost

BFS Number 2

Basic Variables	Nonbasic Variables	Exchange	
x_2, x_3	x_1, x_4		
adjacent to			
x_2, x_1	x_3, x_4	x_3 and x_1	x_1 has pos. reduced cost
and			
x_2, x_4	x_1, x_3	x_3 and x_4	x_4 has pos. reduced cost

BFS Number 3

Basic Variables	Nonbasic Variables	Exchange	
x_2, x_4	x_1, x_3		
adjacent to			
x_2, x_1	x_3, x_4	x_4 and x_1	x_1 has pos. reduced cost
and			
x_2, x_3	x_1, x_4	x_4 and x_3	x_3 has neg. reduced cost

CHAPTER 6

6.1   a. Produce 1000 pounds of Airtex, 533.33 pounds of Extendex, and 400 pounds of Resistex.
       b. Only the constraint for Polymer A is binding because its slack variable has value 0.
       c. An additional demand of 5% for Extendex from 500 pounds to 525 pounds can be met with the current production plan.

6.3   Doubling the profit of either Extendex, E, or Resistex, R, would not affect the current production plan because doubling either of these coefficients yields values that still fall within the allowable sensitivity range for the current plan.

6.5   A *decrease* in demand of 1 pound will *increase* the objective function value by $8. Since the right-hand-side value decreases by 40, the objective function value increases by $40 \times 8 = 320$, yielding a profit of $13,453.33.

6.7   It is not possible to answer this question from the given output. Resolving the problem results in the new optimal production plan in which A = 1020, E = 506.67, and R = 400.

6.9   The production plan changes due to the decrease in the profit per ton of Type C tubes outside the sensitivity range. Resolving the problem results in the following new optimal solution: AP = 0, BP = 0, CP = 4000, AJ = 2000, BJ = 4000, and CJ = 1000, with a profit of $53,000.

6.11   1166.667 ounces of the welding material are not needed in the production plan. This is the amount that should therefore be sold at $32 per pound.

6.13   950 grams.

6.15   An additional 599.9997 milligrams of fat will be included in the optimal meal.

6.17

```
            PARAMETRIC ANALYSIS OF RIGHT-HAND-SIDE VALUE - LAND
       COEF = 50.000        LWR LIMIT = -Infinity     UPR LIMIT = Infinity
             ------- Range -------        Shadow     ---- Variable ----
                 From           To         Price      Leave      Enter
       RHS     50.000       69.333       150.000        S     SLACK    1
       Obj  16940.000    19840.000

       RHS     69.333     Infinity         0.000     ---- No change ----
       Obj  19840.000    19840.000

       RHS     50.000       30.080       150.000        L     SLACK    3
       Obj  16940.000  | 13952.000 |

       RHS     30.080       17.857       206.452        S     SLACK    2
       Obj. | 13952.000 | 11428.570

       RHS     17.857      | 8.000 |      640.000     SLACK    3
       Obj  11428.570     5120.000

       RHS    | 8.000 |   -Infinity   ---- Infeasible in this range ----
```

```
            PARAMETRIC ANALYSIS OF RIGHT-HAND-SIDE VALUE - WATER
       COEF = 100000.000  LWR LIMIT = -Infinity     UPR LIMIT = Infinity
             ------- Range -------        Shadow     ---- Variable ----
                 From           To         Price      Leave      Enter
       RHS  100000.000   149800.000        0.100        L     SLACK    3
       Obj   16940.000    21920.000

       RHS  149800.000   280000.000     7.742E-02       S     SLACK    2
       Obj   21920.000    32000.000

       RHS  280000.000     Infinity        0.000     ---- No change ----
       Obj   32000.000    32000.000

       RHS  100000.000    82600.000        0.100        S     SLACK    1
       Obj   16940.000    15200.000

       RHS   82600.000    44800.000      | 0.267 |        L
       Obj   15200.000     5120.000

       RHS   44800.000    -Infinity   ---- Infeasible in this range ----
```

6.19   10 more acres of land will yield an additional net profit of $1500 and 13,000 liters more of water will yield an additional profit of $1300. It is therefore better to consider obtaining the additional 10 acres of land.

6.21   It is best to lease approximately 20 acres.

6.23   a.

	Airport 1	Airport 2	Airport 3	Airport 4
Vendor 1	0	170	0	130
Vendor 2	150	80	0	0
Vendor 3	0	0	350	350

Total cost = $1,024,000.

b. Vendor 2 has an excess supply of 370 thousand gallons.

c. The cost associated with V1-A2 needs to *decrease* by only $100 per thousand gallons for the shipping plan to change. Likewise, V1-A4 needs to *increase* by only $100 per thousand gallons; V2-A2 needs to *increase* by only $100 per thousand gallons and V2-A4 needs to *decrease* by only $100 per thousand gallons for the shipping plan to change.

6.25 The optimal solution also changes because the new objective function coefficient is outside the sensitivity range. To determine how, however, it is necessary to solve the problem again. On doing so, the new optimal shipping plan is:

	Airport 1	Airport 2	Airport 3	Airport 4
Vendor 1	0	50	0	250
Vendor 2	150	200	0	0
Vendor 3	0	0	350	350

Total cost = $1,180,000.

6.27 A reduction of the demand at Airport 4 to 230,000 gallons is needed to achieve the desired cost reduction to $750,000.

6.29 a. The sulfur and phosphorus content are at their upper limits of 0.0007 grams and 0.0045 grams.
b. The cost of Mississippi crude can increase indefinitely without causing changes in the current blend, but can only decrease from 0.55 to 0.4244 without causing changes in the current blend. For the New Mexico crude, the cost of 0.47 can increase to 0.5657 or decrease to 0.44 without causing changes in the current blend. For Texas crude, the cost of 0.33 can increase to 0.3525 or decrease to 0.1146 without causing changes in the current blend.
c. The shadow price of -375.0 remains valid for right-hand-side values between 0.0007 grams and 0.00081 grams and indicates that each gram of increase in the maximum allowable sulfur content will decrease the cost of the blend by $375.0 per gallon. No change in the objective function occurs for right-hand-side values between 0.00081 and infinity. For right-hand-side values between 0.0007 and 0.000648, the shadow price of -375.0 is again valid. For right-hand-side values between 0.000648 and 0.000567, the shadow price is -3964.289. For right-hand-side values less than 0.0567, the problem is infeasible.
d. A 10% increase in the cost of the Texas crude falls outside the sensitivity range. Therefore, the optimal blend and the objective function value change. The new optimal solution with the associated cost is

```
                  Hexxon Blending Problem
      OPTIMAL SOLUTION - SUMMARY REPORT (NONZERO VARIABLES)
               Variable          Value          Cost
         2          XN           2.0250        0.4700
         4          A1           0.1400        0.0800
         5          A2           0.0500        0.1200
      Slack Variables
         7        SULFUR      5.2000E-05       0.0000
         8       MAX LEAD      1.2200         0.0000
         9       MIN LEAD      0.0300         0.0000
        11       MIN PHOS    2.0000E-03       0.0000

      Objective Function Value = 0.96895
```

e. A decrease in the allowable maximum percentage of additives from 19% to 15% yields an infeasible problem.

CHAPTER 7

7.1 a. Let R = the number of gallons of Regular paint to produce,
P = the number of gallons of Premium paint to produce,
S = the number of gallons of Supreme paint to produce,
P^+ = the profit above the desired goal,
P^- = the profit below the desire goal,
T^+ = the amount of time above the desired goal,
T^- = the amount of time below the desired goal.

i. $2R + 3P + 4S - P^+ + P^- = 100$ profit goal.
ii. $R + 2P + 3S - T^+ + T^- = 60$ time goal.

b. Min $2P^- + T^+$

7.3   a. Let S = the number of gallons of Supreme gasoline to produce,
             E = the number of gallons of Extra to produce,
             R = the number of gallons of Regular to produce,
            C^+ = the cost above the desired goal,
            C^- = the cost below the desired goal,
            R^+ = the production of Regular gasoline above the desired goal,
            R^- = the production of Regular gasoline below the desired goal.

       i. $0.96S + 0.88E + 0.80R - C^+ + C^- = 55000$ (cost goal).
      ii. $R - R^+ + R^- = 40000$ (regular-gasoline goal).

    b. Min $3C^+ + R^-$.

7.5   Constraint (3) corresponds to the objective function: Min $4x_1 + 5x_2$.
        Constraint (4) corresponds to the objective function: Max $2x_2 - 3x_4$.

7.7

$$\begin{aligned}
\text{Min} \quad & 100K^+ \qquad\qquad + C^+ \\
\text{s.t.} \quad & 0.45L + 0.35H & \geq\ & 1{,}260{,}000 \\
& 0.18L + 0.36H & \geq\ & 900{,}000 \\
& 0.30L + 0.20H & \geq\ & 300{,}000 \\
& 0.30L + 0.20H \ -\ K^+ + K^- & =\ & 300{,}000 \\
& 25L + 22H \qquad\qquad - C^+ + C^- & =\ & 75{,}000{,}000 \\
& L,\ H,\ K^+,\ K^-,\ C^+,\ C^- & \geq\ & 0
\end{aligned}$$

b.

	Objective		
	Min cost	Min excess kerosene	Min penalties (Goal programming)
Cost	74,600,000	79,200,000	79,200,000
Kerosene (excess)	480,000	420,000	420,000

7.9

$$\begin{aligned}
\text{Min} \quad & 400S^+ + \quad C^+ \\
\text{s.t.} \quad & 0.35x_M + \ 0.40x_N + \ 0.30x_T + & A_1 + & A_2 & =\ & 1.0 \\
& & 7A_1 + & 6A_2 & \leq\ & 2.50 \\
& & 7A_1 + & 6A_2 & \geq\ & 1.25 \\
& & 0.025A_1 &+ 0.02A_2 & \leq\ & 0.0045 \\
& & 0.025A_1 &+ 0.02A_2 & \geq\ & 0.0025 \\
& & A_1 + & A_2 & \leq\ & 0.19 \\
& .000245x_M + .00032x_N + .0003x_T & & - S^+ + S^- & =\ & 0.0006 \\
& 0.55x_M + \ 0.47x_N + \ 0.33x_T + & 0.08A_1 &+ 0.12A_2 - C^+ + C^- & =\ & 0.95 \\
& x_M,\ x_N,\ x_T,\ A_1, & A_2, C^+, & S^+, C^-, S^- & \geq\ & 0
\end{aligned}$$

	Objective		
	Min cost	Min sulfur	Min penalties (Goal programming)
Cost	0.94945	1.2913	0.9689
Sulfur	0.0007	0.000567	0.000648

7.11   The final mixture has 3 liters. The cost to produce the final mixture is $5.00.

7.13   The final production of 1160 pounds of noodles is 60 pounds above the production goal. The total profit is $530.

7.15   The profit goal must decrease to 450 for the production goal to be met exactly.

7.17   Washington, D.C. receives no gasoline at all. The penalty for not meeting the goal for shipments to Washington, D.C. would have to increase by 10% from 1.0 to 1.1 in order for the current shipping plan no longer to be optimal.

7.19   a. All 50 acres are utilized in the current optimal solution.
       b. Only the profit goal is met.
       c. The corn goal is underachieved by 0.8571 acres.

7.21   The profit goal must decrease to 16940 for both goals to be met exactly.

CHAPTER 8

8.1   a. $P_1 + P_2 \leq 1$.
       b. $P_2 - P_1 \geq 0$.
       c. $P_1 + P_2 + P_3 \geq 1$.

8.3   Max $0.59S + 0.79L$
       s.t.

$1.5S +$	$2L \leq$	8000	(Compound in ounces)
$3.0S + 2.667L \leq$		16000	(Base in ounces)
S ,	$L \geq$	0	and integer

8.5   Let $S_i = \begin{cases} 1 & \text{if machine } i \text{ is tooled for small screws} \\ 0 & \text{otherwise} \end{cases}$ $i = 1, 2, 3, 4$

       $M_i = \begin{cases} 1 & \text{if machine } i \text{ is tooled for medium screws} \\ 0 & \text{otherwise} \end{cases}$ $i = 1, 2, 3, 4$

       $L_i = \begin{cases} 1 & \text{if machine } i \text{ is tooled for large screws} \\ 0 & \text{otherwise} \end{cases}$ $i = 1, 2, 3, 4.$

    Max $5750S_1 + 11250S_2 + 8718.75S_3 + 8700S_4 +$
          $6300M_1 + 10780M_2 + 9660M_3 + 10657.5M_4 +$
          $5280L_1 + 8600L_2 + 7200L_3 + 10440L_4$
    s.t.
       Machine-Assignment Constraints

$S_1 +$	$M_1 +$	$L_1 \leq 1$	(Assign Machine 1 at most once)
$S_2 +$	$M_2 +$	$L_2 \leq 1$	(Assign Machine 2 at most once)
$S_3 +$	$M_3 +$	$L_3 \leq 1$	(Assign Machine 3 at most once)
$S_4 +$	$M_4 +$	$L_4 \leq 1$	(Assign Machine 4 at most once)

       Logical Constraints

$$S_1 , \quad S_2 , \quad S_3 , \quad S_4,$$
$$M_1 , \quad M_2 , \quad M_3 , \quad M_4,$$
$$L_1 , \quad L_2 , \quad L_3 , \quad L_4 = 0 \text{ or } 1$$

8.7   a. The linear program has an optimal solution at $x_1 = 2.2778$ and $x_2 = 3.6111$.
       b. The integer program has an optimal solution at $x_1 = 2$ and $x_2 = 3$, which can be obtained by rounding down the optimal solution in part (a).

8.9   a. The linear program has an optimal solution at $x_1 = 1.1538$ and $x_2 = 1.5385$.
       b. The integer program has no feasible solution.

8.11   a. The linear program is infeasible.
       b. The integer program is infeasible.

8.13

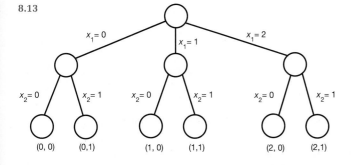

8.15   No nodes can be dropped.

8.17   The current node and all nodes below it can be eliminated.

8.19   a. Max $5x_1 + 3x_2 + x_3$
          s.t. $x_1 + x_2 + x_3 \leq 3$
              $5x_1 \qquad - 2x_3 \leq 2$
              $x_1 , \quad x_2 , \quad x_3 \geq 0$

b. $x_1 = 0.4$, $x_2 = 2.6$, and $x_3 = 0$, with an objective function value of 9.8.

c. There is no lower bound. No nodes can be eliminated yet.

d. The node in which x_2 is fixed to 3 is chosen next.

The following sequence of nodes are visited:

$(-,-,-)$ Forward step to

$(-,3,-)$ The optimal solution to this associated linear program is $x_1 = 0$, $x_2 = 3$, and $x_3 = 0$, with an objective function value of 9. Since this is a feasible integer solution with a value *greater* than the current lower bound, 9 now becomes the lower bound and you can eliminate all nodes below and to the right of this one. Next take a side step to

$(-,2,-)$ The optimal solution to this associated linear program is $x_1 = 0.5714$, $x_2 = 2$, and $x_3 = 0.4286$, with an objective function value of 9.285714. Since this is not lower than the current lower bound of 9, no new nodes can be eliminated. Now take a side step to

$(-,1,-)$ The optimal solution to this associated linear program is $x_1 = 0.8571$, $x_2 = 1$, and $x_3 = 1.1429$, with an objective function value of 8.428. Since this value is less than the current lower bound of 9, this node and all the ones below and to the left of it can be eliminated.

Since nodes below Node $(-,2,-)$ are not eliminated, it is now necessary to fix either x_1 or x_3 to an integer value.

8.21   A maximum profit of $156,790 is attainable when 682 large tents and 1363 small tents are manufactured. None of the constraints are binding.

8.23   The company should manufacture 564 fax-modems, 300 data-compression, and 272 synthesizer boards to achieve the maximum total profit of $10,816.

8.25   The optimal production quantities and the total profit remain the same.

8.27   a. The company should invest in projects P1, P4, P5, and P6. This generates an annual return of approximately 25.05%.

b. The slack variable for the risk constraint is 0.65 and indicates that the total risk factor of the optimal investment plan is $3.0 - 0.65 = 2.35$.

c. All of the investment capital is utilized.

CHAPTER 9

9.1   a.

b. Let x_{ij} = the number of x-ray machines to ship from city i to the hospital located in city j (i = NY, CH, LA; j = DA, DE, PH).

$$\text{Min} \quad 1600x_{NY,DA} + 1800x_{NY,DE} + 2500x_{NY,PH} +$$
$$900x_{CH,DA} + 1000x_{CH,DE} + 1800x_{CH,PH} +$$
$$1400x_{LA,DA} + 1000x_{LA,DE} + 400x_{LA,PH}$$

s.t.

Supply Constraints

$x_{NY,DA} +$	$x_{NY,DE} +$	$x_{NY,PH} \leq 3$	(New York)
$x_{CH,DA} +$	$x_{CH,DE} +$	$x_{CH,PH} \leq 2$	(Chicago)
$x_{LA,DA} +$	$x_{LA,DE} +$	$x_{LA,PH} \leq 3$	(Los Angeles)

Demand Constraints

$x_{NY,DA} +$	$x_{CH,DA} +$	$x_{LA,DA} = 4$	(Dallas)
$x_{NY,DE} +$	$x_{CH,DE} +$	$x_{LA,DE} = 2$	(Denver)
$x_{NY,PH} +$	$x_{CH,PH} +$	$x_{LA,PH} = 2$	(Phoenix)

All variables must be nonnegative integers.

9.3   The new optimal solution is

```
          TRANSPORTATION - OPTIMAL SOLUTION - DETAILED REPORT
      ------- Cell  ------                 Unit        Cell      Reduced
    Row           Column     Amount        Cost        Cost        Cost
    NEW YORK       DALLAS        1    1600.0000   1600.0000      0.0000*
    NEW YORK       DENVER        0    1800.0000      0.0000    200.0000
    NEW YORK       PHOENIX       0    2500.0000      0.0000   1500.0000
    NEW YORK       MIAMI         2    1300.0000   2600.0000      0.0000*
    NEW YORK Subtotal = 4200.0000
    CHICAGO        DALLAS        2     900.0000   1800.0000      0.0000*
    CHICAGO        DENVER        0    1000.0000      0.0000    100.0000
    CHICAGO        PHOENIX       0    1800.0000      0.0000   1500.0000
    CHICAGO        MIAMI         0    1400.0000      0.0000    800.0000
    CHICAGO Subtotal = 1800.0000
    LOS ANGELES    DALLAS        0    1400.0000      0.0000    400.0000
    LOS ANGELES    DENVER        1    1000.0000   1000.0000      0.0000*
    LOS ANGELES    PHOENIX       2     400.0000    800.0000      0.0000*
    LOS ANGELES    MIAMI         0    2700.0000      0.0000   2000.0000
    LOS ANGELES Subtotal = 1800.0000
    Dummy          DALLAS        1       0.0000      0.0000      0.0000*
    Dummy          DENVER        1       0.0000      0.0000      0.0000*
    Dummy          PHOENIX       0       0.0000      0.0000    600.0000
    Dummy          MIAMI         0       0.0000      0.0000    300.0000
    Dummy Subtotal = 0.0000

    Total Cost = 7800.0000                    * Basic cells
```

9.5   Transport 50 cars to Washington, D.C. and 150 cars to Philadelphia by truck. The remaining demand of 200 cars for dealers in Washington, D.C., as well as the entire demand in Cleveland and Chicago, 100 cars and 300 cars, respectively, should be delivered by rail. This shipping plan results in a minimum transportation cost of $43,000.

9.7   The modified network is:

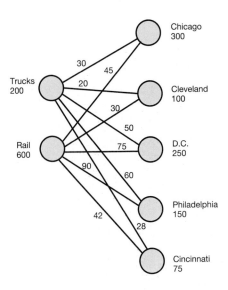

The optimal shipping plan changes (there is also a shortage of automobiles) as indicated below.

```
   TRANSPORTATION - OPTIMAL SOLUTION - SUMMARY REPORT
------- Cell ------                    Unit        Cell
Row             Column     Amount      Cost        Cost
TRUCK             D.C.        125    50.0000     6240.0000
TRUCK            PHILA         75    60.0000     4500.0000
TRUCK Subtotal = 10750.0000
RAIL           CHICAGO        300    45.0000    13500.0000
RAIL          CLEVELAND       100    30.0000     3000.0000
RAIL             D.C.         125    75.0000     9375.0000
RAIL             CINCI         75    42.0000     3150.0000
RAIL Subtotal = 29025.0000
Dummy            PHILA         75     0.0000        0.0000
Dummy Subtotal = 0.0000


Total Cost = 39775.0000
Number of iterations = 5
```

9.9 a. **Supplies**   **Demands**

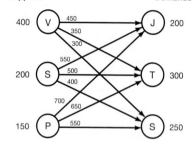

b. Let x_{ij} = the number of tons of lumber to ship from the field outside city i to country j (i = V, S, P; j = J, T, S).

Maximize profit = (Revenues − Costs) =
$$450x_{VJ} + 350x_{VT} + 300x_{VS} +$$
$$550x_{SJ} + 500x_{ST} + 400x_{SS} +$$
$$700x_{PJ} + 650x_{PT} + 550x_{PS}$$

Subject to
Supply Constraints

$$x_{VJ} + x_{VT} + x_{VS} \le 400 \quad \text{(Vancouver)}$$
$$x_{SJ} + x_{ST} + x_{SS} \le 200 \quad \text{(Seattle)}$$
$$x_{PJ} + x_{PT} + x_{PS} \le 150 \quad \text{(Portland)}$$

Demand Constraints

$$x_{VJ} + x_{SJ} + x_{PJ} = 200 \quad \text{(Japan)}$$
$$x_{VT} + x_{ST} + x_{PT} = 300 \quad \text{(Taiwan)}$$
$$x_{VS} + x_{SS} + x_{PS} = 250 \quad \text{(Singapore)}$$

All variables must be nonnegative integers.

9.11   The new optimal solution is:

	Japan		Taiwan		Dummy Customer		Supplies
Vancouver	450		350		−525		400
		200				200	
Seattle	550		500		−420		200
				150		50	
Portland	700		650		−315		150
				150			
Demands		200		300		250	$136,500

9.13 a.

	Saudi Arabia	Venezuela	Indonesia	
U.S.A.	1000	2200	1300	3
Russia	1200	1200	1600	2
Nigeria	1500	1800	1800	1
	2	1	3	

b.

	Saudi Arabia	Venezuela	Indonesia	
U.S.A.	1000 2	2200 1	1300 0	3
Russia	1200	1200	1600 2	2
Nigeria	1500	1800	1800 1	1
	2	1	3	$9,200

c.

Optimal Plan for Consultants

	Saudi Arabia	Venezuela	Indonesia	
U.S.A.	1000 2	2200 1	1300 0	3
Russia	1200	1200	1600 2	2
Nigeria	1500	1800	1800 1	1
	2	1	3	$9,200

d.

```
                    Hexxon Oil
     TRANSPORTATION - OPTIMAL SOLUTION - SUMMARY REPORT
    ------- Cell -------            Unit        Cell
    Row         Column   Amount     Payoff      Payoff
    U.S.        SAUDI        2    1000.0000   2000.0000
    U.S.        VENEZUELA    1    2200.0000   2200.0000
    U.S. Subtotal = 4200.0000

    RUSSIA      INDONESIA    2    1600.0000   3200.0000
    RUSSIA Subtotal = 3200.0000
    NIGERIA     INDONESIA    1    1800.0000   1800.0000
    NIGERIA Subtotal = 1800.0000

    Total Payoff = 9200.0000
    Number of iterations = 1
```

9.15   a.

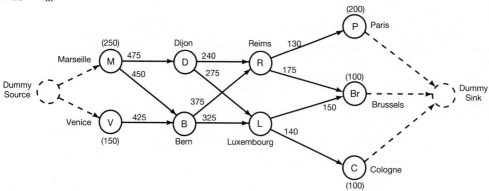

b. Min   475M-D + 450M-B + 425V-B +
          240D-R + 275D-L + 375B-R + 325B-L +
          130R-P + 175R-Br + 150L-Br + 140L-C

   s.t.

    Supply Constraints

        M-D +   M-B   ≤ 250   Marseilles
                          V-B   ≤ 150   Venice

    Demand Constraints

        R-P   = 200   Paris
                  R-Br +   L-Br   = 100   Brussels
                                L-C = 100   Cologne

    Balance Constraints

        M-D −   D-R −   D-L   = 0   Dijon
        M-B +   V-B −   B-R −   B-L =   0   Bern
        D-R +   B-R −   R-P −   R-Br =   0   Reims
        D-L +   B-L −   L-Br − L-C =   0   Luxembourg

    Logical Constraints

        M-D ,   M-B ,   V-B ,
        D-R ,   D-L ,   B-R ,   B-L
        R-P ,   R-Br ,   L-Br ,   L-C ≥   0

9.17   a.

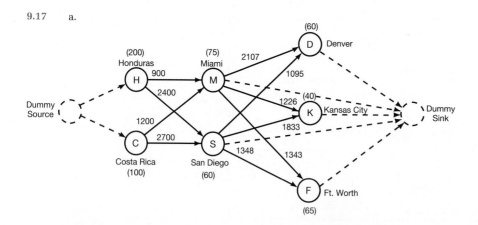

b. Min $900H\text{-}M + 2400H\text{-}S + 1200C\text{-}M + 2700C\text{-}S$
$2107M\text{-}D + 1226M\text{-}K + 1343M\text{-}F +$
$1095S\text{-}D + 1833S\text{-}K + 1348S\text{-}F$

s.t.

Supply Constraints

H-M +		H-S	≤ 200	Honduras
	C-M +	C-S	≤ 100	Costa Rica

Demand Constraints

M-Sink	$= 75$	Miami
S-Sink	$= 60$	San Diego
D-Sink	$= 60$	Denver
K-Sink	$= 40$	Kansas City
F-Sink	$= 65$	Ft. Worth

Balance Constraints

H-M +	C-M −	M-Sink −	
M-D −	M-K −	M-F	$= 0$ Miami
H-S +	C-S −	S-Sink −	
S-D −	S-K −	S-F	$= 0$ San Diego
M-D +	S-D −	D-Sink	$= 0$ Denver
M-K +	S-K −	K-Sink	$= 0$ Kansas City
M-F +	S-F −	F-Sink	$= 0$ Ft. Worth

Logical Constraints

H-M ,   H-S ,   C-M ,   C-S
M-D ,   M-K ,   M-F ,
S-D ,   S-K ,   S-F ,
M-sink ,   S-Sink ,   D-Sink ,   K-Sink , F-Sink ≥ 0

9.19

```
                        Fresh Fruits
            TRANSSHIPMENT - SUMMARY REPORT
                                    Unit        Shipping
Arc          From   To      Flow    Cost        Cost
SOURCE-H      .      1       200     0           0
SOURCE-C      .      2       100     0           0
H-MIAMI       1      3       180     14000       2520000
H - S         1      4        20     24000       480000
C - S         2      4       100     27000       2700000
M-K           3      6        40     12260       490400
M-F           3      7        65     13430       872950
S-D           4      5        60     10950       657000
M-DEST        3      .        75     0           0
S-DEST        4      .        60     0           0
D-DEST        5      .        60     0           0
K-DEST        6      .        40     0           0
F-DEST        7      .        65     0           0

Total cost = 7720350
```

9.21   a.

	Co	Na	Ch	Pi
Wa	173	412	10	0
Cl	0	404	34	0
Lo	29	0	0	219
At	328	0	170	437

b.

	Co	Na	Ch	Pi
Wa	173	412	10	**0**
Cl	**0**	404	34	0
Lo	29	0	0	219
At	328	**0**	170	437

This assignment incurs 892 travel miles.

c.

```
                      Arthur Big
                   OPTIMAL SOLUTION
  Row                    Column              Cost
  WASHINGTON      PITTSBURGH                 247
  CLEVELAND         COLUMBUS                 140
  LOUISVILLE      CHARLESTON                 259
  ATLANTA           NASHVILLE                246

  Total Cost = 82
  Number of Iterations = 3
```

9.23 a. The maximization objective function can be converted to a minimization objective function by changing the sign of each term in the objective function.
   b. Subtracting the smallest value (positive or negative) in each row from every number in that row makes all those elements positive.

9.25 3 of the 5 women and 3 of the 4 men can be paired with compatible partners.

9.27 3 compatible couples can still be paired, only now, Clark has no compatible partner.

9.29 a.

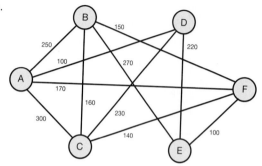

   b. The problem is to determine a sequence for the production of the various compounds in such a way that the profit is maximized. Because the profit for producing a given compound depends on the compound preceding it, the profit can be denoted by arcs in which the nodes are the various compounds. Therefore, the profit for each transition can be considered the length of an arc of a network. Thus, the longest path connecting *all* the nodes corresponds to the largest profit. This is a traveling-salesperson problem.

9.30 a. The cheapest-insertion algorithm yields the following tour: $1 \rightarrow 2 \rightarrow 4 \rightarrow 3 \rightarrow 1$, with a total distance of 29 units.
   b. The two-interchange algorithm performed on the tour: $1 \rightarrow 4 \rightarrow 3 \rightarrow 2 \rightarrow 1$, with a distance of 34 units, yields the following tour: $1 \rightarrow 2 \rightarrow 4 \rightarrow 3 \rightarrow 1$, with a total distance of 29 units.

9.32 A maximization version of the cheapest-insertion algorithm simply involves changing the criterion from minimum to maximum. That is, start with the two nodes whose cycle is the largest. Among all nodes not yet selected, choose the one that, when inserted into its best possible location in the current cycle, produces a new cycle of largest value. Continue until all nodes are included in the cycle.

9.34

Compound	Followed by						
	A	B	C	D	E	F	G
A	—	250	300	100	—	170	—
B	250	—	160	—	270	150	250
C	300	160	—	230	—	140	300
D	100	—	230	—	220	—	100
E	—	270	—	220	—	100	—
F	170	150	140	—	100	—	170
G	—	250	300	100	—	170	—

This problem can be solved by a computer package that determines the longest tour in which the distances between nodes correspond to the profit figures. Using a computer package that computes the shortest tour requires modification of these distance figures in the table. This can be done by subtracting each table entry from the value associated with the largest table entry, in this case 300. Using STORM, the sequence is A, B, E, D, G, F, C, A, with a profit of 1510.

CHAPTER 10

10.1 a. 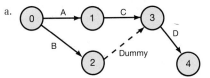 b.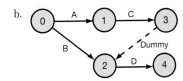

c. 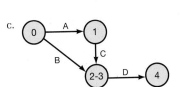 d.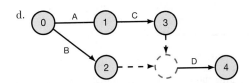

10.3

Task	Immediate predecessors
A	—
B	A
C	A
D	—
E	B
F	C,E

10.5 a.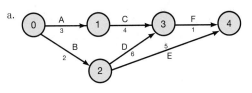

b.

Task	Immediate predecessors
A	—
B	—
C	A
D	B
E	B
F	C,D

10.7 This project can be completed no sooner than 9 weeks. Activity A can be delayed by no more than 1 week. Activity C can be started as late as week 4 (that is, delayed 1 week). Activity E can be started as late as week 4 (that is, delayed 2 weeks). Activities B, D, and E are critical.

10.9 a.

Task	Description	Immediate predecessors
A	Unload passengers	None
B	Unload luggage	None
C	Refuel engines	None
D	Clean interior	A
E	Load meals	A
F	Load luggages	B
G	Board passengers	D
H	Safety check	C,E,F,G

b.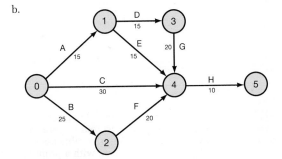

10.11   a.

Task	Description	Immediate predecessors
A	Prepare the wheels	None
B	Mount the wheels	A
C	Assemble sides	None
D	Attach the top	C
E	Attach base	B,C
F	Insert brackets	C
G	Insert shelves	F
H	Attach doors	D,E,G
I	Attach back panel	D,E
J	Paint the unit	H,I

b.

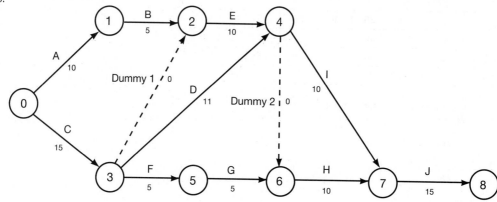

10.13   a, b, c.

Task	Task time	EST	LST	EFT	LFT	Slack	Critical tasks
A	3	0	1	3	4	1	
B	2	0	0	2	2	0	yes
C	4	3	4	7	8	1	
D	6	2	2	8	8	0	yes
E	5	2	4	7	9	2	
F	1	8	8	9	9	0	yes

10.15   a, b, c.

Task	Task time	EST	LST	EFT	LFT	Slack	Critical tasks
A	15	0	0	15	15	0	yes
B	25	0	5	25	30	5	
C	30	0	20	30	50	20	
D	15	15	15	30	30	0	yes
E	15	15	35	30	50	20	
F	20	25	30	45	50	5	
G	20	30	30	50	50	0	yes
H	10	50	50	60	60	0	yes

10.17 a, b, c.

Task	Task time	EST	LST	EFT	LFT	Slack	Critical tasks
A	10	0	1	10	11	1	
B	5	10	11	15	16	1	
C	15	0	0	15	15	0	yes
D	11	15	15	26	26	0	yes
E	10	15	16	25	26	1	
F	5	15	16	20	21	1	
G	5	20	21	25	26	1	.
H	10	26	26	36	36	0	yes
I	10	26	26	36	36	0	yes
J	15	36	36	51	51	0	yes
Dummy 1	0	15	16	15	16	1	
Dummy 2	0	26	26	26	26	0	yes

10.19 a. Let y_i = the number of minutes to reduce task i (i = A, . . . ,J),
x_j = the time at which all tasks emanating from node j can begin (j = 0, . . . , 8).

Min $y_A + 2y_B + y_C + y_D + y_E + 2y_F + 2y_G + 3y_H + 3y_I + 4y_J$
s.t.

$x_0 = 0; x_8 \leq 48; y_A \leq 5; y_B \leq 1; y_C \leq 5; y_0 \leq 5; y_E \leq 3; y_F \leq 1; y_G \leq 1;$
$y_H \leq 2; y_I \leq 2; y_J \leq 5;$

$x_1 \geq x_0 + (10 - y_A)$ $x_5 \geq x_3 + (5 - y_F)$
$x_2 \geq x_1 + (5 - y_B)$ $x_6 \geq x_5 + (5 - y_G)$
$x_2 \geq x_3$ $x_6 \geq x_4$
$x_3 \geq x_0 + (15 - y_C)$ $x_7 \geq x_4 + (10 - y_I)$
$x_4 \geq x_2 + (10 - y_E)$ $x_7 \geq x_6 + (10 - y_H)$
$x_4 \geq x_3 + (11 - y_D)$ $x_8 \geq x_7 + (15 - y_J)$
                                      all variables $\geq$ 0.

b.

```
OPTIMAL SOLUTION FOR ASSEMBLING IN 48 MINUTES
        Variable          Value           Cost
    2       X1           8.0000          0.0000
    3       X2          13.0000          0.0000
    4       X3          13.0000          0.0000
    5       X4          23.0000          0.0000
    6       X5          18.0000          0.0000
    7       X6          23.0000          0.0000
    8       X7          33.0000          0.0000
    9       X8          48.0000          0.0000
   10       YA           2.0000          1.0000
   12       YC           2.0000          1.0000
   13       YD           1.0000          1.0000

        Slack Variables
   22   CONSTR   3       3.0000          0.0000
   23   CONSTR   4       1.0000          0.0000
   24   CONSTR   5       3.0000          0.0000
   25   CONSTR   6       4.0000          0.0000
   26   CONSTR   7       3.0000          0.0000
   27   CONSTR   8       1.0000          0.0000
   28   CONSTR   9       1.0000          0.0000
   29   CONSTR  10       2.0000          0.0000
   30   CONSTR  11       2.0000          C.0000
   31   CONSTR  12       5.0000          0.0000

   Objective Function Value = 5
```

c. The optimal solution indicates that Tasks A, C, and D should each be shortened by 2, 2, and 1 minutes, respectively, at a total additional cost of $5, to achieve a target expected assembly time of 48 minutes.

d. The parametric analysis report indicates that for an additional $19, the cabinets can be assembled in 43 minutes.

10.21   a and b.

```
                   ACTIVITIES IN THE ORDER AS ENTERED

       Activity      Mean Time    Earliest      Latest
         Name   Symb  /Std Dev    Start/Fin    Start/Fin        Slack
       A        UPAS   15.3333      0.0000       0.0000      0.0000  c
                        1.3333     15.3333      15.3333
       B        ULUG   25.8333      0.0000       4.8333      4.8333
                        2.5000     25.8333      30.6667
       C        REFU   31.1667      0.0000      20.3333     20.3333
                        2.1667     31.1667      51.5000
       D        CLEA   15.3333     15.3333      15.3333      0.0000  c
                        1.3333     30.6667      30.6667
       E        MEAL   15.3333     15.3333      36.1667     20.8333
                        1.3333     30.6667      51.5000
       F        LUGG   20.8333     25.8333      30.6667      4.8333
                        2.5000     46.6667      51.5000
       G        BOAR   20.8333     30.6667      30.6667      0.0000  c
                        2.5000     51.5000      51.5000
       H        SAFE   10.0000     51.5000      51.5000      0.0000  c
                        0.0000     61.5000      61.5000




       The computations were based on 8 activities
       Expected project completion time = 61.5000

       Activity std dev = (pessimistic - optimistic) / 6.0
       Std dev of project completion time = 3.1314
```

c. There is a probability of 31.6% that the plane can depart within 60 minutes.

d. A turn-around time of 67 minutes insures that 95% of the flights will depart on time.

10.23   a. The earliest expected project completion time is 60 minutes with an estimated variance of 56.49 (7.5166^2). The critical path and tasks are C, D, I, and J.

b. The probability of completing a cabinet within 65 minutes is approximately 74.70%.

c. The probability of completing two cabinets within 130 minutes is approximately 82.6%.

CHAPTER 11

11.1   a. (1) to rebuild or (2) to settle (and not rebuild).

b. Poor, average, or good.

c.

Economic condition	Rebuild	Settle (do not rebuild)
Poor	0.9M	$1.1M
Average	1.2M	$1.4M
Good	2.0M	$1.8M

d.

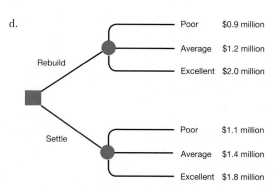

11.3
a. 175, which corresponds to selecting Fund 3.
b. 50, which corresponds to selecting Fund 1.
c. 121, which corresponds to selecting Fund 3.
d. 15, which corresponds to selecting Fund 3.
e. 79, which corresponds to selecting Fund 3.
f.

Criterion	Optimal decision	Criteria value
Optimistic	Fund 3	175
Pessimistic	Fund 1	50
Hurwicz's (0.6)	Fund 3	121
Minimax regret	Fund 3	15
Probabilistic	Fund 3	79

11.4

Criterion	Optimal decision	Criteria value
Optimistic	Fund 3	175
Pessimistic	Fund 1	45
Hurwicz's (0.6)	Fund 3	119.4
Minimax regret	Fund 3	15
Probabilistic	Fund 3	78.2

11.5

Criterion	Low	High
Optimistic	0	175
Pessimistic	0	∞
Hurwicz's (0.6)	0	184
Minimax regret	0	85
Probabilistic	0	73

11.6 As long as the probability of moderate performance of the Dow Jones average is between 0.00 and 0.64 (and hence that of excellent performance is between 0.8 and 0.16), the optimal decision remains Fund 3. At 0.65, the optimal decision becomes Fund 1.

11.7 The range of values for α is 0.1178 to 1.0.

11.8
a.

Outcome	Optimal decision	Payoff
Poor	Fund 1	50
Moderate	Fund 1	75
Excellent	Fund 3	175

b. $79,000.
c. $90,000.
d. $11,000.

11.9
a.

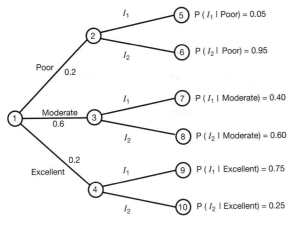

b. i.

Indicator	Joint Probabilities Poor	Moderate	Excellent
I_1	0.01	0.24	0.15
I_2	0.19	0.36	0.05

ii.

Indicator	Marginal Probabilities
I_1	0.40
I_2	0.60

iii.

Indicator	Revised Probabilities Poor	Moderate	Excellent
I_1	0.0250	0.60	0.3750
I_2	0.3167	0.60	0.0833

c. If the indicator is I_1, the optimal decision is Fund 3.
If the indicator is I_2, the optimal decision is Fund 1.
d. 79.
e. 82.55.
f. 3.546.
g. Pension Planners should pay no more than $3,546 for the analysis, so the survey should *not* be done.

11.10 32.27%.

11.19   a.

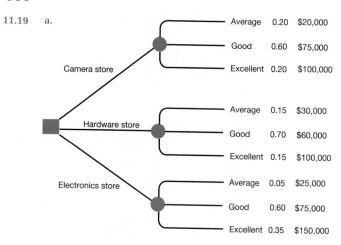

   b. 69.
      61.5.
      98.75.
   c. The optimal decision is to purchase the electronics store.

11.21   a.

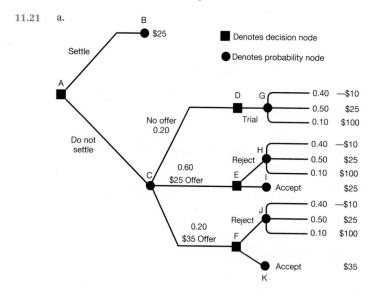

   b. Larry should reject the initial offer.

11.22   The legal expenses can increase up to $18,000.

11.23   An increase of $165,000 over the current $100,000 is needed.

11.24   It is optimal to buy the dealership with no brand-name recognition.

CHAPTER 12

12.1   a. Probabilistic.
        b. Shortages are allowed, but result in lost sales.
        c. Deterministic.
        d. Ordering cost: $110; holding cost: $0.125 per pound; item cost: $0.50 per pound.
        e. There are no quantity discounts.
        f. Continuous review.

12.3 a. Deterministic.
  b. Shortages can be allowed, but cannot be backordered.
  c. 2/52 of a year.
  d. Ordering cost: $220; holding cost: this is based on the annual carrying rate of 30% and the cost per roll, which depends on the quantity ordered; item cost: $425, $400, or $375 per roll.
  e. There are quantity discounts.
  f. The inventory requires neither periodic nor continuous review.

12.5 a. Deterministic
  b. Shortages are not allowed.
  c. Probabilistic.
  d. Ordering cost: $1000; holding cost: $6 per barrel per year; item cost: $20 per barrel.
  e. There are no quantity discounts.
  f. Continuous review.

12.7 a. $Q^* = 1200$ tires per order.
  b. $R = 923.07$ tires ≈ 924 tires.
  c. 40.
  d. The total annual cost (excluding the fixed cost of $960,000 for the tires) is $6000.

12.8 $Q^* = 1252.83 \approx 1253$ tires per order. $R = 1006.15 \approx 1007$ tires. The total annual cost (excluding the fixed cost of $1,046,400 for the tires) is $6264.18.

12.9 The price of the tire would have to increase by $2.16 for the order quantity to decrease by 5%.

12.10 The total annual cost (excluding the fixed cost of $960,000 for the tires) is $7745.96 when the ordering cost is $125.

12.11 a.

Cost per tire	Order quantity	Within allowable range?
20	1200.00	No
18	1264.91	Yes
16	1341.64	No

  b.

Cost per tire	Optimal order quantity	Total annual cost
20	1199.00	6000.00
18	1264.91	5692.10
16	1500.00	5400.00

  c. The lowest total annual cost is for the price of $16 per tire, with an order quantity of 1500 tires. The reorder point is the same as in Exercise 12.7(b), 924 tires. The total annual cost (excluding the fixed cost of $960,000 for the tires) is $5400.

12.12 a. $Q^* = 1200$ tires per order.
  b. The mean demand for one week is 923.07 tires. The standard deviation is 100.
  c. The safety stock S is 164.5 tires.
  d. The total annual cost is $6000 + $822.50 = $6822.50.

12.13 There is an average of 2.7 stockouts per year when the safety stock is 150 tires.

12.14 a. $S = 125$ tires.
  b. Management can expect about $(1 - \alpha)40 = (0.1056)40 = 4.22$ stockouts per year.

12.15 Decreasing the lead time by about 2 days enables management to achieve a 90% service level with a safety stock of only 110 tires.

12.16 a. The demand during this time is 4615.38 tires. The standard deviation during the time $T + L$ is 223.60.
  b. The amount of safety stock is 367.82 tires. Order up to 4984 tires, approximately.
  c. An order should be placed for $4984 - 600 = 4384$ tires.
  d. Annual ordering costs: $975 per year. Annual holding costs: $11,069.86. Annual purchase costs: $960,000. Total annual costs: $972,044.86.

12.17 a. This corresponds to a service level of 79.5%.
  b. Management can afford about 153 tires in safety stock. This yields a service level of approximately 75.3%.

12.30 a. $Q^* = 1861.89$ speakers per production run.
  b. The reorder point $R = 100$ speakers.
  c. The number of production runs per year is 5.58.
  d. The total annual cost (excluding the fixed cost of $312,000 for producing the speakers) is $5582.83.

CHAPTER 13

13.1   a. The customers are the people who call in complaints; the servers are the repairmen.
       b. Infinite.
       c. The arrival process follows a Poisson distribution with $\lambda = 20$ complaints per day.
       d. The queueing process has multiple servers and all are handled on a first-in-first-out basis.
       e. The service time is an exponentially distributed random variable with $\mu = 6.85$ complaints per day.

13.3   a. The customers are the people who come into the bank requesting service; the servers are the bank tellers.
       b. Infinite.
       c. The number of arrivals follows a Poisson distribution with $\lambda = 30$ customers per hour.
       d. The queueing process is a parallel channel system with customers handled in a first-in-first-out manner.
       e. The service time is exponentially-distributed with $\mu = 12$ customers per hour for each teller.

13.5   a. The customers are the cars from which orders are placed; the servers are the two sequential drive-thru windows.
       b. Infinite.
       c. The arrivals at the first window follow a Poisson distribution with $\lambda = 90$ cars per hour. The arrival process at the second window is determined by the rate at which cars leave the first window.
       d. The queueing process is a single channel system with two sequential servers, that is, a queueing network that handles customers in a first-in-first-out manner. The first server has a limited queue capacity of 9 customers. The second server has a limited queue capacity of only 2 customers.
       e. The service time at the first window follows an exponential distribution with $\mu = 3$ customers per minute. The service time at the second window is a normally-distributed random variable with a mean of 30 seconds per order and a standard deviation of 9 seconds.

13.7   a. The average time between arriving calls is $\frac{1}{10}$ of an hour = 6 minutes.
       b. The average number of calls per hour is 15.
       c. 0.0378.
       d. 0.3934.

13.9 $W_q = 10$ minutes $= \frac{1}{6}$ hour (given).

       $W = 0.25$ hour $= 15$ minutes.
       $L = 2$ customers.
       $L_q = 1.3333$ customers.

13.11 $L_q = 1.3333$ calls waiting to be answered.

       $W_q = \frac{2}{15}$ hour $= 8$ minutes.

       $W = \frac{1}{5}$ hour $= 12$ minutes.

       $L = 2$ calls.

       $P_0 = \frac{1}{3}$.

       $p_w = \frac{2}{3}$.

       $P_0 = \frac{1}{3}$

       $P_1 = \frac{2}{9}$.

       $P_2 = \frac{4}{27}$.

       $U = \frac{2}{3}$.

13.13   a. When $\lambda > 12.5$ incoming calls per hour, the average time a customer spends on the phone exceeds 20 minutes.
       b. When $\mu = 13.66$ calls per hour, the average number of calls waiting to be answered is $L_q = 2$.
       c. When $\mu = 12.34$ calls per hour, the probability that there are two calls in the system is $P_2 = 0.125$ (0.1247).

13.15   Since the total hourly cost of $81.25 for using 3 mechanics is more than the total hourly cost of $79.14 for hiring 2 mechanics, the company should hire only 2 mechanics.

13.17   An arrival rate of 74 trucks per hour or more would increase the time each truck remains in the weighing station to at least 10 minutes.

13.19 Each scale would need to weigh 1.6667 trucks more per hour.

13.21 The time required to fix a jammed machine can vary only from 14.4 minutes to 15.6 minutes in order for the optimal crew size to remain at 9.

13.23 40 per hour into each group.

13.24 For two groups. the average time ⬚ ds an average of 8.3 minutes. It is, ther ⬚

13.25 No, the answer is not the same.

CHAPTER 14

14.1   a. When $U = 0.1$, $X = 1$.
           b. When $U = 0.6$, $X = 2$.
           c. When $U = 0.8$, $X = 2$.
           d. When $U = 0.9$, $X = 3$.

14.3 $x = (-1/10)(\ln(1 - U))$
           a. When $U = 0.1$, $X = -(1/10)\ln(1-0.1) = 0.0105$.
           b. When $U = 0.6$, $X = -(1/10)\ln(1-0.6) = 0.0916$.
           c. When $U = 0.8$, $X = -(1/10)\ln(1-0.8) = 0.1609$.
           d. When $U = 0.9$, $X = -(1/10)\ln(1-0.9) = 0.2303$.

14.5 $x = 3U + 2$
           a. When $U = 0.1$, $X = 3U + 2 = 2.3$.
           b. When $U = 0.6$, $X = 3U + 2 = 3.8$.
           c. When $U = 0.8$, $X = 3U + 2 = 4.4$.
           d. When $U = 0.9$, $X = 3U + 2 = 4.7$.

14.7   The expected payoff is $P(\text{Winning } \$0) \cdot 0 + P(\text{Winning } \$1) \cdot \$1 + P(\text{Winning } \$5) \cdot \$5 = 0 + \frac{1}{3} \cdot 1 + \frac{1}{18} \cdot 5 =$

           $\frac{11}{18} \approx \$0.6111$.

14.9   This difference is caused by the fact that these 6 simulations just happened to yield a payoff of $0 for each card. A more accurate estimate could be obtained by simulating a much larger number of lottery cards.

14.11 The expected profit per well is $33.877 million. The expected profit from the 10 wells is $338.77 million.

14.13 a. The output of this simulation is the expected 30-day profit.
           b. The inputs consist of:
             i. Initial conditions: These data consist of the first day of the simulation, the number of video tapes currently in stock, and the number that have been rented at the beginning of that first day.
             ii. Deterministic data: There are 3 copies of the tape. The surcharge of $2 for each day for tapes not returned after the first day, the purchase price of each tape of $25, the charge for renting each tape of $3 per day, and the sales price of $5 for the tapes after one month.
             iii. Probabilistic data: The demand for tapes follows a discrete distribution of 0.15, 0.25, 0.45, 0.10, and 0.05 for 0, 1, 2, 3, and 4 copies, respectively, during the week, and 0.05, 0.10, 0.20, 0.40, 0.25 for 0, 1, 2, 3, and 4 copies, respectively, for the weekend. The number of days that each copy is rented also follows a discrete distribution of 0.75, 0.15, and 0.10 for 1, 2, and 3 days, respectively.
           c. The bookkeeping scheme consists of keeping track of how many copies of tapes are rented, assigning each such copy a random return date and rental fee and tabulating the daily cash flow resulting from renting the tapes and selling them at the end of the month.

14.15 a. The output of this simulation is the average frequency of stockouts.
           b. The inputs consist of:
             i. Initial conditions: The day on which the simulation begins and the inventory level on that day.
             ii. Deterministic data: The lead time of 2 days for orders and the capacities of 1000 and 1100 pounds of the freezers.
             iii. Probabilistic data: The weekly demand for butter is normally distributed with a mean of 100 pounds per day and a standard deviation of 10 pounds.
           c. The bookkeeping scheme consists of keeping track of the current inventory level and the frequency of stockouts.

CHAPTER 15

15.1

Aircraft number	Random number	Interarrival time	Time of entry	Random number	z-value	Amount of landing time
A1	0.710621	2.48	2.48	0.653071	0.39	1.70
A2	0.689315	2.34	4.82	0.407682	0.26	1.63
A3	0.122662	0.26	5.08	0.881552	1.18	2.09
A4	0.151792	0.33	5.41	0.858275	1.07	2.04
A5	0.245387	0.56	5.97	0.570146	0.18	1.59

15.2

Aircraft number	Random number	Inter-departure time	Time of entry	Random number	z-value	Amount of runway time
D1	0.291777	0.34	0.34	0.098975	−1.29	0.86
D2	0.790803	1.56	1.91	0.186970	−0.90	1.05
D3	0.892606	2.23	4.14	0.944184	1.59	2.30
D4	0.361285	0.45	4.59	0.658111	0.41	1.71
D5	0.134913	0.14	4.73	0.281406	−0.58	1.21

15.3

Aircraft number	Time of entry	Runway start time	Runway usage time	Runway finish time	Amount of waiting time
D1	0.34	0.34	0.86	1.20	0.00
D2	1.91	1.91	1.05	2.96	0.00
A1	2.48	2.96	1.70	4.66	0.48
D3	4.14	4.66	2.30	6.96	0.52
D4	4.59	6.96	1.71	8.67	2.37
D5	4.73	8.67	1.21	9.88	3.94
A2	4.82	9.88	1.63	11.51	5.06
A3	5.08	11.51	2.09	13.60	6.43
A4	5.41	13.60	2.04	15.64	8.19
A5	5.97	15.64	1.59	17.23	9.67

15.4   1.37 minutes.

15.8

Car#	Arrival Time	Start order	Order time	Finish order	Leave Window 1	Start fill	Fill time	Leave Window 2
1	10.00	10.00	12.40	22.40	22.40	22.40	38.40	60.80
2	12.30	22.40	10.20	32.60	32.60	60.80	36.60	97.40
3	14.00	32.60	12.60	45.20	45.20	97.40	24.50	121.90
4	16.70	45.20	12.30	57.50	60.80	121.90	18.90	140.80
5	21.20	60.80	12.60	73.40	97.40	140.80	22.50	163.30
6	24.10	97.40	11.10	108.50	121.90	163.30	13.70	177.00
7	36.70	121.90	10.20	132.10	140.80	177.00	14.00	191.00
8	45.80	140.80	23.40	164.20	164.20	191.00	12.30	203.30
9	67.60	164.20	15.20	179.40	179.40	203.30	15.00	218.30
10	76.40	179.40	28.40	207.80	207.80	218.30	16.10	234.40

15.9

Car#	Arrival time	Leave Window 2	Total time at restaurant
1	10.00	60.80	50.80
2	12.30	97.40	85.10
3	14.00	121.90	107.90
4	16.70	140.80	124.10
5	21.20	163.30	142.10
6	24.10	177.00	152.90
7	36.70	191.00	154.30
8	45.80	203.30	157.50
9	67.60	218.30	150.70
10	76.40	234.40	158.00
		Total =	1283.40

The average time a customer spends at the restaurant is 128.34 seconds.

15.14   a. The 95% confidence interval ($\alpha = 0.05$) for the mean assembly time of the product is:
$50 \pm (2.045) * 10/\sqrt{29} = 50 \pm 3.80$.
   b. You must perform $n^* - n = 96.04 - 30 = 66.04$ (approximately 67) more simulations of 8 hours each.

CHAPTER 16

16.1   a. A trend model is appropriate.
   b.

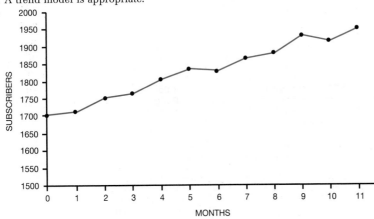

16.3   a. A seasonal model is appropriate.
   b.

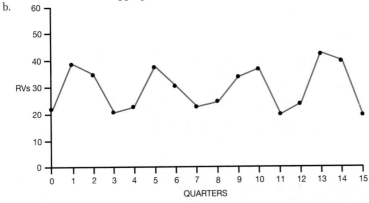

16.5   a. A trend-seasonal model is appropriate.
   b.

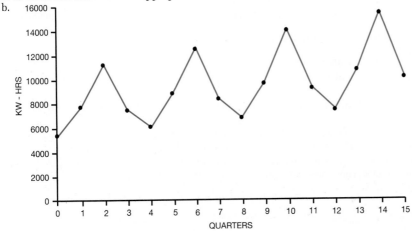

16.7   a. A level model is appropriate.

     b.

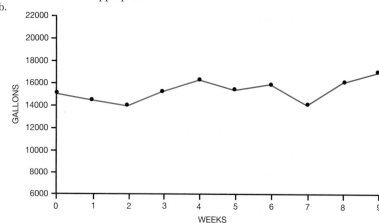

16.9 $F_{10} = F_{11} = 16{,}125$ gallons of milk.

16.11

	Forecast vans	Forecast revenue
$F_{16} = 24$		840,000
$F_{17} = 39$		1,365,000
$F_{18} = 36$		1,260,000
$F_{19} = 21$		735,000

16.13   a. MAE = 8.91.
     b. MPAE = 0.48.
     c. RMSE = 10.68.
     d. 1956 ± 24.88.

16.15

Week	4	5	6	7	8	9
Forecast	14759.5	15077	15313.5	15786.5	15489.75	15427.25

The RMSE for weeks 4 through 9 is 1199.06.

16.17   The final level model has a parameter of $A = 15399.23$. The RMSE is 972.12.

16.19   The initial regression results in A = 1700 and B = 22
     The final trend model has a level parameter $A = 1951.01$ and trend parameter $B = 22.61$.

16.21   The final seasonal model has a parameter of $A = 29.97$ with seasonality indices of $S1 = 0.81$, $S2 = 1.33$, $S3 = 1.16$, and $S4 = 0.75$.

16.23   a. $F_{10} = F_{11} = F_{12} = F_{13} = 15650.92$.
     b. 15,650.92 ± 1592.20.

16.25   a. $A = 29.97$, $S1 = 0.81$, $S2 = 1.33$, $S3 = 1.16$, and $S4 = 0.75$. $F_{16} = 24.27$, $F_{17} = 39.86$, $F_{18} = 34.77$, $F_{19} = 22.47$.
     b. 22.47 ± 7.6275.

16.27   The best level model is $A = 396.40$, with a level smoothing constant of 0.18.
     The best trend model is $L_t = 397.05$ and $B = 2.66$, with a level smoothing constant of 0.45 and a trend smoothing constant of 0.41.
     The level model is best since it has the lowest RMSE.

16.29   The best level model is $A = 3286.10$, with a smoothing constant of 0.01.
     The best trend model is $L_t = 3523.85$ and $B = 28.12$, with a level smoothing constant of 0.01 and a trend smoothing constant of 0.01.
     The best seasonal model is $A = 3382.06$, $S1 = 1.20$, $S2 = 0.80$, and $S3 = 0.99$, with a level smoothing constant of 0.86 and a seasonal smoothing constant of 0.01.
     The best trend-seasonal model is $L_t = 3407.61$, $B = 25.50$, $S_1 = 1.20$, $S2 = 0.80$, and $S3 = 0.98$, with a level smoothing constant of 0.84, a trend smoothing constant of 0.04, and a seasonal smoothing constant of 1.00.
     The best model to use for future forecasts is the one with the lowest RMSE. For the data given, the model yielding the lowest RMSE is the seasonal model. Therefore, this model should be used for future forecasts.

16.31   a. $B = -0.814$ b. $11.829 million.
        $A = 17.934$.
        Tax revenue = $A + B *$ Unemployment rate.

INDEX

898 INDEX

File Name	LINDO	STORM	QSB**
		CHAPTER 10	
PERPUB.DAT	No	Project Management	Project Scheduling
PERPUBLP.DAT*	Yes	Linear and Integer Programming	Linear Programming
HOMECON.DAT	No	Project Management	Project Scheduling
PRIS_1.DAT	No	Project Management	Project Scheduling
PRISLP_1.DAT	Yes	Linear and Integer Programming	Linear Programming
PRISLP_2.DAT	Yes	Linear and Integer Programming	Linear Programming
PRISLP_3.DAT*	Yes	Linear and Integer Programming	Linear Programming
PRIS_2.DAT	No	Project Management	Project Sceduling
		CHAPTER 11	
EX11_1.DAT	No	Decision Analysis	Decision Analysis
EX11_2.DAT	No	Decision Trees	Decision Analysis
SPTREE.DAT	No	Decision Trees	Decision Analysis
HOME_EP.DAT	No	Decision Trees	Decision Analysis
HOME_EU.DAT	No	Decision Trees	Decision Analysis
		CHAPTER 12	
EX12_1.DAT	No	Inventory Management	Inventory Theory
EX12_2.DAT	No	Not Applicable	Inventory Theory
EX12_3.DAT	No	Inventory Management	Not Applicable
EX12_1P.DAT	No	Inventory Management	Not Applicable
ZOO_1.DAT	No	Inventory Management	Inventory Theory
ZOO_2.DAT	No	Inventory Management	Inventory Theory
ZOO_3.DAT	No	Inventory Management	Inventory Theory
ZOO_4.DAT	No	Inventory Management	Inventory Theory
		CHAPTER 13	
EX13_1A.DAT	No	Queueing Analysis	Queueing Theory
EX13_1B.DAT	No	Queueing Analysis	Queueing Theory
OTC_MM2.DAT	No	Queueing Analysis	Queueing Theory
EX13_2A.DAT	No	Queueing Analysis	Queueing Theory
EX13_2B.DAT	No	Queueing Analysis	Queueing Theory
EX13_3.DAT	No	Queueing Analysis	Queueing Theory
EX13_4.DAT	No	Queueing Analysis	Queueing Theory
		CHAPTER 15	
MTGAGE_1.WK1[b]	No	Not Applicable	Not Applicable
MTGAGE_2.WK1[c]	No	Not Applicable	Not Applicable
TPIKE.EXP[d]	No	Not Applicable	Not Applicable
TPIKE.MOD[d]	No	Not Applicable	Not Applicable

File Name	LINDO	STORM	QSB[**]
		CHAPTER 16	
GDTR_MA.DAT	No	Not Applicable	Time Series Forecasting
GDTR_ES.DAT	No	Forecasting	Time Series Forecasting
MHMED.DAT[e]	No	Forecasting	Time Series Forecasting
GASNGO_1.DAT	No	Forecasting	Not Applicable
GASNGO_2.DAT	No	Forecasting	Time Series Forecasting
SUN_1.DAT[e]	No	Forecasting	Time Series Forecasting
SUN_2.DAT	No	Statistics	Not Applicable
		STUDENT STUDY GUIDE	
SGEX_1.DAT[*]	No	Flow Networks	Specialized Network Modeling
SGEX_2.DAT	No	Distance Networks	Specialized Network Modeling
SGEX_3.DAT	No	Distance Networks	Specialized Network Modeling
SGEX_4.DAT	No	Distance Networks	Assignment and Traveling Salesman
SGEX_5.DAT[*]	No	Flow Networks	Specialized Network Modeling
SGEX_6.DAT	No	Distance Networks	Specialized Network Modeling
SGEX_7.DAT	No	Distance Networks	Specialized Network Modeling
SGEX_8.DAT	No	Distance Networks	Assignment and Traveling Salesman
SGCPL_1.DAT	No	Distance Networks	Specialized Network Modeling
SGCPL_2.DAT	No	Distance Networks	Assignment and Traveling Salesman

FOOTNOTES

[*] There are alternative optimal solutions for this problem, so the answers you get may differ from those in the book.

[**] The problems on this disk are prepared and run on QSB+ Version 3.0, which is different from the version used to obtain the answers in the book. Therefore, the format and display of the solutions may not match those in the book precisely.

[a] The constant 12225 is not included in the objective function. To obtain the same answer given in the book, subtract 12225 from the optimal objective function value obtained from the software package.

[b] This file can be run only with the software package LOTUS.

[c] This file can be run only with the software package @RISK.

[d] This file can be run only with the software package SIMAN.

[e] Answers from QSB differ from those of STORM because each package uses different initial conditions for developing the forecasting model.